Readings and
on Financial Acc ...... ठ
Issues and Controversies

Readings and Notes on Financial Accounting

Issues and Controversies

FOURTH EDITION

Stephen A. Zeff
Rice University

Bala G. Dharan
Rice University

McGraw-Hill, Inc.

New York   St. Louis   San Francisco   Auckland   Bogotá   Caracas   Lisbon
London   Madrid   Mexico City   Milan   Montreal   New Delhi   San Juan
Singapore   Sydney   Tokyo   Toronto

READINGS AND NOTES ON FINANCIAL ACCOUNTING
Issues and Controversies
International Editions 1994

1 2 3 4 5 6 7 8 9 0 BJE FC 9 8 7 6 5 4 3

This book was set in Palatino by Better Graphics, Inc.
The editor was Johanna Schmid;
the production supervisor was Richard A. Ausburn.
The cover was designed by Carla Bauer.
Project supervision was done by Tage Publishing Service, Inc.

Library of Congress Cataloging-in-Publication Data

Readings and notes on financial accounting: issues and controversies
    Stephen A. Zeff, Bala G. Dharan.-4th ed.
     p.   cm.
    Rev. ed. of: Financial accounting theory. 3rd ed. c1985.
    Includes bibliographical references.
    ISBN 0-07-016726-5
    1. Accounting.   I. Zeff, Stephen A.   II. Dharan, Bala G.
III. Title: Financial accounting theory.
HF5635.F533   1994
657-dc20   93-36033

When ordering this title, use ISBN 0-07-113781-5

Printed in Singapore

About the Authors

STEPHEN A. ZEFF is Herbert S. Autrey Professor of Accounting, Rice University. He holds B.S. and M.S. degrees from the University of Colorado, M.B.A. and Ph.D. degrees from the University of Michigan, and an honorary doctorate of economics from the Turku School of Economics and Business Administration, in Finland. From 1977 to 1982, he was Editor of *The Accounting Review*, and in 1985–86 he was President of the American Accounting Association. In 1988, he was recipient of the AAA's Outstanding Educator Award, and in 1989 he was selected by Beta Alpha Psi as its Accountant of the Year—Educator. He is author of more than 75 articles in research and professional journals and has written or edited 20 books. He serves on the editorial advisory board of seven research journals. Professor Zeff has been a visiting professor at the University of California, Berkeley, University of Chicago, Harvard University, Northwestern University, and the University of Texas at Austin, and at universities in Mexico, Australia, New Zealand and the Netherlands. In 1977, he served as the AAA's Distinguished International Lecturer in Latin America. He is a member of the executive committee of the European Accounting Association and is the international research adviser to The Institute of Chartered Accountants of Scotland. From 1988 to 1991, he served on the Financial Accounting Standards Advisory Council (to the FASB), and from 1989 to 1992 he was a public member of the planning committee of the AICPA's Auditing Standards Board. Professor Zeff has been the recipient of several awards for superior teaching at Rice University and Tulane University, where he was on the faculty from 1961 to 1978.

BALA G. DHARAN is Jesse H. Jones Distinguished Associate Professor of Accounting, Rice University. He holds a B.Tech degree from the Indian Institute of Technology, Madras, an M.B.A. from the Indian Institute of Management, Ahmedabad, and M.S. and Ph.D. degrees from Carnegie Mellon University, Pittsburgh. He is licensed as a CPA in the state of Texas. He has published a number of articles on financial accounting, auditing, econometrics, and management in such journals as *The Accounting Review*, *Contemporary Accounting Research*, *Journal of Accounting Research*, *Journal of Accounting*,

Auditing & Finance, Management Science, Journal of Business Finance and Accounting, and *The Journal of Small Business Finance*. He serves on the editorial advisory board of *The Accounting Review*. Professor Dharan is active in the national committees of the American Accounting Association and the committees of the Texas Society of CPAs. Professor Dharan has been a visiting professor at the University of California, Berkeley, and was on the faculty of Northwestern University from 1979 to 1982. He has been at Rice since 1982, where he has been recognized for outstanding service for undergraduate student advising and chairs the Master of Accounting curriculum committee.

Contents

Preface

The aim of this collection of notes and readings is to provide a discussion of the issues and controversies relating to contemporary financial accounting topics, using an institutional, historical, and international perspective. The notes and readings are organized into a series of chapters that closely parallel the structure of most intermediate accounting and accounting theory textbooks. This collection is thus designed to be used as a readings supplement in an intermediate accounting course, as well as a resource book in an accounting theory seminar.

The need for such a volume is even greater today than it was in 1985 when the third edition of this book appeared under the title *Financial Accounting Theory: Issues and Controversies*, edited by Stephen A. Zeff and Thomas F. Keller. The number and complexity of accounting pronouncements continue to multiply, forcing accounting curricula to devote an increasing proportion of time to the technical mastery of the numerous utterances of the Financial Accounting Standards Board and other standard-setting bodies, and correspondingly less time to a discussion and debate on the controversies and issues underlying the accounting standards. We believe that a proper professional education is one that attends not only to the particulars of recommended practice but also to conceptual knowledge, research findings, and the historical, institutional, and international factors that collectively set the stage for today's accounting debates. In short, the objective of accounting education is to produce accounting thinkers rather than accounting technicians. It is clear that such a belief is also shared by the Accounting Education Change Commission (AECC), which was created in 1989 by the American Accounting Association, with financial support from all of the Big Six Firms. Seeking to focus accounting education on the *process* of learning, the commission has said that accounting students should *develop the capacity to become* accountants, rather than *be* accountants when they complete their education. Our hope is that this book of notes and readings will serve as a vehicle to enhance the needed critical and analytical thinking in intermediate accounting and theory courses to achieve this goal.

While the book's structure of chapters follows that of many intermediate accounting books, we have departed from tradition in many significant, innovative ways. The development of accounting standards and the objectives of financial reporting are given an early and in-depth coverage in Chapters 1 and 2, including an integrated discussion of U.S. standard-setting and the national standard-setting programs in other countries. A unified discussion of disclosure-oriented developments such as the cash flow statement, Management's Discussion and Analysis (MD&A), summary annual reports, and segment reporting is provided in Chapter 3. The role of uncertainty in financial reports is brought out more clearly by bringing together in a single chapter such topics as contingent liabilities and loan loss provisions, which are typically found dispersed in most books. Major new Financial Accounting Standards Board (FASB) initiatives such as the financial instruments project and stock option valuation are given extensive and critical coverage. The chapter on intangible assets includes a review of the recent efforts in several countries to value brand names. The chapter on accounting changes includes a discussion of the impact of accounting changes on securities markets as well as recommendations for changes in disclosures. Accounting for changing prices is discussed comprehensively in a separate chapter which includes extensive bibliographical notes summarizing worldwide efforts on this topic. Finally, efforts to achieve international harmonization of accounting standards are discussed in a separate new chapter. Other chapters, of course, provide a thorough coverage of traditional financial accounting topics such as revenue recognition, inventories, plant assets and depreciation, long-term liabilities, leases, income taxes, pensions and postretirement benefits, and earnings per share.

The eighty-three readings included in this volume, written by academics, practitioners, financial executives, and financial journalists, have been selected from a broad variety of sources, many of which are not generally available to instructors and students. (In the readings, we have provided the author's current affiliation, rather than the position held at the time the article was written.) In selecting the readings, we have emphasized accessibility of the ideas to accounting students, as well as content. Only ten of the readings also appeared in the previous edition. The sources for the articles include not only accounting journals, business periodicals, and the financial press, but also general interest magazines (*The Economist*), brokerage house newsletters (Bear Stearns *Accounting Issues*, Merrill Lynch *Accounting Bulletin*), Big Six publications (Price Waterhouse *Review*, KPMG Peat Marwick *World*), out-of-print magazines (*Corporate Risk Management, Michigan Business Review*), books (Harvard University Press), lectures (Emanuel Saxe Distinguished Lecture, Stanford Lecture in Accounting), Financial Accounting Standards Board publications, and previously unpublished private correspondence (General Motors Corporation, Business Roundtable, Financial Executive Institute, FASB).

The chapter introductions preceding the readings are extensive, providing not only the settings for the readings, but also a discussion of the issues and controversies related to the topic. The introductory notes in each chapter

also include a review of the historical background and comparative international developments—a unique feature of this book—in order to provide the
student with an institutional framework to understand the debates surrounding current controversies. The chapter introductions conclude with extensive
bibliographical notes containing carefully selected and annotated references
to other useful writings on the subject. The bibliographical references are not
limited to North American authors but include many works written by British, Australian, New Zealand, and Continental European authors. These are
intended to guide students in their research for term papers, and to assist
others who would pursue their inquiries beyond these papers.

We hope that instructors and students alike find the contents of this
volume to be a valuable part of the accounting curriculum.

Stephen A. Zeff
Bala G. Dharan

CHAPTER 1

Development of Accounting Standards

Prior to the 1970s, few academics paid much attention to the standard-setting process in accounting. Beginning in the 1970s, however, it became clear that standard setting was a fascinating process that had become intertwined with the economic self-interests of affected parties. In the 1960s, managers had "discovered" the standard setters, and together with government had sought on several occasions to influence the deliberations of the Accounting Principles Board. It was not until the 1970s that many students of the subject began to study how the standard-setting process actually worked, and they came to the realization that accounting standard-setting was, despite the best efforts of the standard setters themselves, an integral part of the American political process.

Currently, standard-setting boards or committees are active in a number of countries, including the United States, Canada, United Kingdom, Australia, New Zealand, Mexico, the Netherlands, Argentina, Japan, South Africa, Spain, France, Italy, Norway, and Sweden. Securities commissions are particularly powerful in the United States, France, Canada, Italy, Brazil, Australia, and New Zealand. In the Netherlands, there is an Accounting Court.[1] The International Accounting Standards Committee (IASC), whose members represent the accounting bodies of some 78 countries, is active at the international level; and the Fourth and Seventh Directives of the European Community (EC), issued in 1978 and 1983, respectively, deal with accounting matters and have been adopted (with variations) by the legislatures of all 12 EC countries.

The ostensible purpose of each of these standard-setting organizations is to promote the dissemination of timely and useful financial information by companies to investors and certain other parties having an interest in com-

---

[1] For a discussion of the nature and role of the Dutch accounting court, see Jan Klaassen, "An Accounting Court: The Impact of the Enterprise Chamber on Financial Reporting in the Netherlands," *The Accounting Review* (April 1980), pp. 327–341.

panies' economic performance. Standard setters disagree over just what information is likely to be "useful." Differences in the institutions, traditions, and legal systems from one country to another give rise to differences in national accounting standards. But even within a single country, such as the United States or the United Kingdom, leading accountants disagree on what information is "useful." In the United States, the Financial Accounting Standards Board (FASB) completed work on a conceptual framework in 1985, but left several very important policy questions unanswered.[2] In the United Kingdom, Australia and New Zealand, the standard-setting bodies are currently fashioning their own conceptual frameworks.[3]

Formal standard setting has had a longer history in the United States than in any other country. As early as 1932–1934, a committee of the American Institute of Accountants (today known as the American Institute of Certified Public Accountants) collaborated with the New York Stock Exchange in the formulation of five "rules or principles" of accounting, which, together with a sixth, were approved by the Institute's membership in 1934. These were intended to be adopted by companies listed on the Stock Exchange. The next standard-setting initiative occurred in 1938–1939, when the Institute—in response to pressure from the Securities and Exchange Commission (SEC)—authorized its Committee on Accounting Procedure to issue "Accounting Research Bulletins." The bulletins were not binding on Institute members, but since they were in most instances endorsed by the SEC, their influence on the accounting practices of major American corporations was considerable. Between 1939 and 1959, the Committee on Accounting Procedure issued 51 Accounting Research Bulletins. In 1953, Bulletin 43 codified and superseded those of the first 42 bulletins that dealt with accounting principles. (Several of the earlier bulletins discussed terminology.) Today, Bulletins 43 to 51, as modified by subsequent pronouncements, are still in effect.

In 1959, the Institute established the Accounting Principles Board to supplant the Committee on Accounting Procedure. The new Board was to invest heavily in research so as to provide a solid conceptual base for its "Opinions." One of the charges to the Board was to resolve accounting controversies that had perplexed and divided leaders of the accounting profession during the 1940s and 1950s. Examples were: the "current operating performance" versus "all-inclusive" concept of income, price-level accounting, income tax allocation, and accounting for business combinations and intercorporate investments. As it turned out, the Board's early research studies only intensified the controversy and hence failed to unite the Board on conceptual grounds. Nonetheless, the Board addressed a number of difficult accounting issues in a series of major Opinions during the middle and later 1960s. Opinion No. 8 raised the standard of accounting for pensions, Opinion

---

[2] See the next chapter for a discussion of the FASB's conceptual framework project. Also see David Solomons, "The FASB's Conceptual Framework: An Evaluation," *The Journal of Accountancy* (June 1986), p. 114 ff, which is reproduced in that chapter.

[3] These efforts are also discussed in Chapter 2.

No. 9 pleased the SEC by supporting the all-inclusive income concept, and Opinion No. 11 (in a sharply divided Board) endorsed comprehensive income tax allocation. In Opinions 14 (treatment of convertible debt and detachable warrants), 15 (earnings per share), 16 (business combinations), 17 (goodwill), 18 (intercorporate investments), and in Statement 2 (segmental reporting), the Board wrestled with complex issues arising out of the wave of conglomerate mergers during the 1960s. In the end, the Board was defeated by the actions of company managements, government, and the financial community to shape accounting standards in a manner furthering their own special interests. As we have noted, the Board's research program did not fulfill the grandiose expectation that it would furnish the Board with a theoretical underpinning for its rule-making effort. Whether an effective research program would have enabled the Board to counter the pressures of special interest groups cannot be known, but it seems likely that the interest groups would have held considerable sway in any event.

In 1973 the Financial Accounting Standards Board replaced the Accounting Principles Board after the latter had issued 31 Opinions and 4 Statements. Unlike its predecessor, the FASB was not a committee of the Institute.[4] It was set up under the new Financial Accounting Foundation (FAF), an entity independent of the Institute and which was responsible for financing the FASB and choosing its members.

One of the motivations for the above design of the FASB's structure was to bring the Financial Executives Institute (FEI) into the FAF's fold as a cosponsor. During the latter years of the APB, the FEI had actively lobbied the APB on such subjects as tax allocation, business combinations and intangibles. It was believed that the FEI would be less confrontational if it were to become part of the new FASB structure. Yet, not only did the FEI continue to lobby against some proposed FASB standards, a new body representing companies' chief executive officers, known as the Accounting Principles Task Force of the Business Roundtable, surfaced in the 1980s as a vocal and persistent critic of the FASB's composition and operating procedures as well as of many proposed standards.

The articles in this chapter address the standard-setting controversies that are being debated in the 1990s.

The lead-off article by W. T. Baxter renews a warning that he initially sounded in 1953.[5] Baxter argues that standards should be a guide to, and not a substitute for, judgment. "The essence of a profession," he writes, "surely is that each member is willing to think and judge for himself." As practitioners should be expected to weigh alternative theories in the course of their work, accounting students should learn the theories that will be important to them as practitioners. An authoritative literature (FASB standards, etc.) is not

---

[4] For a description of the FASB's due process in standard setting, see Robert Van Riper, "How Accounting Standards are Set," *Journal of Accountancy* (April 1987), pp. 13–136.

[5] See W. T. Baxter, "Recommendations on Accounting Theory," *The Accountant* (October 10, 1953), pp. 404–410.

an excuse for abdicating the use of judgment and thought, and a sound preparation for a career as a professional accountant is not furthered by the rote memorization of standards.

In "Keep It Simple," Walter Schuetze argues that accounting standards have become so complex—as have transactions themselves—that few accountants and users really understand them. He concedes that "by far most of the recent complexity arises because preparers of financial statements and the CPA firms have asked for it." The litigiousness of the U.S. environment explains much of the desire for detailed (and therefore complex) accounting standards. When Schuetze wrote the article, he was an executive office partner in a Big Six public accounting firm. In January 1992, he became the chief accountant of the Securities and Exchange Commission where he would be in a stronger position to make his views known to the FASB.[6]

That Schuetze's concern over complex accounting standards would receive a sympathetic hearing from Corporate America and the SEC is borne out in Linda Keslar's article, "U.S. Accounting: Creating an Uneven Playing Field." For some years, the Business Roundtable's Accounting Principles Task Force has complained of accounting standards that are not only overly complex and detailed but also unfairly depict U.S. corporations as performing more poorly than overseas companies. It is alleged that U.S. corporations are being placed at a competitive disadvantage in international capital markets. It is also argued that the high cost of complying with accounting standards makes the U.S. capital market less attractive to overseas companies.

The bone of contention between the Business Roundtable's Accounting Principles Task Force and the FASB is sketched out more fully in Carol J. Loomis's *Fortune* article, "Will 'FASBEE' Pinch Your Bottom Line?" John S. Reed, the chairman of Citicorp and of the Task Force, is said to argue that the FASB's drive toward "uniformity" prevents companies from telling their financial story the way they want to tell it.[7]

After it became known that SEC Chairman Richard J. Breeden and SEC Commissioner Philip R. Lochner, Jr. favored steps that would lead to the "level [international] playing field" discussed in Keslar's article, the spokesmen for U.S. industry chimed in with letters of support. John S. Reed, the Task Force's chairman, and P. Norman Roy, president of the Financial Executives Institute, criticized the volume and complexity of U.S. accounting standards and took issue with the criteria used by the FASB when pronouncing on standards. In a follow-on letter, Dennis R. Beresford, the FASB chairman, patiently explained the FASB's approach to developing standards and defended its record. These three letters are reproduced in this section.[8]

---

[6] On the changing role of the SEC in accounting standard setting, see William D. Cooper and Ida B. Robinson, "Who Should Formulate Accounting Principles? The Debate within the SEC," *Journal of Accountancy* (May 1987), pp. 137–140.

[7] Also see Lee J. Seidler, "What Ails the FASB?," *The CPA Journal* (July 1990), pp. 46–48.

[8] For a further defense of the FASB, see Dennis R. Beresford, "What's Right with the FASB," *Journal of Accountancy* (January 1990), pp. 81–85.

In an October 1990 talk, "Comparability, Competition, and Cost," FASB Chairman Beresford amplifies his response to the argument in the letters by Reed and Roy that the volume and complexity of U.S. accounting standards are placing U.S. companies at a competitive disadvantage with companies subject to other countries' standard setters. Beresford points out that, in recent years, the FASB has been working with the IASC and other national standard setters toward the end of achieving a level international playing field. The movement toward international accounting comparability, in which the FASB is playing a central role, is further explored in Chapter 18.

Stephen A. Zeff, in "The Rise of 'Economic Consequences'," reviews U.S. standard setting since the 1940s, and identifies several points at which "economic consequences" arguments have been used by supporters or detractors of particular positions. These are special pleadings by parties who have an interest in how a proposed standard might affect people's actions, regardless of the inherent accounting merits of the standard. The acceptance of arguments on the grounds of "economic consequences" would be antithetical to the maintenance of neutrality in standard setting.[9]

BIBLIOGRAPHICAL NOTES

Much has been written in the last 20 years about the standard-setting process. Works collecting the views and research of a number of authors are as follows:

Articles appearing in the Winter 1970 issue of the *Journal of Business Finance*.

Sterling, Robert R. (editor): *Institutional Issues in Public Accounting* (Lawrence, KS: Scholars Book Co., 1974).

Adbel-khalik, A. Rashad (editor): *Government Regulation of Accounting Information*, Accounting Series Number 11 (Gainesville, FL: University Presses of Florida, 1980).

Buckley, John W., and J. Fred Weston (editors): *Regulation and the Accounting Profession* (Belmont, CA: Lifetime Learning Publications—Wadsworth, 1980).

Burton, John C. (editor): *The International World of Accounting: Challenges and Opportunities*, 1980 Proceedings of the Arthur Young Professors' Roundtable (Reston, VA: The Council of Arthur Young Professors, 1981).

Leach, Sir Ronald, and Edward Stamp (editors): *British Accounting Standards: The First Ten Years* (Cambridge, England: Woodhead-Faulkner Ltd., 1981).

"Studies on Standardization of Accounting Practices: An Assessment of Alternative Institutional Arrangements," 1981 Supplement to the *Journal of Accounting Research*.

Bromwich, Michael, and Anthony G. Hopwood (editors): *Accounting Standards Setting: An International Perspective* (London: Pitman Books Limited, 1983).

Flegm, Eugene H.: *Accounting: How to Meet the Challenges of Relevance and Regulation* (New York: Ronald Press/John Wiley & Sons, 1984).

[9] For two opposing views on this subject, see Paul B. W. Miller and Eugene H. Flegm, "Should the FASB be Neutral or Responsive?," *Journal of Accountancy* (March 1990), pp. 35–40.

Bromwich, Michael: *The Economics of Accounting Standard Setting* (London: Prentice/Hall International in association with the Institute of Chartered Accountants in England and Wales, 1985).

For a comprehensive study of the structure, role and functioning of the FASB, see:

Miller, Paul B. W., and Rodney J. Redding: *The FASB: The People, the Process, and the Politics* (Homewood, IL: Richard D. Irwin, Inc., second edition, 1988).

Miller, Paul B. W.: "Financial Accounting Regulation and Organizations," in D. R. Carmichael, Steven B. Lilien and Martin Mellman (editors), *Accountants' Handbook* (New York: John Wiley & Sons, seventh edition, 1991), Chap. 2.

Historical studies of the standard-setting process can be found in the following works:

Storey, Reed K.: *The Search for Accounting Principles: Today's Problems in Perspective* (New York: AICPA, 1964).

Carey, John L.: *The Rise of the Accounting Profession: From Technician to Profession, 1896–1936* (AICPA, 1969), Chaps. 5–6 and 9–11.

Carey, John L.: *The Rise of the Accounting Profession: To Responsibility and Authority, 1937–1969* (AICPA, 1970), Chaps. 1 and 4–6.

Zeff, Stephen A.: *Forging Accounting Principles in Five Countries: A History and an Analysis of Trends* (Champaign, IL: Stipes Publishing Co., 1972).

Zeff, Stephen A.: *Forging Accounting Principles in Australia* (Melbourne: Australian Society of Accountants, 1973).

Moonitz, Maurice: *Obtaining Agreement on Standards in the Accounting Profession*, Studies in Accounting Research #8 (Sarasota, FL: American Accounting Association, 1974).

Chatov, Robert: *Corporate Financial Reporting: Public or Private Control?* (New York: The Free Press, 1975).

Zeff, Stephen A.: *Forging Accounting Principles in New Zealand* (Wellington: Victoria University Press, 1979).

Previts, Gary John, and Barbara Dubis Merino: *A History of Accounting in America* (New York: Ronald Press/Wiley, 1979), esp. Chaps. 5–7.

Zeff, Stephen A.: "Some Junctures in the Evolution of the Process of Establishing Accounting Principles in the U.S.A.: 1917-1972," *The Accounting Review* (July 1984), pp. 447–468.

Zeff, Stephen A., Frans van der Wel and Kees Camfferman: *Company Financial Reporting: A Historical and Comparative Study of the Dutch Regulatory Process* (Amsterdam: North-Holland, 1992).

A conference on the accounting role of the U.S. Securities and Exchange Commission during its first half century is:

Mundheim, Robert H., and Noyes E. Leech (editors): *The SEC and Accounting: The First 50 Years*, 1984 Proceedings of the Arthur Young Professors' Roundtable (Amsterdam: North-Holland, 1986). (Also published in volume 7, issues 3/4, December 1985 of the *Journal of Comparative Business and Capital Market Law*.)

A study of the methodological basis of standard setting is:

Gaa, James C.: *Methodological Foundations of Standardsetting for Corporate Financial Reporting*, Studies in Accounting Research #28 (Sarasota, FL: American Accounting Association, 1988).

On the economic role of accounting standards, written by a well-known economist, see:

Coase, Ronald H.: "Accounting and the Theory of the Firm," *Journal of Accounting and Economics* (January 1990), pp. 3–13.

A work in which the author undertakes a study of the standard-setting process along sociological lines is:

Kelly-Newton, Lauren: *Accounting Policy Formulation: The Role of Corporate Management* (Reading, MA: Addison-Wesley Publishing Company, 1980).

The Dearing Report commissioned by the U.K.'s Consultative Committee of Accountancy Bodies which led to the establishment of the Financial Reporting Council, Accounting Standards Board, and Financial Reporting Review Panel on 1 August 1990 is:

The Making of Accounting Standards, Report of the Review Committee under the Chairmanship of Sir Ron Dearing CB (London: The Institute of Chartered Accountants in England and Wales, 1988).

For a recent review of the Dearing Report by a financial journalist, see:

Griffiths, Ian: "The Dearing Report: Blueprint for a Sound System," *The Accountant's Magazine* (January 1989), pp. 38–40.

A report of the New Zealand Securities Commission containing a proposal for the regulatory reform of financial reporting, together with an extensive comparative survey of accounting standards covering New Zealand, Australia, Canada, the United Kingdom, and the United States, is:

Capital Structure and Financial Reporting in New Zealand, Report of the Securities Commission (Wellington: Securities Commission, December 1989).

A comprehensive study of Canadian standard setting is:

Skinner, Ross M.: *Accounting Standards in Evolution* (Holt, Rinehart and Winston of Canada, Limited, 1987).

A report prepared for the Board of Management of the Australian Accounting Research Foundation on possible reform of the standard-setting structure is:

Peirson, C.G.: *A Report on Institutional Arrangements for Accounting Standard Setting in Australia* (Caulfield, Vic.: Australian Accounting Research Foundation, 1990).

The following articles discuss some of the major policy issues being faced by the newly formed Accounting Standards Board in the United Kingdom:

Tweedie, David, and Geoffrey Whittington: "Financial Reporting: Current Problems and Their Implications for Systematic Reform," *Accounting and Business Research* (Winter 1990), pp. 87–102.

Trotter, Alan: "Accounting Standards Setting: Unresolved Issues," *The Accountant's Magazine* (September 1990), pp. 37–38.

Two addresses on the present and future of standard setting, given by the person who currently serves as the chairman of the U.K.'s Accounting Standards Board, are:

Tweedie, David: *The Accountant: A Crusader or a Prisoner of the Past? Financial Reporting in the Late 1980s*, 75th Anniversary Invitation Research Lecture (Wellington: New Zealand Society of Accountants, 1985).

Tweedie, David: *Setting Accounting Standards: Time for a Radical Change or a Retreat to the Familiar?*, Coopers & Lybrand Deloitte Lecture (Aberystwyth: University of Wales, 1992).

For a personal retrospective on the standard-setting process by a former FASB chairman, see:

Kirk, Donald J.: "Looking Back on Fourteen Years at the FASB: The Education of a Standard Setter," *Accounting Horizons* (March 1988), pp. 8–17.

An influential policy paper presented to the Directorate-General XV of the Commission of the European Community on its future role in shaping company financial reporting in the member countries, is:

Hopwood, Anthony G.: "The Future of Accounting Harmonization in the Community," *European Accounting* (1991), pp. 12–21.

Several books have been written about "creative accounting," by which managements engage in the artful use of accounting principles and disclosure practices in their financial statements in order to improve the image of the company and its prospects. Chapter 16 contains a list of references.

Accounting Standards—
Boon or Curse?

William T. Baxter
Professor Emeritus, London School of Economics

It is fitting that a school should show gratitude to those who have built it, and I am glad to add my tribute to Professor Saxe. A series of lectures is a splendid way with which to acknowledge our debt. Your preceding lecturers have all been outstanding. I feel rather out-of-place—though very honored—to be added to the list.

Most of you, if asked "What is the biggest change in accounting during your lifetime?" would probably point to the emergence of "standards". These were almost unknown before World War II. Now they dominate the accountant's work. They already fill volumes; and fresh ones keep pouring forth with no sign of the stream drying up. They are to be found in many lands; and national standards are being topped up with EEC standards and international standards. They cover accountants, auditors, cost accountants, and probably other species that I do not know about: any accounting group that is not yet emitting standards must feel sadly behind the times, and will no doubt soon be adding its contribution.

We all welcomed standards when we first heard of them, and we all accept that they have great influence. They give us handy rules for our work. We believe that they raise the quality of accounts, make company reports more intelligible, and foster comparability; they dispel doubts, and—we hope—soon will bring harmony of principle. In a world made safe by enough standards, accounting will be plagued by few scandals, and our noisy defamers will have to hunt elsewhere for a quarry.

INDIVIDUALISM VERSUS COLLECTIVE CONTROLS

In passing, we should perhaps dwell for a moment on a rather odd thing.

It is a safe bet that some 90% of accountants are not excessively fond of government. Their political philosophy holds that the state should interfere little in the affairs of good citizens, and that state controls soon reach a point at which they do more harm than good. Such men would scoff at the notion that, by entrusting difficult problems to political authority, we bring the millenium closer.

Yet these men are now happily erecting and submitting to an extra form of authority within their own profession. They hungrily demand more controls over their daily work, and do not doubt that the outcome will be good. Is this not a puzzling paradox?

From *The Emanuel Saxe Distinguished Lectures in Accounting, 1978–79,* The Bernard M. Baruch College, The City University of New York, New York, pp. 25–40. Reprinted by permission of the Department of Accounting, The Bernard M. Baruch College.

ORIGINS OF STANDARDS

It is perhaps worth our while to look back at the origin of standards. They grew from small and inconspicuous beginnings: I doubt if anyone said at the start: "what we accountants need is a set of official rules telling us how to handle every important aspect of our work".

The first milestone of note was the *Statement of Accounting Principles*, published by the American Institute in 1938. Though the Institute commended this book to members in a foreword, it was the work of three authors (Hatfield, Sanders, and Moore) who were not members but had been prompted by the Institute to carry out this task. Such an arrangement seemed excellent: the Institute encouraged research, but did not lend its authority to any of the findings.

Since then, the pronouncements have become more closely linked with the sponsoring bodies, and the latter have tended more and more to back the findings.

Thus the American Institute in 1939 charged its Committee on Accounting Procedure with the task of issuing research bulletins. The committee states its aim as:

> to consider specific topics, first of all in relation to the existing state of practice, and to recommend, whenever possible, one or more alternative procedures as being definitely superior to other procedures.

Bulletin Number 1 stressed the need for good accounts (particularly because of the growth of companies), and the consequent "demand for a larger degree of uniformity in accounting". It said that its rules would be subject to exception, but that "the burden of proof is upon the accountant clearly to bring out the exceptional procedure and the circumstances which render it necessary".

Just after World War II, the biggest group of British accountants, the Institute of Chartered Accountants in England and Wales, took a comparable step. It announced its venture in mild words that do not herald momentous change:

> "The Council has requested the Taxation and Financial Relations Committee to consider and make recommendations to it on certain aspects of the accounts of companies and it is proposed from time to time to publish approved recommendations for the information of members."

The announcement continues with a clear denial of intent to make the new rules mandatory:

> It is, of course, a matter for each individual member to consider his responsibility in regard to accounts presented by directors, but it is hoped that the recommendations to be made will be helpful to members in advising directors as to what is regarded as the best practice.[1]

Thus accounting bodies on both sides of the Atlantic drifted into the new

[1] The Accountant, December 12, 1942, p. 354.

system without clear ideas of where it would take them, and with few, if any, formal motions of consent by the members. A revolution took place with far less fuss than would be needed for a minor change in the bodies' constitutions.

DEVELOPMENT OF STANDARDS

As you will remember, there have been several stages in the evolution of the committees that issue standards.

AMERICAN DEVELOPMENTS

In America, the stages have been as follows:

1. Committee on Accounting Procedure
   Account Research Bulletins (ARBs) were issued by the Committee on Accounting Procedure of the AICPA. The process started in 1939. By 1953, 42 ARBs had come out; in that year, they were consolidated into ARB 43. Only 8 more ARBs were issued during the remaining six years of the committee's life.[2]

   The ARBs had a big impact. But the committee was subject to many pressures and distractions. Its members were part-time. Its staff were inadequate in numbers and kept changing. Its critics claimed that it did not rely enough on research, and it was the cat's-paw of the SEC, that it had no teeth, and that its bulletins were equivocal (e.g., the one on inventories authorized the use of three different methods).

2. Accounting Principles Board
   Because of this dissatisfaction, the committee was scrapped in 1959 and replaced by the Accounting Principles Board. This had more money, and it engaged distinguished men to run a full-time research division. But otherwise it was much the same as its predecessor. It issues 31 "opinions" on a wide range of fundamental topics. Among other things, these tried to narrow areas of difference, and to settle such debatable issues as accounting for the oil and gas industry, research and development, and—most controversial of all—investment credits.

   The APB too failed to placate the critics. They said that it was cumbersome in size, that it was dominated by the profession to the detriment of business, that its 20-odd part-time members met too seldom and did nothing till the research division sent up material. Its opinions aroused violent debate (that on investment credits inspired over a thousand letters of protest). Perhaps the hostility to them was a sign that they were likely

[2] For full details, see John L. Carey, *The Rise of the Accounting Profession*, New York: American Institute of CPAs, 1970.

to be effective: company managers preferred "flexibility" to clear-cut measures.

Dissatisfaction with the APB led to the setting up of yet another group:

3. The Financial Accounting Standards Board (1973)

This is composed of seven full-time members, from widely separated backgrounds. It is generously financed, has a large and able staff, and is independent of the AICPA. It is punctilious about public hearings and first publishing its views as exposure drafts; its final statements are no longer "bulletins" or "opinions", but "standards." We must wait to see how much better this body functions than its predecessors; at least, its organization avoids many of their defects.

BRITISH DEVELOPMENTS

In Britain, the story has been rather different, in part because the profession is split into five major bodies, and has flatly rejected plans for unity. As I said above, the English Institute started the issue of "recommendations"; it continued the process till 1969. Then the other four bodies decided to sail in the same boat; a joint-committee of all (the Consultative Committee of Accountancy Bodies) was set up, and it in turn spawned an Accounting Standards Committee. This has, as I write, issued some fourteen standards.

A noteworthy feature of the British story is that on one occasion—when the date approached for implementing the standard on inflation accounting—unofficial members of the English Institute put up a motion designed in effect to reject the standard. Despite the admonitions of the leadership, the motion was carried at a substantial poll. We could long debate whether this revolt shows the members as deplorable stick-in-the-muds or as men too wise to swallow half-baked proposals.

GROWTH OF MANDATORY POWERS

The disciplinary powers of accounting institutes vary from country to country, but usually are mild. Unaided, institutes could hardly force their own members, let alone outsiders, into complete compliance with a standard. A big body must inevitably contain rebels; even conformists will on occasion find some standards inconvenient and inept. Non-members, including powerful groups such as company directors, are not under the slightest obligation to accounting bodies, and might be expected to brush standards aside whenever it suits them. (And, to complicate matters, the non-members may fall into conflicting sides. Thus the owners of small companies may favor profit rules that minimize early tax. The managers of big companies may favor instead flexible rules that smooth profits from year to year. Ideally, such partisan interests should not influence our reasoning on abstract principle; in the real world, they are likely to carry much weight.)

But the degree of compliance has in fact been substantial. The institutes have high prestige, and can count on the loyalty of members. And the standards boards are reinforced in several ways. First, the auditor of a non-complying company should disclose departures from standards. This threat has been a considerable deterrent. (In Britain, however, there have now been so many qualified reports—with no serious harm to the delinquent companies—that this weapon is losing its edge.) Again, other kinds of (non-governmental) bodies may serve as allies to the accountants. Thus stock exchanges in both America and Britain have threatened to withhold quotations from offending companies. Such threats serve to deter at least companies that are big and want to expand further.

But the above constraints are small beer compared with sanctions imposed by government. Such sanctions may take oblique forms (e.g., tax requirements), or be more direct. In America, the SEC has made the FASB's standards mandatory for companies under its surveillance. The British government hints darkly at a law on inflation accounting if the profession cannot make up its own mind on a standard.

So we have gone far since standards first appeared. They started as gentle guides; they now are becoming firm rules, backed by sanctions.

But they have not yet been tamely accepted everywhere. Perhaps it is correct to say that the most successful rebels are not stray mavericks but powerful companies grouped as an industry and seconded by big auditing firms (e.g., oil companies in U.S. and real estate companies in Britain). Their strident protest—sometimes aided by political action—can win modification of principles. A well-enough financed lobby could probably amend the law of gravity.

THE ANATOMY OF STANDARDS

Let us now look at the structure of standards. Usually they consist of three parts:

a. A description of the problem to be tackled:
b. A reasoned discussion (possibly exploring fundamental theory) of ways of solving the problem. Then, in the light of decision on theory:
c. The prescribed solution.

So here we have an instance of authority telling us how both to think and act.

RULES OF ACTION VERSUS TRUTH

It is important for our argument to distinguish between the two forms of pronouncement by authority.

The first is a bald rule on how we are to act—a command to behave in this or that way. If such commands make life run more smoothly, they may well be good. Thus a law compelling drivers to keep to the right (or left) of the road helps us all; again, the rules of a sports association makes games more enjoyable.

The essence of these good "standards" is that they consist only of part (c) of the above list. They stress *what* we are to do, but say little about *how* and less about *why*. They steer clear of (b), principles. Sporting rules work well though they say nothing about the dynamics of tennis balls or the psychology of footballers. Note that auditing standards can confine themselves to (c), rules of action. This may help to explain why they arouse less criticism than accounting standards.

Admittedly, the men who draft rules of action must sometimes be swayed by theory. A legislature may have to choose between rival theories, e.g., public health law may assume that Pasteur was right. Yet this kind of rule does not set a seal of approval on a theory. It merely enables us to follow a hopeful line of action; if the rule does not work, it can be scrapped without loss of face. A legislature that endorses a theory—as when Tennessee backed fundamentalism—is straying beyond its proper function, and must antagonize all who value freedom of thought.

Sometimes *definitions* are tacked onto rules. They can be helpful if they make the given rules work better—but not if they are regarded as applicable elsewhere, still less if they are viewed as revelations of truth.

With accounting standards, the frontier between (b) and (c) must often be hazy. You may indeed feel that I am pedantic to stress it. But it lies near the heart of our problem. If a standard confines itself to (a) and (c), it may or may not be a useful rule of action; at least, it can be judged by how it works. When it includes (b), it incurs two extra risks: its reasoning may be false, and it will impede other attempts to reach truth.

SUBJECT-MATTER OF STANDARDS

Such ideas are reinforced when one considers the subject matter of standards. These deal with different subjects, and vary in quality accordingly. Four types can be distinguished.[3]

Type 1 states that accountants must tell what they are doing, i.e., their published reports must explain what "accounting policies" have been followed.

Type 2 aims at uniformity of layout and presentation. U.S.A. and Britain have so far tended to by-pass this type. Germany and France, on the other hand, favor standardization of layout, with numbered classifications in balance sheet and income statement. The international standards of the future may well impose similar requirements.

---

[3] I here follow the classification of Harold C. Edey, "Accounting Standards in the British Isles", in Baxter and Davidson, *Studies in Accounting*, 3rd. edition, London: Institute of Chartered Accountants in England and Wales, 1977, p. 294. This, and its companion article by A. M. C. Morison, argue the pros and cons of standards. Rather unexpectedly, the academic author is on balance favorable, whereas the partner in a large firm of chartered accountants is mercilessly hostile.

Type 3 calls for disclosure of specific matters, notably where the reader ought to exercise his own judgment. Examples of such matters are research and development cost, depreciation, and extraordinary items. *Type 3* can perhaps be stretched to cover also the demand for a flow of funds statement.

Type 4 tells us how we should measure economic phenomena—i.e., what are the approved concepts for asset valuation and income assessment. It deals for instance with depreciation methods, inventory values, deferred tax, and foreign exchange.

CRITIQUE OF THE FOUR TYPES

It is hard to quarrel with the aim of *Type 1*—to make accountants explain the assumptions and policies of their published reports: "it is an elementary but fundamental rule of statistical presentation—and indeed of simple good sense, manners and respect for your audience—to make it clear how your figures have been completed."[4]

Standards of *Type 2* are not quite so attractive. Uniform layout has its advantages: thanks to it, we do not need to waste time hunting for given items. But it carries the obvious risk that the layout will become a strait-jacket—that it will not suit all kinds of firms, and will stop experiment. The style of published accounts has improved enormously in recent years, and there is no reason to think that the process cannot go further if left unfettered.

So far as *Type 3* merely calls for more disclosure, it is free from objection (unless indeed the flood of standards leads to an indigestible quantity of details and notes). But of course it will not prevent differences of judgement on e.g., what constitutes "extraordinary."

It is *Type 4* that should arouse most doubt. For here a standards board debates principles (or sometimes tries to think up new ones); it weighs the *pros* and *cons* of different theories, and decides for us that one is the best. In short, authority here informs us where the truth lies.

History suggests that authorities have in the past not been too successful at this task. The most eminent authorities erred persistently on, for instance, the shape of the earth, the origins of life, and the circulation of the blood; more recently, the council of the English Institute has gone badly off the rails with its pronouncements, from 1949 onwards, on inflation accounting. We cannot with complete confidence expect infallibility in the future.

THE GOOD SIDE OF STANDARDS

If we are to criticise fairly, we must spell out the benefits that standards confer.

Standards have greatly reinforced the process of improvement in published reports. They provide stockholders with figures that are fuller, clearer,

---

[4] Edey, *op. cit.*, p. 296.

and more consistent. In this respect, they act rather like additions to company law—supplementing it where it is weak. Often indeed standards have paved the way for new law (e.g., Britain's companies acts) and for new regulations with semi-legal force such as those of the SEC. Standards may thus play a useful role as ways of testing out new methods.

So far as they foster comparability, standards help analysts and potential investors; there is even something to be said for the view that it is better if all firms issue second-rate figures on the same basis than first-rate figures on conflicting bases. Standards are useful also to government, for tasks such as price-control. If Congress is to understand the oil industry, the producers' figures for cost and profit must be presented on the same basis.

Standards deserve some credit for stimulating interest in principles. When new standards are proposed and published as exposure drafts, they often give rise to fierce dispute—and this is surely preferable to apathy.

WHY DO OTHER DISCIPLINES NOT USE STANDARDS?

If standards confer such patent benefits, we should perhaps ask why most other professions fail to produce them.

There seems nothing to stop engineers, doctors, and so on—if so minded—from following our example. Thus a medical body could set up a committee of its distinguished experts to formulate standards for the treatment of this or that intractable disease. Such rules might well spur on wayward doctors to give better treatment; they also would shield doctors accused of negligence. Similarly an engineers' association could produce standards on the design of motor-cars.

But these bodies do not in fact issue standards. Some of the reasons are obvious. A conscientious doctor will wish to use his judgement on each patient; he may feel that diseases show a rich variety, and patients cannot be stretched into a Procrustean bed. Some doctors—including able young innovators—will believe that the standard's treatment is not in fact the best. And knowledge keeps expanding: even the non-controversial best of today will be tomorrow's second- or third-best, so that standard treatment would usually be obsolete treatment. If computer experts complied today with the very best standards of a few years ago, their lives might be more comfortable, but their craft would not have made the giant strides that in fact occurred, and society would be poorer. In these dynamic professions, we may safely conclude, standards would hamper rather than help; and the members would hardly regard themselves as "professional" if they evaded personal responsibility and judgement.

Pure scientists would have even less use for standards. We cannot imagine a society of economists or physicists setting up a committee to issue solutions to puzzling problems. There are several reasons why any such attempt would be laughed out of court. A minor one is that committees, though often useful for collecting facts or deciding on joint action, may not be good at finding ideas: members may think best in solitude; and, sitting in committee, they may be hampered by the need for tact and compromise, or by pressures from outside. More important is respect for scientific method. Presumably a good scientist accepts that his aim is to test and attack hypotheses. He functions best as a Doubting Thomas, not a believer. His knowledge of history tells him that "scientific laws" can never be viewed as final. It tells him too that knowledge flourishes best where there is complete freedom of thought. And this means the absence, not only of crude tyranny, but also of any benevolent authority that makes us respect some ideas and discount others. Ideas should be democratic. As Bacon put it: "Truth is the daughter, not of Authority, but of Time."

DO ANALOGIES APPLY TO ACCOUNTING?

Accountants no doubt concur with such views on scientific standards—and do continue to support accounting standards. We must therefore presume that they regard the analogy with science as imperfect.

How far can one agree that accounting "truth" differs form scientific "truth"? Where some areas are concerned, the argument has strength. Take income realisation. Accounting is here concerned with the growth of wealth. But the size of a firm's wealth can, quite properly, be expressed as a whole range of conflicting figures, varying according to the point at which the bird is deemed to leave the bush and reach the hand; none of these figures may be "untrue," but some will be nearer to "true" than others in the sense of being more useful and reliable for the given user and purpose. In such areas, accounting is more a matter of sound judgement—than of measurement in the physical sense. On the other hand, there are plenty of areas—such as decision budgets and inflation accounting—where strict economic logic applies.

It may be helpful to try to find a closer analogy. Suppose government tells the actuaries of insurance offices to file operating statistics each year; and further, in order to aid understanding and comparability, prescribes the formulae (for assessment of risk, etc.) to be used in calculating the figures. Such a standard seems free from objection. Its rules are a mere matter of convenience. They do not absolve the actuary from the need for judgement on which formulae to use elsewhere, and they do not stop him from experimenting to find better formulae. He does not lose integrity if he dutifully applies the formulae for the government's purpose, and repudiates them elsewhere.

This analogy is perhaps more apt than that of the scientists. But, alas, it too does not fit the facts completely, and should afford us little comfort. Published accounts are not mere incidentals to the accountant's work— something to be filed and forgotten. They are central to it. He cannot shrug off responsibility for their figures, or for the principles on which he prepares them.

THE GROUNDS FOR PESSIMISM

So where has our argument brought us? To their credit, accountants are intent on improvement. They believe that standards are the means (and that accounting differs somehow from other kinds of work, where standards would be useless or disastrous). The belief rests on two grounds. First, if we all keep in step, no one can charge us with inconsistency. Second, and more important, is the view that a committee of leaders can find right principles.

So we demand more and more standards, and accept the big cost of the bureaucracies that will promulgate and police them.

The process of issuing standards has acquired such momentum, and aroused such high expectations, that we must accept it as irreversible—at least for the time being. Presumably it will someday reach a point of equilibrium—where those who call for still more standards are checked by those who are sated.

But if we must willy-nilly live with standards, we should be wide-awake to their defects and dangers. Let us look at these squarely.

1. The most important is concerned with the logic of science. Only god-like creatures know where the truth lies. *Ex cathedra* pronouncements by human authority are pretentious, and inevitably must be wrong sometimes. To trust them is to ask for disappointment.
2. The essence of a profession surely is that each member is willing to think and judge for himself. If members abdicate from such responsibility in favor of a ready-made code, they cease to command respect: in time, moreover, they will become less able to think and judge.
3. Men soaked in rules soon begin to mistake rules for reality. To quote again from Bacon: "The first distemper of learning is when men confuse words with matter". The successful accountant and auditor will be he who is best at hair-splitting and casuistry, not he who best pictures the economic facts.
4. Standard procedures may become petrified procedures.
5. Accounting figures are not docile, and do not lend themselves to standardisation. Industries differ from one another. So do firms within an industry (or, very likely, straddling several industries). The same firm may change from year to year. And the needs of users vary. So, if standards are aimed to suit the "average," they may be quite unsuitable for the fringes.
6. The wording of standards will inevitably bring difficulties of interpretation:

   > If they are broad enough to cover the variety of circumstance, they become platitudinous and admit the very disparity of treatments they were designed to avoid; if they are narrow enough to exclude this, then all sorts of hard cases will come up with a silly result.[5]

[5] Morison, *op. cit.*, page 279.

7. Standard-makers may have to bow to political pressures. Already one hears the argument that standards ought to further desirable political and social ends.[6] Most of us could answer that figures can best further desirable ends by being unbiased and accurate. Note too that a group bound by a rigid code can be manipulated by government far more readily than one where individuals act in freedom.

8. Even if a standard lays down a principle well, it may leave scope for personal estimate: we must still choose the figures to be slotted into the formulae. And many of the figures must be a subjective compromise, with plenty of room for disagreement. In most fields of physical measurement, disagreement over size will rightly suggest that the measures (or their instruments) are at fault. In contrast, we expect some disagreement between judges of (say) ice-skating, or diving, or beauty; such disagreement is far from suggesting incompetence. The estimation of wealth is probably closer to judging in a beauty competition than to physical measurement. Sooner or later, our profession will have to recognize that standards cannot guarantee identical estimates by different accountants, and that we must educate the public on the point. Until we do so, we shall continue to be fair game for our critics.

If you are disposed to agree about any of these dangers, then you must agree too that optimism would be misplaced. Standards will bring many setbacks and much disillusion.

SAFEGUARDS

The possible dangers in accounting standards could be lessened in various ways:

1. As page 13 pointed out, standards normally lead up to their conclusion with a section that explores various principles, and then backs one of them. The briefer this section, the better: authoritative pronouncements on principle are unwise. There would be a strong case for limiting a standard to a bare statement such as that the recommended procedure is already the most usual one.

2. The same reasoning tells us to be wary of the *Type 4* standards of page 15. They are more prone than *Types 1, 2,* and *3* to stray onto thin ice.

3. Pronouncements on theory are less likely to overawe us if they are described as the work of named persons. We all know that individuals can err; we tend to credit institutions with more wisdom. Therefore it would be helpful if standards were signed. Moreover a dissenting opinion adds a valuable dimension. So does an admission that an earlier standard was wrong.

---

[6] Professor David Solomons argues this point with his usual skill in "The Politicization of Accounting", *Journal of Accountancy*, November 1978, page 85.

4. A standard should not pander to political ends.
5. A standard should be explained in terms of *normal behavior*—a rule to be followed so long as it fits the facts. The accountant should be free—indeed obliged—to depart from it when he judges that it will distort the picture. Deviation from standards should of course be described and justified, where possible with a numerical estimate of its effect.

STANDARDS AND INTELLECTUAL TRAINING

My paper has (I fear) done more to list problems than to solve them. But on one point I am clear. Let us agree for argument's sake that standards—particularly if issued with safeguards—may for a time do more good than harm in the world of practice. I still find it hard to feel anything but gloom about their effect on education.

The study of standards now plays a big part in any accounting curriculum. They must have a profound influence on students, just when these are at their most impressionable and uncritical. You have only to look at an up-to-date textbook to see how much weight is given to official pronouncements, how little to the economic reality that accounts are supposed to show. Standards are a godsend to the feebler type of writer and teacher who finds it easier to recite a creed than to analyse facts and to engage in argument. If an official answer is available to a problem, why should a teacher confuse examination candidates with rival views? Thus learning by rote replaces reason; the good student of today is he who can parrot most rules. On this spare diet, accounting students are not likely to develop the habits of reasoning and skepticism that education should instill.[7]

And the student will have little cause to abandon his passive attitude when he leaves the university and enters practice. Here too he must be the respectful servant of standards. We may indeed envisage a brave new world in which an accountant spends his whole life applying rules propounded by others—unless at last, full of years and honors, he himself ascends to the Accounting Principles Board, and then for the first time must face reality.

I am sorry to end so glumly. But the trend in accounting education must make one pessimistic. For many years, academic critics viewed accounting—wrongly, to my mind—as unworthy of a place in higher studies. It got in at last. Now that we are substituting rule-of-thumb for reason, one must sadly admit that our critics were right.

QUESTIONS AND ANSWERS

Question: Professor Baxter, I am particularly intrigued with your analogy with the other professions and their failure to develop standards such as the

---

[7] If this is right, then academic bodies such as the American Accounting Association are naively self-destructive in swimming with the tide—and indeed adding to the output of Holy Writ.

accounting profession has been developing. I'd like to get some elaboration on your thinking on this. Is it not true that the medical profession and the engineering professions are basically based on the physical natural sciences whereas accounting, in essence, is a social science? The interplay in, let us say, medicine, is between the doctor and a single patient, and of course, with the engineer, he might reach more people in the impact of his work, but the accountant really deals with almost the entire world. There is a whole mass of potential in existing investors, and potential in existing creditors that have to deal with an enterprise and they are looking for some order, for some discipline, for some assurance that the representations that they deal with have met the standards agreed upon by people in the know. What is the impact of this on your comparison?

Answer: Well, it's a nice problem whether there is a fundamental difference here. As I said, I think it rather depends on which bit of an accountant's work you are thinking of. The great argument on your side would be, surely, that for the benefit of readers of accounts there should be some uniformity. The instance I cited, that of Congress dealing with oil companies, is perhaps the most persuasive that I can give. But this leads on to the thought that if we all do the same thing we shall in some instances not be giving the best possible picture. As I said, what suits the average won't suit the fringes; and I think we have to see whether experience suggests in the end that figures disciplined in the wrong way are better than ones which are not comparable but nevertheless do show each company in a clearer light. Is it better, in other words, that there are second-rate figures, all prepared on the same basis, or first-rate figures prepared on different bases? This, I think, is one of the questions to which time alone will show the answer.

Comment: Prof. Briloff. Professor Baxter, your presentation was nothing short of inspiring, and as I commented on a number of occasions to Professor Mellman, who was sitting next to me, as a matter of fact, Professor Baxter, I know of only one Saxe lecturer with whom I agree more than I agree with you. I am afraid that as we talk it out you'll see the point I now want to make. It may very well be that the critical flaw lay in the confusion of tongues, and by that I mean by using the very word 'standards' for the kind of mischief that's being perpetrated up in Stamford. No, we know how the term began. It was the word opted for by the Wheat Committee, probably inspired by Professor David Solomons, who undoubtedly read the work by Professors Paton and Littleton, going back some 40 years ago, an inspired work called "An Introduction to Corporate Accounting Standards," where Professors Paton and Littleton made the point that the Wheat Committee study made, that 'principles' is a presumptuous term when used in accounting, therefore we ought to have standards, and they explained it in the most beautiful, soaring terms as to why standards were appropriate. But then, Professors Paton and Littleton made abundantly clear, that standards are not to be implemented as rules. They are, instead, to be guides to more effective, better action. Now what's happened up at the FASB, like with the Accounting

Principles Board, is this pretentiousness of saying that rules are standards, and I believe we fall into their trap by pretending that we are talking about standards. I submit that every profession, including those that you enumerated have standards. As a matter of fact, the very terms that you used, Professor Baxter, scientific method and all that that implies, indicates standards to the scientist. We know the Hippocratic oath, standards for the physician. We know the philosophy of the judicial process, standard for the judiciary. But they are to be severely distinguished from rules. And so it is, that what's been happening is that we've been perpetrating mischief by setting forth a catechism of rules which then are capable of being bent and defied and all the time we are saying to the world, we are moving with standards. Professor Baxter, in sum, I believe that the problem with accounting can best be summarized by saying, it's not a matter of accounting principle, but a matter of principles of the accountants.

Keep It Simple

Walter Schuetze
Chief Accountant, Securities and Exchange Commission

The Financial Accounting Standards Board is getting a lot of advice these days. The advice comes from the American Institute of Certified Public Accountants, The Business Roundtable, the Financial Executives Institute, the chairmen of the large accounting firms, the Financial Analysts Policy Committee, the Securities and Exchange Commission and its staff, and banking and thrift regulators. I will add my voice to the chorus.

My theme (plea) in this piece is for the FASB to Keep It Simple.

Some of the FASB's recent and not-so-recent statements are far too complicated. FASB Statement 96 (Income Taxes), Statement 87 (Pensions), and Statement 13 (Leases) are examples of mind-numbing complexity. Those statements are so complicated that ordinary people cannot understand and apply them. The best analogy that I can think of is one of automobiles. When I look at FASB Statement 96 on Income Taxes, I see a Formula I racing machine. One has to be a Fittipaldi or Luyendyk to drive the racing machine at Indianapolis at an average speed of 167 or 186 mph. Most of us can handle and afford only a production-line automobile, and the speed limit for us is 55 mph (65 mph in certain states) not something in excess of 160 mph.

How did we get here? How did accounting standards get so complex?

Some of the responsibility for the complexity lies with the Securities and Exchange Commission and its staff. *Regulation S-X, Regulation S-K*, the various

From *Accounting Horizons* (June 1991), pp. 113–117. Reprinted by permission of the American Accounting Association and the author. Copyright © 1991 by the American Accounting Association. [This article was written before Schuetze joined the SEC as chief accountant.—Editors]

registration forms, and periodic reporting forms with which public companies must comply are complicated. Over the years, the SEC has layered complexity on top of complexity. The SEC's staff for years has written detailed letters of comments to registrants; it is said that the staff is picking the bugs from the bed linens. Some of the complexity arises because transactions are complex. However, by far most of the recent complexity arises because preparers of financial statements and their CPA firms have asked for it. An example is pension accounting (FASB Statement 87). Pension accounting is complicated because most preparers, and their CPA firms, are unwilling to see changes in market values of plan assets and settlement values of plan liabilities entered into earnings as those values change. Spread those changes, they say. A large part of FASB Statement 87 is devoted to smoothing the hills and valleys of change. FASB Statement 106 on accounting for postretirement benefits other than pensions is complex for the same reason. Income tax accounting (FASB Statement 96) is complicated because the auditing profession was unhappy with a simpler rule that left unanswered a lot of details and because old APB Opinion 11 does not fit into the FASB's Conceptual Framework and had to be changed for that reason.

We have the Emerging Issues Task Force because our current accounting rules are not detailed enough to answer all the accounting questions that arise in a complex business world and the independent auditing profession wants detailed answers to respond to pressures from clients to do things in a less-than-conservative way.

The Board needs to Keep It Simple in future statements. But, the Board cannot just set forth a simple standard, state the objective of the standard, and leave it to the judgment of preparers and their CPAs to implement the standard as it now is in vogue to suggest.[1] That approach will not work. The world needs simple bright-line rules.

We have tried the simple approach that requires judgment. For example, in APB Opinion 5, the Accounting Principles Board said that lessees should recognize on their balance sheet those leases that are in substance installment purchases of property—those that result in creation of a material equity in the property. That was a general standard, requiring judgment to implement. It did not work. Very few leased assets and corresponding lease obligations were recognized by lessees. As a result, the Financial Accounting Standards Board issued very detailed, complex rules on accounting for leases in FASB Statement 13. But now, Statement 13, even with all of its amendments and interpretations, does not work. And, to make things worse, the Securities and Exchange Commission's staff and the Emerging Issues Task Force keep adding layers of complexity to it. The Accounting Principles Board in APB

---

[1] I have heard it said at meetings of the Financial Accounting Standards Advisory Council, "Write simple rules and leave it to the preparer and auditor of the financial statements to use their judgment." What happens under that approach is that the first time that a preparer does not like its CPA's answer, then a way will be found to take the question to the Emerging Issues Task Force in an attempt to overturn the CPA's answer.

ding layers of complexity to it. The Accounting Principles Board in APB Opinion 9 on earnings per share said that an outstanding security is a residual security (now called a *common stock equivalent*) if it derives a major portion of its value from its conversion rights or its common stock characteristics. That was a general standard requiring judgment to implement. It did not work. The CPA firms could not agree on the meaning of "major portion." Some thought 90 percent, others 51 percent. APB Opinion 9 had to be replaced by APB Opinion 15, which is far too complex and needs to be simplified. The predecessor rule (Accounting Research Bulletin 48) to the pooling-of-interest rules in APB Opinion 16 was simple but judgmental. It did not work. And now APB Opinion 16 is not working because its detailed, complex rules do not cover new situations not thought of when it was issued in 1970.

FASB Statements 77 (transfers of receivables) and 80 (futures contracts) are fairly simple but leave a lot of room for judgment. Neither one of them works in practice. What is a sale and what is a financing under Statement 77 is judgmental. A fairly large segment of Wall Street earns a living figuring out how to best the CPA firm and Statement 77. Statement 80 allows for so much judgment about correlation and anticipated transactions that preparers, auditors, and banking and thrift regulators cannot agree on what to do in practice. (One thrift, Franklin Savings, and its regulator, the Office of Thrift Supervision, are in court in a disagreement over how to interpret FASB Statement 80.)

Let's look at some simple, nonjudgmental standards that have been successful. FASB Statement 14 on segments says that if 10 percent or more of total revenues are from a segment, then data for the segment shall be reported separately. No ifs, ands, or buts; 10 percent is 10 percent and FASB Statement 14 has been successful. (Except that many users of financial statements would like segment reporting on a quarterly basis, one seldom hears about problems with Statement 14. Could it be that the success of a standard is measurable by the lack of complaint about it?) FASB Statement 85 says that a convertible bond that has a cash yield of less than two-thirds of the long-term corporate bond rate at the time of its issuance is a common stock equivalent for purpose of earnings per share computations. No ifs, and, or buts; two-thirds of that bond rate is easy to compute and that standard has been successful. APB Opinion 15 says, in a footnote, that if the dilutive feature of a convertible bond or preferred stock or option or warrant does not reduce earnings per share by at least 3 percent, then fully diluted earnings per share need not be reported. The 3 percent rule has been effective. It's simple, and it works.

How might such a simple yet effective bright-line be applied to two live recognition and measurement problems?

Lease accounting by lessees will never be right or correct insofar as all the interested parties (lessees, CPAs, the SEC's staff, and users of financial statements) are concerned. FASB Statement 13, with all of its amendments and interpretations, is not the answer because only a few of us know how to apply Statement 13. (And sometimes we don't know what's "right" until we ring up the SEC's staff and check with them.) We cannot explain the result. We need simple bright-line rules to fix that problem, at least as to lessees.

Either capitalize (recognize) all lease obligations or none of them. If all leases are to be capitalized, specify the rate to be used to discount the lessee's contractual cash outflows: for example, use the 10-year U.S. government bond rate to discount the cash payments. That rate will not correspond exactly with the lessee's incremental borrowing rate, but there is no harm done by using that rate as a surrogate for the lessee's incremental borrowing rate—it's only an estimate, not perfection. We need not measure things to the nth degree. The light is not worth the cost of the candle. Users of financial statements will understand that approach; it is easy to explain and understand.

Deferred tax accounting under FASB Statement 96 is incredibly complex, what with scheduling and hypothetical tax planning strategies for every temporary difference in every taxing jurisdiction. If we must have deferred tax accounting, and I question whether we should,[2] why not just assume that all of the assets are sold for cash at their book amounts and all of the liabilities are settled for cash at their book amounts and the corporation files a final tax return on the day following the balance sheet; the amount of tax payable or recoverable on that hypothetical final tax return would be the deferred tax to be reported in the corporation's balance sheet. Simple. No scheduling. No hypothetical tax planning strategies. Under this approach, there would be no debate about whether to discount the tax asset or liability; no discounting would be necessary. Moreover, that simple answer could be explained to and even understood by ordinary people. The results of APB Opinion 11 and FASB Statement 96 cannot be explained and understood.

We could transport the idea of simplicity to the conceptual framework. Look at the FASB's definition of an asset and its characteristics:

25. Assets are probable[18] future economic benefits obtained or controlled by a particular entity as a result of past transactions or events.
26. An asset has three essential characteristics: (a) it embodies a probable future benefit that involves a capacity, singly or in combination with other assets, to contribute directly or indirectly to future net cash inflows, (b) a particular entity can obtain the benefit and control others' access to it, and (c) the transaction or other event giving rise to the entity's right to or control of the benefit has already occurred. Assets commonly have other features that help identify them—for example, assets may be acquired at

[18] Probable is used with its usual general meaning, rather than in a specific accounting or technical sense (such as that in FASB Statement No. 5, *Accounting for Contingencies*, par. 3), and refers to that which can reasonably be expected or believed on the basis of available evidence or logic but is neither certain nor proved (*Webster's New World Dictionary of the American Language*, 2d college ed. [New York: Simon and Schuster, 1982], p. 1132). Its inclusion in the definition is intended to acknowledge that business and other economic activities occur in an environment characterized by uncertainty in which few outcomes are certain (pars. 44–48).

---

[2] I do not like hypothetical, as-if accounting. Deferred tax accounting is hypothetical, as-if accounting.

a cost[19] and they may be tangible, exchangeable, or legally enforceable. However, those features are not essential characteristics of assets. Their absence, by itself, is not sufficient to preclude an item's qualifying as an asset. That is, assets may be acquired without cost, they may be intangible, and although not exchangeable they may be usable by the entity in producing or distributing other goods or services. Similarly, although the ability of an entity to obtain benefit from an asset and to control others' access to it generally rests on a foundation of legal rights, legal enforceability of a claim to the benefit is not a prerequisite for a benefit to qualify as an asset if the entity has the ability to obtain and control the benefit in other ways.

[19] Cost is the sacrifice incurred in economic activities—that which is given up or forgone to consume, to save, to exchange, to produce, and so forth. For example, the value of cash or other resources given up (or the present value of an obligation incurred) in exchange for a resource measures the cost of the resource acquired. Similarly, the expiration of future benefits caused by using a resource in production is the cost of using it.

Egad! That is mind-boggling stuff. Most accountants do not understand it. Ordinary people are mystified by it. We have not been able to solve accounting problems by using that definition. Almost any expenditure fits into that definition because it does not discriminate. We need a simple definition. How about defining assets as CASH, contractual claims to CASH, and things that can be sold for CASH?[3] That definition would do away with goodwill, preopening costs, employee training costs, and other junk now called assets.[4] The current definition is an abstraction. Under that definition, the asset that I call a truck is not the FASB's asset. The FASB's asset is the present value of the net cash flows that truck will produce by hauling coal or lumber or steel, *viz.* the "probable future economic benefit." I call it a truck. Trucks can be sold for CASH. Abstractions—probable future economic benefits—cannot be sold for CASH. Only real things can be sold for CASH. Only real things can be assets. Mario Gabelli, John Neff, and Martin Zweig will understand and appreciate that approach.[5]

Small and medium-sized companies will understand and appreciate that approach. Many FASB standards are so complex that most small and medium-sized companies do not have the staff to implement the standards. And they do not want to pay their CPA firms to help accumulate the information that is used only to prepare financial statements, but is not understood by or useful to the owners of the company and their bankers. The Alliance of

[3] This definition says nothing about how we might measure assets—cost or current value. I think it ought to be current value, *i.e.*, the price of the assets in a current sale for CASH, at least for financial instruments.
[4] We would have to fix FASB Statement 87 on pensions to do away with intangible assets that arise under that Statement. Deferred tax assets would disappear.
[5] Mario Gabelli (Gabelli Asset Management Company), John Neff (Vanguard's Windsor Fund), and Martin Zweig (Zweig Fund) are investment portfolio managers.

Practicing CPAs has called for a "moratorium on new [FASB] standards" and/ or a "separate, simplified set of accounting principles and standards for nonpublic companies."[6] Small and medium-sized companies and their CPA firms cannot afford to follow the FASB's lead on complex standards.

International standard setters also will not follow the FASB's lead in issuing complex, detailed standards. If the International Accounting Standards Committee were to issue a standard as detailed as FASB Statement 96 on income taxes, IASC would lose its following, which is beginning to grow. That approach would be not only foolhardy but also suicidal for IASC.

Can you imagine a men's shoe manufacturer in Lyon, France who needs money wanting to come to the United States to issue debt or equity securities or American Depository Receipts? This French company has been preparing its financial statements using French francs and the French language and French generally accepted accounting principles and has a French auditor who practices only in France. When the management of the French shoe manufacturer goes to issue securities in the U.S, it will learn that it must reconcile its net income and shareholders' equity to that which would result under U.S. generally accepted accounting principles. The management of the shoe manufacturer will learn that in order to do that reconciliation it and its auditor will have to learn the FASB's accounting pronouncements and those of its predecessors, the Emerging Issues Task Force consensuses, and perhaps even the utterances of the Accounting Standards Executive Committee of the American Institute of Certified Public Accountants. The management of the French company will be dismayed and discouraged. The management will say, "We make shoes; we just want to raise a few dollars; we don't want to be fodder to be crushed by your accounting machines; we will go to Hong Kong or Singapore or Geneva to raise money." Repeat that for shoe makers in Frankfurt, Osaka, Vancouver, and Edinburgh and you begin to see how stifling the complexity is here in the U.S.

Accounting standards have to be implemented by ordinary people. Financial reports are used by ordinary people. The standards and the results of applying the standards have to be understandable to ordinary people. Beyond understandability of new standards, the cost of change to a new standard and the cost of continued compliance should not exceed the benefit. This cost-benefit test is a judgment call, and my judgment is that we have to change the way we write standards. It's perhaps acceptable to have as an objective the construction of a Formula I racing machine, and to state the objective of a standard in that fashion. But, let's remember some practical constraints: automobiles for ordinary people are built on production lines, not in hot-rod high-tech garages. We drive our cars to work, school, and Friday night softball games. The speed limit for us is 55/65 mph on the highway, 30 in town, not 167 or 186 mph. Keep It Simple.

If we keep it simple, then the users of the information will have information that they can use. (What can users do with an intangible asset arising

---

[6] Quoted from the November 30, 1990 issue of *Public Accounting Report*.

from smoothing out pension expense except to ignore the asset?) The smaller CPA firms and their clients will be able to keep up with the rest of the world. Preparers of financial statements can stop fussing over things that cost a lot of money and have little usefulness, like the "corridor" in pension accounting and scheduling temporary differences for deferred income tax computations, and do things to improve the quality of U.S. products in the world marketplace. And the FASB will stand a better chance of promoting its ideas in Australia, Canada, France, Germany, Great Britain, Italy, Japan, Russia, Pacific Rim countries, and at the IASC.

U.S. Accounting:
Creating an Uneven Playing Field?

Linda Keslar

Britain's Midland Bank, swamped by some bad Third World debt, reported a loss of $408 million in its native country last year.

But Midland also files financial information in the United States due to its U.S. operations and stock trading. Forced to follow U.S. accounting standards when it published its numbers in the United States, the $408 million loss reported in Britain ballooned to $868 million—a difference of more than 100%.

That differential is enough to raise most eyebrows in business and finance. And that's just what is happening. Many people think financial statements are losing credibility as deviations of this kind continue.

In fact, increasing controversy surrounds the methods accounting communities of different countries use to arrive at numbers. Issues being raised include what it costs business both directly and indirectly to comply and whether U.S. companies in particular are at a disadvantage to European and Asian competitors. It's no surprise a number of executives are asking if global standards can't be harmonized.

As in most things financial, the United States has more rules on the books than anyone—so many more that some of the country's top executives are crying foul.

Critics say U.S. standards are not only too cumbersome and too costly, but downright unfair compared to those their foreign competitors have to follow. That means U.S. companies face an uneven playing field abroad just

From *Corporate Risk Management* (February 1991), pp. 20–25. Reprinted by permission of Oster Communications Inc. Copyright © 1991 by Oster Communications, Inc., 219 Parkade, P.O. Box 6, Cedar Falls, IA 50613.

as other obstacles to fair competition, such as onerous trade barriers, are being eliminated.

If the critics are right, accounting standards, some say, need to be re-tooled either to provide U.S. competitors with an edge or to make them comparable with those of other nations. Others say standards should be objective measurements, not instruments designed to affect economic events.

And then there's a camp mostly made up of accountants, regulators, politicians and academics who say nothing should be changed. In fact, they think new rules should be added and the current criticism is generated by the self-interests of business.

With so many in the United States expressing different viewpoints, U.S. regulators are stepping in, worried that the nation can hardly influence other codes unless it gets its own act together.

"U.S. companies are required to provide more disclosure on more sub-jects than any other country," agrees Philip Lochner, a commissioner at the Securities and Exchange Commission (SEC), which oversees the standards. "The question is can we bring the rest of the world along and what adjust-ments should we be making?"

At this point, foreign regulators are hardly anxious to imitate a code that is causing so much controversy.

"Foreign countries don't want American rules forced on them," explains Allan Cook, a financial executive with Shell International Petroleum Co. in London. He is studying some of these issues in the United Kingdom. "They want to understand the principles of the rules and pick up what they need for broader application."

In fact, some foreigners are downright critical of the American way.

"The United States is just too bottom-line conscious, an unfortunate preoccupation," says Warren McGregor, an analyst with the Australian Ac-counting Research Foundation in Melbourne. "Australian multinationals are aware of a need for harmonizing our standards with those internationally. But we want our financial statements to reflect economic reality, the impact of events as they occur. We don't want the emphasis just on the bottom line."

For many years, the United States was considered the leader in the development of a comprehensive financial accounting and reporting system. But as foreign economies have grown more advanced, with deeper capital markets of their own and expanding public sectors that demand more infor-mation, they are concocting accounting practices that fit their needs. Thus, U.S. standards are under more scrutiny as countries decide either to copy U.S. rules or invent their own.

The International Accounting Standards Committee (IASC) has issued 29 standards—hardly an accountant's rulesheet of information—with which many foreign multinationals also comply. They are providing an alternative blueprint for foreign regulators looking to update their standards.

Currently, most foreign accounting rules are perceived as less costly to business and certainly less stringent than those in the United States. Even

SEC Chairman Richard Breeden conceded in a letter sent to the Business Roundtable, a group of chief executives, that "some accounting standards developed outside the United States may be superior to U.S. standards."

Complaints from Corporate America about U.S. reporting requirements have become so frequent that the "Supreme Court on Fifth Street" has launched a broad inquiry into ways to reduce the complexity and cost of these rules. This review is part of a broader SEC mandate to examine the competitiveness of U.S. business and U.S. capital markets.

One problem is that fewer and fewer foreign companies are issuing public stocks and bonds in the United States, a sign, some contend, of cumbersome filing requirements. Moreover, because of the code, U.S. companies say they have to spend too much to come up with statistics no one needs—money they say would be better spent in marketing or production. They say the resulting numbers make them look less healthy financially than their competitors overseas.

"Here you have an international marketplace, with companies dealing in many countries, all with different accounting principles," Lochner maintains. "What we all hope for is more agreement on these principles so that the United States is operating on a level playing field."

Of particular interest to the SEC review are domestic issues relating to accounting for income tax, postretirement employment benefits, pensions and leases. These rules are set by the Financial Accounting Standards Board (FASB), a privately financed organization the SEC recognizes as the official accounting standard setter.

Some recent FASB guidelines, corporate executives say, are letting even more air out of their bottom lines. In fact, in a recent letter to the SEC's Lochner, Citibank Chairman John S. Reed says that while the rest of the world moves closer to "meaningful financial reporting, accounting in the United States has taken some serious steps in the wrong direction."

Reed, head of the Business Roundtable's task force on accounting issues, has been a major voice urging reform of these standards, saying they are more theoretical than pragmatic measures of a company's performance and produce many statistics ordinary investors don't use.

The FASB says its job is just to ensure financial disclosure, to make financial data comparable among similar companies and to require companies to disclose the true costs and risks of doing business. Critics claim the quasi-agency is bogged down by technical detail.

"The FASB will compromise anything for technical purity," grouses one chief financial executive.

For example, a pending rule on accounting for retirement benefits other than pensions would require companies for the first time to show on their books the present and future costs of benefits such as medical and insurance coverage for employees after retirement. The extra cost of this rule on company balance sheets has been estimated at more than $200 billion.

"This could result in some dramatic changes in debt-to-equity ratios," confides a top economist at the SEC. "What we need to ask is if these rules lead to a better depiction of reality faced by these firms and their shareholders or creditors."

Among the most sensitive international accounting issues U.S. companies say needs addressing is how goodwill is measured. British firms, for example, have the option of expensing goodwill in the year of the acquisition. U.S. firms are required to expense goodwill for up to 40 years. The result is that UK companies tend to have a capital structure that appears relatively weaker and earnings that look better than those of competitors who amortize goodwill over a period of time.

Critics allege the amortization requirement has been a major factor in the dramatic rise in acquisitions of U.S. companies by foreign investors. The IASC has sought a compromise between the two by proposing mandatory capitalization of goodwill with five-year amortization preferred and 20 years the absolute limit. The FASB, mired in other issues, has yet to formally comment on this idea.

But FASB Chairman Dennis R. Beresford asks: "How many companies would see that as worse than either the U.S. or UK practice?"

Other differences in international accounting practices include everything from accounting for the capitalization of leases (the United States requires it, but Japan, France and Germany do not) and recognizing future tax benefits (the United States doesn't allow this, but German and Swiss companies can bury in hidden reserves). These small differences add up.

"U.S. companies are held to higher standards to such an extent that it becomes a competitive issue when you're competing with a company overseas that is held to much different, less complex standards," adds one banker.

Nevertheless, proponents of the accounting standards say the rules should simply paint a neutral portrait of a company's health. The economic effect of those standards, such as whether foreign companies find them too cumbersome or whether they keep companies from raising financing in the United States, should not be the issue.

Most securities analysts likely agree U.S. rules don't tell enough about a company.

"Analysts are concerned that the SEC is going to dilute U.S. accounting disclosure standards to make U.S. markets more palatable to foreign companies looking to raise capital. Rule 144A is a step in that direction," explains Patricia A. McConnell, a tax analyst and managing director at Bear Stearns & Co. Rule 144A is a new ruling on private placements that loosens filing requirements for issuers.

The criticism of U.S. standards is rising just when pressure is building for international harmonization. As financial flows have grown more interwoven and financial instruments more innovative, demand has exploded for standards facilitating cross-border capital movements reflected in techniques like foreign currency swaps.

Even the United States has failed to keep pace with the kaleidoscopic variety of financial products, particularly when it comes to hedging and speculative purposes. Because many treasury operations have become profit centers, the potential distortion on balance sheets is mushrooming, according to some accountants.

"There could be a difference of over $100 million in how we book a product like a swap and how our competitor might. That's how much gray margin there is with the current rules," confides one U.S. banker. "And with foreign banks, forget it!"

John E. Stewart, a partner at Arthur Andersen in Chicago who is on a global task force examining these issues, adds: "How to account for financial instruments has the potential of becoming the most complex and controversial project government authorities may have to deal with."

Until recently foreign companies—and foreign governments and regulators—have been less concerned about accounting procedures and requirements.

"The demand for detail in U.S. disclosure has been shaped by the highly developed markets here compared to other places," says George Dallas, an analyst with Standard & Poor's in London, who has grown accustomed to working with financial statements shaped by varying country standards. "The philosophy is, 'We'll put up the money and we need to know what's going on.' In Europe, the banks are strong and pervasive financiers, and there has been, at least up to now, less need for a company to bare its soul to the public."

But foreign attitudes are being shaped by similar forces: a demand for more disclosure as new investors enter the picture.

"Companies are going to have to raise capital outside their boundaries, particularly in Germany," Dallas say. "I think the trend is away from the same degree of secrecy to more complex disclosure."

Among those who appear to be lobbying for somewhat looser restrictions are investment banks.

Even the accounting watchdog subcommittee of Congress, headed by Rep. John Dingell (D-Mich.), has urged the SEC to look the other way when it comes to the FASB. In a letter to Breeden, Dingell says he is concerned the FASB "is the target of an external political pressure campaign by certain elements of the business community" that intend to "influence the substance of FASB pronouncements."

There are hard-line objections to the United States making major adjustments to its code, at least for competitive reasons.

"You don't need to compare accounting standards from country to country to determine how a company is doing," says Roman L. Weil, University of Chicago accounting professor. "The market discriminates."

Others disagree. Susan Kroski-Grafter, assistant controller at AT&T's New Jersey offices, has been studying international standards. She says she is overwhelmed by how great some code differences are. The market won't fairly discriminate, she says, due to the many conflicts in measurement.

"I know financial professionals say they look through the accounting rules anyway to focus on the true economics, but what I don't think they are aware of is how economics can be obscured by one form of accounting vs.

another. Only a highly knowledgeable person can ferret all this out," Kroski-Grafter says.

Ironically, pressure is mounting on FASB from regulators and legislators to force greater disclosures on financial risk for financial institutions. The pressure makes political sense given the collapse of the thrift industry and Third World loan problems. In fact, the FASB has launched an extensive new project to figure out how to account for global financial instruments, be they swaps or futures.

Without clear standards, it's difficult to understand the financial health of an institution or, by extension, of the entire banking and thrift industries.

This project is sounding alarms in some quarters. While the FASB has not made a formal ruling, one recommendation coming out of the ongoing study is that companies set more current values on a myriad of financial instruments. Historical cost, transaction-based accounting—the accepted technique that is the basis for U.S. standards—is not timely enough to catch the effects of price and interest rate changes that the more sophisticated financial instruments are designed to manage. Marking to market these products (accounting for them at their current market value on a regular basis) might help.

While many agree accounting for financial instruments is a mess, marking to market provides no quick solutions.

"How to account for marketable securities is dependent on whether it's debt or equity, what industry the company is in, what its intentions are in regard to the security, among other things," Stewart explains. "It's inescapably screwed up."

Manufacturing companies, for example, get to book their marketable equity securities at the lower cost or market value. Banks and some thrifts carry short-term equity portfolios at the lower of cost or market and long-term debt portfolios at cost. Industry executives say marking to market is time consuming, expensive and unworkable because certain instruments (like private placement bonds) by definition have no public market and because results are subjective and can't be compared.

Marking to market, however, would dilute the need for hedge accounting, which now is even more complicated and widely inconsistent. For example, both FASB statements 52 and 80 provide for hedge accounting. Both are designed to achieve some symmetry between accounting for the hedging instrument—forwards, futures, options and swaps—and the assets, liabilities or transactions being hedged. But the rules get inconsistent when transactions do not meet their specific criteria.

One problem is that the users of hedges don't necessarily tie the hedge to a specific asset, so there's no easy quantification of a gain or loss in a specific period. Thus, there is a potential mismatch of earnings from the underlying asset and the hedge.

"A multinational usually has a large portfolio that includes Treasury bills, loans, CDs (certificates of deposit), commercial paper, etc.," says Loretta Moseman, a risk expert at Citibank. "It's a very complicated procedure to show a direct correlation between one of those instruments and a swap."

Instead, accountants rely on a hodge-podge of opinions that have become market practice for instrument dealers.

"I think what's happened is when rules don't fit the circumstances, we tend to come up with something else that makes sense," says Matt Singleton, a partner with Arthur Andersen. Swap dealers in the United States and in the UK are marking swaps to market, although Singleton says in Germany and Switzerland, there's the "greatest degree of resistance against market valuation. Theirs is a conservative, cost-based approach that recognizes income over the life of the swap instead of at the front end."

Uses of contract rate swaps, though, are a different story.

"We don't have rules for swaps, so we have to interpret rules written for futures and apply them to swaps," Moseman says. "And a lot of people say we don't like futures rules, we don't agree with them and we don't use them."

Within regulatory boundaries, she concedes, "We make up our own rules."

Many companies would like to use options to hedge future earnings risk on foreign currency cash flows. Many foreign companies commonly hedge earnings with options. But the SEC questioned this technique in a controversial ruling last year. Options can be used only if they are marked to market as a speculative activity. The rules simply don't allow hedging of anticipated transactions not firmly committed.

"Marking to market, though, adds a lot of potential volatility to operating performance," Stewart notes.

These kinds of constraints are discouraging companies from using many hedging instruments in a variety of scenarios, for better or worse.

"The financial accounting results are discouraging, and companies won't enter into transactions where the accounting result does not reflect the economics of what they're doing," Stewart says.

The experts say the United States and the international community are years away from real standards, though the FASB and the International Accounting Standards Committee have set up a special financial instruments task force to try.

"We are entering a new era with a potential mission of unknown extent," FASB's Beresford has told his colleagues.

So far, they have concluded that to account for the complicated instruments, they first must figure out how to account for the simple ones. FASB has isolated a half dozen instruments it sees as basic, the taproots of more complicated products in the United States. But many foreign markets have just begun to develop the basic products, much less accounting procedures for them or for hybrids.

"There's a sharp learning curve for everyone involved," says McGregor.

Even Beresford questions how involved the FASB should be globally, given the domestic turmoil. Moreover, he ponders what the FASB's position should be.

"Does the recommendation of a special advisory group mean the FASB should sell American—try to increase its influence in international standard-setting activities?" he asked a group at a global conference. "Or buy foreign—consider the conclusions drawn by standard setters in other countries?"

The global search for those answers is likely to last for some time to come.

Will 'FASBEE' Pinch Your Bottom Line?

Carol J. Loomis
Fortune

Warning of "impending crisis," Congressman J. J. "Jake" Pickle opened hearings this fall on the health care liabilities of private employers. In minutes, the Texas Democrat had a monster figure of $221 billion floating in the air: the General Accounting Office's estimate of the present value of retirement health benefits so far promised to active and retired employees. In minutes more, Pickle was looking benignly down at two witnesses from the Financial Accounting Standards Board, or FASB. Drawling out the board's nickname, the Congressman confessed: "I had heard about Frisbees but not fasbees." But in the area of health benefits, he said, "all at once you have become a household word."

Hyperbole, yes. Few Americans have ever heard of this nongovernmental body that sets the rules for corporate financial statements. But in the halls of business, wherever bean counters and their bosses gather, they know FASB well. Endowed with power by the Securities and Exchange Commission and charged with the narrowing of accounting alternatives, the board's seven members are the high priests of their discipline. "Ah, FASB," says a senior partner of a Big Eight accounting firm. "It sits up there by itself, answering only to God."

And, ah, is there ever restlessness below. It is FASB, damn its hide, that is proposing to make corporations open up the closets in which this $221 billion health liability—or, some say, a much larger one—has been hidden, and put the obligation on their financial statements. It is FASB, moreover, that will answer other emotion-fraught questions: Should financial instruments, from receivables to bond portfolios to bank loans—including troubled Latin American debt—be stated at market value rather than historical cost? Should corporations that issue executive stock options have to start "booking" a cost for these on their income statements? The very thought steams many executives, one of whom recently showed his disgust in a Freudian slip: "If it ain't booked," he said, "don't fix it."

To all that FASB may do in the future, add the pain already inflicted: a string of new reporting requirements that amount, says business, to an expensive, oppressive "standards overload." A more graphic description comes from Edmund Coulson, chief accountant of the SEC. Collectively, he says, the new standards are "the big belch."

Among those tasting its effects are insurance and banking executives, who are wrestling with new standards particular to their businesses. Three other recent and radical FASB pronouncements are roiling a wider constituency. One standard, a bow to a growing preoccupation of investors, has created a new cash flows statement. Look for it in 1988 annual reports. Also evident there will be the effects of another standard requiring companies to fully consolidate the books of their finance subsidiaries—General Motors Acceptance Corp., for example—with those of the parent. Had the standard been applicable in 1987, GM's revenues would have been reported as $114 billion instead of $102 billion, and its assets and liabilities would have ballooned.

The most detested new standard of all is one on accounting for income taxes. Many corporations both disagree with the theory behind it and think of it as insanely, onerously complex. FASB, itself a tad bothered by some remaining technical questions, is proposing to put off the standard's effective date by a year, to 1990. But business wants more than that. At a recent Financial Executives Institute conference, Dennis R. Beresford, 50, the tall, lean chairman of FASB, was asked: "Is it possible that the board will rescind this standard in its entirety forever?" Laughter ensued, but Beresford politely flattened hopes: "If I had to place a bet, I would say no."

That's the sort of tough message FASB has often given business—so far living to fight another day. But the corporate community helped kill off two predecessors and in the past couple of years talk of doing the same to FASB has risen as well. The center of discontent is the Business Roundtable, which has sent some of its lead warriors into this battle. The Roundtable's accounting spear from 1985 to 1987 was General Motors Chairman Roger Smith, who was aggressively critical of both FASB and some of its basic objectives. Said Smith, "I believe a lot of good, sensible business practice has been sacrificed on the altar of uniformity."

After Smith came Roundtable lance John Reed, head of Citicorp. For the past year, Reed has spent a lot of his time promoting the notion that FASB is out of control and recklessly unmindful of the costs it is laying on corporations. "An important subsegment" of the Roundtable's executive committee, says Reed, would just as soon scuttle FASB and return standard setting to the SEC. But he himself is pushing a private-sector remedy: some sort of new oversight body, partly composed of businessmen, to monitor the agenda of this rogue accounting body.

Often the outcries of executives focus on the higher operating expenses that attend most new standards, since these may require the capture of new data or a reworking of existing information. But the more fundamental, if sometimes unspoken, grievance concerns the noncash, purely bookkeeping effects—typically bad—that new standards have on reported earnings. Joseph Connor, a top partner of Price Waterhouse and a veteran critic of the board, shakes his head. "A partner of mine says the board seems to hate income like a Southern farmer hates boll weevils."

The board's standards have also added to the volatility of reported earnings. By eliminating one accounting alternative after another, FASB has gradually restricted the ability of managements to smooth their results from one year to the next. The board thinks of itself as simply injecting more realism into financial statements. CEOs see themselves as being robbed of flexibility. Donald Kirk, chairman of FASB before Beresford, says this is particularly maddening to executives because they see earnings as their "personal scorecard," which the numbers just may be in performance-based pay schemes.

On Wall Street some view the feuding between business and FASB as beside the point and having little to do with financial reality. Clearly, the Street's leveraged-buyout artists look right through the published financial statements and see a different picture: a scene in which brand names are worth billions, bad debts are always marked down, and retiree health benefits are sometimes deal-breakers. Does that make the published figures irrelevant for financial engineers or sophisticated investors? Not really, for the findings there are the starting point for all they do.

Today's furor about accounting traces back to the 1930s. That's when the SEC, eager to get the standard-setting monkey off its back, asked the private sector to articulate what we now know as generally accepted accounting principles. The job went to groups drawn from the accounting profession. In the 1960s, Washington put the heat on the then reigning body, the Accounting Principles Board, for its fecklessness in setting rules for mergers. The corporate community joined in to complain that its outside auditing firms—whose partners ran the APB—weren't sufficiently attuned to the concerns of business. Out of the commotion, in 1973, came FASB, new and "independent."

According to the plan, the views of businessmen, accountants, security analysts, and everyone else were to be carefully considered by FASB. The board has since constructed a system of elaborate due process that tends to chew up years. FASB publishes exposure drafts of its standards, solicits comment letters and receives hundreds, holds hearings, and explains in its final standards why it decided what it did. When the board meets—every Wednesday, at its office in Norwalk, Connecticut—it does so "in sunshine," deliberating under the eye of any who care to attend. The same openness applies to meetings of the Emerging Issues Task Force, an FASB offshoot set up four years ago to deal with technical questions crying to be answered promptly.

From the start, FASB's independence was to derive primarily from the makeup of its board. The seven members were to sever their connections with their previous employers, sign on for a five-year term (with the potential of another), and work full time at their board jobs. Helping them out is a staff of 40 professionals.

Besides knowing accounting and financial reporting, the folk who make up the board are supposed to have something akin to the attributes of a Supreme Court justice: intellect, integrity, discipline, a judicial temperament, ability to work in a collegial atmosphere, and communication skills. They are also supposed to come from a mix of backgrounds, which they do. Chairman Beresford came from Ernst & Whinney, and two other board members, Raymond C. Lauver and James J. Leisenring, from other purlieus of public accounting. Two members were formerly high corporate financial officers: Victor H. Brown, from Firestone, and C. Arthur Northrop, from IBM. Academia contributed Robert J. Swieringa, who taught at Cornell. The seventh, and newest, board member, A. Clarence Sampson, was formerly chief accountant of the SEC.

And who appoints this crew? The board's parent, the Financial Accounting Foundation, whose trustees come from the board's various constituencies. As parents go, this one is relatively whipless: The foundation's bylaws forbid the trustees to interfere in standard setting. They are responsible, though, for raising their progeny's spending money: about $11 million annually, a little more than half of which comes from the sale of publications—standards, technical bulletins, and the like—and the rest from contributions. Most big companies chip in.

Also pitching in, though in another way, is the Financial Accounting Standards Advisory Council, whose 30 members meet quarterly with the board to render opinions on FASB's work. Paul Kolton, chairman of FASAC and former chairman of the American Stock Exchange, describes the council as "A microcosm of the board's world—something the board would have to invent if it didn't have it." The key word in FASAC's name, however, is "Advisory."

And then there is the SEC, which in the late 1970s once peremptorily overrode a FASB standard and established rules of its own. Making amends, the two institutions have since forged the closest of working relationships, aimed at what they call "mutual nonsurprise." Says the SEC's Coulson: "Just to meet our statutory responsibilities, we've got to know what FASB's doing, what kind of feedback it's getting, and whether it's coming up with answers we can live with." The SEC's tolerance for FASB's specific conclusions is fairly broad. Says Coulson: "The precise answer doesn't matter that much, as long as it's within a reasonable range of answers."

At bottom, FASB, with its high-priced people handling high-tension questions, is terribly valuable to the SEC. Says Paul B. W. Miller, a University of Colorado professor who has done fellowship work at both FASB and the SEC and written a well-regarded book about the board: "The SEC has got FASB doing all the work, taking all the heat, and getting all the hate mail."

Two years ago the heat even set the pot boiling on the issue of the board's membership, just as Don Kirk was leaving the chairman's post. The betting was that he would be succeeded by Jim Leisenring, then head of FASB's staff, or Arthur R. Wyatt, a board member who had come from Arthur Andersen. But the business community thought of both as unacceptable hard-liners, and

But the business community thought of both as unacceptable hard-liners, and the trustees of the foundation eventually picked Beresford as the compromise candidate. Today he is widely perceived to be a man who will labor to gain peace. Nonetheless, a friend says he "has caught the mission." Translation: He staunchly defends FASB's efforts and independence.

For evidence of FASB's independence, consider the stock option question. Over the eternity this problem has been around, no fewer than 13 board members have agreed, 13 to 0, that the value of options should be recognized as a cost on income statements. But the members have never been able to settle on a way for measuring that cost. Enough, says business, get this crazy item off the agenda. Instead, the board has put it on hold while it pushes ahead on a related project, labeled financial instruments, whose ambit includes currency swaps, collateralized mortgage obligations, reverse repos, and anything else that investment bankers are just this second thinking up.

Where there are financial instruments, there can be some, uh, innovative accounting. All too aware of this, the SEC took the highly unusual step three years ago of asking the board officially, in writing, to scrutinize the subject. The commission also acknowledged that the project would inevitably lead the board into a fundamental examination of whether historical-cost accounting—carrying items on the books at their original cost—is really appropriate for these instruments. The project, says a former board member, is "a cauldron" of mark-to-market questions. Starting gingerly, FASB is expecting first to ask for new disclosures about off-balance-sheet financial instruments.

The new information may be required for 1989 annual reports—but then again it may not. Blasts from critics have made the board acutely aware of the "standards overload" charge. It counters that the bunching was largely accidental, the result of years of due process and a sudden burst of rulings. Nonetheless, the board is likely to exhibit particular caution as it moves ahead.

FASB's standards often reflect caution of a different kind. They tend to be perhaps 80% pure conceptually and 20% pragmatic—reflecting, so the idiom goes, "a practical cut." In its 1985 pension standard, for example, FASB embraced rules that permit earnings to be smoothed. Stricter rules, said the board, might have been conceptually preferable. But FASB thought they would be too sharp a break from present practice.

FASB's controversial new standard on income taxes, however, includes a wrenching change much despised by managers. It relates to deferred taxes, which under all rules—new and old—arise when a company shows costs in its published statements different from those on its tax returns. In the best-known example, a company chooses straight-line depreciation on its income statement for a given piece of equipment and accelerated depreciation for tax purposes. This approach temporarily creates a higher profit on the books than it does on the tax return. It also creates those deferred taxes, which move to the liability side of the balance sheet, there to be extinguished as they are paid.

Meanwhile, a company may accumulate deferred tax assets, which under the old rules could end up on the other side of the balance sheet or be used to offset deferred taxes. Deferred tax assets can arise, for example, if a company books a charge for restructuring, made up primarily of expenses to be paid in the future. The expenses might include severance pay or the costs of closing plants, neither of which become tax deductions until the cash goes out the door. On their books, however, companies have been permitted to "tax-effect" the restructuring charge, reducing it by an amount that anticipated the tax benefits to be realized when the money was actually spent. As it worked out, deferred tax assets were seldom visible on corporate books. Instead, they were normally used as an offset to reduce deferred taxes, which were definitely visible.

Most companies kept buying equipment, depreciating it by straight-line charges, and piling new deferred taxes on top of the old. As the figure on the right-hand side of the balance sheet grew larger, so did its unreality. Because of changes in corporate tax rates, it was not a true liability, representing a precise sum that companies expected to pay. In FASB hearings, William Ihlanfeldt, assistant controller of Shell Oil, referred to this buildup as an "unidentified growing object"—a UGO.

The UGO was acceptable to most companies until tax rates miraculously began heading south, which meant the deferred taxes on their books were overstated. Many businessmen soon were clamoring for a new approach that would let them reduce the UGO to an amount that reflected current tax rates and take the difference as a one-time fillip to earnings.

For once, FASB, which had been brooding over the tax rules for some time, agreed. It proposed a new method of accounting for income taxes that would indeed deflate the UGO. But in thinking hard about the matter, the board reached a conclusion about deferred tax assets that stunned the business community.

It was right, FASB said, to continue making an annual provision for deferred taxes, since these would be truly owed. It was also appropriate to reduce this provision by *certain* tax benefits—those scheduled to hit the tax return in the specific years deferred taxes were to be paid, or that alternatively could be carried back against taxes by then already paid. But companies having future benefits that *exceeded* those taxes could not recognize the difference as a benefit.

FASB's reasoning was simple: It is not appropriate for the books to anticipate events that haven't happened, including the earning of taxable income against which the deductions already made on the books can be taken. We are not making judgments, said FASB, on whether the necessary income will materialize. We are merely saying that until it does, those tax benefits—the effect of the deductions—cannot quality as assets.

The logic is there. But the new standard is a double whammy for companies. First, they must do large amounts of bookkeeping to determine how their deferred taxes will play out in the future, so that they can also determine what tax benefits may be applied against them. Complains Citicorp's Reed: "We're spending millions on this. It's a rip-roaring pain in the behind."

Second, any company that takes large charges on its books today that will become tax deductions only in the future is courting some up-front earnings damage. That is, the charge will often be larger than it otherwise would have been because it will not be reduced by tax benefits that may eventually materialize. At the least, these circumstances will add to the volatility of earnings, pushing them down today and up tomorrow.

The victims will certainly include companies that take large restructuring charges. At one point, the property and casualty insurance industry also looked as if it would be among the whipsawed, because of a two-year-old tax law that delays the deductibility of claims costs. But in the wee hours of October 22, as Congress wrapped up a technical-corrections tax bill, the industry got a provision included that in effect guarantees its ability to use its deferred tax benefits. Because of this maneuver to evade FASB, P&C companies will be able to sidestep the new standard and set up all the deferred tax assets they have available.

Commercial banks, though, are not escaping. Their problem is the big provisions for loan losses that many have made, which will only gradually result in tax deductions, as the loans are written off. In its 1987 annual report, Citicorp estimated that adoption of the new FASB standard would, in its initial effects, crunch earnings hard enough to reduce the stockholders' equity by up to 10%, an assertion implying maximum damage of $880 million. By now, having refined its estimate, Citicorp is thinking the hit can be held to $400 million or less. But in an era in which banks are struggling to build their capital, that is still a wallop.

The shorthand, and perhaps unforgettable, name for this accounting problem is "naked tax debits"—those future benefits that you can't recognize today. Only a minority of companies are bare right now. Many, in fact, are acknowledging the drop in corporate tax rates by shrinking their UGOs and reporting windfall profits. General Electric, for example, adopted the standard the first year it could, 1987, and thereby enjoyed a $577 million special gain.

But down the road for just about every company is that interesting accounting question, retiree health benefits, which is threatening to create whole nudist colonies of naked tax debits. This problem, as is the case with all accounting matters, has to do primarily with bookkeeping, not cash. The implications, though, are immense.

FASB is poised to say that retiree health benefits must be thought of as a form of deferred compensation, of the same variety as pensions. If Joe Employee is earning his retiree benefits today, then their estimated cost must be "accrued," or booked, today. In a catch-up part of the process, costs will also have to be accrued for all the years that Joe has worked up to now and for employees already retired. Booking these costs will be a revolution for most companies, which up to now have not been accruing anything for retiree health benefits. Furthermore, the accruals made today will not produce tax deductions until later years—that is, they will often create naked tax debits.

The unaccrued liability is awesome, as the GAO's estimate of $221 billion would suggest. Corporate America has let health benefits get out of hand, perhaps because up until now the promises made have had so little impact on the income statement. "You manage what you measure," says FASB board member Lauver, and very little measuring has occurred. In effect, the business community has written a blank check, to be filled in over the years, at whatever prices apply.

FASB's new standard is not likely to go into effect before 1992, and exactly what it will say is uncertain. Around year's end, the board is due to publish a draft for public reaction. Next will come a comment period and hearings, probably contentious. In the end, the rules are apt to allow for a long transition period.

The new costs, even so, will be bombs. In the course of doing a study for the Financial Executives Institute, Harold Dankner of Coopers & Lybrand has been accumulating data from 25 big companies, which are refiguring their costs based on what they think FASB's rules will be. The data show that the companies' health costs are likely to jump by three to six times, an explosion that in some instances will crater earnings. Christopher Steffen, vice president and controller of Chrysler, recently said he was expecting at least a doubling of costs, from about $600 million currently to upwards of $1.2 billion under FASB's rules.

In the business community, opinions about FASB's upcoming rules are all over the map. Many executives look at all the variables and contend that future health costs simply cannot be measured. It is ridiculous, they say, to put such "soft" numbers in the financial statements. Other executives argue that the rules will prompt companies to seek some way to avoid paying the benefits they have promised. Some companies have in fact tried this, only to meet stiff resistance from both their employees and the courts. And yes, believe it or not, some executives have even lauded FASB for putting a spotlight on this subject. Says John Ruffle, vice chairman of J.P. Morgan & Co. and president-elect of the Financial Accounting Foundation, FASB's parent: "The board has done American industry a gigantic favor. Over the long term, industry will look back and say thanks."

Even John Reed believes that FASB is right in stepping up to the health benefits question. But specific standards, he says, are not the point. Rather the issue is the totality of FASB's work. As the Roundtable sees it, he says, the board has simply published too many standards. Second, Reed charges that FASB—holed up "in the sticks of Connecticut"—has been insensitive to the practical problems that business faces in putting the standards into place. That doesn't mean, he says, that the people on the board are inherently evil; they appear, in fact, professionally competent. Neither would he ever argue, says Reed, that business lacks access to the board. "We have all we want. But a social scientist would say, I think, that our opinions have not been converted into changed behavior on FASB's part."

Isn't he really quarreling with the answers that FASB arrives at? "Yes," Reed replies. "But it's the cumulative effect of not liking the answers that gets to people. Say you've got a kid that gets into a fight. If he keeps getting into fights, time after time, eventually you're going to say there must be something sour going on at the school."

Which means you might start pushing reforms, as Reed has done. In a September memorandum sent to the Financial Accounting Foundation, Reed proposed a form of emasculation: a new committee that essentially would have control of FASB's agenda, determining what projects were important enough for it to consider and stripping it of "unproductive" undertakings— such as, no doubt, stock options. The committee, as Reed saw it, would have seven members: two CEOs, two senior partners of Big Eight firms, the president of the American Institute of Certified Public Accountants, an SEC commissioner, and the chairman of FASB. This group's decisions would be binding on everyone concerned, including the SEC.

Reed next took up this proposal in a Washington meeting with the chairman of the SEC, David S. Ruder, and Beresford. In a letter to Reed, Ruder said he welcomed the Roundtable's opinions and saw possibilities for improving FASB's procedures, perhaps by the better use of task forces and field tests for new standards. But as to an oversight committee—no. Oversight is the responsibility of the SEC, said Ruder, sounding tough. The SEC chairman also proclaimed himself particularly unhappy that the Roundtable was making suggestions that whacked at FASB's independence. Said Ruder: "The commission has consistently concluded that FASB performs its tasks well."

Ruder's own backbone may have been braced by a letter he had by then received from John Dingell, a powerful Democratic Congressman from Michigan, who had read in the *Wall Street Journal* that Reed was on the attack. In the process of spending years chewing out auditors for failing to catch the bad guys of business, not to mention railing at S&Ls for trying to phony up their books, Dingell has developed a fondness for FASB. In his letter to Ruder, the Congressman commended the board for handling its deeply controversial job well and went on to slap at "self-interested parties" and their complaints.

Count Ruder and Dingell as two ringing rebuffs for Reed. Nonetheless, the Citicorp CEO has stirred things up and put FASB under multiple microscopes. The senior partners of the Big Eight are peering at the board's mindset and the Financial Executives Institute is closely tracking events. Closer to home, the trustees of FASB's parent, toothless tigers up to now, are studying whether a few fangs might be appropriate. As a part of their study, they will be checking in with the Business Roundtable, among others.

They'll find Reed still in there swinging. Replying to Ruder in November, he implicitly dismissed the importance of fine-tuning measures like better use of task forces. More fundamental changes are needed, he said. Perhaps they could be discussed, he suggested, in twice-a-year meetings between the SEC and a new committee to be formed, made up of CEOs and senior partners of accounting firms.

Sometimes when he is spinning the tale of FASB and where it went wrong, Reed mentions that the U.S. has probably the best financial reporting system in the world. He sees this as a source of satisfaction, and as an argument for slowing FASB way down. It could more logically be seen as evidence that we are doing something right. Indeed, if you had a bank you thought was probably the best in the world, you might even be trying to make it better.

Letter from the Accounting Principles Task Force of the Business Roundtable to the Securities and Exchange Commission

August 20, 1990

The Honorable Philip R. Lochner, Jr.
Commissioner
Securities and Exchange Commission
450 5th Street, N.W.
Washington, D.C. 20549

Dear Mr. Lochner:

As you know, the Accounting Principles Task Force of the Business Round-table has expressed concerns about the effects of current U.S. accounting and reporting requirements on U.S. businesses. The Task Force believes that the level of complexity and rapid pace of change in this area have had a seriously negative impact on the efficiency and effectiveness of U.S. businesses and have not improved the quality of information available to investors and other users of financial information. While we strongly support the private sector standard-setting process, we are encouraged by the Securities and Exchange Commission's interest in reducing the burden on U.S. businesses, and welcome this opportunity to offer our views on the subject.

For many years, the U.S. was far ahead of the rest of the world with respect to the development of a comprehensive financial accounting and reporting system. To a very large degree, our success was attributable to the objective of generating general purpose financial statements that would provide relevant and understandable information to a wide variety of potential users. Business itself was a major participant in this process, in its role as both a preparer and a user of financial information.

In contrast, in many other parts of the world, the basis of financial accounting mirrored the local tax or statutory accounts, and lacked a capital markets focus that could equally serve the needs of owners, investors, creditors, employees and other users. However, the accounting profession in many places overseas is rapidly moving away from a local tax and statutory model and closer to a general purpose accounting focus. This process is clearly at work in the attempts to harmonize international accounting standards, and has met with broad support from businesses and accountants both here and abroad.

Unfortunately, while the rest of the world moves closer to meaningful financial reporting, accounting in the U.S. has taken some serious steps in the wrong direction. While we have generally supported the work of the Financial Accounting Standards Board (FASB), recent events indicate that in the quest to develop the perfect theoretical model, it has lost sight of its primary objective—providing useful and meaningful financial information. Instead, U.S. businesses have been burdened with a costly reporting infrastructure that overloads the user with data but provides very little insight into the economic condition or results of the enterprise. For example:

- Financial statement preparers and users have spent the last four years trying to convince the FASB that its statement on accounting for income taxes (SFAS No. 96) results in poor financial reporting and is unnecessarily complicated and costly to implement. While the shortcomings of the FASB's approach were pointed out in detail before the rule was finalized, the FASB pressed on with its inherently flawed approach. Only recently has the FASB agreed to reconsider some of its basic principles.
- Banks counseled the FASB that cash flow statements for their industry would not be meaningful and would be costly to prepare, but the rules were nonetheless imposed. Two years later, after much discussion, the FASB has enacted rules that basically undo much of the gross cash flow reporting initially required. Banks had too incur significant implementation and ongoing reporting costs to provide gross cash flow data until this change was made. It is clear that banks had valid concerns that should have been given greater consideration during the due process period.
- Manufacturing companies were opposed to the FASB's requirement that they commence consolidating their captive finance, real estate and insurance subsidiaries, because presenting these very different activities on a combined basis obscured rather than clarified the financial results of these businesses. Companies were still required to disclose these activities on a separate basis, which increased the reporting burden by showing these

activities on both a consolidated and unconsolidated basis. In addition, many financial analysts have indicated that consolidated information is less useful due to the diversity in activities, and have encouraged a return to prior accounting practice in this area.

In each of these cases, it is clear the rulemakers did not succeed in promulgating "generally accepted accounting principles". To a large degree, few but the rulemakers themselves saw merit in the standards being imposed on U.S. businesses, and their failure was not a surprise to the broad constituencies that—very early in the process—identified and communicated the fundamental problems with the original proposals. Yet these problem-ridden standards were extremely costly in terms of management attention, systems development, and the general sense of uncertainty and confusion that was created among both preparers and users of financial information. All of these examples represent the unproductive utilization of scarce resources that could otherwise have been directed toward business development. While we are not aware of any recent attempts to specifically measure these costs in dollar terms, they clearly are significant.

In order to effectively compete in the global marketplace in the 1990's and beyond, U.S. companies need a more cost-effective approach to financial reporting. The Business Roundtable believes accounting rulemakers need to refocus on the objectives of general purpose financial statements, and provide businesses with needed relief from excessive reporting requirements and unrealistic accounting rules.

In line with these objectives, some of the specific areas which require a careful and thorough reassessment include:

- **Pace and Balance of New Accounting Standards.** It is critical that the recently established FASB oversight committee play an active and effective role in monitoring and influencing the pace of new accounting standards, and in ensuring the appropriate balance between accounting theory and pragmatism.

  Since the beginning of 1985, the FASB alone has issued 23 standards and 13 Technical Bulletins, and the FASB's Emerging Issues Task Force has discussed approximately 180 issues. Many of these items related not to newly developed products or transactions but rather to the reconsideration of previously existing accounting standards. This environment of rapid change is both costly and confusing. The process of adopting new accounting standards every year or so undermines the credibility of previously reported information that was compiled under the prior basis of accounting and is extremely disruptive to users of financial information. Task Force members believe that the need for a new accounting standard should be more carefully evaluated before the process of change is permitted to commence.

In addition, the effectiveness of a new accounting standard must be measured primarily by how fairly it presents economic events and the utility of the information to financial statement users—not by how closely it adheres to a precise theoretical model. To produce reasonable accounting standards, there must be a balance between practical considerations and theory. The needed flexibility to balance these sometimes conflicting objectives has eluded the rulemakers on several recent issues.

- **Lack of Accountability for Policy Implications.** While foreign standard setters consider all of the implications of changes to their accounting rules, the U.S. rulemakers continue to remain neutral to factors outside their narrow, theoretical accounting focus. Recently, Denny Beresford, Chairman of the FASB, stated that ". . . the FASB's main concern will remain neutrality. . . . A given industry's or nation's particular concerns have no place in FASB's role."

    While this might have been an acceptable approach to standard setting in the past when U.S. business dominated the international markets, the FASB's insistence that accounting theory must not be influenced by practical or public policy considerations has hampered U.S. competitiveness. We therefore encourage the FASB and other rulemakers to consider competitiveness issues in evaluating new accounting standards. We are not seeking to give U.S. companies an unfair competitive advantage, but rather to eliminate situations where we are put at a competitive disadvantage.

- **Burden of Implementing New Accounting Rules.** The implementation of new standards places significant pressure on businesses to develop and modify complex reporting systems in a short period of time. Given the current demands of a quarterly reporting cycle, trying to implement major changes to the reporting model strains the capacity of most financial control functions. In addition, since the reporting burden only seems to grow, external financial reporting is overwhelming the balance that used to exist between internal management accounting and external reporting requirements.

    Companies have limited resources and should not be forced to use these resources to implement or maintain unproductive and unnecessary financial reporting. Reasonable effective dates and transition provisions should be a priority at the FASB and changes should be made only when a clear and compelling need can be demonstrated.

- **Burden of Quarterly Reporting.** Although companies have a vital responsibility to provide timely and accurate information to the marketplace, the system of quarterly reporting in the U.S. places an enormous reporting burden on most U.S. businesses and contributes to a counterproductive management focus. A quarter is only about 60 working days, and measuring results for such a short period tends to overemphasize short-term earnings, often at the expense of long-term growth and capital appreciation.

Some foreign companies, particularly those in the United Kingdom, are required to report results only semi-annually. Semi-annual reporting promotes a longer term view of results and counteracts, to a certain extent, the tendency of investors to want an even shorter reporting cycle. Of course, the objective of a semi-annual reporting cycle is not to delay important information from reaching the marketplace, and it would continue to be appropriate for companies to report major events when they occur.

- **Need to Reduce Reporting Overload.** We have gone from a reasonable level of reporting to providing any piece of data that someone thinks might have relevance. However, those requesting additional information are not required to prove that the additional information meets any cost–benefit standard. The Task Force in fact questions how much of the information currently being provided in annual reports, 10-Ks and 10-Qs is actually being used. We are certain that the reporting requirements can be streamlined while still maintaining investor protection.

In addition, greater uniformity among financial, regulatory and tax requirements would greatly simplify the reporting burden on a majority of U.S. businesses. While certain differences may be appropriate or necessary, the task of rationalizing our current system of financial reporting should be a priority for all rulemakers before additional reporting requirements are added to the accounting and reporting roster.

The Task Force would appreciate the opportunity to meet with you to further discuss the issues outlined above. While accounting standard setting belongs in the private sector, we believe that steps can be taken to improve the process in order to produce more efficient and effective accounting and reporting standards. We are available at your convenience.

Very truly yours,

John S. Reed
Chairman
Accounting Principles Task Force, The Business Roundtable

cc: The Honorable Richard C. Breeden, Chairman, Securities and Exchange Commission
Mr. Drew Lewis, Chairman, The Business Roundtable
Mr. William L. Lurie, President, The Business Roundtable
Mr. Dennis R. Beresford, Chairman, Financial Accounting Standards Board
Mr. J. Michael Cook, Chairman, Financial Accounting Foundation Oversight Committee
Mr. Edmund Coulson, Chief Accountant, Securities and Exchange Commission
Accounting Principles Task Force Members

Letter from the Financial Executives Institute to the Securities and Exchange Commission

September 20, 1990

Mr. Philip R. Lochner, Jr.
Commissioner
Securities and Exchange Commission
450 Fifth Street, N.W.
Washington, D.C. 20549

Dear Commissioner Lochner:

Financial Executives Institute appreciates the opportunity to respond to your June 15th letter to John Reed, Chairman of the Accounting Principles Task Force of the Business Roundtable, requesting comments on U.S. accounting standards.

Our Committee on Corporate Reporting, which addresses accounting and financial reporting matters, has compiled a summary of those U.S. accounting standards that are deemed to be most burdensome in terms of complexity and cost benefit considerations. This summary is attached as an appendix to CCR's enclosed position on U.S. accounting complexity. Beyond those enclosures, however, I would like to make some general comments regarding the current state of accounting and financial reporting in the U.S.

FEI recognizes that the accounting standards setting process in the United States is a difficult and complex undertaking that must reconcile and attempt to balance many diverse and often conflicting perspectives. FEI is, however, concerned over the large number of detailed accounting rules that have proliferated, especially in the last ten years, in this country. We do not object to accounting standards. On the contrary, our membership strongly supports the need for high-quality accounting standards and consistent reporting. Because of our responsibilities to shareowners, and since we are also users of financial statements, we recognize that the availability of adequate and reliable financial data is of utmost importance.

FEI also is concerned about "critical mass" of detailed accounting complexities that U.S. managers must deal with on a day to day basis. The focus in this country on detailed financial accounting theory and rules has generated large volumes of data that must be collected, recorded, processed and reported. This situation is consuming enormous amounts of human and financial resources, often with questionable benefit to the public.

Reprinted by permission of P. Norman Roy, President, Financial Executives Institute.

This issue is so widespread that it is difficult to tackle effectively. Our members and our Committee on Corporate Reporting regularly review and respond to accounting proposals, but few organizations can commit the resources needed to develop detailed commentaries on proposed accounting standards that are often viewed as overly theoretical and too detailed to be practical. Comments that we believe are thoughtful, responsive and realistic arguments seem to be largely perceived by FASB as inadequate and self-serving and are often rejected as such. This frustrating outcome is even more perplexing when we consider the excellent professional qualifications of FASB's Board members and staff. We believe that more serious consideration of practical business implications must be made an integral part of the standards setting process.

Once a standard is issued, we have no recourse other than to implement the standard, no matter how costly and burdensome. The fact that there is no independent appeal process places special responsibility on the board to ensure that its pronouncements are pragmatic, workable and cost effective.

While FEI continues to be a strong supporter of the private sector accounting standards setting process and has publicly stated its firm support for the FASB as the U.S. standards setting body, we believe the subject of U.S. accounting complexity is deserving of serious re-examination. In our view, U.S. competitiveness is negatively affected by the volume and complexity of U.S. accounting and financial reporting rules that have become so pervasive and diffuse. We view this as an extremely difficult problem to analyze and resolve. We believe that the SEC should lead an effort to promote and encourage a reduction in the complexity of U.S. accounting and reporting requirements. FEI does not believe that either accounting standards setting or accounting standards compliance should be characterized by such detailed scientific complexity or voluminous specificity.

The interest of the SEC on this important issue is noted with great appreciation by our members, many of whom have devoted long professional careers and many personal hours to advance the cause of ethical, consistent accounting and relevant financial reporting in this country.

Sincerely,

P. Norman Roy,
President
Financial Executives Institute

cc: D. R. Beresford, Chairman, FASB
    E. Coulson, Chief Accountant, SEC
    J. F. Ruffle, President, FAF
    M. Cook, Chairman, FAF Oversight Committee
    FEI Board of Directors
    FEI Committee on Corporate Reporting

Financial Executives Institute
Committee on Corporate Reporting
POSITION ON U.S. ACCOUNTING STANDARDS COMPLEXITY

We are seriously concerned about the increasing complexity and cost of compliance, and the diminishing informational value of current and proposed accounting rules. This paper summarizes the nature of our concerns. The appendix presents specific examples of accounting and reporting requirements deemed to be especially burdensome.

COMPLEXITY ARISES FROM DETAILED THEORETICAL FOCUS AND EMPHASIS ON INTRICATE RULES

In the past decade, we have perceived a trend away from general accounting guidance applied in conjunction with management judgment, a move toward a more highly detailed approach under which specific accounting is minutely prescribed for numerous individual events and conditions. During the same ten-year period, we have seen a trend placing increased emphasis on detailed theory and conceptual purity and moving away from practically oriented, basic accounting principles. These trends have resulted in an accounting standards approach which, while exhaustively carried out, at times belies economic relevance and significance. We believe the result has often been ineffective, overly complex and costly financial reporting. While some measure of complexity is admittedly a function of the business environment in which we operate, it is also a function of the detailed conceptual approach to rulemaking being taken by our rulemakers. A pervasive theme throughout many of the FASB's more recent standards is a reluctance on their part to rely on the use of management judgment to apply general concepts.

VOLUME OF STANDARDS ISSUED ADDS TO COMPLEXITY

Adding to the accounting complexity issue is the sheer volume of total reporting requirements. During the last ten year period:

- The FASB has issued seventy Financial Accounting Standards, comprising in total an extremely lengthy volume of guidance
- The EITF addressed two hundred specific accounting situations
- The SEC issued more than thirty Accounting Series Releases
- The SEC issued more than thirty Financial Reporting Releases
- The SEC issued more than forty-five Staff Accounting Bulletins

In the seventeen years since its formation in 1973, the FASB has issued pronouncements which now comprise more than 1600 pages of guidance— and this figure does not include Emerging Issues Task Force Abstracts, FASB Implementation Guides or other FASB publications designed to explain U.S. accounting rules.

In addition, the Federal Trade Commission, Environmental Protection Agency, Department of Labor, Internal Revenue Service, and various other federal, state and local governmental bodies all have added to the reporting burden by requiring financial information formatted to their own specific needs and guidelines (e.g., FTC survey of manufacturers requiring sales and production by SIC code by location).

COSTS OF COMPLIANCE ARE OFTEN NOT ACCOMPANIED BY COMPENSATING INCREASES IN INFORMATIONAL VALUE OR OTHER BENEFITS

The proliferation of financial reporting requirements has resulted in added costs. While such costs may vary by company, the sheer number and complexity of standards issued in recent years have required increased financial staff resources to analyze and interpret standards, develop implementation guidance, and process and analyze data. More attention needs to be given to whether proposed standards meet cost benefit tests—disclosure requirements often extend beyond reasonable bounds and result in questionable added value to users of the financial statements. There are many situations in which data must be collected that are not used to run the business and that appear to be of marginal value to shareholders and analysts. A prime example would be the pension disclosures required under SFAS No. 87 (other examples are cited in the appendix). Many disclosures have a narrow range of interest and quickly outlive the perceived need that led to their promulgation.

COMPETITIVENESS OF U.S. COMPANIES NEGATIVELY AFFECTED

From a competitive standpoint, the costs of complying with U.S. reporting requirements put companies at a significant disadvantage versus foreign competitors. Also, taken as a whole, the information made freely available to foreign competition in U.S. company financial statements and reports, supplemented by the wealth of information provided in reports to U.S. government agencies and which may ultimately become publicly available under the Freedom of Information Act or otherwise, is unprecedented. U.S. companies do not enjoy equivalent access to information on their foreign competitors.

IASC STANDARDS ARE SIMPLER FROM AN INTERPRETATION AND APPLICATION STANDPOINT

A comparison of FASB standards and those produced by the IASC emphasizes the differences between the two standard-setters. To date, the IASC has issued much briefer and more broadly-based standards and their disclosure requirements have been less extensive and expensive. While we recognize that some additions may need to be made to IASC standards, this overall approach to standard-setting should be encouraged—for both the private and public sector standards setters.

EXAMPLES OF BURDENSOME STANDARDS

We have listed in the attached appendix examples of U.S. accounting rules that are, in our view, the most troublesome in that they require considerable cost and effort to be expended with questionable benefit. We believe this listing should serve as a base for further in-depth study and analysis.

FEI RECOMMENDATIONS

- FASB should be required to consider cost/benefit relationships more comprehensively, prior to issuing any new standards.
- SEC should actively promote and encourage a reduction in the complexity of U.S. accounting and reporting requirements.
- FASB Standards should be written as simply as possible. If accounting rules can not be reasonably understood by senior non-accounting management, they should be subject to challenge and reconsideration.
- FASB should seek to issue the majority of its pronouncements in shorter, more concise standards—preferably in three or four pages, but not more than ten pages.
- Research projects conducted by the Financial Executives Research Foundation and others may provide new perspectives on the subject of U.S. and foreign countries' accounting standards and issues of complexity. One current FERF project, "International Accounting and Reporting", is a broad based study which will focus on accounting and disclosure practices around the world. It will include a literature review and a survey of multinational company financial executives. A second FERF project, currently in the formulation stage, is intended to focus on the North American perspective, i.e., U.S. and Canadian companies' experience with standards around the world.

EXAMPLES OF BURDENSOME ACCOUNTING AND REPORTING REQUIREMENTS

SFAS 13

Lease Accounting

SFAS No. 13 is a prime example of excessive detail and complexity, which some feel can produce an answer which may be correct in form but fails in portraying the true substance of a leasing transaction.

Although this standard revolves around a simple and straightforward concept, i.e., that any lease that transfers all or nearly all of the risks and rewards of ownership should be accounted for as a capital lease, it goes on for almost fifty pages to describe with great specificity, exactly what conditions require capital lease accounting and the numerous disclosures that must be made. Lease accounting has been made so complex by this and other FASB pronouncements that a separate codification over three hundred pages long was deemed necessary.(*)

SFAS 87

Pension Accounting

SFAS No. 87 is a classic example of voluminous data and disclosure that very few people, with the possible exception of actuaries, really understand. The underlying concept in pension accounting seems very simple: record the obligation for pensions to be paid to employees at the time the obligation is incurred and disclose information about basic assumptions used in estimating the future cost. In many annual reports, the footnote on pensions requires more than a full page of disclosures and consumes considerable time and effort to prepare. Yet judging by the number of questions received from financial statement users, relatively few people are interested in this extensive disclosure. Surely the disclosure for pensions can be shortened and simplified and in the process, more useful information can be communicated.

SFAS 94

Consolidation of Subsidiaries

SFAS No. 94 requires consolidation of entities that previously did not need to be consolidated because their operations and financial results were very different from the consolidated enterprise in character and/or form. Previous disclosure practices provided sufficient information to permit users, if they so chose, to produce their own consolidated financial statements which would approximate what is now provided in the financial statements.

However, consolidation of entities whose industry measurement norms are very different from those of the parent and/or other subsidiaries can be totally misleading. Resulting ratios and analyses may be totally meaningless, since the consolidated report mixes "apples and oranges" as if they were the same.

* Comprehensive Publication (Codification) of Pronouncements, "Accounting for Leases, SFAS No. 13 as Amended and Interpreted, Incorporating FASB Statements, Interpretations and Technical Bulletins Issued Through January 1990," FASB.

We believe that a return to previous practice would be more appropriate, since it served so well for many years.

SFAS 95

Statements of Cash Flows

The guidelines of Statement 95 along with the requirements to present the effects of individual transactions have both greatly complicated and increased the cost of preparing external financial statements, when compared with APB 19.

For multinational corporations with many active reporting entities, Statement 95 has required that numerous individuals in different capacities around the world provide input for the computations that are prepared quarterly. In two CCR companies it is estimated that more than one hundred hours are required to comply with each quarterly reporting requirement.

The logistics problems associated with many foreign locations are magnified by the gains and losses on foreign currencies which must be assigned to the various components of the statement. Foreign historical data does not always correspond to cash flow requirements and difficulties arise where source data is not maintained in the United States.

Domestically, this statement has required that separate reporting programs be developed and many departments must provide input to support this reporting. The cost of audit and quarterly review of the data has risen sharply as a result of this requirement. In total, the time and cost necessary to complete the statement of cash flows is very high when compared to the remainder of the external financial statements. In many companies this statement is not used internally or is not used in the same detailed format as is required for external reporting purposes, making the entire effort necessary solely for external reporting. If the SFAS 95 cash flow statement were clearly more useful to financial statement readers, this additional effort would be at least partly justified; however, the fact that the format is not meaningful for management use makes its analytical value to others doubtful as well.

SFAS 95 originally presented even greater difficulties for banks and financial institutions. These problems persisted in the final statement despite input during the development process, necessitating further changes after issuance.

In summary, it is questionable whether the cost of preparing the statement of cash flows in its present form justifies the benefits provided.

SFAS 96

Income Tax Accounting

SFAS No. 96 represents a significant change from the existing method of accounting for income taxes. While some of these changes may have been fairly well thought out, the evaluation and implementation of most of this standard is extremely complex and very time consuming.

For example, SFAS No. 96 requires deferred tax assets and liabilities to be calculated as if a tax return were prepared for each future year using the net taxable or deductible amounts anticipated to occur in each future year as a result of the reversal of existing temporary differences. The scheduling of these temporary differences to the specific years in which they are expected to result in either taxable or deductible amounts will often have to be based on estimates and prediction of future events. Also, certain reversals will require special attention.

For depreciation of fixed assets in service, all future book and tax depreciation will be scheduled by year. This means that the scheduling will not only be concerned with the reversal of the temporary differences at the balance sheet date. For assets in the early part of their tax life and for which annual tax depreciation still exceeds book depreciation, future originations that will increase the temporary difference are scheduled as well as all future reversals.

Needless to say, these scheduling procedures are very complicated, especially since they will have to be done for every tax jurisdiction for both regular and any alternative tax system. From a cost/benefit standpoint, one must seriously question, by performing this detailed scheduling, whether the investor will be provided with a more accurate and understandable set of financial statements. We think not. In preparation for adopting this standard, some CCR companies have already spent in excess of one million dollars. Considering the fact that we are unaware of any abuses of reported earnings under the old tax standard (APB 11), the cost/benefit criteria are totally out of proportion.

While we remain concerned at the vast amounts of time and effort that we and others have and must continue to expend in considering these intricate accounting details, we acknowledge and appreciate that the FASB is reexamining the concepts and provisions of SFAS 96. Furthermore, the rules are so complex that we doubt that anyone, other than technically qualified experts, will understand the reported results.

SFAS 105

Financial Instruments

With respect to the financial instruments project, the voluminous disclosure requirements of the original exposure draft prior to SFAS No. 105 do not bode well for the future direction this project may take. It suggests that there is a substantial potential for excessive disclosure in future phases and that would only exacerbate the problem.

OPEB

Accounting for Other Postemployment Benefits

As we see it, another major problem with the proposed OPEB standard* is the lack of recognition of practical concepts in the proposed transition standards. We foresee OPEB as having the single most stringent effect on the financial statements in recent accounting history. Clearly the effect of transition will distort current and future periods' income and the Board should recognize this by permitting its amortization directly to retained earnings.

It should also be noted that once the standard has been enacted, compliance with OPEB will result in substantial ongoing costs. The proposed OPEB accounting and reporting disclosures are equally as voluminous as those required by SFAS No. 87 and are equally as technically and theoretically focused and thus not easily understandable by the majority of users.

In addition to burdensome complexity, the proposed OPEB standard contains technical requirements which seem illogical or impractical to many CCR members. The problems that CCR companies have faced thus far primarily stem from the proposed measurement methodology for OPEB cost and obligation. It has been our experience that the measurement can be very volatile in that a slight change in any of the major actuarial assumptions will generate significantly different results. We find the FASB's requirement to incorporate health care cost escalation rates into the measurement process particularly troublesome.

While we believe accrual accounting for such costs is conceptually correct, we do not believe the Board's approach to measurement will produce the most useful or reliable information.

* *Editors' note:* The FASB dropped the term "OPEB" in the final standard issued in December 1990, titled "Statement of Financial Accounting Standards No. 106, Employers' Accounting for Postretirement Benefits Other Than Pensions." The FASB opted for the term "postretirement" rather than "postemployment" to refer to the period after retirement or termination of employment.

Letter from the Financial Accounting Standards Board to the Securities and Exchange Commission

November 12, 1990

The Honorable Philip R. Lochner, Jr.
Commissioner
Securities and Exchange Commission
450 5th Street, N.W.
Washington, D.C. 20549

Dear Commissioner Lochner:

The Business Roundtable's Accounting Principles Task Force (BRT) and the Financial Executives Institute (FEI) in their letters of August 20, 1990 and September 20, 1990, respectively, have expressed to you their concerns about the effects of current U.S. accounting and reporting requirements on U.S. businesses. There are matters in their letters that we believe require clarification.

Before addressing certain aspects of those letters, we wish to emphasize that the Board welcomes all responsible suggestions for improvement in its due process and standards. Over the years since 1973, many reviews, studies, and surveys have focused on the Board and have resulted in suggestions for improvement. Incorporating the best of those suggestions has strengthened our due process procedures. We would hope to benefit similarly from the current discussions.

Matters of Balance

Both letters discuss two matters of balance that the Board will continue to struggle with as long as accounting standards are a subject of discussion. One of those matters is the balance of theoretical purity versus practicality and usefulness. The other matter is the appropriate level of detail in accounting standards. These two matters are central to the basic cost-benefit trade-offs in every project. They are often thought to be very closely related, but they are fundamentally different and are more understandable when viewed separately. Indeed, both the BRT and the FEI letters mix the two with confusing results.

The BRT letter asserts that ". . . recent events indicate that in the quest to develop the perfect theoretical model, [the FASB] has lost sight of its primary objective—providing useful and meaningful information." Objective and useful information is the central part of the FASB's mission statement and conceptual framework. Some disagreements over particular accounting issues reflect differences over competing theories; others, however, reflect deliberate sacrifices of the most useful information for other objectives, including reduced cost and a rate of improvement and change perceived to be tolerable. The participants on all sides of major standard-setting debates frequently evoke theory when their interpretation of the appropriate theory is perceived to support the answer they prefer. Put simply, it has often been said, "If you like the answer, you will love the theory."

A theoretically sound answer may also be a very practical answer. The problem is it may not be the *desired* answer. When arguments for competing theories in support of a constituent's desired answer are found without merit, the desired answer may then be supported by being termed a practical solution. The challenge is to identify within a coherent set of theories or concepts the soundest approach (given reasonable cost–benefit considerations) on which to base the standard and account for similar things in similar ways.

The FEI appears to be ambivalent about theory and practicality. In their September 20, 1990 letter referred to earlier, the FEI commented on U.S. accounting rules and stated, ". . . we have seen a trend placing increased emphasis on detailed theory and conceptual purity and moving away from practically oriented, basic accounting principles." Yet, two weeks earlier, in another letter to the SEC dated September 7, 1990, the chairman of the SEC Subcommittee of the FEI stated opposition to a proposal of the International Accounting Standards Committee (IASC) to discontinue the use of LIFO as an acceptable accounting alternative in these words:

> Acceptance of the IASC standards is affected by the strength of the standards' underlying accounting theory. We are not aware of any clear theoretical justification for the superiority of one method over another in all instances.

So, it seems that the FEI does believe theory has a role in standard setting—at least when the theory supports the desired answer.

The issue of the level of detail is often characterized as a choice between detailed complex standards and broad general standards. The former leads to cries of standards overload and to seemingly unending requests to clarify or interpret details of voluminous and specific rules, and for exemption from the rules by entities that find their industries unique. The latter leads to diversity in practice, perceived abuses, and numerous requests for interpretations and for "bright lines" that will insure that like situations are accounted for similarly. Indeed, a standard can be so broad that effectively it is not a standard at all.

The Board and its predecessors have erred in both directions in the past, with ample encouragement and technical assistance from industry, public accountants, and the SEC. Nevertheless, we are extremely sensitive to the pitfalls of the issue, and we continue to seek the appropriate balance in each standard.

Accountability and Neutrality

The BRT and FEI letters point out respectively a "lack of accountability" and a lack of "independent appeal process" for U.S. standards setting. We suggest that in evaluating those comments, you also should consider the Board's commitment to reconsider its positions when necessary and its track record of actually doing so. The Board reconsidered standards on foreign currency and changing prices in response to constituents' requests. More recently, certain aspects of cash flow reporting were changed, and the Board has undertaken to reconsider the income tax standard even before it was fully effective. Of course, each such action provides ammunition for critics who consider it proof that the Board should not have issued the original standard, balanced in part by those who will give the Board credit for continuing to try to listen. As a last and hopefully rare resort, constituents can and do appeal to the SEC, which has the power to overrule the FASB and has done so on one occasion.

The BRT letter attacks the FASB's long-held concept of neutrality as a notion that somehow places U.S. companies at a competitive disadvantage internationally. In making that point, the letter selectively quotes from a statement I made and gives the impression that the Board is insensitive to the concerns about international competitiveness. That is not the case. We are working at the international level toward narrowing differences, but it is a long-term undertaking. In the meantime, we believe that eliminating standards that are seen to cause a competitive disadvantage—segment reporting, for example— would take U.S. accounting to the level of the competitor with the fewest and most flexible standards. We are seeking common ground for international standards, but, in the words of a recent correspondent, "without that common ground being below sea level."

Comments on Specific Standards

The BRT letter specifically criticizes the standards on consolidation, cash flows, and income taxes. We think you should be aware that during the comment periods when those three projects were at the Exposure Draft stage, their Accounting Principles Task Force submitted only one letter, on income taxes.

The project that resulted in the cash flow standard was undertaken by the Board because of a high degree of interest in the subject by many constituent groups. The FEI was the most active. It initiated a drive to encourage its members to convert funds flow statements to a cash basis. The results of that effort provided valuable input to the subsequent project. It was in consideration of the comment letters of the FEI and others on the Exposure Draft that the Board approved the use of the indirect method as an alternative in the final Statement. Further, it was in response to the requests made by FEI and others that the Board reconsidered provisions of this Statement that led to two amendments.

The consolidations standard now criticized by the FEI was supported by its Committee on Corporate Reporting (CCR), which stated in its comment letter on the Exposure Draft that it took "no exception to the basic conclusion reached by the Board that all majority-owned subsidiaries should be consolidated."

The FEI letter gives the impression that the FEI was opposed to all or nearly all aspects of the several standards cited in the September 20 letter. This is simply not the case. Each of the standards cited was the result of a Board agenda project that included many issues. Based on its comment letters, the FEI supported the Board's positions on many, but not all, of those issues.

Number of Pronouncements

The letters cite certain statistics to suggest standards overload. The BRT letter states that 23 standards and 13 Technical Bulletins have been issued since 1985. That is accurate, but counting scarcely tells the story. Of the 23 standards issued since 1985, 9 are amendments or rescissions of existing standards, 3 defer effective dates of existing standards, 2 exempt certain types of organizations from all or part of existing standards, and 2 are applicable only to specialized industries. Thus, of the 23 standards cited, only 7 can be considered to have somewhat general application, a rate of a little over one a year.

The FEI letter notes that FASB Statements total 1600 pages over 17 years and that the EITF has addressed over 200 issues. The raw number of pages issued by the Board over the years overstates the situation considerably. The standard itself—the paragraphs setting forth the procedures that preparers are expected to follow—is usually only a small part of the full package that is included in a FASB Statement. For example, using our Original Pronouncements bound volume and focusing on the Statements the FEI singled out as burdensome as a sample, the following summarizes the number of pages in the standards section of each Statement:

Statement Number	Statement Subject	Number of Pages
FAS 13	Leases	15
FAS 87	Pensions	10
FAS 88	Pensions	3
FAS 94	Consolidation	4
FAS 95	Cash Flows	5
FAS 96	Taxes	8
FAS 96 Appendix A	Taxes	24

(Appendix A of Statement 96 might be regarded as effectively part of the standards section.)

The 1600 pages includes a great deal of material beyond just the standards. Materials such as the basis for conclusions, dissents, and illustrations are intended to be helpful in explaining the standards, and most constituents have found them so. Many Statements include a summary that is intended to be useful to the executive who is not a technical accountant. It is not clear whether the FEI and the BRT are advocating that such materials be excluded in the future.

Of all the FASB Statements issued to date, only 4 include 10 pages or more in the standards section (5 if you include Appendix A of Statement 96 as part of the standard) and 2 of those apply to specialized industries (Statements 19 and 60).

Emerging Issues Task Force

The Emerging Issues Task Force (EITF) is cited as a further example of overload. Since its inception in 1984, the EITF has considered 219 issues. Although its primary purpose is the early identification of implementation concerns and emerging issues, discussion of those concerns and issues helps the Board better understand what topics to consider for its agenda. A consensus by the EITF is achieved when no more than two of the thirteen voting members disagree on the appropriate accounting for a particular issue. A consensus indicates that diversity in practice is not likely to develop and no action by the Board is felt to be needed. A total of 151 issues have resulted in consensus by the EITF; of the remaining 68 issues, only 24 have been accepted for consideration and resolved by the Board, through the issuance of either a standard or a Technical Bulletin. The 151 issues that have resulted in a consensus reduce the likelihood of any significant changes in a particular accounting practice and permit the Board to focus on major issues.

Both the BRT and the FEI nominate members for the EITF and have done so since its inception in 1984. Three of the four industry representatives on the EITF at present were nominees of the BRT and the FEI. The chairman of the group that recommended creation of the EITF was a member of the FEI and was employed by a BRT company. We were under the impression that both groups supported the EITF and believed it to be a useful and constructive addition to the Board's process. We will be working to understand what these two groups might have had in mind by their comments. We have been informed that the SEC looks favorably on the EITF's open meetings and discussions and considers them an improvement over the more informal and less informed procedures used previously.

Conclusion

There were several major standards issued in the period from December 1985 through December 1987. With hindsight, it is clear that the confluence of those standards created a burden of implementation for some entities. The projects in the Board's pipeline make it unlikely that such a situation could recur soon, but the Board will carefully consider the relationships among its projects in deliberating future effective date and transition provisions.

We understand that new standards represent change and that change, as such, will be resisted by some constituents. Nevertheless, the Board has a mission to improve financial reporting, the inevitable result of which will be to effect some change. We are unlikely ever to definitively solve the standard-setting balances of theory versus practicality or the appropriate level of detail. The Board's basic mission is not consistent with pleasing all or even most constituents all of the time. We are dedicated to continuing to balance the conflicting objectives of constituents in standard setting.

We appreciate this opportunity to offer our comments on the letters of the FEI and the BRT. I hope that you will consider our comments as the SEC studies the effects of financial reporting standards on U.S. businesses.

Very truly yours,

Dennis R. Beresford, Chairman

cc: Edmund Coulson
John S. Reed
P. Norman Roy

Comparability, Competition, and Cost

Dennis R. Beresford
Chairman, Financial Accounting Standards Board

My assignment here is to comment on the present state of comparative international financial reporting in the era of more globalized business and finance. I can summarize it in one word: *changing*.

At the international level:

- The International Organization of Securities Commissions (IOSCO) has become active in the last few years with an agenda covering every area of securities regulation including accounting. IOSCO members are in a position to supply enforcement power, heretofore a significant deficiency in the International Accounting Standards Committee structure.
- The IASC, in exchange for potential IOSCO enforcement support, is attempting to eliminate most free-choice accounting alternatives from its standards. Beyond that, its work plan includes new projects to fill in some of the gaps in its body of standards. It is also trying to develop new funding sources to support its more ambitious level of activity.

At the national level, to cite only three countries:

- In the United Kingdom, a new Accounting Standards Board was created on August 1, 1990. It is styled somewhat along the lines of the FASB and includes an innovative new enforcement body.
- In Japan, according to *World Accounting Report*, the Finance Ministry plans to establish a foundation to undertake a fundamental study of the country's accounting system with a view to liberalization and internationalization. Japan also has a recently established Corporation Finance Research Institute, a private organization that aims to stimulate improvements in financial reporting.
- In the United States, the FASB has substantially increased its international involvement over the last three years. We want to be a leader in the internationalization of accounting.

Additionally, the Securities and Exchange Commission is pursuing its own initiative to improve U.S. competitiveness in international markets. It is experimenting with a reciprocal arrangement with Canada whereby for cer-

From Financial Accounting Standards Board Special Report, *Benefits, Costs, and Consequences of Financial Accounting Standards*, pp. 37–47. Reprinted by permission of the Financial Accounting Foundation. Copyright © 1991 by Financial Accounting Standards Board. Copies of the complete document are available from the FASB.

Author's note: This is based on a speech given in October 1990 at the New York University inauguration of an endowment for the study of comparative international financial reporting.

tain cross-border registration purposes each country will accept the other's requirements. The SEC also has issued Rule 144a, which opens a potentially large private-placement market with minimal disclosure requirements.

More recently, the SEC undertook a study of U.S. accounting practices, particularly their cost and complexity. The study has been handled a bit more informally than is usually the case with studies of such potential import, and we have substantial uncertainty about the objectives of the study. But it has stirred resounding applause from the business community and consternation in other quarters. Professor Stephen Zeff, a member of the Financial Accounting Standards Advisory Council, said: "It strikes right to the heart of the standard setting process and the meaning of the terms 'full and fair disclosure' in the Securities Acts." Professor Zeff also suggested that ". . . the SEC seems to be turning on its axis."

Although international accounting comparability has not usually been discussed in terms of the competitiveness of nations, there is a close relationship and that is the topic of this article.

THE NEED FOR COMPARABILITY

Comparable national accounting standards are needed by any multinational company as a matter of internal economy and effectiveness. Complying with national securities registration requirements, training foreign national employees, and converting foreign subsidiary books to parent company accounting methods are all complicated by differing national standards.

Yet, external, rather than internal, needs have come to dominate the debate about the comparability of national accounting. External needs center on certain decision processes. The most obvious external need for international accounting comparability is to help users evaluate corporate performance on a global scale. Cross-country comparisons of traditional indicators such as price–earnings ratios are meaningless, or worse—misleading, if the underlying accounting is not comparable.

Another important external need for comparability concerns financing decisions. World capital markets have developed to the point that corporations have a choice of country for raising capital. It is widely reported that many foreign companies are reluctant to offer their securities in U.S. public markets or list them on U.S. exchanges because they are unwilling to comply with the voluminous and detailed U.S. accounting and disclosure requirements or submit to the SEC's jurisdiction. This is said to put the U.S. exchanges and securities industry at a competitive disadvantage.

International accounting comparability would contribute to leveling the playing field for these and similar kinds of decisions. However, one should not forget that differences in tax law, business regulation, and other factors would continue to contribute plenty of tilts and potholes.

The question I would like to explore is: Should the competitiveness of U.S. companies be factored into the FASB decision process, and if so, how?

COMPETITION AND ACCOUNTING IN
A DOMESTIC SETTING

An Early Case Study: Oil and Gas Accounting

Concern about the impact of financial disclosures on domestic competition has a long history. The mandate of full and fair disclosure in the securities laws of 1933 and 1934 caused widespread concerns at that time that the required disclosures could have a major negative impact on the competitiveness of enterprises. Indeed, as a result of the concern, the Securities Exchange Act of 1934 requires the SEC to consider the burden on competition before adopting its regulations.

However, in dealing with oil and gas accounting in the late 1970s, the SEC issued a classic statement that I would like to quote in part:

> The Commission wishes to make clear . . . its view that attempts to foster particular national economic policies, such as an increase in domestic petroleum production, are not appropriate considerations in formulating financial reporting standards. Financial reporting should seek to provide investors with useful information that is relevant, reliable, comparable, and unbiased. Otherwise, the capital allocation process would be distorted and ultimately the credibility of the information provided by financial reporting would be lost.[1]

The Commission topped that off by stating, "The Commission believes further that allocation of capital in the market place should be based on the competitive performance of companies and not on their accounting methods."[2]

The Neutrality Precept

The SEC's position as articulated in that case is captured both in the FASB's mission statement and in our conceptual framework by the precept of neutrality. In turn, the precept of neutrality is derived from the basic objective of financial reporting—to provide decision-useful information to economic decision makers.

Neutral information is unbiased information; it does not *intentionally* favor one party over another; it is not colored for the purpose of influencing behavior in any particular direction. Like reports on consumer prices, the GNP, or the census, financial statements are meant to serve evenhandedly all users who need that kind of information. Although financial information should be neutral, financial statements are designed to be used by private decision makers who are *not* neutral and who are in competition with one

---

[1] Statement of SEC Chairman Harold M. Williams, "Accounting Practices for Oil and Gas Producers," August 29, 1978, p. 80, fn 32.

[2] Ibid., p. 9.

another in pursuit of private gains. Financial statements also are used by public policy decision makers with constituents who are not neutral and who are in competition with one another in pursuit of shares of public benefits. As a result of these uses, neutral information has economic and social consequences that may advantage some and disadvantage others.

The Cost-Benefit Precept

The neutrality precept often gets tangled up with another central part of the FASB process, the cost-benefit precept. The FASB is charged with the responsibility to evaluate the costs and benefits of every proposed standard and to adopt standards only if they are judged to provide a net benefit. The neutrality and cost-benefit precepts are not in conflict as the FASB applies them, but they are sometimes thought to be by others.

Why is it so often asserted that FASB standards do not pass cost–benefit tests? The answer is rooted in the fact that cost-benefit analysis is a judgmental process involving a range of advantages and disadvantages. Cost-benefit analysis can be done in a highly structured form—as in Defense Secretary Robert McNamara's famous Planning, Programming, Budgeting System—that gives an appearance of precision but still results in judgmental decisions. This is not just because different people put different weights on identified costs and benefits, which they do. It is also because people identify a *different set* of costs and benefits that includes things that the FASB believes are out of bounds for its cost-benefit consideration because of its responsibility to be neutral—for example, the impact of a standard on profitability.

In the broadest sense, the underlying cost of an accounting standard from a reporting entity's perspective is loss of control over information; that is, loss of ability to decide whether, when, or how to present information. It is loss of management flexibility and, to some degree, loss of the advantage of insider information. The counterpart of the reporting entity's loss is the using entity's gain—access to information with analytic power, which is the power to help make better investment decisions. Because at bottom any proposed accounting change activates a power struggle—the power of information—cost-benefit analysis in the standards-setting environment is particularly contentious.

The consequences that may flow from an accounting standard can be put into four categories:

- First, compliance costs accrue to both reporting and using entities for such things as learning how to apply a new standard and starting up and operating data processing systems.
- Second, better investment returns and fewer losses from bad credits and business failures may accrue to using entities because of better investment and credit decisions. As economists put it, better information reduces the asymmetry of information between buyers and sellers.
- Third, a variety of advantages or disadvantages may accrue to reporting entities through the impact reported information may have on such

things as an entity's cost and availability of capital, wage settlements and executive compensation, and attractiveness as a takeover target.

- Fourth, market allocation decisions may have secondary consequences that affect all or a segment of the general populace in some way, for example, dependence on foreign oil as claimed in the oil and gas case cited earlier or curtailment of medical coverage as claimed for our current project on retiree health care benefits.

Of the range of potential consequences, the FASB looks essentially only to compliance costs and capital market efficiency (categories one and two) in its cost-benefit evaluations. Generally, we do not weigh in the potential effects on profitability or competitiveness of reporting entities (category three). Of course, we consider those effects to be sure that accounting standards affect all entities evenhandedly. Beyond that, however, the neutrality precept prevents us from taking actions that favor one competitor over another or over the public interest.

The FASB also does not put indirect economic and social consequences (category four) on its cost-benefit scale. Whether those consequences are beneficial or detrimental to the public interest are issues of public policy, and there are many tools of public policy that can be used to deal with them. The FASB has no public policymaking role. Its job is to set standards that provide neutral decision-useful information for public policymakers and others to act on.

Thus, the competitiveness of individual companies and industries in the domestic economy has not been a factor in the cost-benefit equation at the FASB. Exclusion of competitiveness from cost-benefit consideration is based on the need for neutral financial information to enhance the efficiency of capital markets and the efficacy of public policy. The SEC apparently agrees, based on the oil and gas example cited earlier and the following sentences from testimony of SEC Chairman Richard C. Breeden to the Senate Banking Committee on September 10, 1990.

> The purpose of accounting standards is to assure that financial information is presented in a way that enables decision makers to make informed judgments. To the extent that accounting standards are subverted to achieve objectives unrelated to a fair and accurate presentation, they fail in their purpose.

Let's turn now to the international scene.

COMPETITION AND ACCOUNTING IN AN INTERNATIONAL SETTING

Forbes magazine, in an article about a so-called inventive new way to avoid goodwill charges, took a shot at U.S. accounting, stating, "Having decided the [business combination] case on narrow grounds, the accountants have made it that much more difficult for U.S. business to compete internationally. Is that what they are there for?"[3]

Business Week, under a headline "The SEC Is Relaxing—So Investors Should Be Nervous," took a shot at *foreign* accounting this way:

> Under the new private-placement rules [Rule 144a], securities reliant on dubious foreign accounting practices could reach the U.S. "This type of back-door entry into the U.S. market is going to be an invitation to individuals who can buy accounting opinions more readily overseas," [says an investor].[4]

Those two news clips pretty well bracket the range of views about U.S. accounting and international competition. *Forbes* complained because U.S. rules were *not* bent in the interest of competition; *Business Week* complained because they were. I would like to pose and briefly explore two questions:

- First, is there something different about the *international* setting that provides a rationale for the FASB to factor competitiveness issues into its standards-setting decisions?
- Second, what can the FASB do about the competitiveness problem?

What is Different About International Competition?

I think the logic is compelling for the FASB to be neutral with respect to domestic competitors. However, the logic does not transfer automatically to the international setting. Like domestic competition, international competition is fostered by free markets, and free markets are fostered by a free flow of information. But as some parties have observed, there is no global capital market per se, only a network of national markets. The key difference between international competition and domestic competition is that internationally there is no exclusive regulatory jurisdiction. That changes the competitive implications of accounting standards.

In the domestic economy, U.S. accounting standards apply to all entities, and it is relatively easy to make them competitively neutral. When U.S. companies compete against foreign companies, however, a domestically neutral U.S. accounting measurement can make a U.S. company look better or worse than its foreign competitors who apply different accounting standards. Thus, any U.S. standard that differs from standards applicable to foreign competitors is on its face not neutral. So the questions: Does neutrality stop at the border? If the FASB's neutrality precept is inapplicable in relation to international competition, does that open the cost-benefit equation to the introduction of international competitive impacts on U.S. companies?

To help explore those questions, let's look at the accounting for goodwill. Some have suggested that more liberal accounting in the United Kingdom

[3] Dana Wechsler Linden, "The Accountants versus the Dealmakers," *Forbes* (August 20, 1990): 84.
[4] Dean Foust, "The SEC Is Relaxing—So Investors Should Be Nervous," *Business Week* (July 2, 1990):32.

provides an advantage for U.K. acquirers. They urge the FASB to level the playing field by conforming U.S. goodwill accounting to the British accounting. That sounds simple but it raises several questions.

- First, the complaints center on only the United States and the United Kingdom. What about Japan and others? Japan, for example, is also a major acquirer of U.S. companies; it requires amortization of goodwill over five years.
- Second, the IASC is proposing five-year amortization—20 at most. Would U.S. companies, especially those not concerned with international competition, prefer the IASC proposal to the United States' 40 years?
- And third, tax deductibility of goodwill also varies by country. Does it make sense to attack the accounting but not the tax effect?

What Can Be Done About Competitiveness?

This very brief analysis just scratches the surface of the complexity of the issues involved in trying to modify U.S. accounting in the interest of competitiveness. Several ideas have been floating around about what the FASB might do.

One of these would be to respond ad hoc to specific problems as they arise, such as the goodwill issue. The idea would be to modify U.S. accounting not to give U.S. companies an advantage but simply to remove a disadvantage. A potential problem with this approach is that if several major countries began to pursue a course of removing accounting disadvantages, it might well trigger a race to the most permissive standard—the lowest common denominator.

A second idea is similar to the above but instead of responding on an ad hoc basis to specific identified problems, the FASB would systematically review existing standards to seek out those that might be competitively disadvantageous to U.S. companies. This idea might also run into the race-to-the-bottom problem, and it has a further problem—disadvantageous as compared to what? Any FASB standard is likely to differ from several other countries' standards, and trying to sort out which to adjust to would be difficult.

A third approach would be for the FASB to work with the IASC and others to improve international standards to the point where they would be acceptable for national reporting use. That would solve the comparability and competitiveness problems for everyone. The FASB is already committed to this approach in principle, and we have a number of initiatives under way. However, there is one obvious drawback to the approach: It will be very slow.

There needs to be continuing debate on these issues, and the FASB will be at the forefront of this debate. Let me share some preliminary thoughts. First, I acknowledge that without exclusive jurisdiction, neutrality seems somewhat more problematic. It does not follow, however, that U.S. accounting standards should be shaped to favor U.S. companies or to remove perceived accounting disadvantages. Competitive advantage or disadvantage still does not belong to the cost-benefit equation, in my opinion.

Even if we wanted to take account of competitive advantage, the task would be virtually impossible. The earnings effect of a standard is at best a nebulous indicator of competitive advantage. Negative earnings effects are often judged positively by the market, and vice versa, because the market looks to *quality* as well as *quantity* of earnings. Further, accounting combines with such important factors as tax laws, foreign trade and investment barriers, business regulation, and monetary and fiscal policies to make up a package of competitiveness factors that is unique to each country. Picking out the net effect of any one factor would be a needle-and-haystack exercise.

While my last few comments seem to emphasize the negative side of the competitiveness issue, there are several positive things that can be done. Two broad courses of action are available: unilateral action by the FASB and cooperative action with the IASC and other national standards setters. The FASB will follow both courses.

As to unilateral action, I have already discouraged the urge to design standards either to gain competitive advantages or remove a disadvantage. But there are other possibilities.

- As an overall matter, I think that the FASB and its constituents need to elevate international considerations to a higher level in all FASB projects and activities. We have taken quite a few specific steps already. And though this is a long-range effort, we are taking the time and making the effort to work it into the routine of the process from beginning to end.
- The FASB can monitor complaints about specific standards and use them as a guide to where it should focus its cooperative efforts. Complaints also can be used as a basis for reexamining standards to see if they are currently judged to provide the best measure of economic events. Comparison with IASC and other national standards could yield new insights.
- The FASB can intensify and sharpen its efforts to make FASB standards as simple and cost-effective as possible. For example, recently we sent a questionnaire to our Advisory Council that asks for their views on any standards that are unnecessarily complex or costly. I caution, though, that pressure from all sources—users, auditors, regulators, and even preparers—have traditionally been in the direction of more detailed standards.

As to cooperative efforts, we have already increased our liaison with the IASC, both as a member of its Consultative Group and in connection with specific projects. We see the IASC as the focal point for internationalizing accounting standards, but much depends on the fate of its project to reduce accounting alternatives, its further efforts to fill in gaps in its set of standards, and its success in obtaining a more reasonable level of funding.

I believe there also needs to be more direct consultation and cooperation among *national* standards setters, not to bypass the IASC but as an additional level of cooperation among the bodies that will largely determine the degree to which IASC standards gain worldwide acceptability. National standards setters for the most part are not represented on the IASC, yet they are the ones who call the shots in their domestic settings. International leadership is going to have to be shared if standards are going to become comparable and, equally as important, if they are going to continue to improve in their ability to measure economic activity.

One example of cooperative efforts is a conference on conceptual frameworks now scheduled for June 1991 in Brussels. I first proposed such a conference in an address to the IASC in 1988. Others picked up on it, in particular the European Federation of Accountants (FEE). They and the IASC have brought it along logistically, and several major accounting firms have pledged funding.

In addition to the conference I just mentioned, there are several other specific ideas that we've been considering. One possibility would be a joint project on a topic such as accounting for business combinations with other major countries' standards setters. Another is a research project on the *overall objectives of disclosures* in financial statements, with the idea of rechallenging whether all the standard-specific disclosures are necessary. These are just a couple of examples of "brainstorming," and I encourage all of you to lend your creative thinking to this process.

I think the June 1991 Brussels conference, in particular, will be a step toward developing conceptual measurement objectives and international comparability. Those who think of accounting as a body of arbitrary conventions see the internationalization process as one of negotiation or horse trading. If I held that view, I would be pessimistic about the future of international accounting. Either it would degenerate into a body of inconsistent and toothless generalities or, probably more likely, a substantial stalemate. Accounting standards that are not guided by a conceptual measurement objective are a little like religious maxims—unprovable empirically and therefore accepted on faith. People don't readily negotiate away their articles of faith, hence the potential for stalemate.

Those who view accounting as a process of measuring economic activity have room for a degree of optimism if they have sufficient patience. Economic transactions and events are universal in their effects. They are fundamentally the same in any country, any language, any currency denomination—all are reducible to a measure of past, present, or future cash flows.

Current accounting in the United States, as in all other countries, still falls considerably short of the level of measurement excellence that is achievable. But if there is international agreement on the measurement goal, there is a realistic chance of moving toward international comparability and thereby also removing any possible accounting causes of competitive inequality. If better measurement of economic activity is the objective, not only will comparability and competitive equality be achieved, they will be achieved at a much higher level of financial statement quality.

The Rise of "Economic Consequences"

Stephen A. Zeff
Rice University

In the late 1960s, a literature began to build on the two related subjects of (a) the growing interest by third parties in the establishment of accounting standards, and (b) the impact of accounting standards, and especially changes in those standards, on the behavior of affected parties. In 1968, Moonitz wrote that

> The stake of nonprofessionals in the consequences of any given set of [accounting] principles is too great for them to accept the decisions of a body of technical experts on a voluntary basis, no matter how eminent those experts or how persuasive the research support for their findings [1968, p. 631].

He later urged the standard-setting bodies, to cultivate allies, such as the Securities and Exchange Commission (SEC), in order to secure the enforcement of their pronouncements in the face of political action by "nonprofessionals" [1974, Chap. 7]. In 1969, Hawkins argued that "the time has come . . . to pay greater attention to the possible impact of accounting practices on people's actions" [1969, p. 21]. He referred not only to the possible dysfunctional effect of reported accounting figures on the behavior of managers, but also to the creation of an illusion of managerial performance when none exists [1969, p. 13].

By the mid-1970s, the literature on the politics of the standard-setting process, once a neglected subject, was growing apace [see, e.g., Stamp and Marley, 1970; Gerboth, 1973; Horngren, 1973; Moonitz, 1974; and Chatov, 1975], and the number of articles dealing with various phases of the social and economic consequences of accounting standards was also very much on the rise. Such terms as "feedback effects" [Prakash and Rappaport, 1976], "information inductance" [Prakash and Rappaport, 1977], "economic impact" [Buckley, 1975; Horngren, 1976; Rappaport, 1977; and FAF, 1977], and finally "economic consequences" [FASB, 1977a and FASB, 1978] began to populate the literature. At the same time, and not entirely by coincidence, articles began to appear on the

> fundamental questions of resource allocation and social choice [which] appear to underlie the question of choice among financial reporting alternatives [Demski, 1974, p. 232].

As suggested above, these two developing strains in the literature—the increasing involvement of "nonprofessionals" in the standard-setting process, and the economic (and social) consequences of the accounting standards

Author's note: I gratefully acknowledge the suggestions of Alfred Rappaport, Lawrence Revsine, George J. Staubus, and Joseph G. San Miguel during the planning stage of writing this paper. Responsibility for what has emerged, however, is mine.

themselves—are inextricably related. The very intervention by outside parties in the setting of standards appears to be due, in large measure, to their belief in the fact of economic consequences. The two themes were novel in the accounting literature, and it would not be an exaggeration to label the suggestion that standard-setting bodies take account of economic consequences as nothing less than revolutionary. Judging from accounting textbooks, treatises, articles, and earlier statements emitted from standard-setting bodies and committees of the American Accounting Association, one would have fairly concluded that conventional accounting wisdom supported a resolution of accounting controversies exclusively by reference to some combination of accounting theory, "accounting principles," and "fair presentation." To suggest that accounting policy makers should seriously consider the impact of proposed accounting standards on the micro- and macro-economic welfare of affected parties would have been, only a few years ago, a heresy. Until recently accounting policy making was either assumed to be neutral in its effects or, if not neutral, it was not responsible for those effects. Today neither assumption is unquestioningly accepted as valid, and the subject of social and economic consequences "has become *the* central contemporary issue in accounting" [AAA, 1977b, p. 4]. That the Financial Accounting Standards Board (FASB) has commissioned research papers on the economic consequences of selected standards [see, e.g., FASB, 1977b and c] and has held a conference devoted entirely to the subject [FASB, 1978] underscores the current importance of this mode of inquiry.

In these discussions, the terms "professional" and "nonprofessional" are troublesome. The phrase "accounting profession" is used in a variety of senses. In the United States, it is confined in the strictest sense to independent certified public accountants. But some might include controllers, internal auditors, management accountants, and government accountants. In Great Britain, the term typically refers to a broader array of qualified accountants than in the United States. In the Institute of Chartered Accountants in England and Wales, nonpracticing accountants played leadership roles in the development of accounting principles as long ago as the early 1940s, nonpracticing members have been members of the Council since 1943, and the first nonpracticing president was elected in 1968 [Zeff, 1972, pp. 7–9], while it was not until 1978 that the American Institute of Certified Public Accountants (AICPA) changed its by-laws to permit nonpractitioners to become officers. It is not my intention to endeavor to resolve this problem of definition, but only to suggest that the terms are open to ambiguity. In the ensuing discussion, I will use "third party" or "outside party" in place of "nonprofessional."

Accounting policy makers have been aware since at least the 1960s of the third-party intervention issue,[1] while the issue of economic consequences has

---

[1] In this paper, I am chiefly concerned with third-party intervention in the standard setting for unregulated industries. Accounting policy makers in this country have been alive for several decades to the accounting implications of the rules and regulations of rate-making agencies in the energy, transportation, and communication industries. See, e.g., May [1943, Chap. 7–8], Paton [1944], and Davidson [1952].

surfaced only in the 1970s. Indeed, much of the history of the Accounting Principles Board (APB) during the 1960s was one of endeavoring to understand and cope with the third-party forces which were intervening in the standard-setting process. In the end, the inability of the APB to deal effectively with these forces led to its demise and the establishment in 1973 of the FASB.

The true preoccupations of the intervening third parties have not always been made clear. When endeavoring to understand the third-party arguments, one must remember that prior to the 1970s the accounting model employed by the Committee on Accounting Procedure (CAP) and the APB was, formally at least, confined to technical accounting considerations (sometimes called "accounting principles" or "conceptual questions"), such as the measurement of assets, liabilities, and income, and the "fair presentation" of financial position and operations. The policy makers' sole concern was with the communication of financial information to actual and potential investors, for, indeed, their charter had been "granted" by the SEC, which itself had been charged by Congress to assure "full and fair disclosure" in reports to investors. Third-party interveners, therefore, would have had an obvious incentive to appeal to the accounting model being used by the policy makers, rather than implicitly suggest that the policy makers should adopt an economic consequences model preferred by the third parties.

When management intervened in the standard-setting process, therefore, its true position may well have been disguised. The following three-part classification of management arguments suggests the range of tactical rhetoric employed over the years:

1. Arguments couched in terms of the traditional accounting model, where management is genuinely concerned about unbiased and "theoretically sound" accounting measurements.
2. Arguments couched in terms of the traditional accounting model, where management is really seeking to advance its self-interest in the economic consequences of the contents of published reports.
3. Arguments couched in terms of the economic consequences in which management is self-interested.

If one accepts Johnson's dictum that it requires a "lively imagination" to believe that management is genuinely concerned with fair presentation when choosing between accounting alternatives [1966, p. 91; also see Moonitz, 1968, pp. 628–30], it could be concluded that Argument 1 has seldom been employed in third-party interventions. In recent years, particularly since the early 1970s, management appears to have become increasingly more candid, by electing Argument 3 in discussions with accounting policy makers. That the economic consequences issue was not scrutinized earlier than the 1970s was probably due, at least in part, to the habit of the APB to resolve, and to be seen to resolve, each controversy in the context of the traditional accounting model. Another possible explanation is the predominance of instances of Argument 2, which would have encouraged the Board to confine itself to the traditional model.

THE U.S. HISTORY OF THIRD-PARTY
INTERVENTIONS OF THE "ECONOMIC
CONSEQUENCES" VARIETY (CAP, APB, FASB)

It may be believed by some that third-party intervention coupled with the intrusion into accounting policy debates of economic-consequences considerations are of recent origin. Indeed, if one overlooks the unwitting support which a committee of the American Institute of [Certified Public] Accountants (AIA) gave to Congress as a pretext to impose LIFO inventory accounting on financial reporting [AIA, 1936, p. 465], the first evidence of economic-consequences reasoning in the pronouncements of American policy makers occurred as long ago as 1941. In Accounting Research Bulletin No. 11, "Corporate Accounting for Ordinary Stock Dividends," the CAP, in accordance with "proper accounting and corporate policy," required that fair market value be used to record the issuance of stock dividends where such market value was substantially in excess of book value [AIA, 1941, pp. 102–03]. George O. May, the *de facto* chairman of the CAP at that time, later wrote:

> The phrase 'proper accounting and corporate policy' indicates that the committee went beyond consideration of purely accounting questions. In the early stage of discussion such a step was not contemplated but as the study progressed, the committee came to feel strongly that it had an opportunity, in conjunction with the [New York] Stock Exchange, to take a step in the interest of *financial morality* and to safeguard against recurrence of abuses such as took place in and immediately prior to 1929 in connection with the issue of periodical stock dividends [May, 1952, p. 1; emphasis mine].

Evidently, both the New York Stock Exchange and a majority of the Committee on Accounting Procedure regarded periodic stock dividends as "objectionable" [May, 1941, p. 1], and the CAP acted to make it more difficult for corporations to sustain a series of such stock dividends out of their accumulated earnings. As far as I know, the United States is still the only country in which an accounting pronouncement requires that stock dividends be capitalized at the fair market value of the issued shares [see, e.g., *Price Waterhouse International*, 1975, Table 145], and this position was originally adopted in this country, at least in part, in order to produce an impact on the stock dividend policies of corporations.

A second evidence of economic consequences entering into the debates surrounding the establishment of accounting standards, this time involving management representations, occurred in 1947–48. It was the height of the postwar inflation, and several corporations had adopted replacement cost depreciation in their published financial statements [*Depreciation Policy When Price Levels Change*, 1948, Chap. 14]. Among the arguments employed in the debate involving the CAP were the possible implications for tax reform, the possible impact on wage bargaining, and the need to counteract criticisms of profiteering by big business [see, e.g., "Dual Accounting System Suggested for Depreciation," 1948; "Institute Committee Holds to Depreciation on

Cost," 1948; *Changing Concepts of Business Income*, 1952, p. 64; *Depreciation Policy When Price Levels Change*, 1948, Chap. 13; Storey, 1964, pp. 34–38; and Paton, 1948].[2] Notwithstanding the pressures for accounting reform, the CAP reaffirmed its support of historical cost accounting for depreciation in Accounting Research Bulletin No. 33 and in a letter issued in October, 1948.

A clear use of economic consequences occurred in 1958, when three subsidiaries of American Electric Power Company sued in the Federal courts to enjoin the AICPA from allowing the CAP to issue a letter saying that the Deferred Tax Credit account, as employed in the recently issued Accounting Research Bulletin No. 44 (Revised), should be classified as a liability [see *The AICPA Injunction Case*, 1960]. The three public utility companies were concerned that the SEC, under authority granted by the Public Utility Holding Company Act, would not permit them to issue debt securities in view of the unfavorable debt-to-equity ratios which the proposed reclassification would produce. The case reached the Supreme Court, where *certiorari* was denied. In the end, the clarifying letter was issued. Nonetheless, the SEC accommodated the public utility companies by consenting to exclude the Deferred Tax Credit from both liabilities and stockholders' equity for purposes of decisions taken under the Public Utility Holding Company Act [*SEC Administrative Policy* . . ., 1961, pp. 35–39].

Shortly after the creation of the APB, the accounting treatment of the investment tax credit exploded upon the scene. The three confrontations between the APB and the combined forces of industry and the administrations of Presidents Kennedy, Johnson, and Nixon have already been amply discussed in the literature [see Moonitz, 1966; Carey, 1970, pp. 98–104; and Zeff, 1972, pp. 178–80, 201–02, 219–21, and 326–27]. The Government's argument was not that the accounting deferral of the investment tax credit was bad accounting, but that it diluted the incentive effect of an instrument of fiscal policy.

In 1965, the subject of segmental reporting emerged from a hearing of the Senate Subcommittee on Antitrust and Monopoly on the economic effects of conglomerate mergers. The aim of the Senatorial inquiry was not to promote better accounting practices for investor use, but to provide the Subcommittee and other government policy makers with accounting data that would facilitate their assessment of the economic efficacy of conglomerate mergers. Company managements naturally looked upon such disclosures as potentially detrimental to their merger ambitions. Pressure applied by this powerful Subcommittee eventually forced the hand of the SEC to call for product-line disclosures in published financial reports. The repercussions of this

---

[2] In a survey conducted by the American Institute of [Certified Public] Accountants in 1948, the business executives who replied divided 31–22 in favor of reporting net income after subtracting cost of goods sold and depreciation expense on a current-cost basis *if that were accepted for tax purposes*. The executives divided 31–22 *against* such financial reporting if it were not accepted for tax purposes [AIA, 1948, pp. 1, 10].

initiative which had its origin in a Senate hearing room are still being felt [see, e.g., Plum and Collins, 1976].

In 1967–69, the APB responded to an anguished objection by the startled Investment Bankers Association of America (IBA) (known today as the Securities Industry Association) to a provision, once thought to be innocuous, in APB Opinion No. 10 which imputed a debt discount to convertible debt and debt issued with stock warrants. The IBA was concerned about the impact of the accounting procedure on the market for such securities. In APB Opinion No. 14, the Board rescinded its action in regard to convertible debt, while retaining the rest [see Zeff, 1972, p. 202, 211].

During 1968–71, the banking industry opposed the inclusion of bad-debt provisions and losses on the sales of securities in the net income of commercial banks. Bankers believed that the new measure would reflect unfavorably on the performance of banks. Eventually, through a concerted effort by the APB, SEC, and the bank regulatory agencies, generally accepted accounting principles were made applicable to banks [see Carey, 1970, p. 134; Moonitz, 1974, pp. 38–39; and Zeff, 1972, pp. 210–11].

In 1968–70, the APB struggled with the accounting for business combinations. It was flanked on the one side by the Federal Trade Commission and the Department of Justice, who favored the elimination of "pooling of interests" accounting in order to produce a slowing effect on the merger movement, and on the other side by merger-minded corporations who were fervent supporters of "pooling of interests" accounting. The APB, appearing to behave as if it were a pawn in a game of political chess, disenchanted many of its supporters, as it abandoned positions of principle in favor of an embarrassing series of pressure-induced compromises [see Chatov, 1975, pp. 212–22; and Zeff, 1972, pp. 212–16].

In 1971, the APB held public hearings on accounting for marketable equity securities, leases, and the exploration and drilling costs of companies in the petroleum industry. In all three areas, powerful industry pressures thwarted the Board from acting. The insurance industry was intensely concerned about the possible effects on its companies' stock prices of including the unrealized gains and losses on portfolio holdings in their income statements [see Horngren, 1973, pp. 63–64]. The leasing question was squelched after senators, representatives, and even the secretary of transportation responded to a letter-writing campaign by making pointed inquiries of the SEC and APB. The letter-writers raised the specter of injury which the Board's proposed action would cause to consumers and to the viability of companies in several key industries [see Savoie, 1974, p. 326].[3] The petroleum industry

---

[3] Several of the letters sent to congressmen and senators were in all material respects identical, and although the addresses of those whose names appeared at the bottom of the letters were in different states, the secretary's initials (kh) and the type face used were all the same. These letter writers uniformly claimed the following economic consequences of requiring lessees to capitalize leases: *(cont'd)*

was unable to unite on a solution to the controversy over full costing v. successful-efforts costing, as it was alleged that a general imposition of the latter would adversely affect the fortunes of the small, independent exploration companies [see the testimony and submissions in *APB Public Hearing on Accounting and Reporting Practices in the Petroleum Industry*, 1972]. Using its considerable political might, the industry succeeded in persuading the Board to postpone consideration of the sensitive subject [see Savoie, 1974, p. 326].

On each of the occasions enumerated above, outside parties intervened in the standard-setting process by an appeal to criteria which transcended the traditional questions of accounting measurement and fair presentation. They were concerned instead with the economic consequences of the accounting pronouncements.

Economic consequences have been invoked with even greater intensity in the short life of the FASB. Such questions as accounting for research and development costs, self-insurance and catastrophe reserves, development stage companies, foreign currency fluctuations, leases, the restructuring of troubled debt,[4] domestic inflation and relative price changes, and the exploration and drilling costs of companies in the petroleum industry have provoked widespread interest in their economic consequences [see, e.g., Burns, 1976;

---

[3] *(cont'd)*

    1. Raise the cost of electric power to the public by an estimated $550 million yearly towards the end of the decade.

    2. Raise the cost of freight transportation to industry and the public.

    3. Reduce the inventory of railroad cars and locomotives.

    4. Increase the costs of air fares to the public.

    5. Damage the aerospace industry.

    6. Raise the costs of all goods and services to the public.

    7. Prevent many small and growing businesses from acquiring modern cost-cutting machinery and equipment.

    8. Negatively affect our present adverse international balance of trade.

[4] At the Board's public hearing, some bankers warned of the dire economic consequences of requiring banks to write down their receivables following restructuring. Walter B. Wriston, chairman of Citicorp, said:

> If the banks that held the New York City obligations had been required to record an immediate write-off of say, 25 percent of principal as a result of restructuring, that restructuring just might not have happened. Several of the banks whose cooperation was essential might not have been able to afford it, not from an economic point of view, but in terms of the way that readers of financial statements would interpret such charged earnings. Some New York banks were at that time under severe earning pressure and the prospect of a significant additional charge with a corresponding reduction in capital would have been totally unacceptable [Wriston, 1977, pp. 69–70].

Yet the FASB, in its lengthy "Basis for Conclusions" in Statement No. 15 (in which the feared write-downs were not required), did not refer to bankers' claims about the economic consequences of requiring significant write-downs. Does that omission imply that the Board paid no attention to those assertions? Did the Board conduct any empirical research (as it did concerning the economic consequences claims raised in connection with Statement No. 7, on development stage enterprises) to determine whether there was adequate ground to sustain such claims?

AAA, 1977b, pp. 9–12; Rappaport, 1977, pp. 90, 92; FASB, 1978; U.S. Department of Energy, 1978].[5] The list is both extensive and impressive, and accounting academics are busily investigating the validity of claims that these and other accounting standards are empirically linked with the specified economic consequences.

RESPONSE OF STANDARD-SETTING BODIES TO THIRD-PARTY INTERVENTION AND "ECONOMIC CONSEQUENCES"

What have been the reactions of standard-setting bodies to (a) the intervention by outside parties, and (b) the claim that accounting standards should or should not be changed in order to avoid unhealthy economic consequences? The reactions have been of three kinds: procedural alone, procedural with apparent substantive effects, and explicitly substantive. The first two kinds of reactions predominated until the early 1970s [Zeff, 1972, pp. 167–208]:

1940s. The CAP improved liaison with outside parties and expanded the circulation of early drafts and subcommittee reports.

1950s. The CAP greatly enlarged the list of individuals and organizations to whom exposure drafts were sent.

1957–58. The AICPA appointed a prominent member of the Controllers Institute of America (now known as the Financial Executives Institute (FEI), to the AICPA's Special Committee on Research Program. (The Controllers Institute had complained about its small role in the standard-setting process, and the appointment of a controller to this important AICPA committee was perhaps the first instance in which an individual who was not a practitioner or academic was named to a policy-level AICPA committee.)

1959. The AICPA appointed two financial executives to the first APB. (This was evidently the first appointment of accountants in industry to an AICPA policy-making committee.)

1959–60. The APB began to appoint to the project advisory committees of its research studies some persons who were not members of the Board.

1964–65. For the first time, the APB employed subject-area committees to prepare drafts of proposed pronouncements, and non-Board members began to be appointed to the committees.

1964–65. The Board chairman and AICPA president urged interested

---

[5] Evidence attesting to the attention given by the FASB to economic consequences issues may be found in the "Basis of Conclusions" sections of the applicable statements. In addition to companies and industry groups, government departments (such as the Department of Commerce, in Statement No. 7, and the Departments of Energy and Justice, in Statement No. 19) were actively involved in the discussion of economic consequences.

organizations to collaborate more intensively with the Board, and several important bodies reorganized their liaison activities.

1960s. The Board intensified the exposure process, increasing the number of organizations and individuals to whom exposure drafts were routinely sent. During one period it published exposure drafts in *The Journal of Accountancy*, and later sent drafts to all members of the Institute by separate mail. In the deliberations leading up to Opinions 16 and 17, the Board sent some 20,000 exposure drafts to a wide range of interested organizations and individuals, in addition to sending copies to all AICPA members.

mid–1960s. The Board began to issue "mini-exposure" drafts to interested organizations in order to obtain their views before publishing its formal exposure drafts.

1965–66. The Board's subject-area committees began to hold informal meetings with the representatives of interested organizations.

1966–67. The AICPA created the position of executive vice-president who was to be a spokesman to the press and at meetings of interested organizations.

1968. At the initiative of the AICPA, a two-day symposium was held to exchange ideas between the preparers and users of accounting information; representatives attended from the four co-sponsors: AICPA, FEI, Financial Analysts Federation, and Robert Morris Associates.

1969. In order to fortify the liaison with interested organizations, the Board began to hold symposia on the drafts of proposed pronouncements; attendance was by invitation and the proceedings were closed.

1971. In an effort to meet criticisms of its symposia (e.g., not all interested groups were invited), the Board began to hold public hearings, for which the subject-area committees prepared brief discussion memoranda.

It is evident from the series of steps taken by the AICPA and the APB that they endeavored to bring interested organizations more closely into the standard-setting process, hoping, one supposes, that these organizations would be satisfied that their opinions were given full consideration before the final issuance of opinions. These accommodations were, however, of a procedural sort, although it is possible that these outside opinions did have an impact on the substantive content of some of the resulting opinions. It would appear that the APB was at least somewhat influenced by economic consequences in its prolonged deliberations leading to the issuance of Opinions 16 and 17 [Wyatt, 1977, pp. 92–93]. Yet it is interesting that during the public hearings in 1971 on marketable equity securities and the accounting practices of companies in the petroleum industry, in which management representatives on several occasions asserted economic consequences as relevant considerations, none of the members of the Board's subject-area committees asked questions about the empirical basis for those assertions or, indeed, inquired about their relevance to the setting of accounting standards [see *Proceedings*, 1971; and *APB Public Hearing* . . . , 1972].

In view of the fact that it was the APB's inability to cope with the pressures brought by outside organizations which led to its demise, it is noteworthy that the FASB includes the Financial Executives Institute among its co-sponsors. In my opinion, the incorporation of the FEI in the formal structure of the FASB is one of the most significant advantages which the FASB possesses in relation to its predecessor.[6] Horngren, an APB member in its final years, has said,

> The FEI as an institutional body representing management, by and large, was opposed to the Board, particularly in the latter years, on almost every issue. . . . [T]he FEI seemed in favor of scrapping the APB; to the extent that it could be an institutional force it helped in its termination. They felt . . . that they should have more of a direct voice in the formation of accounting principles [Horngren, 1974, p. 95].

The procedural machinery established for the FASB is even more elaborate than that which existed in the final years of the APB. The object of these additional procedures has been to expand and intensify the interaction between the Board and interested outside parties, notably companies, industry associations, and government departments and agencies. Task forces drawn from a broad spectrum of interested groups are appointed prior to the preparation of each discussion memorandum. The memorandum itself is much bulkier than the modest document which the APB had issued prior to its public hearings; it contains a neutral discussion of the entire gamut of policy issues which bear on the resolution of the controversy before the Board. A Financial Accounting Standards Advisory Council (FASAC), composed of representatives of a wide array of interested groups, was appointed to be a sounding board for the FASB. The Board itself has been composed of members drawn from accounting practice, the universities, companies, and government—again, so that it would be responsive—and would appear to be responsive—to the concerns of those "constituencies." In an effort to persuade skeptics of the merit of its recommendations, the Board includes in its statements a lengthy explanation of the criteria, arguments, and empirical considerations which it used to fashion the recommended standards.

Following criticism from within the profession of the Board's operations and procedures, the Financial Accounting Foundation (FAF), the Board's parent, conducted a study in 1977 of the entire Board operation. Among its many recommendations were proposals that the Board expand its formal and informal contacts with interested groups and that it include an economic impact analysis in important exposure drafts [FAF, 1977, pp. 51, 52]. On this latter point, the FAF's Structure Committee concluded:

---

[6] The inclusion of the FEI could conceivably become the undoing of the Board. If the FEI were to lose confidence in the Board, it is possible that many of the companies which now contribute to the Financial Accounting Foundation might decline to continue doing so, provoking a financial crisis that could threaten the Board's viability.

The Board need not be unduly influenced by the possibility of an economic impact, but it should consider both the possible costs and the expected benefits of a proposal [FAF, 1977, p. 51].

In addition, the Structure Committee recommended actions that would strengthen the roles of the task forces and FASAC [FAF, 1977, pp. 23–25]. In 1978, under pressure from Congress, the Board began to conduct virtually all of its formal meetings (including those of the FASAC) "in the sunshine."

The history of the APB and FASB is one of a succession of procedural steps taken to bring the Board's deliberations into closer proximity to the opinions and concerns of interested third parties. As in the case of the APB, it is possible that an effect of these more elaborate procedures has been a change in the substance of the FASB's conclusions and recommendations.

By the middle 1970s, however, it was decided that the FASB should add economic (and social) consequences to the substantive issues which it normally addresses. The inclusion of "Probable Economic or Social Impact" among the "other qualities of useful information" in the Board's Conceptual Framework discussion memorandum [FASB, 1976, paras. 367–71], coupled with the Board's announcement of its interest in empirical studies of economic consequences [FASB, 1977a] and the recommendation of the FAF Structure Committee that the Board inform itself adequately on the "various impacts its pronouncements might have" [FAF, 1977, p. 31] collectively confirm this new direction. The issue of economic consequences has, therefore, changed from one having only procedural implications for the standard-setting process to one which is now firmly a part of the standard setters' substantive policy framework.

WHAT FACTORS HAVE CONTRIBUTED TO THE EMERGENCE OF "ECONOMIC CONSEQUENCES" AS A SUBSTANTIVE ISSUE?

Economic consequences has finally become accepted as a valid substantive policy issue for a number of reasons:

- The tenor of the times. The decade of the 1970s is clearly one in which American society is holding its institutions responsible for the social, environmental, and economic consequences of their actions, and the crystallized public opinion on this subject eventually became evident (and relevant) to those interested in the accounting standard-setting activity.
- The sheer intractability of the accounting problems being addressed. Since the mid-1960s, the APB and FASB have been taking up difficult accounting questions on which industry positions have been well entrenched. To some degree, companies which are sensitive to the way their performance is evaluated through the medium of reported earnings, have permitted their decision-making behavior to be influenced by their perceptions of how such behavior will be seen through the prism of accounting earnings. Still other such companies have tailored their accounting

practices to reflect their economic performance in the best light—and the managers are evidently loathe to change their decision-making behavior in order to accommodate newly imposed accounting standards. This would also be a concern to managers who are being paid under incentive compensation plans [see Rappaport, 1978].

- **The enormity of the impact.** Several of the issues which have been facing the APB and FASB in recent years have portended such a high degree of impact on either the volatility or level of earnings and other key financial figures and ratios that the Board can no longer discuss the proposed accounting treatments without encountering incessant arguments over the probable economic consequences. Particularly apt examples are accounting for foreign exchange fluctuations, domestic inflation and relative price changes, and the exploration and drilling costs of companies in the petroleum industry.

- **The growth in the information economics/social choice, behavioral, income smoothing, and decision usefulness literatures in accounting.** Recent writings in the information economics/social choice literature have provided a broad analytical framework within which the problems of economic consequences may be conceptualized. Beginning with Stedry [1959], the literature on the behavioral implications of accounting numbers has grown significantly, drawing the attention of researchers and policy makers to the importance of considering the effects of accounting information. The literature on income smoothing has suggested the presence of a managerial motive for influencing the measurement of earnings trends. Finally, the decision usefulness literature, although it is confined to the direct users of accounting information, has served to lessen the inclination of accountants to argue over the inherent "truth" of different accounting incomes, and instead to focus on the use of information by those who receive accounting reports [AAA, 1977a, pp. 5–29].

- **The insufficiency of the procedural reforms adopted by the APB and FASB.** Notwithstanding the succession of procedural steps which both Boards have taken to provide outside parties with a forum for expressing their views, the claims of economic consequences—and the resulting criticisms of the Boards' pronouncements—continue unabated. The conclusion has evidently been reached that procedural remedies alone will not meet the problem.

- **The Moss and Metcalf investigations.** By the middle of 1976, it was known that Rep. John E. Moss and Senator Lee Metcalf were conducting investigations of the performance of the accounting profession, including their standard-setting activities, and it could have reasonably been inferred that the responsiveness of the standard-setting bodies to the economic and social effects of their decisions would be an issue.

- **The increasing importance to corporate managers of the earnings figure in capital-market transactions.** Especially in the 1960s, when capital markets were intensely competitive and the merger movement was fast-paced, the earnings figure came to be viewed as an important element of managerial strategy and tactics.

- Accounting figures came to be viewed as an instrument of social control. The social control of American enterprise has been well known in the rate-regulated energy, transportation, and communications fields, but in recent years the earnings figure has, to an increasing degree, been employed as a control device on a broader scale.[7] Examples are fiscal incentives (such as the investment tax credit and redefinitions of taxable income which diverge from accounting income) which have an influence on debates surrounding financial reporting,[8] the price-control mechanism of Phase II [Lanzillotti et al., 1975, pp. 73–77; and Grayson and Neeb, 1974, pp. 71–76], and the data base which is contemplated by the Energy Policy and Conservation Act of 1975.

- The realization that outsiders could influence the outcome of accounting debates. Prior to the 1960s, accounting controversies were rarely reported in the financial press, and it was widely believed that accounting was a constant, if not a parameter, in the management of business operations. With the publicity given to the accounting for the investment credit in 1962–63, to the fractious dialogue within the AICPA in 1963–64 over the authority of the APB, and to other accounting disagreements involving the APB, managers and other outside parties came to realize that accounting may be a variable after all—that the rules of accounting were not unyielding or even unbending.

- The growing use of Argument 3 (see above) in accounting debates. Mostly for the reasons enumerated above, outside parties began to discard the pretense that their objections to proposed changes in accounting standards were solely, or even primarily, a function of differences over the proper interpretation of accounting principles. True reasons came out into the open, and accounting policy makers could no longer ignore their implications.

It is interesting that economic consequences have become an important issue at a time when accounting and finance academics have been arguing that the American capital markets are efficient with respect to publicly available information and, moreover, that the market cannot be "fooled" by the use of different accounting methods to reflect the same economic reality [see, e.g., Beaver, 1973].

IMPLICATIONS FOR THE FASB

What are the implications of the "economic consequences" movement for the FASB? It has become clear that political agencies (such as government departments and congressional committees) expect accounting standard setters to take explicitly into consideration the possible adverse consequences of pro-

---

[7] D R Scott, though writing in a different context, nonetheless was prophetic in his prediction that accounting would increasingly be used as a means of social control [1931, esp. Chap. 14].
[8] The "required tax conformity" issue of the early 1970s [see Zeff, 1972, pp. 218–19] is another instance.

posed accounting standards. This expectation appears to be strongest where the consequences are thought to be significant and widespread—and especially where they might impinge on economic and social policies being pursued by the government. In these instances, the FASB must show that it has studied the possible consequences and that its recommended standards either are innocent of such consequences or that the benefits from implementing the standards outweigh the possible adverse consequences. Where the claimed consequences have implications for economic or social policies of national importance, the FASB should not be surprised if a political resolution is imposed by outside forces.

But to say that any significant economic consequences should be studied by the Board does not imply that the accounting model—accounting principles and fair presentation—should be dismissed as the principal guiding factor in the Board's determination. The FASB is respected as a body of accounting experts, and it should focus its attention primarily on matters on which its expertise will be acknowledged. While some may suggest that accounting standards should be determined only with regard to their consequences for economic and social welfare, the FASB would assure the termination of its existence if it were to begin to make decisions primarily on other than accounting grounds.

The Board is thus faced with a dilemma which requires a delicate balancing of accounting and nonaccounting variables. Although its decisions should rest—and be seen to rest—chiefly on accounting considerations, it must also study—and be seen to study—the possible adverse economic and social consequences of its proposed actions. As in all micro- and macro-economic policy making, the identification and measurement of possible economic and social repercussions will be exceedingly difficult tasks.[9] In order to deal adequately with the consequences issue, the Board would be wise to develop a staff of competent analysts from allied disciplines, notably economics.

Economic consequences bid fair to be the most challenging accounting issue of the 1970s. We have entered an era in which economic and social consequences may no longer be ignored as a substantive issue in the setting of accounting standards.

REFERENCES

The AICPA Injunction Case: Re: ARB No. 44 (Revised), Cases in Public Accounting Practice No. 1 (Chicago: Arthur Andersen & Co., 1960).

APB Public Hearing on Accounting and Reporting Practices in the Petroleum Industry, Cases in Public Accounting Practice No. 10 (Chicago: Arthur Andersen & Co., 1972).

American Accounting Association, Committee on Concepts and Standards for External Financial Reports, *Statement on Accounting Theory and Theory Acceptance* (Sarasota, Florida: AAA, 1977a).

[9] For a discussion of some of these problems of implementation, see Swieringa [1976, pp. 31–35].

American Accounting Association, *Report of the Committee on the Social Consequences of Accounting Information* (Sarasota, Florida: AAA, 1977b).

American Institute of Accountants, *1936 Year Book of the American Institute of Accountants* (New York: AIA, 1937).

American Institute of Accountants, *Accounting Research Bulletins*, No. 11, "Corporate Accounting for Ordinary Stock Dividends" (New York: AIA, 1941), pp. 99–106.

American Institute of Accountants, "Accounting and Changing Price Levels," unpublished preliminary report, September 1, 1948, 48 pages.

Beaver, William H., "What Should Be the FASB's Objectives?," *Journal of Accountancy*, August 1973, pp. 49–56.

Buckley, John W., "The FASB and Impact Analysis," *Management Accounting* (U.S.), April 1976, pp. 13–17.

Burns, Joseph M., *Accounting Standards and International Finance, with Special Reference to Multinationals* (Washington, D.C.: American Enterprise Institute for Public Policy Research, 1976).

Carey, John L., *The Rise of the Accounting Profession: To Responsibility and Authority, 1937-1969* (New York: American Institute of Certified Public Accountants, 1970).

Changing Concepts of Business Income, Report of Study Group on Business Income (New York: The Macmillan Company, 1952).

Chatov, Robert, *Corporate Financial Reporting: Public or Private Control?* (New York: The Free Press, 1975).

Davidson, Sidney, *The Plant Accounting Regulations of the Federal Power Commission* (Ann Arbor: University of Michigan Press, 1952).

Demski, Joel S., "Choice among Financial Reporting Alternatives," *The Accounting Review*, April 1974, pp. 221–32.

Depreciation Policy When Price Levels Change (New York: Controllership Foundation, Inc., 1948).

"Dual Accounting System Suggested for Depreciation," *The Journal of Accountancy*, February 1948, p. 103.

Financial Accounting Foundation, Structure Committee, *The Structure of Establishing Financial Accounting Standards* (1977).

Financial Accounting Standards Board, *Conceptual Framework for Financial Accounting and Reporting: Elements of Financial Statements and Their Measurement*, Discussion Memorandum (Stamford, Connecticut: FASB, 1976).

_____*Status Report*, No. 45 (February 7, 1977a).

_____*Status Report*, No. 47 (April 19, 1977b).

_____*Status Report*, No. 50 (July 7, 1977c).

_____*Conference on the Economic Consequences of Financial Accounting Standards* (Stamford, Connecticut: FASB, 1978).

Gerboth, Dale L., "Research, Intuition, and Politics in Accounting Inquiry," *The Accounting Review*, July 1973, pp. 475–82.

Grayson, C. Jackson, Jr., and Louis Neeb, *Confessions of a Price Controller* (Homewood, Illinois: Dow Jones-Irwin, Inc., 1974).

Hawkins, David F., "Behavioral Implications of Generally Accepted Accounting Principles," *California Management Review*, Winter 1969, pp. 13–21.

Horngren, Charles T., "The Marketing of Accounting Standards," *Journal of Accountancy*, October 1973, pp. 61–66.

_____, edited dialogue, in Thomas J. Burns (ed.), *Accounting in Transition: Oral Histories of Recent U.S. Experience* (Columbus: College of Administrative Science, The Ohio State University, 1974), pp. 82–100.

_____, "Will the FASB Be Here in the 1980s?," *Journal of Accountancy*, November 1976, pp. 90–96.

"Institute Committee Holds to Depreciation on Cost," Editorial, *The Journal of Accountancy*, November 1948, pp. 353–54.

Johnson, Charles E., "Management's Role in External Accounting Measurements," in Robert K. Jaedicke, Yuji Ijiri, and Oswald Nielsen (eds.), *Research in Accounting Measurement* (American Accounting Association, 1966), pp. 88–100.

Lanzillotti, Robert F., Mary T. Hamilton, and R. Blaine Roberts, *Phase II in Review: The Price Commission Experience* (Washington, D.C.: The Brookings Institution, 1975).

May, George O., letter to J. S. Seidman, July 14, 1941 (Deposited in National Office Library, Price Waterhouse & Co., New York), 2 pages.

_____, *Financial Accounting: A Distillation of Experience* (New York: The Macmillan Company, 1943).

_____, letter to John B. Inglis, August 5, 1952 (Deposited in the National Office Library, Price Waterhouse & Co., New York), 2 pages.

Moonitz, Maurice, "Some Reflections on the Investment Credit Experience," *Journal of Accounting Research*, Spring 1966, pp. 47–61.

_____, "Why Is It So Difficult to Agree upon a Set of Accounting Principles?," *The Australian Accountant*, November 1968, pp. 621–31.

_____, *Obtaining Agreement on Standards in the Accounting Profession*, Studies in Accounting Research No. 8 (Sarasota, Florida: American Accounting Association, 1974).

Paton, William A., "Accounting Policies of the Federal Power Commission—A Critique," *Journal of Accountancy*, June 1944, pp. 432–60.

_____, "Accounting Procedures and Private Enterprise," *Journal of Accountancy*, April 1948, pp. 278–91.

Plum, Charles W., and Daniel W. Collins, "Business Segment Reporting," in James Don Edwards and Homer A. Black (eds.), *The Modern Accountant's Handbook* (Homewood, Illinois: Dow Jones-Irwin, Inc., 1976), pp. 469–511.

Prakash, Prem, and Alfred Rappaport, "The Feedback Effects of Accounting," *Business Week*, January 12, 1976, p. 12.

_____, "Information Inductance and Its Significance for Accounting," *Accounting, Organizations and Society* (1977, No. 1), pp. 29–38.

Price Waterhouse International, *A Survey in 46 Countries: Accounting Principles and Reporting Practices* ([n.p.], PWI, 1975).

Proceedings of Hearing on Accounting for Equity Securities, Accounting Principles Board (New York: American Institute of Certified Public Accountants, 1971), Section A—Transcript.

Rappaport, Alfred, "Economic Impact of Accounting Standards—Implications for the FASB," *The Journal of Accountancy*, May 1977, pp. 89–98.

_____, "Executive Incentives vs. Corporate Growth," *Harvard Business Review*, July-August 1978, pp. 81–88.

SEC Administrative Policy Re: Balance-Sheet Treatment of Deferred Income-Tax Credits, Cases in Public Accounting Practice Nos. 5 and 6 (Chicago: Arthur Andersen & Co., 1961), 2 vols.

Savoie, Leonard M., "Accounting Attitudes," in Robert R. Sterling (ed.), *Institutional Issues in Public Accounting* (Lawrence, Kansas: Scholars Book Co., 1974), pp. 317–27.

Scott, D R, *The Cultural Significance of Accounts* (New York: Henry Holt & Company, 1931).

Stamp, Edward, and Christopher Marley, *Accounting Principles and the City Code* (London, Butterworths, 1970).

Stedry, Andrew C., *Budget Control and Cost Behavior* (Englewood Cliffs, New Jersey: Prentice-Hall, Inc., 1959).

Storey, Reed K., *The Search for Accounting Principles* (New York: American Institute of Certified Public Accountants, 1964).

Swieringa, Robert J., "Consequences of Financial Accounting Standards," *The Accounting Forum*, May 1976, pp. 25–39.

U.S. Department of Energy, Comments before the Securities and Exchange Commission, "Accounting Practices—Oil and Gas Producers—Financial Accounting Standards," unpublished memorandum, April 3, 1978, 53 pages.

Wriston, Walter B., Transcript of Public Hearing on FASB Discussion Memorandum on Accounting by Debtors and Creditors When Debt Is Restructured (1977, Volume 1, Part 2), pp. 57–76.

Wyatt, Arthur R., "The Economic Impact of Financial Accounting Standards," *Journal of Accountancy*, October 1977, pp. 92–94.

Zeff, Stephen A., *Forging Accounting Principles in Five Countries: A History and an Analysis of Trends* (Champaign, Illinois: Stipes Publishing Company, 1972).

CHAPTER 2

Objectives of Accounting

Since the early years of the century, accounting academics and professionals have sought to develop a general theory of accounting. Such works as Charles E. Sprague's *The Philosophy of Accounts* (Sprague, 1908), William A. Paton's *Accounting Theory—With Special Reference to the Corporate Enterprise* (Ronald, 1922), and John B. Canning's *The Economics of Accountancy* (Ronald, 1929) were early efforts by American educators to understand and develop general theories of accounting. An attempt by a professional accountant was Kenneth MacNeal's *Truth in Accounting* (University of Pennsylvania Press, 1939), and in the same year Stephen Gilman, an accounting educator, sought to discover harmonies in a discordant theory literature in *Accounting Concepts of Profit* (Ronald, 1939). In 1940, Paton combined with A.C. Littleton to produce *An Introduction to Corporate Accounting Standards*, which was published by the American Accounting Association. The Paton and Littleton monograph has had a profound effect on the American accounting literature.

This is not to suggest that only Americans were concerned with accounting theory. Such writers as Edwards and Bray in the U.K.; Schmalenbach, Schmidt, and Walb in Germany; Limperg in the Netherlands; Zappa in Italy; and Fitzgerald in Australia were foremost among the pioneers who made major contributions to accounting theory during the first half century.

In the second half of the century, the number of contributors to the theory literature multiplied several times. Beyond the very substantial writings of academics and professionals, working on their own, there have been significant attempts by accounting bodies to fashion an accounting theory. It is these institutional initiatives that are of primary interest here, as the very utterances by accounting bodies have been intended to lead to a direct improvement in the quality of companies' financial reporting.

Probably the earliest attempt by an accounting body to formulate a coherent statement of theory occurred in 1936, when the fledgling American Accounting Association published a five-page "tentative statement" of the "bases upon which accounting standards rest."[1] The leaders of the Association, mostly academics, had hoped to crystallize opinion on accounting principles within the profession, lest the task of establishing accounting principles and practices be left, by default, to the recently created Securities and Exchange Commission. The Paton and Littleton monograph, issued 4 years later, was proposed as an elaboration of the bases set forth in the 1936 AAA principles statement. In 1941 and later years, the Association issued revisions of its 1936 statement.

   An organization composed chiefly of academics seldom can compete with a practitioner body for influence on professional practice. Yet, prior to 1938 no practitioner body anywhere had undertaken, on a continuing, programmatic basis, to issue pronouncements in order to guide the course of accounting practice. It was therefore an event of considerable significance when in 1938 the American Institute of Accountants (as the AICPA was then known) empowered its Committee on Accounting Procedure to issue a series of Accounting Research Bulletins for the edification of practicing accountants and their client companies. The Institute was reacting to pressure from the Securities and Exchange Commission (SEC) to provide "substantial authoritative support" for assistance in limiting the range of "generally accepted accounting principles."[2] From that time forward, the initiative for promoting changes in American accounting practice has been in the hands of the accounting profession, although the public sector (chiefly the SEC) has closely monitored its progress and has occasionally intervened in the profession's decision-making process.

   Although the Committee on Accounting Procedure had, on several occasions in the late 1930s and 1940s, considered expressing itself on fundamental accounting principles, in order to guide its thinking on particular practice issues, it always retreated from the task. In the 1950s, however, it became clear to the committee and to Institute leaders that little progress could be made on the really difficult issues until agreement was reached on fundamental concepts. Such issues as tax allocation, price-level accounting, the all-inclusive versus current-operating-performance concept of the income statement, and accounting for business combinations had either divided the committee or driven a wedge between the committee and the SEC. Underlying these confrontations was a deep philosophical difference over whether a committee that was unable to unite on a single recommended practice could, by the political expediency of a two-thirds majority, impose its will on accounting firms and companies who agreed with the minority. Institute leaders concluded that these differences would best be addressed by a major investment of resources in fundamental research. If agreement could be reached on fundamentals, it was believed, the accounting principles and rules

---

[1] "A Tentative Statement of Accounting Principles Affecting Corporate Reports," *The Accounting Review* (June 1936), p. 187.
[2] See Stephen A. Zeff, *Forging Accounting Principles in Five Countries: A History and an Analysis of Trends* (Champaign, IL: Stipes, 1972), pp. 134–139.

implied by those fundamentals would become evident to all. In 1959, the Institute dramatized the new emphasis on research by terminating the Committee on Accounting Procedure in favor of an impressive-sounding Accounting Principles Board. The new Board was equipped with an accounting research division, and both were charged with divining the "basic postulates" and "broad principles" of accounting.

In 1961–1962, two research studies were published under APB auspices: *The Basic Postulates of Accounting* by Maurice Moonitz and *A Tentative Set of Broad Accounting Principles for Business Enterprises* by Robert T. Sprouse and Moonitz. But the Board found itself unable to accept the "radical" recommendations for accounting reform contained in the two studies, and the first phase of its optimistic search for fundamentals died aborning. Since the APB had to develop opinions on particular issues coming before it, the Board proceeded to face each issue on an ad hoc basis, without a body of fundamental theory to guide it, just as its predecessor, the Committee on Accounting Procedure, had done. This was the first inkling that the task of obtaining agreement on a basic accounting theory—one that would underlie the principles to be applied to the particular problems of accounting practice—was a very difficult one indeed.

The APB made two other attempts at providing a basis for accounting theory development, but both were primarily descriptive rather than normative. In 1965, the Institute published Paul Grady's survey of existing practice and pronouncements, entitled *Inventory of Generally Accepted Accounting Principles for Business Enterprises*, which had been commissioned by the Board. Five years later in 1970, the Board issued Statement No. 4, "Basic Concepts and Accounting Principles Underlying Financial Statements of Business Enterprises," which was, in the main, an enumeration of the concepts and principles reflected in existing practice. (Furthermore, as a Statement, not an Opinion, the pronouncement was only advisory and not mandatory.)

As the accounting profession entered the 1970s, there was a growing and persistent belief that progress on accounting standards could not be achieved without the development of a conceptual framework (as it came to be called). The APB had been issuing opinions in even more controversial areas than had the Committee on Accounting Procedure, and the rising chorus of criticism of the APB's work served to rededicate leaders of the Institute to a search for fundamental principles. In 1971, the Institute, amid criticism from all sides, commissioned a special study to inquire into the objectives of financial statements. Membership in the study group was broadly based: three partners of Big Eight firms, two accounting professors, two financial executives, an investment analyst, and an economist. Robert M. Trueblood, a distinguished practitioner and former Institute president, was named chairman. In its 67-page report entitled *Objectives of Financial Statements* (AICPA, 1973), the study group broke with the traditional orientation of financial statements toward reporting on stewardship and instead emphasized their usefulness in providing investors and creditors with information "for predicting, comparing, and evaluating potential cash flows to them in terms of amount, timing, and related uncertainty."[3] (In a path-breaking principles statement published in 1966, a committee of the American Accounting Association had fore-shadowed the Trueblood Study report by focusing on the usefulness of accounting information for economic decisions, rather than on stewardship.[4])

In 1973, as in 1959, the standard-setting deck was swept clean, and the Financial Accounting Standards Board replaced the beleaguered Accounting Principles Board. In addition to issuing Statements of Financial Accounting Standards (SFASs), which constituted substantial authoritative support of "generally accepted accounting principles," the FASB began a series of Statements of Financial Accounting Concepts (SFACs). The SFACs were intended to be the building blocks of the Board's conceptual framework. SFAC No. 1, issued in 1978, entitled "Objectives of Financial Reporting by Business Enterprises," largely endorsed the recommendations of the Trueblood Study Group, although the Board expanded its concern from financial statements alone to all forms of financial reporting by a company's management, including quantitative and qualitative disclosures.

SFAC Nos. 2 and 3, both issued in 1980, dealt with the "qualitative characteristics of accounting information" and the "elements of financial statements," respectively. In SFAC No. 5, issued in 1984,[5] the Board came to the realization that the really hard decisions on "recognition" and "measurement" defied an easy consensus. For the first time in the Board's series of SFACs, No. 5 contained a dissent. In the more general and abstract SFACs dealing with objectives of financial reporting, qualitative characteristics, and the elements of financial statements, the Board was able to reach agreement on substantive issues. But on recognition and measurement, which are bread-and-butter issues having a direct impact on the contents of financial statements, the Board's conceptual framework ran headlong into the "individual framework" (see Horngren's article) of each board member. Recognition refers to the criteria for determining when changes in assets, liabilities, and owners' equity (including revenues, expenses, and losses) are to be recorded in the accounts. "Measurement" concerns the dollar number to be assigned to these changes, once they are "recognized." These are the fundamental questions of asset and liability valuation and income determination—questions which had bedeviled both the Committee on Accounting Procedure and the

[3] *Objectives of Financial Statements* (AICPA, 1973), p. 20. For a summary of the main conclusions of the Trueblood Study, written by the study's research director, see George H. Sorter, "Objectives of Financial Statements—An Inside View," *CAmagazine* (November 1973), pp.30–33. A set of critiques of the study's conclusions, written by Ross M. Skinner, Edward Stamp, Robert K. Mautz, and R. J. Chambers, may be found in "The Trueblood Report: Promise or Progress?" *CAmagazine* (December 1973), pp. 12–20. A lengthier criticism may be found in K. V. Peasnell, *Accounting Objectives: A Critique of the Trueblood Report*, ICRA Occasional Paper No. 5 (Lancaster, England: International Centre for Research in Accounting, University of Lancaster, 1974).

[4] *A Statement of Basic Accounting Theory* (Sarasota, FL: American Accounting Association, 1966).

[5] SFAC No. 4 deals with the objectives of financial reporting for nonbusiness enterprises, and No. 6 is a revision of No. 3 to expand its application to nonbusiness enterprises. They will not be discussed here.

Accounting Principles Board. Although the FASB closed its book on the conceptual framework in the mid-1980s, the SFACs left a number of central questions unanswered, and several of the readings in this chapter (discussed below) assess what the Board has done to date.

Reports on the objectives of financial statements and on proposed conceptual frameworks have been published by professional accounting organizations and standard-setting bodies in several countries.[6]

Studies on objectives have appeared in Australia and the United Kingdom. In 1972, Australia's Accountancy Research Foundation published a study, entitled *Objectives and Concepts of Financial Statements*, by W. J. Kenley and G. J. Staubus, which was preceded by a 1970 study, *A Statement of Australian Accounting Principles*, written by W. John Kenley and patterned on Paul Grady's 1965 *Inventory* done for the APB. The Australian standard-setting bodies (there were then two) failed to take any action on the two studies. In 1982, the Australian Accounting Research Foundation (the foundation had been renamed) launched a series of Accounting Theory Monographs intended to explore various aspects of the conceptual framework. (See the references at the end of this section for a complete list of the Monographs.) Following several years in which exposure drafts were issued and discussed, in 1990 the Accounting Standards Review Board (today known as the Australian Accounting Standards Board) issued the first three Statements of Accounting Concepts (SACs): "Definition of the Reporting Entity," "Objective of General Purpose Financial Reporting," and "Qualitative Characteristics of Financial Information." These three SACs, drawing heavily on previous work by the FASB, were largely noncontroversial, but the fourth SAC, "Definition and Recognition of the Elements of Financial Statements," issued in 1992, has stirred a great deal of discussion and debate. The two professional accountancy bodies in Australia have declared that their "members who are involved in, or are responsible for, the audit of the general purpose financial report of an entity are required to take all reasonable steps within their power to ensure that the financial report complies with the Statements of Accounting Concepts and Accounting Standards or that a qualified audit opinion is issued."[7] Hence, in Australia, concepts statements are more than just informational documents.

In 1992, New Zealand's Accounting Research & Standards Board issued seven exposure drafts constituting a proposed framework for financial reporting.

An ambitious project was undertaken in the U.K. in 1974–1975, when an eleven-member working party of the Accounting Standards Steering Committee (ASSC) produced an 81-page discussion paper on the "scope and aims of

---

[6] An interesting review of the efforts in several countries appears in K.V. Peasnell, "The Function of a Conceptual Framework for Corporate Financial Reporting," *Accounting and Business Research* (Autumn 1982), pp. 243–246.

[7] "Conformity with Statements of Accounting Concepts and Accounting Standards," APS 1 (Australian Society of Certified Practising Accountants and The Institute of Chartered Accountants in Australia, November 1990), para. 11.

published financial reports in the light of modern needs and conditions.[8] Entitled *The Corporate Report*, the discussion paper contained some daring recommendations, including proposals that management publish a value-added statement and a statement of future prospects, and a suggestion that companies' financial reports incorporate multiple valuation bases (i.e., some combination of historical cost restated for inflation, replacement cost, net realizable value, net present value, and value to the firm). Even though the members of the working party, who represented a wide spectrum of interests and occupations in the accounting profession and the financial community, approved the report unanimously, the parent ASSC never formally addressed its recommendations.

A further U.K. initiative occurred in 1989, when the Institute of Chartered Accountants in England and Wales published a 77-page paper, *Guidelines for Financial Reporting Standards*, by David Solomons, which had been prepared for the Institute's Research Board as guidance to the Accounting Standards Committee.[9] A year earlier, the Institute of Chartered Accountants of Scotland had published *Making Corporate Reports Valuable*, a 108-page discussion document prepared by the Institute's Research Committee. Both Solomons' Guidelines and the Scottish Institute's discussion document proposed a conceptual framework for financial reporting, but they disagreed on the measurement attribute. Solomons recommended a current cost (entry price) model, while the Scottish Institute's Research Committee favored the use of net realizable value (exit price). In 1991, the two Institutes cooperated in the publication of a 36-page booklet, *The Future Shape of Financial Reports*, which called for a redesigned financial reporting package consisting of six statements:

- A statement of objectives and related strategic plan,
- A statement of assets and liabilities,
- An income statement,
- A gains statement,
- A cash flow statement, and
- A statement of future prospects.

The authors of the booklet, who were drawn from both the English and Scottish Institutes, agreed that the existing reporting package, with its use of historical cost accounting, was inadequate.

In 1990, as a result of the Dearing Report,[10] a nine-member Accounting Standards Board (with the chairman and technical director serving on a full-time basis) replaced the wholly part-time Accounting Standards Committee. The new Board's first priority was to develop a Statement of Principles—its

---

[8] *The Corporate Report* (London: Accounting Standards Steering Committee, 1975), p. 1.

[9] In 1976, the ASSC dropped the word "Steering" from its title.

[10] *The Making of Accounting Standards,* Report of the Review Committee under the Chairmanship of Sir Ron Dearing CB (London: The Institute of Chartered Accountants in England and Wales, 1988).

conceptual framework. The Statement of Principles project is divided into chapters. Exposure drafts of three chapters were published in 1991, and two more chapters were issued in discussion draft form in 1992.

In 1980, the Canadian Institute of Chartered Accountants published a major study dealing with both the substance of a conceptual framework and the process by which it might be implemented by a standard-setting body. Entitled *Corporate Reporting: Its Future Evolution*, the study was written at the request of the CICA by Edward Stamp (1928–1986), who was both a U.K. academic and a Canadian chartered accountant. Stamp proposed a number of criteria (the FASB earlier had used a different term, "qualitative characteristics," to describe its own criteria) to be used by preparers, users, standard setters, and others for assessing the quality of financial reporting to users. In regard to the manner of implementing a conceptual framework, Stamp wrote, "It is an integral part of the philosophy of this study that the development of accounting standards should be evolutionary, and that it is not right to adopt a deterministic, authoritarian, or normative approach."[11] He recognized that user needs are not homogeneous and unchanging, and he rejected the view that a conceptual framework might not provide for alternative permissible accounting treatments and even different valuation bases. (Stamp was an influential member of the ASSC working party that gave favorable consideration to multicolumn reporting in 1974–1975, using different valuation bases.) He believed that the FASB's approach to developing a conceptual framework and setting accounting standards might be likened to the codification mentality found in civil law jurisdictions. Stamp favored a common law approach in which the CICA's Accounting Standards Committee would use the knowledge and experience of its members to develop standards based on objectives and qualitative criteria such as those proposed in his study. He also provided for an appeals board to hear problems raised by auditors in the course of their engagements. Stamp's view of the standard-setting process is essentially judicial, while it would seem that the FASB sees itself more as a legislative body.[12]

In 1988, the CICA's Accounting Standards Committee approved a 10-page *Handbook* release (Sec. 1000) on financial accounting concepts which has many points in common with the FASB's framework, including a lack of resolution of the difficult issues relating to recognition and measurement.

---

[11] Edward Stamp, *Corporate Reporting: Its Future Evolution* (Toronto: Canadian Institute of Chartered Accountants, 1980), p. 95.

[12] For a criticism of the Stamp Report, see John Boersema, "Corporate Reporting in Canada and the US," *CAmagazine* (July 1981), pp. 30–35, and Stamp's reply, Letters, *CAmagazine* (October 1981), pp. 13, 15. Also see the papers by T. Ross Archibald, John F. Dewhirst, and Gordon C. Fowler in *Research to Support Standard Setting in Financial Accounting: A Canadian Perspective*, edited by Sanjoy Basu and J. Alex Milburn (Toronto: The Clarkson Gordon Foundation, 1982), pp. 218–253. An article in which Stamp summarizes his approach is "Accounting Standards and the Conceptual Framework: A Plan for Their Evolution," *The Accountant's Magazine* (July 1981), pp. 216–222.

Institutional differences make comparisons between Canadian and American solutions difficult. In Canada, provincial securities commissions and federal and provincial legislative authorities have, in the main, vested substantial autonomy in the CICA. The CICA's Accounting Standards Board (which superseded the Accounting Standards Committee in October 1991) has largely been unfettered by the continuing surveillance of an aggressive regulatory agency, although, in the last few years, the Ontario Securities Commission has become more actively interested in accounting standards.

In 1987, another Canadian accountancy body (which is yet to be recognized by the CICA), The Accounting Standards Authority of Canada (ASAC), published a 50-page booklet, *Conceptual Framework for Financial Reporting*, in which it proposed its own framework for acceptance. ASAC is supported by the Certified General Accountants' Association of Canada, and its proposed framework was heavily influenced by the approach adopted by the FASB.

In 1989, the International Accounting Standards Committee approved a 30-page Framework for the Preparation and Presentation of Financial Statements, which also left unresolved several key questions on recognition and measurement.

It is curious that, before any standard-setting body began to issue drafts of a proposed conceptual framework, two committees composed of both accountants and nonaccountants that were charged with formulating recommendations on inflation accounting found it useful to guide their inquiries with discussions of the aims and uses of financial statements: the Sandilands Report of 1975 (U.K.),[13] and the Richardson Report of 1976 (New Zealand).[14]

Notwithstanding the resources that have been devoted to the development of a conceptual framework by professional bodies, no framework has yet been officially adopted by a standard-setting body that points toward a resolution of the controversies over recognition and measurement—the two critical variables that determine the scope and contents of financial reporting. Why has it been so difficult to make progress on the formulation and acceptance of a conceptual framework?

In "Uses and Limitations of a Conceptual Framework," Charles T. Horngren, an accounting academic who served on the Accounting Principles Board, accepts the view that accounting policy-making is a social-choice problem, and he counsels the FASB on what this view implies for the conceptual framework. Each Board member and each interested party, Horngren maintains, will have his or her own individual "technical framework." An official conceptual framework "may help if it structures the argument and provides a common language when dealing with a complicated issue," but the final decision necessarily will be a reflection of the compatibility of the

---

[13] *Inflation Accounting*, Report of the Inflation Accounting Committee, F. E. P. Sandilands, Esq. CBE, Chairman (London: Her Majesty's Stationery Office, Cmnd. 6225, September 1975).
[14] Report of the Committee of Inquiry into Inflation Accounting, I. L. M. Richardson, Chairman (Wellington, New Zealand: Government Printer, 1976)

collective individual frameworks of those who cast the votes. Horngren contends that it is futile for the Board to attempt to develop a conceptual framework in highly concrete terms, since such a framework is likely to lose the Board a considerable amount of constituent support. It is important that the Board secure acceptance for its policy decisions, and a framework at a fairly high level of generalization (i.e., without seeming to tread on the perceived interests of a great many parties) is most likely to gain that acceptance. Once such a framework is in place, Horngren believes it will be helpful in leading to the resolution of some controversies, but perhaps not others.

In "Building a Better Conceptual Framework," J. Alex Milburn, who is a research partner in the Toronto office of Ernst & Young, addresses some tough questions about the relevance of the well-known conceptual frameworks to countries having very different economies and norms for the conduct of enterprise. He concludes, with considerable justification, that a conceptual framework cannot be viewed as possessing universal validity. It must be explicitly tailored to the conditions and values found in different national environments.

David Solomons, who was an influential member of the Wheat Study, whose report led to the establishment of the FASB in 1972–73, renders a gloomy judgment in his article, "The FASB's Conceptual Framework: An Evaluation." After assessing the Board's four concepts statements dealing with business enterprises, Solomons concludes that the FASB's framework as a whole has been a failure. Above all, he faults SFAC No. 5, on recognition and measurement, which "bypasses all the difficult areas."

BIBLIOGRAPHICAL NOTES

A number of important studies (other than those cited) have proposed general accounting theories, of which the following are among the most prominent:

Edwards, Edgar O., and Philip W. Bell: *The Theory and Measurement of Business Income* (Berkeley, CA: University of California Press, 1961).

Staubus, George J.: *A Theory of Accounting to Investors* (Berkeley, CA: University of California Press, 1961). (Reprinted in 1971 by Scholars Book Co.)

Hansen, Palle: *The Accounting Concept of Profit* (Amsterdam: Einar Harks, 1962). (Second edition was published in 1972 by North-Holland Publishing Company, Amsterdam.)

Mattessich, Richard: *Accounting and Analytical Methods* (Homewood, IL: Richard D. Irwin, Inc., 1964). (Reprinted in 1978 by Scholars Book Co.)

Bedford, Norton M.: *Income Determination Theory: An Accounting Framework* (Reading, MA: Addison-Wesley, 1965).

Chambers, Raymond J.: *Accounting, Evaluation and Economic Behavior* (Englewood Cliffs, NJ: Prentice-Hall, Inc., 1966). (Reprinted in 1974 by Scholars Book Co.)

Ijiri, Yuji: *The Foundations of Accounting Measurement* (Englewood Cliffs, NJ: Prentice-Hall, Inc., 1967).

Sterling, Robert R.: *Theory of the Measurement of Enterprise Income* (Lawrence, KS: The University Press of Kansas, 1970). (Reprinted in 1979 by Scholars Book Co.)

Revsine, Lawrence: *Replacement Cost Accounting* (Englewood Cliffs, NJ: Prentice-Hall, Inc., 1973).

Baxter, William T.: *Accounting Values and Inflation* (London: McGraw-Hill Book Company (U.K.) Limited, 1975).

Anthony, Robert N.: *Tell It Like It Was* (Homewood, IL: Richard D. Irwin, Inc. 1983).

The AICPA's 1961 study on "basic postulates" by Moonitz and 1962 study on "broad accounting principles" by Sprouse and Moonitz, no longer available from the Institute, have been reprinted, together with other articles of the day and some previously unpublished papers, in the following volume:

Zeff, Stephen A. (editor): *The Accounting Postulates and Principles Controversy of the 1960s* (New York: Garland Publishing, Inc., 1982).

A volume containing many of the papers considered by the Trueblood Study Group during the course of its deliberations is:

Cramer, Joe J., Jr., and George H. Sorter (editors): *Objectives of Financial Statements— Volume 2, Selected Papers* (New York: AICPA, 1974).

A study that was undertaken at the request of the U.K. Accounting Standards Committee and that concludes that "A 'conceptual framework' for accounting should be regarded rather as a common basis for identifying issues, for asking questions and for carrying our research than as a package of solutions," is:

Macve, Richard: *A Conceptual Framework for Financial Accounting and Reporting: The Possibilities for An Agreed Structure* (London: The Institute of Chartered Accountants in England and Wales, 1981).

A wide-ranging critique of traditional accounting practice and promulgated standards, which makes a case for an improved set of standards with particular reference to Australia, is:

Company Accounting Standards, Report of the Accounting Standards Review Committee, chaired by R. J. Chambers (Sydney, Australia: Government Printer, New South Wales, 1978).

In the 1960s and 1970s, four Seaview Symposiums were held to discuss the views of preparers and users of financial statements. The proceedings from three of the Symposiums were published in the following volumes:

Burton, John C. (editor): *Corporate Financial Reporting: Conflicts and Challenges* (New York: AICPA, 1969).

Burton, John C. (editor): *Corporate Financial Reporting: Ethical and Other Problems* (New York: AICPA, 1972).

Carmichael, D. R., and Ben Makela (editors): *Corporate Financial Reporting: The Benefits and Problems of Disclosure* (New York: AICPA, 1976).

Numerous conferences have been held to discuss standard setting and the fashioning of a conceptual framework, some of the proceedings from which are as follows:

Berkeley Symposium on the Foundations of Financial Accounting (Berkeley, CA: Schools of Business Administration, University of California, 1967).

Rappaport, Alfred, and Lawrence Revsine (editors): *Corporate Financial Reporting: The Issues, The Objectives and Some New Proposals* (Chicago, IL: Commerce Clearing House, Inc., 1972)

The Conceptual Framework of Accounting (Philadelphia, PA: The Wharton School, University of Pennsylvania, 1977).

Economic Consequences of Financial Accounting Standards: Selected Papers (FASB, 1978).

Basu, Sanjoy, and J. Alex Milburn (editors): *Research to Support Standard Setting In Financial Accounting: A Canadian Perspective* (Toronto: The Clarkson Gordon Foundation, 1982).

Sherman, H. David (editor): *Conceptual Frameworks for Financial Reporting* (Boston: Harvard Business School, 1982).

Standard Setting for Financial Reporting, An International Conference Sponsored by the American Accounting Association with Klynveld Main Goerdeler (KPMG Peat Marwick, 1987).

Shaw, J. C., J. A. Arnold, and M. Cooper (editors): *Financial Reporting: The Way Forward* (London and Edinburgh: The Institute of Chartered Accountants in England and Wales, and The Institute of Chartered Accountants of Scotland, 1990).

For an extensive analysis of the FASB's conceptual framework project in the context of the history of standard setting, see:

Storey, Reed K.: "The Framework of Financial Accounting Concepts and Standards," in D. R. Carmichael, Steven B. Lilien and Martin Mellman (editors), *Accountants' Handbook* (New York: John Wiley & Sons, seventh edition, 1991), Chap. 1.

A study of the development of the FASB's conceptual framework, taken from a doctoral dissertation, is

Gore, Pelham: *The FASB Conceptual Framework Project 1973-1985* (Manchester, England: Manchester University Press, 1992).

The FASB has sponsored two research studies on the "recognition" problem:

Ijiri, Yuji: *Recognition of Contractual Rights and Obligations* (Financial Accounting Standards Board, 1980).

Johnson, L. Todd, and Reed K. Storey: *Recognition in Financial Statements: Underlying Concepts and Practical Conventions* (Financial Accounting Standards Board, 1982).

A valuation framework prepared as a discussion document by the Research Committee of the Institute of Chartered Accountants of Scotland is:

McMonnies, Peter N. (editor): *Making Corporate Reports Valuable,* A Discussion Document by the Research Committee (Edinburgh: The Institute of Chartered Accountants of Scotland/Kogan Page, 1988). (For a specimen annual report reflecting the valuation framework, see *Melody plc Annual Report* (Edinburgh: The Institute of Chartered Accountants of Scotland, 1990.)

A conceptual framework commissioned by the Research Board of the Institute of Chartered Accountants in England and Wales is:

Solomons, David: *Guidelines for Financial Reporting Standards* (London: The Institute of Chartered Accountants in England and Wales, 1989).

A much more extensive argument in support of the views contained in Solomons' *Guidelines* may be found in:

Solomons, David: *Making Accounting Policy: The Quest for Credibility in Financial Reporting* (New York: Oxford University Press, 1986).

A planning document prepared by representatives of the English and Scottish Institutes that proposes a rationale and framework for improved financial reporting is:

Arnold, John, Paul Boyle, Anthony Carey, Malcolm Cooper, and Ken Wild: *The Future Shape of Financial Reports* (London and Edinburgh: The Institute of Chartered Accountants in England and Wales, and The Institute of Chartered Accountants of Scotland, 1991).

Since 1982, the Australian Accounting Research Foundation, based in Melbourne, has published a series of nine Accounting Theory Monographs, intended to explore conceptual matters that are of pervasive relevance to accounting standards, as follows:

1. Bell, Philip W.: *CVA, CCA and CoCoA: How Fundamental are the Differences?* (1982).
2. Barton, A.D.: *Objectives and Basic Concepts of Accounting* (1982).
3. Coombes, Robert J., and Carrick A. Martin: *The Definition and Recognition of Revenue* (1982).
4. Kerr, Jean St.G.: *The Definition and Recognition of Liabilities* (1984).
5. Sutcliffe, P.: *Financial Reporting in the Public Sector—A Framework for Analysis and Identification of Issues* (1985).
6. Newman, Robert L.: *Financial Position: Nature and Reporting* (1988).
7. Miller, Malcolm C., and M. Atiqul Islam: *The Definition and Recognition of Assets* (1988).
8. Ball, Ian: *Definition of the Reporting Entity* (1988).
9. Kerr, Jean St.G.: *The Concept of Equity in Financial Accounting* (1989).

A comprehensive treatise/textbook that demonstrates the relevance of modern finance theory and information economics to accounting theory is:

Bromwich, Michael: *Financial Reporting, Information and Capital Markets* (London: Pitman, 1992).

An early Australian study, which was commissioned and published by the Accountancy Research Foundation (as the AARF was then known), and which continues to be relevant to today's debates, is:

Kenley, W.J., and G.J. Staubus: *Objectives and Concepts of Financial Statements*, Accounting Research Study No. 3 (1972).

Uses and Limitations
of a Conceptual Framework

Charles T. Horngren
Stanford University

My perceptions of the role of a conceptual framework in accounting policy-making are heavily affected by the following definitions:

1. The Financial Accounting Standards Board engages in policymaking, which may be defined as the process by which individuals or groups in power choose general rules for action that may affect others within an organization or perhaps affect an entire society. Raymond Chambers states: "Policy-making is 'choosing which' when the choice is a matter of opinion or taste or some other personal or organizational criterion, and not simply a matter of technology."[1]
2. According to the FASB, its conceptual framework is "a coherent system of interrelated objectives and fundamentals that is expected to lead to consistent standards and that prescribes the nature, function, and limits of financial accounting and reporting."[2]

Why is the board building what I will refer to as a technical framework? Several academicians have recently speculated about why. The why is very important to obtaining overall perspective about this multimillion dollar, multiyear effort. In many people's minds, the framework is responsive to an axiomatic belief—that is, if we only had a foundation, deductive logic would lead us to the correct answer.

Although technology is important, accounting policymaking embraces other considerations too, including the political or educational problems of obtaining general acceptance. So policymaking is enormously complicated. As Albert Einstein once remarked, "Mathematics is hard enough, but political science is far too difficult for me."

A PROBLEM OF SOCIAL CHOICE

The policymaking process has been called a social choice problem by several academicians. That term avoids some of the unfortunate connotations associated with calling it a political process. As an example of the latter, my

From *Journal of Accountancy* (April 1981), pp. 86, 88, 90, 92, 94–95. Reprinted by permission of the American Institute of Certified Public Accountants, Inc. Copyright © 1981 by the American Institute of Certified Public Accountants, Inc. Opinions of the authors are their own and do not necessarily reflect policies of the AICPA.

Author's note: My colleagues at Stanford University, William H. Beaver, CPA, Joel S. Demski, and Paul A. Griffin, provided helpful comments on an earlier draft.

[1] Raymond J. Chambers, "Accounting Principles or Accounting Policies," JofA. May 73, p. 52.
[2] Financial Accounting Concepts Statement no. 2, *Qualitative Characteristics of Accounting Information* (Stamford, Conn.: Financial Accounting Standards Board, 1980). p. 11.

dictionary has five definitions of politics, including one that says "activities characterized by artful and often dishonest practices."

Viewing the policymaking process as a social choice problem entails

"1. An assessment of the consequences of FASB decisions on various constituencies (e.g., analysts, management, auditors, bankers, bondholders, diversified shareholders, undiversified shareholders and the SEC [Securities and Exchange Commission])."

"2. A decision as to which configuration of consequences is most desirable, which involves tradeoffs among the interests of various groups affected (for example, whose ox will get gored?)."[3]

The focus is on power and preference. Joel Demski says: "More precisely, in this view we define one financial reporting system as more valuable than another when some group (1) unanimously regards the one as more valuable than the other in terms of individual value and (2) has the *power*—socially speaking—to guarantee this choice. For example, returning to APB [Accounting Principles Board] days, if the insurance industry prefers historical to current valuation of marketable securities and if they have sufficient power to enforce this desire, we then regard the former as more valuable than the latter."[4]

The key element is the set of individuals or coalitions with sufficient power to force a choice. We should list those who have power. If we know the list, we can often predict how the choices are made.

The FASB's scope and implications document characterizes the conceptual framework as a constitution,[5] which to me clearly implies a social choice perspective. A constitution defines the powers of various groups (that is, constituencies). When a difference of preferences arises, the constitution specifies who will win. For example, under certain circumstances, the president can veto a bill. Under other specified conditions, Congress can override the veto.[6] For a second example closer to policymaking by the FASB, the existing, implied constitution is less clear as to who will win if one of the constituents is the SEC. You can draw your own conclusions.

The FASB has understandably retreated from the social choice perspective in the sense that its conceptual framework emphasizes the technology of accounting. That is, the board is concerned with measuring the financial impact of events in an evenhanded manner. Nevertheless, the ultimate generality or specificity of its technical framework will be heavily affected by the relative importance the FASB attaches to its various constituencies.

Survival is mankind's primary motivation. Standard-setting bodies in the private sector have had various useful lives. The committee on accounting

[3] William H. Beaver, "One Academic's View of the Conceptual Framework Project" (Paper delivered at the Conference of California Society of CPAs. September 1977), pp. 9–10.

[4] Joel S. Demski, "The Value of Financial Accounting" (Work paper, Stanford University, 1980), p. 89.

[5] *Scope and Implications of the Conceptual Framework Project* (Stamford, Conn.: FASB, December 1976), p. 2.

[6] Beaver, p. 10.

procedure lasted about 22 years; the APB, 13 years. I hope the FASB has a long useful life—at least 40 years. The useful life of the FASB is not going to rest on issues of technical competence. The pivotal issue will be the ability of the board to resolve conflicts among the various constituencies in a manner perceived to be acceptable to the ultimate constituent, the 800-pound gorilla in the form of the federal government, particularly the SEC. (Of course, the federal gorilla is also subject to pressure from its constituents.) This ability will be manifested in the FASB's decisions, appointments and conceptual framework. So the conceptual framework is desirable if the survival of the FASB is considered to be desirable.[7] That is, the framework is likely to help provide power to the board. After all, the board has no coercive power. Instead, the board must really rely on power by persuasion.

I wish the conceptual framework could be extended in the form of a constitution, but I can also understand why the development of the more modest technical framework is a more feasible goal for the next two or three or four years. (But no more than four, please.)

Consider another illustration of why the technical framework is the tip of the iceberg. With social choice being conducted in a multiperiod setting, the agenda is important. Note that the present framework is silent about how the agenda is set or what items should be placed on the agenda. Yet the power to control the agenda may be far more critical to the status and life of the FASB than the nature of the technical framework.

At an FASB symposium on the conceptual framework held in New York City last June, FASB Chairman Donald Kirk said he agreed with the views of Louis Harris: "Ultimate achievement rests on the capability of the FASB to set real, workable and sound standards, but at the same time to convince its constituents to accept its work as the reality they must be prepared to live with."

Above all, we should recognize that the process of setting accounting standards includes the gaining of general acceptance and support. A major role of the conceptual framework is ultimately to enhance the likelihood of acceptability of specific statements to be proposed or already in place. The more plausible the assumptions and the more compelling the analysis of the facts, the greater the chance of winning the support of diverse interests—and retaining and enhancing the board's power.

MOVEMENT FROM INDIVIDUAL MEMBERS' VALUES TO BOARD VALUES

Precisely what are the implications of the theory of social choice for accounting policymakers? An essential feature is the movement from individual values and choices to social values and choices. Unfortunately, little research has been conducted in this area. Nevertheless, at least some serious thought

[7] Ibid., p. 12.

is being given to describing the problem less naively now than in 1970. Let's concentrate on some difficulties concerning the frameworks of individuals.

Individual Conceptual Frameworks

Most often, the news stories in the business press refer to the FASB as some sort of monolith. But the board is a collection of individuals, just as the accounting departments in universities are collections of individuals. As our professional careers unfold, each of us develops a technical conceptual framework. Some individual frameworks are sharply defined and firmly held; others are vague and weakly held; still others are vague and firmly held.

For example, I suspect that the board's current proposals regarding Statement no. 8, *Accounting for the Translation of Foreign Currency Transactions and Foreign Currency Financial Statements*,[8] reflect changes in some members' conceptual frameworks, in the membership of the board and in the pressures from constituents. I wonder if the board's decisions would have been different regarding foreign currency (or oil and gas) if its conceptual framework had been in place early in the game.

Of course, in a group setting frameworks are very helpful when they overlap and not so helpful when they clash. At one time or another, most of us have felt the discomfort of listening to somebody attempting to buttress a preconceived conclusion by building a convoluted chain of shaky reasoning. Indeed, perhaps on occasion we have voiced such thinking ourselves. Examples of tortuous reasoning are some vivid justifications of accounting for poolings of interest that frequently involve rivers coming together and then wending onward. (My personal conceptual framework may be showing here.) In my opinion the likening of business combinations to streams of water may be poetic, but it is not a demonstration of applying a technical conceptual framework.

My experience as a member of the APB taught me many lessons. A major one was that most of us have a natural tendency and an incredible talent for processing new facts in such a way that our prior conclusions remain intact.[9] Therefore, no matter what conceptual framework is developed, its success will be heavily affected by individual interpretations.

The role of the framework becomes further complicated by the periodic introduction of new board members. Therefore, the generally accepted framework of the 1974 board may not be the generally accepted framework of the 1980 or 1986 board. Some major difficulties may arise as the conceptual framework moves into the area of earnings recognition and as the board membership changes.

Each person has characteristics that limit the usefulness of a conceptual framework. Receptivity to new ideas and change differs markedly. Given a

[8] FASB Statement no. 8, *Accounting for the Translation of Foreign Currency Transactions and Foreign Currency Financial Statements* (Stamford, Conn.: FASB, 1975).

[9] John Jeuck, "Remarks on the Occasion of the McKinsey Award Dinner," *Issues & Ideas* (Chicago, Ill.: University of Chicago, Winter 1980). p. 11.

set of circumstances, most of us can predict the behavior of people we know well. Thus, various board members' attitudes toward seeing a changing accounting world anew will ultimately determine the degree of influence of the framework. Perhaps we should be as much concerned with developing attitudes toward the use of a common framework as with developing knowledge. However, this is easier said than done.

From time to time, the board pleads with its constituents to swallow hard and defer their judgments to the FASB. Why? Because such behavior will further their constituents' private interests in the long run. Similarly, from time to time, the individual board members may have to swallow hard and defer their judgments to the board as a whole. Why? Again, to further their private interests in the long run in the sense of extending the useful life of the board.

General acceptance among the board's members is the first key to the usefulness of the framework. In itself, this is not a trivial task. The second key is the SEC. As FASB members, SEC commissioners and SEC chief accountants come and go, their attitudes and perceptions will help or hinder the role of the framework.

The fragility of any framework is illustrated by the moves of the regulators regarding FASB Statement no. 19, *Financial Accounting and Reporting by Oil and Gas Producing Companies*,[10] and the remarkable six-year-old Ping-Pong® game between the SEC and the board regarding the role of current costs and constant dollar accounting. That is, the board may be nearly unanimously in favor of constant dollar accounting, serve it softly to the SEC and get a return smash from the SEC consisting of current cost accounting. The theory of social choice tells us that we should not be surprised by such interactions during the multiplay game of continuous policymaking.

Almost everyone says he or she wants a conceptual framework, but his or her conceptual framework may not be yours. For example, four general methods of measuring income and capital are discussed in FASB Statement no. 33, *Financial Reporting and Changing Prices*.[11] Each method has strong advocates, and each method has its variations. Given the historical setting and the diverse interest groups that have real or imagined stakes in the policy decisions and strong preferences for flexibility rather than uniformity, agreement on too concrete a conceptual framework will be hard to achieve. Even the issuance of a statement on a conceptual framework cannot escape political dimensions.[12]

The Varying Influence of a Framework

A conceptual framework can help policymakers. There is no doubt that the use of a generally accepted conceptual framework would make standard

[10] FASB Statement no. 19, *Financial Accounting and Reporting by Oil and Gas Producing Companies* (Stamford, Conn.: FASB, 1977).

[11] FASB Statement no. 33, *Financial Reporting and Changing Prices* (Stamford, Conn.: FASB, 1979).

[12] Charles T. Horngren, "Will the FASB Be Here in the 1980s?" JofA, Nov. 76, p. 96.

setting more efficient and effective, producing faster, more consistent and more defensible answers. The framework definitely can help if it provides a common language, methods of analysis and constraints. However, the degree of help will vary from situation to situation.

Consider this illustration of how a technical framework can help.

APB Opinion no. 21, *Interest on Receivables and Payables*,[13] was adopted by the unanimous vote of the 18 members of the board. The opinion requires the imputation of interest in specified circumstances. One of its introductory paragraphs says that "the primary objective of this Opinion is to refine the manner of applying existing accounting principles in this circumstance. Thus, it is not intended to create a new accounting principle." The members applied some widely held, general concepts such as exchange and present value.

Opinion no. 21 was not preceded by an APB research study. Still, each of the 18 members possessed his own conceptual framework, no matter how ill-defined. My point here is that there was sufficient overlap among the 18 frameworks to lead to a unanimous opinion. Moreover, technology played a dominant role in obtaining an accounting standard. Evidence was gathered, logic was applied and a pronouncement was issued. The job of getting general acceptance by the various constituencies was relatively easy, perhaps because the constituents perceived no major economic impact.

Consider an illustration where a framework did not help much.

APB Opinions no. 16, *Business Combinations*,[14] and no. 17, *Intangible Assets*,[15] were preceded by two research studies. Discussions began and continued intermittently at a highly conceptual level worthy of a first-rate doctoral seminar, but the overlap of individual conceptual frameworks was barely great enough to generate the required support by two-thirds of the APB. Moreover, many of the final votes were not influenced solely by conceptual frameworks, as ordinarily conceived. Therefore, a conceptual framework may help if it structures the arguments and provides a common language when dealing with a complicated issue. Still, the framework may become relatively unimportant in the ultimate deliberations when the votes are counted.

My hypothesis is that many final votes are influenced by individual technical frameworks that are favored over any commonly held framework. Moreover, just as in politics, individuals may cast a positive or negative vote as only one in a series of moves to establish, maintain or enhance power. The thinking may be: "I'll vote for something that is technically unacceptable this time because in the longer run I have to live with my fellow members. I'll give in a little now, but I'll win later on more important policy matters." A favorite rationale is: "I'll vote for this defective standard because at least it is an improvement over existing practice."

Does such kind of thinking exist? Undoubtedly! It is vital to the useful life of the board, but it is not captured in any technical framework.

[13] Accounting Principles Board Opinion no. 21, *Interest on Receivables and Payables* (New York: AICPA, 1971).

[14] APB Opinion no. 16, *Business Combinations* (New York: AICPA, 1970).

[15] APB Opinion no. 17, *Intangible Assets* (New York: AICPA, 1970).

My point in citing these illustrations is that a conceptual framework that deals with the "technology" of accounting may be very helpful in most situations and may be of limited help in other situations. Furthermore, the credibility of the FASB can be hurt by the purported use of a conceptual framework where it does not fit. Arthur Wyatt expressed the situation well: "Research (in this context, a conceptual framework) disregards politics and other compromises necessary in making decisions. Decision makers should acknowledge the political and other required compromises when deviating from the proper research answer, explain their decisions on pragmatic grounds, and not try to justify the answer that they come up with as being the one that is most sound, the best conceptually."[16]

SOME REFLECTIONS AND PREDICTIONS

All regulatory bodies have been flayed because they have used piecemeal approaches, solving one accounting issue at a time. Observers have alleged that not enough tidy rationality has been used in the process of accounting policymaking. Again and again, critics have cited a need for a conceptual framework.

I heartily applaud the FASB's efforts to construct a conceptual framework. Its constituents demand it. Let's get the framework built.

There are two major schools of thought regarding the FASB's pace in the construction of the framework.

The first, which is apparently favored by most board members, is patience and plenty of due process. Like the Egyptian-Israeli peace talks, it may be better for all concerned simply to continue the dialogue without necessarily obtaining complete agreement on both sides. It is not hard for me to see why this point of view has merit. Note that the more complete the closure, the greater the restrictions placed on future plays in the game. Moreover, constituents and present and future board members may be unwilling to restrict freedom of choice.

The second school of thought, which I tend to favor, is to proceed more rapidly. Let's not get bogged down in trying to get too concrete a structure. No matter what effort is expended, the structure will be fragile. Let's not carry due process to an extreme, having too many symposiums and too lengthy exposure periods.

Given the experiences of the APB, the FASB and the nature of policymaking, I predict

- Production of a general framework and acceptance by the board.
- Highly successful application in some cases but not in others.
- Varying interpretations of the framework by individual board members.

---

[16] Arthur R. Wyatt, "Research and the APB," Thomas J. Burns, ed., *Accounting in Transition* (Columbus, Ohio: Ohio State University, College of Administrative Science, 1974), p. 128.

As individual accounting standards are issued, the board will be accused of not properly applying the framework in a consistent way and using a piecemeal approach to standard setting. Nevertheless, I have high hopes (a) that the lack of a conceptual framework will not be cited as often as in the past as a reason for postponing action on accounting standards and (b) that the long-standing clamor for a conceptual framework will diminish because proponents will finally realize that such a framework is only a part of the policymaking process, a part whose prominence fluctuates from standard to standard.

SUMMARY

Many who ardently favor a conceptual framework employ that "if we had a framework, we would know what to do." But there are doubters, including me. A framework that is supposed to provide guidelines for the policymakers may differ, depending on the eyes of the beholder.

Accounting policymaking is obviously complex. Progress will continue to come in fits and starts. It will always be considered as too fast by some critics and too slow by other critics. Most people favor "improvements" in accounting—the quicker the better, but one person's improvement is often another person's impairment. These trade-offs are the nucleus of policymaking.[17]

I hope the framework proceeds and gets in place. There is no doubt that it will help, but let's not expect too much from it. Great expectations and inherent complexity are almost always conflicting terms. A technical conceptual framework is only part of the policymaking process. A framework is desirable, but it is not sufficient.

[17] Horngren, p. 96.

Building a Better
Conceptual Framework

J. Alex Milburn

Ernst & Young, Toronto

It's no secret that financial accounting is under stress. One only has to look at daily newspapers to see reports of alleged accounting failures. Our traditional historical-based model is creaking, if not cracking, under the pressure of coping with highly complex transactions and economic conditions within a volatile global marketplace. It is well recognized that historical-cost accounting loses relevance under inflationary conditions. This can be a serious problem, but in addition, new issues are challenging traditional accounting principles. We are confronted with the need to find acceptable methods of recognition and measurement for modern financial instruments, as well as approaches for determining accrued expenses and liabilities for environmental reclamation, pension and other post-employment benefits. These require the use of advanced estimation and measurement approaches that have not been part of the everyday accountant's experience or training, and their application within generally accepted accounting principles is often unclear.

Add to this the fact that capital is more mobile—that it can be moved quickly across borders in response to perceived changes in costs, risks and income-generating potential. Expectations are rising as sophisticated investors and other external users look for accounting information that will be truly useful in evaluating these risks, costs and income potential.

These challenges are leading some thoughtful accountants to go back to the conceptual foundations upon which accounting measurement and recognition principles have been based. In their view, the profession is not going to be able to resolve the complex issues currently confronting it to the satisfaction of an increasingly sophisticated and demanding public without an improved conceptual framework. David Solomons has observed that "our traditional accounting methods have been deficient and their deficiencies give rise to conflicts between economic interests that could be avoided if accounting's theoretical foundations were more soundly based." (See *Making Accounting Policy: The Quest for Credibility in Financial Reporting*, New York: Oxford University Press, 1986, p. 246.)

Of course, major authoritative accounting bodies, such as the Financial Accounting Standards Board, the Canadian Institute of Chartered Accountants and the International Accounting Standards Committee, have already

From *CAmagazine* (December 1991), pp. 43–48. Reprinted by permission of the Canadian Institute of Chartered Accountants, Toronto. Copyright © 1991 by the Canadian Institute of Chartered Accountants.

Author's note: This article is based on a presentation to the Conference of National, Regional, and International Standard-setting Bodies in Brussels in June 1991.

developed concepts statements. However, these existing statements have not been capable of providing bases for reasoning forward to specific recognition and measurement standards. They have largely left open questions as to the relative merits of different capital maintenance systems and historical cost, current cost, and current value measurement attributes. In short, conceptual frameworks have been incomplete, and only of limited value in the development of accounting standards.

Why has this been? Perhaps conceptual frameworks developed to date have been too heavily geared toward simply codifying traditional accepted conventions that may no longer be fully relevant. Raymond Lauver, a recently retired member of the FASB, would seem to be of this opinion in observing that "It is not enough to do what was possible, expected and accepted in the past." (See "Accountant—Be a Measurer," *The CPA Journal*, January 1991, pp. 12–14.)

With these observations in mind, then, I would like to examine the prospects for improving the conceptual foundations of accounting within an international context.

Let's begin with a definition.

A conceptual framework for financial accounting might be defined as an interrelated structure of propositions and observations that provides a logical foundation for deducing what accounting principles ought to be. While seemingly simple, this definition embodies certain important presumptions that some may wish to debate. First, it presumes that a conceptual framework has a normative purpose—that it provides a basis for determining what accounting principles *ought to be*. Second, it implies that the process of developing accounting standards should be one of deduction, or reasoning forward, within a logical structure of propositions and evidence. This would seem to mean that accounting should be more an applied science than an art, and that its conceptual framework should be much more than a generalization of existing conventions and practices.

An accounting theorist's hope might be that this reasoning forward from basic premises and assumptions would establish unifying principles that could serve as the basis for a financial accounting measurement system that is both internally consistent (that is, always measures and presents like things in like ways), and externally valid (that is, results in values of assets, liabilities, revenues and expenses of business enterprises that represent relevant economic realities).

But we would seem to be doomed to fall significantly short of this ideal. There are limits to how far reasoning forward from economic premises can be expected to take us. In my opinion, a truly comprehensive conceptual framework should factor in these limits and deal with their implications for financial accounting measurement and disclosure. Two types of constraints might be identified:

1. Economic indeterminacy—that is, measurement impossibilities due to incomplete markets, pervasive uncertainties, and allocation problems that cannot be resolved in a nonarbitrary fashion. These are certain to

leave a wide range of measurement/valuation alternatives that cannot be reduced by rational reasoning or estimation processes. Accounting has been described as the art of the possible.

2. Conflicts between user interests and pressures to modify accounting on the basis of perceived economic, social or political effects. Conflicts between competing interests are normally settled on the basis of the users' relative rights to accounting information, and their respective power positions. These relative rights and powers may be a function of the culture of a particular country and its legal, social, political and economic structures, and may differ considerably between nations.

I am proposing, then, three dimensions to a fully defined conceptual framework: first, its economic rationality; second, its recognition of inherent measurement impossibilities (economic indeterminacies); third, its presumption as to the relative rights and powers of competing user interests. Let's examine each of these.

ECONOMIC RATIONALITY

It would seem that accounting standards should at least seek to separate the rational from the irrational decision models and concentrate on the former. For this purpose, attention needs to be paid to the findings of finance and economic theory.
—Ross M. Skinner

Accounting principles rest on principles of economics.
—George J. Staubus

Over the years, a number of accounting scholars have expressed the view that financial accounting should be reasoned forward from premises about the economic purposes of business enterprises and from finance theories related to capital markets (that is, related to the determination of securities prices and interest rates). This, in my view, should be the starting point for developing a conceptual framework. I believe this reasoning process can be taken much further than it has been in conceptual frameworks developed to date—that improvement is possible as a result of developments in capital markets theories and evidence in recent years. I believe these have profound implications for rationally reducing recognition and measurement alternatives. Let me try to illustrate, in general terms, what I mean:

- It is impossible to define a useful conceptual framework without first delineating the economic purpose of profit-oriented enterprises that should be the measurement objective of financial accounting.
- It seems indisputable that the primary purpose of such enterprises is to create wealth, which is expressed in terms of money and ultimately conceived as command over cash, or claims to future cash or cash-

equivalent flows. Thus, an enterprise may be presumed to invest in assets, regardless of their form, for the future cash-equivalent flows they are expected to generate. There is nothing new, or controversial, in this: The FASB Statements of Financial Accounting Concepts acknowledge it, as does the IASC's 1989 Framework for the Preparation and Presentation of Financial Statements. This is not to suggest, however, that the ability to generate cash flows is the only objective that should be accounted for. Many may be interested in other outputs and effects on society and the environment. I am simply asserting that the ability to generate cash flows is a primary objective, one that is at the heart of financial accounting.

- Economic resources (assets), claims upon them (liability and equity contracts), and changes in them (income), are the subject matter of financial accounting. Since it is the cash-expectations property of assets, liabilities and equity that is the objective of business activities, then it would seem appropriate to conclude that this property should be the focus of accounting measurement and disclosure.

- This is where the connection with the theory of capital markets comes in. Capital markets theory, which is accepted and readily evident in the financial marketplace, is based on the premise that rational investors price investments by discounting expected future cash flows and that, under reasonably competitive market conditions, the rational expectation must be that the rate of return will be commensurate with currently available market rates of interest for investments of equivalent risk. I call this the presumption of rational present value expectations.

In my view, accounting should be based on these rational economic expectations, and they should be recognized as a fundamental building block for financial accounting.

To date, the concepts statements of the CICA, FASB, IASC and others have ventured only a little way down this road. For example, "assets" are defined in terms of future economic benefits to result from past events or transactions. If we pushed the rational present value expectations concept to its logical conclusion, "assets" might be redefined as "probable future cash flows to result from past events or transactions discounted at appropriate risk-adjusted market rates of interest."

Many may be highly skeptical of this proposed redefinition. It is turning a generic concept of assets into a concept that has measurement implications. Visualizing assets and liabilities in rational present value expectations terms gives rise to questions as to the validity of certain traditional textbook measurement models and concepts of capital and capital maintenance. In other words, pushing accepted economic premises to their logical accounting conclusions may serve to eliminate so-called measurement systems that are not rational, i.e. that are inconsistent with the economic time-value-of-money presumption. To return to the quotation cited earlier: "It would seem that accounting should at least seek to separate the rational from the irrational decision models."

ECONOMIC INDETERMINACY

It is, of course, naïve to believe that the deductive reasoning process I am proposing can resolve all significant recognition and measurement issues. While it may be expected to serve to eliminate certain irrational alternatives, it is likely to leave a rather large range of choice.

Economic indeterminacy is much more than uncertainty. At its heart is the "allocation problem," which has been the bane of the cost-based accrual accounting model, but can also rear its head in current value models. The allocation problem can arise when one item must be partitioned between two or more objects for accounting purposes. Suppose, for example, that two independent parties agree to join in a business undertaking to provide a service to third parties, and to share the resulting revenues. These revenues could be allocated between the two in a number of ways, none of which may be more defensible in economic theory than any other. Thus we have an economic indeterminacy. It might be expected, however, that if the two parties are going to enter into such a venture, they will have arrived at some agreement on how to share the revenues. If there is a clear contractual basis for this allocation, then accounting should reflect it.

When allocations are determined by arm's-length transactions, then economic indeterminacy is usually resolved for accounting purposes, at least at the dates of the transactions. It is when there are no relevant market exchange transactions that allocations may become indeterminate. But even in such cases, some types of economic indeterminacy might be reduced by way of accepted conventions that define general economic expectations. For example, the allocation of a loan payment between principal (return of capital) and interest (return on capital, that is, income), is, in concept, arbitrary. But in practice, an allocation may be made using certain present value conventions that have general acceptance within the investment community. It might be proposed, then, that in cases of economic indeterminacy, financial accounting should be expected to reflect the accepted measurement expectations of society where such expectations can be demonstrated to exist.

A fully developed conceptual framework should not just sweep economic indeterminacy under the carpet, with the typical general advice that "professional judgment should be applied." Efforts at building a more complete conceptual framework may be usefully focused on examining and understanding the limits of economic reasoning, and on defining the nature and range of economic indeterminacy inherent in it. The objective would be to provide a conceptual basis for developing measurement or allocation approaches in the face of indeterminacy (for example, the development of surrogates that are most consistent with the measurement objective) and appropriate supplementary disclosures. Through such efforts, it might be possible, for example, to develop bases for reporting ranges or other mathematical representations of the extent of an indeterminacy and for identifying and disclosing assumptions. An entity's financial position and income are not fully and fairly represented if pervasive uncertainties or fundamental indeterminacies are not adequately factored into measurements and disclosures.

Indeterminacy issues cannot be productively addressed within a conceptual framework until the deductive reasoning process is taken as far as it reasonably can be, because it is only through this process that the nature and extent of inherent indeterminacies can be defined and understood.

My objective is not to promote particular solutions but, rather, *to make the point that defining and dealing with economic indeterminacy is a basic conceptual issue.*

ECONOMIC EFFECTS AND COMPETING USER INTERESTS

Let's now turn to the balancing of competing interests.

Most existing conceptual frameworks include a set of "qualitative characteristics" or attributes of useful financial statement information. For instance, the 1989 IASC framework states that four main characteristics are understandability, relevance, reliability, and comparability (para. 24). These are similar to the ones set out in the FASB and CICA frameworks. Each of these frameworks recognizes that trade-offs between these characteristics (between relevance and reliability, for example) will be necessary and that professional judgment should be used to determine the relative importance of the characteristics in different cases. The IASC framework is also typical of the other two in observing that "the benefits derived from information should exceed the costs of providing it," but that "the evaluation of benefits and costs is . . . substantially a judgment process" (para. 44).

Such a discussion of the qualitative characteristics of financial information is useful. But it is incomplete because it does not recognize the competing interests that may determine what is considered relevant to whom. If financial information is of value, then those who have private (insider) access to it will probably be reluctant to give up their advantage. The very economic objective of business activities—to maximize wealth—can be expected to lead to protective behaviour. As Paul Miller has observed, "Because users get rich by finding inefficient resource allocations, it is inappropriate for the FASB to expect them to sacrifice their comparative advantage by supporting efforts to turn private information into public disclosures" (see "The conceptual framework as reformation and counter-reformation," *Accounting Horizons*, June 1990, pp. 23–32).

It is important, therefore, to understand the relative rights of different participant interests and their comparative advantages and power positions. It is these relative powers and rights that will dictate the trade-offs between "qualitative characteristics." A conceptual framework is incomplete if it simply passes off these trade-offs as matters of "professional judgment."

The relative rights and powers of different user interests may be defined by law, or simply by custom and practice. In any case, they will most certainly differ between nations and may change over time as conditions change. This could have significant implications for the development of an international conceptual framework that purports to represent a common foundation for financial accounting appropriate to all countries.

For discussion purposes, it may be useful to visualize three orientations that might be expected to exist to some degree in different countries:

1. A free enterprise economy dominated by management and private investors.
2. A free enterprise economy dominated by efficient markets and public investors.
3. A broad public accountability orientation.

ORIENTATION NO. 1

Here, business enterprise management (which may have a significant equity stake in the business) and specific private capital providers (perhaps large banks and other financial institutions) are the dominant forces. These groups may have what might be described as protectionist and paternalistic attitudes toward the dissemination of financial information to outside interests. Larger businesses may take a conservative stewardship attitude, assuming that it is important for external investors and other public interests to see the enterprise as secure; thus, any volatility in financial statement figures should be smoothed out, and undisclosed reserves should be set aside in good times and drawn back into income when times are not as good. The dominant interests may be of the view that outside investors, employees, and others cannot be expected to understand complex financial information and volatility, and may be misled by it to make irrational decisions. They might also believe that shareholders are best served by minimal disclosures in relation to sensitive information that could be used to benefit competitors.

Such attitudes can be witnessed in many countries. They are evident in Canada, for example, with regard to the rights of pension plan members and employees to financial information on their pension plans. The situation may change, however, as employee groups and their representatives become more knowledgeable and press for more complete disclosure. Recently, there have been struggles between business enterprises and their employee plan members over who owns and should benefit from surplus assets in pension plans. This is leading to questions about how surpluses should be measured for financial reporting purposes—on a "best estimate" or conservatively reserved basis.

The internationalization of securities markets may be eroding the basis for this orientation, particularly in industries and countries that need outside capital, and which must therefore meet the increasing information demands of international capital providers and securities exchanges.

ORIENTATION NO. 2

The United States, the United Kingdom and Canada might be examples of this orientation. These countries feature developed securities markets. The accounting and disclosure requirements of securities regulators and accounting standard-setters are aimed at providing "full and fair" disclosure to investors. Trading on the basis of inside knowledge is illegal. The rationale in this type of economy is that extensive disclosure of financial information on business enterprises lays the groundwork for a "fair game" for investors, and in so doing, provides an optimal basis for the efficient allocation of scarce capital resources.

It is understandable within this type of economy that conceptual frameworks for financial accounting give prominence to the decision-usefulness of information for investors. It can also be expected that the objective of financial information will be to reflect best estimates, without any modification to smooth out volatility or to set aside undisclosed reserves against possible adverse deviations. Other users (employees, suppliers, competitors, the general public, etc.) should also benefit from this information, but their rights may be considered secondary to those of the investor.

Although the United States, the United Kingdom and Canada may be held out as examples of this orientation, there are still strong signs of the more restrictive first orientation in these countries, particularly in certain industries. This is evident in the political struggles (most visible in the United States) between industry representatives and standard-setters over, for example, representation on the FASB. It is also seen in the recognition that standard-setting is a political process, and that accounting standards must ultimately reflect the relative power positions of vested interests in the process. In their recent book, *The FASB: The People, the Process and the Politics* (Homewood, Illinois: Irwin, 1988), Paul Miller and Rodney Redding were unequivocal in stating that standard-setting in the United States is a political affair:

> "Politics tend to make generally accepted accounting principles logically inconsistent because the consensus needed to resolve an issue will be shaped by those in power and how important the issues are to them. Thus, inconsistencies will appear between standards issued at different times, under different standard setters, and in different industry settings."

ORIENTATION NO. 3

This orientation might best be illustrated by a discussion paper entitled *The Corporate Report*, published by the Accounting Standards Steering Committee of the Institute of Chartered Accountants in England and Wales in 1975. It proposed a broad public accountability framework for financial accounting. It envisaged a public reporting responsibility on the part of every enterprise that "commands human or material resources on such a scale that the results of its activities have significant economic implications for the community as a whole" (para. 1.2). According to the paper, such organizations should be accountable on a wide range of matters to those whose interests are significantly affected by the organization's activities.

The paper stated that business enterprises should be evaluated against an array of performance indicators, not just income and financial position: "Business enterprises can survive only with the approval of the community in which they operate and they have an interest in revealing information which displays how differing interests are being balanced for the benefit of the whole community" (para. 4.29). And it added: "It is important to keep in mind the pervasive influence of reporting practices on management attitudes. Managements naturally respond to those indicators by which they consider their performance is judged" (para. 4.33).

The discussion paper recommended that, in addition to conventional financial statements, corporate reports should include a statement of value added, an employment report, and statements of money exchanges with governments, transactions in foreign currency, future prospects and corporate objectives. If it had been written now, it would probably have advocated that organizations report on their environmental impacts as well.

At least three questions might be raised against the background of these three orientations:

1. Do differences such as those illustrated by the three orientations undermine the validity of economic rationality as a basis for a conceptual framework?
2. What are the implications of economic indeterminacy?
3. How might the different power and rights scenarios affect the further development of an international conceptual framework?

Let's start with the first question. To the extent that an accounting measurement can be unequivocally deduced from universally accepted economic theory and evidence, it should be expected to represent an "economic reality." Such deductions may be presumed to have broad international applicability if they are founded in premises regarding the economic purpose of business activities and economic theory that are applicable to all business enterprises in all market-based exchange economies. It may be expected, then, that such fundamental principles should be at the basis of accounting standards of individual nations under any of the three orientations mentioned, and that they should therefore provide an appropriate foundation for international standards.

Many will want to debate this conclusion. Proponents of the first orientation may raise arguments for smoothing, reserving and editing financial information to be provided to external interests. Others will contend that accounting standards should take economic effects into consideration and that such considerations may override economic rationality. In their view, standard-setters should be more agents of social change than accounting measurement experts. Those holding either of these views are clearly prepared to modify the accounting that strict economic reasoning would produce. But what frameworks or foundations do standard-setters have for deciding when and how accounting should be adjusted to achieve or avoid economic, social, or political effects?

Some may begin with the premise that a conceptual framework must first and foremost conform with the corporations or tax laws of a country, or with its particular stewardship requirements—and that these must be given priority over any economic rationality-based principles. In order to address this, it would seem necessary to understand the objectives of such legal or stewardship requirements, and how and why they are inconsistent with an economic rationality-based framework.

Advocates of the second orientation might argue that no departures from rational economic expectations deductions should be tolerated (other than perhaps allowing a sufficient transition period for changes), but that the capital marketplace should be left to sort out the effects. To do otherwise, they might claim, is to inject a bias into accounting. Existing conceptual frameworks seem to stand for neutrality. For example, the IASC framework has this provision: "To be reliable, the information contained in financial statements must be neutral, that is, free from bias. Financial statements are not neutral if, by selection or presentation of information, they influence the making of a decision or judgment in order to achieve a predetermined result or outcome." But such simple assertions seem naïve and incomplete in the face of the reality of vested interests.

Let's now turn to the second question, which deals with the implications of economic indeterminacy. Economic effects issues are unavoidable in choosing between alternatives within an area of economic indeterminacy. Let me illustrate. Suppose one is accounting for a utility (a hydro-electric company, for example) whose revenue rates are regulated on the basis of the utility's accounting expenses, plus a rate of return to equity. A major element of the expenses of such a company will relate to the cost of its plant, so it is necessary to determine how this cost should be allocated to the period of use. It may be concluded that this cannot be resolved solely on the basis of economic reasoning. At the same time, the allocation pattern chosen has significant intergenerational equity implications. Should all users of electricity over the life of the plant end up paying the same price per kilowatt hour with respect to the plant cost and, if so, in real or nominal terms? Alternatively, should future generations be expected to pay more, or less? A decision on this issue is implicit in whatever allocation method is chosen, whether it be cost or value based.

Let's now consider the final question, which deals with the different user power and rights scenarios. Each of the three orientations proposed might suggest different consequences within the international environment:

- The first might suggest a multinational company management orientation. Here, the primary purpose would be to standardize, or harmonize, accounting methods and disclosures in order to minimize the costs and confusion of complying with different national requirements. Multinationals might be expected to favour a framework that would not overly inhibit management's freedom to utilize reserves and smoothing mechanisms.

- Under the second orientation, the objective is full and fair disclosure of financial information for investors. It may be expected that, like multinational companies, international investors would welcome harmonized accounting standards, so as to facilitate comparisons of financial statements of enterprises domiciled in different countries. But, unlike multinational companies, investors may be expected to want such harmonization within a framework that is reasoned within capital market-based economic concepts.

- Under the third orientation, emphasis would be placed on public interests. More attention would be focused on the economic impact of international companies on individual national economies—for example, on bases for determining and disclosing transnational transfer pricing between the national components of multinational companies, and on the impact of business activities on the environment. It is interesting that, to date, the IASC has paid scant attention to such issues. The United Nations has, however, devoted a considerable amount of time and effort to examining some of these broader accountability issues.

Where does all of this leave us? Is the further development of the conceptual foundations of accounting a practical possibility or an impossible dream? In my opinion, it is not only possible, but it is essential that financial accounting have a more clearly developed conceptual framework—one that logically links modern capital-based economic theory with accounting recognition and measurement principles, and that provides a foundation for reconciling potentially conflicting national and international user interests.

The FASB's Conceptual Framework: An Evaluation

David Solomons
Professor Emeritus, The Wharton School

Until the publication, in December 1984, of Concepts Statement no. 5, it was reasonable to suspend judgment on the Financial Accounting Standards Board's conceptual framework while waiting for the climax. Now that the

From *Journal of Accountancy* (June 1986), pp. 114–116, 118, 120–122, 124. Reprinted by permission of the American Institute of Certified Public Accountants, Inc. Copyright © 1986 by the American Institute of Certified Public Accountants, Inc. Opinions of the authors are their own and do not necessarily reflect policies of the AICPA.
Author's note: This article is an abridgment and adaptation of the third W. Oscar Neuhaus Lecture, delivered at the Jesse H. Jones Graduate School of Administration, Rice University, on October 9, 1985, and published in the *Jones Journal*, Fall-Winter 1985.

FASB Concepts Statements

Number	Title	Date issued
1	Objectives of Financial Reporting of Business Enterprises	November 1978
2	Qualitative Characteristics of Accounting Information	May 1980
3	Elements of Financial Statements of Business Enterprises	December 1980
4	Objectives of Financial Reporting by Nonbusiness Organizations	December 1980
5	Recognition and Measurement in Financial Statements of Business Enterprises	December 1984
6	Elements of Financial Statements	December 1985

dust has settled, there is no reason to suspend judgment any longer. Though the board has not acknowledged that the statement was its last word on the conceptual framework, it seems unlikely that any further work will be done on it, except perhaps on methods of display of financial information. Whatever real work is going to be done on the framework has been done.

Attempts to formulate a conceptual framework of accounting have been going on now for at least 50 years, and to get the board's project into perspective it is important to see it as only the latest in a series of attempts to formulate what W. A. Paton and A. C. Littleton in 1940 called "a coherent, coordinated, consistent body of doctrine." There have been many steps along the road from the American Accounting Association's 1936 *Tentative Statement of Accounting Principles Underlying Corporate Financial Statements* to Concepts Statement no. 5, with Accounting Principles Board Statement no. 4 (1970) and the American Institute of CPAs' Trueblood report (1973) among the major landmarks.

THE CONCEPTUAL FRAMEWORK— A CONSTITUTION?

The conceptual framework has often been referred to as a constitution. Indeed, the FASB used this language itself when inaugurating the project in 1976: "A conceptual framework can provide a constant thread of reason, a basis for solution—a constitution—to guide the FASB. It will narrow the range of alternatives to be considered by the Board because some alternatives will clearly be 'unconstitutional.'"

I myself used similar language in the 1980 Arthur Young Lecture, which I delivered at the University of Glasgow. Exhorting the British accounting profession to start work on its own conceptual framework in order to give added credibility to the standards promulgated by the Accounting Standards Committee there, I said, "A board or committee setting standards without a conceptual framework is like a legislature making laws without a constitution to protect citizens from arbitrary acts of government." But on closer inspection the analogy can be seen to be an imperfect one, for there are important differences between a constitution and a conceptual framework:

1. A constitution has the force of law. A conceptual framework has no authority except what flows from its intellectual persuasiveness.
2. Constitutions contain many arbitrary elements, for example, the number of senators each state is to have, the length of the interval between elections, and so forth. There is no room for arbitrariness in a conceptual framework.
3. There are significant differences among the nations of the world in their constitutional arrangements. There could be important national differences among conceptual frameworks—this is mere speculation because no country other than the United States has yet made any serious attempt to construct one—but it is doubtful whether the differences would be as fundamental as the constitutional differences between the democracies and the single-party states or, among the democracies, between presidential and parliamentary systems of government.

In short, I do not believe that the case for a conceptual framework is strengthened by likening it to a constitution. The fact is that the FASB already has a constitution—its charter and bylaws. The main source of its legitimacy is the Securities and Exchange Commission and SEC Accounting Series Release no. 150. The case for a conceptual framework must rest on other grounds.

THE CASE FOR A CONCEPTUAL FRAMEWORK

There is widespread skepticism about the need for a conceptual framework of accounting and about the wisdom of the FASB's having spent nine years and a considerable amount of money on it. Though it was reasonable to be skeptical about the outcome, there was, in my view, no question about the need or about the benefits that might have been expected to flow from it. Some benefits are in fact already being reaped.

Economizing of Effort   The most obvious benefit should be to the FASB itself, in the economizing of effort that the framework should make possible. Many accounting problems have common elements, and they should not have to be thought through afresh each time the board encounters them. The definitions of the elements of financial statements formulated in Concepts Statement no. 3 have already been appealed to repeatedly in later board pronouncements.

But we must not be too quick to congratulate the board on its success in this respect, for there have been striking failures to balance the successes. The treatment of executory contracts is one of the grievous failures. The board has never yet been able to decide whether these should be included in financial statements, disclosed in footnotes to the statements or not referred to at all.

The board stumbled over this question in Statement no. 47, *Disclosure of Long-Term Obligations*. It was unable to decide whether unconditional purchase obligations, such as take-or-pay contracts, (1) resulted in ownership interests and obligations to make future cash payments that should be included among the assets and liabilities in a balance sheet or (2) were simply commitments or contingent liabilities that might be noted but not recognized in the balance sheet.

We were promised in Statement no. 47 that this matter would be resolved when the recognition and measurement phase of the conceptual framework was completed. But that promise has never been redeemed, and every time the board confronts an executory contract now, it seems likely to repeat the same fumble.

Gain in Consistency Accounting standards promulgated against the background of an agreed conceptual framework may be expected to be more consistent with one another than standards developed independently of such a framework.

Improved Communication Concepts Statements nos. 2 and 3 have already improved communication among accountants and between the FASB and its constituents. This is the result largely of the definitions handed down, not only of the elements of financial statements but also of other terms, such as "materiality," that have been widely used by accountants but not always to mean the same thing.

Defense Against Politicization If the FASB could show that its standards were derived from a coherent and plausible body of concepts, it would greatly enhance the credibility of financial reporting. I know of no better way to reduce accounting's vulnerability to political pressure. How else can the board demonstrate the superiority of a proposed standard over a counter-proposal from some sectional interest that is self-serving and not in the public interest?

THE FRAMEWORK IN PLACE

It is, of course, much too late to ask whether we need a conceptual framework. The question, rather, is what kind of conceptual framework we should have—for of course we already have one and have been living with it for a long time. The simplest way to characterize it is to call it a historical cost model, but this is an oversimplification. We capture more of its nature if we call it a recoverable cost model, for this notion at least encompasses the "lower of cost or market" rule that is used for stating nonmonetary current assets.

In Concepts Statement no. 5, paragraph 69, the FASB suggests that "'historical exchange price' is more descriptive of the quantity most generally reflected in financial statements in present practice (and 'transaction-based system' would be a better description of the present accounting model than 'historical cost system')."

However we are to describe the present conceptual framework, it is there, in place, and, however imperfectly, it works. The question is whether its imperfections are so serious that the existing framework needs radically to be reconstructed or whether nothing is called for except fine-tuning. We had better give the FASB the benefit of the doubt and assume that the board embarked on the conceptual framework project with an open mind and with no preconceptions about the answer to this question.

There is no doubt about the conclusion they had reached by the end of 1984, when Concepts Statement no. 5 was issued. The conclusion was that, if change was called for, it would have to come gradually, through a process of evolution. It was not to come as a result of the conceptual framework project.

Although there is much of interest in the project besides the part dealing with recognition and measurement, it has always been clear that its success or failure would be judged by what it had to say on these topics. Of course, "success" and "failure" are highly subjective terms. Those who are satisfied with the present state of generally accepted accounting principles will applaud the board for leaving things much as they are. If, like me, you think that radical changes are called for, you will think that Concepts Statement no. 5 is a dismal failure. But I shall come back to this statement later, after looking at the earlier products of the project.

THE OBJECTIVES OF FINANCIAL REPORTING

The first product of the framework project was the concepts statement on the objectives of financial reporting. Much of the board's preparatory work had been done for it by the Trueblood study group, though it is worth noting that, whereas the Trueblood group had reported on the objectives of financial *statements*, the board expanded its perspective to financial *reporting*, of which financial statements are only a part.

On the other hand, while the Trueblood report recognized, however briefly, that business enterprises had a responsibility to society and not just to their stockholders, the board's statement on objectives substantially confines its attention to the needs of investors and creditors, barely recognizes the needs of managers, and ignores altogether the interests of other groups with an interest in enterprise productivity, such as labor and the tax authorities.

It also ignores the last of the Trueblood objectives of financial statements: "to report on those activities of the enterprise affecting society which can be determined and described or measured and which are important to the role of the enterprise in its social environment."

That the board took a narrower view is especially regrettable because of the message transmitted to standard setters in other countries, especially in the less developed ones. In a country like India, for example, private investors play a much less important part in the economy than they do in the United States; government and other public agencies play a larger part. The financial reporting needs of the public sector are more important there, and the objectives of financial reporting in those countries should reflect those needs.

It would be a mistake for the standard setters in the developing countries to embrace the FASB's conceptual framework wholeheartedly, therefore, for this reason if for no other.

It may be doubted whether any statement of objectives would be likely to have much impact on the accounting standards subsequently issued by the board. But one cannot fault the board for starting the conceptual framework with a statement of the objectives of financial reporting, for before a standard can be set for any product, the purpose of the product must be defined. Safety standards for aircraft will be different for passenger-carrying and for freight-carrying planes. Potency standards for drugs will be different for ethical* and for over-the-counter drugs.

In this case, however, the purposes that the board has defined for financial reporting are excessively narrow. For this reason I give Concepts Statement no. 1 no more than a grade of C.

QUALITATIVE CHARACTERISTICS

The next installment of the conceptual framework was Concepts Statement no. 2, which examines the characteristics that make accounting information useful for decision making. The importance of these characteristics is that they constitute the only criteria the board has for choosing among accounting alternatives. And, in fact, the board has leaned on these criteria a number of times in making such choices.

The hierarchy of accounting qualities discussed in the statement first distinguishes between characteristics of the person using information, such as the person's degree of understanding, prior knowledge about a situation, and so forth, and characteristics of the information itself, such as its reliability. Then the principal qualities that make information useful for making decisions are looked at in some detail, under the two broad headings of "relevance" and "reliability."

All the terms used in the hierarchy are carefully defined—a contribution of no small value in itself—and the relationships among the various qualities are considered more carefully than has been done before in an accounting context. Particular attention is given to the idea of a trade-off between the relevance and reliability of information, and this has helped the board to justify the disclosure of relatively "soft" data, such as estimates of oil and gas reserves and the use of a discount rate in Statement no. 69. The gain in

* Editors' note: Prescription drugs.

Representational Faithfulness

The FASB has recently given us a good example of the gap that separates what representational faithfulness requires and what the board thinks it is politically feasible to do. The example is the treatment of actuarial gains and losses in Statement no. 87, *Employers' Accounting for Pensions,* issued in December 1985.

Actuarial gains and losses arise in any pension plan because of the many assumptions that have to be made about the future—about interest rates, mortality, wage rates, stock prices, and so forth. Some or all of these assumptions will prove not to be in accordance with the way things turn out. Under the board's new standard these differences between assumptions and realities will not be immediately reflected in the employer's financial statements when they are capable of being quantified. Rather, they are to be amortized over the future years of service of employees participating in the pension plan.

The board was disarmingly frank about this decision: "The board believes that it would be conceptually appropriate and preferable to recognize a net pension liability or asset measured as the difference between the projected benefit obligation and plan assets, either with no delay in recognition of gains and losses, or perhaps with gains and losses reported currently by comprehensive income but not in earnings. However, it concluded that these approaches would be too great a change from past practice to be adopted at the present time" (paragraph 107).

relevance from these disclosures, the board believed, was more than enough to offset any loss of verifiability in the figures.

It is in the assertion that the concept of reliability is much more than simply verifiability that the concepts statement makes one of its principal contributions. Representational faithfulness, the other ingredient that makes accounting information reliable, has become a powerful tool that the board now uses in formulating standards. (The goal of representational faithfulness is not invariably achieved, however, as the addendum *Representational Faithfulness* indicates.)

Representational faithfulness is defined in the statement's glossary as "correspondence or agreement between a measure or description and the phenomenon that it purports to represent (sometimes called validity)." However many times a measurement can be replicated by independent measurers who verify one another's results, if they are all using the wrong inputs the resulting measurement will not be reliable because it will not represent what it purports to represent.

Not the least important part of Concepts Statement no. 2 is the treatment of neutrality in financial reporting. Neutrality is defined in the glossary as the "absence in reported information of bias intended to attain a predetermined result or to induce a particular mode of behavior." So far the board has not seriously wavered in its espousal of neutrality and its rejection of the "economic consequences" school of thought, though pressures on it to abandon neutrality have been strong from time to time.

Robert T. Sprouse, until recently vice-chairman of the FASB, expressed himself forcefully on this matter in his 1984 W. Oscar Neuhaus Lecture: "According to the by-laws, the individuals serving on the FASB are selected on the basis of 'knowledge of accounting, finance and business.' I do not know about you, but I do not want any part of the notion that the seven individuals appointed as members of the FASB should sit in Stamford, Connecticut, and consciously attempt to slant financial information with the hope and expectation that it will lead to decision makers' acting in ways that those seven individuals believe further national goals. I should be equally alarmed if the seven individuals were elected, no matter what their qualifications might be, if their objective were to tailor financial information in an attempt to influence the decisions that people make."

If, by emphasizing the importance of neutrality, the conceptual framework had done no more than reinforce the credibility of financial reporting, its contribution would not have been negligible.

I shall resist the temptation to give a grade to Concepts Statement no. 2. My close association with the preparation of the document, as a consultant, prevents me from being able to take a detached view of it.

THE ELEMENTS OF FINANCIAL STATEMENTS

The purpose of Concepts Statement no. 3 is to define 10 elements of financial statements: assets, liabilities, equity, investments by owners, distributions to owners, comprehensive income, revenues, expenses, gains and losses. The statement has since been modified, in Concepts Statement no. 6, to apply it to nonbusiness organizations as well.

Whatever may be thought of the definitions put forward, there is no doubt that they are a distinct improvement on the earlier definitions in APB Statement no. 4. Some of the earlier definitions were rightly criticized for circularity and for defining as assets and liabilities any debit or credit balances that current practice treated as assets and liabilities. The FASB's definitions represent progress in three directions:

1. They aid communication by providing more precise terminology.
2. Defining something first requires an analysis and understanding of its nature, and analyzing the nature of an accounting item in order to define it may point to the appropriate way to account for it. The treatment of bond discounts as valuation adjustments to bond liability instead of as assets is a case in point.
3. The definitions have been formulated in such a way as to leave no room for reasonable doubt about the primacy of assets and liabilities and the dependency of the other elements on these two. Thus, revenues are defined in paragraph 63 as "inflows or other enhancements of *assets* of an entity or settlements of its *liabilities* (or a combination of both) during a period from delivering or producing goods, rendering services, or other activities that constitute the entity's ongoing major or central operations" (italics added). Expenses are defined correspondingly, and equity is defined as the residual interest in assets minus liabilities.

These definitions virtually require net income to be viewed as a change in net assets, since revenues and expenses are themselves defined in terms of changes in net assets. This can hardly fail to influence the board's thinking about the nature of profit measurement, and it may already have done so.

But let us not claim too much for the definitions in Concepts Statement no. 3, for there is only so much they can do. Try to apply the definition of "liabilities" to the pension situation. Liabilities are defined in paragraph 28 as "probable future sacrifices of economic benefits arising from present obligations of a particular entity to transfer assets or provide services to other entities in the future as a result of past transactions or events."

Quite apart from the measurement problems resulting from uncertainties, what is an employer's present obligation to the participants in a pension plan? Is it the (discounted) amount of all future payments to all eligible employees, past and present? Or is it the amount that would be payable if the plan were discontinued at the balance sheet date? Or is it the amount of benefits vested at the balance sheet date? Or is it only the amounts currently due and payable to those who have already retired at the balance sheet date?

The term "present obligations" is unfortunately too broad to provide a clear answer to these questions. But in spite of its shortcomings, Concepts Statement no. 3 represents progress, and we should be thankful for that. I give it a grade of B−.

CONCEPTS STATEMENT NO. 4

Whereas most of the conceptual framework is concerned with accounting for business enterprises, Concepts Statement no. 4 discusses the objectives of financial reporting for nonbusiness organizations. I shall pass over it simply because it raises issues of a different kind from those I want to consider here.

RECOGNITION AND MEASUREMENT

The board's long-awaited exposure draft of what was to become Concepts Statement no. 5, on recognition and measurement, was published at the end of December 1983. The board must be given credit for listening to some of the criticisms that were directed at the draft, for the final statement, issued a year later, does represent a modest improvement. But it still falls so far short of what I believe was required that, in spite of the positive contributions made by the earlier parts of the conceptual framework, my judgment of the project as a whole must be that it has failed.

Let me say why I reach this gloomy conclusion.

The conceptual framework was supposed to guide the board in the future formulation of standards. But this concepts statement stands that process on its head. In several places it asserts that concepts are to be developed as the standard-setting process evolves.

Thus, paragraph 51 says, in part, that "future standards may change what is recognized as components of earnings (paragraph 35). Moreover, because of the differences between earnings and comprehensive income, future standards also may recognize certain changes in net assets as components of comprehensive income but not as components of earnings." In paragraph 35 we are told that "the Board expects the concept of earnings to be subject to the process of gradual change or evolution that has characterized the development of net income." And paragraph 108 states that "the Board believes that further development of recognition, measurement, and display matters will occur as the concepts are applied at the standards level."

These appeals to evolution should be seen as what they are—a cop-out. If all that is needed to improve our accounting model is reliance on evolution and the natural selection that results from the development of standards, why was an expensive and protracted conceptual framework project necessary in the first place? It goes without saying that concepts and practices should evolve as conditions change. But if the conceptual framework can do no more than point that out, who needs it? And, for that matter, if progress is simply a matter of waiting for evolution, who needs the FASB?

Let me here quote some words of Professor Alan Williams, of the University of York, speaking in quite a different context in the 1985 Arthur Young Lecture. "For me," he said, "evolution connotes accidental adaptation through uncoordinated innovation. It has got us broadly where we are today (like it or not). With luck it will see us through tomorrow. Planning connotes deliberate adaptation through coordinated innovation. It has had some spectacular results (like them or not) in the last few centuries. With good judgment (and a little luck) it will ensure that tomorrow's world is a better place."

One of the fundamental weaknesses of Concepts Statement no. 5 is to be found in its discussion—or, rather, lack of discussion—of the choice of attributes to be measured in financial statements. In the 1976 discussion memorandum on the conceptual framework, it was appropriate to lay out the alternatives—historical cost, current cost, net realizable value, and so forth—leaving the justification for the choice of one or several of these attributes as an important characteristic of the preferred accounting model to be explained in the later concepts statement. But what do we actually find in the final statement? We find little more than what was in the 1976 discussion memorandum—a description of five different attributes and the circumstances in which they are *presently* used, plus a bland statement in paragraph 70 that "this concepts Statement suggests that use of different attributes will continue. . . ." This is only one of several passages in which the statement is content merely to describe current practice—without analysis, evaluation or justification.

Related to the choice of attributes is the problem of inflation, or accounting for changing prices. This topic should always properly have been a part of the conceptual framework, though the urgency of the problem in the 1970s no doubt justified its separate treatment. But the problem is less urgent now, and it should have been central to the recognition and measurement project. Yet it gets but meager attention and toward the end, in paragraph 90.

It would be tedious to go on listing the deficiencies of this document, which bypasses all the difficult areas, such as an analysis of the concept of earnings, the recognition of executory contracts, the treatment of long-term contracts, inventory valuation, depreciation and other matters. The discussion of capital maintenance is perfunctory. There was a much superior discussion of capital maintenance, comprehensive income and disaggregation of income into components in a 1981 exposure draft, with the title *Reporting Income, Cash Flows, and Financial Position of Business Enterprises.* The draft was subsequently withdrawn, and the recognition and measurement project seems to me to have gone backward from that time.

I am not saying that there is nothing of value in Concepts Statement no. 5. The so-called fundamental recognition criteria in paragraph 63 are worth stating, though they do no more than apply certain criteria from Concepts Statements nos. 2 and 3 to the problem of recognition. The board commissioned three separate research studies on recognition and published the results, yet the concepts statement seems to have benefited little from that work.

Under a rigorous grading system I would give Concepts Statement no. 5 an F and require the board to take the course over again—that is, to scrap the statement and start afresh. This is not going to happen, however, so I give it a grade of D and pass on.

A LOST OPPORTUNITY

There are one or two interesting sidelights on what the board's constituents think about the conceptual framework in the opinion survey conducted last year for the Financial Accounting Foundation by Louis Harris and Associates. Of course, as with all such surveys, the results tell much more about the respondents than they do about the subject, in this case the framework. They certainly give no encouragement to those who think that the FASB's role is to do more than put out fires.

I had hoped that, in the conceptual framework, at least, the board would take its eyes off the ground for a while and look to the horizon. But the opportunity to point the way toward the 21st century has been lost. And most of the board's constituents are content to have it that way.

A passage in a 1971 essay by Friedrich Hayek—"Principles or Expediency?"—well describes the purpose of a conceptual framework: "It is not to be denied that to some extent the guiding model of the overall order will always be a utopia, something to which the existing situation will only be a distant approximation and which many people will regard as wholly impractical. Yet it is only by constantly holding up the guiding conception of an internally consistent model which could be realized by consistent application of the same principles, that anything like an effective framework for a functioning spontaneous order will be achieved."

A "guiding model of the overall order," a "utopia," a "guiding conception of an internally consistent model"—this is what the conceptual framework might have been. In my judgment the result of the board's work falls dismally short of this ideal.

CHAPTER 3

Financial Statements

The contents of financial statements and their accompanying disclosures have undergone fundamental change in the last 30 years. In the 1960s, the funds statement began to appear in company annual reports, and in the 1970s greater emphasis was placed in financial reporting on communicating information about liquidity and solvency. By the mid-1980s, the volume and complexity of disclosures had grown to the point that a call began to be heard for summary annual reports.

CASH FLOW REPORTING

While the funds statement (keyed either to changes in working capital or in cash) has become a staple in the financial statements of many countries, it was rarely seen in company annual reports prior to the 1960s. In Opinion No. 3, issued in October 1963, the Accounting Principles Board (APB), nudged by the New York Stock Exchange, announced its belief that a statement of source and application of funds should be presented as "supplementary information" in financial reports. This first utterance on the subject by a professional accounting body was cautiously expressed: The inclusion of such a statement was not to be mandatory, and it was optional as to whether it should be covered by the auditor's report. In March 1971, the APB—under obvious pressure from the Securities and Exchange Commission and the New York Stock Exchange—declared in Opinion No. 19 that the Statement of Changes in Financial Position (i.e., the funds statement) was a "basic financial statement," although one of the APB members (a partner in a Big Eight firm) filed a dissent that "the Board is going outside its province, if not its authority" by doing so. Both in 1963 and 1971, "funds" was defined as the change in working capital.

The expansion of the financial statements to include a funds statement was driven more by users in the financial community than by the accounting profession. In Australia, the Perth Stock Exchange led a movement to persuade the Institute of Chartered Accountants in Australia to issue a bulletin in 1971 endorsing the publication of a funds statement. In Canada, companies legislation and the policies of the provincial securities commissions required the presentation of a funds statement before the Canadian Institute of Chartered Accountants' Accounting Research Committee finally acted in 1974 to require such a statement. In the United Kingdom and Ireland, it was not until 1975 that a Statement of Standard Accounting Practice was issued to require presentation of a funds statement. In 1977, the International Accounting Standards Committee endorsed the trend. All of these initiatives focused on changes in working capital, not cash. Yet the European Community's Fourth Directive, approved in 1978, was silent on the funds statement, and the Council on Annual Reporting, in the Netherlands, has still not issued a final guideline on the inclusion of a funds statement in company annual reports.

By the late 1970s, a movement began to reorient the funds statement from a working capital analysis to an analysis of cash flow.[1] Inflation and rising interest rates, together with an increasing incidence of corporate insolvencies, led to enhanced concern for liquidity. In December 1981, the Financial Executives Institute urged its members to seek adoption of a cash flow format for the funds statement in their company's annual report. One by one, countries' standard setters began to replace the requirement for a working capital-oriented funds statement with that of a cash flow statement: Australia (1983), Canada (1985), New Zealand and the United States (1987), and the United Kingdom (1991).

CASH FLOW ACCOUNTING
AND EARNINGS DEFINITION

At the same time as funds statements were beginning to make their appearance in company annual reports, several U.S., Canadian, and U.K. accounting academics were arguing that, owing to the numerous arbitrary allocations in accrual accounting as well as the importance of liquidity assessment, cash flow accounting would be a superior measure of enterprise performance for financial reporting purposes.[2]

Harold Bierman, an academic who has a long record of important contributions to finance and accounting, argues that a cash flow analysis, while favored by security analysts, is not a substitute for an earnings measure when assessing the profitability of a company over a short time span. Using an example of a three-period investment in depreciable assets, Bierman con-

---

[1] See "FEI Supports Cash Flows Format for Funds Statement," *FEI Bulletin* (January 5, 1982), p. 1.
[2] For a review of this literature, see T. A. Lee, "Cash Flow Accounting and Corporate Financial Reporting," in Michael Bromwich and Anthony G. Hopwood (editors), *Essays in British Accounting Research* (London: Pitman, 1981), pp. 63–78.

cludes that a cash flow analysis would vastly overstate the rate of return on investment. He argues that accountants should act to improve the usefulness of the earnings figure, and should consider giving explicit accounting recognition to a charge for the use of equity capital.

In "Unreal Accounting," *Forbes* reporter Subrata N. Chakravarty claims that many companies' earnings figures may not be much of a guide to how well the main lines of a business are doing. Special charges and credits, reflecting one-time shocks or windfalls, may or may not be included in earnings. In the United States, companies are not given discretion to omit "extraordinary" items from earnings, else they might include the good news in earnings and classify the bad news as "extraordinary." In the United Kingdom, by contrast, companies have not always been in agreement whether restructuring and reorganization costs should be treated as an "exceptional" item included in operating earnings, or as an "extraordinary" item excluded from operating earnings. As a result, the U.K.'s Urgent Issues Task Force found it necessary to issue guidance on the subject in October 1991.

THE NATURE OF EARNINGS

Should periodic earnings be viewed as an indicator of enterprise performance or as a measure of wealth enhancement? Oscar S. Gellein, who was a research partner of Haskins & Sells (today a part of Deloitte & Touche) and a member of the Accounting Principles Board (1972–1973) and of the Financial Accounting Standards Board (1974–1978), argues in "Periodic Earnings: Income? or Indicator?" that the earnings variable does not perform well as a performance indicator. It can, however, be a meaningful measure of the enhancement of wealth, but only if it is attuned to changes in cash. Gellein recommends several modifications in the way in which companies display earnings in the income statement so as to increase its usefulness as an aid in assessing enterprise performance.

MANAGEMENT'S DISCUSSION
AND ANALYSIS (MD&A)

A distinctive U.S. contribution to financial reporting has been "Management's Discussion and Analysis" (known as MD&A), which is a narrative explanation of the risks and uncertainties implicit in the company's operations, as well as a commentary on future-oriented variables and liquidity considerations. It was imposed as a reporting requirement by the Securities and Exchange Commission (SEC) in 1968, and was amplified in 1974 and 1980. The MD&A has since been introduced as a reporting requirement by the Ontario Securities Commission (OSC) in Canada, and has been proposed for adoption in the United Kingdom and New Zealand. The advent of the MD&A is explicit acknowledgment that the financial statements and footnotes themselves do not tell enough of the story that investors and other interested parties wish to learn.

Both the SEC and the OSC regularly scrutinize companies' MD&As for sufficiency and candor. In their article, "Spotlight on Management's Discussion and Analysis," Richard Dieter and Keith Sandefur, both of Arthur Andersen & Co., highlight the areas in which the SEC has been dissatisfied with specific companies' MD&As in recent years, and advise managements on how to approach the preparation of an acceptable MD&A. At the same time, their discussion alerts investors and financial analysts to the kind of information they can expect to find in the MD&A.

THE SUMMARY ANNUAL REPORT

In the 1980s, following a decade in which the disclosures to be included in the annual reports of the some 11,000 companies subject to the jurisdiction of the SEC grew in number and complexity, the Financial Executives Institute and Deloitte Haskins & Sells launched a campaign to gain acceptance for a "summary annual report" that would adequately serve the needs of the general run of readers of corporate annual reports. In 1987, the SEC gave the go-ahead for companies to distribute summary annual reports to shareholders so long as the full financial statements, as required by the SEC's rules and regulations, were sent to shareholders as part of the annual proxy materials. While General Motors Corporation was the first company to apply to the SEC for permission to issue a summary annual report, McKesson Corporation was the first to send one to its shareholders. Although a number of companies tried out a summary annual report as a means of communicating in a more simplified manner with shareholders and other readers, interest in the experiment seems to have waned in recent years. McKesson, however, continues to issue a summary annual report.

Recent legislation in the United Kingdom allows companies to publish "abridged" financial statements, and a number of major companies have done so. In such cases, shareholders have the right to request a set of the full financial statements.

In their article, "Summary Annual Reports: Is Shorter Better?" Zabihollah Rezaee and Grover L. Porter, two accounting academics, track the experiences of General Motors and McKesson with the summary annual report.

DATA BASES IN PLACE OF FINANCIAL STATEMENTS?

For some years, it has been speculated that, one day, financial statements might be supplanted by users' immediate computer access to companies' data bases. In his article, "The End of the Annual Report? An Events Data Base Alternative," Ken Pratt advocates just such a course of reform. Direct and immediate access to a data base, which stores data relating to transactions or other events in the company's experience, would enable users to develop their own analyses and fashion their own reports and statements. The weights and values—many of which are arbitrary—that are used in accrual accounting could be obviated, having been replaced by the weights and values that the users themselves regard as relevant to their respective decisions.

REPORTING ON "VALUE ADDED"

While U.S. corporate financial reporting has been geared chiefly to the interests of investors, Europeans—and increasingly Americans—have come to place emphasis on a more diverse group of "stakeholders," taking into account not only the interests of all suppliers of capital but also those of employees, government, and the communities that companies serve and in which they conduct their operations. A "value added" report could respond to this broader constituency since it draws attention to the excess of the company's sales revenue over the expense attributable to all materials and services that were purchased from outside suppliers. The difference is therefore the portion of the sales revenue equal to the value added by the enterprise.

The suggestion that companies issue a value added statement was floated in *The Corporate Report*, a discussion paper prepared by a working party of the U.K.'s Accounting Standards Committee in 1975. Two years later, the Labour Government asserted that "the value added statement is [in the Government's view] a useful addition to the financial information produced by companies."[3] (The Conservative Government, since taking over in 1979, has not reasserted this view.)

In their article, "The Value Added Statement: An Innovation for U.S. Companies?" Gary K. Meek and Sidney J. Gray, two academics specializing in international accounting, argue that the introduction of a value added statement as a supplementary disclosure would enable more informed judgments about the broader role that companies play in society.

BIBLIOGRAPHICAL NOTES

Cash Flow Reporting

An AICPA research monograph in which the author advocates a statement of cash flows in place of the funds statement is:

[3] *The Future of Company Reports*, A Consultative Document, Cmnd. 6888 (London: Her Majesty's Stationery Office, 1977), para. 13.

Heath, Loyd C.: *Financial Reporting and the Evaluation of Solvency*, Accounting Research Monograph No. 3 (New York: American Institute of Certified Public Accountants, 1978).

The papers presented at an international conference held in 1980 on cash flow accounting were collected in the following volume:

Hicks, Barry E., and Pearson Hunt (editors): *Cash Flow Accounting* (Sudbury, Ont., Canada: The International Group for Cash Flow Accounting, and The Research and Publication Division, School of Commerce and Administration, Laurentian University, 1981).

An anthology of papers written on cash flow accounting by one of its chief proponents is the following:

Lee, Thomas A.: *Cash Flow Reporting: A Recent History of an Accounting Practice* (New York: Garland Publishing, Inc., 1993).

The Nature of Earnings

An FASB discussion memorandum on earnings that was prepared as part of its conceptual framework project was as follows:

Reporting Earnings (Financial Accounting Standards Board, July 31, 1979).

Management's Discussion and Analysis

The following article examines whether the Management's Discussion and Analysis (MD&A) section in public companies' annual reports provides information about future events:

Pava, Moses L., and Marc J. Epstein: "How Good is MD&A as an Investment Tool?", *Journal of Accountancy* (March 1993), pp. 51–53. The authors conclude, based on an analysis of 25 MD&A disclosures, that while most companies do a good job of disclosing past events, very few provide useful forecasts. The authors find that the prospective data, when provided, are strongly biased toward good news.

The Summary Annual Report

An FERF research study addresses the role played by the annual report in corporate communications with investors:

SRI International: *Investor Information Needs and the Annual Report* (Morristown, NJ: Financial Executives Research Foundation, 1987).

Deloitte Haskins & Sells (today part of Deloitte & Touche) was an early proponent of summary annual reports. General Motors and McKesson are both audit clients of the firm. In 1987, the firm and the FERF published a 48-page booklet promoting the summary annual report, in which the correspondence between both General Motors and McKesson and the SEC was reproduced:

Summary Annual Reports: A New Option to Improve Shareholder Communication (Deloitte Haskins & Sells and the Financial Executives Research Foundation, 1987).

A partner and manager of DH&S conducted a study in which 19 major U.S. corporations rewrote their 1981 annual reports in a more simplified form. The study was published as follows:

Golub, Steven J., and Robert J. Kueppers: *Summary Reporting of Financial Information: Moving Toward More Readable Annual Reports* (Morristown, NJ: Financial Executives Research Foundation, 1983).

In a series of two articles, Gibson and Schroeder review the approaches to the summary annual report by 21 U.S. companies, and assess the effectiveness of 29 companies' summary annual reports, concluding that they "show little of the expected improvement in readability":

Gibson, Charles H., and Nicholas Schroeder: "How 21 Companies Handled Their Summary Annual Reports," *Financial Executive* (November/December 1989), pp. 45–47; see also p. 48.
Schroeder, Nicholas, and Charles Gibson: "Are Summary Annual Reports Successful?", *Accounting Horizons* (June 1992), pp. 28–37.

The Value Added Statement

An article that examines the evolution of value added accounting in the United Kingdom is:

Burchell, Stuart, Colin Clubb, and Anthony G. Hopwood: "Accounting in Its Social Context: Towards a History of Value Added in the United Kingdom," *Accounting, Organizations and Society* (vol. 10, no. 4, 1985), pp. 381–413.

A questionnaire study of value added reporting in South Africa is the following:

Stainbank, L. J.: "Value Added Reporting in South Africa," *De Ratione* (Winter 1992), pp. 43–58.

Two studies on the value added statement are the following:

Morley, Michael F.: *The Value Added Statement* (London: Gee & Co. [Publishers] Limited, 1978).
Gray, Sidney J., and Keith T. Maunders: *Value Added Reporting: Uses and Measurement* (London: Association of Certified Accountants, 1980).

Extending the Usefulness of Accrual Accounting

Harold Bierman
Cornell University

The objectives of this paper are to define the ways in which accrual accounting earnings and cash flow types of measures can be used. Most importantly, accrual earnings are reconciled to the net present value calculation used to make investment decisions.

To understand why there have been misunderstandings, consider the fact that we need:

a. cash flow projections for making investment decisions within the firm.
b. measures of performance for managerial purposes for both individual investments and for the firm (or its subunits).
c. cash flow and earnings projections for valuing a firm by investors in the capital market.

Unless we distinguish between the uses of the measures, we will not be able to understand the importance of both the earnings measures computed in accordance with generally accepted accounting principles, and cash flow measures.

A BASIC PROBLEM AND A SOLUTION

A basic problem in measuring the results of operations for a given time period is that assets are used to service more than one time period, thus the cost of each asset must be allocated to expense somewhat arbitrarily (or at least with uncertainty as to correctness) over the periods of use. Also, revenues and other assets (e.g., inventory) also require judgments as to allocations between time periods. An extreme example is research and development expenditures which may benefit many periods, but which are generally expensed in the period in which they are incurred (in accordance with FAS No. 2).

As a result of the above types of items, some analysts have given up on accrual accounting and concluded that cash flows are a more useful measure. Thus, Ross Watts, in a paper correctly arguing that it does not pay to manipulate EPS, also advocates the use of cash flows in preference to earnings in measuring performance:

From *Accounting Horizons* (September 1988), pp. 10–14. Reprinted by permission of the American Accounting Association and the author. Copyright © 1988 by the American Accounting Association.

Consequently, a company's cash flow rate of return on investment is a more relevant measure of its performance than, say, its rate of growth in EPS.[1]

and also:

. . . structure a management compensation scheme which focuses not on accounting earnings, but on the source of value: cash flow.[2]

Watts (see footnote 1) cites numerous empirical studies that have shown that market prices of securities tend to adjust for accounting peculiarities like different methods of inventory accounting and different methods of depreciation accounting (e.g., flow through and normalization). This implies that the market would see through bad accounting. Certainly, no accounting professor in 1988 familiar with accounting research would argue that security analysts on the average do not adjust accounting earnings for differences in accounting practices.

The objective of this paper is not to fault the appropriate use of cash flow, but to take a position that accounting earnings is a very significant measure that deserves attention both by financial analysts and operating managers. A cash flow statement is not a near substitute for an income statement.

We will next briefly consider some of the explicit differences between accrual income and cash flow.

DIFFERENCES BETWEEN ACCOUNTING ACCRUALS
AND CASH FLOWS

Accounting accruals do not affect a firm's cash flow except through regulatory, contractual, or tax consequences (these considerations are excluded from the paper). We will first consider a set of accounting accruals that affect earnings but would not affect cash flow, and then we will consider a set of transactions which affect cash flow but would not directly affect earnings. For simplicity we will compare cash flows and earnings. The division by the number of shares is trivial, thus defending earnings is equivalent to defending earnings per share (EPS).

Consider the following accruals that affect accounting income but not cash flow:

a. depreciation expense
b. a utility bill not yet paid
c. a sale (with delivery of product) not yet collected

[1] Ross Watts, "Does it Pay to Manipulate EPS?" in *The Revolution in Corporate Finance*, edited by Joel M. Stern and Donald H. Chew, Jr., Blackwell, Oxford, 1986, p. 3.
[2] Ibid., p. 11.

d. a large loan receivable is discovered to be uncollectible
e. the periodic interest on a zero coupon bond.

Do we want to measure a manager's performance using cash flows and neglecting these types of accrual items? Suppose two managers in two different operations both earn $1,300 of cash flows. What does this tell you if you do not deduct the depreciation expense and include the other terms (or other similar items) listed above? Cash basis accounting is not effectively competitive with accrual accounting in determining how well an organization did during a relatively short time period.

Now consider the following items affecting cash flows:

a. the sale of any asset at book value for cash
b. the purchase of any asset for cash
c. the issue of long term debt or equity (or the retirement of debt at face value or the purchase of equity)
d. the collection of accounts receivable
e. the payment of accounts payable

None of these transactions should affect a measure of performance used to determine compensation, but they all affect cash flow.

We do not argue that anyone suggesting the use of cash flow to evaluate a firm would include any of this second list. In fact, we assume that some or all of the items on our accrual list would also be on the list of those advocating the use of cash flow (or cash flow equivalents). But if this is so, then we reconcile the cash flow position to the earnings position, and effectively eliminate the use of conventional cash flow to measure year by year performance. However, it is important to appreciate the fact that many analysts do not accept the accounting conventions and the resulting measures of earnings, and prefer the more objective cash flow measures.

We need to illustrate why cash flow is an extremely valuable tool in finance and is completely consistent with the use of accounting earnings for certain purposes, if accounting earnings are sensibly defined.

THE USE OF CASH FLOWS TO
EVALUATE INVESTMENTS

Cash flows are an invaluable tool for evaluating investment alternatives. The analysis is done by using the cash flows of each year of the asset's life, but the objective is to determine a single overall measure of the investment's acceptability. Several overall measures may be determined (e.g., net present value, internal rate of return, payback, index of present value), but they all have the characteristic of being summary measures, and the year by year evaluation is generally avoided.

Consider an investment with the following set of cash flows:

Time	Cash Flows
0	−3,000
1	1,600
2	1,400
3	1,200

Assuming the appropriate discount rate is .10, we obtain the following discounted cash flow (DCF) measures:

Net Present Value (NPV)	$513.
Internal Rate of Return	.20
Index of Present Value	1.17

All three measures indicate the investment is acceptable. If management earns more cash flows in period one than $1,600, all things equal, this indicates good performance because we know $1,600 is consistent with the targeted cash flow. If we merely indicate a manager earned $1,600 of cash flow without any other information, then we would know very little about that manager's performance, unless we also know that the $1,600 is the forecasted amount.

The theoretical soundness of the net present value calculation is well accepted in the academic community. If the discount rate is correctly chosen (accurately represents the cost of the capital), then the net present value criterion will indicate whether the investment is acceptable.

We want to show that while cash flows are a reliable input into the net present value calculation, we could have shifted to an income measure and obtained exactly the same net present value amount.

ACCRUAL EARNINGS AND NET PRESENT VALUE: MEASURING PERFORMANCE

Now we can translate the expected cash flows to expected accounting earnings. We will first arbitrarily use the straight line depreciation expense method to calculate income (our conclusions are not dependent on that assumption).

	Year 1	Year 2	Year 3
Cash Flow	1,600	1,400	1,200
Depreciation	1,000	1,000	1,000
Interest (.10)	300	200	100
Income	300	200	100

The present value of these income measures is

$$PV = \frac{300}{1.1} + \frac{200}{(1.1)^2} + \frac{100}{(1.1)^3} = \$513$$

which is equal to the net present value of the cash flows determined above. There is no essential conflict in computing net present value between the use of cash flows and the use of earnings as illustrated in the above example. Cash flows are more convenient for the determination of an investment's value over its life. We shall see that earnings can be a better indication of how the investment performed in each year. Note the inclusion of an interest expense based on the book value of the asset. It is reasonable to charge for the capital utilized. In fact, if interest is not charged, the expenses of the period are understated. Capital cannot be committed to a project without there being a capital cost.

If in any year the income is positive we know that management has surpassed the targeted required return.[3] This differs from the use of the annual cash flow where we cannot conclude anything about performance using the cash flow measure, unless we know the expected cash flow for the year.

If we arbitrarily change the depreciation method, the earnings of each year change but the present value of earnings will remain at $513. For example, if we used the Sum of the Years' Digits method we would have:

	Year 1	Year 2	Year 3
Cash Flow	1,600	1,400	1,200
Depreciation	1,500	1,000	500
Interest (.10)	300	150	50
Income	−200	250	650

The present value of these new income measures is:

$$PV = -\frac{200}{1.1} + \frac{250}{(1.1)^2} + \frac{650}{(1.1)^3} = \$513$$

With one assumption (straight line depreciation) we obtain an income of $300 and with a second assumption (accelerated depreciation, SYD) we have a loss of $200 in year one. This example illustrates the frustrations of the financial analyst trying to cope with accrual accounting.

THE EFFECT OF "ECONOMIC DEPRECIATION"

One good solution to the above issue is to use the economic (or present value) depreciation where the depreciation expense is defined to be the change in present value using the internal rate of return (.20) as the discount rate. For the example we have:

---

[3] This assumes that depreciation is being determined using economic (or present value) depreciation, and that the asset's internal rate of return is used as the interest rate.

Time	Present Value Using .20	Economic Depreciation
0	3,000	
1	2,000	1,000
2	1,000	1,000
3	0	1,000

Since the cash flows decrease each year by an equal amount and the amount of the decrease is equal to the straight line depreciation times the internal rate of return, the economic depreciation is equal to the straight line depreciation amount.

If economic depreciation is not used, then we can expect to have situations where the accrual accounting incomes do not reflect the change in the economic welfare of the corporation for the period. The analyst is justified in searching for an alternative objective measure, e.g., the period's cash flow. Sondhi, Sorter, and White suggest a "transactional analysis" approach as an improvement to the traditional cash flow measures but not as a substitute to accounting income.[4]

CASH FLOW RETURN ON INVESTMENT: MEASURING PERFORMANCE

The first quotation cited above makes reference to the use of "a company's cash flow rate of return on investment." We will use the example of the previous section to illustrate one form of this calculation.

Cash Flow Rate of Return on Investment
(CFROI) Calculation

Time Period	Beginning Investment	Cash Flow	Cash Flow Rate of Return on Investment
1	3,000	1,600	53%
2	2,000	1,400	70%
3	1,000	1,200	120%

This investment has an internal rate of return of 20 percent, yet the cash flow rates of return on investment for the three years of its life are 53 percent, 70 percent and 120 percent. The cash flow rates of return on investment as defined all greatly exceed the investment's internal rate of return.

---

[4] A. C. Sondhi, G. H. Sorter, and G. I. White, "Transactional Analysis," *Financial Analysts Journal* (September–October 1987), pp. 57–64.

The cash flow rate of return on investment as defined above, while used in practice, has no sound reliable theoretical relationship to a firm's capital costs or to an investment's net present value or internal rate of return. A cash flow rate of return on investment measure similar to that computed above is extremely difficult to use to measure performance. Conventional frames of reference (e.g., the costs of capital) are not relevant.

Now assume that the asset is replicated through time so that it reaches the following equilibrium:

$$\begin{aligned}
\text{Investment} &= 3{,}000 + 2{,}000 + 1{,}000 = \$6{,}000 \\
\text{Cash Flow} &= 1{,}600 + 1{,}400 + 1{,}200 = 4{,}200 \\
\text{Incomes} &= 600 + 400 + 200 = 1{,}200
\end{aligned}$$

We now have:

$$\text{CFROI} = \frac{4{,}200}{6{,}000} = 70\%$$

$$\text{ROI} = \frac{1{,}200}{6{,}000} = 20\%$$

Even with a mature firm we have the cash flow return on investment, as defined, leading to an absurdly high percentage (compared to the assets' internal rate of return or return on investment).

If the investments each year grow at a rate equal to the internal rate of return of the investment or less, an equilibrium is reached where the annual return on investment is equal to the asset's internal rate of return.

If the investments grow at a more rapid rate than the internal rate of return, then we cannot generalize as easily. The return on investment results will then depend on the method of depreciation.

While it has been argued that internal investments can be evaluated equally well using cash flows or earnings, general practice is to use cash flows. The process seems to be somewhat easier to understand. When we switch to performance measures, return on investment, with all its faults, offers more easily understandable results than a cash flow return on investment that is equal to the period's cash flow divided by the investment.

THE VALUATION OF A CORPORATION

The valuation of a corporation is similar to the evaluation of an investment, thus we should be able to use either expected cash flows or expected earnings to value a corporation.

If cash flows are used, one has to subtract the periodic investments needed to sustain the future cash flows. If no debt flows are subtracted, then the present value is the present value of the firm, and the present value of the debt must be subtracted to obtain the stockholders' equity. If interest and principal payments are subtracted from the cash flows of each year, then the cash flows to the stockholders is obtained and the present value of the cash flows is the value of the stockholders' position.

If earnings are used (computed as illustrated above), the initial book values of the assets that are depreciated have to be added to the present value of the earnings to obtain the present value of the corporation. We want present value, not net present value. To obtain the value of the stock equity, the present value of the debt has to be subtracted.

Assume we start with the following balance sheet:

$$\text{Assets 3,000} \qquad \begin{array}{l} \text{Liability} \quad \text{2,000} \\ \text{Stock equity 1,000} \end{array}$$

Using the same cash flows as above we have:

$$\text{Stock equity} = \frac{1{,}600}{1.1} + \frac{1{,}400}{(1.1)^2} + \frac{1{,}200}{(1.1)^3} - 3{,}000 = \$1{,}513.$$

Using the earnings previously computed and including the $3,000 of depreciable assets and subtracting the $2,000 of debt we have:

$$\text{Stock equity} = \frac{300}{1.1} + \frac{200}{(1.1)^2} + \frac{100}{(1.1)^3} + 3{,}000 - 2{,}000 = \$1{,}513.$$

Both earnings and cash flows give the same present value for the value of the stockholders' position.

The crucial issue for stock valuation is which measure of the past periods' operations, cash or earnings, gives the better estimates of the future. The future projections of cash and earnings should give the same economic value.

CONCLUSIONS

The accountant has the impossible task of determining how profitable a corporation has been for a short period of time (say a quarter or a year). The finance person has the equally difficult, but somewhat different, task of valuing different economic opportunities. For this latter task, cash flows are somewhat easier to use, and since the objective is to determine the worth of the alternative over its useful life, nothing is lost by the use of cash flows.

When the objective is to determine how well a corporation has performed (or will perform) for a shorter period of time than its useful life, then the accounting earnings become a much more useful measure because they attempt a more accurate assignment of revenues and expense to each time period.

The robustness of the accounting earnings measure is illustrated by the fact that the financial markets are able to penetrate the confusion caused by the use of different accounting practices. Market prices do not seem to be influenced by the specific accounting practice but rather by the underlying earnings.

The conclusion is that we should still try to improve the accounting earnings measure so that the temptation is eliminated to recommend the use of the more objective but less theoretically correct cash flow measure for evaluating period performance. No research to date has successfully questioned the value of accrual accounting and of the income resulting from accrual accounting for measuring a firm's operating results for a period of time. This does not mean that all income measures for all periods for all firms are reliable. In fact, we can be sure that there will be situations where the accounting income measures prepared in accordance with generally accepted accounting principles will require adjustment if they are to be useful.

Two important steps towards improvement of accrual accounting earnings are 1) to recognize that accounting depreciation should bear a relationship to value decreases, and 2) to include a charge for all capital that is used to obtain an income measure that more accurately reflects the performance of management. Financial accounting practitioners may choose not to include a charge for stock equity capital, but managerial accountants are deficient if they fail to do so.[5]

[5] Robert N. Anthony of the Harvard Business School has been a long time advocate of including a capital charge for all stock equity capital. This is a sound position.

Unreal Accounting

Subrata N. Chakravarty
Forbes

Suppose your metal-bending company owns an old desk. It's on the books for $100. One day you discover the old desk belonged to Ben Franklin; Sotheby's auctions it off for $50,000.

Comes now the end of the year and you're calculating your company's operating earnings from bending metal. Question: Should you include the $49,900 profit from selling that old desk in "operating earnings"?

Don't laugh. In their reported operating earnings, lots of big companies include gains (and losses) from once-only events. As a result, says David Hawkins, professor of accounting at Harvard Business School, "investors cannot just take the bottom-line numbers before or after extraordinary items and assume that they understand what is going on." Doing so, Hawkins warns, "can be dangerous to your wealth."

Consider Time Inc. For 1986, the august publisher reported income, before taxes, of $626 million. Aftertax net came to $376 million, $5.95 per share, up 89% from 1985. With earnings momentum like that, maybe Time

From *Forbes* (November 16, 1987), pp. 74, 78. Reprinted by permission of Forbes, Inc. Copyright © 1987 by Forbes, Inc.

was worth the $100-plus a share it was selling for before Bloody Monday ripped it to $81. (It recovered to $88 two days later.)

But did Time's ongoing, operating businesses really earn $376 million? Is the figure a good basis from which to project 1987's earnings and buy its stock? Not necessarily.

Look at the $376 million reported profit, and you'll see it includes the equivalent of Ben Franklin's desk. To wit: In 1986, when the stock market was hot, Time sold 20% of a cable television subsidiary, American Television Communications Corp., to the public for a pretax gain of $318 million. Time booked this one-time gain as operating earnings—even though the only way it might realize a comparable gain next year would be to sell off yet another 20%.

Time also threw a $33 million profit on another investment, and $113 million in one-time expenses from relocating offices and reducing staff, into pretax earnings. Eliminate these once-only gains from selling off investments, and Time's aftertax operating earnings from ongoing businesses was around $129 million last year, down over 35% from 1985.

What's going on here? We called John Shank, professor of accounting at Dartmouth's Tuck School. Don't blame Time Inc., said Shank. Blame the accountants. Their rules make companies include such unusual items as stock sale profits and office relocation expenses in income, even though they are unrelated to current, or future, operations.

Sometimes the accounting rules understate a company's earnings from its ongoing businesses. Take Eastman Kodak. In 1985 Kodak decided to get out of the instant photography business, and close some plants. Total writeoff: $563 million. Where should Kodak show this amount? Its accountants made the company deduct it from operating earnings. As a result, Kodak reported earnings on its continuing photographic, copier and chemical businesses of $332 million, whereas in reality those businesses earned $597 million aftertax.

Then, in 1986, Kodak wrote off more assets and sacked people, at a cost of $654 million. Again, this one-time item was deducted from operating earnings, with the result that Kodak reported earnings from ongoing operations at $374 million. But this time the charge made sense: The 1986 writeoff was, after all, associated with Kodak's ongoing businesses. The 1985 writeoff was on a business, instant photography, on which Kodak had irrevocably pulled the plug.

Why do the accountants insist that companies report, as income from operations, gains or losses that will never recur? In essence, because they have come to the conclusion over the years that anything that produces income or expense in a given year must be dragged through the income statement in that year. If a metal-bending company earns $49,900 on an antique desk in 1986, that profit has to show up in 1986's net. Where else, argue the accountants, could it show up?

The accountants have been arguing this so-called dirty surplus problem for years. Back in the go-go accounting of the 1960s, companies had enormous latitude in reporting nonrecurring income and losses. The income they would usually report as income; the losses they would deduct from their retained earnings account, so as to manage earnings better. They could thus avoid acknowledging errors long enough until they could smoothly wipe them off the books. "So there was something called dirty surplus," recalls Dartmouth's John Shank, "which betrayed the bias of those who didn't like it."

The accounting rule writers quickly moved to solve that problem by encouraging companies to report nonrecurring income and loss on their income statements, but labeling them "Extraordinary Items." A new problem was born. "The practice [of reporting extraordinary items] created nothing but confusion because companies would take the good stuff into earnings and call the bad stuff extraordinary," explains Harvard's David Hawkins. The result was a new rule—Accounting Principles Board Opinion 30, issued 1973—which significantly tightened the definition of extraordinary items, defining them as events that were unrelated to the company's business and unlikely to recur. Under Opinion 30, any special event that did not qualify as an "extraordinary event" should be reported as an "unusual item."

Opinion 30 worked all right as long as there weren't too many unusual items. But then came the 1980s and widespread corporate restructuring— office closings, asset sales and all sorts of "unusual" items, some of which are related to operations and some of which are not.

So here the matter stands: By accounting rules, income from nonrecurring events—like selling the old desk, or selling off part of a cable TV system— must be included as part of net income. So must items relating to errors and omissions of past years, even if their effect is to seriously distort current earnings with a one-time adjustment. If investors and other users of financial statements aren't clever enough to read all the explanatory footnotes to see how the company's ongoing businesses are doing—well, too bad for the investors.

The problem becomes more acute when you remember that Value Line, Standard & Poor's and other statistical services generally pick up only a single number—net income—to report a company's profitability.

This single, often meaningless number then gets reflected in return on equity, growth rate calculations, averages and the like.

"There are items that cause earnings to appear to be more volatile than they actually are on a continuing basis," says Hawkins. "But whether they make companies look better or worse, they are, in every case, a poor indicator of the companies' future earnings prospects." More relevant accounting, anyone?

Periodic Earnings:
Income? Or Indicator?

Oscar S. Gellein
Former Member of the Financial Accounting Standards Board

Perceptive observers of the standard-setting process for financial reporting are concerned about the persistent confusion with respect to the meaning and nature of business income, as well as about the role of periodic earnings in evaluating enterprise performance. Introduction by the Financial Accounting Standards Board (FASB) of the terms "comprehensive income" and "earnings," without final resolution of their differences, has refocused attention on some enduring issues:

- What is the nature of business income?
- Should periodic income or earnings be measured in a manner deemed suitable for evaluating the performance of the management of an enterprise?
- If periodic earnings is so measured, will it be essentially different in nature from income for the lifetime of the enterprise?

Comments from different elements of the financial community about proposed financial reporting standards indicate both differences of opinion on those issues and uneasiness about the possible consequences, if they are resolved. Above and beyond this confusion is a cloud of public concern about the usefulness and, at times, the reliability of accounting measurements in general, and of periodic income in particular. Attention to some income theory seems in order. One observer has said:

> Determination of periodic earnings has been a major focus for many accounting writers and for standard setters since the late 1930's. Despite that focus and the centrality of income to financial reporting, the attention given to the nature of periodic earnings has been sporadic and, quite often, has been confined to description.[1]

THE NATURE OF BUSINESS INCOME

The nature of business income is a good place to start because there appears to be considerable agreement on the matter. The prevailing view is that wealth enhancement or, in accounting terms, net asset increase, is the underlying characteristic of business income. There are diverse views about how to

From *Accounting Horizons* (June 1987), pp. 59–64. Reprinted by permission of the American Accounting Association and the author. Copyright © 1987 by the American Accounting Association.
[1] Allan Barton, *An Analysis of Business Income Concepts* (International Centre for Research in Accounting, University of Lancaster, 1975).

measure wealth enhancement, but near unanimity that an increase in net assets attends accounting income. In 1940, Paton and Littleton said it this way:

> Gains and losses are changes in enterprise assets, not in proprietors' assets or stockholders' assets. Accounting theory, therefore, should explain the concepts of revenue and expense in terms of enterprise asset changes rather than as increases or decreases in proprietors' or stockholders' equities.[2]

Thirty-five years later, income was characterized similarly:

> Income is in some sense the *gain in wealth* from being in business. It is the amount that can be spent without encroaching upon the initial wealth, net assets or capital of the firm.[3]

Despite the long-standing consensus about wealth enhancement, or net asset better-offness, as the underlying characteristic of business income, the FASB encountered significant and strongly expressed opposition to the notion of better-offness presented in a discussion memorandum issued in 1976 on a conceptual framework for financial reporting.[4] That opposition appeared to manifest a concern that adoption of the better-offness idea would result in basic changes, with sweeping consequences, in accrual accounting. That concern remains unresolved.

Accrual accounting has been the focus of financial accounting for almost all of this century. Standard setting for financial reporting, since inception, has sought to improve the results of accrual accounting, especially the measure of periodic income, often referred to as earnings—a term used almost exclusively when referring to per-share results. The term has evolved to connote aspects of enterprise performance for a period. Some observers relate earnings to management performance insofar as it affects enterprise performance.

That not uncommon perception of earnings for a period (ordinarily a year) probably accounts for the uneasiness about applying a net asset better-offness notion of income to the determination of earnings in the accrual accounting system.

Net asset better-offness is too abstract, by itself, for direct use in determining earnings. W. A. Paton was quoted as having described in 1922 a concept of income that had common acceptance:

> The most conservative criterion of income is the receipt of cash. Cash— meaning thereby any generally recognized medium of exchange—can be used to purchase any desired commodity or service whatsoever, provided the same is available on the market, to retire obligations, to pay taxes, to pay dividends, to liquidate terminable proprietary investments, etc. Cash is the

[2] W. A. Paton and A. C. Littleton, *An Introduction to Corporate Accounting Standards* (American Accounting Association, 1940).

[3] Barton, 1975, op. cit.

[4] FASB, Discussion Memorandum, *Conceptual Framework for Financial Accounting and Reporting; Elements of Financial Statements and Their Measurement* (FASB, 1976).

asset *excellent*. The receipt of cash for product, consequently, furnishes the ultimate test of revenue realization. From this standpoint the cash sale and the collection of cash following the so-called credit sale constitute the principal income transactions, the important occasion for entries in the revenue account.[5]

Paton may or may not have intended to be defining income, but he did advance an idea about cash consequences that has had a profound, continuing influence on accrual accounting. Business income is ultimately grounded in cash; increases in wealth with a low probability of fruition in cash are suspect as income. From the beginning of an enterprise through its ultimate liquidation, lifetime income is the difference between the amounts of cash (or cash equivalent) invested in the enterprise by owners and the amounts of cash distributed to owners, sometimes called the cash-to-cash notion of better-offness. The question of whether cash should be adjusted for a change in general price levels is separable from the question of the nature of income, and is not dealt with here.

THE NATURE OF PERIODIC EARNINGS

Uncertainty about the probability of cash consequences imposes constraints on financial reporting. Accrual accounting is the response to those constraints. Its characteristics are well known. They are highlighted here simply to provide a context for considering whether earnings of a period should be viewed as an indicator of enterprise performance that may, or may not, have the same nature as lifetime income. Those characteristics are:

1. *A universe for recording.* The universe of things accounted for is generally limited to financial statement elements arising (a) in transactions—that is, in exchanges between the enterprise and other parties; and (b) in connection with certain events, internal or external to the enterprise, that cause existing assets to shrink or, rarely, to grow; liabilities to arise; and the measure to change. Other things are often excluded from the universe for reasons of uncertainty of measure of cash equivalence or cash consequence.
2. *Financial statement focus.* Things on center stage are assets, liabilities, revenues, expenses, income, and equity (ownership interests), and their articulation in a double-entry system. Those factors combine to show and validate a measure of periodic earnings.
3. *Matching.* The matching of costs with revenues produces a measure of periodic earnings. Matching is based on the thought that (a) often there is a discernible association of cost and revenue, and (b) if there is no discernible association with expected future revenue, there is no basis for deferral; accordingly, the cost is borne by current revenue.

[5] Stephen Gilman, *Accounting Concepts of Profit* (The Ronald Press Company, 1939).

4. *Recognition*. Recognition criteria are used to determine the time for initial recognition of assets and liabilities and the time to record revenue; that is, to record a measure for the asset received that is different from the measure of the asset relinquished in exchange. Extensive efforts have been expended on attempts to formulate a workable guideline for realization of revenue, with mixed success. Recognition criteria are the weakest link in accrual accounting, despite significant recent efforts to clarify and strengthen the criteria.
5. *Cost allocation*. Allocation of cost of long-lived assets to periods is an integral part of matching costs with revenues.
6. *Historical measures*. Historical cost is the measure of nonmonetary assets, ordinarily allocated through matching with revenues during asset life. Impairment criteria are applied to recognize impairment of cost—that is, an adverse cash consequence deemed to be permanent.

EARNINGS—INDICATOR? OR INCOME?

Those characteristics of accrual accounting do not address the issue of whether the nature of periodic earnings should be the same as the nature of lifetime income. The view that earnings is different apparently is held by many and has been for many years. The issue can be restated as whether periodic earnings should be an indicator of enterprise performance or a measure of periodic income representing enterprise wealth enhancement during the period, or whether it can fill both roles.

There is a long history, frequently revisited, of standard-setting efforts to change the display of the effects of unusual or extraordinary or nonrecurring happenings. The context has always been a concern about whether the measure or display of earnings is a meaningful and evenhanded indicator of performance. The force tugging on the other side is whether what is represented to be the earnings of the period can be viewed as the income of the period in terms of net asset enhancement.

In the 1940s the opposing views centered on the issue of whether, philosophically, periodic earnings should measure current operating performance or, instead, should be an all-inclusive measure representing an estimated aliquot part of lifetime income. Standard setters, including the Committee on Accounting Procedure, the Accounting Principles Board, and the Financial Accounting Standards Board, have issued more pronouncements dealing with display of the effects of unusual and nonrecurring events than any other subject. Positions taken at various times have tended to erode because of forces stemming from perceptions of abuses, on the one hand, and of unfairness, on the other. That history is not recounted here; it is well known.

At the same time, other manifestations of the persistent controversy about the nature of reported earnings are to be seen in some accounting principles and standards that underlie practice. In short, some financial statement measurements themselves have been affected by the view that earnings is an indicator and, accordingly, that by nature it may not be like lifetime income.

As mentioned previously, the essence of lifetime income is cash realization. Determination of periodic income, however, must deal with uncertainty, since some cash-to-cash cycles are incomplete when the determination of earnings is made. That suggests that periodic earnings will be similar in nature to lifetime income only if assets and liabilities at the end of a period are grounded in cash. But what does that mean? For some assets the carrying amount represents cost, perhaps amortized cost, based on cash (or its equivalent) expended in connection with acquisition. That is a grounding in cash. Other assets await collection of cash. If the carrying amounts of those assets have a high probability of being collected at amounts equalling or exceeding the carrying amount, they are grounded in cash. Similarly, liabilities are grounded in cash if the carrying amount measures a probable outflow of cash (or of assets grounded in cash). If assets and liabilities are grounded in cash, the related revenues and costs will be grounded in cash. If that kind of cost is matched with that kind of revenue, the nature of the resulting measure of periodic earnings will be similar to the nature of income for a lifetime.

FINANCIAL STATEMENT MEASUREMENTS CAUSING EARNINGS TO BE DIFFERENT IN NATURE FROM LIFETIME INCOME

Two kinds of situations result in financial statement amounts that are not grounded in cash. One kind would ignore certain events that have occurred. Instead of recording them at occurrence, their effects are accounted for in the future. The other kind would account currently for the effects of events that might, or might not, occur in the future.

An example of the first kind is the deferred method of accounting for the tax effects of differences in treatments for financial reporting purposes and income tax purposes. Under that method, changes in tax rates are ignored. As a result, earnings after the change in rates is affected by amounts different from expected cash consequences. Earnings for many years after the change could be affected as reversals of the tax effects occur. It should be noted that the FASB had indicated an intention to proscribe the deferred method before a reduction in federal income tax rates for 1987 seemed likely.

Another example of the first kind of situation is the accounting by the creditor for the effects of a restructured troubled debt of a borrower. The adverse effect of the transaction is ignored in determining earnings of the creditor in the year of the restructuring. Instead, the adverse consequence is applied to future years as the newly scheduled collections are received.

An example of the second kind of situation is the recognition of future changes in general price levels in determining current pension costs in plans where pension benefits are based on final pay levels. Recognition of that kind of possible future consequence breaks the link between earnings and cash. Anticipated changes in future price levels do not meet the test of probable and reasonably predictable cash consequences.

Another example of the second kind of situation was the accounting for so-called self-insurance—which, indeed, is no insurance—before issuance in 1975 of Statement of Financial Accounting Standards No. 5, *Accounting for Contingencies*. No insurance does not meet the test of highly probable, predictable cash payments.

EARNINGS VOLATILITY

The unsettled issue of whether periodic earnings is an indicator, rather than a measure of wealth enhancement, feeds controversy about volatility of earnings. Not surprisingly, complaints that a proposed standard of financial reporting would induce improper volatility continue at an increasing rate. In Statement of Financial Accounting Standards No. 87, *Employers' Accounting for Pensions*, for example, eighteen paragraphs (Nos. 173 through 190) are given to describing constituents' concerns about volatility and the Board's conclusions for rejecting or accommodating those concerns.

Those who believe that earnings serve as an indicator see volatility in relation to the role they perceive for earnings. Those perceptions cover a wide range. Among the matters that have been suggested for portrayal by earnings are the following:

- *Enterprise earning power*. That role has a future dimension. Accordingly, it has been suggested that effects of nonrecurring events either be separately displayed or omitted from earnings. Some would say that in fulfilling the role, a broadened group of future events should affect currently reported earnings.
- *Enterprise or management performance*. This role suggests that effects of noncontrollable happenings (like so-called acts of God), although recurring, should either be separately displayed or omitted from earnings.
- *Sustainability of income (or of dividends)*. This perceived role also suggests separate disclosure or elimination from earnings of the effects of unusual, nonrecurring events. A further implication, however, is that unusual losses might be treated differently from unusual gains.

Those perceived roles lead to different norms for identifying volatility or distortion of earnings. Volatility and distortion are sterile terms if unaccompanied by a norm by which to judge their existence. Accrual accounting, as highlighted earlier, has no built-in mechanism for identifying nondistortion or proper volatility.

Perhaps it is fair to say that as an unstated assumption of accrual accounting, the volatility appropriately reflected in earnings is that which is inherent in the ebb and flow of the operating circumstances of an enterprise. Any exaggeration or suppression of that volatility introduced by accounting alone is improper. That idea is so abstract, by itself, as not to be very helpful in identifying the norm.

Yet nonvolatility as an appropriate element of accrual accounting has long had its supporters. Some twenty years ago, Bevis[6] noted that a nondistortion guideline was needed to supplement the theory of the accrual basis of accounting. He proposed this guideline: "From among systematic and rational methods, use that which tends to minimize distortion of periodic income." Despite the acceleration of expressions of concern about accounting-induced volatility in the last twenty years, little effort has been made to identify the norm from which distortion would be measured in that guideline.

SOME OBSERVATIONS, SOME CONCLUSIONS

In the 1940s the first private sector standard-setting body for financial reporting, the Committee on Accounting Procedure, contrasted the all-inclusive and current operating performance views about an income statement. The Committee expressed a leaning toward the all-inclusive view, but left the way open for exclusion of specified kinds of items.

Forty years later, the third standard-setting body, the FASB, left the issue unresolved, and noted further in FASB Statement of Concepts, *Recognition and Measurement in Financial Statements of Business Enterprises*, that the concept of earnings is expected to be subject to the process of gradual change or evolution.

In the intervening forty years, all three standard-setting bodies struggled with the issue of earnings as (a) an indicator or (b) an estimated aliquot part of lifetime income, and with limited success. Several lessons have been learned from that forty years of experience:

- Arbitrary definitions of "extraordinary," "unusual," "infrequent," and "uncontrollable" tend to erode.
- Efforts to make earnings an indicator through measurements affecting reported net income of a period lead to inconsistent treatment of similar things.
- Direct inclusion in equity (ownership interests) of the effects of certain transactions or events results in confusion, as well as inconsistencies.[7]
- As a consequence of such erosion, inconsistencies, and confusion, financial reporting's credibility has suffered.

Credibility of financial reporting is ever so precious, but ever so fragile. Financial reporting has a significant role to play in maintaining an orderly capital market. It has little chance to fulfill the potential of that role without a

---

[6] Herman W. Bevis, *Corporate Financial Reporting in a Competitive Economy* (The Macmillan Company, 1965).

[7] Examples are found in Statement of Financial Accounting Standards No. 12 and 52, *Accounting for Certain Marketable Securities* and *Foreign Currency Translation*, respectively.

sustained perception of evenhandedness and fairness—evenhandedness to enterprises seeking capital and fairness to those providing capital. Order and the attending discipline are necessary to sustain a perception of evenhandedness and fairness. A coordinated general theory of accrual accounting can go a long way in providing the necessary order, if that general theory is sufficiently well articulated to assure consistent treatment of similar matters.

Bottom-Line Earnings, An Indicator

Efforts to measure bottom-line net income so as to indicate operating performance during the period have little or no chance of succeeding. That kind of an effort has never been tried, or even charted. Further, any move toward financial statement measurements that cause earnings to be different in nature from lifetime income should be halted.

Most observers of financial reporting in the financial community will not believe that earnings or net income reported for a period is only an indicator, rather than a measure of wealth enhancement. Most people believe that to have income is to have more wealth. They know that income enhances their wealth, and that a loss eats into it. They transfer that belief to their perception of business income. The belief is so embedded that the risk of continuing the controversy about the nature of bottom-line earnings is intolerable.

As mentioned before, there is nothing in the general theory of accrual accounting that provides the necessary order for heightened general belief in reported periodic earnings. An anchor is needed to provide reasonable assurance that periodic income manifests wealth enhancement.

That anchor is a grounding in cash. Assets and liabilities shown in balance sheets should meet the test of cash grounding, as that notion has been explained in this paper. Matching, recognition criteria, and a grounding in cash for assets and liabilities would then combine to form three sturdy legs undergirding a general theory with considerable operating potential.

Earnings and Performance

At the same time, financial accounting should not neglect assessments of performance. Although financial reporting does not provide a net income measure of performance, a great deal can be done to assist in assessing performance. Certain measurements can be made, displayed, and explained in helpful ways. The scope of this paper does not allow for extensive consideration of ways of improving the presentation of information that will be more useful in assessing operating performance. Instead, only a few guidelines are suggested:

- Separating the results of discontinued operations to show income from continuing operations has proved to be useful. The longer-term success of this display depends on whether the constraints on identification of a discontinued business segment are sustained. Nonetheless, a bottom line in the income statement for overall net income and an intermediate line for net income from continuing operations, if applicable, provide a helpful basic structure.

- Efforts to draw workable lines between ordinary and extraordinary, usual and unusual, and frequent and infrequent have been less than wholly successful. Some arbitrary lines have been drawn and then suffered from erosion. Concern with per-share amounts "before" and "after" a defined class of items has been overriding. A different approach may be needed. Nonrecurrence probably is the central consideration in assessing current performance. Each material effect of nonrecurring transactions and events should be described for what it is in the appropriate place in the income statement.

- Direct inclusion in equity of matters not resulting from transactions with owners should be re-examined. Growing disbelief in financial reporting is inevitable if income effects by-pass the income statement. Designation of income as comprehensive has not been helpful. Income has long been viewed in accounting as broad in concept and in use. If the term "comprehensive income" is to be retained, it would be helpful if all items comprising comprehensive income were brought together in one statement.

Financial accounting may have furthered an excessive concern with short-term enterprise performance, to the virtual exclusion of concern with longer-term performance, by focusing on a display geared to emphasis on different classes of earnings per share. A new look at the display might lead to a better balance between short-term and long-term considerations. Eventually, it might even lead to consideration of rate of return on assets as an important indicator of performance.

Spotlight on Management's Discussion and Analysis

Richard Dieter
Arthur Andersen & Co.

Keith Sandefur
Arthur Andersen & Co.

It's annual report writing time! This year, companies registered with the Securities and Exchange Commission will have to pay special attention to the management's discussion and analysis (MD&A) section of their reports to accommodate the SEC's May 1989 interpretive release (see exhibit 1). This article will focus on how registrants should approach drafting their MD&As.

From *Journal of Accountancy* (December 1989), pp. 64–66, 68, 70. Reprinted by permission of the American Institute of Certified Public Accountants, Inc. Copyright © 1989 by the American Institute of Certified Public Accountants, Inc. Opinions of the authors are their own and do not necessarily reflect policies of the AICPA.

BRIEF HISTORY ON MD&A

The SEC adopted its first requirement for an MD&A in 1968, with the current framework being instituted in 1980. That framework arose from the SEC's concerns that the earlier MD&A requirements had developed into the practice of mechanistic commentary on percentage variations. The 1980 requirements changed the focus—from a summary of earnings to the financial statements as a whole. They required a discussion of

- Liquidity.
- Capital resources.
- Results of operations.
- The future impact of known trends, demands, commitments, events or uncertainties that may affect operations.

The change was intended to give the investor an opportunity to look at the company through the eyes of management.

Although the SEC made many public remarks about the quality of MD&As during the 1980s, no specific action was taken until early 1988 when it began a comprehensive review of MD&A disclosures. The first phase of the review covered 218 companies in 12 industries. The reviews focused on the *registrant* rather than on any one of its reports. The reviews focused particularly on the disclosures made in response to the 1980 MD&A requirements. Of the 218 companies, 206 received letters of comment from the SEC either requesting supplemental information, compliance with the rules in future filings or amendments of existing filings. In fact, 72 of the companies amended their filings.

A second phase of the review program started in late 1988 with 141 companies in another 12 industries. Of this group, 139 received comment letters and another 53 companies filed amendments. More than half of these amendments contained substantively expanded MD&As. Six companies were referred to the SEC's Division of Enforcement—primarily because of accounting issues, but in several instances MD&A disclosures also were affected.

The SEC now has moved into a third phase of its review program with another 12 industries. This phase will focus on form 10-Ks filed for fiscal years ended November 30, 1988, and later.

WHAT DOES THE SEC EXPECT?

A review of selected comment letters (not cited in the interpretive release) during the past 18 months helps to answer the elusive question: "What does the SEC expect?"

1. *Shoe manufacturer* with large domestic manufacturing capacity showing consistent losses: The SEC asked the company to discuss

- Its plans, if any, to return to profitability.

- How management planned to use excess domestic manufacturing capacity.
- Why the percentage of cost of sales had risen in recent years and any plans to reverse the trend.

2. *Biotechnology company* showing flat results and little indication of what the future holds: The SEC asked about

- The company's expectations for continued receipt of contract research and development revenues.
- The consistent decline in research and development expenditures.
- What portion of the increase in product revenue was due to price increases compared with volume increases.

3. *Chemical company* showing reasonable growth and profits: The SEC commented the company should

- Revise its MD&A to provide a more balanced presentation.
- Consider quantification and discussion of divisional performance.
- Discuss long-term prospects for certain chemical products given present environmental concerns.
- Discuss the impact on liquidity and capital resources of recent material acquisitions.

4. *Operator of healthcare facility* experiencing financial difficulty: The SEC asked the company to discuss

- Labor costs, including the impact of the shortage of nurses and the resulting impact on salaries.
- Economic and demographic trends relevant to the company's areas of operation and a comparison of those trends with national trends.
- The impact of regulatory trends, such as rating systems for hospitals and staff.

5. *Computer manufacturer* doing moderately well in its industry: The SEC asked the company to

- Discuss individually the business reasons for the changes in service revenues and equipment sales.
- Analyze the impact, if any, the recent chip shortage had, or was expected to have, on operations.

As these cases demonstrate, the SEC's concerns about the quality of the MD&A applies to mature, successful companies as well as troubled companies.

ENFORCEMENT ACTIONS

In its formal enforcement actions, the SEC has been quick to cite deficiencies in MD&A disclosures. Its comments in this regard are similar to those noted above. Here's a selection of cited MD&A deficiencies noted in the past several years:

In the Burroughs Corporation proceeding, the SEC concluded the MD&A omitted material information about the increase in work-in-process inventory in excess of 30 months' demand and the increase in the amount of unreserved-finished-goods inventory more than two years old. The SEC argued that in the computer industry, where change is rapid, this information was important to shareholders and investors.

Allegheny International, Inc. failed to include information about a sale of real estate in its MD&A. According to the SEC, this caused Allegheny's 1983 annual report to be false and misleading. The SEC contended this sale constituted an unusual and infrequent event that had a material impact on pretax income.

Hiex Development USA, Inc. was cited for failure to disclose a major commitment to purchase equipment over a 10-year period. In addition, the SEC said Hiex didn't disclose certain pertinent information about its ability to remedy a negative working capital situation.

The Charter Company's chief accounting officer and its controller were cited when the SEC concluded the company's MD&A was false and misleading. The SEC claimed the MD&A failed to disclose the company had experienced a continuing loss of its unsecured or open trade credit provided by its suppliers. This affected its ability to make a necessary level of purchases and constituted a threat to operations.

The Baldwin-United Corporation's chief financial officer was the target of an SEC enforcement action because he had reviewed the company's MD&A. That MD&A didn't disclose Baldwin's failure to achieve certain investment assumptions of its earnings model and insufficient taxable income to use the tax benefits inherent in the earnings model.

These enforcement actions—both those against the registrants and individual members of management—clearly demonstrate the SEC believes the MD&A *should provide investors with a realistic assessment of corporate objectives and results.*

DEALING WITH KNOWN TRENDS, DEMANDS, COMMITMENTS, EVENTS OR UNCERTAINTIES

Perhaps the most difficult aspect of the SEC's MD&A regulations is the requirement to discuss *known trends, demands, commitments, events or uncertainties the company reasonably expects will have a material impact on operations or liquidity* or would cause historical "financial information not to be necessarily indicative of future operating results or of future financial condition." Because the SEC often can use hindsight to judge the adequacy of disclosures actually made, companies must assess these factors carefully in preparing their MD&As.

The new interpretive release attempts to explain the difference between a *forecast* (disclosure not required) and a *known trend, demand and uncertainty*. To

EXHIBIT 1 A Summary of the SEC's MD&A Interpretive Release

The SEC's Financial Reporting Release no. 36, *Management's Discussion and Analysis of Financial Condition and Results of Operations*, of May 18, 1989, does *not* change the MD&A requirements. It attempts, however, to explain what's required by certain provisions of its MD&A regulations. Here's a summary of the interpretive release:

- *Prospective information and the discussion of trends, demands, commitments, events and uncertainties.* The release requires management to make two specific assessments:

1. Is the known trend, demand, commitment, event or uncertainty likely to come to fruition? If it's not reasonably likely to occur, no disclosure is required.
2. If management can't make the above determination, it must evaluate objectively the consequences of the known trend, demand, commitment, event or uncertainty, on the assumption that *it will come to fruition.* Disclosure is then required unless management determines there's little likelihood there will be a resulting material effect on the company's financial condition or results of operations.

- *Liquidity and capital resource needs.* The MD&A must address any material deficiency in either short-term or long-term liquidity and capital resources (cash needs) and disclose any proposed remedy. It also must disclose that no remedy has been decided on or that the deficiency cannot be currently addressed. The MD&A must address material capital expenditures, significant balloon payments, payments on long-term obligations and off-balance-sheet items due beyond the next 12 months.
- *Use of statement of cash flows.* Registrants are expected to use their cash flow statements (prepared according to Financial Accounting Standards Board Statement no. 95, *Statement of Cash Flows*) in analyzing liquidity. They should present balanced discussions of the cash flows in terms of investing and financing activities as well as operations. The MD&A must address matters that have materially affected the most recent period presented but that are not expected to have short-term or long-term implications. It must also analyze matters that haven't materially affected the most recent period presented but that are expected to affect future periods materially.
- *Year-to-year financial statement changes.* The interpretive release requires a discussion of the impact of discontinued operations and extraordinary gains and losses that had a material effect or are reasonably likely to have a material effect on financial condition or results of operations. Companies must analyze changes in financial statement line items, particularly when those changes result from two or more factors—for example, price and quantity.
- *Interim period MD&A.* In light of the obligation to update MD&A disclosures periodically, the company must disclose the impact of known trends, demands, commitments, events or uncertainties arising during the interim period that are reasonably likely to have material effects on financial condition or results of operations.
- *Segment data discussion.* An analysis of segment information is required if any segment contributes in a materially disproportionate way to revenues, profitability or cash needs or if the discussion on a consolidated basis would be an incomplete and misleading picture of the company.

some observers, however, this is a circular argument. As a result, the registrant is placed in a difficult position when trying to comply with the new guidance in a meaningful way and maintain its public position of not providing forecasts to the marketplace.

From a practical viewpoint, the best starting point in complying with this aspect of the MD&A interpretive release is the company's business plan for the next year. That plan should provide answers to some, if not most, of the disclosure issues. After considering the business plan, which is often optimistic, management should assess the *downside risks* carefully. Could these risks be tied to a known trend, demand, uncertainty, and so forth? If so, after assessing the probability of occurrence, these factors and their impact may need to be disclosed.

It's also helpful in complying with the SEC release to do a *top-down analysis* of known trends, demands, uncertainties and so forth. A logical starting point is the economy as a whole, then the company's broad industry group and finally company-specific items. Specific product, geographic and customer concentrations also should be analyzed as areas of potential change (positive or negative).

DRAFTING THE MD&A

The guidelines for the MD&A are relatively brief, and the SEC doesn't provide a standard format or cookbook for writing it. Thus, management has flexibility. Nevertheless, before starting the writing exercise, management needs to set a tone that says: If I were an investor, what would I want to know about this company's liquidity, capital resources and results of operations that the financial statements don't spell out clearly? What known trends, demands, commitments, events or uncertainties would affect my judgment about the company?

Making comments about liquidity, capital resources and operations requires input from the company's experienced and knowledgeable managers. In addition, budgets, capital plans, sales reports or other middle management tools become invaluable sources of MD&A information. Top-level executives also must be involved in the drafting because they provide the perspective and judgment needed to meet the SEC's expectations.

Using the SEC's MD&A interpretive release, a company can approach the drafting process by asking the following questions:

- Why did sales and revenues change—volume or price?
- Are there any trends—either favorable or unfavorable?
- What's behind the variations in expense categories?
- What unusual or infrequent events and transactions materially affected operating results?
- Does any segment contribute disproportionately to results or require disproportionate cash needs?
- What planned capital expenditures are material?
- What are the cash needs?

This list can be expanded and tailored to a particular company and its business environment. The point is that in preparing the MD&A, management needs to ask and answer questions about matters affecting *liquidity, capital resources and results of operations*.

A FOCAL POINT OF THE DISCLOSURE SYSTEM

Preparing an MD&A that meets SEC standards requires considerable time and study and involvement by top management. The MD&A should present a discussion of both the positive and negative factors that affected the company's revenues and costs in the past, thus influencing its historical results, as well as the factors that might affect future operations in terms of material changes or impacts on trends. The discussion should not be viewed as a risk disclosure document. Instead, it should be forthright and present in management's words a balanced view of where the company stands today and what it knows about the future given known events, demands, trends and so forth.

Unfortunately, management must be prepared to defend its analysis in hindsight. Nevertheless, if the company has done a forthright job in analyzing its current financial condition and liquidity as of year-end, if it has considered all known factors and if it has made an honest attempt to discuss those factors, it should be in an excellent position to overcome any subsequent SEC challenges.

In the SEC's view, MD&A is a focal point in the disclosure system of the securities acts. The SEC has enhanced and expanded it through recent releases. Although the SEC appropriately concluded no new regulations are required, MD&A drafters must read and understand the SEC's latest interpretive guidance and not simply rely on the initial regulations. The interpretive guidance does provide significant information to assist management in drafting a meaningful MD&A.

Summary Annual Reports: Is Shorter Better?

Zabihollah Rezaee
Middle Tennessee State University

Grover L. Porter
University of Alabama in Huntsville

"I feel like the guy who said, 'The emperor has no clothes,'" says Eugene H. Flegm, assistant comptroller at General Motors. "What we've done is destroy the myth that the SEC [Securities and Exchange Commission] demands a four-color, glossy annual report." Flegm was commenting on the go-ahead

From *Journal of Accountancy* (May 1988), pp. 42, 44, 46, 48, 50, 52, 54. Reprinted by permission of the American Institute of Certified Public Accountants, Inc. Copyright © 1988 by the American Institute of Certified Public Accountants, Inc. Opinions of the authors are their own and do not necessarily reflect policies of the AICPA.

GM received from the SEC on January 20, 1987, to issue a summary annual report (SAR). "Once you've exploded the myth, you've got to rethink the whole concept of the glossy brochure. Why do it at all? You can do everything the SEC requires with a form 10-K and a proxy."

The SEC's support for GM's proposal marked the culmination of a four-year study conducted by Deloitte Haskins & Sells and sponsored by the Financial Executives Research Foundation (FERF). The study was aimed at simplifying the form and content of the traditional compliance-oriented annual report. The magnitude and complexity of the financial information the SEC mandates has resulted in an "information overload" that's of little interest to the average shareholder. Thus, the traditional annual report has become voluminous and overly complex-perhaps too intimidating for most readers. Enter the summary annual report.

Ironically, although GM first ran the idea by the SEC, it was San Francisco-based McKesson Corp. that issued the first SAR in June 1987. "I've received more attention from this than from anything I've ever done before," says Marvin L. Krasnansky, vice-president-corporate relations at McKesson. The Financial Executives Institute (FEI) is strongly encouraging its members to reexamine their annual reporting practices thoroughly and consider switching to an SAR format. In 1987, at least 17 companies, including Sound Advice Inc. and Becton, Dickinson and Co., followed McKesson's lead and issued summary annual reports. It's forecast that almost all companies will be adopting the format in the next 5 to 10 years.

Is this attempt to improve communications a boon or bane for accountants and auditors? What are the guidelines for CPAs and their responsibilities regarding SARs? Is there serious potential for abuse in SARs? This article examines the SAR and provides tentative answers to these questions.

WHAT'S AN SAR?

An SAR is a shareholder report that contains a condensed presentation of a firm's financial statements in a more readable format than the traditional annual report. The reason is that various users of financial information have different needs. These diverse needs can best be met by layering financial reports in terms of the level of disclosure they contain: The most condensed report should be distributed to all readers, with more detailed reports available to others upon request.

The SAR idea really got off the ground with a 1981 research project initiated by the FEI's committee on corporate reporting. In 1983, a pilot research project was conducted by DH&S and sponsored by the FERF to determine whether the content of the traditional annual report could be presented in a shorter, more effective and readable manner to ease and encourage shareholder readership. The results were published by FERF in two volumes entitled *Summary Reporting of Financial Information: Moving Toward More Readable Annual Reports*. As the addendum below illustrates, the FERF proposals contain general and specific guidelines for SAR preparation. While these proposals suggest SARs should include condensed financial statements, they don't recommend any specific format guidelines.

THE FERF STUDY: WHAT SARs SHOULD CONTAIN

The summary annual report (SAR) is based on a study conducted by Deloitte Haskins & Sells in association with the Financial Executives Research Foundation (FERF). According to Thomas B. Simone, McKesson's vice-president and controller, the company reviewed the conclusions of this research and used them as a general guide in issuing the first SAR. According to the FERF study, SARs should include

- A balance sheet and income statement covering at least two years. Funds-flow information should also be presented for a minimum of two years.
- Selected five-year data including trend information, such as rate of return on investment.
- Industry and geographic segment data, if necessary, to give the reader an understanding of the company's business and market interaction.
- The amount of short- and long-term debt, including restrictive covenants, if material.
- Any accounting policies or changes in accounting policies if they are unique to the industry or if alternatives would result in significantly different results.
- Contingencies and uncertainties that have a material effect on operating results.
- Significant acquisitions and dispositions.
- Income taxes, if the effective tax rate differs significantly from the statutory tax rate.
- Financial information on unconsolidated subsidiaries and equity investors and the percentages of ownership.
- Leases, if the maturities cause liquidity problems.
- The number of common and preferred shares outstanding.
- Earnings per share and total dividends declared.
- A breakdown of retained earnings and the amount of treasury stock.
- Extraordinary items affecting financial statements.
- Any additional information that helps the average reader understand reported financial results.

Additionally, the FERF recommends the SAR contain a management report explaining where the financial information comes from and management's objectives in simplifying the presentation of financial information. The report should also state that form 10-K is available on request.

DISCLOSURE SHIFTED TO THE PROXY

The SAR approach effectively removes the traditional annual report from the SEC compliance system by permitting the company to include full audited financial statements and other required financial disclosures *in the proxy materials* sent to all shareholders. This approach gives management more latitude in preparing a summary annual report as a communications tool while ensuring that shareholders receive, on a timely basis, all of the information mandated by the SEC's proxy rules.

The primary purposes of the SAR are to

1. Encourage stockholder readership by making the report easier to read and understand.
2. Provide readers with relevant and concise financial and nonfinancial information without creating information overload.
3. Improve the quality and effectiveness of financial communications.
4. Enhance shareholder relations and management credibility through more effective communications.
5. Reduce the cost of preparing annual reports.
6. Allow companies to design an annual report that doubles as a public relations—as well as marketing and recruiting—document.

SEC REQUIREMENTS FOR ANNUAL REPORTS

As General Motors found out, there has never been anything in the SEC's proxy rules requiring a glossy annual report. The SEC's only two disclosure requirements are:

1. The form 10-K should be filed annually.
2. Complete financial information should be provided to shareholders before or along with the proxy statement.

Since the mid-1960s, however, expanded proxy rules and evolving generally accepted accounting principles have resulted in a hefty annual report. And it's widely perceived that these detailed disclosures must be made in the annual report. *GM did not ask for a change in the disclosure requirements:* The company suggested that the disclosures be shifted to the proxy statement rather than run in the annual report.

WHAT THE SEC SAID

In reviewing General Motors' proposal, the SEC "noted" five points that it apparently favored:

1. The full audited financial statements would be released with the earnings press release, and the information would be circulated extensively to the market.
2. The 10-K would be filed at or prior to the release of the SAR.
3. The SAR would include an auditor's report on the financial information it contained.
4. GM would include its full financial statements and other financial data in the 10-K and in an appendix to the proxy statement.
5. The SAR would state that the 10-K was available on request (GM, of course, has always made it available). The proxy statement would go to all stockholders, as required by law.

The SEC also reminded both GM and McKesson that their SARs must comply with rule 10b-5, which prohibits fraudulent and misleading financial reporting (as must all public statements, including press releases and quarterly reports).

After giving the green light to GM (and shortly thereafter to McKesson), the SEC was flooded with requests for SAR go-aheads. It said it wouldn't respond to any more requests. It argued that the guidance it had already given to GM and McKesson was sufficient. It also said it wished both to save staff time and avoid a whittling down of the standards already set in the two inquiries.

STATUS OF SARs

McKesson was the first major U.S. corporation to issue an SAR, for its fiscal year ended March 31, 1987. As the *Journal* goes to press, McKesson is readying its second SAR (see the exhibit, *How McKesson Is Pioneering the Summary Annual Report*). McKesson's 1987 annual report was 24 pages, compared with 40 pages the previous year. According to Krasnansky, the company saved about $60,000 net in switching to the SAR format. This broke down into an $88,000 savings on the glossy report, offset by an increase of $25,000 on the expanded proxy.

REACTIONS TO SARs

The financial community's reaction to the SAR was, in general, positive and encouraging. According to Thomas B. Simone, McKesson's vice-president and controller, the first SAR was, in fact, a readership "nonevent" largely because of the extensive efforts the company made beforehand to gain acceptance for the idea.

Some members of the financial community are concerned, however, that management may use SARs in a way that conveys only favorable news and buries unfavorable news. The SAR is controversial. Concedes Flegm, "I've been giving speeches, but so far I've received no standing ovations. I've yet to meet a lawyer who likes the idea. They think it presents incomplete data— even though the SAR is similar to the quarterly reports now being published. Even many PR people hate the SAR concept. You've got to keep explaining any major change in tradition. We don't want to surprise anyone—either investors or analysts."

Adds Krasnansky, "If your intention is to obfuscate, you can do it with footnotes just as easily as with an SAR." SARs should improve readability of companies' reports for shareholders by accurately portraying the company's financial position and results of operations from management's perspective. As long as this responsibility is faithfully fulfilled, the SAR holds no more potential for abuse than the traditional annual report.

IMPLEMENTATION OF SARs

Specific guidelines for the form, content and methods of disseminating SARs haven't been established by any authoritative accounting or regulatory body. According to Financial Accounting Standards Board member Victor H. Brown, "The board has not formally deliberated the question of summary annual reports, nor would I expect the board to do so in the near future. Of course, our staff, as well as board members, are following SAR developments with interest."

Some accountants have expressed the fear that use of SARs will create additional legal liability for disclosure in the absence of clear-cut guidelines. Accountants, therefore, should include legal counsel when preparing and disseminating an SAR. Furthermore, the company's secretary should be involved to make sure all proxy requirements are met. Key shareholders should be contacted before going ahead with the idea, and key financial analysts should also be notified. The public relations staff, of course, is also essential.

"I would advise accountants that the program works best if everyone is involved from the start and there are no surprises," says Simone. "Accountants should get together a working group of auditors, the corporate secretary, the law department, public relations and anyone connected with preparing the proxy and the 10-K. The idea is to coordinate all these interests. We worked up a master schedule to integrate all the different functions and to time the release for EDGAR [the Electronic Data Gathering and Retrieval program], the annual press release and the distribution of the SAR. This master schedule enabled everybody to see what was going on all the time.

"It's also important to enter into early discussions with the board of directors to make sure everyone is comfortable with what you're doing," he adds. "We got a very positive response both from our board and from our audit committee."

WHAT SARs MEAN FOR AUDITORS

The SEC clearly indicated it prefers an auditor's statement be included in the SAR. Thus, it's desirable and prudent to seek advance participation of independent auditors in the SAR process. In McKesson's case, its traditional auditor was DH&S, which was backing the SAR concept all the way.

What should auditors look for when examining an SAR? How should their opinions be phrased? Currently, the only guidance provided is in Statement on Auditing Standards no. 42, *Reporting on Condensed Financial Statements and Selected Financial Data*. SAS no. 42 permits an auditor to report on condensed financial statements derived from full audited financial statements. The standard precludes an auditor from being associated with an SAR unless full audited financial statements have previously been made public. SAS no. 42 doesn't cover information presented outside the condensed financial statements contained in the SAR. Therefore, the auditor should

- Ensure that the client's reporting schedule allows distribution of full audited statements prior to dissemination of the SAR.
- Exercise extreme care in determining the adequacy of the extent and nature of disclosures.
- Request necessary modifications of the condensed financial statements if they are materially misleading or inconsistent with the full audited financial statements.
- Take appropriate action upon the client's refusal to make such modifications (such as withdrawing from the engagement).

The auditor's report should also identify the document in which the full financial statements and related auditor's report appear, as well as the type of opinion issued. If the auditor's opinion on the full financial statements was other than unqualified, the report on the condensed financial statements should indicate substantive reasons for, and the nature of, the departure from an unqualified opinion.

An informal survey.   Although the auditor's report doesn't cover information presented outside the condensed financial statements, an informal survey of DH&S and other CPA firms indicates the *auditor's role and involvement in the SAR should be expanded to more comprehensive involvement with all summarized financial data*. The SEC and the auditing standards board of the American Institute of CPAs are considering similar proposals to expand the auditor's role in financial reporting outside the basic financial statements.

WINDOWS OF OPPORTUNITY

The SAR effectively removes the four-color, glossy, traditional annual report from the SEC compliance system by permitting the company to include full audited financial statements and other required financial disclosures in proxy materials sent to all shareholders. This encourages shareholder readership by improving the effectiveness, efficiency and economy of corporate communications with shareholders. As far as McKesson is concerned, says Krasnansky, "there's been no suggestion to drop the SAR. We're issuing another one this year. Once you realize that the annual report is 'deregulated,' all kinds of opportunities open up."

HOW McKESSON IS PIONEERING THE SUMMARY ANNUAL REPORT

In June 1987, San Francisco's McKesson Corp. became the first major U.S. company to issue a summary annual report (SAR). As the *Journal* goes to press, it's about to issue its second one.

According to Thomas B. Simone, McKesson's vice-president and controller, "What you really want to avoid is surprises. What we did was get together a group of people including my boss [Alan Seelenfreund, executive vice-president and chief financial officer], my accounting people, [Marvin] Krasnansky's corporate relations people, the lawyers, our corporate secretary and the guys from DH&S [Deloitte Haskins & Sells] to form a working group to put together a plan of attack. It was a very cooperative effort and needed to be tightly scheduled to dovetail with the SEC filing date of the proxy statement."

The McKesson Timetable

The actual schedule that McKesson followed was:

- March 31, 1987: Fiscal year ended.
- April 23, 1987: Traditional press release issued containing consolidated and segment earnings.
- Week of May 24, 1987: EDGAR transmission of preliminary proxy materials, including appendix with complete audited financial statements, management's discussion and analysis, six-year selected financial data and quarterly information.
- May 28, 1987: Press release of full audited financial statements.
- Week of May 31, 1987: EDGAR transmission of form 10-K with complete audited financial statements, management's discussion and analysis, six-year selected financial data and quarterly information.
- Week of June 14, 1987: EDGAR transmission of definitive proxy material and mailing of the proxy materials and the summary annual report to all shareholders.

What the SAR Contained

"Traditionally," Simone says, "Krasnansky and his people wrote the front of the book and we did the back, and we continued that tradition. Corporate relations did the operating write-up; they showed it to us; we made revisions; they made revisions . . . until it was finished. We did the financial review; they rewrote it; we rewrote it . . . until it was finished."

The result was a two-part 24-page book starting with a letter to share-holders explaining the corporate mission and objectives and containing a brief review of the past year and a discussion of the next year's prospects, includ-ing four specific, quantified goals the company intended to accomplish in the near future. According to Marvin L. Krasnansky, vice-president–corporate relations, "We believe that what everybody wants to know is how the com-pany is going to perform *next year*—not last year."

The next section of the SAR was entitled "Serving America's Independent Retailers" and doubled as a marketing and recruiting document, as well as providing information about the company's market segments and product lines. An informal review of operations detailed the six-year performance of McKesson's various divisions in a simplified statistical presentation.

Next came six-year financial highlights. Says Simone, "We picked the six-year comparison because we found on talking to financial analysts that that's what they like best—a base year plus five years of comparative data."

The "Financial Review and Outlook" was written in more formal, busi-nesslike prose. A discussion of management's goals for the fiscal 1988–92 financial plan was included. And finally, the abbreviated financial statements were presented, including the profit and loss statement, the balance sheet and the statement of changes of financial position. "We talked about includ-ing the stockholder equity table," notes Simone, "but decided against it. I could never understand that table, and I don't think anyone else really can."

"We greatly improved the readability of the report and its use as a communication device," states Krasnansky, "And we cut about 10 pages of footnotes. The pension plan footnote alone occupied one full page in our previous annual report; now it's one paragraph—making the significant point that the pension plan is overfunded."

The SAR also included an auditor's report. "We were fortunate that DH&S was our auditor to begin with, but we would have issued the SAR whoever our auditor was," comments Simone.

WHO KNEW?

Before issuing its SAR, McKesson contacted its 10 biggest institutional inves-tors and ran the idea by them. "If we had run into any flak, we certainly would have reconsidered the whole project," explains Krasnansky. The com-pany also ran the idea by the New York Stock Exchange. "They suggested we explain on the inside of the front cover what we were doing, and we did put in such an explanation." The board of directors and the audit committee also were fully informed of the project and supported it.

In any case, the first SAR was "a nonevent to readers," notes Simone. "You don't get comments unless you ask for comments." But the response from the financial community and other interested companies has been positive. Says Krasnansky, "Since we've done it, I've gotten six requests to speak on this topic and about two calls a week from other companies." And, the company had to go back to press to print another 12,000 copies because of demand.

WHAT'S NEXT?

This year, McKesson will issue another summary annual report as part of a complete communications program. "What we're doing is combining our quarterly report to shareholders and our employee communications quarterly into one quarterly publication called *McKesson Today*—one issue of which will be marked 'annual report,'" says Krasnansky. This year's report may expand to 32 pages and will start with a four-page chairman's letter and the financial and operations review. "Instead of breaking the book into two distinct parts, we'll be combining the financial and operations review," says Simone. "The financial statements themselves will be moved farther forward in the report than last year. They will be more prominent and more integrated than previously," he continues. "There will be no deletions from what we did last year, but we'll be adding a statement of quarterly highlights, including earnings, dividends and share prices. We got some direct feedback from financial analysts who said they wished we had included that table last year. So it'll go in this year."

As Krasnansky notes, "There's been no discussion to drop the SAR." Adds Simone, "Coordination is the key. We had positive response all the way on this. Problems will arise if you don't have internal communication with top management and with the board. Looking back today, I can recommend the summary annual report as a tool for all financial executives who wish to communicate better with their constituents—shareholders, lenders, analysts and employees."

—*Marie Macklin*

The End of the Annual Report?
An Events Data Base Alternative

Ken Pratt
University of Stirling, Scotland

Accounting information is at present provided to shareholders annually, with a more limited and usually unaudited interim report being given half-way through the year. By the time the annual accounts are available to share-

From *Accountants' Magazine* (October 1987), pp. 45, 48–50. Reprinted by permission of the journal and the author. Copyright © 1987 by The Institute of Chartered Accountants of Scotland.

holders the information is often three or more months out of date. Thousands or millions of transactions, each unique and potentially interesting, are aggregated into a few figures. Details of individual financial amounts are lost in the process and there is no information at all on other characteristics such as the timing of the transactions, the parties with whom they were transacted, or the nature of the goods or services given or received. Information in accounts as currently provided to shareholders and other users may be summed up as too little, too late, and too infrequent.

Company directors, managers, accountants and auditors make assumptions about the users and uses of accounts and presume to judge what information is important to those users and uses. Since it is not possible to report every facet of every transaction, the company and its auditors decide which shall be recorded and which discarded; which transactions may be aggregated; and which resulting presentations of information do or do not present a true and fair view.

Accountants presume that users of accounts want to be able to compare the results of different companies. Where existing practice is subject to variation, they make judgments about what is best practice and attempt to impose standards which prescribe this practice to the exclusion of all others. Users of accounts therefore receive accounts which are more comparable, but which will never be wholly so. To enjoy this doubtful benefit, users sacrifice the freedom to choose an accounting method which might better serve their needs. Many man-years of effort are spent in developing accounting standards which are *assumed* but not *known* to be in the general public interest.

Faced with a set of accounts, the enquiring user is likely to derive more questions than answers. If there have been material changes in earnings or turnover he may want to know more about how and why this happened. If there have been material changes in stock or debtors he may similarly want to know how and why. The accounts are not likely to provide the answers.

While most shareholders have access only to the very limited information contained in annual reports, selected financial analysts and advisers, and perhaps large institutional investors, may be privileged to receive much more information, to meet company managers and to seek answers to questions arising from their analyses. It is argued that this practice is in the interests of shareholders and that it contributes to the efficiency of the securities market. Nevertheless, the ability of company managements to decide who shall and who shall not have supplementary information gives cause for concern.

THE ACCOUNTING PROCESS AS IT IS NOW

Accounting records of almost all public companies are stored and processed by computer. Data on individual transactions is captured at source as they occur. Either then or later the entries arising from those transactions are coded with an account number and entered into a transaction or master file. In due course the posted entries in each account are summed and netted-off to strike a balance. It is by this process that transactions are aggregated and lose their individual characteristics such as amounts, dates, references and descriptions. In each of the activities of designing the chart of accounts, coding transactions, making adjustments to the preliminary trial balance, and preparing and presenting final accounts, the accountant exercises judgment about the significance and treatment of items of data and assigns weights and values to them.

The accountant also exercises judgment or personal preference in choosing accounting methods where alternatives are available—for example, in valuation of stocks and work in progress, depreciation calculations, capitalisation of expenditures and provisions for doubtful debts. Many of these chosen methods are incorporated in the suite of programs which make up the computerised accounting system so that they are automatically applied to data as it is processed in each accounting period.

It is increasingly likely that the stored data will be held on a data base from which it is drawn for processing and in which it is accessible to authorised internal users by on-line enquiry. The computer system may be on the same site as the accountant or may be at another remote company site.

THE ACCOUNTING PROCESS AS IT MIGHT BE

Just as the accountant and other authorised internal users do now, any authorised external user, such as a shareholder, could access a company's data base, extract data from it and process that data through his own accounting programs. The data base could be accessed at any time and so, if regularly updated, both the frequency and timeliness of information would be improved.

It would be impracticable to store details of every transaction in the data base, so some aggregation by the company's accountant would be necessary. However, this could be considerably less than that which currently takes place in preparing annual reports. Much more information would be available to users and so the information needs of very diverse groups of users and uses could be satisfied.

Investors, analysts and other groups wanting to compare results of different companies could extract data from each in turn and process it through their own accounting programs. They would thus not only be more sure that the information was comparable but would also be free to choose the basis on which the comparison was made.

There would be no need for the setting of standards aimed at narrowing the range of different accounting methods. Standards to increase the level of disclosure would be more easily achieved. Consider, for example, the ongoing debate about accounting for price-level changes. It would be unnecessary to argue about the relative merits of Current Purchasing Power (CPP) and Current Cost Accounting (CCA). These are different philosophies, each with its own validity and both likely to be of relevance to all users. Much of the debate arising from SSAP 16 has been concerned with the appropriateness of adjustments to historical cost accounts and the extent to which those adjustments result in meaningful approximations of CCA accounts produced *ab initio*. With access to company data bases, choices of methods between and within CPP and CCA would be left entirely to users. Disclosure standards would be concerned only to ensure that temporal aggregation of data in the data base was limited to shorter time periods, say a month. The user could apply his own choice of published indices to produce inflation-adjusted accounts. Alternatively, the data base might be designed to include actual prices or indices in respect of each account in each month or of each category of goods bought or sold during each month.

On analysing the results of processing a company's data through his own accounting model, the user may pose new and unforeseen questions. If he wants to pursue his analysis further he can return to the data which he has already extracted or to the company data base itself. He is not, therefore, confined to making do with the information available in the first set of accounts produced. There is little need to seek further information from officers of the company. Existing inequities in amounts of information available to different groups are reduced or eliminated.

In 1968 Sorter[1] advocated an approach to accounting in which, as far as possible, the accountant reports events without assigning to those events his own weights and values. Sorter referred to this as an "events approach." I will therefore refer to the data bases discussed in this article as "events data bases."

Little research has followed up George Sorter's proposals for an events approach. Two noteworthy contributions, however, are those by Johnson[2] and by Lieberman and Whinston.[3] Johnson seeks, among other things, to define events and characteristics of events which might be reported and he classifies the different ways in which these may be aggregated. Neither Sorter nor Johnson makes specific mention of computers, but the paper by Lieberman and Whinston is a first attempt at a structuring of a computer-based "events-accounting information system."

An approach to financial reporting in which events data bases are maintained by reporting companies could bring significant benefits to users of accounting information. However, a number of problems must be resolved before such a system could be introduced. Some of these are considered in the remainder of this article.

THE SMALL INVESTOR

The use of events data base systems is only likely to be viable for large institutional investors, analysts and advisers. These groups of users will have

[1] Sorter, G. H., "An Events Approach to Basic Accounting Theory," *The Accounting Review*, January 1969.

[2] Johnson, O., "Towards an 'Events' Theory of Accounting," *The Accounting Review*, October 1970.

[3] Lieberman, A. Z. and Whinston, A. B., "A Structuring of an Events-Accounting Information System," *The Accounting Review*, April 1975.

the resources to develop their own accounting programs and to put in place the computers, terminals, network links and other hardware and software needed to operate the system. The investment in these facilities may be justified by their use in providing information about many different companies. The small investor who is unable to use the system must still be provided for. Initially this may be achieved by continuing the annual report in its present form, by publication in the press or other public media such as teletext, or by improved accessibility of returns to the Registrar of Companies. Eventually, however, small investors may be able to choose from a range of information services offered by analysts and advisers using events data base systems.

DEFINITION OF THE DATA BASE

For the system to be economically viable users must be able to use the same programs and procedures for large numbers of companies. This means that company data bases will have to conform to a common definition. Standards will therefore be necessary, and while their development may at first be just as contentious as the current process of standard setting it is likely to be a more attainable goal with a more widespread and lasting effect. The standards will have to specify what characteristics of each event are to be recorded, the nature and extent of permissible aggregation and the chart of accounts or system of codes to be used in storing data. It may not be possible or practical to achieve a single set of codes which applies to all and so a structure may be needed which divides the data base into common and industry-specific segments. In addition to the form and content of the data base, the standards will have to define the frequency and timing of updates to the data and of access to it.

TRUE AND FAIR VIEW

The Companies Act of 1985 requires the directors of every company to prepare a profit and loss account and balance sheet annually. These accounts must give a true and fair view of the profit or loss for the financial year and of the state of affairs of the company at the end of the financial year. The accounts must be audited, must be laid before the company's members in general meeting, and must be sent to the members before that meeting.

The data held in an events data base will be even more factual and objective than accounts in their present form and so, if properly recorded, should satisfy the requirement to be "true and fair." However, an events data base system of the kind outlined here will not give a "view" since it merely provides data which the *user* processes to form his own view. Indeed, since its role is a passive one, merely being available for access, it will not satisfy the requirements of being laid before and sent to members in the sense of tangible statements distributed to them. An auditor's report will still be required but, if there is no printed balance sheet, then the company cannot fulfill the requirement that "the auditors' report shall be attached to it" (Companies Act 1985, s 238(3)). It is therefore likely that changes in the law, or in its interpretation, would be needed before a system of events data bases could replace the existing published annual report.

Despite the preoccupation of accountants with objectivity in financial reporting, there are many matters of uncertainty on which they have to make subjective judgments. These include, for example, incidence and amount of bad debts, obsolescence and net realisable values of stocks, useful lives and residual values of fixed assets, current litigation and outstanding insurance claims. Indeed, it is subjective judgments such as these which make it necessary to express the requirements of accounts in terms of "a true and fair view." It may not be practically or economically feasible for an events data base to provide sufficient information to enable a user to make his own independent assessments of these matters. It is likely that this argument will be strongly promoted by opponents of a move towards a system of events data bases or by those with a vested interest in maintaining the status quo.

ACCESS TO THE DATA BASE

Those who are first to gain access to new information stand a better chance of using it to their advantage—for example, in buying or selling shares ahead of the rest of the market. When a company operating an events data base system adds new information to the data base, all interested parties will want to access it at once. With current technology the cost of a system which would enable them all to access the new information simultaneously is likely to be prohibitive. A system of priority users or a queueing system will inevitably bring accusations of unfairness and is unlikely to be acceptable to stock exchange regulators as a primary method of releasing accounting information. However, recent years have seen significant developments in the technology of making information available to large audiences. Further developments in data bases, networks, teletext and other aspects of information technology should greatly reduce this problem over the next two or three decades.

PUBLIC UNDERSTANDING

One of the major barriers to introducing an events data base system is likely to be the problem of ensuring that users are not misled by subsets of information which are only partially complete. It will be too easy, perhaps, for users to access parts of a data base while ignoring other parts which contain information essential to a reasonable interpretation of the facts.

There is also a problem of the general public's inadequate understanding of accounting. Many believe that accounting is a precise science from which are produced single correct figures for profit or loss and for balance sheet values of assets and liabilities. The widely differing figures which will be produced and reported by different users of an events data base will be confusing to members of the general public and may adversely affect their perceptions of the accounting profession.

GETTING STARTED

Will companies welcome an events data base approach to financial reporting? It is possible that there will be a rush of companies eager to go down in history as the first to make information available in this way. More likely, however, no company will want to take the lead, arguing instead that significant increases in the level of disclosure will give rivals a competitive advantage.

Events data bases might just grow from more modest beginnings, initially containing no more than the information already in published annual reports, as a convenience to enquirers, but later being expanded in response to demands for more information or to new disclosure requirements.

This article has assumed a system in which the events data bases are maintained and accessed within each of the reporting companies. A possible alternative is that the companies prepare the data in a standard form and transmit it to a central data base maintained by the Registrar of Companies, The Stock Exchange or some other agency. Developments in this direction are almost certain to take place as a more efficient means of collecting and disseminating existing company return information. A recent Department of Trade and Industry consultative document[4] on the delivery of annual accounts and returns to the Registrar of Companies discusses potential benefits to companies, the general public and the Companies Registration Offices (CROs) "if the information could be captured in computer manipulative format." The document considers that such a system "would probably in the first instance operate in the CROs' public search rooms, but it is probable the transmission of data on public networks would become economically feasible."

It is unlikely that these developments, at least initially, will achieve either the level of disaggregation or the timeliness of data which would be necessary to yield most of the benefits outlined in this article. In due course, however, users' demands for more detailed information, wider acceptance that higher levels of disclosure are in the public interest, and cheaper methods of data collection, storage and retrieval, may lead to a more disaggregated and timely centralised data base.

Financial reporting by means of events data bases of the kind discussed here could have a major impact upon the profession. If, in due course, such a

---

[4] Department of Trade and Industry, "The Delivery of Annual Accounts and Returns to the Registrar of Companies," 26 August 1986.

development becomes inevitable, or even just desirable, it is to be hoped that accountants will rise to the challenge and demonstrate yet again their ability to initiate and manage change.

The Value Added Statement: An Innovation for U.S. Companies?

Gary K. Meek
Oklahoma State University

Sidney J. Gray
Warwick University, England

INTRODUCTION

A European innovation which may "add value" to U.S. company annual reports is the value added statement, which aims to show the wealth created and attributable to all "stakeholders" rather than just shareholders. In 1975, the Accounting Standards (Steering) Committee (ASSC)—the name at that time of the accounting standards setting body in the United Kingdom—published *The Corporate Report*, which recommended expanded reporting by British companies on a number of fronts. One of the proposals contained in *The Corporate Report* was the publication of a Value Added Statement. The reason for the suggestion was as follows:

> The simplest and most immediate way of putting profit into proper perspective vis-a-vis the whole enterprise as a collective effort by capital, management and employees is by presentation of a statement of value added (that is, sales income less materials and services purchased). Value added is the wealth the reporting entity has been able to create by its own and its employees' efforts. This statement would show how value added has been used to pay those contributing to its creation. It usefully elaborates on the profit and loss account and in time may come to be regarded as a preferable way of describing performance.
>
> . . . We accept the proposition that profits are an essential part of any market economy, and that in consequence their positive and creative function should be clearly recognised and presented. But profit is a part only of value added. From value added must come wages, dividends and interest, taxes and funds for new investment. The interdependence of each is made more apparent by a statement of value added.[1]

From *Accounting Horizons* (June 1988), pp. 73–81. Reprinted by permission of the American Accounting Association and the authors. Copyright © 1988 by the American Accounting Association.

[1] Accounting Standards Steering Committee, *The Corporate Report* (London: ASSC, 1975), p. 49.

The ASSC intended that the value added statement would supplement, rather than supplant, the income ("profit and loss") statement. Since 1975, the value added statement has been researched and discussed by British accountants in both practice and academia, and a sizable minority of U.K. companies have published value added statements in their annual reports. Four of the professional accounting institutes in the U.K. commissioned and issued research reports on value added.[2]

The purposes of this article are to summarize the main issues surrounding the value added statement (VAS) and to suggest that U.S. companies consider including a VAS in their annual reports.[3] On the latter point, it is not the intention to advocate that U.S. companies *ought* to publish a VAS. Rather, the aim is to suggest that corporate accountants weigh the issues in light of their own company's circumstances to decide whether presenting a VAS makes sense from a cost-benefit perspective.

OVERVIEW OF THE VALUE ADDED STATEMENT

Corporate Social Responsibility

In the accounting literature the VAS is normally packaged as a part of "social responsibility reporting" by the business sector, and it is in this context that it was proposed in *The Corporate Report*. Of course the belief that one holds about the relationship between business entities and society at large determines how one views a business entity's social "responsibility." Gray, Owen, and Maunders[4] offer a useful categorization. To paraphrase, these are

1. The "pristine capitalists" who deny that companies have any responsibility beyond efficiently responding to the marketplace.
2. The "expedients" who feel that business can only achieve long-term economic welfare and stability by accepting certain minimal wider social responsibilities.
3. The "proponents of the 'social contract'" who consider that companies exist at society's will and therefore are beholden to society's wishes.

---

[2] B. Cox, *Value Added: An Appreciation of the Accountant Concerned with Industry* (London: Institute of Cost and Management Accountants, 1979); S. Gray and K. Maunders, *Value Added Reporting: Uses and Measurement* (London: Association of Certified Accountants, June 1980); M. F. Morley, *The Value Added Statement* (Edinburgh: Institute of Chartered Accountants of Scotland, 1978); M. Renshall, R. Allan, and K. Nicholson, *Added Value in External Financial Reporting* (London: Institute of Chartered Accountants in England and Wales, 1979).

[3] Computational procedures will not be covered in detail. The interested reader can refer to the four research reports just mentioned, or to M. F. Morley, "The Value Added Statement in Britain," *The Accounting Review* (July 1979), pp. 619–629 and G. J. Harris, "Value Added Statements," *The Australian Accountant* (May 1982), pp. 261–264.

[4] R. Gray, O. Owen, and K. Maunders, *Corporate Social Responsibility: Accounting and Accountability* (Hemel Hempstead: Prentice-Hall International (UK), 1987), pp. 10–12.

4. The "social ecologists" who believe that business has created certain serious social problems (e.g., pollution) and is equally responsible for eliminating them.
5. The "socialists" who wish to break the economic and political power of capital in favor of a collectivist arrangement.

It is probably safe to say that most U.S. opinion tends towards the top of the list (while European sentiment may center a bit further down).

Management's Obligations

Closely related to the concept of corporate social responsibility is the issue of whether the managements of companies owe an obligation to more than shareholder-owners. It seems that the focus of management's duties is subject to some debate in the U.S. at the moment. For example, a recent *Business Week* article quotes the chairman of Avon Products who argues that executives have duties beyond maximizing value for shareholders. "We have 40,000 employees and 1.3 million representatives around the world. We have a number of suppliers, institutions, customers and communities. None of them have the democratic power as shareholders do to buy or sell their shares. They have much deeper and much more important stakes in our company than our shareholders."[5] This view may be contrasted to that of T. Boone Pickens, Jr., who states in a recent issue of *Harvard Business Review* that shareholders' interests should "take precedence over relationships with employees, customers and other corporate constituencies . . . (S)hareholders own the companies. In any public corporation they bear the ultimate financial risk for management's actions."[6]

An Expanded Focus for Financial Reporting

It is argued here that the VAS can be a useful addition to the annual report regardless of the view taken of corporate social responsibility, or whether managers should only manage for owners or for owners as well as other stakeholders. Companies impact society beyond the return they earn for their owners—businesses do create wealth, employ people, and contribute to societal costs through taxes. Indeed, this notion is the crux of Adam Smith's classical argument about the actions of individuals:

> Every individual necessarily labours to render the annual revenue of the society as great as he can. He generally, indeed, neither intends to promote the public interest, nor knows how much he is promoting it . . . he intends only his own gain, and he is in this, as in many other cases, led by an invisible hand to promote an end which is no part of his intention.

[5] "The Battle for Corporate Control," *International Business Week* (May 18, 1987), p. 71.
[6] T. B. Pickens, Jr., "Professions of a Short-Termer," *Harvard Business Review* (May–June 1986), p. 78.

Similarly, in pursuing financial return for the owners, managements of companies necessarily create wealth[7] to pay wages, interest, and taxes, and to fund new investment. The VAS casts corporate activities in this light. In this way the VAS focuses attention on the wider implications of corporate activities. While the income statement reports on the income of shareholders, the VAS reports on the income earned by a larger group of "stakeholders"—all providers of capital, plus employees and government.[8]

The annual report is an important medium by which a corporation communicates information to a diverse set of users. Through supplemental disclosures in the annual report, the company can reach out to a new or expanded audience and thereby enlarge the scope of interest in the company. As an item of supplemental disclosure, the VAS enables the firm to maintain the primary orientation of its traditional financial statements toward shareholders, yet provide information to other groups in a way that may be more meaningful to them. To reemphasize a point made earlier, the VAS is designed to supplement, rather than supplant, the income statement. Though some commentators have argued otherwise, it is not the contention here that value added is a better measure of corporate activity and performance than income—just an additional measure which may be useful in some circumstances.

A Comparison of the Value Added Statement and the Income Statement

Before discussing possible uses of the VAS, it would be helpful to compare the VAS to an income statement. Exhibit 1 is the 1985 VAS for the British firm, Imperial Chemical Industries (ICI), while Exhibit 2 is the same firm's 1985 income statement ("Group Profit and Loss Account").

Exhibit 1 shows that, net of materials and services used in producing its products, ICI added £3,363 million to the world economy in 1985. This added value went to the following groups:

Employees (£1,883 million) in the form of salaries, bonuses, pensions, etc.

Governments (£280 million) in the form of taxes.

Providers of capital (£388 million) mostly as interest to lenders and dividends to stockholders.

The company itself (£812 million) as a reinvestment.

---

[7] Just as "income" measured by accounting conventions does not normally correspond to an economist's notion of income, "value added" based on the same accounting convention is not identical to an economist's calculation. Nor is the value added statement necessarily linked to the value added tax, found in Europe and currently receiving attention in the U.S.

[8] Such a focus is consistent with recent calls for increased cooperation between management and labor in order to improve U.S. productive capabilities vis-a-vis the rest of the world. See, for example, the recent editorial in *International Business Week* (April 20, 1987, p. 184), "The U.S. Must Meet the Challenge."

Comparing Exhibits 1 and 2, it becomes apparent that many of the amounts on the VAS are also on the income statement. However, it is not totally accurate to say that the VAS is merely a re-arranged income statement. Two examples illustrate this point. (1) For the income statement, labor and depreciation are combined with other costs of production and allocated to cost of sales on the basis of finished goods inventory sold during the period.

EXHIBIT 1 1985 Value Added Statement of Imperial Chemical Industries
(Sources and disposal of value added)

	Notes	1985 £m	1984 £m	Percentage change
SOURCES OF INCOME				
Sales turnover		10,725	9,909	+8%
Royalties and other trading income		142	116	+22%
Less: materials and services used		(7,560)	(6,845)	+10%
VALUE ADDED BY MANUFACTURING AND TRADING ACTIVITIES		3,307	3,180	+4%
Share of profits less losses of related companies and amounts written off investments		56	71	−21%
TOTAL VALUE ADDED		3,363	3,251	+3%
DISPOSAL OF TOTAL VALUE ADDED				
EMPLOYEES	1			
Pay, plus pension and national insurance contributions, and severance costs		1,835	1,647	
Profit-sharing bonus	2	48	58	
		1,883	1,705	+10%
GOVERNMENTS	3			
Corporate taxes		308	373	
Less: grants		(28)	(28)	
		280	345	−19%
PROVIDERS OF CAPITAL				
Interest cost of net borrowings		122	100	
Dividends to shareholders		214	186	
Minority shareholders in subsidiaries		52	56	
		388	342	+13%
RE-INVESTMENT IN THE BUSINESS				
Depreciation and provisions in respect of extraordinary items		514	460	
Profit retained		298	399	
		812	859	−5%
TOTAL DISPOSAL		3,363	3,251	

NOTES

1 The average number of employees in the Group worldwide increased by 3 percent. The number employed in the UK decreased by 2 percent.

2 1985 UK bonus rate 8.1p per £1 remuneration (1984 10.1p).

3 Does not include tax deducted from the pay of employees. Income tax deducted from the pay of UK employees under PAYE amounted to £157m in 1985 (1984 £148m).

This table, which is used for calculating the bonus under the Employees' Profit-Sharing Scheme, is based on the audited historical cost accounts; it shows the total value added to the cost of materials and services purchased from outside the Group and indicates how this increase in value has been disposed of.

EXHIBIT 2 1985 Income Statement of Imperial Chemical Industries

GROUP PROFIT AND LOSS ACCOUNT

For the Year Ended 31 December 1985	1985 £m	1984 £m
TURNOVER	10,725	9,909
Operating costs	(9,917)	(8,990)
Other operating income	170	144
TRADING PROFIT (after providing for depreciation 1985 £474m, 1984 £440m)	978	1,063
Share of profits less losses of related companies and amounts written off investments	56	71
Net interest payable	(122)	(100)
PROFIT ON ORDINARY ACTIVITIES BEFORE TAXATION	912	1,034
Tax on profit on ordinary activities	(308)	(373)
PROFIT ON ORDINARY ACTIVITIES AFTER TAXATION	604	661
Attributable to minorities	(52)	(56)
NET PROFIT ATTRIBUTABLE TO PARENT COMPANY	552	605
Extraordinary items	(40)	(20)
NET PROFIT FOR THE FINANCIAL YEAR	512	585
Dividends	(214)	(186)
PROFIT RETAINED FOR YEAR	298	399
EARNINGS BEFORE EXTRAORDINARY ITEMS PER £1 ORDINARY SHARE	86.4p	98.2p

Labor and depreciation costs associated with unsold inventory are placed on the balance sheet. However, the full amounts of labor and depreciation for the period are shown on the VAS. (2) Research and development expense adds materials, labor, and depreciation into a single figure which is deducted in deriving income. On the VAS these items are shown in separate places.[9]

The ability of an annual report reader to come up with, say, total labor and depreciation for the period depends on the kind and amount of information revealed in the income statement and supplemental notes. However, while a reader may be unable to construct a VAS from information published in an annual report, all of the necessary figures are already recorded by a company's accounting system. Similar to the old statement of changes in financial position, the VAS does not require that an accounting system record any new information beyond what is necessary for an income statement and a balance sheet. The VAS is based on identical conceptual foundations as the income statement and balance sheet—historical cost, going concern, consistency, objectivity, etc. Indeed, it is for this reason that the marginal cost to prepare the VAS is unlikely to be significant.

[9] Cost of sales and research and development expense are included in the "Operating costs" amount on ICI's income statement. Note 4 of ICI's financial statements details this information.

USES OF THE VALUE ADDED STATEMENT

To Measure Wealth Created by the Company

The opening quotation from *The Corporate Report* pinpoints several of the alleged advantages of the VAS. The VAS focuses attention on the success of a company to create wealth and generate national income. This would be of general interest to the various stakeholders since a firm can only sustain its payments of wages, taxes, interest, and dividends by creating wealth. By the same token, the levels of these payments can increase by creating additional wealth over what the firm has achieved previously. For the general public, it can lead to a greater awareness of the role of business in producing goods and services and in generating income for society. Income numbers receive a great deal of attention by the media, yet income may be less informative for the public as a measure of a company's performance than value added. After all, profits only measure the owners' share of a company's results of activities. Value added shows another dimension to a company's performance and may as a result put profits in a different perspective. However, as Cox[10] notes, it must also be recognized that value added has the potential to be cynically interpreted as a device to divert attention away from embarrassingly high profits.

To Emphasize Stakeholder Interdependence

The VAS also emphasizes the interdependence of the various stakeholders, and it highlights the interactive effect of policy decisions by any one of these groups on the others. It has been argued that through such an emphasis, the VAS may lead to more cohesiveness among these groups[11] and especially to a more positive attitude by employees toward the company.[12] Greater cooperation is certainly laudable, but it has also been pointed out[13] that showing the relative share received by each stakeholder may only succeed in highlighting an antagonistic relationship (should there be one) since it might be seen that an increased share by one group can only be accomplished by a decreased share from another. Thus, competition among stakeholders can exist. However, there is also no denying some degree of mutual dependence in all companies, and if teamwork and cooperation exist among the stakeholder groups, the VAS can emphasize this point.

---

[10] B. Cox, "There Is No Added Value in the Value Added Statements," *The Accountant* (15 November 1984), pp. 6, 8.

[11] P. D. Bougen, "Value Added," in D. J. Tonkin and L. C. L. Skerratt, *Financial Reporting 1983–84: A Survey of UK Published Accounts* (London: Institute of Chartered Accountants in England and Wales, 1983), p. 152.

[12] Gray and Maunders, op. cit., p. 13; and M. F. Morley, "Value Added Reporting," in T. A. Lee, *Developments in Financial Reporting* (Oxford: Philip Allan, 1981), p. 257.

[13] Gray, Owen, and Maunders, op. cit., p. 51.

To Condition Employee Expectations Regarding Pay and Prospects

By examining the relative share of value added received (over time and compared to other companies) employees may find the VAS useful in forming attitudes about the equity and fairness of their pay levels. It may also indicate a company's ability to pay higher wages in the future. For example, if higher value added were predicted for the future, the amount could be regarded as available for distribution to employees. Thus, value added information could influence the aspirations of employees when engaging in wage discussions with management.[14] Morley[15] also argues that employees have an interest in the wealth created by their company during the year, the share they receive in the form of pay, as well as the proportion reinvested to strengthen the company and enhance future job security. The VAS provides this information in a straightforward and understandable way. Morley notes that the income statement, besides being more complex than a VAS, is not particularly relevant to employees anyway. Employees are interested in information about their own achievements and future prospects, not those of the shareholders.

For Productivity Incentive Schemes

Finally, value added can form the basis for productivity incentive schemes. Morley[16] notes that many U.K. companies have introduced bonus plans based on increases in the ratio of value added to payroll costs or value added per employee.[17] (One company with a value added bonus plan is ICI, whose VAS is reproduced in Exhibit 1.)

Earlier it was observed that supplemental annual report disclosures provide the means for a company to reach out to an expanded audience of users. While the VAS has potential uses by shareholders, financial analysts, lenders, and others, it is likely to be most relevant to the general public and the company's employees. The credibility of value added information can be enhanced by including it in the annual report.

SOME CONCEPTUAL ISSUES IN THE PREPARATION OF THE VALUE ADDED STATEMENT

This section highlights several important conceptual issues which arise in preparing a VAS. Theoretical questions underlie what may superficially appear to be merely questions of format or computation.

[14] Gray and Maunders, op. cit., pp. 10–11.
[15] M. F. Morley, "Value Added: The Fashionable Choice for Annual Reports and Incentive Schemes," *The Accountant's Magazine* (June 1979), p. 235.
[16] Morley, 1981, op. cit., p. 258.
[17] Value added is seen as superior to sales as a measure of output since sales revenue includes the value of work done outside the firm, whereas value added excludes it. Value added is also viewed as better than profits for this purpose since a numerator expressing only the rewards to owners is thought to be less well "matched" to the denominator than one which includes rewards to labor and capital. See Gray and Maunders, op. cit., p. 13.

1. Gross or net value added (the treatment of depreciation).

Note in Exhibit 1 that ICI does not deduct depreciation in calculating value added (i.e., depreciation is included in the value added amount) and shows it as an item reinvested in the business. This is known as the "gross" method of calculating value added and is the one suggested in *The Corporate Report*. Fully 80 percent of U.K. companies disclosing value added statements calculate value added gross of depreciation according to the most recent survey available.[18] This approach is consistent with the idea that the reinvestment of used up productive physical capacity is necessary for a business to continue as a going concern. It has an added advantage in that the value added figure is unaffected by the depreciation method(s) used by the firm. As a result, comparability and consistency are enhanced and the subjectivity involved in determining the depreciation amount is removed from the value added number.

The alternative is the deduction of depreciation along with other "materials and services used" to calculate "net" value added. There are several arguments favoring this approach, the most persuasive being that the fixed assets whose costs are depreciated are purchased from outside the stakeholder group just as materials and services are. Depreciation represents an input cost and not treating it as such is not only inconsistent with how the other inputs are treated but also overstates the wealth created during the period. Moreover, distributing 100 percent of the firm's *gross* value added would eventually deplete its capital base (thus turning the physical capital agrument favoring the gross method on its head!). Finally, the net method avoids the peculiar impression (see Exhibit 1) that depreciation is a member of the stakeholder team.

2. Taxes (the amount of value added distributed to government).

The amount of value added distributed to the government may be limited to corporate income taxes (this is essentially the presentation by ICI) or it may include social security and withholding taxes on employees, and sales and excise taxes paid and/or collected. Most U.K. VAS's treat employee-related taxes, along with pay and pension contributions, as a distribution to employees.[19] Thus employee-related taxes are seen as a benefit enjoyed by employees, paid by the company to the government on their behalf.

Sales and excise taxes paid on materials and services purchased from the outside can be considered a part of the cost of these materials and services, and thus deducted in computing value added. Alternatively, they may be considered a part of value added and subsequently shown as a distribution to government. Similarly, sales and excise taxes collected on products sold may be excluded from sales revenue (and therefore value added), or they may be included in the value of a firm's output and treated as a distribution to

[18] Bougen, op. cit., p. 156.
[19] Ibid., p. 158.

government on the VAS. Excluding sales and excise taxes from value added is consistent with the idea that the government sector has played no role in the wealth created by the firm. By excluding these taxes from the value added amount, only corporate income taxes would be left as the distribution to the government. By contrast, including these taxes as a part of the value added amount and, correspondingly, as a distribution to government represents what McLeay[20] terms the "government as a public sector" view. Here, government presence is seen as contributing to the firm's success in creating wealth, just as capital and labor do. The prevailing attitude in the U.S. on this philosophical point is probably against a "government as public sector" view, suggesting that sales and excise taxes be excluded from value added amount. (Such treatment is also consistent with the way they are customarily shown on the income statement.)

3. Defining the members of the stakeholder group.

The previous paragraph raises the point of why government is included as a member of the stakeholder team in the first place. After all, government is uninvited and does not participate in decision making. On the other hand, a supplier who may serve no other firm is excluded as a member of the group even though the future of this supplier depends on the firm's continued existence. The literature has yet to satisfactorily resolve these issues.

4. Other points.

Gray and Maunders[21] point out that calculating value added on a sales basis and showing total employee costs for the period as a distribution of value added (as is recommended in *The Corporate Report* and practiced by U.K. companies) is conceptually inconsistent in that the latter is reported on a production basis. Thus, if the labor component of unsold inventory is to be shown as a distribution of value added, then the computation of value added itself should likewise consider unsold inventory (i.e., for consistency it should be calculated on a production basis). Such an approach is common among German firms.[22] Despite this conceptual inconsistency, it is unlikely that the difference between the two approaches is material, and there is something to be said for following the same practice in calculating value added as is used for determining sales revenue on the income statement.

A final matter is whether extraordinary, non-operating, and translation gains and losses represent value added. They affect the overall fortunes of the firm but do not arise from normal production activities. Among U.K. com-

[20] S. McLeay, "Value Added: A Comparative Study," *Accounting, Organizations and Society* (Vol. 8, No. 1, 1983), pp. 31–56.
[21] Gray and Maunders, op. cit., pp. 27–28.
[22] McLeay, op. cit., p. 43.

panies there is a wide variation in practice.[23] ICI includes income from associated companies (equity method) and from investments in determining value added as well as extraordinary items (Exhibit 1). This treatment can be justified in that it provides a basis for reconciliation with the income statement.

Underlying the points discussed in this section are conceptual questions about what is value added and which groups contribute to its creation and share in its distribution.

CONCLUSION

According to *Statement of Financial Accounting Concepts No. 2*,[24] relevance and reliability are the two primary qualities that make accounting information useful for decision making. The relevance of the value added statement for certain groups of users was discussed earlier in this paper.[25] The information in the VAS will be just as reliable as that in the other financial statements, given that it is determined on the same basis of accounting. *SFAC No. 2* also stresses that financial reporting should provide information about performance which is understandable to those who use it. The VAS is about performance—albeit more broadly defined than has heretofore been customary in U.S. financial reporting. It also seems straightforward and easy to comprehend. Finally the cost of producing and presenting a VAS is unlikely to be significant since it requires no new information from the accounting system. Moreover, consistent with the requirements of *Statement of Financial Accounting Concepts No. 5*,[26] the VAS articulates with the other financial statements and is derived from the same underlying data. For these same reasons, the VAS raises no new problems for auditors (nor will it add to potential negligence claims against them).

Burchell, Clubb, and Hopwood[27] document the forces which gave birth to the VAS in the United Kingdom. The late 1970s and early 1980s witnessed significant interest in the VAS by British accountants. Recently, however, interest has waned. In part this was due to the debate over accounting for inflation and changing prices preoccupying the profession and dissipating much of its energy during the same period. Burchell, Clubb, and Hopwood also suggest that the election of the Conservative government in 1979 signifi-

---

[23] Bougen, op. cit., p. 156.

[24] Financial Accounting Standards Board, "Qualitative Characteristics of Accounting Information," *Statement of Financial Accounting Concepts No. 2* (Stamford: FASB, May 1980).

[25] Relevance is discussed in more depth in Gray and Maunders, op. cit., pp. 5–18.

[26] Financial Accounting Standards Board, "Recognition and Measurement in Financial Statements of Business Enterprises," *Statement of Financial Accounting Concepts No. 5* (Stamford: FASB, December 1984).

[27] S. Burchell, C. Clubb, and A. G. Hopwood, "Accounting in its Social Context: Towards a History of Value Added in the United Kingdom," *Accounting, Organizations and Society* (Vol. 10, No. 4, 1985), pp. 381–415.

cantly altered relationships in and among business, labor, and government. The VAS was perceived to be less relevant in the new atmosphere of competititon, free markets, and shedding of excess labor.

It might be argued that if the British are losing interest in the VAS then why should accountants in the U.S. show any interest? First of all, the British industrial experience is not the same as that of the U.S. Despite a common accounting heritage, the business conditions contributing to the "rise and fall" of the VAS in the U.K. are not consistent with those in the U.S., as a reading of Burchell, Clubb, and Hopwood reveals. However, it is a mistake to think of the VAS only in the context of reporting about social responsibility. The activities of a business affect more than the owners. Business creates wealth, employs people, rewards investors and creditors for risking their funds, and pays taxes. It is this view of business performance that the VAS portrays. *SFAC No. 5* notes that supplementary financial statements can be useful for introducing or gaining experience with new kinds of information.[28] This paper proposes that as a supplemental disclosure the value added statement can redirect attention to certain wider implications of corporate activity.

---

[28] FASB, *SFAC No. 5*, op. cit., p. 3.

CHAPTER 4

Revenue Recognition

Revenue recognition in conventional accounting is associated with two key notions: earning and realization. Earning implies that substantially all of the effort necessary to secure the revenue has been expended—order-getting, manufacturing, and delivery of the product or rendering of the service. In addition, the selling entity should be able to estimate the cost of the remaining portion of the earning process that might occur after the revenue recognition, for example, the effort to collect a receivable or the effort to provide a warranty coverage. The rationale underlying the importance of earning as a key criterion is that the income statement should be a report on the entity's performance.

The second key notion, realization, requires that the selling entity should either have received cash from the customer or client or have received a valid promise that cash will be received within the near future. Realization plays an important role because managers and investors look to reported profit as an indicator of possible cash dividends. If the profit were to derive from sales transactions that do not promise the receipt of cash for some considerable time, it would be of little value as an indicator of the amount of cash arising from gainful activity that could be paid out as dividends. While academics and some professionals have argued that increases in the values of net assets, also known as unrealized holding gains, should be reflected in the income statement, most such advocates would exclude them from "income from operations."[1]

John H. Myers' classic article, "The Critical Event and the Recognition of Net Profit," originally published in 1959, is the only article in this collection that was also included in the first edition of this book in 1964. In a refreshing manner, Myers tests the usefulness of the assumption that revenue should be recognized at a single moment of time, by examining its application in a

---

[1] See, for example, Edgar O. Edwards and Philip W. Bell, *The Theory and Measurement of Business Income* (Berkeley: University of California Press, 1961), Chapters 7–9.

number of different settings. He reasons that profit is earned "at the moment of making the most critical decision or of performing the most difficult task in the cycle of a complete transaction." In this connection, one is reminded of the sage observation of George O. May, one of the pioneers of the U.S. public accounting profession:

> "Manifestly, when a laborious process of manufacture and sale culminates in the delivery of the product at a profit, that profit is not attributable, except conventionally, to the moment when the sale or delivery occurred. The accounting convention which makes such an attribution is justified only by its demonstrated practical utility."[2]

In "Installment Accounting: Is It Consistent?," Richard A. Scott and Rita K. Scott contend that "[w]hen the installment method is used, a representation is made which can only be true if the proposition on which it is founded is false." Since the installment method is recommended when significant uncertainty attends the collectibility of the receivable, how can a revenue recognition method be used that presupposes the eventual collection of the *full* sales price?

Since the late 1960s, questions have been raised about the practice of some franchisors of retail outlets to front-end their fee revenues. In the case discussed by Penelope Wang, a *Forbes* reporter, in "Claiming Tomorrow's Profits Today," a franchisor was ordered by the Securities and Exchange Commission (SEC) to defer the recognition of certain fee revenues until they were earned. When the franchise agreement requires that an area developer open a certain number of stores within a specified time period, the SEC has argued that the fee revenues will not be earned until the franchise units are open and operating. In the article, the arguments for and against the SEC's position are presented.

BIBLIOGRAPHICAL NOTES

Two research studies on the problem of revenue recognition are the following:

Thomas, Arthur L.: *Revenue Recognition* (Ann Arbor, MI: Bureau of Business Research, Graduate School of Business Administration, University of Michigan, 1966).
Coombes, Robert J., and Carrick A. Martin, *The Definition and Recognition of Revenue*, Accounting Theory Monograph No. 3 (Melbourne: Australian Accounting Research Foundation, 1982).

Two research studies that deal with the recognition decision in accounting, including its application to revenues, are:

---

[2] George O. May, *Financial Accounting: A Distillation of Experience* (New York: The Macmillan Company, 1943), p. 30.

Jaenicke, Henry R.: *Survery of Present Practices in Recognizing Revenues, Expenses, Gains, and Losses* (Financial Accounting Standards Board, 1981).

Johnson, L. Todd, and Reed K. Storey: *Recognition in Financial Statements: Underlying Concepts and Practical Conventions* (Financial Accounting Standards Board, 1982).

A classic article on the realization concept is:

Horngren, Charles T.: "How Should We Interpret the Realization Concept?" *The Accounting Review* (April 1965), pp. 323–333.

An information economics analysis of the rules for revenue recognition is:

Antle, Rick, and Joel S. Demski: "Revenue Recognition," *Contemporary Accounting Research* (Spring 1989), pp. 423–451.

Accounting for revenue recognition often forms the core of court cases in which managers have been accused of financial fraud or auditors of negligence. A celebrated recent case involving both of these issues is ZZZZ Best. The following article describes the extremes to which ZZZZ Best went to report revenues from nonexistent contracts:

Akst, Daniel: "How Barry Minkow Fooled the Auditors," *Forbes* (October 2, 1989).

Revenue recognition practices also show up as the main problem areas when the Financial Accounting Standards Board tries to set standards for specialized industries. Franchising and real estate industries are examples where installment accounting practices are required by the FASB under many situations, even though the Accounting Principles Board Opinion No. 11 (issued in 1966) essentially prohibits the use of installment accounting in most cases. In the motion picture industry, revenue recognition is complicated by the fact that revenue arises from many sources (theatrical release, video, international franchises, cable, network television, etc.) and over many years. In the airline industry, the widespread use of "frequent-flyer" programs poses the problem of estimating an allowance for the cost of these programs while recognizing the associated revenue. In the nonprofit sector, for universities and charitable organizations, an important question is whether "pledges," which are contributions that will be made by a donor at a future date, should be reported as current revenue. The following articles discuss the issues involved in the last two examples:

Zipser, Andy: "Sky's the Limit? Frequent-Flyer Programs Are Ballooning Out of Control," *Barron's* (September 17, 1990).

McMillen, Liz: "Private Colleges Irked by Accounting Plan to Require Fund-Raising Pledges to be Booked as Income," *The Chronicle of Higher Education* (September 26, 1990).

The Critical Event and Recognition of Net Profit

John H. Myers
Professor Emeritus, Indiana University

The matching of cost and revenue has grown during the past fifteen or twenty years into a cardinal principle of accounting. We have learned to postpone or accelerate either cost or revenue, as the case might require, in order to get all the elements of a single transaction into the same period. In spite of such problems as price level fluctuations and requirements of governmental regulatory bodies, we have made considerable headway in sharpening the determination of net income. However, in this effort to sharpen the determination of net income we have given very little attention to the timing of income recognition. We have relied on a variety of rules for specific situations, not on an over-all principle. In this paper I review both the economic concept of net income and the accounting procedure in a number of specific business situations, and then suggest a principle which is compatible with economic theory and at the same time coordinates most current accounting practice. I hope this discussion will provoke further thought on the subject leading to the ultimate refinement and acceptance of a principle which is both (1) as clear and uniform in its applicability as that of matching cost and revenue and (2) sound from an economics standpoint.

Economic theorists since the days of Adam Smith have spoken of land, labor, and capital as the three factors of production. Compensation to these factors has been known as rent, wages, and interest. Under a perfectly functioning system, these three factors receive all the income. Any residual that remains in an actual case is due to the imperfections of the system in the individual case at the particular moment of time. Later economists acknowledged a fourth factor of production: entrepreneurship. Its compensation is known as profit. Profit is the reward for bearing risk—the risk of enterprise, the risk of venturing in business, the risk of owning something in hope of selling it later. This profit may be positive or negative depending upon the entrepreneur's decisions as to the directions in which to risk his capital, his labor, and his land. This profit is very close to what the accountant calls profit.[1]

From *The Accounting Review* (October 1959), pp. 528–532. Reprinted by permission of the American Accounting Association and the author. Copyright © 1959 by the American Accounting Association.

[1] The accountant's profit includes, in addition to the economist's reward for bearing the risks of enterprise, "interest" on the owner's investment and, in some cases, "wages" to the owner of an unincorporated enterprise. However, these two variations do not negate the basic relationship between the profit of the accountant and of the economist. The wage element may be omitted for it is pertinent only in the unincorporated business, and even in such businesses there is a growing tendency to include a fair wage to the owner among the expenses. Interest is seldom if ever set out separately but in profitable corporations it may well be a minor part of the profit.

Let us assume for accounting purposes that profit is the same as the profit of the economist, a reward for having taken the risks of enterprise. This being the case, profit is earned by the operating cycle, the round trip from one balance sheet position back to that position, whether the starting point be cash or inventory or any other factor. Even in a simple merchandising business several steps occur; buying, selling, collecting. The question arises as to when during that cycle any profit should be recognized. Should the profit be recognized when a specific point on the cycle is reached, or should it be spread over that cycle in some manner? If it should be recognized at a point, what is that point? If it should be spread, what criterion should be used? In order to set some limits on this article, I have assumed that profit should be recognized at a single moment of time. This article will be devoted, therefore, to a consideration of the moment of time at which to recognize the profit. Perhaps after considering carefully the implications of the assumption we shall be in a better position to consider the question we have by-passed.

If profit is to be recognized at a moment of time, we must select that moment. The economist gives a clue in the function of entrepreneurship as the function of directing a business, bearing the pain of the risks, and reaping the rewards of astute decisions. This suggests that profit is earned at the moment of making the most critical decision or of performing the most difficult task in the cycle of a complete transaction. Just what event this is may not be easy to distinguish in many cases. Although in most types of business we recognize profit at the moment inventory is converted into accounts receivable, such timing is far from universal.[2]

Let us examine a number of different types of businesses (1) to determine what is done and the apparent theory behind such action and (2) to test the applicability of the critical function theory in that business. In so testing the theory, we must remember that it must not fall merely because the critical function is difficult to determine. A proposed accounting theory must provide the basic objective and leave room for developing means of implementing that theory. Objectivity is one of the desiderata of any means of achieving a goal, but it in itself must not be allowed to be the goal.

Merchandising is one of the most common businesses. The merchant generally performs three steps: (1) wise buying, (2) effective selling, and (3) efficient collecting. If "wise," "effective," and "efficient" permit, there is a profit. We recognize the profit at the time the second step, selling, is performed. Two reasons commonly are given for recognizing profit at this time: (1) an asset has been transferred for a valid claim (transfer); (2) the merchant's opinion as to value is not needed (objectivity). To claim that any profit was realized at the time of purchase would be contrary to our past heritage, but to defer profit until cash has been collected is not uncommon. Major reasons for deferring profit realization until receipt of cash are the risk of collecting in full

---

[2] One clue to the most difficult or crucial task in the operating cycle may be the function of the business from which the president was selected. Was he in sales, manufacturing, collection or something else? A background in sales would tend to confirm most present accounting practice.

and the possibility of incurring additional expense. Bad debt and collection expenses are common, but most businesses feel that they can set up adequate reserves for the estimated expense. Thus, it sounds as if the real principle behind current practice were certainty, but that cannot be so for we do prepare income statements in spite of such major uncertainties as unaudited income tax returns and renegotiable contracts.

The principle of the critical event seems to fit the situation of the merchant very well. Where collection is a critical problem (and I doubt if there are many cases where it is), profit may be taken up at collection time. For most businesses, most of us would agree that selling is the critical event and that profit should be recognized at that time. In rare cases buying might be critical, as where an extremely good price is paid for some rapid-turnover, staple item.

A manufacturer's business is much like that of a merchant except that an extra step is added, converting the purchased raw materials into salable units. This gives an extra point at which profit might be recognized, i.e. time of efficient manufacture. In general we do not use this time because of uncertainty as to eventual sale price. However, in the case of gold refining where the market is assured, profit is recognized at the time of manufacture. The same reasoning as in the case of the merchant seems to apply; again it is the certainty principle. The critical event principle is also pertinent: Selling is very important in most cases; in gold mining it is a mere clerical detail, for the market and the price are assured by the government.

However, in contracting and manufacturing goods to order, especially if the manufacturing time will extend over several fiscal periods, the situation is quite different. In many cases there is no assurance the goods can be made at the contracted price. Therefore, profit is recognized when it becomes certain, when the goods have been made. The critical event theory, if applied to this situation, might be construed to come to the same answer as the certainty theory. In many cases it probably will. However, there may well be cases when profit should be recognized at sale date before the goods are manufactured. If a manufacturer regularly makes standard items for stock, it does not seem right to defer profit recognition beyond sale date merely because the item is temporarily out of stock. Somewhere between these two extremes there will be a twilight zone in which determination of the critical event will be difficult, but knowing that such an event is the determining factor would clarify thinking considerably.

Some people argue that profit can be recognized only when a transaction has been completed, when both purchase and sale have taken place. They argue that both of these elements are necessary and that the sequence of the two is immaterial. This almost assumes that the normal position is to have nothing but cash and that any other position is one of risk. A merchant would consider himself on dangerous ground, assuming he plans to stay in business, if he did not have a stock of merchandise. Anyone who has maintained a heavy cash position in the last decade or so has been assuming a position in which risk (of price level change) has been high. Consider an individual who has accumulated more funds than needed for current living and for an emergency cushion. The normal position for him is to have an investment in stocks or bonds. When he is out of the market, he is assuming substantial risk until he reinvests. There is a real question if he is to measure profit from purchase to sale of a security or to measure from the time he gets out of the market until he again assumes his normal position with respect to the market. Point of view seems all important. What is the critical function in making a profit? This question may be a most useful over-all guide.

Profit is recognized by magazine publishers in the period when the magazines are distributed. In most cases sale occurs and cash is received at the time the subscription is booked. Manufacturing costs are incurred shortly before distribution date. Both advertising revenue and sale price are considered earned at the time of publication. There is serious question if this routine is correct even using the theory of certainty typically followed by manufacturers. Long in advance of publication date, the sales of magazines (by subscription) and of advertising are known. Printing costs are usually incurred under long-term contracts, so no element of uncertainty appears here. The only other element is the editorial one. Since most or all of the editorial staff will be paid fixed salaries, no uncertainty exists here. If the certainty theory is to be used, profit should be recognized at the time the subscription is sold. Among the currently used theories, only the completed contract theory explains the present practice.

Under the critical function theory we must determine whether sales of magazines, sales of advertising, or production of the magazines is the critical function. Without good advertising contracts, the firm cannot prosper. Since advertising rates are based on circulation, sales of magazines seems all important. However, unless the editorial work pleases the subscriber, he soon will fail to renew his subscription. The readers' response will be felt much more quickly in newsstand sales. Choice as to which of these functions is the critical one may well not be unanimous. If it is agreed that editorial work is critical and that editorial work culminates in publication, then the current practice is appropriate.

Lending agencies (banks, small loan companies, etc.) generally recognize profit over the period a loan is outstanding. When the note is discounted at the inception of the loan, the banker has, in a sense, collected the fee in advance. The fact that this fee is called interest might lead the unwary to assume that it should be spread over the period, because the payment is based on time. However, closer inspection shows that the theory behind the lending agency's recognition of gross income over the period of the loan is that many expenses (particularly interest paid or money loaned out and collection and bookkeeping expenses) are spread fairly evenly over the loan period. If expenses of setting up the loan are also spread over the collection period or are minor, the matching of revenue and expenses is well done. The resulting net income is spread over the loan period. In a sense, the situation is somewhat comparable to the contractor and magazine publisher in that the customer has been "sold" at the beginning and only rendering of service is left to be performed. Profit is taken up as each piece of the service contract is completed. However, a fundamental difference exists: the manufacturer and banker have different responsibilities after "sale." The manufacturer or publisher must incur many costs to complete the service to the buyers. The banker's role is much more passive; he has only to wait for payments in the normal order of business.

The current practice of recognizing income during the period the loan is outstanding does not seem to agree with the critical function idea. The only things happening while the loan is outstanding are (1) the money borrowed to lend is incurring interest charges and (2) the economic situation is changing, especially as regards the borrower and his ability to pay. If the loan requires periodic payments there is an additional bookkeeping function. Perhaps in individual cases the critical function is the decision to loan or not to loan. If that is so, profit probably is earned at that time even though collection and exact determination of the amount might be delayed quite some time. This delay is, I am sure, one of the reasons profit is measured over the life of a loan. The service-rendered concept might be another reason for accruing profit over the life of a loan, but my experience is that the borrower receives the greatest service at the time he gets the money. Many merchants selling on the installment plan recognize all profit at time of sale of the merchandise and set up adequate reserves for loss. Their situation is only slightly different from that of a lending agency. The goods are sold and the loan is made in a single transaction. In the merchant's case, more rests upon this event than does in the case of merely making a loan. Nevertheless, a satisfactory or unsatisfactory lending policy, it seems to me, is the one thing that makes loans profitable or unprofitable.

A company owning and renting real estate presents an interesting case. Typically, rents are taken into income in the period to which the rent applies. Expenses are recognized as incurred. A major function of such a firm is providing various building services though payment of taxes, insurance, and the costs of maintenance, heat, and elevator operation. Rental of small dwelling units on a month-to-month basis is very different from rental of large areas for manufacturing or office use. Not only may more service be required for commercial purposes, but also the term of the lease will probably be considerably longer so that the tenant may feel justified in making many improvements to suit his operations. Even though the lease term may be short, there will be a strong presumption to renew because of the large expenses of moving. Under these circumstances, is profit really earned merely by serving the present tenants? When a major tenant occupying a whole floor or two is secured or lost, it would seem a renting firm would have real cause for a feeling of profitability or loss thereof. I would suspect the agent securing a long-term tenant would be well paid in recognition of his great service to the real estate company. The critical function theory would seem to demand that all profit for the term of the lease be recognized at this time. Practical difficulties of determining the ultimate profit from such a contract are large. The basic cause of the problem is the custom of determining profit at least annually. Although this custom is the root of the whole problem discussed in this paper, the problem is larger here because of the length of term of the contract. The practical difficulties of applying the theory in this case must not be the cause of rejecting the theory. If the critical function theory should be correct theoretically, then we must strive to find a way to apply it to the practical situation.

The theory of the critical event as the moment at which to recognize profit or loss on a transaction seems very useful. In the types of business which we have considered, it rather closely matches current practice and gives insight into the true nature of the business. It is a theory based on a fundamental economic process rather than upon such frequently used rationalizations as convenience, conservatism, certainty, tax timing, and legal passage of title. This theory may, at first, seem a radical departure from current practice. Upon further thought it does not seem so different. Perhaps this critical event theory will be rejected in favor of another, but the present status of relying upon many different theories of when to match revenue and expense cannot long stand in a profession. We need to give special attention to the development of a single theory for the timing of profit recognition.

Installment Accounting: Is It Inconsistent?

Richard A. Scott
University of Virginia

Rita K. Scott
Director of Finance, City of Charlottesville, Virginia

The installment method of accounting has been with us for a long time.[1] It is most commonly associated with the retail trade, being an outgrowth of the merchandising tactic, "Buy now—pay later." Just prior to World War II, installment credit to consumers (excluding cash loans and mortgages) was $3.7 billion. By mid-1978 it had exceeded $225 billion.[2] The sheer size and skyrocketing growth of installment selling, in conjunction with the corresponding practice of determining income that was customarily employed by retailers, created an awkward situation for the accounting profession. Recognizing profit piecemeal as cash was collected rather than at the time of sale was a flagrant contravention of the realization principle. In 1932, the Ameri-

From *Journal of Accountancy* (November 1979), pp. 52–59. Reprinted with permission of the American Institute of Certified Public Accountants, Inc. Copyright © 1979 by the American Institute of Certified Public Accountants, Inc. Opinions of the authors are their own and do not necessarily reflect policies of the AICPA.

[1] See, for example, William A. Paton, *Accounting Theory* (Lawrence, Kans.: Scholars Book Co., 1973), pp. 448–49. Originally published in 1922.

[2] United States Department of Commerce, *Survey of Current Business*, July 1978.

can Institute of Accountants (now the American Institute of CPAs) committee on cooperation with stock exchanges stated that

> Profit is deemed to be realized when a sale in the ordinary course of business is effected, unless the circumstances are such that the collection of the sale price is not reasonably assured.[3]

In 1934, the Institute's membership adopted this principle and it remains in force today. By comparison, the installment method of accounting was incongruous. There appeared to be little theoretical justification for permitting some firms to defer profit recognition when the earning process was substantially completed, a legal contract had been executed and customers' accounts were generally beyond reproach or at least within the realm of estimating collectibility. Certainly it might have been argued that collection of the sales price was not reasonably assured in these cases, making them legitimate exceptions to the rule. But then why would sellers consistently engage in many sales transactions where only an unreasonable level of assurance of collection existed? And how would they objectively distinguish them from other reasonable-level-of-assurance sales?

This episode was brought to its inevitable conclusion in 1966. The Accounting Principles Board summarily disposed of installment basis accounting by proclaiming that it was no longer to be considered a member in good standing of generally accepted accounting principles:

> The Board reaffirms this statement [quoted above]; it believes that revenues should ordinarily be accounted for at the time a transaction is completed, with appropriate provision for uncollectible accounts. Accordingly, it concludes that, in the absence of the circumstances referred to above, the installment method of recognizing revenue is not acceptable.[4]

The truth of the matter, however, is that the installment method of accounting is still alive. It is reviving and has been gaining strength. In subsequent parts of this article we trace the rebirth of this aberrant accounting method. In the process we also examine its underlying rationale. By the time our journey is finished we will have been led to the inexorable conclusion that the installment method of accounting is an illogical and contradictory concept that ought to be discarded.

A TINY FOOTNOTE

Installment basis accounting lives on by virtue of an exception contained in microscopic lettering at the bottom of a page. We are told that there will be

---

[3] Committee on Accounting Procedure, Accounting Research Bulletin no. 43, *Restatement and Revision of Accounting Research Bulletins* (New York: American Institute of Accountants, 1953), chap. 1, sec. A, par. 1.

[4] Accounting Principles Board Opinion no. 10, *Omnibus Opinion—1966* (New York: AICPA, 1967), par. 12.

circumstances requiring the services of an invalid accounting procedure. APB Opinion No. 10, *Omnibus Opinion—1966*, left this possibility open by stating

> The Board recognizes that there are exceptional cases where receivables are collectible over an extended period of time and, because of the terms of the transactions or other conditions, there is no reasonable basis for estimating the degree of collectibility. When such circumstances exist, and as long as they exist, either the installment method or the cost recovery method of accounting may be used.[5]

The issue lay dormant until the early 1970s. It emerged from quiescence, awakened by the crisis in financial reporting for franchising operations and retail land sales. Both cases were characterized by small cash down payments and a protracted transaction period. Often, both buyers and sellers were operating without benefit of a historical backdrop in these sorts of undertakings.

ANSWERING THE CALL

Franchisors would sell not only a franchise but a potpourri of related services and assets as well. For starters they might assist in selecting a site or in conducting a feasibility study of a location. They were ready with financing arrangements and would stand at a franchisee's side in negotiating a lease. In later phases they would provide physical facility designs, supervise construction and be suppliers of furnishings and equipment. Finally, when operations were under way, management training, quality control and advertising programs would be made available. The gamut of commitments made by franchisors was widespread in scope, drawn out in time and steeped in uncertainty—factors that would prove troublesome, as the future soon revealed. Complicating matters a bit more, "many contracts have been written to distinctly favor the franchisor. Typically such contracts [were] specific in detailing obligations of the franchisee, but ambiguous regarding obligations of the franchisor or rights of the franchisee."[6]

In return for the franchise a modest down payment ordinarily was accepted along with a long-term note for the balance. Often these notes either did not bear interest or interest was set at an inordinately low rate. The franchise fee in total would then be recorded as revenue ("front-end loading") without regard for the franchisee's ability to pay or the franchisor's capacity to fulfill its promises to perform. "Little or no provision for collection and cancellation losses were being made."[7] Many franchisees and some franchisors subsequently failed, bringing attention to bear on these industry

---

[5] Ibid, ftnt. 8 to par. 12.

[6] P. Ronald Stephenson and Robert G. House, "A Perspective on Franchising," *Business Horizons*, August 1971, p. 38.

[7] Thomas L. Holton and Olden J. Hoover, "The Accountants' Stand on Franchise Reporting," *The New York CPA*, January 1971, p. 50.

accounting practices. The situation as it existed in 1971 was summarily described as follows:

> Considerable public brouhaha currently surrounds the subject of franchising.
> . . . In addition, some franchise organizations are experiencing serious operational and legal problems within the franchisor-franchisee relationship.[8]

In some SEC filings, franchisors were required to leave out earnings per share data and to state in a footnote that omission was because income was from only a few franchise sales and therefore future earnings could not be expected to bear any resemblance to past performance.

In an effort to pour oil on the waters of this maelstrom, the AICPA committee on franchise accounting and auditing issued an industry accounting guide[9] in December 1972. The effect of the committee's recommendations was to postpone revenue recognition until after the sale when the franchisor had "substantially performed" its obligations and the franchisee's operations had commenced. However, the committee at the same time provided that, when no reasonable estimate of collectibility can be made, the installment method of accounting may be used.

A REPEAT PERFORMANCE

Retail land sales companies followed a well-established game plan. They purchased large tracts of unimproved land and proceeded to subdivide them for sale to widely dispersed customers using intensive marketing programs. During the 1950s and 1960s the retail land sales industry developed a tarnished image. Although its image had improved somewhat as the industry moved into the 1970s, it was still far from pristine. *Business Week*, for example, described member firms as being "notorious for high pressure salesmanship" and characterized their methods as "unsavory."[10] Their efforts were concentrated on persuading customers to commit themselves in writing—usually in the form of a land sales contract—to the purchase of a parcel of land. A minimal down payment of as low as 1 percent of the price was accepted, with the remainder plus interest due to the seller over an extended period. The note receivable was routinely accepted by the land company on the basis of the purchaser's personal credit without a credit check being made. Within a prescribed time the buyer might cancel his purchase contract and demand a refund of the down payment under an escape clause in the Truth in Lending Act.

In the event that contract payments were defaulted, the buyer forfeited both land and accumulated equity but was generally able to free himself from

---

[8] Stephenson and House, "A Perspective on Franchising," p. 35.

[9] Committee on Franchise Accounting and Auditing, Industry Accounting Guide, *Accounting for Franchise Fee Revenue* (New York: AICPA, 1973).

[10] "Accounting for Premature Profits," *Business Week*, January 23, 1971, p. 87 and "Land-Sales Companies Refigure Their Books," *Business Week*, May 12, 1973, p. 80.

the balance due. Land sales companies could not seek specific performance or deficiency judgments under the law in these cases and, as a practical matter, were usually content to keep the whole affair quiet rather than alarm prospective buyers. Many buyers did in fact default as well as cancel their contracts.

Land development companies offered to do more than simply carve out parcels from large land tracts. They made some improvements (roads, grading) to the land immediately and promised numerous others ("amenities" such as golf courses, swimming pools and recreation centers). Unfortunately, some companies compounded the tenuousness of retail land sales even further by reneging on their promises to make future improvements.

Again an AICPA committee was established in response to a crisis.[11] Revenue had been recognized by land companies under any of a variety of methods, including complete accrual when the contract was signed, despite the risks associated with collection and the substantial costs yet to be incurred. The committee's directive was to defer revenue recognition until several specified conditions were met which indicated that a buyer seemed committed to completing the contract and the seller appeared able to carry out the promised improvements. Until such time the contract was to be treated as a deposit and as such would be a liability until circumstances made revenue recognition appropriate. Another set of criteria was then stipulated which was to be used in deciding whether to apply the accrual method of accounting. If these were not satisfied, the land company was required to use the installment method of accounting. When the criteria were met after installment basis accounting had commenced, the switch to accrual was to be made in that period and treated as a change in estimate.[12] Installment basis accounting by now had entrenched itself in the accountant's repertoire once again and continued its ascendancy.

OTHER APPLICATIONS

Other real estate transactions were being passed off for sales even though they were something else beneath the surface. Financing, leasing and profit-sharing arrangements were being clothed as real estate sales. A transaction that in legal form was a sale might in economic substance be:

- A construction contract.
- A contract for services for a fee.
- A lease for use of product or property.
- An agreement to loan or borrow funds.

[11] Committee on Land Development Companies, Industry Accounting Guide, *Accounting for Retail Land Sales* (New York: AICPA, 1973).

[12] The AICPA accounting standards division expressed its belief that a switch in methods was not a change in accounting principles. Statement of Position 78-4, *Application of the Deposit, Installment, and Cost Recovery Methods in Accounting for Sales of Real Estate* (New York: AICPA, 1978), p. 10.

- An agreement establishing a joint venture.
- An agreement to divide profits in a specified ratio.
- A deposit on or an option to purchase the asset.
- A sale of something (e.g., depreciation deductions) other than the asset that is the object of the sale.

The AICPA committee on accounting for real estate transactions attacked the problem of profit recognition for all kinds of real estate dealings not covered in the industry accounting guide for retail land sales. In the industry accounting guide[13] entitled *Accounting for Profit Recognition on Sales of Real Estate*, it was concluded that a sale was to be recorded as such only when certain circumventing provisions were absent. Furthermore, accrual of revenue at the time of sale was to take place only when a substantial down payment (25 percent of the sales value of the property is usually sufficient, and it may be lower with less risky properties) was received and subsequent annual payments were scheduled by contract to service the balance due (over 20 years in the case of land and, for other types of real estate, the usual term of a first mortgage loan). If the buyer failed to demonstrate a sufficient initial and continuing investment, revenue recognition was to take place according to the timing prescribed by other accounting techniques. The attendant circumstances would dictate the appropriate alternative from among those available: deposit, cost recovery or installment methods.

In 1976, the Financial Accounting Standards Board issued its standard on accounting for leases. A portion of that document was devoted to leases that were in substance dealer-manufacturer sales arrangements. When a dealer or manufacturer sells or assigns a lease with recourse to a third party, any profit or loss is to be deferred and recognized over the lease term in a systematic manner.[14] That is, as the lessee-purchaser makes periodic payments, the dealer or manufacturer recognizes a portion of the deferred profit or loss. What we have is installment basis accounting in the midst of a three-party transaction. The same treatment is also accorded direct financing leases where the lessor sells a leased asset, with recourse, to a third party.[15]

Throughout the years when the stature of the installment method of accounting was waning and then rejuvenating, the Internal Revenue Service unabatedly considered it an acceptable reporting technique.[16] Section 453(a) permits dealers in personal property who regularly sell on the installment plan to report profits pro rata over the contract term as cash is received. Sec. 453(b) afforded the same opportunity to sellers of real property as long as payments received in the year of sale did not exceed 30 percent of the sales

[13] Committee on Accounting for Real Estate Transactions, Industry Accounting Guide, *Accounting for Profit Recognition on Sales of Real Estate* (New York: AICPA, 1973).
[14] Statement of Financial Accounting Standards, no. 13, *Accounting for Leases* (Stamford, Conn.: FASB, 1976), par. 20.
[15] Ibid.
[16] *Internal Revenue Code* (Chicago: Commerce Clearing House, 1978), sec. 453.

price. Casual sales of personal property for a price exceeding $1,000 were also included under part (b) of the code section. It is commonplace to apply the installment method of accounting when determining tax liability while at the same time accruing revenue in the year of sale for financial reporting purposes. These disparate treatments cause timing differences which require the interperiod allocation of taxes.[17] The rationale of the IRS is to levy taxes when a taxpayer has the cash to make payment. They are not concerned with the proprieties of income determination. Accountants are concerned, however, and ought to scrutinize accounting methods and question their legitimacy.

Not-for-profit entities employing a cash or modified accrual basis of accounting have somewhat of a tendency to regard an asset's valuation as being equal to the cash paid to acquire it. Several cases have come to the attention of the authors where an asset being purchased on an installment payment plan was capitalized in installments. Only when the asset was completely paid for did its total cost finally emerge.

INQUIRING INTO THE THEORY

An installment sale occurs when a contract is signed calling for the purchaser to make (usually equal) payments in accordance with a plan. A protracted schedule of principal and interest payments is a necessary condition if the installment method of accounting is to be employed. When it is, gross profit on the sale is deferred. Each cash payment made toward the principal, including the initial down payment, is then considered to represent a partial recovery of product cost and an element of profit in the same proportion as these two components held in the original total sales price. For example, an item held for resale cost a dealer $900 and had been marked to sell for $1,500. It was sold on January 2, 1978, and an installment contract was signed which called for 36 monthly payments, each due on the first of the month. In 1978 cash collections from this contract were $500[18] and realized gross profit, $200. On December 31, 1978, the installment receivable had a balance of $1,000 and deferred gross profit was $400. The total gross profit is 40 percent of the sales price ($600/$1,500). As each dollar unit of the sales price is collected it is seen as returning $.60 of product cost to the seller and $.40 of profit. Therefore, 1978 cash collections, which represent $500 of the original sales price dollars, also represent $300 of product cost recovery ($.60 × 500) and $200 of profit ($.40 × 500). Every dollar of sales price collected from a customer is looked on

---

[17] Accounting Principles Board Opinion no. 11, *Accounting for Income Taxes* (New York: AICPA, 1967), par. 15a.

[18] In this illustration, interest has been omitted for sake of simplicity. This omission has no effect on the concept in question nor any bearing on the conclusions to which we are led. Including interest would merely alter the pattern of principal amounts included in each equal payment. Instead of being equal in amount as in the illustration above, they would increase gradually as the total debt diminished over time.

individually as being composed of two elements: product cost and profit. Both elements are contained in every dollar collected in proportions that remain unchanged throughout the contract's term.

IN DEFENSE OF THE METHOD

As we have already seen, deferral and piecemeal recognition of profit find support in the federal tax code, which makes it possible for a seller to postpone tax payments until cash is received. Another reason offered in support of the installment method is that profit reporting conforms to the timing of cash flows and, consequently, to the availability of funds for dividend distribution. It is also argued that often there are substantial expenses of collection and administration to be incurred after the sale and that installment recognition of profit permits a matching of income with these expenses. Finally, proponents of the installment method point out that the risk and uncertainty associated with these transactions is far greater than with ordinary credit sales. The collectibility of installment receivables is at question by virtue of the protracted pay-out period, and a "contingent loss" may have occurred.[19] If it is probable that receivables have been impaired and the amount of the loss is estimable, an accrual is required.[20] However, if there is significant uncertainty as to collection and an inability to estimate the loss, accrual is precluded and some other method of revenue recognition such as the installment method or cost recovery method ought to be used.[21] Therefore, employing the installment method of accounting necessarily implies both that significant uncertainty as to collection exists and that the loss cannot be measured. Presumably, these circumstances may be present when accounting for franchisors, land development companies, other sellers of real estate and certain lessors since the installment method has been invoked in response to each situation.

ANALYZING THE DEFENSE

Let us analyze each of these arguments supportive of the installment method of accounting.

Tax Code Support

Unquestionably, benefit may be gained by a taxpayer if the installment method is used for determining taxable income. But that benefit can still be

---

[19] Statement of Financial Accounting Standards no. 5, *Accounting for Contingencies* (Stamford, Conn.: FASB, 1975), par. 1.
[20] Ibid., par. 8.
[21] Ibid., par. 23.

enjoyed no matter how income is determined for financial reporting purposes and, consequently, is not germane to the issue.

Profit Timing Conforms to Cash Flows

This proposition supports the idea that income ought to be recognized so as to conform its timing to cash flows and dividend requirements. Carrying this proposal to its logical conclusion, accrual accounting ought to be abandoned in favor of cash accounting. It appears that the concerns expressed in such an idea have more to do with cash management than with the measurement of income.

Post-Sale Matching

The desire to accomplish matching is offered as an explanation by those who would defer income to offset subsequent costs of administration, collection and improvements construction. These post-sale costs can be material amounts to the seller. The deferral process does not, however, result in a proper matching of expenses with revenue. Not only is revenue being deferred when the installment method is applied, but product cost as well, and the latter has nothing to do with subsequent time periods. Moreover, most selling or administrative costs already incurred are not deferred,[22] thereby leaving the logic of this argument incomplete.

Rather than contributing to an improved matching of revenues and expenses, the installment method can seriously distort the income measurement process. Take, for example, land sales made under a seller's promise to substantially improve the property in a later period.

"In many projects, neither purchaser nor seller expects the lot to be used for any purpose until completion of payment, and therefore some or all of the promised improvements are deferred until later in or after the payment period."[23]

If improvements are undertaken after payment by the purchaser is complete, there will be no deferred income left to reflect in those time periods when the final phase of the earnings process is taking place. All of the deferred income will have been recognized in preceding periods when the cash was collected.[24] It is unlikely that the payment schedule, which in effect establishes the amount of income realized in each time period, is designed with regard for the timing and relative amounts of after-sale expenses that require revenue for matching.

---

[22] Certain direct selling costs are to be deferred by land development companies. Indirect selling costs and administrative costs are charged to the period incurred. See: *Accounting for Retail Land Sales*, par. 43b,c.

[23] Committee on Land Development Companies, *Accounting for Retail Land Sales*, par. 6.

[24] A provision for future improvements costs is included in determining the deferred income. However, the "Liability for Future Improvements" account is based on estimated cost only.

A question arises concerning the proper assignment of revenues to time periods with respect to interest on the note taken on retail land sales. If a sale is recorded by the accrual method, the note receivable is normally discounted to a present value using an imputed interest rate that is higher than the nominal rate. The resulting valuation allowance is thereafter reported as a reduction of the note receivable and systematically amortized to income so that a constant rate of return on the note is experienced. If, on the other hand, the installment method is employed, the nominal rate of the note is accepted as it stands, with the result that interest earned is relatively smaller in amount, both period-by-period and in the aggregate.

Now presumably the land sales company will have certain administrative expenses in subsequent periods when interest is collected, against which the interest revenue will be matched. The implications of different amounts of interest earned that stem from using the two accounting methods are that either there are correspondingly different amounts of administrative expenses or that a smaller profit margin is a natural corollary to use of the installment method. Why either possibility might be so is not clear. However, what is clear is that the installment method, which is enlisted when a more risky transaction is entered into, results in a lower interest rate than the accrual method, which normally characterizes a less risky situation. This incongruous outcome is contrary to the way that lenders ordinarily operate wherein interest rates rise as risk increases.

Another peculiar by-product of the installment method of accounting is how it affects the measure of income over the series of periods when cash is collected. Because of level payments on notes that include a shrinking interest element and an increasing principal component, profit recognition will actually increase as time moves on. A certain portion of each dollar of principal collected is considered realized income. Therefore, as principal amounts of each level payment increase over time, so too will realized income. It is apparent that the proper matching of income to time periods was hardly a consideration when a note's terms were designed.

Unestimable Uncertainty

Finally, let us examine the installment method and its inherent assumptions in light of the conditions under which it is brought into play. We have already observed that the installment method is deemed justified when significant uncertainty as to collectibility exists and losses cannot be measured. This is an indispensable precondition. There is so much doubt and risk surrounding the transaction that accrual accounting is inadequate to deal with it.

Let us return for a moment to the illustration given earlier. In it we witnessed that every dollar of sales price collected from a customer is looked on as being made up of product cost recovery and profit. Each dollar represented $.60 of product cost being recovered by the seller and $.40 of profit. In 1978, $200 of profit was recognized. But this representation is true only under one condition. It is true only if every single dollar of the $1,500 sales price is collected. If a lesser amount is collected, the profit will be correspondingly reduced (offset by the value of repossessed collateral) and, at some point, even wiped out completely. Were $1,200 ultimately collected, profit would be $300, or $.25 on the dollar. If only $900 were recovered, there would be no profit. Only on conclusion of the contract, when all $600 of profit has been collected, can we contend that $.40 of every sales dollar represents profit. When the installment method is used, a representation is made which can only be true if the proposition on which it is founded is false. Only if we are absolutely certain that the total sales price will be collected and the installment receivable is risk-free should the assertion be made that every dollar has a profit component. In other words, the fundamental premise underlying the method contradicts the condition of great risk and uncertainty which justified its use in the first place.

CONCLUSIONS

What must we conclude? If an installment receivable is so shrouded in doubt as to render accrual accounting ineffectual, it would seem that the only reasonable procedure to follow is to view every dollar received as representing product cost until the total is recovered. Thereafter, recognition of profit would be appropriate. This is still a less than satisfactory solution. For one thing, what is the nature of a deferred income account? It certainly isn't a liability although it may be classified as such on the balance sheet. In financial reporting for retail land sales under the installment method, deferred income is to be deducted from the note receivable balance with only the remainder being shown as the asset's valuation. But what exactly does such a remainder represent? The balance that is left after several payments have been received on the notes is even more enigmatic than at the outset. It is not the estimated collectible balance of the notes, their discounted present value or the land's value or cost. What meaning can a banker, for example, attach to these balances? And, in addition, if some form of net asset valuation is the objective, why preclude offsetting the note receivable with a deferred income tax balance that arises when the accrual method is used for financial reporting and the installment method for tax reporting?

It is questionable that accrual accounting must be set aside because accountants are unable to satisfactorily estimate doubtful installment receivables. They have proved themselves able to cope with too many extremely difficult estimation problems in the past to warrant such a conclusion. The installment method of accounting is illogical, internally inconsistent and riddled with flaws. It ought to be abandoned as an acceptable accounting practice; abandoned entirely and unequivocally.

The FASB has now taken the responsibility for dealing with the specialized accounting and reporting principles and practices in current AICPA industry accounting and audit guides and statements of position. It is hoped that the FASB will seriously reconsider any of the authoritative literature that sanctions installment basis accounting, including the currently outstanding industry accounting guides.

Claiming Tomorrow's Profits Today

Penelope Wang
Forbes

Last February Jiffy Lube International, a Baltimore-based franchiser of quick-oil-change centers (fiscal 1988 revenues, $78 million), was ordered by the Securities & Exchange Commission to change its accounting. The surprise order resulted in a staggering earnings hit for the first quarter of Jiffy's 1989 fiscal year: net income of $95,000, less than 25% of what Jiffy would have reported. Why the SEC order? Because the commission said Jiffy was claiming income it hadn't yet earned.

Over the past two years, the SEC has made similar charges against about half a dozen other fast-growing startups in the franchise field. Among them: Moto Photo, Inc., Swensen's Inc. and Le Peep Restaurants, Inc.

The accounting issue involves the tricky problem of revenue recognition from the sale of so-called area development rights. These are contracts that are sold by the company granting a developer the exclusive right to open franchises in a particular territory. In return, the developer traditionally pays the company a nonrefundable fee up front.

For years some franchisors have been reporting these upfront fees as current income. But the SEC argues that the increasing complexity of the contracts no longer makes doing so permissible. These days, area developers are often required to open a certain number of stores within a set time period. In some cases, the franchisor also agrees to provide training and advertising support services to the developer. By imposing such conditions on the agreement, the SEC argues, the franchisor changes the nature of the fee paid in the deal.

The SEC's position is based on two long-held accounting principles: Revenue must be earned in order to be recognized; and costs must be matched with revenues as they are earned. Says Peter Knutson, associate professor of accounting at the Wharton School: "If some effort or sacrifice isn't put forth, then the revenue hasn't been earned."

In publishing, for example, magazines collect fees for subscriptions up front, but until the magazine publishes those future issues, the money cannot be recognized as revenue. Instead, the funds must be recorded as a balance sheet liability, often labeled "unearned income." When the issues are published, the revenues are taken into income and the costs of publishing are deducted.

In the case of area development fees, the SEC argues that companies have not truly earned the revenues until the franchise units are open and operating. Moreover, the SEC argues that franchise companies sometimes use area development fees to meet the costs of servicing the developer, and therefore that this income should not be recognized until the costs are incurred as well.

One of the first companies to draw the attention of the SEC to this issue was Le Peep Restaurants, a Denver-based brunch chain, which filed for an initial public offering in mid-1986. Originally the company planned to sell about 1.7 million shares at up to $10 per share. But after the SEC determined that Le Peep had overstated income from area development fees, the company had to revise its financials. As a result, Le Peep's offering was delayed and the company sold only 1.3 million shares at 6½. [Currently the stock is selling at a bid price of 1¾.]

Not surprisingly, the SEC's position has dismayed the franchise industry. "The economic substance of the transaction—selling exclusive rights to develop an area—is being ignored," contends David Mason, executive vice president of Moto Photo. Agrees Ronald Diegelman, a partner at Ernst & Whinney: "It seems unreasonable to say that the right of exclusivity does not have real value."

But the SEC rightly responds that the right of exclusivity has value up front only when it is granted to a developer without conditions. If an agreement says, for instance, that a franchisee must open ten stores in five years in order to preserve his exclusivity rights, then the exclusive right should have value only as the stores are actually opened.

Franchisors complain that the SEC's position will particularly hurt startup companies, which depend on area development agreements to attract sophisticated entrepreneurs to their businesses, as well as to provide them with much-needed cash. "In the long run, this could have a major financial impact," says Neil A. Simon, counsel for the International Franchise Association.

That way overstates the case. After all, fee income will still be realizable—just not up front all at once. In fact, the SEC's position may well have a salutary long-term effect in preventing small franchisors from trying to grow too quickly. In any case, this seems to be one area in which the SEC, much criticized in recent years for its dozing oversight of the securities markets, is proving itself both wide awake and on the ball.

CHAPTER 5

Integrating Uncertainty Into Accounting: Receivables and Contingencies

In the 1970s, issues of uncertainty surrounding receivables began to be raised in standard-setting circles and in the accounting literature. The confidence that financial institutions had in the collectibility of their loan receivables was shaken in 1973–1974, when the City of New York seemed to be at the brink of defaulting on its payments of interest and principal to major banks throughout the United States. In a climate of crisis, the creditor banks "restructured" New York City's troubled debt, by agreeing, in the main, to a postponement of the city's principal payments to points further in the future. At the same time, the Financial Accounting Standards Board inquired whether such a restructuring meant that the banks' receivables should be written down to lower present (or current) value.

At a public hearing held by the Financial Accounting Standards Board (FASB) on the issue, Walter B. Wriston, the chairman of Citicorp and the most influential banker in the country, jarred his audience by declaring that,

> "If the banks that held the New York City obligations had been required to record an immediate write-off of say, 25 percent of principal as a result of restructuring, that restructuring just might not have happened."[1]

Wriston added that future restructurings might be in jeopardy if the Board were to adopt a standard requiring that restructured receivables be stated at current values. The banking industry proceeded to lobby the FASB not to require a new basis of accounting for restructured receivables. Finally, in 1977 the FASB issued Statement No. 15, "Accounting by Debtors and Creditors for Troubled Debt Restructurings," in which it did not require a writedown of receivables in the event of a restructuring involving a modification of terms (i.e., where the principal payments by the debtor were postponed) unless the

---

[1] Testimony of Walter B. Wriston, Transcript of Public Hearing on FASB Discussion Memorandum on Accounting by Debtors and Creditors When Debt is Restructured (1977, Volume 1, Part 2), pp. 69–70.

sum of the debtor's interest and principal payments would be less than the recorded amount of the receivable. (para. 31) This Statement, which passed by the minimum majority of 5 to 2, in effect employed a standard of undiscounted future cash flows for determining the amount of a loss or gain. It allowed financial institutions to engage in restructurings without the need to give accounting recognition to any of the economic loss that all parties would have acknowledged was confirmed by the restructuring transaction. Statement No. 15 is, we believe, the most lamentable statement ever issued by the FASB, and in the 1980s it served as a source of support to which the regulators and auditors of U.S. financial institutions could point when, as a result of restructurings, they accepted the practice of leaving receivables at their recorded values. Statement No. 15 did not represent a sound approach to coping with uncertainty relating to financial institutions' restructured loan receivables.[2].

Another FASB statement that deals with uncertainties is No. 5, "Accounting for Contingencies," which was issued in March 1975. Its principal concerns were: loss contingencies resulting from overstated asset values, the uncertain effects of contingent obligations entered into by the company (e.g., product warranties and guarantees of other entities' indebtedness), and the risks of loss from lawsuits, government expropriations, or Acts of God. The FASB identified two conditions that justified loss recognition: that it is probable that an asset has been impaired or a liability has been incurred, and that the amount of the loss can be reasonably estimated. Both conditions had to be met.

In part, Statement No. 5 was a reaction to the practice by some companies of accruing losses that could be expected to materialize from the ordinary run of risks and uncertainties to which businesses are exposed. Some companies would accrue vague "losses from contingencies," while others had opted to cancel their insurance coverage and instead become "self-insurers" with respect to possible losses from fires, floods, earthquakes, volcanic eruptions, tornadoes, hurricanes or typhoons, or other Acts of God. In each period in which the "loss" was accrued, an entry such as the following might be made:

Expected Loss from Acts of God 1,000,000
Reserve for Self-Insurance 1,000,000

When such a loss actually occurred, the book value of the assets actually destroyed would be charged to the reserve account, and the company's reported profits for the period would be unaffected. Self-insurance, many

---

[2] In June 1992, the FASB issued an exposure draft, "Accounting by Creditors for Impairment of a Loan," in which it proposed to require that, in instances of restructurings involving a modification of terms, a receivable should be remeasured at fair value, by discounting total future cash flows "at a market interest rate commensurate with the risks involved." (para. 16) In February 1993, the Board retreated to the use of the interest rate implicit in the original loan contract, instead of the market interest rate. In May 1993, Statement No. 114 confirmed this position over the objection of two dissenters.

argued, was a means of "smoothing" profits and thus of protecting a period's results from the distorting effects of a single, devastating Act of God.

In the annual survey of 600 major companies' financial statements conducted by the American Institute of Certified Public Accountants, the practice of maintaining self-insurance reserves was already on the decline during the 1960s, from 78 companies in 1960 to 45 in 1969.[3] Among the large companies that, at one time, used the practice, were General Motors, U.S. Steel, Johns-Manville, A&P, National Gypsum, F.W. Woolworth, and International Paper.

One of the questions raised in regard to general loss accruals was the proper balance-sheet classification of the reserve: are they liabilities, shareholders' equity, or "what-you-may-call-its"?[4]

Over the years, there has been a lively debate over whether such accruals are a part of sound accounting. The classic argument against such accruals was given by the late Professor William A. Paton (1889–1991) in 1971. Paton, who was one of the most respected U.S. accounting academics from the 1920s to the 1980s, argues, in "Do Casualties Accrue?," that "self-insurance" is a misnomer and that casualty losses are properly given accounting recognition only upon the actual occurrence of the casualty.

In a 1987 article, "Self-Insurance Should be Accrued," Jack F. Truitt and Thomas R. Nunamaker, two accounting academics, marshal several arguments in favor of recognizing self-insurance losses. They cite the "tremendous growth of self-insurance that has been caused by the lack of available or affordable insurance coverage" as justification that the FASB reconsider its position on self-insurance. Among the issues they raise is whether, as under FASB Statement No. 5, shareholders at the time a casualty befalls a company should "have to bear the entire brunt of the loss while from an economic perspective both past and future shareholders should bear a portion of it."

The impact of FASB Statement Nos. 5 and 15 on the incidence of loan loss recognition by financial institutions is treated in the short article, " 'RAP-Man'—It's Devouring GAAP," by Gilbert Simonetti, Jr. and Andrea R. Andrews. RAP stands for Regulatory Accounting Principles, which were invented by bank and thrift regulators in order to cushion the accounting impact of financial adversity on their regulated financial institutions. In the end, the adversities did not disappear in the ensuing weak economy, and the financial vulnerability of the banks and thrifts was laid bare before an unbelieving Congress and public—who were understandably incensed that regulators would allow the accounting facts to be shielded from public view by the instruments of creative accounting.

---

[3] *Accounting Trends & Techniques* (New York: American Institute of Certified Public Accountants, 1970), p. 126.

[4] For the classic article on what-you-may-call-its, see Robert T. Sprouse, "Accounting for What-You-May-Call-Its," *The Journal of Accountancy* (October 1966), pp. 45–53, which was reproduced in volume II of the first edition of this book, published in 1969.

Another application of FASB Statement No. 5 deals with pending litigation, and the late Edward B. Deakin (1943–1992), in "Accounting for Contingencies: The Pennzoil-Texaco Case," illustrates how parties on opposite sides of the largest dollar value lawsuit in U.S. legal history interpreted their respective obligations to disclose the contingent outcomes. The differences in the nature and timing of their disclosures were attributable, in some degree, to whether they were anticipating a gain or a loss.

Probably the most daunting class of contingencies, both in terms of measurement and disclosure, relates to potential environmental liabilities. In "Messy Accounting," from *Forbes*, one gains some impression of the reporting difficulties confronting companies that are faced with environmental risks. The FASB's Statement No. 5 is cited in the article as the "applicable accounting rule," but its criteria are not easy to apply to such ill-defined contingencies.

BIBLIOGRAPHICAL NOTES

Two FASB discussion memoranda summarized the issues and cited relevant literature on restructured receivables/payables and on loss contingencies:

Accounting by Debtors and Creditors When Debt is Restructured (Financial Accounting Standards Board, May 11, 1976).

An Analysis of Issues Related to Accounting for Future Losses (Financial Accounting Standards Board, March 13, 1974).

An FASB research study on the effect of Statement No. 5 on companies' risk and insurance management decisions, with particular attention to companies that had used self-insurance reserves before the promulgation of the statement, is as follows:

Goshay, Robert C.: *Statement of Financial Accounting Standards No. 5: Impact on Corporate Risk and Insurance Management* (Financial Accounting Standards Board, October 1978).

A Canadian research study that considers the implications for accounting of risk and uncertainty is

Boritz, J. E.: *Approaches to Dealing with Risk and Uncertainty* (Toronto: Canadian Institute of Chartered Accountants, 1990).

The following is a volume of proceedings from a conference dealing with the differences between Regulatory Accounting Principles (RAP) and GAAP:

Arnold, Jerry L. (editor): *Proceedings of the October 8, 1987 Roundtable Discussion on Generally Accepted Accounting Principles and Regulatory Accounting Practices* ([Los Angeles:] SEC and Financial Reporting Institute, School of Accounting, University of Southern California, 1988).

An Australian research study on liabilities has addressed issues related to contingencies:

Kerr, Jean St.G.: *The Definition and Recognition of Liabilities*, Accounting Theory Monograph No. 4 (Melbourne: Australian Accounting Research Foundation, 1984).

A discussion of accounting policy issues related to environmental reporting, including a commentary on 20 disclosures in the annual reports of major U.K. companies, is the following:

Butler, David, Ceri Frost and Richard Macve: "Environmental Reporting," in L. C. L. Skerratt and D. J. Tonkin (editors), *Financial Reporting 1991–92: A Survey of UK Reporting Practice* (London: The Institute of Chartered Accountants in England and Wales, 1992), pp. 53–76.

Two publications that treat the diverse impacts of environmental issues on accounting are:

Gray, R. H.: *The Greening of Accountancy: The Profession After Pearce*, Certified Research Report No. 17 (London: Certified Accountant Publications Limited, 1990).
Gray, Rob, and Richard Laughlin (editors): "Green Accounting," special issue of the *Accounting, Auditing & Accountability Journal* (vol. 4, no. 3, 1991).

Do Casualties Accrue?

Willian A. Paton
Late Professor, University of Michigan

The view that losses due to casualties should be predicted, and should be accounted for systematically in periodic income reckonings, continues to be encountered in financial management and accounting circles. This position is often supported by an assumed similarity between the conventional practice of accruing depreciation of plant assets over an estimated service life and a policy of recognizing and spreading the burden of anticipated fires, floods, and other disasters.

I have long taken the position that casualty losses do not *accrue*, in any reasonable sense of the term, and that it is not sound accounting to include in current expenses the estimated impact of calamities that have not occurred as yet—and may indeed never occur. Moreover, I have not been able to find substantial merit in the argument that the accrual of possible fire losses, for example, is on all fours with the established practice of charging the cost or value of structures and equipment to operations, by some reasonable method of allocation, as the capacity to render service is exhausted.

On the ground that where muddy concepts and questionable procedures persist there is a need for continuing emphasis on clear thinking and sound policy, it may be permissible to make a brief restatement of the case for the negative side of the question posed.

TO BE OR NOT TO BE INSURED

To begin with, I'd like to emphasize the serious objection to the misleading label "self-insurance." Use of this term tends to block the door to a sensible, realistic discussion of the treatment of casualty losses. Strictly speaking, there is no such thing as "self-insurance." The basic question that management has to face in a particular situation is: Should we insure or should we not insure? The act of insuring consists of hiring some entity specializing in the field of risk-bearing to assume part or all of the risk of loss by fire or other casualty. (Only where the insurer is financially sound, of course, is the element of risk covered by the contract effectively transferred.) The price paid for this shifting of a risk is the cost of insurance, and is a bona-fide expense of operation—as is the cost of any service deemed necessary. The alternative for the property owner is to shoulder the risk of loss—take his chances. And by deciding not

From *Michigan Business Review* (November 1971), pp. 20–24. Reprinted by permission of the School of Business Administration, The University of Michigan. Copyright © 1971 by the University of Michigan.

to buy protection, the operating entity does not thereby "insure" its assets against losses; instead, it undertakes to get along without insurance, in whole or in part. Thus the first step in dealing with the problem is to get rid of a ridiculous, confusing term.

Certain conditions should, of course, be present to justify minimizing or entirely avoiding the use of casualty insurance. The major requirements are: (1) ownership of a substantial number of units of property subject to damage or destruction by fire or other type of casualty; (2) the value of each unit of such property should not be large relative to total assets or periodic earnings; (3) the units of property should be so located that there is little likelihood of many being damaged or destroyed by a particular fire, flood, tornado, earthquake, or other calamity. With these conditions, a management may well decide *not* to insure or to insure for some minimum amount. If, for example, a particular land company owns 100,000 cedar fence posts, installed on 100 farm tracts scattered over 10 states, a decision by management not to insure the posts against loss by fire would probably be justified. On the other hand, the management of a company owning a chain of fifty hotels and motels with an average value, exclusive of land, of $4,000,000 each, could be criticized for failure to carry fire insurance, even if the properties were in separate locations scattered over the country.

Having a bearing on decisions as to the extent to which risks should be covered by insurance are the possibilities, in some situations, of taking steps to guard against or minimize hazards to which the business is subject. Thus the danger of fire may be abated by installing sprinkler systems, fireproofing roofs, and so on, and flood menace may be limited by building embankments and taking other precautionary measures. Where it is technically and financially practicable to incur expenditures for reducing casualty risks, such costs may be regarded as an alternative to at least a portion of the expense of insurance. It may be added that preventing fire loss, for example, has an inherent advantage over relying on insurance coverage. If an important building burns, the fact that it is insured for full value doesn't spare the insured from the disruption of operation by the casualty. This point needs to be taken into account in considering the cost of the installation of protective devices and all other programs for reducing casualty risks.

COMPARISON OF INSURED
AND UNINSURED CASES

Let's now focus attention directly on the question posed in my title. For this purpose, let's begin by imagining two business concerns, A and B, that are identical as to amount and character of employed resources, and in every other respect (including prevention and abatement measures), except that the management of A remains committed to carrying full casualty insurance while the management of B, after a careful review of the pertinent conditions, has decided to cancel all casualty policies. For simplicity, it will be assumed that the only insurable hazard in both companies is the risk of destruction or damage by fire; and, to have a definite insurance cost figure in view, it will also be assumed that the current annual expenditure required for full fire loss coverage is $50,000. This item of cost will continue to be incurred by A and will be included in operating expenses, but no such expenditure will appear in the records of B. No conclusion need be reached at this point as to which management is on the right track, and there is of course the possibility that there is no net advantage in either course of action.

With these arbitrary conditions, the question at issue becomes: what, if any, periodic charges should appear in the accounts and statements of concern B in lieu of the regular cost of fire insurance? The advocates of "self-insurance"—so-called—generally insist that there should be a regular recognition of some substitute for the expense of casualty insurance. One possibility, sometimes recommended, is to charge to expense the precise amount of the expenditure that would be made if full insurance coverage were continued, or $50,000, with a corresponding credit to an appropriate "reserve." Any actual casualty losses incurred are then charged to the "reserve" account rather than being included in current deductions from revenue. This recommendation, obviously, has little or no merit from the standpoint of effective protection from loss. Assume, to illustrate, that during the year the procedure is initiated, a fire occurs that results in a loss of $150,000. The existence of the "reserve" balance of $50,000 in such circumstances has no significance. Accounting for the loss will require the cancellation of the "reserve" credit and the inclusion of an additional charge of $100,000 in expenses or losses, and the net effect will simply be the recognition of the total loss of $150,000 in two parts. For another possibility, assume that no fire loss whatever occurs during the year. The accounts and statements of B will then show a deduction from income of $50,000, although no expenditures have been made and no loss suffered. Here we come upon the nub of the problem. Is the charge of $50,000 a proper deduction, or is the current net earnings figure understated by this amount, and the total of retained earnings correspondingly understated if the "reserve" balance is excluded therefrom? And those who insist that the deduction is proper are confronted with the interpretation and treatment of the "reserve" credit of $50,000. Are they prepared to regard this balance as some kind of shadowy contra to the existing assets? Presumably, they will hesitate to contend that this item is an outright liability. And to throw it into a limbo of "reserves" of indeterminate character is, of course, equivalent to no decision as to the actual meaning of the account.

Another and somewhat more sophisticated "accrual" procedure is found in the proposal to estimate the average annual fire loss anticipated and to charge this amount to expense year by year, again crediting some kind of "reserve" account. Assume, for example, that a review of the history of our twin companies for the past decade shows that in each concern three losses by fire were suffered totaling $300,000, or an average of $30,000 per year, and that it is reasonable to assume that this average loss is a fair estimate of what may be expected, as an annual average, over the next few years. This method of determining the periodic charge, however, does not cure the difficulties of treatment and interpretation encountered as already pointed out. In other words, changing the amount of the accrual leaves the basic question unresolved.

The conclusion indicated is that if casualty insurance is abandoned as a means of dealing with fire hazard or other risks, the result is a shift from an actual expenditure, which may be readily spread on the basis of policy terms, to the shouldering of losses if and when they occur.

DEPRECIATION PRACTICE AND CASUALTY LOSSES

In the light of the persistence of the idea that accruing prospective casualty losses is a close relative of the practice of accruing depreciation, as mentioned earlier, some comments on this questionable stance are needed.

The propriety of spreading the cost or value of depreciable assets over an assumed period of use, with due attention to probable salvage value at retirement, seems very clear. The alternatives are charging the depreciable amount to operation at date of acquisition, or postponing such action to date of retirement, and such practices—although not unknown—are generally regarded as quite unrealistic, at least for major items. It is true that service lives are often uncertain, conjectural, and in extreme cases the estimates made may be no better than intelligent guesses, but experience shows that business buildings and equipment do have limited periods of use and this requires the assumption that capacity to render service tends to expire as time passes. It is also true that there has been a great deal of discussion and argument regarding the methods of allocation to be employed, and the impact of price changes on the dollar amount to be absorbed in operating costs. But all this is a far cry from accruing the estimated effect of mishaps, calamities, that have not occurred, and which may never be encountered. There are many examples of business concerns, especially among the host of small and medium-sized enterprises, that have never experienced a substantial fire for a half-century or more. Accruals of fire losses through the years in these cases, however labeled, would have simply loaded revenue deductions with spurious charges. On the other hand the need to recognize depreciation systematically is present wherever depreciable resources are employed, in small concerns or in large, and the practice of spreading over the prospective period of use is well established.

The fact is that casualty losses are contingent, although common, and that charging to expense estimated losses that have not been suffered is not at all comparable to a policy of accruing depreciation.

A CLINCHING ILLUSTRATION

I recall a visit I had many years ago with an executive of a major trucking company who was an enthusiast for casualty accrual (and was also addicted to the use of the "self-insurance" description). For some time I made no headway in my effort to make him see the case for nonaccrual. Finally, I cornered him with an example that went somewhat as follows:

> Assume that a trucking company starts in business at the beginning of a year with 1,000 new trucks which cost $6,000,000. On the basis of data compiled by a trade association or some governmental agency, it is estimated that, according to the average for the industry, 5% of the fleet will be completely destroyed by collisions, fires, etc., with no net recoverable value, during the first year of operation. The actual casualty loss for the year, however, turns out to be 10 trucks rather than 50. As of the end of the year negotiations are in progress, looking to a possible merger with another trucking concern. An officer of the other company suggests that the balance of the "reserve for casualties" that had been set up should be deducted in determining the value of the remaining trucks, despite the fact that 990 trucks were still on hand and in good condition. He admitted that the loss to date was below average; but argued that the excess had been properly accrued.

On the basis of this illustration I asked my executive friend if he would agree to make a deduction for the 40 trucks, since they were placed in a sort of statistical jeopardy, or would he insist on including them in existing assets and treating the balance of the "reserve" as a part of retained earnings. Not surprisingly, he chose the latter position. He also admitted that he would have no objection to deducting a reasonable amount to cover depreciation for one year. He left my office a firm convert to the view that casualties do not accrue, and he never backslid. Such is the power of a good example.

ABSORBING LOSS ACCRUALS IN DEPRECIATION

Trying to make a case for casualty loss accruals by referring to depreciation practice is bad enough, but even more objectionable is the attempt to modify and redefine "group" depreciation procedure for the purpose of routing such accruals into expenses in the guise of depreciation charges.[1]

This kind of undertaking founders, in the first place, because of the implication that only depreciable assets are exposed to casualty. This, obviously, is not the case. All kinds of inventories are subject to loss by fire, flood, theft, and other casualties throughout the period of holding, and in many

---

[1] For a recent example, see "Depreciation Accounting and the Anomalous Self-Insurance Cost" by Professors J. J. Cramer, Jr. and W. J. Schrader in the October, 1970, issue of the *Accounting Review*.

enterprises this risk overshadows that associated with the relatively minor investment in structures and equipment. It follows that if possible casualty losses are to be embodied in depreciation charges, they should also be absorbed, somehow, in the amount of inventoriable assets periodically charged to revenues. But nobody has yet proposed this, and I doubt if anyone will. If a big department store, for example, has not had a fire in a particular year the management would surely not take kindly to the idea that a slice of the stock of goods on hand, computed by applying an average loss percentage of some kind, should be regarded as worthless.

Estimating the useful life of a particular depreciable asset or a group is, as already admitted, in some degree a guessing game. Service life is affected by the physical factors, including the conditions of use, by market developments, by the technological march. It must also be admitted that an accident (such as collision on the highway—in the case of vehicles—or serious damage from an explosion in the plant) or other type of casualty may bring the period of use to an abrupt end. But such considerations fail to justify regarding possible losses by casualty as a component of periodic depreciation charges (aside from the fundamental objection that casualty risk is not confined to depreciable resources, already made). Broadly viewed, over a considerable period, all costs—including actual losses—are on the same plane; that is, all are deductions in the overall process of measuring earnings. But we can't get along with a single account labeled "All Deductions." Breakdown and classification is essential in recording, tracing, applying, and finally disposing of the costs incurred in business operation, including those described as losses. Thus there is a general presumption to the effect that the important and distinctive burden resulting from casualties—man-made and "natural"—should be segregated, rather than obscured by absorption in such areas as depreciation of structures and equipment or the cost or value of the inventoriable factors periodically consumed. Certainly the burden of proof rests squarely on anyone proposing to do this.

CONCLUSIONS

The plain fact is that until a casualty occurs, there is no loss. The results of fires, floods, earthquakes, and other disasters do not accrue. This is true of an aggregate as well as for a particular asset. Casualties occur irregularly through time, and in many cases—as already emphasized—no major loss is suffered for a long period, or even during the life of the particular enterprise. In some cases, good judgment indicates the need for insurance to cover certain risks and dangers; in others, the assumption of risk by the operating company makes sense. There is no such thing as "self-insurance." Casualty losses, either as anticipated or as suffered, are not a component of depreciation, or periodic absorption of inventoriable resources.

Supporters of the view that prospective or possible losses should be accrued, I'm afraid, have succumbed to the widespread and persistent inclination to deal with the burdens of business in such a manner as to make their impact on periodic income statements smooth or stable. But the fact remains that there are fluctuations in the affairs of most enterprises, and in some cases such variations and swings are of major moment. I don't believe anyone has yet proposed that in the case of a fleet of oil tankers there should be a regular charge for a possible sinking (perhaps amounting to the value of a quarter of one tanker), but I won't be too surprised if such a proposal appears on the scene one of these days. The longing for a bit of stability and order is not unnatural, but business, like the weather in most places, is inherently subject to ups and downs, favorable and unfavorable changes. And perhaps the uncertainties and misfortunes that plague us have a stimulating and invigorating influence.

Self-Insurance Should Be Accrued

Jack F. Truitt
Washington State University

Thomas R. Nunamaker
Washington State University

The argument that self-insurance is a legitimate expense that should be recognized in the financial statements is based on the classical accounting concept of matching and a changed environment for the insurance industry since the Financial Accounting Standards Board issued Statement No. 5 in 1975.

Proponents cite a number of advantages of recognizing self-insurance expense. The accrual of self-insurance expense would enhance comparability between commercially insured and self-insured entities and provide full disclosure of the risk level that the various firms have assumed. Such recognition of self-insurance expense also would properly match costs and revenues which would be analogous to other after-costs such as warranties and bad debts.

The business climate has changed a great deal since the FASB issued Statement No. 5, which provides general guidelines for accounting for contingencies. The statement requires that an estimated loss from a contingency be accrued by a charge to income if both of the following conditons exist:

A. It is probable that an asset has been impaired or a liability incurred at the date of the financial statements, and
B. The amount of the loss can be reasonably estimated.

From *Management Accounting* (March 1987), pp. 62–65. Reprinted by permission of the Institute of Management Accountants. Copyright © 1987 by the Institute of Management Accountants, Montvale, NJ.

Later, in Appendix A, the Board stresses that self-insurance does not satisfy the aforementioned conditions; thus, is not an acceptable expense. Paragraph 28 specifically states, "The absence of insurance does not mean that an asset has been impaired or a liability has been incurred at the date of an enterprise's financial statements."

The rising cost and in many cases the inability to obtain insurance coverage has taken its toll on businesses, professionals, and local governments across the United States. The insurance crisis has forced many companies to modify their operations, raise product prices or accept lower profit margins, and, in some instances, discontinue product lines and/or services.

THE INSURANCE CRISIS

The current insurance crisis has been caused by excessive capacity, the legal system, dollar underwriting, and greed.

Increased capacity in both the direct and reinsurance markets has resulted in too many players competing for a limited amount of insurance dollars.[1] Part of the increased capacity resulted from the dramatic increase in captive insurance companies. A captive insurance firm is a subsidiary firm that writes insurance primarily for the parent corporation. During the five-year period ending in 1983, 538 new captives were formed to bring the total number of captives to 1,426 companies that insure some $7 billion worth of business.[2]

Insurance executives and many business people blame the current insurance crisis on rising costs of defending and settling law suits. Last year settling liability claims in and out of court cost more than $70 billion. In fact, for commercial property liability policies in 1985, claims and administrative costs exceeded investment income by $5.5 billion even though premiums were increased 21% to $142 billion.[3] Insurance trade associations have banded together with other business groups to lobby for changes in liability laws and the placement of caps on jury awards and lawyers' fees.

The liability insurance crisis is pervasive; it has affected manufacturers, service industries, municipalities, the health care industry, financial institutions, and professional firms. For example, the Cessna Aircraft Co. stopped manufacturing five types of small aircraft because the product liability premiums accounted for 30% of the plane's cost, thereby driving the price of the planes out of the range that most consumers could afford.[4]

Another prime cause of the current insurance crisis has been dollar underwriting. Dollar underwriting involves the utilization of investment returns during periods of high interest rates to subsidize premium rates. Histor-

---

[1] G. Buddy Nichols, "Who's Really to Blame For the Current Insurance Crisis?," *Risk and Management*, July 1985, p. 44.

[2] Richard Morais, "The Elusive Captives," *Forbes*, November 19, 1984, p. 250.

[3] "Business Struggles to Adapt as Insurance Crisis Spreads," *The Wall Street Journal*, January 21, 1986, p. 33.

[4] Ibid, p. 33.

ically, insurance companies did not consider maximizing investment income as one of their major objectives. However, in the mid-seventies the insurance industry shifted from investing in blue chip stocks to short-term investments with high interest rates. The goal structure of the insurance firms changed from writing profitable insurance to gathering all the money possible in order to invest in the short-term, high-return market.[5]

Greed then set in as underwriters began to cut premiums and accept levels of risk that were undesirable with apparently little consideration given as to what would happen in the future. Wanting a larger share of the market, insurance firms became very competitive with one another, accepting policies with very high limits and any type of risk in exchange for unrealistically low premiums.

Then, in 1985, dollar underwriting disappeared as interest rates dropped, yet insurance claims continued to rise. As the insurance companies attempted to return to profitable underwriting, premiums soared because of the unrealistic rates that had been charged in the past. In some cases, the insurance companies simply refused to underwrite some risks because of potential lawsuits.

THE SELF-INSURANCE DECISION

The sudden shift in the structure of insurance rates has prompted many companies to examine the practicality of self-insurance. One obvious drawback is the unacceptability of recording self-insurance expense. It is perhaps time for the FASB to reexamine FAS 5 and the self-insurance question. There is a strong possibility that what was suitable for a 1975 business environment is inappropriate for 1986 and beyond. Commercial insurance coverage for many business risks is rapidly becoming unobtainable or unaffordable because of large court awards that have stunned the insurance industry.

Self-insurance is a firm's deliberate program of exposing itself to risk because it is economically advantageous to accept that element of risk.[6] Under a program of self-insurance (with or without a captive insurance company), it can be argued that an asset has been impaired or a liability incurred. For instance, when a national chain store decides to self-insure its various outlets against a possible loss due to a fire, the firm has met the two basic conditions that are necessary for a self-insurance program. The two basic conditions are:

- The firm should have a large number of homogeneous assets, and
- These assets should not be subject collectively to a catastrophic loss.

For example, the moment the firm decides to self-insure against fire losses at its various locations, the value of the stores collectively is diminished by the expected value of the possible loss due to fires. Similarly, when a firm decides

---

[5] Nichols, p. 45.
[6] Jules I. Bogen, Editor, *Financial Handbook*, 4th Ed., Ronald Press Co., New York, 1965.

to self-insure instead of obtaining outside insurance for product liability, the firm has incurred a liability equivalent to the expected value of future payments for defective products.

A company's profit and loss statement should reflect a charge for self-insurance so that current and potential stockholders can see how assets have been impaired or liabilities incurred as a result of the company accepting new levels of measurable risk. The large increase in self-insurance either by going bare, creating a captive, or joining a pooled insurance group should be disclosed in order to provide comparability between insured and self-insured firms.

Self-insurance should be recognized as an expense in order to be consistent with the current treatment of other after-costs such as pensions, bad debts, and warranties. An after-cost is an expense that does not actually occur until after the revenue it helped generate has been recognized. For matching purposes, after-costs are estimated and recorded as expenses in the period of revenue recognition. There would appear to be little difference between estimating how many receivables will prove to be uncollectible versus how many stores will be destroyed by fire because both can be estimated on a statistical basis within a relatively narrow range. Actuaries could be employed to determine the expected number of stores that would be destroyed as a result of fire.

One of the prime arguments put forth by the FASB for not accruing a self-insured loss is that there has not been a transfer of risk. Without a transfer of risk, the FASB contends that a contractual obligation to reimburse the insured for losses is not present and therefore no liability is present. The Internal Revenue Service (IRS) has taken a similar position on the tax deductibility of premium payments to captive insurers by their parent corporation. That is, the IRS argues that no insurance exists unless there is a transfer of risk.

In the case of a firm that self-insures against a fire loss there can be no transfer of risk. However, an asset has been impaired. The transfer of risk concept dates back to a 1940 Supreme Court decision (Le Gierse, 41-1USTC para. 10,029 [1940]), which stated that insurance requires the transfer of an economic risk of loss and the distribution of such risk. A 1940 definition of insurance may not be appropriate for our current business environment.

The transfer-of-risk argument has not been applied consistently by the accounting profession. Consider the case of warranties versus product liability. Many believe that warranties are merely business agreements to repair or replace a defective product and thus are different from insurance because insurance involves outside perils. However, insurance and after-costs are more similar than such a view would suggest. For example, product liability insurance provides protection to the insured party against claims concerning defective design, production, and performance of a product that may cause serious harm to the product user. Both a warranty on an automobile and product liability insurance result in guarantees to the consumer concerning the performance of a product.

The acquisition of product liability insurance by a manufacturer results in a transfer of risk to the insurance company. When a consumer purchases an automobile, however, the car manufacturer provides the purchaser with a warranty. If the automobile proves to be defective, the manufacturer is responsible for repairing the automobile. The accounting profession would accrue an expense in both the product liability and warranty situations, yet there is a transfer of risk in the case of product liability and no transfer of risk in the warranty situation. Thus, as a criterion for recognizing a liability and related expense, the accounting profession should not use the transfer-of-risk concept to distinguish between after-costs such as warranties and self-insurance.

The transfer-of-risk argument also does not appear applicable to captive insurance companies. Most captives purchase protection from reinsurers, who generally deal only with insurers.[7] Generally, reinsurers sell coverage to the captive that its parent would have a hard time obtaining from a general insurer. The utilization of reinsurers allows the captive to transfer risk. In addition, many captives are selling insurance to unrelated parties as well as reinsuring other insurers, which makes the captive very representative of a normal insurance firm. Other business firms that have found insurance protection unavailable or too expensive to carry have pooled their risks by forming group or mutual captive insurance companies. Thus, the contention that estimated self-insurance losses should not be accrued because there has not been a transfer of risk seems to be inappropriate for most captives.

The comparability of firms is hindered under FAS 5 because firms that insure internally instead of obtaining external insurance will have no periodic charge for insurance expense. Under the provisions of FAS 5, a self-insuring firm's income statement will probably be overstated in the early years and understated during the years when the actual loss occurs. It may be that after a number of years of operating the self-insurance program the actual amount of loss will approximate a normal accrual of the estimated insurance expense.

Further, the comparability of firms that insure internally instead of externally may be decreased because the self-insurers may decrease the lives of the assets in order to make an allowance for self-insurance. In a footnote to FAS 5, the FASB acknowledges the possibility of dysfunctional expense comparisons between firms could result if the lives of assets are shortened. In addition to improving comparability and consistency, the accrual of expected future losses would provide a better matching of costs and revenues, which is one of the major goals of the current accounting model.

Another argument for accruing losses from self-insurance is that the data are already available and could be easily incorporated into the financial statements. Firms that are self-insuring would normally have had to establish a realistic estimate for self-insurance expense in order to price their product.

[7] C. Arthur Williams, Jr., and Richard M. Heins, *Risk Management and Insurance*, Fifth Ed., McGraw-Hill Book Co., New York, 1985.

The fact that companies are considering the cost of insurance in their pricing decisions is well illustrated by the current insurance situation facing Lederle Laboratories, one of two manufacturers of DTP (Diphtheria, Tetanus, Pertussis) vaccine in the United States.[8] As of June 30, 1986, Lederle will be unable to obtain any insurance for DTP vaccines because of insurance carriers' concerns about the number of claims and the costs associated with these claims. In a letter to pharmacists and physicians, Lederle announced that the company will continue to supply DTP vaccine but the price will increase to $171 per vial. The letter notes that this price increase is due solely to liability claims associated with the use of the vaccine and that $120 of the price per vial will be reserved for product liability claims. For financial reporting purposes, verifiability can be obtained by the actuaries employed by CPA firms through an examination of management's assumptions concerning the amount of estimated self-insurance expense.

The last argument for allowing the accrual of self-insurance expense concerns price discrimination among the stockholders of a particular firm over time.[9] Self-insurance losses will definitely occur but there is uncertainty in terms of when these losses will occur. Under FAS 5, shareholders at the time the actual loss occurs will have to bear the entire brunt of the loss while from an economic perspective both past and future shareholders should bear a portion of it.

When a stockholder buys stock, the price will probably not reflect the future losses that will occur from a prior decision by the firm because there is currently no mechanism for revealing the self-insurance arrangement of a firm. Therefore, accrual of self-insurance should permit equitable sharing of expected losses by shareholders over time. In addition, the periodic accrual of self-insurance losses would produce a smoother earnings stream, which is probably a better reflection of the firm's long-run earnings picture.

Our proposed accounting treatment for self-insurance is dichotomized into the property insurance case and the liability insurance situation. In the property insurance situation, an estimated insurance expense account would be debited and a contra-asset account called "allowance for self-insurance" would be credited. Thus, the asset would be reduced on the balance sheet by the estimated cost of self-insurance to date. The property insurance situation would include insurance for fire, vandalism, water damage, and so on.

In the liability insurance situation, an estimated insurance expense account would be debited and a liability account called "liability for self-insurance" would be credited. Therefore, the balance sheet would reveal to the user the estimated liability that the company has undertaken as a result of assuming more risk. The liability insurance situation would include coverage for product, director, automobile, professional and general liabilities.

---

[8] *Re Ipsa Loquitor*, Vol. 13, Number 6, June 1986.
[9] Richard J. Keintz and J. Finley Lee, "Accounting for Future Losses: The Risk Management Problem," *Risk Management*, Jan. 1975, pp. 7–14.

As a result of the tremendous growth of self-insurance that has been caused by the lack of available or affordable insurance coverage, the FASB should reconsider its position on self-insurance. For many firms, self-insurance meets all the requirements put forth in FAS 5 and is truly a contingency that can be estimated. The separate treatment afforded after-costs such as warranties and self-insurance does not appear to be realistic given today's business environment. Inter-firm comparison and financial statement reporting would be greatly enhanced if companies were allowed to book self-insurance expense. In the final analysis, self-insurance is a real expense that should be accrued.

'RAP-Man'—It's Devouring GAAP

Gilbert Simonetti, Jr.

Price Waterhouse

Andrea R. Andrews

Price Waterhouse

Regulatory Accounting Principles—or RAP—seemed like a good idea at the time. They were originally created to meet the specialized accounting and reporting needs of U.S. government agencies that regulate financial institutions.

But the good idea has gone awry—in terms of RAP's departure from Generally Accepted Accounting Principles, in terms of their increased utilization as a bailout mechanism, and in the degree to which RAP-based information intended only for regulators has been publicly disseminated with little or no qualification as to its reliability or basis of presentation.

Until recently, there was little significant difference between financial reporting under RAP and GAAP. But in the early 1980s, major problems in the financial services industry gave rise to a number of RAP departures from GAAP intended to improve, on paper, the financial condition of troubled institutions.

THE TROUBLE BEGINS

The Federal Home Loan Bank Board (FHLBB) was the first and most aggressive user of RAP for this purpose. It reasoned that if ailing thrifts were given a chance to bring themselves back from the brink of failure, the resources of the

From Price Waterhouse *Review* (1987, No. 3), pp. 55–58. Reprinted by permission of Price Waterhouse. Copyright © 1987 by Price Waterhouse.

already hard-pressed Federal Savings and Loan Insurance Corporation (FSLIC) fund would not have to be employed. It didn't work out that way.

To quote David Mosso, Vice-Chairman of the Financial Accounting Standards Board, "The numbers you see are the numbers you manage by." FHLBB regulators were hypnotized by RAP and lost sight of financial reality.

The General Accounting Office has contended that reliance on RAP by the FHLBB systematically and significantly overstated the net worth of savings and loan institutions. Results? The true financial condition of some institutions was masked until it was too late to save them, and potential claims on the FSLIC were seriously understated. The FSLIC fund was declared insolvent in late 1986. There were, of course, a variety of causes, but RAP-inflated net worth was surely an important contributing factor.

To make matters worse, the availability of RAP-based information is not confined to regulators. Such information finds its way into reports issued by financial institutions, financial analysts' reports, press reports, and footnotes to GAAP financial statements. In addition, financial institutions not subject to SEC reporting requirements may issue only RAP financial statements, often failing to label them as such or to highlight departures from GAAP. Thus, the numbers that mislead the regulators are disseminated to also confuse and mislead the public, investors, and depositors, and undermine the credibility of financial reporting.

Moreover, encouraging the use of RAP to shore up troubled financial institutions has spread from the Bank Board to other regulatory agencies and to Congress. There is a pronounced trend toward using or twisting certain accounting standards for that purpose, and ignoring other standards that get in the way. The probable results are more financial mismanagement and public confusion, and less faith in the financial reporting system.

GOOD GUY, BAD GUY

An excellent example of this trend is the saga of Financial Accounting Standard No. 15, "Accounting by Debtors and Creditors for Troubled Debt Restructurings," and FAS No. 5, "Accounting for Contingencies." It's a clear case of "good guy" versus "bad guy."

FAS No. 15 is a good guy. Ostensibly, in the words of one member of Congress, it allows financial institutions to "avoid loan loss recognition where economic conditions require that borrowers restructure or work out their loans." But FAS No. 15 must be used in concert with FAS No 5, a bad guy. It requires lenders to take into account the effects of restructuring on loan profitability and consider the potential for collectibility. After all, restructuring an uncollectible loan hardly makes it collectible.

This bad guy also interferes with another practice that has become popular in Congress—deferral or amortization of loan losses. Under FAS No. 5, a loss must be recognized immediately when a loan is impaired and the amount of the loss can be reasonably estimated.

SELECTIVE AMNESIA

Since FAS No. 5 is so troublesome, regulators and Congress have largely chosen to forget its existence. The FASB and the AICPA, among others, have been vigorously battling this selective amnesia. But it has been an uphill fight.

In April 1986, for example, the federal bank regulatory agencies announced a three-point program to help banks whose survival was threatened by heavy involvement in loans to the agricultural and energy sectors. One element of the program was to encourage such banks to restructure problem loans and account for the restructuring in accordance with FAS No. 15. There was no mention of FAS No. 5.

Critics contended that the regulators were endorsing accounting gimmickry that would "turn bad loans into good loans overnight." This perception pervaded the financial community and the financial press, undermining the credibility of FAS No. 15.

In late 1986, in legislation applying a Band-Aid to the Farm Credit System's financial wounds, Congress revised strict provisions in the Farm Credit Act Amendments of 1985 prohibiting any departures from GAAP. Under the Farm Credit Act Amendments of 1986, the FCS was permitted to defer and amortize certain amounts of interest expense and provisions for loan losses for periods of up to 20 years. This use of RAP was subject to stringent requirements, including disclosure in footnotes to the GAAP financial statements. Nevertheless, the impression was created that the System was going to be able to, as one newspaper headline put it, "Paper Over Its Red Ink."

1987: RAP VS. GAAP SCORECARD

This year has brought a mixed scorecard for RAP vs. GAAP. A spate of highly publicized failures, scrutiny from some Congressional Committees and the GAO, and the financial crisis facing the FSLIC have apparently caused the Federal Home Loan Bank Board to become disenchanted with RAP. In May, the Board approved a final rule first proposed in April 1986 which requires GAAP reporting by insured thrifts effective January 1, 1988.

Meanwhile, Congress has persisted in its collective mental blackout on FAS No. 5. As the legislation to recapitalize the FSLIC fund made its way to the President's desk, several provisions for loan loss deferral and amortization were proposed for inclusion.

In the House, provisions were proposed to (1) allow thrift institutions to amortize loan losses over a five to ten year period, and (2) allow thrifts to restructure problem loans under FAS No. 15.

The final FSLIC legislation dropped the loan loss deferral provision for thrift institutions and specified that loan restructuring has to be accounted for using *both* FAS No. 15 and FAS No. 5. Also added was a requirement for insured thrifts to utilize GAAP effective December 31, 1987, with two qualifiers.

First, GAAP is to be required only to the extent required by commercial bank regulators. Second, if an institution can show that compliance with GAAP by the specified deadline is not feasible, it may submit a plan for compliance by a later date—up to December 31, 1993.

But with the type of logic that arises when controversial legislation requires countless quid pro quos, the FSLIC bill also contains a Senate proposal allowing small agricultural banks with resources under $100 million to amortize loan losses over seven years. Those who set out to give small, financially threatened banks in depressed agricultural regions a break may get a surprise. A large number of bank holding companies with assets over a billion dollars own small agricultural banks which meet the legislation's eligibility criteria. Thus, the loan loss deferral is available to them as well.

GOING INTERNATIONAL?

Loan loss deferral has also threatened to "go international." Both the House and Senate considered including provisions in their omnibus trade bills to allow deferral of losses on Third World debt. The House Banking Committee stopped short of developing legislative language. The Senate Banking Committee produced S.898, "The International Lending Institution Safety Act of 1987," which would have required banking institutions to establish reserves for probable losses from foreign loans over a ten-year period.

As the FASB pointed out in a letter to the Senate Banking Committee, this is tantamount to amortizing a loan loss over ten years in contradiction to— you guessed it—FAS No. 5. If a bank can identify a loan loss and reasonably estimate the amount, the entire loss must be recognized at once. If it is not yet clear or probable that a loss has been incurred, there is no need to establish a reserve.

NOT SO INNOCUOUS LANGUAGE

The final House and Senate trade bills contain seemingly innocuous provisions calling for a study of regulatory and accounting barriers to amortization of loan losses. But the language regarding the study in the Senate Banking Committee's report on its portion of the trade bill is hardly innocuous:

> . . . the Committee desires to have the regulatory agencies identify any policies and practices by either bank accountants and auditors, or the bank regulatory authorities themselves, which inhibit banks from developing on a voluntary basis, loan restructurings which involve reductions in current debt payments by borrowers. In this regard, examination of the applicability of Financial Accounting Standards Board Standard No. 15 to Third World debt restructurings might be appropriate.

If the private sector were to suggest that certain accounting rules be changed or ignored because they are making life difficult, while others are enshrined because they serve a useful purpose, cries of "foul," would ring through Congress.

But "RAP-man" appears to be everywhere—devouring not only GAAP, but our legislators' sense of perspective. It's time to end this risky game before the entire financial reporting system gets swallowed.

It's time to "put the wraps on RAP."

Accounting for Contingencies: The Pennzoil–Texaco Case

Edward B. Deakin
Late Professor, University of Texas at Austin

In 1984, Texaco acquired Getty Oil Company, an event that was to have far reaching consequences for the acquiring company, the rules by which mergers and acquisitions were carried out, and the perception of the Texas and federal legal systems. The disclosures provided in the annual reports of the two parties to this litigation provide insight into the implementation of the FASB's terms "reasonably possible" and "probable" as criteria for accounting and disclosure of contingencies. Moreover, a side-by-side comparison of the disclosures by the two parties illustrates the difference in practice between accounting for gains and for losses. An additional issue that comes to light from this case is that Pennzoil had apparently deferred its legal costs during the lawsuit. This amounts to capitalization of the "costs" of contingent assets, an issue that has not been previously addressed in the literature. This issue, together with the disclosures during the period when the case was in litigation, points out some interesting matters with respect to accounting for contingencies and the costs related thereto.

CONTINGENCY REPORTING RULES

Under generally accepted accounting principles, companies subject to contingent claims or with contingent assets, such as those arising from litigation, are required to disclose such claims in their financial statements when they become "reasonably possible," regardless of whether they can be reasonably estimated. An accrual for a liability is required when the contingency is both "probable" and the amount can be "reasonably estimated." By contrast, companies with contingent gains are not permitted to report such contingent assets in the income statement or balance sheet until realization criteria have

From *Accounting Horizons* (March 1989), pp. 21–28. Reprinted by permission of the American Accounting Association. Copyright © 1989 by the American Accounting Association.

been met.[1] SAS 1 states that when a material contingency can have a "probable" adverse effect on a company, an auditor should issue a "subject to" opinion.[2] Thus, the accounting disclosures and auditors' reports rely on similar criteria. However, the official pronouncements do not provide practical guidance concerning when an event is "reasonably possible" or when it is "probable." The differential application of these criteria in a contingent gain and contingent loss situation are illustrated by the Pennzoil-Texaco disclosures.[3]

The case itself is of interest because it was the largest dollar value judgment in history and led to the largest bankruptcy in history. Also, because of the magnitude of the case, disclosures were made in the financial reports of both parties. This rarely occurs. This case was an exception. This article presents a year-by-year comparison of the events related to the litigation in this case together with each company's financial statement disclosures about the litigation. The reporting of these events in the financial statements of Texaco and Pennzoil provides an interesting history about this case and about contingency reporting in general.

BACKGROUND

In 1983, Pennzoil approached Getty Oil Company to discuss the possibility of Pennzoil purchasing Getty. Negotiations proceeded throughout the year, with a merger agreement being reached with a degree of finality that was to be the subject of later litigation. The process started when Pennzoil issued a tender offer for 20 percent of Getty's shares at a price of $100 per share. This agreement ultimately called for Pennzoil to pay $3.4 billion for three-sevenths of the outstanding common stock of Getty Oil Company.

At around the same time, Texaco decided to bid for the purchase of Getty. In Texaco's view, it was a "white knight" offering to extricate Getty from an unfriendly takeover. Texaco agreed to pay $10.2 billion for all of the common stock of Getty Oil Company. The bid amounted to $128 per share. Texaco and Getty entered into a definitive merger agreement and the merger was consummated in the first quarter of 1984. Texaco's 1984 financial statements include the following note:

> Texaco acquired all of the outstanding common stock of Getty Oil Company for $10.2 billion. Getty was an integrated petroleum and natural gas company involved in the exploration for and production, transportation, refining and marketing of crude oil and petroleum products, operating primarily in the United States.
>
> The acquisition has been accounted for as a purchase and the financial statements for the year 1984 reflect the incorporation of Getty assets and

---

[1] These criteria are discussed in the FASB's *Statement No. 5: Accounting for Contingencies*.

[2] *Statement on Auditing Standards No. 1*, §547.

[3] A summary of the history of the litigation and the related disclosures by each party is presented in Appendix 1.

liabilities at fair market value on a fully consolidated basis beginning March 1, 1984.

Shortly thereafter, Pennzoil filed suit, claiming that Texaco had unlawfully interfered with Pennzoil's definite merger agreement with Getty. Pennzoil sought damages of approximately $14 billion. This was clearly the largest dollar value lawsuit in the history of U.S. litigation.

The litigation proceeded for over four years. During that time, Texaco filed for protection under Chapter 11 of the Bankruptcy Code, making it the largest failed firm in history. In 1988, Texaco and Pennzoil reached a settlement agreement under which Texaco paid Pennzoil $3 billion. The year-by-year history of these events as discussed in the company financial statements is presented in the following sections of this article.

1984: Merger and Start of Litigation

As noted above, the Texaco-Getty merger was completed in 1984 and the Pennzoil-Texaco litigation was initiated that year. Pennzoil filed suit in Delaware in January and in Houston in February of that year. Because the suit was filed between the date of the financial statements and the date when the statements were issued, it was a post-balance sheet event that was reported in the 1983 statements.. The filing of the lawsuit apparently met the test of "reasonably possible" for Texaco since a footnote disclosure was made. The 1983 Texaco Annual Report included this item in the fifth paragraph of its note on contingent liabilities. The text of the note was as follows:

> *Other Contingent Liabilities*— . . . In related actions commenced in the Delaware Chancery Court in January 1984 and in the Houston, Texas, District Court in February 1984, Pennzoil Company (Pennzoil) has asserted claims totaling $14 billion as a result of its unsuccessful attempt to acquire a minority interest in Getty Oil Company. Pennzoil's earlier attempt in the Delaware action to block Texaco's acquisition of Getty was rejected by the Court. Exercising rights granted under Getty indemnity agreements with the Sarah C. Getty Trust and the J. Paul Getty Museum, Texaco will continue to oppose Pennzoil's claims that those parties and Getty Oil Company breached an agreement which it alleges would have resulted in it acquiring the desired minority interest. Similarly, Texaco will continue to vigorously defend Pennzoil's Texas action which is brought on a theory that Texaco tortuously interfered with Pennzoil's alleged contractual rights.

There was no other mention of the litigation in the Texaco 1983 annual report. The same note reappeared in Texaco's 1984 annual report.

Pennzoil made no mention of the litigation in its financial statements until 1986. Prior to that time, its discussions of the litigation were included in the President's letter. In its 1983 Annual Report, Pennzoil discussed the events leading up to the proposed Pennzoil-Getty merger. The note further stated that Pennzoil had initiated a $14 billion lawsuit against Texaco for interfering with its Getty acquisition.

Pennzoil made only brief mention of the litigation in its 1984 President's letter. Thus, according to Pennzoil, the "reasonably possible" criterion had not been attained at this point. The note, reproduced below, contained few details relative to the ultimate impact that the litigation would have on the company. It stated:

> Despite repeated efforts by Texaco Inc. to prevent a trial by jury in Texas, Pennzoil's $14 billion lawsuit against Texaco Inc. is scheduled to be heard before a jury in Houston beginning July 8, 1985.

The differences in disclosure are of interest. Texaco began disclosing the contingent liability from the date when the litigation was filed. It apparently believed that the criterion of "reasonably possible" was met at the time of filing. By contrast, Pennzoil's lack of disclosure suggests that it did not view the outcome as "reasonably possible," despite its President's letter and other public statements.

1985: Trial Court Judgment Entered

1985 was the watershed year for this litigation. The Texas District Court in Houston decided that it held jurisdiction for the litigation and the trial began in June. The trial lasted for $4^{1}/_{2}$ months. On December 10, 1985, the jury decided to award $10.5 billion to Pennzoil. The judge later increased the award to $11.1 billion.

The entry of judgment by the trial court changed the significance and the extent of the disclosure for Texaco. In its 1985 Annual Report, Texaco included a two-page discussion of its version of the litigation and the events related thereto. The Pennzoil-Texaco litigation moved up to first place in the contingencies note and was expanded to three paragraphs. The text of the note follows:

> *Pennzoil Litigation*—On December 10, 1985, the District Court of Harris County, Texas, entered judgment for Pennzoil Company against Texaco Inc. in the amount of $10.5 billion as actual and punitive damages and $600 million as prejudgment interest in *Pennzoil Company vs. Texaco Inc.*, an action in which Pennzoil claims that Texaco tortuously interfered with Pennzoil's alleged contract to acquire a minority interest in Getty Oil Company. Interest will accrue on the total $11.1 billion judgment at a simple rate of 10% per annum from the date of judgment. Texaco believes that there is no legal basis for the judgment, which it believes is contrary to the weight of the evidence and applicable law. Texaco is pursuing all available remedies to set aside or to reverse the findings. In this connection, Texaco will expeditiously file its appeal in the Texas Court of Appeals.
>
> On January 16, 1986, the United States District Court for the Southern District of New York granted Texaco a preliminary injunction which enjoins Pennzoil from taking any action to enforce or attempt to enforce the $11.1 billion judgment, pending Texaco's appeal. To satisfy the $1 billion security requirement established in connection with the preliminary injunction, on February 5, 1986, Texaco placed 65 million shares of Texaco Canada Inc.

common stock with the Clerk of the U.S. District Court. On February 20, 1986, the United States Court of Appeals for the Second Circuit affirmed the grant of a preliminary injunction.

The ultimate outcome of the Texaco-Pennzoil litigation is not presently determinable. A final decision of Texaco's appeal that affirms all or a significant part of the $11.1 billion judgment could have a material adverse effect on the consolidated financial position and results of operations of Texaco Inc. and its subsidiaries.

One key aspect of the note was Texaco's assertion that the judgment "had no legal merit" and was "contrary to the weight of the evidence and applicable law." This phraseology appears frequently in litigation disclosures. However, Texaco also noted that "The ultimate outcome of the Texaco-Pennzoil litigation is not presently determinable," and that if the judgment were upheld, it would have a material adverse effect on Texaco's operations. This admission only appeared after the trial court had ruled against Texaco, even though this statement was factual from the date that the suit was filed.

After entry of the trial court's judgment, the problem for Texaco was aggravated by the Texas appeal bond requirement. Under Texas law, to appeal an adverse judgment, the appealing party must post a bond equal to the amount of the judgment. The amount of the appeal bond was slightly in excess of $11 billion. At the time, Texaco had cash and cash equivalents of $1.7 billion. It had shareholders' equity of $13.6 billion and total assets of $37.7 billion. If Texaco were to borrow the $11.1 billion required for the appeal, its debt to equity ratio would trigger defaults on several of its loan agreements. Moreover, if Texaco had lost the appeal, the company would emerge with approximately $2.5 billion of equity (i.e., $13.6 billion less $11.1 billion) on assets of $37.7 billion. The resulting debt/equity ratio would also trigger defaults in its loan agreements. It was, therefore, considered unlikely that Texaco would be able to raise the bond money necessary to pursue its appeal.

Once the trial court judgment was entered, Texaco's auditors issued an opinion that was subject to the results of the litigation.[4] The relevant text of the opinion is as follows:

> As more fully discussed in Note 16 of the Notes to Consolidated Financial Statements, on December 10, 1985, the District Court of Harris County, Texas, entered judgment against Texaco and awarded the plaintiff substantial damages. While the Company intends to pursue all available remedies to set aside or to reverse the findings, the ultimate outcome of this litigation is not presently determinable.

Given the auditor's "subject to" opinion, one would conclude that the likelihood of an actual liability for Texaco increased to the "probable" stage within the meaning of SAS 1.

Texaco appealed the bond requirements and obtained temporary injunctive relief which enabled it to pursue its appeal while posting $1 billion bond

---

[4] It is worth noting that Arthur Andersen & Co. was the auditor for both Pennzoil and Texaco.

in the U.S. District Court. If the appeal to the U.S. District Court failed, Texaco would be required to post the $11.1 billion bond with the Texas courts or lose its right to appeal.

Pennzoil's view of the litigation was, as expected, substantially different from Texaco's. The 1985 Annual Report President's Letter contained a three paragraph section headed "Pennzoil Victory in Texaco Trial." The text of the note is as follows:

> In November, . . . a jury unanimously decided that Texaco Inc. had knowingly interfered with Pennzoil's agreement to acquire $3/7$ths of Getty Oil Company. The jury set actual damages at $7.53 billion and punitive damages at $3 billion, for a total of $10.53 billion. Subsequently, State District Judge Solomon Casseb upheld both the verdict and the damages, increasing the award to $11.12 billion to include accrued interest.
>
> Texaco subsequently attempted to shift the conflict from state to federal jurisdiction, suing Pennzoil in federal district court in White Plains, New York. The district judge granted Texaco a favorable ruling on all seven issues it raised in district court. On February 20, 1986, the U.S. Court of Appeals for the Second Circuit reversed his ruling on five of those issues and affirmed him on two of them. The decision makes it clear that Texas is the only proper forum available to Texaco to appeal the existing judgment. The Second Circuit Court upheld the jurisdiction of the Federal district court to enjoin Pennzoil from protecting its judgment with liens and the district court's right to set the amount of a bond in lieu of a supersedeas bond. In so doing, the circuit court removed any possible reason for Texaco's having to declare bankruptcy or attempting to delay the appellate procedure further. The court stated, "The grant of preliminary injunctive relief, as modified, is affirmed on condition that Texaco promptly and diligently prosecute its appeal in the Texas appellate courts."

This note by Pennzoil was the first mention of Texaco's possible need to seek bankruptcy protection: a topic that was avoided in the Texaco Annual Reports.

Although the contingent liability appeared both in Texaco's notes to its financial statements and in the auditor's report, it still did not appear in Pennzoil's financial statements. This would suggest that there was either an imbalance in the two parties' view of the probability of the likely realization or that the accounting for contingent assets uses more strict definitions for the terms "reasonably possible" and "probable" than for contingent liabilities, even though the terms are defined equivalently for gains and losses in SFAS 5. This disparity in assessment of the degree of certainty on the two sides of the litigation is even more significant given that both companies had the same auditor.

1986: Appellate Maneuvering

The 1985 financial statements of Texaco discussed some of the early 1986 legal activities that were taking place with respect to this litigation. On March 7, Texaco filed an appeal from the trial court's ruling with the Texas Court of

Appeals. Oral argument was held before the Texas Appeals Court in July 1986.

Meanwhile, Texaco was pursuing relief through the Federal courts in New York. That court system was more sympathetic to Texaco's cause, and effectively stayed the Texas appeal bond requirement. Pennzoil appealed the Federal court judgment to the U.S. Supreme Court, seeking to reinstate the $11.1 billion bond requirement.

At this point, Texaco's future was clearly in the hands of the Supreme Courts of Texas and of the United States. If the U.S. Supreme Court were to reverse the Circuit Court ruling, Texaco would be required to post the $11.1 billion bond or else forfeit its right to appeal. Since Texaco was unable to raise the funds for the bond requirement, its appeal would be lost if the U.S. Supreme Court reversed the Circuit Court.

On the Texas litigation front, the state Court of Appeals had affirmed the trial court's judgment, but reduced the judgment to $9.1 billion plus interest at 10 percent.[5]

Texaco's 1986 Annual Report contained a two-page discussion of the litigation which was highly critical of the judgment and the Texas court system. The first paragraph of that discussion gives a flavor of the tenor of Texaco's comments:

> The decision by the appeals court to uphold the judgment and reduce by a small percentage the total dollar amount is essentially just an acceptance of the capricious lower court action, is not responsive to the applicable law on the key issues, and has no foundation in justice. The court's action leaves standing major portions of a judgment that is contrary to reason, contrary to fair play, and contrary to Constitutional and legal principles governing business activity.

Meanwhile, Texaco's contingency note expanded dramatically. The Pennzoil-Texaco litigation covered over a full page of the notes. One part of the note discussed the issue of settlement for the first time. It is reproduced below:

> Efforts by Texaco Inc. and by an intermediary to secure a reasonable and economic settlement of the Pennzoil litigation have not been successful to date.

More interestingly, the discussion about the effect of the outcome of the litigation on Texaco was more bleak than had been presented earlier. For the first time, Texaco mentioned the possibility of bankruptcy. This section of the note read:

> *Effect on Texaco Inc.*—If at any time during the pendency of the full appellate review of the judgment, Texaco Inc. no longer were to have the protection from the imposition of liens or other enforcement of the judgment—whether that protection is provided by the District Court's preliminary injunction, or

---

[5] Pennzoil had the opportunity to avoid the reduction in the judgment by requesting a new trial. As expected, Pennzoil decided not to start over in the trial courts.

alternatively, by the Texas courts pursuant to representations made to various federal courts on behalf of Pennzoil, by agreement with Pennzoil, or otherwise—or the availability of credit were to become so restrictive as to impair operations, Texaco Inc. would face prospects such as having to seek protection of its assets and business pursuant to the bankruptcy and reorganization provisions of Chapter 11 of Title 11 of the United States Code and being subject to liquidation of significant assets. Texaco Inc. would face similar prospects if, following all available appellate review, the judgment were to be affirmed in whole or significant part.

The outcome of the appeal on the preliminary injunction and the ultimate outcome of the Pennzoil litigation are not presently determinable, but could have a material adverse effect on the consolidated financial position and the results of the consolidated operations of Texaco Inc.

Arthur Andersen again issued a "subject to" opinion, with a more comprehensive paragraph on the nature of the litigation and the possibility of bankruptcy protection. This note was as follows:

A judgment against Texaco Inc. has been rendered by the District Court of Harris County, Texas, and substantially affirmed by the Court of Appeals for the First Supreme Judicial District of Texas. The Federal courts have granted a preliminary injunction which enjoins the Texas plaintiff from taking any action to enforce or attempt to enforce the judgment during the appeals process. A United States Supreme Court decision is pending regarding the Texas plaintiff's appeal to have the preliminary injunction overturned. Certain developments, as more fully explained in Note 17 to the Consolidated Financial Statements, could cause Texaco Inc. to face prospects such as having to seek protection of its assets and business pursuant to the bankruptcy and reorganization provisions of Chapter 11 of Title 11 of the United States Code and being subject to liquidation of significant assets. While Texaco Inc. intends to pursue all available remedies to set aside or to reverse the judgment entered by the Texas District Court, the ultimate outcome of this litigation is not presently determinable.

No amount was recorded for the potential liability in Texaco's financial statements. This suggests that at this point, the amount could not be "reasonably estimated."

Meanwhile, Pennzoil presented its view of the history of the litigation in its 1986 Annual Report. A five-paragraph section of the President's Letter headed "Texaco Verdict, Damages Upheld" cited several quotes from the Court of Appeals opinion that are reproduced below:

In its ruling, the court said, "Though the compensatory damages are large, they are supported by the evidence and were not the result of mere passion, prejudice or improper motive." The court noted that the jury could have concluded from the evidence that "Texaco deliberately seized upon an opportunity to wrest an immensely valuable contract from a less-affluent competitor by using its vast wealth to induce the Museum, Gordon Getty and Getty Oil to breach an existing contract.

> "The evidence shows that the wrongful conduct came not from servants or mid-level employees, but from top-level management," the judges wrote. They added: "Apparently the jury believed that the conduct of Texaco's top-level management was less than the public was entitled to expéct from persons of such stature."

As expected, Pennzoil's view of the Texas court system and of the resulting judgment varied substantially from Texaco's.

For the first time, Pennzoil included a note in its financial statements concerning the litigation. The note was nearly a page long and recited much of the history of the case. The note also addressed the issue of settlement by noting:

> Pennzoil believes that the Judgment will be upheld if again appealed. However, there can be no assurance as to the final outcome or the timing of final judicial action or the result of any settlement discussions between the parties nor assurance that there will ultimately be any recovery, pursuant to the Judgment, by settlement or otherwise, from the Lawsuit.

Apparently, by 1986 Pennzoil believed that the contingent asset had become at least "reasonably possible" and thus met the requirements for disclosure. The timing is of interest because it was over one year after the trial court judgment. The Texas Court of Appeals had affirmed the verdict and most of the award, but the appeal process had not been completed. An appeal was still pending before the Texas Supreme Court and both parties made it clear they would appeal an adverse ruling there to the U.S. Supreme Court. Hence, there was no evident objective criterion associated with Pennzoil's determination that the contingent asset had become "reasonably possible" in 1986.

Pennzoil's auditors made no note of the litigation, even though if it had a favorable final outcome, it would have been a very material item. However, there is no requirement that auditors take note of material contingent gains.

1987: Texaco Bankruptcy

Events in 1987 took a turn for the worse for Texaco. The Texas Supreme Court upheld the judgment of the Texas Court of Appeals. This meant that Texaco owed Pennzoil $9.1 billion plus interest from the date of the judgment. Moreover, it rendered Texaco's proceedings in the New York Federal courts moot. The appeals bond was no longer an issue since Texaco had lost the appeal. At this point, Texaco's only hope was that the U.S. Supreme Court would agree to hear its appeal of the trial court judgment. U.S. Supreme Court observers note that the court rarely becomes involved in issues involving two private parties.

Given the high probability that Texaco would be forced to pay Pennzoil $9.1 billion plus interest, Texaco began to experience problems with suppliers and with dealers in its commercial paper. The markets perceived that Texaco would be devastated if it had to pay the full amount of the judgment.[6] Texaco also realized that so far, Pennzoil was an unsecured creditor. By filing under Chapter 11 of the Bankruptcy Code, Texaco could reassure its creditors and suppliers.[7] This would buy the company time to seek resolution of the dispute.

Of greater importance to Texaco, though, the company would be in a stronger negotiating position with respect to the Pennzoil claim. Pennzoil could seek settlement of the judgment, or enforce the judgment (assuming it was upheld by the U.S. Supreme Court) and force Texaco into liquidation. Given the poor market for oil and gas related assets, Pennzoil could very well have received a relatively small amount after liquidation. For these reasons, Texaco filed for protection under Chapter 11 of the U.S. Bankruptcy Code on April 12, 1987.

During the remainder of 1987, the two parties were involved in settlement negotiations. On December 19, 1987, the two parties agreed to settle the litigation with Texaco agreeing to pay Pennzoil $3 billion in early 1988. On December 12, 1987, Texaco's creditors (including Pennzoil) and Texaco filed a joint plan for reorganization with the court. Among other things, the plan required approval of the court and of two thirds of Texaco's shareholders. Final settlement of the matter was still a technically open issue as of the end of 1987.

Nonetheless, the Texaco 1987 financial reports reflected the view that all of the criteria for loss recognition had occurred. Texaco included a line item in its income statement for the $3 billion settlement with Pennzoil.

Pennzoil included an extensive note in its 1987 financial statements which discussed the history of the case, Texaco's bankruptcy filing, and the agreement which the two parties had reached. A statement about the expected effect of the settlement on Pennzoil was as follows:

> If the Joint Plan is confirmed in its existing form, based on present estimates, management expects to have pretax net cash recovery after all expenses incurred in connection with the Lawsuit and the bankruptcy proceedings of approximately $2.6 billion. The current and deferred tax liability related to this amount is presently difficult to estimate and will depend largely on how and when the recovery funds are reinvested. As of December 31, 1987, Pennzoil has deferred approximately $29 million of legal and other direct and indirect costs associated with the Lawsuit and related proceedings.

At this time, Pennzoil's shareholders' equity totaled $621 million. The settlement would, therefore, amount to approximately four times the company's existing capital. Even at this late stage in the process when the

---

[6] Brigham and Gapenski, pp. 841–2.

[7] Obligations incurred after a bankruptcy filing have precedence in the order of settlement of claims. Therefore, creditors from post-bankruptcy transactions are more likely to obtain full value for their claims.

settlement plan was agreed upon and when Texaco had recognized the liability, Pennzoil did not include the settlement amount in its balance sheet or income statement. Hence, even at this point, Pennzoil did not believe that either the amount was "probable" or Pennzoil did not believe it could be reasonably estimated. Since the settlement terms had been agreed to by both parties and Texaco had the funds to pay the $3 billion, the remaining approvals were viewed as relatively minor. However, they were perceived as sufficient to preclude recognition by Pennzoil on December 31, 1987. Apparently, the criteria for recognizing contingent assets is stricter in practice than the term "probable" would imply.

There is no specified accounting treatment for the costs associated with litigation. It is interesting to note that Pennzoil had deferred $29 million of "legal and other direct and indirect costs" associated with the litigation and had not expensed these costs currently. A review of Pennzoil's balance sheet does not reveal where this amount was recorded. There is a $13 million amount under "Other" current assets and a $137 million reported under other property plant and equipment. Presumably the deferred charge was included with the property plant and equipment account. One might assert that the $29 million was a cost of the contingent asset and, therefore, was properly a long-term asset. However, by the end of 1987, with settlement in sight, the amount could have been reclassified to the current assets section.

1988: Settlement

On April 7, 1988, Texaco paid $3 billion to Pennzoil, thus settling the litigation. Four days later, Texaco issued an amendment to its 1987 financial reports which disclosed settlement of litigation and provided a pro forma balance sheet reflecting the settlement. The amendment also included a revised auditor's report which indicated that the "subject to" provision of earlier reports had been removed.

CONCLUSIONS

The accounting disclosures about the largest lawsuit in history provide an interesting comparison of the views of the litigation by each party to the action throughout its history as well as an indication of the operative definitions of the FASB's criteria for gain and loss contingencies although the extreme materiality of this case makes it difficult to draw general conclusions. On the contingent liability side, the criterion of "reasonably possible" was considered to be met at the time of filing of the lawsuit. The "probable" criterion seemed to appear when judgment was entered against the defendant. However, entry of a liability did not occur until actual payment was agreed upon. On the contingent asset side, the criterion of "reasonably possible" was considered to be met sometime after judgment was issued but before final resolution of all appeals. However, recognition of the specific dollar amount in the accounts does not seem to occur until payment of the settlement.

The case also raises the question about the accounting treatment for legal costs. Pennzoil deferred its litigation costs and first disclosed this deferral in 1987. The accounting treatment for such costs is not specified in FASB rules, nor does it appear elsewhere in the literature. Pennzoil's treatment, though, raises the question of accounting for the "costs" of a contingent asset. Given the often high costs involved in litigation, accounting for these legal costs may be an issue that is more widespread than evident to date.

While this was but one case in an environment characterized by frequent litigation, the way each party treated the events is of interest.

REFERENCES

American Insitute of Certified Public Accountants, *Statement on Auditing Standards* (New York: AICPA, 1973).

Brigham, E., and L. Gapenski, *Financial Management: Theory and Practice*, 5th ed. (New York: Dryden Press, 1988).

Financial Accounting Standards Board, *Statement No. 5: Accounting for Contingencies* (Stamford, Conn.: FASB, 1975).

APPENDIX 1 Summary of Legal and Financial Disclosure History
Pennzoil v. Texaco Inc.

| Year-End | | Financial Statements | |
12/31	Litigation Status	Pennzoil	Texaco
1983	Suit filed post-balance sheet date	No disclosure	Brief contingency disclosure
1984	Litigation underway	No disclosure	Extensive contingency disclosure
1985	Trial court rules for Pennzoil	No disclosure	Primary item in contingency disclosures: "subject to" opinion
1986	Appellate Court upholds judgment	Contingency note	Primary contingency note; expanded "subject to" opinion
1987	Texas Supreme Court upholds judgment; Texaco files for bankruptcy protection; settlement proposed	Expanded contingency disclosure	Loss recognized; "subject to" opinion
1988	Settlement finalized	Gain recognition	Revised 1987 financial statements issued; "clean opinion" obtained

Messy Accounting

Reed Abelson
Forbes

American Cyanamid is involved in legal proceedings over cleaning up pollution at approximately 60 sites. How do we know? Because we searched through the notes tucked away in the back of Cyanamid's latest annual report. The note informs us the $4.6 billion (1990 revenues) biotechnology and chemical company may face "substantial" cleanup costs.

Substantial? What does that mean? Ten million dollars, perhaps? Or several hundred million dollars, enough to wipe out an entire year's earnings? The company doesn't say.

We're not picking on Cyanamid. It has plenty of company. Such reticence on the subject of environmental liabilities isn't rare, unfortunately. Most companies offer some kind of boiler-plate in their annual report, but they differ widely on how promptly to reveal a problem, or how much to say about it. In most cases, says chemical analyst William Young of Donaldson, Lufkin & Jenrette, "we don't get very much specific disclosure."

Smith Barney's Tobias Levkovich puts the problem more bluntly: "It's obviously something that can come bite you in the butt." Specialty materials company Dexter Corp. (1990 revenues, $907 million), for instance, disclosed in 1989 that it faced possible environmental troubles at its Windsor Locks, Conn. facility. But this was specifically disclosed in the 10-K and not in the annual report, giving the impression that the problem was minor. Since then, Dexter has accrued $9.1 million in pretax charges for settlement costs and legal fees. Earnings were down almost 50 percent from last year, to only $12 million, in part because of these charges. Is there more bad news in the offing? Dexter won't comment.

Houston-based consulting firm Pilko & Associates recently surveyed 200 manufacturing executives representing a broad range of industries. About two-thirds had discovered an environmental problem just within the last year. Half were already involved in some sort of environmental litigation.

Yet the nation's accounting rule-makers have not provided guidelines on when and how to disclose the mess in your backyard. The applicable accounting rule is an old (1975) standard on the broad subject of contingent liabilities. A company must disclose a liability, it decrees, as soon as there is a "reasonable possibility" the liability has been incurred.

"Reasonable possibility," of course, is a bit vague, and practice diverges widely. Late last year a survey of 125 industrial companies by accountants Price Waterhouse found that just over a third disclosed their environmental problems to shareholders as soon as federal or state regulators tapped them on the shoulder. Some others disclosed before such notification.

Accounting guidelines say that as soon as a company considers a liability is "probable" and can reasonably be estimated, it must start accruing charges—that is, deducting amounts from today's earnings to cover the future expense.

But "reasonably estimated" is just as vague as "reasonably possible." Some companies seem to take advantage of this by taking the hits to earnings when it's most convenient. Last year Occidental Petroleum lumped $720 million of environmental charges into a $2.2 billion pretax big bath for "restructuring costs." Others wait for strong earnings to let out the news.

Not all the blame rests with the companies or their accountants. It sometimes takes the bureaucrats at the Environmental Protection Agency as long as 18 to 30 months to come up with estimates for different cleanup alternatives. There's also uncertainty as to whether the company's insurer will cover some or all of costs. And lawsuits with vendors or neighbors have yet to be resolved.

Still, the looming threat is a matter that greatly concerns investors, and they deserve better than they are getting in the way of timely warning. Consider the natural gas transmission company Panhandle Eastern (1990 revenues, $3 billion). In early 1989 Panhandle acquired Texas Eastern, which tentatively expected a contingent liability of $400 million for the cleanup of 89 sites contaminated by polychlorinated biphenyls (PCBs). There was no estimate for other associated costs, like third-party claims.

The day after the merger Panhandle gave security analysts the impression that the $400 million estimate was "not only sufficient but generous." Yet in the second quarter of last year the company revised its estimate to $480 million. With the extras, which Panhandle said could add "more than $250 million," the total cost could come to $730 million.

Alan Gaines of New York's Gaines, Berland Inc., who is short the stock, thinks Panhandle is giving only the best-case scenario. "With their debt load [68% of capitalization], it would be important to know" the worst case, too, says Gaines. He says the total cost could easily top $1 billion.

Of course, you can't entirely blame managements for being coy about these numbers, which can hurt their stock badly. For years, industrial-equipment maker Duriron Co., Inc. said in its annual report it would have to clean its Dayton, Ohio landfill, and the cost "is difficult to project but could be substantial." Many investors shunned the stock, which never broke the $20 range. Last year a study of the site was completed, and the company finally announced it anticipated no "material" expense.

Still, environmental risks are part of the landscape today, and corporate management will have to face the risks. Dennis Beresford, chairman of the Financial Accounting Standards Board, agrees "there will be a call for more standard setting." Beresford warns that the task is a difficult one. Every oil leak, asbestos or landfill situation varies. Nevertheless, he hopes the standard setters will address the issue sometime within the next few years. We'd suggest sooner.

"In the end, it's all judgment," argues Norman Strauss of accounting firm Ernst & Young. True, but investors are entitled to some help in judging the risks.

CHAPTER 6

Inventory

Since the late 1930s, when LIFO became an acceptable method of inventory valuation for federal income tax purposes, many American companies have adopted it for both tax and financial accounting purposes. Section 472 of the U.S. Internal Revenue Code provides that taxpayers may use the LIFO method only if they have used

> no procedure other than [LIFO] to ascertain the income, profit, or loss . . . for the purpose of a report or statement covering [the] taxable year
>
> (1) To shareholders, partners, or other proprietors, or to beneficiaries or
> (2) For credit purposes.

Accounting Research Bulletin (ARB) No. 29, issued in 1947 by the American Institute's Committee on Accounting Procedure, formally endorsed LIFO as being among the "generally accepted accounting principles" for inventory valuation, and in 1953 the same Committee, in ARB No. 43, Chapter 4, reaffirmed that position. In 1972, one-quarter of the 600 companies surveyed by the American Institute in its annual volume entitled *Accounting Trends and Techniques* used LIFO for at least some of their inventories; in 1982, owing chiefly to the spurts of inflation in the middle and late 1970s, two thirds of the 600 companies reported at least some use of LIFO.[1]

Until the last several years, the use of LIFO was confined largely to the financial statements of U.S. companies, and typically only for those inventories held by the American parent and by any American subsidiaries. Inventories held by foreign subsidiaries of U.S. parents have usually been accounted for by other methods. The main reason for using LIFO has evidently been to reduce taxes, for, if companies were convinced that it produced a more informative measure of income, they would be using it for *all* of their group inventories, not solely for those eligible for the U.S. tax benefit. In periods of

---

[1] In 1992, 60 percent of the companies surveyed reported at least some use of LIFO.

248

rising prices, companies would probably prefer the larger FIFO profit, except where the tax benefits conferred by LIFO are a dominant factor.

A proposal made in 1990 by the International Accounting Standards Committee (IASC) to remove LIFO from the set of its allowed alternative treatments was expected to be opposed only by the United States. In the end, however, the IASC proposal was defeated by a group of European and Asian countries—Germany, Italy, Japan and Korea—where, evidently, LIFO has become an active accounting/tax option in recent years.[2] Hence, LIFO, as a fiscal instrument for eliminating most of the inventory holding gain from taxable income so long as it is used for financial reporting purposes, is spreading.

Whether LIFO or FIFO promotes a better measure of inventory value and cost of goods sold is a debatable question. It seems likely that many companies that have adopted LIFO have sought to eliminate most of the "holding gain" from their reported net income (and taxable income). Although LIFO is nominally a method of historical cost accounting, one can argue that its tendency to exclude most of the "holding gain" from net income, while FIFO would include much of the "holding gain" in net income, qualifies it as being similar in its effect on net income to current value accounting with a physical-capital-maintenance interpretation (see the introduction to Chapter 17). Indeed, the Financial Accounting Standards Board's Statement No. 33 on changing prices notes that "Cost of goods sold measured on a LIFO basis may provide an acceptable approximation of cost of goods sold, measured at current cost, provided that the effect of any decreases in inventory layers is excluded" (para. 60, footnote 3).

Since, for more than a decade, the Securities and Exchange Commission has required companies using LIFO to disclose the excess of replacement cost over the LIFO cost (the so-called "LIFO reserve") of their beginning and ending merchandise inventories (see Regulation S-X, Rule 5-01-6(c)), it is a simple matter for readers to estimate a LIFO company's net income according to FIFO, as well as the tax savings to the company from using LIFO. This has prompted many researchers to ask why more company managements have not made the switch to LIFO and thus reap the tax benefits of showing a lower taxable income during periods of rising merchandise prices.

In his brief article, "Paying FIFO Taxes: Your Favorite Charity?" Gary C. Biddle draws on his prior research to suggest that companies staying on FIFO are wittingly making avoidable contributions to the federal coffers. Why do companies retain FIFO? Is it to bolster the profits on which a management compensation plan is based?[3]

Michael H. Granof and Daniel G. Short, writing in *The Wall Street Journal* 18 months later in a brief article entitled, "For Some Companies, FIFO Ac-

---

[2] For a brief summary of the contending views on the LIFO question, and an account of the IASC board's deliberations on LIFO at its October 1992 meeting, see "Comparability/Improvements Project: Board Approves First Three Revised Standards," *IASC Insight* (newsletter of the IASC) (December 1992), pp. 14–16.

[3] See the bibliographical notes below for more on research studies examining this issue.

counting Makes Sense," report on a questionnaire survey of corporate controllers in which justifications for staying on FIFO inventory accounting are
suggested.[4] In a letter commenting on the findings reported by Granof and
Short, Biddle professes disbelief.

BIBLIOGRAPHICAL NOTES

A history of LIFO, including both its use in taxation and in financial statements, is as follows:

Davis, Harry Zvi: "History of LIFO," *The Accounting Historians Journal* (Spring 1982),
    pp. 1–23. (Reprinted in the *Journal of Accountancy* (May 1983), pp. 96–98, 101–102,
    104–106, 108, 110, 112, 114.)

A study of the legislative history of the LIFO provision in the U.S. income tax
law is:

Pincus, Morton: "Legislative History of the Allowance of LIFO for Tax Purposes," *The
    Accounting Historians Journal* (June 1989), pp. 23–55.

A research study conducted by a retired partner of a major public accounting
firm deals with the valuation of inventories:

Barden, Horace G.: *The Accounting Basis of Inventories*, Accounting Research Study No.
    13 (New York: American Institute of Certified Public Accountants, 1973).

A comprehensive study done by three public accounting practitioners is:

Janis, C. Paul, Carl H. Poedtke, Jr., and Donald R. Ziegler: *Managing and Accounting for
    Inventories: Control, Income Recognition, and Tax Strategy*, (New York: John Wiley
    and Sons, 1980). (Previous editions were published by The Ronald Press Com-
    pany in 1962 and 1970.)

Many researchers have studied the effect of taxes, inflation, interest rates,
inventory turnover, and other economic variables on the manager's choice of
inventory methods. In addition, several empirical studies have been conducted to understand investors' reactions to the impact on earnings of a
change in inventory valuation method from FIFO to LIFO. These include the
following:[5]

Sunder, Shyam: "Optimal Choice Between FIFO and LIFO," *Journal of Accounting
    Research* (Autumn 1976), pp. 277–300. This was the first major article on this topic.
Abdel-khalik, A. Rashad, and James C. McKeown: "Understanding Accounting
    Changes in an Efficient Market: Evidence of Differential Reaction," *The Accounting
    Review* (October 1978), pp. 851–868.
Abdel-khalik, A. Rashad, and Thomas F. Keller: *"Earnings or Cash Flows: An Experiment*

---

[4] See also Michael H. Granof and Daniel G. Short, "Why Do Companies Reject LIFO?," *Journal of
Accounting, Auditing & Finance* (Summer 1984), pp. 323–333.
[5] Additional bibliographical notes on the capital market reaction to accounting changes are given
in the introduction to Chapter 16.

on Functional Fixation and the Valuation of the Firm, Studies in Accounting Research #16 (Sarasota, FL: American Accounting Association, 1979).

Biddle, Gary C.: "Accounting Methods and Management Decisions: The Case of Inventory Costing and Inventory Policy," *Journal of Accounting Research* (Supplement 1980), pp. 235–280.

Ricks, William E.: "The Market's Response to the 1974 LIFO Adoptions," *Journal of Accounting Research* (Autumn 1982, Part I), pp. 367–387. The author examines the market reaction to the large number of LIFO adoptions in the years 1974–1975. He concludes that "LIFO adopters suffered negative abnormal return performance during the period surrounding" their earnings release.

Lee, Chi-wen Jevons, and David A. Hsieh: "Choice of Inventory Accounting Methods: Comparative Analyses of Alternative Hypotheses," *Journal of Accounting Research* (Autumn 1985) pp. 468–485.

Stevenson, Francis L.: "New Evidence on LIFO Adoptions: The Effects of More Precise Event Dates," *Journal of Accounting Research* (Autumn 1987), pp. 306–316. The author finds no correlation between excess stock returns and LIFO tax savings. This result, together with Ricks's findings, suggests that the stock market ignores the tax benefit of LIFO at the time the LIFO adoption is announced by companies.

Dopuch, Nicholas, and Morton Pincus: "Evidence on the Choice of Inventory Accounting Methods: LIFO versus FIFO," *Journal of Accounting Research* (Spring 1988), pp. 28–59.

Lindahl, Frederick W.: "Dynamic Analysis of Inventory Accounting Choice," *Journal of Accounting Research* (Autumn 1989), pp. 201–226.

Hand, John R. M.: "Resolving LIFO Uncertainty: A Theoretical and Empirical Re-Examination of 1974–1975 LIFO Adoptions and Non-Adoptions," *Journal of Accounting Research* (Spring 1993), pp. 21–49. This comprehensive study confirms the above findings on the noncorrelation between stock returns and LIFO tax savings. Hand reports a mean 2-day price decline of 1.38 percent around the earnings announcement date.

Bar-Yosef, Sasson, and Pradyot K. Sen: "On Optimal Choice of Inventory Accounting Method," *The Accounting Review* (April 1992), pp. 320–336.

Cushing, Barry E., and Marc J. LeClere: "Evidence on the Determinants of Inventory Accounting Policy Choice," *The Accounting Review* (April 1992), pp. 355–366. The authors confirm prior research that shows that anticipated tax savings are the primary reason for firms to choose LIFO. The authors also survey financial executives and find that firms do not choose LIFO when other factors such as the method's complexity diminish the potential tax savings from LIFO.

Jennings, Ross, David P. Mest, and Robert B. Thompson II: "Investor Reaction to Disclosures of 1974–75 LIFO Adoption Decisions," *The Accounting Review* (April 1992), pp. 337–354. The authors show that firms that could have adopted LIFO, but did not, experienced a strong negative price response, whereas firms that did adopt LIFO experienced a weak positive price response.

For a review of the large literature on the management motivations for, and the capital market's reaction to, LIFO adoption, see:

Lindahl, Frederick W., Craig Emby, and Robert H. Ashton: "Empirical Research on LIFO: A Review and Analysis," *Journal of Accounting Literature* (1988), pp. 310–331.

Paying FIFO Taxes:
Your Favorite Charity?

Gary C. Biddle
University of Washington

In one of the most puzzling rituals of American business behavior, thousands of U.S. companies are once again preparing their annual reports using FIFO rather than LIFO inventory accounting. By so doing, they will pay as extra taxes funds which could be used for expansion, capital replacement or dividends.

Under FIFO, or the first-in, first-out assumption, inventory costs flow through the firm as if on a conveyor belt. Costs are assigned to units sold in the same order the costs entered inventory. As a result, during periods of rising prices, older and thus *lower* costs are subtracted from revenues when determining reported (and taxable) earnings.

In contrast, under LIFO, or the last-in, first-out assumption, inventory costs are accumulated as if on a coal pile, with the newest costs being removed from the top and assigned to units sold. Unless a cost layer is liquidated by depleting inventories, it can remain in the base of the pile indefinitely. Thus, during periods of rising prices older and lower costs can remain in the balance sheet inventory accounts while the newer and *higher* costs are used to calculate earnings. Compared to FIFO, reported earnings in most cases drop. But so do taxable earnings. The company can keep more cash for itself and for shareholders.

According to their latest annual reports, three long-time LIFO users—Amoco, General Electric and U.S. Steel—have together saved more than $3 billion in taxes compared to what they would have paid using FIFO.

LIFO was deemed acceptable for tax purposes in 1939, and it's been used widely in selected industries, notably steel and petroleum, since the late 1940s. A large number of firms switched to LIFO in 1974, a year of high inflation. And for 1980, American Hospital Supply, Eli Lilly, Clorox and Williams Cos., among others, have announced they're making the switch.

Yet the vast majority of companies continue to use FIFO. Some managers are perhaps reluctant to incur additional LIFO bookkeeping costs. Some have perhaps dismissed LIFO's tax advantages in light of variable year-end inventory levels or less than galloping prices. Others may believe that since LIFO would result in lower reported earnings, stockholders are content to pay the extra FIFO taxes.

How much extra are stockholders willing to pay? In a forthcoming study in the "Supplement to the Journal of Accounting Research, 1980," I compare the inventory levels and accounts of 106 New York Stock Exchange firms which used FIFO, with those of 106 competitors that adopted LIFO between 1973 and 1975. From 1974 to 1978, by my estimates, the 106 FIFO firms paid an average of nearly $26 million each in additional federal income taxes, thanks to their policy of sticking with FIFO. For 1974 alone, these additional taxes averaged nearly $12 million per firm—more than 1 1/2 percent of their sales.

Indeed there are good reasons to suspect that the additional taxes paid by FIFO firms put them at a competitive disadvantage. The accompanying table compares estimates of the additional taxes paid by six FIFO firms, with the amounts saved by direct competitors that adopted LIFO or extended its use in 1974.

FIFO firms, of course, do not typically disclose the additional taxes they have paid. I have estimated these amounts, however, using industry specific price indexes and assumptions about procurement to come up with the differences between FIFO and LIFO based earnings. The additional FIFO taxes shown in the table equal these differences multiplied by the corporate income tax rate (then 48%).

The estimates of additional FIFO taxes assume that LIFO is applicable to all of a FIFO firm's inventories. As a result, these amounts may be overstated for firms like Smith International which hold significant portions of their inventories in other countries where LIFO is not permitted. However, the amounts that have been saved by LIFO competitors may understate the potential savings in cases like American Stores where LIFO has been adopted for only a portion of domestic inventories.

*FIFO firms LIFO competitors	1974–1978	
	Additional FIFO taxes (in millions	LIFO tax savings of dollars)
* Federal Paper Board	$8	
Mead Corp		$46
* J.P. Stevens	29	
Burlington Inds		44
Cone Mill		28
* Jewel Companies	36	
American Stores		18
* Masco Corp	15	
Wallace-Murray		13
* Minn. Mining & Mfg.	118	
Eastman Kodak		204
* Smith International	32	
Dresser Inds.		125
Hughes Tool Co.		22

The amounts presented suggest that a number of firms have paid millions of dollars each in additional taxes by using FIFO rather than LIFO for domestic inventories. It is unlikely that bookkeeping costs could account for such sums. And fears of negative stockholder reaction appear unfounded in light of the efficient markets research documenting investor preferences for cash flows. While there are some unusual circumstances (like falling prices or inventory levels) in which LIFO could yield smaller cash flows, it is puzzling why so many firms in so many industries have continued to use FIFO.

Perhaps companies sticking to FIFO are showing their support for some worthy federal program. But wouldn't it make more sense to contribute some LIFO tax savings to a favorite tax-deductible charity? Or perhaps I have ignored an important LIFO cost or FIFO benefit. If so, please let me know.

For Some Companies, FIFO Accounting Makes Sense

Michael H. Granof
University of Texas at Austin

Daniel G. Short
Kansas State University

The use of FIFO, or the first-in first-out inventory accounting method, may not be so puzzling after all.

It is frequently argued that LIFO, the last-in first-out method, provides companies with substantial tax savings by permitting them to determine their cost of goods sold as if the items purchased last—at presumably higher prices—were in fact the ones sold. Financial analysts and business school professors often wonder why companies using FIFO, or another method called the weighted average, are paying millions of dollars in extra taxes— funds that would otherwise be available for expansion, capital replacement and dividends. The conventional explanation is that companies use FIFO in order to boost their reported earnings, even at the expense of their after-tax cash flow. But we have just concluded a survey that makes clear this interpretation is usually wrong.

We asked the controllers of 380 corporations that have not adopted LIFO why they haven't. We received 213 answers. Our survey convinces us that many companies have legitimate reasons for not climbing aboard the LIFO bandwagon.

For one thing, we found that most non-LIFO companies are *not* incurring a tax penalty. On the contrary, in a number of circumstances, the FIFO or weighted-average method can reduce tax payments.

Over 16 percent of our respondents indicated that the prices of their goods held in inventory have been declining. This was especially true of firms in high technology industries, but was also reported by firms in less glamorous industries such as steel and meat packing. In periods of declining prices, LIFO serves to accelerate recognition of taxable gains and, therefore, results in higher tax payments.

Many controllers—17%—told us that their firms as a whole or various of their subsidiaries are using tax loss or tax credit carryforwards. These carryforwards make it advantageous for the firm to accept the currently higher earnings that go with FIFO in order to have correspondingly lower earnings in the future, when the firm will again be in a tax-paying position.

Some managers explained that adoption of LIFO would prevent them from taking advantage of the "lower of cost or market" rule. This feature of the tax code (which is not available to firms that use LIFO) enables firms that have incurred losses on selected inventory items to give them immediate tax recognition. When LIFO is adopted, inventory must be stated at original cost. Previously recorded losses must be recovered and taxes must be paid on that amount.

Many managers have already taken advantage of a recent relaxation of the LIFO conformity rule. Normally a firm that uses LIFO for tax purposes must do so for financial reporting purposes. As a result of a ruling last year by the Second Circuit Court of Appeals in a case involving Insilco Corp., a parent company may now report the results of a subsidiary in its financial statements based on a method other than LIFO even though its subsidiaries calculate their taxable earnings using LIFO.

In addition, many controllers focused on various drawbacks of LIFO that could outweigh possible tax benefits. If a company's inventory balances fluctuate from year to year, LIFO increases the difficulties of cash planning. This is because LIFO subjects the company to the risk of dipping into its LIFO base—valuing for tax purposes its goods sold at the artificially low prices of past years. The company might then report artificially high profits and have to repay in a single year the accumulated tax savings of several previous years. Other controllers emphasized that the record-keeping requirements of LIFO are burdensome and costly.

While our study uncovered a number of legitimate reasons for not using LIFO, several responses seemed to lack economic support. One company said it did not use LIFO because it is "trying to maintain a record of year-to-year growth in profits, and though the impact of the change would not be material in relation to total profits in the first year, it would be significant in terms of year-to-year profit improvement." Another did not use LIFO because it thought that "such a switch would depress the market price of our stock. Such a switch would reduce the book value of our stock and would depress reported earnings . . . these considerations are more significant to our stock price than cash flow."

These explanations are somewhat surprising in light of the persuasive evidence that the capital markets are able to understand and compensate for differences in earning attributable solely to choices between accounting principles. But only 9 percent of the controllers gave such explanations.

Our study has convinced us that when it comes to paying taxes, most managers know what they are doing. But managers who have justification for not adopting LIFO need to be careful to explain these reasons to investors. We found that often the justification is not apparent from an analysis of financial statements. Companies that do not use LIFO for sound economic reasons should avoid being confused with companies that do not adopt LIFO for merely cosmetic reasons.

Taking Stock of Inventory Accounting Choices

Gary C. Biddle
University of Washington

Based on their survey of corporate controllers, Granof and Short (*Manager's Journal*, Aug. 30) are convinced "that many companies have legitimate reasons for not climbing aboard the LIFO bandwagon." Their evidence, however, is far from convincing.

A firm facing declining inventory costs would generally pay lower taxes by using FIFO rather than LIFO. Yet only 16 percent (of the 56% who responded) cited declining costs. Another 17 percent justified their non-use of LIFO in terms of tax-loss carryforwards and credits. However, this argument applies only when there is some danger that the carryforwards and credits will expire. Otherwise a firm can "lock in" its LIFO tax savings in the form of larger carryforwards in future years. Other controllers explained that the adoption of LIFO would prevent them from taking advantage of "lower of cost or market" writedowns. Yet writedowns below original LIFO costs will be infrequent if inventory costs are rising. Moreover, LIFO can be selectively adopted to avoid inventory items whose costs fluctuate. While it is also noted that previous writedowns must be reversed at the time of a LIFO adoption, the Thor Power Tool Co. decision (which disallowed the writedowns of many FIFO firms) has significantly weakened this LIFO disincentive.

Granof and Short cite other respondents who avoid LIFO because of additional planning and record-keeping costs. For these firms, the value of potential tax savings is apparently small enough to be offset by increased administrative costs. A follow-up questionnaire would provide welcome evidence on this hypothesis (and may reveal some lucrative employment opportunities for cost accountants). Still other respondents were concerned about the impact of LIFO on reported earnings. Surprisingly, Granof and Short are comforted by the fact that "only 9 percent of the respondents gave such explanations." Recent interest in the Insilco Corp. decision suggests that concern with LIFO's earnings impact is not limited to these few firms.

Granof and Short conclude from their survey that "the use of FIFO may not be so puzzling after all." What is puzzling, however, is how they drew this conclusion from their evidence. Managers undoubtedly have motives for their accounting choices. Yet to judge them as "legitimate" requires both the identification of motives and their reconciliation with optimizing behavior.

CHAPTER 7

Plant Assets and Depreciation

Accounting for long-lived, tangible assets has been contentious since the dawn of the Industrial Revolution. In earlier times, the main issues were: (1) distinguishing between expenditures that should be capitalized and those that should be expensed, (2) using historical cost or current value, (3) estimating the asset's useful life, and (4) choosing the most appropriate method of depreciation. In the last few decades, new questions have been added to the list: (1) should interest on debt and equity capital be added to the cost of assets?, (2) what should be the criteria for recognizing asset impairments?, and (3) should a way be found for avoiding arbitrary allocations?

CAPITALIZED INTEREST

On the first of the new questions, the Financial Accounting Standards Board (FASB), in Statement No. 34 issued in 1979, decided that, for certain long-lived tangible assets, the interest incurred on debt should be capitalized. Interest, the FASB reasoned, is one of the costs necessarily incurred to bring an asset "to the condition and location necessary for its intended use." The qualifying assets are, in the main, self-constructed capital assets and assets held "for sale or lease that are constructed or otherwise produced as discrete projects (e.g., ships or real estate developments)."[1] Statement 34 would not alter the total amount of interest that may be charged against revenues over the life of the enterprise—since the amount to be capitalized is limited to the interest actually incurred—but it would affect the year-to-year timing of expense recognition of interest in companies' income statements. The standard does not address the important issues of the treatment of (a) interest associated with routinely produced inventories, standing tracts of timber, aging spirits, and other assets not comprehended by the definition in State-

[1] "Capitalization of Interest Cost," *Statement of Financial Accounting Standards No. 34* (Financial Accounting Standards Board, October 1979), paras. 6 and 9(b).

ment No. 34, and (b) imputed interest on equity capital. In 1983, the International Accounting Standards Committee approved a standard that was substantially the same as the FASB's Statement No. 34, and quite a number of countries follow the capitalization practice with respect to interest on debt.

In "Equity Interest—Its Time has Come," Robert N. Anthony, a professor of management control at the Harvard Business School from 1940 to his retirement in 1983 and a onetime Assistant Secretary of Defense (Controller), makes the case for recognizing interest on owners' equity as a cost of doing business. He argues that his proposal would increase the comparability of the income numbers reported by companies with different debt/equity ratios. While Anthony acknowledges the difficulty of determining the cost of equity capital, he does not believe the task is insurmountable.[2]

THE MYSTERY OF CHANGING ASSET LIVES

A continuing controversy is asset lives, and especially corporate decisions to make changes in those lives. In "The Long and Short of Asset Lives," Don Egginton, an accounting professor at Bristol University, in England, inquires into companies' policies and practices for reviewing asset lives, and comments on the hidden reserves of profits when companies underestimate—as apparently many do—their useful lives for accounting purposes. If asset lives are understated, depreciation per year is consequently overstated, so that, in the years after which the assets are fully depreciated, bountiful profits will emerge. Egginton gives an indication of the several accounting options available to U.K. companies that revise their asset lives, including the possibility of charging (or crediting) such adjustments directly against reserves (i.e., owners' equity). In the United States, companies are required to spread the effects of such changes over the remaining life of the asset.

General Motors Corporation has been known to revise the lives of its depreciable assets. In October 1987, GM announced a revision of the estimated service lives of its plants and equipment and special tools retroactive to January 1, 1987, having the effect of increasing its annual earnings per share from $8.51 to $10.06. Moreover, since GM's decision was announced at the time of publication of the third-quarter earnings report, the combined effect of the changes applicable to the year's first *three* quarters was credited entirely to the third quarter's earnings (in accordance with U.S. generally accepted accounting principles on changes in an estimate made in interim periods other than the first period[3]), boosting GM's traditionally weak third-quarter EPS of $0.46 to a very respectable $2.28. That this decision fell in the third quarter may have been a coincidence, but it was a very happy coincidence for GM's reported performance. Even as sophisticated a newspaper as *The Wall*

---

[2] A fuller statement of Anthony's views may be found in Robert N. Anthony, *Accounting for the Cost of Interest* (Lexington, MA: Lexington Books, 1975).

[3] See "Interim Financial Reporting," *APB Opinion No. 28* (New York: American Institute of Certified Public Accountants, May 1973), para. 26.

Street Journal did not comment on the three-in-one accounting bonus in the third quarter's earnings.

Three years later, Howard P. Hodges, a GM shareholder, wrote a letter to the company's chairman in which he contrasted the $1.2 billion reduction in depreciation and amortization charges of 1987 with the $2.1 billion (after tax) "special restructuring charge" announced in 1990 to cover a contraction of manufacturing operations. Hodges' letter was circulated widely in accounting and regulatory circles. He was no ordinary shareholder. In fact, he was the retired chief accountant of the Securities and Exchange Commission's corporation finance division, which scrutinizes the annual reports of all corporations subject to the Commission's jurisdiction. In his letter, Hodges wrote, "a closer look at General Motors financial statements in recent years raises a question as to the integrity of its financial reporting, either for 1987 or 1990." In 1987, GM had recorded a change in estimate that increased earnings, and three years later it announced a curtailment of certain operations that depressed earnings. In the reply from GM, Robert T. O'Connell, the chief financial officer, contended that the two events were not contradictory and were the inevitable consequence of reviewing manufacturing needs in a highly competitive climate. As is usual in such cases, the auditors did not register a dissent either to the change in asset lives or to the restructuring charge. In Egginton's study, one auditor observed that "there is not much the auditor can do about" changes in asset lives, other than to be sure that the proper disclosures are made.

ASSET IMPAIRMENTS

During the 1980s, as companies were cutting back operations and acknowledging unproductive investments, the issue of when, and at what amount, asset impairments should be recognized was anxiously debated. In "Disclosure and the Impairment Question," Walter Schuetze raises a series of key questions concerning the accounting recognition of impairments, and suggests that, as an interim measure, the FASB require companies to disclose the fair value of nonmonetary assets when it falls below cost. He believes that "such disclosure also would alleviate considerably the surprise that frequently accompanies business failures." The FASB has added the large and complicated question of accounting for asset impairments to its agenda, but it has not yet acted on Schuetze's disclosure proposal. At the time of writing the article, Schuetze was a partner in the executive office of Peat Marwick Main & Co. (known today as KPMG Peat Marwick), but in January 1992 he became chief accountant of the Securities and Exchange Commission. Today, his views carry even more weight.

Penelope Wang, in the *Forbes* article titled "You Know It When You See It," discusses the broad range of discretion enjoyed by company managements that have suffered asset impairments. For assets that are still in service, companies possess considerable freedom when deciding both on the timing and on the amount of a writedown in the amount at which impaired assets are carried.

ARBITRARY ALLOCATIONS

Allocations of one kind or another are inherent in income accounting. Yet, as Arthur L. Thomas so aptly discusses in "The FASB and the Allocation Fallacy," the practice of making allocations by whatever means is inevitably arbitrary.[4] If one can identify the information that is of service to users, what schemes of cost and revenue assignment can be devised that would avoid arbitrary allocations and thus provide meaningful information?

As Thomas points out, current value accounting (where depreciation calculations are absent) and funds flow accounting where funds are defined as "net quick assets" are alternatives that are free of allocation problems. In this context, the trend toward cash flow statements may lead to the presentation of financial information that is less open to criticism on allocation grounds.

BIBLIOGRAPHICAL NOTES

Depreciation

Four thoughtful studies of the depreciation question are:

Goldberg, Louis: *Concepts of Depreciation* (Sydney: The Law Book Co. of Australasia Pty Ltd., 1960).
Wright, F. K.: "Towards a General Theory of Depreciation," *Journal of Accounting Research* (Spring 1964), pp. 80–90.
Baxter, W. T.: *Depreciation* (London: Sweet & Maxwell, 1971).
Lamden, Charles W., Dale L. Gerboth and Thomas W. McRae: *Accounting for Depreciable Assets*, Accounting Research Monograph No. 1 (New York: American Institute of Certified Public Accountants, 1975).

Interest Capitalization

A comprehensive study of the role of interest in accounting is

Milburn, J. Alex: *Incorporating the Time Value of Money Within Financial Accounting*, A Research Study (Toronto: Canadian Institute of Chartered Accountants, 1988).

The FASB's Discussion Memorandum that preceded Statement No. 34 on interest capitalization was

---

[4] Those who wish to pursue Thomas' logic more fully are encouraged to read his major works: *The Allocation Problem in Financial Accounting Theory*, Studies in Accounting Research No. 3 (Sarasota, FL: American Accounting Association, 1969) and *The Allocation Problem: Part Two*, Studies in Accounting Research No. 9 (Sarasota, FL: American Accounting Association, 1974).

Accounting for Interest Costs (Financial Accounting Standards Board, December 16, 1977).

An early advocacy of including interest in the cost of production, a practice that was summarily rejected by the American Institute of Accountants, may be found in

Scovell, Clinton H.: *Interest as a Cost* (New York: The Ronald Press Company, 1924).

Asset Impairment

A recent study of impairment practice is

Fried, Dov, Michael Schiff and Ashwinpaul C. Sondhi: *Impairments and Writeoffs of Long-Lived Assets* (Montvale, NJ: National Association of Accountants, 1989).

An FASB Discussion Memorandum on the subject of impairment is

Accounting for the Impairment of Long-Lived Assets and Identifiable Intangibles (Financial Accounting Standards Board, December 7, 1990).

Arbitrary Allocations

Dialogue involving Arthur L. Thomas and two critics may be of interest:

Himmel, Sid: "Financial Allocations Justified," *CAmagazine* (October 1981), pp. 70–73; and Arthur L. Thomas, "Why Financial Allocations Can't Be Justified," *CAmagazine* (April 1982), pp. 28–32.
Eckel, Leonard G.: "Arbitrary and Incorrigible Allocations," *The Accounting Review* (October 1976), pp. 764–777; and Arthur L. Thomas, "Arbitrary and Incorrigible Allocations: A Comment," *The Accounting Review* (January 1978), pp. 263–269.

Equity Interest—Its Time Has Come

Robert N. Anthony
Professor Emeritus, Harvard University

Informed readers understand what the numbers on a balance sheet mean— right? Wrong! I shall show that no explanation of the numbers now reported on the right-hand side is consistent with reality. However, with one change in accounting—the explicit recognition of equity interest cost—a meaningful balance sheet can be prepared. This change also would provide more useful information about an entity's performance, its assets and the sources of its funds.

From *Journal of Accountancy* (December 1982), pp. 76–78, 80, 82, 84, 86, 88, 90, 92–93. Reprinted by permission of the American Institute of Certified Public Accountants, Inc. Copyright © 1982 by the American Institute of Certified Public Accountants, Inc. Opinions of the authors are their own and do not necessarily reflect policies of the AICPA.

THE PROBLEM

Do the items on the right-hand side of the balance sheet represent obligations, that is, claims against the assets? Some of them do, but others do not. Although most of the liabilities are claims, and the amount reported for preferred stock is sort of a claim, shareholder equity is not. Except by coincidence, shareholders will never claim or receive the amount reported as this equity. In a going concern, they have no claim at all unless the corporation is liquidated, but the balance sheet doesn't purport to state liquidation values.

Does the right-hand side report the sources of the entity's funds? This is closer to reality than the idea of a "claim." The liabilities do report the amount of funds furnished by various parties: lenders, vendors (in the form of accounts payable), employees (in the form of accrued salaries), even the government (in the form of deferred incomes taxes).

The shareholder equity section, however, doesn't report the amount of funds supplied by shareholders. Although the paid-in capital item shows the amount shareholders supplied initially, the retained earnings number doesn't represent a shareholder contribution. "Earnings" were earned by the entity itself, not by the shareholders. The shareholders in a publicly owned corporation have little to say about what fraction of these earnings is retained. (The idea that shareholders "consented" to this retention is true but naïve.)

Moreover, the right-hand side of the balance sheet purports to make a basic distinction between liabilities and shareholder equity, a distinction so basic that the concepts for the measurement of income depend on it. Can an operational distinction be made? I don't think so. Financial Accounting Standards Board Concepts Statement No. 3, *Elements of Financial Statements of Business Enterprises*,[1] defines liabilities as future sacrifices arising from present obligations as a result of past transactions or events. Unfortunately, this definition doesn't distinguish items that properly are included within the defined category from those that are outside it. This is an essential characteristic of any good definition.

Although bonds are classified as liabilities, many convertible bonds don't fit this definition of liabilities because there is no likelihood that the stated amount will ever be "sacrificed"; the bonds will be converted into stock. Conversely, redeemable preferred stock clearly is a liability under this definition, although it isn't treated as such in practice. The amount reported as deferred income taxes doesn't represent a probable future sacrifice of the stated amount.

THE SOLUTION

How can the right-hand side of the balance sheet be described in a meaningful way? The "sources of funds" idea is the most fruitful approach. Liabilities

---

[1] Financial Accounting Standards Board Concepts Statement No. 3, *Elements of Financial Statements of Business Enterprises* (Stamford, CT: FASB, 1980).

already reflect sources of funds. If the shareholder equity section could be reconstituted so that it also reports sources of funds, the right-hand side would report a conceptually consistent set of facts.

They desired result can be achieved by recognizing that there are three, rather than two, types of sources of funds: (1) liabilities; (2) funds supplied by shareholders, here labeled *shareholder equity*; and (3) funds generated by the entity's own efforts, here labeled *entity equity*.

Shareholder Equity

The amount of funds supplied by shareholders is greater than the amount the entity reports as paid-in capital. In addition to their direct contributions, shareholders also have furnished funds to the extent that the cost associated with the use of these funds hasn't been repaid to them in the form of dividends. I refer to the cost of using shareholder equity funds as equity interest. Unpaid equity interest is a source of funds, just like unpaid debt interest, but it appears nowhere on the balance sheet. The amount reported as shareholder equity should include both paid-in capital and unpaid equity interest.

Entity Equity

Both liabilities and shareholder equity represent funds supplied by outside parties. In addition to these external sources, a profitable entity also generates funds by its own operating activities. However, the amount of these internally generated funds isn't identified on the balance sheet. Retained earnings overstates this amount because the net income that adds to retained earnings overstates the entity's economic profitability; it omits the cost of equity interest. A new category is needed to report the amount of funds that the entity has generated through its own efforts after recovering all the associated costs. This category is entity equity.

Entity equity would report the cumulative amount of net incomes for all years to date.[2] Net income for a year would be the difference between revenues (including gains) and expenses (including losses and equity interest). Each year's net income would be added to entity equity, just as net income is added to retained earnings in current practice, but, because equity interest is recognized as a cost, the amount of entity equity would be much smaller than the amount of retained earnings as currently reported.

Recognition of Interest Cost

Both equity interest and debt interest are costs, and they should be accounted for just like other costs. Since interest is the cost of using funds for specified

---

[2] Entity equity also will increase by the amount of funds contributed for nonoperating purposes, such as additions to endowment and plant funds in nonprofit organizations. It will increase or decrease by entries such as the change in the valuation allowance of noncurrent equity securities.

time periods, interest cost should be charged to cost objects in proportion to the funds used by cost objects. Specifically

1. Interest is an element of the cost of newly acquired plant and equipment (and is now treated as such under FASB Statement No. 34, *Capitalization of Interest Cost*[3]). The cost should include the interest cost of funds tied up during the construction period for self-constructed plant and the interest cost of advance payments or progress payments on purchased plant.
2. The interest cost of funds used during the production process is an element of product cost and should be assigned to products in the same way that depreciation on plant and equipment is assigned.
3. When assets are held in inventory for significant lengths of time, an interest cost is incurred that should be added to the cost of the inventory items. As used here, *inventory* is interpreted broadly to include projects, mineral reserves, timber, nursery stocks and similar assets as well as material, work in process and finished goods. (Interest is now included as a cost of projects under FASB Statement No. 34.)
4. That part of the interest cost of a period that isn't capitalized for one of the above reasons is an expense of the period, just as other noncapitalized overhead costs are expenses.

The mechanics of accounting for these items are described in the appendix.

The amount reported for inventory would be larger than the amount now reported because of the inclusion of an interest component. (It wouldn't be excessively large because the lower-of-cost-or-market rule limits the reported amount to the realizable value of the inventory.) The amount for plant would be similar to the amount reported under FASB Statement No. 34 except that the amount of interest charged to the plant account would not be limited to the total amount of debt interest. (Under current concepts, this limitation is necessary because, without the explicit recognition of equity interest, any excess of capitalized interest cost over debt interest would end up as an item of income. An entity cannot earn income by dealing with itself.)

Revised View of the Balance Sheet

With the proposed changes, each item on the balance sheet gives a meaningful message, as summarized in Exhibit 1. Each item on the right-hand side represents the amount of funds supplied by the indicated source. Liabilities are amounts supplied principally by creditors but also by the government and other nonowner parties. (The issue of how, if at all, the gross amounts should be discounted is outside the scope of this article.) Shareholder equity represents the amount supplied by equity investors, both directly (as paid-in capital) and indirectly (as that portion of equity interest cost that hasn't been paid them as dividends). Liabilities and shareholder equity together represent

---

[3] FASB Statement No. 34, *Capitalization of Interest Cost* (Stamford, CT: FASB, 1979).

EXHIBIT 1 Schematic Balance Sheet as of December 31, 19X1 (As Proposed)

Assets*	Sources of funds
Items on this side report the forms in which the entity's funds exist and the amount tied up in each form as of December 31, 19X1.	Items on this side report the sources of the entity's funds and the amount obtained from each source as of December 31, 19X1.
Assets consist of	Fund sources consist of
1. Monetary assets These are money or claims to specified amounts of money. The amounts are the present value of these claims. 2. Unexpired costs These are nonmonetary assets to be used in future periods. The amounts are that part of these assets' costs that hasn't yet been charged as expenses. 3. Investments These are investments in other entities. The amounts are the amounts originally invested plus unpaid debt and equity interest on these amounts.	1. Liabilities Funds supplied by external parties other than equity investors. These parties include, among others a. Lenders (amounts supplied directly plus unpaid debt interest). b. Vendors. c. Employees (accrued wages and unfunded benefits). d. Government (deferred income taxes). 2. Shareholder equity Funds supplied by equity investors (amounts supplied directly plus unpaid equity interest). 3. Entity equity Funds obtained by the entity's own efforts. The cumulative difference through December 31, 19X1, between revenues (including gains) and expenses (including losses).

*For display, assets may be classified as either current or noncurrent.

the funds supplied by outside parties. The new section, entity equity, represents the amount of funds generated by the entity's own activities.[4]

The items on the left-hand side of the balance sheet report the forms in which the capital acquired with these funds exists as of the balance sheet date. This is, I submit, what the amounts reported as assets actually represent in current practice.

Some have said that the net effect of these changes would be merely to divide the amount now labeled *retained earnings* into two parts. As the appendix demonstrates, this is by no means the case. The change would affect the amount reported as net income and the amounts reported for many asset items. Also, the sum of shareholder equity and entity equity would not correspond to the amount now reported as shareholder equity, nor would any items in these two categories add up to the amount now reported as retained earnings.

The capitalization of interest also would recognize certain economic realities that aren't acknowledged in current practice. Goods that are held for a long time in inventory do incur additional costs as do holding growing

---

[4] In the unusual case in which dividends exceeded the cumulative amount of equity interest cost, the excess would reduce the amount of entity equity.

timber, mineral reserves or similar assets. These very real costs aren't currently recognized. One reason why the profits of petroleum companies appear to be "obscenely" high is that the costs of holding oil and gas reserves weren't recognized in earlier periods.

Revised View of the Income Statement

Recognition of equity interest as a cost would reduce the amount of net income, as compared with the amount currently reported. More importantly, it would increase the comparability of the income reported by companies with different debt-equity ratios and with assets that are held for different lengths of time. There is no way of taking the effect of these differences into account under current practice except by a laborious and inherently inexact adjustment of income statement amounts.

The proposed income statement also clarifies two concepts that are fuzzy in the current accounting model: (1) the meaning of income, or earnings, and (2) the meaning of financial capital maintenance.

The Income Concept. FASB Concepts Statement No. 3 defines income as the increase in net assets during a period, with net assets being the difference between assets and liabilities. The practical problem with this definition is that it requires a clear distinction between liabilities and shareholder equity. With the proliferation of financial instruments that are almost but not quite debt or almost but not quite equity, this line is almost impossible to draw. Under the proposed arrangement, however, income would be measured directly as the difference between revenues (including gains) and expenses (including losses). The problem of distinguishing between liabilities and equity doesn't arise.

Financial Capital Maintenance. Viewing the income statement as an explanation of changes in entity equity also leads to a clear way of reflecting the central accounting concept of financial capital maintenance. The conventional income statement implies that an entity has maintained its capital if it earns at least zero net income. This isn't so. With zero income, an entity hasn't provided anything for the cost of using shareholder equity funds. Such an entity is not viable. The use of shareholder equity funds involves a cost, and the entity hasn't maintained its capital unless its revenues are at least equal to all items of cost, including this one.

MEASURING EQUITY INTEREST COST

Shareholders wouldn't furnish funds unless they expected to earn a return, and the expected return is the cost of using these funds. Critics assert that there is no reliable way of measuring this cost. (In most companies, dividends far understate the cost.)

The absence of an accurate measurement method doesn't, however, deter accountants from reporting such items as the cost of employee pension plans. Measuring this cost involves assumptions about the service life and mortality of plan participants, interest rates, inflation rates (and, hence, future benefits) and other factors. Differences in expert judgments can easily result in pension cost estimates for a given company that differ significantly.[5]

Although the shareholder equity interest rate should correspond conceptually to the cost of using shareholder equity funds, an accurate number can be found only in special circumstances, principally in rate-regulated companies whose securities are publicly traded. The capital asset pricing model has been used to estimate the cost of using shareholder equity funds. There are difficult conceptual and practical problems in applying this model to actively traded companies; for any company whose stock isn't actively traded, such an approach isn't possible.

The FASB has at least two practical alternatives, however. It could require either that each company use its own pretax debt interest rate as the rate for both debt and equity or that all companies use a rate obtained from some published source.

The first approach is implicit in FASB Statement No. 34. This standard specifies that the interest cost charged to qualifying assets be calculated by applying the entity's pretax debt interest rate to the funds used in acquiring such assets.

The other approach was used by the Cost Accounting Standards Board in Cost Accounting Standard (CAS) No. 414, *Cost of Money as an Element of the Cost of Facilities Capital*.[6] That standard states that the cost of using facilities capital is to be calculated at a rate specified semiannually by the U.S. Treasury. In contrast to the FASB approach, the CASB standard doesn't link the rate to a particular company's actual interest cost. It has the advantage, however, of being applicable even to companies that have no debt; moreover, no judgment is permitted in arriving at the rate used.

ADEQUACY OF THE APPROXIMATION

The funds used to finance assets are a mixture of debt and equity. The theoretically correct interest rate for measuring the cost of using these funds is an average of the aftertax debt and equity interest rates, weighted by the

---

[5] See, for example, Sara A. Lutz, "Pension Plan Disclosures: What They Mean," *Management Accounting*, April 1982, pp. 48–54. As a case in point, Lutz states that General Electric Company reported a pension liability on its balance sheet as of December 31, 1980, of $124 million, which it computed as the actuarial present value of accumulated benefits less net assets available. It disclosed in a note that the liability calculated by the actuarial method actually used by the company was $964 million. Use of the latter amount would have increased its liabilities and decreased its retained earnings by $840 million.

[6] Cost Accounting Standard No. 414, *Cost of Money as an Element of the Cost of Facilities Capital* (Washington, D.C.: Cost Accounting Standards Board, 1976).

proportions of each. Using the pretax debt rate for both debt and equity, as required in FASB Statement No. 34, results in a satisfactory approximation of this ideal. The pretax debt rate overstates the real cost of the debt component, but it correspondingly understates the cost of the equity component.

These relationships can be illustrated by an example. Assume that a company obtains 40 percent of its permanent funds from debt and 60 percent from equity, that the pretax cost of debt is 12 percent and that the tax rate is 50 percent. The cost of equity funds is higher than the pretax cost of debt, but by an unknown amount. Assume that the equity cost, if it could be calculated, is 15 percent. The theoretically correct cost of using funds is then 11.4 percent, calculated as follows:

	Pretax cost	Aftertax cost	Weight	Weighted amount
Debt	12%	6%	4	2.4%
Equity	15	15	6	9.0
True interest cost				11.4%

In this example the pretax debt cost, 12 percent, is within six tenths of a percentage point of the true interest cost of 11.4 percent. Exhibit 2 shows how closely the pretax debt rate approximates the theoretically correct rate under a variety of assumptions as to the mix of debt and equity capital and as to the spread between debt and equity interest costs.

In the great majority of companies, the proportion of debt is between 20 percent and 50 percent of total permanent funds, and in the great majority the risk premium for shareholder equity over debt is between two and four percentage points. For such companies, the use of a pretax debt rate produces a maximum error of two percentage points. This is less than the probable error (not the maximum error) inherent in the calculation of pension fund expenses.

Studies by J. W. Bartley and L. F. Davidson[7] show that small variations in the interest rate don't have a significant effect on intercompany comparisons in any case. A good approximation is preferable to assuming that equity interest cost is zero, which is the implication of current practice.

PRACTICAL ADVANTAGES

Accounting is supposed to report economic reality, and the basic reason for the proposed change is that it will lead to more realistic and more understandable financial statements. For example, many readers think that "net worth"

[7] J. W. Bartley and L. F. Davidson, "Accounting for the Cost of Capital: An Empirical Examination" (University of North Carolina Working Paper, March 1980).

EXHIBIT 2 Difference Between True Interest Cost and Pretax Debt Cost
of 12% Under Various Assumptions

Assumed percent of debt	Assumed equity cost			
	14%	16%	18%	20%
10%	−1.2	−3.0	−4.8	−6.6
			*	
20	−.4	−2.0	−3.6	−5.2
30	.4	−1.0	−2.4	−3.8
40	1.2	1.0	−1.2	−2.4
50	2.0	1.0	0	−1.0
60	2.8	2.0	1.2	.4
70	3.6	3.0	2.4	1.8
80	4.4	4.0	3.6	3.2
90	5.2	5.0	4.8	4.6

Example
Assume 10% debt (90% equity) and 14% true cost of equity:

	Aftertax cost	Weight	Weighted percentage
Debt	6%	.1	0.6
Equity	14	.9	12.6
Actual cost			13.2
Pretax debt cost			12.0
Understatement of actual cost			1.2

*The capital structure of most companies is within this box.

reports what the company is worth. Many others don't realize that reported
income greatly overstates the real profitability of a company. Practical people
may regard this as merely a theoretical point, however, and for them several
eminently practical consequences are described briefly in this section.

Comparability

If two companies differ in their debt-equity ratios but otherwise are identical,
under current practice the company with more debt will report lower net
income than the other company because the amount of debt interest is
reported as a cost while the amount of equity interest isn't reported at all.
Because interest is not a component of production cost, a company with a
large amount of capital tied up in plant understates its inventory and hence
overstates its income compared with a company that is less capital-intensive.
Similarly, companies with low inventory turnover, or with large mineral
reserves, growing timber and other assets that require the use of much
capital, understate the real cost of these assets and correspondingly overstate
income.

Some financial analysts attempt to adjust the financial statements to allow for these differences, but the process is complicated and the results are crude at best. Recognition of equity interest automatically makes these adjustments and therefore improves the comparability of financial statements. Several studies show that the explicit recognition of equity interest makes a significant difference in reported net income.

D. W. Young reconstructed the financial statements of three timber companies, going back at least 17 years, to recognize the cost of interest tied up in growing timber and to recognize equity interest as a period expense.[8] The effect was to increase the reported ending value of timberland by 83 percent, 46 percent, and 50 percent, for the three companies and to reduce their reported total income for the period by 60 percent, 51 percent, and 176 percent. Analysts could have arrived at a similar conclusion only by repeating this complicated year-by-year analysis.

J. A. Hayes adjusted the 1970 financial statements of 22 integrated oil companies to incorporate interest as a cost.[9] The change in their reported net income ranged from +11 percent to −292 percent. A decrease occurred in most cases, but other than that there was no consistent pattern to these changes.

C. J. Casey adjusted the 1974 retained earnings amounts of 189 companies in 16 industries.[10] There was no consistent pattern to the revised numbers, either across industries or within an industry.

Studies such as the above are time-consuming and, in the absence of detailed data, assumptions have to be made about some of the numbers. They are therefore approximations, but they are better approximations than analysts are likely to make, given the constraints on their time. In any event, analysts shouldn't be required to make these adjustments; accountants should report the appropriate numbers in the financial statements.

Correspondence With Investors' Decisions

The studies described above demonstrate that the inclusion of interest as a cost has a significant effect on reported income, assets and retained earnings. They don't by themselves demonstrate that the adjusted numbers are better. Such a conclusion is supported by studies made by J. W. Bartley and by J. W. Bartley and L. F. Davidson.[11] These studies tested whether income as con-

[8] D. W. Young, "Accounting for the Cost of Interest: Implications for the Timber Industry," *Accounting Review*, October 1976, pp. 788–799.

[9] J. A. Hayes and R. N. Anthony, "Accounting for the Cost of Interest" (Harvard Graduate School of Business Administration, Working Paper HBS 75-47, 1975).

[10] C. J. Casey, "Capitalization of Interest Costs: Empirical Evidence of the Effect on Financial Statements" (Harvard Graduate School of Business Administration, Working Paper HBS 78-59, 1978).

[11] J. W. Bartley, "Accounting for the Cost of Capital and the Assessment of Market Risk" (Paper presented at the American Accounting Association Annual Meeting, Boston, Massachusetts, August 1980). Bartley and Davidson, "Accounting for the Cost of Capital: An Empirical Examination."

ventionally reported corresponds more closely to the actual behavior of stock market prices than income as adjusted for equity interest. The capital asset pricing model was used, and it was applied to 200 companies in one study and to 210 companies (over a period of 13 years) in the other. The results indicate that, judged by the behavior of stock market prices, investors do tend to allow for the effect of equity interest in the price they pay for stock.

Income Tax Implications

Debt interest is allowed as a deductible expense on corporate income tax returns, but equity interest is not. The effect is to encourage the use of debt financing and to penalize equity financing. Since companies must maintain a prudent debt-equity ratio, the equity penalty inhibits a company's willingness to raise equity capital, hurts new and growing companies and reduces the total amount of capital formation in the economy. The drying up of equity capital formation is a serious problem.

Furthermore, a different tax treatment of debt interest and equity interest encourages companies to devise securities that are almost like equity but that nevertheless qualify as debt. The Internal Revenue Service has wrestled for years with the problem of drawing a line between these two sources of capital but with no success.

Recognition of equity interest as a deductible expense on the corporate income tax return would solve all these problems. Influential people in Congress recognize this fact, but they are unwilling to advocate the change. They say, "How can you expect us to recognize equity interest for income tax purposes when the accounting profession won't recognize it for financial reporting purposes?" This is a reasonable question.[12]

Consistency With Management Accounting

Many companies recognize equity interest as a cost in measuring the profitability of profit centers. Top management wants profit center managers to understand that no real profit has been earned until equity interest has been recouped.

Moreover, explicit recognition of equity interest cures a serious problem that can arise under conventional accounting. Assume a company accepts capital expenditure projects if the time-adjusted rate of return is at least 15 percent. If a proposed project requires an investment of $1,000 and is estimated to produce earnings of $300 a year for five years, it should be accepted; the time-adjusted return on such a project is slightly more than 15 percent. If such an investment is accepted, however, and if straight-line depreciation of $200 a year is charged, reported income in the first year will increase by only

---

[12] For a discussion of the advantages of allowing equity interest as a tax-deductible expense, compared with other proposals for correcting this inequity, see R. N. Anthony, "Recognizing the Cost of Interest on Equity," *Harvard Business Review*, January-February 1982. pp. 91–95.

$100 ($300 − $200), which indicates a return of only 10 percent ($100 ÷ $1,000).

Conventional accounting always understates the true return in the early years and overstates the true return in later years. Managers know this, and, if their performances are measured on the conventional basis, they are reluctant to propose an investment that reduces next year's reported profits, even though the investment is worthwhile. Recognition of equity interest, together with annuity depreciation, solves this problem. For the above example, this method reports a profit, after allowing for both interest and depreciation, every year.

Investors focus on reported net income, however, and many companies won't use for internal purposes a practice that gives a different result from that reported on the published income statement.

Consistency with Nonbusiness Accounting

A nonbusiness organization doesn't ordinarily obtain capital from equity investors, and its revenue therefore needn't provide for the recovery of equity interest. If businesses included equity interest as a cost, their reported net income would be comparable to that of nonbusiness organizations.

Many government-controlled organizations, especially in Europe, do have equity capital and do record the interest on that capital as a cost. There are practical advantages in having a single set of accounting principles applying to all organizations—business and nonbusiness, in the U.S. and elsewhere.

Legitimacy of Interest

Until a decade or so ago, the federal government maintained that interest wasn't a cost, except in public utility rate making. Consequently, governmental contractors couldn't recover interest costs, as such, in cost-reimbursement contracts. This attitude is changing. Interest on capital tied up in plant is specifically allowed by CASs No. 414 and No. 417, *Cost of Money as an Element of the Cost of Capital Assets Under Construction.*[13] Office of Management and Budget (OMB) Circular A-21, *Cost Principles for Educational Institutions,*[14] was revised in 1982 to provide for partial recognition of interest as a cost. OMB Circular A-87, *Cost Principles for State and Local Governments,*[15] was revised in 1980 to permit interest as an element of the cost of using buildings. Medicare and Medicaid regulations permit the recovery of debt interest and, in some circumstances, equity interest by health care providers. However, OMB Cir-

[13] CAS No. 417, *Cost of Money as an Element of the Cost of Capital Assets Under Construction* (Washington, DC: CASB, 1980).
[14] Office of Management and Budget Circular A-21, *Cost Principles for Educational Institutions* (Washington, DC: OMB, 1979).
[15] OMB Circular A-87, *Cost Principles for State and Local Governments* (Washington, DC: OMB, 1981).

cular A-122, *Cost Principles for Nonprofit Organizations*,[16] doesn't permit interest as an allowable cost.[17]

Thus, the government is gradually changing its long-standing opposition to the recognition of interest. A financial accounting standard requiring such recognition would give impetus to this movement.

CONCLUSION

Full recognition of equity interest as an element of cost and of entity equity as a source of funds will require major changes in accounting, probably too drastic to be adopted all at once. The FASB's first step in this direction was Statement No. 34. Its next step should be to incorporate interest, on both debt and equity, as an element of cost in long-lived inventories, including growing timber, petroleum and other mineral reserves and nursery stocks.

The final step, which should be salable within a few years, is to recognize equity interest as a cost whenever it is appropriate and to reconstruct the right-hand side of the balance sheet so that unpaid equity interest is reported separately from the equity that the entity has generated through its own efforts. Opposition can be expected from those who believe that (1) the change is of no consequence or (2) there is no satisfactory way of measuring equity interest cost. I have tried to show that neither of these objections is valid.

APPENDIX: Accounting Procedures and Their Effect on the Financial Statements

This appendix describes the mechanics of accounting for the cost of interest and contrasts financial statements prepared on the basis of this accounting with those prepared in accordance with current practice. It is based on Chapter 7 of my book *Accounting for the Cost of Interest* (Lexington, MA: D. C. Heath and Company, 1975), modified to incorporate improvements that have been suggested since the publication of that book.

THE INTEREST POOL

Think of an "interest pool" account that is analogous to the conventional overhead pool. Elements of interest cost are debited to the interest pool

---

[16] OMB Circular A-122, *Cost Principles for Nonprofit Organizations* (Washington, DC: OMB, 1980).
[17] For an excellent description of the historical development and current status of interest recognition in contracts of all types, see the 130-page opinion in the *Pennsylvania Blue Shield* case (ASBCA no. 21113), July 20, 1982. The traditional attitude about interest is in 28 U.S.C. section 2516(a): "Interest on a claim against the United States shall be allowed in a judgment of the Court of Claims only under a contract or Act of Congress expressly providing for payment thereof."

account, and the total amount accumulated in it during an accounting period is allocated to various asset and expense accounts. Assume that entries to the interest pool account for 19X1 are as follows (omitting $000 or $000,000, as you wish):

Interest Pool			
Debits		**Credits**	
Debt		To cost of sales	$32
Interest	$25	To inventory	8
Equity		To plant	4
interest	35	To general expense	16
Total	$60	Total	$60

Debits to the Interest Pool

Debt interest ($25) is the actual amount of debt interest cost incurred during the year.

Equity interest ($35) is the cost of using shareholder equity funds. The amount is calculated by applying a rate to the amount of shareholder equity. The $35 is credited to shareholder equity.

The rate is here assumed to be 10 percent, the same as the pretax rate for long-term debt. (Alternatively, this rate might be designated by the Financial Accounting Standards Board.)

The amount is here taken as the amount of shareholder equity at the beginning of the year. It would be increased if new shareholder equity funds were obtained during the year. Conceivably, it could be adjusted by the difference between additions (equity interest) and subtractions (dividends) during the year; however, this refinement, which is analogous to compound interest, probably isn't warranted.

An unsettled point is whether this rate should be applied to entity equity funds as well as to shareholder equity funds. Such a treatment assumes that there is a cost of holding entity funds, which some people dispute. On the other hand, it can be argued that there is an opportunity cost of investing entity equity funds in a given project. The counter to this argument is that accounting doesn't recognize opportunity costs.

Interest Chargeout Rate

Interest is charged to cost objects at a rate similar to an overhead rate. The rate is established at the beginning of the year by dividing the estimated interest cost ($60) by the estimated average amount of capital employed during the year. It is assumed here that the average capital employed during 19X1 was as follows:

Inventory	$105
Other current assets	168
Plant under construction	44
Other assets (at book value)	350
Total capital employed	$667

These average asset levels are estimated in a manner similar to that used in developing the basis of overhead allocations.

The allocation rate is therefore

$$\frac{\text{Annual interest cost}}{\text{Capital employed}} = \frac{\$\ 60}{\$667} = 9\%$$

This 9 percent rate is less than the assumed debt and equity interest rate because some funds (such as accounts payable) are obtained at zero explicit interest cost.

A good conceptual case can be made for establishing two allocation rates, one for current assets and a higher rate for noncurrent assets, which have a lower turnover and hence a higher risk exposure. This possible refinement is omitted here.

Charges to Cost Objects

The principal items to which an interest cost is charged are inventory, plant under construction and expense.

Inventory ($40).   Interest is a component of production cost. It is allocated to products in the same way that depreciation is charged. In most circumstances, the best basis of allocation is the sum of annual interest cost and annuity depreciation, which is a level total each year. An interest charge also is added to the cost of products that remain in inventory for a relatively long time. (For items that turn over rapidly, the charge would be immaterial.) *Inventory* is used here in a broad sense to include mineral reserves, growing timber and nursery stock, and projects in process, such as motion picture films and real estate developments.

Plant Under Construction ($4).   Interest is a component of the cost of constructing plant. It is charged to construction in progress in the manner prescribed in FASB Statement No. 34, *Capitalization of Interest Cost*.[18] No interest is added to plant account after the plant goes on stream. The cost of using the funds committed to the plant is an element of the inventory cost (and eventually cost of sales) of products produced in the plant.

---

[18] Financial Accounting Standards Board Statement No. 34, *Capitalization of Interest Cost* (Stamford, CT: FASB, 1979).

Expense ($16). The balance in the interest pool account, after the above charges have been made, is an expense of the period. The amount of interest associated with the capital used in marketing, administrative and other non-manufacturing activities could be charged as a cost of these activities, but the effect on net income is the same whether interest expense is shown separately or charged to these cost objects.

FINANCIAL STATEMENTS

Table 1 shows how financial statements will look when interest is recognized as a cost, compared with those prepared according to current practice. The adjustments assume that this is the first year under the new system. Differences between the two sets of statements and the effect on future years are explained.

Operating Statement

Cost of sales on the operating statement increases by the amount of the interest component. The total interest cost charged to production was $40, of

TABLE 1 Current and Proposed Financial Statements

	As now reported		As proposed	
Operating statement, 19X1				
Sales revenue		$1,000		$1,000
Cost of sales	$700		$732	
Selling, general and administrative expense	220		211	
Income tax expense	40	960	40	983
Net income		$ 40		$ 17
Balance sheet, December 31, 19X1				
		Assets		Assets
Inventory		$135		$143
Plant and equipment (net)		300		304
Other assets		300		300
Total assets		$735		$747
		Equities		Sources of funds
Current liabilities		$115		$115
Long-term debt		250		250
Shareholder equity		370		365
Entity equity		*		17
Total		$735		$747

*No such item on current balance sheet.

which $8 remains in inventory, so the additional cost of sales is $32. In subsequent years the amount reported as cost of sales will be higher than under current practice, by the amount of the interest component.

Selling, general and administrative expense decreases by $9. This is the net of two items: (1) a decrease of $25 because debt interest, as such, is no longer charged; and (2) an increase of $16 representing the interest cost not charged to asset accounts.

Income tax expense is unchanged. It is assumed that, at least initially, equity interest won't be allqwed as a tax deductible item.

Net income decreases by $23, primarily because equity interest is recognized as a cost. The decrease does not correspond to the amount of equity interest because some equity interest ends up in asset accounts. In subsequent years, the reported net income will be lower than is the case under current practice.

Balance Sheet

On the balance sheet, inventory increases by $8—the amount of interest cost charged to products that remain in inventory. In subsequent years the reported inventory amount will be higher than under current practice because of the inclusion of this cost element.

Plant increases by $4, the amount of interest capitalized in plant under construction.

On the present balance sheet, shareholder equity isn't separated from entity equity. In the proposed balance sheet, it is assumed, for simplicity, that entity equity at the beginning of the first year was zero; therefore, shareholder equity was $350. Changes in shareholder equity during the year are as follows:

	Present	Proposed	Difference
Beginning balance	$350	$350	$ 0
Net income	+40	*	-40
Equity interest	*	+35	+35
Dividends	-20	-20	0
Ending balance	$370	$365	$ -5

*Not included in shareholder equity

Since it is assumed that entity equity starts at zero, the balance at the end of the year is equal to the net income, $17. The balance in entity equity will increase in years in which there is a positive net income.

The Long and Short of Asset Lives

Don Egginton

University of Bristol, England

Failure to review the lives of fixed assets distorts accounts. The recently revised depreciation standard SSAP 12 calls for a regular review of lives, which may lead companies to reconsider their policies. Don Egginton examines some evidence on company practice and questions whether SSAP 12 goes far enough.

Certainty is said to be confined to death and taxes, but for death the timing is uncertain. How long life will last is a matter of estimation. Where a fixed asset is concerned, actual life may well prove longer or shorter than was forecast for depreciation.

Estimation errors can be corrected during asset life, and in principle continuous revision could ensure that book value matches disposal value at the end of life. Failure to revise will give messy endings; either assets will continue in use despite nil book values, or undepreciated amounts will have to be written off at disposal.

If there were no bias in estimation, the errors of lives which are longer or shorter than forecast would roughly cancel out. But *on average* U.K. companies understate the lives of their assets, so that many companies have hidden reserves of fully depreciated assets which remain in use. The U.K. is not alone in this respect, but we cannot blame our tax rules for influencing depreciation in financial accounts, as can some other countries. The reasons may be conservatism, crude attempts to bring the depreciation charge nearer to current costs, or tardiness in replacing old assets.

Whatever the reasons, the asset lives recorded in official U.K. statistics are thought to be about twice as long as those in company accounts (*Economic Trends*, August 1984, p. 98). To anyone who really believes in straight-line depreciation, that would imply enormous hidden reserves roughly equal to the disclosed net book values of depreciable assets. Although such an extreme view can be excluded, the scale of the discrepancy on lives raises serious doubts about the meaning of the true and fair view in company accounts.

The average understatement of asset lives must mean that the majority of companies have been less than diligent in revisions. In fact the old depreciation standard SSAP 12 (1977) made no direct requirement for the systematic revision of asset lives, but stated: "Where there is a revision of the estimated useful life of an asset, the unamortised cost should be charged over the revised remaining useful life" (paragraph 17). This charging method remains in SSAP 12 (1987 paragraph 18); it modifies straight-line depreciation into a reduced charge when life is extended, and into an increased charge if revision shortens life. But the new version says that "where, however, future results would be materially distorted, the adjustment to accumulated depreciation should be recognised in the accounts in accordance with SSAP 6 Extraordinary Items and Prior Year Adjustments". Thus there is now an option to treat the effects of revision as an extraordinary item. For the user of accounts the extraordinary item approach does have the merit of explicitly requiring the amount and nature of the adjustment to be shown; for the preparer of accounts it will have the attraction of keeping the adjustment out of the earnings per share calculation.

Previously the only possibility of softening the blow to the P & L account occurred when a dramatic change in estimated lives could be regarded as part of an overall correction of fundamental errors or change in accounting policy, qualifying for treatment as a prior year adjustment under SSAP 6.

In this case the effect of the change goes to reserves, avoiding the unfavourable impact on the P & L when revision shortens lives. This route is still strictly available but companies may be less concerned to take it now that the extraordinary items approach has been approved.

There is a new specific requirement in paragraph 18 that "lives of assets should be reviewed regularly and, where necessary, revised". But there is no rule on the *frequency* of the review; the explanatory note does suggest a review "would normally be undertaken at least every five years", but that is neither very demanding nor part of the standard.

The exposure draft ED 37 proposed a safety net, requiring companies to reinstate fully depreciated assets where necessary for a true and fair view. This rule would have acted as a check on failures to revise lives upwards, but unfortunately it did not reach SSAP 12. The ASC bowed to the weight of objections; it was said that the proposal was unnecessary if realistic estimation and review of lives were carried out, and omission would rarely impair a true and fair view anyway. The very strength of the protests suggested that the rule would have had an impact, and the view that fully depreciated assets are rarely material is contradicted by the U.K. statistical evidence. The findings below show that rigorous review procedures cannot be taken for granted.

COMPANY PRACTICE

Senior accountants in 12 large companies from different industries were interviewed on fixed asset policies. Six companies were in the top 100 of the *Times* 1000 and three others were substantial public companies. The remaining three companies were in the public sector, but their responses were well distributed through the range of private sector answers.

Questions were asked on the review policy for asset lives, on the scale of fully depreciated assets in use, and on revisions which had occurred in the previous four years. In two cases respondents in holding companies gave answers on the diverse practices of subsidiaries, so that answers relating to 15 "companies" were obtained. These answers are summarised in Table 1,

TABLE 1 Company Policies and Practices on Revision of Asset Lives

Review policy on asset lives	Number of companies	Fully depreciated assets still in use				Revisions in preceding 4 years		
		None	Some	Moderate	A lot	None	Minor	Major and minor
Very formalised, annual or less	3	a,d	F				a,d	F
Fairly formalised, annually	3		b,G,H				b,G,H	
Fairly formalised, every 2–3 years	2		I	e		I	e	
"Kept under review"	7		J,K	c	L,M,N,O	c,J,K,N	L,O	M
Number of companies	15	2	7	2	4	5	8	2

NOTE: Companies a, b and c are subsidiaries in the same group; d and e are subsidiaries in another group.

where subsidiaries are shown in lower case and other companies in upper case.

Although the grouping of the answers is inevitably subjective, the differences proved reasonably clear-cut. On review policy, subsidiaries a and d were both in extractive industries with well-established procedures for recalculating unused resources. The other company which was very assiduous in its revisions was F, where a special committee met regularly to review experience on lives of plant and made quite fine adjustments. At the other extreme were those companies which claimed to keep lives under review, but gave no indication of the process by which this was done.

The central columns of Table 1 tabulate fully depreciated assets in historical cost accounts against the company's review policy. In only one case was a quantified answer obtained on fully depreciated assets; this was from company H, where most of the assets were physically similar and about 8 percent had been fully depreciated. In the other cases answers were qualitative, and although respondents may have been secretive, it seemed that explicit information was not available. The answers of "none" for subsidiaries a and d related to their main extractive assets; there may have been some minor items fully depreciated.

Among the practices not fully reflected in Table 1 was the approach adopted by company L. This company continued to provide depreciation on assets which had been fully depreciated, a strong case of correcting the P & L account at the expense of the balance sheet. However, the excess depreciation was not allowed to go beyond 10 percent of the historical cost of company assets. When the need arose to reduce the lives of other assets, the company wanted to treat the adjustment as a prior year adjustment under SSAP 6. The solution agreed with the auditors was that the reduction of lives would be offset against the excess depreciation accumulated for fully depreciated assets.

As might be expected, the pattern of responses shows that greater amounts of fully depreciated assets tended to remain in use as review policies became less formalised. The companies with the "kept under review" policy were generally conservative in their estimates of asset lives, and it seemed that lives were unlikely to be revised so long as they remained on the cautious side.

The right hand side of Table 1 summarises revisions to asset lives during the preceding four years. Two companies reported major adjustments, which involved more than 5 percent of the historical cost of assets in the balance sheets of the companies. Both the major revisions were treated as adjustments to reserves under SSAP 6 rather than as changes to future depreciation charges under SSAP 12. All the other revisions were considered minor (for example, in two cases vehicle lives were reduced from 5 years to 4 years) and adopted the SSAP 12 procedure.

It might be thought that companies with rigorous review policies would make frequent minor revisions but would be able to avoid major adjustments.

That is not supported by the major revision of company F. In fact the cause of this revision was not a failure of the normal procedures to deal with gradual change, but a need for adjustment arising from a major "one-off" external change. The most careful internal review procedures cannot deal with dramatic external change in an undramatic way.

Company M's major revision seemed to be more in the nature of a spring-cleaning in the face of market changes which had taken place over a few years. However, the auditors considered the adjustments to be eligible for the SSAP 6 prior year adjustment rule.

The tentative conclusions must be that review policy can eliminate hidden reserves, but cannot avoid the occasional dramatic impact of external changes. The less comfortable observation must be that companies with hazy review policies are not put at a noticeable accounting disadvantage. Those with conservative depreciation policies have a cushion if future adjustments should prove necessary, and those who do not respond swiftly to market changes may be able to make reserve adjustments like company M.

AUDIT CASES

Another view of asset life revisions is given by some audit cases, unconnected with any of the companies considered above. Three major audit firms gave information on revisions which had been examined with nine public company clients. Most of the cases also involved current cost accounts, but the decisions for the historical cost accounts are summarised in Table 2.

Only one out of six who contemplated reductions in asset lives made the revision, but all three upward revisions examined were carried out. Details of the rejected reductions were available in only two cases. Both of these companies had idle and underused assets; one faced the advent of technically superior assets and the other had falling demand and had been making losses for two years. It may therefore seem surprising that asset lives remained unrevised.

Assuming that all the cases were validly examined by the auditors, the pattern of the decisions might be explained by lives which were originally underestimated. A review would then reveal that there was scope for revising upward but relatively little need for reducing lives. None of the auditors said that asset lives had originally been too conservatively estimated but disap-

TABLE 2 Audit Cases on Revision of Asset Lives

	Downward revision of asset lives	Upward revision of asset lives
Seriously examined with client but not made	5	0
Revision made in accounts	1	3

proving remarks by auditors on two of the upward revision cases support that possibility. One auditor commented: "They did not like the results they were getting on their accounts. . . . They have been able to go to a substantially longer life, and there is not much the auditor can do about it, other than giving SSAP 12 disclosure in the notes." On the other case a different auditor said "The sole reason was not to present their figures in a worse light than was either necessary or adopted by other companies."

The comments imply that the auditors were unhappy but powerless to prevent a movement away from conservative lives. Perhaps their views arose from ideas of prudence or from a belief that hidden reserves were being used for creative accounting purposes. Whatever the motives in those two cases, the auditor responses generally revealed little enthusiasm for revising asset lives.

CONCLUSIONS

The cases which have been considered suggest that an average bias towards conservative lives and a tardiness in revising asset lives go hand in hand. The effect on company balance sheets cannot be quantified in financial terms. However, there is evidence that hidden reserves may be substantial, and a suspicion in at least two cases that hidden reserves were drawn upon at convenient times.

In an ideal world companies would review asset lives as part of their overall investment planning, taking into consideration changes in demand and technology which affect the lives of their existing assets. The evidence suggests that such an approach is the exception rather than the rule. It therefore becomes particularly important that accounting standards and the attentions of auditors should ensure that the needs of users of accounts are satisfied. Three measures which could help would be a maximum review period of (say) three years, fuller disclosure of the lives assumed, and adoption of the safety net requiring fully depreciated assets to be reinstated where that is necessary for a true and fair view.

Letter from Howard P. Hodges
to General Motors Corporation

November 14, 1990

Chairman Robert C. Stempel
General Motors Corporation
3044 West Grand Boulevard
Detroit, Michigan 48202

Dear Chairman Stempel,

The Wall Street Journal (11/1/90) reports that third quarter 1990 earnings for General Motors reflects a $2.1 billion charge to cover the cost of closing several plants, including plant closings that won't actually occur for two to three years. The story quotes you as saying that this is "a major element in GM's long-term strategic plan to improve the competitiveness and profitability of its North American operations." Whether or not it improves competitiveness remains to be seen. But, it is clear that charging expense today for the cost of $2.1 billion of plant that would otherwise have to be depreciated as a cost of future years operations will reduce expense in future accounting periods, and improve reported profits in future periods by a like amount.

The announced write off in the initial quarter in which a new person assumes the Chairmanship might be accepted if it is a big bath to clear the books of costs incurred by the previous Chairman associated with projects that the new Chairman will scrap. But a closer look at General Motors financial statements in recent years raises a question as to the integrity of its financial reporting, either for 1987 or 1990. The question: Is General Motors using depreciation, amortization and restructuring charges to control reported income?

A note regarding depreciation in the financial statements in the 1987 annual report to shareholders states that:

> In the third quarter of 1987, the Corporation revised the estimated service lives of its plants and equipment and special tools retroactive to January 1, 1987. These revisions, which were based on 1987 studies of actual useful lives and periods of use, recognized current estimates of service lives of the assets

Reprinted by permission of Howard P. Hodges, CPA (New York), formerly the Chief Accountant of the Division of Corporation Finance, Securities and Exchange Commission. The letter was written after the author's retirement from the SEC.

and had the effect of reducing 1987 depreciation and amortization charges by $1,236.6 million or $2.55 per share of $1-2/3 par value common stock.

So far, there have not been any newspaper reports explaining what studies support the proposed $2.1 billion write off in the third quarter of 1990, nor any explanation as to why it was necessary to shorten the lives of plants so soon after the 1987 depreciation study which resulted in lengthening the lives of plant. If the $2.1 billion write off was effected in the third quarter of 1990, it seems reasonable to assume that some study had commenced well before that date. Why was the 1987 study obsolete so soon?

Is it possible that General Motors knew or should have known in 1987 that its study was faulty? The Chairman's Message to Stockholders in the 1987 annual report states that:

> GM earned $3.6 billion for the year, up 21 percent from 1986 despite a 9 percent reduction in worldwide unit sales.

Without the $1.2 billion increase in income arising from the reduced depreciation charge in 1987, net income would have been lower than in 1986 and the Chairman's Message to Stockholders less ebullient. If unit sales were down in 1987, what consideration was given at that time to the possibility that excess capacity existed, and that such write offs should have been used to offset, in part at least, the then planned increases in lives of assets and the reduced depreciation charges in 1987 and future years?

It is probably less obvious to most shareholders that the $1.2 billion reduction in depreciation expense in 1987 carries forward into future years and that cumulatively through the third quarter of 1990, the new depreciation rates may have increased income by an estimated $4.5 billion ($1.2 billion in each of 1987, 1988, 1989, and 3/4 of that amount for the first three quarters of 1990), an amount in excess of the $2.1 billion write down taken in the third quarter of 1990. If no adjustment of depreciation rates had been made in 1987, would a $2.1 billion write down have been necessary in 1990?

It is also noted that in 1986 a provision was made for scheduled plant closings and other restructuring of $1.2876 billion. However, through 1989, only $.518 billion has been charged against this provision. In understanding General Motors financial statements, it would be helpful in understanding cost of sales figure trends to know whether the 1986 and 1990 charges are for the estimated amount of book value of the plants at the date they are to be closed and that depreciation on plants still in use is being recorded as a cost of sales, or whether the charges represent a full write off of the book value of the plants at the date the charges were recorded, with the result that cost of sales is relieved of any depreciation charges during the future years that the plants are in use.

I would appreciate a response to my questions, and hope that my questions will focus your attention on the dilemma a shareholder faces when they must rely on published financial information to understand the financial condition of their investment. I would prefer that a response be made in a format that makes answers to my questions available to all shareholders.

Notwithstanding my serious questions about the financial reporting of General Motors, I wish you success as the new Chairman and hope that you are successful in restoring General Motors to the position of prominence it once held.

Yours very truly,

Howard P. Hodges

cc: Mr. George P. Shultz, Finance Committee, General Motors
Chairman Richard C. Breeden, U. S. Securities & Exchange Commission
Chairman Charles C. Cox, United Shareholders Association
Prof. Abraham J. Briloff, Bernard Baruch College
Messrs. Joseph B. White and Paul Ingrassia, Wall Street Journal
Mr. A. Clarence Sampson, Financial Accounting Standards Board

Letter from General Motors to Howard P. Hodges

February 13, 1991

Mr. Howard P. Hodges
604 Allison Street
Alexandria, Virginia 22302

Dear Mr. Hodges:

Let me start by thanking you for taking the time to research and prepare your recent letter to Mr. Stempel. If more public shareholders would display the interest in their companies as you have, our free enterprise system would certainly be enhanced. Please forgive the time it has taken to respond to your thoughtful letter. However, as you can undoubtedly tell from media reports, we have been intensely focused on the business itself.

As your letter displays a significant knowledge of accounting concepts, you are probably aware of the requirement under generally accepted accounting principles that a loss of the nature provided for in our 1990 third quarter be recognized at the point in time that management, with the approval of the Board of Directors, commits itself to a formal plan. It is for this reason that the provision was recorded in the third quarter. We do not view it as a "big bath" related to "projects that the new Chairman will scrap." Nor, as I will discuss further below, do we agree that a closer look at the General Motors financial statements should raise any questions as to the integrity of our financial reporting.

As Chief Financial Officer, I can assure you that General Motors' reported income is based on sound accounting principles concurred with by our independent public accountants. The revisions to the estimated service lives of certain assets made in 1987 were based on studies made of actual experience. We have no reason today to question the findings of the 1987 studies. Those studies reflected the effect of an extensive modernization program on plants which were almost fully depreciated. The programs greatly extended the useful lives of the plants. The third quarter 1990 action does not shorten the lives of plants, but reflects management's conclusion with respect to current and future plant capacity requirements. As you might expect, we review plant capacity requirements continually. Over time, it has been more common to find a need for greater capacity. Unfortunately, that was not the conclusion reached in 1990.

It is impossible to determine accurately to what extent the 1990 restructuring charge would have been less had the depreciation rates not been adjusted in 1987. However, the impact would not have been significant, since a substantial portion of the 1990 restructuring charge related to people costs on which the 1987 depreciation adjustment would have no effect.

We hope these comments provide additional insight into the decisions made by the management of General Motors. If you have further questions, I would be pleased to respond to them.

We at General Motors are confident our new leadership will indeed be successful in directing the Company through the challenging times ahead. We appreciate your good wishes and continued support.

Sincerely,

Robert T. O'Connell
Executive Vice President
General Motors Corporation

cc: Mr. R. C. Stempel

· Disclosure and the Impairment Question

Walter Schuetze

Chief Accountant, Securities and Exchange Commission

Accounting for impaired long-lived, nonmonetary assets is an old problem, one of the acknowledged imperfections of financial accounting and reporting. The problem is when to recognize "impairment"—the inability to recover the carrying amount—by a write-down and how to measure it. Practice is inconsistent, and rules that would establish consistency thus far have eluded standard setters. In view of the confusion, this article proposes an interim solution: required disclosure of the fair value of nonmonetary assets when fair value is less than cost.

IMPAIRMENT AND THE WINDS OF CHANGE

The first feature of the problem is its urgency. Economic change is now so rapid that various assets all too frequently lose some or all of their capacity to recover cost. This is obvious in the case, say, of a dramatic drop in the price of oil that impairs the cost, or value, of oil- and gas-drilling rigs. The conditions that lead to such events can be treated as unique, but ongoing conditions also lead to asset impairment. Technological advances that create obsolescent plant, equipment, patents, and licenses are common events today, and rapid technological progress is a condition that will continue to be with us. Similarly, intense competition and rapid changes in market demand are standing rather than temporary conditions, and both can impair asset values. Still other conditions that can impair asset values—most notably, volatile interest and foreign-exchange rates—have been around long enough to make their disappearance hard to anticipate.

All these factors suggest that users of financial statements would benefit from information on impaired long-lived assets.

The urgency of the problem is also illustrated by the sense of surprise sometimes expressed when huge write-downs are reported. Many believe that either the management or the independent auditors, or both, should have warned users of financial statements about the possibility of these write-downs or foreseen the necessity for write-downs and reported them earlier. Such beliefs erode confidence in financial reporting.

From *Journal of Accountancy* (December 1987), pp. 26–28, 30, 32. Reprinted by permission of the American Institute of Certified Public Accountants, Inc. Copyright © 1987 by the American Institute of Certified Public Accountants, Inc. Opinions of the authors are their own and do not necessarily reflect policies of the AICPA. This article was written when Schuetze was a partner in Peat Marwick Main & Co.

LITTLE CLARITY IN THE LITERATURE

The second feature of the problem is that the authoritative literature contains no clear, operational guidance on accounting for impaired long-lived assets.

In fact, the absence of a rule on when to write down impaired long-lived assets was acknowledged explicitly by the Financial Accounting Standards Board in 1977 in Statement no. 19, *Financial Accounting and Reporting by Oil and Gas Producing Companies:* "The question of whether to write down the carrying amount of productive assets to an amount expected to be recoverable for future use of those assets is unsettled under present generally accepted accounting principles. This is a pervasive issue that the Board has not addressed."

Despite the support one can find in various places in the literature for the concept of mandatory write-downs of impaired long-lived assets, serious practical problems have made it difficult to establish a rule for consistent practice:

- How does one know when the cost of an asset is sufficiently impaired to necessitate a write-down?
- Should the write-down be mandatory if there is a chance that the asset will regain its stature or only when impairment is permanent?
- How does one distinguish with confidence between temporary and permanent impairments?
- How does one disaggregate impaired individual assets from other elements in an operating unit?
- Should write-ups be permissible for assets that have become unimpaired?
- Under what circumstances, if any, would a shortened amortization period or an accelerated depreciation method coupled with a reduction in residual value be more appropriate than a write-down (for example, a change from units-of-production depreciation to an accelerated depreciation method for facilities operating significantly below normal levels)?
- How should write-downs to recognize impairments be measured?

The measurement alternatives include fair value, replacement cost, undiscounted future cash flows, and discounted future cash flows using a choice of several possible interest rates. The measurement base can assume break-even, a normal profit margin, or less than a normal profit margin. The discount rate can be the enterprise's incremental borrowing rate, its cost of capital, a risk-free rate, or some other rate.

INCONSISTENCIES IN PRACTICE

Current practice is marked by two types of inconsistency. There is no uniform practice in selecting the circumstances that justify or require a write-down, and there is no uniform practice in measuring the amount of such write-downs. As of this writing, the FASB's emerging issues task force has discussed the issue three times but reached a consensus on only one point—that the dominant practice is to recognize permanent rather than temporary impairment.

There are some hard data on inconsistencies in practice. The Financial Executives Institute (FEI) surveyed a number of companies reporting unusual charges in 1985. Of 24 companies reporting write-downs of fixed assets retained by the business (either idle or still in use), 60 percent of the decisions to write down the asset were based on a probability test similar to that in FASB Statement no. 5, *Accounting for Contingencies,* and 36 percent of the decisions were based on the permanent decline test. Thirteen of the write-downs (46%) were measured by net realizable value, 5 (18%) by undiscounted expected future cash flows, 4 (14%) by the net present value of future cash flows, and 3 (11%) by some combination of the former methods. The remaining three write-downs were based on current replacement cost, percentage of historical cost based on expected long-term capacity, and historical cost reduced by the cost of holding a building that could not be sold.

These and other data in the FEI survey show inconsistencies in practice, but a plurality of the participating companies (48%) responded in the negative to a question asking whether additional guidance from the FASB on accounting and reporting on the impairment of fixed assets was desirable. Thirty-eight percent responded that additional guidance would be useful. What the survey does not point out explicitly is that, in the absence of a decision to abandon or dispose of assets at a loss, the timing and amount of any write-down are largely discretionary.

PROPOSALS AND PROJECTS

In 1980 the AICPA accounting standards executive committee (AcSEC) recommended that the probability approach in FASB Statement no. 5 be used to determine whether to report the inability to recover fully the carrying amounts of long-lived assets. Under this approach, declines would be recorded in the accounts if the inability to recover cost is probable and the amount can be reasonably estimated. This proposal was an explicit rejection of the concept that declines should be recognized only if the assets are permanently impaired. AcSEC concluded that the concept of permanent decline in value was too subjective and restrictive. AcSEC also recommended, however, that no one method of measurement be prescribed for determining the amount of the write-down.

Looking back on AcSEC's conclusions in 1980—which I endorsed at the time—one can understand the rejection of subjective determinations of permanent impairment. But it is harder, now that our experience with Statement no. 5 has more than doubled, to agree that its probability test could serve as a replacement because it is sufficiently less subjective than the permanent-impairment test. In both cases, the preparer of the financial statements and the independent auditor must foretell the future.

ROADBLOCKS TO RECOGNITION AND MEASUREMENT CRITERIA

In order to develop operational criteria as to *when* to recognize and *how* to measure impairments of long-lived assets, the Financial Accounting Standards Board will have to answer the following questions, among many others.

1. For an investment type of asset, for example, a common stock, how long should the quoted market price stay below cost before a write-down is required? Six months? One year? Three years? May a write-down be reversed if the quoted price later bounces back?

2. For operating-type assets, such as plant, equipment and patents,

- Should the presence of an operating loss (assuming "operations" is clearly defined) for some period of time require a write-down? How long? Six months? One year? Two years? When does an asset become *operational*?
- Should the management of an enterprise be entitled to assume improved future cash flows from the asset or from reasonable groupings of assets?
- Should the future cash flows be discounted? At what rate?
- Once write-downs have been made, may those write-downs be reversed if cash flows improve?
- Should the question of a write-down be considered in tandem with the amortization/depreciation policy related to the assets? Estimated useful lives? Residual values?

3. How does one deal with the intangible asset that arises from the application of FASB Statement no. 87, *Employers' Accounting for Pensions,* in relation to pensions?

4. For how long should losses or "subnormal" earnings be allowed to run before goodwill should be written down?

5. May assets be grouped? (This question, in and of itself, is larger than it may seem, involving more than just write-downs.) What is the unit of accounting—individual assets or groups of assets?

The FASB's staff is now considering whether to recommend that the board add to its agenda a project on accounting for the inability to recover fully the carrying amounts of long-lived assets. One immediate issue for the FASB's staff is to define the project's objective. The objective could be to develop guidance on recognition and measurement of impairment of long-lived assets, or it could be to develop disclosure requirements that minimize the likelihood that users are taken by surprise when long-lived assets are written down. Unless the board simply requires that assets be written down to fair value whenever fair value is less than cost, the task of developing definitive, operational criteria for recognition and measurement of write-downs will be extremely difficult to complete. The board will have to answer many difficult questions, some of which are offered in the addendum "Road-blocks to Recognition and Measurement Criteria."

AN INTERIM SOLUTION

I suggest an interim solution while the FASB works on the recognition and measurement problems or before it adds the item to its formal agenda: The FASB should require disclosure of the fair value (estimated price in an immediate, but not forced, sale for cash) of a nonmonetary asset, or reasonable groupings of such assets, whenever the fair value of the asset at the date of the most recent balance sheet is less than its cost.

This proposal has several things going for it:

1. The rule would be unambiguous. Whether fair value of an asset is less than cost is—at least in theory—a question of fact, not a judgment. I do not deny that the facts may be hard to come by (and perhaps in some instances costly), but at least we know how and where to look for facts. And in some instances the facts are easy to come by, for example, price quotations in newspapers for marketable equity securities. From the independent auditor's perspective, this would be a tremendous improvement over the current state of affairs. As it is today, we do not search for facts. Rather, we rely on management's assertions about its judgment about recoverability of cost, and then we apply our judgment to that judgment.

   I also acknowledge that fair value of an asset often is not a clear-cut, indisputable fact, but at least we would be making judgments about facts, not speculating about future events and their outcomes, as we do today in trying to decide when and by how much to write down assets.

2. The disclosure would not be discretionary.

3. If there were no disclosure about cost being in excess of fair value, the user of the financial statements would be entitled to assume that fair value of the asset at least was equal to or in excess of cost at the date of the balance sheet. (One day later, however, fair value might be less than cost.)

4. If there were no disclosure and if the auditor's report were unqualified, the user of the financial statements would be entitled to assume that the independent auditor was satisfied that fair value of the asset was at least equal to or in excess of cost. This would mean that the preparer of the financial statements would have to produce evidential matter about the fair value of assets to satisfy the auditor.

5. Preparers and their independent auditors would not have to speculate, as they do today in assessing the need for write-downs, about future events and their outcomes, such as:

- Will the fair value—for example, the quoted market price of a common stock listed on the New York Stock Exchange—bounce back above cost? How likely is it to bounce back? How long will it take?
- Will cash flows from operations, but before interest charges, improve for an asset such as plant? Even if such cash flows do improve, will interest rates hold steady, decline or rise?
- How will cash flows from operations be affected by local, regional, national, and international competition?
- How will cash flows from operations for operating assets be affected by foreign exchange rate changes?

This proposal probably cannot be applied to goodwill, or most goodwill. Unless goodwill attaches to specific assets or groupings of assets (for example, to separate divisions), it cannot be sold and has no separate value. I would exclude goodwill from the disclosure requirement.

How much would it cost to implement this proposal? I don't know. Business people generally know, sometimes only intuitively, the fair value of their assets; they know what the marketplace would pay for the assets. I doubt, however, that independent auditors will accept intuition and unsupported assertions by management. The degree of auditor association with the disclosure will have to be worked out. If, however, auditor association appears to be a significant hurdle, it should be sacrificed, at least at the outset. The disclosures could be labeled "unaudited" or could be placed outside the basic financial statements and notes.

A PRACTICAL ALTERNATIVE

Because getting objectively determined fair values of nonmonetary assets often is difficult and costly, I suggest an alternative required disclosure that would be more practical for some assets. The alternative would be a standardized measure of cash flow to be disclosed in all cases when it is negative, along with the cost of the asset. The standardized measure of cash flow would be the net amount of annual operating revenue of the asset minus the annual related cash operating costs, both based on the most recent year's results, minus one year's hypothetical interest to carry the cost of the asset with that interest to be measured by using the 30-year U.S. Treasury bond rate at the balance sheet date.

This disclosure would allow users to make their own subjective determinations about fair value of the asset and whether a write-down is necessary.

A FIELD TEST FOR DISCLOSURE

Given the support for mandatory write-downs of impaired long-lived, non-monetary assets, the serious practical problems already cited must be considered the major obstacle to achieving a definitive, operational standard that would result in consistent practice and comparability for recognizing and measuring write-downs. The FASB may solve these problems, but we cannot assume that the answers will come quickly. Until the answers are in hand, users of financial statements would benefit from disclosures. However, the disclosures will not be comparable or consistent if they entail the same practical problems that have beset recognition and measurement in the accounts. In other words, the disclosures cannot be based on predicting future events and their outcomes. For this reason, I suggest consideration of required disclosures of fair value when it is below cost.

The relationship of costs to benefits for this disclosure may or may not be favorable, but we need to find out. One way to do this would be to subject the proposal to a test in the field.

I believe that such disclosure also would alleviate considerably the surprise that frequently accompanies business failures. A business failure almost always is preceded by a decline in the fair value of the assets of the enterprise. Disclosure of those declines should help to serve as a harbinger of failure and thus reduce surprise and shock, unless the declines are sudden, as in the case of the price of oil in 1986. Such disclosure should all but eliminate surprise related to write-downs, sometimes involving huge amounts, in the absence of a business failure.

You Know It When You See It

Penelope Wang
Forbes

Last winter wasn't a particularly good one for Pillsbury Co., and a footnote in the company's third-quarter report to shareholders showed why: a $113 million loss on the sale or shutdown of several restaurant operations, including its money-losing Godfather's Pizza chain. But precisely how did Pillsbury, which saw its stock jump nearly 10 percent in value on the day of the announced write-offs, wind up with the $113 million figure? You'll search Pillsbury's financials in vain for an answer, as indeed you would in the case of almost any other company engaged in writing off failed (or failing) assets.

The 1980s are clearly the decade of business restructurings and write-offs. But, ironically, accounting provides few rules to protect shareholders regarding when management can (or must) write off an "impaired asset," and by how much.

Since 1986 the Dow Jones industrials alone have taken at least $10 billion in writedowns, much of it related to impairment questions. A recent study by the National Association of Accountants reports that these impairment write-offs are one of the fastest-growing categories of all asset writedowns. Further, the study concludes that behind the numbers lurks "a climate of vague accounting standards" that gives companies too much leeway in choosing when and how to write down assets. That feeling was echoed in a survey of accountants by the Financial Accounting Standards Board who ranked impairment at the top of outstanding issues warranting new standards.

Yet many corporations don't seem eager for tightened standards, arguing that management is the best guide for when an asset becomes worthless. Even so, lax accounting standards can lead to abuses. In 1986, for example, the Securities & Exchange Commission took action against Charter Co. for attempting to sell a refinery at well below book value without first writing it down on its balance sheet. Warns Edmund Coulson, chief accountant at the SEC: "There are many other such cases in the pipeline."

What are the rules governing impairment? Under current accounting principles, a long-lived asset (plant, property and so on) should be labeled "impaired" when there is no hope of recovering its book value. Of course, hope, or lack of it, is in the eye of the beholder. Comments Wayne Kolins, partner at accounting firm Seidman & Seidman/BDO: "In these situations, it's often a case of people saying, 'You know it when you see it.'"

Once an asset has been judged impaired, companies also have considerable leeway in determining what balance sheet value to assign to it. Among the acceptable methods: net realizable value (what the asset will bring if sold); a total of projected future cash flows over the life of the asset; and "discounting"—the present value of those future cash flows based on a given rate of return. Since future cash flow is worth less than cash in hand, discounting can result in lower valuations and larger writeoffs.

To complicate matters, businesses have begun announcing partial writedowns based on "probable" impairment. This includes assets whose return no longer meets carrying costs but which might recover their value in the future. Thus in 1986 Squibb Corp. decided that political and economic conditions in South America and Asia had impaired its pharmaceuticals operations there. Squibb took a writedown of $68 million on those assets, declaring them "permanently" impaired. But are they really? Since Squibb concedes that there remains a "small probability" that those assets will recover, it is operating those facilities on a reduced scale.

With writedowns becoming such a common—and costly—feature of a business scene that is complex enough already, such accounting doublespeak is hardly to be welcomed. But without a clarification of the rules, there seems little doubt that it will continue.

The FASB and the Allocation Fallacy

Arthur L. Thomas
Professor Emeritus, University of Kansas

Off to an impressively active start, the Financial Accounting Standards Board has already wrestled with a broad range of accounting issues. Topics on its active agenda or on which it has issued Standards include

1. Accounting for leases.
2. Accounting for research and development costs.
3. Contingencies and future losses.
4. Gains and losses from extinguishment of debt.
5. Interest costs and capitalization.
6. Accounting for pensions.
7. Segment reporting.
8. Business combinations.
9. Interim financial statements.
10. Reporting by development stage entities.
11. Reporting in units of general purchasing power.
12. Translation of foreign currency transactions and financial statements.
13. The recommendations of the Trueblood Report.[1]

All these topics involve some kind of *allocation*, which is the assignment of a total to one or more locations or categories. A thesaurus gives "division," "partition," "slicing," "splitting," and "apportionment" as synonyms of "allocation." Accounting's allocations include assignment of a lease's costs to the individual years of its life, assignment of R&D costs to the single year of their expenditure and assignment of long term investment interest to successive annual revenues. All the FASB topics listed above fall into one of the following two classes of allocations, with items seven through nine falling into both:

1. The first nine topics require deciding when to recognize revenues, expenses, gains or losses—that is, deciding to what periods they should be assigned. For example, the FASB may eventually specify how to allocate pension costs to successive annual pension expenses.
2. The last seven topics involve ways of preparing financial statements composed mainly of allocated data. For example, this is implicit through-

From *Journal of Accountancy* (November 1975), pp. 65–68. Reprinted by permission of the American Institute of Certified Public Accountants, Inc. Copyright © 1975 by the American Institute of Certified Public Accountants, Inc. Opinions of the authors are their own and do not necessarily reflect policies of the AICPA.

Author's note: I'm grateful to Paul Rosenfield for his comments on an earlier draft of this article.
[1] "Objectives of Financial Statements," Report of the Study Group on the Objectives of Financial Statements, Robert M. Trueblood, chairman (New York: AICPA, October 1973).

out the Trueblood Report and explicit in its position statement and income statement recommendations.

In fact, almost all of our revenue recognition and matching efforts require allocation.

THE ALLOCATION PROBLEM

The foregoing is background to a problem that we accountants acknowledge, but whose severity we usually misjudge. To use a term from formal logic, recent research indicates that, unfortunately, our allocations must almost always be *incorrigible*—that is to say, they can neither be refuted nor verified.[2] Incorrigibility will be a central concept in this discussion, and it is well to give a few examples even if doing so may initially seem to be a detour.

Let's suppose that someone claims that beings live among us who look and act exactly like humans, but who actually are aliens, seeded on this planet by flying saucers. We ask: do they come equipped with authentic looking birth certificates? Yes. Would tests of their internal structure, chromosomes or the like expose them? No. Could psychiatrists unmask them? No. The horrible thing is that they have such good counterfeit memories that even the aliens themselves don't know their real nature—you may be one yourself.

Such claims are incorrigible, for no experiment could prove either that such aliens exist or that they don't. Here are some other incorrigible claims:

- Charles Dickens may not have been a greater author than Shakespeare, but he was more of a person.
- Our bourbon is mellower.
- The official state flower of Unicornia is the marsh mallow.
- Even if the colonists had lost their war of independence, by now America would be independent of Britain.
- Since I've lost weight, I've become more spiritual.

Now, if our allocations are incorrigible, practicing accountants should be deeply concerned. We attest that financial statements present fairly the positions of companies and the results of their operations. But if both our revenue recognition and matching are founded upon allocations that we can neither refute nor verify, *we have no way of knowing whether these attestations are true.*

Are they incorrigible? I'll begin with matching and for brevity will disregard extraordinary items (and other nonoperating gains and losses), lower-of-cost-or-market writedowns and the like. Our matchings assign costs of a firm's nonmonetary inputs (inventories, labor, other services, depreciable assets, etc.) to the expenses of one or more accounting periods, temporarily reporting as assets costs assigned to future periods. We're all familiar with the theory behind these matching assignments: each input's purchase price should be allocated to successive periods in proportion to the contribution it

[2] Arthur L. Thomas, Studies in Accounting Research No. 9, *The Allocation Problem: Part Two* (American Accounting Association, 1974), hereafter SAR 9.

should be allocated to successive periods in proportion to the contribution it makes to each period's revenues. Academics and most practitioners also know that an equivalent matching theory can be developed around contributions to net cash inflows.

The allocation problem has several dimensions, some of which are subtle. But one is easily described: to match costs with revenues, we must know what the contributions of the firm's individual inputs *are*. Unfortunately, as I'll illustrate below, there's no way that we can know this.

Seeing why this is so requires introducing a final concept, *interaction*. Inputs to a process interact whenever they generate an output different from the total of what they would yield separately. For instance, labor and equipment interact whenever people and machines working together produce more goods than the total of what people could make with their bare hands and machines could make untended. As this example suggests, interaction is extremely common. Almost all of a firm's inputs interact with each other— their failure to do so would ordinarily signal their uselessness.

Surprising as it may seem, it can be proved that whenever inputs interact, calculations of how much total revenue or cash flow has been contributed by any individual input are as meaningless as, say, calculations of the proportion of a worker's services due to any one internal organ: heart, liver or lungs. Thus, despite all textbooks and American Institute of CPAs or FASB releases to the contrary—despite what you've been trained to believe—our attempts to match costs with revenues must almost always fail. The next section tries to demonstrate this.

A SIMPLE EXAMPLE

A complete demonstration, meeting all possible counterarguments, is very lengthy.[3] But a simple example reveals the kernel of the matter. What follows is offered in the same spirit as Robert Sterling's recent illustration in these pages that only price-level-adjusted current-value financial statements are fully relevant and interpretable:

> A highly simplified case will be considered in this article. The advantages of simplified cases are that they are easily understood by both the reader and the author and they are more easily solved. If we cannot solve the simplified cases, then we can be fairly certain that we also cannot solve the complex cases. Thus, if a particular approach fails to provide a solution for simplified cases, then we can avoid wasting effort by trying that approach on complex cases.[4]

However, instead of Sterling's cash, securities, bread and milk trading economy, I'll describe a production process for bread alone and confine the

[3] See SAR 9, Chapters 1–6, for the attempt.
[4] Robert R. Sterling, "Relevant Financial Reporting in an Age of Price Changes," JofA, Feb.75, p.42.

discussion to strictly physical measures (to avoid complications introduced by monetary valuations).[5] If individual contributions are necessarily incorrigible even in the following example, it's hard to imagine how they could be otherwise in the vastly more complex processes by which business enterprises generate their product, services, revenues and cash flows.

A prospector manufactures sourdough bread by a three-stage process:

1. He makes leaven by mixing flour, sugar and water in a crock, then keeps it in a warm place for about a week (until it bubbles).
2. He makes bread by transferring all but a cup of leaven to a large pot, where he mixes it with soda and additional flour, sugar and water, kneads it slightly and then lets it rise. He digs a shallow pit, fills it with coals from his camp fire, covers the pot, places it in the pit, buries it in hot coals and keeps it there until the bread is baked.
3. He replenishes the leaven (for the next baking) by adding enough flour and water to restore the crock to its original level.

Water, airborne yeasts and wood are free goods here. We accountants would be concerned with the following inputs to this process: flour, sugar, soda, labor, the crock, the pot and a shovel. Finally, part of the flour and sugar leaven for one loaf becomes included in the leaven for the next. The output of each baking is one loaf of bread.

Although its manufacture is simple, the moment we try to calculate the contributions of any individual input to this output we face a dilemma. Each input (except, perhaps, the soda and the shovel) is essential. Therefore, we could plausibly assign all of the output to any individual input. For example, we could assign all of the output to the flour, reasoning that were flour withheld from the process there would be no bread. Yet we could equally well assign all of the output to the pot, since without it the loaf would have been incinerated.

Having assigned all output to any one input, we've implicitly assigned zero to each other input. But if either all or zero is appropriate for each input, any intermediate allocation will be equally appropriate—say, half the loaf to the flour and a sixth each to the pot, labor and the crock.

I'm unable to prove which of the infinitely many possible ways of allocating the loaf is correct. Therefore, I can't specify the individual contributions of the inputs; instead, all I'm entitled to say is that they generate the loaf jointly. Research shows that other writers on economics and accounting—even efficient-markets investigators—are equally unable to solve this problem. Perhaps the reader can. But until someone does, any contributions calculated for these inputs must be incorrigible:

1. One can't verify them, because any other calculation is just as good.
2. One can't refute them, because their calculation is just as good as any other.

---

[5] As a technical point, I've also simplified by discussing only incremental contributions of inputs. See SAR 9, especially pp. 32–40, 47–48, and 141–44, for the parallel problems that arise for their marginal contributions.

Therefore, any attempts at matching based on these contributions (say, depreciation of the pot or calculation of a value for the ending leaven inventory) will also be incorrigible. But the sourdough process is so much simpler than the productive process of business enterprises, that *matching must necessarily be incorrigible for them, too*—unless, again, the reader can show how complications ease the calculations. To generalize, when a company tries to match costs with revenues there's no way either to refute or to verify the results. Instead, all possible ways of matching will be just as good—or bad— as each other.

If it's any consolation, I don't like this conclusion either, and have spent years trying to disprove it. Nor should you accept it without further inquiry. But I urge you at least to suspend disbelief in it (and in what follows) until you've read the detailed research, cited earlier, that backs it up.

And please notice that the difficulty here isn't one of being unable to allocate—there might be some way of getting around that problem. Instead, we're drowned in possible allocations, with no defensible way to choose among them. To be sure, since we must prepare reports, we eventually do pick one set of figures or another. Long before completing our training, we became accustomed to do this with few (if any) pangs. First, we narrow the possibilities by looking to generally accepted accounting principles and then select one of the survivors according to industry custom, apparent advantage to the company, apparent appropriateness of the method to the firm's circumstances or some other plausible rationale. But how can the incorrigible results be useful to decision makers?

Unless you (or someone) can suggest ways in which calculations that can neither be verified nor refuted assist decisions,[6] our allocations of the costs of depreciable assets, inventories, labor and other inputs are irrelevant to investor needs. Indeed, although it's painful to say this, they are mere rituals— solemn nonsense—and our beliefs in them are fallacies. This should trouble all of us, because practitioners spend much time conducting such rituals, and theorists much time elaborating on such fallacies.[7]

The Accounting Principles Board was well aware of this, but, underrating its severity, was satisfied to claim that exact measurements are seldom possible and that allocation often requires informed judgment.[8] With all due respect, acknowledging that few allocations are exact is like replying, "Few animals are ever completely healthy," in response to the statement, "Sir, your cow is dead."

Finally, since what's true of individual inputs also holds for groups of inputs, I'm forced to conclude that our revenue recognition practices are rituals, too. For revenue recognition allocates the firm's *lifetime* output to the groups of inputs that constitute its resources during the individual years of its life. Once again, the details of this appear in SAR 9.

---

[6] Assistance that goes beyond the unsatisfactory, short run utilities is described on pp. 8–9, 40–46, 65–70 and 163–74 of SAR 9.

[7] For examples of the latter, see SAR 9, pp. 94–110, 116–19 and 128–55.

[8] For examples, see APB Statement No. 4, pp. 11, 13–15, 21–22, 46–48, and 102.

THE FASB'S RESPONSIBILITY

What, then, of the FASB? We've seen it worry, or propose to worry, about which allocations are most appropriate for various accounting situations. The FASB should stop doing this. Instead, whenever possible, it should *eliminate* allocations. Such incorrigible figures don't do readers of our reports any real good, and they

1. Cost money.
2. Strain relations between auditors and clients (when they disagree about which incorrigible figures to report).
3. Cause much of the nonuniformity problem that plagues us (since allocations are incorrigible, naturally GAAP conflict—there's no way to settle which rules are right).
4. Thereby confuse individual readers, thus violating what the Trueblood Report designates as the basic objective of financial statements.
5. Generally breed distrust in our profession.

When their elimination isn't possible, the FASB should keep allocations unsophisticated (if we must be incorrigible, at least let's be simple), choose allocation rules on expedient, political grounds (ceasing to worry about theory) and be candid about what it's doing. In particular, the FASB should actively

1. Try to convert conventional reporting practices to allocation-free ones. There are two main allocation-free alternatives to conventional accounting: current value reporting and the type of funds statement reporting that defines "funds" as net quick assets.[9] Certainly, Sterling is correct that merely adjusting allocated historical costs for changes in purchasing power serves little purpose: adjusted ritual remains ritual. The same is true of foreign currency translations.
2. Meanwhile, avoid launching any new incorrigible allocations in such areas as interim and segment reports, leases, contingencies, interest and pensions. And eliminate the more flagrantly incorrigible allocations that we now commit. A prime example of the latter (despite its being one of the APB's greatest political triumphs) is tax deferral: we take the difference between an incorrigible book allocation and an incorrigible tax allocation and allocate it, incorrigibly.

In conclusion, I would emphasize that none of these remarks are intended to disparage accounting practitioners. As SAR 9 points out (p. 157), practitioners have honestly believed that allocations are appropriate and have struggled to cope with them, while we academics saddled practitioners with a

---

[9] See SAR 9, Chapter 7.

matching theory that requires such assignments, then failed to provide defensible ways for their calculation. But the hard fact remains that so long as we continue to certify that incorrigible allocations present fairly a firm's financial position and the results of its operations, we're making claims that we just can't back up. Professional responsibility urges that we, and the FASB, cease to tolerate this.

CHAPTER 8

Goodwill and Other Intangible Assets

Some years ago, Ambrose Bierce, the social cynic who compiled *The Devil's Dictionary*, might have defined intangible assets as "those assets a company wants to have so long as they do not appear in the balance sheet." The "ideal," as seen by the managements of takeover-minded companies, would be to prevent the introduction of intangible assets into the accounts, as under "pooling of interests" accounting in the United States and merger accounting in the United Kingdom. If there were no way of avoiding their booking, they should preferably be removed by a direct charge against owners' equity, as with goodwill in the United Kingdom. Failing that, as with research and developments costs in the United States, they should be expensed immediately. Above all, a company must avoid an accounting recognition of intangible assets that could penalize future years' earnings.

In recent years, attitudes have changed toward showing intangible assets in the financial statements, although the opposition to burdening earnings with their eventual amortization remains undiminished. Partly owing to the balance sheet orientation favored by the Financial Accounting Standards Board (FASB), there has been a greater willingness to display the values, both tangible and intangible, developed by the enterprise. Mark-to-market accounting for securities entails showing gains as well as losses (see Chapter 9). And U.K. companies' hasty writeoffs of goodwill against their owners' equity ("reserves" in British parlance) left them with embarrassingly high debt/equity ratios, so that their managements have found it necessary to resuscitate most of the written-off goodwill under the heading of "brand names." *But* be oh, so careful not to allow the brand names to be amortized against earnings; instead, as their value falls, charge the "loss" directly to the revaluation reserve account (in owners' equity) that was created when the brand names were placed on the balance sheet.

Acquisition-minded companies are not alone in favoring the direct writeoff of goodwill against owners' equity. In 1992, a major user group, the Association of Investment Management and Research, formerly the Financial Analysts Federation, recommended that all unidentifiable intangibles be written off to owners' equity. Moreover David Solomons, in an appendix to his proposed conceptual framework for the former U.K. Accounting Standards Committee, favors the immediate writeoff of goodwill against owners' equity, as it would promote consistency with the treatment of self-developed goodwill.[1] Yet in a recent study solicited by the U.K.'s Accounting Standards Board (ASB), five leading academics concluded that "in no circumstances should any part of 'goodwill' be written off against [owners' equity]."[2] In the annual report for 1992 of the Financial Reporting Council (FRC), the parent body of the ASB, it is stated that "goodwill is an increasingly important part of the assets of companies, and financial reporting has to recognise that,"[3] perhaps being a clue to the FRC's thinking about the proper treatment of goodwill. It is evident that informed views are widely at variance on this contentious reporting issue.

That goodwill amortization is not deductible for income tax purposes in either the United States or the United Kingdom makes it an expense that company managements find particularly distasteful. In the case of expenses that have tax consequences (e.g., costs of goods sold, salaries), their negative impact on the bottom line is relieved by a corresponding reduction in income tax expense equal to the marginal tax rate multiplied by the amount of the expense. In the case of goodwill amortization, however, net income is reduced by 100 percent of the expense. During 1991 and 1992, efforts were made in the U.S. Congress to allow goodwill to be amortizable for income tax purposes over a 14-year life, but the proposed tax legislation of which it was a part was vetoed twice by the President.[4] In Canada, goodwill amortization is partially tax deductible.

RESEARCH AND DEVELOPMENT

The FASB's second standard, issued in 1974, declared that R&D must be expensed in the year of expenditure. The apparent reason was that "evidence of a direct causal relationship between current research and development expenditures and subsequent future benefits generally has not been found."[5]

---

[1] David Solomons, *Guidelines for Financial Reporting Standards* (London: The Institute of Chartered Accountants in England and Wales, 1989), p. 69.

[2] John Arnold, Don Egginton, Linda Kirkham, Richard Macve, and Ken Peasnell, *Goodwill and Other Intangibles: Theoretical Considerations and Policy Issues* (London: The Research Board of The Institute of Chartered Accountants in England and Wales, [1992]), p. xi.

[3] *The State of Financial Reporting: Second Annual Review* (London: Financial Reporting Council, November 1992), p. 36.

[4] In August 1993, President Clinton signed the Omnibus Budget Reconciliation Act of 1993, which, among many other things, made the amortization of purchased goodwill deductible for income-tax purposes over a 15-year period. Not all purchased goodwill, however, is eligible for this treatment. As there are tax disadvantages as well as advantages to this eligibility, it is not clear how widely corporations will avail themselves of this new provision.

[5] "Accounting for Research and Development Costs," *Statement of Financial Accounting Standards No. 2* (Financial Accounting Standards Board, October 1974), para. 49.

Immediate expensing was also a way of preventing company managements from choosing arbitrary useful lives and thus manipulate their earnings streams. In the United Kingdom, the standard-setting body was initially inclined to adopt the U.S. standard, until the aerospace and electronics industries registered vigorous protests over the immediate expensing of development costs, a sizable category of expenditure in both industries. On second thought, the U.K. body opted for an immediate expensing of research but provided greater scope for capitalizing and amortizing development costs.[6] The standards in Canada and Australia are closer to the American position.

In "Accounting for Research and Development Costs," Harold Bierman, Jr. and Roland E. Dukes, two accounting academics, question the rationale offered by the FASB. They recognize the difficulty and arbitrariness of allocating the cost over an assumed useful life, but they disagree with the FASB's conclusion that a causal link between R&D costs and future benefits is yet to be demonstrated.

In an empirical study of the impact of the FASB's standard on the behavior of small, high-technology firms, Horwitz and Kolodny found that the immediate expensing requirement seemed to lead to a decision to incur reduced R&D expenditures.[7] Not a few U.S. accounting academics remain unconvinced that the FASB's standard on R&D is soundly based.

GOODWILL AND BRAND NAMES

The United States was the first country, in 1970, to require systematic amortization of goodwill, and established an (arbitrary) maximum useful life of 40 years. Four years later, Canada also decided on a maximum life of 40 years. Australia has opted for 20 years and Japan for 5 years. The International Accounting Standards Committee (IASC) has proposed a maximum of 20 years. Regardless of the limit placed on useful life, the standards of all of the foregoing countries and of the IASC require that the amortization be charged against earnings. The United Kingdom and the Netherlands, on the other hand, permit companies to charge goodwill against owners' equity at the time of acquisition. In the United Kingdom, where this is the officially encouraged practice, virtually all large listed companies have done so.

In recent years, many acquisitions have been of service companies, which tend to have little in the way of long-lived tangible assets. Goodwill, therefore, has been one of the largest assets in the acquisition package. Takeover-minded managements, especially when service companies are being ac-

---

[6] For a study of the influences on the U.K. standard-setting process for R&D, see Tony Hope and Rob Gray, "Power and Policy Making: The Development of an R&D Standard," *Journal of Business Finance and Accounting* (Winter 1982), pp. 531–558.

[7] Bertrand Horwitz and Richard Kolodny, "The FASB, the SEC, and R&D," *The Bell Journal of Economics* (Spring 1981), pp. 249–262.

quired, assiduously seek to avoid burdening future years' earnings with a charge for goodwill amortization. In the United States and Canada, the intangible assets must be amortized, and the amortization must be charged to earnings. But in the United Kingdom, companies typically charge goodwill immediately against owners' equity, thus circumventing the income statement. For U.K. companies active in the takeover market, however, their debt/equity ratios are seen to grow to disproportionately high levels as a result of the depression of their owners' equity balances. Beginning in 1988, a number of enterprising U.K. companies created asset accounts for their brand names, at the same time crediting a revaluation account as part of owners' equity. In this way, the written-off goodwill could be restored to the balance sheet (in the guise of brand names), and the owners' equity balance could be augmented correspondingly. As the values of the brand names diminish over time, the charge would be made against the revaluation account rather than against earnings. These ultraliberal policies for the treatment of intangibles are currently under intensive review by the U.K.'s Accounting Standards Board.

In "Accounting for Goodwill," J. Ron Colley and Ara G. Volkan show how the accounting effects of capitalizing and amortizing goodwill against earnings can be "reversed out" in order to discern the effect of a policy of direct charge-off of goodwill against owners' equity on the debt/equity ratio and the return on total assets. Somewhat surprisingly, the authors found that the issue of capitalization versus noncapitalization does not matter that much when making these two calculations.

Arguments have circulated in the U.S. financial community that, owing to the differences between U.S. and U.K. accounting standards on the treatment of goodwill, U.K. companies are favored over U.S. companies when seeking to buy U.S. companies where a substantial amount of goodwill is involved. It's an interesting example of how differences between countries' accounting standards can lead to an "uneven playing field." This U.S./U.K. differential is discussed in two articles from the financial press: "Goodwill Is Making a Lot of People Angry," from *Business Week*; and "Accounting Rules Favor Foreign Bidders," a column in *The Wall Street Journal* written by an investment banker who deals with mergers and acquisitions.

In "Accounting for Goodwill: A Case Analysis of the U.S., U.K. and Japan," Kathleen M. Dunne and Theresa P. Rollins compare the accounting and tax rules for the treatment of goodwill in several countries, and construct a case to show how the different rules in the United States, United Kingdom, and Japan would affect the price paid to acquire a company as well as the figures in the post-acquisition financial statements. While the U.K. Acquirer would report the highest post-acquisition accounting income and rate of return if goodwill is written off against owners' equity immediately on acquisition, the Japan Acquirer would show the highest post-acquisition cash flow since goodwill may be amortized over 5 years for tax purposes (in a high-tax country).

In "Britain's Goodwill Games," an article from *Forbes*, the U.K. practice of capitalizing brand names so as to restore intangible values to the balance sheet, and to repair debt/equity ratios following massive goodwill writeoffs, is explored in the context of the very different U.S. and U.K. standards on treating intangibles. A large U.K. bakery conglomerate, Ranks Hovis McDougall (RHM), added £678 million of internally developed brand names, without any dissent expressed by the company's external auditor, to its balance sheet at the close of its 1987–1988 financial year. The company's overt booking of self-developed intangibles, not purchased intangibles, was without precedent in the United Kingdom, and it shocked leaders of the accounting profession and the financial community. RHM's motivations to build up its recorded assets and owners' equity may have been externally induced. It was noted that RHM had recently been under attack in a hostile takeover bid by an Australian food group.[8]

The Economist, which is a close observer of the accounting scene, asserts that "Putting brands on a balance sheet is like trying to trap a ghost." Now that RHM has capitalized internally developed brands, where will it all lead? Branding whole corporations and organizations? In addition to being an accounting issue, brands are an important variable in marketing, organization studies, and finance.

In their article, "Accounting for the Value of Brands," British academics Tony Arnold and Michael Sherer refer to the RHM case, as well as to recent acquisitions in which the economic importance of brand names was evident. Their sympathy is with the use of "exit price accounting" (net realizable value accounting) as a means of obviating the "arbitrary and incorrigible" allocations associated with historical and current costs. They harken back to the argument of Arthur L. Thomas (see Chapter 7).

The foregoing articles are a small sample of the literature that has been spawned by recent actions in the United Kingdom (as well as in the Netherlands and Australia) to give explicit accounting recognition to brand names and, in the case of newspapers and publishers, to titles and editorial rights. Perhaps for the wrong reasons, values are returning to the balance sheet.

BIBLIOGRAPHICAL NOTES

Intangible Assets—In General

An inquiry into a number of thorny conceptual issues relating to intangibles, including the warrant for recognizing intangibles as assets in the light of four different valuation models, is

Egginton, Don A.: "Towards Some Principles for Intangible Asset Accounting," *Accounting and Business Research* (Summer 1990), pp. 193–205.

---

[8] L. G. Campbell, *Accounting for Brands* (Edinburgh: The Institute of Chartered Accountants of Scotland, 1989), p. 25.

Two related books on intangibles are

Intangible Assets: Their Value and How to Report It (London: Coopers & Lybrand Deloitte, 1990).

Intangible Assets: A Survey of Senior Businessmen's Views (London: Coopers & Lybrand Deloitte, 1990).

An extensive study on the valuation of intangibles is

The Valuation of Intangible Assets, Special Report No. P254 (London: The Economist Intelligence Unit and Arthur Andersen & Co, SC, January 1992).

Research and Development

Two research studies undertaken for standard-setting bodies are the following:

Gellein, Oscar S., and Maurice S. Newman: *Accounting for Research and Development Expenditures*, Accounting Research Study No. 14 (New York: American Institute of Certified Public Accountants, 1973).

McGregor, Warren J.: *Accounting for Research and Development Costs*, Discussion Paper No. 5 (Melbourne: Australian Accounting Research Foundation, 1980).

Conceptual arguments and empirical evidence relating to the standard-setting process for segment reporting and research and development costs are couched in a public policy framework in the following work:

Horwitz, Bertrand, and Richard Kolodny: *Financial Reporting Rules and Corporate Decisions: A Study of Public Policy* (Greenwich, CT: JAI Press Inc., 1982).

A study of the historical development of the U.S. literature and practice on accounting for R&D costs, with an extensive bibliography is

Nix, Paul E., and David E. Nix: "A Historical Review of the Accounting Treatment of Research and Development Costs," *The Accounting Historians Journal* (June 1992), pp. 51–78.

Goodwill and Brands

A historical study of goodwill accounting in the United States from 1884 to 1980 is

Hughes, Hugh P.: *Goodwill in Accounting: A History of the Issues and Problems*, Research Monograph No. 80 (Atlanta, GA: College of Business Administration, Georgia State University, 1982).

A case study of self-interested lobbying on a goodwill pronouncement (ED 47) issued in 1990 by the U.K.'s Accounting Standards Committee is

Grinyer, John R., and Alex Russell: "National Impediments to International Harmonization: Evidence of Lobbying in the U.K.," *Journal of International Accounting Auditing & Taxation* (vol. 1, no. 1, 1992), pp. 13–31. This article is reproduced in Chapter 18.

Several studies on goodwill have been published by professional accounting organizations or standard-setting bodies, as follows:

Arnold, John, Don Egginton, Linda Kirkham, Richard Macve, and Ken Peasnell: *Goodwill and Other Intangibles: Theoretical Considerations and Policy Issues* (London: The Research Board of The Institute of Chartered Accountants in England and Wales, [1992]).

Catlett, George R., and Norman O. Olson: *Accounting for Goodwill*, Accounting Research Study No. 10 (New York: American Institute of Certified Public Accountants, 1968).

Accounting for Goodwill, A Discussion Paper (London: Accounting Standards Committee, 1980).

Russell, A., J. R. Grinyer, M. Walker, and P. A. Malton: *Accounting for Goodwill*, Certified Research Report 13 (London: Certified Accountant Publications Limited, 1989).

A comprehensive study of the several sides of the brand accounting controversy is

Barwise, Patrick, Christopher Higson, Andrew Likierman, and Paul Marsh: *Accounting for Brands* (London: London Business School and The Institute of Chartered Accountants in England and Wales, 1989).

Other books on brands are the following:

Campbell, L. G.: *Accounting for Brands* (Edinburgh: The Institute of Chartered Accountants of Scotland, 1989).

Power, Michael (editor): *Brand and Goodwill Strategies* (Cambridge: Woodhead-Faulkner, 1990).

Murphy, John (editor): *Brand Valuation* (London: Business Books Limited, 1991).

For a view from the financial community on proper accounting for intangibles, placing emphasis on the role of value in accounting measurements, see:

Donaldson, T. H.: *The Treatment of Intangibles: A Banker's View* (London: St. Martin's Press, 1992).

Accounting for Research and Development Costs

Harold Bierman, Jr.
Cornell University

Roland E. Dukes
University of Washington

The accounting profession has four basic choices available as to the method of accounting for assets:

- Use cost of acquisition.
- Use value estimations.
- Use price level adjusted cost.
- Implicitly assume the value is zero and expense the costs associated with the acquisition of the asset.

In its Statement of Financial Accounting Standards No. 2, "Accounting for Research and Development Costs" (October 1974), the Financial Accounting Standards Board concludes that "all research and development costs encompassed by this Statement shall be charged to expense when incurred." This practice implicitly assumes the expected value of R&D is zero. The Board reached its conclusion as a result of a reasoning process in which several preliminary premises were accepted as true. It may be possible to conclude for pragmatic reasons that the expensing decision reached by the Board is a reasonable practice, but we object to the process the Board used in arriving at the conclusion that R&D should be expensed. Specifically, the following five factors that were covered by the Board as support for its conclusion will be considered:

- Uncertainty of future benefits.
- Lack of causal relationship between expenditures and benefits.
- R&D does not meet the accounting concept of an asset.
- Matching of revenues and expenses.
- Relevance of resulting information for investment and credit decisions.

Following are descriptons of these factors and evaluations of their relevance.

From *Journal of Accountancy* (April 1975), pp. 48–55. Reprinted by permission of the American Institute of Certified Public Accountants, Inc.

UNCERTAINTY OF FUTURE BENEFITS

The primary justification offered by the FASB[1] for expensing the R&D expenditures is the level of uncertainty associated with the benefits. It is argued that R&D expenditures have considerable risk where risk is defined as a large probability of failure for an individual project. In reaching its conclusion to expense R&D costs when incurred, the Board states (p. 15) that the "high degree of uncertainty about the future benefits of individual research and development projects" was a significant factor in reaching this conclusion. In elaborating on this conclusion, the Board cites several studies that indicate a high failure rate for research and development projects. Although the Statement is not specific on this point, it appears that because a large proportion of research and development projects are "failures," the Board concludes that all R&D should be treated as failures and expensed. There are several fallacies with this conclusion.

First, it is not clear that the risks and uncertainties of company-sponsored research and development are as formidable as corporate publicists and the references cited by the Board would have us believe. In 1963, Mansfield and Hamburger[2] studied 22 major firms in the chemical and petroleum industries and found that the bulk of the R&D projects carried out by these firms were relatively safe from a technical point of view. Most of the projects were regarded as having better than a 50–50 chance of technical success. In an analysis of 70 projects carried out in the central research and development laboratories of a leading electrical equipment manufacturing company, Mansfield and Brandenburg[3] found that in more than three-fourths of the cases, the ex ante probability of technical success had originally been estimated at .80 or higher, and only two projects had predicted success probabilities of less than .50. After the projects were completed, 44 percent were fully successful technically, and only 16 percent were unsuccessful because of unanticipated technical difficulties.

These findings are consistent with the hypothesis that business firms do not generally begin new product or process development projects until the principal technical uncertainties have been resolved through inexpensive research, conducted either by their own personnel or by outsiders. They are also consistent with the notion that managers are averse to risk and are reluctant to pursue high risk projects when their own reputations and the funds of the company are involved. On the other hand, research and development projects sponsored by the federal government are likely to be more risky than industrial R&D because the federal government bears the financial risk. This point is also made by Scherer.[4]

---

[1] Financial Accounting Standards Board, Statement of Financial Accounting Standards No. 2, "Accounting for Research and Development Costs" (Stamford, CT: FASB, 1974).

[2] E. Mansfield, "Industrial Research and Development: Characteristics, Costs, and the Diffusion of Results," *American Economic Review*, May 1969, p. 65.

[3] E. Mansfield, *Industrial Research and Technological Innovation* (New York: Norton, 1969).

[4] F. M. Scherer, *Industrial Market Structure and Economic Performance* (Chicago: Rand McNally, 1970), pp. 354–56.

Second, one has to be careful as to the definition of risk. Because of the historically high profitability of R&D efforts, it may well be that risk defined in terms of expected loss or expected monetary value may be less than many types of plant and equipment expenditures (the different tax treatments afforded the different types of expenditures also affect risk).

Bailey,[5] who computed the rate of return from R&D expenditures in the U.S. pharmaceutical industry, found a rate of return (pretax) of 35 percent in 1954 and 25 percent in 1961. Bailey explains the decrease in rate of return as being the result of increased R&D expenditures (170 percent increase between 1954 and 1961) as firms realized the high profitability of R&D in this area. Bailey does forecast decreasing returns in this industry after 1962 as a result of more stringent regulations associated with introducing new products and warns of the difficulty of isolating causal relationships. Also, the measurement of profitability of R&D is difficult because there are many factors affecting earnings. But if Bailey is close to being correct, there may be less risk with R&D expenditures (if a large amount of expenditures are made, spread over a large number of projects) than with plant and equipment.

Bailey's findings are reinforced by studies by Minasian and Mansfield. Mansfield[6] found that "among the petroleum firms, regardless of whether technical change was capital-embodied or organizational, the marginal rates of return average about 40–60 percent." He found other industries also high, but not as high as for the period 1946–62. Minasian,[7] in studying firms in the chemical industry (1948–57), found the gross return on research and development to be 54 percent as compared to 9 percent for the physical capital. While Minasian defines this as a social return and not a private return, it is again evident that R&D has been very profitable. Moreover, the expected profitablity affects the risk of the expenditure.

This is inconsistent with the definition of risk apparently used by the FASB, which defines risk only in terms of probability of failure. The Board does not consider the reduction in uncertainty that can be achieved by pursuing a portfolio of research and development projects. A simple example will help to illustrate this point. Suppose a firm is pursuing 100 independent R&D projects. For computational ease, we assume each project costs $10,000, that each has a probability of "success" of .10 and a probability of "failure" of .90. Success results in a $200,000 present value accruing to the firm; failure results in no benefits.

Each individual project has 1 chance in 10 of being successful; this is consistent with the point made by the Board that for any individual project the probability that it will generate future benefits for the firm seems dismally low. However, the more important question is, what is the probability of making a profit from the portfolio of projects? Since each R&D project repre-

[5] Martin Neil Bailey, "Research and Development Costs and Returns: The U.S. Pharmaceutical Industry," *Journal of Political Economy*, January-February 1972, pp. 70–85.

[6] E. Mansfield, "Rates of Return from Industrial Research and Development," *American Economic Review*, May 1965, pp. 310–22.

[7] Jora R. Minasian, "Research and Development, Production Functions, and Rates of Return," *American Economic Review*, May 1969, pp. 80–85.

sents an independent event with two possible outcomes, the number of successes in 100 trials is a random variable whose distribution is the binomial distribution. For this example, the probability that there will be one or more successes is equal to .99997.[8] That is, the firm is virtually assured that it will realize 1 or more successes from a portfolio of 100 R&D projects.[9] This is a substantial reduction in uncertainty when compared to the .10 probability of success attached to individual projects. Moreover, the expected future benefits from the portfolio is $2 million.[10] Thus, while the Board claims a large probability of failure associated with individual projects, it fails to consider the change in the uncertainty (defined in terms of probability of failure) associated with undertaking a portfolio of independent R&D projects.

In the above example, the $20,000 expected future benefit of each project (equal to its probability of success, .10, times the expected future benefit of success, $200,000) is greater than the $10,000 cost of each project. The expected payoff from the portfolio is twice the total cost of $1 million for all 100 research and development projects. To break even, the firm needs 5 or more successes out of 100 projects, and there is .9763 probability of this happening. Thus, rather than .10 probability of success (defined in terms of the individual project), there is .9763 probability of success (defined in terms of the profitability of the portfolio).

Since the firm does not know before it investigates which of the projects will be successful, the appropriate cost of finding the successful projects is the total cost of pursuing the portfolio of projects. Bierman, Dukes and Dyckman[11] discuss this point further with specific reference to accounting for exploration costs in the petroleum industry.

The FASB cites the low probability of success with new products. We argue that this low probability has not been proved. Moreover, it is not a valid measure of risk. The Board needs to define uncertainty and risk more exactly before risk of R&D can be offered as the reason for an accounting treatment. Even if it were agreed that R&D had more risk (a position we do not accept), it

---

[8] The probability that there will be 1 or more successes is equal to 1 minus the probability there will be zero successes. The probability of zero success is given as

$$P \text{ (0 successes)} = \frac{100!}{0! \ 100!} [.10]^0 [.90]^{100} = .00003$$

[9] If the probability of success for an individual project is .05, .02, or .01, then the portfolio probabilities of one or more successes are .989, .905, and .633, respectively.

[10] The expected present value from the portfolio is the sum of the expected payoffs for the individual projects:

$$\text{Expected present value from portfolio} = \sum_{i=1}^{100} \text{Expected present value of project } i$$

$$= \sum_{i=1}^{100} [(.10)(\$200,000) + (.90)(0)]$$

$$= 100 \ (\$20,000) = \$2,000,000$$

[11] Harold Bierman, Jr., Roland E. Dukes and Thomas R. Dyckman, "Financial Reporting in the Petroleum Industry," JofA, Oct. 74, pp. 58–64.

is still not clear that this leads to the policy conclusion of expensing the costs of R&D.

There is some uncertainty of future benefits associated with every asset currently recorded on balance sheets. Even the future real benefits that can be realized from holding cash are uncertain, especially during these times of "double-digit" inflation. More analogous to research and development, there is a high degree of uncertainty associated with investments in long-lived plant and equipment, especially in fields where the assets are extremely specialized in nature and where there is rapid technological advance. It is not clear that investments in these kinds of projects are any less uncertain in terms of the probability of making a profit than an investment in a portfolio of R&D projects. If both are uncertain, why should one be recorded differently from the other? It does not appear that using the "degree of uncertainty of future benefits" is an appropriate factor or criterion to employ in helping to resolve this issue. So long as the project has a net positive expected future benefit, uncertainty should not lead automatically to a conclusion that cost factors should be expensed.

We argue that at the portfolio level there is the possibility of a substantial reduction in uncertainty vis-à-vis the individual project level. Moreover, expected future benefits will in general be equal to or greater than the total cost of pursuing the research and development portfolio. Thus, the existence of a probability of failure cannot be used to justify the expensing of R&D expenditures.[12]

LACK OF CAUSAL RELATION BETWEEN EXPENDITURES AND BENEFITS

In its Statement the FASB cites (p. 16) three empirical research studies that "generally failed to find a significant correlation between research and development expenditures and increased future benefits as measured by subsequent sales, earnings or share of industry sales." The Board does not specify what conclusion is to be drawn regarding the accounting treatment of research and development costs from the above statement, although it appears to consider this lack of evidence of a direct relationship between research and development costs and specific future revenue as an important factor in its conclusions.

Several points can be made regarding this factor. First, even though the studies cited by the Board were unable to detect a significant relationship

---

[12] An irrelevant argument is offered in paragraph 52 of the FASB Statement. It is stated that companies have the philosophy that "research and development expenditures are intended to be recovered by current revenues rather than by revenues from new product." This philosophy (if it does exist) should in no way affect the accounting for R&D. In addition, in evaluating new projects any sensible method of evaluation will consider the revenue (benefits) associated with the new projects. The current product revenues are irrelevant to the decision to go ahead except to the extent that they supply the cash that is used for the financing of the R&D.

between costs of research and subsequent benefits, this does not imply that such a relationship does not exist. That is, when logical deductive reasoning leads to a hypothesized relationship that cannot subsequently be empirically observed, the scientist will generally "suspend judgment" regarding the hypothesis rather than embrace the alternative hypothesis that no relationship exists. It is more appropriate to draw conclusions upon the observation of the phenomena under study rather than upon the inability to observe the phenomena.

Second, considerable research in economics does provide support for the hypothesis that research and development efforts do produce benefits for the firm. Scherer[13] reviews much of this literature when he discusses the relationship between market structures and technological innovation. Subsequent to the Scherer review, several additional studies have contributed to the evidence on the relationship between research and development and various measures of benefit to the firm. Bailey[14] found pretax rates of return from investments in research and development in the vicinity of 25 to 35 percent for the pharmaceutical firms included in his study. He also found that "earnings of the companies over time are clearly related to the number of patents held by the company." The number of patents held by a firm is an often-used surrogate for research output. In a related study, Angilley[15] found pharmaceutical sales to be significantly related to "innovative output," where innovative output was defined in terms of several measures of new pharmaceutical compounds produced by the company. Equally important, he found that his measures of innovative output were all significantly related to the amount of research and development expenditures incurred by the firm. In a more recent study, Grabowski and Mueller[16] investigated the rates of return on investments in physical capital, in research and development and in advertising. They conclude that their result "indicates that R&D does increase the profitability of the firm over competitive levels." For the 86 firms included in their sample, "additional R&D did increase the rate of return on total capital."

Given this brief review of some of the contrary evidence, the FASB's statement (p. 16) that "a direct relationship between research and development costs and specific revenue generally has not been demonstrated . . ." is confusing and somewhat misleading. Clearly, management expects to generate positive returns from R&D. Moreover, the expected profit from large, expensive research and development portfolios is larger than the expected benefits from smaller, less costly portfolios of research and development. An inexpensive plant may turn out to be more profitable than a much

---

[13] Scherer, especially Chapters 15 and 16.
[14] Bailey, op. cit.
[15] Alan Angilley, "Returns to Scale in Research in the Ethical Pharmaceutical Industry: Some Further Empirical Evidence," *Journal of Industrial Economics*, December 1973, pp. 81–93.
[16] Henry Grabowski and Dennis Mueller, "Rates of Return on Corporate Investment, Research and Development and Advertising," unpublished working paper, Cornell University, 1974.

more expensive plant, but this outcome does not "prove" that the plants' costs should have been expensed in both cases.

It is probably true that there is a higher variance of benefits arising from the research and development expenditures. But higher variance does not necessarily imply a higher risk is associated with such expenditures (the capital asset pricing model of Sharpe[17] is of relevance here). Applying the capital asset pricing model, the important measure of risk is the covariability of expected return between the individual project and the overall portfolio of securities. Expenditures on R&D to develop new products or improve old ones are likely to be less correlated with market returns than expenditures for expansion into new markets or expanding market capacity. Thus, it seems likely that many R&D expenditures will have relatively desirable risk characteristics compared to expenditures in physical capital.

In sum, it is incorrect to conclude that, because it has been difficult to observe a significant correlation between expenditures and subsequent benefits, future benefits are not generated by research and development expenditures. Moreover, considerable research does exist in which the findings support the hypothesis that research and development does generate substantive future benefits for the firm. While the Board may still determine that the expensing of research and development expenditures is an appropriate accounting policy, it is not clear that the lack of benefits argument is an appropriate supporting factor in this conclusion.

THE ACCOUNTING CONCEPT OF AN ASSET

The Board appears to be close to requiring the capitalization of research and development when it describes (p. 17) economic resources as those scarce resources for which there is an "expectation of future benefits to the enterprise either through use or sale." While R&D would qualify using this definition, the Board then discusses the criteria of measurability. We argue that the cost of R&D is subject to reasonable measurement. However, the FASB states (p. 17)

> The criterion of measurability would require that a resource not be recognized as an asset for accounting purposes unless at the time it is acquired or developed its future economic benefits can be identified and objectively measured.

Can the economic benefits of an automobile plant be objectively measured at the time it is acquired? This criterion opens the door to the reclassification to expense of many "asset" types of expenditures.

Also, the values of many assets are relatively independent of their costs.

---

[17] W. F. Sharpe, "Capital Asset Prices: A Theory of Market Equilibrium Under Conditions of Risk," *Journal of Finance*, September 1964, pp. 425–42.

A nonregulated pipeline immediately after it has been constructed has value that is independent of its cost. As soon as any cost is incurred, it is a sunk cost and is not price or value determining.

It is probably true that R&D ranks high in variance of relationship between cost and value on specific expenditures. The lack of a one-to-one relationship between benefits and costs tends to argue in favor of a value type of accounting. But if value is excluded from consideration, at least for now, and the choice is between zero (expensing) and cost, lacking other information cost will on the average be a better estimator of value than the zero asset value resulting from the expensing of R&D.[18]

EXPENSE RECOGNITION AND MATCHING

Surprisingly the matching of revenues and expenses of earning those revenues is used as an argument by the Board in favor of expensing R&D (p. 19) because of "the general lack of discernible future benefits at the time such costs are incurred. . . ." The only reason R&D expenditures are made is to benefit future time periods by generating new revenues in those time periods. It is unlikely that R&D will increase the operating revenues of the immediate time period given the time necessary to implement R&D. To argue in favor of immediate expensing is to ignore completely one of the basic principles on which accounting stands—namely, the necessity of matching revenues and expenses. If the Board had chosen to argue that matching was not an important criterion (it wisely did not do so), then its conclusion might be understandable. But to argue that expensing of R&D is consistent with matching is a conclusion that is difficult to comprehend.

RELEVANCE OF RESULTING INFORMATION
FOR INVESTMENT AND CREDIT DECISIONS

In paragraph 50 of the Statement, the Board refers to APB Statement No. 4, which indicates that certain costs are immediately "recognized as expenses because allocating them to several accounting periods is considered to serve no useful purpose." Citing evidence of the high degree of uncertainty associated with research and development and the views of security analysts and other professional investors, the Board states that "capitalization of any research and development costs is not useful in assessment of the earnings potential of the enterprise." The Board concludes that "therefore, it is unlikely that the investor's ability to predict the return on his investment and the variability of that return would be enhanced by capitalization."

There are two points to be made regarding the above reasoning and

---

[18] For an expansion on this point, see the article by Bierman, Dukes and Dyckman in the October 1974 *Journal of Accountancy*.

conclusions. First, the usefulness of accounting data regarding the amount of research and development costs to investors is an empirically testable question. In a study related to this issue, Dukes[19] found that the amount of research and development cost incurred and expensed during the period was significantly related to the security price of the firm. All of the firms in the Dukes study followed the accounting policy of expensing research and development costs, yet results were consistent with investors making capitalization adjustments to research and development costs in estimating the future earnings potential of the firm. That is, the "research intensity" of the firm (more precisely, the research intensity of the industry in which a firm found itself) was a significant explanatory variable in explaining the market value of the firm.

The Dukes study suggests that capitalization may serve a useful purpose in aiding the investor to predict the future return of a security. At a minimum, the study provides support to the Board's conclusion that disclosure of the amount of research and development costs is information relevant to the investment decision.

A second significant issue deals with who would be served by the requirement that research and development costs be expensed. If the results of the Dukes study are accepted, then security price behavior is more closely related to earnings computed with research and development capitalized rather than expensed. It is probably reasonable to expect security analysts and other professional investors to be able to make adjusting calculations to the reported earnings numbers, where sufficient information is supplied to adjust the basic accounting data. One is less confident, however, about the ability of nonexpert investors to make the adjustments. For example, consider an investor who takes the accounting measures seriously and does not adjust the information, analyzing two firms both of which have reported earnings of $2 per share. However, one firm has expended (and expensed) $3 per share on R&D and the other firm has spent zero. The R&D firm would have had $5 per share of earnings if it had not purchased any R&D. The expensing of the R&D expenditures results in the two firms having the same earnings per share, thus implying equal value based on this one measure. These earnings are not comparable and the investor who views them as equivalent will be misled. There is another, related problem. Managers are very concerned with earnings per share, and they assume these numbers are used in the investment decision process. The first firm can stabilize its earnings at $2 per share by varying the amount of R&D it purchases. Thus earnings become a function of decisions to buy or not to buy R&D. It is difficult to see why the decision to buy or not to buy R&D should affect the earnings of the current year. A loss firm can reduce its loss by $1 for $1 of R&D it stops buying. This is a relatively easy way to reduce losses. The result of expensing of R&D may distort

[19] Roland E. Dukes, *Market Evaluation of Accounting Information: A Cross Sectional Test of Investor Response to Expensing Research and Development Expenditures*, unpublished Ph.D. dissertation, Stanford University, 1974.

corporate decision making and lead to faulty measure of income and changes in income through time.

CONCLUSIONS

The primary purpose of this critique is to question the rationale employed by the FASB in arriving at its conclusion. It may well be that requiring all firms to disclose the amount of their research and development costs and to expense these costs is the best feasible solution. Capitalizing of such costs may not be feasible because of attendant lawsuits when the R&D is found to have less value than the recorded cost. But the resulting practice should not then be justified on the grounds that it is good accounting theory.

Virtually every time an accountant records expenditures he or she runs the risk that a later development might, with the aid of hindsight, show that the recording was "wrong." The asset may turn out to be worth much less than cost. The obvious solution for avoiding this sort of situation and resulting criticisms is to expense all costs associated with the acquisition of assets where there is some significant probability that the asset will turn out to be worth less than the cost of the asset. This "conservative" approach to asset measurement is consistent with the Board's recommendation to expense R&D expenditures. The policy decision to expense R&D costs does not appear to be based on sound accounting theory but, rather, appears to be motivated by a desire to avoid the criticism and problems resulting from situations where, after the fact, an asset is found to be worth less than the amount reported by the accountant. It ignores completely the types of errors that arise from a systematic expense overstatement, income misstatement, asset understatement and stock equity understatement. Unfortunately, criticism and lawsuits may force the adoption of such conservative practices. The way to avoid criticism that past earnings and assets have been overstated is to expense all factors associated with assets whose value is uncertain. Such a solution, however, is really a way of avoiding responsibility and is a too easy solution to an extremely difficult problem. The accountant does exercise judgment; he is an estimator and should be willing to face up to the existence of uncertainty, rather than expensing items because their ultimate value is difficult to forecast at the time the cost is incurred.

Theoretically, the accountant should provide the information most useful to society, considering the costs and benefits of the alternative accounting policies. However, the measurement of these costs and benefits is extremely difficult. Currently, all we can do is offer qualitative evaluations of alternatives rather than explicit measures.

However, Dukes[20] has offered empirical evidence of the importance of the disclosure of R&D expenditures. This evidence supports the Board's recommendation that more information relative to the magnitude of R&D

---

[20] Ibid.

expenditures be disclosed. Whatever accounting procedure is finally adopted, the disclosure of the amounts of expenditures by year will enable the analyst using the information to make the adjustments that he sees fit. If one accepts the hypothesis that capital markets are efficient in the processing of information, disclosure of the amount of the research and development expenditure is an extremely important first step. Given the basic data regarding the amount of the expenditure, an assumption of efficient capital markets implies market prices will reflect appropriate adjustments to the reported accounting numbers. The Dukes study reports findings consistent with this conclusion. However, we are not suggesting that the ability of the market to digest data should be used as a justification for neglecting accounting practices. In the first place, the adjustment process has a cost. Second, there are many other uses of accounting data besides financial analysis for the evaluation of common stock.

When a firm suffers economic difficulty, it is likely that the accounting (book) value of its assets will exceed their economic value. Technological and social change can cause assets to lose value suddenly. It is virtually impossible for the accountant to anticipate and report these value changes and at the same time use cost-based accounting principles of asset and income measurement in a theoretically correct manner. It would be possible to expense all cost factors whose benefit stream has an element of risk, but this would result in reports that were essentially cash flow statements. The income statement prepared in accordance with theoretically correct accrual concepts is an extremely important report. While it is true that later events may indicate that estimated writeoffs of assets were too rapid or not rapid enough, the accountant has an obligation to attempt to estimate the expenses of earning the revenues of a period rather than reporting as expenses the expenditures made during the period. From the point of view of accounting theory, the expenditures of R&D, which are made in the expectation of benefiting future periods, should not be written off against the revenues of the present period. Justification for such practice must be found elsewhere, if it is to be found.

Accounting for Goodwill

J. Ron Colley
West Georgia College

Ara G. Volkan
West Georgia College

INTRODUCTION

The Financial Accounting Standards Board (FASB) has placed accounting for business combinations and goodwill in its list of current issues. Thus, the profession will once more debate this century-old controversy, and reexamine the accounting principles and procedures mandated by the various Opinions of the Accounting Principles Board. Whether the final standards resulting from the review of this subject area will contain any changes in the present accounting rules remains to be seen. If the past is a good predictor of the future, the capitalization of goodwill issue will be at the center of intense discussions since major revisions of the accounting rules for business combinations cannot occur without a change in the profession's view of goodwill.

The purpose of this paper is to analyze the goodwill issue within the framework established by the pronouncements of the FASB. First, the two basic views of goodwill are presented. This discussion is followed by an examination of the factors underlying goodwill. The feasibility of using these factors to eliminate the goodwill account is examined next. We conclude that complete elimination of goodwill will not occur since the interaction of its components results in synergism. This section is followed by an argument for not capitalizing goodwill based on the measurability criterion advocated by the FASB. Finally, the financial consequences of this accounting alternative for goodwill on the risk and return ratios of a sample of firms are examined.

TWO VIEWS OF GOODWILL

Excess Earnings View

Two basic views of goodwill can be distinguished from a review of the literature. The first view holds that goodwill represents an above normal earnings capacity.[1] A price is paid in excess of the market value of net assets acquired (excess or goodwill hereafter) because profits in excess of a normal return on these net assets are anticipated. Thus, goodwill can be viewed as

From *Accounting Horizons* (June 1988), pp. 35–41. Reprinted by permission of the American Accounting Association and the authors. Copyright © 1988 by the American Accounting Association.
[1] George R. Catlett, and Norman O. Olson, *Accounting Research Study No. 10* (New York: AICPA, 1968).

the present value of the anticipated excess earnings discounted over a certain number of years. The discount period will reflect the estimated life or duration of the reason(s) underlying the excess returns.

For example, a firm may decide to acquire the net assets of another in order to add certain production capabilities to its existing product lines. An alternative would have been to develop these products internally. If the firm can estimate the dollar amounts of the expenditures over the time period necessary to develop these production and sale capabilities, and the income lost due to waiting for the sales to start, then the amount of goodwill paid will, ideally, be equal to the difference between the present value of these amounts computed using the project time horizon, the internal rate of return of the acquiring firm, and the anticipated return on the market value of the identifiable net assets of the acquired firm.

Therefore, determination of goodwill will depend on the estimates of future earnings or cash flows, normal rate of return, value of identifiable net assets, and the discount period. Under this approach a proper assessment of the judgments used in the determination of the excess price paid over the value of the identifiable net assets of a company is not possible if one disagrees with any of the estimates used by the purchaser. Both the transaction itself and the excess payment which is a part of it are unique in the sense that one is dealing with imperfect markets where, generally, there is only one buyer and one seller.

Hidden Assets View

The second view states that goodwill represents various assets of the acquired firm which are not currently disclosed in its balance sheet. Tearney[2] offers excellent arguments in support of this view when he suggests that goodwill consists of many intangible assets which are separately identifiable and that such identification would enable the amortization of each asset over its useful life eliminating the need for the term "goodwill." If this view can be operationalized, a proper assessment of management's judgment in arriving at the excess payment amount can be made since the assumed values of the assets underlying the excess can be compared to values recorded in instances when these assets are bought and sold individually.

FACTORS UNDERLYING GOODWILL

In order to examine the feasibility of implementing either of these two views, a list of the components of goodwill would be most helpful. Such lists have been proposed in various studies that employ either the survey or deductive/normative methodologies, with or without empirical analysis.

---

[2] M. G. Tearney, "Accounting for Goodwill: A Realistic Approach," *The Journal of Accountancy* (July 1973), pp. 41–45.

Survey and Deductive Studies

An example of a list of factors supporting the first view of goodwill is a study by Mace and Montgomery[3] that identified five major factors affecting a firm's decision to purchase another firm. The most important reasons for business acquisitions were found to be "market factors." Firms purchase other businesses in order to acquire their "market share" or their excess earnings and cash flow capacity that derive from marketing success. Mace and Montgomery cite the following reasons for acquisitions:

a. Accomplishing market objectives (9.8 percent),
b. Saving time in expanding into a new area (4.3 percent),
c. Acquiring management skills (5.6 percent),
d. Achieving product diversification (40.1 percent), and
e. Achieving integration (33.2 percent).

On the other hand, Nelson,[4] supporting a middle ground between the first and the second views, argues that goodwill generally consists of the following "elements."

a. Customer lists,
b. Organization costs,
c. Developmental costs,
d. Trademarks, trade names, and brands,
e. Secret processes and formulas,
f. Patents,
g. Copyrights,
h. Licenses,
i. Franchises, and
j. Superior earnings power.

A comparison of the above two lists may suggest a lack of agreement as to the identity of the components of goodwill. But the differences mainly lie in the level of aggregation of these components. While the first list contains general factors underlying goodwill, the second list specifies individual items, which taken together, may underlie these general factors. Thus, it is entirely possible that the reality is in between these two views and an accounting procedure common to all business acquisitions involving goodwill can be established.

An Empirical Study

A study conducted by Falk and Gordon[5] (hereafter F&G) contains the most comprehensive list of empirically identifiable factors as well as elements

---

[3] M. L. Mace, and G. E. Montgomery, *Management Problems of Corporate Acquisitions* (Boston: Harvard University Press, 1962).

[4] R. H. Nelson, "The Momentum Theory of Goodwill," *Accounting Review* (October 1953), pp. 491–499.

[5] Haim Falk and L. A. Gordon, "Imperfect Markets and the Nature of Goodwill," *Journal of Business Finance and Accounting* (April 1977), pp. 443–463.

TABLE 1 Factors Underlying Goodwill

Factor A: Increasing Short-run Cash Flows
Production economies
Raise more funds
Cash reserves
Low cost of funds
Reducing inventory holding cost
Avoiding transaction cost
Tax benefits

Factor B: Stability
Assurance of supply
Reducing fluctuations
Good government relations

Factor C: Human Factor
Managerial talent
Good labor relations
Good training programs
Organizational structure
Good public relations

Factor D: Exclusiveness
Access to technology
Brand name

(characteristics) of goodwill we have encountered in the literature. F&G conducted in-depth interviews with top executives to select 17 characteristics for use in a questionnaire sent to a sample of financial executives. These 17 characteristics were expressed in four groups (factor categories) established through the use of cluster analysis. This methodology first identifies the many elements of goodwill and then mathematically determines the interrelationships of these elements to form a set of factors (clusters). The four factors thus identified are labeled as: (a) Increasing short-run cash flow; (b) Stability; (c) Human factor; and (d) Exclusiveness. The characteristics within each cluster are presented in Table 1.[6] A recent article by Anderson[7] lists some of the items in Table 1 as the focal points of the acquisition strategy of Johnson & Johnson. In the next section an attempt will be made to employ these factors and characteristics as a means of eliminating the need for the goodwill account.

ATTRIBUTES OF GOODWILL AND SYNERGISM

The F&G study can be used as a means of implementing both views of goodwill if the useful life and dollar value of each factor can be determined for amortization purposes. However, the useful life of a factor can only be determined if its individual characteristics are examined. For example, the

[6] Ibid., p. 453.
[7] C. M. Anderson, "1 × 1 = 3," *Management Accounting* (April 1987), pp. 28–31.

"exclusiveness" factor has "brand name" and "access to technology" as individual characteristics. But, a purchased brand name will likely have a different useful life than purchased technology.

An a priori classification of factors also has similar problems. For example, to say that a major objective of many acquisitions is "achieving integration" is not enough. An acquisition which "achieves integration" can have characteristics which are included in all four of the F&G clusters. The benefits of integration may include reducing inventory holding costs, assurance of supply, and access to technology and managerial talent (among others).

Moreover, the characteristics must not only be identified, but also must be assigned meaningful dollar values. For acquisitions in which the excess consists of only one or two characteristics this may be feasible. However, it is likely that most acquisitions will involve an excess consisting of a multitude of characteristics and the problem of assigning meaningful dollar values to interrelated characteristics will render the exercise hopeless.

For example, characteristics such as organizational structure, good training programs, and good labor relations may be correlated resulting in a purchase price that is based upon the interaction of these characteristics rather than a separate consideration of each characteristic. The F&G study[8] resulted in the following correlation matrix for these three variables which shows some degree of interdependence:

	OS	TP	LR
Organizational Structure (OS)	1	.45	.40
Training Programs (TP)		1	.49
Labor Relations (LR)			1

Thus, in most cases, the assignment of individual dollar values to a group of purchased intangibles may not be meaningful. Rather, the purchased entity can be evaluated only as a whole because the value of the entity is based on the proper functioning of the interrelated parts to achieve some objective. Furthermore, the value of an acquired firm as a separate entity may be less than its value to an acquiring firm for which there is a particularly good fit. That is, the combination of the two firms may result in synergism.[9,10] Viewing an acquisition as synergistic is illustrated by the 1984 annual report of Black & Decker[11] which states:

> We are proceeding to integrate the acquired operations . . . in order to capitalize on synergistic possibilities including lower costs, increased brand awareness and an even greater number of new product opportunities.

Therefore, it is quite possible that the goodwill that is recorded in acquisitions consists of many identifiable elements. However, such identification is

---

[8] Haim Falk and L. A. Gordon, p. 459.
[9] Malcolm C. Miller, "Goodwill—An Aggregation Issue," *Accounting Review* (April 1973), pp. 280–291.
[10] C. M. Anderson, p. 28.
[11] Black & Decker, 1984 *Annual Report*, p. 3.

not likely to result in the clear assignment of the entire purchase price to all identified assets (tangible and intangible). Some residual and the problem of how to account for this residual will remain. Thus, neither of the two views of goodwill can be used to obtain an independently verifiable measure of the entire excess payment since the nature of the residual included in it defies such verification.

AN ARGUMENT FOR NOT CAPITALIZING GOODWILL

Should the unidentified portion of the excess payment (hereafter "goodwill" means the unidentified portion of the excess or the residual) be capitalized? This question has been debated for several decades. The decision of whether to capitalize goodwill is usually supported by a theoretical discussion of whether goodwill is an asset.

However, the discussion of whether goodwill is an asset is a moot point if the amount of goodwill cannot be measured for capitalization purposes. Guidance in the issue of capitalization of goodwill can be found in past pronouncements of the FASB.

The Measurability Criterion

In 1974, the FASB decided against capitalization of R&D expenditures because of the uncertainty of future benefits. The decision of the FASB to expense all R&D costs was not in conflict with the idea that, theoretically, some R&D expenditures did have future benefit and should have been capitalized. Rather, the Board stated that "not all of the economic resources of an enterprise are recognized as assets for financial accounting purposes."[12]

One of the reasons used by the Board as the basis for the decision not to capitalize R&D expenditures was the "measurability" criterion. The future benefit of R&D expenditures is so difficult to measure that expensing R&D costs was viewed as more appropriate than even partial capitalization of these expenditures.

The criterion of measurability was given further support in Statement of Financial Accounting Concepts No. 5. The Statement required that four fundamental criteria should be met in order for an item to be recognized in the financial statements. One of these criteria is measurability. To be recognized, an item must be ". . . measurable with sufficient reliability."[13] Thus, in order to be capitalized, goodwill must meet the measurability criterion

---

[12] Financial Accounting Standards Board, *Statement of Financial Accounting Standards No. 2* (Stamford: FASB, 1974), par. 43.
[13] Financial Accounting Standards Board, *Statement of Accounting Concepts No. 5* (Stamford: FASB, 1975), par. 63.

established by the FASB which requires that a verifiable (reliable) estimate of the dollar value of the asset be known.

Moreover, a decision to capitalize goodwill will require an estimate of its useful life for amortization purposes. (Nonamortization is a possibility, but this still requires an estimate of a useful life into perpetuity.) As mentioned earlier, goodwill appears to consist of many factors and elements and each transaction creating goodwill may involve a unique mix of these. Therefore, the determination of the useful life of goodwill requires that the dollar value and useful lives of these factors and elements be identified.

Post-Acquisition Problems

The failure to identify and measure the value of the elements underlying the residual creates problems with capitalizing goodwill both at the acquisition date and after the date of acquisition. As an example of the latter, assume that a premium is paid for a firm partly because of contracts the firm possesses which give exclusive access to a customer base. The acquiring firm has purchased the contracts for the exclusive rights they provide. If the contracts are expected to remain in effect for 20 years, then they should be separately capitalized and amortized over a 20-year period. If for some reason, the contracts are unexpectedly terminated and their value lost, the unamortized cost of the contracts should immediately be written off.

However, if the contracts are not separately identified and thus are included as a part of goodwill, it is unlikely that a portion of goodwill will be written off upon the termination of the contracts. This is one of the major problems with the current method of accounting for goodwill. A periodic determination of whether the current market value of the goodwill asset is lower than its unamortized cost is not likely to occur. Thus, the impairment of the asset is next to impossible to determine.

Even if one assumes that the factors and elements underlying goodwill can be identified and objective measures of their useful lives are available, their continued existence is subject to serious reservations. For example, in a competitive environment, any advantage that a business has because of its reputation and relations with its customers must be regenerated by new efforts and expenditures. If the customers are left unattended, it will not take long for them to go elsewhere. Thus, within a short time after the purchase of goodwill, the meaning of its recorded value (whether amortized or not) is subject to serious doubts. When does the purchased goodwill expire and the internally generated goodwill come into effect?

Problems At the Date of Acquisition

There are also problems with measurement at the acquisition date. It is not uncommon for firms to be acquired at a market price per share that is far in excess of the price per share before information of the impending acquisition was available. If the markets are efficient, the market price per share prior to the release of information concerning the takeover attempt should be a valid representation of the value of the stand-alone firm. If investors are willing to pay a substantially higher price for the firm than was determined by market forces, they must expect that the value of the acquired firm to be greater to their company than its value as a stand-alone firm.

Thus, a premium is being paid for synergism based upon the judgment of the management of the acquiring firm. In most instances, the transaction is at an arm's length and independent observers (e.g., auditors) can easily verify the purchase price. However, the verification of the value of the premium included in this purchase price is not possible since the only source of goodwill measurement is management representations. That is, the estimates used in the computation of the price paid are the only evidential matter available and an independent appraiser engaged by the auditor will probably arrive at a different amount for the excess payment.

ACCOUNTING ALTERNATIVES

The discussion presented so far leads to the conclusion that goodwill cannot be capitalized because the auditor cannot attest to its measured amount. If this argument is supported by the FASB, then accounting for the unidentified portion of the excess (goodwill or residual) must reflect the substance of this transaction by debiting equity. In this matter management will have to prove the validity of its assumptions, and amounts that do not belong in a balance sheet will be disposed of.

However, the FASB may decide that, in the case of business acquisitions, the measurement process is sufficiently objective and the measured amount itself is verifiable and reliable. It may also be argued that the management would not have paid for the excess if it did not have future benefit, especially when the amount is determined through negotiations between a willing buyer and a willing seller. Therefore, regardless of the nature of the excess, the FASB may decide to capitalize the residual under the caption of goodwill arguing that the management intent and the price paid for the investment indicate the existence of some future benefit. Moreover, one can argue in favor of using management intent as evidence by indicating that management would not voluntarily try to allocate any portion of the excess to goodwill since its amortization is not tax deductible.

If the residual is capitalized as goodwill, then an amortization period or useful life must be determined. Since the nature of the residual under consideration is analogous to the first view of goodwill, a logical choice would be the time period selected by management to compute the present value of the excess earnings or cash flows. Thus, management's estimates may be used in the amortization process as it was done when the decision was made to capitalize goodwill.

As previously stated, the reasons for the excess payment, specifically the acquisition of market share or market factors, have relatively short useful lives as they relate to projects that can be accomplished within, for example, a five-year period.[14] Thus, the 40-year amortization period used in current practice is too long and cannot be supported on either theoretical or technical grounds. Consequently, a rapid amortization (specifically if the use of the present value amortization method is permitted by the FASB) of capitalized goodwill over a relatively short period of time should occur and the reported financial indicators of companies with material amounts of capitalized good-will will be affected.

FINANCIAL CONSEQUENCES
OF NONCAPITALIZATION

If the FASB agrees with the contention that the amounts presently capitalized and reported on the balance sheets under the caption of "goodwill" need to be amortized quite rapidly and/or written off immediately, there will be an impact on the total assets (decrease), total equity (decrease), and net income (increase slightly) reported in the financial statements. The impact will even be greater if we assume the worst and the entire amount of goodwill currently present on the balance sheet is written off immediately. Since the FASB is generally concerned with the financial consequences of its standards, it is worthwhile to examine the magnitude of the impact of such an accounting policy change on the risk (debt-to-equity) and performance (return-on-investment) ratios. These ratios are extensively used by financial analysts to determine the credit ratings and stock prices of companies.

To accomplish this objective we first obtained from the COMPUSTAT tapes a list of all firms with total assets of $100 million or more for the years 1980 through 1984, a period of high merger activity. We assumed that large asset bases indicated well diversified and mature firms that may have gone through a number of mergers and accumulated substantial amounts of goodwill.[15] Thus, we biased the sample selection in order to obtain the maximum possible impact of the accounting policy change. This step yielded 359 firms that had sufficient data for the time period chosen.

Second, we obtained the goodwill amount reported on the annual and/or 10-K report balance sheets of the firms in our sample. After eliminating all firms with insufficient data (for many firms the amount was immaterial or zero), our final sample sizes ranged from 59 (1980) to 65 (1984). In some cases the goodwill amount was incorporated in "other assets" or "other intangibles" and could not be separately identified. In such instances the amount representing these general categories was used. Thus, a positive error in the

---

[14] See, for example: A. H. Rosenbloom, "How to Determine the Value of a Business: A Case Study," *The Practical Accountant* (March 1983), pp. 28–34; and P. Anthony, "Goodbye Goodwill—Hello Share of the Market," *Management Accounting* (June 1977), pp. 31–40.

[15] Including all the firms in the *Compustat* tapes in our sample resulted in a ratio of goodwill (or other assets) to total assets of .018 compared to a ratio of .034 if only "large" firms are included in the sample. Thus, we tried to obtain the largest possible impact.

measured financial consequences may exist. (A list of companies is available from the authors.)

Next, we computed the debt-to-equity (DTE) and net income-to-total assets (ROA) ratios of the firms in our sample for each of the five years. Finally, we repeated this step assuming that the goodwill (or other assets) amount was deducted from total assets and total equity and its amortization was added back to net income (NEWROA and NEWDTE, respectively).

It is important to note that the distributions of the ROA and DTE ratios are not symmetrical about their means (i.e., these two distributions are not normal). Therefore, it is necessary to have another measure in addition to the mean and standard deviation in order to adequately describe these two distributions. The coefficient of skewness (CS) provides a measure of the direction and extent of skewness or lack of symmetry. A positive CS means that most observations forming the distribution are to the left of the mean, indicating a long tail to the right. The larger the numerical value of the CS, the more skewed is the distribution.

The results of our observations show (see Table 2) that:

1. Average ROA is .0804 while average NEWROA is .0844 indicating an increase of .4 percentage points with a range of 0 to 1.7 percentage points,
2. Average DTE is .9481 while average NEWDTE is 1.0310 indicating an increase of 8 percentage points with a range of .2 to 110.0 percentage points,
3. The average ratio of goodwill (or other assets) to total assets is .034,
4. The average ratio of goodwill (or other assets) to retained earnings is only .089, and
5. All of the coefficients of skewness in Table 2 are positive numbers, indicating that the bulk of each distribution is to the left of the mean. Therefore, most of the observed differences between the DTE and NEW-DTE and ROA and NEWROA ratios are smaller than the mean. Alternatively, very few differences between the two ratios are substantially larger than the mean.

It follows that the average impact of the suggested change in accounting policy on ROA may be viewed as immaterial (according to a five percent materiality criterion) while the impact is modest on DTE, indicating an increase in these ratios of 4.9 percent versus 8.7 percent, respectively. This is not a surprising result, since goodwill is much larger in proportion to equity than it is to total assets.

CONCLUSIONS

The measurability criterion has been clearly established as one of the main principles of asset recognition by the FASB and should be given primary consideration in the selection of a method of accounting for goodwill. There is a problem of uncertainty of future benefits when acquisitions involve pur-

TABLE 2

Year	Number of Firms	ROA	NEW ROA	Difference Amount	Difference Percent	Standard Deviation	Coefficient of Skewness	Goodwill to Asset Ratio
1980	59	.0840	.0878	.0038	4.5	.0039	2.7	.0318
1981	60	.0838	.0875	.0038	4.5	.0037	2.2	.0320
1982	62	.0749	.0790	.0041	5.5	.0041	2.2	.0373
1983	64	.0762	.0800	.0038	5.0	.0036	2.2	.0350
1984	65	.0833	.0875	.0042	5.0	.0036	2.2	.0359

Year	Number of Firms	DTE	NEW DTE	Difference Amount	Difference Percent	Standard Deviation	Coefficient of Skewness	Goodwill to R/E Ratio
1980	59	.9090	.9811	.0721	7.9	.1096	3.1	.0807
1981	60	.9277	.9943	.0666	7.2	.1217	2.2	.0785
1982	62	.9817	1.0837	.1020	10.4	.2358	6.7	.0913
1983	64	.9298	1.0117	.0819	8.8	.1460	5.6	.0960
1984	65	.9924	1.0843	.0919	9.3	.1424	5.9	.0988

chase prices based upon management's judgment regarding synergistic possibilities. Extensive efforts to identify the elements of the purchased intangibles may reduce the amount of the unidentified portion that has commonly been labeled as goodwill, but will not eliminate it. Application of the measurability criterion to business combinations suggests that this residual amount must not be capitalized.

We, therefore, proposed a two-step approach to accounting for goodwill. First, all intangible and tangible assets that form the basis for the excess payment over fair values of net assets acquired must be identified, capitalized, and amortized over their useful lives. Second, any remaining unidentifiable portion of the excess must be written off against equity on date of acquisition.

Direct writeoff of goodwill against equity produces minimal impact on the ROA and a modest impact on the DTE ratios of the companies included in our sample. However, one must note that even this modest impact is overstated. For approximately 40 percent of the observations, goodwill is not separately identified but is included with other intangibles in the other assets category. Therefore, the amount of time and effort spent by the profession to resolve the debate on whether or not to capitalize goodwill must be in proportion to the relatively small economic consequence of this problem.

Goodwill Is Making a Lot of People Angry

Jeffrey M. Laderman
Business Week

When Philip Morris Cos. gobbled up Kraft Inc. for $12.9 billion last year, it acquired a passel of prizes that are household names to nearly every shopper in America: Velveeta cheese and Chiffon margarine, to mention just a few. Wall Street has applauded vigorously, sending Philip Morris stock up more than 50%. But according to accountants, Philip Morris was taken to the cleaners. The fair value of the Kraft assets, say the bean counters, was only $1.3 billion. The difference, a staggering $11.6 billion, or 90% of the purchase price, is a wispy, intangible asset known as goodwill.

There are scores of issues on which investors and accountants part company, but few are as contentious—or important—as the treatment of goodwill. And in an era of megadeals, the balance sheets of U.S. companies are piling it up at a torrid pace. Because of the Kraft deal, Philip Morris' goodwill climbed to $15 billion from $4 billion. That's nearly triple its net worth (table). And for many other companies, especially those in consumer products and media, goodwill is becoming an ever larger piece of the balance sheet. At Gannett, Dow Jones, and PepsiCo, goodwill and other intangibles make up more than 80% of net worth.

'SLIPPERY CONCEPT'

All that goodwill is bad news for reported earnings. U.S. corporations must "amortize" or write it off—without the benefit of a tax deduction. That puts American companies at a disadvantage when bidding against foreign buyers for acquisitions. In Britain, companies don't amortize goodwill at the expense of earnings. In Japan, West Germany, and Canada, they do, but the write-off is cushioned by tax breaks. "If there's a more slippery concept [in accounting,] I don't know of it," says Robert Willens, an accounting analyst at Shearson Lehman Hutton Inc.

No one's advocating doing away with goodwill entirely. Indeed, it's a "plug" number that makes a balance sheet balance. When one company buys another, the fair value of the physical assets go into the inventory or plant, property, and equipment accounts. The remainder is called goodwill, also known as "going concern value," and is classified as an intangible asset. In that light, it makes sense. Kraft spent decades building up its food products, and consumer loyalty to the Kraft label is a valuable asset.

But will the value of the Kraft name decline to zero in 40 years? That's how Philip Morris has to treat it, deducting $290 million a year from earnings—about $1.25 a share. While assets such as machines deteriorate visibly, it's not so easy to pinpoint when an intangible is losing value. The write-off is "ludicrous," says Hans G. Storr, Philip Morris' chief financial officer. "It's camouflaging real income."

The goodwill rules also have a vastly different impact on different industries. In capital-intensive businesses, the bulk of the purchase price can be attributed to physical assets. Goodwill is not a major factor, and the write-off does not chew up earnings.

But in consumer products and media, the bulk of the purchase price is goodwill. If Time Inc. succeeds in buying Warner Communications Inc., nearly $11 billion of its $14 billion bid will result in goodwill. The write-off— and it could be more than $300 million annually—will throw Time's reported earnings into the red for several years, even though it takes no cash out of the till. "We have an accounting system that works fine for bricks and mortar," says Lee Seidler, senior managing director at Bear, Stearns & Co. "But it penalizes service companies."

Companies didn't always have to write down their goodwill. Prior to 1970, goodwill was carried at cost and cut only when there was evidence that the asset's value was diminishing. That's essentially what some would like to see today. "If you take care of it, the asset lasts indefinitely," says Roman L.

How Goodwill Weighs on the Balance Sheets

When one company buys another the difference between the purchase price and the fair value of the physical assets is goodwill. Most companies put it under the heading of intangible assets.

Company	Intangible assets	
	Millions of dollars	Percentage of net worth
VIACOM	$2,468	721%
FRUIT OF THE LOOM	908	352
TELE-COMMUNICATIONS	3,143	261
PHILIP MORRIS	15,071	196
COCA-COLA ENTERPRISES	2,935	188
BAXTER INTERNATIONAL	2,705	87
GANNETT	1,526	85
DOW JONES	964	83
PEPSICO	2,582	82
SHEARSON LEHMAN HUTTON	1,758	76
CAPITAL CITIES/ABC	2,217	73
EASTMAN KODAK	4,610	68
McGRAW-HILL	507	55
GENERAL ELECTRIC	8,552	46
WASTE MANAGEMENT	838	38
CHRYSLER	2,688	35
AMERICAN HOME PRODUCTS	643	22
XEROX	1,089	20
GENERAL MOTORS	5,392	15
IBM	717	2

Data: Standard & Poor's Compustat Services Inc.

Weil, professor of accounting at the University of Chicago Graduate School of Business. "But bad management can destroy it quickly, too."

Accountants made the write-off of goodwill mandatory because some managers were loathe to recognize that the value of intangibles, such as brand names, had eroded. "The goodwill write-off is only a compromise," says Arthur R. Wyatt, a partner at Arthur Andersen & Co. "But no one's yet come up with a better solution."

UNFAIR ADVANTAGE

U.S. companies can also be hurt by the goodwill write-off in international deals. Seidler, among others, thinks that goodwill helped two British advertising giants, Saatchi & Saatchi PLC and WPP Group PLC, swallow up U.S. advertising agencies. As service businesses, nearly all the purchase price of the companies would up as goodwill. The British don't have to charge it off before reporting earnings on their profit-and-loss statement. Instead, they turn directly to the balance sheet and deduct the goodwill from retained earnings. That can make a company look precariously leveraged. To remedy that problem, a few aggressive British companies have begun to shore up their balance sheets by creating an entry called intangible assets, just as it's called in the U.S. But they don't have to amortize it. The bottom line: Since the accounting for acquisitions doesn't penalize earnings, the British can outbid the U.S.

That advantage is under fire in Britain. The British Accounting Standards Committee is weighing a proposed move to a U.S.-style treatment of goodwill. That would coincide with a proposal from the International Accounting Standards Committee, which has proposed a goodwill rule that would write off the asset over five years, though the period could be extended to as much as 20 years if the company could justify it. If adopted in the U.S., that standard would be even more punishing on reported profits.

Of course, some dealmakers say that goodwill's distortion of profits doesn't matter much, because the smart money knows what's going on anyway. "We've never backed off an acquisition because of the goodwill," says Douglas H. McCorkindale, chief financial officer of Gannett Co., the media giant.

Still, McCorkindale says it has taken a long time for Wall Street to realize that goodwill "is an accounting charge without any substance." That could be true for Gannett, Philip Morris, and a few others. But if scores of companies started reporting big losses just because of goodwill, shareholders would surely start screaming.

Accounting Rules Favor Foreign Bidders

Sanford Pensler
Pensler Capital

Americans, weary of losing many markets to foreign competitors, are currently losing the battle for the most important market, the market for corporate control. In large measure, it is our own fault. Would-be U.S. purchasers of U.S. firms are burdened by accounting rules that favor foreign buyers.

Acquisition of U.S. corporations by foreign companies has grown dramat ically over the past 5 years, rising to $41.9 billion in 1987 from $5.9 billion in 1983. The pace is accelerating this year. While forbidding foreign corporations to buy U.S. corporations is not advisable, a leveling of the playing field is to be desired. The "good-will" accounting rules of different countries are a case in point.

Good will is the excess of the purchase price over the fair value of the actual "hard" assets of the company. Since most going concerns are worth more than the value of their underlying assets, most corporate acquisitions involve some good will. Indeed, companies with the strongest management, performance and market position usually have the most good will in their sectors.

Of the major industrial nations, only the U.S. requires its companies to amortize, or write off, good will against earnings but doesn't allow any tax deductions. In other words, there are both earnings effects and no tax benefits.

In most European countries, including Britain, good will is treated entirely on the balance sheet and has no earnings effects. A group led by British-based Beazer Co. is in the midst of a hostile offer for Pennsylvania-based Koppers. At a price of $56 a share, the good will in this transaction would be about $1.1 billion. A French company, Hachette, has launched a hostile tender offer for Connecticut-based Grolier; at a final price of about $25 a share, the good will would be about $350 million.

U.S. companies bidding for these companies would be at a disadvantage to their foreign competitors. A U.S. purchaser of Koppers would have lower incremental reported earnings than its British counterpart of approximately $30 million a year; a U.S. purchaser of Grolier would have lower incremental reported earnings than its French counterpart of approximately $10 million a year, or roughly half of Grolier's latest 12-month earnings. This is no slight disadvantage, since U.S. companies are valued to a significant degree on a multiple of reported earnings.

Canada, Japan and West Germany require good will to be amortized against earnings. However, the good-will charges are in large measure tax deductible, which gives companies from these countries a cash-flow advantage over a U.S. purchaser. In effect, the governments of Japan, Germany and Canada provide a subsidy for the purchase of U.S. companies.

The improved after-tax cash flow resulting from good-will tax deductions helps companies bid higher than a U.S. counterpart could. In the battle for Federated, there are two bidders, Canadian Campeau Corp. and Macy's. At the prices currently contemplated, there will be about $3.5 billion of good will. If this good will were deducted according to the Canadian rules, Campeau would have an after-tax cash advantage in year one of approximately $60 million and a total tax advantage of approximately $600 million. Japanese and German companies' tax deductions for good will are even more advantageous.

Given this American disadvantage, it has become very difficult for publicly traded companies to compete in the bidding for prime U.S. corporate properties. The acquisition of Sterling Drug is the exception that proves the rule. Hoffmann-LaRoche, a Swiss pharmaceutical company, bid for Sterling Drug early this year. Most industry analysts believed that the possibility of a U.S. company buying Sterling was low due to the large amount of good will that would be created in the transaction. Sterling was, however, ultimately acquired by a U.S. buyer, Kodak, for approximately $5.2 billion, with an estimated good will of more than $4 billion or a charge of about $100 million a year—more than half of the amount of Sterling's latest 12-month earnings of $190 million.

Kodak's stock dropped about $3 billion in value following the announcement, reflecting in large measure Wall Street's distaste for the earnings dilution caused predominantly by the good-will charge from acquiring Sterling.

U.S. accounting rules, as well as those of other nations, were designed for domestic use. It is only as markets have become more international that differences in the rules have taken on importance. The rules should now be adjusted so that similar accounting standards are used worldwide.

The current U.S. rules were adopted in 1970 by the Accounting Principles Board. The logic for deducting the value of good will from earnings was that any price paid for a company above the value of its physical assets was for "intangibles." Since the value of these intangibles would eventually become zero, the argument went, if the intangible assets were used up in generating earnings, there should be some way of expensing the price paid for these intangibles against earnings. The board, arguing that it was better to take some arbitrary standard of expensing intangible assets than to reflect nothing, established an expensing period of 40 years to expense long-lived assets with no discernible lifetime.

Prior to 1970, U.S. corporations were allowed to leave good will on their balance sheets indefinitely if it was not used up in creating earnings. This standard should be reinstated. Not only does it better reflect economic reality, it also would make U.S. companies more competitive in bidding for corporate properties. It would not, however, balance the situation with those countries that allow tax deduction for good will—Canada, Japan and West Germany.

To put companies from those countries on an even footing with U.S. bidders, perhaps a tariff or foreign corporation tax should be imposed on their U.S. operations. While the optimum solution would be the elimination of the subsidy by foreign countries, the tariff or tax could provide an interim solution.

The accounting standards under which the U.S. operates are established by self-regulatory accounting review boards. If the profession can formulate an internationally unified set of rules without U.S. government involvement, that is fine; otherwise, these rules should be established through trade negotiations. The alternative is for the U.S. to forfeit control of many of its major corporations to foreign buyers, when if given a level playing field, U.S. corporations would pay as much if not more to own them.

Accounting for Goodwill: A Case Analysis of the U.S., U.K. and Japan

Kathleen M. Dunne

Rider College

Theresa P. Rollins

Villanova University

This paper discusses the international differences in accounting for goodwill, for financial reporting, and tax purposes. Financial publications have often discussed a bidding disadvantage that the U.S. firms face, because they must amortize goodwill, whereas British firms may write off goodwill directly to stockholders' equity. The effect of these differences on acquisitions is investigated within the specific environments of the United States, Great Britain, and Japan. Using a case analysis, the paper demonstrates that the different financial reporting rules should not put U.S. firms at a disadvantage. However, Japanese firms may have a bidding advantage over the other two countries.

Foreign firms have entered the bidding competition for American companies. Recently, some of the largest acquisitions have involved British and Japanese acquirer firms, including Grand Metropolitan's acquisition of Pillsbury, and Japanese acquisitions of CBS Records, MGM, and Firestone Tire. Most of these acquisitions have resulted in the recognition of large amounts of goodwill. *Forbes* noted that Grand Met's original offer of $60 per share would have resulted in over four billion dollars in goodwill (Jereski, 1989). Jereski suggested that the U.S. firms were at a disadvantage stating, "unencumbered by U.S. accounting rules (foreign companies) need not amortize goodwill, or if they must, they deduct it from their taxes" (Jereski, 1989, p. 41). This quote summarizes the major complaint of most U.S. firms that compete with foreign companies for U.S. takeover candidates.

The financial press has repeatedly stressed the British advantage. For example, Laderman (1989) noted in *Business Week*:

> All that goodwill is bad news for reported earnings. U.S. corporations must 'amortize' or write off goodwill without the benefit of a tax deduction. That puts American companies at a disadvantage when bidding against foreign buyers for acquisitions. In Britain, companies don't amortize goodwill at the expense of earnings (Laderman, 1989, p. 65).

From *Journal of International Accounting Auditing and Taxation* (1992, No. 2), pp. 191–207. Reprinted by permission of JAI Press Inc. Copyright © 1992 by JAI Press Inc.

Authors' note: The authors wish to acknowledge the assistance of David Stout, Don Wygal, and Saburo Narada of DRT International for their helpful comments.

Lee Berton, of *The Wall Street Journal*, discussed a similar British bidding advantage. While noting that the British accounting standards for goodwill are being revised, Berton stated:

> Until now, the normally acquisitive British have held an enormous advantage over any American suitor in bidding for a U.S. company. In deciding how high to bid, the British never had to worry about penalizing future profits. They could write off goodwill . . . against reserves. . . . The British invasion has been no small potatoes, and so any letup is bound to dampen acquisition demand in the U.S., investment bankers say.

As the above illustrates, the U.S. is considered to be at a disadvantage as compared with the British because the U.S. must amortize goodwill, but the British are able to deduct it directly from stockholders' equity (through a reserve account[1]). More importantly, however, what the literature fails to point out is that neither the U.S. nor Great Britain allows a tax benefit for the amortization of goodwill. The different financial statement treatment of good-will does not directly affect the cash flow of firms in either country and, consequently, should not, in theory, give the British a significant price advantage in the bidding process.[2] The major issue that should concern management is the deductibility of goodwill for tax purposes, which would positively affect firm cash flow.

Goodwill impacts the financial statements in a number of ways. For financial reporting purposes, goodwill resulting from an acquisition is capitalized in most countries. In some cases, it is written off immediately. If an asset is recognized, it is usually amortized on a systematic basis over a specific number of years, though there is a significant variation in the useful life used among countries. (See Table 1.)

The international tax treatment of goodwill also differs significantly. In the United States and Great Britain, no tax deduction is allowed for amortization of goodwill. This impacts both the taxes paid and the tax expense reported on the financial statements. Other countries, notably Japan, allow goodwill to be amortized over a short time period for tax purposes, thereby reducing current tax expense and taxes paid. Ultimately, if the subsidiary is sold, the tax basis will differ between countries, eliminating some of the difference in taxes paid.

The different capitalization and amortization policies for financial reporting purposes will result in different balance sheet and income statement results (Corry, 1990). However, as noted earlier, if countries are compared

---

[1] Many foreign countries, including Great Britain, use "reserve" accounts. These accounts are part of stockholders equity and usually have credit balances. One major use of reserve accounts is to indicate portions of retained earnings that are not available for dividends (Stickney, Weil, and Davidson, 1991).

[2] Agency theory, or positive theory, suggests that firms may be motivated to choose accounting procedures that enhance certain financial ratios, even if there are no favorable cash flow benefits (Watts and Zimmerman, 1986). The non-cash effects of different accounting treatments may affect the price, which will be discussed later.

TABLE 1 Accounting and Tax Treatment for Goodwill[a]

Country	Accounting Treatment	Tax Treatment
United States	If the acquisition is accounted for as a purchase, goodwill is amortized over no more than 40 years. A permanent decline in value should be expensed in the current period.	Not deductible for tax purposes.
Canada	Goodwill should be capitalized and amortized over no more than 40 years. A permanent decline in value should be expensed in the current period.	Seventy-five percent of the balance is deductible for tax purposes at the rate of 7 percent per year.
Great Britain	Goodwill should be written off immediately against stockholders' equity. Some excess value of the acquisition can be capitalized as trademarks.	Not deductible for tax purposes.
France	Goodwill is capitalized and amortized over a 5- to 10-year period.	Not deductible for tax purposes.
Germany	Goodwill can be capitalized or written off immediately.	Deductible over 15 years.
Japan	Goodwill is capitalized and amortized over no more than 5 years.	Deductible over a 5-year life.
Italy	Goodwill is capitalized and amortized over a period of 5 to 20 years.	Deductible over a 5- to 10-year life.
Netherlands	Goodwill can be capitalized or written off immediately. If it is capitalized it must be amortized over a period of 5 years, unless 10 years can be justified.	Deductible over a 5-year life.
Spain	Goodwill must be capitalized and amortized over a 10-year period.	Deductible if it can be proven that it declines in value.

[a] AICPA, *The Accounting Profession in Japan* (1988) and Nobes, C. and R. Parker (eds.) *Comparative International Accounting* (1985).

that have the same tax treatment of goodwill, the cash flow generated by the acquisition should be the same, *ceteris paribus*. In fact, there is increased focus on cash flow information (Kochanek and Norgaard, 1988). In discussing the leveraged buyout of Reynolds and Nabisco, Henry Kravis, of Kohlberg, Kravis and Roberts noted, "We forget about reported earnings. . . . You have all new accounting adjustments, including goodwill which you have to write off. It's not a cash charge . . ." (Briloff, 1990, p. 17).

The purpose of this paper is to explore international differences in accounting for goodwill. In addition, the paper demonstrates, using a case study, that the difference in tax treatment of goodwill must be considered in evaluating the competition posed by international firms. The case is suitable for presentation or assignment in an undergraduate advanced accounting course, an MBA course, or a multinational CPA firm training course. The case allows for the integration of a financial and an accounting topic, and provides an opportunity to discuss the international marketplace.

INTERNATIONAL TREATMENT OF GOODWILL

Accounting standards are almost exclusively national in character and origin, usually developed by government regulation, or through accounting bodies with government oversight. Large discrepancies exist as to the treatment of many assets. Moreover, because goodwill is intangible in nature, the differences have been intensified. With capital markets becoming increasingly international, the lack of consistent international accounting practices is problematic (Watters & Collins, 1989).

In 1973, the International Accounting Standards Committee (IASC) was established to promote consistency. The standards issued by the IASC are strongly influenced by the developed countries and closely resemble U.S. GAAP (Rivera, 1989). International Accounting Standard 22 (IAS 22, 1984), *Accounting for Business Combinations*, calls for either the immediate write off of goodwill against stockholders' equity or the capitalization and amortization of goodwill. IAS 22 proposes a goodwill life of 5 years, unless a longer life can be demonstrated. A 20-year life would be the maximum allowed. In 1989, the IASC released an exposure draft entitled *Comparability of Financial Statements*, recommending the elimination of the option of writing off goodwill against stockholders' equity. IAS 27 was issued in the same year, recommending the issuance of consolidated statements and the changing of the definition of subsidiary.

While the IASC has issued many statements, most have not been adopted internationally. Rivera (1989) notes that the IASC has not been successful in obtaining consensus or use of standard accounting practices, because of a lack of a common theoretical structure and the nonenforceability of international standards. A more successful group than the IASC, the European Economic Community (EEC), is attempting to "harmonize" accounting principles among member nations. The group attempts to achieve harmonization through directives which must be adopted by member nations. The Seventh Directive, adopted in 1983, recommends that goodwill on consolidation be depreciated or immediately written off against stockholders' equity. In addition, a European Accounting Forum has been established to address the issue of common accounting standards, and met for the first time in 1991 (Rutteman, 1990). Because wide variation in accounting principles exists within Europe, a consensus through the European Accounting Forum may make the IASC's job easier.

Table 1 summarizes the accounting and tax treatment for acquisitions and goodwill. Although countries differ as to the capitalization policy, most countries require some capitalization of goodwill. The policy differences range from the option for immediate write-off (Italy) to a practice of amortization over a 40-year period (U.S.). There is a wide variation in the tax treatment of goodwill amortization.

U.S. Accounting for Goodwill

U.S. accounting practice requires that goodwill be recognized in acquisitions accounted for as purchases (APB 16, 1970).[3] Goodwill represents the excess of the purchase price over the fair market value of all identifiable net assets for both financial reporting and tax purposes. The company must recognize goodwill, even if it cannot identify the reasons or attributes of the acquired company that make up the goodwill. All intangibles, including goodwill, must be amortized over a useful life of no more than 40 years (APB 17, 1970). In future periods, if the carrying value of the goodwill is diminished, it must be written off against earnings (APB 17, 1970). For tax purposes, no deduction is allowed for goodwill amortization (Internal Revenue Code, 1989). In addition, Congress is considering a bill that would limit amortization of franchises, trademarks and tradenames acquired from third parties (Coopers & Lybrand, 1991). Currently, non-goodwill intangibles can be amortized for tax purposes, if they can be shown to have a limited life.

Presently, the FASB has a multi-phase project on consolidations on its agenda. In September 1991, the FASB issued the *Discussion Memorandum*, "Consolidation Policy and Procedures," (FASB, 1991). The FASB has not indicated that it is considering a change in goodwill as part of this project. The Discussion Memorandum deals primarily with the issue of control and intercompany transactions.

British Accounting for Goodwill

The United Kingdom currently is changing its accounting for goodwill. Statement of Standard Accounting Practice No. 22 (SSAP 22), *Accounting for Goodwill* (1984) allows goodwill to be amortized over its useful life, an unspecified period. However, the standard encourages that goodwill, because of its intangible nature, be removed from the balance sheet immediately by reducing stockholders' equity. Unlike the U.S., the British may attribute some of the excess cost to "Brands," which currently may have an indefinite life and, thus, would not be amortized. For tax purposes there is no deduction for goodwill amortization.

In an attempt to reduce the choices allowed under SSAP 22, the British Accounting Standards Committee issued *Exposure Draft 47* (ED 47, ASC, 1990) that would require capitalization and amortization of goodwill. A 20-year life

---

[3] Per APB Opinion No. 16, a purchase is defined as any acquisition that does not qualify as a pooling. Generally, this means that more than 10% of the purchase price was paid in cash or debt. The tax rules for a tax-free exchange are similar to that of a pooling, but not identical. We are assuming the acquisition is accounted for as a purchase for both financial reporting and tax purposes.

would be mandated, and in exceptional cases up to 40 years could be used. While this standard would bring the U.K. more in line with the U.S. treatment, there has been considerable opposition to this. In fact, the opposition has been so great that one accounting firm noted that its support of ED 47 was "news" in the *Financial Times* (Hastie, 1990).

Some predict, firms will be more likely to allocate the excess cost to brand assets, an option not open to U.S. firms. This would result in little or no amortization (Stobart, 1989). Many are opposed to the option of capitalizing brands, though this is an accepted practice in Australia (Rutteman, 1990). Recently, some have predicted that the Accounting Standards Board would revise ED 47 because of the near total opposition to it (*Accountancy*, 1990).

Japanese Accounting for Goodwill

Very little is written on the Japanese treatment of goodwill. The AICPA summary of Japanese accounting (1988) notes that intercorporate purchases are rare in Japan. For tax purposes, Japanese firms must capitalize and amortize goodwill over a maximum of 5 years. Japanese firms must account for goodwill on a consistent basis for financial reporting purposes. While acquisitions within Japan may be rare, Japanese acquisitions of U.S. firms are increasing.

Although the Japanese may not have addressed the specific question of goodwill, they are focusing more on U.S. GAAP. The Japanese finance ministry recently postponed an effort to require "American-style" consolidated financial statements (Shida, 1991). As part of the Structural Impediments Initiative Talks, the Japanese are being encouraged to produce statements in conformity with the SEC requirements. Currently, 29 companies, including Hitachi and Sony, produce such statements, because they are listed on U.S. stock or bond markets. Over 60 percent of the 1,300 other Japanese firms provide some consolidated data, though not in nearly as much detail as U.S. GAAP requires. Japan hopes to implement U.S. style consolidated reporting by 1995 [Shida, 1991].

Japanese firms release little information about goodwill resulting from acquisitions. Goodwill arising from the Sony acquisition of CBS records was estimated by reviewing Sony's financial statements prepared for the SEC, Form 20-K, in which Sony followed U.S. GAAP. The goodwill may have exceeded 700 million dollars.[4] For the SEC statements, Sony uses a 40-year life. In terms of the tax treatment, Sony could have an annual tax deduction of $140 million for 5 years compared to no tax deduction in the U.S. or Great Britain. Clearly, this large difference could significantly affect the price a firm could pay. The tax difference will be demonstrated in the case.

---

[4] Specific information was not provided in the financial statements. The number was estimated using the change in the Intangibles account for 1988 and 1989, which was stated in yen, and converting the information to dollars. The change in the account was also affected by other acquisitions and amortization. While not precise, the calculation indicates that goodwill from the acquisition was significant.

CASE ANALYSIS

This case study addresses two critical issues in international accounting. The first part of the analysis examines the increase in cash flow to an acquiring firm in three different countries, assuming they purchase the same target. The second section illustrates the impact of the international differences in accounting treatment for goodwill on the financial statements of an acquiring company in three different countries. Table 2 presents the unconsolidated financial statement information for Acquirer Company and Target Company that is used throughout the case. Both parts of the case consider three examples. The difference between each example is the country of origin of Acquirer Company and, consequently, the difference in accounting and tax treatment of goodwill after the acquisition. The first example assumes the acquirer to be a U.S. firm while the next two examples assume the acquirer to be from the United Kingdom and Japan, respectively.

TABLE 2 Unconsolidated Financial Statements

	Acquirer	Target
Balance Sheet December 31, 19x1 (Dollars in Millions)		
Cash	$ 70.0	$10.0
Accounts Receivable (net)	50.0	5.0
Inventory	200.0	15.0
Plant and Equipment (net)	700.0	50.0
Investment in S	100.0	
Total Assets	1120.0	80.0
Current Liabilities	10.0	10.0
Long Term Liabilities	110.0	10.0
Total Liabilities	120.0	20.0
Common Stock, par $1 (100,000,000 shares)	100.0	10.0
Additional Paid-in-Capital	400.0	20.0
Retained Earnings	500.0	30.0
Total Stockholders' Equity	1000.0	60.0
Total Liabilities and Stockholders' Equity	$1120.0	$80.0
Income Statement Year ending December 31, 19x1 (Dollars in Millions)		
Sales	$ 300.0	$20.0
Expenses:		
Depreciation	70.0	5.0
Other	130.0	6.0
Total Expenses	200.0	11.0
Income Before Taxes	$ 100.0	$ 9.0

I. Analysis of the Cash Flow Generated by the Acquisition

The purchase decision should be made primarily as an investment decision. One way to analyze the benefits of a potential acquisition and determine an appropriate price is to evaluate the incremental cash flow that would be generated by the acquisition using the discounted free cash flow method. This method requires the acquiring firm to assess the target firm's cash flow over a specified period of time. An appropriate discount rate is selected, and the present value of the cash flows is calculated. The present value represents the value of the target to the acquiring company in terms of cash flow and may indicate an approximate price the acquirer would be willing to pay for the target. For this example, cash flow is analyzed over three time frames: 5-year, 10-year, and 20-year horizons. The case assumes a discount rate of 10 percent for all three time frames. Earnings are assumed to be constant over the time period studied to limit the impact of other variables.

Table 3 presents the data that the acquiring company would use to make the investment decision. To simplify the example, a goodwill amount of $40 million is assumed for each acquirer. A 37 percent overall tax rate in the U.S., comprised of a federal rate of 34 percent, and state and local rate of 3 percent is used. For Great Britain an overall rate of 35 percent, and 55.2 percent for Japan is used (Coopers and Lybrand, 1990). All three countries allow acceler-

TABLE 3 Analysis of Acquirer's Incremental Cash Flow as a Result of the Acquisition

	Acquirer		
	U.S.	U.K.	Japan
Computation of target firm's after tax cash flow:			
Pre-acquisition income before tax[a]	$ 9.0	$ 9.0	$ 9.0
Acquisition adjustment:			
goodwill amortization	1.0		8.0
Pre-tax income	8.0	9.0	1.0
Income tax	3.3	3.2	.6
Net income (loss)	4.7	5.8	.4
Adjustments to income:			
Depreciation	5.0	5.0	5.0
Goodwill amortization	1.0		8.0
Cash flow	$10.7	$10.8	$ 13.4
Computation of income tax expense:			
Pre-tax income	$ 8.0	$ 9.0	$ 1.0
Permanent difference:			
U.S. goodwill amortization	1.0		
Taxable Income	9.0	9.0	1.0
Tax rate	37%	35%	55.2%
Income tax expense	$ 3.3	$ 3.2	$ .6

[a] Pre-acquisition income represents the income that the target company would earn regardless of who purchased it. We are assuming the goodwill amortization would be the only adjustment to earnings after the acquisition.

ated depreciation for tax purposes. Both the United States and Great Britain allow firms to use other methods for financial reporting, while Japanese firms must use the same method for both purposes. Therefore, in order to keep the focus of this example on the goodwill issue, all three acquiring firms use straight-line depreciation for both tax and financial reporting purposes.

ACQUIRER IS U.S. FIRM

The first step in the analysis is to determine the incremental cash flow to the acquirer as a result of the acquisition. Starting with the income of the target before taxes (shown in Table 2) an adjustment is made for the amortization of goodwill that is required under U.S. GAAP (APB Opinion No. 17, 1970). However, because the amortization of goodwill is a permanent difference between accounting and taxable income it must be added back to pre-tax income to determine taxable income of $9.0 million. The income tax expense of $3.3 is computed and deducted from pre-tax income to arrive at net income of $4.7 million.

The incremental cash flow to U.S. Acquirer is calculated by adjustments to net income for depreciation and goodwill amortization because these expenses do not require a cash outlay. The incremental cash flow to U.S. Acquirer as a result of the acquisition is $10.7 million. The present value of the cash flow assuming a 10 percent discount rate and three different time horizons is shown in Table 4. As Table 4 indicates, the cash flow generated by

TABLE 4 Present Value Calculations of Cash Flow Annuity per Table 3

Five-Year horizon:
    Assuming a 5-year cash flow (the life of the Japanese tax deduction) with no growth in earnings (all numbers in millions of dollars).
      Present value of an annuity assuming a 10% discount rate:

Price paid by U.S. firm	= $40.6
Price paid by British firm	= $40.9
Price paid by Japanese firm	= $50.8

Ten-year horizon:
    Assuming a 10-year cash flow, with no growth in earnings.[a]
    Present value of an annuity assuming a 10% discount rate:

Price paid by U.S. firm	= $65.8
Price paid by British firm	= $66.4
Price paid by Japanese firm	= $72.0

Twenty-year horizon:
    Assuming a 20-year cash flow with no growth in earnings.[a]
    Present value of an annuity assuming a 10% discount rate:

Price paid by U.S. firm	= $91.1
Price paid by British firm	= $92.0
Price paid by Japanese firm	= $93.3

[a] After the fifth year, the Japanese firm will no longer have a tax advantage from the goodwill deduction. Therefore, for years six through ten (or six through twenty), the Japanese cash flow from the acquisition will be $9.0 (pre-tax income of $9.0, tax expense of $5.0, plus the add back of depreciation of $5.0). The present value of the cash flows is the sum of the present value of two different cash streams.

the acquisition for U.S. Acquirer increases from $40.6 million to $91.1 million as the time period lengthens.

ACQUIRER IS BRITISH FIRM

Examination of the cash flow analysis for UK Acquirer in Table 3 indicates that there is no charge against the target's income for the write off of goodwill. Similarly, there is no deduction for the write off in computing taxable income and tax expense. The statement of cash flow for the UK target firm includes an add back for depreciation only. Therefore, the incremental increase in cash flow for UK Acquirer as a result of the acquisition is $10.8 million. The difference in the cash flows between the United States and the United Kingdom is caused by the difference in tax rates and not by the difference in accounting treatment between the two countries.

The present value computation in Table 4 shows that the incremental cash flow of the U.S. and British firms is almost the same, assuming a 5-year time horizon, $40.6 million and $40.9 million, respectively. The difference of less than 1 percent is caused by the higher overall tax rate in the U.S., and not by the goodwill. It is unlikely that the immediate write off of goodwill in the U.K. creates a purchase advantage. As the time period increases, U.K. Acquirer continues to receive greater cash flow increases relative to the U.S., but only by a small amount.

ACQUIRER IS JAPANESE FIRM

An analysis of the investment decision for Japan Acquirer shows that the incremental cash flow to the Japanese firm is the greatest. Japan is the only country of the three that allows the amortization of goodwill to be deducted for tax purposes. Given the high tax rate in Japan and the fact that goodwill must be amortized over a brief period of time (5 years) the cash flow advantage to Japan Acquirer is significant—especially given the relatively high marginal income tax rates existing in Japan. The additional cash flow that the Japanese firm would experience is $50.8 which is 25.0 percent higher than the U.S. Clearly, the increase in cash flow relative to the U.S. and U.K. companies gives Japan Acquirer a purchase advantage in the merger game.[5] Japan Acquirer can afford to pay more than U.S. Acquirer or U.K. Acquirer for Target Company because of the cash flow advantage. Therefore, while Japanese firms must amortize goodwill for financial reporting purposes, similar to the U.S., they are at a distinct advantage because of the tax law.

---

[5] The Japanese firms have a much higher tax rate than U.S. or U.K. firms. In acquisitions with relatively small amounts of goodwill, the Japanese acquirer would be at a disadvantage. While the case focuses on acquisitions with large amounts of goodwill, the point should be made that the specific characteristics of both the acquirer and the acquired company will determine which country offers an advantage.

The differences between the U.S. and U.K. versus Japan narrow, significantly, as the time frame is extended, but the Japanese firm continues to receive greater benefits than the other two countries using a 10-year horizon. In this time period, Japan Acquirer experiences an increase in cash flow that is 9 percent higher than the U.S. Over a 20-year period the Japanese have only a 2 percent advantage.[6]

Frequently, the discounted cash flow method is used to determine the price paid for the target company. While it is unlikely that a purchase decision would be made based on 5 years, the short-term cash flow is very important to most firms. If the acquisition is leveraged in any way, sufficient cash must be generated immediately to pay for the acquisition. As stated above, Table 4 shows that the present value of the target firm's cash flow with either a U.S. or British parent is almost identical, while the increase in cash flow to Japan Acquirer is significantly greater (approximately 25% greater than U.S. or U.K. Acquirer). This difference puts the Japanese firm at a distinct advantage when bidding for Target Company.

II. Financial Statement Impact of Goodwill

This section considers three examples that illustrate the impact of the international differences in accounting treatment for goodwill on the financial statements of the consolidated firm. Each example assumes that on January 1, 19x1, Acquirer Company purchases Target Company, a U.S. firm, for $100 million in cash. The fair market value of the identifiable net assets of Target Company on the date of acquisition is equal to their book value of $60 million.[7] The business combination is accounted for as a purchase, with the difference between fair market value of the acquired net assets and the price paid resulting in goodwill of $40 million.

Table 2 presents the financial information for Acquirer Company and Target Company for 19x1. Each example assumes the same financial data. Table 5 shows the consolidated balance sheet and income statement for the three companies as of December 31, 19x1.

ACQUIRER COMPANY IS U.S. FIRM

Under U.S. GAAP the capitalization and amortization of goodwill over a period not to exceed 40 years is required (APB No. 17, 1970). Therefore, goodwill is stated as an asset of $40 million on the post-combination balance sheet of U.S. Acquirer, increasing total assets and stockholders' equity by the

---

[6] The results are sensitive to the interest rate assumption. Ten percent was chosen because it represents a reasonable rate in today's market. However, at higher rates, such as 14 percent, the Japanese advantage would be small in the long run, though the cash savings in the early years would remain high for the Japanese firm.

[7] This assumption allows one to concentrate on the financial statement impact of goodwill. When the market value of the fixed assets is different from the book value, there will be tax and financial statement differences between countries here as well.

TABLE 5 Post-Combination Financial Statements

	Acquirer		
	U.S.	U.K.	Japan
Consolidated Balance Sheet December 31, 19x1 (Dollars in Millions)			
Cash	$ 80.0	$ 80.0	$ 80.0
Accounts Receivable (net)	55.0	55.0	55.0
Inventory	215.0	215.0	215.0
Plant and Equipment (net)	750.0	750.0	750.0
Goodwill	39.0		32.0
Total Assets	1139.0	1100.0	1132.0
Current Liabilities	20.0	20.0	20.0
Long Term Liabilities	120.0	120.0	120.0
Total Liabilities	140.0	140.0	140.0
Common Stock, par $1 (100,000,000 shares)	100.0	100.0	100.0
Additional Paid-in Capital	400.0	400.0	400.0
Retained Earnings	499.0	460.0	492.0
Total Stockholders' Equity	999.0	960.0	992.0
Total Liabilities & Stockholders' Equity	$1139.0	$1100.0	$1132.0
Consolidated Income Statement year ending December 31, 19x1 (Dollars in Millions)			
Sales	$ 320.0	$ 320.0	$ 320.0
Expenses:			
Depreciation	75.0	75.0	75.0
Amortization Charges	1.0		8.0
Other	136.0	136.0	136.0
Total Expenses	212.0	211.0	219.0
Net Income Before Taxes	$ 108.0	$ 109.0	$ 101.0

same amount. This also results in a charge against income of $1 million a year for 40 years, assuming that the maximum amortization period is used. Table 5 illustrates the effect of capitalization and amortization of goodwill on the financial statements of U.S. Acquirer.

Table 6 compares selected financial ratios before and after the acquisition. Return on investment (ROI) and return on total assets (ROA) are increased for U.S. Acquirer as a result of the acquisition. Earnings per share (EPS) increases from $1.00 to $1.08 per share and the long-term debt to stockholders' equity ratio (debt/equity) is raised from 11.0 percent to 12.0 percent.

ACQUIRER COMPANY IS BRITISH FIRM

The accounting principles in the United Kingdom do not require the amortization of goodwill. Goodwill can be capitalized and written off immediately against stockholders' equity. Therefore, the consolidated balance sheet of

TABLE 6 Comparison of Financial Ratios for Acquiring Firms Before and After the Acquisition

		Acquirer		
		U.S.	U.K.	Japan
ROI	Before Acquisition	10.0%	10.0%	10.0%
	After Acquisition	10.8%	11.4%	10.2%
ROA	Before Acquisition	8.9%	8.9%	8.9%
	After Acquisition	9.5%	9.9%	8.9%
EPS	Before Acquisition	$1.00	$1.00	$1.00
	After Acquisition	1.08	1.09	1.01
Debt/Equity	Before Acquisition	11.0%	11.0%	11.0%
	After Acquisition	12.0%	12.5%	12.1%

ROI = Net Income before Taxes/Stockholders' Equity
ROA = Net Income before Taxes/Total Assets
EPS = Net Income before Taxes/Shares of Common Stock Outstanding
Debt/Equity = Long-term Debt/Stockholders' Equity

U.K. Acquirer (Table 5) reflects a write off against stockholders' equity of $40 million.[8] Examination of the consolidated income statement in Table 5 for U.K. Acquirer indicates that there is no charge against income for this write off. The write off against stockholders' equity increases the ROI and ROA for the British company relative to U.S. Acquirer (see Table 6) because it decreases the asset base with no decrease in reported income. The British ROI and ROA are 11.4 percent and 9.9 percent, respectively, compared to the U.S. firm's ROI and ROA of 10.8 percent and 9.5 percent, respectively. The increase in EPS from $1.00 to $1.09 per share is similar to the change for the U.S. firm. However, the debt/equity ratio of the British firm is higher, at 12.5 percent, compared to 12.0 percent for the U.S. firm.

ACQUIRER COMPANY IS JAPANESE FIRM

According to accounting principles in Japan, goodwill must be treated in a consistent manner for both financial reporting and tax purposes. Therefore, the case assumes that Japan Acquirer amortizes goodwill over a 5-year period. Consequently, Table 5 shows goodwill of $32 million on the post-combination balance sheet of Japan Acquirer as well as an amortization expense of $8 million on the income statement for the first year. Table 6 illustrates the effect the amortization has on the financial ratios of Japan Acquirer. The ROI and ROA ratios are the lowest of the three companies, at 10.2 percent and 8.9 percent, respectively. Also, EPS is increased only 1 percent from $1.00 to $1.01 per share while the debt/equity ratio is increased from 11.0 to 12.1 percent.

---

[8] In practice, the format and account titles of the financial statements for British and Japanese firms will be different. However, for clarity of discussion, the same presentation for all three countries is used.

Thus, at the date of acquisition, the balance sheets of U.S. Acquirer and Japan Acquirer are similarly affected by the capitalization of goodwill. Only the total assets and stockholders' equity of U.K. Acquirer are reduced at the date of acquisition because of the goodwill write off. While this reduces the amount for total assets and stockholders' equity, the rates of return for U.K. Acquirer are increased, *ceteris paribus*. Comparatively, the U.S. and Japanese firms do not experience the same beneficial effects regarding their rates of return because the capitalization and amortization of goodwill negatively affect the ratios by lowering net income (due to the amortization charges) and increasing the asset base (because the capitalization of goodwill increases assets). U.S. Acquirer's ROI and ROA increase to 10.8 percent and 9.5 percent while Japan Acquirer's ratios increase to only 10.2 percent and 8.9 percent, respectively. Also, while the EPS for U.S. and U.K. Acquirer increase by 8 percent and 9 percent, respectively, Japan Acquirer experiences little increase in EPS. However, the debt/equity ratio of the British firm is the highest because of the decrease in stockholders' equity due to the write off of goodwill.

These changes in financial ratios as a result of differential accounting treatments for goodwill may indirectly affect cash flow through the effects that reported accounting earnings have on management compensation plans and bond covenants (Watts and Zimmerman, 1986). For example, because profitability measures such as ROI or ROA are often used to award bonuses, an increase in these ratios may result in greater wealth to management in the form of increased compensation at the firm's expense (Healy, 1985). Additionally, a higher debt/equity ratio may affect a firm's ability to borrow additional funds or place a firm close to violation of lending agreement restrictions (Smith and Warner, 1979). This could result in additional costs to the firm. From this perspective, U.K. Acquirer appears to be at the greatest disadvantage; while that firm experiences the greatest increase in ROI and ROA, it also has the largest increase in the debt/equity ratio. On the other hand, U.K. Acquirer reports the highest percentage increase in EPS. This financial ratio, because of its widespread use, is considered an important measure of past operating performance (APB No. 15, 1969).

CONCLUSION

The case analyzes the impact that international differences in the accounting and tax treatment for goodwill could have on the price an acquirer is willing to pay for a target company and on the post-combination financial statements of firms in three countries: the United States, the United Kingdom, and Japan. The actual purchase decision that a firm makes is very complex. Many factors, in addition to the overall tax rate and tax treatment of goodwill, will impact the outcome of any comparison of firms. The foreign exchange rates and post-combination environment of the acquiring firm will also affect the decision. While certain simplifying assumptions were made, the main point is that one cannot say that British firms have a significant advantage over U.S. firms. In fact, it appears they may have no real advantage.

Moreover, a comparison of the tax accounting treatment of goodwill across firms suggests that Japan Acquirer experiences a cash flow advantage. Of the countries included in this case, only Japan allows the amortization of goodwill to be deducted for tax purposes. Table 3 and Table 4 show that, because of the high tax rate in Japan and the fact that goodwill must be amortized over a 5-year period, the cash flow advantage to Japan Acquirer over the first 5 years is significant. Clearly, this increase in cash flow gives Japan Acquirer a competitive edge in the bidding process. Japan Acquirer may be willing to pay more than U.S. Acquirer or U.K. Acquirer for Target Company because of the advantage caused by the difference in tax laws across countries.

This study also shows that U.K. Acquirer experiences the highest reported income and rates of return because goodwill is written off immediately against stockholders' equity. U.S. Acquirer does not experience a cash flow advantage or a reported earnings advantage compared to either U.K. or Japan Acquirer.

The IASC and EEC are seen as a means of "harmonizing" accounting principles. However, if the goal of the international market place is to create an equitable business environment, then additional focus must be placed on the different tax environments.

BIBLIOGRAPHY

Accountancy, 1990, "New Goodwill ED Likely," (October):9.

Accounting for Goodwill, 1984. London: Institute of Chartered Accountants in England and Wales.

Accounting Principles Board, 1969. *Opinion No. 15: Earnings per Share*, New York: American Institute of Certified Public Accountants.

————. 1970. *Opinion No. 16: Business Combinations*, New York: American Institute of Certified Public Accountants.

————. 1970. *Opinion No. 17: Intangible Assets*, New York: American Institute of Certified Public Accountants.

Accounting Standards Committee. 1990. *Exposure Draft 47: Accounting for Goodwill*, London: Institute of Chartered Accountants in England and Wales, February.

American Institute of Certified Public Accountants. 1988. *The Accounting Profession in Japan*, New York: American Institute of Certified Public Accountants.

Berton, L., 1990. "Heard on the Street: Merger Scene Strafed by U.K. Accountants," *The Wall Street Journal*, (February 6):C1-C2.

Briloff, A. 1990, "Accounting and Society," *Critical Perspectives on Accounting*: 4-30.

Coopers & Lybrand. 1991. "Congressional Proposal Would Disallow Amortization of Certain Intangible Assets," *Executive Briefing*, (March):6.

————. 1990. *International Tax Summaries*, New York: John Wiley.

Corry, J. 1990. "Accounting Aspects of Takeovers," *Management Accounting*, (September):47-51.

Financial Accounting Standard Board. 1991. "Consolidation Policy and Procedures," *Discussion Memorandum*, Stamford, Conn.

Hastie, S. 1990. "Goodwill—Are We Really Making Progress?" *Accountancy*, (October):28.

Healy, P. 1985. "The Impact of Bonus Schemes on the Selection of Accounting Principles," *Journal of Accounting and Economics 7*, (April):85–107.

Internal Revenue Code. 1989. Chicago: Commerce Clearing House:Sec. 1060.

International Accounting Standards Committee. 1983. *Accounting for Business Combinations*, London: IASC.

Kochanek, R., and C. Norgaard. 1988. "Analyzing the Components of Operating Cash Flow: The Charter Company," *Accounting Horizons*, (March):58–66.

Jereski, L. 1989. "Ill Will," *Forbes*, (January 23):41–42.

Laderman, J. 1989. "Goodwill is Making a Lot of People Angry," *Business Week*, (July 31):73, 76.

Moulin, D., and M. Solomon. 1989. "Practical Means of Promoting Common International Standards," *The CPA Journal*, (December):38–48.

Nobes, C., and R. Parker. 1985. *Comparative International Accounting*, New York: Philip Allan/St. Martins Press.

Rivera, J. 1989. "The Internationalization of Accounting Standards: Past Problems and Current Prospects," *International Journal of Accounting*, 4 (24):322–341.

Rutterman, P. 1990. "Can We Leap the Harmonization Hurdles?" *Accountancy*, (November):29.

Shida, T. 1991. "MOF Adopts Lax Rule on Disclosure," *Japan Economic Journal*, (January):1.

Smith, K. V., and J. B. Warner. 1979. "On Financial Contracting: An Analysis of Bond Covenants," *Journal of Financial Economics 7*, (June):117–161.

Stickney, C.P., R. Weil, and S. Davidson. 1991. *Financial Accounting*, New York: Harcourt, Brace & Jovanovich, Inc.

Stobart, P. 1989. "Brand Valuation: A True and Fair View," *Accountancy*, (October):27–28.

Walters, R., and S. Collins. 1989. "The Globalization of Accounting Standards," *Australian Accountant*, (September):22–27.

Watts, R., and J. Zimmerman. 1986. *Positive Accounting Theory*, New York: Prentice Hall.

Britain's Goodwill Games

Dana Wechsler
Forbes

In July 1988 John Murphy got a flash that is changing the face of British accounting and of deal-making throughout the world. Murphy, chairman of the London marketing consulting firm Interbrand Group Plc., was visiting Australia. He picked up the newspaper and saw that Australian food giant Goodman Fielder Wattie had made a hostile bid for Britain's Ranks Hovis McDougall Plc.—the "Pillsbury of the U.K.," as Ranks Hovis is known. The

£1.7 billion bid was aimed at getting hold of Ranks Hovis' valuable brands—
including Mothers Pride sliced bread and Mr. Kipling fruit pies—whose
values were nowhere reflected on the balance sheet.

Seizing the moment, Murphy shot off a note to Ranks Hovis McDougall
Chief Executive Stanley Metcalfe, suggesting that Interbrand be called in to
figure out just how much those brands were really worth and put that value
on Ranks Hovis' balance sheet. Metcalfe readily agreed.

As it turned out, Goodman Fielder Wattie withdrew its bid. But Ranks
Hovis continued its brand valuation process. In its 1988 annual report, Ranks
Hovis McDougall included £678 million, or $1.2 billion, of new asset values.
This stemmed from putting a current value on over 40 brands.

As a result, the company's fixed assets jumped to £1.1 billion, nearly two-
and-a-half times what they had been before the revaluation. Thanks to the
writeup, just before Ranks Hovis McDougall purchased RJR Nabisco's U.K.
cereals late last year, its debt came to 14% of equity. Without the writeup, the
ratio would have been nearly 50%.

Nor is Ranks Hovis planning to amortize that $1.2 billion in new intan-
gible assets (though it will review the amount annually), because the brands
ostensibly have indefinite lives. This frustrates and angers many American
businessmen who are forced, under U.S. accounting rules, to amortize goodwill and other intangibles.

Goodwill gets on a company's books when it pays more for assets than
the book value of those assets—a typical occurrence in purchasing branded
goods, for example. Our rules say this goodwill must be amortized over no
more than 40 years.

Now, clearly, this amortization penalizes earnings. Take a case where a
company pays $1 billion for assets with a book value of just $500 million. The
transaction creates $500 million worth of goodwill; writing it off over 40 years
bites into aftertax earnings to the extent of $12.5 million a year. Because many
analysts value companies on the basis of their earnings, acquisitions involving lots of goodwill can really hurt an expanding company's stock price, and
make acquisitions for stock more expensive.

British businesses, by contrast, can charge the entire amount of goodwill
directly against shareholders' equity without penalizing their earnings at all.
And with the new British practice, even the reduction to shareholders' equity
can be reversed.

Take London's WPP Group, run by Martin Sorrell. WPP snapped up New
York's JWT Group, parent of advertising agency J. Walter Thompson, in 1987.
Goodwill on the deal: $465 million, which WPP took out of its shareholders'
equity account. That gave the company a negative $120 million net worth at
the end of that year.

But following quickly in Ranks Hovis McDougall's footsteps, in 1988 WPP
said that J. Walter Thompson and JWT's Hill & Knowlton public relations firm
were worth $317 million. Presto! At the end of 1988, WPP reported that
shareholders' equity was a positive $110 million.

Is this cricket? London's accounting rulemakers, the Accounting Standards Committee, don't think so. They have appealed to all companies to hold

off on brand valuation until they have a chance to come up with a standard that addresses the issue. But many executives—probably fearful of being taken over if they don't revalue their balance sheets, or on the prowl themselves—are ignoring the appeal. They can do that because the Accounting Standards Committee hasn't come up yet with a formal ruling.

The British companies to embrace brand valuation so far are "the most acquisitive of companies," observes Robert Willens, senior vice president in Shearson Lehman Hutton's mergers and acquisitions department. Grand Metropolitan Plc. is a good example. It added $1 billion in brand values, mostly for Smirnoff vodka, to its 1988 balance sheet after buying Heublein. Then Grand Met used its weightier balance sheet and acquired Pillsbury for $5.7 billion in January.

Rumor has it that British brewer Bass Plc., which just snapped up Holiday Corp.'s U.S. properties, plans to put a value on the Holiday Inns name. WPP itself swallowed Ogilvy Group for $864 million just after restoring its balance sheet by putting a value on J. Walter Thompson.

WPP's Martin Sorrell bristles at the suggestion that the new accounting offers his firm any strategic advantage. "No bank is going to attribute value to intangible assets just because we've written them up by £175 million," he says. "I can't understand why there's such a fuss about it."

So why did Sorrell write up his company's assets? Replies he: "The balance sheet should give a true and fair view of value, and traditional accounting concepts don't do that for service companies."

Which brings up another interesting question: How does a company put a monetary value on something so ephemeral as a brand name? With historical cost accounting, a company knows how much it actually paid for something. But, in valuing intangibles like goodwill, approaches differ wildly. Coopers & Lybrand's valuation department, for example, usually adds up all the future income attributable to a brand name and then discounts it into today's dollars.

Interbrand's method involves a complex set of calculations: First, Interbrand isolates the earnings of the brand name from any other business factors like distribution or manufacturing economics. It then applies a multiple to those earnings, reflecting things like the brand's market leadership and how international it is. A product like Coca-Cola would be awarded the highest possible multiple, an 18 or 19. Most brands score closer to 12. In the last 12 months, Interbrand has done valuations for 40 corporations around the world; most clients are in the midst of takeover battles for brands, and others are simply shopping. Some U.S. companies are evaluating their brand values to be ready with a defensive response in case of an unwanted takeover bid.

Will U.S. companies be able to put higher brand values on their balance sheets? Not soon. Says Edmund Coulson, chief accountant of the Securities & Exchange Commission: "Valuing brands is extremely subjective. Basically they're worth what your investment banker tells you."

"Besides," he adds, "if we are going to start marking assets to market, why stop at brands? There are a lot of things you could revalue in a business.

including management." Managers writing themselves up and down—now there's a sobering thought.

The Name's the Game

The Economist

"Buildings age and become dilapidated. Machines wear out. Cars rust. But what lives on are brands," argues Sir Hector Laing of Britain's United Biscuits. How long does a product-brand live and how much money will it make? In 1988 thousands of businessmen's calculators tried to tap out a value for brands. In all probability, few of them got it right.

Rules vary on how companies can record brands as intangible assets on their balance sheets. Americans can value them only after they acquire them —and then they have to depreciate the value over 40 years. Australians are more cavalier. Mr. Rupert Murdoch, for instance, often revalues the worth of his newspaper mastheads.

Now shareholders may see many more trademark valuations in annual reports—particularly in Britain. Grand Metropolitan has decided that all the brands it has acquired since 1985 are worth £588m. Ranks Hovis McDougall (RHM), the maker of Hovis bread and Mr. Kipling cakes, has recently set a value of £678m for all its brands.

Why the change? Some companies are afraid that the stockmarket fails to value them correctly and leaves them open to a takeover. RHM recently shrugged off a £1.7 billion bid from Goodman Fielder Wattie of New Zealand. Predators like GrandMet resent allocating so much of the value of an acquisition as "goodwill"—the difference between the net book value of their target and the price they paid. The acquirer either has to depreciate the goodwill against profits or write it off against net worth (in America they have to take the former course).

A balance sheet is supposed to give shareholders a true and fair view of the company: in many cases a company's foremost assets are its brands. Nestlé did not buy Rowntree because it thought that industrial property in York was due for a boom. Many accountants support brand valuation. But:

- The balance sheet is now becoming a mess of assets, all valued at different times. RHM, for example, records property at a historic value of £170m. Accountants worldwide need to sort out which system to follow: either a balance sheet based on historical cost or on present valuation.
- There is no easy way to value a brand. RHM, advised by Interbrand, took each brand's average earnings from the past three years and multiplied it

by a "power" factor. RHM stressed that its value was a "current cost value" (ie, the value of replacing the brands), not a market value. The latter, which would presumably be based on the net-present-value of all the earnings from a brand, would tell the shareholder much more. But it would also set a price on the company. Shareholders would have learnt more if RHM had simply recorded how much profit each brand had made: the stockmarket might then have decided whether RHM's "brand" profits were consistent enough to increase the company's market value.

TWENTY-FIRST CENTURY BRAND

While techniques for valuing brands evolve, what will happen to the objects of all this attention? Will product-brands remain the gold that they are made out to be? The signs are that in the area where branding has been most successful—consumer-goods and food products—brands will be weeded out. Powerful retailers, some specialised, others not, learning how to use scanners and develop good quality own-label brands, will claw away at the third, fourth, and fifth brands in each type of product in any country. So will purveyors of multinational brands, once they learn how to act local. The Japanese may yet, in their indefatigable way, show that creating new brands is easier than western companies think.

As product brands come under pressure, however, there will remain another area in which branding can fight back—the branding of whole corporations and organisations. According to Professor John Quelch of the Harvard Business School, "brands of the highest stature are likely to be those coincident with the company's own name." Thus, Heinz, Kellogg's and Quaker have an extra value that Unilever does not. Cadbury's Flake has a double value: first the individual brand, Flake, and second the company name itself. Most Japanese companies are also strong corporate branders.

In contrast, every American's kitchen probably includes a General Food's product, but few react to it as a brand. It also owns Brazil's favourite ice cream, Kibon, and France's leading chewing gum, Hollywood. Its decaffeinated coffee sells as Sanka in America and Haag in Europe. As a result General Foods is nothing more than the sum of its parts. In marketing speak, there is no added value in its name.

Branding a company name has its limitations. Unilever is now displaying "Lever Brothers" more prominently on its detergents, but, understandably, it is keeping it away from its food and health products. Other names are simply not attractive: Wire and Plastic Products (WPP) is a less glamorous name for an advertising agency than J. Walter Thompson. Westpac, an Australian Bank, sounds as though it ships corrugated cardboard. Rhone-Poulenc, a French chemicals group, wondered long and hard whether it needed to change its name before promoting it worldwide. It stuck with it.

Mr. Simon Gulliford, programme director at Ashridge Management College in Britain, argues that companies can go a stage further and brand the "experience" that they purport to sell. BMW gives all its cars numbers, not names—so you buy "a BMW". But it also checks that the garages which sell and service BMWs are clean; it sells expensive leather jackets and briefcases to expensive-looking drivers. None of this means that a BMW is any better than its rivals: but proud owners are left with a feeling that they have joined some sort of elite. Other examples of branded experiences are flying with Singapore Airlines or shopping in Marks & Spencer. Others should try: name a bank or an insurance company whose products could be called familiar brands.

Commodity-to-product; product-to-brand. Is brand-to-experience the next and even more insubstantial step in the affluent adding of value? A good hunch is that the winners will continue to be those brands (or experiences) that keep their appeal as intangible as possible. Coca-Cola has never advertised itself on price. No matter how efficient producers become, consumers still relate to "names" in the same way as the author of an old Brazilian bossa nova song: "There is no patent on love; but you have a trademark on my heart."

Accounting for the Value of Brands

Tony Arnold
University of Essex, England

Michael Sherer
University of Essex, England

The accounting policy treatment of brand names has recently become a matter of debate and some controversy, prompted largely by the decisions of Grand Metropolitan and Ranks Hovis McDougall to include the value of brand names in their most recent consolidated balance sheets. For Grand Metropolitan this change of accounting policy has added over £500 million to the assets of the group at 30 September 1988; for Ranks Hovis McDougall the inclusion of brand names has increased the balance sheet value of its business at 30 September 1988 by £678 million.

Grand Metropolitan and Ranks Hovis McDougall are not alone in adopting this accounting policy. Reckitt & Colman includes trademarks of subsidiaries acquired during the last three years in its consolidated balance sheet, and several publishers—for example, Reed International, United Newspapers and Maxwell Communications—include in their balance sheets amounts paid for publishing rights.

Before the Ranks Hovis McDougall 1988 balance sheet was published there did seem to be a growing consistency in the accounting treatment of

From *Accountants' Magazine* (February 1989), pp. 12–14. Reprinted by permission of the journal and the author. Copyright © 1989 by The Institute of Chartered Accountants of Scotland.

brand names, even though this is an area of accounting policy where there is a great deal of scope for alternative treatments. Once brand names were included in the balance sheet, the amount was not upvalued. Few companies have provided for systematic amortisation of brand names, although most review the amounts regularly to assess whether there has been any permanent diminution in value. Finally, no company had included internally developed brand names as a balance sheet asset.

This semblance of consistency has been destroyed by RHM's decision to put balance sheet values on all its brands, whether purchased or internally developed. The value was determined by a specialist consultancy group, who took account of each brand's earnings and market position. Also, in contrast to other companies which include brand names in their balance sheets, RHM states that it will be revaluing its brands every three years.

Marketing managers have always recognised the importance of brand names. A brand name can refer to a specific product or service—for example, Kit Kat, Smirnoff Vodka and Mother's Pride—or to the company itself—for example, Rowntree Mackintosh, Grand Metropolitan and Ranks Hovis McDougall.[1] The financial and economic importance of brand names has been apparent in Nestlé's recent take-over of Rowntree Mackintosh, where the values placed upon the company's brand names were a significant part of the total consideration. It has also been said that RHM's decision to value its brand names is primarily a defensive measure to ward off potential predators.[2]

In view of their importance in marketing operations in takeovers it is perhaps surprising that until recently in the UK so little attention has been paid to the accounting treatment of brand names. Both the USA and Canada have positive policy recommendations that acquired, but not internally generated, brand names should be shown separately in group balance sheets.[3]

Brand names are intangible fixed assets as defined in Schedule 4 of the Companies Act 1985, which category includes concessions, patents, licences, trademarks and similar rights and assets. In common with the other examples, brand names are recognised as separable net assets when fair values are ascribed to assets on the acquisition of a subsidiary. The only intangible fixed asset which is not regarded as a separable net asset is goodwill, which by definition is simply the residual when the cost of acquisition is compared with the fair values of the net assets acquired.

The recognition by Grand Metropolitan and other companies that a separate value can be placed on brand names reduces the amount which is likely to be classified as goodwill.

---

[1] As reported in the *Guardian* on 17 November 1988 the top ten UK brand names, in terms of public awareness and respect, were: Marks & Spencer, Cadbury, Kellogg, Heinz, Rolls-Royce, Boots, Nescafé, BBC, Rowntree Mackintosh, Sainsbury. As a matter of comparison the top five world brand names were: Cola-Cola, IBM, Sony, Porsche, McDonald's.

[2] *The Times*, 23 November 1988, p 25 and p 27.

[3] APB Opinion No. 16: "Business Combinations" in the USA and "Accounting Recommendations on Business Combinations" in Canada.

It is not logical, however, for companies to treat internally developed brand names differently from purchased brand names in their balance sheets. If brand names are separable assets for the purpose of acquisition accounting they should be treated as separable, and hence capable of having a separate value, in all balance sheets. Until the announcement of Ranks Hovis McDougall's new policy it had been said that, while auditors were willing to concur with a valuation of purchased brand names, they would not be so amenable to a valuation of internally developed brand names. The auditors' argument had been that an objective figure could be used for putting an amount on purchased brand names, but that no such basis existed for internally developed brand names. The principles for valuing brand names, however, should be the same whether or not an acquisition has taken place, and the auditors of Ranks Hovis McDougall have accepted this.

Interestingly, no distinction is made in the Companies Act 1985 between acquired and internally developed brand names. Indeed, the Act provides one set of accounting principles for all fixed assets with the sole exception of goodwill. Hence, under the historical cost accounting rules, brand names should be valued at their purchase or production price.

The Companies Act 1985 also allows companies to value brand names at their current cost under the alternative accounting rules. This effectively means that the balance sheet amount for brand names can be upvalued, as well as reduced in the case of a permanent diminution in value. It appears, therefore, that the provisions of the Companies Act 1985 do not prevent companies recording internally developed brand names in their balance sheets and revaluing the amounts on a regular basis.

In this rather confused context the recent ASC discussion paper on fair value accounting[4] is to be welcomed as a helpful contribution to the debate on the accounting treatment of brand names. The discussion document takes as its starting point the criteria laid down in the Companies Acts and the relevant accounting standards, and then attempts to review the main areas of fair value accounting where alternative treatments are possible.

In particular it argues strongly for an acquirer's perspective to be adopted, with the consequence that the recommended valuation basis should be the entry-based one of replacement cost, defined in items of service potential. If, however, the asset is to be disposed of or is not worth replacing, then the net realisable value or the recoverable amount respectively is to be used. The document does not discuss whether there should be regular revaluations of assets recorded at fair values, but it does recommend that write-downs due to estimating errors should be charged directly to the profit and loss account.

The clear implication of this discussion document is that brand names should be recorded at the amount it would have cost the acquiring company to obtain them—normally their replacement cost. It seems, however, that this provisional recommendation does not accord with the current accounting

---

[4] Accounting Standards Committee: "Fair value in the context of acquisition accounting: a discussion paper," 1988.

treatment adopted by Ranks Hovis McDougall, a treatment which has been agreed with its auditors. We shall argue below that the arguments in the discussion document as they relate to brand names and other intangibles are fundamentally flawed.

The current controversy over the presentation and treatment of brand names in financial reports is symptomatic of the difficulties involved in attempting to accommodate new problem areas within the existing reporting framework. Although these various pronouncements are of some help to companies which own brand names, they do not provide an accounting "solution" that is consistent with the economic and financial realities of business life.

This is primarily because financial accounting derives asset and expense figures, and thus measures profit, by allocating "entry-side" costs. The effectiveness and utility of the accruals or allocation process has too rarely been questioned and the possibility of "exit-side" solutions has not, until recently, received consideration from any of the professional bodies.

Allocation procedures are an unsatisfactory basis for reporting because they are "arbitrary and incorrigible." Although any system of profit measurement requires the making of estimates, allocation estimates are objectionable because they are "assertions that cannot be proven correct nor refuted by reference to any real world external events."[5]

The accounting standards programme has not significantly reduced the arbitrary nature of the allocation process; even in so central an area as depreciation, the relevant standard can only recommend that the cost (or revalued amount) should be allocated "as fairly as possible to the periods expected to benefit from their use."[6]

SSAP22 "Accounting for goodwill" discusses the issue of when an intangible asset is a separable asset. Paragraph 13 argues that a separable net asset is an asset which can be identified and sold separately without disposing of the business as a whole. It therefore excludes goodwill as a separable net asset since by definition it cannot be identified and sold separately. The standard does, however, specifically include in separable net assets those categories of intangible fixed assets, other than goodwill, mentioned in the Companies Act.

SSAP22 also makes it clear that a separable net asset can be recognised by the acquirer in the balance sheet of the new group even though it was not recorded in the acquired company's accounts. This is exactly the treatment for brand names which has been adopted by Grand Metropolitan. Because this accounting standard deals with goodwill there is no discussion of internally developed brand names. If, however, an acquiring company can "discover" a valuable separable net asset then, to maintain economic or financial consistency, this accounting treatment should be available to all companies.

---

[5] A. L. Thomas. "The Allocation Problem Part II: Studies in Accounting Research No 9," The American Accounting Association, 1974.
[6] SSAP12 "Accounting for Depreciation," para 15.

When it comes to the carrying value of brand names, SSAP12 "Accounting for depreciation," like the Companies Act 1985, makes no distinction between tangible and intangible fixed assets (other than goodwill, of course). This implies that brand names should be shown on the balance sheet net of depreciation, although most of the companies which recognise brand names in their published accounts argue that no depreciation is required because such assets have infinite lives. SSAP12 also makes it clear that a provision should be made and charged to the profit and loss account for any permanent diminution in the value of fixed assets, thus including brand names.

Moreover, the combined use of historical costs and accruals adjustments prevent balance sheets being proper statements of *financial* position. Replacement, or current cost, accounting would not remedy this; the costs would be up-dated, but the importance of accruals adjustments involving unverifiable assumptions about the future would increase.

There are two alternative possibilities: either to report the "economic value" of assets, calculated as the present value of the future cash flows they are expected to generate; or to include assets (and liabilities) on the balance sheet at their exit price (or net realisable value).

The calculation of an asset's economic value is an important part of the investment appraisal process within the company, but is probably not sufficiently objective for inclusion in published balance sheets. The other approach, exit price accounting, does not, however, rely on any assumptions about the future as it includes assets on the balance sheet at their present "opportunity cost" to the company as a whole, obtained by estimating their current market value on an orderly disposal.

However many alternative uses there are for an asset within the company, for the business as a whole, which is the focus for financial reporting, there is only one opportunity foregone—the opportunity to have sold the asset. The market value, or sale price, foregone is therefore the opportunity cost of the asset to the company as a whole. Under an opportunity cost approach assets are included on the balance sheet at realisable values, not because there is any intention of sale but merely because at the balance sheet date they had not been sold.

This exit price approach would create a logical framework for all separable assets, intangible as well as tangible. We have already discussed the "separable assets" criteria which would apply to all assets except goodwill; an exit price approach would, by focusing on the sale proceeds that were foregone at the balance sheet date, also render irrelevant the "purchased/internally developed" distinction. This means that all separable assets, internally generated or purchased, could be treated on a uniform basis and one that reflected the financial state of the asset.

Moreover, exit price accounting can be combined with cash flow statements, which makes possible a closer relationship between financial reporting and management accounting. Such an approach now forms the basis of the current recommendations of the Research Committee of The Institute of Chartered Accountants of Scotland, set out in their recent publication, "Making Corporate Reports Valuable."[7] Alternative combinations of exit prices and cash flows have also been put forward as "Cash Flow Reporting" or "CFR accounting" by Lee[8] and as "Cash Flow and Exit Price" or "CaFE accounting" by Arnold and Wearing.[9]

The use of exit prices does require some change in the way that profit is conceptualised. The annual depreciation charge for an asset is, using an exit price approach, intended to reflect the asset's financial cost over the year, which is the change in the sunk-cost not recoverable through resale, rather than the amount of the asset which has been physically consumed (which cannot in any case be estimated with any degree of precision).

The changes between successive balance sheets can be set out and analysed in a number of different ways. Here there are important differences between the systems that combine exit prices and cash flows.

The Scottish Institute proposals certainly do place exit prices in a central position. However, while they view cash flow statements as "essential for any board of directors and for investors"[10] they do not make cash flows one of their "four basic statements,"[11] and in consequence the realised and unrealised components of the changes between successive balance sheets are not clearly distinguished.

If the word "realised" is used correctly—*i.e.*, as meaning "converted into cash"—then the realised changes must be by definition cash flows, which can be readily reported and audited, and also reconciled with information routinely presented to management.

Under CaFE accounting total annual changes are segregated into their factual (*i.e.*, realised or converted into cash) and estimated (*i.e.*, unrealised) components, which should be of benefit to investors, creditors and other users who are attempting to appraise the risk level attaching to a particular set of reported results.

In conclusion, although the Companies Act 1985, SSAPs 12 and 22, and the fair value discussion paper all provide some guidance on how to account for brand names, they do not provide a consistent framework for the valuation of both purchased and internally developed brand names. They also fail to establish coherent principles for dealing with changes in brand name valuations and how these changes should be reported in financial statements.

We argue that the use of exit prices on corporate balance sheets would provide a logical framework for the recognition of brand names and other intangibles. Brand names have the same characteristics as trade marks, patents, publishing rights and other intangibles. Hence, the exit price approach can provide a solution not only to the brand names problem but also to the problem of valuing other intangibles and indeed all other assets.

---

[7] Published by Kogan Page, 1988. Available from the Institute.
[8] T. A. Lee. "Cash Flow Accounting," Van Nostrand Reinhold, 1984.
[9] A. J. Arnold and R. T. Wearing. "Cash Flows, Exit Prices and British Airways", *Journal of Business Finance and Accounting*, Autumn 1988, pp. 311–33.
[10] "Making Corporate Reports Valuable," p. 76.
[11] ibid., p. 85–7.

The current debate on the accounting treatment for brand names also has implications for the amount of goodwill that needs to be shown in the balance sheet. The more separable net assets that can be identified and the more often exit price values can be used for these assets the less will be the amount for goodwill that needs to be dealt with in the financial statements. In particular, this approach may reduce the incidence of creative accounting techniques designed to minimise the write-off of goodwill on consolidation.

The exit price approach, given prominence by the Scottish Institute's "Making Corporate Reports Valuable," would entail carrying assets on balance sheets at their opportunity cost, namely the market price foregone by the decision to retain the asset concerned. This would render irrelevant the "purchased/internally developed" distinction and put brand names and other separable assets, whether tangible or intangible, on a consistent basis.

We further suggest that annual changes between balance sheets should be reported under two headings, realised and unrealised, which would articulate fully with the balance sheet. Any change in the balance sheet value attached to brand names would then change the profit for the year, but, unless actual disposals took place, through the unrealised "track."

We believe that the approach we have suggested would provide a framework for asset recognition in company reports which would inform users about the current financial state of all assets, including brand names and other intangibles, and about the risk profile of the company's earnings.

CHAPTER 9

Intercorporate Investments

Since economic activity is carried out in the form of legal entities, some fundamental questions in accounting are (1) how is the accounting entity to be defined, and (2) how should the financial position and the results of operations of the various legal entities constituting the accounting entity be reported?

On the latter question, intercorporate investments have been reflected via consolidated financial statements, the equity method of accounting, the cost method, and lower of cost or market, depending on the significance and degree of ownership interest or degree of control. In the United States, investments in marketable equity securities not qualifying for the equity method have been accounted for at the lower of cost or market.

An ages-old controversy in accounting for intercorporate investments in equity and debt securities is whether, and to what degree, they should be accounted for at historical costs or current values.[1] In regard to debt securities, U.S. financial institutions (commercial banks, savings and loan associations, insurance companies, credit unions, etc.) have been permitted to use historical cost, as adjusted for the amortization of premiums and discounts, for securities held for investment, while those held for trading are generally accounted for at market value. The Achilles' heel in this classification scheme is that it depends entirely on management's judgment. It is not unusual to find debt securities on which large gains or losses have accrued to be classified in the investment portfolio, so as to avoid accounting recognition of the unrealized gains and losses. The dual classification also allows financial

---

[1] In 1971, the Accounting Principles Board issued an exposure draft in favor of immediate income statement recognition of accrued gains and losses on marketable securities, whether realized or not. The initiative was defeated by strong opposition from the insurance industry. See Charles T. Horngren, "The Marketing of Accounting Standards," *The Journal of Accountancy* (October 1973), pp. 61–66.

institutions to engage in "gains trading," or "cherry picking," by which they elect to sell "investment" securities on which large gains have accumulated in order that these gains may be recognized in the financial year of choice.

In September 1990, Securities and Exchange Commission (SEC) Chairman Richard C. Breeden gave Congressional testimony in which he advocated mark-to-market accounting (i.e., current value accounting) for the debt securities held by deposit-accepting financial institutions.[2] He argued that the failure to recognize the accounting losses on such securities masked the seriousness of the financial condition of the savings and loan (also known as thrift) industry during the 1980s. An interview with Breeden held shortly after his Congressional appearance is reported in the *Forbes* article, "If Life Is Volatile, Account for It."

The consequences of Breeden's advocacy for the Financial Accounting Standards Board (FASB) are captured in a pair of articles by Arthur R. Wyatt, a former FASB member, and Donald J. Kirk, a former FASB chairman. In "The SEC Says: Mark to Market!" Wyatt recounts the recent developments in the context of the many years of dominance of the historical cost model. He notes that "the focus on mark-to-market accounting for investment securities reflects the emerging conceptual focus on the balance sheet," a change in focus that has been fostered by the FASB.

Kirk's article addresses two concerns. First, he reacts to the argument by an SEC Commissioner that accounting standards are too costly if they place U.S. companies or U.S. capital markets at a competitive disadvantage with those in other countries. Kirk argues that the FASB should be concerned only with neutral financial reporting, not with preserving the international equilibrium of competitive conditions. The second concern deals with the momentum toward mark-to-market accounting for certain financial institutions' investment portfolios of debt securities. In this regard, he examines the dialogue between the SEC and the bank regulators, as well as the follow-on actions by the FASB.

In July 1991, a month following the publication of Kirk's article, the FASB added a project to its agenda that would address marketable equity and debt securities. In December 1991, the FASB issued Statement No. 107 (the first standard to emerge from its broad-ranging financial instruments project launched in 1986), calling for the disclosure of the fair values of financial instruments that are either assets or liabilities, both on and off the balance sheet. In September 1992, the FASB issued an exposure draft that would allow entities having a "positive intent and ability" to hold debt securities until maturity to continue to account for them at amortized cost. Other debt securities and all equity securities would be reported at fair value: The gains and losses on those held for current resale would be included in earnings, while the gains and losses on other debt and equity securities would be reported as a part of shareholders' equity. The Board's struggle to determine

[2] See Kevin G. Salwen, "What's It Worth? Tackling Accounting, SEC Pushes Changes with Broad Impact," *The Wall Street Journal* (September 27, 1990).

whether, and to what degree, fair values should be used for debt and equity securities has not been an easy one, as banks and bank regulators have been persistently opposed to a mark-to-market requirement for securities included in an investment portfolio. If fair value were applied to such securities, the banking industry and its regulators have predicted adverse behavioral effects on banks' investment and lending policies.[3] Charting the course of neutral financial reporting is never easy when the political stakes are high.

ACCOUNTING FOR DIFFERENT LINES OF BUSINESS

Two broad (and controversial) issues appear under this heading: consolidation of all subsidiaries, including the finance subsidiaries of industrial companies; and segment reporting.

In 1987, the Financial Accounting Standards Board issued Statement No. 94, in which, among other things, it repealed an earlier standard, adopted in 1959, that permitted industrial companies that were the parents of banks, insurance companies or finance companies—even if they were 100%-owned—to exclude those nonhomogeneous subsidiaries from the consolidated financial statements. Under the former standard, the parent was to present separate or combined financial statements for the excluded subsidiaries. An argument made by many respondents to the FASB's exposure draft was that the inclusion of nonhomogeneous subsidiaries in the consolidation

> would impair comparability of the financial data between enterprises and that it would confuse the expected debt-equity (and other) ratios of manufacturing and financial components of diverse business enterprises, resulting in ratios that would accurately reflect neither component.[4]

Many other respondents, however, believed that comparability would be enhanced by consolidation. Partially to overcome the possible problem of lack of comparability, the FASB specified that "summarized information about the assets, liabilities, and results of operations (or separate statements) shall be provided" for the subsidiaries that were formerly omitted from consolidation.[5]

While Canadian, Australian, and U.S. standards are in agreement on the required inclusion of nonhomogeneous subsidiaries in the consolidation,

---

[3] For example, see Kevin G. Salwen, "SEC Renews Call for Pressure on Banks and S&Ls to Update Accounting Rules," *The Wall Street Journal* (January 8, 1992); Lee Berton, "FASB Balks on Current-Market Rules For Banks as Member Switches His Vote," *The Wall Street Journal* (January 16, 1992); Lee Berton, "Accounting Body Backs Modified Rule On the Valuation of Securities by Banks," *The Wall Street Journal* (July 16, 1992); Alison Leigh Cowan, "Accounting Asset Rule is Backed," *The New York Times* (July 16, 1992); Ford S. Worthy, "The Battle of the Bean Counters," *Fortune* (June 1, 1992); and "Uncook the Books," *The Economist* (May 9, 1992).

[4] "Consolidation of All Majority-owned Subsidiaries," *Statement of Financial Accounting Standards No. 94* (Financial Accounting Standards Board, October 1987), para. 45.

[5] *Ibid.*, para. 14.

their exclusion is permitted, in varying degrees, in the United Kingdom and Japan. Although the International Accounting Standards Committee's (IASC) Standard 27, "Consolidated Financial Statements and Accounting for Investments in Subsidiaries," adopted in 1988, does not countenance the exclusion of nonhomogeneous subsidiaries, the European Community's Seventh Directive, which was approved in 1983, requires that subsidiaries be excluded when their inclusion would be incompatible with giving a "true and fair view." It is clear that an international consensus is lacking on this question.

"Mishmash Accounting," an article from *Forbes*, provides evidence that analysts prefer disaggregation to aggregation, and that the FASB's Statement No. 94 has imposed a considerable cost on companies.

Spurred by the conglomerate merger movement of the 1960s, the reporting of financial information by segment of business activity—product lines and geographic areas—has become commonplace in the annual reports of diversified U.S. corporations. Comparable standards have been issued in Canada, Australia, and the United Kingdom, and by the IASC. Much latitude is left to company managements to determine how broadly or narrowly a "segment" is defined. In "An Innate Fear of Disclosure," another article from *Forbes*, examples are given of company decisions to opt for broad definitions of product line segments, thus placing a heavier burden on analysts (and competitors) to locate the principal sources of profitability within a conglomerate enterprise.

BIBLIOGRAPHICAL NOTES

Two articles on the nonconsolidation of finance subsidiaries are:

Benis, Martin: "The Non-Consolidated Finance Company Subsidiary," *The Accounting Review* (October 1979), pp. 808–814.
Burnett, Tom, Thomas E. King, and Valdean C. Lembke: "Equity Method Reporting for Major Finance Company Subsidiaries," *The Accounting Review* (October 1979), pp. 815–823.

The literature on segment reporting is considerable. Book-length works are listed in chronological order:

Mautz, R. K.: *Financial Reporting by Diversified Companies* (New York: Financial Executives Research Foundation, 1968).
Rappaport, Alfred, Peter A. Firmin, and Stephen A. Zeff (editors): *Public Reporting by Conglomerates* (Englewood Cliffs, NJ: Prentice-Hall, Inc., 1968).
Backer, Morton, and Walter B. McFarland: *External Reporting for Segments of a Business* (New York: National Association of Accountants, 1968).
Rappaport, Alfred, and Eugene M. Lerner: *A Framework for Financial Reporting by Diversified Companies* (New York: National Association of Accountants, 1969).
Rappaport, Alfred, and Eugene M. Lerner: *Segment Reporting for Managers and Investors* (New York: National Association of Accountants, 1972).
Analysed Reporting, A Background Study (London: The Institute of Chartered Accountants in England and Wales, 1977).

Barefield, Russell M., and Gary L. Holstrum: *Disclosure Criteria and Segment Reporting* (Gainesville: University Presses of Florida, 1979).

Miller, Malcolm C., and Mark R. Scott: *Financial Reporting by Segments*, Discussion Paper No. 4 (Melbourne: Australian Accounting Research Foundation, 1980).

Emmanuel, Clive, and Neil Garrod: *Segment Reporting: International Issues and Evidence* (London: Prentice Hall in association with The Institute of Chartered Accountants in England and Wales, 1992).

Boersema, John M., and Susan J. Van Weelden: *Financial Reporting for Segments*, A Research Study (Toronto: Canadian Institute of Chartered Accountants, 1992).

If Life Is Volatile, Account for It

Dana Wechsler Linden

Forbes

A rumble went through the sleepy world of accounting in September when the Securities & Exchange Commission's new chairman, Richard C. Breeden, 40, told a Senate committee that financial reporting for banks and thrifts should move toward "market-based measures of valuation at the earliest possible date." Translation: Financial institutions should write assets and liabilities up and down as their market values change. Next Breeden will want *all* companies to abandon historical cost accounting, speculated reporters, accountants and nervous corporate controllers.

They can relax. Breeden, a New York lawyer who became the architect of President Bush's savings and loan legislation, says he plans no revolution. FORBES talked with him in his Washington office bedecked with three photographs of George Bush and three computer terminals enabling him to keep a constant watch on the markets. We asked Breeden about that Senate testimony that started so many tongues wagging.

Breeden: We have merely spoken up about a particular accounting standard that was being reconsidered by the American Institute of Certified Public Accountants. That standard allows historical cost accounting for debt securities in the investment portfolios of banks and thrifts. In a world in which interest rates change—sometimes quite considerably in a short period of time—that is fictitious accounting.

Are you thinking about the S&L crisis?
Certainly. If you look back at the financials, thrifts were reporting almost $33 billion of net worth at the end of 1980, in accordance with generally accepted accounting principles. But if you marked their portfolios to market,

their actual net worth at that time was as much as $118 billion negative. That's a $150 billion swing!

Many people ask how the problem went undetected. It's easy. Presented with financial statements certified by Big Six accountants, most people presumed they bore some resemblance to reality. Really they were prepared in accordance with a set of rules, but those rules didn't measure reality.

Many people are afraid you intend to push for market value accounting for nonfinancial corporations, such as IBM, McDonald's or Du Pont.
We haven't reached any conclusions about market value accounting for industrial companies. For liquid assets of financial institutions, market value accounting has enormous benefit and virtually no cost. If you have a portfolio of $1 billion worth of Treasury bonds, the market price for those bonds is immediately determinable down to the penny. We want to tell creditors and investors what it is.

But any other change, even for less liquid financial instruments, will require careful study. People have misread what I've said if they think I have preconceptions. Certainly I would not suggest it would be an improvement for industrial companies to get appraisals of all their personal computers every year. I don't find fault with having the depreciated value of that office equipment on the books.

Many financial company executives complain that being forced to adopt market value accounting will result in terribly volatile earnings. Your response?
If you are in a volatile business, then your balance sheet and income statement should reflect that volatility. Furthermore, we have seen significant abuse of managed earnings. Too often companies buy securities with an intent to hold them as investments, and then miraculously, when they rise in value, the companies decide it's time to sell them. Meanwhile, their desire to hold those securities that are falling in value grows ever stronger. So companies report the gains and hide the losses.

This is a terribly important issue today. The banks need to raise capital. But investors disbelieve their financial statements, which raises the cost of capital even for strong institutions. And it undermines confidence in the stability of the banking system.

If the private sector's rulemakers vote against market value accounting for financial institutions' investment portfolios, will you overrule them?
Well, the testimony that I gave before the Senate was the unanimous testimony of the Commission, so let that speak for the record. We do have the final authority over what must be disclosed in accounting statements by public companies.

What time frame do you have in mind?
I don't see any particular obstacles to having the year-end 1991 financial statements include market values.

How do you think the Financial Accounting Standards Board has done in making the bottom line a more reliable measure of corporate performance?
Over the past few years, FASB has put out increasingly technical, detailed and costly standards.

On pensions, companies go through a fantastically complicated calculation to come up with one number to put on a balance sheet or income statement. But the truth is that the amount of the ultimate pension liability is unknown and unknowable. How can you know how long your employees will live, or whether they will quit before retirement time, or how much medical costs will go up over the next 50 years? The one thing you do know is that that single number isn't going to be accurate.

Our financial statements become costlier to prepare, and you end up with a number that isn't much better than you could have had by going through a much simpler process.

And you think this hurts us in competing against foreign financial markets?
Unquestionably, the differences in accounting principles between the U.S. and other major countries create a significant disincentive for foreign companies to list in U.S. markets. Greater conformity is long overdue.

Are there are any other major accounting initiatives coming soon from the SEC?
The whole question of the ethics of the profession is a subject we're concerned about. We're looking at the possible involvement of accounting firms in some of the most egregious frauds of financial institutions.

And over the next year we will be looking at the profession's rules precluding accounting firms from doing work on commission for the clients they audit. The rules may be too tough. But there are some circumstances, which I'm not free to talk about but which will eventually become public, where we may have to take action against accountants who disregarded the rules.

The SEC Says: Mark to Market!

Arthur Wyatt
University of Illinois at Urbana-Champaign

No, this title is not intended for the lead article in an April Fool's Day publication. Neither is it designed to attract attention but have little relationship to the thrust of this commentary. Rather, it reports a fact, possibly the most significant initiative in accounting principles development in over 50

From *Accounting Horizons* (March 1991), pp. 80–84. Reprinted by permission of the American Accounting Association and the author. Copyright © 1991 by the American Accounting Association.

years. That great bastion of historical cost accounting, the Securities and Exchange Commission, has encouraged, some might say dictated, the use of market-based measures to value certain debt securities, a new level of relevance in financial reporting.

The dramatic change in SEC thinking culminated in testimony of SEC Chairman Richard C. Breeden before the Committee on Banking, Housing and Urban Affairs of the United States Senate on September 10, 1990. That testimony was presented in connection with hearings concerning issues involving financial institutions and accounting principles that arose out of the savings and loan industry deterioration in the United States. While the specifics of that testimony will be dealt with more thoroughly in subsequent paragraphs, in substance Chairman Breeden called for use of market-based measures of valuation for debt securities held as assets by financial institutions.

MARK TO MARKET CONSIDERED—
AND REJECTED—BY OTHERS

Before considering some of the ramifications—and opportunities—of the Breeden initiative, some background is helpful to develop the setting in which the initiative was introduced. The issue of mark-to-market[1] accounting is certainly not new. The Accounting Principles Board considered moving to a mark-to-market valuation approach for investments in certain financial instruments in the early 1970s, but no agreement was reached. The FASB undertook a limited project involving the same issues in the mid-1970s and eventually issued SFAS 12 dealing with marketable equity securities in late 1975.

The principal concerns with historical cost accounting for investment securities are that gains can be recognized as income is needed to meet earnings projections by selectively selling appreciated securities (so-called "gains trading"), and that recognition of losses can be delayed almost indefinitely by holding depreciated securities and representing that the decline in value is only temporary. Some have argued that the historical cost model promotes an unsound investment management policy—sell the winners and hold the losers. Others have noted that the model permits an overstatement of shareholders' equity because of delays in the recognition of losses.

The principal concerns expressed about the mark-to-market approach are that market values are often not reliable and are sometimes costly to obtain, that inappropriate volatility is reported in the income statement, and that the approach is often suggested for use on a piecemeal basis, that is, only certain

---

[1] Throughout this commentary the terms "mark to market" and "fair value" are used somewhat interchangeably. As attention is focused more on specific applications, the distinctions in these terms will become more significant. At the general level of the current discussion, however, the imprecision should be of little consequence.

assets are proposed to be so accounted for or only certain types of entities would be affected. Until Chairman Breeden's testimony these concerns, among others, have been sufficient to forestall recognition of mark-to-market for investment securities except for limited circumstances or in certain specialized industries.

CERTAIN INDUSTRIES USE MARK TO MARKET IN SOME SITUATIONS

Specific accounting guidance on investment securities is limited, and even that which exists is inconsistent among industries. Thus, banks divide their investment securities into two categories, trading and investing. Trading securities are marked to market with gains and losses reported in income. Investing securities are reported at historical cost, with a provision required for permanent impairment. Permanent impairment is deemed to exist when market value is lower than carrying amount and the bank no longer "has the ability and intent to hold these securities on a long-term basis." Savings and loans have a similar classification system, and permanent impairment is recognizable when a market decline has occurred and the savings and loan no longer has "both the ability and intent to hold the debt instrument to maturity." Credit unions have similar guidance, but such guidance uses "hold to maturity," "long-term basis," and "foreseeable future" as the intended holding period. The insurance industry guidance uses "ability and intent to hold the bonds until maturity." The result of these differences in the various existing AICPA audit guides and FASB standards is that an unlevel playing field is perceived to exist among entities that are competitors for at least certain kinds of business.

THE SAVINGS AND LOAN INDUSTRY ACCOUNTING SHORTCOMING

Of particular concern recently has been the experience of savings and loans even before the massive failures occurred. In earlier times savings and loans' regular operating activities generated mortgage loan receivables, generally on single family residences or up to four unit apartment buildings. The mortgages were serviced monthly and often held to maturity. When interest rates began to rise in the late 1960s, savings and loans began to package mortgages to sell them, a process that accelerated during the late 1970s and 1980s. Even during the package-and-sell process, however, some low rate mortgage receivables continued to be held. Sale of them would have generated losses and thereby reduced capital, with the consequent limitation under Federal regulations on the ability to write new mortgages.

Thus, the notion of "selling winners" and "holding losers" was applied not only to investments in stocks and bonds, but also to mortgage receivables in the savings and loan industry. Some have argued that on a real economic basis, that is, if the losses on underwater mortgages had been recognized at an earlier date, many savings and loans would have been recognized as insolvent years prior to the time they eventually failed. Some speculate that had such accounting been required the magnitude of the current savings and loan bailout would be markedly lower.

The issue of valuing investment securities at historical cost or on a fair value basis has generally been approached as a conceptual issue, wherein the arguments have focused on the objectives of financial accounting, or on practical grounds, wherein assertions have been made regarding lack of reliability and the cost to arrive at market values. Little attention has been directed to the economic consequences flowing from each alternative. With the savings and loan debacle projected to cost taxpayers $500 billion or more, new focus is directed at this accounting issue and the role it may have played in contributing to the savings and loan losses. One assertion that merits study is that the accounting information produced for savings and loan managers under the historical cost model, combined with the banking regulatory restrictions on capital adequacy, helped generate bad management decisions, decisions to sell securities on which gains has arisen but to hold securities with inherent losses. In any event, the issue of marking investments to market has clearly emerged from a principally academic environment to become an issue of pressing practical significance.

BREEDEN TESTIMONY IS UNEQUIVOCAL

The focus on this accounting issue was highlighted by the testimony of SEC Chairman Richard C. Breeden before the Committee on Banking, Housing and Urban Affairs of the U.S. Senate in September 1990. That testimony dealt with a number of matters involving the savings and loan industry and its accounting requirements. A final section dealt with "The Proper Role of Financial Reporting: Market Based Accounting." A few quotations from this testimony, while admittedly out of context, convey the principal thrust of the Breeden testimony.

> Financial institutions are in the business of buying and selling financial instruments, all of which have a value measured in terms of current market conditions. Determining the current value of an institution's assets, not recording their original cost, should increasingly be the goal toward which we must work.
>
> The Commission recognizes that transforming the accounting standards of banks and thrifts from a cost to a market-based standard is a complex undertaking, and we realize that studies are currently under way concerning these issues. The objective of these efforts should be to achieve financial reporting that uses appropriate market-based measures of valuation at the earliest possible date.
>
> [Historical cost accounting] . . . was developed in a vastly different economic environment than the one in which most institutions function today.

Today financial institutions actively manage their interest earning asset and interest bearing liability portfolios to maximize net income and to manage interest rate risk. This "asset/liability" management often requires frequent buying and selling of investment securities to restructure asset and liability maturities. The continued use of the historical cost model in this environment is inappropriate because of the diminished relevance of the resulting financial information.

Chairman Breeden also recognized that any move to increase the use of market-based measures in the accounts requires "careful and deliberate planning." Concerns exist over the reliability of market-based measures and the costs of implementation and ongoing compliance. Even so, recognition is increasing that historical cost amounts for many monetary items can be misleading to financial statement users and lead to economically unsound decisions by business managers. Clearly it is the obligation of accountants to seek improvements in the reporting process.

FEDERAL RESERVE BOARD INTERVENTION DERAILED EARLIER MARK-TO-MARKET MOVE

In early October 1990 *The Wall Street Journal*, reporting on these developments, noted:

The SEC has been down this road before. John C. Burton, a Columbia professor and former SEC chief accountant, recalls that in 1974, when bank portfolios "were very much underwater," the (AICPA) Accounting Standards Executive Committee was ready to shift those holdings to current prices. Mr. Burton says he lined up the five commissioners to vote for the plan.

Arthur Burns, then the Federal Reserve Chairman, called Mr. Burton to a special meeting to discuss the plan—on Christmas Eve. The Federal chief praised Mr. Burton, his former student, as an accounting theorist. Then he informed Mr. Burton that he "should advise the commissioners that they were taking a grave risk with the economic future of the U.S. in the interest of a somewhat dubious accounting principle."

The next day, the commissioners withdrew their support for the plan.

In retrospect, many now believe that it is clear that the grave risk undertaken was to continue a measurement system for certain financial instruments that lacked both relevance and correspondence to underlying economics. The lesson has been a costly one.

FOLLOW-UP ACTIVITY TO BREEDEN INITIATIVE

The immediate result of the Breeden testimony was a meeting involving representatives of the AICPA, the FASB, and the SEC. At this meeting, it was decided that the AICPA Accounting Standards Executive Committee (AcSEC) would undertake the responsibility to develop an appropriate accounting standard to meet the concerns of Chairman Breeden. AcSEC already had a project under way involving these issues and was more likely than the FASB to meet the time deadline of the end of 1991.

The top accounting policy makers of the six largest public accounting firms expressed concern, however, about whether AcSEC was the most appropriate body to deal with these issues. They noted, for example, that it was likely a final standard would conflict with various FASB pronouncements dealing with marketable securities, insurance accounting, and possibly other areas as well. In late October agreement was reached that the FASB should undertake a limited project dealing with debt instruments and attempt to accelerate its procedures to meet the SEC time constraints. Such a project could conceivably involve an amendment to SFAS 12. The FASB would also continue to develop its pending exposure draft calling for increased disclosure of fair values for financial instruments.

MARK-TO-MARKET ACCOUNTING— AN EVOLUTIONARY DEVELOPMENT

Any move to mark-to-market (or fair value) basis for a significant part of the variety of investment securities held by business enterprises will be a dramatic development in the evolution of accounting. For over 50 years many have asserted that the relevance of the information reported in financial statements has been suspect because of the suffocating influence on current practice of accounting inadequacies prior to the 1929 stock market crash and ensuing depression. Under the historical cost model accounting has become increasingly divorced from economics. Too many came to rely on accounting numbers as if they reflected economic reality when only those trained in accounting (and a few others) understood well the actual basis for the reported numbers, and thus any defects they may have contained. The savings and loan crisis simply provided new evidence of existing accounting inadequacies that some had been pointing to for a number of years.

The focus on mark-to-market accounting for investment securities reflects the emerging conceptual focus on the balance sheet, on the critical nature of asset and liability measurements if balance sheets are to reflect faithfully the resources and obligations of the reporting entity. While this focus is of equal concern for unregulated entities and for nonfinancial entities, it is vital for the partially regulated financial institutions. Such regulation historically has been based in part on the magnitude of capital, or shareholders' equity. Any accounting which artificially enhances capital is subverting the intent of the regulation. Up to now, regulators have used (and misused) accounting in order to make it appear that capital adequacy standards had been met. Mark-to-market accounting will force regulators to focus more attention on their own capital adequacy guidelines and reduce the artificiality of the regulatory process.

Of course, one of the by-products of a focus on the balance sheet is that the income statement results will demonstrate increased volatility. That might be a concern if such volatility were artificial, but it is the relatively smooth patterns of reported income by business enterprises over the past 50 years or so that many believe are artificial. While managers tend to desire smoothness rather than volatility, the role of accounting is to approximate the real world as closely as possible. Too many existing accounting standards artificially smooth real world volatility.

It is possible, of course, that the FASB may try to achieve the appropriate balance sheet improvement while at the same time minimizing volatility by reporting market value fluctuations directly in equity. While that approach has some conceptual shortcomings, it may have some merit in the short run, particularly if the FASB deals only with certain investment securities and not with any liabilities. That approach would also be more palatable to those who desire to achieve the appearance of smoothness in reported earnings for those who use income statements. In the past (e.g., SFAS 12, 15, 52, 87) the Board has faced the same pressures and decided to reflect the market variations in equity. Clearly, the principal focus in the current concern on remeasurement of financial instruments is on the balance sheet and not on the income statement.

OPPORTUNITIES FOR NEW RESEARCH INITIATIVES

The new initiative by the SEC to embrace mark-to-market valuation for investment securities of financial institutions provides new incentives for academic research and involvement. Many practical issues will arise for which research assistance can be significant. The conceptual ramifications need additional exploration as well.

Should the immediate project be limited to investment assets and omit liabilities? If so, what are the ramifications for highly leveraged entities with significant investment assets? Should investment assets include mortgage (and loan) receivables? What surrogates are reliable (and reasonable from a cost perspective) for investment assets that have no ready markets? What basis, if any, exists to limit any new standards only to financial institutions? If such a limitation is desirable, how does a complex entity report, if it is partly a financial institution? What levels of capital adequacy will meet regulatory needs if mark-to-market measures are adopted? What are the benefits, and shortcomings, of limiting mark-to-market to investment securities? What are the ramifications of the artificial smoothing created under the historical cost model? What are the ramifications of reporting value fluctuations directly in equity?

These, and many other, issues will require careful thought as the change to a market valuation model is considered. It has taken more than 50 years to see a major crack in the armor of historical cost accounting. The research avenues to explore as we move toward a more relevant measurement system in accounting are varied and exciting. For this, Chairman Breeden and the SEC merit great credit in their call to "mark to market."

Competitive Disadvantage and Mark-To-Market Accounting

Donald J. Kirk

Columbia University

This commentary is two parts: one, on the competitive disadvantages of U.S. accounting standards that differ from foreign accounting practices; and the other, on the need for mark-to-market accounting for U.S. financial institutions. There is a connection between these two seemingly conflicting issues. They both have been the subject of recent communications from the Securities and Exchange Commission to the Financial Accounting Foundation and the Financial Accounting Standards Board.

COMPETITIVE DISADVANTAGE

In my commentary in the December 1990 issue of this journal it was noted that the Securities and Exchange Commission in a communication to the Financial Accounting Foundation had endorsed the need for "reasonable, cost-effective standards that maintain the integrity of financial reporting." Such a position is not a surprising statement from a regulatory agency charged with protecting investors and is consistent with the mission statement of the Financial Accounting Standards Board, the organization to whom the accounting profession and the SEC look to for leadership in the establishment of accounting standards. In that same communication, however, the SEC introduced what seemed to be a *new factor* into their weighing of the costs and benefits of accounting standards—the suggestion that accounting standards "not undercut the competitive position of U.S. companies or the U.S. capital markets."

The FASB has on occasion heard similar messages from some companies affected by a proposed accounting standard, that is, the proposal would have a devastating effect economically or competitively. Although often skeptical about such claims, the Board considers them in weighing costs and benefits, and, if persuaded that the proposal does not mislead readers about the underlying economics, concludes that such predicted results, if they eventuate, result from better, not misleading, information. If some public policy, other than neutral financial reporting, suggests a different action, that is the responsibility of legislators or their designated regulators, not the FASB. The FASB's attitude had been endorsed by the SEC, even though that agency's actions on occasion have conflicted with those of the FASB. I observed in the December commentary that only time will tell what was the intention of this

From *Accounting Horizons* (June 1991), pp. 98–106. Reprinted by permission of the American Accounting Association and the author. Copyright © 1991 by the American Accounting Association.

latest message from the SEC and expressed the hope that the SEC do nothing that would undercut neutrality as a foundation for standard setting.

Evidence that FASB members do not ignore a wide range of potential costs of accounting changes is presented in the September 1990 issue of this journal. That issue includes two excellent commentaries on how standard setters assess the potential costs and benefits of accounting standards. Former FASB member Arthur Wyatt and Board member Victor Brown in separate commentaries both describe from personal experience the standard setters' efforts to identify sound and useful concepts and to weigh the costs and benefits of proposed accounting changes. Victor Brown's commentary, "Accounting Standards: Their Economic and Social Consequences," identifies a wide range of social and economic costs that are considered in the standard setting process.

The question addressed in the first part of this two-part commentary is what did the SEC have in mind when sending the message to the Financial Accounting Foundation that the FASB's standards should "not undercut the competitive position of U.S. companies or U.S. capital markets"? Vic Brown's analysis suggests that the *competitive position* or costs of U.S. companies might be impacted negatively in three ways by accounting and disclosure requirements that are not applicable to foreign companies:[1]

1. There would be additional cost to comply with the requirements.
2. There might be a loss of economic advantage from disclosure of information useful to foreign competitors.
3. There might be an increase in the costs of capital and loss in investor appeal when a standard would increase recorded expenses and recorded liabilities, or would increase volatility of reported earnings. Closely related is the alleged loss in ability to compete for acquisitions caused by existing U.S. standards concerning accounting for goodwill, which differ from foreign practices.

Which of these categories of cost was the SEC concerned about in its communication to the Financial Accounting Foundation? Is it the third type of costs noted above? If so, was the SEC suggesting that the FASB, by acts of omission or commission, enhance through accounting standards the competitive position of U.S. companies or capital markets? Was the SEC asking that neutrality be downplayed as was suggested by the Business Roundtable?[2]

The SEC's communication has been expanded upon by Commissioner Philip R. Lochner, Jr. in a speech at a conference on financial reporting sponsored by the University of California at Berkeley. Commissioner Lochner

---

[1] Brown identifies other categories of cost but they do not appear to have import to the international competitiveness issue raised by the SEC. For the views of the Chairman of the FASB on this subject see, Dennis R. Beresford, "Financial Reporting: Comparability and Competition," *FASB Viewpoints*, Nov. 8, 1990.

[2] Letter dated August 20, 1990 from John S. Reed, Chairman, Accounting Principles Task Force of the Business Roundtable, to Commissioner Philip R. Lochner, Jr.

made the point, although in a rather indirect manner, that the SEC is not suggesting that the FASB abandon or downplay neutrality in standard setting when he remarked:

> One hears that accounting standard setters should not consider the more broadly defined costs of standard setting because the purpose of accounting standards should not be to reach results that favor one company over another, one industry over another, or one country over another. This assertion is so evidently correct as to defy contradiction. . . .

What then is meant? Commissioner Lochner stated that he does *not* believe "that attempting to avoid unnecessary regulatory costs is the same as intentionally crafting regulations to bestow favors on a particular economic interest." He describes the costs of complying with accounting and disclosure requirements as a tax on the issuers of financial reports and includes those costs along with "all other types of regulatory costs" in his call for "public and private standard setters to provide an explicit and systematic cost/benefit analysis of their actions."

Lochner went on to comment, "the potential for accounting standards to cause competitive disparities has increased in recent years as a result of a dramatic expansion in the financial reporting requirements applicable to U.S. companies." Commissioner Lochner describes what he means by "competitive disparities" as follows:

> When all competitors are not subject to the same regulatory scheme, a *new factor* must be added to the cost/benefit analysis: the extent to which regulated companies will be disadvantaged in their competition with similarly-situated competitors that are not subject to similar regulatory requirements. (Emphasis added.)

His point is that in these times of international markets and competition, regulatory costs imposed only on U.S. companies should add more weight to the cost side of the standard setters' deliberations, because those costs do not also apply to foreign competitors. Lochner sums it up in the following quotation:

> Obviously, there are many costs, in addition to accounting costs, that affect a business' financial health. I am not suggesting that accounting costs are in any way determinative of the outcome of the competitive struggle. Nevertheless, I believe that it is important to look at accounting costs as *an* element affecting competition, and that these costs, like all other types of regulatory costs, should not be imposed on U.S. companies unnecessarily or without sufficient thought and analysis.

Lochner's point is unexceptionable. Complying with regulations and standards is not costless. Regulators and standard setters, public or private, have a responsibility to explain both the benefits and costs of their proposals and requirements.

However, Commissioner Lochner goes on to claim that the FASB turns a blind eye and takes a narrow view in assessing the costs of accounting standards—one that ignores the *loss of competitive advantage*.

As evidence of the FASB's supposedly narrow view, Lochner states, with reference to FASB Concepts Statement No. 2: "While the loss of competitive advantages is mentioned, its cost is referred to as 'clearly in a different category' from other costs involved, and is said to be a cost that is nearly impossible to begin to quantify." His conclusion is that this dimension of regulatory costs, what he describes as the needed *new factor* in cost-benefit analysis, is in this *different category*, not believed to be quantifiable and, thus, ignored by the FASB.

Lochner's analysis is faulty in two respects. First, regulatory costs imposed on U.S. companies but not foreign ones, what Lochner refers to as the *new factor*, are in the *compliance costs* considered by the FASB, i.e., the first of the three types of cost noted above. They are *not* in what FASB Concepts Statement No. 2 refers to as a *different category*. Second, the *different category* of costs as defined by the FASB, although difficult, if not impossible, to measure is *not* to be ignored. Let me explain.

FASB Concepts Statement No. 2 includes in what is categorized above as *compliance costs*, the costs of collecting, processing, auditing, and disseminating information, as well as the cost to users of analysis and interpretation, and, at times, rejection of redundant information. These would seem to be the type of cost, particularly when imposed on U.S. companies only, that Lochner would include among regulatory costs that must be weighed against benefits in order "to avoid imposing unnecessary . . . costs."

Concepts Statement No. 2 (par. 137) also makes reference to the second type of cost noted above by acknowledging that there might be an economic cost of complying with some disclosure requirements "in the form of a *loss of competitive advantages* vis-a-vis trade competitors, labor unions (with a consequent effect on wage demands), or foreign enterprises." Disclosures of, for example, major customers and line-of-business profitability, might have a detrimental economic impact on particular companies, but the disclosure of proprietary information might also have a greater detrimental impact on society as a whole. It is that latter impact—on society, not the economic impact on an individual company or industry—that is the *different category* of cost referred to in FASB Concepts Statement No. 2. Here is how that societal concern is expressed in Concepts Statement No. 2 (par. 139):

> From the point of view of society, the loss of competitive advantage that is said to result from some disclosure requirements is clearly in a different category from the other costs involved. Although the loss to one business may be a gain to another, the Board is aware of and concerned about the economic effects of the possible discouragement of initiative, innovation, and willingness to take risks if reward to risk taking is denied. That is another cost that is impossible to begin to quantify.

Whether you view the *loss of competitive advantage* discussion in its narrow, entity effect or in a broader societal context, paragraph 139 quoted above notes that the "Board is aware and concerned about the economic effects." Paragraph 140, quoted below, reinforces that it is not to be ignored.

> The burden of the costs and the incidence of benefits fall quite unevenly throughout the economy, and it has been observed that ". . . the matter of establishing disclosure requirements becomes not only a matter of judgment but also a complex balancing of many factors so that all costs and benefits receive the consideration they merit. For example, a simple rule that any information useful in making investment decisions should be disclosed fails as completely as a rule which says disclosure should not be required if competitive disadvantage results." The problem is to know how to accomplish that "complex balancing." (Footnote reference omitted.)

In Commissioner Lochner's remarks, there are four messages to the FASB.[3] One is that the cost of complying with a new standard that differs from practices of foreign companies adds more weight to the cost side of the cost-benefit scale than does a standard that complies with foreign practices. That should be no surprise to the FASB. The second is that the FASB's cost-benefit assessments have been incomplete. That results, as explained above, from a misreading of FASB Concepts Statement No. 2. The third is that the assessments should be more explicit and done more often during the consideration of a proposed standard. That is a reasonable, low-cost suggestion. The FASB has reorganized its explanation in its most recent Statement (No. 106) to be more explicit about its cost-benefit considerations and undoubtedly will do the same at earlier stages of other projects.

The fourth message is in somewhat reluctant, from my reading, recognition that the benefits of some proposed accounting change might outweigh its costs. In closing his remarks, Commissioner Lochner acknowledges that "full and fair disclosure has been an integral part of the development of our efficient and successful securities markets, which has enhanced the capital-raising ability of U.S. business, among other benefits." While certain that past

---

[3] Interestingly, Lochner did not mention anywhere in his remarks concern about the impact of accounting standards on the competitive position of U.S. capital markets. Regulating those markets is, of course, the responsibility of the SEC and complying with U.S. accounting standards is part of the mandated costs of that regulatory scheme. The SEC is feeling the effects of competition from other markets whose regulatory system is less costly. For example, Chairman Richard C. Breeden in an interview reported in *Forbes* (November 12, 1990) makes the point that complying with U.S. accounting standards is "unquestionably . . . a significant disincentive for foreign companies to list in U.S. markets."
Breeden's view about the costs of accounting standards and their competitive effect among securities markets is different from Lochner's description of those costs as just *an* element of regulatory cost in the economic competition among companies. In trying not to lose out in the securities market competition the SEC is on the horns of a dilemma trying to lessen the costs for foreign registrants without abandoning its legislated mandate for "full and fair disclosure" by all registrants. One way for the SEC to alleviate the problem is to prod the U.S. accounting standard setters to slow down, stop or conform U.S. practices with those in the rest of the developed world. Recently, until the push for mark-to-market accounting, the SEC seemed to be doing all of the above.

cost-benefit tests have not been rigorous enough, he closes with uncertainty about how to deal with accounting issues that pass the cost-benefit test by posing and not answering a familiar question: "Does the solution to better understanding of the financial conditions of companies lie in financial statements or in other forms of disclosure such as the MD&A?"

MARK-TO-MARKET ACCOUNTING

The question posed by Commissioner Lochner has been answered in part by the Chairman of the SEC, Richard C. Breeden.

Chairman Breeden's testimony before the Senate Committee on Banking, Housing and Urban Affairs in September 1990 in which he called for mark-to-market accounting[4] *in the financial statements*, not the MD&A, is described by Art Wyatt in the March 1991 issue of this journal. In summary, the Chairman urged a concerted effort "to achieve financial reporting that uses appropriate market-based measures of valuation at the earliest possible date" for deposit-accepting financial institutions and noted that "serious consideration must be given to reporting all investment securities at market value." In a letter forwarding his testimony to the FASB, the Chairman elaborated: "At a minimum, the Commission does not perceive any justification for maintaining the current distinction between trading and investment portfolios given that this permits portfolios of securities to be reflected at values higher than their true worth at any given time."

THE BANK REGULATORS' REACTIONS

Robert Clarke, Comptroller of the Currency, and Chairman Alan Greenspan of the Federal Reserve Board have made their views known.

Robert Clarke, in a speech before the AICPA National Conference on Banking, noting that "bankers oppose any change to current standards," sums up the arguments as follows:

> The argument in favor of a mark-to-market standard is simple: It assumes that the mark-to-market standard would provide the best possible information to users of financial data—investors, depositors, the market place, even regulators.
>
> In opposing the mark-to-market standard, bankers argue that it would create too much volatility in bank earnings and capital. They also object to applying a mark-to-market standard to assets without taking into account the other side of the balance sheet.

---

[4] The term *mark-to-market, market value* and *fair value* accounting are used in this commentary somewhat interchangeably. As Art Wyatt noted in his March commentary, any imprecision in their use at this stage is of little consequence.

Clarke went on to note that mark-to-market accounting "has the potential of lessening the appetite of banks for . . . [U.S. Government] securities," and "it would drive business decisions by bankers." He concluded: "In short, the potential for market distortions and for behavior that is not in the long-run best interest of the banking industry and the economy should be measured and factored into the decision."

Chairman Greenspan in a letter to Chairman Breeden urged caution and questioned the relevance of market values of loans in measuring the success of commercial banking. On the narrower subject of marking-to-market only investment securities, Chairman Greenspan objected to a partial valuation that could result in volatility and a measure of capital "that is not indicative of the bank's true financial condition." In addition Greenspan noted, "the adoption of market value accounting for investment securities . . . might also affect the amount of securities that banks are willing to hold, . . . thereby having the undesired effect of reducing the liquidity of banking organizations."

THE 1938 ACCORD—WILL IT SURVIVE?

Greenspan in his letter to Breeden noted "that prior to 1938, banking organizations were required for supervisory purposes to use market value accounting for their investment securities" and that "serious concerns on the part of the U.S. Treasury and the bank regulators over how this affected the banks' financial performance and investment decisions led the agencies to abandon in that year the use of this accounting convention. . . ."

Researchers who have studied the actions of the regulators in 1938 point out the concerns at that time were about the liquidity of U.S. businesses. It was believed that the then existing regulatory practices that valued securities at market when below ultimately collectible amounts and that categorized loans as "slow" even though ultimate collection was expected had a dampening effect on banks' capital and, therefore, on lending. Concerns about the consequences of such valuations and categorizations, and skepticism about the fairness of market values, led the regulators in 1938 to abandon market values, ignore the time value of money, and to adopt what has been called the *doctrine of ultimate collectibility*.

While more than 50 years have passed, similar concerns are again being voiced by banks and regulators about the liquidity problems of U.S. businesses and the relevance of market values. Mark-to-market accounting is again seen as having dire consequences.

Newspapers have contained frequent reports of accounting proposals being considered by regulators that would ease the problems of the banks. For example, the headline of a March 1 *Wall Street Journal* article is: "Bank Regulators Are Set to Announce Accounting Changes to Ease Credit Pinch." The article makes it clear that the *doctrine of ultimate collectibility* is not dead; it just needs a little interpretation. The article says the proposals will "highlight that current rules allow bank examiners to look at the expected cash flow from a property that collateralizes a loan, rather the lower liquidation value of the property." The article also notes that the regulators are moving cautiously, putting one proposal out for public comment. The article juxtaposes the report of that action with a quote from Chairman Breeden of the SEC: "The worst mistake in the thrift disaster was the move to weaken accounting rules."

SEC RESPONSES TO THE REGULATORS

Evidence of the steadfastness of the SEC is in testimony of the SEC General Counsel James Doty before the Senate Judiciary Antitrust Subcommittee in December 1990. That testimony includes the following:

> Market-value accounting for debt securities is a reflection of a simple but important principle: no publicly held entity should knowingly misstate the value of its assets to its creditors and public shareholders. It is important to note, however, that Chairman Breeden's testimony did *not* call for immediate market value accounting for the *loan portfolios* or *real estate holdings* of banks or other financial firms. . . . (Emphasis in original.)
>
> The current historical-cost accounting convention was established in 1938. The economic environment in which financial institutions now operate, which has resulted in sophisticated asset-liability management strategies, has undermined whatever original strength there may have been in the 50-year-old presumption that investment securities will be held to maturity. (Footnote reference omitted.)
>
> The Commission has urged that market value accounting for investment securities be considered in the near term because this step toward more meaningful financial statements could be implemented with *little or no cost* to reporting entities. . . . (Emphasis added.)

That *little-or-no-cost* assertion had been challenged by bankers and their regulators, and Doty had the opportunity to rebut the challengers in that same testimony:

> Banks will likely not eschew the liquidity afforded by the government securities markets and the advantages of hedging techniques, all in order to avoid stating as a financial statement line item the information now set forth in the accompanying notes. . . .
>
> Finally, objections that market value accounting for investment portfolios will exacerbate a 'credit crunch,' if one in fact exists, borders on the absurd. . . .

WHAT IS THE VIEW OF THE U.S. TREASURY?

The last of the federal government organizations to be heard from was the U.S. Treasury. The Financial Institutions Reform, Recovery and Enforcement Act of 1989 (FIRREA) included "the feasibility of market value accounting" in a long list of topics to be included in a mandated study of the federal deposit insurance system. The study, issued in February 1991, contains a comprehensive analysis of the arguments for and against market value accounting (MVA). The report's recommendations are consistent with the views of the bank regulators and are excerpted below:

> Despite the theoretical appeal, comprehensive MVA has a number of problems that argue against its adoption at this time. Because active trading markets do not exist for the bulk of the assets and liabilities of depository institutions . . . fair market values would have to be estimated. . . . The subjectivity inherent in such procedures would reduce . . . comparability . . . and render it difficult to verify valuations. . . . Such reliability problems would make financial statements more prone to manipulation. . . . Although it is possible that reasonably specific standards could be developed to provide the basis for appropriate accounting and auditing practices in this area, such a process is likely to require considerable time.
>
> A second concern is the cost of developing and implementing a comprehensive MVA system. Such costs could be substantial, and would likely fall disproportionately on smaller banks and thrifts. . . .

Nothing in the recommendations quoted above would have surprised the SEC for it has acknowledged the difficulty and potential costliness of a comprehensive MVA system. However, before concluding in favor of "more detailed disclosures" of market values, the Treasury study had this to say about the SEC's *little-or-no-cost* project that the SEC and the AICPA had urged the FASB to take on.

> An often-mentioned alternative would be to adopt MVA only for those assets that have clear secondary market values, such as marketable securities and certain residential mortgages. However, recording some balance sheet items at market and others at historical cost would fail to reflect certain hedging positions undertaken to minimize interest rate sensitivity. As a consequence, the partial MVA approach could result in volatility and distortion in reported income and capital that are misleading indicators of a firm's true financial condition. *Adoption of the partial MVA approach would appear premature at this time, as well.* (Emphasis added.)

WHAT IS THE NEXT STEP?

The lines have been drawn. What happens next? The regulators can, of course, require whatever is necessary for fulfilling their responsibilities and that can be done outside the framework of GAAP and the requirements of the SEC for reports to shareholders. However, the regulators would not like reporting to shareholders that cast doubt on the relevance of their requirements and, undoubtedly, more attempts will be made to try to bring the SEC in line with the views of the bank regulators and the U.S. Treasury.

The spotlight is turning toward the FASB. In a three-way understanding, the AICPA has withdrawn from the arena after issuing a Statement of Position (No. 96-11) requiring what its title suggests: "Disclosure of Certain

Information by Financial Institutions About Debt Securities Held as Assets"
and urging the FASB to take on market-value-based accounting for investment in debt securities; the SEC has stopped criticizing the FASB for issuing
too many standards and performing inadequate cost-benefit analyses, and
agreed to run interference on the Washington scene; and, the FASB is considering the scope of a project that would require limited use of market-value-
based accounting.

WHAT IS THE FASB DOING?

In 1986 the FASB added to its agenda a comprehensive, multi-phased project
on accounting for financial instruments. Only the first phase, described
below, has been completed. The last phase was to be the determination of
how financial instruments should be measured—for example, at market
value, amortized cost, or the lower of cost or market. The SEC had been
among those that urged that this project be undertaken.

Here is what the FASB has done to date:

• issued in March 1990 Statement No. 105, *Disclosure of Information about
  Financial Instruments with Off-Balance Sheet Risk and Financial Instruments
  with Concentrations of Credit Risk*. That Statement does not include a
  requirement for disclosure of market or fair value of financial instruments, as had been proposed in a 1987 Exposure Draft. The Statement
  does, however, include a promise that Statements dealing with recognition and measurement (as distinct from disclosure) issues, including
  "How financial instruments should be measured—for example, at market
  value, amortized original cost, or the lower of cost or market . . . will be
  issued only after extensive Board deliberation, including discussion documents, public hearings, and Exposure Drafts."

• issued in December 1990 an Exposure Draft, *Disclosure about Market Value
  of Financial Instruments*. The proposal is to extend market value disclosures
  practices by requiring *all* entities to disclose the market value of *all*
  financial instruments, both assets and liabilities on and off balance sheet,
  for which it is practicable to estimate market value. It is to be effective for
  companies with more than $100 million in total assets for calendar year
  1991; for smaller companies, 1992. A public hearing is scheduled for May
  29–31.

• has been considering the scope of a project requiring market-value based
  accounting for debt securities held as assets and perhaps for certain other
  financial assets and financial liabilities. The original expectation of the
  AICPA and SEC was that this project would result in a Statement of
  Financial Accounting Standards effective for the calendar year 1991.

The planned sequence of the Board's project has been disrupted and the
proposed or expected effective dates, the result of trying to be responsive to
pressure from the AICPA and SEC, are unrealistic for subjects of such scope,

complexity and controversy. However, this is not something new to the standard setting process, for events often overtake the best of plans and force consideration of issues out of the most logical sequence (e.g., FASB Statement Nos. 12, 15, and 76). The question is: can the FASB act prudently and neutrally in technical areas that have become an intragovernmental policy dispute?

The December 1990 proposal, of course, is not new, for a similar proposal was included in a November 1987 Exposure Draft. The Board undoubtedly considered what it heard in response to the earlier proposal in the drafting of the 1990 proposal. Also, generally accepted accounting principles already require market value disclosure or recognition for many classes of financial instruments, particularly investments with quoted market prices.

The complexity and controversy relates to financial instruments that do not have quoted prices, such as loans, and to liabilities, particularly of nonfinancial institutions. Challenges to both the relevance—remember the doctrine of ultimate collectibility—and reliability of the information will have to be considered. In addition the FASB will again be told that allowing the preparers of financial statements to judge whether it is too costly and, therefore, not practicable to estimate market value will diminish the quantity and comparability of data.

While there may have been pressure on the Board to set a 1991 effective date for the disclosure proposal, the ultimate resolution of this phase of the project should be able to proceed from this point forward without undue pressure. While all parties are not convinced of the relevance of the information, there is wide recognition of the implementation problems associated with it. More market value disclosures will be the ultimate outcome and it will be the usefulness and use of those disclosures and their demonstrated superiority in measuring financial position that will dictate when consideration is given to recognizing those values in financial statements.

More pressure exists on the FASB to complete its yet-to-be defined, limited-scope recognition project. Even though AICPA Statement of Position No. 90-11, effective for 1990, requires extensive disclosures by all types of financial institutions about market values and unrealized gains and losses in debt securities held as assets, the SEC uncharacteristically continues to insist that disclosure is not enough.

The SEC's position continues to be that a more "accurate" statement of financial position can be achieved at *little or no cost* by marking-to-market debt securities that are held as investments. It wants to eliminate from the income statement the benefit of "gains trading," that is, selling profitable and holding losing positions, but has declared neutrality on whether the unrealized gains and losses from marking-to-market are to be included in net income or directly in equity. Its testimony has addressed the accounting of depository financial institutions such as insurance companies.

At the time of the writing of this commentary, the FASB had not yet decided whether or not to undertake a limited scope recognition project. If there continues to be an urgent need for some immediate change in recognition practices, evenhandedness may be impossible in a limited-scope project for it is improbable that the scope would include liabilities. Not including liabilities, suggests that marking-to-market assets only for financial institutions with related liabilities, such as insurance companies, would be unlikely. Including recognized unrealized gains and losses in net income, would be unlikely as well.

So what is the most that might be achieved by a limited-scope project? Under the best of circumstances, it would be marking-to-market debt securities held as assets by deposit-accepting financial institutions with changes in unrealized gains and losses bypassing net income and being recognized directly in equity. Realized gains (possibly the result of "gains trading") and losses would continue to be recognized in net income.[5]

Conceptually such a partial solution is troublesome; it is not even handed in its result. However, when considerations other than purely technical ones dictate the need for a project and the support for the project remains steadfast, it is best to keep the scope of a project as narrow as possible, find a solution that improves financial reporting and get on with it. Marking-to-market debt securities held as assets for some financial institutions would be an improvement, albeit a small one. The big question is whether support from the accounting profession and SEC will continue, for without it the project will not pass anyone's cost-benefit test.

HAS TIME RUN OUT ON THE HISTORICAL COST MODEL?

The General Counsel of the SEC concluded his December 1990 testimony to a subcommittee of the Senate Judiciary Committee with following:

> As the Commission's earlier testimony on this matter has made clear the time has run out on "once upon a time accounting."

Old ways die slowly, however, and the *doctrine of ultimate collectibility* may prove to be more durable than the SEC thinks, and not just because of technical problems in developing reliable estimates of fair value. T. S. Eliot described the nontechnical reason with poetic brevity: "Human kind cannot bear very much reality." A banker put a similar thought into an accounting context:

> Mark to market your balance sheet frequently. . . . This will always tell you the truth about your condition. . . . I would be as truthful in developing this

---

[5] The SEC is troubled by "gains trading" but is willing to accept unrealized gains and losses being recognized directly in equity. Acceptance of the latter implies acceptance of the former, i.e., realized gains would be in net income. To avoid the former, Chairman Breeden has suggested an approach that would "disallow the firm from recognizing gains on sales of 'investment' securities until their maturity." This cure, which I confess I do not fully understand, sounds worse than the ill.

as possible even if it proves embarrassing. But be careful who sees the figures. They should not be shown to outsiders. . . .[6]

Mishmash Accounting

Dana Wechsler

Forbes

Did you know that General Electric's assets have ballooned to $110 billion as of Dec. 31, up from $40 billion at the end of 1987? Or that General Motors' debt is now 47% of capitalization, up from 10% at the end of 1987?

No, these blue chips have not turned into speculative plays. What's going on is just the sort of nonsense that the critics predicted from the Financial Accounting Standards Board rule on consolidation. Under this rule, approved after much contention in October 1987, all majority-owned subsidiaries must be folded into the parent's financial statements, no matter what business the subs are in. Before the rule took effect with 1988 annual reports, companies with subsidiaries outside their core business—such as finance, insurance or leasing subs—were not forced to fold the subs' assets and liabilities into the parent's consolidated balance sheet. That made sense because manufacturing and finance companies use capital so differently that their balance sheets are not really comparable.

Justification for the rule was that companies could bury liabilities in their subsidiaries. But the cure is worse than the disease. "Now GM looks like a finance company with a car division," quips Norman Strauss, a partner at Ernst & Young.

The old rule wasn't so terrible for investors. A company could exclude a subsidiary from its main balance sheet only if it also reported a balance sheet for the subsidiary. If there's any reforming to be done it should take place in Europe. In Germany a public company can bury so much in unreported subsidiaries that its true profit remains a secret.

Finance companies typically have huge receivables, huge liabilities and relatively small revenues. So investors measure their performance by stand-ards quite different from those of manufacturing companies.

What irks Robert Richter, vice president of administration of Dana Corp., is the thought of all those investors who screen for stocks using financial ratios: return on assets, operating margins, debt-to-equity and the like. When Dana was forced to consolidate its finance sub, virtually all of its ratios changed, even though the fundamentals did not. Someone spending a fair amount of time with the annual report would be able to figure this out. But an

---

[6] Wes Lindow, *National Thrift News*, September 6, 1988.

investor using a computer to filter for investment candidates would never get this far.

"A year ago, any list of companies with less than 50% debt would have had Dana on it," says Richter. "We should be there now, but we aren't."

What's more, ratios are only helpful when one can draw comparisons across similar companies. "After you lump financial services with the manu-facturing operations, what companies is it comparable to?" asks Richter. "What's the appropriate debt-to-equity ratio, or interest coverage? There aren't any answers because there aren't any comparables."

Securities analysts don't like the change any more than the companies do. Their instinct is to evaluate a company piecemeal—whence all the talk these days about breakup value. Now that job is much tougher.

"I had one fellow pleading with me to tell him what was long-term debt," says Eugene Flegm, assistant controller of GM. "I went back to the traditional number and gave it to him. He said, 'That's it!' like he'd found an old friend."

He goes on: "Try to find one person who uses the new data. So what are we giving it to them for?"

Indeed, many companies with finance subsidiaries now feel compelled to present the numbers both ways, the old and the new. General Electric added 33 pages to the financial section of its annual report. "We felt we had to," explains Bernard Doyle, manager of corporate accounting services. "Other-wise the old GE would have disappeared."

In some cases, the consolidated number for liabilities is downright mis-leading. Dana's 1988 balance sheet shows $3.7 billion of liabilities. But the company is on the hook for only $1.8 billion; the remaining $1.9 billion represents liabilities of Dana's finance sub, Diamond Financial Holdings, for which the parent is not liable. Lenders who extend credit to Diamond gener-ally rely on Diamond's own financial statements. If Diamond failed, Dana's shareholders would likely be out only $128 million, their equity in the subsid-iary.

GM, which used to release its earnings figures three weeks after the end of each quarter, now needs four weeks to compile the results. All calculations have to be made twice. What's the cost to GM in man-hours? "No one is impressed if it costs GM another few hundred thousand dollars," replies Flegm. "But if the benefit is zero, I don't even want to spend $10 on it."

The new consolidation rule has been one resounding flop. The solution is simple: Repeal it.

An Innate Fear of Disclosure

Dana Wechsler
Forbes

Katarzyna Wandycz
Forbes

Jessica Reif, an industrious media securities analyst at First Boston Corp., explains what she does for a living: "I spend a good part of my time trying to get numbers that aren't reported."

In this day of information overload, aren't people like Reif drowning in numbers? In numbers, yes. But in useful numbers, not necessarily— especially when analysts and other investors try to disaggregate a large corporation to see how each of its important segments is doing.

Consider IBM. As befits its size, the $63 billion (estimated 1989 sales) computer company is in several lines of business, including personal computers, mainframes, electronic mail systems and semiconductors (IBM's semiconductor facilities rank among the world's largest). How is each of these segments doing? That's hard to say. IBM reports figures for a grand total of one segment, called "information processing systems, software, communications systems and other products and services."

At first glance, $17 billion (sales) Eastman Kodak is more forthcoming. Kodak lists three segments in its annual report: imaging, chemicals and health. But don't expect much enlightenment. With an aggregate $11 billion of revenues, the "imaging" segment includes everything from cameras to batteries to a giant copier business. The group as a whole earns $1.7 billion, 60 percent of Kodak's operating earnings. How much of that comes from copiers or other businesses, nobody outside Kodak knows for sure.

Does anybody care? They should. Says Eugene Glazer, technology analyst at Dean Witter Reynolds: "Investors need to know how a company is doing in each major business. Maybe one business is so dominant and earning such huge profits that it's masking errors in other businesses."

In theory, companies are supposed to report line-of-business financial information. Segment reporting came into being after a vicious battle waged between the Federal Trade Commission and big corporations in the mid-1970s. The corporations fought the FTC's demands for income statements and balance sheets on each of their different lines of business all the way to the Supreme Court, and they lost.

In 1976, the Financial Accounting Standards Board decreed that all companies must break out the industry segments that constitute more than 10% of sales, and must report revenues, profits, assets, depreciation expenses and capital expenditures for each. But no sooner was the rule printed than companies began blurring distinctions among segments.

CBS is a good case in point. A lot of people are poring over CBS' financial statements these days, trying to understand why the company's operating profits dropped by $173 million between 1984 and 1988. Most important, they want to know just how badly the company's television network—traditionally CBS' bread and butter—is doing. But CBS, which operates the television network, 5 television stations, 2 radio networks and 20 radio stations, reports only two segments: broadcasting and other. All the networks and stations are lumped together under broadcasting.

"We know that the network has done badly," says Salomon Brothers media analyst Edward Atorino, "but we don't know how badly." Instead, Atorino and his peers must deduce what they can from such annual report phrases as "Network sales declined slightly" and "Television station sales rose modestly," plus management's hints and industry research.

Will CBS consider increasing the number of segments it reports? "Historically, we have always reported this way," bristles CBS spokeswoman Ann Morfogen. "We are an integrated company, and we don't plan to start doing it any other way."

Typically, companies voice two objections to providing information on their separate lines of business. First, they say, it would give an advantage to their competitors. Second, it would cost too much. But neither objection holds much water.

"I'm not aware of anyone who ever lost a nickel giving this kind of information to their competitors," says Sidney Spencer, a finance executive at General Electric. "Nevertheless, there's an innate fear of disclosure."

Some executives are less fearful than others. For an example of more useful reporting, look at Knight-Ridder's latest annual report. The $2 billion (sales) company reports two segments, newspapers and financial information products, and lists each of its major newspapers' contributions to revenues. And Lin Broadcasting, which still derives most of its sales and earnings from television and publishing assets, early on disclosed how its rapidly growing cellular telephone division was doing. It was this segment that attracted McCaw Cellular, which recently agreed to pay $3.4 billion for about 40 percent of Lin (McCaw already owned 10%), giving investors who understood the disclosures a huge profit.

How should a company determine how many segments to report? Wayne Kolins, a partner of the accounting firm BDO Seidman, has a sound idea: If a company has businesses that respond differently to changes in the economy, or if they face different kinds of competitors, or earn different levels of profits, then the company probably should report the businesses separately.

"It really comes down to the risks and the rewards," says Kolins. "Ask yourself: Are the risks different? Are the rewards different? If either answer is a significant yes, then you've got two segments."

Securities & Exchange Commission officials say their agency is certainly interested in good segment reporting. The SEC has required several companies—including Amfac and Duty Free International—to split their segments more narrowly. "It's a key component of financial reports," says SEC chief accountant Edmund Coulson. "Auditors ought to challenge the companies, and if investors believe a company is doing inappropriate segment reporting, they ought to write us." Coulson's address: Office of the Chief Accountant, Securities & Exchange Commission, 450 Fifth St., N.W., Washington, D.C. 20549.

CHAPTER 10

Long-Term Liabilities

Recognition and measurement of long-term liabilities have been active topics for research and standard-setting in recent years due to the phenomenal growth in the amount of financial assets and liabilities in corporate balance sheets and the proliferation of financial instruments (known as derivatives) used by corporations. Existing accounting standards seem inadequate to handle these new financial items, particularly those that seem designed to bring about "off-balance sheet" liability exposures to the firm. These developments, as well as the U.S. savings and loan industry debacle, have led the Financial Accounting Standards Board (FASB) to launch a series of "financial instruments" projects since 1986 to search for new standards for the measurement and reporting of financial assets and financial liabilities.[1]

On the liability side, there are at least two major topics covered by these projects:[2]

- Accounting for the impairment of a loan, and
- Measuring and reporting of off-balance sheet liability items.

The first of these was previously addressed by the FASB in Statement No. 15. This statement has been controversial from the beginning for the way it ignores the economic substance of most loan restructuring transactions. According to Statement 15, the creditor (or the debtor) involved in a troubled debt restructuring does not have to report a loss (or a gain) as long as the

---

[1] One of the financial instrument projects, a controversial one, deals with the reporting of market values of investments in marketable debt and equity securities. The FASB issued Statement No. 115, *Accounting for Certain Investments in Debt and Equity Securities*, in May 1993, requiring the reporting of fair market values for certain debt and equity securities. (See the introduction to Chapter 9.)

[2] There have been, of course, other recent accounting developments affecting specific long-term liability accounts such as deferred income taxes, pensions, post-retirement benefits, equity-like debt securities, and leases. These are discussed elsewhere in this book. Issues related to current liabilities and contingent liabilities are discussed in the introduction to Chapter 5.

undiscounted sum of expected future cash flows after the restructuring at least equals the current carrying value of the obligation. For example, a $300,000, 12 percent debt in arrears could be restructured as a $250,000 four-year loan with a 5 percent interest per year (for a total undiscounted future cash flow, of principal and interest, of $300,000), with no loss reported by the creditor. This accounting treatment clearly ignores the economic losses to the creditor and gains to the debtor.

The history of the development of Statement No. 15, which was issued in 1977, indicates that the FASB agreed to this procedure after initially proposing the more conceptually defensible alternative of using the estimated market value of debt at the time of restructuring. But financial institutions and federal regulators opposed the use of market value owing to its substantial negative effect on the financial institutions' balance sheets and income statements. In June 1992, the FASB issued an exposure draft addressing loan impairment (including troubled debt restructuring) in which it proposed to require that the expected future cash flows be discounted at the effective interest rate (i.e., the rate implied in the original loan contract) for impaired loans and the market interest rate for restructured loans. While the conceptually sound solution would have been the market interest rate in both cases, the FASB's choice of the market interest rate for restructured loans represented a vast improvement over its position in Statement No. 15. In the final standard issued as Statement No. 114 in May 1993, however, apparently as a result of pressures from financial institutions, the FASB called for the use of the effective interest rate for restructured loans as well. That the Board has opted to recognize the revision of the amount and timing of future cash flows but not the market interest rate that is inextricably part of this revision has led to a flawed solution.

The other major focus of the financial instruments projects is the liability risk posed by various new off-balance sheet financing instruments. Examples of such instruments include interest rate swaps, project financing arrangements, joint ventures, forward contracts, and various hedging transactions. The FASB issued Statement No. 105 in 1990 to require increased disclosure of these items. Nevertheless, accounting procedures for the recognition of gains and losses on these transactions remain unresolved, as well as the basic question of whether such transactions should result in the reporting of a financial liability.

In "Accounting for Interest Rate Swaps—A Critical Evaluation," R. D. Nair, Larry E. Rittenberg, and Jerry J. Weygandt discuss the accounting alternatives with respect to interest rate swaps, an industry that grew from zero to over a trillion dollars per year of market transactions within the past decade. They recommend treating swaps as executory contracts and recognizing an asset and a liability.

In "Managing Off-Balance-Sheet Financing," Samuel Laibstain, David Stout, and Larry P. Bailey describe some of the common financing arrangements that lead to off-balance sheet liabilities and discuss the management incentives to engage in such transactions. They note that off-balance sheet financing could lead to an improved debt-equity ratio, improved borrowing capacity, lower borrowing costs, and better risk-sharing arrangements. There is, however, no clear empirical evidence that these hoped-for benefits are actually realized by companies that engage in off-balance sheet transactions.

A common type of transaction with off-balance sheet liability exposure is hedging. John E. Stewart, in "The Challenge of Hedge Accounting," notes that there is a need to develop what he calls "hedge accounting" to properly handle the explosion of transactions that involve risk sharing in foreign currency markets, financial markets or commodity markets. He notes that, while the FASB has addressed some of the hedge accounting issues for foreign currency transactions in Statement No. 52 and for futures contracts in Statement No. 80, the constant evolution of new hedging instruments such as interest rate swaps, options and interest rate forwards requires accountants to develop a broad conceptual approach to hedge accounting rather than settle for a piecemeal approach of putting out specific rules for specific instruments.

There are other controversial issues related to long-term liabilities that, despite having been addressed somewhat incompletely by prior FASB rules, are not being addressed by the current financial instruments projects. An example is the accounting for early extinguishment of debt. While Accounting Principles Board (APB) Opinion No. 26 required that gains and losses from early retirement of debt be recognized in current earnings, it did not require the classification of the gains and losses as extraordinary. In response to concerns expressed by the Securities and Exchange Commission and others that some firms might employ debt retirement to manipulate reported earnings, the FASB ruled in Statement No. 4 that a gain or loss from early extinguishment of debt be classified by the debtor as an extraordinary item. This unusual amendment diluting APB Opinion No. 30, which had virtually eliminated all items that might be classified as extraordinary, may have been an overly heavy-handed response to an ill-documented management disclosure problem. The high frequency of early debt extinguishment transactions in current financial reports despite FASB Statement No. 4 may be proof that firms undertake these transactions for other economic reasons and not for income manipulation.[3]

A new procedure for early extinguishment of debt evolved in the Eighties which involves an "in-substance defeasance" rather than legal retirement of debt. After some initial confusion and concern about the motivation for such transactions, the accounting profession has now come to accept in-substance defeasance as a legitimate financing tool.[4] The FASB issued Statement No. 76 in 1983, defining the allowable circumstances for in-substance defeasance and prescribing the application of Statement No. 4 to such transactions. Statement No. 76 is broad in its applicability, and allows in-substance defeasance to remove any kind of liability, for example, lease obligations, from the balance

---

[3] A search of *Disclosure's* CD-ROM database of annual reports shows that over 200 such transactions, with material extraordinary item disclosure, were reported in 1991.

[4] The FASB's first exposure draft on this topic in 1982 ruled against in-substance defeasance as constituting debt extinguishment. The FASB reversed its position in 1983.

sheet, and not just bonds and notes. Some critics, however, remain opposed to the accounting treatment of in-substance defeasance. In "In-Substance Defeasance: Costs, Yes; Benefits, No," Bruce R. Gaumnitz and Joel E. Thompson raise both accounting-theoretical and legal issues to argue against the removal of debt from the balance sheet after an in-substance defeasance. They note that bankruptcy courts are not likely to agree with the accounting view presented in Statement No. 76 and would look to the debt's contractual terms to decide on its defeasance status. It is this point that caused three of the seven FASB members to dissent from Statement No. 76.

BIBLIOGRAPHICAL NOTES

An Australian contribution to the development of a conceptual framework for liabilities is

Kerr, Jean St.G.: *The Definition and Recognition of Liabilities*, Accounting Theory Monograph No. 4 (Melbourne: Australian Accounting Research Foundation, 1984).

Papers from a conference on off-balance sheet financing, appearing in the *Journal of Accounting, Auditing & Finance*, volume 4, number 2, 1989, are also published as

Ronen, Joshua, Anthony Saunders and Ashwinpaul C. Sondhi (editors): *Off-Balance Sheet Activities* (New York: Quorum Books, 1990).

For more on the practice of off-balance sheet debt financing, see:

Andrews, Suzanna, and Henry Sender: "Off-Balance-Sheet Risk: Where is It Leading the Banks?," *Institutional Investor* (January 1986), pp. 75–84.

Berton, Lee: "Loose Ledgers: Many Firms Hide Debt to Give Them an Aura of Financial Strength," *The Wall Street Journal* (December 13, 1983).

Dieter, Richard, and Arthur R. Wyatt: "Get It Off the Balance Sheet!" *Financial Executive* (January 1980), pp. 42–48.

Stewart, John E., and Benjamin S. Neuhausen: "Financial Instruments and Transactions: The CPA's Newest Challenge," *Journal of Accountancy* (August 1986), pp. 102–113.

Wang, Penelope: "Accounting for an Albatross," *Forbes* (June 13, 1988). (Opening sentence: "Frequent-flier coupons may be a bonus for the customer, but what do they mean for the airlines that promote and issue them?")

The following articles provide an analytical analysis of off-balance sheet financing arrangements:

Donegan, Jim, and Shyam Sunder: "Contract Theoretic Analysis of Off-Balance Sheet Financing," *Journal of Accounting, Auditing & Finance* (Summer 1989), pp. 203–216.

El-Gazzar, Samir, Steven Lilien and Victor Pastena: "The Use of Off-Balance Sheet Financing to Circumvent Financial Covenant Restrictions," *Journal of Accounting, Auditing & Finance* (Summer 1989), pp. 217–231.

For a conceptual discussion and critique of the in-substance defeasance accounting rule, see:

Cason, Roger: "Conceptual Framework Begins to Affect Current Standards," *Journal of Accounting, Auditing & Finance (Summer 1984), pp. 369–373.*

An empirical analysis of management motivations for in-substance defeasance is given by

Hand, John R. M., Patricia J. Hughes and Stephen E. Sefcik: "In-Substance Defeasance: Security Price Reactions and Motivations," *Journal of Accounting and Economics* (May 1990), pp. 47–89.

Additional articles on in-substance debt defeasance:

"How 'Defeasance' Will Help Companies and the Treasury," *Business Week* (February 6, 1984), pp. 12, 16.

Blumstein, Michael: "Pros and Cons of Defeasance," *The New York Times* (January 12, 1984), pp. 27,33.

Chaney, Paul K.: "Defeasance: Financial Tool or Window Dressing?," *Management Accounting* (November 1985), pp. 52–55.

Gup, Benton E., and Maurice S. Newman: "Defeasance: What is Its Effect on Your Firm?," *Financial Executive* (December 1984), pp. 34–37.

Gray, Dahli, and Mary Alice Seville: "In-Substance Defeasance: Altering the Shape of Debt Management," *Journal of Accountancy* (January 1985), pp. 100–107.

Kay, Robert S.: "Extinguishment of Debt—SFAS 76," *The CPA Journal* (April 1984), pp. 62–65.

Mielke, David E., and James Seifert: "A Survey on the Effects of Defeasing Debt," *Journal of Accounting, Auditing & Finance* (Winter 1987), pp. 65–78.

Peterson, Pamela, David Peterson and James Ang: "The Extinguishment of Debt Through In-Substance Defeasance," *Financial Management* (Spring 1985), pp. 59–67.

Roden, Peyton Foster: "The Financial Implications of In-Substance Defeasance," *Journal of Accounting, Auditing & Finance* (Winter 1987), pp. 79–89.

The following article examines the computational procedures related to bond valuation, something not often found in the literature:

Spurrell, A. C. Lloyd: "Calculating the Present Value of a Bond: An Alternative Approach," *Issues in Accounting Education* (Spring 1990), pp. 120–122.

For a general discussion of the use of time value of money in accounting procedures, see:

Milburn, J. Alex: *Incorporating the Time Value of Money Within Financial Accounting* (Toronto: Canadian Institute of Chartered Accountants, 1988).

Boritz, J. E.: *Approaches to Dealing with Risk and Uncertainty* (Toronto: Canadian Institute of Chartered Accountants, 1990).

A paper by Weil, similar to Milburn's work, is part of a broader FASB project on this topic:

Weil, Roman L.: "Role of the Time Value of Money in Financial Reporting," *Accounting Horizons* (December 1990), pp. 47–67.

Present Value-Based Measurement in Accounting, Discussion Memorandum (Financial Accounting Standards Board, December 7, 1990).

The FASB's financial instruments projects and the possible accounting requirement to "mark" financial assets and liabilities to "market" have attracted a large number of articles in professional and academic journals. Here is a selection:

Levites, Jim B.: "Mark-To-Market: Freddie Mac's Fourth Financial Statement," *Journal of Accountancy* (October 1990), pp. 78–87.
Woods, Clifford C. III, and Halsey G. Bullen: "An Overview of the FASB's Financial Instruments Project," *Journal of Accountancy* (November 1989), pp. 42–47.
Wyatt, Arthur: "The SEC Says: Mark to Market!" *Accounting Horizons* (March 1991), pp. 80–84. (This article is reproduced in Chapter 9.)

For an interesting case study of how the economic consequences of reporting a liability from a transaction could dictate its accounting treatment, see:

Zeff, Stephen A., and Sven-Erik Johansson: "The Curious Accounting Treatment of the Swedish Government Loan to Uddeholm," *The Accounting Review* (April 1984), pp. 342–350.

Accounting for Interest Rate Swaps— A Critical Evaluation

R. D. Nair
University of Wisconsin-Madison

Larry E. Rittenberg
University of Wisconsin-Madison

Jerry J. Weygandt
University of Wisconsin-Madison

There has been a remarkable explosion in the number of new financial instruments[1] in recent years creating an equal number of new accounting issues. Usually these issues arise because the accounting for these new financial instruments is not addressed in the accounting literature, or the literature itself provides conflicting guidance. Recognizing the complexity of

From *Accounting Horizons* (September 1990), pp. 20–30. Reprinted by permission of the American Accounting Association. Copyright © 1990 by the American Accounting Association. This version is a December 1992 update of the article supplied by the authors. Reprinted by permission of the authors.
[1] Financial instruments include both financial assets and liabilities now carried on balance sheets (for example, bonds, loans, and trade receivables and payables) and obligations, commitments, and guarantees often not recognized in balance sheets (for example, interest rate swaps, forward contracts for government bonds, and loan commitments).

these instruments and the potential for varying accounting treatments, the Financial Accounting Standards Board (FASB) added a major long-term project to address the accounting for financial instruments and other off-balance sheet financing issues to its agenda in May 1986.[2]

An example of the new financial instruments is the interest rate swap.[3] Interest rate swaps are agreements between two counterparties to exchange interest rate payments based on a notional (defined) principal amount for a term of years in order to convert the periodic payments on an asset or liability from a fixed rate to a floating rate, a floating to a fixed rate, or from one type of floating rate to another. Swaps are used by financial and investment managers to minimize borrowing costs, create attractive returns on assets, hedge portfolio risk, to speculate, or raise capital in foreign currency markets.[4] Major swap market participants include domestic and foreign securities firms, commercial and investment banks, savings and loan institutions, corporations, and sovereign and supranational entities.

The purpose of this article is to critically examine the current accounting for swaps and to recommend improvements. Articles on interest rate swaps[5] have described swaps and summarized the current consensus among swap participants as to how to account for and disclose information about swaps. Bierman[6] defined some of the accounting issues raised by swap transactions and suggested increased use of notes to the financial statements to reveal the changes in risk of the parties involved in the swap. Cummings, Apostolou, and Mister[7] described interest rate swaps and offered recommendations for

---

[2] As an initial, interim step, the FASB, in November 1987, issued an Exposure Draft of a proposed Statement of Financial Accounting Standards, *Disclosures about Financial Instruments*, that would require improved disclosures about financial instruments. The Exposure Draft proposes disclosures of the credit risks, cash flows, interest rates, and market values of financial instruments but does not address issues related to recognition and measurement. As noted later in this article, the FASB, in March 1990, issued SFAS 105 to address disclosures about financial instruments with off-balance-sheet risk. The provisions of this Statement are summarized later in the article. Also, as noted later in this article, FASB has issued SFAS 107 to address disclosures of fair values of financial instruments.

[3] Interest rate swaps are a financial instrument that have undergone remarkable growth since they were introduced in 1982. According to John Stewart, "The Challenges of Hedge Accounting," *Journal of Accountancy* (November 1989), p. 49, the market for interest rate swaps has grown to over $1 trillion. The focus of this paper is exclusively on "plain vanilla" interest rate swaps, excluding an important and rapidly growing segment of the swap market which deals with combined interest rate and currency swaps.

[4] Credit risk in swaps markets seems to be low. "Losses in Derivative Market Are Reported to be Small," *Wall Street Journal* (July 31, 1992) reports that losses from defaulted swap transactions have totaled approximately 0.46% of the market value outstanding, relative to 1.9% on loans. The bankruptcy filing of Olympia & York Developments Ltd. in 1992 highlighted the potential credit risk in this market.

[5] W. Riley and S. Smith, "Interest Rate Swaps: Disclosure and Recognition," *CPA Journal* (January 1987), pp. 64–70; K. Wishon and L. Chevalier, "Interest Rate Swaps—Your Rate or Mine?", *Journal of Accountancy* (September 1985), pp. 65–84.

[6] H. Bierman, "Accounting for Interest Rate Swaps," *Journal of Accounting, Auditing and Finance* (Fall 1987), pp. 396–408.

[7] B. Cummings, N. Apostolou, and W. Mister, "Accounting for Interest Rate Swaps: An Emerging Issue," *Accounting Horizons* (June 1987), pp. 19–24.

their accounting treatment based on authoritative pronouncements applicable to similar financial instruments. One of their recommendations, based on analogies to SFAS 80, *Accounting for Futures Contracts*, was that the gain or loss on the early termination of a swap (through sale, or reversal, of the swap) should be deferred and amortized if the swap qualifies as a hedge. However, current practice defines basically all swaps as hedges except those that are clearly speculative and are therefore marked to market. For example, in a recent survey of the accounting and reporting practices of major U.S. banks, Comiskey, Mulford and Turner[8] found that they may be inappropriately treating interest rate swaps as hedges.

This article evaluates the accounting for interest rate swaps and develops a theoretical framework for analyzing the accounting for swaps—including the identification of specific conditions under which an interest rate swap would qualify as a hedge. Three different accounting perspectives on swaps —synthetic instruments (current practice), refinancing, and separate instruments—are described. Issues addressed in the paper include recognition of swaps at inception, recognition of gains and losses on swaps subsequent to inception, recognition of gains and losses at terminations of swaps, and disclosures of information about swaps. One of the major conclusions of the paper is that only swaps that meet all the hedging criteria of SFAS 80 should be treated as hedges.

ACCOUNTING FOR INTEREST RATE SWAPS— CURRENT PRACTICES

Despite the growth of interest rate swaps and the size of the transactions, no authoritative pronouncements address the accounting for interest rate swaps. The following accounting, however, appears to be generally accepted:

- Changes in the market value of the swap are not recorded except when the original asset or liability is reported at market value, or the swap is unmatched (i.e., there is no underlying asset or liability and the swap is a speculation).[9]
- Changes in the market value of speculative swaps are recognized as gains and losses each period. While the predominant practice is to carry these swaps at market value, some practitioners believe it is acceptable to carry such swaps at lower of cost or market.

---

[8] E. Comiskey, C. Mulford, and D. Turner, "Bank Accounting and Reporting Practices for Interest Rate Swaps," *Journal of Bank Accounting and Finance* (Winter 1987–88), pp. 3–14.

[9] SFAS 107, *Disclosure about Fair Value of Financial Instruments*, requires the disclosure of fair values of financial instruments for which it is practicable to estimate fair value. In paragraphs 24 and 31 of that pronouncement, the FASB indicates that fair value may be estimated by adjusting the market price of a similar instrument, or the estimated replacement cost of the swap, or the amount the entity would receive or pay to terminate the swap agreements at the reporting date, taking into account current interest rates and the current creditworthiness of the swap counterparties.

- "Settlement accounting" is followed, that is, interest income or expense on the original asset/liability is adjusted for the net difference on the swap from period to period and reported as an adjustment to interest income or expense on the income statement.
- Gains and losses on early termination of swaps are deferred and recognized when the offsetting gain or loss is recognized on the hedged transaction.

SFAS 105, *Disclosure of Information about Financial Instruments with Off-Balance-Sheet Risk and Financial Instruments with Concentrations of Credit Risk*, requires certain disclosures about financial instruments, such as interest rate swaps, with off-balance-sheet risk. Off-balance-sheet risk exists if the risk of accounting loss to the entity exceeds the amount recognized in the balance sheet. Disclosures include the nature and terms of the instrument and a discussion of the related credit and market risk, cash requirement and related accounting policy; contract or notional principal amount of the instrument; the accounting loss the entity would incur if any party to the instrument failed completely to perform and any collateral proved to be worthless; information about collateral; and credit risk concentrations. SFAS 105 is effective for financial statements issued for fiscal years ending after June 15, 1990.

Accounting issues with respect to swaps include the recognition of swaps at inception, recognition of gains and losses subsequent to inception but prior to termination, recognition of gains and losses at termination, and disclosures about swaps. We address these issues by examining alternative transactions or approaches which may be analogous to an interest rate swap transaction. The next section describes these analogous approaches. The appropriate analogy is then selected by determining which comes closest to the economics of the transaction and the appropriate accounting treatment is then derived. In examining interest rate swaps, we do so from the perspective of either counterparty so that our conclusions are applicable to all the parties involved in the transaction.

ALTERNATIVE APPROACHES

Synthetic Instruments Approach

One approach that may be used to describe the current accounting for interest rate swaps is a "synthetic instruments approach."[10] Under this approach, a swap is seen as transforming the original liability or asset with a fixed or

---

[10] L. T. Johnson and V. L. Wall, "Might Synthetic Instrument Accounting be Substituted for Hedge Accounting for Some "Hedging" Relationships," *Highlights of Financial Reporting Issues* (September 30, 1992), FASB Financial Accounting Series No. 119-B, pp. 4–9, describe a synthetic instrument as one that hypothetically combines or synthesizes two or more conventional instruments to replicate a desired instrument. Synthetic instrument accounting then accounts for the combination of financial instruments like the financial instrument it replicates.

variable rate into a "new" liability or asset with a variable or fixed rate. (This is often referred to as a "matched" swap because the swap is matched against a related asset or liability.) The original instrument and the swap are viewed as one unit, with the swap changing the interest rate characteristics of the original instrument and thus the original instrument is effectively synthesized into a new instrument. For example, a fixed-rate liability paired with a variable-rate swap effectively becomes a "synthetic" variable-rate liability. Under "synthetic instruments accounting," the swap is seen as changing only the interest rate characteristics of the matched asset or liability for the period of the swap. Consequently, the interest effect of the swap is to be recognized only as interest is paid or received.

As an example of this approach, in Issue 84-36, "Interest Rate Swap Transactions," the Emerging Issues Task Force (EITF) discussed the accounting for a swap transaction if the purpose of entering into the transaction is to change the nature of a liability (for example, from a fixed to a variable interest obligation). The Task Force agreed that, if there is an underlying debt obligation on the balance sheet of the company entering into the swap transaction, the company should account for the swap arrangement like a hedge of the obligation and record interest expense using the revised interest rate, with any fees or other payments amortized as yield adjustments.

Refinancing Approach

In this approach, the swap might be seen as the equivalent of a refinancing, resulting in a possible gain or loss to be recognized at the inception of the swap.[11] An analogous situation would be a refinancing where fixed (variable) rate debt is extinguished and refinanced with variable (fixed) rate debt. Under APB Opinion No. 26, *Early Extinguishment of Debt* and SFAS 76, *Extinguishment of Debt*, a gain or loss is recognized and is measured as the difference between the amount the debt is extinguished for (its market value) and its carrying amount. Under this view, an interest rate swap is a bargained arm's-length transaction with the same economic substance as a refinancing. In a swap the gain or loss would be calculated by comparing the value of the debt using market interest rates (implied in the swap) with the carrying amount of the debt.

Separate Instruments Approach

Alternatively, the original liability or asset could be viewed as one instrument, and the interest rate swap as a second instrument, with the accounting

---

[11] Gain or loss treatment would result only if the swap took place subsequent to the original issuance of the underlying asset or liability. If the debt were issued, and a swap immediately occurred, no gain or loss results. However, the underlying terms of the debt are changed and should be reported in the financial statements.

issues for each instrument being addressed separately and independently.[12] It is argued that interest rate swaps are financial instruments which, like bonds, have markets in which they can be bought and sold; they can be entered into at, or after, or even before the issuance of the debt or purchase of an asset; they can be terminated at any time; the swap term may be different from the maturity of the debt or asset; and the notional amount of the swap may be different from the principal amount of the debt. These features of swaps support viewing them as separate instruments whose accounting treatment should be viewed separately and independently from the accounting treatment of the underlying asset or liability.

ARGUMENTS FOR SEPARATE INSTRUMENTS APPROACH

Interest rate swaps are executory contracts and we believe that under certain specified conditions they should be recognized in the financial statements. This section discusses those conditions and examines whether interest rate swaps satisfy them. Satisfaction of the conditions for recognition of executory contracts would provide support for the separate instruments approach to accounting for interest rate swaps.

An interest rate swap is initially a wholly executory contract since neither party has made any payments at the inception of the swap. Under current accounting, executory contracts are generally not recognized in the financial statements with the exception of capital leases and stock option grants at below market prices which vest later. Foreign currency forward contracts are recognized to the extent that exchange gains and losses on the contract at the settlement date and at intervening financial statement dates must be recognized. Thus, the net exposure on this executory contract is measured by changes in a specified exchange rate.

Although executory contracts are generally not recognized at inception, compelling arguments are often made for their recognition. For example, Ijiri[13] states that the majority of the articles on recognition of executory contracts conclude that all executory contracts should be recognized. The arguments in favor of recognition of executory contracts are that the exchange of promises at the signing of the contract represents an exchange of rights to future service potentials and a corresponding obligation and thus is a valid point at which to recognize assets and liabilities.

---

[12] This approach is analogous to the fundamental financial instrument approach proposed in *Recognition and Measurement of Financial Instruments* (FASB, 1991). In that Discussion Memorandum the fundamental financial instrument approach is based on the premise that all financial instruments are made from a set of fundamental financial instruments, and that determining how to recognize and measure those fundamental financial instruments will lead to reaching consistent solutions for the more complex financial instruments.

[13] Y. Ijiri, *Recognition of Contractual Rights and Obligations* (FASB, 1980), pp. 86–89.

In discussing executory contracts, Ijiri[14] states that the first test that must be applied to contractual rights and obligations is whether or not they meet the definitions of assets and liabilities. The FASB defines assets as probable future economic benefits obtained or controlled by a particular entity (the interest to be received in an interest rate swap) as a result of past transactions or events (the signing of the swap contract). Liabilities are defined as probable future sacrifices of economic benefits arising from present obligations of a particular entity to transfer assets or provide services to other entities in the future (the interest to be paid in an interest rate swap) as a result of past transactions or events (the signing of the swap contract).

Ijiri[15] then states that recognition of contractual rights and obligations as assets and liabilities also must be justified on the basis that doing so produces information useful for decision making. Interest rate swaps have the potential to change both the amount and the pattern of future cash flows, thus making them relevant to investors and creditors. Ijiri[16] further states the recognition principle for executory contracts as: A contractual right of obligation should be recognized when it becomes firm. A commitment is said to be firm if it is unlikely that its performance can be avoided without a severe penalty. A penalty is considered to be severe if in the normal course of business an enterprise would perform what is required under the commitment rather than incur the penalty. An example of the importance of a penalty in the recognition and measurement of an executory contract is provided in SFAS 98, *Accounting for Leases: Sale-Leaseback Transactions Involving Real Estate; Sales-Type Leases of Real Estate; Definition of the Lease Term; Initial Direct Costs of Direct Financing Leases*. In that pronouncement, the fixed noncancellable term of the lease is defined to include all periods for which failure to renew the lease imposes a penalty on the lessee in such amount that a renewal appears, at the lease's inception, to be reasonably assured. A penalty is defined to be a requirement to disburse cash, incur or assume a liability, perform services, surrender or transfer an asset or rights to an asset or otherwise forego an economic benefit, or suffer an economic detriment.

Penalties are an important part of a swap contract. According to Marshall and Kapner,[17] the process for measuring penalties is one of the most important clauses in a swap agreement. The International Swap Dealers Association's code of swaps describes three methods for measuring penalties in the event of early termination. These three methods are the agreement value method, the indemnification method, and the formula method. The use of the agreement value method is nearly universal. Under this method, the penalty is based upon market quotations obtained by the nondefaulting

---

[14] *Ibid.*, p. 65.
[15] *Ibid.*, p. 66.
[16] *Ibid.*, p. 67.
[17] J. F. Marshall and K. R. Kapner, *Understanding Swap Finance* (South-Western Publishing Co., 1990), p. 117.

party from swap market makers to approximate the replacement cost of the swap.[18]

Upon examination of the terms of the interest rate swap contract, it appears that such contracts represent economic assets and liabilities in their own right. They are separate financial instruments in which a company may make an investment just as it does in other financial instruments such as bonds or stocks. They represent more than just a transformation of an existing liability into a synthetic instrument or just a refinancing of an existing liability. We therefore conclude that a separate instruments analogy for interest rate swaps is appropriate.

Right to Offset

A further issue in analyzing the separate instruments approach is the fact that the receipts and payments in an interest rate swap offset. If a company does not make its payments, the counterparty will not make its payments.[19] In these circumstances, it would seem that current accounting should permit the offsetting of the asset and liability.

APB Opinion No. 10, *Omnibus Opinion—1966*, states that "it is a general principle of accounting that the offsetting of assets and liabilities in the balance sheet is improper except where a right of setoff exists." FASB Interpretation 39, *Offsetting of Amounts Related to Certain Contracts*, states that a "right of setoff" exists when each of two parties owes the other determinable amounts; the reporting party has the right to set off the amount owed with the amount owed by the other party; the reporting party intends to set off; and the right of setoff is enforceable by law. Generally, interest rate swaps satisfy the above conditions.[20] Thus, it is appropriate to set off the present value of the interest to be paid against the present value of the interest to be received.

---

[18] An alternative perspective on swaps developed by Harold Bierman, "Accounting for Interest Rate Swaps," *Journal of Accounting, Auditing and Finance* (Fall 1987), pp. 396–408 is that each payment by a firm that enters into a swap is contingent upon receipt of a payment from the other party to the swap. He therefore concludes that it is reasonable to limit the swap liability shown by a firm to the present value of the interest payment to be made by the firm for the next period, i.e., until it is to receive interest from the other party to the swap. This approach would have merit if the liability of a party walking away from a swap is limited to the next payment. However, such contracts would usually not be feasible since, if interest rates rose, variable rate payers would renege at the cost of having to make one additional payment. As noted, interest rate swaps normally include penalty clauses in order to make them effective long-term contracts and to offer protection against interest rate fluctuations.

[19] Although a penalty is imposed in the event of nonpayment, that penalty is a contingency at the inception of the swap.

[20] As pointed out in "Taming the Derivatives Beast," *The Economist* (May 23, 1992), pp. 81–82, the "legal aspects of derivatives are hazy, as banks were shocked to find after entering into swaps with British local authorities. The contracts were voided by the courts because the authorities had no right to enter into them."

RECOGNITION OF CHANGES IN MARKET VALUE OF INTEREST RATE SWAPS

Given the above conclusion that swaps should be treated as separate instruments, the next question to be addressed is how they should be valued. This issue involves both whether changes in the market value of swaps should be recognized and whether those changes in the market value should be included in income. This issue is complicated by the fact that in many cases interest rate swaps serve as hedges for other financial instruments. Current practice requires that changes in the market value of a financial instrument (such as a futures contract) used as a hedge of an existing asset, liability or firm commitment are generally not recognized in income but are instead deferred and offset against or added to the carrying value of the hedged item (unless the hedged item is carried at fair value).

The requirements for hedge accounting are defined in SFAS 80, SFAS 52, *Foreign Currency Translation*, and the AICPA Issues Paper 86-2, *Accounting for Options*. Three criteria must be met in order for hedge accounting to be used:

1. The item to be hedged presents an exposure to risk. Under SFAS 52 and the Issues Paper, risk assessment is made on a transaction-by-transaction basis. SFAS 80 requires that, in a futures hedge, the hedged item must expose the enterprise as a whole to price or interest rate risk. SFAS 80 defines risk as the sensitivity of an enterprise's income for one or more future periods to changes in market prices or yields of existing assets, liabilities, firm commitments, or anticipated transactions. In determining whether this condition is met, SFAS 80 requires consideration of whether other assets, liabilities, firm commitments and anticipated transactions already offset or reduce the exposure.

2. Management must designate the hedging instrument as the hedge of a specific item or a group of essentially similar items.

3. The hedging instrument should reduce the exposure to risk. SFAS 80 requires that at the inception of the hedge and throughout the hedge period, high correlation of changes in the market value of the hedged item (or the interest income or expense associated therewith) and the hedging instrument shall be probable so that changes in the value of the hedging instrument will substantially offset the effects of the price or interest rate changes on the exposed item.

Stewart[21] points out some of the inconsistencies between SFAS 80, SFAS 52 and the Issues Paper relating both to the conditions necessary to qualify for hedge accounting and the application of hedge accounting when the criteria actually are met. In the absence of any authoritative guidance on accounting

---

[21] J. Stewart, "The Challenges of Hedge Accounting," *Journal of Accountancy* (November 1989), pp. 48–60.

for interest rate swaps, practice has tended to draw analogies to SFAS 80.[22] In our analysis, we too rely on the guidance provided in SFAS 80.

Comiskey, Mulford and Turner[23] report on a survey of the accounting and reporting practices for interest rate swaps of the 100 largest U.S. commercial banks. One of their findings was the deferral of gains and losses on swaps may be practiced even where identifiable hedges are not in effect. The surveyed banks made many references to hedge accounting in the absence of any reference to identifiable hedge swaps. It is possible that hedge swaps did exist but were not disclosed. If that were not the case, however, then they conclude that "evolving GAAP in the area of swaps is at odds with the related promulgated GAAP found in SFAS No. 80."[24]

Given the criteria for hedges in SFAS 80, an interest rate swap should qualify for hedge accounting only if it reduces an enterprise's exposure to interest rate risk. A swap does not qualify for hedge accounting if it only meets the second criterion above, that is, that management designates the swap as a hedge, or as a match, of a specific asset or liability. All three hedge accounting criteria would be satisfied by a swap when three securities—an existing asset, an existing liability, and the interest rate swap if it reduces the enterprise's exposure to risk—are involved. Table 1 presents examples of when hedge accounting for swaps is or is not appropriate. As can be seen from the four examples, an interest rate swap cannot be classified as a hedge of a specific liability only by looking at its effect on that matched liability. For example, in situation C, Company DEF swaps its variable rate payments for fixed rate payments. This may appear to have reduced its risk. However, the opposite has happened. Since the company has variable rate assets, it was protected from interest rate risk before but is now exposed to risk if interest rates drop. To call such a swap a hedge is inappropriate since it does not satisfy either the first or third criterion above.[25] Interest rate swaps should be considered hedges only after considering any existing hedging relationships between assets and liabilities.[26] Matching a swap with an asset or liability does not necessarily result in a hedge.

---

[22] H. Bierman, Jr., L. T. Johnson, and D. S. Peterson, *Hedge Accounting: An Exploratory Study of the Underlying Issues* (FASB, 1991), point out that SFAS 52 and SFAS 80 are the only two pronouncements in which hedge accounting is considered. However, hedge accounting was not the focus of either of those pronouncements. Taken together, those two pronouncements cover only a portion of the set of possible hedging activities. Moreover, the two pronouncements are inconsistent in certain respects. These factors have created problems for practitioners who try to make analogies to one or both pronouncements.

[23] E. Comiskey, C. Mulford, and D. Turner, "Bank Accounting and Reporting Practices for Interest Rate Swaps," *Journal of Bank Accounting and Finance* (Winter 1987-88), pp. 3–14.

[24] *Ibid.*, p. 9.

[25] Many would indicate that practice embraces the separate instruments viewpoint, and then denies recognition of changes in the value of a swap, other than a speculative swap, on the basis that it hedges the underlying asset or liability. Such reasoning is fallacious because it implies that these types of swaps always hedge.

[26] It appears that many companies, especially financial institutions, use interest rate swaps as hedges of general firm-wide interest rate risk rather than as hedges of specific assets, liabilities, or

TABLE 1 Illustration of "Three Securities Approach" for Hedge Accounting for Swaps

A. Company XYZ has $100 million of fixed rate assets financed by $100 million of variable rate debt. The company swaps its variable rate payments for fixed rate payments.* The company is now insulated from interest rate risk. The swap qualifies as a hedge.

B. Company ABC has $100 million of fixed rate assets financed by $100 million of fixed rate debt. The company swaps its fixed rate payments for variable rate payments in the expectation that rates will drop. The company is not insulated from interest rate risk. The swap does not qualify as a hedge.

C. Company DEF has $100 million of variable rate assets financed by $100 million of variable rate debt. The company swaps its variable rate payments for fixed rate payments. The company is not insulated from interest rate risk (on the asset side). In fact, the swap removed its protection against that risk. The swap does not qualify as a hedge.

D. Company KLM has $100 million of variable rate assets financed by $100 million of fixed rate debt. The company swaps its fixed rate payments for variable rate payments. The company is insulated from interest rate risk since its assets and liabilities are now both variable. The swap qualifies as a hedge.

* In all these examples, the swaps involve the company's liabilities. The company may also engage in swaps related to its assets. The conclusions, however, will be similar to the above analysis.

If an interest rate swap qualifies as a hedge, then changes in its value should be deferred and reported as an adjustment of the carrying value of the hedged item if carried at amortized cost. If an interest rate swap does not qualify as a hedge, then changes in the market value of swaps should be included in income. Rationales for carrying swaps at market include:[27]

- Concepts Statement No. 5, *Recognition and Measurement in Financial Statements of Business Enterprises* (paragraph 90), recommends market value accounting when current price information "is sufficiently relevant and reliable to justify the costs involved and more relevant than alternative information."

anticipated transactions. As noted above, a strict application of the criteria in SFAS 80 would prevent the use of hedge accounting for such swaps. It may be difficult to identify the specific item being hedged or to determine whether, after considering the offsetting effects of existing assets and liabilities, that enterprise risk has been reduced. Changes in the criteria for the use of hedge accounting may be necessary as more innovative financial instruments are developed.

[27] Similar arguments for carrying options at market value are stated in W. P. Hauworth II and L. Moody, "An Accountant's Option Primer: Puts and Calls Demystified," *Journal of Accountancy* (January 1987), pp. 87–97.

- SFAS 80 requires market value accounting for futures contracts, with changes in market value included in income in the period of change, unless the contract qualifies for hedge accounting and the hedged item is carried at amortized cost.
- SFAS 52 requires market value accounting for foreign exchange contracts. Like swaps, such contracts are not settled in cash daily.

The principles and criteria in Concepts Statement No. 5 and SFAS 52 and 80 provide strong justification for the use of market value in accounting for interest rate swaps. We therefore recommend that swaps that do not qualify for hedge treatment be carried at market.[28, 29]

Terminations of Interest Rate Swaps

In current practice, the EITF consensus in Issue 84-7, "Termination of Interest Rate Swaps," is that gains and losses on terminated interest rate swaps accounted for as hedges should be deferred and amortized over the life of the original instrument under the assumption that such a swap is closely analogous to a similar transaction described in SFAS 80. In SFAS 80, the Board took the view that gains and losses on a hedge transaction deferred before termination should continue to be deferred following termination, pending disposition of the hedged item, because the company has taken the position that the futures contract cannot be viewed by itself, but is to be viewed as an integral part of the accounting for the hedged item. The argument is that the futures contract has been linked with another asset, liability or transaction, and therefore the accounting should continue to be consistent with this view. In Issue 84-36, the EITF reiterated its consensus in Issue 84-7 that gains and losses on terminated interest rate swaps that were accounted for as hedges should not be recognized immediately in income.

---

[28] FASB Interpretation 39, *Offsetting of Amounts Related to Certain Contracts*, states that fair value amounts related to interest rate swaps executed with the same counterparty under a master netting arrangement may be offset. Offsetting the fair values recognized for swaps outstanding with a single counterparty results in the net fair value of the position between the two counterparties being reported as an asset or a liability in the statement of financial position.

[29] Since swaps are not standardized like futures contracts, they do not have readily quoted prices like futures. However, market values can be derived usually by reference to market makers in swaps. E. Comiskey, C. Mulford, and D. Turner, "Bank Accounting and Reporting Practices for Interest Rate Swaps," *Journal of Bank Accounting and Finance* (Winter 1987-88), pp. 3–14, state that market value, which could be an asset or liability, is estimated as the present value of the current favorable or unfavorable spread between the interest streams. Changes in the interest rate determine changes in the market value and result in the reported gains and losses. Also, an example of a valuation technique is provided in R. Kopprasch, J. Macfarlane, D. Ross and J. Showers, *The Interest Rate Swap Market: Yield Mathematics, Terminology and Conventions* (Salomon Brothers, Inc., 1985). As mentioned earlier, SFAS 107, *Disclosures about Fair Value of Financial Instruments*, also provides examples of how to measure the fair value of swaps. John Stewart, "The Challenges of Hedge Accounting," *Journal of Accountancy* (November 1989), pp. 48–60, and Touche Ross, *Accounting and Auditing Manual for Options and Interest Rate Swaps* (1987), indicate that, in current practice, swaps that do not qualify as hedges are carried at market or lower of cost or market.

If the swap is viewed as a separate instrument as recommended above, then the gain or loss on termination of a swap that qualifies for hedge treatment should be deferred, and, consistent with SFAS 80, amortized over the remaining life of the debt. If the swap did not qualify for hedge treatment, then changes in the market value of the swap would have already been recognized in income. The only gain or loss to be recognized would be that relating to the period from the last reporting date, and the firm would also record the disposition of its investment in the swap. We should emphasize that deferral of gains and losses should not be based on the criteria in the EITF consensus in Issues 84-7 and 84-36 because to do so would incorrectly imply that all swaps are futures contracts that hedge.[30]

INFORMATION NEEDS OF INVESTORS

As was pointed out earlier, there does not seem to be any consensus in the literature or conformity in practice about the level of detail that should be disclosed about swaps. For example, in 1984, AMAX entered into a variable-rate loan of seven years with the Canadian Imperial Bank of Commerce (CIBC). It then immediately entered into three $25 million swaps with CIBC to fix the interest rate. The 1986 financial statements of AMAX[31] had the following disclosures with respect to interest rate swaps:

(a) In the *Summary of Accounting Policies*, AMAX disclosed:
Interest rate swaps are entered into primarily as a hedge against interest rate exposure of floating rate debt, although swaps may be entered into as speculative contracts. Gains or losses related to changes in the value of speculative swaps are recognized currently. Gains or losses related to changes in value of swaps designated as hedges are deferred and reported as components of the related transactions.

(b) Under *Interest Expense, Net*, AMAX disclosed:
At December 31, 1986 and 1985, interest rate swap agreements which hedge interest rate exposure on floating rate debt were $140 million and $120 million, respectively. Net payments or receipts under these agreements are included in interest expense.

(c) Under *Long-Term Debt Excluding Current Maturities*, AMAX disclosed:

---

[30] In an interest rate swap, the fixed rate is typically negotiated to eliminate any need for a cash payment at the outset. Sometimes, however, swaps are accompanied by a cash payment at initiation, if the swap is entered into at a fixed rate that is different from the market rate. In that case, the economic substance of the payment must be analyzed to determine if the receipt of the up-front payment is a borrowing. Any such borrowing would be written off to interest expense over the life of the swap. Touche Ross, *Accounting and Auditing Manual for Options and Interest Rate Swaps* (1987), paragraph 23.100, presents an example of such a transaction. Also, transaction costs are usually incurred in a swap. The EITF consensus in Issue 84-36 is that fees or other payments are to be amortized as yield adjustments.
[31] AMAX, Inc., Annual Report (1986).

	1986	*1985*
Retractable facsimile bonds	75.0	75.0
1991—11.2% (1985—11.5%)		

No mention was made about the swaps relating to that debt. These notes do not indicate that part of AMAX's interest rate swaps related to the $75,000,000 of retractable facsimile bonds listed in the long-term debt note. Changes in the nature of the debt—from variable to fixed and vice-versa—as interest rate swaps are entered into and then reversed are not disclosed. Such information is essential for assessing the future liquidity and solvency of a company. Also, the assessment of whether the swaps qualified as hedges seems to have been made only by considering the effect on the debt—that is, whether the swap was matched—without looking at whether AMAX had any variable rate assets which would now expose it to interest rate risk. This seems to be a clear case of where evolved practice with respect to swaps is at odds with promulgated GAAP.

Uniform disclosures should be required of all companies for interest rate swaps. Such disclosures should include the term of the swap, the contracted rates for receipts and payments, the indexes used, the base for floating rates, the notional amounts involved, the identity of the counterparty, the market value of the swap, whether that swap is being treated as a hedge and any gains or losses on terminations. As noted earlier, some of these disclosures are not required by SFAS 105, *Disclosure of Information about Financial Instruments with Off-Balance-Sheet Risk and Financial Instruments with Concentrations of Credit Risk*, and SFAS 107, *Disclosures about Fair Value of Financial Instruments*. Also, Bierman[32] gives examples of the kinds of notes that should be given in the financial statements of the parties to a swap contract in order to reveal the effect of the swap on the firm's risk. He suggests notes of the following general nature:

1. BB has engaged in a $100-million interest rate swap. It has effectively exchanged its floating-rate debt for a fixed-rate debt. Given the nature of $100 million of BB's assets (fixed-rate investments), this transaction will tend to be risk reducing.
2. AA has engaged in a $100-million interest rate swap. It has effectively exchanged its fixed-rate debt for a variable rate debt. Given the nature of $100 million of BB's assets (fixed-rate investments), this transaction will tend to be risk increasing (if interest rates increase) but will be beneficial if interest rates decrease.

It is interesting that in both of these situations described by Bierman the assessment of whether a swap is risk reducing or risk increasing is done by examining the relationship between three securities: the interest rate swap, the debt, and related assets. For example, in situation 1, the swap is considered risk reducing not because floating-rate debt has become fixed-rate debt

---

[32] H. Bierman, "Accounting for Interest Rate Swaps," *Journal of Accounting, Auditing and Finance* (Fall 1987), p. 403.

TABLE 2 Comparison of Different Accounting Approaches to Interest Rate Swaps

The journal entries given in the table are those that would be made for each of the major events in the life of a swap under the different approaches discussed in the text. The situation assumes a swap involving a notional amount of $75,000,000. We assume interest expense on the outstanding debt to be $10,000,000 each period, that at the end of the first period the company received $1,000,000 as a net receipt under the swap and that the market value of the swap then was $4,500,000. The swap was terminated 2 years later with the company receiving $6,800,000.

Event	Swaps (Current Practice—Synthetic Instruments)	Swaps (Separate Instruments—Not Hedged)	Swaps (Separate Instruments—Hedged)
1. Recognizing interest rate swap at inception	No recognition	Recognition but no entry because of offset	Recognition but no entry because of offset

2. Recording gain/loss due to interest rate change subsequent to inception of swap	*On Debt*
	Interest Exp. 10,000,000
	  Cash 10,000,000
	On Swap
	Cash 1,000,000
	  Interest Exp. 1,000,000
		On Debt
		Interest Exp. 10,000,000
		  Cash 10,000,000
		On Swap
		Cash 1,000,000
		  Interest Exp. 1,000,000
			On Debt
			Interest Exp. 10,000,000
			  Cash 10,000,000
			On Swap
			Cash 1,000,000
			  Interest Exp. 1,000,000

3. Changes in market value of swap $4,500,000	No income recognition*	*Valuation of Swap* Net investment in swap 4,500,000 Gain on Swap 4,500,000	No income recognition

4. Swap termination	Cash 6,800,000
	  Premium on Liability 6,800,000
		Cash 6,800,000
		  Net Investment in Swap 6,800,000
			Cash 6,800,000
			  Premium on Liability 6,800,000

*Current practice does not recognize gains and losses on those swaps that are not treated as hedges and are, therefore, considered to be speculative.

but because the assets held are fixed-rate investments. In situation 2, the swap has transformed fixed-rate debt into floating-rate debt. The assets are still fixed-rate investments. Therefore, in situation 2, the swap is not a hedge because it reduces risk if rates decrease, but increases risk if rates increase. Bierman's analysis is thus consistent with the three-security approach suggested in this paper and implies that a swap does not automatically qualify for hedge accounting.

SUMMARY AND CONCLUSIONS

Table 2 summarizes the entries that would be made for different events in the life of a swap under current practice and the approach discussed in this paper.

Our conclusions are that swaps are executory contracts that meet the definition of an asset and a liability. As such, they are separate instruments and merit recognition in the financial statements since the penalty for failure to honor the contract may be severe. However, because the rules of offset are applicable to a swap contract, the practical effect is not to recognize an interest rate swap at inception. Thus, this approach yields the same answer as current practice (synthetic instruments accounting) but for different reasons.

If an interest rate swap qualifies as a hedge by satisfying all the criteria for hedge treatment listed in SFAS 80, then changes in its value should be deferred and reported as an adjustment of the carrying value of the hedged item. This would represent a departure from current practice in that swaps would have to satisfy more stringent criteria to qualify as hedges. Changes in the market value of swaps that do not qualify for hedge treatment should be included in income. At the termination of a swap that qualifies as a hedge, the gain or loss on termination should be deferred and amortized over the life of the hedged instrument. Gains and losses on termination of swaps that do not qualify as hedges would not be deferred.

Finally, disclosures about interest rate swaps should be increased significantly from current practice. Present disclosures are minimal and do not permit users of financial statements to assess the impact of interest rate swaps on a company's liquidity, solvency and exposure to interest rate risk.

Managing Off-Balance-Sheet Financing

Samuel Laibstain
Rider College (Retired)

David E. Stout
Villanova University

Larry P. Bailey
Rider College

Off-balance-sheet financing is the term used to describe the nonreporting by a company on its balance sheet of debt related to costs incurred (but likewise not reported), or ownership, or control, or at least the use of, cash or other assets.

Over the years, many different methods of achieving off-balance-sheet financing have been developed. All have one thing in common: They enable a company to leave certain obligations off the balance sheet without violating current GAAP.

Off-balance-sheet financing methods range from some that are clearly sanctioned by current GAAP to others whose accounting propriety is not so clear. Many off-balance-sheet financing methods rely on the careful structuring of or emphasis on:

1. Separate entity relationships, or
2. The executory nature of certain transactions where it can be argued that the actual receipt of goods or services has not yet occurred, or
3. Innovative financial instruments or arrangements.

In May 1986, the Financial Accounting Standards Board announced its Financial Instruments and Off-Balance-Sheet Financing project. A strong impetus for this project has been innovations in financial instruments. The FASB addressed related accounting and disclosure issues in its recently issued Exposure Draft on "Disclosures about Financial Instruments."

It has become evident that accounting for some transactions related to off-balance-sheet financing is in a state of disarray, with many companies accounting and disclosing differently for similar transactions. Furthermore, some of the authoritative pronouncements that could be helpful in these areas are contradictory in some respects, enabling companies to engage in a kind of "pick and choose" accounting.[1]

From *Management Accounting* (July 1988), pp. 32–39. Reprinted by permission of the Institute of Management Accountants. Copyright © 1988 by the Institute of Management Accountants, Montvale, NJ.

[1] For illustrations and elaboration, see John E. Stewart and Benjamin S. Neuhausen, "Financial Instruments and Transactions: The CPA's Newest Challenge," *Journal of Accountancy*, August 1986, pp. 102–112.

BENEFITS TO COMPANIES

Many companies are strongly motivated to keep liabilities off their balance sheets, especially when they can do so and still accomplish their operating and financing objectives at little or no additional cost or even at a lower cost. Some of the advantages of off-balance-sheet financing are:

- Improvement in the company's debt-to-equity ratio. For many companies this is important not only for borrowing purposes but also for reducing the perceived "riskiness" of their stock, thus affecting the market value of their stock favorably.
- Borrowing capacity. Sometimes, preventing liabilities from appearing on the balance sheet will enable a company to borrow more than it otherwise could, especially if there are contractual debt limit restrictions related to what actually appears on the company's balance sheet.
- Borrowing costs. A more attractive-looking financial position may result in lower borrowing costs. Lower borrowing costs also may result from certain off-balance-sheet financing methods such as project financing arrangements and interest rate swaps.
- Management compensation. To the extent that management compensation plans are tied to ratios or reported earnings that are affected favorably by off-balance-sheet financing, management benefits directly from the use of these arrangements.
- Risk-sharing and tax management. The use of limited partnership arrangements and in-substance debt defeasance provides means, respectively, for a company to spread the risk associated, for example, with research and development activities and to defer tax payments.

The main concerns about off-balance-sheet financing activities have to do with the basic goals of financial reporting—whether the information *not reported* on the financial statements lessens their usefulness. The amount of a company's debt could be reaching alarming proportions without users, even sophisticated users, being aware of it. In periods of economic downturn, companies with hidden debt may not be able to meet their *total obligations*, with the result that unsuspecting creditors and investors may suffer unanticipated losses.

SEPARATE ENTITY RELATIONSHIPS

Captive Finance Companies and Other Unconsolidated Subsidiaries

In the past, accounting practice almost invariably has excluded finance company subsidiaries (often referred to as "captive finance companies") from consolidations and has reported them by the equity method of accounting. The nonconsolidation of these companies was expressly sanctioned in the AICPA's Accounting Research Bulletin (ARB) 51, issued in 1959.

In the consolidated balance sheet, under the equity method, the various assets and liabilities of the unconsolidated subsidiary were not included with the various assets and liabilities of the parent company and its consolidated subsidiaries. Instead, the investment in the common stock of the unconsolidated subsidiary generally was reported in the consolidated balance sheet of the parent company as a single amount captioned "Investment in Unconsolidated Subsidiary" or similarly.

Thus, under the equity method, the liabilities of the unconsolidated finance subsidiary were not included in the consolidated financial statements. This omission was a form of off-balance-sheet financing.

Because the current ratios of finance subsidiaries are usually lower than normal current ratios reflected in consolidated balance sheets, the failure to consolidate the finance subsidiary has been not only a form of off-balance-sheet financing but also a method of improving the current ratio of the consolidated balance sheet. In addition, because the parent company's consolidated net worth is normally not affected by the use of the equity method instead of consolidation, the omission of the debt of the unconsolidated subsidiary from the consolidated balance sheet decreases the debt-to-equity ratio.

In compliance with APB Opinion 18, *The Equity Method of Accounting for Investments in Common Stock*, disclosures have been required that caused at least a summary of the various assets and liabilities of the finance subsidiary to be available in the notes to financial statements. Sometimes, data pertaining to two or more unconsolidated subsidiaries have been combined in these notes.

For many accountants, nonconsolidation of finance subsidiaries has not been just a way of keeping liabilities off the balance sheet. These accountants have regarded such nonconsolidation as good, sound accounting practice. They have argued that the nature of the assets and the liabilities, the nature of the revenues and expenses, and the magnitudes of the various financial and operating ratios pertaining to these subsidiaries are so different from most other types of companies that consolidating them would create confusion and misinformation rather than understanding about the parent company.

The opposing view has been that the differences between finance subsidiaries and other companies are not sufficient to invalidate the basic thrust of consolidating stated in ARB 51, which is that "consolidated financial statements are more meaningful than separate statements. . . ." and, furthermore, that confusion can be prevented by adequate disclosure.

In developing its continuing project on "The Reporting Entity, Including Consolidations and the Equity Method," the FASB clearly indicated in its December 1986 Exposure Draft, "Consolidation of All Majority-owned Subsidiaries," that it intended to require finance subsidiaries to be consolidated rather than reported by the equity method. In October 1987, the Board issued FAS 94 with the same title as the Exposure Draft. This Statement amends ARB 51 to require consolidation of virtually all majority-owned subsidiaries. Consolidation is required even if the subsidiary has "nonhomogeneous" operations, a large minority interest, or a foreign location.

Statement 94 requires that summarized information about the assets, liabilities, and results of operations (or separate statements) of previously unconsolidated majority-owned subsidiaries continue to be provided after those subsidiaries are consolidated. However, the FASB indicated in the Statement that its continuing project on the reporting entity, including consolidations and the equity method, will consider the question of what disaggregated information should be disclosed with consolidated financial statements in the future.

One effect of this required disclosure is that it enables users of financial statements to determine the effect on the consolidated financial statements of including the finance subsidiary (and other "nonhomogeneous" subsidiaries) in the consolidation. This should overcome most of the objections of people who believe that such consolidation will be confusing.

In our opinion, companies should be preparing pro-forma statements now to see what the effect on consolidating their finance subsidiaries will be on their consolidated financial statements. The same applies to insurance, real estate, and leasing subsidiaries that usually are not consolidated under present rules because FAS 94 calls for consolidating *all* majority-owned subsidiaries unless:

1. Control is temporary, or
2. Control does not rest with the majority owner, or
3. Control is significantly impeded by a foreign government's exchange restrictions, controls, or other uncertainties.

Some companies have "current GAAP" protective clauses in their loan agreements that state certain violations of their loan contracts that are due to changes to GAAP are not a reason for default. Others do not. Companies that do not have these protective clauses need to negotiate with their lenders to modify their contracts. Some companies that have state government contracts must meet certain solvency tests that relate to the content of their financial statements. Some of these companies may have to go back to the state and renegotiate the particulars of the solvency tests. For reasons such as these, the FASB has decided to delay the effective date of FAS 94 to fiscal years ending after December 31, 1988.

One of the oldest expressly sanctioned off-balance-sheet reporting methods (going all the way back to ARB 51) is about to disappear.

In the future, unless the FASB prohibits it, companies may resort to corporate joint ventures or even trusts in their efforts to create entities that will not have to be consolidated. In 1980, for example, Avis Rent-A-Car, at that time a subsidiary of Norton Simon, Inc., set up a trust to borrow money for the purchase of automobiles that were leased to Avis for its rental fleet. Because the trust was separate from both Avis and Norton Simon, neither company reported the debt incurred by the trust. As a result, Norton Simon, Inc. was able to keep $400 million of liabilities off its consolidated balance sheet.

Research and Development (R&D) Limited Partnerships

Funding for an enterprise's R&D costs can be arranged either through traditional debt or equity issues (through "in-house" sources) or through various arrangements with external parties. Although the form and legal structure of external arrangements can vary, one of the more popular arrangements in the recent past has been the R&D limited partnership. The U.S. Department of Commerce estimates that during the period 1981-84, over $2.3 billion of R&D funds were raised through this arrangement. Firms most likely to form R&D limited partnerships are those in the pharmaceutical, drug, medical, electronic, and computer (high technology) industries.[2]

The details of such R&D partnerships can be elaborate, but the essential ingredients of the arrangement are shown in Figure 1. A "sponsor firm" creates the off-balance-sheet financing of its R&D costs through the creation of a limited partnership in conjunction with a group of outside investors. The sponsor transfers rights to develop a certain "basic technology" to the partnership, but, as general partner, the sponsoring firm acts as manager (decision maker) for the partnership. Any successfully developed technology is purchased (or leased) by the sponsor firm from the partnership.

The R&D partnership generally contracts development work out to an R&D contractor (which can be, and often is, the sponsor firm itself). Payments to the R&D contractor generate tax losses by the partnership that are passed on to the partners. The partnership retains rights to any technology successfully developed by the contractor and generates income through the sale or lease of rights to any successfully developed technology. This income is subsequently passed through to the partners.

The R&D limited partnership form of funding avoids some of the financial statement effects of in-house funding. Because most sponsor firms disclose limited partnership details only through notes to financial statements, funds raised through the partnership do not appear as debt on the balance sheet *and* the partnership-funded R&D expenditures do not appear as expenses on the income statement of the sponsor firm. In the short run (specifically, until the sponsor firm must pick up expense resulting from the purchase or lease of any successfully developed technology), the limited partnership may be used by the sponsor firm to avoid the negative effects of in-house funding on leverage, interest coverage, and the unrestricted pool of retained earnings.

FAS 68 provides guidance for the accounting for R&D arrangements (limited partnerships and other forms as well). In the case of an R&D limited partnership, the key issue is whether or not a substantive and genuine transfer of financial risk from the sponsor firm to the outside partners has occurred. If the sponsor firm is obligated to repay any of the funds provided by the outside partners, regardless of the outcome of the research and devel-

[2] Terry Shevlin, "Taxes and Off-Balance Sheet Financing: Research and Development Limited Partnerships," *The Accounting Review*, July 1987, p. 491.

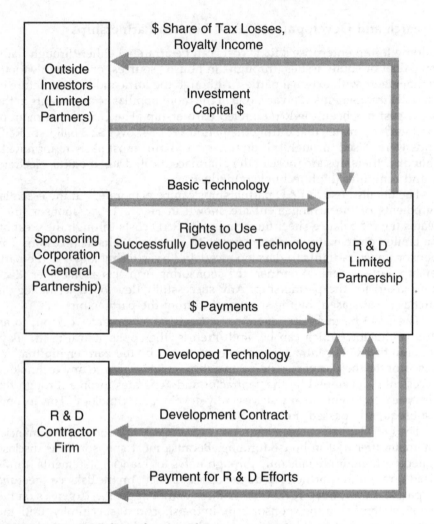

FIGURE 1 How R&D limited partnerships are arranged

opment, the financial risk is presumed not to have been transferred. In such case, the sponsor firm must estimate and recognize its liability to the outside partners. Thus, if properly structured (the sponsor firm does not guarantee funds contributed by the outside partners to the partnership), an R&D partnership agreement can result in an off-balance-sheet financing activity from the standpoint of the sponsor firm.

WHEN GOODS AND SERVICES ARE NOT RECEIVED

Business entities enter into a variety of executory contracts—contracts where the actual receipt of goods or services has not occurred—that often are not reflected in the firm's financial statements. Some accountants believe that many executory contracts result in off-balance-sheet financing.

Project Financing Arrangements

One type of contract that has gained popularity in recent years is a purchase agreement that enables a business entity to finance a capital project for long-term productive capacity without having to report the related obligation on its balance sheet. This transaction is a financing arrangement for both the supplier and the business entity. It is a supplier's financing arrangement in that the business entity either arranges financing for a supplier's facility or arranges financing for the cost of producing a supplier's goods or services. It is a financing arrangement for the business entity because the business, in effect, gains long-term productive capacity through the arrangement.

Two examples of purchase obligations for suppliers' financing arrangements are *take-or-pay contracts* and *throughput contracts*. A take-or-pay contract requires that a business entity (the purchaser) make payments for a minimum number of units of a supplier's goods or services, even if delivery is not taken by the purchaser. A throughput contract is similar in concept to a take-or-pay contract but calls for a service rather than a product to be provided by the facility involved, such as a pipeline or processing plant.

Take-or-pay contracts and throughput contracts become project financing arrangements for the supplier when the earnings from the contracts become the basic security for the lender who supplies funds for the construction of the supplier's capital project. For the business entity that needs the product or service of the facility and, therefore, initiated the project, the use of a take-or-pay contract or a throughput contract becomes an off-balance-sheet financing arrangement because the production *capacity* is acquired even though the facilities are not owned by the business. Furthermore, the related unconditional purchase obligation is not recorded as a liability because it represents an executory contract for future goods or services.

Alternatively, if the business entity had constructed its own facility, the facility as well as the related debt would have to be reported on the entity's balance sheet.

FAS 49, *Disclosure of Long-Term Obligations*, establishes disclosure requirements for certain unconditional purchase obligations, but the Statement does not require that the obligation and property rights related to the obligation be reported on a business entity's financial statements. As illustrated by the following example, disclosure requirements consist of a general description and term of the obligation, amounts purchased under the obligation for the current year, and amounts committed for each of the five succeeding years.

Standard Oil Company (1984 Statement)
The Company has contracted on a take-or-pay basis to purchase certain quantities of materials used in oil and gas producing activities. The contracted quantities are not in excess of anticipated requirements and will be acquired at prevailing market prices at the time of shipment. Minimum semi-annual

payments of $6.3 million are required through June 1993. The Company made purchases of $12.6 million in 1984 under this minimum obligation. The present value of future payments at December 13, 1984, was $62 million.

Lease Agreements

Leasing is a prevalent method of off-balance-sheet financing. Although a lease contract is an executory contract, the FASB requires that lease agreements that transfer substantially all of the benefits and risks related to ownership be capitalized. Specifically, a lessee must report on its balance sheet an obligation arising from a lease if any one of the following conditions exists:

- Ownership of the leased property is transferred to the lessee by the end of the lease term.
- A bargain purchase option is contained in the lease agreement.
- The lease term covers 75 percent or more of the economic life of the leased property (not applicable to lease contracts that begin during the last 25 percent of the economic life of the leased property).
- The present value of the minimum lease payments is 90 percent or more of the fair market value of the leased property (not applicable to lease contracts that begin during the last 25 percent of the economic life of the leased property).

The above criteria were specified in FAS 13, *Accounting for Leases,* but the application of this Statement to lease agreements has been more difficult and less successful than the FASB anticipated. The difficulty of prescribing which lease contract characteristics represent the transfer of substantially all benefits and risks of ownership is demonstrated by the fact that Statement 13 has been amended by nine more FASB Statements and explained further by six FASB Interpretations.

Lease transactions are a significant off-balance-sheet financing method because they often are specifically structured so as not to meet any of the criteria that would require capitalization on the lessee's financial statements. Strategies used to avoid lease capitalization follow.

- Do not include a clause in the lease agreement that transfers title to the lessee.
- Do not include a bargain purchase option in the lease agreement.
- Identify the lease term as less that 75 percent of the economic life of the leased property.
- Establish a high incremental borrowing rate so that the present value of minimum lease payments will be less than 90 percent of the fair value of the leased property at the inception of the lease.
- Lease property where the lease term begins during the last 25 percent of the economic life of the leased property.

An additional strategy illustrates the ingenuity of those companies that wish to avoid capitalization. According to FAS 13 [para. 5(j)(i)], "minimum lease payments" are defined as those payments made *by the lessee* and may include the guaranteed residual value of the leased property. Therefore, when the residual value of leased property is guaranteed by a third party, the present value of the residual value is not included in the definition of "minimum lease payments." This technique may be used to avoid the fourth criterion (90% rule) specified by Statement 13. Using a third-party guarantor (and, often, substantial residual values) frequently results in the lessee not capitalizing the lease whether or not the lessor accounts for the lease as an in-substance sale of the leased property.

Thus, lease arrangements remain a frequently used off-balance-sheet financing method.

CERTAIN FINANCIAL ARRANGEMENTS AND TRANSACTIONS

Receivables Sold with Recourse

Business enterprises can transfer their notes and accounts receivable to a third party for collection for the purpose of raising funds, avoiding collection problems associated with the receivables, or shifting collection risk to an outside party. Such receivable transfers are common to certain industries such as textile and clothing manufacturing. Transfers of receivables can be accomplished in one of three ways: assignment (a borrowing arrangement in which the receivables are pledged as collateral), factoring (sale of receivables without recourse), or transfer of receivables with recourse.

The accounting for the first two methods is straightforward. In an assignment of receivables, a liability is recorded on the balance sheet of the transferor for the amount of the promissory note (backed by the pledged receivables) given to the lender. In a factoring arrangement, an outside party "buys" certain accounts receivable on a nonrecourse basis from the transferor.

When a transfer of receivables is made with recourse (that is, when the transferee has the right to receive payment from the transferor in the event debtors fail to pay), a question exists as to whether the substance of the transaction is a *loan* secured by the receivables (as in an assignment) or a *sale* (as in a factoring arrangement). The distinction is an important one, for only in the former case is a liability entered on the balance sheet of the transferor.

Accounting for transfers of receivables with recourse is governed by FAS 77. This Statement specifies that the substance of the transaction is presumed to be a sale (in which case no liability is recorded on the balance sheet) if *all* of the following three conditions exist:

- Control of the future economic benefits of the receivables has been transferred to the transferee,
- The cost of the transferor's obligations under the recourse provisions (e.g., collection and repossession costs) is subject to reasonable estimation, and

• The transferee (buyer) cannot force the transferor to repurchase the receivables by means other than through the recourse provisions.

Proper structuring of the receivables transfer, therefore, is important. When the transfer is treated as a sale, no liability would be recorded on the balance sheet of the transferor. Details of the financial arrangement, however, would be presented in the notes to financial statements in a manner similar to the following note, which accompanied the 1985 consolidated balance sheet of Ingersoll-Rand Company:

Note 14 (in Part) Commitments and Contingencies
Receivables sold during 1985 with recourse amounted to $30,200,000. At December 31, 1985, $33,100,000 of receivables sold remained uncollected.

Any loss contingency relating to receivables sold with recourse would be disclosed according to the provisions of FAS 5, *Contingencies,* in a manner similar to the following note taken from the 1984 annual report of CPC International, Inc.:

Financing Arrangements—Short-Term (in part)
In several countries outside the United States, notes and accounts receivable are discounted with banks. The contingent liability under such arrangements amounted to $25.3 million in 1984, $44.5 million in 1983, and $36.8 million in 1982 at the respective year ends.

Interest Rate Swaps

The innovation that has occurred in financial instruments in recent years has been due primarily to deregulation and competition in financial markets, advances in computer and telecommunications technology, unprecedented volatility in foreign exchange and interest rates, and tax law changes. While many of these matters concern financial institutions primarily, innovative financial instruments and transactions have raised financial reporting issues for all types of business enterprises.

One type of financial transaction that may occur in virtually any type of business is an interest rate swap. The most basic type of interest rate swap involves two companies, both with outstanding debt. One has fixed rate of interest on its debt, and the other has a variable rate tied to some interest index such as the bank prime rate. For various reasons, these companies may consider it beneficial to exchange interest rates. Almost always, these exchanges are made through a financial intermediary. Sometimes one or both companies may find themselves obligated to pay amounts substantially in excess of the interest cost elements reflected in their balance sheets or in their notes to financial statements. The present value of these additional interest costs, especially if such amounts are not viewed as executory costs, is considered by some to be a form of debt whose omission from the balance sheet is a form of off-balance-sheet financing.

In-Substance Defeasance of Debt

There are several ways business entities can extinguish long-term debt before scheduled maturity. Bonds can be refinanced, redeemed, or converted. In each case, the original bond issue is retired in the transaction. One of the more controversial ways to extinguish debt before scheduled maturity, however, is through "in-substance defeasance."[3] Unlike refinancing, redemption, or conversion, in-substance defeasance does not involve a legal *retirement* of the original debt issue.

With an in-substance defeasance, a business entity can extinguish certain types of debt (specifically, debt with specified maturities and fixed payment schedules, including capitalized lease obligations) by transferring "risk-free" assets (cash and/or certain government securities) to an irrevocable trust. In turn, the trust uses these assets *solely* to service the principal and interest obligations as specified in the original debt agreement. In such a situation, FAS 76, *Extinguishment of Debt*, permits the transfer of assets to be treated as a debt extinguishment even though the debtor is not legally released from its liability under provisions of the debt covenant. Thus, the debt is removed from the balance sheet without actually being retired. In this sense, in-substance defeasance represents a form of off-balance-sheet financing.

A company may choose to extinguish debt through an in-substance defeasance rather than an actual retirement of the liability for a number of reasons. Finance considerations may be of primary importance: call provisions on the original debt may be costly, transaction costs (for example, broker's fees for a bond redemption) may be prohibitive, or current market conditions may not be favorable (in the case of a refinancing). Equally important, and sometimes more important, removal of the debt from the balance sheet has a beneficial impact on the company's debt-to-equity and return-on-assets ratios. In the case of a gain realized on the in-substance defeasance, earnings per share for the current period are increased as well.[4]

There may be secondary reasons for an in-substance defeasance. For example, the in-substance defeasance of debt maturing within the coming year usually improves the company's current ratio. In addition, there may be tax motivations because the taxes on any gain realized are deferred until the debt actually matures. Also, companies can use in-substance defeasance to rid themselves of certain onerous debt covenants. By receiving the additional security of government bonds placed in an irrevocable trust, debt holders may be more willing to remove or modify restrictive covenants. Finally, in-substance defeasance can be used to help avert a hostile takeover. A company with excessive cash can be an acquisition target. In some cases, one way to

---

[3] The term "defeasance" connotes the debtor's release from *legal* liability.

[4] FAS 4, "Reporting Gains and Losses from Extinguishment of Debt," requires that any difference between the carrying value of the assets placed in trust and the extinguished debt be reported as an extraordinary gain or loss.

make the acquisition less attractive would be to use such cash to effect an in-substance debt defeasance. The associated increase in earnings (which may result) can make shareholders less inclined to sell their shares in a takeover attempt.

Disclosure requirements for in-substance defeasances are minimal. Beyond the information the FASB requires to be disclosed in the notes to financial statements, little information is available to investors and creditors to assist them in evaluating the impact of these transactions on their risk and return.[5] All that is currently required for external reporting purposes is a general description of the transaction and specification of the amount of debt considered to be extinguished as of the balance sheet date.

TWO SPECIAL CASES

Certain Post-Employment Benefits

Many employers provide benefits to employees that include life insurance and health care insurance coverage after retirement. Such benefits can represent a significant liability for a business entity. For the *Fortune* 500 companies, this liability for future benefits has been estimated to be 150 percent of total assets.[6] But, under current accounting standards, the obligation related to these future post-employment benefits does not have to be reflected on an employer's balance sheet.

Post-employment insurance and health care insurance benefits are earned by an employee during the periods in which that employee works for an employer. From a conceptual perspective, post-employment insurance and health care insurance benefits are similar to pension benefits; however, the accounting for these post-employment benefits, unlike the accounting for pension cost, is not standardized.

The lack of standardization arises because accounting standards and concepts established by FAS 87, *Employers' Accounting for Pensions*, are specified as not applicable to plans that provide only life insurance or health care insurance benefits to retirees. In addition, Statement 87 stipulates that it does not apply to post-employment health care benefits provided by a pension plan.

Thus, under current GAAP, post-employment insurance and health care insurance benefits can be accounted for in much the same way as pension cost in an employer's financial statements. They also can be accounted for on a pay-as-you-go (cash) basis. When post-employment insurance and health care insurance benefits are accounted for on a cash basis (by far, the prevalent method at the present time) or in some other manner that does not reflect the full accrual concept, the accounting method employed becomes a method of off-balance-sheet financing.

[5] David E. Mielke and James Seifert, "A Survey on the Effects of Defeasing Debt," *Journal of Accounting, Auditing and Finance*, Winter 1987, pp. 65–78.

[6] Thomas G. Nelson, "Post-retirement Benefits: The Tip of a Financial Iceberg," *Management Accounting*, January 1987, p. 53.

The FASB has the accounting for post-retirement benefits on its agenda, but until standards are promulgated, the liability arising from these benefit plans is not being reported as a liability in many companies' financial statements.* Rather, as illustrated by the example below, disclosure of these commitments is to be found in the notes that accompany the financial statements.

Ex-Cell-O Corporation (1985 Statement)
In addition to pension benefits, the company also provides certain health care and life insurance benefits for both active and retired North American employees. During 1985, there were 14,473 active and 4,738 retired employees eligible to receive these benefits. The costs of these benefits, which amounted to $35,720,000 in 1985, are charged to expense as applicable claims or insurance premiums are paid.

In recent years, through analysis and projections, a large number of companies have come to realize the magnitude of their commitment in this area. All companies should seriously consider making such analyses. Many will be unpleasantly surprised by the size of their commitment. Some companies are already taking steps to reduce this commitment in the future.

Defined Benefit Pension Plans

FAS 87, issued in 1985, standardized the accounting methods for defined benefit pension plans. However, certain accounting methods promulgated by that Statement continue to result in the nonreporting of a portion of the pension liability.

Prior service cost occurs when an employer initially adopts or amends its pension plan so that benefits are earned by employees for periods prior to the adoption or amendment date of the plan. Generally, prior service costs significantly increase the present value of pension benefits earned to the date of the adoption or amendment.

Nonetheless, the FASB has taken the position that prior service costs that arise in a particular accounting period should not be fully recognized as a liability, expense, or deferred charge, in that period. Prior service costs must be amortized over the remaining future service periods of those employees for whose benefit the prior service pension costs were incurred. The result is that often a significant liability for prior service cost is not shown as an obligation of the employer.

Although the FASB did not require the immediate recognition of a liability resulting from prior service cost, there is an exception to this approach called "minimum liability rule." In general, a minimum liability must be recorded when the pension plan's "accumulated benefit obligation" is greater than the fair value of the pension plan's assets. When this occurs, the minimum liability is recorded with an adjustment equal to the minimum liability (the

---

* Editors' Note: Accounting for postretirement benefits is the subject of FASB Statement No. 106, *Employers' Accounting for Postretirement Benefits Other Than Pensions,* issued in December 1990. See Chapter 12 for a discussion.

difference between the accumulated benefit obligation and the fair value of
the plan's assets) less any pension liability or plus any prepaid pension
amounts already reflected in the company's accounts.

Even when a minimum liability must be recognized, there is an understatement of the liability because the computation does not take into consideration future salary increases in determining the present value of future
benefit payments—the accumulated benefit obligation. In this respect, the
minimum liability computation is inconsistent with the general philosophy
reflected in FAS 87: that the computation of pension cost should take into
consideration future compensation levels.

Thus, even with the recent adoption of FAS 87, pension plans remain an
area in which a business may engage in off-balance-sheet financing. It should
be noted, however, that the FASB has served notice (Paragraph 5, Statement
87) that pension accounting is still in a transitional stage. Nevertheless, given
the long struggle between the FASB and the many companies that resisted
the FASB's initial suggestion that the entire liability for prior service costs be
recorded at the time of their incurrence (and expensed over the remaining
service lives of the employees), we believe that it is unlikely that this accounting method will be changed in the foreseeable future.

OPPORTUNITY AND RESPONSIBILITY

Management must be aware of the various forms of off-balance-sheet financing and where to look for information related to these transactions in company financial statements. As we have shown, most of the information is
disclosed through notes accompanying the financial statements.

Off-balance-sheet financing offers many advantages, and many companies will continue to take advantage of the opportunities it offers. In fact, they
would be foolish not to. This places an added burden on managers and
management accountants to know what off-balance-sheet financing methods
are available and under what circumstances their company should consider
using them. Also, companies must be certain that adequate disclosures of
these activities are made so their financial statements are not misleading.

The Challenges of Hedge Accounting

John E. Stewart
Arthur Andersen & Co.

Increased volatility of interest rates, foreign exchange rates and other prices
has elevated hedging to an important business necessity. A tremendous
variety of hedging products has sprung up in recent years to meet this need.

From *Journal of Accountancy* (November 1989), pp. 48–50, 52, 54, 56. Reprinted by permission of
the American Institute of Certified Public Accountants, Inc. Copyright © 1989 by the American
Institute of Certified Public Accountants, Inc. Opinions of the authors are their own and do not
necessarily reflect policies of the AICPA.

How should these products be reported in financial statements? Because traditional guidance fails to answer this question satisfactorily, the challenge of hedge accounting is here. This article describes hedging and why it's important, some of the financial reporting issues involved, the accounting profession's response and the significant problems that exist.

WHAT'S HEDGING AND WHY IS IT IMPORTANT?

Hedging is a tool for transferring price, foreign exchange or interest rate *risk* from those wishing to avoid it to those willing to assume it. Specifically, hedging is the act of taking a position in a hedging instrument—such as in the futures, forward, options or swap market—opposite to an actual position that's exposed to risk. (See exhibit 1 for definitions.) Hedging reduces the risk of loss from adverse price or rate fluctuations that may occur in owning or owing items over a period of time. Conversely, hedging may limit the gain from favorable changes. Among the items hedged are

- Owned assets including financial instruments or commodities such as grains, metals and livestock.
- Existing liabilities such as foreign currency-denominated borrowings.
- Contractual (firm) commitments to buy or sell items such as commodities or financial instruments.
- Anticipated, but not contractually committed, transactions such as purchases or sales or the issuance or refinancing of debt.

EXHIBIT 1 Definitions of the basic hedging instruments

Forward	An agreement between two parties to exchange specific items—for example, two currencies—at a specified future date and at a specified price.
Futures	An exchange-traded contract for future delivery of a standardized quantity of an item at a specified future date and at a specified price. Changes in the market value of the futures contract are settled in cash daily.
Option	A contract allowing, but *not* requiring, its holder to buy (call) or sell (put) a specific or standard item at a specified price during a specified time period or on a specified date. Options may trade on exchanges or over-the-counter.
Interest rate swap	An agreement between two parties to exchange one interest stream—for example, floating rate—for another—fixed rate—based on a contractual or notional amount. No principal changes hands.
Currency swap	An exchange of two currencies according to an agreement to re-exchange the currencies at the same rate at a specified future date. During the term of the agreement, exchanges of interest payments denominated in the respective currencies also may occur.

Volatility in interest rates, foreign exchange rates and other prices has created a demand for instruments that could help borrowers, lenders, financial institutions, manufacturers and other industrial companies reduce their risks—risks that if not properly managed could threaten the very survival of their companies. This volatility—combined with increased internationalization, competition, global deregulation, technology, sophisticated analysis techniques and tax and regulatory changes—has promoted an almost unbelievable explosion of innovative financial instruments that may be used as hedging vehicles.

WHY THE NEED FOR HEDGE ACCOUNTING

The need for some special accounting for hedges arises in part because of our historical cost, transaction-based accounting system. Under that system, the effects of price or interest rate changes on many existing assets and liabilities aren't recognized in income until realized in a later transaction. If the gains or losses on the underlying assets or liabilities are reported in a time period different from that of the losses and gains reported on the instruments used to hedge these assets and liabilities, the accounting result could be reporting related, offsetting accounts in income during different reporting periods. This reporting would tend to cause fluctuations in income, implying increased exposure to price or interest rate changes when, in fact, the exposure has been reduced.

A somewhat similar result would occur if gains or losses were recognized currently for instruments entered into to hedge firmly committed or probable transactions *not* involving existing assets or liabilities. Under traditional accounting, the unrealized gains or losses associated with these future transactions may not be reflected in the financial statements until realized.

The accounting challenges are to develop special or different accounting (hedge accounting) that addresses these issues and then to specify the conditions under which this hedge accounting is appropriate.

THE FASB'S RESPONSE

How have accounting standard setters, primarily the Financial Accounting Standards Board, responded to the challenge? In general, the standard setters' response has been slow, ad hoc and inconsistent; but there's some hope in the long run with the FASB's financial instruments project.

In 1981, the FASB issued Statement no. 52, *Foreign Currency Translation*, which deals with hedge accounting for foreign exchange forwards, futures and currency swaps. In 1984, it issued Statement no. 80, *Accounting for Futures Contracts*, which addresses all types of exchange-traded futures, except foreign currency.

However, problems persist. *For many of the new instruments and transactions, the problem is a total absence of accounting guidance.* Not covered are

- Interest rate forwards.
- Almost all types of options.
- Interest rate swaps.

Interest rate swaps were born in the early 1980s and the market has grown to over $1 trillion. The accounting standards say virtually nothing about how either users or market makers should account for these swaps. Similarly, the market for options of all types—exchange-traded and over-the-counter—on commodities, foreign currencies, financial instruments and futures contracts has soared in recent years, but existing accounting standards address only accounting for options on common stocks (FASB Statement no. 12, *Accounting for Certain Marketable Securities*).

A second problem is that the standards promulgated are *inconsistent.* To the extent instruments covered by existing standards seem analogous to the new financial instruments, the inconsistencies create uncertainty about which rules to follow.

WHAT'S HEDGE ACCOUNTING?

Both Statements nos. 52 and 80 provide for hedge accounting. The underlying broad concept of both statements is to achieve some sort of symmetry between accounting for the hedging instrument and the assets, liabilities or transactions being hedged. If specified criteria are met (reduction of risk, designation, effectiveness and so forth), gains or losses on the hedging instrument are recorded at the same time and in the same manner as the losses or gains on the hedged item. If the losses or gains on the item being hedged are *deferred*—for example, assets carried at cost or a future transaction—then the gains or losses on the hedging instrument are *deferred* as part of the carrying amount of the hedged item rather than recognized currently in income.

Similarly, if unrealized changes in the market price of the hedged item are included in income or in a separate component of stockholders' equity (for example, net investment in a foreign entity), gains or losses on the hedging instrument also are recognized as they occur in income or in the separate component of stockholders' equity—thus providing a match.

If the hedging instrument doesn't meet the specified criteria for hedge accounting, it's accounted for separately at value with gains and losses recorded currently in income.

Despite the similarities in concept between Statements nos. 52 and 80, important inconsistencies exist. These inconsistencies relate both to the conditions necessary to qualify for hedge accounting and the application of hedge accounting when the criteria actually are met.

EXHIBIT 2 Hedge accounting comparison

	FASB 52[1]	FASB 80[2]	AICPA issues paper on options[3]	Interest rate swaps in practice[4]
Hedge accounting criteria:				
Designation as a hedge	Yes	Yes	Yes	Frequently but not always
Risk reduction basis	Transaction	Enterprise	Transaction	Sometimes
Degree of correlation	Not explicit	High	High	Matching
Ongoing assessment	Not explicit	Yes	Yes	Usually
Hedge of anticipated transaction (not firm commitment)	No	Yes	Yes	Yes
Cross hedges	Usually not	Yes	Yes	Yes
Hedge of an asset carried at cost	N/A	Yes	No	Yes
Application of accounting:				
Split accounting for inherent elements (premium or discount)	Yes	Usually not	Yes	Frequently not necessary
Amortization of premium on hedge of net investment in a foreign entity	Income or equity	N/A	Income	N/A
Cap on deferred losses to fair value	No	No	Yes	No
Accounting if hedge criteria not met	Formula value	Market	Market	Market or lower of cost or market

[1] Statement no. 52 covers foreign exchange forwards, futures and swaps—but not options explicitly.

[2] Statement no. 80 covers all (and only) exchange-traded futures except foreign currency futures, which are covered by Statement no. 52.

[3] The recommendations included in the AICPA issues paper cover all options (whether or not exchange traded). These recommendations do *not* constitute authoritative generally accepted accounting principles. The chart covers only purchased options.

[4] There's no authoritative GAAP for interest rate swaps, although the emerging issues task force has dealt with several swap issues. Existing practice for interest rate swaps is not uniform. Summarized here is the author's perception of practice. The federal banking regulators are working on a release that would provide guidance for regulatory accounting.

434

CONFLICTS BETWEEN STATEMENTS nos. 52 AND 80

Exhibit 2 compares the provisions of Statements nos. 52 and 80 in several key areas. Also included are comparisons with the advisory conclusions in the American Institute of CPAs' issues paper, *Accounting for Options*, and interest rate swap accounting as applied in practice. It's apparent many conflicts exist, some of which are discussed below.

Risk Reduction

One criterion for hedge accounting is that hedging instruments must reduce exposure to risk. The statements, however, take different approaches to the determination of risk reduction. Statement no. 80 requires an *enterprise approach:* A futures contract should reduce the enterprise's overall exposure to risk. If the enterprise's other positions already offset the exposure the futures contract is supposed to hedge, the contract won't qualify for hedge accounting. Statement no. 52 provides for a *transaction approach:* Foreign exchange forward contracts or futures need only hedge particular transactions, even if other positions already offset the exposure.

Hedges of Anticipated Transactions

Statement no. 80 allows the designation of futures contracts as an accounting hedge of an anticipated probable transaction (a transaction that an enterprise expects but isn't obligated to carry out in the normal course of business). Statement no. 52 forbids designating foreign currency forward and futures contracts as an accounting hedge of an anticipated foreign currency transaction.

Cross Hedging

Cross hedging involves hedging an exposure, such as commercial paper, with an instrument whose underlying basis differs from the item being hedged, such as U.S. Treasury bill futures. Statement no. 80 permits cross hedging if a clear economic relationship exists and high correlation is probable. Statement no. 52, however, usually does not permit using one currency to hedge another.

Split Accounting for Inherent Elements
(premium or discount)

Futures and forward contracts incorporate a premium or discount representing the difference between the current spot price of the underlying commodity or instrument and the future or forward price. This difference reflects, among other things, the time value of money. For futures and forward contracts accounted for as hedges, Statement no. 52 requires the premium or discount be accounted for separately from the changes in value of the futures or forward contract (split accounting). Statement no. 80 forbids separate accounting for the premium or discount except in rare circumstances.

Valuation of Speculative (nonhedge) Positions

Statement no. 80 requires futures positions that don't qualify for hedge accounting to be valued at market value. However, Statement no. 52 provides for a formula value that ignores the time value of money. (Note that the FASB's emerging issues task force [EITF] reached a consensus in Issue no. 87-2, *Net Present Value Method of Valuing Speculative Foreign Exchange Contracts*, which says that discounting is allowed but not required in applying Statement no. 52.)

FILLING THE VOID

As discussed above, many hedging instruments aren't covered by authoritative generally accepted accounting principles—that is, standards issued by the FASB or its predecessors. To fill the void until the FASB addresses hedge accounting as part of its financial instruments project, accountants have to improvise. They can do this by looking to nonauthoritative guidance and by drawing analogies to existing GAAP. Some of the sources of help and problems in analogizing are described below.

OTHER SOURCES OF INFORMATION

In 1986, the AICPA accounting standards executive committee (AcSEC) finalized an issues paper, *Accounting for Options*, whose conclusions incorporate many of the concepts of FASB Statements nos. 52 and 80. However, because the FASB statements' conclusions are inconsistent, AcSEC had to make choices and develop some new ideas along the way, in some cases *adding* to the inconsistencies. (See JofA, Jan. 87, page 87, for how options work and AcSEC's conclusions.)

The options issues paper has been submitted to the FASB. Although not authoritative, it represents a source of information for practitioners. However, because some of the issues paper's conclusions are inconsistent with existing authoritative literature (for example, Statement no. 12), care must be taken in using it.

Other sources of hedge accounting information CPAs may find useful include

- Another AICPA issues paper published in 1980, *Accounting for Forward Placement and Standby Commitments and Interest Rate Futures Contracts*.
- Articles describing how hedging products work, the accounting issues and current practice. An example is the article on interest rate swaps in the September 1985 *Journal of Accountancy* (page 63).

Further, the EITF has dealt with several hedging issues (see exhibit 3), but the solutions sometimes have been ad hoc, and in some cases no consensus was reached.

THE PROBLEMS OF INCONSISTENCIES

Despite the fact that some information exists, the inconsistencies among existing FASB standards, AICPA recommendations and EITF consensuses make it difficult to address accounting for new products by analogy. The result is uncertainty about which accounting should be followed. It's particularly difficult and confusing to resolve practice problems because the instruments—futures, forwards, options, swaps and so forth—have similarities. Here are some accounting dilemmas:

What Does a CPA Do with Foreign Currency Options?

Does the CPA

- Follow Statement no. 52 and *not* permit hedge accounting for anticipated probable (but not firmly committed) transactions?
- Follow the more recent Statement no. 80 and the AICPA options issues paper and permit it?

Statement no. 52 does not mention options partially because it was written before options became a factor in the market. And even if anticipatory hedge accounting is acceptable for foreign currency options, what does the CPA do with instruments such as foreign exchange participating forwards and range forward contracts that have elements of both options and forwards? Statement no. 52 clearly prohibits anticipatory hedge accounting for foreign currency forwards, futures and swaps.

EXHIBIT 3 Hedging issues dealt with by the Emerging Issues Task Force

Issue no.	Topic
84–7	Termination of Interest Rate Swaps
84–14	Deferred Interest Rate Setting
84–36	Interest Rate Swap Transactions
85–6	Futures Implementation Questions
86–25	Offsetting Foreign Currency Swaps
86–26	Using Forward Commitments as a Surrogate for Deferred Rate Setting
86–28	Accounting Implications of Indexed Debt Instruments
86–34	Futures Contracts Used as Hedges of Anticipated Reverse Repurchase Transactions
87–1	Deferral Accounting for Cash Securities That Are Used to Hedge Rate or Price Risk
87–2	Net Present Value Method of Valuing Speculative Foreign Exchange Contracts
87–26	Hedging of Foreign Currency Exposure with a Tandem Currency
88–8	Mortgage Swaps
88–18	Sales of Future Revenues

What Does the CPA Do with Interest Rate Forwards or Interest Rate Swaps?

Does he or she follow

- The designation and enterprise-risk-reduction criteria of Statement no. 80?
- The designation and transaction-risk-reduction criteria of Statement no. 52 and the AICPA recommendations?
- None of these?

As indicated in exhibit 2, practice is not uniform. What about an option on an interest rate swap? What about hedging anticipated, but not firmly committed, transactions with interest rate swaps?

What Does a CPA Do with Synthetic Instruments?

Does the CPA

- Analogize to existing hedge accounting criteria and rules?
- If so, which ones?
- Simply account for the instrument?

Synthetic instruments are created in several ways. For example, an entity issues fixed-rate debt to creditors and at the same time enters into an interest rate swap with a third party. It receives fixed-rate interest and pays floating-rate interest on a notional principal amount that equals the principal on the debt. The combination of the debt and the swap converts fixed-rate debt to "synthetic" floating-rate debt.

Synthetic instrument accounting is accounting for that which the synthetic instrument is meant to replicate—in this case, floating-rate debt. Other examples of synthetic instruments include

- Callable debt synthetically changed to noncallable debt through writing (selling) an option on an interest rate swap.
- Synthetic puttable debt created from callable debt.
- Synthetically shortening the mandatory maturity of callable debt.
- Synthetic yen debt created from dollar-denominated debt and a currency swap.

All of these synthetic instruments behave like basic identifiable financial instruments in the market place, but they're created synthetically because the total cost is perceived to be lower. Synthetic instrument accounting is frequently used in practice. Sometimes the same results could be achieved by applying hedge accounting, but in other cases the criteria for hedge accounting aren't satisfied. For example, the synthetic instrument may well *increase* transaction and enterprise risk.

What Does the CPA Do with Hedging Using Cash Instruments?

Statement no. 52 permits hedge accounting when the *hedging instrument* is a cash instrument, such as foreign currency-denominated debt or time deposits. However, opinions differ about the acceptability of hedge accounting using cash instruments in other areas, such as U.S. government bonds. In Issue no. 87-1, *Deferral Accounting for Cash Securities That Are Used to Hedge Rate or Price Risk*, the EITF did not reach a consensus, although a majority of the EITF members would prohibit hedge accounting in these other areas.

Compounding Problems

Further compounding the problem are some aspects of Statements nos. 52 and 80 that many believe just don't make sense—that is, they don't follow economic substance:

- The prohibition of anticipatory hedge accounting in Statement no. 52.
- The general absence of split accounting for futures in Statement no. 80.
- The effective prohibition of cross hedging (tandem currency) in Statement no. 52.
- The procedures in Statement no. 52 for valuing speculative foreign exchange positions at formula rather than market value.

HOPE FOR RESOLUTION

There's hope for a resolution of these practice problems, but probably not in the near term. That hope is the FASB's project on financial instruments, which includes one segment addressing instruments that transfer risk.

I believe the goals of that project should be to

- Create a level playing field by developing a conceptually based approach that will account for similar instruments similarly and different instruments differently.
- Achieve accounting consistent with economic substance.
- Modernize and generalize accounting standards to deal with new products.
- Address the needs of both product users and market makers.

Any solution should be able to handle existing instruments as well as instruments that will be developed in the future. Many of the new hedging products will be permutations of existing products.

It's worth noting again that the need for hedge accounting is in part—but not completely—driven by our historical cost system. The more *market value accounting* is used for existing assets and liabilities (and that issue also is part of the FASB's project), the less need for special hedge accounting rules. But until the FASB issues new, comprehensive standards, CPAs will have to solve problems by analogizing to existing literature and current practices and by relying on the EITF.

In-Substance Defeasance: Costs, Yes; Benefits, No

Bruce R. Gaumnitz
University of Cincinnati

Joel E. Thompson
Northern Michigan University

As a part of a project addressing financial instruments and off-balance sheet financing issues, the Financial Accounting Standards Board will have an opportunity to reverse its position in Statement no. 76, *Extinguishment of Debt*. In this statement, the FASB permits special accounting treatment for a transaction known as "in-substance defeasance."

In such a transaction, the reporting entity irrevocably places in trust some cash and U.S. government securities (or securities guaranteed or backed by the U.S. government) whose amounts and timing will cover the interest and principal payments of a specified debt of the reporting entity. This accounting treatment removes both the assets placed in trust and the debt from the balance sheet and recognizes the difference between the book value of the assets placed in trust and the book value of the debt, net of administrative costs, as an extraordinary gain or loss when the irrevocable transfer is made.

We believe this practice permits potentially unacceptable costs and provides no discernible benefits. Unless compelling new evidence arises regarding the benefits of in-substance defeasance, therefore, the practice should be halted and the assets and liabilities that have been affected should be reinstated on the balance sheets.

HOW IT WORKS

Assume that on January 2, 1971, a corporation issued 20-year 6 percent bonds at par, with a total principal amount of $1 million and with interest payable semiannually on July 1 and January 2. The management of the corporation did an in-substance defeasance transaction on January 2, 1986, by (1) paying $845,562 for U.S. government securities that at that price yielded 10 percent to maturity and whose due dates and amounts match those of the debt's interest and principal payments and by (2) irrevocably placing the securities in a trust designated to meet the interest and principal payments of the debt. The corporation's gain before tax is $154,438 ($1 million minus $845,562), assuming no administrative costs.

Provided the debt wasn't incurred at the same time the in-substance defeasance transaction was completed, there is no restriction on the source of the trust investment. Instead of using available cash, investment funds could be borrowed or existing qualified securities could be used.

Thus, for example, if the company borrows $845,562 at 12 percent a year, the gain of $154,438 is still recognized, but the effect of the treatment on the balance sheet merely reduces reported liabilities by $154,438. Reported assets aren't affected. In any case, the trust assets aren't included in the balance sheet. Notes describing the in-substance defeasance transaction and the amount of debt considered extinguished are provided in the financial statements in the period in which the transaction occurred and in subsequent periods as long as the debt is unpaid.

A DIFFICULT DECISION

FASB Statement no. 76 was issued as a result of the FASB's review of the American Institute of CPAs' Statement of Position no. 78-5, *Accounting for Advance Refundings of Tax-Exempt Debt*. The FASB statement required two exposure drafts and passed with only four affirmative votes.

In the first (1982) exposure draft, in-substance defeasance wasn't considered in an extinguishment of debt. In the second (1983) exposure draft, the FASB reversed its position and considered in-substance defeasance an extinguishment of virtually any debt instrument. This reversed position became Statement no. 76.

EQUIVOCAL DEFINITIONS

The board justified its final decision principally in terms of the definitions of "assets" and "liabilities" given in Concepts Statement no. 3, *Elements of Financial Statements of Business Enterprises*. An FASB *Status Report* of 1983 said that in-substance defeasance was permitted because " . . . the Board believes that by placing the risk-free assets irrevocably in trust solely for paying the debt, the debtor no longer has 'a probable future sacrifice of economic benefits,' which is the general definition of a liability for accounting purposes."

But three members of the board dissented to Statement no. 76, claiming that the debt " . . . continues to be a liability of the original debtor until satisfied by payment or by agreement of the creditor that the debtor is no longer the primary obligor." In addition, they claimed that, "though dedicated to a single purpose, assets in the trust continue to be assets (that is, probable future economic benefits) of the debtor until applied to payment of the debt" and that "for a debt to be satisfied, the creditor must be satisfied."

The asset and liability definitions are so broad that they can reasonably be interpreted as support for conflicting positions. This is a consequence of attempting to cover a wide variety of circumstances. Their equivocal nature, however, renders them almost useless in deciding how to account for in-substance defeasances.

This is unfortunate because it was precisely to help make close calls that the FASB's conceptual framework project, including the definitions of the financial statement elements, was started in the first place. When the definitions provided in Concepts Statement no. 3 aren't sufficiently concrete and specific to be helpful in these critical situations, decisions have to be based on such factors as management's stewardship, accountants' legal liability and accounting theory.

MANAGEMENT WEAKENED

It isn't clear whether the in-substance defeasance provisions of Statement no. 76 help foster effective management stewardship. In fact, they may do just the opposite. In an in-substance defeasance, the securities must be irrevocably placed in a trust. Thus, these securities can neither be used to help finance future investment opportunities nor be recovered in the event of a financial emergency.

This condition is also undesirable from the stockholders' point of view. Simply by holding the securities and not placing them in an irrevocable trust, they could still be used to service the debt. Management could then use the assets in other ways if holding them was no longer advisable or if an emergency occurred. Buying riskless securities and squirreling them away solely to pay designated debt only increases the reporting entity's risk and provides no compensating benefits.

Also, an in-substance defeasance causes the reporting entity to incur opportunity costs. Irrevocable long-term commitment of funds to riskless assets usually is poor management. Unless they provide the highest rate of return that management expects to achieve while bearing a reasonable amount of risk, other investments are preferable.

Moreover, if returns on riskless investments are the most attractive alternative for management, then that management isn't needed. The corporation should be liquidated, allowing the former stockholders to save considerable costs by investing directly in riskless assets.

Thus, the only beneficiaries of in-substance defeasance transactions are the debt holders, who may have their security enhanced but give up nothing in return.

ACCOUNTANTS' LIABILITY

What if the trustee holding the government securities proves to be unreliable and the securities are lost, stolen, destroyed or misappropriated? Examples of major defaults involving government securities include Drysdale Government Securities, Lombard-Wall, Lion Capital Associates and ESM. Should the trustee default, the liability would have to be reinstated on the balance sheet because the original debtor remains primarily liable.

The extent of an accountant's liability in the event of defalcations or bankruptcy has yet to be established. If the debt has to be reinstated, the accountant may face legal consequences. Investors who relied on audited financial statements that excluded the liability could suffer substantial losses that might be attributed to the accountant's actions. If it is held that financial statements excluding the liability aren't sound, a CPA's liability could be substantial.

Accounting principles aren't sacrosanct. A defense based on conformity with an FASB statement might not hold up. The AICPA Code of Professional Ethics Rule 203—Accounting Principles requires adherence to an FASB statement only if doing so doesn't cause financial statements to be misleading. How the courts would resolve this issue is an open question.

Another ambiguity involves the bankruptcy of the debtor corporation. The courts may not accept the FASB's definition of "liabilities" or its application in this area and may hold that the debt hasn't been extinguished. The courts might be more impressed with the terms of the contract, under which the debtor remains the primary obligor, and return both the debt and the assets to the debtor's balance sheet. CPAs might then be liable to creditors who relied on representations that their receivables were secured. It is still unclear whether the courts would uphold the irrevocable nature of the trust or would set it aside under the Bankruptcy Act.

By adopting Statement no. 76 amid these unresolved issues, the FASB appears to have exposed CPAs to potentially large liabilities to which they wouldn't have been exposed if both the assets and the liabilities had been left on the balance sheet. In addition, if the FASB's position in Statement no. 76 is reversed by the courts, support would go to those who believe that setting accounting standards should be a governmental activity, not left to the private sector.

All these potential problems could have been avoided had the FASB maintained the status quo, prohibited in-substance defeasance accounting, and not removed this kind of legal liability from the balance sheet.

DEPARTURES FROM TRADITIONAL ACCOUNTING THEORY

In view of the risks involved, it is reasonable to assume that the FASB had some compelling theoretical justification for introducing a revolutionary new method of eliminating debt from balance sheets. After all, the subject of accounting for debt had been previously covered by Accounting Principles Board Opinion no. 26, *Early Extinguishment of Debt*, and by FASB Statement no. 15, *Accounting by Debtors and Creditors for Troubled Debt Restructurings*.

The propriety of offsetting assets and liabilities was addressed in APB Opinion no. 10, *Omnibus Opinion—1966*, which states that "it is a general principle of accounting that the offsetting of assets and liabilities in the balance sheet is improper except where a right of setoff exists."

But Statement no. 76 presents no new conceptual justification for extinguishment of debt. This may explain the board's difficulty in issuing the statement. Had there been compelling evidence, a quickly agreed-on unanimous decision would surely have resulted.

FALLING SHORT

The in-substance defeasance provisions of Statement no. 76 fall short of the FASB's typical high standards. The drawbacks are clear, but the benefits aren't apparent. Aside from placating corporate treasurers, the provisions don't appear to compensate for their substantial deficiencies. They encourage questionable stewardship practices, may mislead users of financial statements, raise questions about accountants' legal liability, and depart from traditional accounting practice without clear justification.

We believe the in-substance defeasance provisions of Statement no. 76 should be repealed and are encouraged that the board will be reconsidering its position. Although there are numerous issues to be addressed on financial instruments and off-balance sheet financing, the arguments related to in-substance defeasance are straightforward and demand a speedy resolution.

CHAPTER 11

Leases

Companies lease assets for all sorts of sound economic reasons. But they also often tend to lease because the alternative of borrowing and buying will mean showing a liability in their balance sheets. Worried about this off-balance sheet financing appeal of leases, the Financial Accounting Standards Board (FASB) attempted, in Statement No. 13, "Accounting for Leases," to distinguish between leases that were operating programs and those that were financing programs. The basic aim of Statement No. 13 is that a lease that is effectively like borrowing and buying should be shown in the balance sheet as an asset and a corresponding liability. In addition, Statement No. 13 seeks symmetrical accounting treatment of leases by lessees and lessors.

The heart of Statement No. 13 is a set of four criteria that it lays out for lessees to identify capitalizable, or capital, leases. The objective of the criteria is to identify the situations where the lessee is the prime beneficiary of the asset over the bulk of its life. If any one of the criteria is met, then the lease is a capital lease for the lessee and a sales-type or direct-financing lease for the lessor (subject to certain other revenue-recognition criteria for the lessor). But the arbitrary cutoffs between operating and capital leases reflected in these criteria have visited a series of headaches on the FASB. Numerous interpretations and amendments have been adopted by the FASB to clarify ambiguities and close loopholes in a pronouncement that has veritably created a "cottage industry" in how to design a long-term lease contract that will escape the capitalization requirements of Statement No. 13.[1] An FASB-sponsored research study found that a majority of the companies surveyed "indicated that

---

[1] FASB Statements 17, 22, 23, 26, 27, 28, 29, 71 and 98 are major amendments to Statement No. 13. In addition, Statements 66, 67, 86, 91 and 92 amend or expand on Statement No. 13's lease rules. Within years after Statement No. 13's release, the FASB had also issued Technical Bulletins 79-10, 79-11, 79-12, 79-13, 79-16 and 79-17 as well as Interpretations 19, 21, 23, 24, 26 and 28 dealing with issues raised by Statement No. 13. Additional FASB releases on Statement No. 13 rules include Technical Bulletins 85-3, 86-2, and 88-1.

the terms of new lease contracts were structured to avoid capitalization."[2] Moreover, a large number of companies indicated that existing leases were renegotiated to avoid capitalization.

A main lesson from the FASB's messy experience with Statement No. 13 may be that accounting standard-setters should avoid prescribing arbitrary cutoffs or break-points to govern the choice between alternative accounting methods, especially where one method is strongly preferred by management. If arbitrary rules must be used, it is important to make the rules simple and objective.

In his widely quoted article, "Is Lessee Accounting Working?," Richard Dieter, a partner in Arthur Andersen & Co., concludes that the objectives of Statement No. 13 are being lost in a climate in which the Board's arbitrary cutoff rules are being followed to their finest detail. Rather than clinging tenaciously to the idea that assets must be recognized when attributes of ownership are signalled by arbitrary cutoff rules, the Board might instead focus on the acquisition of economic resources in exchange for a long-term lease contract. Dieter reviews several of the implementation problems under Statement No. 13 and expresses concern over the anomalous results sometimes produced. Some of the problems cited by Dieter have since been subjected to further FASB releases intended to close suspected loopholes in Statement No. 13.[3] Nevertheless, there is still merit today in Dieter's conclusion that "While arbitrary rules may work when the objectives are at the extremes of available options, they rarely work if the position sought is on middle ground."

Given the evidence that many companies structure their leases to qualify as operating leases, a question that arises is whether financial statement analysis is enhanced by "constructive capitalization" of operating leases by the analyst. This issue is studied by Eugene Imhoff, Robert Lipe and David Wright in "Operating Leases: Impact of Constructive Capitalization." They find numerous industries in which companies report very large noncancelable operating lease commitments extending over many years. They demonstrate a technique to capitalize the operating leases, and show that operating leases have a significant impact on risk and return measures. For their sample of seven pairs of firms in different industries, they find that, when operating leases are constructively capitalized for "high lease firms," the return-on-asset ratio declines by 34 percent and the debt-to-equity ratio increases by 191 percent. They conclude that "The off-balance-sheet effects of operating

---

[2] A. Rashad Abdel-khalik (principal researcher), *The Economic Effects on Lessees of FASB Statement No. 13, Accounting for Leases* (Financial Accounting Standards Board, 1981), p. ii.

[3] For example, loopholes involving contingent rent were addressed by FASB Interpretation No. 19, "Lessee Guarantee of the Residual Value of Leased Property" (1977), and by Technical Bulletin 85-3, "Accounting for Operating Leases with Scheduled Rent Increases" (1985). Similarly, the "part-of-the-building" loophole cited by Dieter was partially addressed by FASB Interpretation No. 23, "Leases of Certain Properties Owned by a Governmental Unit or Authority" (1978) and by Interpretation No. 24, "Leases Involving Only Part of a Building" (1978).

leases . . . are too material to ignore for meaningful analyses and comparisons of financial statement data."

BIBLIOGRAPHICAL NOTES

For a comprehensive handbook on the current standards and other authoritative statements on leases, see:

Accounting for Leases (Chicago: Arthur Andersen & Co., Third Edition, 1992).

Two discussion documents on the subject of accounting for leases are:

*An Analysis of Issues Related to Accounting for Leases,*Discussion Memorandum (Financial Accounting Standards Board, July 2, 1974).

Accounting for Leases, Discussion Paper No. 1 (Melbourne: Australian Accounting Research Foundation, Second Edition, 1983).

The following normative research study was commissioned by the Accounting Principles Board:

Myers, John H.: *Reporting of Leases in Financial Statements.* Accounting Research Study No. 4 (New York: American Institute of Certified Public Accountants, 1962).

As noted earlier, a major FASB-sponsored empirical study on the economic effects of leases is the following:

Abdel-khalik, A. Rashad (principal researcher): *The Economic Effects on Lessees of FASB Statement No. 13, Accounting for Leases* (Financial Accounting Standards Board, 1981).

The following articles provide additional empirical evidence on the management use of various kinds of leases and the impact of lease disclosures on financial markets:

El-Gazzar, Samir, Steve Lilien, and Victor Pastena: "Accounting for Leases by Lessees," *Journal of Accounting and Economics* (October 1986), pp. 217–237.

Finucane, Thomas J.: "Some Empirical Evidence on the Use of Financial Leases," *Journal of Financial Research* (Winter 1988), pp. 321–334.

Smith, Clifford W., Jr., and L. MacDonald Wakeman: "Determinants of Corporate Leasing Policy," *Journal of Finance* (July 1985), pp. 895–908.

Taylor, Peter, and Stuart Turley: "The Views of Management on Accounting for Leases," *Accounting and Business Research* (Winter 1985), pp. 59–68.

Many researchers have examined the issue of the effect of leases, capitalized or operating, on financial statement analysis, particularly risk measures. The following is a sample:

Bowman, Robert G.: "The Debt Equivalence of Leases: An Empirical Investigation," *The Accounting Review* (April 1980), pp. 237–253.

Davidson, Sidney, and Roman L. Weil: "Inflation Accounting and Leases," *Financial Analysts Journal* (November-December 1975), pp. 22–29, 57.

Grimlund, Richard A., and Robert Capettini: "A Note on the Evaluation of Leveraged
    Leases and Other Investments," *Financial Management* (Summer 1982), pp. 68–72.

The following articles describe behavioral studies that examine the impact of
lease disclosures on user decisions:

Hartman, Bart P., and Heibatollah Sami: "The Impact of the Accounting Treatment of
    Leasing Contracts on User Decision Making: A Field Experiment," *Advances in
    Accounting* (1989), pp. 23–35.
Munter, Paul, and Thomas A. Ratcliffe: "An Assessment of User Reactions to Lease
    Accounting Disclosures," *Journal of Accounting, Auditing & Finance,* (Winter 1983),
    pp. 108–114.
Wilkins, Trevor, and Ian Zimmer: "The Effect of Leasing and Different Methods of
    Accounting for Leases on Credit Evaluations," *The Accounting Review* (October
    1983), pp. 749–764.

The following articles provide supplementary discussion of various technical
issues raised by Statement No. 13:

Grant, Edward B., and Raymond C. Witt: "A Look at Leveraged Leases under FAS
    No. 13," *Management Accounting* (February 1979), pp. 49–52.
Harmelink, Philip J., and Robert Capettini: "Income Tax Consequences in Leasing,"
    The CPA Journal (March 1979), pp. 29–34.
Stickney, Clyde P., Roman L. Weil, and Mark A. Wolfson: "Income Taxes and Tax-
    Transfer Leases: General Electric's Accounting for a Molotov Cocktail," *The Ac-
    counting Review* (April 1983), pp. 439–459.
Swieringa, Robert J.: "When Current is Noncurrent and Vice Versa!" *The Accounting
    Review* (January 1984), pp. 123–130.

Is Lessee Accounting Working?

Richard Dieter

Arthur Andersen & Co.

While the objectives of FASB Statement 13 "Accounting for Leases" appear
meritorious, the arbitrary rules, sub-rules, subsequent interpretations and
amendments (both official and unofficial) for implementing these objectives
have created substantial problems for the independent CPA and for financial
management. This article analyzes many of the implementation problems;
offers reasons why they have arisen; and finally suggests a solution to the
dilemma, primarily with respect to accounting for leases by lessees.

The objective of Statement 13, as described in its Appendix (Basis for
Conclusions) was that:

A lease that transfers substantially all of the benefits and risks incident to the ownership of property should be accounted for as the acquisition of an asset and the incurrence of an obligation by the lessee and as a sale or financing by the lessor.

The Board believed that Statement 13 would remove most "if not all, of the conceptual differences in lease classification as between lessors and lessees and that it provides criteria for such classification that are more explicit and less susceptible to varied interpretation than those in previous literature."

Based on actual results of Statement 13 for over two years, its objectives and the assertion of "less susceptibility to varied interpretation" have not been reached. In fact, there continues to be a significant number of long-term leases that pass substantially all risks and rewards of ownership of property to the lessee and yet continue to be accounted for as operating leases. In addition, while drafters of new leases may have to sharpen their pencils a bit, it is common to find agreements negotiated that provide a finance lease for the lessor and an operating lease for the lessee.

STATEMENT NO. 13—AN OVERVIEW

In studying the lease classification rules of Statement 13, one quickly concludes that the major stumbling block to noncapitalization is in overcoming the test of paragraph 7d. While this paragraph represents only one of four distinct tests that, if met, requires a lessee to capitalize a lease, it is the only new rule that is, in most instances, quantifiable. This rule, commonly referred to as the 90 percent recovery test, requires a lessee to capitalize a lease if the present value, at the beginning of the lease term, of the minimum lease payments equals or exceeds 90 percent of the excess of the fair value of the leased property over any related investment tax credit retained by the lessor and expected to be realized by him.

The other lessee capitalization rules, referred to in paragraphs 7a, b and c of Statement 13 are not significant hurdles to overcome. For example, paragraphs 7a and 7b require a lessee to capitalize a lease if "the lease transfers ownership of the property to the lessee by the end of the lease term" or if "the lease contains a bargain purchase option." Both of these tests are substantially unchanged from APB Opinion No. 5 and, except for possible varying interpretation of what constitutes a bargain purchase option, few, if any, leases not capitalized under APB Opinion No. 5 would be capitalized under these rules of Statement 13.

The test in paragraph 7c of Statement 13 is also similar to the underlying thrust of APB Opinion No. 5; however, it does differ in that Statement 13 is more specific. It provides that if the lease term (as defined) equals or exceeds 75 percent of the estimated economic life of the leased property, the lessee is required to capitalize the lease. Most practitioners realize that estimates of useful lives of assets are judgmental and, if an estimate is within a given range, they are not apt to object. Accordingly, a building lease of 30 years will commonly not be required to be capitalized under paragraph 7c, because arguments that a building life often exceeds 40 years are easily sustainable and reasonable. Similarly, estimates of economic lives of 12 to 15 years are not uncommon for equipment covered by an eight-year lease. Thus, for all practical purposes, a lessee is able to overcome the numerical test of paragraph 7c and in clear conscience justify it to himself and his independent auditor. There are, however, extremes that have been taken in this regard, particularly by some major retailers. These assertions and the questions raised by the SEC are discussed in this article.

Nevertheless, the 90 percent recovery test remains the focal point of lease capitalization from the lessee's viewpoint. Accordingly, the implementation problems discussed in this article focus on what the issues are, why there are varying interpretations, to what extremes people are willing to go and what they are willing to give up in negotiating leases that do not meet this test.

One of the best approaches to analyze implementation problems that have beset the practitioner is to study carefully specific issues that the FASB has faced or is facing through issuance of official interpretations and amendments to Statement 13. As of May 1, 1979, FASB had amended Statement 13 four times, had issued six interpretations and had in the exposure stage three additional amendments. In addition, the Board has authorized its staff to develop interpretations on two other lease problems.

PART-OF-THE-BUILDING PROBLEM

Certain perceived measurement problems exist in performing lease classification tests for leases involving only part of a building (e.g., floors of a multistory office building and retail space in a shopping mall). As a result, FASB devised special rules to assist a user of Statement 13 in obtaining objectively determinable costs or fair market values of leased space. It provided without any specificity that, with respect to the lessee:

> If the fair value of the leased property is not objectively determinable, the lessee shall classify the lease according to the criterion of paragraph 7(c) only, using the estimated economic life of the building in which the leased premises are located.

In practice lessees uniformly asserted that it was never practical to estimate the fair value of a part of a building and thus the 90 percent recovery test was not applicable. Accordingly, only the useful life test was to be applied, and, as discussed previously, this was quickly overcome by applying subjective judgment to estimated useful lives.

Subsequent to the issuance of Statement 13, FASB was asked to clarify when fair value can be objectively determined for a lease involving only part of a building if there were no sales of similar property. The FASB responded by issuing its Interpretation No. 24 in September 1978. It provides that other evidence (e.g., independent appraisal or estimated replacement cost information) may provide a basis for an objective determination of fair value. The Board also acknowledged that (a) it was not imposing a requirement to obtain an appraisal or other similar valuation as a general matter and, (b) a meaningful estimate of fair value "of an office or a floor of a multi-story building may not be possible whereas similar information may be readily obtainable if the leased property is a major part of that facility." This interpretation has had little or no impact on lessee capitalization decisions since Statement 13 continues to be applied literally and information as to fair value remains elusive. Consequently, for the vast majority of leases involving only part of a building or structure, no capitalization is occurring.

RESIDUAL VALUE GUARANTEES

In performing the 90 percent recovery test of Statement 13 a lessee is required to include, in the determination of minimum lease payments, guarantees of the residual value of leased property at expiration of the lease. Lessee guarantees of the residual value, while not uncommon, occur most frequently in leases involving personal property such as automobiles. Since the question of residual value guarantees was not a criterion of lease capitalization prior to Statement 13, it was commonplace to find the residual value guarantee at the end of an automobile lease term equating to the balance of undepreciated cost. Consequently, in performing the lease capitalization tests of Statement 13, many lessees initially found themselves in the unhappy position of having to capitalize most of their automobile leases. Almost immediately after this consequence became known to the car lessors, they set out to amend and rectify lease agreements to overcome the capitalization requirements. This was accomplished primarily through a specific limitation on the amount of the residual value deficiency that a lessee would be required to make up and, in some cases, by limiting the guarantee to situations beyond normal wear and tear.

In addition, the Board assisted lessees in this effort through the issuance of Interpretation No. 19 "Lessee Guarantee of the Residual Value of Leased Property." It dealt with lease provisions that require the lessee to make up a residual value deficiency only in cases where the shortfall in residual value is attributable to damage, extraordinary wear and tear, etc., and whether this type of provision constitutes a lessee guarantee of residual value as that term is used in defining minimum lease payments under Statement 13. The interpretation stated that (1) a residual value guarantee is limited to the specific maximum deficiency the lessee can be required to make up, and (2) a lessee that is required to make up a residual value deficiency attributable to extraordinary wear and tear does not constitute a lessee guarantee of residual value for purposes of defining minimum lease payments.

The practical effect of this interpretation, as it relates to the specified maximum deficiency, can best be demonstrated with an example. Assume a lessee enters into a one-year lease for a current model year Volvo for a monthly rental of $300. The fair market value of the Volvo at the inception of the lease is $10,000. The lessee agrees, at the conclusion of the one-year lease, to make up any residual value deficiency on the car between $3,000 and $8,000. Thus the lessor takes the risk that a one-year-old Volvo would not be worth at least $3,000. In computing minimum lease payments, the lessee would compare the $10,000 to the present value of $3,600 (1 year's monthly payments) and the $5,000 residual value guarantee ($8,000 minus $3,000). The mechanics of the present value computation lead to a conclusion that the minimum lease payments are less than 90 percent of the fair market value of the car at the inception of the lease. While the mechanical test of Statement 13 for capitalization has not been met, it is clear that the lessor has given up very little and yet has been able to achieve an operating lease for the lessee. Thus this interpretation applied literally allows lessees, through a modification of terms that are not economically substantive, to alter substantially the accounting treatment by converting an otherwise capital lease to an operating lease.

CONTINGENT RENT

Statement 13 provides that contingent rentals, from the lessee's viewpoint, are to be charged to expense as incurred, and not considered part of minimum lease payments for the purpose of performing the 90 percent recovery test. Since many leases contain a base rent and an override based on sales, the override rent is excluded from minimum lease payments in determining lease classification. For example, retail space is often leased at a base rate per month plus a fixed or variable percentage of sales over a predetermined amount. Drafters of lease agreements were quick to realize that by a slight reduction in base rent and a minor increase in percentage rent or simply a decrease in the base sales amount, minimum lease payments could be reduced to enable the present value calculation to equal 89 percent of the fair value of the leased property with a miniscule increase in risk to the lessor.

In other circumstances a rental cost is based on the prime interest rate. The following hypothetical example demonstrates the problem. A lease agreement provides that yearly rent will be a function of the prime interest rate times a given principal amount, with a limitation on the absolute amount of rent per year. The limitation would equate to a prime rate of 4 percent. This yearly amount over the lease term would qualify the lease as a capital lease. Nevertheless, the practical interpretation of Statement 13 would be to classify all payments as contingent and consequently the lease would be treated as an operating lease.

Situations such as the above were brought to the Board's attention and in December 1978, it issued an exposure draft of an amendment to Statement 13 providing that:

> Lease payments that depend on an existing index or rate, such as the prime interest rate, shall be included in minimum lease payments based on the index or rate existing at the inception of the lease; any increases or decreases in lease payments that result from subsequent changes in the index or rate are contingent rentals.

This proposed amendment would appear to correct many of the perceived abuses in using the contingent rental clause based on indexes to avoid capitalization.

IMPLICIT INTEREST RATE IN THE LEASE

Statement 13 provides that when a lessee is computing the present value of the minimum lease payments for the purpose of measuring whether a capital lease exists, it should use its incremental borrowing rate unless "it is practicable for him to learn the implicit interest rate computed by the lessor and the implicit rate computed by the lessor is less than the lessee's incremental borrowing rate." If both these conditions exist, the lessee is required to use the implicit rate. By and large, the lessor's implicit interest rate in the lease is lower than the lessee's incremental borrowing rate. This is due to several factors including the lessor's estimate of the residual value. In addition, in determining an appropriate rate of return the lessor considers the additional tax benefits that flow to the lessor (e.g., cash flow benefits of accelerated depreciation for tax purposes); these benefits are not considered in the lease evaluation criteria of Statement 13. As most practitioners realize today, a lessee request from the lessor for the implicit interest rate will "reluctantly" be declined. In most situations, the lessee will not press the lessor because the direction of the answer is known in advance. As a result, many lessees represent to their CPAs that although they have requested information from the lessor, the lessor has refused to respond. Consequently, when performing the 90 percent recovery test, the incremental borrowing rate is used. As is readily apparent, in a long-term lease, when a present value computation is performed using an interest rate of approximately 10 percent (a rate representative of most companies' incremental borrowing rate today), rentals due after ten years have little or no present value.

This problem was brought to the Board's attention and it has proposed to amend Statement 13 to require the lessee, where practicable, to estimate the interest rate implicit in the lease. In so doing, the lessee is forced into an evaluation of the residual value. This unfortunately raises the issue of how to handle inflation, particularly for leases involving real estate. Should the residual value be viewed as a percentage of original cost based on a depreciable life of 30 or 40 years? Should it take into account trends of the past eight years of significant inflation? Should it take an historical approach that shows real estate values have increased at a rate, in many instances, that exceed normal inflation? The Board has not answered these questions in its proposed amendment.

Through the comment letters the Board has received on its exposure draft of the amendment of Statement 13 entitled "Lessee's Use of the Interest Rate Implicit in the Lease" it became aware of the problem of estimating residual values. As a result, the Board has directed its staff to address the question of whether expected future increases in value should be considered in estimating residual values. They have also reached the conclusion to defer a decision on the amendment covering the lessee's use of the interest rate implicit in the lease until that question is solved.

In analyzing how the impact of inflation should be considered in determining residual values, many would argue that this judgment should be consistent with the other provisions of Statement 13. For example, the Board has emphasized in Statement 13 that upward revisions of residual value are not acceptable. While this appears to relate primarily to the notion that once property is "sold" (capital lease), additional profit recognition by the lessor should not be permitted prior to end of the lease term, it also seems to preclude giving recognition to inflation. It should also be borne in mind that inflation, in general, is not accounted for under the historical cost framework presently used. Others argue that the interest rate (e.g., approximately 10 percent today) used to discount residual values reflects inflation, as that rate far exceeds a pure cost of money, and therefore, in estimating residual values, inflation should also be considered. They further believe that by not assuming inflation for real estate leases, the lease capitalization test and the use of the implicit interest rate of Statement 13 are avoiding economic reality.

THE RETAILERS' ARGUMENTS

Perhaps in no other industry are the potential effects of lease capitalization as significant to the balance sheet as they are to large retail chains. The majority of these retailers lease substantially all their facilities under long-term leases, particularly in shopping malls and strip centers.

Readers of large retailers' financial statements were given a warning of the magnitude of the impact of lease capitalization by the disclosures required under Accounting Series Release No. 147. Most readers assumed that the "noncapitalized financing leases," disclosed in accordance with ASR No. 147 would become capital leases under Statement 13. How wrong they were! In fact, less than one half, and in some cases only a small percentage of the "noncapitalized finance leases," have been treated as capital leases under Statement 13.

For example, one large retailer reported over 160 leases with a present value of approximately $50,000,000 meeting the SEC's definition of a "noncapitalized finance" lease. Reporting under Statement 13, that retailer reported only 50 leases with a present value of $25,000,000 as capital leases. The major reasons for certain "noncapitalized finance leases" not meeting the capital lease test of Statement 13 were (a) option periods were considered in the lease term for purposes of the ASR disclosures but are excluded in

Statement 13's tests; (b) the inability to estimate fair market value where the leased premise was part of a large shopping mall; and (c) the exclusion of leases of a property located in government facilities.

The retailing industry has carefully analyzed the criteria for lease classification under Statement 13 and has sought to take consistent and aggressive positions in interpreting the rules. Recently, the Office of the Chief Accountant of the SEC commented that it would be carefully reviewing the assertions and conclusions reached by the industry since it also was taken aback by the lack of capitalization of leased stores and facilities under Statement 13 compared to the disclosures of "noncapitalized finance leases" under ASR No. 147.

The following conclusions reached by several large retailers in implementing Statement 13 have led to many long-term leases being classified as operating leases.

Economic Life

Statement 13 defines economic life as:

> The estimated remaining period during which the property is expected to be economically usable by one or more users, with normal repairs and maintenance, for the purpose for which it was intended at the inception of the lease, without limitation by the lease term.

The conclusion reached by certain larger retailers was that the life of the property should be measured in terms of a retail enterprise or otherwise. Since alternative uses (warehouses, etc.) exist, they conclude it is reasonable to assume, for purposes of Statement 13, economic lives of 50 to 75 years. Accordingly, the interpretation leads one to conclude that most real property leases should not require capitalization in accordance with paragraph 7(c) of Statement 13. Literally applied, retailers with a 50-year lease could argue a life of 75 years and fail the capitalization test of paragraph 7c. Without arguing the merits of a 75-year life or the apparent inconsistency with the treatment adopted by nonretailers for economic lives of real property, one wonders whether this interpretation is consistent with the words "for the purpose for which it was intended at the inception of the lease." Namely, is it appropriate to consider the additional useful life as a warehouse that occurs beyond its retail life in determining the economic life under Statement 13?

Part of a Facility

FASB Interpretation No. 24 attempts to rectify a problem of Statement 13, as covered previously, dealing with leases involving only part of a building (space in a shopping mall) by indicating that other evidence may provide an objective determination of fair value. One of the factors to be considered is whether the lessee occupies a major part of the facility. The retailers have concluded that a major part would be equivalent to more than 50 percent of the available space which would be an extreme rarity in a shopping mall. Some believe this was not the intent of the FASB and that a more appropriate interpretation would be that an anchor tenant would be assumed to have information to estimate fair market value. This argument appears to have merit, since anchor tenants are an integral part of the mall and the developer's plans, and it would seem reasonable that the anchor tenant would often have this information available, though it may only occupy 10 to 20 percent of the mall space.

LEASES INVOLVING GOVERNMENT FACILITIES

Just prior to finalizing the issuance of Statement 13, FASB added a section under the rules covering leases involving only part of a building. It read as follows:

> Because of special provisions normally present in leases involving terminal space and other airport facilities owned by a governmental unit or authority, the economic life of such facilities for purposes of classifying the lease is essentially indeterminate. Likewise, the concept of fair value is not applicable to such leases. Since such leases also do not provide for a transfer of ownership or a bargain purchase option, they shall be classified as operating leases. Leases of other facilities owned by a governmental unit or authority wherein the rights of the parties are essentially the same as in a lease of airport facilities described above shall also be classified as operating leases. Examples of such leases may be those involving facilities at ports and bus terminals.

This special exemption had a tremendous impact on the airline industry by allowing them to classify their airport terminal space as operating leases. Many took this exemption also to apply to free standing airline hangars, including maintenance hangars, since the property was on government land and subject to the same considerations as airport terminal space. The SEC raised questions on whether the exemption applied to free standing structures since the exemption provided by Statement 13 was in a subsection covering "Leases Involving Part of a Building." This demonstrated that the SEC was also interpreting Statement 13 literally, although in this case it appeared a bit absurd.

In response to problems such as the one cited in the previous paragraph, the FASB issued an official interpretation—No. 23, "Leases of Certain Property Owned by a Governmental Unit or Authority." The interpretation specifies certain conditions that must be met if the leases in question are to be considered operating leases. One of those is that the lessor has the explicit right to terminate the lease at any time. Since such a right often does not exist, at least certain leases in this area may now require capitalization.

The Board, in response to many comments received that these leases should be subject to the same rule as other leases, gave serious consideration to eliminating the exemption entirely. However, it concluded that further consideration of an amendment should not delay the issuance of the interpretation.

WHERE DOES THIS LEAVE STATEMENT NO. 13?

It now appears likely that Statement 13 will rank fourth in number of interpretations and amendments of an authoritative document, ranking behind only APB Opinion No. 15, "Earnings per Share," APB Opinion No. 11, "Accounting for Income Taxes" and the all-time leader APB Opinion No. 16, "Accounting for Business Combinations." In terms of frustration it may rank higher. These distinctions are not without certain redeeming qualities—countless hours of billable professional time are spent in analyzing lease transactions in light of Statement 13, but one wonders whether this is really productive.

Clearly, from a practitioner's viewpoint, Statement 13 has created practice problems and difficulties by forcing one to rummage through rules, amendments and interpretations when analyzing a lease. Conclusions on lease accounting seem to reach the lowest common denominator in practice, so that most practitioners have concluded that the objectives of Statement 13 and substance over form give way to a literal interpretation of the rules of Statement 13. No white knights are appearing to invoke the Board's objectives, since the Board itself, through its amendments and interpretations, has opted, for the most part, to apply the arbitrary rules and percentages literally. To answer the question of why Statement 13 has failed to achieve its objective, one must first question the objective itself. From the author's viewpoint, it is questionable whether the objective could ever have been expected to be achieved, since the basis of Statement 13 represented a compromise between capitalizing all leases and capitalizing only those where title passes. Thus, Statement 13 is aimed at a position in between, and the break points are arbitrary. While arbitrary rules may work when the objectives are at the extremes of available options, they rarely work if the position sought is on middle ground.

What then is the solution? Would it not be more workable to require capitalization of all leases that extend for some defined period (such as one year), not on the premise that the lease transfers substantially all the risks and rewards of ownership of the property, but that the lessee has acquired an asset, a property right, and correspondingly has incurred an obligation? Using this criterion the necessity for most of the rules of Statement 13 would be eliminated, and the lessee's balance sheet would give a better picture of its assets and liabilities.

What are the possibilities of such a scenario? It is difficult to predict but certain events seem to indicate that a rethinking of Statement 13 is probable. In March 1979, the Board met to consider the underlying concepts in accounting for leases. The subject matter was placed on the Board's agenda in view of the number of amendments and interpretations of Statement 13 and the inordinate amount of time the Board has spent on Statement 13 problems since its issuance. It is generally acknowledged that, with the present complement on the Board, and the hindsight of the Statement's difficulties, if Statement 13 were submitted to the Board in its present form, a majority vote to issue would not be sustained.

At its March 6, 1979 meeting, a majority of the Board expressed "the tentative view that, if Statement 13 were to be reconsidered, they would support a property right approach in which all leases are included as 'rights to use property' and as 'lease obligations' in the lessee's balance sheet."

The other recent developments comes out of the Board's exposure draft on accounting concepts. Many believe that the Board deviated from the definition of an economic obligation given in that document when it defined a capital lease. Eventually this inconsistency must be removed. If one uses the definition of a liability in the proposed statement on accounting concepts, it is not difficult to reach the conclusion that all leases represent obligations to transfer enterprise resources and should therefore be reflected on the balance sheet.

Statement 13 has not achieved its goal in terms of the degree of lease capitalization that its drafters believed would be accomplished or in eliminating most of the inconsistencies between accounting for leases by lessors and lessees. This practitioner believes the cause of failure is with the objective the Board used—an objective, as has been demonstrated, not capable of practical implementation. The Board should recognize its obligation to rethink the issue and its objective, taking into account its new definition of assets and liabilities, and recognize that, while compromise in the setting of accounting principles is necessary in many circumstances, a compromise that doesn't work should be discarded.

Operating Leases:
Impact of Constructive Capitalization

Eugene A. Imhoff
University of Michigan

Robert C. Lipe
University of Michigan

David W. Wright
University of Michigan

The purpose of this article is to document the importance of long-term operating lease commitments on commonly used measures of risk and performance. Under generally accepted accounting principles (GAAP), operating leases do not affect assets or liabilities, but are simply reported as rent

From *Accounting Horizons* (March 1991), pp. 51–63. Reprinted by permission of the American Accounting Association and the authors. Copyright © 1991 by the American Accounting Association.

Authors' note: Financial support for this paper was provided by the University of Michigan, the KPMG Peat Marwick Foundation, and the Ernst & Young Foundation.

expense for the amount of the current period's payments. Accounting texts typically describe operating leases as short-term rental arrangements. We find numerous firms in many different industries who report very large noncancelable operating lease commitments extending many years into the future. These firms are, in effect, using significantly more assets than they report on their balance sheets under GAAP to generate revenues, and are also much more levered than their reported debt to equity ratios suggest.

The presence of material long-term noncancelable operating lease commitments for many firms encouraged us to develop a method for constructively capitalizing these commitments. This method allows key financial statement ratios to be calculated as if the operating leases had been capitalized at their inception. Although the concern over off-balance sheet financing via operating leases has long been recognized by financial analysts, it should be noted that widely utilized databases of financial information and ratios such as Dun & Bradstreet, Value Line, and Compact Disclosure do not routinely adjust for its effects. Here, the impact of constructive capitalization on the return on assets and the debt to equity ratios is illustrated for a sample of firms. Our evidence suggests that operating leases have a significant effect on these risk and return measures, and that the magnitude of the effect varies within and across industries in which operating leases are an important form of off-balance sheet investing/financing activity. Thus, constructive capitalization of long-term operating lease commitment, enhances the relevance and comparability of firm-specific measures of risk and performance.

REASON FOR CONCERN
ABOUT OPERATING LEASES

Leasing has historically been an attractive vehicle for obtaining the use of productive assets. The popularity of leasing is due, in part, to management's ability to keep the leased asset and its associated financial obligation off the balance sheet.[1] Despite efforts by accounting policymakers to develop rules which require the substance of lease transactions to be reported,[2] managers have found ways to record most leases as rental arrangements (operating leases) instead of asset purchases (capitalized leases). Evidence from around the time of the adoption of SFAS 13 suggests that the terms of most capital leases were restructured to avoid the new capitalization requirements.[3] By avoiding capitalization of their leases, managers improve their firm's reported performance and leverage ratios. Although it may be possible to undo the

---

[1] A. R. Abdel-khalik, *The Economic Effects on Lessees of FASB Statement No. 13: Accounting for Leases* (Stamford, CT: FASB, 1981).

[2] Financial Accounting Standards Board (FASB), *Statement of Financial Accounting Standards No. 13: Accounting for Leases* (Stamford, CT: FASB, 1976).

[3] E. Imhoff and J. Thomas, "Economic Consequences of Accounting Standards: The Lease Disclosure Rule Change," *Journal of Accounting and Economics* (December 1988), pp. 277–310.

effects of such off-balance sheet financing/investing activities, most public databases do not do so.

Many corporations continue to commit significant future cash flows to long-term operating leases,[4] circumventing FASB rules intended to reduce management's ability to acquire effective ownership control over assets which do not appear on the balance sheet.[5] The procedures explained in the following section show how failure to capitalize these operating lease commitments can materially distort the risk and performance measures of the firm.

CONSTRUCTIVE CAPITALIZATION

In this section, we present a method for constructively capitalizing the non-cancelable commitments embodied in a firm's operating leases. The effects of constructive capitalization on reported assets, liabilities, and net income are each examined separately. The techniques of constructive capitalization are later used to investigate the effects of unrecorded assets and debt on the return on assets and leverage ratios for a sample of lessee firms in seven industries.

Constructive capitalization requires estimating the amount of debt and assets that would be reported on the balance sheet if the operating leases had been treated as capital leases from their inception. To estimate the debt, we employ the schedule of minimum future cash flows required to be disclosed by SFAS 13 for operating leases with remaining noncancelable lease terms in excess of one year. The cash flows are reported for each of the next 5 years, followed by a single amount for all payments more than 5 years hence.[6] Note

---

[4] As one possible motive, we point to the evidence of R. Antle and A. Smith, "An Empirical Investigation of the Relative Performance Evaluation of Corporate Executives," *Journal of Accounting Research* (Spring 1986), pp. 1–39. They find (book) return on asset ratios to be most important in explaining the relative performance of corporate executives. When managers are compensated based on return on assets (per books) they have financial incentives to keep assets used to generate profits off their books.

[5] Some common reasons why a material long-term lease may fail to meet the capitalization criteria include: (1) The exclusion of contingent rental payments in determining the present value of future minimum lease payments. This is especially prevalent in the retail industry where rental payments are often based, in part, on sales in the rental space. (2) Rental of part of a building, such as floor space in a large shopping mall, which has no determinable fair market value, thereby rendering the fourth (market value based) criterion of SFAS 13 not applicable. (3) Rental of space in a government facility, such as a municipally-owned airport, so that the third and fourth criteria of SFAS 13 are not applicable under Financial Accounting Standards Board *Interpretation No. 23: Leases of Certain Property Owned by a Governmental Unit or Authority* (Stamford, CT: FASB, 1978). (4) Obtaining third party insurance coverage for guaranteed residual values to reduce the present value of minimum lease payments. Under SFAS 13, any lease which does not meet the capitalization criteria must be an operating lease. Thus, some long-term leases will be classified as operating due to standard industry practices instead of management's manipulations.

[6] When capital leases are disclosed, operating lease data will normally be contained in the lease footnote. However, the scheduled future operating lease cash flows might also be reported in the "contingencies and commitments" footnote or similar footnote disclosure.

that the future cash flows which are used in our constructive capitalization technique represent the same minimum lease payments which would have been used to measure the liability had they been classified as capital leases. Thus, for example, expected (nonbargain) rental payments during optional renewal periods would not be included by either SFAS 13 or our technique. These minimum future cash flows are then discounted using an estimate of the firm's incremental secured borrowing rate and an estimate of the remaining life of the leased asset. The result is our estimate of the off-balance sheet debt represented by the present value (PV) of the remaining noncancelable obligations under operating leases.

Once the PV of the debt is measured, we estimate the related unamortized off-balance sheet assets by examining the relation between assets and debt. Assuming that the leased assets are 100 percent financed with debt,[7] we show how estimates of the firm's incremental secured borrowing rate and the remaining life of operating leased assets may also be used to estimate the asset balance had the operating leases been capitalized from their inception.

Estimating the Unrecorded Liability

To illustrate constructive capitalization, consider the data reported in Table 1 for McDonald's Corporation, the world's largest chain of fast food restaurants. Panel A summarizes key information from the 1988 balance sheet and income statement, and Panel B provides the leasing footnote from the 1988 annual report. McDonald's scheduled minimum future operating lease cash flows total about $2,236 million. To estimate the PV of these future cash flows, we need to estimate the appropriate interest rate and the pattern of payments for the $1,402,357,000 of total nominal cash flows scheduled beyond 1993.

The appropriate interest rate should be the average of the historical marginal secured borrowing rate of McDonald's at the inception of the operating leases, weighted by the relative size of each lease in comparison to all operating leases. This rate should be similar to the average historical interest rate for reported secured long-term debt, and can normally be estimated by examining the debt footnote. Although McDonald's historical interest rates average about 9 percent, we use 10 percent to produce a conservative measure which avoids overstating the liability.[8] Similarly, we conservatively assume that all cash flows occur at year-end versus throughout the year.[9]

---

[7] Because of the rules stipulated in SFAS 13 and the related pronouncements, this is a reasonable assumption. To avoid capitalization, it is necessary for the depreciation/amortization of the unrecorded leased assets to end as the lease payments end. Also, assuming no material down payment, the initial unrecorded asset will equal the initial unrecorded liability. The implications of this assumption are illustrated later in the paper.

[8] As an alternative one might use the weighted average interest rate on the company's capital leases, which is sometimes disclosed in the footnotes.

[9] Another built-in conservatism is the fact that the scheduled future cash flows are minimums. As noted in most lease footnotes, actual rent expense will usually be greater. For example, McDonald's 1987 annual report had minimum scheduled 1988 operating lease payments of $157 million and in 1988's report they revealed that 1988 rent expense was $190 million. Some of this difference is probably due to contingent rental payments.

TABLE 1 McDonald's Corporation Financial Statement Data
and Leasing Footnote

Panel A

	($ in 000,000)
Reported Total Assets	$8,159
Reported Total Liabilities	$4,746
Reported Total Stockholders' Equity	$3,413
Reported Net Income	$ 646
Reported Effective Book Tax Rate	38.3%

Panel B

At December 31, 1988, the Company was lessee at 1,636 restaurant locations under ground
leases (the Company leases the land and constructs and owns the buildings) and at 1,922 locations under improved leases (lessor owns the land and buildings). These leases are operating
leases except for the building portions of 485 leases, which together with certain restaurant
equipment leases, are capital leases. Land and building lease terms are generally for 20 to
25 years and, in many cases, provide for rent escalations and one or more five-year renewal
options with certain leases providing purchase options. The Company is generally obligated
for the related occupancy costs which include property taxes, insurance and maintenance. In
addition, the Company is lessee under noncancelable operating leases covering offices and
vehicles.

At December 31, 1988, future minimum payments under capital leases and noncancelable
operating leases, with initial terms of one year or more, are as follows:

		Operating leases		
(In thousands of dollars)	Capital leases	Restaurant	Other	Total
1989	$ 17,047	$ 152,834	$ 28,289	$ 181,123
1990	15,209	151,897	26,422	178,319
1991	13,926	147,962	20,199	168,161
1992	10,214	143,556	13,864	157,420
1993	6,983	138,142	10,234	148,376
Thereafter	52,504	1,336,377	65,980	1,402,357
Total	115,883	$2,070,768	$164,988	$2,235,756
Less imputed interest	50,196			
Present Value at December 31, 1988	$ 65,687			

Rent expense was as follows: 1988—$190 million; 1987—$160 million; and 1986—$143 million. Included in
these amounts were percentage rents based on sales by the related restaurants in excess of minimum rents
stipulated in certain capital and operating lease agreements as follows: 1988—$15 million; 1987—$12 million; and 1986—$11 million.

The pattern of the operating lease payments beyond 1993 is a more
ambiguous issue to address. Footnote disclosures suggest that most of the
operating leases are for equipment, facility improvements/renovations, offices and vehicles. Most of these classes of assets would have useful lives of 30
years or less. If we assume that the remaining life is 14 years, the $1,402
million lump sum would be spread over nine years, resulting in an average
cash flow per year beyond 1993 of $155.7 million ($1,402 million/9 years =
$155.7 million per year). Since the estimated annual cash flow of $155.7
million is greater than the reported payment scheduled for 1993 ($148.4
million), it is likely that the average actual remaining life of the operating

TABLE 2 McDonald's Operating Leases: Equivalent Present Value
($ in millions)

Panel A: PV of Operating Leases

	Scheduled Cash Flows[a]	×	10% Present Value Factor	=	PV of Cash Flows
1989	181.1	×	.9091	=	$ 164.6
1990	178.3	×	.8264	=	147.3
1991	168.2	×	.7513	=	126.4
1992	157.4	×	.6830	=	107.5
1993	148.4	×	.6209	=	92.1
1994 to 2003	140.2[b]	×	3.8153[c]	=	534.9

$1,172.8 Estimated unrecorded debt

[a] Rounded to the nearest $100,000, and assuming all payments occur at the end of each year.
[b] $1,402.357/10 years = $140.2 per year
[c] This factor is the present value of a 15-year annuity at 10% less the present value of a 5-year annuity at 10%, based on assumed $140.2 million at the end of each year from 1994–2003.

Panel B: Sensitivity Analysis

Assumptions as above except—	Estimated Unrecorded Debt
1. If interest rate is 8 percent (not 10 percent)	$1,311.0 million
2. If interest rate is 12 percent (not 10 percent)	$1,057.3 million
3. If total remaining life is 20 years (not 15 years)	$1,079.4 million
4. If total remaining life is 25 years (not 15 years)	$1,008.6 million

leases is greater than 14 years.[10] For simplicity we assume that these distant cash flows occur equally over the ten years beyond 1993, resulting in an average total remaining life of 15 years and an average cash flow of $140.2 million each year beyond 1993.

Panel A of Table 2 reports calculation of the PV of the operating lease cash flows using the assumed 10 percent interest rate and 15-year average remaining lease life. The results suggest that the PV of McDonald's unrecorded liability for operating lease commitments is about $1.17 billion. This is more than one-third of McDonald's total reported long- and short-term debt, clearly a material amount of off-balance sheet debt. To test the impact of changes in our assumptions, we varied both the interest rate (± 2 percent) and the remaining life of the leases (+ 5 years and + 10 years). The results of these sensitivity tests, reported in Panel B of Table 2, provide a range of estimates from $1.01 billion to $1.31 billion for the unrecorded debt attributable to operating leases.

The estimated $1.17 billion for McDonald's operating lease debt reflects important assumptions about lease lives and interest rates. To provide a

---

[10] This conclusion is based on the fact that scheduled future minimum cash flows are virtually always decreasing. We note that the rate of decline in scheduled future cash flows, as measured by the ratio of the 5 years-ahead amount over the 1 year-ahead amount, is a good indicator of both the stability or growth in leased assets (e.g., growth firms would have the highest ratios) and the average remaining life of the operating leases (e.g., those with the shortest average remaining life will have the lowest ratios).

limited test of the reasonableness of this estimation procedure, we found a rare disclosure of the PV of operating lease commitments reported in the footnotes of Pillsbury (parent of Burger King) for 1988. Pillsbury's lease footnote for the year ended May 31, 1988 revealed:

> The present value of the net minimum future obligations under operating leases, calculated using the Company's incremental borrowing rate at inception of the leases, is $423 million.

We used Pillsbury's scheduled cash flows to estimate their operating lease liability using the procedures illustrated above for McDonald's. These computations, not reported here, indicate that the estimated PV of about $440 million is within 4 percent of the reported actual PV of $423 million. Accordingly, we believe the error in estimating the liability using the approach illustrated here will generally be less than 5 percent.

Estimating the Unrecorded Asset

The preceding discussion illustrates a technique for assessing the magnitude of a firm's off-balance sheet debt from noncancelable operating leases. However, in order to fully address the overall balance sheet effects of constructive capitalization, an estimate of the associated unrecorded asset must also be made. The unrecorded asset measurement depends on the scheduled cash flows, incremental borrowing rate, and remaining life of the lease used above. In addition, it requires an estimate of the weighted average *total* life of the leased assets and an assumed depreciation method. The total life is the key additional unknown, since straight-line depreciation is used for most long-term assets. These additional assumptions make the estimated unrecorded asset somewhat more difficult to measure than the liability, and the error may exceed ± 5 percent. Even so, it is likely that the estimate will still be within tolerable limits and should be superior to ignoring the effects of constructive capitalization altogether.

Table 3 provides a mechanism for estimating the unrecorded asset after estimating the unrecorded liability in the manner described in the previous section. The tabled percentages express the unamortized unrecorded operating lease asset as a percentage of the remaining unrecorded operating lease liability at various stages of the assets' weighted average remaining useful life. The underlying assumptions for these tabled values are:

1. Straight-line depreciation is used for all assets.
2. The unrecorded lease asset and unrecorded lease liability both equal 100 percent of the PV of the future lease payments at the inception of each lease.
3. The unrecorded lease asset and unrecorded lease liability are both zero after the last lease payment is made for each lease.

These assumptions should be appropriate in most instances and should not be unreasonably binding in the subsequent analysis.

TABLE 3 Constructive Capitalization of Operating Leases: Relation Between Unrecorded Liability and Unrecorded Asset Over Time

Total Lease Life	Marginal Interest Rate	Ratio of Asset Balance to Liability Balance[a] % of Original Lease Life Expired							Point of Maximum Difference Between Asset and Liability
		20%	30%	40%	50%	60%	70%	80%	
10	.08	93%	90%	87%	84%	81%	78%	75%	53%
15	.08	91	86	82	78	74	70	66	55%
20	.08	89	83	78	73	68	64	59	56%
25	.08	87	81	75	69	64	58	53	58%
30	.08	86	79	72	66	60	54	49	59%
10	.10	92	88	85	81	78	74	71	54%
15	.10	89	84	79	74	70	65	61	56%
20	.10	87	81	75	69	64	59	54	58%
25	.10	85	78	72	65	59	53	48	59%
30	.10	84	76	69	62	55	49	43	61%
10	.12	91	87	82	78	74	71	67	55%
15	.12	88	82	77	71	66	61	57	57%
20	.12	86	79	72	66	60	55	49	59%
25	.12	84	76	69	62	56	49	44	61%
30	.12	83	75	67	59	52	45	39	63%

[a] Ratio equals (RL/TL) times PV of annuity for TL at i%, divided by PV of annuity for RL at i%, where RL = remaining life, TL = total life and i% = marginal borrowing rate.

All percentages in Table 3 are below 100 percent because, after the first payment, the unpaid balance in each (unrecorded) operating lease liability is greater than the balance in its respective (unrecorded) operating lease asset. For any interest bearing debt being repaid in equal payments, the early payments are primarily interest payments and the principal is reduced at a slower than straight-line rate. In later periods, the debt payments become mostly principal, and the opposite effect occurs. But until the lease is terminated, the balance in the unrecorded lease debt is always greater than the net book value of the unrecorded asset. This relation between the net book value of the unrecorded asset and the unrecorded liability over time is depicted in Figure 1.

To apply the percentages in Table 3 to the McDonald's data requires an estimate of the weighted average total life of the operating leases and the percentage of the life that has expired. Previously we assumed a weighted average total life of 30 years with 15 years remaining (i.e., 50 percent expired). Using the 10 percent interest rate category in Table 3, the implied net book value of the unrecorded asset is 62 percent of the estimated unrecorded liability balance. Alternatively, staying within the 10 percent interest category, if the weighted average total life is 25 years with 15 years remaining (i.e., 10/25 = 40 percent expired), the unrecorded asset would be 72 percent of the unrecorded liability amount. The asset percentage will generally be between 60 and 80 percent in most cases, and it is not unreasonable to simply use 70 percent as a rule of thumb in estimating the unrecorded asset.

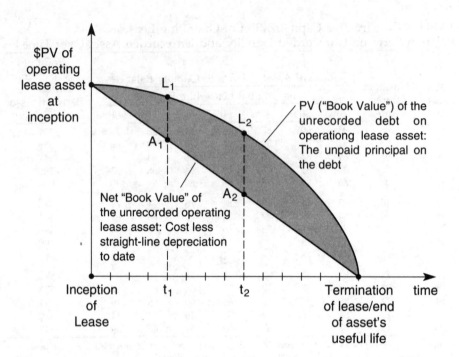

FIGURE 1 The relation between the unrecorded operating lease asset and the unrecorded operating lease liability.

Using Table 3 as a guide, we estimate that the unrecorded asset value is 67 percent of the unrecorded liability for McDonald's. This estimate is between the 62 percent (30 years, 50 percent expired) and the 72 percent (25 years, 40 percent expired) tabled values assuming a 10 percent interest rate. The result is that McDonald's leased assets would have increased by $785.8 million if the operating leases had been capitalized. This is about one tenth of total assets, but it is more than ten times larger than the capitalized leases under SFAS 13 (see Table 1).

Effects on Net Income of Constructive Capitalization

As mentioned, the unrecorded liability will exceed the unrecorded asset. The last column in Table 3 reports "Point of Maximum Difference . . ." between these two balances, which is the stage in the lease's life where net income is the same when measured under either the operating lease or capital lease accounting convention. Prior to this point, the depreciation plus interest expenses under the capital lease method will exceed the rent expense under the operating lease method. After this point, the reverse is true. For example, for a leased asset with a 20-year life and a 10 percent interest rate, Table 3 indicates that the point of maximum difference occurs after 58 percent of the

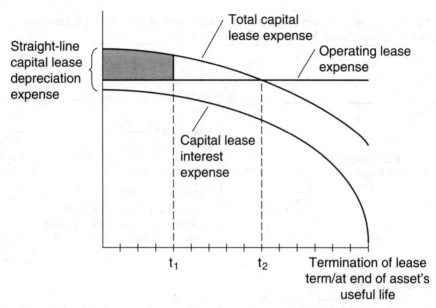

FIGURE 2 The relation between the total annual expense from operating versus capital leases.

20-year life, or during the 12th year of the lease. After this point, the amount of the operating lease rent expense (the cash payment) per month becomes greater than the sum of the depreciation expense plus interest expense per month that would have been reported if the same operating lease had been capitalized.

Figure 2 further establishes the relationship between the balance sheet and income statement effects of capital versus operating lease accounting treatments. Figure 2 depicts the recognized expenses for capital versus operating leases over the life of the lease. The cumulative excess of capital lease expenses over operating lease expense up to time t_1 (the shaded area in Figure 2) equals the difference between the capitalized liability and asset at time t_1 (also represented by the distance $A_1—L_1$ in Figure 1). In Figure 2, time t_2 represents the breakeven point where the periodic capital lease expenses equal the periodic operating lease expenses, and it also identifies the point of the maximum difference between the capital lease liability balance and the capital lease asset balance. As reported in the last column of Table 3, this point generally occurs past the halfway point in the lease's life, after between 53–63 percent of the asset has been depreciated.

The insight from Figure 2 is that constructive capitalization will have only a minimal effect on the current period's income if the weighted average age of a company's operating leases is near t_2. For a company with a stable portfolio of leases, this is normally the case since the average lease is 50 percent of the

TABLE 4 Impact of Constructive Capitalization of Operating Leases on McDonald's Balance Sheet and Financial Ratios

Panal A: Balance Sheet Impact

Balance Sheet
December 31, 1988
($ in millions)

Assets		Liabilities:	
		Unrecorded Lease Liabilities (See Table 2 Details)	$1,172.8[a]
Unrecorded Lease Assets (.67 × Liability)	$785.8[b]	Tax Consequences (.4 × $387)	(154.8)[d]
		Net Liability Effect	$1,018.0
		Stockholders Equity:	
		Cumulative Effect on Retained Earnings Net of Tax Consequences ($1,172.8 − $785.8 = $387) × (1 − .4)	(232.2)[c]
	$785.8		$ 785.8

a Step 1—see Table 2 calculation
b Step 2—using Table 3
c Step 3—based on combined total marginal tax rate of 40 percent
d Step 4—either deferred income taxes or taxes payable depending on tax treatment of lease

Panel B: Impact on Financial Ratios

	Return on Assets (ROA)	Total Debt to Total Equity (D/E)
1) As reported based on annual report	$\frac{\$646}{\$8,159} = 7.9\%$	$\frac{\$4,746}{\$3,413} = 1.39$ times
2) As revised per panel A adjustments to balance sheet only	$\frac{\$646}{\$8,945} = 7.2\%$	$\frac{\$5,764}{\$3,181} = 1.81$ times
3) Percentage change $\left(\frac{(1-2)}{1}\right)$	9% Decrease in ROA	30% Increase in D/E

way through its life.[11] The remaining analysis assumes the effect on the current period's income of constructive capitalization is minimal, and hence, examines only the effects of balance sheet capitalization as described above.

Table 4 provides a summary of McDonald's assets, liabilities and retained earnings based on our constructive capitalization technique and the assumptions used above. The analysis further assumes that the appropriate combined tax rate is 40 percent (actual effective tax expense in 1988 was 38.3 percent per Table 1), and the calculation or return on assets (ROA) assumes that the impact on the current period's (1988) income is negligible. Note that

[11] An indication of the average age of a company's portfolio of leases can be obtained by considering the historical pattern of the actual annual operating lease expense disclosed in the footnotes. If the operating lease rent expense (excluding contingent rentals based on sales) has been dramatically increasing, this is indicative of the company's growing activity in operating leases, implying a relatively young age for the portfolio. A relatively stable rent expense is consistent with a portfolio of leases which are, on average, 50 percent through their useful lives. A series of declining annual rent expenses signals a mature portfolio of operating leases.

because we assumed the weighted average percentage of the original life for McDonald's operating leases to be between 40 and 50 percent expired, or sometime *before* the point of maximum difference between the asset and liability (see Table 3), the analysis of the impact on ROA reported in Panel B of Table 4 should *understate* the impact of constructive capitalization on ROA. That is, 1988 net income under constructive capitalization will *decrease* if the weighted average age of the leases is earlier than the point of maximum difference. Ignoring the 1988 net income effect will not materially affect the debt to equity (D/E) ratio analysis. Based on the Table 4 results, we find that if McDonald's had capitalized their operating leases, their ROA ratio for 1988 would have been about 9 percent less and their D/E ratio would have been about 30 percent higher. These are material effects, and it would be difficult to conduct a meaningful analysis of McDonald's performance or leverage without considering the potential impact of their operating leases.

EVIDENCE ON THE EFFECTS OF CONSTRUCTIVE CAPITALIZATION

How prevalent is the use of operating leases as an important source of off-balance sheet financing and investing activity? Although we find certain industries with virtually no long-term lease commitments of any kind, operating leases do appear to be an important source of financing in a significant number of industries. At the same time, the use of operating leases within these industries varies across firms. For these reasons, constructive capitalization is an important ingredient in both inter- and intra-industry comparisons. In the detailed financial statement analyses made by security analysts, intra-industry comparisons would be most relevant. Inter-industry comparisons are frequently made in accounting research, where the D/E ratio is often used to capture leverage differences between industries. Thus, constructive capitalization can be fruitfully used in both endeavors.

To demonstrate that both intra- and inter-industry effects can be significant, we applied the constructive capitalization techniques to a sample of seven pairs of firms in different industries for the 1987 fiscal year. The sample pairs were selected by first identifying those four-digit SIC Code Industries where the average ratio of operating lease cash flows for years 1–5 to total reported assets was relatively high. Within each of these industries, we sought firm pairs which were relatively similar in size, measured by total reported assets, but were relatively different in their use of operating leases.[12]

---

[12] Because COMPUSTAT does not report scheduled minimum operating lease cash flows beyond 5 years into the future, these sample data were collected from actual annual report footnotes. COMPUSTAT was used to screen for firms based on two important ratios: 1) cash flows for operating leases scheduled for years 1–5 divided by total assets; and 2) the 5-year-ahead cash flow divided by the 1-year-ahead cash flow. This latter criterion assessed the likelihood that the operating lease commitments are long-term in that the amount scheduled for years beyond year 5 are more likely to be material when the fraction is large.

TABLE 5 Impact of Constructive Capitalization of Operating Leases on Seven Industry Pairings

Industry/Company	As Reported ($ in millions)			Reported ROA	Revised ROA	% Change[b]	Reported D/E Multiple	Revised D/E Multiple	% Change[b]
	Total Assets	Total Debt	Net Income[a]						
Home Furnishings									
Pier 1 Imports	$ 257.9	$ 163.8	$ 16.1	6.2%	4.0%	-35%	1.7	6.0	+243%
Rhodes, Inc.	261.5	152.0	11.9	4.6	4.1	-9	1.4	1.8	+30
Food Stores									
Winn-Dixie	1,417.7	678.3	112.3	7.9	5.3	-33	.9	2.8	+204
A&P (Great Atl. & Pac.)	2,248.2	1,391.9	103.4	4.6	4.0	-14	1.6	2.5	+50
Fast Food									
Foodmaker (Jack-in-box)	470.5	352.9	13.9	2.9	2.4	-19	3.0	5.6	+85
Church's Fried Chicken	344.8	86.3	9.5	2.8	2.6	-4	.3	.4	+25
Semi-Fast Food									
TGI Friday's	178.6	70.6	7.9	4.4	2.7	-38	.7	2.6	+302
Luby's Cafeteria	162.2	36.6	23.7	14.6	13.4	-8	.3	.4	+54
Clothing									
The Limited	1,587.9	858.8	235.2	14.8	9.6	-35	1.2	3.8	+222
Petrie Stores	1,134.3	595.8	47.5	4.2	3.5	-16	1.1	1.8	+64
Drug/Food Stores									
Walgreen Co.	1,362.0	739.6	103.5	7.6	5.6	-27	1.2	2.8	+134
American Stores	3,650.2	2,764.5	154.3	4.2	3.9	-9	3.1	4.0	+29
Airlines									
Delta	5,342.4	3,404.5	263.7	4.9	3.5	-29	1.8	4.4	+150
TWA	4,224.2	3,931.7	45.3	1.1	1.0	-9	13.5	23.8	+77
Average Percentage Changes									
High Lessee						-34%			+191%
Low Lessee						-10%			+47%

[a] Excluding Extraordinary Gains/Losses
[b] Based on non-rounded ratio values: (Actual-Revised)/Actual.

Constructive capitalization could have been conducted on a firm-by-firm basis, as with McDonald's. However, we elected to employ a uniform set of assumptions in order to ensure that the resulting changes and differences can be attributed strictly to differences in the operating leases and not to differences in our assumptions. Although these uniform assumptions may not be equally appropriate for all 14 companies examined, sensitivity tests indicate these results are robust. The constructive capitalization for these seven pairs of firms are based on the following six uniform assumptions:

1. an appropriate interest rate is 10 percent for each company;
2. the average remaining life of the operating leases is 15 years;
3. all scheduled cash flows occur at year-end;
4. the unrecorded asset equals 70 percent of the unrecorded debt;
5. the combined effective tax rate is 40 percent;
6. the effect on the current period's net income is zero.

Based on these six assumptions, we measured the impact of constructive capitalization of operating leases on the return on assets and debt to equity ratios. The results reported in Table 5 are consistent with the premise that operating leases can materially affect interfirm comparisons of key financial statement ratios. The average decrease in ROA for the high lessees is 34 percent compared to 10 percent for the low lessees. The average increase in D/E for the high lessees is 191 percent compared to only 47 percent for the low lessees. These differences are real and material under a wide range of alternative firm-specific assumptions concerning interest rates, asset lives, and so on. The off-balance sheet effects of operating leases in these and numerous other cases are simply too material to ignore for meaningful analyses and comparisons of financial statement data.

SUMMARY

The results reported here strongly suggest that constructive capitalization of material long-term operating lease commitments may be necessary before an accurate evaluation of financial results within or across firms and industries can be performed. Although the method of constructive capitalization illustrated here has some limitations, these limitations do not undermine the general usefulness of this approach to estimating financial statement effects. Financial statement users with sufficient economic incentives may obtain additional nonfinancial statement information in order to improve the precision of their estimates of the key constructive capitalization variables, such as interest rates and asset lives. This method should prove very useful for (1) in-depth comparisons and analyses involving relatively small groups of firms for which operating leases are significant to some or all and (2) broad-based empirical studies in which balance sheet data are a relevant component of the underlying economic analysis. Future research may reveal whether these off-balance sheet effects are being incorporated by the capital markets.

CHAPTER 12

Pensions and Post-Retirement Benefits

The off-balance sheet financing question arises also in the area of pension accounting and the related area of accounting for post-retirement benefits other than pensions. Historically, pensions and other post-retirement benefits were accounted for on a pay-as-you-go basis in the income statement, with the reported expense equalling the cash paid out to retirees. No liabilities were recognized in the balance sheet for future obligations. In 1966, the Accounting Principles Board (APB) issued Opinion No. 8, mandating accrual accounting for the pension liability and expense. Though flawed in many ways, the rule did bring a greater degree of uniformity in the measurement of annual pension expenses. It did not, however, address the issue of balance sheet recognition of the pension liability. It also did not address the matter of retiree health benefits, which did not become an issue of great importance until the run-up of the cost of medical care in the 1970s and 1980s.

After considerable effort (following two discussion memoranda, two public hearings, and a number of sponsored research studies), the Financial Accounting Standards Board (FASB) issued Statement No. 87 in 1985, incorporating new rules for the balance sheet disclosure of pension liability as well as bringing more uniformity into the calculation and disclosure of pension expense. Here are highlights of Statement No. 87's main provisions:

- The pension expense calculation resembles more closely the economic cost of providing pension coverage to current employees, and avoids the arbitrary "minimum" and "maximum" provisions of APB Opinion No. 8.
- Companies are required in some cases to disclose a liability in the balance sheet, called the "minimum liability," to reflect underfunded pension obligations.
- Detailed footnote disclosures are required to reconcile the liabilities reported in the balance sheet with unrecognized amounts.

While the disclosure rules are a clear improvement over the earlier standard, Statement No. 87 ended up compromising on the balance sheet recognition of unfunded pension liability. Rather than requiring the recognition of the excess of *projected* benefit obligations over the market value of plan assets as a liability, the FASB opted instead to require the recognition of a related, but smaller, amount representing the excess of *accumulated* benefit obligations ·over plan assets.

Unlike lease accounting rules, Statement No. 87 has been generally well received by corporate managers, for many reasons. It helped that Statement No. 87 became effective during a period of strong U.S. stock and bond markets. As a result, few firms were forced to report a balance sheet liability. Moreover, Statement No. 87 included a variety of "smoothing" rules, such as the "corridor" approach to the amortization of gains and losses, which minimized the likelihood of reporting unexpectedly large pension expenses or liabilities. Finally, corporations made the best use of a controversial policy shift by the FASB to allow a very long window in which to adopt the more difficult provisions of Statement No. 87. While Statement No. 87 was issued in 1985, the recognition of minimum liability was required only by 1989. The FASB argued that an extended adoption period was needed to reduce companies' costs of implementing new accounting rules. However, an unintended effect of Statement No. 87's extended adoption period may have been some "earnings management" by corporations.[1]

In "The Effect of Statement No. 87 on the Financial Reports of Early Adopters," Mary Stone and Robert Ingram document the financial statement effects of Statement No. 87 on 227 companies that elected to adopt the statement early. They also provide statistical data on the financial characteristics of the early adopters. They find that Statement No. 87 "generally had a favorable effect on the income statements of most of the early adopters." They also find that the initial balance sheet effect of Statement No. 87 was "minimal." Only ten companies in their sample recognized a minimum liability. Their data suggest that it was less the cost of implementation than the direction of the effect of Statement No. 87 in financial reports that was the main factor influencing the timing of adoption.

Accounting for post-retirement benefits other than pensions was covered for the first time by an "interim" FASB rule in Statement No. 81, followed later by the much more comprehensive Statement No. 106, "Employers' Accounting for Postretirement Benefits Other Than Pensions."[2] This statement follows the general doctrine of Statement No. 87 and in fact resembles Statement No. 87 in many of its expense computation provisions. However, unlike Statement No. 87, Statement No. 106 does not require companies to

---

[1] See Russell Langer and Baruch Lev, "The FASB's Policy of Extended Adoption for New Standards: An Examination of FAS No. 87," *The Accounting Review* (July 1993), pp. 515–533.

[2] The FASB initially used the terminology "other post-employment benefits" or OPEB, to refer to post-retirement benefits, but no longer. Instead, "post-employment benefits" now means benefits offered by employers subsequent to the beginning of one's employment and before retirement.

report a "minimum liability" in the balance sheet. Moreover, the transition obligation, or the amount of the unfunded obligation at the time of adopting Statement No. 106, can optionally be written off as expense in one lump sum as a cumulative effect of an accounting change in the year of the adoption or be amortized (generally over 20 years) as an ordinary expense as in the case of Statement No. 87. The vast majority of adopters of Statement No. 106 have chosen the one-time write-off option, presumably because analysts tend to discount the cumulative effect disclosure as a one-time non-cash event of no valuation consequence.

The impact of Statement No. 106 on the financial statements of some adopters has been substantial. The largest after-tax transition amount was reported by General Motors, $20.8 billion. By comparison, its December 31, 1991 owners' equity was $27 billion. Chrysler's after-tax charge of $4.7 billion is greater than its retained earnings. Ford Motor took a $7.5 billion write-off, American Telephone & Telegraph took a $7 billion charge, and IBM took a charge of $2.3 billion. Many adopters of Statement No. 87 have also announced reductions in their future benefits coverage. For example, Primerica said it would ask 7,800 retirees to start paying the cost of continuing health benefits. Not surprisingly, some practitioners have sought relief from Congress and the Securities and Exchange Commission to modify or mitigate the alleged economic effects of Statement No. 106.[3]

Pat McConnell, a noted Wall Street financial analyst, documents the financial statement impact of Statement No. 106 adoption in "Retiree Health Care Accounting: Impact on 70 Companies." She notes that the health care obligation as a multiple of the former pay-as-you-go expense shows wide variations among the companies sampled, from a low of eight times to a high of 60 times. All 70 companies took an immediate charge to income rather than electing to spread the transition amount over 15 years. Unlike the case of the early adopters of the FASB's pension rule studied by Stone and Ingram, McConnell concludes that the early adopters of Statement No. 106 had little to gain from their early adoption. These firms thus raise an interesting issue: Why did they not take advantage of the extended adoption period of Statement No. 106 and use the time to amend their health coverage rules and thereby lower the transition amounts?

BIBLIOGRAPHICAL NOTES

The FASB's discussion documents on the subject of pensions and post-retirement benefits are:

Employers' Accounting for Pensions and Other Postemployment Benefits, Discussion Memorandum (Financial Accounting Standards Board, February 1981).

---

[3] See Robert G. Ripston, "Wrongheaded Hit at Retiree Benefits," *The Wall Street Journal* (December 28, 1992).

Employers' Accounting for Pensions and Other Postemployment Benefits, Preliminary Views (Financial Accounting Standards Board, November 1982).

Employers' Accounting for Pensions and Other Postemployment Benefits, Discussion Memorandum (Financial Accounting Standards Board, April 1983).

An Australian issues paper on pensions is:

Hubbard, Graham: *Accounting and Reporting for Superannuation Plans*, Discussion Paper No. 7 (Melbourne: Australian Accounting Research Foundation, 1982).

See also a Canadian study on this subject:

Archibald, T. Ross: *Accounting for Pension Costs and Liabilities* (Toronto: Canadian Institute of Chartered Accountants, 1980).

A study of pension accounting by a leading Canadian practitioner is:

Skinner, R. M.: *Pension Accounting—The Problem of Equating Payments Tomorrow with Expenses Today* (Toronto: The Clarkson Gordon Foundation, 1980).

Also see Skinner's discussion of his research project in

Basu, Sanjoy, and J. Alex Milburn (editors): *Research to Support Standard Setting in Financial Accounting: A Canadian Perspective* (Toronto: The Clarkson Gordon Foundation, 1982), pp. 177–202.

The following articles provide supplementary discussion of various technical issues raised by Statements 87 and 106:

Bline, Dennis M., and Ted D. Skekel: "Effective Classroom Presentation of FAS 87 Footnote Reconciliation," *Issues in Accounting Education* (Fall 1988), pp. 215–227.

Lucas, Timothy S., and Paul B. W. Miller: "Pension Accounting: Impacting the Financial Statement," *Journal of Accountancy* (June 1983), pp. 90–92, 94, 96, 99–102, 105–106.

Searfoss, D. Gerald, and Naomi Erickson: "The Big Unfunded Liability: Postretirement Healthcare Benefits," *Journal of Accountancy* (November 1988), pp. 28–39.

Thomas, Paula B., and Larry Farmer: "OPEB: Improved Reporting or the Last Straw?" *Journal of Accountancy* (November 1990), pp. 102–112.

Wilbert, James R., and Kenneth E. Dakdduk: "The New FASB 106: How to Account for Postretirement Benefits," *Journal of Accountancy* (August 1991), pp. 36–41.

The following articles discuss the management reaction to, or the financial statement impact of, the FASB rules:

Berton, Lee: "Profit Volatility Rises After Rule Change: Some Earnings Said 'Created' by Bookkeeping," *The Wall Street Journal* (May 6, 1986).

Berton, Lee: "New Benefits-Accounting Rule Yields Fresh Red Tape," *The Wall Street Journal* (January 29, 1991).

Crossen, Cynthia: "Dreaded Disclosure: New Accounting Rule May Affect Pensions of Millions of People," *The Wall Street Journal* (January 18, 1988).

Gillespie, Richard J.: "FASB 87 Produces $1 Billion Swing at AT&T," *Pensions & Investment Age* (July 7, 1986), p. 22.

McConnell, Pat: "Pension Accounting Boosts Corporate Earnings: Aerospace Takes Off," *Accounting Issues* (Bear Stearns, July 17, 1990).

McConnell, Pat: "FASB No. 106—Retiree Health Care Accounting: Early Adopters and Footnote Disclosures Reviewed," *Accounting Issues* (Bear Stearns, April 18, 1991). (This is a predecessor to the article that is reproduced in this chapter.)

More articles on the timing of adoption of Statement No. 87:

Norton, Curtis: "Transition to New Accounting Rules: The Case of FAS 87," *Accounting Horizons* (December 1989), pp. 40–48.

Sami, Heibatollah, and Mary Jeanne Welsh: "Characteristics of Early and Late Adopters of Pension Accounting Standard SFAS No. 87," *Contemporary Accounting Research* (Fall 1992), pp. 212–236.

The following articles focus on management choices resulting from the FASB rules:

Mackie, James Jay, and Minica E. Oss: "Reducing Retiree Health Care Liabilities," *Management Accounting* (April 1989), pp. 21–26. Subtitle: "In the wake of FASB's rule, hard choices and 10 options."

Petertil, Jeffrey: "Ignore the Retiree Health Benefits Rule," *The Wall Street Journal* (February 21, 1992).

Ross, E. Chadwick: "FAS 87—What It Means For Business," *Management Accounting* (March 1986), pp. 20–24.

Wallis, Charles T.: "FASB Statement No. 87 And The Bottom Line," *Corporate Accounting* (Fall 1987), pp. 38–41.

Researchers have started to examine the impact of the pension and post-retirement disclosures on the financial markets as well the impact of the disclosures on financial statement analysis. Here are some articles:

Amir, Eli: "The Market Valuation of Accounting Information: The Case of Post-Retirement Benefits Other than Pensions," *The Accounting Review* (October 1993), pp. 703–724.

Barth, Mary: "Relative Measurement Errors Among Alternative Pension Asset and Liability Measures," *The Accounting Review* (July 1991), pp. 433–463.

Harold Danker *et al.* of Coopers & Lybrand: *Employer Accounting for Pension Costs and Other Post-Retirement Benefits* (New York: Financial Executives Research Foundation, 1981).

Landsman, Wayne R.: "An Empirical Investigation of Pension and Property Rights," *The Accounting Review* (October 1986), pp. 662–691.

Thomas, Jacob K.: "Why Do Firms Terminate Their Overfunded Pension Plans?," *Journal of Accounting and Economics* (November 1989), pp. 361–398.

The Effect of Statement No. 87 on the Financial Reports of Early Adopters

Mary Stone
University of Alabama

Robert W. Ingram
University of Alabama

OVERVIEW

Despite claims of adverse economic consequences, the Financial Accounting Standards Board (FASB) issued *Statement No. 87*[1] in late December 1985.[2] Some of the more controversial provisions of the statement require all companies sponsoring defined benefit pension plans (1) to use a uniform method for computing pension expense rather than selecting from several equally acceptable alternatives, (2) to disclose the service cost, interest cost, actual return, and amortization components of pension expense, (3) to provide additional disclosures about the funding status of the company's pension plans, (4) to narrow the range of actuarial assumptions used in computing pension expense and valuing promised benefits, (5) to recognize a balance sheet liability for underfunded pension plans, and (6) to begin applying the new pension accounting rules within two years.

Because the new pension accounting standard requires many computational changes and new disclosures, it has been impossible to predict exactly how its initial application would affect the income statements and balance sheets of plan sponsors or the pension plan presentations in the footnotes to the corporate annual reports. A number of companies responding to the *Exposure Draft*[3] and the *Preliminary Views*[4] that preceded *Statement No. 87* predicted negative impacts on earnings, pension funding, borrowing capacity, and other corporate activities. Because a substantial number of companies have begun applying *Statement No. 87*, it is now possible to assess the accuracy of those predictions for companies that chose to apply the statement early rather than to wait until the 1987 deadline for initial application.

From *Accounting Horizons* (September 1988), pp. 48–61. Reprinted by permission of the American Accounting Association and the authors. Copyright © 1988 by the American Accounting Association.

Authors' note: The authors gratefully acknowledge the financial support of a University of Alabama Research Grant and the Peat, Marwick, Mitchell Foundation.

[1] FASB, "Employers' Accounting for Pensions," *Statement of Financial Accounting Standards No. 87* (FASB, December 1985).

[2] For a summary of the predicted adverse consequences of *Statement No. 87*, see "How Damaging Will the New Accounting Laws Be?" *Institutional Investor* (April 1986), pp. 131–142.

[3] FASB, "Employers' Accounting for Pensions," *Exposure Draft* (FASB, March 1985).

[4] FASB, *Preliminary Views* (FASB, November 1982).

Analysis of the disclosures and financial statement effect of *Statement No. 87* on these early adopters will provide a basis for later comparison with the effects of initial application on companies that deferred application. Arguably, the companies that chose to apply *Statement No. 87* early would be the ones that were favorably or less adversely affected by the new pension accounting rules. The results reported in this paper substantiate this argument. Thus, the importance of the results of the paper is not in the identity of the adopters but in the number of adopters and in the nature and magnitude of the effects of *Statement No. 87* on the adopters.

The objective of this paper is to describe the effect of *Statement No. 87* on the financial reports of corporations that adopted the statement in 1986 and to assess the usefulness of the new pension information for evaluating the cost of plan sponsorship and the funding sufficiency of large corporate pension plans. Examining the actual pension disclosures provides a much clearer picture of how the components of pension cost and the projected benefit obligation are computed and related to one another than is provided by reading *Statement No. 87* or the texts and professional literature that have been written to explain the statement.

Questions Addressed by the Study

To achieve its objective, the paper addresses the following questions:

1. What are the pension plan and operating characteristics of the companies that chose to apply *Statement No. 87* early?
2. What is the effect of *Statement No. 87* on pension expense? What insights do the disclosures of the components of pension expense provide about the cost of using pension promises to compensate employees?
3. Has *Statement No. 87* narrowed the range of actuarial assumptions selected by employers?
4. What do the *Statement No. 87* disclosures show about the funding status of U.S. pension plans? To what extent do the new funding measures that can be calculated from the *Statement No. 87* data provide a different picture of plans' funding status than was provided under FASB *Statement No. 36*?[5]
5. What was the effect of the initial application of *Statement No. 87* on corporate balance sheets?

After a brief summary and a description of the companies whose pension disclosures are studied, the remaining sections of the paper are devoted to addressing each of the questions listed above. Each section begins with a brief discussion of the provisions of *Statement No. 87* that are relevant to the question addressed.

---

[5] FASB, "Disclosure of Pension Information: An Amendment of APB Opinion No. 8," *Statement of Financial Accounting Standards No. 36* (FASB, May 1980).

Summary of Answers From the Study

Analysis of pension data relevant to answering each of the questions indicates that (1) a substantial number of large companies with overfunded pension plans elected to apply *Statement No. 87* early, (2) for all but five companies, the initial application of *Statement No. 87* had no material effect on income or resulted in a decrease in pension expense and an increase in after-tax income, (3) the service cost component of net periodic pension cost is small relative to the interest cost and amortization/deferral components, (4) application of *Statement No. 87* did not significantly narrow the range of assumptions used to compute pension expense and obligations, (5) there are relatively significant differences in the funding status of the different plans sponsored by an individual employer, and (6) the initial balance sheet impact of *Statement No. 87* was minimal.

COMPANIES STUDIED

The study began with the 650 companies surveyed by the American Institute of Certified Public Accountants (AICPA) for the 1986 and 1987 editions of *Accounting Trends & Techniques*.[6] Under the extended transition period allowed by *Statement No. 87*, none of the companies would have had to begin applying *Statement No. 87* until 1987. However, information obtained from the AICPA indicated that 18 of the companies surveyed had applied *Statement No. 87* in preparing their 1985 annual reports and that another 265 had first applied the statement in preparing their 1986 annual reports. The remaining 367 companies did not sponsor defined benefit pension plans or were deferring application of the statement until 1987.

Because plan funding status and other pension information may be affected by general economic and stock market conditions that vary from year to year, this paper focuses primarily on the 265 companies that began applying *Statement No. 87* in 1986. The 1986 annual reports for 243 of these companies were available in the university library. Initial examination of the pension footnotes for these companies indicated a high degree of compliance with the specific requirements of *Statement No. 87* and the use of a presentation format very similar to the illustration provided in the appendix of the statement. Only four companies had to be dropped from the study because of the insufficiency of their pension disclosures. Full pension data were available for the remaining 239 companies and the 319 defined benefit pension plans they sponsored.

These companies are the data base for the parts of the paper that focus only on pension information. Whenever the pension information is analyzed along with other company financial or industry data, the data base is reduced

---

[6] AICPA, *Accounting Trends and Techniques* (AICPA, 1986, 1987).

to the 227 companies that also have data available on the 1987 version of the Compustat Annual Industrial Tape.

CHARACTERISTICS OF COMPANIES CHOOSING EARLY ADOPTION

Although *Statement No. 87* was issued in December 1985, initial application of the statement's expense and disclosure provisions could be deferred until 1987. The recognition of an additional liability for underfunded plans could be deferred until 1989. The extended transition period was allowed "to give time for employers and their advisors to assimilate the (Statement's) requirements. . . . to obtain the information required" and "to arrange to renegotiate or to obtain waivers of provision of some legal contracts."[7] To date, only FASB *Statement No. 19*[8] has had as lengthy a transition period.

The Board's justification for the extended transition period suggests that transition was expected to be difficult, at least for some corporations. The results of a survey by *Institutional Investor*[9] published shortly after the issuance of *Statement No. 87* are consistent with this reasoning. They indicated that only 20.4 percent of the managers surveyed definitely planned to adopt *Statement No. 87* early. However, the AICPA data on the timing of initial application, which was discussed earlier in this paper, indicate an early adoption rate more than twice as high. According to the AICPA data, 283 or 44 percent of the 650 companies surveyed adopted *Statement No. 87* in 1985 or 1986.

A comparison of sample companies with an FASB data base of large firms sponsoring defined benefit pension plans and Pension Benefit Guaranty Corporation (PBGC) lists of companies terminating plans indicates that only 267 of the companies not listed as early adopters are likely to be sponsors of defined benefit pension plans subject to the requirements of *Statement No. 87*. Thus, the early adoption rate may be as high as 60 percent. This higher adoption rate may indicate that the transition process was not as difficult as anticipated or that under 1985 and 1986 stock market conditions adopting *Statement No. 87* had a favorable effect on the companies' financial statements.

The Board did not discuss the characteristics of the companies that it thought would need additional time for transition. Discussion in *The Wall Street Journal*,[10] however, suggested that companies in the smokestack, heavy

---

[7] FASB, *Statement No. 87*, paragraph 259.

[8] FASB, "Financial Accounting and Reporting by Oil and Gas Producing Companies," *Statement of Financial Accounting Standards No. 19* (FASB, December 1977).

[9] "Assessing the New Accounting Rules," *Institutional Investor* (August 1986), pp. 137–138.

[10] "Concessions to Industry Critics on the Issues of Pensions and Taxes are Expected at the FASB" (Business Bulletin), *The Wall Street Journal* (January 10, 1985), p. 1, column 5. For additional discussion also see articles on p. 8 of the March 22, 1985, p. 6 of the December 6, 1985 and p. 2 of the December 27, 1985 editions.

manufacturing industries would be the most reluctant to begin applying the new statement becuase it would increase pension expense and, by 1989, lead to the recognition of a balance sheet liability for unfunded accumulated benefits.

This line of reasoning is not supported by data in Table 1, which compares the number of early and deferred adopters included in the 2000 and 3000 Standard Industrial Classification (SIC) codes used for companies engaged in manufacturing. Approximately half of the manufacturing companies adopted *Statement No. 87* early and approximately half deferred application.

Table 1 also does not suggest a pattern of either early or deferred adoption by companies in specific industries within the manufacturing classification. The largest concentration of early adopters was in the chemicals industry (SIC code 2800), which accounts for approximately 14 percent of the early adopters in Table 1. The largest concentration of deferred adopters was in the electrical

TABLE 1 Timing of the Initial Adoption of FASB *Statement No. 87* by Firms in the Manufacturing Industries, SIC Codes 2000 and 3000[a]

2-digit SIC Code and Industry Name	Number of Firms Adopting in		
	1985	1986	1987[b]
20 Food and Kindred	0	12	23
21 Tobacco Products	0	2	0
22 Textile	0	4	7
23 Apparel	1	2	5
24 Lumber and Wood Products	0	1	1
25 Furniture	0	0	2
26 Paper and Allied Products	1	15	3
27 Printing and Publishing	0	9	10
28 Chemicals	2	27	18
29 Petroleum Refining	3	15	7
30 Rubber	0	4	8
31 Footwear	0	1	1
32 Stone, Clay, Glass, and Concrete	0	7	8
33 Primary Metals	3	10	3
34 Fabricated Metals	0	16	7
35 Machinery	1	16	16
36 Electrical Equipment and Supplies	1	24	34
37 Transportation Equipment	0	16	14
38 Professional, Scientific Equipment	0	7	5
39 Toys and Amusements	0	4	7
Total	12	192	179 = 383
As a percent of 383 of 650 AICPA-surveyed companies classified in manufacturing industries	3%	50%	47%

[a] Because this table omits companies in nonmanufacturing industries, the column totals do not equal the total number of companies adopting in each year discussed in the text.
[b] Numbers in this column reflect firms which are expected to adopt *Statement No. 87* in 1987.

equipment and supplies industry (SIC code 3600), which accounts for approximately 19 percent of the deferred adopters.

The funding status of a company's pension plans appears to have had an effect on the timing of the initial application of *Statement No. 87*. All but 19 (less than eight percent) of the 1986 adopters sponsored at least one plan in which the fair value of plan assets exceeded the projected benefit obligation at the beginning of the transition year. The average amount of excess, which was the net transition asset, was $165.6 million. Because this transition asset will be amortized over the longer of the average remaining service lives of plan participants or 15 years, future pension expense will be lower for these companies than it would have been if they had first applied the statement at a time when the projected benefit obligation exceeded the fair value of plan assets.

Approximately 23 percent of the early adopters curtailed (i.e., reduced the size of their pension commitment) or terminated a plan in the same year they initially applied *Statement No. 87* and, therefore, also applied *Statement No. 88*.[11] Because *Statement No. 88*, which could not be used until after the company had begun applying *Statement No. 87*, often would accelerate gain recognition for companies terminating pension plans, some companies may have been motivated to adopt *Statement No. 87* early so that *Statement No. 88* could be used to account for anticipated curtailments or terminations.

INCOME STATEMENT EFFECTS OF STATEMENT NO. 87

Under *Statement No. 87*, pension expense is the sum of service cost, interest cost, return on plan assets, amortization of unrecognized gains or losses, amortization of unrecognized prior service cost, and amortization of the transition net asset or obligation. The statement requires all companies to use the benefits/years-of-service method for determining service (normal) cost rather than any of five actuarial cost methods that were previously acceptable.

The FASB did not conduct a formal study to predict the effects of *Statement No. 87*'s initial application. However, the results of its study of the likely effects of implementing the statement's predecessor, *Preliminary Views*, indicated that few companies already used the benefits/years-of-service method and that it would be impossible to develop general rules for predicting which companies would report higher pension expense and lower income under *Statement No. 87*.

Table 2 summarizes disclosures of (1) the amount of 1986 pension expense reported by companies initially adopting *Statement No. 87* in 1986, (2) the change in amount of pension expense attributable to the change in *Statement No. 87*, (3) the change in after-tax income caused by the accounting change,

---

[11] FASB, "Employers' Accounting for Settlements and Curtailments of Defined Benefit Pension Plans and for Termination Benefits," *Statement of Financial Accounting Standards No. 88* (FASB, December 1985).

TABLE 2 Income Statement Impact of FASB *Statement No. 87*
(in millions except for percents and per share amounts)

Panel 1 All Companies (*n* = 227)	Average	Standard Deviation
Pension Expense	$ 5.40	$58.75
Decrease in Pension Expense	− 22.49	75.40
Increase in Income (after-tax)	14.39	61.61
Increase in Income as a Percent of Income Before 　Extraordinary Items	21%	1.76%
Increase in Income Per Share	$ .18	$ .24

Panel 2 Companies For Which FASB *Statement No. 87* Decreased Pension Expense (*n* = 190)		
Pension Expense	$ 4.13	$62.48
Decrease in Pension Expense	− 27.05	81.60
Increase in Income (after-tax)	17.31	66.97
Increase in Income as a Percent of Income Before 　Extraordinary Items	26%	1.92%
Increase in Income Per Share	$ .22	$ .24

Panel 3 Companies For Which FASB *Statement No. 87* Increased or Did Not Materially Change Pension Expense (*n* = 37)		
Pension Expense	$ 11.94	$33.53
Increase in Pension Expense	1.07	4.73
Decrease in Income (after-tax)	− .60	2.60
Increase in Income as a Percent of Income Before 　Extraordinary Items	− 5%	0.28%
Increase in Income Per Share	$ − .04	$ .15

(4) the change in after-tax income as a percent of income before extraordinary items, and (5) the change in after-tax income on a per share basis. Disclosures are summarized for the 227 1986 adopters with pension and Compustat data, for the 190 of these companies for which the accounting change resulted in a decrease in pension expense, and for the 37 companies for which the change did not materially affect or increase pension expense.

As the data in Table 2 indicate, the income statement impact of the initial application of *Statement No. 87* was favorable for most early adopters. The relatively small average pension expense of $5.4 million is attributable to the fact that 96 of the companies earned net pension income rather than incurred pension expense.[12] Companies recognize pension income whenever the return and gain components of net periodic pension cost exceed the cost and loss components. The average amount of pension income reported by these companies was $12.75 million. The average amount of pension expense for the 131 companies that incurred pension expense was $19.63 million.

---

[12] In the full sample of 239 companies, 101 companies recognized pension income.

The average decrease in pension expense for all companies was $22.49 million. This translated into an increase in after-tax income of approximately $14.39 million (21 percent) or 18 cents per share. The significance of the change is indicated by the fact that the auditors' opinion for 53 percent of the companies contained a consistency exception for the change to *Statement No. 87*.

As the second panel of the table indicates, the income statement effect was even more favorable for the 190 companies for which the change decreased pension expense. The after-tax income of these companies increased by approximately 26 percent.

Only five of the 37 companies in Panel 3 of the table disclosed the dollar amount of the increase in pension expense caused by the change to *Statement No. 87*. The remaining 32 companies indicated that the change had no material effect on pension expense. Because a change in method of determining pension expense generally would have a material effect on pension expense, these 32 companies are likely to be the ones that voluntarily were applying the benefits/years-of-service method or a closely related method prior to *Statement No. 87*.

Table 3 separates average pension expense or income into the four com-

TABLE 3 Components of Net Periodic Pension Cost

Panel 1 All Firms Disclosing Components (*n* = 238)[a]	Mean	Standard Deviation
Service Cost	$ 23.51	$ 67.74
Interest Cost	64.59	211.92
Actual Return on Plan Assets	(152.82)	567.42
Net Amortization and Deferrals	69.88	332.51
Net Periodic Pension Cost	$ 5.16	

Panel 2 All Firms Reporting Pension Expense and Disclosing Components (*n* = 137)		
Service Cost	$ 29.33	$ 80.78
Interest Cost	76.36	247.98
Actual Return	(172.87)	655.93
Net Amortization and Deferrals	85.95	401.34
Net Periodic Pension Cost	$ 18.77	

Panel 3 All Firms Reporting Pension Income and Disclosing Components (*n* = 101)		
Service Cost	$ 15.62	$ 43.50
Interest Cost	48.64	149.51
Actual Return	(125.62)	420.28
Net Amortization and Deferrals	48.09	205.28
Net Periodic Pension Income	$ (13.27)	

[a] Because this table uses only data from the pension footnotes and no Compustat data, it is based on the 239 companies with footnote data minus one company that did not disclose all of the components of pension expense.

ponents that must be disclosed separately—service cost, interest cost, actual return on plan assets, and net amortization and deferrals. With few exceptions, the companies followed disclosure formats very similar to the illustrations in the appendices of *Statement No. 87*.

As the data in the table indicate, the service cost component is the smallest component of pension expense. This component measures the cost of benefits earned by employees during the year and represents a previously undisclosed component of the company's labor cost.

Interest cost, which measures the financing cost of deferring payment to employees, is more than twice as large as service cost. The higher service cost, interest cost, and actual return of the companies reporting pension expense rather than pension income suggest that companies in the former group generally sponsor plans that are larger and probably older.

The net amortization component, which is relatively large, reflects the deferral of the current period difference between actual and expected returns and the amortization of the net transition amount, which for these companies was most frequently an asset. The fact that this component is being added rather than deducted in the computation indicates that the actual return on plan assets was substantially greater than the expected return and that the deferral of this difference more than offset the amortization of the net transition asset.

The size of the average actual return on plan assets, $152.82 million, reflects the favorable stock market conditions of 1986. It represents a return of approximately 17 percent on the beginning-of-the-year value of plan assets,[13] a rate of return substantially greater than the average long-term expected rate of return of 9.26 percent disclosed by the companies.

EFFECT ON RANGE OF ACTUARIAL ASSUMPTIONS

Because most pension benefits will not be paid for many years, the computation of pension expense and benefits is based on assumptions about future interest rates, rates of return on plan assets, and annual increases in salary levels. Under the authoritative accounting standards prior to *Statement No. 87*, the assumptions had to be reasonable overall and only the expected average long-term rate of return on plan assets had to be disclosed. The lack of disclosure of individual assumptions and the wide range of rates of return documented in several studies by actuarial firms led to claims of diminished comparability. This criticism was particularly troublesome because of the

---

[13] *Statement No. 87* does not require disclosure of the fair value of plan assets at the beginning of the year of the initial application of *Statement No. 87*. Therefore, the actual rate of return was computed by dividing the actual rate of return reported in the 1986 annual report by the year-end fair value of assets reported in the 1985 annual report. In some cases, this latter amount actually was based on a valuation made earlier in the year. For these cases, the computed rate of return is likely to be an overstatement of the actual return for the year. Despite this measurement error, it is valid to conclude that the actual return was much higher than the expected return.

dramatic effect of the rate of return or discount rate assumptions on accumulated benefit computations. Trowbridge and Farr[14] provide a rule of thumb used by actuaries which attributes a 20 percent decrease in the accumulated benefit obligation to a one percent increase in the discount rate used in the calculation.

FASB *Statement No. 87* requires that each individual assumption be realistic and requires separate disclosure of (1) the discount rate used to determine the interest component of pension expense and the projected and accumulated benefit obligations, (2) the expected rate of return on plan assets used to compute expected return for use in the pension expense computation, and (3) the expected annual increase in salaries for final pay and average pay plans that base benefits on employees' future salary levels. Table 4 shows the range of assumptions used by the 1986 adopters.

As the table indicates, the range of assumptions being made continues to be relatively wide. Panel 1 of the table shows the discount rates that were selected. *Statement No. 87* defines the discount rate as the rate at which the plan's pension obligations currently could be settled. This is a rate that could be approximated by the discount rate used by the Pension Benefit Guaranty Corporation (PBGC) to calculate the termination liabilities of plans that are being terminated. The discount rates selected by the companies represented in the table ranged from 6.50 percent to 11 percent. However, the average of 8.48 percent is very close to the average PBGC 1986 settlement rate of 8.60 percent.

The expected rates of return selected by the companies are shown in Panel 2 of Table 4. These rates reflect the companies' long-term earnings expectations for existing plan assets. As the table indicates, the expected rates of return ranged from seven to 14 percent, with the majority in the range of eight to 10.5 percent. This range is not appreciably narrower than the range of six to 12.5 percent selected by these companies in 1985 under *Statement No. 36* and shown in Table 5. However, the 1986 average rate of return of 9.26 percent is higher than the 1985 average of 8.33 percent. This suggests some movement away from the selection of the comparatively low rates that companies were criticized for under *Statement No. 36.*

Some of the early analyses of *Statement No. 87* suggested that companies might select discount rates and rates of return that were equal so that net interest cost (i.e., the difference between interest cost and the expected return on plan assets) would be close to zero or negative for well-funded plans and would be equivalent to interest on the unfunded projected benefit obligation for companies sponsoring underfunded plans.[15] The rates selected by the companies studied do not indicate that the companies actually follow such a strategy. Using simple regression analysis to study the relationship between the discount rate and rate of return selected by the companies indicates that

[14] C. L. Trowbridge and C. E. Farr, *The Theory and Practice of Pension Funding* (Irwin, 1977).
[15] For a discussion of factors a benefits consulting firm thought that companies might be considering in planning to implement *Statement No. 87*, see "What FASB Statements 87 and 88 Will Mean to Employers—A Mercer-Meidinger Commentary" (William M. Mercer-Meidinger, Inc., 1986).

TABLE 4 FASB *Statement No. 87* Distributions of Discount Rate, Expected Rate of Return, and Salary Rate Assumptions

Panel 1
Discount Rate—used to compute present value of pension obligations and interest cost component of pension expense

Rate	Number of Companies	Percent of Companies	Cumulative Percent
Less than 7%	1	.40	.40
7–7.9%	21	8.80	9.20
8–8.9%	144	60.20	69.50
9–9.6%	61	25.50	95.00
10–10.5%	11	4.60	99.60
11%	1	0.40	100.00
			Average = 8.48%

Panel 2
Expected Rate of Return—used to compute expected rate of return on plan assets

7–7.5%	9	3.80	3.80
8–8.9%	59	24.60	28.40
9–9.7%	100	41.90	70.30
10–10.5%	51	21.30	91.60
11–11.8%	15	6.30	97.90
12%	4	1.70	99.60
14%	1	0.40	100.00
			Average = 9.26%

Panel 3
Salary Progression—used in determining service cost component for salary related plans

1.5%	1	0.40	0.40
3.0%	1	0.40	0.80
4.0–4.8%	10	4.30	5.10
5.0–5.95%	80	35.70	38.80
6.0–6.8%	114	48.10	86.90
7–7.5%	23	9.70	96.60
8–8.5%	8	3.40	100.00
Not disclosed	2		Average = 5.92%

TABLE 5 Expected Rates of Returns Selected by Companies in 1985 Under FASB *Statement No. 36*[a]

Rate	Number of Companies	Percent of Companies	Cumulative Percent
6–6.8%	10	4.20	4.20
7–7.9%	53	22.20	26.40
8–8.8%	101	42.20	68.60
9–9.9%	57	23.90	92.50
10–10.7%	12	5.00	97.50
11.2–11.5%	4	1.70	99.20
12.0–12.5%	2	0.80	100.00
			Average = 8.33%

[a] FASB, "Disclosure of Pension Information: An Amendment of APB Opinion No. 8," *Statement of Financial Accounting Standards No. 36* (FASB, May 1980).
Source: 1985 annual report footnotes for 239 companies initially applying *Statement No. 87* in 1986.

knowing the value of one of the rates explains only 10 percent of the variation in the selection of the other. This suggests that the rates are being selected independently and that companies are looking to different economic indicators in their selection.

These rates also are not correlated with the assumed rate of salary increase. As Panel 3 indicates, the assumed rates of salary increases selected range from 1.5 percent to 8.5 percent, with an average rate of 5.92 percent selected.

FUNDING STATUS

FASB *Statement No. 87* increases the information that is available for assessing the funding status of a company's pension plans by requiring (1) disclosure of plans' projected benefit obligations as well as their accumulated and vested benefit obligations and (2) separate disclosures of assets and benefits for plans with assets in excess of the accumulated benefit obligation and for plans with assets less than the accumulated benefit obligation (i.e., overfunded and underfunded pension plans).

The projected benefit obligation is computed on the basis of employees' service to date and the future salary levels that are expected to be in effect when benefits are paid to the employees. The obligation is intended to approximate the plan's and, in turn, the company's obligation as a going concern. The obligation is computed using a method referred to by actuaries as the projected unit credit method. Because this obligation was not a required disclosure prior to *Statement No. 87* and the actuarial method for computing it was not frequently used for funding purposes, information on the projected benefit obligation generally was not available prior to companies' initial applications of *Statement No. 87*.

Table 6 reports the average fair value of plan assets and average projected benefit obligation for the plans of the early adopters. It also reports the average accumulated benefit obligation and vested benefit obligation of the companies' plans. The accumulated benefit obligation is based on employees' service to date and current rather than future salary levels. The portion of this obligation for which all age and service requirements have been satisfied is referred to as the vested benefit obligation.

The relatively large standard deviations reported in Table 6 indicate that there was considerable variation in the size of the pension plans sponsored by the companies. Several of the companies sponsored very large pension plans that caused the distributions of plan assets and obligations to be positively skewed.

The accumulated benefit obligation is computed on the basis of employees' salaries to date rather than their expected future salaries but otherwise is computed in the same way as the projected benefit obligation. The vested benefit obligation is the portion of the accumulated benefit obligation to which employees have earned an inalienable right by satisfying all age and

TABLE 6 Plans' Assets and Obligations Under
FASB *Statement No. 87* (in millions)

Panel 1

All Plans (n = 319)	Average	Standard Deviation
Fair Value of Plan Assets	$715.99	$2,518.90
Projected Benefit Obligation	622.77	2,073.09
Accumulated Benefit Obligation	528.49	1,820.41
Vested Benefit Obligation	487.13	1,643.48

Panel 2
Overfunded Plans (n = 192)

Fair Value of Plan Assets	980.61	3,021.64
Projected Benefit Obligation	783.32	2,326.70
Accumulated Benefit Obligation	650.40	1,957.12
Vested Benefit Obligation	604.31	1,815.28

Panel 3
Underfunded Plans (n = 127)

Fair Value of Plan Assets	315.93	1,380.15
Projected Benefit Obligation	380.05	1,594.25
Accumulated Benefit Obligation	344.18	1,581.30
Vested Benefit Obligation	309.50	1,329.14

service requirements of the plan's vesting provisions. On average, the projected benefit obligation is approximately 18 percent larger than the accumulated benefit obligation and 28 percent greater than the vested benefit obligation.

Dividing the fair value of plan assets by the different pension benefit obligation measures provides a basis for assessing the funding status of the companies' pension plans. Table 7 shows the different funding status ratios that can be computed from *Statement No. 87* data and their average values for all plans of early adopters. The first ratio, fair value of assets at year-end divided by the projected benefit obligation at year-end, gives a picture of the plans' funding status assuming the plans will be continued. The average for all plans for early adopters is 1.07, which indicates that the plans of the early adopters were slightly overfunded at the end of 1986. However, expressing this funding surplus (i.e., fair value of assets—projected benefit obligation) as a percent of the obligation indicates that a 7 percent decrease in the fair value of plan assets could eliminate the appearance of overfunding.

The second ratio, fair value of assets at year-end divided by the accumulated benefit obligation, indicates the status of the companies' pension plans on a termination basis. The average of 1.30 indicates that companies have accumulated 30 percent more assets than would be necessary to settle the plans' termination liabilities. Under current pension law, these assets could revert to the company if the overfunded plans were terminated. These assets represent a potential source of financing that is not reflected on the companies' balance sheets.

The third ratio, fair value of assets at year-end divided by the vested

TABLE 7 Plans' Funding Status Under FASB *Statement No. 87*

Panel 1

All Plans (*n* = 316)[a]	Average	Standard Deviation
Funding Status on a Going-Concern Basis: Fair Value of Plan Assets/Projected Benefit Obligation	1.07	0.42
Funding Status on a Termination Basis: Fair Value of Plan Assets/Accumulated Benefit Obligation	1.30	0.59
Funding Status in Relation to Vested Benefits: Fair Value of Plan Assets/Vested Benefit Obligation	1.43	0.69

Panel 2
Overfunded Plans (*n* = 191)

	Average	Standard Deviation
Funding Status on a Going-Concern Basis: Fair Value of Plan Assets/Projected Benefit Obligation	1.33	0.27
Funding Status on a Termination Basis: Fair Value of Plan Assets/Accumulated Benefit Obligation	1.63	0.47
Funding Status in Relation to Vested Benefits: Fair Value of Plan Assets/Vested Benefit Obligation	1.80	0.60

Panel 3
Underfunded Plans (*n* = 125)

	Average	Standard Deviation
Funding Status on a Going-Concern Basis: Fair Value of Plan Assets/Projected Benefit Obligation	0.69	0.30
Funding Status on a Termination Basis: Fair Value of Plan Assets/Accumulated Benefit Obligation	0.80	0.34
Funding Status in Relation to Vested Benefits: Fair Value of Plan Assets/Vested Benefit Obligation	0.88	0.40

[a] Excludes three plans with values more than six standard deviations from the mean.

benefit obligation at year end, indicates the extent to which the firm has provided for the benefits which employees have earned by satisfying all age and service requirements of the plan. An average ratio of 1.43 indicates that the vested benefits of the employees of the early adopters are relatively secure. A fairly dramatic decline in values would be needed for these employees' vested benefits to be at risk.

Because *Statement No. 87* requires separate disclosure of asset and benefit information for overfunded and underfunded plans, the analysis of overall funding status can be refined to focus on overfunded and underfunded plans separately, as is done in Panels 2 and 3 of Table 7. Prior to *Statement No. 87*, assets and benefits of different plans of a single company (e.g., Plan A for salaried employees and Plan B for hourly workers) routinely were aggregated for disclosure purposes even if the assets of one of the plans could not be used to settle the liabilities of the other.

Eighty-seven (36 percent) of the early adopters sponsored both overfunded and underfunded plans. As the data in the bottom panels of Table 7 indicate, there are substantial differences in the funding status of the overfunded and underfunded plans. The ratio that indicates funding status on a going-concern basis is 1.33 for the overfunded plans but only 0.69 for the underfunded plans. On average, the underfunded plans are underfunded in terms of both the accumulated benefit and vested benefit obligations, with, on average, only 80 percent of the former and 88 percent of the latter being funded. Because *Statement No. 87* does not require disclosure of the identity of the groups participating in the overfunded and underfunded plans, it is impossible to tell whether the underfunded plans cover management employees, hourly employees, or a mixture. Data that are available from other sources indicate that underfunding tends to occur more frequently in plans involving unionized employees.[16]

The full funding limitation of current tax law, which denies tax deductibility for contributions to plans with assets in excess of their projected benefit obligations, may discourage additional funding of currently overfunded plans and encourage increased funding of currently underfunded plans.[17] Over time this would reduce the disparity in the funding statuses of the plans. This would benefit employees in currently underfunded plans but could be detrimental to the retirement security of employees in plans which are only minimally overfunded on a going-concern basis.

BALANCE SHEET EFFECT

The effect of *Statement No. 87* on the 1986 balance sheets of early adopters is minimal. The majority of companies show an amount of prepaid or accrued pension cost in their footnote reconciliation of plans' funding status with pension amounts on the corporate balance sheet. However, the amount generally is quite small and never appears on the balance sheet as a separately identifiable item.

Ninety-five of the plans had an accumulated benefit obligation that exceeded the fair value of plan assets at the end of 1986. The average minimum liability for these plans would have been approximately $62 million. However, only ten of the companies indicated that an additional pension liability and deferred charge had been recognized. This is not surprising because *Statement No. 87* allows the minimum liability recognition requirement to be deferred until 1989. What is surprising is that, for the companies that stated in their footnotes that the minimum liability provision was being implemented, there is no straightforward, easy-to-identify disclosure of the amount on the companies' balance sheets. Presumably, this is because the minimum liabilities recognized are relatively insignificant and have been aggregated with other amounts on the balance sheet.

---

[16] For further discussion of this point, see R. A. Ippolito, "The Economic Function of Underfunded Pension Plans," *Journal of Law & Economics* (October 1985), pp. 611–651.

[17] See IRC Sec. 412(c)(7).

SUMMARY AND CONCLUSIONS

This paper (1) documents the financial statement impact of the initial application of *Statement No. 87* and (2) demonstrates how the pension information disclosed under the statement can be used to analyze (a) the cost of compensating employees with defined benefit pension promises and (b) the funding status of U.S. pension plans.

Data analyzed in the paper provide the following insights into the major topic areas identified in the five questions stated in the introduction to the paper.

1. Characteristics of Early Adopters

The analysis shows that a large percentage of companies with pension plans chose to begin complying with the expense and disclosure requirements of *Statement No. 87* prior to the 1987 deadline. Overall, the early adopters were not concentrated in specific industries and there was no indication of widespread deferral of adoption by companies in the smokestack industries that had claimed they would be most adversely affected by the statement.

2. Income Statement Effect of Initial Application

Statement No. 87 generally had a favorable effect on the income statements of most of the early adopters. Application of the statement increased pension expense for only five companies. For the other companies, application did not materially affect income or increased after-tax income. For 101 of the companies studied, the change in the method of determining pension expense resulted in pension income.

3. Effect on Range of Actuarial Assumptions

There is little indication that *Statement No. 87* significantly narrowed the range of assumptions used in computing pension expense and obligations. The separate disclosure of the discount rate, expected rate of return, and expected rate of increase in salaries, however, makes it easier to assess the extent to which disclosures for different companies or different years are comparable.

4. Funding Status

Examination of funding ratios computed using *Statement No. 87* data indicates that the plans of the early adopters are generally well funded but that there are some relatively significant differences in the funding statuses of the different plans sponsored by an individual employer.

5. Balance Sheet Effect

The initial balance sheet effect of *Statement No. 87* was minimal. Most companies disclosed prepaid or accrued pension costs in their pension footnotes. However, the amounts generally were too small to warrant separate disclosure on the balance sheet. This was also true of the minimum liability, which ten of the companies indicated was being recognized in 1986.

FASB No. 106—
Retiree Health Care Accounting:
Early Adopters and Footnote
Disclosures Reviewed

Pat McConnell
Bear Stearns & Co. Inc.

IBM took a $2.3 billion after-tax charge to implement FASB No. 106. A few other companies have also adopted the new methodology, but the list of early adopters is likely to remain short. However, some managements have disclosed the expected impacts of adoption. This ACCOUNTING ISSUES describes the initial and future impacts the new accounting rule will have on earnings and balance sheets of 32 companies that have either adopted the new standard or were courageous enough to make meaningful disclosure.

Most companies currently account for retirement benefits (except pensions) on a "pay-as-you-go" basis. As claims are made, they expense and disclose the amount. FASB Statement No. 106, "Employers' Accounting for Postretirement Benefits Other Than Pensions," requires the expected cost of these benefits (primarily retiree medical) to be accrued. The liability is recorded during the years the employee works using the familiar pension accounting model. However, unlike pensions, other retirement benefits are rarely funded. Thus, adopting FASB No. 106 will create a significant unfunded liability for many companies as well as negative impacts on income.

From *Accounting Issues* (April 18, 1991), pp. 1–8. Reprinted by permission of Bear Stearns & Co. Inc. Copyright © 1991 by Bear Stearns & Co. Inc.

EARLY ADOPTERS

The FASB has given companies until 1993 to adopt Statement No. 106, but a few managements have elected to adopt the new methodology early. Tables 1A and 1B give the impacts for six of these companies. Table 1A lists the unfunded liability, the immediate after-tax earnings charge and the percentage impact on shareholders' equity. Table 1B compares the FASB No. 106 expense to the company's previous charge and relates the increase to pre-tax income.

When FASB No. 106 is adopted, the unfunded liability (Table 1A, Column 4) may be recorded in the balance sheet by taking a one-time charge to earnings. Alternatively, management has the option of recording the liability over twenty years. All of the companies in Table 1A elected to take a one-time charge to earnings (Column 5). Three of the companies (Abbott Labs, Dayton Hudson, and General Mills) conveniently had nonrecurring gains in the same period so that reported net income and equity were unaffected.

The $2.3 billion after-tax charge taken by IBM (Table 1A, Column 5) represents the after-tax cost of establishing the liability for IBM's active employees only. Prior to the adoption of Statement No. 106, IBM followed a policy known as "terminal accrual." Under "terminal accrual," the entire future cost of providing benefits, other than pensions, is recorded when an employee retires. Thus, IBM had previously recorded the liability for retired workers' benefits.

As shown in Table 1B, LTV's annual retiree health care expense (Column 5) is more than twice the "pay-as-you-go" amount (Column 4). For General Mills, doubling the expense reduces pre-tax income by 1 percent. First Empire State had no material change in its annual retiree health care expense. Abbott Labs and IBM did not provide information about the increase in expense but IBM disclosed that the impact on future earnings would be immaterial.

FASB NO. 106 IMPACTS DISCLOSED

When a new accounting pronouncement is issued, if it has not been implemented, the SEC requires companies to discuss the potential impacts of the required change. Frequently, the disclosure is "boiler plate", briefly describing the new requirements and indicating the general direction of the income statement or balance sheet impact or both.

Tables 2A and 2B include nine companies that had the fortitude to quantify the expected impacts of the accounting change in their 1990 annual reports.

Table 2A (Column 3) shows the disclosed unfunded liability. Management has the option of spreading this liability over 20 years. Alternatively, if management elects to recognize the liability immediately, the "one time" charge to earnings is estimated in Column 4.

General Electric currently accrues the cost of retirement benefits other than pensions on the employee's retirement date (the same policy followed

TABLE 1A Companies That Have Adopted FASB No. 106 Methodology

Balance sheet impact ($ millions)

(1) Company	(2) Industry	(3) Year Adopted	(4) Unfunded Obligation	(5) Immediate Earnings Charge	(6) Charge as a Percent of Equity	(7) Liability as a Multiple of Pay-As-You-Go Expense
Abbott Labs	Health Care	1991	$ 214 (a)	$ 128	5%	n/a
Dayton Hudson	Specialty Stores	1990	80 (a)	48	3%	20
First Empire State	Banking	1989	16	9	2%	16
General Mills	Food	1989	116	70	11%	23
IBM	Computers	1991	3,767 (a)	2,260	5%	39
LTV	Steel	1988	2,363	2,263	(b)	22

Notes:

n/a: Not available

(a) Estimated by dividing after-tax earnings charge by one minus an assumed 40% tax rate.

(b) Equity was negative prior to charge.

TABLE 1B Companies That Have Adopted FASB No. 106 Methodology
Impact on expense ($ millions)

(1)	(2)	(3)	(4)	(5)	(6)	(7)	(8)
		Year	Pay-As-You-Go	FASB No. 106	Percent Increase	Pre-Tax	Percent Decrease in Pre-Tax
Company	Industry	Adopted	Expense	Expense	in Expense	Income	Income
First Empire State	Banking	1989	$ 1	n/a	n/m	$ 76	n/m
General Mills	Food	1989	5	12	126%	518 (c)	1%
IBM	Computers	1991	96 (a,b)	n/a	n/a	10,203 (a)	n/m
LTV	Steel	1988	107	239	124%	(865)	n/a

Notes:

n/a: Not available

n/m: Not material

(a) Adopted in the first quarter of 1991; amount given is for year preceding adoption.

(b) Unlike most companies that currently use "pay-as-you-go" accounting for retiree medical cost, this company used a method which fully accrued the cost of retiree medical benefits at the employees' retirement date.

(d) Continuing operations

TABLE 2A Companies Disclosing FASB No. 106 Effect
Potential balance sheet impact ($ millions)

(1) Company	(2) Industry	(3) Unfunded Obligation	(4) "One Time" Charge to Earnings	(5) Charge as a Percent of Equity	(6) Liability as a Multiple of Pay-As-You-Go Expense
AMR	Airline	$ 700	$ 420 (a)	11%	26
ALCOA	Aluminum	1,000	600 (a)	12%	19
Dominion Resources	Elec. Utility	340	204 (a)	6%	38
GE	Diversified	4,200 (b)	1,620 (a)	7%	17
Honeywell	Computers	230	138 (a)	8%	n/a
Lockheed	Aerospace	1,000	660	29%	23
United Techologies	Aerospace	500 to 600	300 to 360 (a)	6% to 7%	n/a
USX	Steel/Oil	2,000 to 3,000	1,200 to 1,800 (a)	20% to 30%	13 to 20

Notes:
n/a: not available
(a) Estimated by multiplying unfunded obligation by one minus an assumed 40% tax rate.
(b) See discussion in the text.

TABLE 2B Companies Disclosing FASB No. 106 Effect
Potential impact on expense ($ millions)

(1) Company	(2) Industry	(3) Pay-As-You-Go Expense	(4) Estimated FASB No. 106 Expense	(5) Percent Increase in Expense	(6) Pre-Tax Income	(7) Percent Decrease in Pre-Tax Income
AMR	Airline	$ 27	$108 to $136	300% to 400%	$ (33)	n/a
ALCOA	Aluminum	53	n/a	"substantial"	1,047	n/a
American Brands	Tobacco	10	30 to 40	200% to 300%	1,048	2% to 3%
Dominion Resources	Elec. Utility	9	54	500%	642	n/m
Lockheed	Aerospace	43	86	100%	430	n/m
United Technologies	Aerospace	n/m	n/a	n/a	1,230	n/a
USX	Steel/Oil	150	317 to 483	111% to 222%	1,216	14% to 27%

Notes:
n/a: Not available
n/m: Not material

by IBM before it adopted Statement No. 106). GE has even funded some of the accrued amount. Thus, GE's unfunded and unrecorded obligation for retirement benefits of current workers is $2.7 billion computed as follows:

$4.2 billion obligation for retired and current employees

Less: 1.5 billion recorded liabilities and assets held in trust for ___ retired workers

$2.7 billion transition obligation for current workers

Table 2B lists the disclosed "pay-as-you-go" expense (Column 3), the estimated expense under Statement No. 106 when provided (Column 4), the percent increase in the expense (Column 5) and the impact on pre-tax income on a recurring basis (Column 7).

CASH FLOW UNCHANGED

Despite the potentially large liabilities and significant expense increases, rating agencies indicate that they will continue to monitor companies' annual cash expenditures for retiree medical. Companies' cash flows are unchanged by the new FASB rule. Since there is no ERISA-like legislation governing post-retirement health benefits, companies are not required to put money aside in a fund to pay for these future benefits. In addition, there are few tax incentives to do so. There is no indication that this will change. Retirees receiving health care benefits from corporations are also generally receiving pensions protected by ERISA and guaranteed by the PBGC. There is little support in Washington for legislation that will protect additional benefits of a segment of the elderly population that is better off than those receiving no benefits at all.

NOW FOR THE GOOD NEWS—COMPANIES THAT WILL BE UNAFFECTED

Some companies, while not quantifying the impacts, disclosed that adoption of FASB No. 106 will not impact them materially. Table 3 lists some of these lucky ones.

About half the companies listed in Table 3 are financial institutions, but generalizations may be dangerous. U.S. Bancorp, for example, disclosed that it expects the accounting change "to be material to operations."

The reasons these companies will be unaffected by FASB No. 106 are disparate. For example, Philips Petroleum explains that "essentially retirees pay their own way" while Colgate "intends to utilize a portion of its leveraged ESOP to reduce its current and future obligation." Lockheed, Martin Marietta, Dominion Resources and Pinnacle West plan to pass the increased cost on to their customers.

TABLE 3 Companies Not Materially
Impacted by FASB No. 106

BankAmerica	Banking
Barnett Bank	Banking
Colgate	Household Products
CoreStates Financial	Banking
Dominion Resources	Electric Utility
First Chicago	Banking
Harsco	Steel Recovery
Lockheed	Aerospace
Martin Marietta	Aerospace
NBD Bancorp	Saving Bank
Philips Petroleum	Oil
Pinnacle West	Electric Utility
Tultex	Sportswear Manufacturer

PUBLIC UTILITIES—INCREASED RECEIVABLES RATHER THAN INCREASED EXPENSE

Dominion Resources discloses in its 1990 annual report that

> [a] transition obligation of approximately $340 million would result from the application of this standard. The transition obligation would be amortized over a 20-year period. . .[A]pplication of this Standard in 1993 will increase annual expenses by approximately six times the currenty pay-as-you-go amount (emphasis added).

However, rather than increased cost reducing the bottom line it will be recorded as a receivable.

The FASB allows rate regulated enterprises like Dominion and Pinnacle West to capitalize rather than expense a cost if it is probable that the cost will be recovered through rates in the future. The Statement No. 106 expense in excess of amounts currently collected will be recorded as a receivable representing the amount to be collected in the future through rate increases.

Pinnacle West explains:

> Accordingly, this statement should not have a significant impact on Pinnacle West's financial position or results of operations . . .[since] management expects that most of the increased benefits expense will either be recovered currently through APS rates or that a regulatory asset will be recorded to reflect amounts to be recovered through rates in the future as the costs are paid.

Most utilities should be in a similar position.

GOVERNMENT CONTRACTORS—GUESS WHO ABSORBS THE HIGHER COST?

Table 2A shows that Lockheed expects its obligation under FASB No. 106 to be $1 billion. The change in accounting will also double Lockheed's annual expense for retirement benefits other than pensions from $43 million to approximately $86 million (Table 2B) but Lockheed concludes that this "should not have a meaningful impact on reported income on a recurring basis." Lockheed intends to annually fund an amount approximately equal to the FASB No. 106 expense. This will allow Lockheed to include the cost in government contracts.

Martin Marietta, another defense contractor, also plans to pass the increased cost on to the government. Its 1990 annual report explains that

> reported annual cost (under Statement No. 106) is expected to be significantly greater than current claims-paid method outlays. . . . [A]n accrual method also is allowable under U.S. Government Cost Accounting Standards, and hence, [Martin Marietta has] elected to use accrual accounting in pricing work to be performed in 1993 and thereafter.

Martin Marietta concludes that "[a]doption is not expected to have a material effect upon reported earnings."

THE LIST OF EARLY ADOPTERS WILL STAY SHORT

Many 1990 annual reports indicate management is undecided about how and when to adopt but some, such as Eastman Kodak, Union Carbide and Goodyear, say they will wait until 1993.

The list of companies electing to adopt FASB No. 106 before January 1, 1993, the effective date for calendar year companies, is not likely to grow significantly. Some managements simply need the time to accumulate the data required for the calculation. Others are using the time to restructure their retiree medical plans, shifting more of the cost to the retiree, thus lowering the companies' obligation. Still others remember that the effective date of another unpopular pronouncement on accounting for taxes, has been delayed several times. They are keeping their fingers crossed that history will repeat itself. Early adopters are likely to be companies with nonrecurring gains to soften the impact or those already having a bad year and trying to get all the negative news behind them.

CHAPTER 13

Income Taxes

Accounting for corporate income taxes has been a topic of debate that has divided accountants for more than 40 years. Before the Accounting Principles Board (APB) addressed the issue in its Opinion No. 11, there was basic disagreement among accountants regarding the critical event in the recognition of the tax obligation. One view was to hold the legal position that the obligation arises when the tax calculation is made each year. The APB adopted the alternative, the economic view, that the obligation to pay arises with the earning of income.[1] In the United States, this position led to comprehensive tax allocation.

Many problems remained with the procedure required by Opinion No. 11. The rule differed from an "asset-liability" method in that the computed deferred tax amount was not based on an assessment of the tax situations and tax rates expected to be in effect during the periods in which the tax is expected to be paid. Rather, the computation was based on a concept called the "deferred" method in which only the tax rates of the originating period are taken into consideration. On a practical level, the reported deferred tax liability (or more properly deferred tax "credit") amount seemed to keep growing in magnitude for most reporting corporations rather than reverse to zero as predicted by theory.[2] This and other reporting and conceptual consid-

---

[1] See William C. Dent and Paul Rosenfield, "No More Deferred Taxes," *Journal of Accountancy* (February 1983), pp. 44–45, for a defense of the legal view. A rebuttal favoring the economic view is provided by Philip L. Defliese, "Deferred Taxes—Forever," *Journal of Accountancy* (August 1983), pp. 94–98, followed by a reply from Dent and Rosenfield.

[2] See Sidney Davidson, Steven F. Rasch, and Roman L. Weil, "Behavior of the Deferred Tax Credit Account, 1973–82," *Journal of Accountancy* (October 1984), pp. 138–142, and Ted Skekel and Charles Fazzi, "The Deferred Tax Liability: Do Capital Intensive Companies Pay It?," *Journal of Accountancy* (October 1984), pp. 142–150. The first article reports that about 76% of the changes in deferred tax accounts were increases and only 24% were decreases. The dollar amount of the increases was eight times that of the decreases.

erations led the Financial Accounting Standards Board (FASB) to issue a new standard in 1987, Statement No. 96, *Accounting for Income Taxes,* to replace APB Opinion No. 11.

From the very beginning, Statement No. 96 met with sharp criticism from managers and practitioners owing to its computational complexity. While the new rule, mandating the liability method as the standard, was said to be an improvement over APB Opinion No. 11, it required a complex forecasting of tax positions in future periods. Additionally, the procedure made it almost impossible to record deferred tax assets. Learning from its experience with the foreign currency translation rule (Statement Nos. 8 and 52), the FASB responded to the criticisms from its constituents quickly and positively, first by repeatedly postponing the effective date of Statement No. 96, and later by replacing it with Statement No. 109 in early 1992. The new rule, also reflecting the asset-liability method, allows the recognition of deferred tax assets based on estimated future deductions and operating loss and tax credit carryforwards. To alleviate the concern that deferred tax assets may violate the usual norm of conservatism, the new rule requires the creation of a valuation allowance account to approximate the amount that is "more likely than not" to be realized.

The long and controversial history of deferred tax assets is the underlying theme in Carol Loomis's *Fortune* article, "Behind the Profits Glow at Aetna." The article criticizes Aetna Life and Casualty for recognizing as a deferred tax asset and a corresponding reduction in current tax expense the tax benefit of a loss carryforward. Such a practice was strongly discouraged in APB Opinion No. 11 by its requirement that tax benefit realization must be assured "beyond any reasonable doubt." It is worth noting that, under Statement No. 109, the practice is currently permissible under the less rigorous "more likely than not" standard. Loomis's article, questioning Aetna's reporting practice, led to a subsequent Securities and Exchange Commission (SEC) investigation of Aetna.[3] The article by John A. Elliott and Robert J. Swieringa (now an FASB board member), "Aetna, The SEC and Tax Benefits of Loss Carryforwards," complements Loomis's article, and fills in the details of the complex interaction between Aetna's managers, the accounting profession and the accounting regulators: in all, a fascinating case study.

Statement No. 109, like its predecessor rules, stops short of requiring the discounting of future deferred tax amounts when computing the balance sheet liability. Frank R. Rayburn, in "Discounting of Deferred Income Taxes: An Argument for Reconsideration," notes that the discounting of deferred taxes is "theoretically consistent with current GAAP," especially given the asset-liability method as the theoretical basis for the new Statement No. 109. In its deliberations preceding the issuance of Statement No. 109, the FASB encountered strong opposition from practitioners to the discounting of deferred taxes, principally due to fears of added computational complexity—

---

[3] In the end, the company restated its financial statements to conform more closely to APB Opinion No. 11.

fears that were no doubt fanned by the complex procedural requirements already present in Statement No. 96.[4] With the complexity question mostly put to rest by the simpler procedures of Statement No. 109, the FASB might face less resistance to a future project on the discounting of deferred taxes.

With the ascendancy of the Clinton Administration, one of the hottest accounting topics from the days of the Kennedy, Johnson, and Nixon Administrations seems ready to resurface: the investment tax credit (ITC). In 1962, the U.S. Department of the Treasury devised the credit as a means of stimulating investment in capital goods and therefore expanding employment. In its simplest form, the plan provided that an amount equal to a flat percentage (usually 7% or 10%) of the cost of the production facilities acquired would be a direct credit against that year's federal income tax. The accounting question was whether the credit should be included entirely in the accounting income of the year of purchase (flow-through) or whether it should be amortized over the life of the purchased facilities (deferral).[5] The U.S. accounting profession's past efforts in setting a standard for the recognition of ITC have been embarrassingly unsuccessful. The APB issued three exposure drafts on this topic (in 1962, 1967, and 1971), as well as Opinion No. 2 in 1962, requiring in each case the deferral method for the recognition of ITC in the income statement. Even though the SEC was sympathetic to the APB's position, pressure from industry led the SEC, and later Congress, to allow companies to continue to use the flow-through method. What began as an accounting issue thus became a political issue. Against the background of an expected revival of the ITC in early 1993, Stephen A. Zeff wrote to the FASB to urge the Board, in concert with the SEC and the U.S. General Accounting Office, to make every effort to discourage Congress from dictating the accounting standard for ITC's treatment in the financial statements. Zeff's letter is reproduced in this chapter.

BIBLIOGRAPHICAL NOTES

The literature on income tax allocation is fairly extensive. Here are some studies on the conceptual issues:

Arnold, Anthony J., and Brian J. Webb: *The Financial Reporting and Policy Effects of Partial Deferred Tax Accounting* (London: The Institute of Chartered Accountants in England and Wales, 1989).

Beechy, T. H.: *Accounting for Corporate Income Taxes: Conceptual Considerations and Empirical Analyses* (Toronto: Canadian Institute of Chartered Accountants, 1983).

Beresford, Dennis R., Lawrence C. Best, Paul W. Craig, and Joseph V. Weber:

---

[4] See Roman L. Weil, "Role of the Time Value of Money in Financial Reporting," *Accounting Horizons* (December 1990), pp. 47–67, and James O. Stepp, "Deferred Taxes: The Discounting Controversy," *Journal of Accountancy* (November 1985), pp. 98–108, for discussions of this topic.
[5] Under the deferral method, the tax credit is either deducted from the cost of the asset (thus reducing future depreciation amounts) or credited to a liability account and amortized to income over the life of the asset.

Accounting for Income Taxes: A Review of Alternatives (Financial Accounting Standards Board, 1983).

Chaney, Paul K., and Debra C. Jeter: "Accounting for Deferred Income Taxes: Simplicity? Usefulness?," *Accounting Horizons* (June 1989), pp. 6–13.

Jeter, Debra C., and Paul K. Chaney: "A Financial Statement Analysis Approach to Deferred Taxes," *Accounting Horizons* (December 1988), pp. 41–49.

Nair, R. D., and Jerry J. Weygandt: "Let's Fix Deferred Taxes," *Journal of Accountancy* (November 1982), pp. 87–102.

Wheeler, James E., and Willard H. Galliart: *An Appraisal of Interperiod Income Tax Allocation* (New York: Financial Executives Research Foundation, 1974).

Wolk, Harry I., Dale R. Martin and Virginia A. Nichols: "Statement of Financial Accounting Standards No. 96: Some Theoretical Problems," *Accounting Horizons* (June 1989), pp. 1–5.

Wyatt, Arthur R., Richard Dieter and John E. Stewart: "Tax Allocation Revisited," *The CPA Journal* (March 1984), pp. 10–18.

A review of the circumstances and discussions attending the issuance in the United Kingdom of two accounting standards on tax allocation accounting within the space of but 3 years is:

Hope, Tony, and John Briggs: "Accounting Policy Making—Some Lessons from the Deferred Taxation Debate," *Accounting and Business Research* (Spring 1982), pp. 83–96.

The following book contains a collection of both old and recent articles on deferred taxes:

Wise, Trevor D., Claudio A. Romano and Victoria J. Wise (editors), *Readings in Income Tax Allocation* (Melbourne: School of Economics, La Trobe University, 1988).

As noted, the large, unexpected growth in the deferred tax account under APB Opinion No. 11 is documented in the following articles:

Davidson, Sidney, Steven F. Rasch and Roman L. Weil: "Behavior of the Deferred Tax Credit Account, 1973–82," *Journal of Accountancy* (October 1984), pp. 138–142.

Skekel, Ted, and Charles Fazzi: "The Deferred Tax Liability: Do Capital Intensive Companies Pay It?," *Journal of Accountancy* (October 1984), pp. 142–150.

The following article examines firms that adopted Statement No. 96 early:

Gujarathi, Mahendra R., and Robert E. Hoskin: "Evidence of Earnings Management by the Early Adopters of SFAS 96," *Accounting Horizons* (December 1992), pp. 18–31.

Many articles have appeared criticizing Statement No. 96 and recommending changes to it. Some are:

Bierman, Harold Jr.: "One More Reason to Revise Statement 96," *Accounting Horizons* (June 1990), pp. 42–46.

Means, Kathryn M.: "Accounting for Income Taxes: FAS 96—Unexpected Results," *Journal of Accounting, Auditing & Finance* (Fall 1989), pp. 571–579.

Nurnberg, Hugo: "Deferred Tax Assets under FASB Statement No. 96," *Accounting Horizons* (December 1989), pp. 49–56.

The following articles provide supplementary information on the accounting procedures in Statement Nos. 96 or 109:

Accounting for Income Taxes: An Analysis of FASB Statement No. 109 (New York: Deloitte & Touche, 1992).

Hawkins, David F.: "General Electric Co.: A Case Study in Adopting SFAS No. 96," *Accounting Bulletin* (Drexel Burnham Lambert, June 1988).

Klingler, John P., and James B. Savage: "Deciphering the New Accounting for Income Tax Rules," *Management Accounting* (August 1988), pp. 32–38.

McConnell, Pat: "FASB No. 109: Accounting for Income Taxes Explained," *Accounting Issues* (Bear Stearns, June 4, 1992).

Parks, James T.: "A Guide to FASB's Overhaul of Income Tax Accounting," *Journal of Accountancy* (October 1988), pp. 24–35.

Read, William J., and Robert A. J. Bartsch: "The FASB's Proposed Rules for Deferred Taxes," *Journal of Accountancy* (August 1991), pp. 44–53.

Behind the Profits Glow at Aetna

Carol J. Loomis

Fortune

Like every other company in the business, giant Aetna Life & Casualty has been swamped by a viciously competitive swing in the property and casualty insurance market. But Aetna's responses to this sea of troubles have been unique.

The dynamics of the business are inexorable. When interest rates are high, the insurance crowd fights for premiums to sink into investments. As the claims from this cut-rate business come due, cash flow needs become compelling. Now, in the depths of an unusually long and low trough, the insurers are writing policies in a spirit of abandon—asking all the while when it will ever end.

Aetna has acted with less abandon than most. In early 1981, like King Canute trying to hold back the waves, it even made a jawboning effort to firm up prices. Canute couldn't do it and neither could Aetna.

The company has meanwhile been an amazingly active diversifier, putting more than $1 billion into four separate ventures in the last year. One move, the acquisition of Geosource, a large oil-field services company, seemed so inappropriate that Wall Street hammered Aetna's stock.

Even so, Aetna is mighty. With more than $40 billion in assets, it is the largest publicly owned U.S. insurer, and its business spread-eagles the field, embracing not only property and casualty but also the life, health, and pension markets. Accordingly, analysts continue to respect the company's

From *Fortune* (November 15, 1982), pp. 54–58. Reprinted by permission of Time Inc. Copyright © 1982 by Time Inc. All rights reserved.

earning power. At a round-table discussion staged by the *Wall Street Transcript* last May, five insurance analysts all lamented Aetna's property and casualty troubles, yet went on to predict that the improved first-quarter results already reported would be followed by improved results for the year. One analyst, Donald Franz, then at Smith Barney and now with Donaldson Lufkin & Jenrette, framed his prediction memorably. Recalling that Aetna's chairman, John H. Filer, had recently made some positive statements about 1982, Franz said that earnings would quite likely rise "to ensure that the chairman will not be called a liar."

Some of the statements Franz had in mind appeared in Aetna's first-quarter report, in a letter signed by Filer and William O. Bailey, the company's president. They spoke of "increased balance and stability," of earnings improvements over the last three quarters, and of "our belief that Aetna will maintain reasonable and improving profits this year."

The remarkable thing about that letter, about a second-quarter letter that followed, and about the analysts' forecasts to boot is that none of these declarations about Aetna mentioned the overwhelming and extraordinary reason why its 1982 earnings are up. The reason, made visible only by a terse footnote to Aetna's financial statements, is tax benefits that the company has been plugging into its earnings even though at best it will not realize the benefits until sometime in the future.

TWO SETS OF BOOKS

Like most companies, Aetna prepares one set of accounts for the Internal Revenue Service and another for its shareholders. In its shareholder accounts, Aetna reports large amounts of income from municipal bonds and dividends. In the company's filings with the IRS, most of this income escapes taxation. During the suicidally competitive phase of the property and casualty business, Aetna has been reporting operating profits to its shareholders and large operating losses to the IRS—a legal and not unusual dichotomy.

These tax losses can be carried forward to offset future taxable profits. In Aetna's case, the operating loss carry-forwards, as they are called, came to a huge $736 million at the end of 1981 and apparently topped $1 billion in midyear. If Aetna realizes taxable operating profits within 15 years, which is the time limit on carry-forwards, its tax losses will be available as offsets, and taxes on the profits will be avoided. This potential deliverance from future taxes is what Aetna is recognizing in today's profits.

The effects on the company's 1982 earnings have been dramatic. In the first 6 months of the year, Aetna took $138 million of these anticipated tax benefits into its earnings, an amount accounting for no less than 62 percent of reported operating earnings of $222 million. Without this boost, the company's operating earnings would have been 60 percent lower than in 1981. Had they been reported in this skimpy form, the earnings would not have even covered Aetna's first-half dividends.

And just how unusual are Aetna's tactics? Extremely and undeniably so, to the degree that it is almost impossible to overstate the point. It is not that operating tax-loss carry-forwards are scarce; lots of companies have them and would no doubt be delighted to convert them immediately into current earnings. But generally accepted accounting principles come close to prohibiting the practice. The problem is addressed in Opinion No. 11, a pronouncement issued by a predecessor of the profession's self-regulatory body, the Financial Accounting Standards Board. The opinion declares that realization of the tax benefits ordinarily is not "assured" because a company can't know with absolute certainty that it will have taxable profits in the future against which the loss carry-forwards can be used. Therefore, says the opinion, tax benefits arising from loss carry-forwards should not be recognized in profits until they are realized, except in unusual circumstances when realization is assured "beyond any reasonable doubt."

A company might pass this test, the opinion then says, if three conditions, each and all, are satisfied. The first concerns the character of the loss being carried forward: it must have resulted from "an identifiable, isolated, and nonrecurring cause." The second concerns the character of the company: it must have been continuously profitable over a long period or have suffered occasional losses that were more than offset by taxable income later on. The third concerns the character of the taxable income expected: it must with near certainty be large enough to offset the loss carry-forward and must come along fast enough to deliver the tax benefits within the carry-forward period.

Some accountants, among them Aetna's auditors, Peat Marwick Mitchell, have interpreted this listing of conditions as providing "such as" guidance; that is, if a company can meet tests "such as" the ones stated, it may consider its tax benefits to be realizable beyond a reasonable doubt. The problem with this interpretation is that the accounting office of the Securities and Exchange Commission doesn't agree with it. The SEC regards the conditions as absolute requirements that must be met. That makes the standard of "beyond any reasonable doubt" terribly difficult to satisfy. As an FASB staff member says, "Those are tough words."

So strong are the SEC's feelings about Opinion 11 that it has on occasion forced a company to restate its earnings and remove the offending tax benefits. One such occasion in the mid-1970s involved Rapid-American Corp., a trouble-prone company run by a controversy-prone chairman, Meshulam Riklis.

Instances in which the SEC has allowed future tax benefits to worm their way into earnings are hard to find. Stumped to name examples, a Big Eight partner who often handles questions from the press excused his nonhelpfulness by stressing the unacceptability, and therefore rarity, of the accounting practice: "The language in Opinion 11 creates a very strong presumption that one doesn't do that."

THE FRANKLIN HAD THE HABIT

Further digging, however, turned up about a dozen companies that at one time or another have shown future tax benefits in earnings. Some dignify the practice still more poorly than Rapid-American. Two were Detroit's Bank of the Commonwealth, which fell into deep trouble in the early 1970s, and Franklin New York Corp., which with its subsidiary, Franklin National Bank, went bankrupt in 1974.

The dozen specimens, however, also include a few companies of a vastly different and significantly higher financial character, among them none other than Aetna itself. A second example is another big (and, like Aetna, Hartford-based) multiline insurer, Travelers Corp. Aetna took future tax benefits into its earnings in 1975. Travelers did so in 1975 and 1976, years when the property and casualty business was ensnarled in another traumatic down-cycle.

These Hartford-hewn accounting aberrations did not pass the SEC un-challenged. As Robert H. McMillen, a Travelers senior vice president, remem-bers things, the SEC noticed in a 1975 Travelers quarterly report that the company had begun to book tax benefits related to a tax-loss carry-forward and promptly requested Travelers to justify its action. The SEC wanted to know, first, just how Travelers knew it was going to earn taxable profits sufficient to realize the tax benefits and, second, how cyclical losses could be construed as rising from "isolated and nonrecurring causes."

Travelers gave this matter some deep thought, McMillen says, and then replied. The answer to the first question, the company told the SEC, is that we have experienced depressed conditions in the property and casualty business before and these always come to an end, whereupon we begin to earn profits that exceed our earlier losses; you should assume, therefore, that this pattern will repeat. The answer to the second question, Travelers contin-ued, is harder to substantiate, since we are not fortune-tellers and cannot say definitely that our current variety of tax-loss carry-forwards will not crop up again. But we can tell you we have never before had tax-loss carry-forwards of any kind and that they arose now because of a wicked, two-fisted punch: double-digit inflation rates that ballooned our claim costs and price controls that prevented our raising premiums. We argue, said Travelers, that these causes are "isolated and nonrecurring."

John C. ("Sandy") Burton, then chief accountant of the SEC and now dean of Columbia's Graduate School of Business, says he listened to Trav-elers' presentation and came reluctantly to the conclusion—"I was sullen but not mutinous"—that the company should be allowed to recognize the future tax benefits it wished to. Aetna says it had similar dealings with Burton and also received permission to proceed.

Only a short time later, however, in mid-1976, the SEC suddenly braced itself in regard to Opinion 11, issuing an accounting bulletin that reminded the corporte and accounting communities of the opinion's "restrictive tests." Edmund Coulson, assistant chief accountant of the SEC, explains the bulletin's origins: "We had noted in some filings with us that there was laxity in applying Opinion 11 and we wanted to make it clear that shouldn't happen." One point in the bulletin concerned losses attributable to "a general economic or industry decline," which would seem to describe the cyclical variety. The bulletin indicated that such losses would not normally justify the recognition of future tax benefits in earnings.

Since that 1976 milestone, the number of instances in which future tax benefits have been recognized seems to have dwindled from few to mini-few. The conclusion arises from a search of annual reports that *Fortune* made through the National Automated Accounting Research Service (NAARS), a computerized data base. NAARS provides access to the financial statements (and accompanying footnotes) of 4,000 public corporations and allows a search for all the companies using a given accounting practice. To query NAARS, a trained searcher feeds key words into a computer. Within seconds the computer identifies all companies using those words in a certain fashion and proclaims itself ready to deliver, via videoscreen and printout, the relevant sections of their annual reports.

A STANDOUT IN THE CROWD

The expert performing this small miracle for *Fortune* was Hortense Goodman, a staff member of the American Institute of Certified Public Accountants. Spending 43 minutes and 9 seconds at a computer terminal (cost to *Fortune*: $155.65), Mrs. Goodman interrogated the 1981–82 file of annual reports. She found a good number of companies that said they were *not* recognizing future tax benefits because their realization was open to at least some doubt. She found only one company among the entire 4,000 that *was* recognizing future tax benefits in 1981, and that was Aetna (which began the practice in the fourth quarter). "In the opinion of management," Aetna's footnote said, utilization of the company's loss carry-forwards to offset future taxable income "is assured beyond any reasonable doubt."

One point needs to be made about Aetna's lonely prominence in the NAARS data base: the data are being updated gradually and still contain some 1980 annual reports. So complete 1981 data might show other companies booking future tax benefits.

Donald Conrad, Aetna's executive vice president, says its 1981 decision to begin recognizing future tax benefits was not accompanied by consultation with the SEC—though, he adds, "we would be perfectly willing to talk to the SEC about the issue now." But Conrad also points out that Aetna has filed three registration statements with the SEC during 1982. The fact suggests, he says, that the commission has observed what Aetna is doing and decided it is okay.

In fact, the SEC hasn't decided any such thing. Because of budget constraints, the agency is engaged these days in "selective review" of registration statements. That means some filings get virtually no attention at all, and that's what happened to Aetna's three 1982 registrations. No one at the SEC appears to have known that Aetna was recognizing future tax benefits in current earnings until *Fortune* called to ask whether the registrations were reviewed. Howard P. Hodges, chief accountant of the Division of Corporation Finance, said then that he certainly planned to look at Aetna's financial statments now that he knew of the situation. He may look with a jaundiced eye, since his view of "beyond any reasonable doubt" appears to be hardline. He says, "We think the test is very difficult to meet."

THE FOCUS OF AETNA

Aetna says nevertheless that it meets the test—absolutely and positively. John Filer, its chairman, sounds patiently impatient about the whole matter: "My view is that that interpretation is correct. My view is that the certainty of using the loss carry-forward over a 15-year time span is absolute." In forming that opinion, he says, Aetna relied on lawyers, accountants, and its own judgment. He goes on: "The numbers are large, but I don't think that's the focus of what's going on at the Aetna."

Why, he is asked, did he not render an explanation of these large numbers—60 percent of reported earnings—to the shareholders in the quarterly reports? "That's the simple answer I gave you a moment ago. I don't think this is one of the urgent, important issues at the Aetna. This is an accounting issue. I think the important issues are operational issues, strategic issues, changes of markets, acquisitions and divestitures, financings."

The company is equally categorical in discussing a related matter: Aetna's mode of presenting future tax benefits in its balance sheet. When such a benefit is taken into earnings, it must also make an appearance on the balance sheet, since it is an asset realizable down the road. Indeed, Opinion 11 states that in those rare cases when future tax benefits are recognized, an asset shall be set up and amortized as the benefit is realized.

But Aetna has not set up an asset. Instead, a detailed June 30 balance sheet—included in a recent Aetna prospectus though not in the quarterly report to shareholders—copes with $144 million in tax benefits by displaying them in the liability column. They are called deferred federal income taxes and presented as negative numbers—that is, they are enclosed in parentheses. Sorting out all these double negatives is a challenge. Think about it for a moment, however, and you will see that a "negative liability" is an asset.

But since not all readers of the prospectus might make that semantic leap, and since Opinion 11 does not remotely contemplate the presentation of tax benefits on the liability side, *Fortune* asked Aetna why it had handled the matter that way. One of the company's accounting executives, Heath Fitzsimmons, explains that Aetna believed that the expected tax benefit would be more visible as a separately stated item on the liability side than it would be if lumped into miscellaneous assets on the asset side. Well, perhaps—except why could it not be stated as a separate item on the asset side, possibly captioned as "future tax benefits" (a label that other companies have used in the past)? Fitzsimmons said that treatment was not justified because the amount of $144 million was a lower order of magnitude than the other huge asset numbers on the books. But, said *Fortune*, are there not also huge numbers on the liability side, among which you are saying the future tax benefits are nicely visible?

This colloquy, conducted in a telephone conference call, was joined by a Peat Marwick partner, Walter P. Schuetze, vice chairman of the firm's committee on accounting practice. Refreshingly, Schuetze said straight out that putting future tax benefits on the liability side of the balance sheet does not meet the directives of Opinion 11. He said, however, that Peat Marwick believed the treatment permissible.

The overriding question, of course, concerns Aetna's decision to include the tax benefits in its current statements in any form at all. The company's alternative would have been to wait until the tax benfits are actually realized, assuming they are, and then to present them as extraordinary items, which is the procedure directed by Opinion 11. That approach would have clobbered Aetna's earnings in the first half and would continue to clobber them until the moment the tax benefits begin to arise, which could be several years out. Even then the damage would not be entirely redressed, since investors ordinarily do not value extraordinary earnings as highly as they do the consistently delivered variety. These complications help explain why Aetna's executives do not take questions about their tax-benefit policies lightly.

THE ACCOUNTANT FOR THE DEFENSE

If Aetna's accounting is now challenged by the SEC, the point man in the defense may turn out to be Schuetze of Peat Marwick. It is not clear how he felt about Aetna's decision to book the tax benefits, but it is clear that he now has the accounting defenses mustered. He is familiar, he says, with the original intentions of Opinion 11—its legislative history, so to speak—and he says that the criteria the opinion sets forth, such as "isolated and nonrecurring causes," were never meant to be more than examples. "Opinion 11," he says, "prescribes just one test and that is 'beyond any reasonable doubt.' "

Suppose the SEC does not agree with that reading of history or says its policies, in any case, supersede history? On the phone, Schuetze seems to draw in a deep breath: "Then I will convince Clarence"—that's Clarence Sampson, the SEC's chief accountant—"that I am right."

If Aetna is allowed to defend itself on the ground of "beyond any reasonable doubt," it is likely to haul out an arsenal of talking points. Its inside and outside accountants mention two recent changes in the tax law as important. One, by extending the tax-loss carry-forward period from seven years to 15, supplies Aetna with more maneuvering room in which to realize the taxable profits it needs. The other tax change gives a multiline insurance company increased freedom to consolidate the results of its life insurance subsidiaries, which might be earning operating profits today, with those of property and casualty subsidiaries, which almost certainly are earning operating losses. The problem with this bit of help is that Aetna's life insurance business is itself feeling profit pressures, the result of huge shifts in consumer attitudes toward life products.

Several Aetna executives, accounting and otherwise, also mention the company's ability to boost taxable income by shifting its property and casualty portfolio away from tax-exempt securities toward the taxable variety, whose higher yields would be tax-sheltered by the carry-forwards. This shift, however, cannot be accomplished by a wholesale shedding of tax-exempts, since most holdings in the portfolio could only be disposed of at a loss. Instead the shift must be accomplished gradually, as tax-exempts mature and income from investments and new cash flow is plowed into taxables.

Unfortunately, Aetna may even now be suffering from "negative cash flow." That is, premium revenues may not be supplying the cash needed to meet claims payments and other expenses. In part Aetna's weak cash flow position reflects its 1981 decision to try to stiffen its prices while encouraging the whole industry to do likewise. The effort was premature and, in any case, the industry is too fragmented to accept price leadership. In short, the effort didn't work. It did, however, cost Aetna some market share, a loss it is still feeling.

Still another source of possible taxable profits for Aetna is the flock of non-insurance businesses it has been pursuing. Its U.S. deals include the purchase of Geosource and the formation of a real estate partnership with Twentieth Century-Fox Film; an acquisition in process is Federated Investors, a mutual-fund management company. Aetna has also bought an interest in a British merchant bank, Samuel Montagu, but the taxable U.S. profits it will generate are apt to be minor.

Aetna's Conrad says each venture looks good as an investment and that the taxable income coming along will look "very attractive" also. But the immediate income may be limited: even at their best the acquired businesses do not produce huge profits, and one, Geosource, is right now caught up in the oil-patch slump.

WAITING FOR THE TURN

The strongest hope of Aetna's executives, not surprisingly, is that the property and casualty cycle will turn upward and begin to shower the company with profits, an event that would be signaled by firming prices. The key to that hope is interest rates, which in the 4-year-old downward leg of the cycle have encouraged insurers to "buy" business so that they could sink the premiums into high-yielding investments—or at least avoid the necessity of selling holdings at a loss to meet current expenses. If interest rates stay down at their current levels or decline still further, that proposition would begin to seem a whole lot less interesting and prices should begin to firm. But there is no telling when all this is going to happen or what the durability of the upward leg of the cycle will be. To state matters simply, this is a business about which there are "reasonable doubts."

Aetna, The SEC and Tax Benefits of Loss Carryforwards

John A. Elliott
Cornell University

Robert J. Swieringa
Member, Financial Accounting Standards Board

Aetna Life & Casualty Company, the largest stockholder-owned insurance company in the United States, disclosed in its 1982 annual report that the company's accounting for future tax benefits in 1982 was under formal investigation by the Securities and Exchange Commission (SEC). The dispute centered on the accounting recognition of tax losses which may lead to expected tax benefits in the future. These benefits provided $203 million, or 39 percent, of Aetna's 1982 operating profit of $522 million. The SEC believed that Aetna could not be assured of being able to use the tax-loss benefits "beyond any reasonable doubt." Aetna and its auditors, Peat, Marwick, Mitchell & Co., believed that it had met this test. The SEC began its formal investigation in March 1983. In July 1983, Aetna announced that it had decided to restate its 1982 financial results to eliminate the tax benefits questioned by the SEC. In a prepared statement, Aetna stated that "we have now concluded that it no longer serves any useful purpose to remain in a continuing, expensive and distractive controversy with the SEC and have agreed in settlement with the SEC to restate our 1982 financial results."[1]

This article explores several of the issues involved in the dispute between Aetna and the SEC. Tax-loss carryforwards provide economic benefits in

From *The Accounting Review* (July 1985), pp. 531–546. Reprinted by permission of the American Accounting Association and the authors. Copyright © 1985 by the American Accounting Association. Swieringa was an accounting professor at Cornell University when this article was written. *Authors' note:* The authors gratefully acknowledge the comments and suggestions of Harold Bierman, Jack Robertson, Walter Schuetze, Clyde Stickney, Mark Wolfson, Arthur Wyatt, and the reviewers.

[1] "Aetna Restates Results for All of '82, Ending Tax Dispute with SEC," *The Wall Street Journal*, Friday, July 8, 1983.

future periods of taxable income.[2] The next section discusses accounting for the tax benefits of loss carryforwards under current generally accepted accounting principles. The interpretation of these principles, as specified in APB *Opinion No. 11* [APB, 1967], created the conflict between the SEC and Aetna.

We also examine and evaluate Aetna's accounting for its tax benefits and the performance of its share price during this period. A negative relative performance of Aetna's share price is identified in general over the period, significant portions of which are associated with specific references to the accounting controversy in the financial press. We do not believe that Aetna's share price was devalued because of a change in accounting for an unchanging, underlying economic reality. Rather, we believe that the underlying economic reality itself was changing. We use a simple decision rule and Aetna's public statements to describe how the cycle associated with profitable underwriting in property and casualty insurance appears to have changed such that underwriting losses were greater than before and persisted longer. This change is important in deciding how to account for the uncertain benefits of tax-loss carryforwards.

We conclude with some suggestions for improving accounting for tax benefits of loss carryforwards.

TAX-LOSS CARRYFORWARDS

Operating losses for tax purposes (e.g., deductions exceed gross income) arising in one period may be carried back three years to generate refunds of taxes paid in those years and/or carried forward for up to 15 years, providing deductions from taxable income in those subsequent years. Generally accepted accounting principles require that the tax effects of any realized operating loss carrybacks be recognized in the determination of net income of the loss periods, since the refund "is both measurable and currently realizable" [APB, 1967].

When a tax-loss is carried forward, the future benefits are neither certain nor objectively measurable. Generally accepted accounting principles require that the future tax benefits due to loss carryforwards be recognized in the determination of net income in the period in which they are realized, "except in unusual circumstances when realization is assured beyond any reasonable doubt at the time the loss carryforwards arise" [APB, 1967]. Future recognition of tax-loss carryforward benefits should be reported as extraordinary items.

---

[2] Insurance companies are covered by unique tax provisions. They can affect their tax status by the structure and timing of loss settlements and by investment strategies. Recent changes in the industry have led to unprofitable underwriting activity offset by (perhaps) profitable portfolio management. The taxability of portfolio gains is controllable by the composition of the portfolio and the timing of trades.

The Accounting Principles Board (APB) apparently believed that, in accounting for the tax benefits of loss carryforwards, a strict interpretation of the realization concept should take precedence over the matching concept [AICPA, 1974]. The matching concept suggests that these benefits should be recognized in the period the losses arise. The benefits are generated in the loss periods and ideally should be matched with (reduce) these losses. Otherwise, the losses are overstated and a potentially important asset (the ability to reduce taxes) is not recorded. The realization concept suggests that these benefits should be recognized only in the later period in which they are received, because realization of these benefits is uncertain. Such conflict between recognition and realization has affected the development of generally accepted accounting principles for many years [Horngren, 1965].

APB *Opinion No. 11* [APB, 1967] provides "that the future tax benefit of a loss carryforward should be recognized as an asset during the loss period if realization is 'assured beyond any reasonable doubt.' " It was the APB's intention that such recognition should be restricted to unusual cases. APB *Opinion No. 11* [APB, 1967] states that "in those rare cases in which realization of the tax benefits of loss carryforwards is assured beyond any reasonable doubt, the potential benefits should be associated with the periods of loss and should be recognized in the determination of results of operations for those periods." Realization was considered to be assured beyond any reasonable doubt when both of the following conditions existed: (a) the loss resulted from an identifiable, isolated, and nonrecurring cause and the company either had been continuously profitable over a long period or had suffered occasional losses which were more than offset by taxable income in subsequent years; and (b) future taxable income was virtually certain to be large enough to offset the loss carryforward and would occur soon enough to provide realization during the carryforward period [APB, 1967].

The use of the words "identifiable, isolated, and nonrecurring" in the above quotation was intended to rule out recognition of loss carryforwards resulting from generally unsuccessful business operations of an entity [AICPA, 1974]. Operating losses resulting because of depressed economic conditions or because of changes in consumer preferences or in technology would not give rise to a situation where a future tax benefit might be recognized currently. Loss carryforwards resulting from the introduction of products or services which had not achieved sufficient acceptance to produce profits also would not qualify for recognition prior to realization [AICPA, 1974].

Two examples of loss carryforwards that might qualify for recognition during the loss period are (a) losses resulting from the expropriation of a foreign subsidiary, or from the abandonment of one of several operations where the continuing operations are and have been profitable and are virtually certain to be profitable enough to offset the loss carryforwards; and (b) losses of one or more subsidiaries of a profitable parent company where the carryforward will be made available as an offset against other taxable income by filing a consolidated income tax return, or by claiming a bad debt deduction, or by some other means [AICPA, 1974]. It would not be appropriate, however, to record the tax benefit of a loss carryforward of a subsidiary company, even though the parent and other subsidiaries are profitable, if there are no specific plans to obtain the tax benefit from the loss [AICPA, 1974]. In those rare cases where operating loss carryforwards are expected to be realized beyond any reasonable doubt as offsets against future taxable income, the potential tax benefits would be reflected in the balance sheet as assets and should be classified as current or noncurrent depending on the extent to which realization is expected to occur within the current operating cycle [AICPA, 1974].

APB *Opinion No. 11* [APB, 1967] also discusses a situation in which it may be necessary to recognize a portion or all of the tax benefits of the loss carryforward as an offset to net deferred tax credits:

> Net tax credits should be eliminated to the extent of the lower of (a) the tax effect of the loss carryforward, or (b) the amortization of the net deferred tax credits that would otherwise have occurred during the carryforward period. If the loss carryforward is realized in whole or in part in periods subsequent to the loss period, the amounts eliminated from the deferred tax credit accounts should be reinstated (at the then current tax rates) on a cumulative basis as, and to the extent that, the tax benefit of the loss carryforward is realized.

The justification for recognizing loss carryforwards as an offset to deferred tax credits was that it would be unrealistic to require recognition of deferred tax credits while at the same time denying recognition of deferred tax charges, in the form of a loss carryforward. This follows because both the deferred credits and the deferred charges will reverse during the same future accounting periods. However, net deferred credits that will not be amortized until after the expiration of the loss carryforward period cannot be offset by loss carryforwards [APB, 1967].

AETNA'S ACCOUNTING FOR TAX BENEFITS

In 1982, Aetna included $203 million attributable to tax benefits of tax-loss carryforwards in its operating earnings. Aetna essentially made the following entry to record these benefits:[3]

Federal income taxes:
tax benefits recoverable   203,000,000
    Federal income tax expense   203,000,000

The "federal income taxes: tax benefits recoverable" account appeared in the asset section of Aetna's December 31, 1982 Consolidated Balance Sheet; the

---

[3] These tax benefits are for tax-loss carryforwards in excess of amounts deducted from existing deferred taxes.

"federal income tax expense" account appeared as a credit in Aetna's 1982 Consolidated Statement of Income.

The tax-loss carryforwards were generated by Aetna's property-casualty companies. To maximize shareholder returns over time, funds held for future property-casualty claim payments were invested primarily in tax-exempt securities. Taxable bonds were purchased as necessary to assure that the tax benefits arising from property-casualty underwriting losses could be used to offset current taxable investment income well before the 15-year carryforward period for tax-losses expired. The disputed tax-loss carryforwards arose primarily from the fact that property-casualty underwriting losses substantially exceeded the taxable investment income.

Aetna's management stated that it was "assured beyond any reasonable doubt, that the tax benefits of these tax-loss carryforwards will be realized."[4] Aetna's management identified several factors which reinforced its assurance. First, Aetna elected to consolidate its life companies, which generate substantial taxable income, with non-life companies for tax purposes.[5] This provided a partial offset against non-life losses. Second, investable funds generated by property-casualty operations and by property-casualty investment portfolios have been and are being directed toward taxable investments. Third, Aetna's non-insurance operations were expected to generate increasing amounts of taxable income in future years. Fourth, Aetna has undertaken several steps to accelerate recovery of these tax benefits, including selective additional sales of tax-exempt securities for reinvestment in taxable bonds. The timing, manner, and extent of these sales will be governed by market conditions and the development of other sources of taxable income within Aetna. Fifth, the company was considering the redeployment of other assets for which the current market value was higher than the carrying value. Finally, Aetna was considering various reinsurance programs which would allow it to accelerate the realization of taxable income through the release of reserves for claims far in the future.[6]

Peat, Marwick, Mitchell & Co. stated that "we concur with the Company's application of generally accepted accounting principles with regard to the recognition of such benefits."[7] The SEC's staff advised Aetna in February 1983 that, although the realization of the tax benefits by Aetna may be more likely than not, it had not, in the staff's view, met the accounting test of assurance beyond any reasonable doubt, and therefore, Aetna should appropriately adjust its financial statements. Aetna's management continued to believe that realization of these benefits was assured beyond any reasonable doubt, but did not wish to continue applying an accounting principle in the

---

[4] This statement and the following factors were included in Aetna's SEC Form 10-K for 1982.

[5] Life insurance taxation is complex. This consolidation may not be as simple as it seems. Moreover, continuing changes in the tax law make all plans for future benefits somewhat problematic.

[6] Reinsurance provides income because loss relief is recorded at the face value of the future settlement while the premium to the insurance company providing the reinsurance is at a lower, present value.

[7] This statement was included in the independent auditor's report dated February 18, 1983.

face of an SEC staff assertion that its application was not appropriate. Aetna's response was to discontinue current recognition of these tax benefits after the third quarter of 1982, but not to adjust prior quarters. In March 1983, the staff of the SEC began a formal investigation of Aetna's accounting for these benefits.[8]

Aetna first recognized tax benefits from loss carryforwards in the loss periods in 1975. At that time, the staff of the SEC reviewed this practice and after consideration took no exception to it. Tax-loss carryforwards again were generated by Aetna beginning in the third quarter of 1981 and their recognition in the loss period was disclosed in Aetna's notes to its consolidated financial statements for 1981 as follows:

> For financial statement purposes, a tax benefit of $26.6 million related to operating loss carryforwards, in excess of amounts deducted from existing deferred taxes, has been recognized in 1981. In the opinion of management, the utilization of these losses to offset future taxable income is assured beyond a reasonable doubt.

The impact of Aetna's accounting for these tax benefits in 1982 was disclosed in management's discussion and analysis of financial condition and results of operations as follows:

	1982 Operating Earnings (millions)	1982 Operating Earnings per Share
Operating earnings as reported (tax benefits recognized for first three quarters only)	$522	$5.80
Operating earnings if tax benefit of tax loss carryforwards was not recognized at all for 1982	$319	$3.50
Operating earnings if tax benefit of tax loss carryforwards was recognized for entire year	$538	$5.98

THE SEC POSITION

The staff of the SEC has taken a hard line in situations involving accounting for the tax benefits from loss carryforwards. *Staff Accounting Bulletin No. 8* [SEC, 1976] states: "It is the staff's opinion that the 'assured beyond any reasonable doubt' criterion established in APB *Opinion No. 11* is one of the most restrictive tests contained within the authoritative literature. Accordingly, the staff will expect the evidence supporting current recognition of a tax-loss carryforward to be highly persuasive."

In response to a question about what are the key elements necessary to demonstrate that "future taxable income is virtually certain to be large enough to offset the loss carryforward . . . ," *Staff Accounting Bulletin No. 8* notes that

---

[8] Aetna's discussion of its position and response is included in its SEC Form 10-K for 1982.

numerous factors are to be considered and the relative significance will vary somewhat from case to case. However, the staff believes the following are particularly important:

(a) A very strong earnings history.
(b) Clear evidence that the loss was not attributable to a general economic decline.
(c) The availability of reasonably feasible alternative tax strategies, such as the conversion of a tax-exempt portfolio to taxable securities.
(d) Forecasts based upon realistic assumptions which indicate future earnings substantially in excess of the recorded loss carryforward.

Staff Accounting Bulletin No. 8 also states that "normally, the registrant should be able to demonstrate the existence of all of these factors. Seldom, if ever, would any one element, such as forecasts of future earnings, standing alone be sufficient to demonstrate that future earnings will meet the 'virtually certain' test" [SEC, 1976].

A *Business Week* article dated February 28, 1983 provides some insight into the SEC's position:

> "We don't think Aetna met the test that says future profits must be beyond a reasonable doubt," says an SEC accountant. "We think the test is much more severe, and we're concerned because we know a lot of companies are moving in Aetna's direction." The company and the commission can pursue a variety of administrative and legal procedures to resolve the conflict, but the SEC would appear to have the upper hand because the securities laws give it the power to set accounting standards.[9]

This article also noted that the SEC acted against Aetna only after questions about the insurer's accounting practices were raised publicly.

DISCUSSION OF AETNA'S POSITION

Aetna may have been able to make a good case for each of the factors listed in *Staff Accounting Bulletin No. 8*. It had reported earnings in each of the last ten years; the tax-benefits were generated by its nonlife companies, principally the property-casualty operations, and not by a general economic decline; the company had several feasible tax strategies available to it, including converting tax-exempt securities to taxable securities; and it is likely that the company could have provided forecasts for 15 years which reflected future earnings in excess of the recorded loss carryforwards.

Earnings History

First, consider the strong earnings history factor or criterion. Aetna reported earnings in each of the last 10 years and these earnings have ranged from a low of $107.3 million in 1975 to a high of $585.4 million in 1979. Its earnings in 1982 for the employee benefits division, the life, health, and annuity lines of

---

[9] "Profits the SEC Wants to Deflate," *Business Week*, February 28, 1983.

the personal financial security division, and the American Re-insurance Company were at or near their highest levels, but the earnings for the property-casualty operations were well below their highest levels.

Even though Aetna has had a consistent record of earnings, it is important to recognize that a large proportion of the earnings in each year has been tax-exempt. Casualty companies historically have concentrated their investments in tax-exempt securities and have purchased or held taxable securities only to the extent needed to provide enough taxable income to offset tax losses from underwriting. Because of these investment practices, earnings in each year reflect a large proportion of nontaxable earnings (e.g., tax-exempt interest and dividends eligible for the 85 percent dividend-received deduction).

At December 31, 1983, over half of Aetna's investments of $7,950 million related to property-casualty operations were state and municipal bonds. The net investment income from these investments was sufficient to cover underwriting losses for financial accounting purposes; but, since most of this income was tax-exempt, it was not sufficient to cover these losses for tax purposes. Tax-exempt interest and dividends eligible for the 85 percent dividend-received deduction represented about 80 percent of the difference between the expected federal income tax expense of $97.8 million based on the 46 percent federal income tax rate and the actual tax credit of $189.8 million in 1982. Aetna reflected net tax credits for both 1981 and 1982 and tax return operating loss carryforwards increased from $78.7 million at December 31, 1980 to $736.5 million at December 31, 1981 and to $1,312.9 million at December 31, 1982. At December 31, 1983, Aetna had tax return operating loss carryforwards of $1,613.9 million. Although Aetna consistently has generated earnings, it apparently has not consistently generated taxable earnings. And it is the history of taxable earnings that is relevant in assessing its ability to realize tax benefits from loss carryforwards.[10]

Economic Decline

Aetna's tax loss carryforwards were generated by its property-casualty operations rather than by a general economic decline. Thus, Aetna apparently met the second test for current realization. However, the property-casualty oper-

[10] Concern about Aetna's ability to generate taxable earnings also was expressed by Denis J. Callaghan and Jeffrey Cohen of Dean Witter Reynolds Inc. in a research note dated February 15, 1983. Tax losses in the property-casualty operations and consolidated companies in 1982 and estimated losses in 1983 and 1984 primarily were created by underwriting losses less taxable investment income. The life insurance companies generated taxable income. The diversified operations reported positive earnings to shareholders, but they currently generate large tax losses. Callaghan and Cohen observed that Aetna was accelerating its taxable income by (1) selling tax-exempt bonds and reinvesting the proceeds in taxable securities, (2) re-insuring some of its very long-term reserves, and (3) shifting tax credits back to its partners in return for taxable income. Callaghan and Cohen estimated declining tax losses in the property-casualty companies in 1983 and 1984, due to increased taxable investment income and re-insurance transactions. An estimated decline in the diversified operations tax loss in 1983 reflected the inclusion of a full year's pretax earnings for Geosource and Federated Investors and assumed that Aetna would shift some tax credits to its partners.

ating problems were severe. Aetna acknowledged in its SEC Form 10-K for 1982 that the company and the insurance business generally "have been operating in a period of dramatic change and intense competition compounded by a volatile economy. . . . Commercial casualty and property is highly price competitive. . . . Underwriting profitability in the property-casualty industry has tended to fluctuate considerably over cycles ranging from 5 to 7 years."

Yet, a research report dated February 15, 1983 concluded that the fundamental outlook for Aetna's group and property-casualty insurance business was relatively favorable:

> Aetna's property-casualty loss ratio has already stabilized, due to the better pricing and underwriting disciplines that were implemented well over a year ago. Loss reserves appear to be in good shape, especially in relation to the favorable trend established in paid losses during the past 15 months or so. Group health pricing remains very strong. The combination of an economic recovery and better pricing in the commercial insurance markets, which we expect to emerge later this year, suggests that Aetna's earnings could begin to improve cyclically as much as a year sooner than many other companies.[11]

Alternative Tax Strategies

Aetna appears to have several feasible alternative tax strategies for realizing its loss carryforwards. Aetna has announced its intention to generate sufficient taxable income to benefit from the tax losses. One of the planned alternatives involves the redirection of tax-exempt investments into taxable ones. There is little doubt that such a strategy could succeed, but there are economic implications to its adoption. Such a strategy implies an economic environment in which historical relations between underwriting profitability and investment income have changed.[12]

The long-standing practice of the casualty insurance industry is to hold most of the loss reserves in tax-exempt securities. This is optimal as long as

---

[11] Report by Denis J. Callaghan and Jeffrey Cohen of Dean Witter Reynolds Inc. dated February 15, 1983.

[12] The property-casualty business essentially consists of the receipt of premiums, payment of expenses and losses, and investment of the cash in the interim. The profitability of the underwriting side of the business is commonly reflected in the combined ratio of expenses and losses to premiums. When underwriting is profitable, the combined ratio is less than one and much of the portfolio is invested in tax-exempt securities. The following table presents some related data for the property-casualty portion of Aetna's operations:

Year	Combined Ratio	Percentage in Tax-Exempts
1983	108.1	51.1
1982	107.8	55.8
1981	106.4	56.9
1980	102.2	60.4
1979	94.9	64.5

the underwriting activity generates taxable income and the yield on tax-exempt securities exceeds the after-tax yield on taxable securities:

$$R_{TE} > (1 - t)R_T, \tag{1}$$

where R_{TE} is the yield on tax-exempt securities, R_T is the yield on taxable securities, and t is the corporate tax rate (typically 46 percent). The condition in equation (1) has historically held for firms subject to a 46 percent marginal tax rate. If we introduce tax losses from underwriting and delay the realization of tax benefits from future underwriting profitability, the decision to invest in tax-exempt securities is optimal provided:

$$R_{TE} > [1 - \frac{t}{(1 + k)^n}]R_T, \tag{2}$$

where k is the time discount rate and n is the years to realization of the tax benefit. As the number of years before realization of current tax losses increases—that is, as n increases—or the time discount rate increases, the bracketed expression in equation (2) approaches one, and taxable investments become more attractive since the right-hand side increases.

The use of a mixed portfolio of taxable and tax-exempt securities with the proportions chosen based on the profitability of the underwriting activity is appropriate. Given a short, stable cycle of profitability, the proportions would be stable as well. Tax losses have been large and growing since 1980. Aetna began a substantial restructuring of assets in 1982 coincident with the SEC dispute and concerns over current realization of tax benefits for financial reporting purposes. With the benefit of hindsight it can be argued that the restructuring should have occurred earlier, but Aetna's management made decisions in 1980 and 1981 which reflected its expectations. At that time the price competition and resulting underwriting losses on property-casualty operations were not expected to persist. Forecasting is always problematic. The opinions of analysts and others ranged from predictions of a return to shorter historical profitability cycles, to predictions of a permanent change in the nature of the business. The SEC correctly predicted that other insurers would soon generate tax-loss carryforwards as Aetna did.[13]

Assuming that Aetna's management made a correct strategic choice to generate taxable income, there are still tactical questions. For example, Aetna announced a plan to actively rearrange the portfolio rather than simply to direct new funds to taxable investments. This implies transaction costs and recognition of capital gains or losses on sales of current holdings. Aetna's 1982 SEC Form 10-K revealed unrealized losses on average for the tax-exempt portfolio. A corporate taxpayer can use these only to offset capital gains with a three-year carryback and a five-year carryforward.

A second announced strategy involved the transfer of existing long-term liabilities in the re-insurance market. Aetna has booked losses at their future

---

[13] See "Insurer Takes Novel Steps to Avoid Loss," *The Wall Street Journal*, June 4, 1984 which describes the plight of USF&G Corporation.

expected value and has stated the liability in these terms. However, other insurers can be paid the present value of the obligation to accept the responsibility for future payment. In the process, Aetna generated book and taxable income in the amount of the difference between the present value and the future (nominal) value of these liabilities. This technique has gained attention recently and is currently the subject of debate in the tax committees of Congress.[14]

Aetna has reported several other alternatives which can be used to generate taxable income, including consolidation of life and nonlife companies for tax purposes, increased profits from noninsurance businesses, and redeployment of assets with unrealized gains. These alternatives are all subject to uncertainty about tax laws and possible changes, the ability to attain stated goals and predictions, and the ability to replace assets in a favorable manner. Transaction costs may be especially large for redeployment of assets. These strategies, while feasible, are not without risk and do not seem to meet the requirements of APB *Opinion No. 11* [APB, 1967] for virtually certain taxable income.

MARKET REACTIONS TO THE DISPUTE

The economic events confronting Aetna and the related dispute with the SEC are reflected in Aetna's share price performance in this period.[15] Figure 1 graphs price indices for Aetna, the S&P 500, multi-line insurance companies, and property-casualty companies from September 30, 1982 (prior to the tax benefits controversy) through September 30, 1983 (after the controversy was resolved). Each index is defined with September 30, 1982 equal to 100.[16] A substantial divergence is apparent between Aetna and the S&P 500 beginning in early October 1982 and reaching a 27-point difference in late January 1983. The divergence increases again in late May and June of 1983 to almost 35 points. The indices for the multi-line and property-casualty insurance companies suggest that while the relative decline was not unique to Aetna, it was more pronounced for Aetna. The patterns are similar for Aetna and the property-casualty and multi-line insurance companies after the divergence which took place early in the time period covered.

---

[14] Callaghan and Cohen observe in their report dated February 15, 1983 that "the effect of the reinsurance transactions could be quite large. Because of the time value of money, the cost of reinsuring very long-term reserves could be only one-third the amount currently held in those reserves. For example, reinsuring $150 million in long-term reserves might cost $50 million, and $100 million would be released from reserves into taxable income. Each transaction produces a one-time gain, but Aetna could do a series of these transactions in 1983 and 1984 as it needs the taxable income."

[15] Callaghan and Cohen note in their report dated February 15, 1983 that they "now see the stock in a bottoming trend, with limited downside risk. Moreover, the tax issue has probably run its course in terms of having a major market impact on the stock."

[16] The Aetna index is not dividend adjusted, but neither is the S&P 500. Aetna's dividends could explain one-day ex-dividend differences, but not long-term patterns.

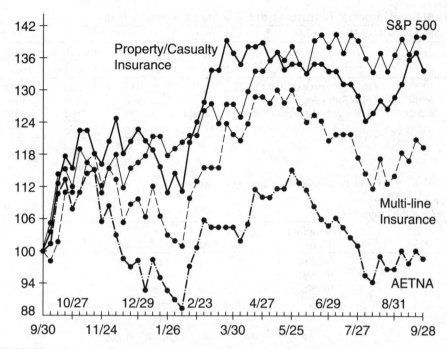

FIGURE 1 Prices indices for Aetna, S&P 500, and property/casualty and multi-line insurance companies   9/30/82 = 100

To examine the effects of the tax benefits controversy on Aetna's market value more directly, the abnormal returns were calculated from the daily, dividend-adjusted returns of Aetna using the market model. Returns from September 30, 1982 through February 29, 1984 (360 observations) were regressed on the corresponding values of the S&P 500 and the prediction errors were recorded. The results are summarized in Table 1. Panel A of Table 1 reveals that a cumulative, abnormal, six-day return of approximately 5.2 percent was associated with three *Wall Street Journal* announcements about the tax benefits issue in February and March of 1983. The flow of news about this issue, and more generally about Aetna, was substantial.[17] A chronology of major announcements in the general business press is provided in Table 2. The first public discussion of the effects of the accounting method appears to have been a *Fortune* article dated November 15, 1982 (and available two weeks

---

[17] These three dates were selected because they represented news items about this issue which were free of unrelated disclosures and *ex ante* seemed to represent changes in the likelihood that Aetna eventually would have to restate all of the results for 1982. Confounding information appears, for example, on May 2, 1983, when the WSJ announced that the SEC ordered abandonment of the method together with announcement of an 18 percent rise in the first-period profit. Similarly, the February 24, 1983 "Heard on the Street" column discussed the issue and speculated that the accounting method requirement would lead insurers to end the current price war. *Ex ante*, the implications of this speculation are ambiguous.

TABLE 1 Abnormal Returns at the Release of News Articles

Panel A—*The Wall Street Journal*

Publication Date	Subject	Abnormal Returns		
		Day -1	Day 0	Total
2/1/83	Ruling Expected from SEC	− .0114	− .0111	− .0225
2/9/83	SEC Rules Against Aetna	− .0032	− .0101	− .0133
3/22/83	SEC Formally Probes Refusal to Restate	− .0069	− .0093	− .0162
		− .0215	− .0305	− .0520

t-statistic = 1.647
One-tailed alpha = .05

t-statistic calculated as cumulative return ÷ $\sqrt{6 \times \text{daily variance}}$

Panel B—*Fortune*
"Behind the Profits Glow"

Availability Dates	Abnormal Return
10/27/82	− .0108
10/28/82	− .0229
10/29/82	− .0163
11/1/82	+ .0088
	− .0412

t-statistic = 1.600
One-tailed alpha ≈ .055

TABLE 2 Chronology of Aetna's Tax Carryforwards in the General Business Press

Date	
11/15/82	*Fortune* article "Behind the Profits Glow at Aetna" includes consideration of the impact of tax loss carryforwards.
2/1/83	*WSJ* discloses imminent SEC ruling on Aetna's accounting.
2/9/83	*WSJ* reveals SEC order to abandon accounting practice.
2/10/83	*WSJ* reports Aetna's plans to offset the SEC ruling.
2/24/83	*WSJ* "Heard on the Street" discusses implications of SEC ruling for existing price war in casualty insurance.
3/7/83	*Fortune* article "Battle over Earnings: The SEC vs. Aetna" appears.
3/22/83	*WSJ* announces formal SEC probe into Aetna's refusal to restate earnings for first three quarters of 1982.
5/5/83	*WSJ* announces FASB has included tax loss carryforwards as a major component of "Accounting for Income Taxes."
7/8/83	*WSJ* reveals that Aetna ended dispute with SEC by restating all of 1982 results.
8/1/83	*Business Week* article "Profit Pains at the New Aetna" appears.
9/7/83	*WSJ* questions Aetna's moves to lift profits.

earlier). Panel B of Table 1 reveals a significance level of just over 5 percent on a four-day abnormal return of -4 percent associated with the *Fortune* article.[18]

The results in Figure 1 and Tables 1 and 2 are consistent with negative evaluations by investors of Aetna's controversy with the staff of the SEC about accounting for tax-loss carryforwards. The linkage between the accounting method and the market's reactions is not clear, since market reactions could reflect reassessments of the economic significance of reported earnings, the costs associated with the regulatory conflict, or anticipation of subsequent management reactions by Aetna.

Aetna's accounting for the tax benefits of loss carryforwards had its defenders in addition to Peat, Marwick, Mitchell & Co. Callaghan and Cohen of Dean Witter Reynolds Inc. made the following observations in a careful analysis on February 2, 1983, just following the *Wall Street Journal* disclosure of the pending ruling:

> We are comfortable with Aetna's accounting methods. We believe that recognizing the full benefit of tax credits against underwriting losses is the appropriate procedure under the current accounting and tax regulations and represents a fair presentation of current earnings. It seems quite likely that Aetna will be able to generate sufficient taxable income over 15 years to offset its 1981 and 1982 tax losses. However, we do worry about the potential cumulative effect of a substantial buildup of a deferred tax asset if large tax losses are produced year after year. Obviously, there is a point where Aetna would no longer be able to demonstrate "beyond any reasonable doubt" its ability to earn off the deferred tax asset. We also worry about how much of a premium Aetna will have to pay for taxable income in order to earn off the tax asset, especially if the cumulative buildup of the asset is substantial. . . . We should stress that regardless of which way the SEC rules, the use of tax-loss carryforwards will have no effect on future operating earnings once Aetna is no longer in a current tax-loss position. If the SEC ruling is negative, the effect of using the tax-loss carryforwards in future years will be reported below the line as an extraordinary item. If the SEC ruling is positive, Aetna will be allowed to continue to fully tax effect its underwriting losses in its income statements and will build up a deferred tax asset on its balance sheet. As the tax credits are earned off, the deferred tax asset will be reduced, with no impact on the income statement.

When Aetna released annual results, Callaghan and Cohen updated their analysis, observing that the fourth-quarter income effect was less than their expectations (February 15, 1983):

> It seems reasonable to assume that Aetna is now willing to accept some financial loss in its strategy to generate taxable income. Otherwise, it would not have waited until now to reposition itself along the lines described above.

---

[18] These dates were chosen based on *Fortune*'s publication schedule where Monday, November 1, 1982 corresponds to the newsstand availability of the November 15, 1982 issue and the previous Wednesday, Thursday, and Friday represent receipt by mail subscribers.

We suspect, however, that much of the penalty may be in the form of
opportunity costs and/or stretched out over many years. . . .

CONCLUSIONS

Aetna's accounting for its tax benefits from loss carryforwards in 1982 provides a classic example of the role of judgment in the application of generally
accepted accounting principles. Aetna's management and the staff of the SEC
had different reasons for becoming involved in this dispute and they interpreted existing criteria differently.

Why did Aetna choose to recognize these tax benefits in periods of tax
losses? Aetna's management may have believed that this recognition was
correct given Aetna's circumstances, and it may have wanted to recognize the
effects of these tax benefits in earnings for 1982.[19] Why did the staff of the
SEC choose to question Aetna's accounting for these tax benefits in 1982? SEC
accountants may have believed that recognition of these tax benefits in 1982
was incorrect given Aetna's circumstances and may have wanted "to make an
example" of Aetna because other insurance companies were poised to follow
its precedent if it was successful.[20] Why did Aetna refuse to change its
accounting method and restate its earnings for 1982? Aetna's management
may have believed that it had a good case for its position. It also may have
been concerned about the legal status of published financial statements which
reflected the tax benefits in earnings for 1982. Aetna included financial statements which reflected tax benefits in earnings for 1982 in prospectuses for
securities offerings. Aetna also was involved in acquisition and merger activity during this period.

Aetna's stock values declined sharply in relative terms during the period
of dispute. It is reasonable to associate this decline with real economic charac-
teristcs of the property-casualty insurance industry and also with various
choices of Aetna's management. It may be that the public controversy itself
induced investors to modify their assessments of Aetna and of the industry.

The dispute focused on interpretations of criteria provided in APB *Opinion No. 11* [APB, 1967]. These criteria were framed and interpreted when the
carryforward period was five years and later extended to seven years [AICPA,
1974; SEC, 1976]. A 5- or 7-year period constrained management's opportunities to realize the tax benefits of loss carryforwards and reasonable forecasts of taxable earnings could be meaningfully interpreted for such a time
period. The carryforward period is now 15 years. This longer carryforward
period provides managements with increased opportunities to realize the tax
benefits of loss carryforwards by implementing various alternative tax strate-

[19] Aetna's SEC Form 10-K for 1982 provides a very complete discussion of management's
position.
[20] See "Profits the SEC Wants to Deflate," *Business Week*, February 28, 1983.

gies. Increased opportunities do not necessarily provide sufficient assurance that the tax benefits will be realized, but a company can be changed dramatically in the pursuit of tax benefits over a 15-year period.

The FASB currently is reassessing accounting for income taxes, including the issue of in what periods the tax effects of net operating loss carryforwards should be recognized in financial reporting income [FASB, 1983]. The FASB has raised several salient points: (1) the current 15-year carryforward period is much less restrictive than the former 5-year period; (2) the current requirement for recognition is that realization of the benefits be assured beyond a reasonable doubt; and (3) guidelines for recognition of the benefits could be established which more closely parallel existing practices for receivables and similar assets [FASB, 1983].

The FASB's conceptual framework provides the basis for some questions which can be used to structure the issue of when to recognize the tax benefits of loss carryforwards in financial reporting income. Elements of financial statements, such as assets, liabilities, revenues, and expenses, are defined in FASB *Statement of Financial Accounting Concepts No. 3* [FASB, 1980]. Recognition and measurement criteria are set forth in FASB *Statement of Financial Accounting Concepts No. 5* [FASB, 1984].

First, are these tax benefits assets? Do these tax benefits meet the definition of an element of financial statements? The FASB has defined assets as "probable future economic benefits obtained or controlled by a particular entity as a result of past transactions or events" [FASB, 1980, para. 19]. Three characteristics have been associated with assets: (1) they embody a probable future benefit that involves a capacity singly or in combination with other assets, to contribute directly or indirectly to future net cash inflows; (2) a particular enterprise can obtain the benefit and control others' access to it; and (3) the transaction or other event giving rise to the enterprise's right to or control of the benefit already has occurred [FASB, 1980, para. 20]. The tax benefits of loss carryforwards appear to qualify as assets under the FASB definition. They are future economic benefits which have arisen because of past events and which can be controlled by a particular enterprise.

Second, how uncertain are these tax benefits? Do these tax benefits meet the criteria of measurability, relevance, and reliability which bear directly on the matter of uncertainty [FASB, 1984, para. 63]? Uncertainty exists about whether an enterprise can obtain these benefits. The tax benefits are probable, but not certain. The existence and amount of these tax benefits do not need to be certain for the benefits to qualify as assets [FASB, 1980, para. 39], but whether these benefits are formally recognized and measured as assets depends on how uncertain they are. That is, accounting for these benefits requires an assessment of the probability that they will be realized. The FASB has defined realization as "the process of converting resources and rights into money" [FASB, 1980, para. 83]. An enterprise that can be characterized as a going concern and that is accounted for on that basis can reasonably be expected to obtain at least some of the tax benefits of loss carryforwards. This realization may occur in the normal course of events or because of responsive changes in the economic structure of the company, such as those instituted by Aetna and others.[21]

Aetna's accounting for its tax benefits of loss carryforwards reflects the interactions among tax accounting, financial reporting, and economic choices. With a 15-year carryforward period, Aetna and other companies have substantially more time in which to restructure their asset positions or to institute other tax strategies to obtain these tax benefits. The staff of the SEC was aware of these strategies but did not find them persuasive in meeting the requirements of APB *Opinion No. 11* [APB, 1967].

We believe that the requirement for realization of these tax benefits "to be assured beyond any reasonable doubt" is more restrictive than the criteria suggested by the FASB conceptual framework and in most cases has precluded the recognition of these benefits as assets.[22] This requirement also seems to be inconsistent with the treatment of other assets, which are recognized and measured as assets on the expectation that they will have future value and will be written down only when evidence arises which negates their future value. The well-established requirements of full disclosure and reasonable assurance of realization have been adequate in accounting for most assets. A similar perspective should be taken with the tax benefits of loss carryforwards. These benefits should be recognized and measured as assets in the loss period unless specific doubts exist about their future realizability. Current recognition of these benefits should be disclosed separately and footnotes should describe the probability of realization. Changes in accounting estimates then should be used to reflect changes in the probability of realization [APB, 1971].

REFERENCES

Accounting Principles Board (APB), "Accounting for Income Taxes," *Accounting Principles Board Opinion No. 11* (AICPA, 1967).
———, "Accounting Changes," *Accounting Principles Board Opinion No. 20* (AICPA, 1971).
American Institute of Certified Public Accountants (AICPA), "Assurance Beyond Any Reasonable Doubt," *AICPA Accounting Interpretation No. 13* (AICPA, 1974).
Financial Accounting Standards Board (FASB), "Elements of Financial Statements of Business Enterprises," *Statement of Financial Accounting Concepts No. 3* (Financial Accounting Standards Board, 1980).

---

[21] Like Aetna, USF&G Corporation, a multi-line insurer, has incurred substantial tax-loss carryforwards. See "Insurer Takes Novel Steps to Avoid Loss," *The Wall Street Journal*, June 4, 1984 and the company's 1983 annual report.

[22] The propensity to not recognize assets may create problems in recognizing losses of future economic benefits [FASB, 1980, para. 42]. Is it better to recognize these tax benefits as assets and then recognize losses of these benefits if events or circumstances cause such losses, or is it better to not recognize either the assets or the losses?

————, "Accounting for Income Taxes," *FASB Discussion Memorandum* (Financial Accounting Standards Board, 1983).

————, "Recognition and Measurement in Financial Statements of Business Enterprises," *Statement of Financial Accounting Concepts No. 5* (Financial Accounting Standards Board, 1984).

Horngren, Charles T., "How Should We Interpret the Realization Concept?," *The Accounting Review* (April 1965), pp. 323–333.

Securities and Exchange Commission (SEC), "Changes in Bulletin No. 1 and New Interpretations," *Staff Accounting Bulletin No. 8* (SEC, 1976).

Discounting of Deferred Income Taxes: An Argument for Reconsideration

Frank R. Rayburn
University of Alabama at Birmingham

In *Status Report No. 166* (April 8, 1985), the Financial Accounting Standards Board (FASB) presented its tentative conclusions on accounting for income taxes. The Board has concluded that the effects of tax timing differences are assets and liabilities (liability method), rather than deferred debits and credits (deferred method).[1] A change from the deferred method to the liability method is consistent with the definitions of the elements of financial statements of business enterprises (Statement of Financial Accounting Concepts No. 3, paras. 163–165). At the same time, however, the Board concluded that assets and liabilities recognized by the effects of tax timing differences shall be measured without discounting the future cash flow to arrive at the present value of that cash flow. Specifically, "the Board . . . has deferred a decision on when or in what context to address discounting." Measurement of tax

From *Accounting Horizons* (March 1987), pp. 43–49. Reprinted by permission of the American Accounting Association and the author. Copyright © 1987 by the American Accounting Association.

Author's note: I wish to acknowledge the helpful comments of Mike Dugan, Mary Stone, and two anonymous reviewers.

[1] APB Opinion No. 11 currently requires the deferred method of comprehensive interperiod tax allocation. Under the deferred method, deferred taxes are computed using the tax rates in effect when the timing differences originate and are not adjusted to reflect subsequent changes in tax rates or the imposition of new taxes. Conceptually, the difference between income tax expense and income taxes payable in the periods in which the timing differences originate are treated as either deferred charges or deferred credits.

Under the proposed liability method, deferred taxes are computed using the tax rates expected to be in effect in the period in which the items are expected to be included in taxable income (reversal period) and are subject to future adjustment if the tax rates change or new taxes are imposed. Conceptually, the difference between income tax expense and income taxes payable in the periods in which the timing differences originate are either liabilities for taxes payable in the future or assets for prepaid taxes.

assets and liabilities without discounting their future cash flows is inconsistent with current GAAP and the economics of delaying payment of taxes. Additionally, the FASB has rejected the notion of "indefinite reversal" as presented in APB Opinion No. 23.

The purpose of this paper is to argue that discounting of deferred income taxes is theoretically consistent with current GAAP and with the other tentative conclusions of the Board and that to ignore discounting of taxes is to ignore economic facts that should be reflected in the measurement of tax assets, tax liabilities, and income. Additionally, I suggest that the decision to defer consideration of discounting is nonresponsive to major concerns about tax allocation and is impossible to reconcile conceptually.

To make the argument, I will review the reasons the FASB added the project on accounting for income taxes to its agenda; identify the issues involved in discounting deferred taxes; argue that discounting of deferred taxes is theoretically consistent with the liability method; illustrate the effect of discounting of deferred taxes on the balance sheet and the income statement; and then relate the Board's decision to ignore discounting to the major concerns about tax allocation under the current (deferred) method.

RATIONALE FOR RECONSIDERING ACCOUNTING FOR INCOME TAXES

With the enactment of the Economic Recovery Act of 1981 that introduced a new "accelerated cost recovery system" (ACRS) for depreciable assets, renewed efforts were directed toward reconsideration of comprehensive interperiod tax allocation based on the deferred method. The literature suggests the major concerns about interperiod tax allocation are as follows:

1. Perhaps the greatest concern is the increasing magnitude of the amount of deferred income taxes reported.[2] Compounding this already empirically validated phenomenon is the notion that under ACRS, not only are current deferred income tax balances expected to accelerate, they also appear on some enterprises' balance sheets that had not previously had different amounts of depreciation for book and tax purposes.
2. Another concern is the complexity of applying the deferred method comprehensively. Recognition of the interplay of deferred income taxes and unused investment tax credits (see FASB Interpretation 25) has significantly increased that complexity.[3]
3. A third issue is the concern of many managers and users about how to interpret deferred taxes. Moreover, considering the complexity of calculation and the difficulty of interpreting the meaning, does the cost exceed the benefits?[4]

[2] Robert T. Sprouse, "Deferred Income Taxes," Unpublished paper presented to members of the IASC Working Party on Deferred Income Tax, 1981, p. 7.
[3] Ibid., p. 8.
[4] Ibid.

4. The deferred method does not fit the definition of liabilities in the FASB conceptual framework. Specifically, in Concepts Statement No. 3, the Board said that only the net of tax and liability methods are compatible with the definitions therein.[5]

In response to the above concerns, the FASB added a major project on "Accounting for Income Taxes" to its agenda on January 27, 1982.

ISSUES ASSOCIATED WITH DISCOUNTING

The present value concept inherent in discounting taxes is relatively simple, but the implementation issues may be somewhat more burdensome. The basic implementation issues are predicting timing difference reversals, selecting an appropriate discount rate, and selecting a method to schedule timing difference reversals (LIFO, FIFO, etc.). Predicting timing difference reversals is intrinsic to implementing the liability method tentatively selected by the Board. Thus, this is not an issue unique to discounting.

To apply the liability method, information about specific reversal periods will be necessary when: (1) rate changes have been enacted to take effect in some future period, therefore applying to some but not all reversals; or (2) carryforwards exist and it must be determined whether reversals will occur within or beyond the carryforward period.[6] Stepp suggests that discounting of deferred taxes would require a schedule of cumulative timing differences by the expected year of reversal at the balance sheet date; that such a requirement would go well beyond the information about the period of reversal of timing differences required by the liability method; and concludes that this computational complexity argues against discounting of deferred taxes. The FASB apparently has concluded that an entity can predict reversal periods accurately enough to apply the liability method. If one accepts that position, it is inconsistent to argue that discounting of taxes should be ignored because of the implementation problem noted above.

Selection of an appropriate discount rate has been debated at some length in the literature.[7] Because interest on deferred taxes would not be tax deductible and most corporations are debt-leveraged—or at least, without benefit of

---

[5] Ibid., p. 9.

[6] James O. Stepp, "Deferred Taxes: The Discounting Controversy," *Journal of Accountancy* (November 1985), p. 106.

[7] Homer A. Black, *Interperiod Allocation of Corporate Income Taxes*, Accounting Research Study No. 9 (AICPA, 1966); Thomas F. Keller, *Accounting for Corporate Income Taxes*, Michigan Business Studies Volume XV (The University of Michigan, 1961); Kenneth W. Lemke and Paul R. Graul, "Deferred Taxes—an 'Explicit Cost' Solution to the Discounting Problem," *Accounting and Business Research* (Autumn 1981); Hugo Nurnberg, "Discounting Deferred Tax Liabilities," *The Accounting Review* (October 1972); James E. Wheeler and Willard H. Galliart, *An Appraisal of Interperiod Income Tax Allocation* (Financial Executives Research Foundation, 1974); Edward E. Williams and M. Chapman Findlay III, "Discounting Deferred Tax Liabilities: Some Clarifying Comments," *Journal of Business Finance and Accounting* (Spring 1975); Harry I. Wolk and Michael G. Tearney, "Discounting Deferred Tax Liabilities: Review and Analysis," *Journal of Business Finance and Accounting* (Spring 1980).

deferred taxes an entity would require additional borrowing—I believe the after-tax cost of debt to be the preferable discount rate. The fact that accretion of a discounted deferred tax liability is in after-tax dollars also supports using an after-tax discount rate. In any event, the literature is replete with research that the Board could evaluate in selecting an appropriate discount rate if it elects to study discounting of deferred taxes.

Stepp[8] has identified some other questions regarding the discount rate: (1) Should an investment or a borrowing rate be used? (2) Should a company-specific or an external rate be used? (3) Should a single rate or multiple rates be used? These are relevant issues, but they are not unique to discounting deferred taxes. The Board most recently has wrestled with those same issues in the accounting for pensions project. Also, these same issues relate to discounting of long-term receivables and payables (currently required GAAP; see APB Opinion No. 21). Thus, it is useful to identify these issues, but they are not new problems of a magnitude to defeat the concept of discounting deferred taxes.

Discounting the tax effects of timing differences suggests that the time value of money has important economic effects that should be recognized in financial reporting. In addition to the issues of predicting timing difference reversals and selecting an appropriate discount rate, discounting deferred taxes also requires selection of a method to schedule timing difference reversals (LIFO, FIFO, etc.). While the literature is silent on the issue, FIFO appears the appropriate method for scheduling timing difference reversals. Any other method would approximate the real economic effects of delaying tax payments only by coincidence. Thus, both balance sheet and income statement presentation would appear enhanced by the use of FIFO.

DISCOUNTING IS CONSISTENT WITH LIABILITY METHOD

Under the liability approach, deferred taxes are either assets or liabilities, with the balance in the account determined by timing differences and the tax rate expected to be in effect in the reversal periods. Current GAAP dictates presenting long-term receivables and payables in the balance sheet at their present values (see APB Opinion 21 and FASB Statements 13 and 87). Accounting for deferred tax liabilities should be consistent with current measurement theory for other assets and liabilities.

While tax deferral does not change the total taxes a company pays over its legal life, there are cash flow impacts that should be reflected in the financial statements. Nurnberg[9] has pointed out that to be consistent with Sprouse and Moonitz's argument for the valuation of a liability, ". . . a deferred tax liability should be measured by the present value of a theoretical fund which

[8] Op. cit., p. 102.
[9] Op. cit., p. 657.

would accumulate to its maturity value, and interest expense thereon represents the increase in the present value due to the passage of time." Nurnberg's arguments were predicated on an assumption that the deferred method of tax allocation is an aberration of the liability method. Now that the FASB has selected the liability method, that assumption can be dropped and the power of his logic is enhanced.

In Statement of Financial Accounting Concepts No. 3, the FASB noted that "A common feature of liabilities is interest—the time value of money or the price of delay." To be consistent with this concept, the price of delaying payment of income taxes should be recognized, as with other liabilities, by carrying deferred taxes in the balance sheet at their present value and accruing the interest expense thereon.

One of the primary reasons for reconsidering accounting for income taxes is the inconsistency of the deferred method and the FASB conceptual framework. Adoption of the liability method is responsive to this concern. To reject discounting would be theoretically inconsistent with the liability method of computing deferred taxes and would create a new controversy. The Board's conclusion that the effects of tax timing differences are assets and liabilities and its rejection of discounting are conceptually irreconcilable.

ILLUSTRATION OF EFFECT OF DISCOUNTING DEFERRED TAXES ON FINANCIAL STATEMENTS

Assumptions:

Pretax accounting income before depreciation	$3,000
Asset Cost (Equipment)	10,000
Book Life	10 years, straight-line depreciation
Tax Life	5 years, ACRS depreciation
Salvage Value	-0-
Tax Rate	46%
Discount Rate (After-tax cost of debt)	7%

Pretax accounting income before depreciation is a constant over the 10-year horizon, the investment tax credit is ignored, cash flows occur at the end of the year, and the tax rate is not expected to change over the ten-year period. Timing differences reverse on a FIFO basis.

In Exhibit 1, the tax liability for each year and in total is in column 4. In this one-asset case, reversals start in year 6. Columns 5 and 9 reflect the deferred tax provision without and with discounting, respectively. The impact of discounting on the balance sheet is illustrated by the balance in the deferred tax account in columns 6 and 10. With discounting, the deferred tax balance is increased by the accretion of interest on the balance at the beginning of the period at the assumed rate of seven percent, as shown in column 8. Note in column 12 that the percentage change in the deferred tax account when

EXHIBIT 1 Illustration of Effect of Discounting Deferred Taxes on Financial Statements

	(1)	(2)	(3)	(4)	(5)	(6)	(7)	(8)	(9)	(10)	(11)	(12)
	Pretax Accounting Income Before	Book	ACRS	Taxes	Without Discounting Deferred Taxes		Net	Interest	With Discounting Deferred Taxes		Net	Percent Change In Deferred
Year	Depreciation	Depreciation	Depreciation	Payable	Provision	Balance	Income	Expense	Provision	Balance	Income	Taxes[a]
1	$ 3,000	$ 1,000	$ 1,500	$ 690	$230	$ 230	$ 1,080	$ 0	$164	$ 164	$ 1,146	29
2	3,000	1,000	2,200	368	552	782	1,080	11	405	580	1,216	26
3	3,000	1,000	2,100	414	506	1,288	1,080	41	368	989	1,177	23
4	3,000	1,000	2,100	414	506	1,794	1,080	69	365	1,423	1,152	21
5	3,000	1,000	2,100	414	506	2,300	1,080	100	363	1,886	1,123	18
6	3,000	1,000	0	1,380	(460)	1,840	1,080	132	(460)	1,558	948	15
7	3,000	1,000	0	1,380	(460)	1,380	1,080	109	(460)	1,207	971	13
8	3,000	1,000	0	1,380	(460)	920	1,080	85	(460)	832	995	10
9	3,000	1,000	0	1,380	(460)	460	1,080	58	(460)	430	1,022	7
10	3,000	1,000	0	1,380	(460)	0	1,080	30	(460)	0	1,050	0
	$30,000	$10,000	$10,000	$9,200			$10,800				$10,800	

[a] (Column 6 – Column 10) ÷ Column 6

deferred taxes are discounted ranges from 29 to 18 percent over years one through five and is a positive number through year nine. Longer-lived assets and/or higher discount rates would have a more significant impact whereas shorter-lived assets and/or lower discount rates would reduce the impact.

Columns 7 and 11 present the net effect of discounting deferred taxes on the income statement. By discounting deferred tax liabilities and accreting interest thereon, the economic consequences and the operational advantages of deferring taxes are disclosed separately in the income statement.

BOARD'S RESPONSIVENESS TO MAJOR CONCERNS

Approximately 88 percent of the respondents to the discussion memorandum, "An Analysis of the Issues Related to Accounting for Income Taxes," opposed discounting of deferred taxes. Thus, the Board's tentative decision to exclude consideration of discounting may appear to be very popular with its constituents. I submit, however, that the FASB's tentative conclusions not only are nonresponsive to the reasons cited above for reconsidering the subject, but also have the potential to produce results that are as theoretically deficient as current accounting for deferred taxes and will perpetuate the debate over accounting for income taxes.

Unless corporate tax rates are expected to decrease in the future, the liability method without discounting will give rise to deferred tax account balances equal to or greater than those generated under the deferred method. Thus, a change to the liability method could provide little or no relief to the great concern about the increasing magnitude of deferred taxes. On the other hand, rejection of the "indefinite reversal criterion"[10] (a move I believe to be theoretically sound) could significantly increase deferred tax account balances. If, for example, the FASB should decide that all the undistributed earnings of a subsidiary included in consolidated income or in income of the parent company should be accounted for as a timing difference, significant instantaneous increases in deferred taxes and instantaneous charges to income or retained earnings could result. The same potential impact exists for investments in certain corporate joint ventures. Discounting is a theoretically sound alternative that would be responsive to the current concern about the increasing magnitude of deferred taxes. As illustrated above, discounting could significantly reduce the balance in deferred tax accounts, and in so doing, reflect more accurately the economics of deferring tax payments.

---

[10] In APB Opinion No. 23, there is a presumption that all undistributed earnings of a subsidiary will be transferred to the parent company and that the undistributed earnings included in income of the parent company should be accounted for as a timing difference. That presumption may be overcome and no income taxes should be accrued by the parent company if sufficient evidence shows that the subsidiary has invested or will invest the undistributed earnings indefinitely or that the earnings will be remitted in a tax-free liquidation (indefinite reversal criterion). When the indefinite reversal criterion applies, the undistributed earnings are treated as permanent differences and no deferred taxes are recorded.

Sprouse[11] stated that another major concern that argues for reconsideration of accounting for income taxes is the complexity of applying the deferred method comprehensively. A change to the liability method of comprehensive tax allocation appears to be nonresponsive to the complexity-of-application issue. Deferred tax computations under the liability method are just as complex and perhaps more so than under the deferred method. Discounting would add more complexity, but I believe discounting can be implemented.

The concern of many managers and users about how to interpret deferred taxes does not appear to have been alleviated by the Board's tentative conclusions. It is difficult to argue that changing the labels from deferred debits to assets and deferred credits to liabilities significantly enhances one's ability to interpret deferred taxes. On the other hand, adjusting the deferred tax balance to reflect expected tax rates for the period the item is to be included in taxable income will more nearly reflect anticipated cash flows than is currently the case. Discounting of those future cash outflows would more accurately reflect the cash-flow impacts of deferring tax payments.

The inconsistency of the deferred method and the FASB conceptual framework is partially addressed by the Board's decision to propose the liability method. The liability method is compatible with the definitions of elements in SFAC No. 3, whereas the currently mandated deferred method is not. Rejection of discounting, however, is theoretically inconsistent with the measurement of liabilities as presented in current GAAP and as implied in SFAC No. 3. Thus, the Board has resolved one major theoretical conflict but has created another. In an attempt to be sensitive to the standards overload issue and the apparent disdain for discounting by its constituents, the FASB appears to have made a political decision that may serve it well in the short run but that may eventually crumble from a lack of conceptual support.

CONCLUDING COMMENTS

In 1966, Black[12] concluded that to avoid overstating liabilities and misstating periodic net income, deferred income taxes should be discounted. Later that year, the Accounting Principles Board (APB) rejected Black's recommendation and in APB Opinion No. 10 said "deferred taxes should not be accounted for on a discounted basis," a position that was reaffirmed in APB Opinion No. 11. In rejecting discounting of deferred taxes at that time, the APB said it was considering the broader implications of discounting on financial accounting in general and implied it would readdress the issue at the conclusion of the process. Wheeler and Galliart[13] summarize the APB's study of the subject as follows:

[11] Op. cit., p. 8.
[12] Op. cit., para. 114.
[13] Op. cit., p. 40.

At its September 1966 meeting the Board recommended the creation of a sub-committee to study discounting in general. Such a sub-committee was formed with Donald Bevis as chairman. He reported the committee's recommendation for a research study on the subject to be completed within two years. The Board authorized the study as recommended by Bevis' committee at the Board meeting in December 1966, but no study has been forthcoming.

Discounting of deferred taxes has been an issue in accounting for at least 20 years, but no authoritative body has ever studied the subject.[14] I have demonstrated that discounting of deferred taxes is theoretically consistent with current measurement of liabilities and would be responsive to major concerns about interperiod income tax allocation. The Board's tentative positions that the tax effects of timing differences are assets and liabilities and that those tax effects should not be discounted are conceptually irreconcilable. As a minimum, the FASB should undertake a comprehensive study of the discounting issue and then make an informed decision as it relates to deferred taxes.

[14] It should be noted that the Accounting Standards Executive Committee (AcSEC) of the AICPA has recommended discounting if the liability method is selected. See "FASB Income Tax Hearings Show Diverse Opinions Still Exist on 1960s APB Opinions," *Journal of Accountancy* (June 1984), p. 50.

Letter from Stephen A. Zeff to the Financial Accounting Standards Board

December 2, 1992

Mr. Timothy S. Lucas
Director of Research and Technical Activities
Financial Accounting Standards Board
401 Merritt 7
P.O. Box 5116
Norwalk, CT 06856-5116

Dear Tim:

In the interest of sound financial reporting, I am writing to urge the FASB to play a role in the proper accounting for the investment credit. A revival of the investment credit, which was repealed in 1986, has been mentioned by a number of sources close to the Clinton transition team, and it would be highly desirable if we could close the book on flow-through accounting for the credit and instead account for it as subsidy, which evidently is the government intent.

As is well known, following the third of three exposure drafts issued by the Accounting Principles Board (in 1962, 1967 and 1971), the Treasury, apparently with a strong push from industry, persuaded Congress to provide in the Revenue Act of 1971 that no taxpayer shall be required to use "any particular method of accounting for the credit." (Sec. 101 (c) of P.L. 92–178, Stat. 499 (1971).) In all three exposure drafts (and in Opinion No. 2, issued in 1962), the APB rejected the flow-through approach. In the Senate Committee Report of November 9, 1971, it was stated that "The committee, as was the House, is concerned that the investment credit provided by the bill have as great a stimulative effect on the economy as possible. Therefore, from this standpoint it would appear undesirable to preclude the use of 'flow through' in the financial reporting of income." (92d Congress, 1st Session, Report No. 92–437, p. 45.) The argument for this provision in the bill does not appeal to the accounting merits but only to the economic consequences.

It hardly needs to be said that it has been an embarrassment that Congress dictated an accounting standard over the heads of the SEC and the APB. In November/December 1971, when Congress was heading toward adoption of the accounting amendment to the tax bill, the APB issued a statement deploring Congressional involvement in the establishment of accounting principles, a view that was echoed in editorials in *The Wall Street Journal* and *Business Week*.

Prior to repeal of the credit six years ago, the passage in the law referring to the accounting treatment of the investment credit occupied "non-Code" status, since it was not formally a part of the Internal Revenue Code. It was, as a member of the Congressional Joint Committee on Taxation recently told me, a political provision, not a tax provision.

Should Congress seek to revive the investment credit, it is not currently known whether this political provision will be included. I think it is in the interest of investors and creditors who depend on the usefulness and credibility of financial reporting that the FASB use its resources to persuade the tax-writing committees not to substitute their judgment for that of accounting standard setters. I suspect that the FASB could count on Walter Schuetze and Charles Bowsher as allies in this cause. But it should not be a cause that is forsaken simply because a law of the land precluded the use of sound accounting for the credit in prior years.

You are probably aware that, in 1985, the Accounting Standards Committee of the Canadian Institute of Chartered Accountants declared that "Investment tax credits should be accounted for using the cost reduction approach," (*Handbook* sec. 3805.12). If flow-through accounting is used for a reconstituted U.S. investment credit, a gap between American and Canadian accounting standards would be opened.

I encourage the Board to move on this matter before a bill is drafted.

Sincerely,

Stephen A. Zeff

cc: Mr. Walter Schuetze [SEC Chief Accountant]
    Mr. Charles A. Bowsher [Comptroller General of the United States]

CHAPTER 14

Shareholders' Equity

New financing and compensation arrangements involving equity-like instruments constantly turn up over time, posing accounting questions about how they should be reported in the shareholders' equity section and the income statement. A particularly vexing problem has been the accounting for employee stock options which are commonly used to compensate managers so that their compensation is, in theory, tied to the performance of the company.[1] The main accounting issue related to employee stock options is the measurement (and timing of recognition) of compensation expense: what is the value of the option granted, and, accordingly, what is the cost to the company of the service acquired from the employee? Unlike options and warrants that are actively and regularly traded in the securities markets and therefore have a readily determinable value, employee stock options are not transferable and in most cases may not be exercised until a specified holding period has expired. Nevertheless, employee stock options do share an essential economic characteristic with traded options, namely, the "option" to acquire a share of the company at a specified exercise price during a specified period of time.

The accounting controversy predates the development of options valuation models in the finance literature, which in the last two decades have been widely adopted by finance professionals and are now an essential tool in the securities industry. The position of the Accounting Principles Board in Opinion No. 25, for example, was that the compensation expense was to be measured by the difference between the option exercise price and the market price of the stock on the date of grant. The computation excluded the consideration of the time value of money and the uncertainty regarding the future share value, which are the principal variables affecting option value in the options valuation models. Since most employee stock options are issued at an

---

[1] "Stock" is used in this chapter to mean equity shares. In some countries, the word refers to merchandise inventory.

exercise price greater than or equal to the market price on the date of grant, they are assigned an accounting value of zero by the computation of APB Opinion No. 25, and no compensation expense is reported in the determination of net income.

The Financial Accounting Standards Board (FASB), recognizing a need for change in the current accounting policy for employee stock option plans, added the topic to its agenda in 1984.[2] In 1986, it reached the "tentative conclusion" that the compensation cost associated with stock options should be measured on the grant date using a "minimum value" model. The model is less complex and is more easily implemented than the valuation models used in finance. Nevertheless, the reaction to the FASB's proposal was strongly negative from industry, including small and medium-sized high-tech firms where stock options are a principal way of compensating senior executives. After a long hiatus, the FASB's interest in accounting for stock option plans revived in early 1992, following revelations in the press of huge capital gains from the sale of option shares by top executives of several large companies, without any compensation expense appearing in the companies' income statements. Sen. Carl Levin of Michigan threatened legislative action if the FASB or the SEC didn't act promptly to mandate expense recognition for stock option plans. In October 1992, the SEC imposed greater disclosure requirements for stock option plans, and in June 1993 the FASB issued an exposure draft, "Accounting for Stock-based Compensation," in which it called for an explicit recognition of compensation cost, measured by reference to an option-pricing model, ordinarily on the grant date.

The evolution of the profession's views on the measurement of the compensation implicit in stock options can be seen in Michael P. Bohan's "Measuring the Compensation Element in Employee Stock Option Plans." Bohan notes that the issuance of employee stock options should result in a compensation cost to the issuing company, but argues that the cost can be measured only at the exercise date, based on the cash outlay of the employee, and not on the grant date. This view, while an improvement over Opinion No. 25, ignores the fact that the motivating element in a stock option is the employee's ex-ante expectation, as of the date of grant, of realizing some large gains. This "options valuation" viewpoint, however, is absent in Eric W. Noreen's "Comment: Measuring the Compensation Element in Employee Stock Option Plans." Instead, his criticism of Bohan revolves around whether an "out-of-pocket" economic loss is incurred by the issuance of stock options: that is, Bohan's approach was acceptable if a firm used cash to acquire shares on the open market on the exercise date, but not on the grant date.

Noreen does note that the options valuation models in finance and the minimum value model, originally proposed by Clifford W. Smith and Jerold L. Zimmerman, represent an improvement over APB Opinion No. 25. The minimum value model is described in detail by Robert J. Swieringa, an FASB

[2] See *Accounting for Compensation Plans Involving Certain Rights Granted to Employees*, An Invitation to Comment (Financial Accounting Standards Board, 1984).

member, in "Accounting for Stock Options." Finally, in "FASB's Long Look at Stock Compensation Plans," Barry P. Robbins summarizes the alternatives faced by the FASB in its attempts to revise APB Opinion No. 25.

In addition to employee stock options, at least two major disclosure issues related to shareholders' equity have aroused controversies in recent years. One deals with the accounting and disclosure rules for stock splits and stock dividends. Many writers have noted that the current accounting rules on this subject, which date back to Accounting Research Bulletin (ARB) No. 11 (later incorporated in Chapter 7B of ARB No. 43), are arcane in that they treat small and large share distributions differently (including the effect on retained earnings), regardless of the economic effects of the transaction. This is particularly true for share distributions just below or just above 25 percent: a share distribution smaller than 25 percent requires a transfer from the retained earnings in the amount of the market value of shares distributed, while a 25 percent or larger share distribution requires a transfer equal only to the par value of the shares distributed.

The other issue deals with the variety of new equity-like instruments issued by firms to raise capital. Securities such as redeemable preferred shares and many convertibles are often subjected to different and conflicting accounting rules: whether the security is debt or equity, whether a cash distribution on the security qualifies as interest or dividend, and how to report the gain/loss from disposal of the security. The conflicting reporting issues related to redeemable preferred shares are discussed by R. D. Nair, Larry E. Rittenberg and Jerry J. Weygandt in "Accounting for Redeemable Preferred Stock: Unresolved Issues." The authors show that, while current U.S. generally accepted accounting principles require the classification of these securities as nonequity (reported between liabilities and shareholders' equity), "dividend" declarations on the securities are charged to retained earnings and not reported as interest expense. Moreover, any "dividends" in arrears on the securities are disclosed in a footnote rather than accrued as a liability. The authors recommend a consistent treatment based on the premise that these securities are debt and not equity.

The basic approach to shareholders' equity reporting has been to focus on the sources of equity, for example, contributed capital at par, paid-in capital in excess of par and retained earnings. It is generally known that the reporting of par value provides no substantive information to investors. Yet accountants have continued to require the separate reporting of par value, additional paid-in capital, and so on, on the justification that state laws require such disclosure for determining distributable dividends. It should come as a surprise, therefore, to find in "The Stockholders' Equity Section: Form Without Substance?" by Michael L. Roberts, William D. Samson and Michael T. Dugan that state laws now generally base distributable dividends on the *fair value* of assets, not on demarcations of capital such as par value. They conclude that current reporting practice "is based on an outmoded understanding of legal concepts." The authors urge a new reporting format for the shareholders' equity section that keeps pace with changing legal requirements on distributable dividends.

BIBLIOGRAPHICAL NOTES

For a book containing "a current summary of the accounting rules and the practices followed in applying the current framework for compensation accounting," see:

Accounting for Compensation Arrangements in the United States (Chicago: Arthur Andersen & Co., Second Edition, 1991).

Employee stock option plans and bonus plans have attracted the attention of accounting researchers less for the reporting issues than for the impact that the plans have on management decisions, including the choice of accounting methods. The literature on this topic, and on the impact of stock options on companies' performance, is vast. Some examples:

Larcker, David F.: "The Association Between Performance Plan Adoption and Corporate Capital Investment," Journal of Accounting and Economics (April 1983), pp. 3–30.
Healy, Paul: "The Effect of Bonus Schemes on Accounting Decisions," Journal of Accounting and Economics (April 1985), pp. 85–107.
Waegelein, James F.: "The Association Between the Adoption of Short-Term Bonus Plans and Corporate Expenditures," Journal of Accounting and Public Policy (Spring 1988), pp. 43–63.
Lambert, Richard A., William N. Lanen and David F. Larcker: "Executive Stock Option Plans and Corporate Dividend Policy," Journal of Financial and Quantitative Analysis (December 1989), pp. 409–426.

A recent paper on the FASB project on stock options is:

Rosenfield, Paul, and Mitchell Jaiven: "Reporting on Employee Stock Compensation Plans: Case Not Closed," Journal of Accountancy (December 1990), pp. 73–78.

This paper, however, makes the debatable argument that, because employee stock options do not result in cash payments or similar economic "loss" to the firm, there is no expense to report. One could argue, by a similar reasoning, that there would be no expense to report whenever the company pays a vendor in shares of stock in return for services acquired.

In many ways, employee stock options and stock appreciation rights (SARs) are economically equivalent compensation arrangements. SARs evolved to eliminate the need for the employee actually to acquire shares when exercising the option and then to sell the shares to realize cash income. Under an SAR, the employee receives a cash payment from the company for the difference between the stock's market value and the SAR's exercise price. Despite the economic equivalence, SARs and stock options are accounted for very differently. The following articles and book discuss these differences:

Wallace, Wanda A.: "The Effects of Delays by Accounting Policy-Setters in Reconciling the Accounting Treatment of Stock Options and Stock Appreciation Rights," The Accounting Review (April 1984), pp. 325–341.
Thomas, Paula Bevels, and Larry E. Farmer: "Accounting for Stock Options and SARs: The Equality Question," Journal of Accountancy (December 1984), pp. 92–98.

Wallace, Wanda A., and S. Duane Smith: *Accounting for Options: No Longer an Option* (Toronto: The Canadian Certified General Accountants' Research Foundation, 1991).

A historical study of the influence of stock dividends on the development of accounting is:

Tucker, James J., III: "The Role of Stock Dividends in Defining Income, Developing Capital Market Research and Exploring the Economic Consequences of Accounting Policy Decisions," *The Accounting Historians Journal* (Fall 1985), pp. 73–94. (Contains an extensive bibliography.)

Stock splits and stock dividends have also been the subject of many empirical research studies examining the stock market's reaction to announcements and to the long-term valuation impact of the stock distributions. The following studies are illustrative:

Grinblatt, Mark S., Ronald W. Masulis and Sheridan Titman: "The Valuation Effects of Stock Splits and Stock Dividends," *Journal of Financial Economics* (December 1984), pp. 461–490.
Lakonishok, Josef, and Baruch Lev: "Stock Splits and Stock Dividends: Why, Who, and When," *Journal of Finance* (September 1987) pp. 913–932.

These articles provide additional discussion on the reporting issues related to shareholders' equity:

Scott, Richard A: "Owners' Equity, The Anachronistic Element," *The Accounting Review* (October 1979), pp. 750–763.
Selling, Thomas I., and Clyde P. Stickney: "Disaggregating the Rate of Return on Common Shareholders' Equity: A New Approach," *Accounting Horizons* (Winter 1990), pp. 9–17.

An area of shareholders' equity that has been the subject of controversies in the past and may require the future attention of accounting regulators is the accounting for treasury shares. The following articles discuss the issues involved:

Paton, W. A.: "Postscript on 'Treasury' Shares," *The Accounting Review* (April 1969), pp. 276–283.
Meyer, Philip E.: "Some Accounting Ramifications of Treasury Stock," *The CPA Journal* (November 1973), pp. 1018–1020.
Priest, Alice L.: "Why Corporate Stock Buybacks Don't Really Pay Off," *Business Week* (June 25, 1984), p. 33.

Measuring the Compensation Element in Employee Stock Option Plans

Michael P. Bohan
BP America, Cleveland

This article discusses the deficiencies of current generally accepted accounting principles for determining and recording compensation expense under employee stock option "compensatory plans" as defined by the Accounting Principles Board (APB) Opinion No. 25, "Accounting for Stock Issued to Employees." This discussion does not deal with companywide employee stock purchase plans, since such plans generally are not intended to be compensatory but serve other valid corporate purposes, such as raising capital and enhancing employee loyalty; the issue of compensation for services rendered is not usually relevant for these plans. However, the conclusions of this article would be equally applicable to companywide employee stock purchase plans if the discount from market price at the exercise date is greater than would be reasonable in a sale of previously unissued stock of the same class on the open market.

HISTORY

Stock options have long been a staple of executive perquisites. The use of stock options in executive compensation packages increased significantly with the amendments to the Internal Revenue Code in 1950, which granted specialized tax treatment to certain types of stock option plans.

The accounting profession first dealt very generally with options through the issuance in 1948 of Accounting Research Bulletin (ARB) No. 37, "Accounting for Compensation in the Form of Stock Options." In response to the effect of the Internal Revenue Code modification, ARB No. 37 was revised and reissued in 1953, ultimately to become chapter 13B of ARB No. 43.

The accounting rules generated at that time were quite attuned to the tax rules. Generally, a plan which qualified for the special tax treatment would not require the recording of compensation by the company.

Over the years, the tax rules have changed, allowing more deductibility to the company and reducing the sheltering of an employee's income. Although the tax deductibility rules for employers have changed substantially over the years, as have the basic option plans, the accounting profession did issue APB Opinion No. 25 in 1972 to tighten the measurement rules, but that merely closed some loopholes (by specifying the use of market instead of a surrogate in measuring compensation and by specifying the attributes necessary for measurement, a fixed number of shares and a fixed price).

Reprinted by permission of the *Journal of Accounting, Auditing and Finance* (Spring 1979), pp. 261–264. Copyright © 1979 by Research Institute of America, Inc., Warren Gorham Lamont Professional Publishing Division, 210 South St., Boston, MA 02111. All rights reserved.

compensation element in a stock option plan and still realize some related tax benefits. Fortunately, such tax benefits do not further distort operations because they are treated as a credit to paid-in capital.

Currently, due to the relatively recent appearances of more exotic but still basically stock-related plans, the Financial Accounting Standards Board proposed an interpretation of APB Opinion No. 25, to clarify the manner in which it is to be applied, but which does not disturb the conclusions of the original opinion.

CURRENT PRACTICE

Let's look at the current requirements of APB Opinion No. 25 and see how it is being applied. The Opinion calls for compensation to be measured by the difference between the option price and the quoted market price at the "measurement date." The measurement date is the earliest date at which both of the following are known:

(1) The number of shares the employee is entitled to receive, and
(2) The option price per share.

This information is typically, but not always, known at the date the option is granted. Current practice varies as to the actual time the expense is recognized. If the compensation is "earned" throughout the option period, it is often allocated over the estimated period benefited. However, the purpose of this article is to challenge the determination of aggregate compensation under a compensatory plan, and not to discuss the appropriate allocation of these costs to periodic income.

The anomalies of the accounting measurement principles are best understood by studying several examples of the accounting for some plans that have been popular in the last few years.

Example I.   XYZ Corporation, which operates on a calendar year, provides an incentive to certain key executives in the form of an executive stock purchase plan. On January 1, 1978, under this plan, Mr. J was offered 10,000 shares of the company's common stock at $15 per share, exercisable immediately and continuing until December 31, 1982. On January 1, 1978, the company's common stock was trading for $15 per share. Mr. J exercised his option on April 14, 1980 when the stock was selling for $18.75 per share.

The following are the key factors in the above example:

Event	Date	Market Price
Grant	January 1, 1978	$15.00
Measurement	January 1, 1978	15.00
Exercise	April 14, 1980	18.75
Option price $15		

In this example, no compensation is recorded because the option price ($15) and the market price at the date of measurement ($15) were identical. The measurement date is the date of grant because the number of shares and option price are known at that time.

Example II. Occasionally, the measurement date will differ from the grant date due to a "floating" or "variable" option price. Assume the facts as in *Example I* except that the option price is to be 80 percent of the market price at the exercise date. If the option is exercised on April 14, 1980, when the market price is $18.75, the option price on that date will be $15 (.8 × $18.75). In this example, the compensation ultimately to be recorded is $37,500 (($18.75 − $15.00) × 10,000). Compensation is not measured until the exercise date because that is the first date the option price is known.

Example III. Another example of a "variable" option price is an "inversely variable" plan whereby the option price decreases as the market price increases (usually the exercise price will not be permitted to go below zero).

Assume the facts as in *Example I* except that the option is granted on August 31, 1978 at an option price of $16.875 (the then market). The option price of $16.875 decreases on a dollar-for-dollar basis with increases in market value. If the option is exercised on April 14, 1980, when the market price is $18.75, the option price on that date will be $15 ($16.875 − ($18.75 − $16.875)). In this example, the compensation ultimately to be recorded is $37,500 (($18.75 − $15.00) × 10,000). As with *Example II,* measurement does not take place until exercise because that is the first time the option price is known.

Example IV. There is still another type of plan that is designed to accomplish the same end result as the "inversely variable" plan, but through the use of cash reimbursement to the employee for the income tax effect of the unrealized appreciation (a reimbursement plan), if the employee exercises the option to purchase the shares.

Assume the same facts as in *Example III* except that the employee is to receive the unrealized appreciation in cash upon the exercise of the option. The option price at the exercise date is $16.875 (the date-of-grant price). In this example, the date of grant and the measurement date are the same date because at that time both the number of shares and option price are known, so compensation is measured only to the extent of the cash payment of $18,750 (($18.75 − $16.875) × 10,000), as provided by paragraph 18 of APB Opinion No. 25.

The following schedule summarizes the compensation elements (as seen by the author) and the amounts of compensation required to be recorded under current generally accepted accounting principles for *Examples I, II, III,* and *IV.*

While the aggregate compensation element is $37,500 under all four plans, the accounting charge varies from zero to $37,500. This is because APB

| | EXAMPLE | | | |
PER SHARE:	I	II	III	IV
Market price at date of grant	$15.00	$15.00	$16.875	$16.875
Market price at date of exercise	$18.75	$18.75	$18.75	$18.75
Cash paid by employee at exercise price	$15.00	$15.00	$15.00	$16.875
Less cash paid employee by company				1.875
Net exercise price	$15.00	$15.00	$15.00	$15.00
Compensation element	$ 3.75	$ 3.75	$ 3.75	$ 3.75
Number of shares obtained by option	10,000	10,000	10,000	10,000
Aggregate compensation element	$37,500	$37,500	$37,500	$37,500
Aggregate compensation recorded in accordance with APB Opinion No. 25	0	37,500	37,500	18,750

Opinion No. 25 establishes a premature compensation measurement point, which does not always measure all of the compensation which inures to the employee at the exercise date.

CONCLUSION

When an enterprise and a key executive negotiate a compensation arrangement, many factors must be taken into consideration, not the least of which is form of payment. The inclusion of stock options in an executive compensation package is not uncommon and can be very beneficial to both parties. An employee receives compensation for services rendered and a stock option is only a form of payment. However, present accounting rules fail to adequately measure the compensation element. Measuring compensation at a date prior to exercise, and on a basis other than the net cash outlay by the employee (on a pre-tax basis), ignores the realities and clearly leads to differing accounting results in similar economic circumstances.

In this author's opinion, the only date that makes sense for the measurement of compensation under an option plan is the date of exercise. Only then is the actual amount of compensation known. This position does recognize that there are measurement problems for the intervening period between the date of grant and exercise date, but that is not an uncommon accounting problem and no worse a problem than estimating the cost of a pension plan. The charge of modern accounting is to accurately reflect the economic substance of a transaction. A change in the relative components in an executive compensation package (i.e., insurance, deferred annuities, stock option, or straight salary) should not alter the economic reality or the accounting measurement of the economic cost of the package to the enterprise or ultimately to its stockholders.

Let's tell it like it is.

Comment: Measuring the Compensation Element in Employee Stock Option Plans

Eric W. Noreen
University of Washington

In his column in the Spring issue of this *Journal*, Michael Bohan proposes that compensation expense from an employee stock option plan be measured on the date of exercise of the option and not on the date the option is granted as is now ordinarily the case. The amount of compensation expense to declare would be measured by the difference between the market price and option price at exercise.[1]

A contrary opinion is held by others who believe that compensation expense should be measured at the time of the grant.[2] To a large extent, this disagreement is probably due to differences in perceptions of the practicality of objectively measuring an option's value before it is exercised. Advances in the theory of option valuation in finance have raised the hopes of those who would measure compensation expense prior to the exercise of an option.[3] Unfortunately, none of the option valuation models now available appears to be accurate enough for financial accounting purposes.[4] Nevertheless, it is certainly conceivable that a model could be constructed that would provide reasonably accurate estimates of the value of the option before the exercise date.

If such a practical model were developed, most accountants would probably agree that the value of the option on the grant date represents compensa-

---

Reprinted by permission of the *Journal of Accounting, Auditing and Finance* (Fall 1979), pp. 67–69. Copyright © 1979 by Research Institute of America, Inc., Warren Gorham Lamont Professional Publishing Division, 210 South St., Boston, MA 02111. All rights reserved.

[1] This is not the first time that such a proposal has appeared in the accounting literature. E. R. Dillavou, "Employee Stock Options," *Accounting Review*, July 1945, pp. 320–326, proposed essentially the same treatment for options.

[2] See, e.g., Daniel L. Sweeney, *Accounting for Stock Options* (Michigan Business Studies, 1960); Edwin D. Campbell, "Stock Options Should Be Valued," *Harvard Business Review*, July/Aug. 1961, pp. 52–58; Taylor William Foster, III, "An Empirical Investigation of the Accounting for Stock Options" (Ph.D. dissertation, Pennsylvania State University, 1974); Clifford W. Smith, Jr. & Jerold L. Zimmerman, "Valuing Employee Stock Option Plans Using Option Pricing Models," *Journal of Accounting Research*, Autumn 1976, pp. 357–364.

[3] See Jerry J. Weygandt, "Valuation of Stock Option Contracts," *Accounting Review*, Jan. 1977, pp. 40–51.

[4] See Eric Noreen, "Assessing the Market Value of an Executive Stock Option" (unpublished, University of Washington, School of Business Administration, Sept. 1978), for an empirical test of the various models' abilities to predict the market values of traded warrants.

tion expense and should be allocated to those periods when the related services are performed.

After the grant date, the question would be whether to recognize changes in the value of the option, and if so, how those changes should be accounted for. Some accountants would argue that no change in the value of the option should ever be recognized in the income statement since the value of the option is tied to the value of the firm's own stock. This position is consistent with the current accounting treatment of marketable warrants.

Others, on the other hand, would argue that changes in the value of the option should be recognized in the income statement (but perhaps only when the option is exercised). They would interpret the option as a liability of the firm whose amount is contingent upon the value of the firm's stock. If it turns out that the size of the liability is greater (less) than originally anticipated, then a loss (gain) should be recognized. Some would advocate that the loss (gain) be recorded as additional (a reduction of) compensation expense, whereas others prefer that it be recorded explicitly as a loss (gain) without affecting the amount of compensation expense.

It should be noted that recognizing the difference between the market price and the option price at exercise on the income statement would be inconsistent with current practice in accounting for marketable warrants. It would also violate the general rule in accounting that transactions involving the firm's own stock cannot give rise to income or expense.[5]

Apart from the lack of consistency between Bohan's proposal and required practice in accounting for transactions involving a firm's own stock, there are sound economic reasons for questioning the proposal.

The argument for the Bohan approach would perhaps be strongest if firms fulfilled their obligations at execution by using cash to acquire shares on the open market. In such a case, one can argue that the firm suffers an economic loss. However, if the firm had purchased stock on the open market on the grant date, there would be no economic loss when the stock is subsequently exercised. If the option price is the same as the stock price on the grant date, the firm would collect from the executive upon exercise precisely the amount paid by the firm to purchase the stock on the earlier date. There would then be no economic loss.[6] It would seem, therefore, that

---

[5] See, e.g., AICPA, Accounting Research Bulletin No. 43, Ch. 1, Sec. B.

[6] An analogy may be helpful. Suppose a trading firm sells an option to deliver 100 ounces of gold any time within the next three years for $200 per ounce, the current market price of gold. Suppose further the option sells for $2,200 and the firm buys 100 ounces of gold on the open market on the day the option is sold. Ignoring interest charges, if the option is subsequently exercised, the firm's net gain on the transaction will be precisely $2,200 and this gain would be irrespective of the market value of gold at exercise. If the option expires without being exercised, the firm's net economic gain or loss will be the cash collected from sale of the option ($2,200) plus the market value of the 100 ounces of gold at expiration less the market value of the gold on the date it was purchased ($200 × 100 oz.). Thus, if executive stock options are viewed as hedged options from the standpoint of the firm, there would be an apparent economic loss only if the option is *not* exercised. Since the apparent economic loss occurs because the value of the stock held in anticipation of exercise has declined, conventional accounting would dictate that no loss be recognized in the income statement because gains and losses on holding the firm's own stock can never be recognized.

there is an economic loss if the firm buys stock on the exercise date, but not if it buys the stock on the grant date in anticipation of eventual exercise.

Additionally, firms do not always purchase on the open market the stock that is transferred to the executive upon exercise. Rather, the stock often comes out of authorized, but unissued shares. Since the choice of whether to earmark unissued shares for option exercise on the grant date or to wait until the exercise date to create or segregate such shares is essentially arbitrary and devoid of economic substance, I see little basis for choosing between the competing accounting methods. Accordingly, I see little reason to change from present policy which is essentially not to record the spread at exercise as a loss or expense and, by SEC rules, to disclose sufficient information in footnotes so that one could convert to another method if desired.

On the other hand, the present method of estimating the value of the option at its inception is clearly deficient. A first step in the direction of improving the valuation model would be adoption of the Smith and Zimmerman proposal.[7] Their valuation method underestimates the value of an option before its exercise, but so does the valuation method presently required. And since their valuation method never estimates a value lower than that estimated by the required method, the Smith and Zimmerman method is clearly more accurate.

---

[7] Using simple and powerful arbitrage arguments developed by Robert C. Merton, "Theory of Rational Option Pricing," *Bell Journal of Economics and Management Science*, Spring 1973, Smith and Zimmerman, note 2 *supra*, show that the value of an option can never be less than the maximum of zero or $S - (X + D)B$, where S is the market value of the stock on the grant date, X is the option price, D is the present value of anticipated future dividends, and B is the amount that would have to be invested today at the riskless rate to obtain \$1 on the expiration date.

Accounting for Stock Options

Robert J. Swieringa

Member, Financial Accounting Standards Board

I'll be happy to accept a lottery ticket as a gift—but I'll never buy one.[1]

The Financial Accounting Standards Board is in the process of reconsidering APB Opinion No. 25, "Accounting for Stock Issued to Employees," because of perceived inconsistencies in this pronouncement and related pronouncements.[2]

As of early January 1986, the Board had "tentatively agreed that compensation cost for stock option and stock award plans should be measured at the

---

From FASB *Status Report* No. 183 (January 20, 1987), pp. 6–10. Reprinted by permission of the Financial Accounting Foundation. Copyright © 1987 by the Financial Accounting Standards Board. The views in this article are those of the author.

[1] Warren Buffett, "Capital Sin: Warren Buffett on Incentive Stock Options," *Barron's* (April 7, 1986), 28.

[2] Accounting Principles Board Opinion No. 25, *Accounting for Stock Issued to Employees* (New York: American Institute of Certified Public Accountants, October 1972).

date of grant" and "tentatively adopted a model of computing the minimum value of a stock option for use in measuring the compensation cost of stock option plans. The model measures compensation as the difference between (a) the market price of an enterprise's stock at grant and (b) the present values of the exercise price and estimated dividends during the period."[3]

As of early April 1986, the Board had "tentatively agreed that compensation cost for stock option and stock award plans for which (a) the number of shares that an individual is entitled to receive and (b) the option or purchase price, if any, are known at the date of grant ("fixed plans") should be measured at the date of grant. All other plans ("variable plans") should be measured on the first date that both of those facts are known."[4]

As of early July 1986, the Board had "tentatively agreed that compensation cost for stock option and stock award plans should be measured at the later of the vesting date (the first date on which an employee is entitled to receive and retain or purchase and retain a stock award or has unconditional rights to a stock option) or the date on which certain measurement factors, including number of shares and purchase price, are known. The Board has also tentatively agreed that the measurement method is fair value with the rebuttable presumption that it is not less than the value determined by applying the minimum value model."[5]

As these excerpts reveal, the FASB has reconsidered its tentative conclusions about both the measurement date (from grant date to vesting date) and the measurement method (from minimum value to fair value) for employee stock options.[6] This paper places these changes in measurement dates and methods in the context of various alternative approaches for accounting for employee stock options.

OPTION VALUATION

An employee stock option is a call option contract. Cox and Rubinstein define a call option contract on common shares as "giving its owner the right to buy a fixed number of shares of a common stock at a fixed price at any time on or

[3] FASB, "FASB Plan for Technical Projects, Research, and Other Technical Activities as of January 1, 1986," *Status Report* No. 173 (January 13, 1986), 3.

[4] FASB, "FASB Plan for Technical Projects, Research, and Other Technical Activities as of April 1, 1986," *Status Report* No. 174 (April 7, 1986), 3.

[5] FASB, "FASB Plan for Technical Projects, Research, and Other Technical Activities as of July 1, 1986," *Status Report* No. 177 (July 7, 1986), 3.

[6] APB Opinion 25 distinguishes between noncompensatory and compensatory stock option plans. No compensation expense is recognized for noncompensatory plans. For compensatory plans, total compensation expense is measured by the quoted market price of the stock at the measurement date less the amount, if any, that the employee is required to pay. The measurement date is the first date on which both (1) the number of shares that an employee is entitled to receive and (2) the option or purchase price, if any, are known. The measurement date may be the date of grant or may be later than the date of grant in plans in which the number of shares, the option price, or both depend on events after the date of grant.

before a given date."[7] The option holder has the right, but not the obligation, to exercise the option. The value of the option at expiration will be either zero or the stock price minus the exercise price, whichever is larger.

The upper limit on the value of a call option on stock is the current price of the underlying stock. The call option is less desirable than a share of stock and should never sell at a higher price. However, the value of a call option on stock can never be negative, because the call option cannot be so unattractive that an individual will have to be paid to take it. If Po is the current value or price of the call option and Ps is the current price of the underlying stock then the upper and lower limits on a call option's value or price are as follows:

$$0 \leq Po \leq Ps \tag{1}$$

Within these limits, the least amount one should pay for a call option on stock can be determined by considering the following portfolios: Portfolio A comprises one call option for one share of stock with an exercise price equal to the current price of the stock; portfolio B comprises one share of the stock. Portfolio B is created by purchasing the one share of stock by borrowing an amount equal to the present values of the option's exercise price (E) plus the present value of all dividends (D) to be paid prior to the option's expiration at an interest rate equal to the risk-free rate. The out-of-pocket cost of purchasing the share is the current stock price minus the amount borrowed.

Portfolio A is as good as or better than portfolio B and should sell for as much or more than portfolio B. If the stock price goes up, both portfolios have the same value. If the stock price goes down, portfolio A is worth more than portfolio B. Thus, portfolio A, the option, cannot be worth less than portfolio B and may be worth more. The minimum value of the option should not be less than the cost of creating portfolio B: the stock price (Ps) minus the sum of the present value of the option price (E) and the present value of the dividends (D): [Ps − PV(E) − PV(D)]. The relationships among the minimum value of the call option, the current value or price of the call option, and the current price of the underlying stock can be summarized as follows:

$$0 \leq [Ps - PV(E) - PV(D)] \leq Po \leq Ps \tag{2}$$

Ps is observable only for stock traded in securities markets; Ps is not observable and must be estimated for stock that is not traded. Po for employee stock options is not observable because they are not traded in securities markets. Estimates of Po attempt to determine the value that a security with identical terms would have if it were offered for sale in the securities markets. Estimates of Po can be obtained from appraisers or specialists, such as investment bankers, or from the use of option-pricing models.[8]

---

[7] John C. Cox and Mark Rubinstein, *Options Markets* (Englewood Cliffs, N.J.: Prentice-Hall, 1985), 1.

[8] Many specialists use option-pricing models in developing their estimates of current value.

MEASUREMENT METHODS

The Board initially embraced the minimum value method because it was believed to be conceptually sound, objectively determinable, and easily computed. The minimum value method, [Ps − PV(E) − PV(D)], focuses on five determinants of option value: (1) current stock price, (2) exercise price, (3) time to expiration, (4) interest rate, and (5) cash dividends. Consider the following example:

> Assume that a company grants 100 options to executives. The options vest in one year and have a 10-year term. Assume that the market price of the stock at the date of grant is $100 per share, the exercise price is $100 per share, the risk-free rate is 10 percent, and the dividend yield is 2 percent.

The minimum value of each option at the date of grant is calculated as follows:

Market Price, Ps	$100.00
Less:	
Present Value of Exercise Price, PV(E)	38.55
Present Value of Dividends, PV(D)	12.29
Minimum Value	$ 49.16

Options having the same stock price, exercise price, time to expiration, exercisable period, interest rate, and cash dividends will have the same minimum value. However, the minimum value method does not focus on volatility, a critical determinant of option value. The higher the volatility, the greater the likelihood that the stock will do either very well or very poorly. An option holder benefits from favorable outcomes (by exercising the option) and can avoid unfavorable outcomes (by not exercising the option). As a result, two options, A and B, may have identical minimum values, but if option A is on a stock with high volatility and option B is on a stock with low volatility, option A should have a higher option value than option B.

An exact option-pricing model, such as the Black-Scholes option-pricing model, includes volatility as a determinant of option value and can be used to estimate the current value of a call option (Po).[9] The Black-Scholes model is widely used, but assumes no cash dividends, that exercise occurs only on the expiration date, that the volatility of the stock is constant, and that the interest rate is constant. To be used for estimating the fair value of employee stock options, this model has to be modified to deal with cash dividends, the probability of early exercise, changes in volatility, uncertain interest rates, longer times to expiration, insider trading restrictions, delayed exercisability, sequential exercise requirements of incentive stock options, continued employment provisions, nontransferability, and so forth. These modifications

---

[9] See F. Black and M. Scholes, "The Pricing of Options and Corporate Liabilities," Journal of Political Economy (May/June 1973), 637–54.

suggest that considerable care must be exercised in using an exact option-pricing model to estimate Po.

Why would the FASB move away from the minimum value approach that is more objective and easier to use to a fair value approach that is more subjective and more difficult to use? A major concern with the use of the minimum value method was the extent to which it provided a surrogate for the fair value of a stock option. As indicated in equation (2) above, the minimum value of an option is expected to be less than or equal to its current value:

$$[Ps - PV(E) - PV(D)] \leq Po$$

Table 1 provides information about the percent discount of the minimum value from exact value for different risk-free rates, dividend yields, and levels of volatility.[10] The minimum value calculated above was for a 10 percent risk-free rate and a dividend yield of 2 percent. If volatility is .10, the minimum value of $49.16 is a very good surrogate for the option's exact value. However, as volatility increases, the minimum value of $49.16 significantly understates the option's exact value. The information in Table 1 provides some evidence about the situations in which an option's minimum value is likely to underestimate its exact value.

In using an exact value model to estimate an employee stock option's fair value, several important modifications have to be considered. For example, a specialist might reduce the calculated exact value to reflect nontransferability of the option in estimating the option's fair value.[11] The exact values used to calculate the percent discounts in Table 1 do not reflect this or other modifications. As a result, Table 1 overstates the extent to which minimum value may understate an option's fair value. Various modifications of an option's exact value could result in the option's calculated minimum value exceeding its estimated fair value. In other words, the following result could be obtained: $[Ps - PV(E) - PV(D)] > Po$. This result is contrary to equation (2).

The Board's current position is that the appropriate measurement method is fair value with the rebuttable presumption that it is not less than minimum value. This position reflects the Board's attempts to deal with factors not adequately captured by the minimum value method (such as volatility) as well as with factors not adequately captured by exact value models (such as nontransferability) in estimating an employee stock option's fair value.

In July 1986, the FASB staff asked several investment bankers to estimate the fair value of employee stock options for a sample of companies from various industries. The investment bankers were given the market price of each company's stock at June 30, 1986 and were asked to value hypothetical

---

[10] Table 1 was developed by FASB staff and outside consultants to help the Board assess the usefulness of the minimum value method.

[11] It can be argued that no adjustment should be made for nontransferability. The company could have issued an unrestricted option and therefore has foregone the value of an unrestricted option in granting it to employees.

TABLE 1 Minimum Value as a Percent Discount from Exact Value

Volatility	Dividend Yield							
	0%		2%		5%		8%	
	10-year Term	5-year Term	10-year Term	5-year Term	10-year Term	5-year Term	10-year Term	5-year Term
Risk-free Rate 15%								
.10	0	0	0	0	2	3	9	8
.20	0	1	1	3	8	9	25	24
.30	2	6	4	10	16	20	38	39
.40	5	13	10	18	26	30	48	49
.50	8	19	15	25	33	38	55	56
.60	11	24	20	31	39	44	60	61
.70	14	29	24	36	43	49	64	65
.80	17	33	27	40	47	53	66	68
.90	19	36	30	43	49	56	68	71
1.00	20	39	32	43	52	59	70	73
Risk-free Rate 10%								
.10	0	0	0	2	5	11	46	51
.20	2	6	5	12	23	30	68	71
.30	7	16	13	24	38	45	77	79
.40	13	25	22	34	48	55	82	84
.50	18	32	29	42	55	62	85	87
.60	23	38	35	48	60	66	87	89
.70	27	43	40	52	63	70	88	90
.80	30	47	43	56	66	73	89	91
.90	32	50	46	59	68	75	90	92
1.00	34	52	48	61	70	76	91	93
Risk-free Rate 5%								
.10	2	6	10	21	100*	100*	100*	100*
.20	14	25	32	45	100*	100*	100*	100*
.30	26	39	47	58	100*	100*	100*	100*
.40	35	44	56	67	100*	100*	100*	100*
.50	42	56	63	72	100*	100*	100*	100*
.60	47	61	67	76	100*	100*	100*	100*
.70	51	65	70	78	100*	100*	100*	100*
.80	54	68	72	80	100*	100*	100*	100*
.90	56	70	74	82	100*	100*	100*	100*
1.00	58	72	75	83	100*	100*	100*	100*

* Minimum value is zero.
Boxed areas represent the normal range of volatility and dividend yields for publicly traded companies.

stock options as of that date assuming that the options were exercisable immediately and for a period of seven years, that the exercise price was equal to the stock's market price at June 30, 1986, that the options were not transferable, and that the options must be exercised on or shortly after termination of employment.

The values the investment bankers assigned to these employee stock options were significant, ranging from an average of 15 percent to 48 percent of the June 30, 1986 market price for each stock. All of the investment bankers used option-pricing models, but different models were used, different estimates were made for dividend yields, interest rates, and volatility, and different adjustments were made for nontransferability and termination provisions. The FASB staff is performing additional research to understand the valuation processes used by these investment bankers, to determine those factors that significantly caused observed differences in the option values assigned, and to ascertain if clarification or guidance is feasible and appropriate to narrow these differences.

MEASUREMENT DATE

The Board initially focused on the grant date as the measurement date for employee stock options. Grant date accounting assumes that the important factors affecting these options (such as the exercise price and the number of options) are known at this date and that compensation expense can be measured as the fair value of the options at this date. An analogous situation is accounting for a warrant at its fair value at the date of issuance. Grant date accounting also avoids reflecting future changes in stock prices in compensation expense.

Consider again the example described above and assume that the minimum value of $49.16 for each option approximates the fair value of each option at the date of grant. The fair value of the 100 options granted would be $4,916 ($49.16 × 100 options). The $4,916 would be recognized as compensation expense over the service period. The following entry would be made at the end of the one-year vesting or service period:

Compensation expense	4,916	
Additional paid-in capital		4,916

To record compensation expense for 100
  employee stock options.

The recognition of compensation expense over a service period focuses attention on the vesting date. The vesting date reflects the date on which the employees have completed service requirements. It is also the date the employees have earned the right to exercise the stock options they have been granted. The stock options become contractual obligations of the company only on the vesting date. Prior to the vesting date, the stock option contract is an executory contract because one party must still perform. Not all employees will complete the service requirements and earn the right to exercise stock options awarded to them. Before the vesting date, uncertainty exists about which employees will earn the right to exercise the stock options awarded.

The Board changed its focus from grant date to vesting date because the rights awarded on grant date are uncertain. The stock options awarded are contingent on fulfilling a service requirement. Employees are not just awarded the right to exercise these stock options; they have to earn this right. The analogous situation is accounting for a warrant that is contingent on a future uncertain event.

Let us extend the earlier example as follows:

Assume that a company grants 100 options to executives. The options vest in one year and have a 10-year term. Assume that the market price at the date of grant is $100 per share, the exercise price is $100 per share, the risk-free rate is 10 percent, and the dividend yield is 2 percent. In addition, assume that the market price at the date of vesting is $120 per share.

Again, for convenience, assume that the minimum value of each option is a good approximation of its fair value. The minimum value of each option at the vesting date is calculated as follows:

Market Price, Ps	$120.00
Less:	
Present Value of Exercise Price, PV(E)	42.41
Present Value of Dividends, PV(D)	11.52
Minimum Value	$ 66.07

Note that the calculation of each option's minimum value at the vesting date includes the market price of the stock at vesting date. As a result, changes in the market price of a company's stock for the period from grant date to vesting date are reflected in compensation expense. Also note that the calculations of PV(E) and PV(D) reflect 9 years instead of 10 years.

The compensation expense of $6,607 would be recorded as follows on the vesting date:

Compensation expense	6,607	
Additional paid-in capital		6,607

To record compensation expense for 100
employee stock options.

This entry assumes that vesting of all shares takes place at the end of the first year (cliff vesting). However, some employee stock option plans provide for pro rata (graded) vesting, which greatly complicates the recognition and measurement of compensation expense.

A FURTHER COMPLICATION

Almost all employee stock option plans include a continued employment or termination provision that requires that employees exercise their options upon or shortly after termination. Such a provision does not take away the rights employees have earned by meeting vesting requirements, but it is subject to different considerations in valuing employee stock options. Some argue that such a provision effectively extends the service period requirement and that employees do not have options with fixed or known terms. Others argue that such a provision does not extend the service period requirement and is intended to preclude ex-employees from holding stock options and to facilitate administration of employee stock option plans.

Let us extend the earlier example as follows:

> Assume that a company grants 100 options to executives. The options vest in one year and have a 10-year term. Assume that the market price at the date of grant is $100 per share, the exercise price is $100 per share, the risk-free rate is 10 percent, and the dividend yield is 2 percent. In addition, assume that the market price at the date of vesting is $120 per share. Executives must be employed to retain the vested options. The market value at the date of exercise (or termination) is $150 per share.

If the continued employment or termination provision is viewed as extending the option's term, the executives do not have a call option as defined earlier but merely have an employment-contingent right to a positive difference or spread between the market price and the exercise price or strike price. If this spread is $50 at the date of exercise ($150 − $100) and 100 options are exercised, compensation of $5,000 would be incurred and amortized over the extended service period. This interpretation results in exercise date accounting because the term is only known at the exercise date or the expiration date. In addition, compensation expense would be accrued over the service period using a mark-to-market approach.[12] However, the number of options exercised could be very different from both the number of options granted and the number of options vested.

The Board's tentative conclusion is that the continued employment or termination provision does not extend the service period and that an option's maximum term can be used in measuring its fair and minimum values at vesting date.

CONCLUSIONS

The Board's continuing in-depth analysis of employee stock options has resulted in changes in its tentative conclusions about the measurement methods and measurement dates to be used as a basis for accounting for these options. Changes in these conclusions are likely to continue as additional issues and types of stock compensation plans are considered.

The factors determining the fair value of employee stock options go well beyond the number of shares and the option price factors discussed in APB Opinion 25. The important factors included in both the minimum value method and the exact models include (1) the current stock price, (2) exercise price, (3) time to expiration, (4) interest rate, and (5) cash dividends. Exact

---

[12] FASB Invitation to Comment, *Accounting for Compensation Plans Involving Certain Rights Granted to Employees* (Stamford, Conn.: FASB, May 31, 1984).

models also include the volatility of the stock price. In addition, the provisions and requirements of employee stock option plans include features that are not dealt with in the accounting literature. Attempting to value employee stock options focuses attention on issues of delayed exercisability, sequential exercise requirements, nontransferability, continued employment provisions, and so forth. By viewing many plans as noncompensatory and focusing only on the number of shares and exercise price for compensatory plans, APB Opinion 25 does not capture the effects of different time-to-expiration and exercisability provisions. Viewing all employee stock option plans as compensatory and attempting to value employee stock options involves detailed consideration of these and other provisions.

Accounting for employee stock options would be much less difficult if companies sold these options to employees instead of granting them without cash consideration. But, as suggested by the quote at the beginning of this paper, many executives would likely assert that they "are happy to accept a stock option, but they would never buy one."

FASB's Long Look at Stock Compensation Plans

Barry P. Robbins

Price Waterhouse

The stock compensation project currently on the Financial Accounting Standards Board's agenda is important to a large cross section of American business. The controversy the project has engendered thus far can be expected to increase as more attention is focused on it. Indeed, the fascination and preoccupation with executive compensation virtually assures significant interest.

Although the stock compensation project has received less publicity than the pension and income tax projects, it nevertheless is active and has used considerable resources of the FASB over the past few years.

This article provides a background on the project, including an overview of the major accounting issues involved and an appreciation of the difficulty of resolving them.

REASONS FOR THE PROJECT

The FASB's vote to add the stock compensation project to its agenda in March 1984 was unanimous but noticeably unenthusiastic. There was concern that the very difficult issues that had stymied the Accounting Principles Board

From *Journal of Accountancy* (August 1988), pp. 60–62, 66, 68. Reprinted by permission of the American Institute of Certified Public Accountants, Inc. Copyright © 1988 by the American Institute of Certified Public Accountants, Inc. Opinions of the authors are their own and do not necessarily reflect policies of the AICPA.

roughly 12 years earlier would again prove intractable. Nevertheless, the board added the project to its agenda for three reasons:

1. Dissatisfaction with current accounting literature on the subject (APB Opinion no. 25, *Accounting for Stock Issued to Employees*, and FASB Interpretation no. 28, *Accounting for Stock Appreciation Rights and Other Variable Stock Option or Award Plans*).
2. The introduction of new types of stock compensation arrangements.
3. The development of option pricing models.

Opinion no. 25.   Critics claim this opinion emphasizes form—sometimes at the expense of substance. Various stock compensation arrangements with similar effects on both employer and employee can receive very different accounting treatments. The classic examples are a stock option and a stock appreciation right payable in stock. The economic effects of both arrangements are quite similar, but the accounting for them is dramatically different.

Additionally, under Opinion no. 25 compensation expense isn't usually recognized for employee stock options (provided the exercise price equals or exceeds the market price of the stock on the date of grant). Although most financial statement preparers aren't bothered by this accounting, its results are viewed by many as unsound. Opinion no. 25 suggests that employee stock options have no value or, conversely, that a company incurs no cost in granting the options.

New Stock Compensation Arrangements.   Since Opinion no. 25 was issued in 1972, new types of stock compensation arrangements have proliferated. Innovations include

- Stock depreciation rights.
- Permanent discount restricted stock purchase plans.
- Pyramiding arrangements.
- Junior stock plans.

Although APB Opinion no. 25 and FASB Interpretation no. 28 determine the accounting for these and other arrangements, how the application is made often isn't very clear. The most visible example is the junior stock plan, which came into vogue in the late 1970s primarily at high-technology companies. These plans' initial accounting, which had become accepted in practice, came into question as junior stock arrangements became more and more complex. At the Securities and Exchange Commission's urging, in August 1984 the FASB issued Interpretation no. 38, *Determining the Measurement Date for Stock Options, Purchase and Award Plans Involving Junior Stock.* The board discussed junior stock plans at the same March 1984 meeting at which it voted to add the stock compensation project to its agenda.

Option Pricing Models.   The third reason the board undertook the project was the introduction of option pricing models. These are mathematical formulas, developed by the financial and academic communities, that estimate the value of nonemployee, traded stock options and warrants. The best known of these models is the Black-Scholes option pricing model (see the addendum, "Two Option Pricing Models," for more information), first described in the *Journal of Political Economy* (May/June 1973).

Few would contend that employee stock options have no value. The problem confronting the APB when formulating Opinion no. 25 was how to determine the value of these employee stock options. The FASB believed that option pricing models might provide a useful tool for doing this.

In May 1984, the FASB issued an invitation to comment entitled *Accounting for Compensation Plans Involving Certain Rights Granted to Employees*, which identified the issues to be considered, the alternatives available and the arguments for and against each alternative.

The FASB began deliberating the issues in the spring of 1985, and it continues to do so. It has reached several tentative conclusions; it has changed several tentative conclusions; and it has many tentative conclusions still to reach.

TYPES OF PLANS

In its invitation to comment, the FASB classified compensation arrangements into three categories:

1. *Market performance plans.* Plans in which the value ultimately received by the employee depends solely on the market price, or movements in the market price, of the employer's stock. The most widespread market performance plan is the traditional stock option—that is, the employee receives the right to purchase a specified number of company shares, at a specified price, over a specified period.
2. *Enterprise performance plans.* Plans in which the value ultimately received by the employee depends solely on company performance. Long-term enterprise performance plans (as opposed to short-term plans, such as annual bonuses based on company performance) are typified by the performance unit plan. The employee is awarded performance units, each unit carrying a specified dollar value. The number of units ultimately earned by the employee depends on the extent to which the company meets certain specified performance goals during the performance period (typically three to five years).
3. *Combination market-enterprise performance plans.* Plans in which the value ultimately received by the employee depends on both company performance and the market price of the company's stock. A performance share plan is similar to the performance unit plan described above except that the employee receives performance shares which, if earned, entitle the holder to a specified number of shares of company stock rather than cash. The number of shares the employee receives depends on company per-

A Sampling of Stock Compensation Plans

The FASB stock compensation project has divided stock compensation plans into three broad categories. One hopes this broad classification will make it easier to develop broad accounting standards.

Market performance plans
   Incentive stock options.
   Nonqualified stock options.
   Stock appreciation rights.
   Restricted stock award plans.

Enterprise performance plans
   Performance unit plans.
   Book value plans.

Combination market-enterprise performance plans
   Performance share plans.
   Junior stock plans.
   Stock options with performance requirements.

formance and the value of those shares depends on the stock market price. (See the addendum, "A Sampling of Stock Compensation Plans.")

One hopes this broad classification of plans will make it easier to develop broad standards of accounting; the efficacy of such broad standards then could be tested by assessing their results when applied to specific plans.

As can be seen, certain stock compensation arrangements—such as performance unit plans—have nothing to do with stock. Nevertheless, they fall within the scope of the FASB's stock compensation project. A more accurate title for the project might be "long-term executive supplemental incentive compensation arrangements," but "stock compensation plans" trips off the tongue more easily. This points up, however, a distinction between cash plans and stock plans.

Cash plans are those in which the employee ultimately receives cash from the company; stock plans are those in which the employee ultimately receives stock. Accounting for cash plans isn't controversial; essentially, compensation cost equals the amount of cash paid to the employee. The idea that cash paid by an employer to an employee should be charged to expense is accepted almost without question, even if the amount depends on the company's stock price. Accounting for cash plans is unlikely to change.

The difficult accounting issues, then, relate to stock plans. They're simple to state, simple to understand, but extremely difficult to resolve. There are only two basic questions:

* When should compensation cost be measured?
* How should it be measured?

Resolution of these two questions would impel the project to a speedy conclusion. In its deliberations thus far, the FASB has considered them primarily as they relate to employee stock options.

WHEN TO MEASURE

There are three key dates in the life cycle of an employee stock option:

1. The date the option is granted.
2. The date the option vests.
3. The date the option is exercised or lapses unexercised.

Valid conceptual arguments support each of these as the date on which compensation cost should be measured. But there's simply no way to demonstrate the superiority of one over the other two.

Grant Date.   Supporters of grant date measurement point out that this is when the employer decides the number of options to give the employee and the terms of those options. The employer commits to the transaction at that date, because the employee, by continuing to work the required number of years, controls whether the options are exercised. Presumably, the company grants the options based on its grant date assessment of the value of the services to be rendered by the employee-recipient. Furthermore, compensation measurement subsequent to the grant date would allow changes in the company's stock price to affect reported compensation cost, even though those stock price changes may bear no relationship to the value of the services rendered by the employee.

Vesting Date.   Supporters of vesting date measurement contend that, before the vesting date, the option contract is merely an executory contract between the employer and employee. The employer isn't committed to allowing option exercise until the employee renders the required years of service. Generally, executory contracts aren't recognized in accounting until performance occurs. In that sense, the stock option is only a contingency until the employee vests in the right.

Exercise Date.   This also has its proponents, who argue that the stock option is a contingency until it's exercised or lapses. The ultimate value of the option can't be determined until the exercise date. Furthermore, exercise date measurement produces symmetry between the compensation cost recognized by the employer and the value received by the employee.

Not surprisingly, the FASB has had great difficulty choosing among these three alternatives. Its present tentative conclusion is that compensation cost for employee stock options should be measured at the vesting date. This is a rather surprising conclusion, since vesting date measurement was certainly not a front-runner at the inception of the project. Indeed, the arguments for and against vesting date were tucked away in an appendix of the invitation to comment rather than in the main body of the document.

Using the vesting date would constitute a major switch from APB Opinion no. 25's required use of the grant date for most stock options. Under the opinion, grant date measurement is required unless either or both of two key measurement criteria—the number of shares an employee is entitled to receive and the price, if any, to be paid for those shares—are unknown at the grant date. In these cases, compensation is to be measured as soon as those two factors are known. This is the distinction Opinion no. 25 makes between fixed and variable plans—with compensation cost measured at the exercise date for most variable plans.

HOW TO MEASURE

The question of how to measure compensation cost is, perhaps, even more difficult than the question of when. The difficulty, though, is a practical one, rather than a conceptual one.

The *fair value* of a stock option consists of two elements:

- Intrinsic value.
- Time value.

Intrinsic Value. This is easy to calculate: It's the difference between the exercise price of the option and the market price of the underlying stock on any given date. Intrinsic value can be positive or negative, but the fair value of an option can't be negative. This is because the option holder can benefit from upward price movements; unfavorable price movements simply mean the holder won't exercise the option.

Time Value. This one-sided risk-reward characteristic of options—the ability to benefit from stock appreciation without having to purchase the underly-

---

Two Option Pricing Models

Minimum value method

The minimum value option pricing method is expressed by a fairly straightforward mathematical formula. To the layman, the equation means the value of a stock option can't be negative and must be at least equal to the difference between the market value of the underlying stock and the present value (at a risk-free discount rate) of the sum of the exercise price and expected dividends during the exercise period.

Thus, the "minimum value" of a stock option will increase with

1. An increase in the market value of the underlying stock.
2. A decrease in the exercise price.
3. A decrease in dividends paid by the company.
4. An increase in the exercise period.
5. An increase in the risk-free rate of return.

Black-Scholes option pricing model

The Black-Scholes option pricing model also is expressed mathematically, but the formula is significantly more complicated. The main difference between the Black-Scholes model and the minimum value method is that the Black-Scholes model incorporates probability estimates relating to the future variation of the market price of the underlying stock: The riskier the stock, the more valuable the option.

ing stock—gives options their time value. Time value decreases as the remaining exercise period shortens. It equals zero on the final day of the exercise period.

The first consideration in determining how to measure the compensation cost of an employee stock option is whether to use fair value (intrinsic value *plus* time value) or intrinsic value. Conceptually, fair value is far superior to intrinsic value; it's used when options or warrants are given to nonemployees in exchange for goods or services and when debt is issued with detachable warrants.

The problem, however, is that *there's no clear, objective method by which to calculate fair value.* This problem plagued the APB and continues to plague the FASB.

The option pricing models mentioned previously (two of which are illustrated in the addendum, "Two Option Pricing Models") might prove useful. But there is one potentially serious drawback: These models were developed to estimate the fair value of publicly traded nonemployee stock options. Their accuracy can be validated by the prices at which options trade in the market. However, employee stock options have two important characteristics that distinguish them from publicly traded nonemployee options:

1. Employee stock options cannot be transferred.
2. They generally lapse three months after an employee leaves the company (whether by decision of the company or the employee).

Both of these features reduce the value of employee stock options compared with nonemployee options, but it's impossible to determine by how much.

As part of its research, the FASB's staff requested several investment banking firms to estimate the value of various hypothetical stock options unencumbered by employee option restrictions. The results were fairly consistent. But when the exercise was repeated, with nontransferability and accelerated lapsing restrictions attached, there was considerable disparity in the estimated fair values.

The FASB faces a hard choice:

- It can choose intrinsic value, but that lacks conceptual merit.
- It can choose fair value, specifying use of a particular option pricing model, but that endorses an arbitrary formula whose accuracy can't be tested.
- It can choose fair value and specify only that the company make its best estimate of fair value (perhaps with the assistance of an investment banker), but that could lead to disparate results for similar cases.
- It can choose to measure compensation cost at exercise date and avoid the problem, since fair value equals intrinsic value at the exercise date.

The FASB has tentatively concluded it's better to be approximately correct than precisely wrong. Thus, it believes that compensation cost for employee stock options should be measured at fair value, based on the best good faith estimate available. This differs from Opinion no. 25's requirements prescribing the use of intrinsic value.

STILL AN ADOLESCENT

Roughly four years old, the stock compensation project is only in its adolescence. Its final shape is unknown. Currently, all interested parties have the opportunity and, indeed, the responsibility to work with the FASB in molding that shape.

Accounting for Redeemable Preferred Stock: Unresolved Issues

R. D. Nair
University of Wisconsin-Madison

Larry E. Rittenberg
University of Wisconsin-Madison

Jerry J. Weygandt
University of Wisconsin-Madison

In July 1979 the Securities and Exchange Commission (SEC) issued Accounting Series Release No. 268 "Redeemable Preferred Stocks" which addressed the balance sheet classification of such stocks. That release required SEC registrants to exclude redeemable preferred stock from stockholders' equity.[1] The release stated that "The rules . . . do not attempt to deal with the conceptual question of whether such a security is a liability. Further, the rules do not attempt to deal with the income statement treatment of payments to holders of such a security or with any related income statement matters, including accounting for its extinguishment." The Commission was cognizant of the conceptual problems in determining the appropriate accounting for and reporting of redeemable preferred stock, and indicated that these matters should best be addressed by the Financial Accounting Standards Board (FASB). Subsequently, the SEC has addressed ancillary issues such as increasing rate preferred stock, but not the basic accounting issues described above.

Since 1979, redeemable preferred stock issuances have become more

From *Accounting Horizons* (June 1990), pp. 33–41. Reprinted by permission of the American Accounting Association and the authors. Copyright © 1990 by the American Accounting Association.

[1] The SEC rule does not require classification as a liability, only that it not be classified as equity.

common.[2] A search of 1987/88 National Automated Accounting Research System (NAARS) file indicates that 485 companies (approximately 12 percent of all companies in the database) had some form of redeemable preferred stock outstanding.[3] Since 1979, the FASB has completed work on the major portion of the conceptual framework and has provided definitions of the elements of financial statements. The definitions developed by the FASB can now be used to deal with the conceptual question of when, if ever, such securities are liabilities. Further, those concepts can be used to address important income statement issues associated with redeemable preferred stock, such as accounting for dividends and early redemption costs. This article examines these issues.

CURRENT PRACTICE

The SEC, in ASR No. 268, stated that redeemable preferred stock should be excluded from stockholders' equity. In developing its position, the SEC took a narrow approach in defining redeemable preferred stock as preferred stock that:

1. has a fixed or determinable redemption date,
2. is redeemable at the option of the holder, or
3. has conditions for redemption that are not solely within the control of the issuer.

The SEC also formally defined nonredeemable preferred stock as preferred stock that is not redeemable or is redeemable solely at the option of the issuer, for example, callable preferred stock.[4]

An example of the accounting for redeemable preferred stock for an SEC registered company is shown in Exhibit I. The Toro Company has redeemable preferred stock outstanding which is classified between debt and equity with disclosure of the redemption requirements. An early redemption premium of $508,000 was incurred when a portion of the stock was retired early. This redemption premium was charged directly to retained earnings. Dividends were accounted for as a distribution of retained earnings and thus did not affect reported net income. However, like all preferred dividends they were deducted from income to determine earnings per share of common stock.

---

[2] Redeemable preferred stocks have been issued to finance operations, consummate mergers and acquisitions, or to restructure existing debt arrangements. Absent SEC regulation, they allow firms to raise money in a form that is classified as equity. This, in turn, improves firms' debt-equity ratios, as well as capital ratios for financial institutions, and avoids violation of loan covenants that may restrict the incurrence of additional debt.

[3] As another example of the magnitude of these types of securities, a recent article noted that approximately $4.1 billion of the RJR Nabisco leveraged buyout was financed by mandatory redeemable and exchangeable preferred stock. See Abraham Briloff, "Shame on You, Henry Kravis," *Barron's*, March 6, 1989 pp. 18–20.

[4] The SEC's rule does not provide criteria for handling items that may have some, but not all, of the mandatory characteristics noted above. In addition, the SEC did not address income statement issues, nor did it address other variations of redeemable preferred stock such as those that have recently been developed as part of anti-takeover provisions.

EXHIBIT I Example of Accounting for Redeemable Preferred Stock

The Toro Company—1986

Redeemable Preferred Stock
(Classification is Between Liability and Equity)

Redeemable Series A Preferred Stock, par value $1.00; authorized 150,000 shares; issued and outstanding 105,000 shares.	$ 105,000
Additional paid-in capital	10,395,000
Total Redeemable Series A Preferred Stock (Note 6)	$10,500,000

Note 6

The Company has outstanding 105,000 shares of redeemable, cumulative, nonvoting Series A Preferred Stock, par value $1.00. Mandatory redemption terms provide for a $100 per share redemption of 15,000 shares annually from May 15, 1988 to May 15, 1991, and 22,500 shares on May 15, 1992, and May 15, 1993. The shares are callable by the Company at $100 per share plus accrued dividends and a premium computed on a 10-year declining basis. In 1985, the Company redeemed 45,000 shares in cash for $5,008,000. The aggregate purchase price included a redemption premium of $508,000 which was charged to retained earnings. The redemption premium had no effect on earnings per share. Dividends on Series A Preferred Stock have preference over dividends on common stock and are payable quarterly. The preferred stock has a stated annual cumulative dividend rate of $11.28 per share.

The Toro example highlights many of the characteristics of redeemable preferred stock:

- The stock is nonvoting.
- The stock calls for a mandatory schedule of periodic redemption at par over a fixed period, in this case from 1988 through 1993, that is, the stock has a fixed or determinable life.
- The stock may be redeemable (callable) at the option of the company at par plus accrued dividends and a redemption premium. In this case, shares were redeemed at an average premium of $11.28 per share. This premium is the same as the dividend rate.
- The stock's dividends are cumulative and have preference over common stock dividends.
- The stock has a fixed, annual dividend rate of 11.28 percent which is similar to the interest rate on debt issued at the same time with similar maturity.

Most SEC registrants now classify such stock as neither debt nor equity, but within a middle area between debt and equity. The SEC ruling, however, does not apply to non-registered companies and many of these companies continue to classify redeemable preferred stock as part of stockholders' equity on the grounds that such a classification is generally accepted accounting practice.[5]

---

[5] Support for this observation is based upon our discussions with partners in the national offices of major international accounting firms. These individuals all confirmed the difference in practice in accounting for redeemable preferred stock between SEC registrants and other companies. Also, a source for classroom case materials, *The Trueblood Professors' Seminar, Accounting and Auditing Case Studies* (Touche Ross Foundation, 1983, p. 30) states: "The state of the art, at least for private companies, is that redeemable preferred stock is classified as an equity security. This is its legal definition and accounting for private companies follows this definition for most circumstances."

In Staff Accounting Bulletin No. 64, the SEC addressed the issue of the carrying amount at which redeemable preferred stock should be reported, and how changes in the carrying amount should be reported. The conclusion was that the initial carrying amount of redeemable preferred stock should be its fair value at date of issue. When that value is less than the mandatory redemption amount, the carrying amount should be increased by periodic accretions, using the interest method, so that the carrying amount will equal the mandatory redemption amount at the redemption date. Similarly, the carrying amount should be increased by dividends in arrears that will be payable under the mandatory redemption features. However, the increase in carrying amount is charged against retained earnings or, in the absence of retained earnings, by a charge against paid-in capital. Further, in calculating earnings per share such an increase in carrying amount should be treated in the same manner as preferred dividends.

The SEC also briefly addressed the issue of increasing rate preferred stocks in Staff Accounting Bulletin 68 and ruled that such stocks should be carried at fair market value at the time of issuance. In addition, the fair market rate at the time of issuance should be used in recording dividend distributions. The difference between the fair market rate and the stated rate would be accreted to the carrying value of the stock over the security's life.

Although the accounting for redeemable preferred stock was briefly discussed by the Accounting Standards Executive Committee, there have been no direct authoritative pronouncements on the subject matter by either the FASB or the Accounting Standards Executive Committee. Redeemable preferred stock is briefly addressed from the investor side in SFAS 12, "Accounting for Certain Marketable Securities." In defining equity securities, SFAS 12 states:

> The term does not encompass preferred stock that by its terms either must be redeemed by the issuing enterprise or is redeemable at the option of the investor. . . . [paragraph 7]

Also, from the investor side, SFAS 60, "Accounting and Reporting by Insurance Enterprises," requires that redeemable preferred stock, along with bonds and mortgage loans, be reported at amortized cost. On the other hand, nonredeemable preferred stock, along with common stock, should be reported at market. In mandating disclosures about liabilities, the FASB in SFAS 47, "Disclosure of Long-Term Obligations," required disclosure of the amount of redemption requirements for all issues of capital stock that are redeemable at fixed or determinable prices on fixed or determinable dates, for the next five years from the balance sheet date.

The FASB's Emerging Issues Task Force (EITF) addressed the early extinguishment of a subsidiary's redeemable preferred stock and reached the consensus that it should be accounted for as a capital stock transaction. The consolidated entity would not recognize any gain or loss from the acquisition of the subsidiary's redeemable preferred stock (Issue 86-32). In Issue 86-45, the EITF considered preferred stock with a below-market-rate dividend for an initial period after issuance. The EITF concluded that if the preferred stock was, in substance, redeemable, the SEC regulations (as stated in SAB 68) would require accrual of a market dividend on the preferred stock.

ACCOUNTING ISSUES

The current accounting for redeemable preferred stock is both incomplete and inconsistent. There is one set of rules for SEC registered companies and a different practice for non-SEC registered companies.[6] The current SEC rule provides for a "no-man's land" whereby redeemable preferred stock is excluded from equity but not included in liabilities. There are inconsistencies between the balance sheet and income statement treatments of dividends and early redemption costs. The stock is excluded from equity, but dividends and redemption costs are charged directly to retained earnings or paid-in capital. Finally, there are no guidelines to account for redeemable preferred stock when the redemption is contingent upon activities not controllable by either the issuing corporation or the holder of the security.

This paper addresses issues related to redeemable preferred stock as a basis for determining:

1. The proper balance sheet classification of the security.
2. The proper treatment (income statement or retained earnings) of dividends when such stock is excluded from equity for financial reporting purposes.
3. The proper treatment of any difference between issuance price and mandatory redemption price.
4. The proper treatment of the gain or loss on early redemption of the stock.
5. The treatment of preferred stocks that become mandatorily redeemable only on the occurrence of some specified event, such as a takeover.

CONCEPTUAL NATURE OF EQUITY AND LIABILITIES

The FASB defines equity as the "residual interest in the assets of an entity that remains after deducting its liabilities."[7] Further insight into the nature of equity is provided by the FASB's description of the owner's right to assets:

> the essential characteristics of equity center on the conditions for transferring enterprise assets to owners. Equity—an excess of assets over liabilities—is a

---

[6] Although not the only criteria in determining proper accounting, the auditor is encouraged to determine whether the "accounting principles selected and applied have general acceptance." Since preferred stock has been classified as equity, it has become generally acceptable to continue that classification when redeemable preferred stock is issued for companies not subject to SEC regulations. A *Technical Practice* answer to a question in the *Journal of Accountancy* (September 1988, p. 126) encouraged adoption of the SEC rule for non-publicly held entities.

[7] Statement of Financial Accounting Concepts No. 6, "Elements of Financial Statements" (Stamford, CT: FASB, 1985).

necessary but not sufficient condition; *distributions to owners are at the discretion and volition of the owners or their representatives* after satisfying restrictions imposed by law, regulation, or agreements with other entities. Generally, an enterprise is not obligated to transfer assets to owners. . . unless the enterprise formally acts to distribute assets to owners, for example by declaring a dividend (emphasis added).[8]

In forming their view, the FASB reasoned that no class of equity carries an unconditional right to receive future transfers of assets from the organization except in liquidation, and then only after liabilities have been satisfied.[9]

In the absence of restrictive provisions, each share of stock carries the right to share in profits and losses, share in management, and share in assets upon liquidation. Since equity represents a residual ownership interest in the entity, the owners bear the ultimate risks and uncertainties, as well as the benefits, of the enterprise operations. Transactions of the entity with shareholders involving distributions of corporate assets or changes in ownership do not result in any gains or losses. The rights of different classes of stockholders, such as preferences to dividends or preferences in liquidation, are generally disclosed in the financial statements.

Liabilities represent claims on the assets of an entity. Sprouse and Moonitz define liabilities as ". . . obligations resulting from past or current transactions and requiring settlement in the future."[10] The definition has been further refined by the FASB as "probable future sacrifices of economic benefits arising from present obligations of a particular entity to transfer assets or provide services to other entities in the future as a result of past transactions or events."[11] The following are identified as essential features of liabilities:

1. A required transfer of economic resources to the other entities in the future.
2. An obligation identified with a particular enterprise.
3. A result of past transactions or events.
4. Amounts are susceptible to reasonable estimation.

Once incurred, a liability remains until the entity settles it, or another event or circumstance discharges it or removes the entity's responsibility to settle it.

Liabilities require transfer of economic resources in the future, and they must be satisfied by specified or reasonably estimated amounts. The amount of the transfer, and in many cases the timing of the transfer, is usually fixed by contract. Changes in the amount and the timing of the transfers can be made but they usually involve a renegotiation or restructuring of the contract. The priority of claims among liabilities may be determined by law or contract. However, with every liability, its claim precedes those of equity. In summary,

---

[8] Ibid., para 61.
[9] Ibid., para. 62.
[10] Robert T. Sprouse and Maurice Moonitz, "A Tentative Set of Broad Accounting Principles for Business Enterprises," *Accounting Research Study No. 3* (New York, AICPA, 1962), p. 37.
[11] Statement of Financial Accounting Concepts, No. 6, op. cit., para. 36.

liabilities involve nondiscretionary future sacrifices of economic benefits generally on demand or at a specified or determinable date, whereas equity is a residual interest.[12]

CHARACTERISTICS OF PREFERRED STOCK

Preferred stock has generally been viewed as equity, differing from common stock only by its preferences. These preferences are generally offered in lieu of some other feature that might be associated with common stock. For example, a stock may be preferred as to dividends, but the holders may forego the possibility of sharing increased dividends beyond the preference amount. Although preferred stock, unless otherwise prohibited, possesses all the basic rights of stock ownership, it is often restricted as to voting rights or dividend participation. Most preferred stock issuances have cumulative dividend preferences as well as liquidation preferences over common stock. Preferred stock claims are subordinate to those of debt.

Consistent with its characteristics, most preferred stock issuances are accounted for as equity: dividends are treated as distributions of earnings, and the stock is shown as part of stockholders' equity with disclosure of preferences. Even though dividends may be cumulative, they are not normally accrued under the premise that such dividends do not become a legal obligation until declared by the Board of Directors.

Since preferred stock has been viewed as equity, the accounting for traditional preferred stock issuances with dividend or liquidation preferences has been noncontroversial. However, as Vatter[13] notes:

> Under common law shares of stock are entirely equivalent unless made different by specific provisions. Human ingenuity has created a great many varieties of shares, however, and there are many questions that arise in connection with the special features attached to each. (p. 267)

Vatter identified preferences related to dividends, dissolution, dividend priority, cumulation, and participation. Although such preferences did cause potential problems in classification and disclosure, Vatter did not question the appropriateness of treating preferred stock as part of equity. However, Vatter did not anticipate the ingenuity that would result in redemption preferences that did not contemplate a full or partial liquidation of the entity.

---

[12] The FASB acknowledges that although the line between equity and liabilities is clear in concept, it may be obscured in practice. Applying the definitions to particular situations may involve practical problems because several kinds of securities seem to have characteristics of both liabilities and equity in varying degrees or because the names given some securities may not accurately describe their essential characteristics. For example, convertible debt instruments have both liability and residual-interest characteristics which may create problems in accounting for them.

[13] William Vatter, "Corporate Stock Equities: Part 1," in Morton Backer, editor, *Modern Accounting Theory* (Englewood Cliffs, NJ, Prentice-Hall, Inc., 1966).

EFFECT OF MANDATORY REDEMPTION
CHARACTERISTICS

The addition of the mandatory redemption feature appears to change the nature of preferred stock from one of residual interest to one of a liability. Redemption is specified as to both amount and time. Dividends are cumulative and any dividends in arrears must be satisfied as of the mandatory redemption date. These characteristics are evident in the Toro preferred stock which contractually must be redeemed serially between 1988 and 1993. There is no option regarding the redemption. The Company can only alter the timing of the redemption by calling the stock early or by purchasing the shares on the open market. The redemption provisions constitute both an economic and a legal obligation, leading to our belief that such stock ought to be classified as a liability.[14]

Although some accountants would agree that redeemable preferred stock contains all the characteristics of debt, they may still argue that since it is legal capital it should be classified as equity. Vatter, for example, notes that "Accounting has never been able to throw off the yoke of legal capital from corporate stock equity reporting." In our view, the legal determination should not dictate the accounting classification. Rather, the underlying characteristics of the security should dictate whether it represents an obligation or a residual interest in the organization. The legal requirements can be disclosed if the company considers such disclosure necessary.

The FASB, in Concepts Statement No. 6, further supports this point of view by recognizing that "some liabilities rest on equitable or constructive obligations, including some that arise in exchange transactions" (para. 40). The FASB recognized that applying the concepts of constructive or equitable obligations may be troublesome, but "to interpret equitable and constructive obligations too narrowly will tend to exclude significant actual obligations of an entity" (para. 40). Examples of this concept's application are evident in the current accounting for leases and consolidations. A lease does not represent a legal purchase of an asset although we may account for it as such. Financial statements of controlled entities are consolidated even though the entities retain separate legal identities.

ACCOUNTING TREATMENT OF DIVIDENDS

When redeemable preferred stock is classified as a liability, a question arises as to whether the related dividends should be treated as expenses. For example, should Toro have recorded redeemable preferred dividends as an

---

[14] The stock would normally be classified as a long-term liability and would be grouped with other long-term debt except in the case where the redemption term is current and the redeemable stock should be classified as a current liability.

expense in determining net income? If the redeemable preferred stock is classified as debt then related dividends should be treated as expenses and appropriately classified with other financing expenses on the income statement. In contrast, if preferred stock does not have mandatory redemption features or other features that indicate debt treatment, the dividends should be treated as distributions of equity.

The payment of dividends on redeemable preferred stock is similar to paying interest on long-term debt.[15] Both represent periodic payments for the use of resources (money) loaned to the organization. Dividends on redeemable preferred stock differ from dividends on other preferred stock in that they must be paid upon redemption.

TREATMENT OF DIVIDENDS IN ARREARS

A dividend arrearage on redeemable preferred stocks meets the conceptual definition of a liability: there is a required transfer of resources, there is an economic obligation, the obligation results from past transactions (issuance of the security), and the amounts can be reasonably estimated. Since the dividends on redeemable preferred stock are contractually mandated, it follows that dividend arrearages should also be accrued and recognized as a liability of the corporation.

Since, in most cases, dividends can be paid to the extent of retained earnings, we believe that the amount of the liability recognized should not exceed the amount of retained earnings. We recommend that the amount of earnings restricted for payment of preferred dividends be disclosed in the financial statements whenever retained earnings are not sufficient to cover the accrual of the liability.

ACCRETION OF DISCOUNT OR PREMIUM

Market conditions and underwriting costs often result in a stock issuance at other than the stock's redemption value. In addition, many redeemable preferred stock issues have provisions whereby the stock is redeemed at specified prices which may increase or decline over time. In a number of instances, the issuer may force early retirement of the preferred stock by utilizing call or conversion features or by buying the stock in the open market. The differences between the issuance price and the redemption price of

[15] There is one major difference. Most bond indentures indicate that the bond is immediately due whenever there is a default in meeting current interest payments. Most mandatory redeemable preferred stock issuances, particularly when issued by companies in financial distress, do not carry such provision. However, they will often include other provisions such as allowing the preferred stockholders to elect a majority of the Board of Directors when such a default occurs.

mandatory redeemable preferred stock raise two additional accounting issues: (1) the appropriate accounting for differences between issuance price
and the mandatory redemption price; and (2) the appropriate accounting
when the redemption price and timing can be decided by the shareholder
according to a prespecified schedule of redemption dates and prices.

Difference Between Issuance Price and Redemption Price

In a situation where the redemption price does not vary, we recommend that
the difference between the issuance price and the mandatory redemption
price be treated as a dividend rate adjustment and amortized over the life of
the liability in the same manner that a premium or discount is amortized for
bonds. Such treatment is consistent with the recommendation of Staff Accounting Bulletin No. 68 issued by the SEC. Complexity is added when
redeemable preferred stock contains a serial schedule of retirements and
retirement value. The serial schedule often results in differing effective dividend rates for some shares according to the length of time the shares will be
outstanding. It is our view that the discount or premium be allocated to the
shares of stock based on the effective interest rate required to amortize the
discount or premium to its redemption date.

Variable Redemption Prices

A somewhat more complex situation exists when the redemption price varies
depending on the shareholder's actions. For example, there may be one
redemption price if the shareholder redeems the stock within the first ten
years. Otherwise, the redemption value changes between years 10 and 15,
with mandatory redemption at year 15. Such provisions are sometimes found
in stock issued by companies experiencing financial problems. For example,
Beehive International's 1986 annual report disclosed a redeemable preferred
stock with a schedule of redemption prices which varied from $11.30 per
share to $18.42 per share depending on when the stock was redeemed.
Absent evidence to the contrary, we recommend the premium or discount be
amortized as an adjustment to the effective dividend rate over the minimum
period to redemption.

GAINS AND LOSSES UPON REDEMPTION

Most companies follow the approach of the Toro Corporation in treating gains
and losses on early redemption as an adjustment to retained earnings or
paid-in capital. Such treatments do not affect reported income or earnings
per share. We find such a treatment to be inconsistent with the underlying
nature of most redeemable preferred stock. Using the analogy to early redemption of debt, we recommend that gains and losses upon redemption be
recognized immediately in the income statement and treated as an extraordinary item.

CONTINGENT REDEMPTIONS

Some companies have adopted anti-takeover provisions whereby preferred stock becomes mandatorily redeemable only if another company acquires a majority ownership of the issuing corporation. The SEC's definition in ASR 268 focused on stocks that "have conditions for redemption that are not solely within the control of the issuer." Thus, stocks issued with these anti-takeover provisions meet the SEC's criteria for redeemable preferred stock, and would be excluded from equity. The SEC's rule in such a situation is not consistent with the FASB's concept of a liability. We believe the accounting for such issuances should be guided by SFAS No. 5, "Accounting for Contingencies," and should consider the probability of redemption of the stock in determining its classification. If the probability is remote, the stock retains the essential characteristics of equity and should be classified as such. Full disclosure of the nature of the contingency should be included in the financial statements.

IMPLICATIONS FOR PRACTICE

A summary of differences between current practice and our recommendations is contained in Exhibit II. The recommended treatment differs significantly from both the SEC guidelines and current practice. The first two columns of Exhibit II present current practice as prescribed by the SEC and generally accepted practice for non-SEC companies.

Column 3 presents our conclusions for redeemable preferred stock. Whereas the SEC dictated only that such stock be excluded from equity, our recommendation is that it be classified as a liability. The remainder of column 3 accounts for income-related factors on a basis consistent with the balance sheet treatment and is analogous to treatments of related expenditures incurred with long-term debt.

Our recommendations differ significantly from both current practice and SEC guidance regarding the income statement treatment of dividends and early redemption provisions. In substance, the dividends represent a financing cost associated with a liability and should be reported as such in the income statement. Amortization of the difference between issuance price and the mandatory redemption price would utilize the effective interest method. Premiums on early redemptions would be treated in the same manner as premiums on early extinguishments of debt and would be reported as extraordinary items. Our recommendations parallel the SEC's approach of accruing dividend arrearages when the arrearages must be paid either on or before redemption.

SUMMARY

This paper has analyzed the appropriateness of alternative accounting treatments for redeemable preferred stock. Current practice is not logically consistent with the FASB's conceptual framework. Our recommendations deal with

EXHIBIT II Mandatory Redeemable Preferred Stock Accounting Treatment

Accounting Treatment	Current Practice		Our Recommendations
	(1) SEC Treatment	(2) GAAP (Non-SEC Clients)	(3)
Balance Sheet Classification	Excluded from equity	Equity, although it could also be excluded from equity	Liability
Dividend Treatment	Charge to retained earnings	Charge to retained earnings	Charge to income—financing expense
Early Redemption (Premium) Costs	Adjustment to retained earnings or paid-in capital	Adjustment to retained earnings or paid-in capital	Income—extraordinary item
Accretion of Issuance Premium or Discount	Charge to retained earnings	Charge to retained earnings	Charge to income—financing expense
Dividend Arrearages	Disclosure	Disclosure	Accrue as a liability and disclose

fundamental accounting issues and can be used as a basis for dealing with more complex problems that continue to arise in accounting for preferred stock. Improvements are suggested which classify the stock according to its underlying characteristics and treat dividends consistently with the underlying classification model. The proposed treatment is consistent with both the FASB's conceptual framework and with prior FASB pronouncements dealing with substantive issues of debt and equity. The recommendations would continue the accounting convention of reporting transactions in accordance with their economic substance.

The Stockholders' Equity Section: Form Without Substance?

Michael L. Roberts
University of Alabama

William D. Samson
University of Alabama

Michael T. Dugan
University of Alabama

The takeover fever of the 1980s produced hundreds of leveraged buyouts, debt-financed dividend distributions, and treasury stock repurchases involving massive distributions of corporate assets to stockholders. In many of these restructurings, distributions to stockholders exceeded the net book value of the corporation's assets and were possible only because corporate managers and creditors relied on the fair values (i.e., the current appraised values) of the assets to maintain a positive net worth. These distributions would not have been possible under traditional state legal capital requirements which restricted distributions to earned and contributed capital in excess of the par value of the corporation's outstanding stock. Indeed, the resulting effect of many of the debt-financed restructurings on corporate stockholders' equity sections has been to produce deficit balances not only in retained earnings, but also in total stockholders' equity. This phenomenon leads us to question the relevance of current stockholders' equity disclosures, which focus attention on the source of capital but ignore the capacity of the corporation for making distributions to stockholders.

This article describes the recent changes in state laws regulating corporate distributions which have made these distributions possible and offers alterna-

From *Accounting Horizons* (December, 1990), pp. 35–46. Reprinted by permission of the American Accounting Association and the authors. Copyright © 1990 by the American Accounting Association.

Authors' note: The authors gratefully acknowledge the contributions of two anonymous reviewers and suggestions provided by Barney Cargile, Frank Rayburn, Keith Shriver, and Mary Stone.

tive accounting presentations that will better inform users of financial statements about (1) corporations' compliance with state laws and (2) their capacity for making distributions. Because of recent changes in state legal restrictions on corporate distributions new disclosures are necessary for financial statement users to be informed about the fair values of net corporate assets—the basis upon which corporate distributions now may be made in many states.

Existing balance sheet presentations of stockholders' equity segregate the various components according to whether they are contributed or earned. Thus, the typical equity section reports the par value of outstanding stock, additional paid-in capital, and retained earnings.[1] This segregation has its roots in state legal capital requirements designed primarily for the protection of creditors. The traditional view of minimum legal capital is that some amount of assets (usually an amount equal to the par or stated value of outstanding stock) must be maintained to buffer the claims of creditors against bankruptcy.[2] To protect this buffer, the dollar amount of distributions that a corporation is able to make to stockholders typically has been limited to assets earned by the corporation (i.e., current or retained earnings) or to assets contributed in excess of the minimum legal capital (e.g., additional paid-in capital). However, as this paper reveals, the traditional view is outdated given the recent changes in state corporation codes that govern distributions to stockholders.

While the legal capital concept evolved from the desire to protect creditors against prejudicial distributions to corporate stockholders, disclosures about legal restrictions on corporate distributions are important to all the parties who have a financial interest in a corporation, including government, suppliers, employees, management, and stockholders. Each of these parties has an interest in the continued viability of the business entity as well as an interest in protecting their own rights relative to the other groups in the event of reorganization or liquidation. Both the continuity of the business enterprise and liquidation rights may be affected by illegal distributions of corporate assets. However, current financial statement disclosures do not include such basic information as what legal restrictions exist regarding distributions to stockholders (e.g., dividends, redemptions, and treasury stock purchases), whether or not a corporation is in compliance with state legal requirements, or the corporation's capacity for making distributions.

As an example of the inadequacies of existing accounting disclosures, consider the 1987 and 1988 stockholders' equity balance sheet sections of Holiday Corporation, the parent corporation of Holiday Inns of America (see Exhibit 1). The January 2, 1987 stockholders' equity section reports the traditional segregation of stockholders' equity items: par value of common stock, additional paid-in capital, and retained earnings, less treasury stock at cost,

---

[1] AICPA, *Accounting Trends and Techniques*, 43rd ed., J. Shohet and R. Rikert (eds.) (NY:AICPA, 1989).

[2] M. A. Miller, *Miller Comprehensive GAAP Guide 1990* (New York: Harcourt Brace Jovanovich, 1989), p. 38.01.

EXHIBIT 1 Holiday Corporation and Consolidated Subsidiaries Balance Sheets

(In thousands, except share amounts)	January 1, 1988	January 2, 1987
Stockholders' equity		
Preferred stock, $100.00 par value, authorized— 150,000 shares, none issued	—	—
Special stock, authorized—5,000,000 shares		
Series A—$1.125 par value, redeemable at $105.00, convertible into 1.5 shares of common stock, outstanding—none and 170,171 shares (excluding none and 98,072 shares held in treasury)	—	$ 191
Series B—$1.25 par value, none issued	—	—
Common stock, $1.50 par value, authorized— 120,000,000 shares, outstanding—26,225,980 and 23,592,569 shares (excluding 14,613,417 and 17,246,828 shares held in treasury)	$ 39,339	35,389
Capital surplus	12,625	205,717
Retained earnings (deficit)	(791,021)	404,655
Cumulative foreign currency translation adjustment	7,972	(63)
Restricted stock	(38,861)	(7,156)
Total stockholders' equity	(769,946)	638,733
Total liabilities and stockholders' equity	$2,399,272	$2,278,189

and foreign currency adjustments. Total stockholders' equity is $639 million. However, the January 1, 1988 stockholders' equity section reveals a *$770 million deficit* in Holiday's *total stockholders' equity*. How did this deficit occur? The explanation lies in the $65 per share dividend that Holiday distributed in 1987 to prevent a hostile takeover. This aggregate $1.55 billion dividend, financed with borrowed funds, not only exceeded the corporation's retained earnings but total stockholders' equity as well by more than three quarters of a billion dollars.

Holiday was able to borrow a large portion of the amount required for the dividend by using the fair value (i.e., appraised value) of its real estate assets as collateral. Holiday was able to distribute the dividend (legally, according to Delaware law) because the fair value of its assets exceeded its liabilities after the distribution, and therefore it had positive equity on a fair value basis. However, the traditional accounting disclosures of par value, additional paid-in capital, and retained earnings do not contain any information (either before or after the dividend distribution) enabling financial statement users to assess the corporation's capacity for making such distributions. While stockholders and other interested parties may have had notice of Holiday's intent to leverage its assets to make the massive dividend, only Holiday's management had information about the fair values of the assets involved.

The point of the Holiday example is that state laws governing a corporation's ability to make distributions to stockholders have continued to evolve from the time when minimum legal capital was considered to be equivalent to the par value of the corporation's stock. That traditional equivalency of minimum legal capital and par value no longer holds in many states. Thus, the traditional stockholders' equity presentation of par value, additional paid-in capital, and retained earnings is obsolete because it implies that some amount, represented by a portion of stockholders' equity, exists to protect creditors. Furthermore, Holiday's situation is by no means unique.[3] In recent years, hundreds of other large corporations have engaged in leveraged buyouts, debt-financed dividends, treasury stock purchases and other corporate restructurings also financed largely by debt.[4] Thus, the issues of stockholders' equity presentation and disclosure are both timely and relevant.

The remainder of this paper is organized as follows. In the next section, we discuss the evolution of minimum legal capital requirements for corporations that influenced existing accounting presentation and disclosure practices. In the following section, we describe recent trends in legal restrictions on corporate distributions to stockholders. Finally, we provide recommendations for changes in reporting stockholders' equity that include disclosures regarding the corporation's compliance with applicable laws and the corporation's capacity to make distributions to stockholders.

DEVELOPMENT OF LEGAL CAPITAL REQUIREMENTS AND ACCOUNTING DISCLOSURES

Development of Legal Capital Requirements

The concept of legal capital evolved during the 18th Century as businesses began to require large amounts of capital for long-term ventures.[5] Early charters for long-term ventures such as banking and insurance businesses included restrictions that limited distributions to owners to the amount of profits, thus preserving the owners' original investment as permanent, non-distributable capital to provide a buffer to protect creditors. These prudent business practices were copied from charter to charter and became the basis for judicial decisions involving corporations. With the advent of the corporation as a separate legal entity and the limited liability of stockholders, the legal capital concept became important for protecting corporate creditors. Stockholders were to be both the shock absorbers for bumps in the business cycle and the recipients of any residual assets in the event of business failure. On

---

[3] See, for example, the annual reports for Shoney's and Interco for 1987 and 1988.
[4] During 1988, these corporations engaged in stock repurchases of more than $1 billion each: UAL, IBM, CSX, Sears Roebuck, Digital Equipment, Gillette, Schlumberger, Dow Chemical, and GTE. In addition, there were over 300 LBOs in 1988; 17 LBOs were in excess of $1 billion. The RJR-Nabisco acquisition was the largest LBO, at $25.3 billion.
[5] B. Manning, *A Concise Textbook on Legal Capital*, 2nd ed. (Mineola, NY: Foundation Press, 1981) provides a complete treatment of the development of legal capital.

the other hand, creditors were given a preferred legal status because they were external investors, whose control over the success or failure of the business was more limited.

According to Manning,[6] five judicial theories evolved concerning stockholders' liability for stock issued at less than par value: (1) the trust fund theory (stockholders hold the contributed capital in trust for creditors, retaining a residual interest upon liquidation), (2) the fraud theory (capital contributions were required to avoid a fraud upon other investors, that is, creditors), (3) the statutory obligation theory (stockholders held liable on the basis of state statutory requirements for maintaining minimum capital), (4) the contract by subscription theory (stockholders' liability was based on their subscription contract), and (5) the balance sheet misrepresentation theory (classic tort misrepresentation that shares were fully paid when, in fact, they were not). As Hendriksen[7] notes, the trust fund theory found its way into corporate accounting by the separate classification of capital stock and additional paid-in capital. Originally, the par value of capital stock was equivalent to legal capital and thus was unavailable for distribution to stockholders. The par value served as a buffer for the protection of creditors, ensuring that the stockholders, rather than creditors, would in fact bear the residual risk of bankruptcy.

The earliest state statutes governing corporations gave substance to the accounting disclosure idea, restricting distributions based on two requirements: insolvency and capital impairment. Capital was assumed to be equal to the total par value of stock. For example, the 1825 Corporation Act adopted in New York made it unlawful for directors or managers "to divide, withdraw, or in any way pay to the stockholders, or any of them, any part of the said capital stock . . . without consent of the legislature.[8] However, restrictions on corporate distributions varied widely among the states even after the American Bar Association's Committee on Corporate Laws released the first Model Business Corporation Act (MBCA) in 1950. According to the 1950 Model Act, a corporation was permitted to make distributions to stockholders so long as the corporation was not insolvent.[9] Significantly, distribution in the form of dividends still had to come from retained earnings or, according to a 1965 amendment, from current earnings. Other distributions, such as treasury stock purchases, could be made directly from paid-in capital in excess of par value if the source of the distribution was disclosed, the corporation was not insolvent, and the articles of incorporation permitted such distribution. Thus, a solvent corporation could make a distribution to its stockholders even though the corporation had a deficit in retained earnings.

---

[6] Ibid.
[7] E. S. Hendriksen, *Accounting Theory*, Fourth Edition (Homewood, IL: Irwin, 1982), pp. 464–465.
[8] D. Kehl, "The Origin and Early Development of American Dividend Laws," 53 *Harvard Law Review* 36 (1939), p. 56.
[9] American Bar Association Committee on Corporate Laws, *Model Business Corporation Act* (rev.) (Philadelphia: ABA, 1979), p. v.

Insolvency was not defined in most early state corporate statutes. Confusion often arose about whether insolvency meant a deficiency of assets over liabilities and legal capital (the traditional bankruptcy definition developed by courts of law) or an inability to pay debts (the definition developed by courts of equity). In the 1950 Model Business Corporation Act, insolvency was defined as the inability to pay debts as they come due in the normal course of business. As discussed below, insolvency is now defined by the 1984 Revised Model Business Corporation Act as either (1) the inability to pay debts as they come due or (2) an excess of liabilities over asset *fair values* (i.e., appraised values). This latter interpretation allows corporations, such as Holiday, to make distributions even when the book value of total stockholders' equity is a deficit.

In this century, restrictions on corporate distributions based on legal capital have had little impact because the practice of using nominal amounts for par or stated values of capital stock has evolved, thereby giving corporate directors much latitude in declaring distributions to stockholders. The recent wave of corporate restructurings has resulted in distributions in which the impairment of capital, at least as measured by GAAP, is clear-cut. Given the large number of restructuring transactions that have occurred, and the fact that many of these have been possible only because of the new flexibility of corporate laws, the relevance of the traditional accounting disclosures about a corporation's compliance with state law and the corporation's capacity for making distributions to stockholders merits reconsideration. These issues have become even more critical, as some recently restructured, highly leveraged corporations have begun defaulting on their obligations.

Development of Current Accounting Disclosures for Stockholders' Equity

Accounting Research Bulletin No. 43 and Accounting Principles Board Opinions Nos. 9, 12 and 14 describe required disclosures for stockholders' equity. The treatment of capital transactions and disclosures in these pronouncements is brief and may be summarized as follows: (1) capital transactions shall be excluded from the determination of net income, and (2) disclosure of changes in the separate accounts comprising stockholders' equity is required. No mention is made in Accounting Research Bulletins, Accounting Principles Board Opinions, or Financial Accounting Standards Board Statements of the need to disclose the minimum legal capital amount or the state statutes that restrict distributions. However, legal capital is discussed in other non-authoritative literature.[10]

In Technical Practice Aid Section 2210.18,[11] a corporation purchased such a large amount of treasury stock that its entire retained earnings and addition-

---

[10] AICPA Committee on Terminology, *Accounting Terminology Bulletin No. 1* (NY: AICPA, 1953); FASB, *Statement of Financial Accounting Concepts No. 6* (Stamford, CT: FASB, 1985), ftnt. 29.

[11] L. Lindenberg, ed., *AICPA Technical Practice Aids* (Chicago: Commerce Clearing House, 1986), p. 1171.

al paid-in capital balances were exhausted. In that case, the relevant state law prohibited such purchases where capital was impaired, so the corporation inquired whether or not it was proper to write up asset values to fair value. The reply cites APB Opinion No. 6 to the effect that write-ups of asset values are not appropriate apart from reorganizations or quasi-reorganizations.[12]

In addition, Issues Paper 88-1, "Quasi-Reorganizations," contains some interesting comments on existing stockholders' equity disclosures.[13]

> Because subdividing equity according to its sources appears to be *based on legal concepts and not accounting concepts,* there is no reason to prohibit a change in that subdivision if the law permits it. . . . *Apart from providing some inconclusive information about legal restrictions on payments of dividends, statistics about the sources of a reporting entity's equity provide little useful information.* For many reporting entities these statistics have already been affected by capitalizations of earnings in connection with stock distributions, business combinations accounted for by the pooling of interests method, and the like. Further, though a deficit in reported retained earnings could result from cumulative losses from operations, a deficit is also a function of the reporting entity's dividend policy and the extent of, and the accounting for, its treasury stock transactions. The fact that there is a deficit, or its amount, may provide little useful information by itself (emphasis added).

The observation that segregating stockholders' equity according to its sources—par or stated value, additional paid-in capital in excess of par or stated value, and retained earnings—"appears to be based on legal concepts and not accounting concepts" is true historically, but it ignores the trend in state corporation codes away from using par or stated value to limit distributions to stockholders. This statement might better have said that the accounting practice is based on an outmoded understanding of legal concepts. Furthermore, the statement that "statistics about the sources of a reporting entity's equity provide little useful information" also is a telling indictment of current stockholders' equity disclosures.

Exhibit 2 shows a representative stockholders' equity presentation and accompanying note for Potlatch Corporation taken from *Accounting Trends and Techniques.*[14] This example was included in *Techniques* to illustrate the accompanying note describing the convertibility features of the preferred stock and voting rights. We include it here because the stockholders' equity section shows the traditional source of equity divisions among preferred and com-

---

[12] Since the inquiry by the corporation's accountants was post hoc, the distribution apparently was illegal and would have subjected the individual members of the corporation's board of directors to personal liability. Such a result could have been avoided had the corporation simply reorganized by reincorporating in a state that has adopted the 1980 or later provisions of the MBCA.

[13] AICPA, Accounting Standards Division, Issues Paper 88-1, *Quasi-Reorganizations* (NY: AICPA, 1988).

[14] AICPA, *Accounting Trends and Techniques*, 43rd ed., J. Shohet and R. Rikert (eds.) (NY: AICPA, 1989).

EXHIBIT 2 Example of Current Disclosure for Stockholders' Equity

Potlatch Corporation
December 31
($000)

	1988	1987
Stockholders' Equity (Note 8):		
Preferred Stock, $3.75 Series B convertible exchangeable, without par value		
Authorized 4,000,000 shares, issued and outstanding 999,996 shares	$ 50,000	$ 50,000
Common Stock, $1 par value		
Authorized 40,000,000 shares, issued 30,812,380 shares	30,812	30,812
Additional paid-in capital	73,623	73,847
Retained Earnings	650,974	567,900
Common shares in treasury 3,904,399 (3,958,769 in 1987)	(83,368)	(84,525)
Total stockholders' equity	$722,041	$638,034

NOTES TO FINANCIAL STATEMENTS
Stockholders' Equity

The preferred stock, which has a liquidation value of $50 per share, is convertible at the option of the holder at any time, unless previously redeemed, into common stock of the company at the rate of 1.8868 shares of common stock for each share of preferred stock, or a conversion price of $26.50 per share of common stock. On any dividend date beginning April 15, 1989, the preferred stock is also exchangeable at the option of the company, in whole but not in part, for 7.5 percent convertible subordinated debentures. The debentures, if issued, will be convertible into common stock of the company at the conversion price in effect for the preferred stock. The preferred stock may not be redeemed prior to April 15, 1989. On or after such date, it will be redeemed at the option of the company, in whole or in part, at redemption prices declining to $50 per share on April 15, 1996, plus accrued and unpaid dividends. Dividends on the preferred stock are paid quarterly.

In general, all holders of Potlatch common stock as of December 12, 1985, and stockholders after that date who own shares 48 consecutive months or longer ("long-term holders") are entitled to exercise four votes per share of stock so held, while stockholders who are not long-term holders are entitled to one vote per share. All stockholders are entitled to only one vote per share on matters arising under certain provisions of the company's charter.

Source: Accounting Trends and Techniques, 43rd ed., J. Shohet and R. Rikert (eds.) (NY: AICPA, 1989).

mon stock, additional paid-in capital, and retained earnings, less treasury stock. However, what the example from *Techniques* fails to reveal, and what is disclosed nowhere in the annual report, is the amount legally available for distribution to stockholders. Although not disclosed in the annual report, Potlatch Corporation is incorporated in Delaware (though it has no operations there). According to Delaware law, as noted in the next section, capital surplus (i.e., the amount available for distribution to stockholders) consists of the excess of net assets (*at fair value*) over par value. Therefore, the amount that Potlatch may legally distribute is at least equal to Potlatch's $722 million book value of stockholders' equity less $81 million par value. The *book value* is irrelevant, however, since the actual amount distributable is the *fair value* of Potlatch's assets in excess of $81 million (and Potlatch owns approximately $250 million in land, which could well have a higher fair value). This actual amount cannot be determined from the traditional stockholders' equity presentation and disclosures. Neither creditors nor stockholders are provided with information about the corporation's compliance with Delaware law (or even in which state Potlatch is incorporated) or its capacity for making distributions.

CURRENT TRENDS IN LEGAL RESTRICTIONS ON DISTRIBUTIONS

Since 1950, the American Bar Association's Committee on Corporate Laws' Model Business Corporation Act has been very influential in shaping state laws governing corporations. This model act was eventually adopted, at least in part, by 35 states. The MBCA has been revised many times over the years. However, the 1980 revisions were particularly noteworthy with regard to the concept of legal capital. The Committee's report on the 1980 revisions to the Model Business Corporation Act reflects the dramatic nature of the changes in the financial provisions that were adopted at that time:[15]

> The amendments. . . reflect a complete modernization of all provisions of the Model Act concerning financial matters, including (a) *the elimination of the outmoded concepts of stated capital and par value,* (b) the definition of "distribution" as a broad term governing dividends, share repurchases and similar actions that should be governed by the same standard (c) the reformulation of the statutory standards governing the making of distributions, (d) the elimination of the concept of treasury stock, and (e) the making of a number of technical and conforming changes. . . .
>
> It has long been recognized by practitioners and legal scholars that the pervasive statutory structure in which "par value" and "stated capital" are basic to the state corporation statutes does not today serve the original purpose of protecting creditors and senior security holders from payments to

---

[15] The Report of the Committee on Corporate Laws," *The Business Lawyer* (July 1979), pp. 1867–1889.

junior security holders, and may, to the extent security holders are led to believe that it provides some protection, *tend to be misleading*. In light of this recognized fact, the Committee . . . deleted the mandatory concepts of stated capital and par value . . . (emphasis added).

The 1980 Model Act retained the same equity definition of insolvency as the 1950 Act, i.e., the requirement that in order to make distributions the corporation must be able to pay its debts as they come due. However, a major change was introduced in Section 45(b) that includes a second substantive test prohibiting distributions if the corporation's total assets would be less than the sum of total liabilities plus any liquidation preferences of preferred stock. This requirement, by itself, does not seem troubling. The next paragraph, though, "contains the big bomb":[16]

Determination [of net assets] may be based upon (i) financial statements prepared on the basis of accounting practices and principles that are reasonable in the circumstances, or (ii) *fair valuation* or other method that is reasonable in the circumstances (emphasis added).

The Committee report discusses at length the decision to allow fair valuation in addition to GAAP. "This does not mean that the statute is intended to reject the use and reliance upon generally accepted accounting principles; on the contrary, it is expected that their use would be the basic rule in most cases."[17] However, the report also states that "the statute . . . specifically authorizes departures from historical cost accounting and sanctions the utilization of appraisal methods for the purpose of determining the funds available for distributions."[18] Accordingly, it seems that attorneys have resolved, for their purposes, the debate that has raged for years among accountants as to which measurement basis is appropriate: the legal profession has resolved that, when push comes to shove, fair values are more appropriate, at least for purposes of determining the measurement of asset values for distributions to stockholders.[19] The legal standard now appears to favor historical cost (i.e., GAAP) as a routine matter, but also permits fair values to be used. The important questions for accounting disclosure are: when and how are these fair values to be disclosed? We address these questions in the section below.

Currently, the 50 states may be classified into one of three groups for purposes of comparing restrictions on distributions.[20] The least restrictive

---

[16] Manning, op. cit., p. 171.
[17] "The Report of the Committee on Corporate Laws," op. cit.
[18] Ibid.
[19] There is some judicial support for allowing corporations to make distributions based on excess net fair values of assets even aside from the revised MBCA (see *Randall v. Bailey*, 288 N. Y. 280 (1942)), although the decision has not been followed by any other court.
[20] P. McGough, "The Legal Significance of the Par Value of Common Stock: What Accounting Educators Should Know," *Issues in Accounting Education* (Fall 1988), pp. 330–350, at p. 341.

group consists of 18 states, including 17 that either follow the 1984 Revised Model Business Corporation Act or have similar uniform tests for distributions, that is, (1) the corporation must be solvent, and (2) distributions must not exceed the fair value of net assets plus liquidation preferences.[21] Because solvency is defined in these state statutes as the ability to pay debts as they come due, the concept of par or stated value as minimum legal capital has been deleted from these state corporation codes. Accordingly, existing accounting presentation of stockholders' equity by source for corporations incorporated in these states can be explained only by tradition.

The largest group, consisting of 22 states, also has a solvency requirement but, in addition, has separate requirements for distributions that take the form of dividends, treasury stock purchases, redemptions, and partial liquidations in accordance with the 1950 Model Business Corporation Act and subsequent modifications. Generally, these states require that dividends must come from earned surplus (i.e., retained earnings). In some cases, however, this second group of states permits distributions from capital surplus (i.e., additional paid-in capital). Par value or stated capital is never directly available for distribution. However, in many states the board of directors is statutorily granted the authority to reallocate stated capital to additional paid-in capital by resolution. Thus, distributions may come from any one of the following sources: retained earnings, additional paid-in capital, or stated capital. The remaining states use various hybrid restrictions, usually consisting of solvency and balance sheet tests.

Exhibit 3 contains excerpts from three state corporation statutes to illustrate the different legal restrictions that currently exist. As shown in the exhibit, California is one of the hybrid states, and it relies on two tests. Distributions may come either from retained earnings or may be paid exclusive of retained earnings if a balance sheet solvency test is met. California does not permit valuing assets other than marketable securities at fair value. Delaware, on the other hand, grants the corporation's directors the authority to rely on appraised values of assets in determining the amount of available surplus.[22] Delaware law thereby permits distributions from capital surplus (defined as the excess of net assets [*at fair value*] over stated capital) or from current net profits. Hawaii's provisions governing distributions are similar to the 1980 MBCA that was discussed in the previous section and, thus, specifically authorizes distributions up to the excess net fair value of assets.

---

[21] American Bar Association Committee on Corporate Laws, *Model Business Corporation Act Annotated* (3d Ed.) (Englewood Cliffs, NJ: Prentice-Hall, 1989), p. xxxiv.

[22] Del. Code Ann. Cum. Supp. (1988). Sec. 172 states that board members are fully protected when they rely in good faith on information provided by professionals or experts "as to the value and amount of the assets, liabilities and/or net profits of the corporation or any other facts pertinent to the existence and amount of surplus. . . ." Delaware has been called "the Liechtenstein of the United States" because its liberal business laws have attracted 56 percent of *Fortune* 500 corporations and 45 percent of corporations listed on the New York Stock Exchange to incorporate in the state. P. M. Barrett, "Delaware Moves Closer to Adopting Law to Deter Hostile Takeovers," *The Wall Street Journal* (December 9, 1987).

EXHIBIT 3 Selected Statutes Limiting Corporate Distributions

California:

Sec. 500. Distributions; retained earnings or assets remaining after completion.

Neither a corporation nor any of its subsidiaries shall make any distribution to the corporation's shareholders except as follows:

(a) The distribution may be made if the amount of the retained earnings of the corporation immediately prior thereto equals or exceeds the amount of the proposed distribution; or

(b) The distribution may be made if immediately after giving effect thereto:

(1) The sum of the assets of the corporation . . . would be at least equal to 1¼ times its liabilities . . . ; and

(2) The current assets of the corporation would be at least equal to its current liabilities . . . .

West's Ann. Cal. Code (1988 Supplement)

Delaware:

Sec. 170. Dividends.

(a) The directors of every corporation . . . may declare and pay dividends . . . either (1) out of its surplus . . . or (2) in case there shall be no such surplus, out of its net profits for the fiscal year in which the dividend is declared and/or the preceding fiscal year.

Sec. 154. Determination of amount of capital; capital, surplus and net assets defined.

Any corporation may, by resolution of its board of directors, determine that only a part of the consideration which shall be received by the corporation for any of its capital stock . . . shall be capital; but [capital shall not be less than par value for any stock having a par value]. . . . The excess, if any, at any given time, of the net assets of the corporation over the amount so determined to be capital shall be surplus.

Del. Code Ann. (1983)

Hawaii:

Sec. 415-45. Distributions to shareholders.

Subject to any restrictions in the articles of incorporation, the board of directors may authorize and the corporation may make distributions, except that no distribution may be made if, after giving effect thereto, either:

(1) The corporation would be unable to pay its debts as they become due in the usual course of its business; or

(2) The corporation's total assets would be less than the sum of its total liabilities and . . . the maximum amount that then would be payable, in any liquidation, in respect of all outstanding shares having preferential rights in liquidation.

Determination under paragraph (2) may be based upon (a) financial statements prepared on the basis of accounting practices and principles that are reasonable in the circumstances, or (b) a fair valuation or other method that is reasonable in the circumstances.

Haw. Rev. Stat. (1985)

Thus far, we have summarized the development of existing accounting presentation and disclosures and the new legal restrictions on corporate distributions to stockholders. In the next section, we suggest some alternatives for reporting a corporation's compliance with statutory restrictions on distributions to stockholders as well as the corporation's capacity for making distributions.

RECOMMENDED PRESENTATION
AND DISCLOSURES

To make stockholders' equity presentation and disclosures more relevant, attention must be given to the purpose of the disclosures. Should the purpose simply be to report the sources of capital, or should the purpose be to inform readers (1) *what* state legal restrictions exist and whether or not the corporation has made any distributions to stockholders in *violation* of the laws of the state of incorporation, and (2) the amount of capital, if any, that the directors *may distribute* legally without violating state law? If the purpose is to disclose compliance and capacity to make distributions, then identification of the source of capital, whether from earnings or paid-in sources, is irrelevant.

We agree with the statement in AICPA Issues Paper 88-1 that "Apart from providing . . . information about legal restrictions on payments of dividends, statistics about the sources of a reporting entity's equity provide little useful information."[23] Reporting capital stock, additional paid-in capital, and retained earnings in the traditional manner provides little useful information except for corporations incorporated in states that continue to follow the 1950 Model Business Corporation Act. For corporations incorporated in states that have adopted the 1980 or 1984 MBCA (allowing assets to be valued at fair value for determining the capacity for distributions), the traditional reporting based on source of capital is no longer relevant.

What information should be reported? At a minimum, disclosure of the corporation's compliance with restrictions on distributions according to the applicable state law should be provided in a footnote to the financial statements. Presentation of the stockholders' equity section in the balance sheet could be reduced to a single line item. Of course, other balance sheet presentations are possible and should be explored. Accompanying notes should specify the number of shares authorized, issued, and outstanding for each class of stock and the rights associated with each class. For determination of compliance, the notes should clearly describe the state requirements, including whether the applicable test is solely an insolvency standard or more restrictive, and should specify how the law applies to the corporation. For example, if the state law contains an insolvency test and, in addition, requires the distribution to come from retained earnings or current earnings, then the note should so indicate and also should reveal the dollar amount necessary to meet current obligations as they come due.

In addition to disclosing the corporation's current compliance with state legal restrictions, the note also should indicate the corporation's capacity for current distributions. As with the compliance disclosure, the corporation's

---

[23] AICPA, Accounting Standards Division, Issues Paper 88-1, *Quasi-Reorganizations* (NY: AICPA, 1988).

capacity to make distributions will depend on the particular legal requirements of the state of incorporation. For solvency states, the disclosure should
indicate the corporation's current ability to meet obligations as they come
due, for example, its quick asset ratio. Other information, such as the existence of any nonrecurring obligations that are expected to come due in the
foreseeable future or short-term borrowing capacity, also would be useful.
For states that restrict distributions based on an excess of net assets at either
book or fair value, the corporation's capacity to make current distributions
within these limits should be disclosed. This would necessitate a disclosure of
the excess of either book value or fair value of assets over liabilities, depending on the applicable state law.

While disclosure of the excess fair value of assets may seem heretical to
some accountants, the legal and financial communities already have adopted
this approach to measure a corporation's ability to make current distributions
to stockholders. Shouldn't this information be provided to stockholders,
creditors, and other parties who have an interest in the continuity of the
corporation? Consider the position in which the stockholders and creditors of
Holiday Corporation found themselves at the end of 1987. Did they have any
inkling that the Company had the capability of paying out a $65 per share
dividend? And, consider those who bought and sold the stock when rumors
of a takeover were rife. Had those stockholders been informed of the possibility of a large payout, would these investors have sold their stock? Unfor-

EXHIBIT 4 Recommended Presentation of Stockholders' Equity and
Disclosures of Distribution Limitations

(For Corporations Incorporated in States Following the 1980 or 1984 Model Business
Corporation Acts)

XYZ Corporation
Balance Sheet
December 31
Stockholders' Equity Section

	1990	1989
Stockholders' Equity	$xxx,xxx	$xxx,xxx

Note xx: Stockholders' Equity

As of December 31, 1990, there were 1,000,000 shares of common stock authorized; 500,000
issued; and 400,000 outstanding. Total contributed capital at December 31, 1990 was $xxx,xxx.
Total retained earnings at December 31, 1990 was $xxx,xxx. There were no changes in contrib-
uted capital during 1990. For changes in retained earnings, see the accompanying statement.

Note xx: Distributions to Stockholders

XYZ Corporation is incorporated in the State of X. State law requires all corporations to meet
several requirements before distributions can be made. The corporation must be solvent, and the
corporation's assets (measured on a fair value basis) must exceed its liabilities and any liquidation
preferences both before and after the distribution. As of December 31, 1990, the corporation's
financial position meets both of these requirements. The fair value of the corporation's net assets
is $xxx,xxx at December 31, 1990.

(If the corporation's charter prohibits the use of the fair value basis or if the corporation's board of
directors has adopted an equivalent resolution, the footnote should acknowledge that fact and
then state that distributions are limited to the value of the corporation's net assets on an historical
cost basis, which is $xxx,xxx at December 31, 1990.)

tunately, the investors were not given the choice because the accounting disclosures for stockholders' equity did not describe Holiday's capacity for making distributions permitted by state law.

Finally, it seems critical to update the disclosures of distribution compliance and capacity after such a restructuring has occurred so that investors can monitor the progress of the restructured entity. For example, in the case of Holiday Corporation, subsequent disclosures were made regarding the gains on sales of hotel properties, but not about discrepancies between amounts realized and appraised values. The appraisals were the basis for the extra-large dividend—and to its related refinancing. Given the events subsequent to the recapitalization (i.e., a class action suit, debt refinancing, and, ultimately, sale of the company to a foreign corporation), such disclosures undoubtedly would have been useful to stockholders, suppliers, regulators, and other interested parties.

In Exhibits 4 and 5, we provide two examples of how disclosures of compliance with state restrictions on distributions and distribution capacity might look. Exhibit 4 presents the disclosure for a corporation that is incorporated in a state that follows the approach of the 1980 and 1984 Model Business Corporation Acts. Exhibit 5 presents a sample stockholders' equity presentation and footnote disclosure for a corporation incorporated in a state that follows the earlier 1950 MBCA. In both situations, the current balance sheet

---

EXHIBIT 5 Recommended Presentation of Stockholders' Equity and Disclosures of Distribution Limitations

(For Corporations Incorporated in States Following the 1950 Model Business Corporation Act)

XYZ Corporation
Balance Sheet
December 31
Stockholders' Equity Section

	1990	1989
Stockholders' Equity	$xxx,xxx	$xxx,xxx

Note xx: Stockholders' Equity

As of December 31, 1990, there were 1,000,000 shares of $1 stated value common stock authorized; 500,000 issued; and 400,000 outstanding. Total contributed capital at December 31, 1990 was $xxx,xxx. Total retained earnings at December 31, 1990 was $xxx,xxx. There were no changes in contributed capital during 1990. For changes in retained earnings, see the accompanying statement.

Note xx: Distributions to Stockholders

XYZ Corporation is incorporated in the State of X. State law requires all corporations to meet several requirements before distributions can be made. The corporation must be solvent, dividends may be distributed from retained earnings or from current earnings, and redemptions and treasury stock purchases may be made from retained earnings, current earnings, and/or additional paid-in capital. In addition, the Board of Directors is authorized to make changes in the stated value of common stock to transfer capital to additional paid-in capital for the purpose of making distributions. As of December 31, 1990, the corporation has complied with these requirements. Based on the above legal restrictions, distributions in the form of dividends are limited to no more than $xxx,xxx; distributions in the form of redemptions or treasury stock purchases are limited to no more than $xxx,xxx.

stockholders' equity sections have been replaced with a single line reporting total stockholders' equity. The accompanying footnotes would disclose the usual information about the number of shares authorized, issued and outstanding, and also would indicate the corporation's compliance with restrictions on distributions to stockholders imposed by state law and the corporation's capacity for making such distributions. Regardless of the form of presentation, the disclosures should provide relevant information to potential investors, creditors, stockholders, management, employees, etc., about the ability of the corporation to make distributions to stockholders within the applicable legal boundaries.

One further point should be noted regarding disclosures about limitations on corporate distributions. Corporations with substantial debt often enter into agreements with their creditors to limit distributions to shareholders. These limitations usually are described in a note to the financial statements and may be even more restrictive than the limitations imposed by state law. However, these restrictions are not always very specific, and furthermore may be changed at any time by agreement between the corporation and the creditors. Thus, even when such debt-related restrictions are present, the recommended disclosures in Exhibits 4 and 5 should be made.

CONCLUSION

The legal capital concept has recently undergone significant change, and it will continue to change as more states adopt the provisions of the 1984 Revised Model Business Corporation Act. The new concept is to restrict the ability of corporations to make distributions to stockholders based on an equity definition of insolvency and on the excess fair value of assets over liabilities. This change in legal standards has eliminated the concept of par or stated value.

Accounting for stockholders' equity, long associated with the reporting of par or stated values as equivalent to legal capital, needs to keep pace with the changing legal requirements. Reporting capital by source is now irrelevant given the changes in many state corporation codes. Thus, a single line amount for stockholders' equity could be presented along with a footnote providing additional disclosures that are targeted to the new restrictions on distributions to stockholders. At a minimum, the notes to the financial statements should indicate whether or not the corporation is complying with legal restrictions and the amount that is currently distributable under state law. Especially in situations in which restructuring transactions (e.g., excessive debt-financed dividends, stock repurchases, or leveraged buyouts) have occurred or may occur, and are financed based on the fair values of assets, preparers should disclose the fair value of assets as supplemental information to financial statements prepared on an historical cost basis.

CHAPTER 15

Earnings Per Share

The current accounting rules for the computation and disclosure of earnings per share (EPS) data are very complex and detailed. Given that managers, financial analysts, and investors use EPS data to measure a firm's financial performance, the reporting complexity mainly reflects accountants' concern that managers have a strong incentive to manipulate the calculation of EPS numbers. For example, if EPS were to be defined as simply net income divided by the average number of common shares outstanding, managers could issue equity-like financing instruments such as convertible debt, stock options and appreciation rights, warrants, etc., and keep the denominator of EPS small. It is this kind of concern that led the Accounting Principles Board (APB) to issue Opinion No. 15 in 1969, providing for very specific, if arbitrary, procedures to handle such securities in the computation of EPS.

APB Opinion No. 15 requires two types of EPS disclosures for companies with complex capital structures: primary and fully diluted. The former includes in the denominator potentially dilutive securities that are "common stock equivalents" while the latter requires the inclusion of all potentially dilutive securities in the computation. APB Opinion No. 15 does not require the disclosure of a "simple" or "basic" EPS, though a calculation of one is needed to apply its materiality standards. In practice, companies tend to vary greatly in the nature of the EPS presentation, with dual presentation of primary and fully diluted EPS numbers more the exception than the rule. Those that disclose just one EPS number (owing to the materiality criterion) do not always give sufficient information to determine whether the number is the basic EPS or one of the two computed EPS numbers. In addition to this disclosure diversity, financial media and financial analysts show a lack of consistency in the way in which they report primary and fully diluted EPS data.

There is very little empirical evidence on the question of the relative informativeness of the two EPS measures. Anecdotal evidence suggests that most financial analysts refer to the primary and not the fully diluted EPS in their forecasts and analyses. At least one paper shows that the basic EPS is, in fact, more correlated with security returns than is either primary or fully diluted EPS.[1] However, the paper's methodology is weak and more work needs to be done in this area.

In "Earnings Per Share Reporting: Time for an Overhaul?" R. David Mautz and Thomas Jeffery Hogan argue that APB Opinion No. 15, in focusing on the effect of dilution on EPS, ignores the historical, undiluted EPS completely, and they call for replacing the primary EPS with the basic EPS. They also argue that the procedures required by APB Opinion 15 to determine the dilutive effect of options are not substantiated by empirical evidence, and specifically call for the elimination of the treasury stock method for warrants and options.

Julie S. Sobery, in "An Empirical Evaluation of SFAS No. 55," also questions the underlying assumptions in the current standard's EPS computation. She specifically examines the "common stock equivalence" classification rule for a convertible debt, given by Financial Accounting Standards Board's (FASB) Statement of Financial Accounting Standards (SFAS) No. 55. The standard, amending APB Opinion No. 15, requires convertible debt to be classified as a common stock equivalent if its cash yield at the time of issuance is less that $66^2/3$ percent of the average Aa corporate bond yield. The use of this arbitrary rule eliminates the need for management to make a subjective assessment of the probability of conversion of the debt, but this type of information may well be what the shareholder wants to learn from the primary and fully diluted EPS data. Examining the actual conversion experience of a large sample of convertible debt, Sobery shows that the FASB Statement 55 rule classifies the subsequent conversion only about half the time, a large error rate indeed.

The computational complexity of current EPS disclosure rules is nicely illustrated by Lee J. Seidler in "Ralston Purina: Computing Earnings Per Share for Leveraged ESOPs." An ESOP, or employee stock option plan, is an accounting entity used by a corporation to invest employees' pension or wage contributions in the firm's own shares. Since ESOPs typically use borrowed funds to buy convertible preferred stocks, the APB's "if-converted" method to determine the dilution requires the consideration of both the potential conversion of the security and the repayment of the associated debt with a corporate cash contribution. The article illustrates the way Ralston Purina handles this computation.

BIBLIOGRAPHICAL NOTES

Another article in which APB Opinion No. 15's computational assumptions are questioned is:

[1] James A. Millar, Thakol Nunthirapakorn and Steve Courtenay, "A Note on the Information Content of Primary and Fully Diluted Earnings Per Share," *Financial Analysts Journal* (September-October 1987), pp. 77–79.

Coughlan, John W.: "Anomalies in Calculating Earnings Per Share," *Accounting Horizons* (December 1988), pp. 80–88.

Using examples similar to those used by critics of the return on investment ratio, the author argues that a firm with a large current EPS of, say, $10 would be better off turning down investments (requiring additional equity) that earn less than $10 per share, even if they are beneficial to the firm's value, because of the current procedure for calculating the weighted average of shares outstanding during a period. For additional critiques of the computational assumptions of APB Opinion No. 15, see:

Barlev, Benzion: "Contingent Equity and the Dilutive Effect on EPS," *The Accounting Review* (April 1983), pp. 385–393.
Barlev, Benzion: "Theory, Pragmatism and Conservatism in Reflecting the Effects of Warrants on Diluted EPS," *Abacus* (June 1984), pp. 1–15.
Dudley, Lola Woodward: "Should We Junk the Common Stock Equivalence Test?" *The Woman CPA* (October 1986), pp. 12–14.

These articles deal with empirical tests or analytical arguments about APB Opinion No. 15's procedures:

Rice, Steven J.: "The Information Content of Fully Diluted Earnings Per Share," *The Accounting Review* (April 1978), pp. 429–438.
Dudley, Lola Woodward: "A Critical Look at EPS," *Journal of Accountancy* (August 1985), pp. 102–111. The author evaluates the EPS disclosure rules in the context of the FASB's Concepts Statement No. 2.
Gaumnitz, Bruce R., and Joel E. Thompson: "Establishing the Common Stock Equivalence of Convertible Bonds," *The Accounting Review* (July 1987), pp. 601–622. This paper follows up on Julie Sobery's work and proposes a test based on the market value of the common stock at the time of issuing the convertible bond.
Wiseman, Donald E.: "Holding Loss/Gain as an Alternative to EPS Dilution," *Accounting Horizons* (December 1990), pp. 18–34. The author argues that current value accounting provides superior information than APB Opinion No. 15 on the dilutive effect of options.

The following articles provide supplemental reading material to illustrate various computational aspects of APB Opinion 15:

Matulich, Serge, Loren A. Nikolai and Stevan K. Olson: "Earnings Per Share: A Flow Chart Approach to Teaching Concepts and Procedures," *The Accounting Review* (January 1977), pp. 233–247. The paper illustrates the EPS procedures using a flow chart approach and applies it to a complex capital structure problem based on a CPA exam question.
Swieringa, Robert J., and Dale Morse: "Accounting for Hybrid Convertible Debentures," *The Accounting Review* (January 1985), pp. 127–133. Hybrid securities are convertible into the common stock of a firm other than the issuer. The authors recommend a method for valuing the special conversion feature.
Kilpatrick, Bob, Karl Putnam and Harold Schneider: "Convertible Securities and Earnings Per Share: A Competitive Ranking Algorithm," *The Accounting Review* (July 1985), pp. 526–530.
Curatola, Anthony P., David B. Vicknair and Suzanne R. Pinac Ward: "Earnings Per Share: Alternative Interpretations of the Three Percent Provision of APB 15 in

Intermediate Accounting Textbooks," *Issues in Accounting Education* (Spring 1988), pp. 17–26.

Chasteen, Lanny G., and Marvin S. Keener: "Ranking Convertible Securities for Earnings Per Share: A Graphical Analysis," *Issues in Accounting Education* (Fall 1988), pp. 241–247.

Earnings Per Share Reporting: Time for an Overhaul?

R. David Mautz, Jr.
University of North Carolina at Greensboro

Thomas Jeffery Hogan
University of Massachusetts at Boston

INTRODUCTION

The preparation of earnings per share (EPS) disclosures for public companies with complex capital structures is much more complicated than dividing income by outstanding common shares.[1] Much of this complexity results from the efforts of standard setters to make EPS disclosures reflect the effects of potentially dilutive securities. A critical evaluation of current EPS disclosures suggests that they are of questionable usefulness. This paper concludes that EPS reporting standards are deficient and sets forth a proposal to modify those standards. The proposed changes are intended to improve the usefulness of EPS reporting without increasing the burden placed upon preparers of financial statements.

A prominent feature of the proposal is the recommendation that primary EPS be replaced by an undiluted measure of EPS which we call basic EPS.[2] The following section focuses on issues surrounding the computation of diluted EPS, such as common stock equivalency, the treasury stock method, and the three percent materiality standard. The next section details the

From *Accounting Horizons* (September 1989), pp. 21–27. Reprinted by permission of the American Accounting Association and the authors. Copyright © 1989 by the American Accounting Association.

Authors' note: We are indebted to Robert K. Mautz and an anonymous reviewer for their helpful comments and suggestions.

[1] The principal authoritative guidance for EPS reporting is: Accounting Principles Board, "Accounting Principles Board Opinion Number 15: *Earnings Per Share*," New York: May 1969.

[2] Henceforth in this paper, the term "basic EPS" is used to describe the statistic obtained by dividing historical earnings available to common shareholders by weighted average common shares outstanding.

proposed changes in EPS reporting requirements and provides an illustration and explanation of the recommended disclosure format. It is followed by a brief summary and conclusions.

CONVERTIBLE SECURITIES, POTENTIAL DILUTION, AND EPS REPORTING

Finance theory suggests that investors attempt to maximize expected utility. With respect to investments in debt securities, utility can be assumed to be a function of the expected future cash flows associated with those investments and the uncertainty surrounding those cash flows. Market participants evaluate debt characteristics and determine the effective return they are willing to accept. Debt issues which incorporate conversion features complicate this evaluation, since the market must also consider the potential increased returns available if the issuing company performs better than expected.

Conversion features also complicate external financial reporting since they represent a potential dilution of EPS. Just as the default risk associated with a pure debt security is unobservable to investors, debtholders' intentions with respect to exercising conversion features are unobservable to preparers of financial statements. Accounting standard setters have sought a linkage between investors' intentions and an observable phenomenon. Lambert terms such linkages "bridge assumptions."[3] The linkage currently made involves the comparison of a security's yield upon issuance with a market-based standard. This benchmark, the average Aa corporate bond yield, is intended to surrogate for the risk-adjusted rate of return that the security would yield absent the conversion feature. When a security's yield rate is significantly lower than this benchmark, accountants assume that investors value the conversion feature highly and are more likely to exercise it.

Current reporting standards for public companies with complex capital structures require presentation of two pro forma EPS numbers on the face of the income statement when potential dilution is material. The first number, commonly referred to as primary EPS, is prepared assuming that those dilutive securities most likely to be converted are converted on the first day of the fiscal year. The second pro forma disclosure, fully diluted EPS, is computed assuming that *all* dilutive securities are converted to common stock on the first day of the fiscal year.

This paper focuses on three major concerns related to the usefulness of EPS as currently reported. First, under current standards, historical EPS numbers may be completely supplanted by pro forma disclosures designed to illustrate possible future effects of conversions to common stock.[4] The impor-

---

[3] Samuel Joseph Lambert, III, "Basic Assumptions in Accounting Theory Construction," *Journal of Accountancy*, February 1974, p. 43.
[4] This is the case whenever potential dilution exceeds three percent.

tance of information about potential dilution is apparent.[5] However, that acknowledgment does not necessarily lead to the conclusion that historically based EPS data are of no use to readers.

Second, current standards require the presentation of only two discrete EPS numbers. The possible levels of EPS actually span a range from no dilution to maximum possible dilution. Thus, financial statements currently present a severely truncated disclosure of EPS. Furthermore, the two EPS numbers presented do not represent the endpoints of the range of possible dilution levels.

Third, authoritative standards for EPS reporting incorporate three bridge assumptions which are either untested or unsupported in the empirical literature. These are (1) the assumption that common stock equivalency tests are accurate indicators of conversion likelihood, (2) the assumption that option and warrant proceeds are used to acquire treasury shares (the so-called "treasury stock method"), and (3) the assumption that potential dilution of less than 3 percent is immaterial.

Lambert points out that bridge assumptions may be established in light of empirical evidence, or they may result from arbitrary stipulation.[6] The cash yield test for common stock equivalency established by Accounting Principles Board Opinion 15 (APB 15) has repeatedly been tested for its predictive power and found to be lacking. Amendments to the APB 15 test and a handful of rival tests have, likewise, proven poor predictors of conversion.[7] These conclusions suggest that the designation "common stock equivalent" is not meaningful as it is currently defined. That being the case, the adjustment of basic EPS for the assumed conversion of common stock equivalents produces a statistic that is, at best, difficult to interpret. The usefulness of primary EPS is considered in greater detail in the following section.

Both the treasury stock method and the three percent dilution test appear to fall into the category of unverified bridge assumptions. The authors are not aware of any direct evidence that either assumption contributes to the useful-

[5] For an empirical study of market reaction to potential dilution, see:
Lerner, Eugene M., and Rolf Auster, "Does the Market Discount Potential Dilution," *Financial Analysts Journal,* July-August 1969, pp. 118–121.

[6] Lambert, p. 44.

[7] See for example:
Arnold, Donald F., and Thomas E. Humann, "Earnings Per Share: An Empirical Test of the Market Parity and the Investment Value Methods," *The Accounting Review,* January 1973, pp. 23–33.

Frank, Werner G., and Jerry J. Weygandt, "A Prediction Model for Convertible Debentures," *Journal of Accounting Research,* Spring 1971, pp. 116–26.

Fulmer, Jr., John G., and James E. Moon, "Tests for Common Stock Equivalency," *Journal of Accounting, Auditing, and Finance,* Fall 1984, pp. 5–14.

Givoly, Dan, and Dan Palmon, "Classification of Convertible Debt and Common Stock Equivalents: Some Empirical Evidence on the Effects of APB Opinion 15," *Journal of Accounting Research,* Autumn 1981, pp. 530–543.

Hofstedt, Thomas R., and Richard R. West, "The APB, Yield Indices, and Predictive Ability," *The Accounting Review,* April 1971, pp. 329–337.

ness of EPS disclosures. Yet, both practices have important effects on reported EPS. Use of the treasury stock method minimizes the dilutive effect of the assumed exercise of options and warrants. The result is that EPS numbers do not reflect the maximum possible dilution. The 3 percent materiality standard permits the presentation of a single, undiluted EPS statistic when the difference between basic and fully diluted EPS is less than 3 percent. The effect of this assumption on users' decisions is not known. The following section outlines a proposal to modify EPS reporting. The issues of common stock equivalency, the treasury stock method, and the 3 percent materiality standard are discussed in greater detail in that section.

POLICY RECOMMENDATION

The introduction to this paper calls into question the usefulness of the complex EPS disclosures that are currently mandated for public companies. The previous section focused on some individual problem areas within those disclosures. In this section, we recommend four specific amendments to the accounting standards governing EPS. We believe that each is a step toward meeting our stated objective of improving the usefulness of EPS disclosures without materially increasing the computational burden associated with their presentation. The proposed amendments are:

1. Discontinue the presentation of primary EPS in favor of basic EPS;
2. Modify the computation of fully diluted EPS to eliminate the treasury stock method;
3. Eliminate the 3 percent materiality standard for dual presentation; and,
4. Require the presentation of supplementary information about all potential diluters to assist financial statement readers in assessing the impact on EPS of assumed conversion.

The balance of this section considers the benefits of each proposed change.

Replacing Primary EPS with Basic EPS

As discussed previously, the importance of anticipating future dilution is evident. It is the authors' belief that the merits of presenting historical EPS data are equally apparent. The issue, then, is why primary EPS ought to be discarded rather than reported as part of a three-level disclosure (i.e., basic, primary, and fully diluted EPS).

Research findings have repeatedly demonstrated that common stock equivalency testing, a critical element in the primary EPS computation, does not produce interpretable results. This leads to the conclusion that the primary EPS statistic conveys a noisy signal. Performing such a garbled transformation of the basic EPS statistic is unlikely to yield incremental information. Thus, the cost of preparing primary EPS must almost certainly exceed any benefit.

The usefulness of primary EPS can also be examined analytically. Ijiri and Jaedicke provide a mathematical definition of reliability, one of the principal characteristics of useful information.[8] Employing their definition of reliability and assuming that dividend policy is a direct function of earnings, it can be demonstrated that, in the circumstances described, basic EPS is a more reliable measure than primary EPS. Put another way, a financial statement reader attempting to determine a relationship between EPS and dividends will be more successful employing basic EPS.

Actual dividends probably change only in response to long run changes in income levels. Even under this "sticky" dividend policy, it seems likely that a lagged model employing basic EPS would outperform primary EPS. In a more complex dividend generating scheme, potential dilution might also be an important factor. While the basic EPS statistic does not incorporate information about dilution potential, the supplementary disclosures recommended in point four of this proposal do. Comprehensive raw data of that type are almost certainly more useful than limited disclosures prepared using questionable assumptions.

Finally, the usefulness of primary EPS can be considered in light of empirical findings. A recent study by Millar, Nunthirapakorn, and Courtenay examines the correlations between five per-share measures and stock returns.[9] The measures examined are primary EPS, fully diluted EPS, simple (basic) EPS, and two forms of cash flow per share. The results indicate ". . . that, for explaining stock returns, primary and fully diluted EPS are the least informative of the earnings numbers studied. Simple and cash flow forms of earnings are significantly more closely related to stock returns than those earnings reported according to APB 15."[10] Considered collectively, these arguments make a strong case for replacing primary EPS with basic EPS.

Discarding the Treasury Stock Method

The issuance of stock in exchange for options and warrants produces cash inflows for the issuing company, but has no direct effect on income. In terms of calculating diluted EPS, an assumed issuance of stock yields an increase in the denominator and no change in the numerator. The result is a reduction in reported EPS. The treasury stock method dampens this effect by assuming that the cash proceeds are used to acquire the company's own shares. Thus, only the net issuance is reflected in the denominator of the EPS calculation. When the shares obtainable under the treasury stock assumption exceed 20 percent of the common shares outstanding, APB 15 recommends the

---

[8] Ijiri, Yuji, and Robert K. Jaedicke, "Reliability and Objectivity of Accounting Measurements," *The Accounting Review*, July 1966, pp. 474–483.

[9] Millar, James A., Thakol Nunthirapakorn and Steve Courtenay, "A Note on the Information Content of Primary and Fully Diluted Earnings Per Share," *Financial Analysts Journal*, September–October 1987, pp. 77–79.

[10] Ibid, p. 79.

modified treasury stock method. The modification involves the additional assumption that funds in excess of those used to acquire 20 percent of the common shares outstanding are applied to reduce debt or purchase government securities. This, or course, generates additional income in the numerator of the EPS calculation.

The purchase of treasury shares and government securities is not the only investment strategy available to management. While these are reasonable choices in given circumstances, expanding plant facilities, building up inventories, and funding pension obligations are also potentially worthwhile uses for option and warrant proceeds. Selecting a use for cash inflows is the prerogative of management and is likely to involve the consideration of numerous factors.

Eliminating the treasury stock method from the calculation of fully diluted EPS has the same effect as assuming the most conservative investment choice, holding a cash balance. Two principal advantages are evident in this treatment. One is that no speculation about management choices is involved in the preparation of the financial statements. The second is that fully diluted EPS then represents the maximum dilution scenario. Presentation of basic and fully diluted EPS is, thus, a disclosure of both endpoints of the range of dilution possibilities.

The distortive effects peculiar to the modified treasury stock method are explored in detail by Barlev.[11] These include the assumption that ". . . funds obtained through the exercise of options and warrants are invested in projects which yield returns lower than the cost of equity capital."[12] Barlev also cites the influences of market and economic conditions on EPS and the potential for management manipulation as shortcomings of the modified treasury stock method. Shank, too, points out the potential problems resulting from the use of market prices in calculating EPS.[13]

In summary, the treasury stock method and its modified form are predicated upon a series of unsupported assumptions. Their use introduces elements of speculation into the calculation of EPS and restricts the range of EPS numbers presented in the financial statements. Eliminating the treasury stock method and presenting supplementary information about potentially dilutive securities should permit financial statement readers to adjust EPS to incorporate their own judgments about the use of option and warrant proceeds.

Abandoning the Three Percent Materiality Standard

SFAC Number 2 discusses materiality guidance, and points out that "The more important a judgment item is, the finer the screen should be that will be

---

[11] Barlev, Benzion, "Contingent Equity and the Dilutive Effect on EPS," *The Accounting Review*, April 1983, pp. 385–393.

[12] Ibid, p. 392.

[13] Shank, John K, "Earnings Per Share, Stock Prices, and APB Opinion No. 15," *Journal of Accounting Research*, Spring, 1971, pp. 165–170.

used to determine whether it is material."[14] The importance of the EPS statistic and its potential dilution suggest that the screen for materiality ought to be very fine. Whether 3 percent dilution is an appropriate threshold is an empirical question that can only be answered with reference to decision makers. Research efforts have not established universally appropriate levels of materiality. Given that the fully diluted EPS calculation must be made before a materiality test can be performed, the only saving apparent in permitting a single, undiluted presentation is in printing costs. Requiring dual presentation by all companies with complex capital structures places all the facts in the hands of those who ultimately define materiality, the financial statement readers, at minimal or no cost. It also lessens the urgency associated with attempts to develop quantitative materiality standards.

Presenting Supplementary Information about Potential Diluters

The presentation of detailed information about potentially dilutive securities makes the proposed EPS reporting format a comprehensive disclosure of historical earnings per share and the full range of future dilution possibilities. The principal additional information envisioned in the supplementary disclosures consists of the dilutive effects of individual securities on basic EPS. Ready access to such information facilitates the calculation of all points in the range of potential dilution and permits analysts to make their own assumptions about conversion timing and likelihood. This disclosure is possible at a relatively small marginal cost, because this information is needed to calculate fully diluted EPS. Additionally, our proposal concentrates currently required capital structure disclosures in the EPS footnote.[15]

Summary

Exhibit 1 illustrates the presentation of EPS disclosures incorporating the suggested amendments to current practice. The background information and calculations necessary to prepare Exhibit 1 are available from the authors.

While the proposed changes in EPS reporting standards would result in an expansion of printed material, they would not require accounting practitioners to employ sophisticated financial modeling techniques or gather large amounts of additional data.[16] Nor would they necessitate speculation about

---

[14] Financial Accounting Standards Board, "Statement of Financial Accounting Concepts Number 2: *Qualitative Characteristics of Accounting Information*," Stamford, CT: May 1980, para. 128.

[15] See APB 15, paragraph 19.

[16] At least two proposals have been advanced which recommend the use of more sophisticated procedures for predicting conversion. These are:

Gaumnitz, Bruce R., and Joel E. Thompson, "Establishing the Common Stock Equivalence of Convertible Bonds," *The Accounting Review*, July 1987, pp. 601–622.

Vigeland, Robert L., "Dilution of Earnings per Share in an Option Pricing Framework," *The Accounting Review*, April 1982, pp. 348–357.

EXHIBIT 1

(on the face of the income statement)
Earnings per share (see Note X)

Without dilution, basic EPS	($8,140,000/900,000)	$9.04
Assuming maximum dilution, fully-diluted EPS	($9,280,060/1,580,000)	$5.87

(among the notes to the financial statements)
Note X:

Both basic and fully diluted EPS were calculated based upon 900,000 weighted average shares outstanding. This estimate reflects the stock split as though it had occurred on January 1. Basic EPS is calculated using historical data about earnings and equity. Fully diluted EPS is a pro forma disclosure presented to illustrate the minimum earnings that would have been available to common shareholders had the holders of other securities exercised their rights to obtain common stock. Management makes no assertions about the likelihood, timing, or amounts of future conversions to common stock. The following table presents information to assist in assessing the dilution potential of individual convertible securities.

Convertible Security	Other Information Available	Income (Numerator) Effect on Basic EPS (in dollars)	Equity (Denominator) Effect on Basic EPS (in common shares)	Assumed Converted in Fully-Diluted EPS?
Stock Options	Note A	$0	30,000[a]	Yes
Convertible Bonds	Note B	$840,060	500,000	Yes
Convertible Preferred Stock	Note C	$300,000	150,000	Yes
Contingent Issuance	Note D	$560,000	75,000	No

[a] The actual shares available under options totaled 30,000. Had all options been exercised, Example Company would have received cash totaling $1,350,000. A common assumption regarding the assumed exercise of options is that the company uses the cash proceeds to acquire treasury shares. Had that assumption been applied in this case, the net issuance of shares would have been 4,038 if treasury shares were purchased at the 1987 average price of $52. 5,893 shares would have been assumed issued had the treasury stock purchases been made at $56, the 1987 ending market price.

management's reactions to possible future exercises of convertibles. SFAC Number 1 states that "The role of financial reporting in the economy is to provide information that is useful in making business and economic decisions . . ."[17] In contrast, as Beaver states, "The analyst community is an industry whose product is information, analysis and interpretation."[18] It is the authors' belief that the proposals set forth in this section would move preparers of EPS disclosures away from the role of financial analysts and

---

[17] Financial Accounting Standards Board, "Statement of Financial Accounting Concepts Number 1: *Objectives of Financial Reporting*," Stamford, CT: November 1978, para. 33.
[18] Beaver, William, "Current Trends in Corporate Disclosure," *Journal of Accountancy*, January 1978, p. 48.

toward the role of financial reporters without increasing the already considerable burden of EPS reporting.[19]

CONCLUSIONS

APB 15 was issued nearly 20 years ago. Since that time, researchers have devoted considerable attention to the calculation and presentation of EPS. This literature suggests widespread concern over the extent to which current reporting standards result in useful disclosures. For example, Boyer and Gibson cite a survey of the readers of *Financial Executive* in which almost three-fourths of the respondents indicated disagreement with the residual security concept. The preferred presentation among that majority was a basic EPS number supplemented by pro forma disclosures incorporating potential dilution. Perhaps more disconcerting are their findings that substantial minorities of practitioners and academics are unable to correctly answer questions about the calculation of EPS under current standards.[20]

Numerous specific changes to the APB 15 format have been proposed, and a few have been incorporated into accounting standards. However, the basic structure and assumptions of APB 15 remain intact. The authors believe that, when considered as a whole, the literature examining EPS suggests the need for a comprehensive evaluation and overhaul of EPS reporting standards. This paper details a proposal to modify EPS reporting to improve its usefulness without significantly increasing the related computational burden. The specific changes proposed include the elimination of primary EPS, the treasury stock method, and the 3 percent materiality standard for dual presentation. Restoration of basic EPS to the face of the income statement and the supplementary disclosure of the effects of individual dilutive securities are also important features of this proposal. While the format proposed and illustrated in this paper is only one of the many possible, the authors strongly believe that EPS reporting should move from selective, pro forma disclosure to comprehensive historical disclosure supplemented by information to assist in anticipating possible future dilution.

[19] The magnitude of this burden is evidenced by the fact that non-public companies are exempted from the requirements of APB 15. See:
Financial Accounting Standards Board, "Statement of Financial Accounting Standards Number 21: *Suspension of the Reporting of Earnings Per Share and Segment Information by Nonpublic Enterprises*," Stamford, CT: April 1978.
[20] Boyer, Patricia A., and Charles H. Gibson. "How About Earnings Per Share?" *CPA Journal*, February 1969.

An Empirical Evaluation of SFAS No. 55

Julie S. Sobery
Southern Illinois University, Carbondale

1. INTRODUCTION

The Accounting Principles Board's *Opinion No. 15* requires publicly held companies which have issued certain common stock equivalent securities to report two earnings-per-share figures, primary earnings per share and fully diluted earnings per share. Primary earnings per share is based on the number of common shares outstanding and the equivalent number of common shares of those securities which *Opinion No. 15* defined to be substantively equivalent to common stock and which have a dilutive effect. Securities treated as common stock and which have a dilutive effect. Securities treated as common stock equivalents and included in the computation of primary earnings per share are those which have a ". . . cash yield to the holder at time of issuance significantly below what would be a comparable rate for a similar security of the issuer without the conversion option" (APB [1969, para. 23]).[1]

APB *Opinion No. 15* defined significantly below a comparable rate as less than 66²/₃ percent of the prime rate. The Financial Accounting Standards Board's *SFAS No. 55* changed the cash yield definition to less than 66²/₃ percent of the average Aa corporate bond yield. The cash yield test involves a one-time classification determination made at the issuance date.

The cash yield to prime interest rate test of common stock equivalency was initially selected as a means of measuring the value of a convertible bond derived from the related common stock; the selection was not conditioned on any assessment of the probability of future conversion. Prime was chosen as the benchmark interest rate because it was believed to be a "practicable, simple, and readily available basis on which to establish the criteria for determining common stock equivalency" (APB [1969, para. 34]).

The FASB amended the calculation of the cash yield test, but did not modify its original function. Because the prime rate is susceptible to such factors as interest rate inversion and market turbulence, its disadvantages become obvious over time. In contrast, the average Aa corporate bond yield is also useful, practical to apply, but more economically related to yields of corporate convertible securities.

From *Journal of Accounting Research* (Autumn 1983), Volume 21, No. 2, pp. 623–628. Reprinted by permission of the Institute of Professional Accounting, Graduate School of Business, University of Chicago. Copyright © 1983 by the Institute of Professional Accounting.
[1] Fully diluted is a pro forma calculation which does not require any subjective assessment of yields (interest rates); rather, all outstanding convertible securities are used in the calculation.

Neither the APB nor the FASB recommended a method for determining common stock equivalency that requires an assessment of the probability of future conversion. The APB stated in *Opinion No. 15:* "neither conversion nor imminence of conversion is necessary to cause a security to be a common stock equivalent" [1969, para. 25]. *SFAS No. 55* did not even mention probability of future conversion, which suggests that the FASB concurred with the APB.

Yet the primary significance of convertible securities to common stockholders is the probability of conversion and the consequent earnings dilution. Actual earnings impairment occurs only upon a real conversion, so the common stock equivalency status of a convertible bond should depend on the probability of future conversion.

This was the criterion employed in several empirical tests of *Opinion No. 15,* for example, Frank and Weygandt [1970], Gibson and Williams [1973], and Rhodes and Snavely [1973]. A review of these studies suggests that the cash yield to prime interest rate test required by *No. 15* has not been an effective measure of common stock equivalency, since it has not been a good predictor of future conversion. Several alternative tests for determining the common stock equivalency status of convertible bonds have been proposed, such as the ratio of conversion value to call price (Frank and Weygandt [1971]), conversion value to market price (Arnold and Humann [1973]), and cash yield to Moody's Baa average interest rate (Holfstedt and West [1971]).

The purpose of this paper is to report the results of tests of whether the cash yield to average Aa corporate bond yield test can distinguish between those convertible bonds which will be converted and those which will not on an ex ante basis. The results indicate that the cash yield test recommended in *SFAS No. 55* has some predictive ability, particularly when applied on a year-to-year basis.

2. DATA AND TESTS

The sample data used consisted of convertible bonds issued in 1975 through 1979 by New York Stock Exchange corporations. Convertible bonds included in *Moody's Bond Record* provided the initial list of convertible bonds. Reported new issues of convertible bonds and amounts were obtained and subjected to annual review. A decrease in face value of bonds outstanding indicated that either conversion or redemption had occurred. Bonds which decreased in amount outstanding were identified in the bimonthly Moody's supplement *News Report,* and convertible bond issues which had experienced either partial or full conversion were retained for further study. *Moody's Bond Record* was used to obtain the bonds' coupon rate and market price in order to compute the cash yield. The average Aa corporate bond yield was obtained from *Moody's Industrial Manual.*

For the first test, I compared the relationship between the average Aa corporate bond yield and the cash yield in order to predict which bonds would be converted in the future and which would not. The accuracy of this

TABLE 1 Accuracy of the Cash Yield to Average Aa Bond Yield Test at Issuance Date

	Convertible Bonds Issued in 1975–79					
	CSE*		Non-CSE**		Total	
Correct	11	19.64%	17	30.36%	28	50.0%
Incorrect	6	10.71%	22	39.29%	28	50.0%
Total	17	30.35%	39	69.65%	56	100.0%

* Common stock equivalent.
** Noncommon stock equivalent.

common stock equivalency test was determined for each class of convertible bonds and as an overall rate. The results appear in Table 1.

Recall that *SFAS No. 55* defines a convertible bond as a common stock equivalent if, at the time of issuance, its cash yield based on its market price is less than 66²/₃ percent of the then-current average Aa corporate bond yield. This is a one-time test to be made only at the date of issuance. Fifty-six convertible bond issues were examined in this study. Twenty-eight (50%) of the convertible bonds were correctly classified employing the *SFAS No. 55* test. For a convertible bond to be correctly classified it either qualified as a common stock equivalent and exhibited full or any partial conversion in future years through 1980, or it qualified as a noncommon stock equivalent and exhibited no conversion. A misclassification was defined as either a convertible bond qualifying as a common stock equivalent that had no conversion or a convertible bond qualifying as a noncommon stock equivalent that experienced conversion.

Seventeen convertible bonds qualified as common stock equivalents, of which 11 issues experienced at least partial conversion. Thirty-nine convertible bond issues were classified as noncommon stock equivalents, of which 17 were not converted. Hence, 50 percent of the bonds were correctly classified, 19.6 percent as common stock equivalents and 30.36 percent as noncommon stock equivalents. Six convertible bonds were incorrectly classified as common stock equivalents (Type I error), that is, each had a cash yield of less than 66²/₃ percent of the average Aa corporate bond yield, but experienced no conversion through 1980. This type of error resulted in an overstatement of the number of common equivalent shares included in earnings per share, resulting in an understatement of earnings per share. Twenty-two convertible bonds were incorrectly classified as noncommon stock equivalents (Type II error) in that they did not have a cash yield equal to or greater than 66²/₃ percent of the average Aa corporate bond yield, but still experienced conversion. This error resulted in an understatement of the number of common equivalent shares included in earnings per share, resulting in an overstatement of earnings per share.

Table 2 provides a detailed analysis of the latter (Type II) error. For each of the 22 issues misclassified as a noncommon stock equivalent, I determined the year(s) of conversion and the percentage of each issue converted. Twelve of these were fully converted by the end of 1980, and four others experienced conversion of over 45 percent of their original issue. It is apparent from these

TABLE 2 Convertible Bonds Misclassified as Noncommon Stock Equivalents

7 Convertible Bonds Issued in 1975 and Misclassified as Non-CSE*		5 Convertible Bonds Issued in 1976 and Misclassified as Non-CSE*		4 Convertible Bonds Issued in 1977 and Misclassified as Non-CSE*		5 Convertible Bonds Issued in 1978 and Misclassified as Non-CSE*		1 Convertible Bond Issued in 1979 and Misclassified as Non-CSE*	
Year	% Converted	Year	% Converted	Year	% Converted	Year	% Converted	Year	% Converted
1977	10.33	1980	2.00	1978	100.00	1980	31.00	1980	100.00
1979	38.66		2.00		100.00		31.00		100.00
1980	23.70	1980	100.00	1980	3.00	1980	100.00		
	72.69		100.00		3.00		100.00		
1977	97.00	1978	100.00	1978	17.70	1980	100.00		
1980	3.00		100.00		17.70		100.00		
	100.00	1978	100.00	1978	100.00	1980	100.00		
1980	100.00		100.00		100.00		100.00		
	100.00	1979	3.80			1979	53.10		
1980	100.00	1980	6.00			1980	40.00		
	100.00		9.80				93.10		
1978	1.60								
1979	20.70								
1980	16.60								
	38.90								
1979	3.75								
1980	56.50								
	60.25								
1977	1.50								
1978	31.50								
1979	1.10								
1980	11.00								
	45.10								

* Noncommon stock equivalent.

TABLE 3 Accuracy of the Cash Yield to Average Aa Bond Yield Test at Year-End

		Convertible Bonds Issued in 1975–1979				
		CSE*		Non-CSE**		Total
Correct	19	12.03%	87	55.06%	106	67.09%
Incorrect	24	15.19%	28	17.72%	52	32.91%
Total	43	27.22%	115	72.78%	158	100.00%

* Common stock equivalent.
** Noncommon stock equivalent.

results that the use of the cash yield to average Aa corporate bond rate common stock equivalency test would have resulted in an overstatement of common stock earnings per share.

It is apparent from the above results that the one-time common stock equivalency test used in APB *Opinion No. 15* and *SFAS No. 55* may not identify as common stock equivalents those convertible bonds which will be converted, and as noncommon stock equivalents those which will not be converted. As a further test, I determined the accuracy of using the cash yield to Aa bond yield based on year-end market variables. The cash yield to Aa bond yield ratio was calculated at year-end for every year the convertible bond was outstanding through 1979. The amount of conversion experienced by the bonds per year was obtained through 1980, and the results are presented in Table 3.

Using an annual common stock equivalency test based on year-end variables, 67 percent were correctly classified as either common stock equivalents (12 percent) or noncommon stock equivalents (55 percent). A Type I (alpha) error occurred for 15 percent of the cases, and a Type II (beta) error for 18 percent of the cases. Overall, the results substantially improved when the yield test was employed on a year-by-year basis.

3. SUMMARY AND CONCLUSIONS

In this paper I have provided results on the accuracy of the present one-time common stock equivalency test, and of a similar test applied on a year-to-year basis using the cash yield to average Aa corporate bond yields. The one-time test correctly classified 50 percent of the convertible bonds as either common stock equivalents or noncommon stock equivalents based on future conversion. The 50-percent error broke down into an 11-percent alpha error and a 39-percent beta error. The beta errors resulted in overstatements of primary earnings per share, violating the conservatism principle.

The results improved when common stock equivalency was determined yearly using year-end estimates for cash yield and average Aa rate. This annual determination of common stock equivalency resulted in correctly classifying 67 percent of the convertible bonds as either debt or equity.

Although the alpha error increased to 15.2 percent, the more serious beta error decreased to 17.7 percent.

One may also conclude from my results and those of other studies in this area that there is probably no reliable indicator of future conversion that yields consistent results over time. Bondholders' decisions to convert or to hold are made independently by individual bondholders. Their decisions are definitely influenced by their perception of current and future common stock prices, so it is unlikely that the accounting profession can formulate a uniform rule to determine common stock equivalency status which will correlate with investors' decisions.

Mr. Halvorson of the APB dissented to the issuance of *Opinion No. 15* for this reason, stating that the problem of predicting conversion of convertible bonds was for financial analysis and not accounting principles. Mr. Walters of the FASB dissented to the issuance of *SFAS No. 55* for the same reason. He believed there was no reason to modify an unsound concept, and that the FASB should amend *Opinion No. 15* to require actual earnings per share instead of pro forma figures of primary earnings per share based on assumptions of common stock equivalency. Such an amendment would be a large undertaking and would require a major reconsideration of *Opinion No. 15*, including not only convertible securities but also stock options, warrants, and rights. There is no present evidence that the FASB intends to do any more in this area.

REFERENCES

Accounting Principles Board. *Opinion No. 15: Earnings per Share*. Stamford, Conn.. APB, 1969.

Arnold, D. R., and T. E. Humann. "Earnings Per Share: An Empirical Test of the Market Parity and the Investment Value Methods." *The Accounting Review* 48 (January 1973): 23–33.

Financial Accounting Standards Board. *Statement of Financial Accounting Standards No. 55: Determining Whether a Convertible Security Is a Common Stock Equivalent—An Amendment of APB Opinion No. 15*. Stamford, Conn.: FASB, 1982.

Frank, W. G., and J. J. Weygandt. "Convertible Debt and Earnings per Share: Pragmatism vs. Good Theory." *The Accounting Review* 45 (April 1970): 280–89.

———. "A Predictive Model for Convertible Debentures." *Journal of Accounting Research* 9 (Spring 1971): 116–26.

Gibson, C. H., and J. D. Williams. "Should Common Stock Equivalents Be Considered in Earnings per Share?" *The CPA Journal* 43 (March 1973): 209–13.

Hofstedt, T. R., and R. R. West. "The APB, Yield Indices, and Predictive Ability." *The Accounting Review* 46 (April 1971): 329–37.

Rhodes, L., and H. F. Snavely. "Convertible Bonds and Earnings per Share." *The CPA Journal* 43 (December 1973): 1116–19.

Ralston Purina: Computing Earnings Per Share for Leveraged ESOPs

Lee J. Seidler

Bear Stearns & Co. Inc.

She stood for some moments . . . with affection beaming in one eye, and calculation shining out of the other.

—Charles Dickens, *Martin Chuzzlewitt*

Computing the fully diluted earnings per share (FDEPS) of an ESOP sponsor can be complicated. Ralston Purina's most recent six- and nine-month EPS computations, appended here, provide a good example. Fully diluted EPS computations of companies with leveraged ESOPs, such as RAL's, include unique adjustments. For RAL, we estimate the adjustments reduced FDEPS for the nine months ended June 30, 1989 by $0.13 (2.4%). These adjustments present a "worst case" rather than a realistic picture of a company's earnings per share. In most situations, analysts can disregard these adjustments. However, the dilutive effect of the common shares underlying the preferred is real and should not be ignored.

In a typical transaction, an ESOP borrows from a financial institution and uses the funds to purchase securities of the sponsor, usually convertible preferred stock. The ESOP debt will be repaid by the preferred dividends and by sponsor contributions.

Since the ESOP is a shell, for accounting purposes, the debt owed to the financial institution is shown in the sponsor's balance sheet. Correspondingly, the preferred shares do not increase equity of the sponsor except to the extent the debt is paid down.

The ESOP convertibles are generally designed not to be dilutive for **primary EPS.** The only impact, as seen in the RAL examples, is subtraction of the preferred dividend, $3.4 million in the March 31 6-month results, from net income in the numerator of the earnings per share computation.

The "if converted" method is used to calculate fully diluted EPS. For a traditional convertible preferred net income is divided by the weighted average number of common shares outstanding plus the common shares assumed issued. This adjustment is also necessary for an ESOP convertible preferred and its dilutive effect should not be ignored. The preferred will eventually be converted into common. For the RAL 9-month computation, we estimate that this adds 2.5 million shares to the denominator and reduces FDEPS by $0.15. The adjustment will add approximately 3.0 and 4.5 million shares to the

From *Accounting Issues* (September 7, 1989), pp. 1–3. Reprinted by permission of Bear Stearns & Co. Inc. Copyright © 1989 by Bear Stearns & Co. Inc.

Ralston Purina Company and Subsidiaries
Computation of Earnings Per Share
(in millions, except per share data)

	6 Mos. ended 3/31/89	9 Mos. ended 6/30/89
Earnings per share of common outstanding		
Earnings from continuing operations	$222.2	$306.0
Dividend on Series A ESOP convertible preferred stock, net of tax	(3.4)	(8.6)
Net earnings from continuing operations	218.8	297.4
Earnings from discontinued operations	71.3	71.3
Net earnings	$290.1	$368.7
Weighted average number of shares outstanding applicable to earnings per common share calculation	65.3	64.1
Earnings per common share outstanding:		
Net earnings from continuing operations	$3.35	$4.64
Earnings from discontinued operations	1.09	1.11
Net earnings	$4.44	$5.75
Earnings per share assuming full dilution		
Earnings from continuing operations	222.2	$306.0
Earnings from discontinued operations	71.3	71.3
Dividend yield differential on converted ESOP preferred shares		(6.1)
Net earnings for fully diluted earnings per share calculation	$293.5	$371.2
Weighted average number of shares outstanding	65.3	64.1
Dilutive effect of stock options..........................	.3	.5
Shares issuable on conversion of debentures	.1	.1
Dilutive effect of deferred compensation awards..........	.1	.1
Convertible preferred stock............................	1.5*	2.5*
"Floor" put	.5*	.5*
Weighted average number of shares and equivalent shares applicable to fully diluted earnings per share calculation	67.8	67.8
Earnings per share assuming full dilution:		
Earnings from continuing operations	$3.28	$4.43
Earnings from discontinued operations	1.05	1.05
Net earnings	$4.33	$5.48

* Bear Stearns estimates.

denominator for the full years 1989 and 1990, respectively. The increase is due to the effects of weighting for the period outstanding.

EPS ADJUSTMENT FOR PREFERRED AND COMMON DIVIDEND DIFFERENTIAL

To repay its loan, the ESOP has two sources of cash: the sponsor corporation's annual contribution and the dividends on the preferred stock. If the preferred were converted, the lower common dividends would have to be supplemented by an additional corporate contribution. It is difficult to hypothesize a conversion of a significant amount of the preferred before the ESOP loan is substantially repaid. Nevertheless, the FASB's Emerging Issues Task Force (EITF) believes that the possibility should be reflected in FDEPS computations. Under the EITF interpretation, since the FDEPS calculation assumes the conversion of the preferred, the numerator must also be adjusted for an assumed additional after-tax corporate contribution. RAL followed that opinion in its 9-month computation, but not in the earlier 6-month figures.

This adjustment, which will decrease as the ESOP loan is repaid, cost RAL $6.1 million in the numerator, reducing 9-month FDEPS by an additional $0.09. However, since the possibility of early conversion is illogical and remote, we believe that analysts should not reduce earnings by the impact of this adjustment.

EPS ADJUSTMENT FOR "FLOOR PUT"

ESOP convertible preferreds have unique provisions that most conventional convertibles do not. One is the "floor put." Since the convertible preferred is typically nontransferable, when a vested employee leaves the plan, the shares in his account must be converted to common. To guarantee a minimum value if the conversion feature is not in the money, the trustee may put the stock to the company at its liquidation value or "floor." The "floor" for Ralston is $110.83 per share. The company can satisfy the "floor put" with cash or additional shares of common stock. The EITF has, at least tentatively, concluded that since the EPS calculation assumes the preferred are converted, it should also assume the "floor put" is exercised if the company's stock price is below the floor. Thus, the denominator in RAL's 6- and 9-month FDEPS calculation was increased by approximately 500,000 additional shares. The number of shares needed for this adjustment will vary from period-to-period with the company's share price. The adjustment is not required when the stock price is above the floor. In addition, prior periods' EPS will be restated if the number of shares contingently issuable subsequently changes because the market price changes. **Analysts should generally ignore this adjustment as well.**

CHAPTER 16

Accounting Changes

Consistency in the use of financial accounting procedures between account-ing periods as well as comparability of financial reports between companies are considered to be essential to a reasonable understanding of the activities of an enterprise. Not surprisingly, consistency and comparability were identi-fied as basic qualities of financial reporting by the Financial Accounting Standards Board (FASB) in its Concepts Statement No. 2.[1] Since there is a general assumption by readers of financial reports that accounting methods have been and will be applied consistently over time, when this is not the case there is need for full disclosure that a change in accounting method has occurred.

The need for disclosure is amplified by the fact that changes in accounting methods could have a material effect on the financial statements, as shown by the case of General Motors Corporation which increased the useful lives of its depreciable assets in 1987 and boosted its income for the year by $1.237 billion (resulting in a reported net income of $3.551 billion). While these types of discretionary accounting changes (i.e., those not mandated by the FASB or regulatory agencies) are commonly undertaken by companies, we do not have a good understanding of why companies do so. With the exception of the adoption or abandonment of LIFO, accounting changes in the U.S. gener-ally do not have mandatory tax-related cash flow consequences to a firm. Hence some other non-cash flow related reasons must motivate a firm to decide to implement an accounting change.

One possible motivation for accounting changes is income management. For example, without the above accounting change, General Motors would have reported a decrease in its 1987 earnings relative to the previous year. Bala G. Dharan and Baruch Lev report that 65 percent of income-increasing accounting changes were made by firms experiencing a decrease in their pre-

[1] "Qualitative Characteristics of Accounting Information," *Statement of Financial Accounting Con-cepts No. 2* (Financial Accounting Standards Board, May 1980).

accounting change earnings, while 70 percent of income-decreasing account-ing changes were made by firms reporting an increase in pre-accounting change earnings.[2] These statistics point to an income-smoothing motivation for accounting changes.

Another possibility is that accounting changes are managers' responses to changes in their environment. For example, it is possible that GM's manage-ment had no choice but to increase the asset lives given the decreased capacity utilization of their plant and equipment as a result of falling sales.[3] A problem with this explanation is that it does not adequately explain the timing of GM's accounting change. It may be that, while changes in a firm's environ-ment create the basic premise for an accounting change, the timing is still a discretionary managerial decision based on income management.[4] As an example, Jennifer Jones finds that companies that sought import relief from the U.S. International Trade Commission made income-decreasing accruals during the agency's investigation period.[5] Finally, it is often postulated that accounting change decisions are influenced by the presence of management compensation and bonus plans that reward the reporting of earnings in-creases. Paul Healy found that the presence of upper and lower limits on earnings growth or similar performance measures in bonus plans partially explained the amount of "accounting accruals" made by companies.[6] Healy's work is one of a large number of articles that examine the "contract" theory of accounting choice postulated by Ross Watts and Jerold Zimmerman.[7] While recent research in understanding accounting changes has been promising, much work remains to be done. A better understanding of the managerial motivations would likely lead to improved disclosure requirements for ac-counting changes.

The current disclosure rules for accounting changes date back to 1971, when the Accounting Principles Board (APB) issued Opinion No. 20. In it, the APB distinguished between a change in accounting principle and a change in an estimate.[8] While both result in footnote disclosures, a change in accoun-ting principle (such as a change in the depreciation method used) also leads to

---

[2] Bala G. Dharan and Baruch Lev, "The Valuation Consequence of Accounting Changes: A Multi-Year Examination," *Journal of Accounting, Auditing & Finance* (Fall 1993), pp. 475–494.

[3] A frequent proponent of this "benign" view of accounting changes is Ray Ball. See his "Discussion of Accounting for Research and Development Costs: The Impact on Research and Development Expenditures," *Journal of Accounting Research* (Supplement 1980), pp. 27–37.

[4] This was a main finding of Bala G. Dharan and Briance Mascarenhas, "Determinants of Accounting Change: An Industry Analysis of Depreciation Change," *Journal of Accounting, Auditing & Finance* (Winter 1992), pp. 1–21.

[5] Jennifer Jones, "Earnings Management During Import Relief Investigations," *Journal of Account-ing Research* (Autumn 1991), pp. 193–228.

[6] Paul M. Healy, "The Effect of Bonus Schemes on Accounting Decisions," *Journal of Accounting and Economics* (April 1985), pp. 85–107.

[7] Ross L. Watts and Jerold L. Zimmerman, "Towards a Positive Theory of the Determination of Accounting Standards," *The Accounting Review* (January 1978), pp. 112–134.

[8] APB Opinion No. 20 also deals with accounting for a change in the accounting entity, and with corrections of errors.

an explanatory paragraph in the auditor's report, while a change in an accounting estimate (such as the depreciation period) is not flagged by the auditor.[9] Moreover, accounting estimate changes are applied prospectively, while accounting principle changes, with a few exceptions, are applied retroactively with the prior periods' income effect shown as an item in the current-period income statement. This distinction in APB Opinion No. 20 between a "principle" change and an "estimate" change ignores the fact that firms might use either kind of accounting change for income management. When the APB issued Opinion No. 20, six of its eighteen members dissented, giving its passage a bare two-thirds majority, the minimum needed. Among the Big Eight representatives on the Board, the vote was split 4-4. One's difficulty in understanding sections of the Opinion is probably related to the trade-offs that had to be made within the Board in order to arrive at a version that would garner the necessary two-thirds approval for passage.

It may be time for the FASB to reexamine many aspects of APB Opinion No. 20. One such area is the disclosure a firm needs to make about the impact on a current year's figures of *prior years'* accounting changes. Using GM's accounting change as an example, adequate disclosures were made by GM about the depreciation estimate change in its 1987 annual report, including the effect of the change on 1987 earnings. However, its 1988 annual report included only a footnote referring to the 1987 change and did not provide the impact of the change on 1988 earnings. Thus GM's shareholders had no way of knowing how much lower the 1988 earnings would have been without the 1987 accounting change. In the following year (1989), the 1987 change was not even mentioned in GM's annual report. Given the long-term earnings impact of accounting changes, it would be useful to require companies to disclose pro forma pre-accounting change earnings data for at least 2 or 3 years following material accounting changes.

A consistent policy for implementation rules for mandated accounting changes also needs to be addressed by a future accounting standard. Recent FASB rules for pensions, post-retirement benefits and deferred taxes allow wide windows of adoption periods for companies to implement the new rules, with each standard specifying a different width of adoption window. The extended adoption periods for these standards caused additional problems for investors in terms of comparability between companies. In addition, while the FASB's reasons for providing extended adoption periods were different, in practice income management may have been an important factor affecting the firm's choice of adoption year.

In their article, "Reporting Changes in Accounting Principles—Time for a

---

[9] "Reports on Audited Financial Statements," *Statement on Auditing Standards No. 58* (New York: American Institute of Certified Public Accountants, April 1988), para. 34, requires the auditor to add an explanatory paragraph following the opinion paragraph of the auditor's report, whenever "there has been a change in accounting principles or in the method of their application that has a material effect on the comparability of the company's financial statements." In practice, explanatory paragraphs are added only for accounting principle changes and not for accounting estimate changes.

Change?" D. Jacque Grinnell and Corine T. Norgaard argue that existing requirements for reporting changes in accounting principles are inadequate. In particular, they criticize the "cumulative effect" and "prospective application" methods of accounting for such changes as being disruptive of the year-to-year comparability so essential in financial statements. The authors' preference is for retroactive application. Their argument is that present standards do not even reflect any general principles of disclosure for such changes but instead are an amalgam of arbitrary rules that may not serve the reader of financial statements well. It is interesting that the authors' policy recommendation—namely, that retroactive application is the best method for reflecting changes in accounting principles, whether voluntary or mandatory—accords with the view expressed by three of the six dissenting Board members in APB Opinion No. 20.

A characterization of the standard-setting environment that allows accounting changes is presented by Lawrence Revsine in "The Selective Financial Misrepresentation Hypothesis." Accounting changes are made possible, of course, by the wide variety of alternative accounting methods permitted by generally accepted accounting principles for many business situations. Revsine argues that this permissive regulatory environment "is not accidental," but instead results from the fact that both the regulators and the regulated benefit from the resulting latitude in presenting firms' performance. Not only do managers prefer "loose" financial reporting standards, shareholders also benefit when accounting manipulations by firms lead to a "smoother" earnings stream which is perceived by the market as a proxy for lower default risk. The advantages to regulators is less clear-cut, but Revsine cites the case of troubled-debt restructuring (FASB Statement No. 15) as an example of regulators' benefits from loose accounting standards.

While academic researchers seem undecided on the motivations for accounting changes, the financial press is generally convinced that income smoothing is the prime motivation. In a *Fortune* article, "Manipulating Profits: How It's Done," Ford S. Worthy says that "most executives prefer to report earnings that follow a smooth, regular, upward path" and would "bank" earnings by "depositing" them in good years and "withdrawing" them in bad years. He groups income manipulation techniques into three classes—accounting method changes, changes in the amounts of discretionary accounting accruals, and changes in the timing of expenses and revenues. Interestingly, only the first type is broadly covered by APB Opinion No. 20. Investors have to resort to sophisticated analytical techniques to identify the second and third types of income manipulation.

Dana Wechsler's "Earnings Helper," a *Forbes* article, is another example of the financial press's interpretation of accounting changes as income manipulation techniques. She focuses on the wide latitude companies have in selecting, and changing, depreciation periods. Blockbuster Entertainment's increase of its amortization period for video tapes from 9 months to 36 months is a clear case of excessive discretion in accounting estimate changes. One might also point out that Blockbuster used a 40-year amortization period for goodwill, although one could safely bet that changes in technology would make video rental stores obsolete long before that.

If we want to find out why managers make accounting changes, perhaps a good place to start is to ask managers. Krishna G. Palepu, a Harvard Business School professor, does just that, in "The Anatomy of an Accounting Change." His case study of Harnischfeger's accounting changes shows that the firm's managers explicitly considered the stock market's reactions to its accounting changes. The managers felt that, while analysts would not be fooled by the accounting changes in the current year, "given the difficulty in tracing the effects of these changes in subsequent years, management did not believe that profits in subsequent years would be adjusted." Our recommendation to amend APB Opinion No. 20 to require the disclosure of pro forma pre-accounting change earnings data would specifically address such concerns. Palepu also provides anecdotal support for the "contract" theory of accounting choice. Harnischfeger's managers felt that their lenders did not provide relief to the firm when it violated some debt covenants, and wanted to avoid similar situations in the future by adopting liberal accounting methods.

BIBLIOGRAPHICAL NOTES

On the topic of income manipulation, see also:

Griffiths, Ian: *Creative Accounting: How to Make Your Profits What You Want Them to Be* (London: Sidgwick & Jackson, 1986).

O'glove, Thornton L., with Robert Sobel: *Quality of Earnings: The Investors' Guide to How Much a Company Is Really Making* (New York: The Free Press, 1987).

Jereski, Laura: "You've Come a Long Way, Shareholder," *Forbes* (July 13, 1987), p. 282. Leading sentence: "Today's mischief with financial reporting pales beside the accounting rascality that was common—and legal—70 years ago."

Jameson, Michael: *A Practical Guide to Creative Accounting* (London: Kogan Page, 1988).

Smith, Terry: *Accounting for Growth: Stripping the Camouflage from Company Accounts* (London: Century Business, 1992).

The Securities and Exchange Commission (SEC) has been more active in the setting of accounting policies in areas where issues of income manipulation arise. An example is the reporting of loan loss allowances by banks. For a discussion, see:

Salwen, Kevin G., and Robin Goldwyn Blumenthal: "Tackling Accounting, SEC Pushes Changes with Broad Impact," *The Wall Street Journal* (September 27, 1990).

APB Opinion No. 28 contains complex rules for interim reporting of accounting changes. For a discussion, see:

Nurnberg, Hugo: "Annual and Interim Financial Reporting of Changes in Accounting Estimates," *Accounting Horizons* (September 1988), pp. 15–25.

In an interesting extension of the income-manipulation research, the following studies focus on the choice of accounting methods by firms facing financial difficulties:

Schwartz, Kenneth B.: "Accounting Changes by Corporations Facing Possible Insolvency," *Journal of Accounting, Auditing & Finance* (Fall 1982), pp. 32–43. The author finds that firms facing possible insolvency tend to make four times as many income-increasing accounting changes as other firms.

Elliott, John A., and Wayne H. Shaw: "Write-Offs as Accounting Procedures to Manage Perceptions," *Journal of Accounting Research* (Supplement 1988), pp. 91–119.

Lilien, Steven, Martin Mellman and Victor Pastena: "Accounting Changes: Successful versus Unsuccessful Firms," *The Accounting Review* (October 1988), pp. 642–656.

DeAngelo, Harry, Linda DeAngelo and Douglas J. Skinner: "Accounting Choice in Troubled Companies," Working Paper, University of Southern California (January 1992).

Reporting Changes in Accounting Principles—Time for a Change?

D. Jacque Grinnell
University of Vermont

Corine T. Norgaard
University of Connecticut

A change in an accounting principle used by a reporting entity may significantly affect financial statement measurements and other related accounting data. Proper interpretation of financial data may be difficult, and the comparability of such data diminished, without adequate accounting and disclosure of the effects of such a change. The objective of reporting the effects of a change in an accounting principle should be to enhance understanding and interpretation of the change.

The adequacy of the current system of reporting the effects of changes in accounting principles has been questioned by the Accounting Standards Executive Committee of the American Institute of CPAs. In a letter to the Financial Accounting Standards Board, AcSEC called for a reconsideration of those provisions of Accounting Principles Board Opinion No. 20, *Accounting Changes*.[1] The purpose of this article is to analyze and evaluate the current

From *Journal of Accountancy* (December 1979), pp. 64–72. Reprinted by permission of the American Institute of Certified Public Accountants, Inc. Copyright © 1979 by the American Institute of Certified Public Accountants, Inc. Opinions of the authors are their own and do not necessarily reflect policies of the AICPA.

[1] Letter from Raymond C. Lauver, chairman, Accounting Standards Executive Committee, to Marshall S. Armstrong, chairman, Financial Accounting Standards Board, March 25, 1977.

reporting requirements for accounting principle changes in order to determine whether alternative practices should be adopted.

BACKGROUND

Current treatment of a change in accounting principle is governed by whether the change is voluntary (made at the discretion of management) or mandatory (necessitated by a pronouncement of an authoritative body). In the first case, the manner in which the change is reported is governed by APB Opinion No. 20.[2] In the second case, the appropriate treatment is prescribed by each specific pronouncement.

Voluntary Changes

Opinion No. 20 requires that, in general, the change's cumulative effect on retained earnings for years prior to the year of change be computed and reported as part of the change year's income. Pro forma income calculations, together with related earnings per share data, must be disclosed for all periods presented as if the newly adopted accounting principle had been applied retroactively. Disclosure of the new principle's effect on the change year's income and earnings per share must also be made.

Opinion No. 20 cited three specific exceptions to the general cumulative effect treatment, and it requires, for these cases, retroactive application of the new principle through restatement of the financial statements of prior periods.[3] The APB justified these exceptions to the general cumulative effect treatment by stating that certain changes in accounting principles are such that the advantages of retroactive application outweigh the disadvantages. In these cases, the effect of the new principle on income and earnings per share of the change year and of all prior years for which income statements are presented must be disclosed.

In addition, Opinion No. 20 recognized that, in some cases, the cumulative effect may not be determinable, and it cited, as an example, the change in inventory cost from the FIFO to the LIFO method. The prescribed treatment of changes of this type is to disclose the effect of the change on income and earnings per share of the change year and to explain the reasons for omitting the cumulative income effect and pro forma income and per share data for prior years.

In still other cases, while the total cumulative effect on prior years' income is determinable, the identification of the effect with specific prior years may not be possible due to lack of adequate information. An example cited in Opinion No. 20 concerns changing from the completed contract to the per-

---

[2] Accounting Principles Board Opinion No. 20, *Accounting Changes* (New York: AICPA, 1971).
[3] The three cases cited are (1) a change from LIFO to another inventory costing method, (2) a change in accounting for long-term construction projects and (3) a change to or from the "full cost" method used by extractive industries. See APB Opinion No. 20, par. 27.

centage-of-completion method of accounting for long-term contracts. In such cases, the reasons for not showing pro forma information for prior years should be disclosed.

Mandatory Changes

APB Opinions. The accounting and reporting requirements of Opinion No. 20 do not extend to certain accounting principle changes made to implement recommendations of specialized industry pronouncements of the AICPA or to mandatory accounting principle changes made to conform with APB opinions and FASB statements of financial accounting standards.

When APB Opinion No. 20 was issued in 1971, it permitted AICPA industry audit guides, which dealt with auditing procedures and accounting practices for specialized industries, to prescribe methods of reporting the effects of changing to recommended principles applicable to these specialized industries.[4] Subsequently, the AICPA issued a new series of specialized industry accounting guides, with each guide specifying the manner of reporting the effects of accounting principle changes to conform with its recommendations. The industry accounting guide series has now been replaced by statements of position concerning specialized industry accounting practices. The FASB has issued Interpretation No. 20, *Reporting Accounting Changes Under AICPA Statements of Position*, which states

> For purposes of applying *APB Opinion No. 20*, an enterprise making a change in accounting principle to conform with the recommendations of an AICPA statement of position shall report the change as specified in the statement. If an AICPA statement of position does not specify the manner of reporting a change in accounting principle to conform with its recommendations, an enterprise making a change in accounting principle to conform with the recommendations of the statement shall report the change as specified by Opinion No. 20.[5]

The general policy of the APB was that its opinions, unless otherwise stated, were intended to be applied prospectively, not retroactively. This general policy did not necessarily rule out retroactive application at the election of the accounting entity. For example, Opinion No. 11, *Accounting for Income Taxes*, stated that "the Board recognizes that companies may apply this Opinion retroactively to periods prior to the effective date to obtain comparability in financial presentations for the current and future periods."[6]

In other instances, the APB did rule out retroactive application by provision in the specific opinion. For example, Opinion No. 8, *Accounting for the Cost of Pension Plans*, stated that "the effect of any changes in accounting

---

[4] Ibid., par. 4.

[5] FASB Interpretation No. 20, *Reporting Accounting Changes Under AICPA Statements of Position* (Stamford, Conn.: FASB, 1977), par. 5.

[6] Accounting Principles Board Opinion No. 11, *Accounting for Income Taxes* (New York: AICPA, 1967), par. 67.

methods made as a result of the issuance of this Opinion should be applied prospectively . . . and not retroactively by an adjustment of retained earnings or otherwise."[7] Similar prohibitions of retroactive application are provided in several other opinions.

In still other cases, the APB prohibited the prospective approach by specifically calling for retroactive application. Examples include APB Opinion No. 18, *The Equity Method of Accounting for Investments in Common Stock*, and two related opinions, Nos. 23 and 24, dealing with income tax considerations. In Opinion No. 23, as well as No. 24, the APB stated that "the conclusions of the Board . . . represent a clarification of current practice" and "accordingly, this Opinion should be applied retroactively. . . ."[8] In elaborating, the board stated further that "an adjustment resulting from a change in accounting method to comply with this Opinion should be treated as an adjustment of prior periods, and financial statements presented for the periods affected should be restated."[9]

In short, all the APB opinions call for either prospective or retroactive application of the provisions, or permit either. In no case, either with respect to opinions issued prior or subsequent to Opinion No. 20, did the APB stipulate the use of the cumulative effect method for implementing a mandated accounting principle change.

FASB Statements. The method of transition to conform with new requirements is prescribed by each specific statement. The statements selected for comparison in this article are those which are concerned with financial statement measurement alternatives as opposed to mere disclosure of information or statement classification. In cases where changes in accounting measurement principles are mandated, three basic transition methods exist as potential choices for implementing the changes: retroactive application through prior period restatement; prospective application; and the cumulative effect method in accordance with APB Opinion No. 20. All three transition methods have been selected at various times, although retroactive application has been the dominant choice. Further, the choice of transition method has frequently been changed between exposure draft and final statement.

Only once, in the case of Statement No. 5, *Accounting for Contingencies*, was the cumulative effect method prescribed in a final statement as the basis for implementing a mandated accounting principle change. However, in Statement No. 11, *Accounting for Contingencies—Transition Method*, the FASB reversed its position and displaced the cumulative effect method by requiring a modified retroactive application approach for implementing Statement No.

---

[7] Accounting Principles Board Opinion No. 8, *Accounting for the Cost of Pension Plans* (New York: AICPA, 1966), par. 49.
[8] Accounting Principles Board Opinion No. 23, *Accounting for Income Taxes—Special Areas* (New York: AICPA, 1972), par. 32.
[9] Ibid.

5. The FASB stated that the decision to change the transition method was reached after a "reconsideration of all the circumstances."[10] However, the change was brought about primarily, it would appear, because of inconsistencies in the transition method originally required for Statement No. 5 versus that for Statement No. 8, *Accounting for the Translation of Foreign Currency Transactions and Foreign Currency Financial Statements.* Statement Nos. 8 and 11 recognized a hybrid approach that combines prior period restatement with the cumulative effect method. "[I]nformation presented shall be restated for as many consecutive periods . . . as is practicable, and the cumulative effect . . . on the retained earnings at the beginning of the earliest period restated . . . shall be included in determining net income of that period."[11]

A further modification of the hybrid approach taken in Statement Nos. 8 and 11 is associated with Statement No. 13, *Accounting for Leases.* In implementing the provisions of Statement No. 13, only prospective application is initially required. Retroactive application is required after 1980, although earlier adjustment is encouraged. After retroactive application is accomplished, post-1976 income statements and balance sheets as of year-end 1976 and thereafter must be restated when presented. Earlier financial statements, when presented, must also be retroactively adjusted to the extent practicable with the cumulative effect on retained earnings at the beginning of the earliest period restated included in the net income of that period.

In Statement No. 9, *Accounting for Income Taxes—Oil and Gas Producing Companies,* the FASB added an additional shade of gray to the accounting for its mandated accounting principle changes by "permitting" as opposed to "requiring" retroactive application in certain specified situations. If the reporting entity does not choose to restate, it must prospectively apply the new provisions; the cumulative effect method is not permitted as an alternative to retroactive application.

JUSTIFICATION FOR TRANSITION METHODS ADOPTED

Voluntary Changes

When it issued Opinion No. 20, the APB clearly was concerned with abuses developing from a switch in accounting principle when circumstances did not warrant such a switch. The APB stated

> The Board concludes that in the preparation of financial statements there is a presumption that an accounting principle once adopted should not be changed in accounting for events and transactions of a similar type. Consis-

---

[10] Statement of Financial Accounting Standards No. 11, *Accounting for Contingencies—Transition Method* (Stamford, Conn.: FASB, 1975), par. 6.

[11] Ibid., par. 10.

tent use of accounting principles from one accounting period to another
enhances the utility of financial statements to users by facilitating analysis
and understanding of comparative accounting data.[12]

The presumption that an entity should not change an accounting principle may be overcome only if the enterprise justifies the use of an alternative
acceptable accounting principle on the basis that it is preferable.[13]

Accordingly, Opinion No. 20 requires that the justification for a principle
change be disclosed in the financial statements in terms of "why the newly
adopted accounting principle is preferable."[14]

Since the cumulative effect method highlights, as a special item in the
income statement, the retroactive impact on income of an accounting principle change, it may be reasoned that the method was adopted as a punitive
measure to inhibit arbitrary or inappropriate principle changes. In fact, three
members of the APB dissented to the issuance of the opinion on the basis of
their belief that this method was adopted as a disciplinary measure rather
than as a way of enhancing the usefulness of financial statements.

Mandatory Changes

While the expressed policy of the APB was that its opinions, unless otherwise
stated, were intended to be applied prospectively and not retroactively, the
board apparently was not disposed to provide reasons for adopting this
policy. It might be presumed that fear of dilution of public confidence in
previously reported financial statements was a prime factor militating against
retroactive application. As noted earlier, there were some exceptions to this
general approach, such as in the case of Opinion No. 11 where the board did
permit retroactive application to obtain comparability in financial presentations.

Although no stated policy on transition methods has been adopted by the
FASB, there appears to be a growing propensity to select the retroactive
application approach unless special circumstances dictate otherwise. The
selection of the retroactive application method has been made on the basis
that it will provide the most useful information for comparing financial data
for periods after the effective date of a particular statement with data presented for earlier periods. This presumption that retroactive restatement
through prior period adjustment provides the most useful information is
clearly acknowledged in several final statements (including nos. 2, 7, 8, 11, 13
and 19). This view also was acknowledged as the basis for selecting the
retroactive application method in the exposure drafts for Statement Nos. 5
and 12, although the choice of method was later altered in the final statements.

Departures from the retroactive application approach generally have been

---

[12] APB Opinion No. 20, par. 15.
[13] Ibid., par. 16.
[14] Ibid., par. 17.

made on the basis of extenuating circumstances. In Statement No. 5, the cumulative effect method was selected, in part because there might be "significant difficulties involved in determining the degree of probability and estimability that had existed in prior periods."[15] The amendment of that statement by Statement No. 11, as noted earlier, was justified by the FASB on the basis of a "reconsideration of all circumstances," but primarily on the basis of inconsistencies with the treatment required by Statement No. 8. In Statement No. 8, the FASB required the use of retroactive application to the extent practicable since "restatement requires the availability of records or information that an enterprise may no longer have or that its past procedures did not require."[16]

Again in Statement No. 13, based on similar reasoning, retroactive application is required to the extent practicable, but is coupled with a 4-year transition period before full implementation is necessitated. The purpose of this 4-year grace period is to give companies time to resolve problems of data accumulation and issues relating to restrictive covenants in loan agreements.

In the case of applying Statement No. 12, *Accounting for Certain Marketable Securities*, retroactive application was initially proposed in the exposure draft, but prospective application was ultimately selected in the final statement. The prospective approach was justified as follows:

> The Board has obtained information . . . that a number of companies have in past years made substantial reclassifications of marketable equity securities as between current and noncurrent assets. With the Board's decision to provide for separate portfolios of current and noncurrent marketable equity securities with different accounting for changes in carrying value of the two portfolios, the number of and seemingly divergent bases for reclassifications that have occurred in recent years would, in the case of retroactive restatement, result in less rather than more comparability.[17]

The FASB also required prospective application of Statement No. 15, *Accounting by Debtors and Creditors for Troubled Debt Restructurings*, on the basis that comparability would not be greatly enhanced by prior period restatement and of the difficulty in generating the information required for restatement.

In summary, a marked contrast in transition methods for implementing voluntary and mandatory accounting principle changes is apparent. While the cumulative effect method serves as the general approach for implementing voluntary changes, this method has not been considered appropriate for implementing mandatory changes. Failure to adopt the cumulative effect method for implementing mandatory changes adds additional credibility to

---

[15] Statement of Financial Accounting Standards No. 5, *Accounting for Contingencies* (Stamford, Conn.: FASB, 1975), par. 104.

[16] Statement of Financial Accounting Standards No. 8, *Accounting for the Translation of Foreign Currency Transactions and Foreign Currency Financial Statements* (Stamford, Conn.: FASB, 1975), par. 241.

[17] Statement of Financial Accounting Standards No. 12, *Accounting for Certain Marketable Securities* (Stamford, Conn.: FASB, 1975), par. 41.

the view that the method was intended as a punitively oriented way of treating voluntary accounting principle changes.

Further, a marked difference in attitude toward implementing mandatory changes exists between the APB and the FASB. The general approach of the APB was one of prospective application whereas the FASB tends to prefer the use of the retroactive approach to the extent practicable.

MANDATORY VERSUS VOLUNTARY ACCOUNTING CHANGES

In determining if it is appropriate to change the existing system for implementing accounting principle changes, a basic question that must be answered is that of whether we should distinguish between voluntary changes and mandatory changes. The AICPA Accounting Standards Executive Committee has pointed out three factors in support of more congruence in implementing voluntary and mandatory accounting principle changes: the financial accounting and reporting environment has changed substantially since the issuance of Opinion No. 20; inconsistencies result under the current system; and management may be reluctant to voluntarily adopt different accounting principles considered by it to be preferable.[18]

There can be little doubt as to the validity of the first factor. Since Opinion No. 20 was issued, the range of acceptable accounting and reporting alternatives has significantly narrowed and continues to diminish through the issuance of pronouncements by authoritative bodies. For example, the range of permitted practices has been reduced in the important and controversial areas of research and development costs, leases and investments.

Further, another inhibitor to inappropriate changes in accounting principles has been established by the Securities and Exchange Commission. Accounting Series Release No. 177, *Notice of Adoption of Amendments to Form 10-Q and Regulation S-X Regarding Interim Financial Reporting*, requires the independent accountant to state whether or not a voluntary principle change by a client in certain SEC filings is to an alternative which in the accountant's judgment is preferable under the circumstances.[19] The SEC holds that the justification of a voluntary principle change by management is inadequate unless it is sufficient to persuade an independent accountant that the new principle results in better measurement of business operations in the particular circumstances.[20] In addition, SEC requirements concerning the reporting

[18] Letter from AcSEC to FASB.

[19] Securities and Exchange Commission, Accounting Series Release No. 177, *Notice of Adoption of Amendments to Form 10-Q and Regulation S-X Regarding Interim Financial Reporting*, September 10, 1975; also see Securities and Exchange Commission, Staff Accounting Bulletin No. 6, *Interpretations of ASR No. 177, Relating to Interim Financial Reporting*, March 1, 1976, and Staff Accounting Bulletin No. 14, *Amended Interpretations Relating to Reporting Requirements for Accounting Changes*, February 3, 1977.

[20] For an excellent discussion of the preferability issue see Lawrence Revsine, "The Preferability Dilemma," JofA, Sept. 77, pp. 80–89.

of client disagreements with auditors when there is a change in auditors may help to curb abuses brought about by undesirable principle changes.[21]

The contention that inconsistencies arise because of current reporting requirements also is legitimate. For example, if a company adopts a change voluntarily, it may have to account for the results of the change using the cumulative effect method. On the other hand, if another company made the same change, but did so at a later date as the result of an FASB statement, the change would undoubtedly be accounted for in a manner other than that based on the cumulative effect method. Under these circumstances, it appears logical that the manner of implementing accounting principle changes should provide the same result irrespective of whether such changes are voluntary or imposed through an authoritative pronouncement.

A third argument concerns the behavioral effect of the cumulative effect method on management decisions. A company that is considering the voluntary adoption of a different accounting principle could well be penalized by having to absorb a lump-sum charge to income in the year of change. As a result, management may be reluctant to adopt a new principle which it genuinely considers to be preferable. Conversely, management might be motivated to adopt a less desirable accounting principle, if such adoption was to result in a lump-sum credit to income in the year of change.

In summary, one can hardly take issue with the position that voluntary accounting principle changes which endanger the credibility of financial accounting and reporting and facilitate manipulation should be discouraged. However, the objective of restraining inappropriate accounting principle changes should not be accomplished through the imposition of transition rules which seemingly are intended as disciplinary measures, but which may well have a dysfunctional effect. Accounting rules for implementing accounting principle changes should serve to improve, rather than impair, the quality of financial measurements. The professional judgment and expertise of the independent auditor must be relied on as the basis for monitoring the validity of accounting principle changes. Since the issuance of APB Opinion No. 20, the range of available accounting principle alternatives has been reduced and new safeguards have been built into the system to restrain the adoption of inappropriate accounting principle changes. Consequently, little support can be found for the view that voluntary and mandatory accounting principle changes should be accounted for differently.

ESTABLISHING TRANSITION METHOD GUIDELINES

Questions of merit aside, APB Opinion No. 20 does provide a general frame of reference for implementing voluntary accounting principle changes. No similar basic framework exists for implementing mandatory accounting prin-

---

[21] Securities and Exchange Commission, Accounting Series Release No. 165, *Notice of Amendments to Require Increased Disclosure of Relationships Between Registrants and Their Independent Public Accountants*, December 20, 1974.

ciple changes; rather, transition approaches are established on a case-by-case basis without reference to an established policy. To provide more consistency between voluntary and mandatory changes, and to ensure consistency within the context of mandatory changes, the need exists for replacing that portion of APB Opinion No. 20 concerning accounting principle changes with new guidelines for implementing all accounting principle changes.

Cumulative Effect and Prospective Application Methods

In developing policy guidelines for implementing accounting principle changes, a preference for one of the three basic transition methods must be established. The cumulative effect method has little theoretical support as a general implementation approach. The primary deficiency of the cumulative effect method concerns its failure to maintain comparability of financial measurements over time. This lack of comparability is particularly acute over the 3-year period spanning the change year. Income for the year preceding the change year would be based on the old principle; income for the change year would be based on the new principle and also would include the cumulative effect of the change; and income for the year subsequent to the change year would be based on the new principle.

A related criticism of the method concerns that of distortion of the results of current year's operations through inclusion in the change year's income, as a current period item, of the "catch-up" adjustment which is applicable to prior years. The distortion of the change year's income could be avoided, and comparability of income of the change year with that of subsequent years obtained, by including the cumulative effect as an adjustment to the beginning balance of retained earnings for the change year. However, noncomparability with income of years prior to the change year would remain.

Although prospective application avoids the problems of determining and reporting a cumulative effect adjustment, it also is subject to criticism on the basis of noncomparability of results of the change year and subsequent years with those of the years preceding the change year. In addition, the measurement of operating results for the change year, and for a number of years following, is based on a combined use of the old and new principles.

Retroactive Application

While practical problems of estimating and reconstructing past data may exist, the retroactive approach to implementation of accounting principle changes has a conceptual advantage over the other approaches. The retroactive application method is the only approach which provides complete comparability of financial statements generated over time by a company. The FASB has frequently stressed the benefits of retroactive application in terms of providing more meaningful and comparable financial statements. The APB also acknowledged the merits of retroactive application. It stated in APB Opinion No. 9:

> A change in the application of accounting principles may create a situation in which retroactive application is appropriate. In such situations, these changes should receive the same treatment as that for prior period adjustments.[22]

While recognizing a difference between accounting principle changes and prior period adjustments, the APB also acknowledged that the same accounting treatment was applicable to both, namely, retroactive application. Subsequently, this Opinion No. 9 position was altered by Opinion No. 20 with the following comment:

> Paragraph 25 of APB Opinion No. 9 is superseded. Although the conclusion of that paragraph is not modified, this Opinion deals more completely with accounting changes.[23]

It is also interesting to note that the APB in the original exposure draft of Opinion No. 20 stated:

> The Board concludes that where changes in accounting methods are appropriate, consistency of treatment is overriding and that accounting changes, except in the instances explained hereinafter, should be computed and applied retroactively by restating financial statements presented for any period affected by the change.[24]

This position was subsequently changed in a second exposure draft leading to the final opinion.

A major criticism of the retroactive application approach is that it might lead to erosion of public confidence in the independent auditor who reported on the original statements and in financial reporting in general. Conversely, one may argue that, without retroactive application, financial presentations lead to investor confusion and make comparisons difficult or impossible. This, in turn, might lead to greater dilution of public confidence.

While past decisions by users of financial statements were made on the basis of the old numbers which the auditors approved, this does not justify prohibiting retroactive restatement for changes to preferable accounting principles. Financial statements should be viewed as tentative and subject to revision if judgments and subjective assessments are subsequently altered in light of further information and the development of improved accounting methods. Although not directly related to accounting principle changes, there

---

[22] Accounting Principles Board Opinion No. 9, *Reporting the Results of Operations* (New York: AICPA, 1966), par. 25.

[23] APB Opinion No. 20, par. 5.

[24] Accounting Principles Board Exposure Draft, *Proposed APB Opinion: Changes in Accounting Methods and Estimates* (New York: AICPA, February 16, 1970), par. 11.

is a precedent for revision in another area of accounting, namely, the audit function. Because of new information or changed circumstances, the auditor, in updating his report on previously issued financial statements, may express an opinion different from that expressed in an earlier report.[25]

Past decisions by users of financial statements cannot be altered. It is current and future decisions which are relevant. These new decisions should be based on the best possible information available which includes measurements based on the application of different, if preferable, accounting principles. Ideally, for current decision-making purposes, comparative financial statements should be presented on a consistent basis using that set of accounting principles considered to be the best under the existing circumstances. Of course, a full and complete disclosure of the impact of a principle change on the current and previously issued financial statements is appropriate. If firms and their auditors, relative to voluntary changes, and the FASB and other authoritative bodies, relative to mandatory changes, genuinely believe that a different principle improves the quality of financial measurements, then it should, in most cases, improve the measurement of past as well as current and future results.

In the final analysis, the comparability of financial data which results through retroactive application and restatement is a compelling argument in support of this transition method for implementing accounting principle changes. Having a set of internally consistent statements and related statistics based on a common set of accounting principles is a strong reason for the adoption of this method as the general mode for implementing accounting principle changes.

While the authors believe that retroactive application represents the best approach for implementing accounting principle changes under normal circumstances, it is not practicable to prescribe a single approach for implementing all changes. However, exceptions to retroactive application should be made only when special circumstances exist to justify modification or which preclude its use. For example, the lack of information relating to prior periods or other problems of data accumulation may preclude strict retroactive application; in such cases, a modified or hybrid approach might be in order, possibly along the lines taken in Statement Nos. 8 and 11, or No. 13. In other rare situations, determining the impact of a principle change on prior years' statements may require arbitrary assumptions, for example, when adopting the LIFO method of inventory costing; prospective application would appear necessary under these circumstances.

Although this discussion has been concerned exclusively with accounting principle changes which influence financial statement measurements, many pronouncements of authoritative bodies deal with information disclosure and statement classification. In these situations, implementation by retroactive

---

[25] Statement on Auditing Standards No. 15, *Reports on Comparative Financial Statements* (New York: AICPA, 1976), par. 6–7. Also found in *AICPA Professional Standards*, "Report With an Updated Opinion Different From a Previous Opinion" (Chicago, Ill.: Commerce Clearing House, 1977), AC sec. 505.06–07.

application might also serve as the ideal norm, with limited retroactive application or prospective application justified in particular circumstances.

SUMMARY AND CONCLUSIONS

There appears to be little theoretical justification for maintaining the existing framework for implementing voluntary accounting principle changes in a manner different from those which are mandated by authoritative bodies. From a practical viewpoint, the continuing development of new standards by authoritative bodies which tend to reduce the range of acceptable accounting alternatives, and the development of new safeguards by the SEC, serve to restrain alleged abuses stemming from inappropriate accounting principle changes.

The need exists to develop new guidelines for implementing voluntary and mandatory accounting principle changes in a consistent and logical manner. Based on the importance and utility of statement comparability and trend analysis, the retroactive application and restatement approach should serve as the general means of implementing principle changes, with special circumstances dictating departures from this norm.

The Selective Financial Misrepresentation Hypothesis

Lawrence Revsine
Northwestern University

Before the advent of modern technology and communication, decisionmaking was simpler in one critical respect—direct observation provided the basis for most judgments. For example, manufacturing efficiency was assessed by an owner who personally monitored the workforce; similarly, municipal decisions were made in town meetings by citizens who debated individually experienced events.

As business and society grew more complex, it became difficult to make financial decisions by directly observing the important variables. This com-

From *Accounting Horizons* (December 1991), pp. 16–27. Reprinted by permission of the American Accounting Association and the author. Copyright © 1991 by the American Accounting Association.

Author's note: The author gratefully acknowledges the helpful comments of James R. Boatsman, Ronald A. Dye, Dan Givoly, James J. Leisenring, Thomas Lys, Paul B. W. Miller, Arthur R. Wyatt and Stephen A. Zeff and financial support from the KPMG Peat Marwick Foundation. The viewpoints expressed in this paper are not necessarily those of the above named individuals and organization.

plexity gave rise to financial reporting since "abstractions" (or surrogates) became necessary to summarize events and to provide information for more complex analyses. Although originally a *consequence* of societal complexity, the surrogates—by facilitating broader spans of control—eventually bred even more complexity. Today virtually all financial decisions in both the private and the public sector use accounting surrogates rather than directly observed events as the basis for action. Not surprisingly, managers, as well as public policy makers, gradually learned that while the events that affect performance often cannot be controlled, the way that people *perceive* these events can be controlled. Manipulating the surrogates provides decision-makers with a means for influencing people's perceptions of managerial performance.

Financial reporting rules in both the private and public sector are often arbitrary, complicated, and misleading. Most critics view this situation as accidental, a result of bad judgments by standard setters and regulators. By contrast, this paper advances the hypothesis that the problem is not accidental, but instead results from contrived and flexible reporting rules promulgated by standard setters who have been "captured" by the intended regulatees and others involved in the financial reporting process.[1] Regulatees desire such rules because the resulting latitude allows them flexibility in depicting their performance.[2] Interestingly, other participants—shareholders, auditors, standard setters/public policy makers, and even academics—frequently derive simultaneous benefits from these misrepresentations. Thus, the often articulated financial reporting objective (FASB, 1980, para. 63)—correspondence between accounting numbers and the events those numbers purport to represent—is not always followed in practice.

---

[1] For those unfamiliar with the term, regulatory "capture" describes a process where the ostensible purpose of regulation—protection of consumers—is eventually reversed and regulatees become the beneficiaries (Stigler, 1971). This happens largely because of personnel movement between the regulatory agency and the regulatees.

While it regrettably conjures a pejorative image, the phrase "regulatory capture" is not intended to impugn the integrity of standard setters. Instead, the point is that everyone is influenced by their background and becomes comfortable with familiar perspectives and experiences. This is inevitable and natural. Unfortunately, in the regulatory sphere, it is also antithetical to the intended purpose of regulation.

[2] Those who transact with managers understand that flexible financial reporting standards facilitate opportunistic behavior (see Jensen and Meckling, 1976). Contracts are presumably adjusted to reflect these anticipated costs. Since the cost of the anticipated opportunistic behavior is borne by the presumed perpetrators (in the form of lower salaries, etc.), there is an incentive on the part of managers and others to lower these "agency costs." Detailed reporting standards and audited statements can be viewed as mechanisms for reducing the costs by tying contract terms to the agreed-upon standards.

All parties to the transaction also understand that monitoring contracts is costly. Because of this, there is evidence that contracts are simply linked to GAAP and not adjusted for "artificial" effects like the impact of changed reporting rules (e.g., Simon, 1983; Healy et al., 1987). If contracts are simply linked to GAAP, there is an immediate incentive on the part of potential perpetrators to favor reporting standards that facilitate opportunistic behavior. Thus, a preference for flexible reporting rules is plausible even where agency costs are totally borne by the prospective perpetrators.

Instead, I argue that financial reporting is sometimes better characterized by the phrase *selective financial misrepresentation*. This selective financial misrepresentation hypothesis cuts across both public[3] and private sectors since participants in both sectors are motivated to support standards that selectively misrepresent economic reality when it suits their purpose.

I will illustrate the incentives that motivate various parties to misrepresent financial events. One must understand these incentives in order to appreciate the pitfalls that confront financial standard setters.

THE PROBLEM

Managers, shareholders, auditors and standard setters all derive benefits from selective financial misrepresentation. The motives for misrepresentation by each of these groups are presented in this section.

Managers

Virtually all U.S. companies have management compensation plans tied to reported earnings numbers; consequently, managers have a natural incentive to increase reported profit since higher profit means higher compensation. However, external factors that are beyond managers' control sometimes drive real economic performance to levels too low for bonus attainment. But if flexible accounting rules are permitted, managers can shift income between years and thereby increase total bonus payouts. To facilitate these income shifts, managers prefer "loose" reporting standards over "tight" standards.[4]

Historical cost accounting for investments in marketable securities exemplifies a required "loose" financial reporting standard. To illustrate, under historical costing, real economic gains from investment activities do not appear in the financial statements when they occur. Instead, such gains are recognized only when managers choose to sell the securities, perhaps years after the gains initially arose. By adroitly timing sales of appreciated investments, managers can use the belatedly reported gains to offset current period operating shortfalls.

---

[3] As used in this paper, "public sector financial reporting" extends beyond reporting by government agencies. It also includes accounting rules for enterprises whose performance can lead to direct economic losses for individuals who are neither owners nor direct transactors. Publicly regulated enterprises like S&Ls are a prime example. The distinguishing feature in such settings is that the market forces by which individuals can protect themselves from financial misrepresentations are limited. Specifically, an investor with superior analytic ability could have avoided S&L stocks (or sold them short) in response to the misleading regulatory accounting principles (or RAP accounting) statements. However, once the securities market as a whole impounds these effects, there is no convenient, efficient market mechanism for knowledgeable individuals to protect themselves from the social costs (e.g., higher taxes) occasioned by the S&L bailout. Thus, "public sector" refers to those areas in which market mechanisms are either partially or totally ineffective.

[4] A loose standard is defined as one that provides managers with income timing latitude.

The LIFO inventory method also exemplifies potential "looseness" benefits. Although LIFO lowers earnings in periods of rising prices (relative to
FIFO and average cost), the existence of LIFO "reserves" and other characteristics provides a reservoir for inter-period income shifts. That is, dipping
into LIFO layers and carefully timing purchases at year-end provide opportunities for managers to achieve desired income targets.

Managers' preferences for "loose" financial reporting standards also arise
for reasons other than bonuses. These include, for example, enhancing reported performance in an attempt to (1) impress shareholders and (2) protect
their jobs by forestalling takeovers.

"Loose" reporting methods have been repeatedly criticized; however, the
alternatives that are more closely related to economic reality (e.g., market-
value accounting for marketable securities and inventories) have been consistently and overwhelmingly rejected by the financial community. The selective
misrepresentation hypothesis helps us understand why these economically
rational arguments are repeatedly rejected; specifically, various sectors of the
financial community simply do not want reporting "improvements" since the
changes reduce possibilities for opportunistic behavior. It is obviously politically unacceptable for them to say so; as a result, innovative smokescreens are
used to defeat proposals for change. (A typical smokescreen is that market
value numbers are either unauditable or too volatile, depending upon the
context.) Standard setters frequently acquiesce to the smokescreens, perhaps
because they have been "captured" by their constituency.

In summary, the selective misrepresentation hypothesis argues that managers prefer reporting methods that provide latitude in income determination
(e.g., requiring choices among mutually acceptable alternatives) rather than
methods that tightly specify statement numbers under given economic conditions. By providing managers with control over when they can report externally driven events, loose reporting standards can be used by managers to
increase compensation, and to hide perquisite consumption, incompetence,
or laziness. Whether these efforts are totally successful is unclear. It is reasonable to presume that those who negotiate managers' employment contracts
anticipate such opportunistic behavior and reduce the compensation package
accordingly.[5] Notice that the demand for "loose" standards is further increased insofar as managers bear some or all of the agency costs. Since they
have already been "charged" for the anticipated opportunistic actions, they
must now engage in them in order to achieve the benefits they "paid" for.
Since loose standards facilitate opportunistic actions, the demand for such
standards increases.

Shareholders

One might initially presume that shareholders would object to reporting
methods that allow managers to receive unwarranted rewards. However, the

---

[5] This perspective is consistent with the "agency theory" view of managerial behavior. See
Jensen and Meckling (1976) and Watts and Zimmerman (1986).

financial misrepresentation hypothesis suggests otherwise since shareholders often derive simultaneous benefits from these "loose" reporting methods. To illustrate, consider the following. Most earnings-based incentive plans have maxima and minima: for managers to receive a bonus, earnings must exceed some threshold level; but there are simultaneous upper limits on bonus payments. Given these incentive plan characteristics, it is often surmised that managers will try to smooth reported earnings in order to maximize their bonuses.[6] If they do so successfully, the *reported* earnings pattern would appear less volatile than the *real* earnings pattern. This appearance of lower volatility could, perhaps, lower the market's perception of default risk. The lower is the perceived default risk, the higher is firm value. As a consequence, shareholders would also benefit from managers' choices of "loose" accounting standards. Indeed, following the misrepresentation hypothesis, rather than objecting to such standards, shareholders might have a decided preference for them.

The flexibility afforded by "loose" reporting standards also provides opportunities to circumvent loan covenant and bond indenture restrictions. If covenants are successfully evaded, these activities would lower actual default risk and, again, convey positive benefits to shareholders. Recent theoretical papers (e.g., Dye, 1988) have used variations on this theme to explain why shareholders continue to allow managers to write employment and bonus contracts tied to "loose" numbers; while managers might utilize this "looseness" to enhance their remuneration, simultaneous benefits also accrue to shareholders.

Auditors

Following the selective misrepresentation hypothesis, auditors may likewise prefer reporting rules that sometimes distort economic reality. The explanation relates to auditors' obvious preferences for retaining clients: repeat audit engagements are especially profitable owing to the steepness of the learning curve. Thus, the hypothesis suggests that auditors' preferences for reporting methods will be influenced by the degree of client harmony elicited by various alternatives.

Depending upon the issue, these auditor preferences can take one of two forms. First, there will be instances where auditors will push for rigid standards that make no pretense of capturing economic circumstances. The immediate expensing of research and development expenditures (FASB, 1974) illustrates this avenue. This rigid approach reduces possibilities for frictions with clients where future outcomes are highly uncertain. When reporting

---

[6] There is some research evidence that demonstrates income smoothing behavior by managers. Additionally, there are numerous well-publicized incidents where managers have been willing to misrepresent financial performance (via misdated invoices and manipulation of purchase and sales cut-offs) in order to achieve income smoothing objectives. Getschow (1979) describes such activities by managers at H. J. Heinz over the period 1972–1978; Guyon (1983) reports on similar smoothing activities at PepsiCo from 1978 through 1982; finally, Ingersoll (1984) discusses other types of manipulations at Datapoint Corp. during fiscal year 1981.

procedures *require* immediate expensing, the threat of client loss arising from disputes is eliminated since all other auditors are compelled to apply the same standard.

Second, in instances where the reporting dilemma is driven more by theory debates rather than by uncertain future events, auditors will opt for reporting standards that simultaneously encompass *both* rigid computational metrics and flexibility. Historical cost accounting provides a perfect illustration of such a system. Readily auditable, "objective," past events measured using well-defined computational procedures (e.g., sum-of-years-digits depreciation) form the basis for historical cost statement numbers. Such numbers are defensible in court and, as such, would be preferred by auditors in the litigious climate they face (Arthur Andersen, 1984, p. 6). However, because of its simultaneous reliance on arbitrary allocations, historical cost accounting presents numerous alternatives for reporting similar phenomena. Full cost versus successful efforts accounting in the oil and gas industry provides one familiar example. Measurement and reporting latitude of this sort allows auditors flexibility and thereby facilitates more harmonious relations with clients.

Historical cost based inventory options like LIFO and FIFO also illustrate the simultaneous confluence of rigid computational metrics and flexibility. The alternative financial measures inherent in the initial LIFO/FIFO choice and the ability to periodically change methods, provide the negotiating room which enables auditors to placate clients and thereby avoid losing future billings.

The preceding analysis helps explain a curious anomaly. Sometimes auditors welcome certain inflexible methods (e.g., mandatory charge-offs of R&D expenditures) that don't necessarily capture economic circumstances. At other times, they reject methods that nicely capture the relevant economics, for instance, market value accounting for inventories and marketable securities. Why? The selective misrepresentation hypothesis suggests one explanation: client harmony. Sometimes harmony requires "slack" in the system as a desirable safety valve, while under other circumstances rigidly specified rules provide a convenient shield for the auditor to hide behind.

Standard Setters

Even standard setters have sometimes revealed a preference for reporting methods that obscure reality. Following the selective misrepresentation hypothesis, the motive here is a combination of self-protection and altruism.

The issue of troubled loan restructuring provides an example. Statement Number 15 (FASB, 1977) has been widely, repeatedly, and justifiably attacked for ignoring real economic losses in certain loan restructurings. However, many believe that this misrepresentation was purposeful. The issue arose after renegotiation of loan terms because of the New York City financial crisis in the mid 1970s. A candid recognition of the amount of genuine economic losses owing to the renegotiations would have eliminated much of the reported bank capital that must be maintained under regulatory guidelines. If the FASB had required realistic accounting rules for these restructurings, additional capital infusions might have been necessitated, lending limits exceeded, and potential use of Federal funds required to honor deposit insurance guarantees at failed banks.[7] The FASB's apparent agenda was to avoid precipitating a capital crisis for banks while simultaneously giving the appearance of having dealt with a highly visible problem. Notice that the general public is the ostensible beneficiary in this scenario since the avoidance of a bank capital crisis presumably made continued credit available to the economy. Indeed, the Office of the Comptroller of the Currency implicitly utilized the FASB (1977) model to achieve similar misrepresentation objectives in assessing adequacy of loan loss reserves for Third World debt (*Comptroller's Handbook*, 1990, Section 215.1). As before, the selective financial misrepresentation led to outcomes that, one surmises, were deemed by the standard setters to enhance aggregate social welfare.

While the troubled loan restructuring example illustrates financial misrepresentation actions precipitated by standard setters, a more familiar example of public policy manipulation using selective misrepresentation is provided by the savings and loan accounting rules. Regulatory accounting principles (RAP) are widely acknowledged to have been politically motivated mechanisms invented by regulators to misrepresent S&L financial performance and thereby delay the closing of insolvent associations (e.g., Berton, 1985). Keeping these insolvent S&Ls open avoided increasing the Federal budget deficits of the early 1980s. As the economic performance of S&Ls worsened, eventually even the notoriously lenient RAP rules could not disguise the unhealthy financial conditions confronting numerous thrifts. Consequently, additional misrepresentations were necessary. One example is provided by a 1984 stock dividend that was declared and paid to member associations by the Federal Home Loan Mortgage Corporation (Freddie Mac). The intent of the dividend, critics charge, was to bolster regulatory capital of the recipient S&Ls.[8] To achieve this end, the Federal Home Loan Bank Board and other interested parties lobbied the FASB to allow the stock dividend to be treated as income.

Not surprisingly, seven of the then Big Eight accounting firms also advised the Board to permit income treatment for the stock dividend (Berton, 1985); they argued that the stock dividend conveyed ownership rights that the thrifts did not previously have. Despite the conflict between income treatment and established accounting principles relating to stock dividends,

---

[7] In the 1970s, capital adequacy was not determined by strict formulae; instead a range of factors—some subjective like management quality—were used by regulators (see, for example, Crosse and Hempel, 1980, pp. 78–79).

[8] This objective was stated openly by the Federal Home Loan Bank Board, which initiated the transaction:

> "Transferring the appreciated value of Freddie Mac in the form of a stock dividend to these institutions will allow them to recognize on their balance sheets a substantial portion of the value of the Corporation" (U.S. League, 1984).

the FASB (1985a) ultimately permitted the stock dividend to be included in income. This incident illustrates perhaps best of all the breadth of the benefits conveyed by accounting standards that permit selective misrepresentation. Here the beneficiaries included S&L managers (they kept their jobs), shareholders (the S&Ls stayed in business), auditors (they were able to placate their clients), standard setters (they thought they performed a social service), and public policy makers (they were able to avoid increasing the Federal deficit).

The undiscounted cost of the S&L industry collapse to be borne by taxpayers over the next forty years is currently estimated to be between $750 billion and one trillion dollars (Veribanc, 1991, p. 3). A considerable portion of the blame must be attributed to selective financial misrepresentations. Despite this, regulators and public policy makers continue to repeat the mistakes. Consider Federal Reserve Board Chairman Alan Greenspan's reaction to the SEC proposal that banks use current market value accounting for financial assets. In opposition, Greenspan raises the familiar argument that mark-to-market accounting injects volatility (Duke and Salwen, 1990). Of course, that is precisely the justification *for* the proposal. According to the SEC's chairman, "if you are in a volatile business, then your balance sheet and income statement should reflect that volatility" (Linden, 1990). Obviously, volatility in reported bank earnings and reported capital creates potential problems for the Federal Reserve Board; this apparently motivates the opposition since the Fed's latitude in responding to other economic conditions could be restricted by the mark-to-market volatility.

Academics

It has even been suggested (Watts and Zimmerman, 1979) that accounting theories and proposals for "improvements" in financial reporting advanced by the academic community are also sometimes motivated by a demand for selective misrepresentation. Succinctly, the argument is that the financial community understands that accounting rules can be used to effect wealth transfers. As events dictate, a demand for theories that facilitate such transfers emerges; in this view, academic (and other) accounting writers succumb to standard market forces and supply the demanded theories. Their remuneration is in the form of enhanced prestige and consulting fees.

To summarize, the selective misrepresentation hypothesis is dramatically inconsistent with the accounting profession's publicly articulated description of the financial reporting process. Because selective misrepresentation potentially leads to a resource allocation that is very different from the more traditional view implied by financial reporting standards, it is important to examine which view is more consistent with available evidence.

THE EVIDENCE

Obtaining evidence about embarrassing activities is difficult, especially when the subject is selective financial misrepresentation; after all, the perpetrators have professional reputations to uphold. Despite the obstacles, piecemeal evidence supporting the hypothesis has been accumulated. In addition, the behavior of participants in the financial reporting process allows observers to make inferences that are often very consistent with the misrepresentation hypothesis.

Before summarizing the evidence, it is important to understand that the primary purpose of financial reporting is to provide a basis for contracting and decision making. Therefore, the degree and frequency of misrepresentation must indeed be selective. Some reasonably close correspondence between economic events and accounting messages must predominate in order to instill confidence in affected parties. Without this correspondence, accounting numbers are unlikely to play any major role in contracting (Holmstrom, 1979). Stated somewhat differently, the fact that existing financial reporting rules predominantly reflect underlying economics is *not* inconsistent with selective misrepresentation. If the misrepresentations were pervasive, accounting would be discredited and the opportunity to use the numbers to effect wealth transfers would be limited.

Empirical evidence regarding selective misrepresentation must be inferred. One cannot easily discover the motives prompting advocacy of controversial, income increasing reporting methods for things like debt-for-debt swaps, debt-for-equity swaps, or defeasances. Empirical researchers are limited to studying the circumstances in which managers have utilized these (and other) devices and determining whether their adoption is consistent with the motivations for misrepresentation.

Research of this sort has been undertaken. Watts and Zimmerman (1978) and Deakin (1989) provide evidence consistent with the notion that managers lobby standard setting bodies to approve reporting methods that maximize managers' welfare. Similarly, Dhaliwal (1980) found that managers in highly leveraged firms lobbied against accounting standards that decreased reported income and (presumably increased risk of covenant violation.) Further evidence suggests that once desired methods are permitted, managers adopt them in circumstances under which they derive benefits. For example, debt-for-equity swaps that increase earnings tend to occur during periods of low profitability (Hand, 1989) and are most likely "when the earnings 'shortfall' is small and transitory" (Lys and Sivaramakrishnan, 1988); furthermore, these swaps are associated with increases in executive compensation (Defeo, Lambert and Larcker, 1989). Discretionary transactions frequently associated with income management were also found to increase compensation of bank executives (Clinch and Magliolo, 1991). A study of in-substance defeasances suggests that firms undertook these controversial transactions in order to smooth annual earnings or avoid bond covenant restrictions (Hand, Hughes and Sefcik, 1990). Johnson and Dhaliwal (1988) find that, in their sample, firms abandoning LIFO are characterized by low earnings performance and strained financial conditions. Healy (1985) found that when managers' bonuses are tied to profits, income-decreasing accruals tend to occur where upper and lower bonus constraints are binding; by contrast, income-increasing accruals are concentrated in periods where these constraints are not binding. This behavior is consistent with bonus maximization across periods. Using a different methodology, McNichols and Wilson (1988) focused on income decreasing accruals. They found that, for their sample, income-decreasing accruals tend to occur when income is unusually high or low; these results are again consistent with multiperiod bonus maximization. Similarly, DeAngelo (1988) found that incumbent managers engaged in a proxy fight use income-increasing accruals. She suggests that this behavior is motivated by self-protection. In a study that examines factors influencing the choice of RAP by S&L managers, Blacconiere et al. (1991) report results that are also consistent with managerial self-protection. Elliott and Shaw (1988) examined discretionary accounting write-offs and found that managerial behavior conforms to "big bath" bunching of expenses and losses. Givoly and Revsine (1991) found evidence that the timing of the adoption of new reporting principles is consistent with income smoothing and acceleration of "good" earnings news.

To summarize, research evidence is consistent with the notion that managers use latitude in existing financial reporting to benefit themselves. In several of these studies, this behavior simultaneously benefits shareholders. This reinforces the point that misrepresentation conveys potentially widespread benefits. Indeed, this characteristic of "shared benefits" may be crucial to the survival of selective misrepresentation.

Academic research on auditors' preferences for principles that facilitate selective misrepresentation is sparse. One exception is Puro (1984). She finds that auditors' FASB lobbying activity regarding standardization of accounting treatment (i.e., eliminating alternatives) is consistent with self-interest. Another example is provided by Hill and Ingram (1989, p. 678) who infer from their results that auditors' willingness to let their S&L clients adopt RAP rather than GAAP accounting was "influenced by their perceptions of [RAP's] key role in maintaining the continued existence of their S&L clients." Less rigorous scrutiny of auditors' behavior on other issues also provides evidence that is consistent with selective misrepresentation. Perhaps the clearest illustration is in the area of accounting for marketable securities. By definition, market prices exist for these assets; despite the existence of such non-arbitrary non-manipulatable measures, lower of cost or market is the accepted reporting method. In addressing this anomaly, Arthur Wyatt, a former member of the FASB, stated (Wyatt, 1989):

> One can question why so little progress has been made in this [marketable securities] accounting problem area. The answer certainly goes beyond a simple resistance to change. Preparers of financial statements, and many auditors, are adamantly opposed to any accounting practice that injects volatility into the measure of reported earnings. It might be more accurate to say that the opposition is to volatility in reported earnings over which the preparer has no control. My perception is that today there can be little optimism that any research, whether undertaken by academics or others, would persuade preparers and many practitioners to agree that marketable securities should be measured at market rather than at historical cost.

Wyatt thus contends that existing practice is dictated by a desire to minimize volatility in income determination. Favoring reporting methods that minimize volatility, of course, is simply another way of describing a preference for selective misrepresentation.[9]

Another example that has already been discussed simultaneously illustrates both auditors' and standard setters' occasional preferences for misrepresentation. The issue relates to the lobbying to obtain income treatment for the Federal Home Loan Mortgage Corporation preferred stock dividend. As noted previously, there are also other inexplicable, apparently politically motivated, pronouncements and regulatory rules of this sort.

IMPLICATIONS AND A PROPOSAL FOR CHANGE

In the private sector, accounting and financial reporting evolved as a consequence of increasingly complex industrial structures, sophisticated contracting, and diffused ownership. Similarly, in the public sector as laws and regulatory policies grew more and more intricate and significant, accounting gradually assumed greater importance as a means for assuring compliance.

Inevitably, decision-makers in both sectors learned that clever manipulation of the surrogates—financial accounting data—could be utilized to perpetrate wealth transfers or circumvent social controls. Because accounting cannot be perfect, and because it is too costly to monitor each event, transfers of this sort must be accepted as an unavoidable element of modern contracting.[10] In the private sector, market forces anticipate and ameliorate important aspects of the transfers through the pricing process. For example, managers' salaries are presumably adjusted downward to absorb the expected losses associated with perquisite consumption, bonus manipulation and other wealth transfers. Accordingly, some of the losses discussed in this paper are not always a "surprise" to those on the other side of the transaction.

The moderating effect of these offsetting market forces coupled with the existence of selective financial misrepresentation requires reconsideration of the benefits of standard setting in the private sector. Standard setting is costly.[11] The financial community has previously borne this cost willingly since accounting standards facilitate contracting. But given the growing use of selective financial misrepresentation and the increasingly successful efforts to add standards that allow misrepresentation, the resulting rules may, at best,

[9] Another example of this desire to minimize volatility is illustrated by Statement Number 87 on pensions (FASB, 1985b). Numerous exceedingly complicated smoothing devices permeate this standard. Eliminating volatility is explicitly discussed in the Statement, e.g., paragraphs 173–190.
[10] Following Jensen and Meckling (1976), these are now widely referred to as "agency costs."
[11] Funding the operations of the SEC and the FASB is only a small part of the total cost of standard setting. In addition, there are the costs associated with individual comprehension of the new standards, formal training, implementation of the standard, and adaptive behavior (including opportunistic adaptive behavior) on the part of market participants and other affected parties.

merely facilitate wealth transfers and, at worst, lead to dead-weight social losses.

Since the costly reporting standards allow misrepresentation, logic suggests that we should consider reducing the resources devoted to developing these complicated standards. If the task is fruitless, and countervailing market forces exist in the private sector, why should society expend resources? Instead, existing standards could effectively be "frozen" and used as the basis for all future contracting and reporting. (Indeed, the FASB's new "supermajority" voting rule might have been conceived as a step in this direction.) The resources saved by down-scaling the often ineffective private standard setting process could be redeployed to bolster the standard setting process in the public sector. (Recollect from footnote 3 that the definition of "public sector" used in this paper includes private enterprises whose performance can lead to direct economic losses for individuals who are neither owners nor direct transactors. Examples include publicly regulated banks and S&Ls.) Developing financial reporting rules for this sector should be the FASB's prime responsibility.

This redeployment of FASB effort is justified since market discipline is muted in the public sector and perpetrators of financial misrepresentations confront fewer obstacles. Accordingly, standards serve a more critical role here as is evidenced by the fact that the S&L misrepresentations identified in this paper have been used to circumvent social contracts underlying deposit insurance. That is, in exchange for the deposit guarantee, thrifts were compelled to maintain a cushion of capital. The manipulation of the accounting rules used to measure this capital subverted the intent of the agreement and raised the social risk of the insurance to unintended levels. As the costs of these accounting misrepresentations escalate, it becomes evident that something must be done. Nations built upon the rule of law must do more than just provide safety and environmental protection for their citizens. Fiscal misdeeds must also be prevented.

But can public sector financial reporting standards be upgraded without repeating the selective misrepresentation mistakes from the private sector? Realistically, the answer is "not completely." However, clear improvements are possible. To accomplish this, the FASB (or whatever other group assumes the primary public sector standard setting role) must be insulated from regulatory capture. This requires a four-step process: (1) educating the public, (2) improving the process for selecting and monitoring standard setters, (3) establishing new funding arrangements, and (4) creating independence for the standard setters.

Educating the Public

The public must first understand the losses that financial misrepresentation causes. As one example, the role of selective misrepresentation in the Savings and Loan fiasco is unclear to many, even in retrospect.[12] Part of the blame rests with accounting educators since misrepresentation issues receive little attention in most university courses and few academics try to alert the public as abuses unfold. Once we do a better job of communicating the problem in our various constituencies, more sophisticated public policy control devices will be widely demanded.

Take the case of the Gramm-Rudman-Hollings budget deficit law. The clear intent here was ultimately to bring Federal *operating* deficits down. Yet the law is easily circumvented because of the naïve accounting rules that it utilizes (Bowsher, 1990). Asset sales (Conrail, etc.) and commingling of disparate activities (e.g., Social Security surpluses) have been used as accounting devices to subvert its objective. When the general public understands the true extent of financial misrepresentation, more sophisticated and less manipulatable control devices will be perceived to be necessary and ultimately implemented. This is the first step.

Improving Selection and Monitoring

The phenomenon of regulatory capture compounds the problem of selective financial misrepresentation; accordingly, certain changes in the selection and monitoring of financial regulatory bodies are urgently needed. As an example of existing insensitivity to such concerns, a majority of the composition of the FASB is comprised of former regulatees, specifically, individuals from CPA firms and industry. The oversight board that reviews the activities of the FASB—the Financial Accounting Foundation—is comprised primarily of *current* regulatees, thereby exacerbating the problem (Miller and Redding, 1988).[13] A more notorious public regulatory example is the Federal Home Loan Bank Board, the originator of many of the RAP rules that precipitated the S&L debacle. As public understanding grows, so too will pressure to reform the regulatory appointment and oversight process. An effort to balance representation between those knowledgeable about financial issues and others possessing a broader perspective can lead to clear improvements.

Establishing New Funding Arrangements

Since business organizations fund the FASB, it is not surprising that these regulatees expect to participate in oversight activities. But this intrusion worsens the selective misrepresentation problem. One solution is to continue the existing FASB funding arrangement but bar the funding organizations

---

[12] A recent, supposedly exhaustive, review of the S&L crisis (Rosenbaum, 1990) failed even to mention manipulation of accounting regulatory rules as one of the culprits.

[13] A longstanding, prominent observer of the FASB recently wrote a blistering letter to the President of the Financial Accounting Foundation accusing the Foundation of damaging the standard-setting system (Miller, 1991).

Chapter 16   Accounting Changes

(and their members) from oversight activities. However, those who pay the
bill usually expect accountability; therefore, if this approach were enforced,
funding would inevitably cease.

Another approach is to have the relatively modest (under $20 million)
annual FASB operating costs funded by user fees. For example, a small
Federal tax on all security market transactions, private placements, loans and
other financing contracts would easily fund standard-setting operations.
Since the FASB's operating costs pale in comparison to the recent costs arising
from public sector selective financial misrepresentation, once the social benefits of improved standards are understood, it should be relatively easy to alter
the funding base.

(Of course, Federal funding raises the possibility of Congressional intrusion since, as stated above, those who pay the cost expect to influence the
outcome. But Congressional intrusion already exists in the form of government hearings, SEC oversight of FASB activities, and similar pressures. Since
the ultimate responsibility for formulating financial reporting rules already
resides in the governmental sector, i.e., through the SEC,[14] Federal funding is
unlikely to drastically alter the degree of Congressional intrusion.)

Creating Independence

Above all else, those who set public sector financial standards must be
insulated from the regulatees—that is, from ourselves and our elected representatives. After all, it was Congress that instigated the S&L RAP rules that
kept insolvent associations open in the early 1980s and thereby deferred
(and worsened) the problem. It was also Congress that acquiesced to putting
more than half of the initial Resolution Trust financing "off-budget," thereby understating the true deficit and circumventing the budget deficit law
(Thomas, 1989).

Mechanisms for establishing the requisite independence for standard
setters already exist in the public sector. Examples include life-tenure for
Supreme Court justices and 14-year terms for Federal Reserve Board gover-
nors. By providing similar continuity for public sector financial standard
setters, the public might be somewhat better protected from Congressional
pressure for politically inspired financial misrepresentations. That is, long-

---

[14] These powers are given to the SEC in Section 19(a) of the Securities Act of 1933 as Amended:

> [T]he Commission shall have authority, for the purposes of this title, to prescribe the
> form or forms in which required information shall be set forth, the items or details to be
> shown in the balance sheet and earning statement, and the methods to be followed in
> the preparation of accounts, in the appraisal or valuation of assets and liabilities, in the
> determination of depreciation and depletion, in the differentiation of recurring and
> nonrecurring income, in the differentiation of investment and operating income, and in
> the preparation, where the Commission deems it necessary or desirable, of consoli-
> dated balance sheets or income accounts of any person directly or indirectly controlling
> or controlled by the issuer, or any person under direct or indirect common control with
> the issuer. The rules and regulations of the Commission shall be effective upon
> publication in the manner which the Commission shall prescribe.

648

term job protection should insulate these individuals from pressures to initi-ate opportunistic standards advanced by interested parties. Making standard setters impervious to such pressures is an important element in reducing the incidence of selective financial misrepresentation.

CONCLUSION

Financial reporting standards should enhance economic efficiency, rather than aiding those who wish to gain at another's expense. But the repeated wealth transfers perpetrated using financial standards in the private sector call into question the justification for incurring these standard-setting costs. Since market forces anticipate and ameliorate elements of the private sector wealth transfers, further refinement of existing reporting rules in that sector seems less urgent than a tightening of standards in the public sector.

In outlining the selective financial misrepresentation hypothesis, this paper advances the notion that society may have overinvested in standard-setting activities in the private sector and underinvested in these activities in the public sector. One can hope that a better understanding of selective financial misrepresentation will motivate important reforms.

REFERENCES

Arthur Andersen & Co., *Objectives of Financial Statements for Business Enterprises*, 1984.

Berton, Lee, "Accounting at Thrifts Provokes Controversy As Gimmickry Mounts," *The Wall Street Journal*, March 21, 1985.

Blacconiere, Walter G., Robert M. Bowen, Stephen E. Sefcik, and Christopher H. Stinson, "Determinants of the Use of Regulatory Accounting Principles by Sav-ings and Loans," *Journal of Accounting and Economics* (June, 1991), pp. 167–201.

Bowsher, Charles A., "Cooking the Books Is a Bad Recipe To Cool Deficit," *Journal of Accountancy* (February, 1990), pp. 23, 25.

Clinch, Greg, and Joseph Magliolo, "Executive Compensation Effects of Accounting-Oriented Discretionary Transactions in Commercial Banks," working paper, Uni-versity of Pennsylvania (May 1991).

Comptroller's Handbook for National Bank Examiners, March 1990.

Crosse, Howard, and George H. Hempel, *Management Policies For Commercial Banks*, 3rd ed. (Englewood Cliffs, N.J.: Prentice-Hall, Inc., 1980).

Deakin, Edward B., "Rational Economic Behavior and Lobbying on Accounting Is-sues: Evidence from the Oil and Gas Industry," *The Accounting Review* (January, 1989), pp. 137–151.

DeAngelo, Linda E., "Managerial Compensation, Information Costs, and Corporate Governance: The Use of Accounting Performance Measures in Proxy Contests," *Journal of Accounting and Economics* (January, 1988), pp. 3–36.

Defeo, Victor, Richard Lambert, and David Larcker, "The Executive Compensation Effects of Equity-for-Debt Swaps," *The Accounting Review* (April, 1989), pp. 201–227.

Dhaliwal, Dan S., "The Effect of the Firm's Capital Structure on the Choice of Accounting Methods," *The Accounting Review* (January, 1980), pp. 78–84.

Duke, Paul Jr., and Kevin G. Salwen, "SEC Proposal Draws Criticism From Greenspan," *The Wall Street Journal*, November 8, 1990.

Dye, Ronald A., "Earnings Management in an Overlapping Generations Model," *Journal of Accounting Research* (Autumn, 1988), pp. 195–235.

Elliott, John, and Wayne Shaw, "Write-Offs as Accounting Procedures to Manage Perceptions," *Journal of Accounting Research*, Supplement, 1988, pp. 91–119.

Financial Accounting Standards Board, "Accounting for Research and Development Costs," *Statement of Financial Accounting Standards No. 2* (1974).

_____, "Accounting by Debtors and Creditors for Troubled Debt Restructurings," *Statement of Financial Accounting Standards No. 15* (1977).

_____, "Qualitative Characteristics of Accounting Information," *Statement of Financial Accounting Concepts No. 2* (1980).

_____, Technical Bulletin No. 85–1, "Accounting for the Receipt of Federal Home Loan Mortgage Corporation Participating Preferred Stock" (March, 1985). (1985a)

_____, "Employers' Accounting for Pensions," *Statement of Financial Accounting Standards No. 87* (1985). (1985b)

_____, "Statement of Cash Flows," *Statement of Financial Accounting Standards No. 95* (1987).

Getschow, George, "Initial Study of Some Heinz Units Finds $5.5 Million in Profit-Juggling Practices," *The Wall Street Journal*, July 2, 1979.

Givoly, Dan, and Lawrence Revsine, "Managerial Opportunism and the Adoption Timing of New Accounting Principles," working paper, Northwestern University (May, 1991).

Guyon, Janet, "PepsiCo Chief Kendall Steps Up Role at Firm Before '86 Retirement," *The Wall Street Journal*, July 29, 1983.

Hand, John, "Did Firms Undertake Debt-Equity Swaps for an Accounting Paper Profit or True Financial Gain?" *The Accounting Review* (October, 1989), pp. 587–623.

_____, Patricia J. Hughes, and Stephen E. Sefcik, "Insubstance Defeasances: Security Price Reactions and Motivations," *Journal of Accounting and Economics* (May 1990), pp. 47–89.

Healy, Paul, "The Impact of Bonus Schemes on the Selection of Accounting Principles," *Journal of Accounting and Economics* (April 1985), pp. 85–108.

_____, Sok-Hyon Kang, and Krishna G. Palepu, "The Effect of Accounting Procedure Changes on CEOs' Cash Salary and Bonus Compensation," *Journal of Accounting and Economics* (April 1987), pp. 7–34.

Hill, John W., and Robert W. Ingram, "Selection of GAAP or RAP in the Savings and Loan Industry," *The Accounting Review* (October, 1989), pp. 667–679.

Holmstrom, Bengt, "Moral Hazard and Observability," *The Bell Journal of Economics* (Spring, 1979), pp. 74–91.

Ingersoll, Bruce, "SEC Accuses Datapoint of Overstating Revenue and Net Income for Fiscal 1981," *The Wall Street Journal* (June 19, 1984).

Jensen, Michael, and William Meckling, "Theory of the Firm: Managerial Behavior, Agency Costs and Ownership Structure," *Journal of Financial Economics* (1976), pp. 306–60.

Johnson, W. Bruce, and Dan S. Dhaliwal, "LIFO Abandonment," *Journal of Accounting Research* (Autumn, 1988), pp. 236–272.

Linden, Dana Wechsler, "If Life is Volatile, Account for It," *Forbes*, November 12, 1990, pp. 114–115.

Lys, Thomas, and Konduru Sivaramakrishnan, "Earnings Expectations and Capital Restructuring: The Case of Equity-for-Debt Swaps," *Journal of Accounting Research* (Autumn, 1988), pp. 273–299.

McNichols, Maureen, and G. Peter Wilson, "Evidence of Earnings Management From the Provision for Bad Debts," *Journal of Accounting Research*, Supplement, 1988, pp. 1–31.

Miller, Paul B. W., and Rodney J. Redding, *The FASB: The People, the Process and the Politics*, 2nd ed. (Homewood, IL: Richard D. Irwin, Inc., 1988).

_____, Letter to Shaun F. O'Malley, February 13, 1991.

Puro, Marsha, "Audit Firm Lobbying Before the Financial Accounting Standards Board: An Empirical Study," *Journal of Accounting Research* (Autumn, 1984), pp. 624–646.

Rosenbaum, David E., "A Financial Disaster With Many Culprits," *The New York Times*, June 6, 1990.

Simon, Daniel T., "Compensation Effects and Accounting Changes: An Empirical Examination" (Unpublished Ph.D. dissertation, Northwestern University, 1983).

Stigler, George J., "The Theory of Economic Regulation," *Bell Journal of Economics and Management Science* (Spring 1971), pp. 3–21.

Thomas, Paulette, "Thrift Regulators Could Further Raise Bailout Debt Apart From U.S. Budget," *The Wall Street Journal*, October 10, 1989.

U.S. Congress, "Securities Act of 1933 as Amended" [H. R. 5480] 73d Congress.

U.S. League of Savings Institutions, *Washington Notes* (Washington, D. C., December 7, 1984).

Veribanc, Inc., *Veribanc News Release* (Wakefield, Massachusetts, April 4, 1991).

Watts, Ross, and Jerold Zimmerman, "Towards a Positive Theory of the Determination of Accounting Standards," *The Accounting Review* (January 1978), pp. 112–134.

_____, "The Demand For and Supply of Accounting Theories: The Market for Excuses," *The Accounting Review* (April 1979), pp. 273–305.

_____, *Positive Accounting Theory* (Englewood Cliffs, N.J.: Prentice-Hall, Inc., 1986).

Wyatt, Arthur, "Interface Between Teaching/Research and Teaching/Practice," *Accounting Horizons* (March, 1989), pp. 125–128.

Manipulating Profits: How It's Done

Ford S. Worthy

"Life is not smooth," as an auditor for a large accounting firm restates the truism. Neither are the year-to-year performances of corporations, but that doesn't keep executives from trying to purge the wiggles and spikes from the lines that chart their profits. Managers don't have to cook the books to manipulate earnings; they often have all the power they need in the leeway built into accounting rules.

Sometimes flexibility in calculating earnings comes from having several strikingly different ways to account for a single set of facts. Sometimes managers have leeway because situations call for highly subjective estimates. While there is a lot less room to manipulate earnings today than a decade ago, the rules still are mighty spacious.

The bailout of the Continental Illinois National Bank has focused new attention on the extraordinary discretion that banks have in establishing loss reserves and accruing interest on shaky loans. The present system allows banks to report rising earnings even as loans sour. The Securities and Exchange Commission has made inadequate bank loss reserves a top enforcement priority.

Figuring out which companies fine-tune profits is difficult, but the practice appears widespread. Extreme efforts to manage earnings occasionally surface. As *Fortune* disclosed in 1982, Aetna Life & Casualty was boosting results by including anticipated tax benefits in earnings. The SEC subsequently required Aetna to stop the practice and restate 1982 earnings.

Most well-known instances of managed earnings involve companies trying to make profits look robust. But the process often is considerably subtler. Most executives prefer to report earnings that follow a smooth, regular, upward path. They hate to report declines, but they also want to avoid increases that vary wildly from year to year: it's better to have two years of 15 percent earnings increases than a 30 percent gain one year and none the next. As a result, some companies "bank" earnings by understating them in particularly good years and use the banked profits to polish results in bad years.

Fortune asked experts at several Big Eight accounting firms to calculate how much some of the most common tools for managing earnings could pump up the income of a mythical $10-billion-a-year conglomerate. (This company, it's assumed, runs a specialty steel division, a consumer products company, and a property and casualty insurance subsidiary.) The experts say that such a company, using a combination of techniques that do not have to be disclosed in financial statements could easily raise earnings by 10 percent to 15 percent—enough booster power to transform a modest profit decline into a small increase.

To perform such alchemy, executives sometimes pay more heed to the accounting consequences of major decisions than to the economics. Management might sell off the headquarters building, for example, to enhance current income by realizing a big gain, even though it might be more sensible over the long run to keep the building. One auditor describes that as "letting the accounting tail wag the economic dog."

Managers devote such attention to earnings because they think that's what matters most to shareholders. What the stock market likes, says Abraham Briloff, a professor of accounting at Baruch College in New York City and one of the most vociferous critics of the accounting profession, "is a

nice, smooth, predictable earnings trajectory." Reports that please shareholders serve the managers' self-interest. "Why do they manage the bottom
line?" asks Briloff. "Because it's their report card. Executives like their bonuses and the other perquisites" that are tied to reported earnings.

A recent study by accounting professor Paul Healy of the Massachusetts
Institute of Technology bolsters Briloff's assertions. Healy documents a connection between bonus schemes and the accounting choices executives make.
Executives whose bonus plans rewarded them up to a ceiling tended to
choose accounting options that minimized reported profits, while executives
on bonus plans without upper limits chose profit-boosting options. In other
words, if no additional bonus is paid once profits hit a certain level, it's not in
the executive's interest for reported earnings to exceed that amount. He's
better off deferring any profits above the maximum bonus level until he needs
them to sustain his own income.

Most techniques for managing earnings can be grouped in three broad
classes—changing accounting methods, fiddling with managers' estimates of
costs, and shifting the period when expenses and revenues are included in
results.

Choosing a different accounting method gives rise to the greatest and
most permanent impact on earnings. The impact is also the most easily
recognizable because changes in accounting procedures usually are disclosed
in a company's reports.

The oil industry offers one of the best examples of how different accounting options can drastically alter reported income. In mid-1978 Occidental
Petroleum changed the way it accounted for the costs of finding oil and gas.
The change, which was merely a different way to record the same economic
events, slashed reported profits by a third. Under the old method Oxy's
earnings per share were $2.92 in 1977. Restated, 1977 earnings dropped to
$1.93 a share.

Companies can't switch back and forth between accounting methods. But
the fact that they can change to "preferable" methods stirs up critics who
argue that if there is a preferable way, there ought not to be another way.
Says John C. Burton, a former chief accountant for the SEC and now dean of
Columbia University's Graduate School of Business: "I feel very strongly that
there should be fewer areas where alternative accounting principles are
permitted."

When companies change accounting methods, they often pick one that
gives reported earnings a lift. Most academic researchers doubt that investors
are fooled by higher accounting income that doesn't bring any extra cash flow
along with it. But Thornton O'glove, an independent security analyst, takes a
different view. For the past 15 years O'glove has published a newsletter for
institutional investors called the *Quality of Earnings Report*, in which he dis-
sects income statements, pointing out "soft" earnings that investors should
be wary of. Ordinarily, earnings that arise purely from accounting changes go
in the flabby category. But when the changes are great, O'glove thinks the
earnings may harden over time.

He cites the case of Union Carbide, which in 1980 lengthened depreciation periods for machinery and equipment, and started taking the benefits of
investment tax credits into accounting profits in the year they arose instead of
spreading the credits over time. Both changes increased reported earnings.
O'glove figures the new procedures contributed 18 percent of Union Carbide's earnings per share in 1980 and 15 percent, 28 percent, and 26 percent
the following three years, but "did not affect income tax payments or cash
flow," as the company stated in its 1980 annual report.

O'glove has tracked Union Carbide's stock price, and the stock prices of
six competitors, since the changes. Ranked by price-earnings multiples,
Union Carbide shot from last place to second. "What these efficient-market
professors don't realize," says O'glove, "is that the higher earnings are
embedded for infinity, but Wall Street forgets about the accounting change
after a couple of years."

The second broad category of ways to manage earnings is dominated by
one particularly malleable element: judgment. Any company with a substantial inventory, for example, must estimate how much of it is obsolete. The
answer gets deducted from current income. Companies must predict what
portion of their accounts receivable will be uncollectible. Future costs of
honoring warranties must be projected. Many companies must also estimate
how much it will cost to settle pending litigation.

But the opportunity for judgment in accounting matters to affect earnings
is most potent in two industries—banking and property and casualty insurance. Banks must make a provision to cover loans that will ultimately go bad.
Property and casualty companies establish reserves to cover claims they
ultimately will pay out on current insurance policies. These amounts are
deducted from profits in the year they are added to reserves, not in the year a
claim is paid or a loan becomes worthless. When a loan is written off, for
example, the bank removes it from assets and deducts an equal amount from
the pool of loss reserves; that's a bookkeeping entry that doesn't affect the
income statement.

Ideally, the total amount held in reserve should be just enough to cover
all loans on the books that the bank has reason to believe will eventually go
bad. The addition to reserves that is charged against income each year should
be just enough to keep total reserves at the appropriate level.

A company's management and its auditors sometimes have different
opinions about what level of reserves is appropriate. But they can generally
agree on a range of acceptable estimates. Within this range earnings can be
managed. Since total reserves can exceed a bank's annual earnings, "a small
percentage variation in the loan loss estimate can have a huge effect on the
bottom line," says Roger Cason, a partner at Main Hurdman/KMG, a New
York accounting firm.

John Gutfreund, co-chairman of Philbro-Salomon, the securities and commodities firm, characterizes reserve juggling thus: "My guess is that when
things are going well executives try to legitimately squirrel away reserves."
Those squirreled-away reserves, which reduce reported profits, are kept in
places like the "cupboard" and the "corporate sugar bowl." When earnings

turn down, managers can reach into the sugar bowl by cutting back on the reserve provision for the current year. The lower that reserve provision, the higher net income.

The only thing wrong with Gutfreund's description is the word "legitimately." When managers over-reserve to fill the sugar bowl, they are understating earnings and misleading shareholders and creditors, just as much as they are when they overstate earnings. They also are misleading the Internal Revenue Service, since additions to reserves are deducted from taxable income. Equally important, they are misleading themselves if they treat the managed numbers as though they were real. Accounting information can provide crucial guidance in business decisions, but it's useless if the figures are phony.

Executives rarely acknowledge that the sugar bowl exists. But Allied Bancshares, a Houston-based amalgamation of banks that turned in a string of 31 quarterly earnings increases before a decline in the final quarter of 1983 (*Fortune*, June 11), apparently got so proud of its record that it couldn't resist talking about it. In an interview a year ago with three Goldman Sachs security analysts, one of the bank's senior officers said, "We believe it is entirely appropriate to use high-profit opportunities to build special reserves for cycles such as the current one."

The bank's treasurer, Thomas C. Clausen, recently explained what Allied meant by special reserves: "When you are bumping along with such good earnings, you don't get any benefit by showing extraordinary increases. Some years we could have reported extremely higher earnings than we did. In fact, we were building our reserves quite high in late 1980 and early 1981. Our outside accountants, Peat Marwick Mitchell, began raising questions. 'Golly, folks,' they told us, 'as clean as y'all are looking, this is getting a little ridiculous!'"

Did Peat Marwick mean that Allied was over-reserving? "Exactly," says Clausen. "But we went over the Houston manager's head to the New York office. We said, 'Look, this is kind of unusual, to say that we're too high.' The reply that came back from New York to the Houston office was something to the effect of: 'There's nothing wrong with erring as long as you err on the side of the angels.'" According to Clausen, the bank stuck with its original "special reserves."

Peat Marwick, which rendered an unqualified opinion that Allied's financial statements "present fairly" the condition of the company, says its Houston partner made the final decision on Allied's reserves after consulting with partners in New York.

Auditors apparently will tolerate sugar-bowling so long as companies don't materially misrepresent results. That gives managers enormous latitude in matters of judgment, and they don't always err on the side of the angels. Many big banks, for instance, are under a cloud for presumably *under*-reserving.

Judgment calls can have profound effects on profits in other industries as well. When the Washington Public Power Supply System suspended construction of a nuclear plant last year, two Oregon utilities had to decide how to value their investments in the project. Pacific Power & Light, coming off a strong operating performance in 1983, wrote off over half its $292-million investment. Portland General Electric, which posted flat operating results last year, kept its full $266-million investment on the balance sheet.

Chrysler kept an unsuccessful investment in Peugeot on its books at the full original cost until finally taking a $224-million earnings hit last year. Al Nelson, an auto analyst with A.G. Becker Paribas, contends that Chrysler should have taken the write-down two or three years ago but "wanted to put the best foot forward for the bankers and investors." Chrysler maintains there was no proof of a permanent reduction in the value of the investment in earlier years.

The third category of earnings manipulations encompasses the things executives do to alter the timing of expenses and, to a much lesser degree, revenues. They might defer expenses for maintenance or research until the following quarter. That would boost earnings in the current quarter and might not cause any harm. A company could delay an ad campaign in order to give current earnings a kick. But deferring promotional expenses might also result in lost sales and market share. Once an ad runs, its cost must be charged against income. McCormick, the spice company, got into trouble with the SEC two years ago for, among other things, allegedly asking its ad agency not to mail invoices until later periods. Without admitting the charges, McCormick agreed not to engage in that practice in the future.

Companies with order backlogs can ship products a little earlier (or later) to tinker with earnings. Capital expenditures can be timed to give a company the benefit of the associated investment tax credit in either the current year or the next one. Just as individuals scramble in the last few days of the year to reduce their taxes, a lot of corporate efforts to add to or subtract from earnings also seem to occur in December.

Not long ago a senior executive at a large New York-based company ordered his subordinates to do whatever was possible to incur expenses by the end of the year. Profits were going to be robust no matter what, he told them, so it would be wise to save a little for an encore the following year. One middle manager received an edict in mid-December to spend $12 million. The manager bought $12 million worth of postage metering, an item that could be deducted immediately even though the benefits would last for millions and millions of letters.

Juggling a company's portfolio of stocks and bonds is another way to smooth earnings. Analysts pay close attention to the relationship between income generated by financial investments—T bills and stocks, for example—and income from a company's basic operations. If the relationship fluctuates significantly from year to year, it could be a signal that management is using financial assets to straighten out the trend line—taking big stock gains in periods when operating income sags, for instance. A burst in financial income can be meaningful because it might not be repeatable. In April Ted O'glove flagged TIE Communications, a high-stepping telecommunications equipment company. The company's income from financial investments in 1983 accounted for over half of a big jump in pretax earnings. "They're actually earning a higher return on their investment portfolio than on their basic business," says O'glove.

One of the more ingenious, controversial, and unambiguously legal ways to create earnings is by erasing old debt from the balance sheet without actually paying it off. Known as in-substance defeasance, the technique has been labeled a charade by a former SEC commissioner but won a narrow endorsement last November from the accounting profession's rule-making body, the Financial Accounting Standards Board.

An in-substance defeasance works like this: A company decides it wants to clear $20 million of its 9 percent bonds off its books. It sets up a trust and irrevocably funds it with 9 percent U.S. Treasury bonds at the same par value but purchased at a discount for $17 million. The interest received on the government securities has to cover the interest payments on the debt, and the maturity value of the government securities must be sufficient to repay the debt when it eventually comes due. The company records a profit equal to the difference between the book value of its bonds and the price of the Treasury bonds it buys for the trust.

Investment bankers have been hawking various defeasance packages ever since they sold Exxon on the idea two years ago. Exxon "defeased" $515 million of debt, reported a gain of $132 million on the transaction, and improved its debt-to-equity ratio. But critics say that shareholders lose on such deals. In effect, the bondholders own somewhat risky corporate bonds prior to defeasance that are backed by virtually risk-free government securities afterward. The bondholders get this extra safety without having to pay for it. Who pays? The shareholders, because the cost of the Treasury bonds exceeds the present value of the interest and principal the company would otherwise have to pay on its bonds. They also pay fees to the investment banker who handles the transaction and possibly higher bonuses to executives because of the resulting bulge in earnings.

Strategies to manage earnings via inventories can also cost a company money, but accountants say their clients occasionally find it worthwhile to pay a real price for unreal profits. Companies using LIFO (last-in-first-out) inventory accounting face myriad legal and ethical questions because the LIFO rules are not well-defined. Under LIFO the last inventory purchased is considered the first sold, so that the inventory costs deducted from earnings tend to be close to current replacement costs. But the inventory on the balance sheet is the oldest inventory purchased and often is valued at prices in effect years ago.

A LIFO company can generate higher earnings by letting inventory levels drop and dipping into the low-cost layers. As those layers are sold, the lower costs pass through the income statement and inflate earnings. But inventory profits actually decrease cash flow unless the inventory reduction is permanent. Companies have to pay current prices for replacement goods, and they also have to pay taxes on accounting profits.

Executives usually are most eager to boost earnings in hard times, just when they also are especially anxious to reduce inventories. As a result, it is difficult for auditors and SEC investigators to know whether a company is liquidating inventory for sound business reasons or to manipulate earnings. L. Glenn Perry, the chief accountant for the enforcement division of the SEC, wants the LIFO rules tightened.

U.S. Steel has reported $1.7 billion in LIFO profits since 1976, while the company's steel business has been shrinking. "The magnitude of their liquidations is so large that you wonder if they're not doing it purposely," says Ted O'glove. "I don't think it's an indication of real profit." U.S. Steel has broken out the accounting profits each year and says they resulted from a long-term program to reduce inventories permanently.

Figuring out just who manages earnings and by how much requires a glimpse inside the chief executive's mind. Lacking that insight, it certainly is useful to take a close look at what a company will tell you about itself in the detailed reports it files with the SEC. A lot of the flabbiness is right there on display. And some companies are probably fitter than they appear. By all the economic signals, 1984 should be a bumper year for earnings. If the sugar-bowl strategy of earnings management operates according to theory, companies ought to be socking away a lot of unreported profits this year.

Earnings Helper

Dana Wechsler

Forbes

No one ever said accounting was an exact science. How inexact it can be has been illustrated in two recent cases: Cineplex Odeon (*Forbes*, May 29) and Blockbuster Entertainment. Both companies minimized the amortization of assets to the benefit of reported earnings.

In the case of Cineplex Odeon, the movie theater circuit, amortizes its leasehold improvements—seats, carpet, equipment and the like—over an average of 27 years, despite the fact that many of these assets will almost certainly be on the scrap heap long before 27 years have elapsed.

In Blockbuster's case, the aggressive videotape rental store chain recently spread the amortization period for its tapes from a fast writeoff over 9 months to a slow one over 36 months. That bookkeeping gimmick added $3 million, or nearly 20 percent, to Blockbuster's reported 1988 income. Last month a Bear, Stearns report critical of Blockbuster's accounting policies sliced over $226 million off the company's market value within 2 days.

Questions about proper amortization and depreciation schedules even involve companies that have never been accused of dubious accounting

From *Forbes* (June 12, 1989), pp. 150, 152. Reprinted by permission of Forbes, Inc. Copyright © 1989 by Forbes, Inc.

practices, as Cineplex and Blockbuster have. Consider General Motors. Until 1987 GM wrote off tools and dies at by far the fastest rate in the car business. But in that year the company slowed amortization of its tools and dies down to a level comparable with those of Ford and Chrysler. GM was in no wise cooking the books, but the move did increase GM's reported earnings by $2.55 per share; total earnings came to $10.06 per share that year.

In 1984 IBM shifted from accelerated depreciation to the straight-line method for its rental machines, plant and other property. According to Thornton O'glove, author of the *Quality of Earnings Report*, the change increased IBM's reported earnings by $375 million, or 37 cents a share.

What's going on here? When it comes to amortization and depreciation, Generally Accepted Accounting Principles provide only the vaguest of guidelines. Management is supposed to write off assets over their estimated useful lives. But asset life expectancy is highly subjective, and is influenced by a myriad of factors. A state-of-the-art computer that will function mechanically for 50 years could become technologically obsolete in 5. Is its estimated useful life 5 years, 50 years or somewhere in between?

Another tough question: If something happens that will reduce (or lengthen) an asset's useful life, should management be required to change the depreciation schedule, to better reflect economic reality?

In a situation like this, where there can be honest differences of opinion, there is clearly room for the kind of abuse that prevailed in the Cineplex case. Many depreciation abuses are probably going undetected. Howard Hodges, chief accountant for the SEC's corporation finance division, cites lump sum writeoffs. "All of the restructuring charges—with big, lump sum writeoffs— are recognition that companies haven't been depreciating fast enough," says Hodges.

Why doesn't the SEC insist upon more conformity in companies' depreciation and amortization policies? Hodges replies: "We try to be observant, but when a company says it's depreciating its plant over 3 to 40 years, we don't know the intimate details. And there's no practical way we could. I'd like the accountants to take more responsibility for it."

For their part, the accountants retort that they're doing the best they can—that when reviewing depreciation, they look at engineering reports, industry practices and the company's historical use of its assets. Even so, they say, it is difficult to pass judgment on how much value can be squeezed from the assets. As Robert Fenimore, a partner at the accounting firm KPMG Peat Marwick, puts it: "You can count fixed assets and make sure they're there, but what are they worth? It's hard to say. There could be numerous studies done, all of which could give you reasonable answers with different conclusions."

As a result, the corporation's auditors will probably go along with management's judgment as long as the writeoff period doesn't diverge too much from general industry practice. Yet the permissible variations are so great as to make it difficult to compare two companies' earnings without intimate knowledge of their accounting practices.

Take the case of the airlines, which write off the same kinds of equipment over very different periods, with significant consequences for their bottom lines. Delta Air Lines depreciates its planes over 15 years and figures on a 10 percent residual value. Pan Am estimates a life of 25 years for the same 727s that Delta writes off in 15—and assumes a 15 percent residual value. Texas Air also writes off its planes over up to 25 years.

Are Pan Am and Texas Air being too aggressive? Is Delta too conservative? "There is a justification for lives well beyond 20 years, if the planes are properly maintained," says KPMG Peat Marwick's Fenimore, an airline specialist. "But in reality, it's obvious that the airlines with less financial strength are the ones with longer depreciation lives."

What can an investor do? Under Generally Accepted Accounting Principles, whenever a company stretches out the lives of its assets, management must note (but not justify) any material change in the reported earnings in the footnotes to the annual report. And an accounting shift from accelerated to straight-line depreciation must be both footnoted and justified—although the justification can be vague. When IBM changed its depreciation schedule on its rental machines five years ago, for example, it cited only "evolving changes in our operations, maintenance costs and technology."

In December 1987 the SEC asked the American Institute of Certified Public Accountants to consider having any change in the length of depreciation highlighted in the auditor's report accompanying financial statements. Presumably this would draw attention to the change and put investors on the alert.

But the accountants retort that disclosure in the footnotes is enough. Says Daniel Guy, vice president for auditing for the American Institute of Certified Public Accountants: "Footnotes are very important. Why is it necessary to highlight them? I can't imagine anyone being hoodwinked by changes in depreciation anyway." Maybe so, but some pretty smart investors were taken in by the Cineplex Odeon and Blockbuster Entertainment amortization schedules.

The Anatomy of an Accounting Change

Krishna G. Palepu
Harvard University

INTRODUCTION

Generally accepted accounting principles allow companies a wide latitude in the choice of accounting policies. There is some evidence that firms often choose accounting policies to reflect managements' financial reporting strategy. After a firm chooses a set of accounting policies, current accounting rules also permit it to change from one policy to another at the discretion of the management.

Reported accounting numbers are used by all parties that have contractual and regulatory relationships with the firm. Investors use accounting information in assessing the investment potential of a firm's stock; lenders use accounting numbers in specifying debt covenant agreements; boards of directors employ accounting performance measures in determining top management compensation; and regulators and politicians use reported accounting numbers in enforcing existing laws as well as in the formulation of new laws. Given such a wide use of accounting data by various external parties, accounting researchers have posited that managements have incentives to choose accounting policies to influence the behavior of these parties.

Much of the empirical research dealing with accounting policy choice has analyzed large samples of firms, using conventional statistical methods. Here, in contrast, I examine in depth the case of one company that made major changes in its financial reporting strategy. The factors identified as important in this particular instance are compared with those proposed in the current accounting literature. By examining the case of one company in considerable detail, this study attempts to provide data that will help interpret the conclusions of the earlier studies. In addition, the study identifies avenues for further research.

This chapter examines a number of accounting changes made by Harnischfeger Corporation, a large New York Stock Exchange company. It appears that the factors hypothesized in the literature seem to have played some role in the company's decision to change its accounting policy. In addition, a

From William J. Bruns, Jr. and Robert S. Kaplan (editors), *Accounting and Management: Field Study Perspectives* (Harvard Business School Press, 1987), pp. 73–94. Reprinted by permission of Harvard Business School Press. Copyright © 1987 by the President and Fellows of Harvard College. All rights reserved.
Author's note: I am grateful to the management of Harnischfeger Corporation for help in gathering information for this chapter. I wish to thank Bill Bruns for help in the field research process, and Ray Ball, Robin Cooper, Paul Healy, Robert Kaplan, Ross Watts, and the participants of the colloquium for their comments.

variety of internal management considerations, and management's belief that it was costly (and perhaps impossible) for external users of accounting to adjust for differences in accounting policies across firms, seem to have been significant reasons behind the company's change in accounting policy. Since my analysis is based on a single case, the ability to generalize from these observations is seriously limited.

The first section of the chapter gives a brief overview of the accounting literature dealing with the determinants of accounting policy choice. This is followed by a detailed description of the case study. The last section compares the important factors in the case study with those hypothesized in the literature and discusses the implications of the similarities and differences between the two sets of factors.

ACCOUNTING POLICY CHOICE: A REVIEW OF THE LITERATURE

Early studies investigating the accounting policy choices of firms focused on the stock price behavior of firms that switched accounting policies.[1] These studies investigated whether the stock market is systematically misled by the effect of accounting changes on reported earnings. The studies attempted to discriminate between two competing hypotheses on how the stock market reacts to reported earnings: the "mechanistic" hypothesis, which states that the stock market reacts mechanically to changes in earnings due to accounting policy changes, and the "efficient market" hypothesis, which holds that the stock market does not react to changes in earnings due to accounting policy changes unless the accounting changes affect the cash flows of a firm (e.g., tax payments in FIFO/LIFO changes).

Among the accounting changes investigated by earlier studies were changes from accelerated depreciation to straight-line depreciation, from deferral of investment tax credits to flow through, and from FIFO inventory method to LIFO. Researchers studied the reaction of stock prices to earnings announcements immediately following a change in accounting policies. The evidence reported by these studies is generally inconsistent with the hypothesis that the stock market reacts mechanically to the accounting numbers by ignoring the effects of the accounting changes. Based on this evidence, some researchers have argued that it is unlikely that firms switch accounting policies to fool the stock market.

In light of the above conclusion, recent studies investigating the choice of accounting procedures by firms have examined the following question: If the stock market is not fooled by accounting changes, why do managers care about the accounting policies of their firms? This literature (the positive accounting theory literature) analyzes the use of accounting numbers by

---

[1] See Watts and Zimmerman (1986) for a comprehensive review of the literature.

various parties that have contractual and regulatory relationships with firms: namely, bondholders, managers, and regulators. The proponents of the positive accounting theory hypothesize that if there are nonzero costs associated with writing and enforcing various contracts that use accounting numbers, managers have reasons to care about the policies used in defining and computing accounting numbers. This concern exists even if the stock market can "see through" the differences in accounting policies of a given firm across time and among different firms at any point in time.

The most frequently stated hypotheses in the positive accounting theory literature deal with the effect of the choice of management compensation plans, debt covenants, and political costs on accounting policies. Most management compensation plans make the awards contingent upon meeting or exceeding performance as measured by accounting numbers. Hence, it is hypothesized that managers have incentives to choose or switch accounting policies to affect their compensation awards. This, of course, assumes that the compensation committees of the boards of directors do not adjust the reported numbers for the effect of accounting changes.

Similarly, since debt covenant restrictions are often stated in terms of accounting numbers, it is hypothesized that firms have incentives to choose or change accounting policies to meet restrictions they would otherwise violate. Finally, it is argued that, since reported accounting numbers are used by politicians and other regulators, firms threatened with increased political costs (for example, the windfall profits tax levied on oil companies) choose policies that reduce current reported earnings and thus minimize political costs.

Empirical studies of the validity of the above hypotheses have analyzed statistically large cross-sectional samples of data. Simple proxy variables were used to represent each of the factors considered important. Among the variables used were debt/equity ratio, a 0/1 dummy variable for the existence of a management compensation plan tied to accounting numbers, and firm size (as a proxy for political visibility). There were two frequently found empirical regularities: firms with management compensation plans and high debt/equity ratios were most likely to choose liberal accounting procedures, and larger firms were likely to choose conservative accounting procedures.

But today's understanding of the determinants of a firm's accounting policy choices and changes is still limited. Interpretation of the empirical evidence is difficult because simple proxies have been used to test rich and complex hypotheses. For example, the debt/equity ratio is often used as a proxy to test the hypothesis that firms facing tight debt covenant restrictions are likely to choose liberal accounting policies. Holthausen and Leftwich (1983), in a recent review of this literature, state that "further progress depends on innovation in theory and empirical tests rather than continued application of the current state of the art." It is in this spirit that I undertook a descriptive analysis of a single company to gain further insights into the accounting policy decisions of firms.

REPORTING POLICY CHANGES AT
HARNISCHFEGER: A CASE STUDY

This section describes the circumstances surrounding the major reporting policy changes that occurred at Harnischfeger Corporation and analyzes the reasons for the changes. The section begins with a brief description of the site-selection and data-collection processes. Following this, some background information on Harnischfeger's business and products is presented. Next, the financial crisis that the company experienced in 1982 and the subsequent management and strategic changes are described. Finally, I discuss the specific accounting changes that the company made and the management's stated reasons for instituting them.

Site Selection and Data Collection

The search for a site started with a NAARS data base listing of companies that made an accounting change in fiscal 1984. From among these companies, I chose Harnischfeger Corporation for two reasons. First, in terms of the number of changes, as well as their effect on the reported profits of the corporation, the accounting changes of Harnischfeger were far more significant than those of any other corporation on the list. Second, and equally important, Harnischfeger's management was willing to discuss the reasons for their accounting decisions and to provide access to the relevant data. Thus, the site selection was not random.

The data for the analysis presented in this chapter were obtained from two sources. First, public documents, including the company's annual reports, proxy statements, 10-K statements, analysts' reports, and articles from the financial press were used to gather information on the company's background and its accounting policy changes. Next, semistructured interviews with top management were conducted. Information gathered in these interviews was supplemented by internal documents obtained from the firm.

Company Background

Harnischfeger Corporation is an industrial machinery manufacturer based in Milwaukee, Wisconsin. The company was originally started as a partnership in 1884 and was incorporated in Wisconsin in 1919 under the name Pawling and Harnischfeger. Its name was changed to the present one in 1924. The company went public in 1929 and is currently listed on the New York Stock Exchange. In the fiscal year ending October 31, 1984, the company reported a net income after tax of $16 million from $489 million revenues and $640 million total assets.

The company has two major operating segments: the P&H Heavy Equipment Group, and the Industrial Technologies Group. The heavy equipment group consists of the construction equipment and the mining and electrical equipment divisions; the industrial technologies group consists of the material-handling equipment and the engineering divisions.

Harnischfeger is a leading producer of construction equipment. Its products, bearing the widely recognized brand name P&H, include hydraulic cranes and lattice boom cranes. These are used in bridge and highway construction and for cargo and other material-handling applications.

Electric mining shovels and excavators constitute the principal products of the mining and electrical equipment division of Harnischfeger. The company has a dominant market share of the mining machinery market. The company's products are used in coal, copper, and iron mining. A significant part of the division's sales in recent years came from the sale of spare parts.

The material-handling division of Harnischfeger is the fourth-largest U.S. supplier of automated material-handling equipment. The division's products include overhead cranes, portal cranes, hoists, monorails, and components and parts. Since an increasing number of manufacturing firms have been emphasizing cost-reduction programs involving automation, the material-handling equipment business of the company appears to be a growth business.

Harnischfeger also provides engineering-systems services through its subsidiary, Harnischfeger Engineers. The subsidiary engages in design, custom software development, and project management for factory and distribution center automation projects. While revenues from the division accounted for only 12 percent of the total for the company in 1985, management expects this business to be a major source of the company's future growth.

Harnischfeger's operations extend worldwide through a number of subsidiaries, affiliated companies, and licensees. Export and foreign sales constitute a significant portion of the company's total revenues.

Financial Difficulties of 1982

The machinery industry experienced a period of explosive growth during the 1970s. Harnischfeger expanded rapidly during this period, with sales growing from $205 million in 1973 to $644 million in 1980. To fund its growth, the company relied increasingly on debt financing. The firm's debt/equity ratio rose from 0.88 in 1973 to 1.26 in 1980. The worldwide recession in the early 1980s caused a significant drop in demand for the company's products starting in 1981 and culminated in a series of events that shook the financial stability of Harnischfeger.

Reduced sales and the high interest payments led to poor profit performance; a loss of $77 million was reported in 1982. Management commented on its financial difficulties in the 1982 annual report.

> There is persistent weakness in the basic industries, both in the United States and overseas, which have been large, traditional markets for P&H products. Energy-related projects, which had been a major source of business of our Construction Equipment Division, have slowed significantly in the last year as a result of lower oil demand and subsequent price decline, not only in the U.S. but throughout the world. Lack of demand for such basic minerals as iron ore, copper and bauxite had decreased worldwide mining activity, causing reduced sales for mining equipment, although coal mining remains

relatively strong worldwide. Difficult economic conditions have caused many of our normal customers to cut capital expenditures dramatically, especially in such depressed sectors as the steel industry, which has always been a major source of sales for all P&H products.

The significant operating losses recorded in 1982 and the credit losses experienced by its finance subsidiary caused Harnischfeger to default on certain covenants of its loan agreements. The most restrictive provisions of the company's loan agreements required it to maintain a minimum working capital of $175 million, consolidated net worth of $180 million, and a ratio of current assets to current liabilities of 1.75. On October 31, 1982, the company's working capital (after reclassification of about $115 million long-term debt as a current liability) was $29.3 million, the consolidated net worth was $142.2 million, and the ratio of current assets to current liabilities was 1.12. Harnischfeger Credit Corporation, an unconsolidated finance subsidiary, also defaulted on certain covenants of its loan agreements; this was largely due to significant credit losses related to the financing of construction equipment sold to a large distributor. Because of these covenant violations, Harnischfeger's long-term debt of $124.3 million became due on demand, the unused portion of its bank revolving credit line of $25.0 million became unavailable, and the unused short-term bank credit lines of $12.0 million were canceled. In addition, the $25.1 million debt of Harnischfeger Credit Corporation also became immediately due. The company stopped paying dividends and began negotiations with its lenders to restructure its debt to permit the company to continue to operate. Price Waterhouse, the company's audit firm, issued a qualified audit opinion in the company's 1982 annual report.

Corporate Recovery Plan

Harnischfeger responded to its financial crisis by developing a corporate recovery plan. The plan had four elements: (1) changes in top management, (2) cost reductions to lower the break-even point, (3) reorientation of the company's business, and (4) debt restructuring and recapitalization. The company's actions in each of these four areas are described below.

Following the advice of a reputable management consulting firm, Henry Harnischfeger, then chairman of chief executive officer of the company, created the position of chief operating officer. After an extensive search by Harnischfeger, William Goessel, who had considerable experience in the machinery industry, accepted the position in August 1982. Jeffrey Grade was another important addition to the management team; he joined the company in 1983 as senior vice president of finance and administration and chief financial officer. His appointment followed the early retirement in 1982 of the previous vice president of finance. The engineering, manufacturing, and marketing functions were also restructured to streamline the company's operations.

At the time he joined the company, Goessel was aware of the financial problems facing Harnischfeger. He knew, however, that the company had a strong market position in several of its businesses and felt he could manage the company out of its difficulty. To deal with the short-term liquidity squeeze, the company initiated a number of cost-reduction measures. These included (1) reducing the workforce from 6,900 to 3,800; (2) eliminating management bonuses, reducing benefits, and freezing wages of salaried and hourly employees; (3) liquidating excess inventories and stretching out payments to creditors; and (4) permanently closing the company's construction equipment plant at Escanaba, Michigan. These and other related measures improved the company's cash position considerably and helped reduce the rate of loss during fiscal 1983.

Simultaneously with these cost-reduction measures, the new management made some critical strategic decisions to reorient the company's businesses. First, it entered into a long-term agreement with Kobe Steel, Ltd. of Japan. Under this agreement, as Harnischfeger phased out its own manufacture of cranes, Kobe agreed to supply it with construction cranes for sale in the United States. This step was expected to reduce significantly the manufacturing costs of Harnischfeger's construction equipment, enabling it to compete effectively in the domestic market. Second, the company decided to emphasize high-technology markets by targeting the material-handling equipment and systems businesses for future growth. To facilitate this strategy, the company created a new group called the Industrial Technologies Group. As part of this new emphasis, the company stated that it would develop or acquire new products, technology, and equipment to expand its abilities in providing computer-integrated solutions to material-handling, storing, and retrieval applications hitherto not pursued by the company in industries such as distribution warehousing, food, pharmaceuticals, and aerospace.

As the company was implementing its turnaround strategy, it was also engaged in complex and difficult negotiations with its bankers. On January 6, 1984, the company entered into agreements with lenders to restructure its debt obligations into 3-year term loans secured by fixed as well as other assets, with a 1-year extension option. The agreement specified, among other restrictions, minimum levels of cash and unpledged receivables, working capital, and net worth.

The company reported a net loss of $35 million in 1983, down from the $77 million loss the year before. Based on the actions taken during the year, management expressed confidence that the company would soon return to profitability. The 1983 annual report stated this belief:

> We approach our second century with optimism, knowing that the negative events of the last three years are behind us, and with a firm belief that positive achievements will be recorded in 1984. By the time the corporation celebrates its 100th birthday on December 1, we are confident it will be operating profitably and attaining new levels of market strength and leadership.

During 1984, the company reported profits during each of the four quarters, ending the year with a pretax operating profit of $5.7 million and a net income after tax and extraordinary credits of $15 million. During the year, the company raised substantial new capital through a public offering of debentures and common stock. Net proceeds from the offering, which totaled $150 million, were used to pay off all the company's restructured debt.

Changes in Financial Reporting Policies

While Harnischfeger Corporation was undergoing significant operational and financing changes, its management also changed financial reporting policies. These included changes in accounting principles as well as changes in accounting estimates. Collectively, these changes accounted for most of the reported profits of the company in 1984 and, more important, changed significantly the reporting philosophy of the company. The accounting changes will likely affect the company's reported numbers in all future periods.

During fiscal years 1984 and 1985, the company made the following major accounting policy changes:

1. The depreciation method was changed from accelerated to straight line, applied retroactively to all assets. The cumulative effect of this change, not including the reduction in the current year's depreciation expense, increased net income for 1984 by $11.0 million; this was reported as one-time gain on the income statement. The company reported that the impact of the new method on the depreciation expense for 1984 was insignificant.
2. The company also changed its estimated depreciation lives for certain U.S. plants, machinery, and equipment and the estimated residual values on certain machinery and equipment effective the beginning of the fiscal year 1984. This change increased the pretax reported profit by $3.2 million.
3. In 1984, the company changed its rate of return assumption for determining pension expense. The rate assumed was 9 percent, compared to 8 percent in 1983 and 7.5 percent in 1982. During the year, the company also restructured its pension plan. The effect of the changes in the rate of return assumption for the pension plan, and the plan restructuring, reduced the pension expense by approximately $4.0 million in 1984. In addition, the company recaptured $39.3 million in excess plan assets from the pension-plan restructuring. This $39.3 million cash gain was treated, as required by accounting rules at that time, as an actuarial gain; it is being amortized over the 10-year period that commenced in 1984. This led to a $3.93 million pretax gain in 1984.
4. Effective fiscal 1984, for certain foreign subsidiaries the company changed the fiscal year ending from July 31 to September 30. Thus the 1984 consolidated income statement of Harnischfeger included the results of 15 months of operations for these subsidiaries. This action increased 1984 net sales by $5.4 million; the profit effect of this change was reported to be immaterial.

5. During 1985, the company changed its accounting for durable patterns and tooling. Previously, the cost of patterns and tooling was expensed in the year of acquisition. Under the changed method, these assets are capitalized and their cost amortized over their estimated useful lives. The cumulative effect of the change on fiscal years prior to 1985 increased the 1985 net income by $2.85 million. The impact of the change on the annual expense in 1985 was not disclosed, but was described as "insignificant."
6. In 1985, the company also changed the pay increase assumption used for computing the pension expense from 6.5 percent to 5.5 percent. This change reduced the 1985 pension expense by approximately $0.4 million.

A number of points related to these changes are worth mentioning. First, the cumulative effect of the decisions accounts for most, if not all, of the reported 1984 profits. Second, all the changes affect reported profits not only in the year of the accounting change but also in several future periods; given the current disclosure requirements, it is quite difficult to estimate these future effects. Third, the only accounting changes among the above that had a direct cash-flow effect were the pension accounting changes.

Management's Reasons for Accounting Changes

The impetus for the changes in Harnischfeger's accounting policies seems to have come from two major events: the financial crisis of 1982 and the change in top management. Within the company, the accounting policy-change process was initiated by the chief financial officer, who first consulted the external auditors on whether the proposed changes would be acceptable to them. After the external auditors gave their approval, the rest of the top management of the firm was informed of the proposal. The role of the audit committee and the rest of the board of directors was quite limited. The board's primary concern was apparently to make sure that the external auditors approved of the proposed changes. The auditors pointed out that the changes represented a shift in the company's reporting philosophy, but they were willing to recommend them, given the circumstances of the company.

In explaining the decision to change its depreciation policies, the company disclosed (in a footnote to the financial statements) that "the changes in accounting for depreciation were made to conform the corporation's depreciation policy to those used by manufacturers in the corporation's and similar industries and to provide a more equitable allocation of the cost of plants, machinery, and equipment over their useful lives." Similarly, the company explained its decision to capitalize the tooling and patterns costs by stating that "the change was made to recognize the corporation's investment in these assets and to provide a better allocation of their cost over their useful lives." The company did not disclose the reasons for its other accounting changes.

During my visit to the company, management gave three specific reasons for the accounting changes: the management's belief that external parties could not fairly compare Harnischfeger's performance with that of its competitors; the firm's recent experience with its debt covenant requirements, which were based on reported accounting numbers; and the internal management consequences of accounting policies chosen for external reporting purposes. These three reasons are discussed below in detail.

Prior to the recent changes, most competitors had used more liberal accounting policies than Harnischfeger. The company listed its significant competitors as Dresser Industries, Caterpillar, Eaton, Bucyrus-Erie, Marion Power Shovel, and Litton Industries. With the exception of Caterpillar, all these companies used straight-line depreciation in 1983. Similarly, with the exception of Dresser Industries, which assumed an 8 percent rate of return in determining its pension expense, the others assumed a return of 7.5 percent or less. Harnischfeger's management felt that, because of its conservative accounting policies, the company had been consistently reporting lower profits than its competition. The chief financial officer of the company emphasized that, given the current disclosure requirements, he believed external users did not make appropriate adjustments for accounting differences. He pointed out that no clear evidence existed to show that external parties adjusted reported accounting numbers for accounting policy differences. Given this belief, Harnischfeger's management felt that its conservative accounting policies had impaired the company's ability to compete effectively with other firms for capital, customers, and talented employees. In fact, management felt that the implementation of major strategic changes for the survival and growth of the company would not have been possible under its previous financial reporting policies.

As mentioned above, a major part of the company's recovery plan was to issue fresh debt and equity to retire the restructured debt, which carried very strict covenants and a very quick repayment schedule. In 1984, the company issued $150 million in senior debt, subordinated debentures, and common stock. Just before these public issues, the company announced its return to profitability after the substantial losses reported in the prior 2 years. While management attributed its success in raising substantial new capital to the sound strategic changes made in the company's operations, it nonetheless strongly believed that its efforts had been greatly aided by the company's return to profitability.

The management of Harnischfeger did not believe that it was fooling the stock market through its accounting changes. On the contrary, the company took a proactive role by explaining its accounting policy changes to the analysts. The company knew that the analysts would adjust the company's reported numbers for the effect of the accounting changes in the year of the change. But given the difficulty in tracing the effects of these changes in subsequent years, management did not believe that profits in subsequent years would be adjusted. In fact, it was this belief that had initially made management worry about the ability of investors to compare Harnischfeger with its competitors on a fair basis.

Management's accounting changes were also influenced by its experience with the recent violation of debt covenant restrictions and the consequent financial crisis. Management felt that during its financial difficulties the company had not received any special beneficial treatment from its lenders when they enforced the debt covenant restrictions—even though the company had used conservative accounting policies. The traumatic experience resulting from the consequences of violating these covenants made the company determined to avoid any future violations. To this end, management felt that violations were less likely if more liberal accounting policies were adopted.

Some internal management factors also appear to have influenced the company's accounting decisions. The company had used the same accounting rules for external reporting and for internal management accounting. The company's pricing was based on fully allocated product costs, and therefore its accelerated depreciation policies apparently caused its products to be overpriced relative to competition.[2] In addition, the higher depreciation charges led its divisions to demand increased capital reinvestment for maintaining and replacing fixed assets.

A similar internal management reason was cited as a factor in the decision to capitalize the company's tooling and patterns expense. Under the company's previous capital-budgeting system, capitalized costs were subject to top management approval, whereas decisions regarding other costs were decentralized. Since tools and patterns were expensed, these costs were not controlled by the top management even though they accounted for a significant amount of investment. As part of its overall cost-control effort, the new management felt that it needed better control over tooling and patterns costs. The most practical way to accomplish this objective was to start treating the item as a capital expenditure. Once this treatment was adopted for internal purposes, the company believed that it should use similar treatment for external reporting as well.[3]

In sum, a belief about the inability of the external users of accounting data to adjust for Harnischfeger's conservative financial reporting, the unpleasant experience with its debt covenant restrictions, and the interaction between management accounting and external reporting were the major reasons for the company's change in its accounting policies.

Underlying all the accounting changes was a reporting philosophy outlined by the chief financial officer (now president) of the company:

> In accounting, there is no such thing as absolute truth. The same underlying reality can be accounted for using a range of assumptions. The earlier philosophy of this company was to choose the conservative alternative whenever there was a choice. Now we have decided to change this. We would like to tell the world that we are alive and well. We wish to tell the truth but do not want to be overly conservative in doing so.
>
> When the outside world compares our financial performance with that of other companies, they may or may not take the time and effort to untangle the effects of the differences in financial policies that various companies follow. My own belief is that people adjust for the obvious things like one-time gains and losses but have difficulty in adjusting for ongoing differences.

---

[2] See Cooper and Kaplan (1987) for a discussion of the prevalence of this practice.
[3] Internal management factors were also cited by another company that I visited as a reason for a recent change in its depreciation policies for equipment leases.

In any case, these adjustments impose a cost on the user. If people adjust for the differences in accounting policies when they compare us with other companies, then it should not matter whether we follow conservative or liberal policies. But suppose they do not adjust. Then clearly we are better off following the more liberal policies than conservative policies. I am not sure whether people make the adjustments or not, but either way we wish to present an optimistic version of the picture and let people figure out what to do with those numbers.

As a company you have to put the best foot forward if you want to raise capital, convince customers that you are a viable company, and attract talented people to work for the company. I feel that the financial reporting should help rather than hinder the implementation of our operating strategy. In my opinion, the changed accounting format highlights the effectiveness of our strategy better than the old policies do.

Role of Accounting Literature Hypotheses

As I mentioned earlier, the positive accounting theory literature hypothesizes two primary factors leading to income-increasing accounting changes of the type made by Harnischfeger: debt covenant restrictions and management compensation plans specified in terms of accounting numbers. In Harnischfeger's case, these two factors seem to have played only a minor role in the company's accounting policy decisions.

Harnischfeger did not change its accounting policies to avoid an anticipated violation of debt covenant restrictions. Rather, the changes were a reaction to the painful experience of having violated such covenants. Management felt that the company's lenders had not distinguished between conservative and liberal accounting policies in specifying and administering debt covenant restrictions. It also knew, however, that an accounting policy change, solely made to avoid debt covenant restrictions, would be detected by the lenders who would then take appropriate action. By choosing to change its accounting policies when the company was not in immediate danger of violating any restrictions, the management felt it would avoid future problems.

Although Harnischfeger has an executive incentive plan under which senior executives of the company are awarded bonuses based on accounting earnings, the desire to achieve short-term profit targets for bonus purposes does not appear to have been a factor in management's accounting policy changes. The company's bonus awards had been linked to the achievement of profit budgets specified annually at the beginning of the year. Since all the accounting policy changes documented in this study were made at the beginning of the year, the profit budget for each year was prepared using the same accounting policies as the ones employed in calculating the actual profits. This led to an automatic adjustment of the profit performance for the effects of the accounting policy changes in the determination of the management bonus awards.

Harnischfeger's management did expect to receive an indirect (and, in its view, a legitimate) benefit from its accounting decisions. It felt that the accounting changes would enhance the company's ability to raise the resources necessary to implement its new operating strategy. The company's shareholders would benefit from the improvements in the company's long-term profitability. Management clearly expected to be rewarded for this achievement.

SUMMARY AND DISCUSSION

As noted, the analysis presented in this chapter, being based on a single case study, cannot be uncritically generalized. The following discussion therefore focuses on identifying areas for further research rather than on drawing definite conclusions.

The single most important reason for Harnischfeger's financial reporting philosophy appears to have been management's belief that it is costly, if not impossible, for the external users of accounting data to adjust for the effects of accounting policy differences across firms. Despite the substantial evidence on the efficiency of the capital markets, the managers I talked with at Harnischfeger were unconvinced of the stock market's ability to "see through" accounting policy differences.[4]

The efficient capital markets literature is by no means conclusive on the nature of the relation between accounting earnings and stock prices. Much of the research deals with stock returns and not the levels of stock prices.[5] Also, the studies that analyze the stock price reaction to accounting changes do not examine the recurring earnings effects of these changes. Instead, they examine the stock price behavior only in the year of the accounting change—the period in which the earnings effects can be ascertained most easily. There is a clear need for additional research in this area. Without such research, it is difficult to present convincing evidence to managers as to whether their current beliefs are valid or not.

Even if the stock market sees through the effects of pure accounting decisions, there still may be other reasons for managers to care about their accounting policy choices when dealing with public capital markets. Auditors, underwriters, and trustees in bond offerings have reasons to prefer dealing with profitable firms, all else being equal. For example, the trustees in a bond offering may believe that they have a better chance to defend themselves successfully against potential law suits if the offering company is profitable.[6] This may explain why the management of Harnischfeger felt that

---

[4] A recent article, entitled "Manipulating Profits: How It's Done," *Fortune*, 25 June 1984, indicates that this belief is widespread among managers.

[5] See Lev and Ohlson (1982).

[6] I am grateful to Ross Watts for this example and this general hypothesis. See Watts (1977).

it was quite necessary for the company to report a profit, however modest, before the firm could successfully issue public debt and equity offerings. (This line of argument, of course, assumes that the legal system does not see through the complexities of financial reporting as easily as the capital markets do.) We currently have little understanding of the influence of the financial intermediaries on the accounting decisions of firms, and further research in this direction would be quite useful.

It may be appropriate to reexamine whether managers do make accounting decisions believing that capital markets are fully efficient.[7] Many managers, in fact, seem unconvinced by the impressive evidence academic literature has compiled on stock market efficiency. The question then is whether there are significant penalties for a manager who makes an accounting decision with an erroneous belief about its impact on the firm's stock price. If such penalties exist, sooner or later managers will learn what the penalties are. Otherwise, they may continue to believe (correctly or not) that the capital markets cannot see through the effects of pure accounting decisions and may make decisions accordingly. At present, we have little empirical evidence to show whether penalties exist for such behavior.

A second factor that influenced Harnischfeger's accounting policy decisions was the link between accounting policies used for external reporting and those used for internal planning and control purposes. Whether such linkage between financial and managerial accounting systems is a good practice is debatable. But given that it exists, the factors that affect the choices for one system are likely to be important for the other system.[8] The opportunity therefore exists to explore the linkage of financial reporting policy choices with management accounting and control systems.

Debt covenant restrictions and management compensation plans seem to have played only a minor role in Harnischfeger's accounting policy decisions. One explanation for this is that the links between opportunistic accounting decisions and debt and compensation contracts may be more valid for accounting accrual decisions than for the highly visible accounting policy changes.[9]

In summary, a variety of internal management considerations, and management's belief that it is costly for external users to adjust for the recurring effects of accounting policy differences across firms, seem to have been the significant reasons for Harnischfeger's accounting policy changes. While other researchers have also noted the importance of such factors in accounting decisions, further research is needed to better understand their role.

REFERENCES

Ball, R. 1985. "Accounting, Auditing and the Nature of the Firm." Manuscript, Australian Graduate School of Management, Sydney, Australia.

[7] Wyatt (1983) provides a similar argument.
[8] Watts (1977), Zimmerman (1979), Ball (1985), and Watts and Zimmerman (1986) also point out this possibility.
[9] See Healy (1985).

Cooper, R. C., and R. Kaplan. 1987. "How Cost Accounting Systematically Distorts Product Costs." Ch. 8 in this volume.

Healy, P. 1985. "The Impact of Bonus Schemes on the Selection of Accounting Principles." *Journal of Accounting and Economics* 7, 85–107.

Holthausen, R. W., and R. W. Leftwich. 1983. "The Economic Consequences of Accounting Choice: Implications of Costly Contracting and Monitoring." *Journal of Accounting Economics* 5:2, 77–117.

Lev, B., and J. A. Ohlson. 1982. "Market-Based Empirical Research in Accounting: A Review, Interpretation, and Extension." *Journal of Accounting Research* 20, Supplement, 249–322.

Watts, R. L. 1977. "Corporate Financial Statements, A Product of the Market and Political Process." *Australian Journal of Management* 2, 53–75.

Watts, R. L., and J. L. Zimmerman. 1986. *Positive Accounting Theory.* Englewood Cliffs, NJ: Prentice-Hall.

Wyatt, A. R. 1983. "Efficient Market Theory: Its Impact on Accounting." *Journal of Accountancy* (February), 56–60.

Zimmerman, J. L. 1979. "The Costs and Benefits of Cost Allocations," *Accounting Review* (July), 504–21.

CHAPTER 17

Changing Prices

The topic of accounting for the impact of changing prices on financial statements consists of two broad areas: accounting for relative price changes and accounting for general price-level (GPL) changes. Although many commentators have argued that the GPL and relative price proposals should be seen as complementary, and not competitive, there has been disagreement over this view. As a result, standard setters in many countries have often been confronted with a choice between the two systems, yet, in many cases, their final pronouncements have embodied elements of both relative and general price-level solutions. In the United States, for example, the Financial Accounting Standards Board (FASB) issued Statement No. 33 in 1979, requiring supplementary disclosures using both current cost (relative price changes) and constant dollar (GPL) accounting. Statement No. 33 disclosure requirements were subsequently suspended by the FASB, by a four-to-three vote, in Statement No. 89 issued in 1986. The FASB concluded that its brief "experiment" in accounting for changing prices did not warrant continuing mandatory disclosure requirements, and that "further supplementary disclosures should be encouraged, not required."[1]

While many factors were responsible for the early demise of the FASB experiment, including low single-digit inflation rates in the United States during much of the period when Statement No. 33 was effective, the dual presentation requirement of Statement No. 33, covering both current cost and constant dollar data, probably was a major factor, contributing to investors' confusion over the use of Statement No. 33 data.[2] Acknowledging this prob-

---

[1] "Financial Reporting and Changing Prices," *Statement of Financial Accounting Standards No. 89* (Financial Accounting Standards Board, 1986), para. 1.

[2] For an early, and prophetic, view of the dual presentation requirement of Statement No. 33, see Tom Herman, "New Standard on Inflation-Adjusted Data Is Seen Causing Confusion in Accounting," *The Wall Street Journal* (October 5, 1979). Herman found financial analysts fearing that "the average investor won't know which figures to rely on, if any, and won't understand how they were computed."

lem, the FASB issued Statement No. 82 in 1984 by the unanimous vote of its seven members, eliminating the constant dollar disclosure requirement. The FASB said it "decided to eliminate the historical cost/constant dollar disclosure requirements of Statement No. 33 because the evidence has indicated that reporting effects of changing prices using two different methods may detract from the usefulness of the information and that the historical cost/constant dollar information is less useful than the current cost/constant purchasing power information" (Statement No. 82, para. 8). By then, however, the damage from the dual presentation experiment was done. As noted, a subsequent FASB pronouncement (Statement No. 89) made the non-GPL disclosure requirements of Statement No. 33 voluntary as well.

Historically, the standard setters' interest in a non-GPL solution is a relatively recent phenomenon. Though standard-setting bodies have shown an active interest in "inflation accounting"[3] at least since the 1960s, until 1975 their interest was confined mainly to general price-level solutions. During this period, the standard setters in the following countries issued one or another form of tentative proposal that GPL accounting be given consideration: Argentina, the United States, Chile, the United Kingdom and Ireland, Australia, New Zealand, Mexico, and Canada. But standard setters' enthusiasm for a GPL solution (known as CPP, or current purchasing power, in the United Kingdom) declined precipitately in 1975–1976. It was then that the Sandilands Committee,[4] appointed by the U.K. government to render a comprehensive report on "inflation accounting," as well as the Securities and Exchange Commission (SEC) in the United States, declared their preference for a relative price solution over any kind of GPL.[5] As a result, in the United Kingdom and Ireland, a provisional exposure draft in favor of CPP accounting was scrapped, and, in the United States, the FASB shelved its 1974 exposure draft on GPL accounting. Influenced by these developments, standard setters in most countries shifted their focus from GPL/CPP toward relative price solutions.

In the end, final pronouncements embodying elements of relative and general price-level solutions were issued in (the then) West Germany, the United Kingdom and Ireland, the United States, New Zealand, Canada, Australia, and Mexico. Each country's solution is different in one or more respects from those of the others. For example, Mexico allows companies to use either relative or general prices. Only countries plagued by hyperinfla-

---

[3] The term "inflation accounting" has been applied to the general area of the study of the impact of changing prices on accounting reports. However, the term strictly refers to only a general price-level solution, and is a misnomer when applied to a combination of general price-level and relative price solutions. The term seems to have entered usage with the publication in the United Kingdom of the Sandilands Report (see below) in 1975, and, for reasons that are not clear, it came to be applied to whatever solution might be found to accounting for general inflation and for relative price changes.

[4] *Inflation Accounting*, Report of the Inflation Accounting Committee, F. E. P. Sandilands, Esq, CBE, Chairman (London: Her Majesty's Stationery Office, Cmnd. 6225, September 1975).

[5] During the same period, the standard-setting body in Australia also proposed a current value solution.

tion, such as Argentina, Brazil and Chile, have favored a general price-level solution. The International Accounting Standards Committee (IASC), confronted by this array of solutions from country to country, has declined to take a position, recommending only that companies disclose which approach they have adopted.[6]

At a conceptual level, the debate over the methodology of "inflation accounting" reflects not only the assumed underlying conceptual framework of accounting (including beliefs about the objectives of financial reporting) but also one's judgment concerning the supposed economic consequences. Hence, the debate has, at times, centered on "technical" issues such as the preferred capital maintenance concept (financial versus physical), and at other times on how particular accounting measures could tilt the behavior of affected parties such as management, employees, investors, creditors, and government. Policy recommendations have also been conditioned by standard setters' belief or nonbelief in the efficiency of the capital markets.

Partly responding to the confusion over the methodology of "inflation accounting," and partly because of the experimental nature of the methods used, the FASB and other standard setters have generally required only supplementary disclosures on changing prices' impact rather than alterations in the main financial statements. The standard setters also seem to be concerned with the likely disruption that a complete change to relative price accounting or general price-level accounting (or a combination) would provoke. Unlike most controversial problem areas in accounting, which potentially affect a limited number of accounts, the policy making on "inflation accounting" could have a pervasive effect throughout the financial statements. As an example of the "economic consequences" concern, some governments fear that an accounting regimen of generally lower reported profits under "current cost accounting" would lead to intensified pressure for a concomitant reform of the corporate income tax law.

In addition to these methodological concerns, the FASB and other standard setters have found that there is no strong demand among their constituents for the continued reporting of supplementary disclosures on changing prices.[7] Indeed, during the years between 1980 and 1985, when companies were subject to FASB Statement No. 33, many of them registered complaints in the narrative material in their supplementary disclosures, asserting that the adjusted information was misleading and not useful to investors. As noted, this lack of demand led the FASB to issue Statement No. 89 in 1986 suspending the mandatory reporting requirements of Statement No. 33.[8] In that same year, in the U.K., the Accounting Standards Committee (ASC) recommended

---

[6] IASC Standard 29, issued in 1989, does require the use of a general price-level adjustment for an "enterprise that reports in the currency of a hyperinflationary economy, whether [its financial statements] are based on a historical cost approach or a current cost approach."

[7] See the discussion below on the empirical studies on managements' and investors' use of current value information.

[8] Voluntary reporting of supplementary current cost/constant purchasing power data is still permitted, although few companies do so.

the withdrawal of Statement of Standard Accounting Practice No. 16 on "Current Cost Accounting" (issued in March 1980), after removing it from its "mandatory list" in 1985.

Though the GPL and relative price solutions have received only lukewarm endorsements from standard setters thus far, some commentators would like the FASB and other bodies to return to the "inflation accounting" experiment. As Robert K. Elliott, an executive office partner at the U.S. accounting firm of KPMG Peat Marwick, notes in "Dinosaurs, Passenger Pigeons, and Financial Accountants," even at a 4-percent inflation rate, "a company will have to pay more than twice as many dollars to replace a 20-year asset and nearly five times as many dollars to replace a 40-year asset." Thus, reliance on a historical cost financial system could distort long-term financial performance even when inflation rates are low. Elliott concludes that, if accountants continue to emphasize historical data and do not provide the more relevant "value" data, they could suffer the same fate as dinosaurs and passenger pigeons.

The distortion in measuring financial performance is also the concern of John L. Grant, then a senior executive at American Standard Inc., in the *Business Week* article, "Inflation's Full Impact on the Bottom Line." He laments the "corporate complacency about inflation-adjusted data" as well as the lack of attention paid to FASB Statement No. 33 data by the financial press and financial analysts. He bluntly warns that "managements, far more than investors, are courting disaster" by not using the Statement No. 33 supplementary disclosures in their dividend and investment decisions.

A small number of companies, both in the United States and in other countries, have made extensive "inflation accounting" disclosures, even during periods when there was no regulatory requirement to do so. Henry Schwarzbach and Richard Vangermeersch, in "The Current Value Experiences of The Rouse Company, 1973–1989," describe the innovative reporting approach taken by one real-estate developer, The Rouse Company (TRC). From 1976, TRC included in its annual reports an *audited* supplementary balance sheet based on current value accounting. The authors point to a *Forbes* article's analysis of the similarity between TRC's share price and its current value-based shareholders' equity per share (see Exhibit I) as evidence that TRC's current value reporting influenced, or at least tracked, the market's valuation of the company.

Since 1976, when the SEC issued Accounting Series Release (ASR) No. 190 requiring supplementary data on replacement cost, and particularly following the release of FASB Statement No. 33,[9] researchers have tried to find out the extent of investors' use of current value data, and the effect of the supplementary disclosures on stock returns. Surveys of financial analysts[10] show very little use of Statement No. 33 data, suggesting that stock market

[9] The SEC withdrew ASR No. 190 after the FASB's issuance of Statement No. 33.
[10] See Robert W. Berliner, "Do Analysts Use Inflation-Adjusted Information? Results of a Survey," *Financial Analysts Journal* (March–April 1983), pp. 65–72, and related articles in that issue.

returns were perhaps unaffected by Statement No. 33 data as well. William H. Beaver and Stephen G. Ryan confirm this inference in "How Well Do Statement No. 33 Earnings Explain Stock Returns?" In this article, they report the findings from their empirical analysis of stock returns during the period 1979–1982, extending an earlier study by Beaver and Wayne R. Landsman.[11] They find that, while historical cost earnings add to the "explanatory power" provided by the FASB's data, "knowledge of Statement No. 33 data does not significantly increase the ability of historical cost earnings to explain stock returns." In other words, while Statement No. 33 data are informative, in the aggregate they are no more informative than the historical cost earnings data.[12]

The use of Statement No. 33 data by managers, particularly for dividend policy decisions, is the subject addressed by Bala G. Dharan in "The Association Between Corporate Dividends and Current Cost Disclosures." The FASB noted in Statement No. 33 that the current cost income information "provides a basis for users' assessment of distributable income," that is, dividends.[13] Many authors have likewise suggested that managers should use current cost data in designing a proper dividend policy that preserves a company's capital.[14] To see whether corporate dividend policies were affected by Statement No. 33 data, Dharan examined the association between dividend changes and changes in historical cost and current cost earnings for 325 companies. Using the data from 1979 to 1982, Dharan concludes that "current cost data possess no incremental explanatory power for dividend decisions," although he finds "evidence of some learning effect [by managers] with respect to the use of current cost data" over the period examined. It may be that financial analysts, investors and managers needed more time (than given by the FASB) to learn how to interpret the current cost information and incorporate it in their decision models.

BIBLIOGRAPHICAL NOTES

Some of the works advocating historical cost, general price-level (i.e., constant dollar) systems, relative price systems, or dual combinations thereof,

[11] See William H. Beaver and Wayne R. Landsman, *Incremental Information Content of Statement 33 Disclosures*, Research Report (Financial Accounting Standards Board, 1983).

[12] This is not to imply that Statement No. 33 earnings were similar to historical earnings. Indeed, there was a substantial variation between the two sets of earnings across different industries. See Kristine Evans and Robert Freeman, "Statement 33 Disclosures Confirm Profit Illusion in Primary Statements," *FASB Viewpoints* (Financial Accounting Standards Board, June 24, 1983); "A Real-World Test for the New Inflation Rules," *Business Week* (April 14, 1980); and *FASB Inflation Accounting: The First Year—An E&W Survey* (Ernst & Whinney, 1980).

[13] However, the Accounting Standards Committee in the United Kingdom explicitly discouraged the use of current cost income for dividend decisions.

[14] For example, see Lawrence Revsine, "Let's Stop Eating Our Seed Corn," *Harvard Business Review* (January–February 1981), pp. 128–134. For a different perspective, see Alfred Rappaport, "Inflation Accounting and Corporate Dividends," *Financial Executive* (February 1981), pp. 20–22.

propose general accounting frameworks and are therefore listed in the Chapter 2's Bibliographical Notes. The following works, classified according to valuation concepts, are representative of the major normative arguments:

Historical Cost/Nominal Dollar

Paton, W. A., and A. C. Littleton: *An Introduction to Corporate Accounting Standards* (American Accounting Association, 1940). This is a classic work that has had a profound effect on the literature and practice.

Littleton, A. C.: *Structure of Accounting Theory* (American Accounting Association, 1953).

Kolter, Eric L.: "Why Not Retain Historical Cost?" *The Journal of Accountancy* (October 1963), pp. 35–41.

Ijiri, Yuji: "A Defense for Historical Cost Accounting," in Robert R. Sterling (editor), *Asset Valuation and Income Determination* (Lawrence, KS: Scholars Book Co., 1971), pp. 1–14. For a fuller statement of Ijiri's views, see his *Historical Cost Accounting and Its Rationality*, Research Monograph Number 1 (Vancouver, B.C.: Canadian Certified General Accountants' Research Foundation, 1981).

Anthony, Robert N.: *Tell It Like It Was* (Homewood, IL: Richard D. Irwin, Inc., 1983).

Historical Cost/Constant Dollar

Sweeney, Henry W.: *Stabilized Accounting* (New York: Harper & Brothers, 1936). (Reprinted in 1964 by Holt, Rinehart and Winston, Inc., and in 1978 by Arno Press.) This classic work has been highly influential in the movement for GPL accounting in the United States. In his Chapter III, Sweeney exhibits a preference for replacement cost valuation. His views in support of Current (Entry) Value/ Constant Dollar accounting, with a financial-capital-maintenance interpretation, may be found in his several articles, most of which are reproduced in Stephen A. Zeff (editor), *Asset Appreciation, Business Income and Price-Level Accounting, 1918–1935* (New York: Arno Press, 1976).

Schmalenbach, Eugen: *Dynamic Accounting*, originally published in 1955 and translated from the German by G. W. Murphy and Kenneth S. Most (London: Gee & Company (Publishers) Limited, 1959). (Reprinted in 1980 by Arno Press.)

Staff of the Accounting Research Division: *Reporting the Financial Effects of Price-Level Changes* (New York: American Institute of Certified Public Accountants, 1963). This work contains an especially rich pair of appendices which refer to actual applications and case studies.

Current (Entry) Value/Nominal Dollar
(Physical Capital Maintenance)

Matthews, Russell, and John Mc.B. Grant: *Inflation and Company Finance* (Sydney: The Law Book Co. of Australasia Pty Ltd., 1958). (A second edition was published in 1962.)

Revsine, Lawrence: *Replacement Cost Accounting* (Englewood Cliffs, NJ: Prentice-Hall, Inc., 1973).

Current (Entry) Value/Constant Dollar
(Real Financial Capital Maintenance)

Edwards, Edgar O., and Philip W. Bell: *The Theory and Measurement of Business Income* (Berkeley, CA: University of California Press, 1961). This classic work has had a major influence on the literature dealing with relative prices and GPL accounting.

Bell, Philip W.: *CVA, CCA, and CoCoA: How Fundamental are the Differences?* Research Monograph No. 1 'Melbourne: Australian Accounting Research Foundation, 1982). This monograph compares the author's preferred method with Chambers' Continuously Contemporary Accounting (CoCoA) and with the physical-capital-maintenance interpretation of Current (Entry) Value Accounting (CCA).

Current (Exit) Value/Constant Dollar
(Real Financial Capital Maintenance)

Chambers, Raymond J.: *Accounting, Evaluation and Economic Behavior* (Englewood Cliffs, NJ: Prentice-Hall, Inc., 1966). (Reprinted in 1974 by Scholars Book Co.) Also see Chambers's "Second Thoughts on Continuously Contemporary Accounting," *Abacus* (September 1970), pp. 39–55; and "Third Thoughts," *Abacus* (December 1974), pp. 129–137.

Sterling, Robert R.: *Theory of the Measurement of Enterprise Income* (Lawrence, KS: The University Press of Kansas, 1970). (Reprinted in 1979 by Scholars Book Co.)

McMonnies, Peter N. (editor): *Making Corporate Reports Valuable*, A Discussion Document by the Research Committee (Edinburgh: The Institute of Chartered Accountants of Scotland/Kogan Page, 1988).

Chambers, Ray: "A New Era in Corporate Reporting?" *The Accountant's Magazine* (February 1989), pp. 26–28. The author favorably reviews the above Scottish Institute publication.

Discounted Cash Flow

Canning, John B.: *The Economics of Accountancy* (New York: The Ronald Press Company, 1929). (Reprinted in 1978 by Arno Press.)

Staubus, George J.: *A Theory of Accounting to Investors* (Berkeley, CA: University of California Press, 1961).

Market Value/Nominal Dollar
(Financial Capital Maintenance)

MacNeal, Kenneth: *Truth in Accounting* (Philadelphia, PA: University of Pennsylvania Press, 1939). (Reprinted in 1970 by Scholars Book Co.)

Deprival Value (Value to the Business)/Nominal Dollar
(Physical Capital Maintenance)

Wright, F. K.: "A Theory of Inventory Measurement," *Abacus* (December 1965), pp. 150–155. (Reproduced in the second edition of this book.)

Solomons, David: "Economic and Accounting Concepts of Cost and Value," in Morton Backer (editor), *Modern Accounting Theory* (Englewood Cliffs, NJ: Prentice-Hall, Inc., 1966), pp. 117–140.

Inflation Accounting, Report of the Inflation Accounting Committee, F. E. P. Sandilands Esq, CBE, Chairman (London: Her Majesty's Stationery Office, Cmnd 6225, 1975).

Parker, R. H., and G. C. Harcourt: "Introduction to the First Edition," in R. H. Parker, G. C. Harcourt and G. Whittington (editors), *Readings in the Concept and Measurement of Income* (Deddington, Oxford: Philip Allan Publishers Limited, Second Edition, 1986), esp. pp. 28–31.

Deprival Value (Value to the Business)/Constant Dollar (Physical Capital Maintenance)

Stamp, Edward: "Income and Value Determination and Changing Price-Levels: An Essay Towards a Theory," *The Accountant's Magazine* (June 1971), pp. 277–292. (Reproduced in the second edition of this book.)

Baxter, W. T.: *Accounting Values and Inflation* (London: McGraw-Hill Book Company (U.K.) Limited, 1975).

Report of the Committee of Inquiry into Inflation Accounting, I. L. M. Richardson, Chairman (Wellington, New Zealand: Government Printer, 1976).

Several volumes are available in which the authors review and analyze the competing approaches to relative prices, general price-level applications, or both, and these include the following:

Sprouse, Robert T.: "Adjustments for Changing Prices," in Sidney Davidson (editor), *Handbook of Modern Accounting* (New York: McGraw-Hill Book Company, 1970), Chapter 30.

Rosen, L. S.: *Current Value Accounting and Price-Level Restatements* (Toronto: Canadian Institute of Chartered Accountants, 1972).

Hanna, John R.: *Accounting Income Models: An Application and Evaluation* (Hamilton, Ontario: The Society of Industrial Accountants of Canada, 1974). Examines the experience of Imperial Tobacco Company of Canada, Limited with replacement cost accounting during the years 1961–1968.

Barton, Allan: *An Analysis of Business Income Concepts,* ICRA Occasional Paper No. 7 (Lancaster, England: International Centre for Research in Accounting, University of Lancaster, 1975).

Anderson, James A.: *A Comparative Analysis of Selected Income Measurement Theories in Financial Accounting,* Studies in Accounting Research #12 (Sarasota, FL: American Accounting Association, 1976).

Davidson, Sidney, Clyde P. Stickney, and Roman L. Weil: *Inflation Accounting: A Guide for the Accountant and the Financial Analyst* (New York: McGraw-Hill Book Company, 1976). Also contains a discussion of the impact of GPL accounting on the financial numbers reported by major U.S. companies.

Scapens, Robert W.: *Accounting in an Inflationary Environment* (London: The Macmillan Press Ltd., Second Edition, 1981).

Whittington, Geoffrey: *Inflation Accounting: An Introduction to the Debate* (Cambridge: Cambridge University Press, 1983).

Lee, Tom: *Income and Value Measurement: Theory and Practice* (Wokingham, Berks: Van Nostrand Reinhold (UK) Co. Ltd., Third Edition, 1985).

A comprehensive review and analysis of the standards and other literature on "inflation accounting" is:

Tweedie, David, and Geoffrey C. Whittington: *The Debate on Inflation Accounting* (Cambridge: Cambridge University Press, 1984).

A series of research studies on current cost accounting appears in

Carsberg, Bryan, and Michael Page (editors): *Current Cost Accounting: The Benefits and the Costs* (London: Prentice-Hall International in association with The Institute of Chartered Accountants in England and Wales, 1984).

A review of some of the historical milestones in the work of academics and accounting bodies in the search for a resolution of the inflation accounting controversies is provided by the following article, reproduced in the third edition of this book:

Rosenfield, Paul H.: "A History of Inflation Accounting," *Journal of Accountancy* (September 1981), pp. 95, 98, 100, 102–104, 106, 108, 110, 112, 114, 116, 118–120, 122, 124, 126.

A discussion and description of the operation of a full-scale system of Historical Cost/Constant Dollar accounting is:

Stickler, Alan D., and Christina S. R. Hutchins: *General Price-Level Accounting: Described and Illustrated* (Toronto: Canadian Institute of Chartered Accountants, 1975).

A discussion and description of the operation of a full-scale system of Current (Entry) Value/Constant Dollar accounting, with a physical-capital-maintenance interpretation, is:

Drummond, Christina S. R., and Alan D. Stickler: *Current Cost Accounting: Its Concepts and Its Uses in Practical Terms* (Toronto: Methuen Publications, 1983).

An elaborate illustration of the operation of a full-scale system of Current (Entry) Value/Constant Dollar accounting, with a real financial-capital-maintenance interpretation, can be found in:

Edwards, Edgar O., Philip W. Bell, and L. Todd Johnson: *Accounting for Economic Events* (Houston: Scholars Book Co., 1979), Chapter 12. In Chapter 13, the authors draw comparisons among the several competing systems.

Several collections of previously published articles on relative price accounting, GPL accounting, or both, have been issued, of which the following are the best examples:

Dean, G. W., and M. C. Wells (editors): *Current Cost Accounting: Identifying the Issues—A Book of Readings* (Lancaster, England: International Centre for Research in Accounting, and Sydney, Australia: Department of Accounting, University of Sydney, 1977). (A second edition was published in 1979.)

Parker, R. H., G. C. Harcourt, and G. Whittington (editors): *Readings in the Concept and Measurements of Income* (Deddington, Oxford: Philip Allan Publishers Limited, Second Edition, 1986).

Three proceedings volumes from conferences held primarily to discuss the "inflation accounting" controversy are:

Sterling, Robert R. (editor): *Asset Valuation and Income Determination* (Lawrence, KS: Scholars Book Co., 1971).

Sterling, Robert R., and Arthur L. Thomas (editors): *Accounting for a Simplified Firm Owning Depreciable Assets* (Houston: Scholars Book Co., 1979).

Sterling, Robert R., and Kenneth W. Lemke (editors): *Maintenance of Capital: Financial versus Physical* (Houston: Scholars Book Co., 1982).

These papers cover recent international efforts in implementing "inflation accounting" rules:

Doupnik, Timothy S.: "The Evolution of Financial Statement Indexation in Brazil," *The Accounting Historians Journal* (Spring 1986), pp. 1–18.

McConnell, Pat: "Los Fundamentos de la Contabilidad en Mexico: The Basics of Mexican Accounting," *Accounting Issues* (Bear Stearns, October 11, 1991), pp. 2–26.

A proceedings volume from a conference sponsored by the FASB at which the effects of changing general and relative prices on decisions by managers, investors and creditors were examined in the light of possible improvements in financial reporting is as follows:

Griffin, Paul A. (editor): *Financial Reporting and Changing Prices: The Conference* (Financial Accounting Standards Board, June 1979).

For a FASB-sponsored capital markets study which found that "Statement 33 earnings variables provide no incremental information over and above that already provided by historical cost earnings," see:

Beaver, William H., and Wayne R. Landsman: *Incremental Information Content of Statement 33 Disclosures* (Financial Accounting Standards Board, 1983). A related article by Beaver and Stephen G. Ryan is reproduced in this chapter.

The following articles on the capital market impact of ASR 190 data appeared in a special journal issue:

Gheyara, Kelly, and James Boatsman: "Market Reaction to the 1976 Replacement Cost Disclosures," *Journal of Accounting and Economics* (August 1980), pp. 107–125.

Beaver, William H., Andrew A. Christie, and Paul A. Griffin: "The Information Content of SEC Accounting Series Release No. 190," *Journal of Accounting and Economics* (August 1980), pp. 127–157.

Ro, Byung T.: "The Adjustment of Security Returns to the Disclosure of Replacement Cost Accounting Information," *Journal of Accounting and Economics* (August 1980), pp. 159–189.

For an introduction to the above studies, see:

Watts, Ross L., and Jerold L. Zimmerman: "On the Irrelevance of Replacement Cost Accounting Information," *Journal of Accounting and Economics* (August 1980), pp. 95–106.

For follow-up studies, see:

Beaver, William H., Paul A. Griffin, and Wayne R. Landsman: "The Incremental Information Content of Replacement Cost Earnings," *Journal of Accounting and Economics* (July 1982), pp. 15–39.

Lustgarten, Steven: "The Impact of Replacement Cost Disclosure on Security Prices: New Evidence," *Journal of Accounting and Economics* (October 1982), pp. 121–141.

A summary of the empirical studies examining the use of current cost data can be found in:

DeBerg, Curtis L., and Keith A. Shriver: "The Relevance of Current Cost Accounting Data: A Review and Analysis of Recent Studies," *Journal of Accounting Literature* (1987), pp. 55–87.

For a critique of the FASB's suspension of Statement No. 33 requirements, see:

Swanson, Edward P., and Keith A. Shriver: "The Accounting-for-Changing-Prices Experiment: A Valid Test of Usefulness?" *Accounting Horizons* (September 1987), pp. 69–78.

The FASB's proposals for disclosing the market values of financial instruments (see the introduction to Chapter 10) have once again spotlighted the current value-historical cost debate. For a summary of the issues involved in this debate, see the following related articles:

"Market Value: The Debate Rages," *Financial Executive* (January–February 1993), pp. 30–36. A panel discussion with Thomas E. Jones, executive vice-president, Citibank; Patrick W. Kenny, group executive-finance and administration, Aetna; James J. Leisenring, vice chairman, FASB; and Walter Schuetze, chief accountant, SEC. Donald J. Kirk, professor at Columbia University and former FASB chairman, moderated.

Sutton, Michael H., and James A. Johnson, "Current Values: Finding a Way Forward," *Financial Executive* (January–February 1993), pp. 39–43.

Dinosaurs, Passenger Pigeons, and Financial Accountants

Robert K. Elliott

KPMG Peat Marwick

Imagine yourself the manager of a professional football team. You've built your team for years, and you've finally made it to the Super Bowl. You're ahead 52 to 16 at the end of the third quarter and feeling mighty good.

From *World*, The Magazine for Decision Makers, Vol. 20, No. 5 (1986), pp. 32–35. Reprinted by permission of KPMG Peat Marwick. Copyright © 1986 by KPMG Peat Marwick.

Suddenly, an official runs onto the field and shouts that the rules have been changed: Effective immediately, the low score wins!

Similarly, business people today have worked hard and built their prospects under one set of rules for measuring the results—generally accepted accounting principles (GAAP)—and it's reasonable to believe they'd be just as nonplussed if the measurement rules were changed in the middle of their game. Yet, the current rules are not serving us as well as they must in order for our economy to thrive and for the United States to meet the international competitive challenges of the coming decades.

The historical cost-reporting model mandated today is, in large measure, reactive to the Industrial Revolution of the nineteenth century. As such, it makes a number of assumptions that may not reflect present economic realities. First, it assumes that what is being measured is the production and distribution of goods. In reality, what we have today—especially in the United States—is an information-based economy increasingly producing services. This inadequacy makes accurately measuring the service economy difficult.

Second, the accounting model assumes, erroneously, that money has constant purchasing power. Third, it assumes that executory contracts, in general, require no accounting recognition. And, fourth, it continues to assume annual or, at best, quarterly financial reporting.

The principal method for entities to report their results remains through periodic, historical, cost-basis financial statements. Each of the four adjectives preceding the word "statements" implies a limitation of relevance from the user's perspective.

IS "PERIODIC" OFTEN ENOUGH?

In an era when communications had to be physically prepared and transmitted, annual statements were all that was feasible. Lately, we have progressed to quarterly statements, but the essential mechanism is still the same.

Economic, political, and technological events affect our economy with increasing speed, and the need for timelier information grows apace. Securities markets do the best they can to impound new information, but the results are necessarily crude in the absense of timely, company-specific information. More frequent reporting would result in more refined, accurate securities prices.

Technology now provides users of financial statements with the means to access data in real time through telecommunications. People are becoming accustomed to using public, real-time data bases, and companies now have the means to provide users with a "view" into their data bases. Users could access raw data and apply their own analytic and accounting models. This development could radically alter the character of financial reporting in the near future.

Companies will be under growing demand to make real-time access to their data bases available to sophisticated users, and they should be starting to address the questions of which types of data would be relevant to users and continuously accurate but, at the same time, not too revealing to competitors.

DOES HISTORY PREDICT THE FUTURE?

Users are not interested in history per se, but only in its usefulness in making predictions. Managers and companies that have succeeded in the past are considered more likely to succeed in the future. Future results are expected to resemble the past, adjusted for known and expected economic and company-specific changes. Critics of accounting have focused on surprises—mostly unexpected bankruptcies. Yet, financial accounting delivers, as its core product, historical statements. In an attempt to meet user demands, we have tacked some predictive information—such as maturities of long-term debt—onto historical financial statements, but the result is ad hoc and confuses the meaning of historical statements.

SOME THOUGHTS ON UNCERTAINTY

The accounting model is based on measuring things with a degree of certainty. A person buys a horse for $100. That transaction can be measured with near certainty: that's one horse, not two; $100, not $50. But, what of transactions in which the components of measurement are imprecise? More and more current transactions fall into this category of uncertainty or risk.

The accounting model assumes that transactions are essentially complete when booked, yet more and more of what actually goes on is future-oriented. Company A agrees to rent space from company B. The transaction is not booked when the agreement is made, but rather as the payments come due. Thus, the historical cost model does not do a good job of capturing executory contracts, that is, contracts that have been entered into but not yet completed. Certain executory contracts, including leases, are subject to disclosure in the financial statement notes, but almost as an afterthought.

The financial accounting model could easily be expanded to capture and report executory contracts. The resulting statements would be to accrual-basis statements as accrual-basis statements are to cash-basis statements. But, under current GAAP, executory transactions are not booked except as "exceptions."

Another example: Before FASB No. 2, companies were, in effect, free to determine whether to write off or capitalize research-and-development expenditures. What happened was that some companies with excellent R&D, but conservative accounting methods, wrote off what was clearly an asset. Others, whose R&D was of distinctly dubious value, decided to capitalize it. FASB Statement No. 2 resolved the issue by saying that everyone would write off R&D. Thus, a situation of uncertainty was resolved arbitrarily. The net effect was a diminution of the information value of the financial statements.

Still another example of inadequately dealing with uncertainty is FASB Statement No. 5 on contingencies. Company A has been sued for $100 million. If it is lucky, it will win and be out only legal costs. If it loses, it may be out the whole amount plus legal costs. Another possibility is that the suit will be settled somewhere in between. In short, the outcome is uncertain.

In situations like this, FASB Statement No. 5 makes the following policy determination: If the loss of the suit is probable, and the amount of loss can be reasonably estimated, it is reported in the financial statements. If either of those conditions is not met—if it is not probable or if it is probable but cannot be measured—it is left out of the financial statements and discussed in a footnote. Once again, the current accounting model is deficient in dealing with uncertainty.

DEALING WITH UNCERTAINTY

The growing market for financial forecasts is an indication that the business community is interested in addressing the issue of uncertainty. A financial forecast is management's best estimate of future financial results, reflecting the conditions it expects to be existent and the course of action it expects to take. The information content of a financial forecast goes well beyond the expected earnings per share, since it also discloses the key actors that are expected to influence a company's future results and the likely magnitudes of those effects.

Given the limited utility of historical costs information as a predictor of future events, the accounting model is going to have to deal with uncertainty—perhaps through mandated creation and publication of prospective information—if the model is to remain relevant.

There are growing demands for other ways to convey more information about uncertainty to financial-statement users. Possibilities now being discussed include an enhanced "management's discussion and analysis"; disclosure of the existence and effect on the financial statements of judgments, estimates, and assumptions inherent therein; and disclosure of risks and uncertainties existing at the balance sheet date that could lead to adverse consequences in the ensuing year, given the occurrence of reasonably possible adverse events.

COST-BASIS VERSUS VALUE

Another implicit and troublesome assumption in the historical cost model is that the monetary unit is fixed and constant over time. However, there are three components of the modern economy that make this assumption less valid than it was at the time the model was developed.

One component is specific price-level changes, occasioned by such things as technological advances and shifts in consumer preferences; the second component is general price-level changes (inflation); and the third component is the fluctuation in exchange rates for currencies. Thus, the book of value of a company, as reported in its financial statements, only coincidentally reflects the current value of assets.

Some have said that now that inflation is under control, there is no need to worry about its effect on financial statements. However, at a 4 percent inflation rate, a company will have to pay more than twice as many dollars to replace a 20-year asset and nearly five times as many dollars to replace a 40-year asset. Fixed assets and LIFO inventories, for example, can become very distorted, even at such "low" inflation rates as 4 percent.

One proposed, but controversial, approach to this problem is current-value accounting. Current value is a concept that has been around for many years. Indeed, it was Adam Smith who made the distinction between value in use (user value) and exchange value, and that remains the fundamental delineation of value theorists.

There are many concepts of value. Value in use is most likely the best basis for assessing the value of productive assets in a going concern. However, exchange value is more likely relevant for assets not in use, for example, vacant land. The value of an object to its user can only be subjectively determined, and subjective measurements are not considered acceptable for external financial reporting. In embracing the historical cost concept, financial accountants have chosen to ignore the problem of value and changes in value, and use cost as a surrogate for value. However, under the traditional accounting model, rising prices usually result in an overstatement of real income and an understatement of asset values. Many critics see this gap between historical costs and current value as a source of imperfect decision making by report users. Still others view it as an opportunity for insiders—particularly in the instance of management buyouts—to manipulate their superior knowledge of the value of a company's assets for personal gain at the expense of the public shareholders.

Columbia University law professor Louis Lowenstein raised this point in an article called "No More Cozy Management Buyouts" in the January–February [1986] issue of the *Harvard Business Review*. Professor Lowenstein wrote: "Insiders choose the timing of the buyout and can take advantage of important differences in the way the stock market, with its very high turnover rates, fixes the prices of the shares of a company and the way it prices the company as a whole. The temptation to profit from these differences, as well as to depress if not manipulate reported earnings or stock prices, is continuing and compelling. It's time we reappraised LBOs."

Defenders of the traditional historical cost system contend that the data generated are relatively objective and can easily be verified. They also argue that the built-in conservative bias resulting from failure to recognize unrealized gains and adherence to the lower of cost or market rule is supported by the business and investment communities.

The latter contention may well be valid. FASB Statement No. 33 requires the disclosure of value information on one or two bases, either price-level adjusted or current cost. Surveys taken since this rule became effective suggest that users do not find the information helpful, don't use it, and say it doesn't tell them anything they didn't already know. Preparers of the information complain that it is a nuisance to assemble.

For advocates of expanded-value reporting, these are disturbing findings, but there are possible explanations. Since FASB Statement No. 33 data are not audited, users may believe the information to be unreliable. Management, which is the preparer, may have motives for objection other than simply the nuisance factor.

For example, as pointed out earlier, there is a tremendous potential for manipulation in the difference between costs and value because management gets to sit on assets that are carried at amounts different from their values, and can use that gap to affect financial statements. A simple example is a case where a company bought stocks several years ago for $50 million that are now worth $100 million. That means management can take $50 million into income any time it chooses. If it has a bad quarter and needs $10 million, management can simply sell one-fifth of that stock and, presto, it has a good quarter. There are other, more complex, examples. It is possible that management opposes value accounting because it would eliminate this sort of financial flexibility.

Another objection to value reporting may be that the present accounting model allows management to fool itself into making suboptimal business decisions. What would have happened in the savings and loan industry if, for example, at the end of each quarter, managements had been required to mark their loan portfolios to market value? It can be speculated that the practice of lending long and borrowing short, which nearly buried many S&Ls when interest rates skyrocketed, would not have happened. Instead, managements would probably have done what banks have done in recent years, that is, balance their asset and liability portfolios so that they are prudently hedged.

Other management objections to value reporting are that it costs additional money to prepare, over and above the historical cost information, and that value numbers are "soft," and subject to errors, which paves the way for criticism of management should it turn out to be wrong.

Placing a current value on assets and liabilities involves varying degrees of difficulty. Financial instruments and cash are fairly easy to estimate, as is inventory that is turning over regularly. Buildings or equipment are more difficult to estimate, as are intangibles such as patents, rights, leaseholds, and goodwill.

Because the most difficult of these estimates are extremely complex, there is a tendency not to report current values. However, it would be better—even if theoretically impure—to report current values for those assets and liabilities that can be "current valued." Some companies already do: The mutual fund industry uses current values, as do certain real estate firms, such as The (pioneering) Rouse Company.

FINANCIAL INFORMATION IS NOT ENOUGH

There are many types of information beyond financial information that are relevant to economic decision making. As a result of the deficiencies of the historical cost-basis accounting model, there has been a tremendous growth in demand for collateral, supplemental information. Examples include data about the physical plant, present and prospective products, personnel, and operating and planning systems and strategies.

Users who attempt to base their entire decision-making process on financial statements are bound to be disappointed. Because of the limitations already noted on the usefulness of the financial information to make their decisions, historical cost-basis financial statements are an ever-decreasing component of the relevant information set.

HOW DO WE GET THERE FROM HERE?

As noted at the beginning of this article, companies have a legitimate interest in being measured under a stable set of rules. Even though financial executives can see the theoretical merits of some revisions in the model—whether those discussed above or others—they understandably place their company's interest ahead of the common wealth. They can, therefore, be expected to lobby to retain existing rules. The FASB, quite properly, considers such lobbying in setting standards; thus it is unlikely to alter accounting rules precipitously. Yet, as described above, those rules are increasingly obsolete. How do we break out of this fix?

Luckily, there exists a means. It is not necessary to jettison the present accounting rules and the financial statements that result from them. Because the securities markets can, and do, absorb supplementary information, evaluate its effects, and reflect it in securities prices, the route to change is supplementary disclosures in the financial statements. The basic financial statements would continue as they are, providing comparability over the years and allowing companies to report results on the basis they anticipated when they laid their plans.

Obviously, the costs and benefits of these proposals need analysis. This article is predicated on the assumption that the benefits would be extensive and the costs reasonable, given the increasing power of the computer to process information cheaply. However, accounting policy setters cannot act upon mere assumptions. Proper study of costs and benefits would have to precede adoption of the suggested changes.

THE WAY OF THE HORSE AND BUGGY?

Sandy Burton, former chief accountant of the SEC, now dean of the Columbia Business School, tells of an informal survey he has been conducting. He asks CFOs—who are generally CPAs—who within their organizations is the most likely candidate to be the next CFO. In most instances, he reports, the likely candidate is not a CPA. From this, he infers that companies are beginning to regard CPAs, and the type of historical cost information they deal with, as of declining utility.

Burton's point is anecdotal, of course, but there is growing evidence in the marketplace that he is on to something—that historical cost-basis information is of ever-declining usefulness to the modern business world. The issue for the financial accounting profession is to move the accounting model toward greater relevance or face the fate of the dinosaur and the passenger pigeon.

Inflation's Full Impact on the Bottom Line

John L. Grant

It is entirely possible for a corporation to show a profit when it is actually going out of business. This anomaly exists because the financial community has not developed a consensus on the definition of profits and the degree to which inflation erodes the financial firepower they represent. Instead, we face corporate complacency about inflation-adjusted data, something akin to silence from the business press, and indifference on the part of most securities analysts.

Recent reports celebrating the slowing of inflation threaten to dampen even the most enthusiastic support of inflation-adjusted data. That would be a serious mistake. Whether the rate of inflation is 6 percent or 16 percent, there can be no meaningful corporate scorekeeping without an accurate restatement of financial results to reflect inflation's impact. If anything, the drop from the superheated rates of recent years makes it all the more important for astute managers to seek out undistorted sales and earnings figures. Unadjusted data can show fat boosts in profits in an inflationary era but far

From *Business Week* (February 7, 1983), p. 8. Reprinted by special permission of *Business Week*. Copyright © 1983 by McGraw-Hill, Inc.

smaller rises in times of lower inflation. When the underlying economic structure is shifting, as is the case now, this rollercoaster effect yields highly erratic, and highly misleading, earnings patterns. Indeed, there is considerable evidence that only about half of reported corporate earnings are "real": The other half must be reinvested for companies just to jog in place. Consider these points:

- Because inflation swells revenues, managers often cannot tell whether a company turned out more or fewer units than in the prior period.
- Because inflation raises the value of goods produced, profits from selling the older, cheaper inventory are worthless to the extent that they must pay for costlier replacement goods.
- Because inflation increases the cost of new plant and equipment, conventional historical-cost depreciation fails to ensure that a company is retaining enough profits to replace old capacity.
- Because conventional reporting fails to show how much of "profits" should be earmarked for maintenance of the business and how much remains for real growth, a management that pays out dividends on the basis of unadjusted data may be returning capital, not profits, to shareholders and letting the company drift toward liquidation.

The dimensions of the situation are becoming increasingly clear. The Financial Accounting Standards Board's Statement 33 requires many corporations to compute inflation's effects on profit-and-loss figures. An FASB report on 846 industrial companies showed that their 1980 paid-out dividends, when restated on a current-cost basis, exceeded profits by 2.4 percent. Such disturbing reports underline the critical need for management to know at least whether a corporation under its stewardship is liquidating itself and, if not, to what extent it is generating funds for real growth. Yet in a survey of 201 companies last year by Arthur Young & Co., only slightly more than a third indicated an intention to adopt the FASB's Statement 33 data for internal management purposes. If a management is not even being honest with itself, how can it be expected to embrace more realistic public reporting?

Nowhere is this delusion more evident than in the refusal of managements to adopt last-in-first-out (LIFO) inventory accounting instead of first-in-first-out (FIFO). LIFO not only removes the majority of so-called inventory profits from reported earnings but also husbands corporate cash by reducing U.S. taxes. Yet approximately a third of the companies listed on the New York Stock Exchange have failed to adopt LIFO, preferring instead to maintain artificially high reported earnings. Such skittishness is understandable, for there is little evidence that the higher-quality LIFO earnings are recognized by securities analysts and in market price-earnings ratios. After almost 20 years of dealing with securities analysts, I am convinced that all but a few pay scant attention to the impact of inventory accounting on the quality of earnings per share.

Yet managements, far more than investors, are courting disaster by failing to ferret out and use inflation-adjusted data. The pitfalls are myriad. For example, resources may be misallocated. A division with aging plant and equipment may seem to be earning a high return on investment because the cost of that equipment was far lower when the investment was made. As a result, managers of divisions with newer, more efficient equipment are penalized in performance evaluations. Responding to such dangers, a handful of companies, including my own since the mid-1970s, have adopted internal management procedures that assess replacement depreciation to all operating units, remove inventory profits from results reported by operating units, assess a capital charge to operating units, and develop gauges for return on investment or return on net assets that reflect inflation-adjusted capacity to grow.

Such calculations have helped immeasurably to point up or prevent errors of judgment. At my company, for example, we realized a few years ago that a small manufacturing division had not earned $1.9 million in operating profits, as conventional accounting would show, but had actually lost $2.6 million and had lost money in each of the previous four years. Such data led to a decision to dispose of the business.

My purpose in raising these issues is to endorse the efforts of the FASB to insist on inflation-adjusted data that will become even more useful in assessing a company's "real" results. I urge securities analysts to wake up and start assessing inflation-adjusted price-earnings ratios as they compare the relative merits of various companies. Most of all, I urge corporate managements to start facing the facts.

The Current Value Experiences of The Rouse Company, 1973–1989

Henry Schwarzbach
University of Rhode Island

Richard Vangermeersch
University of Rhode Island

The Rouse Company (TRC) was voted the most creative/innovative real estate developer in a recent survey of the retail members of the International Council of Shopping Centers.[1] TRC has also been creative in its accounting for real estate through its strong advocacy of current value accounting. This article describes the innovative approach taken by TRC to disclose current value information in its financial statements.

TRC has been a leader in current value accounting among real estate

From *Accounting Horizons* (June 1991), pp. 45–54. Reprinted by permission of the American Accounting Association and the authors. Copyright © 1991 by the American Accounting Association.
[1] "Retailers Pick Favorite Developers: 1st Annual Survey Lists Top 5 in Six Categories Plus Best Overall," *Chain Store Age Executive*, August, 1988, p. 38.

companies, but is not alone in its belief that historical cost-based financial statements do not provide a fair representation of either financial performance or financial position for real estate firms. For example, companies such as Hilton, Holiday Inn, Marriott, Bay Financial, BTR Realty, and Sonesta have cautioned against the use of historical cost-based financial statements and supported a current value basis. Excerpts on current value reporting from the annual reports and 10-Ks of these companies appear in the Appendix.

TRC disclosed a version of current value reporting for fixed assets in its 1973 annual report within the "Letter to Shareholders" section. In its 1976 annual report, TRC upgraded both the method of determining the current value of fixed assets and the place of disclosure to a current value column in its formal balance sheet. TRC has continued to disclose current values in its annual balance sheets. With the decline of inflation and cessation of mandatory inflation reporting, one might disregard any attempts at current value reporting. Searfoss and Weiss, in their recent article, explained why many real estate companies support current value reporting even in times of low general inflation:

> Real estate assets traditionally have tended to fluctuate widely in value. Since inflation is currently under control, the increased interest in current value reporting is not due to changes in general price levels. Instead, the interest reflects a perceived need for better information about a real estate entity's assets and liabilities as well as the capacity of these assets to benefit the entity economically.[2]

Traditional historical cost reporting is especially inappropriate for real estate. Unrealized holding gains and losses are not reported and depreciation is provided on assets that are often appreciating in value. Current value reporting enables the major activity of a developer, improving the value of real estate, to be disclosed and evaluated.

A review of TRC's current value reporting is timely in view of the discussion on "Real Estate: The Impact of Current Value Reporting" at the 1989 AICPA annual meeting and the AICPA Real Estate Committee's continuing efforts to develop a policy statement. This Committee is reviewing the needs of users to determine an appropriate valuation model for that industry. In *SFAS 89*,[3] the Financial Accounting Standards Board (FASB) discontinued the mandatory inflation reporting of *SFAS 33*.[4] The FASB, however, encouraged firms to disclose supplementary information on the effects of changing prices.

Richard C. Breeden, chairman of the U.S. Securities annd Exchange Commission (SEC), is also recommending that the accounting profession

---

[2] D. Gerald Searfoss and Judith F. Weiss, "Current Value Reporting for Real Estate: An Industry Perspective," *Journal of Accountancy*, October 1990, p. 69.

[3] FASB, SFAS 89, *Financial Reporting and Changing Prices*, December, 1986.

[4] FASB, SFAS 33, *Financial Reporting and Changing Prices*, September, 1979.

review generally accepted asset valuation principles. He was quoted in *The Wall Street Journal*:

> If accounting standards aren't adequate to give an accurate picture of a firm's condition, they're not doing the job they need to do.[5]

Given the strong interest, by both the AICPA and the SEC, in investigating the usefulness of current value accounting, the pioneering experiences of TRC deserve review.

EVENTS LEADING TO THE INITIAL CURRENT VALUE DISCLOSURES

Three events had a significant impact on TRC in 1973. The first event was the AICPA Industry Accounting Guide, "Accounting for Retail Land Sales," which was approved for publication by the Accounting Principles Board.[6] One of TRC's major subsidiaries had to defer recognition of a $15,700,000 profit until the more stringent tests established by "Accounting for Retail Land Sales" were met. A second event affecting TRC was the continued losses on the development of low income housing by the Rouse-Wates subsidiary. For instance, in 1973, $1,500,000 was included as a loss in the "Operation Breakthrough" project sponsored by the U.S. Department of Housing and Urban Development (HUD). Net Income went from $2,340,000 in 1971 to a Net Loss (restated) of $897,000 in 1972 to a Net Loss of $5,791,000 in 1973. A third event was the SEC action of limiting disclosure of "cash flow per share" and similar data on the grounds that "these and other means of presenting financial data appear designed to decrease the credibility of conventional financial statements as a measure of business activity."[7]

Since "Earnings before Non-Cash Charges" and "Net Cash from Operations" were key figures in TRC's 1972 annual report, management felt that not being able to disclose these items would tend to depress the stock prices of TRC and other companies in its industry. At this point, the Chief Financial Officer concluded that there was a need to inform investors, in some other way, that net income on the historical cost basis was not a useful performance indicator. The CFO wanted to disclose evidence of economic *appreciation*, not economic *depreciation*. The 1973 decision to display current value information in the "Letter to Shareholders" section reflected more of a defense of the "Earnings before Non-Cash Charges" and "Net Cash from Operations" figures, rather than a purely aggressive move to current value reporting.

---

[5] Kevin G. Salwen and Robin G. Blumenthal, "What's It Worth? Tackling Accounting, SEC Pushes Changes with Broad Impact," *The Wall Street Journal*, September 17, 1990, p. 1.

[6] AICPA, *Accounting for Retail Land Sales*, 1973, pp. 39–41.

[7] "SEC Position on Reporting Cash Flow and Other Related Data: Excerpts from SEC Accounting Series Release No. 142, March 15, 1973," *The CPA Journal*, July, 1973, p. 616.

DISCLOSURES IN THE 1973
"LETTER TO SHAREHOLDERS"

Two items in the "Letter to Shareholders" section of the 1973 annual report require analysis. One was a defense of the continued use of "Earnings before Non-Cash Charges" and "Net Cash from Operations":

> In the meantime, we continue to consider "earnings before non-cash charges" (whatever it ultimately may be called) the most significant measure of our financial performance. We have consistently used this figure in our Financial Highlights statement, and, in the past, have reported it on a per share basis.
>
> We also report "net cash from operations" (after mortgage principal payments). Both measurements are traditionally used in the industry—by lenders, appraisers, assessors, and investors—in estimating values of income-producing properties and the performance of companies engaged in developing and owning such properties (p. 3).

The computations of "Earnings before Non-Cash Charges" and of "Net Cash from Operations" are in line with computations published in 1967 by the Special Technical Committee of the Education Committee of the American Institute of Real Estate Appraisers.[8]

The second explanation was found in the "Value Added Above Cost Now $40,200,000" subsection of the "Letter to Shareholders":

> Some important elements of these realities of real estate development are not reflected in our balance sheet, because standard accounting principles are not designed to reflect these conditions. In an attempt to communicate this aspect of our company, we have consolidated into a single set of figures the net available before debt service ("net available") from all of our properties with at least a full year of operations, as if they were a single asset. We have capitalized that "net available" at a nine percent rate to indicate a composite value of the properties. We have reported the total cost of the properties and the total outstanding mortgage debt. The net result is to report for the first time an estimated "Value Added Above Cost" and "Value Equity Above Debt" for all our properties taken as a whole.
>
> A principal goal of our company is to expand and improve our existing properties and add, through new development, to our pool of operating projects, thus increasing "earnings before non-cash charges," "net available," and "value added above cost." This is how our company grows (p. 6).

INCLUSION OF CURRENT VALUES IN THE
1976 BALANCE SHEET

Top management believed that TRC stock prices during 1975 were undervalued and feared a takeover attempt at a price below the underlying value of the company's real estate portfolio. They wanted security analysts to recog-

---

[8] American Institute of Real Estate Appraisers, *The Appraisal of Real Estate*, 5th Ed. (Chicago: American Institute of Real Estate Appraisers, 1967), pp. 282-3.

nize that TRC stock was undervalued and to see the market adjust the price of the stock upward. In order to promote this recognition, TRC changed its emphasis from reporting of "Earnings before Non-Cash Charges" and "Net Cash from Operations" to reporting the current value of assets in the Balance Sheet. TRC's auditors, Peat, Marwick, Mitchell & Co. (PMM), supported this change. Discussions were held with the Chief Accountant of the SEC and his staff, and TRC was advised by a leading academic. The Chief Accountant was quite insistent that, if current value procedures were to be utilized, they be followed consistently in good times and bad. The prime topic of contention with the SEC was TRC's desire to avoid accruing an amount for Estimated Taxes Payable on the Estimated Gain on Revaluation. Although the SEC first agreed to accept no accrual, it subsequently insisted on one. The accrual is currently included in the company's deferred tax liability reported in the current value column of the balance sheet. An explanation of TRC's method for computing the deferred income tax liability is included in the footnotes to their 1989 annual report:

> Because the current value financial statements presume that values will be realized over the long-term through operating cash flows and not through liquidation, the deferred income taxes on a current value basis is an estimate of the present value of income tax payments which may be made based on projections of taxable income through 2047. The projections of taxable income include projects presently under development and future, unnamed development projects and reflect all allowable deductions permitted under the Internal Revenue Code. The inclusion of future unnamed projects in the projections reduced the estimated present value of potential tax payments. . . . The discount rates used to compute the present values of income taxes are based on the internal rates of return used to compute the current values of assets, adjusted to reflect the Company's assessment of the greater uncertainty with respect to the ultimate timing and amounts of income tax payments (p. 32).

This approach is one of three possible methods mentioned in the 1984 AICPA Real Estate Accounting Committee report, "Guidance for an Experiment on Reporting Current Value Information For Real Estate."[9] There are a number of issues in TRC's computation of the deferred tax liability that need analysis. First, should the tax liability be discounted to its present value? Second, if discounting is used, should future unnamed development projects be included? Third, should a single discount rate be used for both assets and the deferred tax liability? Since TRC did not want to disclose deferred taxes at all, it is not surprising that they chose options that reduced their deferred tax liability. Because *SFAS 96* implementation is currently postponed and the topic of discounting the deferred tax liability has not been resolved by the FASB, companies reporting current values are left with a lack of guidance on this controversial issue.

In March 1976, the SEC issued *ASR 190*, requiring certain large corpora-

---

[9] Real Estate Accounting Committee, Accounting Standards Division, AICPA, *Guidanc‹ for an Experiment on Reporting Current Value Information for Real Estate*, December 31, 1984, p. 16.

tions to disclose the current replacement cost of inventories and property, plant and equipment.[10] TRC used *ASR 190* as the rationale for a change in both the computation and placement of current value data in the balance sheet, as explained on page 2 of the Special Report insert in its May 31, 1976 annual report:

> For the past three years, the letter to shareholders has included a "Value Added" table summarizing the company's estimate of value in its operating properties. This year, with the promulgation of replacement cost/current value accounting by the Securities and Exchange Commission, a new and important opportunity became apparent. With the concurrence of our auditors, the company developed a process for estimating and presenting current values in its financial reports. This process has met SEC requirements and has been accepted by our auditors—producing valuations that are a part of the certified financial statements.

The focal point for the valuation of capital assets in *ASR 190* was "replacement cost (new) of 'productive capacity' and depreciated replacement cost of such assets shown in the annual balance sheets."[11] TRC did not follow *ASR 190* but merely used it as support for the disclosure of current value information in the financial statements. TRC did not use replacement cost, as defined in *ASR 190*, to value its assets nor did it calculate replacement cost depreciation as required by *ASR 190*.

In order to estimate the current value of its real estate portfolio, TRC contacted real estate appraisal companies and received bids ranging from $250,000 to $400,000—much too high for the purpose. TRC then met with James D. Landauer Associates to discuss a procedure in which TRC's professional market research department would estimate fair market value and Landauer would review and analyze the computations. The valuation material was sent to Landauer, whose appraisers visited certain sites. Hence, Landauer was able to report on page 26 of the 1976 annual report that "As a result of our review and analysis of the data and the appraisal reports, we concur with this estimate of the total value of the property interests appraised." This approach enabled TRC to obtain what it believed to be credible current value measures at a reasonable cost.

Although PMM supported this process, it took some time for PMM and TRC to find a mutually acceptable wording for the audit opinion. TRC felt that PMM's wording was crucial if readers were to rely on the current value information; any hint of negativism would create a high level of uncertainty for readers. The section of the 1976 audit report dealing with the current value amount and its placement in separate columns in the Balance Sheet addressed this point directly:

> As described in Note 1, the financial statements include a consolidated balance sheet as of May 31, 1976 prepared on a current value basis to

---

[10] U.S. Securities and Exchange Commission, "Accounting Series Release No. 190," March 1976.
[11] "ASR 190—The Experiment," from the SEC Commentary Section, *The CPA Journal*, November, 1976, p. 70.

supplement the financial statements prepared on the cost basis. The current value basis of presentation provides relevant information about the current financial position of the company which is not provided by financial statements prepared on the historical cost basis. The current value basis of presentation differs significantly from the historical cost basis required by generally accepted accounting principles.

In our opinion, based upon our examination and the report of the other auditors and subject to the effect on the financial statements of the company of the matters underlying the qualification taken by the other auditors, the aforementioned consolidated financial statements stated on a cost basis present fairly the financial position of The Rouse Company and its subsidiaries at May 31, 1976 and 1975 and the results of their operations and the changes in their financial position for the years then ended, in conformity with generally accepted accounting principles applied on a consistent basis; and the consolidated current value basis balance sheet as of May 31, 1976, is presented fairly on the basis indicated in the preceding paragraph and the note referred to therein (p. 25).

The May 31, 1976 statements reported $112,873,000 of Revaluation Equity in the Shareholders' Equity section of the Current Value Basis column. The Revaluation Equity account balance has grown steadily to $1,677,124,000 at December 31, 1989, and reports unrealized holding gains, less deferred taxes, on the company's real estate assets. Holding gains are not reported in the income statement until they are realized through the sale of these assets.

REACTION TO THE CURRENT VALUE
BALANCE SHEET

David L. Tripp, Vice President and Director of Investor Relations for TRC, stated that analysts needed about two years after 1976 to become comfortable with TRC's current value approach and presentation. Since TRC is an over-the-counter stock with very significant institutional holdings, its stockholders are more sophisticated than those of many other companies. While there was some initial suspicion by statement users, acceptance of the valuation procedure by federal bank examiners who reviewed TRC's mortgage loans led to greater credibility. The 1976 decision was intended to be an important attention-getting device; it directed attention to the deficiencies of historical cost reporting and to the value added by real estate development activities. The company contends that realized gains on the sales of certain properties helped confirm the reliability of the valuation amounts.

Two items demonstrate that the 1976 decision has been very positively received by the investing community. The first was an October 11, 1976 article in *Business Week*. TRC was credited with becoming "the first U.S. public company to issue a balance sheet in which current values of its properties are set out alongside the more familiar historical costs of assets, liabilities, and equities. It went far beyond the requirements of ASR #190. Both PMM and

James D. Landauer Associates attested to the current value figure."[12] TRC Chairman James W. Rouse was quoted in the article as follows:

> The shareholder will have a much more dependable image of our business, in language he can understand—arithmetic," adds Chairman James W. Rouse. "It says we are worth $10 a share. Yet we're selling at less than $5. It was not fair not having some way to communicate that. Now we do.

The second item was a published analysis of TRC by Green Street Advisors, Inc., as of January 19, 1989. The quote below provides evidence that Green Street's financial analysts used TRC's current valuation information in evaluating the company. It is also interesting to note the view taken about the appraisal value of TRC.

> The Company's next appraisal (to be dated 12/31/88) is due to be released in mid-February, and will probably come out near $30.50, an increase of 12.4% over last year's estimate. It is reasonable to assume that cap rate assumptions will remain fairly constant while sales growth assumptions at most properties may be steady to slightly down from prior growth levels. Most of the increase in value will come as a result of improved performance and lower cap rates at renovated/expanded properties. We feel that the Company's appraisal is very sound, but probably errs on the side of conservatism by about 10 percent due to conservative cap rate and discount rate assumptions. In a reorganization/ liquidation/takeover analysis of the Company's value, the number would be perhaps 30 percent greater than the reported current value (primarily because of the conservative appraisal assumptions and the value of the Company's developmental franchise).[13]

We found additional evidence that TRC's current value balance sheet is being used. Roger Lowenstein, in the "Heard on the Street" column of *The Wall Street Journal*, wrote about analysts' use of TRC's current value equity per share. In discussing how corporate raiders are looking for undervalued real estate assets as a way to spot low-priced firms, he said:

> Analysts say railroads have even more real estate value than hotels and retailers, because they own properties, such as old freight yards, that are no longer needed for the basic business.
>   And analysts have few clues as to what railroad properties are worth. Railroad lands are so immense and scattered that most say they have no way of putting a value on them.
>   By contrast, Rouse is a pure real estate play. The mall developer's 1987 estimate of its real estate equity is scheduled to be released in March, and analysts predict it will be $27 a share, or $3 a share higher than the previous year. That would be some 40 percent above its share price. Rouse is 25 percent controlled by Trizec Equities and conservatively managed, so patience is advised. However, says Kenneth Campbell of Audit Investments, "There is enormous value there."
>   David Tripp, head of investor relations at Rouse, agrees that "if you get

---

[12] "Rouse Pioneers More Realistic Numbers," *Business Week*, October 11, 1976, p. 124.
[13] Green Street Advisors, Inc., "The Rouse Company—Update," January 19, 1989, p. 8.

too big of a discount somebody can say 'we can take those assets and come out way ahead.' It's a problem."[14]

Another reference to TRC's current value reporting appeared in "Malled," a recent *Forbes* article suggesting that TRC's shareholders' equity computed on a current value basis may be overstated. Although the article is critical of TRC's appraisals, it does report that many of the company's investors see TRC's current value shareholders' equity as a good proxy for the firm's breakup value.[15] This article and the comments by Green Street Advisors point to the difficulty of obtaining credible appraisals.

In Exhibit I the authors modified a graph provided by TRC to show the relationship between year-end stock price and common shareholders' equity per share at current value and historical cost. TRC believes that the strong relationship between stock price and the current value shareholders equity per share is adequate justification for its decision to report current values in its balance sheet. The authors added common shareholders' equity per share at historical cost to the Exhibit. The graph shows a high correlation between year-end stock price and Common Shareholders' Equity—Current Value per

[14] Roger Lowenstein, "Raiders Focus on Real Estate Assets as a Way to Spot Low-Priced Firms, Finance Takeovers," *The Wall Street Journal*, January 29, 1988, p. 43.
[15] Tatiana Pouschine in the October 30, 1989 issue of *Forbes*, p. 46, suggests that "asset values look overinflated; many properties are unprofitable." The article claims that "nothing is wrong with Rouse's practice of providing its own appraisal of assets." The author, however, cites examples of certain shopping malls where the current values appear to be inflated.

EXHIBIT I The Rouse Company Year-End Common Stock Price vs. Common Shareholders' Equity—Current Value per Share and Common Shareholders' Equity—Historical Cost Per Share

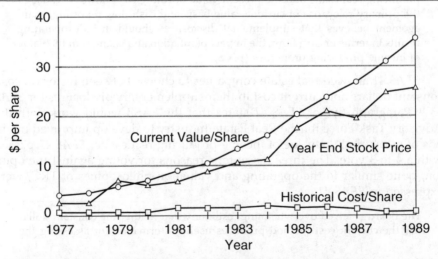

Note: The data have been adjusted for a 2 for 1 stock split in 1985 and a 3 for 2 split in 1987.

share. There is a much lower correlation between stock price and Common Shareholders' Equity—Historical Cost per share. The wide disparity between historical cost book value per share and common stock prices over this 14-year period makes the historical cost figures appear to be meaningless and perhaps misleading.

THE IMPACT OF *SFAS 33* AND *SFAS 41* ON TRC

SFAS 33 required large publicly held companies to report both historical cost/constant dollar measurements and current cost measurements for Property, Plant and Equipment and for depreciation thereon. However, paragraph 53 stated that *SFAS 33* ". . . does not contain provisions for the measurement, on a current cost basis, of income-producing real estate properties . . . and related depreciation . . . expense." Although not required by *SFAS 33* to disclose current cost data, TRC continued reporting current values on its balance sheet. The company explained its valuation philosophy in the 1979 annual report:

> The economic characteristics of income producing real estate provide an opportunity for the Company to achieve the objectives of financial reporting identified above. Based on stable, long-term rents which generate a high quality cash flow stream for the Company's income producing properties and the ability to identify this cash flow stream with specific properties, the objectives of financial reporting can be achieved by reporting net cash generated by properties and the value of properties measured by the present value of prospective net cash flows. Lenders and investors in income producing properties are generally not concerned with "Income" measurements which include a deduction for recovery of cost (depreciation and amortization). Lenders and investors are concerned with cash flow generated by income producing real estate and the present value of future cash flows. Because of the primary relevance of current value basis and cash flow reporting, management believes that supplemental disclosures should include operating results in terms of cash flow, the impact of inflation and changes in the value of income producing properties (p. 38).

SFAS 41 allowed real estate companies to choose between historical cost/constant dollars and current cost in their supplementary disclosures for *SFAS 33*.[16] Paragraph five of *SFAS 41* states that the FASB would work with the Advisory Task Force for the Real Estate Industry to develop improved methods of measuring the value of income-producing real estate. *SFAS 41* passed with a 4-to-3 vote. The three dissenters' reasons for voting against the opinion, quite similar to the operating and valuation philosophies of TRC, were expressed in *SFAS 41*:

> The Board received overwhelming testimony that neither the constant dollar nor the current cost method produces useful information for assessing the

---

[16] FASB, SFAS 41, *Financial Reporting and Changing Prices: Specialized Assets—Income Producing Real Estate*, November, 1980, p. 2.

impact of specific price changes on real estate investment properties, yet this Statement permits either method to be used in current cost presentations. Of special concern is the relevance of deducting current cost depreciation to measure income from a property that is being maintained to last indefinitely and that is continuing to appreciate in value. Because income-producing real estate is generally held as an investment rather than as an operating capability involving continuous disposals and replacements of components, the effect of changing specific prices on depreciation is not a significant concern. Cash flows and value changes are the critical factors just as they are with other kinds of marketable investments. The relevant accounting analogy is to an investment portfolio not, as implicit in this Statement, to property, plant, and equipment. Estimated fair values and changes in fair values are the most relevant information that can be provided about the effects of changing prices on income-producing real estate; those estimates are sufficiently reliable to be required as supplementary information (pp. 4–5).

THE FUTURE OF CURRENT VALUE REPORTING FOR REAL ESTATE DEVELOPERS

In addition to addressing the topic of current value reporting for real estate at the 1989 Annual Meeting of the AICPA, in that same year the Planning Subcommittee of the AICPA's Accounting Standards Executive Committee approved a project to develop a statement of position on current value reporting for real estate. An important part of this process will, undoubtedly, be the December 31, 1984 report of the Real Estate Accounting Committee of the Accounting Standards Division.[17] The report discusses many of the issues handled by TRC and once more illustrates the strong acceptance of many aspects of TRC's 1976 current value approach.

SUMMARY AND CONCLUSIONS

Progress in the development of professional guidance has been slow since the 1973 discussion in TRC's "Letter to Shareholders" section and the company's 1976 decision to report current values in its Balance Sheet. TRC management, and comments by some financial analysts, lead the authors to believe that the TRC experiment has provided useful information to the investment community. It is, however, quite clear that a major reason for TRC's desire to report current value information and to continue to report it has been its significant positive impact on the book value per share. Management felt that historical cost financial statements did not reflect how management had added value for the shareholder. Such feelings are not new. MacNeal in *Truth in Accounting* expressed a similar view when he stated that "present accounting principles prescribe that most assets be carried at original cost. . . . Its effect is to

---

[17] Real Estate Accounting Committee, Accounting Standards Division, AICPA, *Guidance for an Experiment on Reporting Current Value Information for Real Estate*, December 31, 1984.

sanction the misrepresentation of profits and to conceal from shareholders profits of which they should be informed."[18] TRC management believed that Cash Flow statements and Current Value Balance Sheets could present the company in a much more positive and realistic light. TRC's current value balance sheet is more subjective than historical cost, yet some users find it more relevant. Further study of the users of TRC financial statements could add to our knowledge about the usefulness of current value financial statements.

The TRC story shows that constructive innovation in financial reporting is not dead. Corporate accountants can initiate new presentations supplementary to GAAP-basis statements in order to improve communication with investors and creditors and provide information useful for evaluation and decision making. Such presentations can also receive favorable treatment by auditors and regulators.

But the TRC story presented in this article should be only the beginning of a much deeper analysis of the need for current value reporting. The AICPA and the FASB should utilize TRC as the basis for an in-depth analysis of users of TRC's annual reports. Researchers should closely examine the relationships between TRC and such organizations as its public auditor, its appraiser, the SEC, and the investment community. Other real estate developers could be studied to determine why they did not follow TRC's lead. It would be unfortunate for the AICPA to start studying "from scratch" and to ignore the current state of the art developed by TRC.

A review of TRC's financial statements over the past 17 years certainly shows that, although *SFAS 33* is no longer mandatory, current value reporting lives on. Further research on valuation and new reporting standards is needed because historical cost-based financial statements do not always fairly report financial position or the results of operations.

---

[18] Kenneth MacNeal, *Truth in Accounting*, (Philadelphia: University of Pennsylvania Press, 1939), p. 42.

APPENDIX I Examples of Disclosures of Current Value Information From Annual Reports and 10-Ks of Selected Companies in the Real Estate Industry

Bay Financial Corporation, 1989 10-K
The company discloses current values under the sectional heading "Current Fair Market Value." It is interesting that this company reported decreases in current values due to several factors including "the continued deterioration in real estate values in certain geographic markets. . . ." (p. 5)
Ernst & Young was the auditor and did not reference the current value in its report. (p. 15)
Like TRC, Bay retains Landauer Associates to review the estimate of fair market value. (pp. 40–41)

BTR Realty, Inc. 1989 Annual Report
It is evident from looking at the cover of the 1989 annual report that BTR management is a proponent of current value reporting. The following quote appears in the center of the cover.

Experience indicates that, over time, quality real estate projects appreciate in value. More importantly, current value stockholders' equity reached $11.88 per share in 1989, a 13 percent increase over 1988.

The majority of the letter to the stockholders and discussion of the company's operations is devoted to explaining why the company is reporting current values in its balance sheet. The company includes examples of its valuation procedures as well as a tutorial on valuation methods (pp. 6, 7, 20, 21). Two paragraphs are excerpted below: (p. 5)

In the Company's last Annual Report, the current value of BTR's assets and net worth were reflected, for the first time, in its financial statements. This important reporting change marked a watershed in the company's existence.

Current value reporting is believed preferable because experience indicates that, over time, quality real estate projects appreciate in value. Generally accepted accounting principles based on historical cost require annual depreciation charges against operations, and related accumulated depreciation is deducted from such cost in reporting balance sheet values. While it is clear that asset values are rising, traditional accounting procedures simply do not give investors enough relevant information.

BTR's current values were attested to by Lee Mason Realty Group, Inc., independent appraisers. Deloitte & Touche, the company's auditors, include the following two paragraphs in their audit opinion (p. 12):

As more fully described in Note A to the consolidated financial statements, the current value basis financial statements supplement the financial statements prepared on a cost basis. They are not intended to present financial position and results of operations in conformity with generally accepted accounting principles but to provide relevant financial information about BTR Realty, Inc., and Subsidiaries which is not provided by the cost basis financial statements.

In our opinion, the consolidated current value basis financial statements referred to above present fairly, in all material respects, the information set forth therein. . . .

Hilton Hotels, 1988 Annual Report

Barron Hilton in his letter to stockholders explained why Hilton discloses current values in a supplementary schedule. "There are several ways to define value. We provide three measures in this report. The first, 'stockholders' equity per share,' gives the book or historical accounting basis for our assets. . . . The deficiencies of stockholders' equity per share are apparent. For a hotel such as the Waldorf-Astoria that was acquired many years ago, the historical accounting basis bears little relationship to its value today. Therefore, since 1976 we also have presented supplementary information on the current value of our assets and liabilities. . . . A third measure of value is reflected in the public securities markets. . . . The distortion of historical cost has never been more evident than today." Hilton obviously arrived at this conclusion due to the wide disparity of historical cost value per share of $17.03 and the current value per share of $62.00. (pp. 7, 8)

The supplementary information on current value is noted in Arthur Andersen's audit report, which states that it "also audits the accompanying condensed consolidated balance sheets—current value basis of Hilton's Hotel Corporation. . . ." (p. 43)

Hilton's current value balance sheet appears after the footnotes to the financial statements and does not include deferred income taxes on the difference between historical cost amounts and the current value amounts. (pp. 43, 44)

—1989 Annual Report

Hilton Hotels did not report current values this year. There was no reason given for this change.

Holiday Inns, 1981 Annual Report

". . . [We] engaged an independent firm in 1981 to appraise the appreciated value of the company's tangible assets and certain contract rights. [T]he study indicated a market value of $1.86 billion, or nearly 2.5 times the $.77 billion reported shareholders' equity shown on our balance sheet. We believe this information will be welcomed by lenders, investors and rating agencies as a clearer definition of the true financial condition of our company . . ." (p. 3)

"Present financial reporting based on historical dollars does not reflect economic changes caused by inflation. . . . During periods of high inflation, even though the book value of the company's property and equipment may decrease because of depreciation charges, these assets tend to increase in value if properly maintained. . . ." (p. 23)
This comment was included in the FAS #33 footnote. "Also, neither the constant dollar nor current costs methods purport to represent the fair market value of the company or the financial statement items considered in the calculations. . . ." (p. 36)

—1988 Annual Report
Since 1984, the company pursued a strategy of asset dispositions. In 1987, it was recapitalized. During this period there was no mention of current values, except for a brief comment stating "inflation tends to increase the value of the company's real estate assets and franchise and management contracts." (p. 35)

Marriott, 1980 Annual Report
In their letter to shareholders, J. Willard Marriott and J. W. Marriott, Jr., stated "Marriott's ability to operate hotels profitably under management agreements is a strength not reflected in traditional accounting reports. . . . Our balance sheet does not reflect approximately $326 million in value developed from our existing hotel management agreement. Nor does it show that most of our existing hotels, currently valued at $634 million could be sold and converted to long-term management agreements." (p. 3)
Marriott included a condensed consolidated Current Value Balance Sheet in the "Financial Review" section of its annual report. It did include a brief description of the "basis of valuation" and defer taxes on the increase of current value over book value of its net assets. (Note: the Statement first appeared in 1979.) (p. 19)
The Statement was not mentioned in Arthur Andersen's audit report. (p. 30)
The company included a FAS #33 footnote. They stated however that the current cost/constant dollar information required by FAS #33 "distorts Marriott's economic performance because historical cost depreciation is further increased for changes in general price levels and the company's specific prices . . . management believes that the Current Value information on page 19 is more meaningful in evaluating Marriott's performance and financial condition in an inflationary environment." (p. 31)

—1981–84 Annual Reports
Same reporting policies as 1980.

—1985 Annual Report
During this year the senior J. Willard Marriott died and J. W. became Chairman and President. There was no mention of current values in the letter to shareholders, no Current Value-Balance Sheet and no reference to current value in the FAS #33 footnote.

Sonesta International Hotels, 1988 Annual Report
Ron and Paul Sonnabend, Chairman and President, criticize periodic historical cost net income. "Unfortunately, annual financial statements cannot show, in a truly meaningful way, the long term nature of Sonesta's financial results. Capital transactions, costs of real estate ownership and varying tax provisions often overwhelm our operating results. The substantial profit reported in . . . 1986 [on the sale of their Bermuda Hotel] was actually achieved over many years while the hotel was increasing in value." (p. 1)
"The company's consolidated balance sheets reflect a significant investment in hotel properties which, under generally accepted accounting principles, are carried at historical cost. In the opinion of management, and based on prices paid for equivalent hotels, and on the Company's recent and anticipated real estate transactions, management believes the value of the Company's real estate interests significantly exceeds their balance sheet carrying values." (p. 2)

How Well Do Statement No. 33 Earnings Explain Stock Returns?

William H. Beaver
Stanford University

Stephen G. Ryan
New York University

Previous research has indicated that replacement cost earnings derived from disclosures mandated by the Securities and Exchange Commission's Accounting Series Release No. 190 (ASR 190) do not have explanatory power for stock market returns beyond that provided by historical cost earnings.[1] Since 1979, the Financial Accounting Standards Board's Statement No. 33 has required disclosure of the effects of changing prices in annual reports. But there is little evidence that analysts use such data.[2] This study concentrates on the ability of various earnings measures derived from FASB Statement No. 33 data to explain stock returns for the years 1979 through 1982.[3]

From *Financial Analysts Journal* (September/October 1985), pp. 66–71. Reprinted by permission of the *Financial Analysts Journal* and the authors. Copyright © 1985 by the Association for Investment Management and Research.

[1] See, for example, William H. Beaver, Paul A. Griffin and Wayne R. Landsman, "How Well Does Replacement Cost Income Explain Stock Return?" *Financial Analysts Journal*, March/April 1983, pp. 26–39.

[2] See Robert W. Berliner, "Do Analysts Use Inflation-Adjusted Information? Results of a Survey," *Financial Analysts Journal*, March/April 1983, pp. 65–72, and William C. Norby, "Applications of Inflation-Adjusted Accounting Data," *Financial Analysts Journal*, March/April 1983, pp. 33–39.

[3] Our study differs from earlier work reported in this journal in three respects. First, it focuses on Statement No. 33 data rather than ASR 190 data. Statement No. 33's reliance on current costs rather than replacement costs could result in improvements in the quality of the disclosures relative to ASR 190 data. This is because current cost differs from replacement cost in that it reflects adjustments for the value of operating advantages of replacement assets (e.g., anticipated cost savings from newer technology). (See, for example, Financial Accounting Standards Board, "Invitation to Comment: Supplementary Disclosures about the Effects of Changing Prices," December 27, 1983, pp. 11–12.) Second, it examines more recent years than those covered by the ASR 190 data. Third, it includes additional earnings variables derived from the more comprehensive Statement No. 33 disclosures.

    The study extends an earlier investigation of Statement No. 33 data based on the years 1979 through 1981 (see William H. Beaver and Wayne R. Landsman, "Incremental Information Content of Statement 33 Disclosures: Research Report" (Stamford, Conn.: Financial Accounting Standards Board, November 1983)). The inclusion of 1982 is of particular importance for two reasons. First, our experience with Statement No. 33 data is brief, and an additional year's data can be informative. Second, 1982 differed markedly from earlier years. Stock prices rose dramatically in late 1982, both short and long-term interest rates declined substantially, and the magnitude of unanticipated inflation (negative, in this case) was larger than it was in the 1979–1981 period.

THE THEORY

According to the FASB, the purpose of financial reporting in general, and income measurement in particular, is to provide investors with information on the magnitude, timing and uncertainty of prospective cash flows.[4] Thus earnings information can affect analysts' and investors' judgments, which in turn can affect stock prices. At any point in time, stock prices reflect the collective, or consensus, judgment of analysts and others as to the future earning power of a stock. Changes in stock price (i.e., returns) reflect changes in investors' expectations regarding future earning power.

Two conditions must be met if earnings are to convey information. First, reported earnings must differ from expected earnings. Second, the unexpected portion of earnings must be capable of changing expectations about future earning power. Prior research has demonstrated that unexpected changes in historical cost earnings explain a significant portion of changes in stock prices. This finding, one of the most robust empirical results observed in security price research, is consistent with the perception that earnings provide information about prospective cash flows and future earning power.

It has been asserted that various forms of earnings adjusted for inflation (and for changes in prices of specific assets) provide information on operating performance beyond that provided by historical cost earnings.[5] In particular, historical cost earnings do not reflect the effects of inflation upon certain assets such as inventory, property, plant and equipment.

The merits of Statement No. 33 data rest upon two major considerations. The potential value of such data lies in their ability to provide information about the effects of inflation upon the prospective cash flows, hence the value of firms' securities. But measurement errors can creep into the data and impair their potential informational content. Which effect dominates? The answer depends upon the magnitude of unanticipated inflation relative to the magnitude of the measurement errors. We conducted an empirical analysis to provide evidence on this issue.

THE DATA

From the 1,137 nonfinancial firms recorded on the FASB's Statement No. 33 research tape, we chose those firms with December 31 fiscal year-ends and with the components necessary to compute all seven of the earnings variables (to be described below) in a given year.[6]

For each firm, stock return was calculated as the annual cash dividend

---

[4] For further discussion see *Concepts Statement No. 1: Objectives of Financial Reporting by Business Enterprises* (Stamford, Conn.: Financial Accounting Standards Board, November 1978).

[5] Statement No. 33 provides for disclosures related to inflation and to changes in prices of specific assets. For brevity, the article will merely refer to inflation, but it is intended to apply to changes in prices of specific assets as well.

[6] Observations were also deleted if earnings in that year were negative or if the percentage change in earnings was extremely large (i.e., greater than 300 percent in absolute value).

plus capital gains or losses divided by price at the end of the previous year. Seven variables were used to explain stock returns—historical cost earnings (HC) plus six earnings measures based on Statement No. 33 (PRE, PREP, CD, CDP, POST, POSTP).[7]

PRE represents percentage change in per share *income from continuing operations under current cost;* adjustments are made here for the current cost of depreciation and cost of goods sold. CD is the percentage change in per share *income from continuing operations under constant dollar,* with adjustments made to depreciation and the cost of goods sold to reflect changes in the general price level since the date of acquisition of the assets.

PREP and CDP represent *adjustments for purchasing power gain (or loss).* Purchasing power gain or loss is added to income from continuing operations under both current cost (PREP) and constant dollar (CDP), and the new earnings number expressed in terms of percentage change in a per share figure.

POST is a current cost *adjustment for holding gains.* Income from continuing operations under current cost does not include the holding gain or loss due to the change in current costs of assets during the year. A more comprehensive measure of income would include such gains. The *gross* holding gain (before reflecting the effects of changes in the general price index) is added to income from continuing operations under current cost, and the resulting number is divided by net assets (essentially stockholders' equity) under current cost to obtain the variable POST.

Income from continuing operations *after* the purchasing power gain and loss adjustment is also further adjusted by adding the *net* holding gain (after reflecting the effects of the change in the general price index). The resulting number is then divided by net assets under current cost to obtain the variable POSTP.

Historical cost earnings available for common shareholders before extraordinary items are expressed in percentage change in the per share figure, for the variable HC.

As noted, the merits of Statement No. 33 data rest on a tradeoff between the magnitude of unanticipated inflation and measurement errors in the data. Each earnings measure represents an imperfect alternative. The issue is not which earnings measure possesses the greatest information content. Rather, the issue is whether Statement No. 33 earnings variables provide information that historical cost earnings do not.

THE RESULTS

We initially conducted cross-sectional correlations between stock returns and each of the income measures. Table 1 reports the correlation coefficients,

---

[7] The reason for the variable names, further rationale for each of the variables, and a precise definition of the variables are discussed in William H. Beaver and Wayne R. Landsman, "Incremental Information Content of Statement 33 Disclosures: Research Report," *op cit.,* pp. 48–52.

TABLE 1 Correlation Between Annual Security Returns and Various
Earnings Measures, 1979–1982[a]

	1979	1980	1981	1982
Percentage Change In Historical Cost Earnings (HC)	0.48	0.47	0.30	0.46
Percentage Change In IFCO: Current Cost (PRE)[b]	NA[c]	0.32	0.30	0.35
Percentage Change In IFCO: Current Cost Plus Purchasing Power Gains (PREP)	NA	0.33	0.24	0.39
Percentage Change In IFCO: Constant Dollar (CD)	NA	0.33	0.20	0.39
Percentage Change In IFCO: Constant Dollar Plus Purchasing Power Gains (CDP)	NA	0.35	0.19	0.36
IFCO: Current Cost Plus *Gross* Holding Gains Divided by Net Assets: Current Cost (POST)	−0.04	0.29	0.02	0.12
IFCO: Current Cost Plus *Net* Holding Gains Plus Purchasing Power Gains Divided by Net Assets: Current Cost (POSTP)	0.46	0.35	0.03	0.18
Number of Observations	368	301	298	260

[a] The correlation coefficients are Pearson (product moment) correlations. The correlation coefficient is significant at the 5 percent level if it is larger than 0.11 in absolute value.
[b] IFCO denotes income from continuing operations.
[c] NA = not available, because percentage change variables require previous year's data. Statement No. 33 data start in 1979.

which indicate the extent to which differences in stock return across firms in a given year can be explained by each of the earnings variables. HC has a higher correlation than any of the six Statement No. 33 variables across all four years. The only exception is the behavior of PRE in 1981, which has the same correlation with stock returns as HC does. PRE is unable to sustain this performance in the other years.[8] The explanatory power of historical cost is remarkable in that it had to compete against six challengers and might be expected to lose occasionally simply by chance.

These simple correlations suggest that historical cost income has greater explanatory power with respect to stock returns than any of its rivals. However, this perspective treats the other earnings variables as competitors and does not address the question of gains from using more than one earnings measure. Once we have knowledge of HC, do we gain further explanatory power by also knowing the Statement No. 33 variables?

[8] Further analysis indicated that PRE failed to perform as well as HC in 1981 on a larger set of data (common to both PRE and HC only) and on a smaller set of nonutility firms. For further discussion, see William H. Beaver and Wayne R. Landsman, "Incremental Information Content of Statement 33 Disclosures: Research Report," *op. cit.*, p. 59.

To answer this question, we compared the proportions of variance explained (R-squared) under two regressions. The first regression used only HC earnings to explain cross-sectional differences in returns. The second regression included both HC earnings and one additional Statement No. 33 earnings variable. We tested to determine if the increase in R-squared was significant.[9]

Table 2 compares the R-squared attained by using HC only with the R-squared attained by adding each of the Statement No. 33 variables. For the years 1979 through 1982, HC has R-squares of 23, 22, 9 and 21 percent. Adding POSTP increases these by 8, 3, zero and 1 percent, respectively.

No one Statement No. 33 variable is able to add significant explanatory power on a consistent basis.[10] PRE, PREP, CD and CDP do not provide significant additional explanatory power in any of the 4 years. POST provides a significant addition in only 1 year. POSTP is significant in the first 2 years, but insignificant in the 2 most recent years. Although not reported here, the signs of the regression coefficients on the Statement No. 33 variables also fluctuate over time.[11]

We also performed a multiple regression analysis, where all the variables were included in a single equation. The results were similar to those reported in Table 2. There was essentially no increase in the proportion of variance explained beyond the results reported in Table 2, largely because the Statement No. 33 variables are correlated with one another and little is added by including all six instead of just one.

We also addressed the question of the incremental explanatory power of

[9] The test is an F test on the reduction in sum of the squared residuals as a result of using two instead of one earnings variable. This approach is not the econometrically unique way to test for incremental explanatory power. For further discussion see William H. Beaver and Wayne R. Landsman, "Incremental Information Content of Statement 33 Disclosures: Research Report," op. cit., p. 57; William H. Beaver, Paul A. Griffin and Wayne R. Landsman, "Testing for Incremental Information Content in the Presence of Collinearity: A Comment," Journal of Accounting and Economics, December 1984, pp. 219–223; and A. Christie, M. Kennelly, J. King and T. Schaeffer, "Testing for Incremental Information Content in the Presence of Collinearity," Journal of Accounting and Economics, December 1984, pp. 205–217.

[10] The F test assumes normality and independence of the regression residuals. Empirical evidence indicates that positive correlation in the residuals may be present (e.g., due to industry effects). If so, the tests of significance are biased against accepting the null hypothesis of no incremental explanatory power. For convenience, levels of significance rather than F ratios are reported, and the conventional 5 percent significance level has been used here. The results reported for 1979 through 1981 are essentially the same as those reported in William H. Beaver and Wayne R. Landsman, "Incremental Information Content of Statement 33 Disclosures: Research Report." The only exception is for POSTP in 1979 and 1980. Qualitatively, the conclusions regarding the performance of POSTP are the same, but we cannot literally replicate the results for 1979 and 1980 using the latest version of the Statement No. 33 research tape. After further investigation, we are convinced that the results reported here for POSTP are the correct ones. We are indebted to Professor James McKeown of the University of Illinois for alerting us to this difference.

[11] The statement regarding the stability of the signs has to be tempered somewhat because each of the Statement No. 33 variables is correlated with the HC variable. However, as we shall see, the sign of the HC variable is consistent over time, even in the presence of the correlation.

TABLE 2 Contribution To Proportion of
Variance Explained (R²) Attained by Adding
Statement No. 33 Variable, 1979–1982

Variable in Addition to HC	PROPORTION OF VARIANCE EXPLAINED AFTER ADDING VARIABLE			
	1979	1980	1981	1982
PRE	NA	0.22	0.10	0.21
PREP	NA	0.22	0.09	0.21
CD	NA	0.22	0.09	0.21
CDP	NA	0.22	0.09	0.21
POST	0.24	0.24[a]	0.09	0.22
POSTP	0.31[a]	0.25[a]	0.09	0.22
HC only[b]	0.23	0.22	0.09	0.21

[a] Increase in R² relative to the R² of the HC-only regression is
significant at the 5 percent level.
[b] The R² refers to the proportion of variance explained by a
regression which includes only HC.

HC over and above that provided by the Statement No. 33 variables. The
results reported in Table 2 may arise because the HC and the Statement No.
33 variables are so highly correlated with each other that nothing is gained by
adding a second variable.

From one perspective, knowing the incremental explanatory power of HC
may seem of little importance, since HC is already provided in the primary
financial statements and Statement No. 33 data are merely intended to be
supplemental. From a purely statistical point of view, however, if HC provides no additional explanatory power beyond that provided by the other
variables we might be indifferent as to which were used. More importantly,
examining the incremental explanatory power of HC earnings may provide
insights about the extent to which the results reported in Table 2 are merely
due to high correlation between HC and each of the Statement No. 33
earnings variables. If the results *are* due to high correlation, then HC earnings
would not be expected to provide incremental explanatory power beyond that
already provided by the Statement No. 33 variables.

We compared the R-squared of one Statement No. 33 variable with the
R-squared obtained when that variable was used in conjunction with HC.
Table 3 reports the results. For 1979 through 1982, POSTP has R-squares of 21,
12, 0.04 and 3 percent; adding HC increases these R-squares by 10, 13, 9 and
19 percent, respectively.

Whatever the Statement No. 33 variable used, adding HC earnings significantly increased the R-squared in all four years, with only one exception. In
1981 the increase in R-squared with respect to PRE was significant at the 5.3
percent level (i.e., it "just misses" the conventional 5%). HC earnings data do
provide significant incremental explanatory power beyond that provided by

TABLE 3 Contribution To Proportion of Variance Explained (R^2) Attained by Adding the Historical Cost Variable, 1979–1982[a]

	1979		1980		1981		1982	
	No. 33 Variable	Both Variables	No. 33 Variable	Both Variables	No. 33 Variable	Both Variables	No. 33 Variable	Both Variables
PRE	NA	NA	0.10	0.22	0.09	0.10	0.12	0.21
PREP	NA	NA	0.11	0.22	0.06	0.09	0.15	0.21
CD	NA	NA	0.11	0.22	0.04	0.09	0.15	0.21
CDP	NA	NA	0.12	0.22	0.04	0.09	0.13	0.21
POST	0.0016	0.24	0.08	0.24	0.0004	0.09	0.01	0.22
POSTP	0.21	0.31	0.12	0.25	0.0004	0.09	0.03	0.22

[a] The increase in R^2 relative to using the Statement No. 33 variable only is significant at the 5 percent level in all cases, except for PRE in 1981. Here, the level of significance is 0.053.

Statement No. 33 earnings. Moreover, the regression coefficients on HC (not reported here) are positive without exception.

These results and those reported in Table 2 indicate that it is not a matter of indifference which set of data is used to explain stock returns. HC data "dominate" Statement No. 33 data in this context. The explanatory power of historical cost earnings is significant, whether or not Statement No. 33 variables are included in the regression. By contrast, none of the Statement No. 33 variables is able to explain stock returns beyond historical cost earnings.

The combined results suggest that high correlation between Statement No. 33 variables and HC is not the sole reason for the poor performance of the FASB variables. To be sure, there is correlation. Despite it, however, HC demonstrated significant incremental explanatory power; the FASB data did not. Furthermore, in contrast to the Statement No. 33 variables, the HC data demonstrated stability in the sign of the regression coefficient over time. Differences in the quality of the data may be another explanation for the differences in incremental explanatory power.

IMPLICATIONS

Statement No. 33 variables provide no incremental information beyond that already provided by historical cost earnings, when explanatory power is defined in terms of the ability to explain cross-sectional stock returns.

Negative results are usually difficult to interpret. Is there really no incremental explanatory power or have we failed to detect it because of some flaw in our research design? Previous research using a variety of other analyses has found no effect.[12] Moreover, our finding is consistent with earlier research on ASR 190 data and analyst nonusage of Statement No. 33 data.

It is important to state what these results do *not* imply, however. They do not imply that it is unimportant to make adjustments for inflation in an analysis of security prices. They do *not* imply that analysts are not making adjustments for inflation in their analysis. They do imply that, if the adjustments are being made, either Statement No. 33 data are not capturing that adjustment process very well or the magnitude of the adjustment is small.

While it was possible that the results could have differed for 1982 relative to earlier years, they do not. Either the magnitude of unanticipated inflation is still too small to be material, even in 1982, or the magnitude of the measurement errors in the Statement 33 data is large enough to overwhelm the potential informational value.

---

[12] The variations include examining a larger set of observations, which requires that the data be available only for the one Statement No. 33 variable currently being examined, instead of requiring that they be available for all of the variables. Another extension was to repeat the regression analysis on a smaller set of firms, which excluded the utility firms. Under both analyses, the results are essentially the same as those reported here. Further discussion appears in William H. Beaver and Wayne R. Landsman, "Incremental Information Content of Statement 33 Disclosures: Research Report," *op cit.*

What does the future hold for the Statement No. 33 disclosures? The FASB has voted to extend changing prices disclosures beyond 1984. Will the data perform better in the future? The answer depends upon the magnitude of future unexpected inflation and upon improvements in the quality of the data.

The Association between Corporate Dividends and Current Cost Disclosures

Bala G. Dharan
Rice University

INTRODUCTION

Since 1979, large and medium-sized U.S. firms meeting certain size requirements have been disclosing current cost earnings data in accordance with the requirements of Statement of Financial Accounting Standards No. 33 (FASB, 1979). This paper examines the extent to which SFAS-33 data explain firms' dividend decisions.

Many researchers and practitioners have argued that current cost earnings data would provide management with the necessary information to establish a dividend policy consistent with prudent capital maintenance. This view is also expressed by the FASB in Statement No. 33: "The information on current cost income from continuing operations required by this Statement provides a basis for users' assessment of distributable income" (FASB, 1979, para. 124). The argument is that dividends based on historical cost earnings might not preserve capital and that dividends should be less than current cost earnings, which implies that changes in dividends should be explained by current cost earnings changes rather than historical cost earnings changes.

However, the Accounting Standards Committee in the United Kingdom explicitly proscribed such an interpretation of the current cost income. In Statement of Standard Accounting Practice No. 16, it said in determining dividend policy one must also consider "factors such as capital expenditure plans, . . . funding requirements . . . , liquidity, and new financing arrangements. The current cost profit . . . should not be assumed to measure the amount that can be prudently distributed" (ASC, 1980, para. 23). This view is consistent with the investment opportunity model of dividends,

From *Journal of Business Finance and Accounting* (Summer 1988), pp. 215–230. Reprinted by permission of Basil Blackwell Ltd. and the author. Copyright © 1988 by Basil Blackwell Ltd., Oxford, England.

viz., firms with good investment opportunities would pay less dividends. If current cost earnings proxy for expected future operating profits, an implication is that there may be a negative cross-sectional association between changes in dividends and changes in current cost earnings. On the other hand, the classic target payout and partial adjustment models of dividends postulate that firms try to maintain a stable long-term relationship between dividends and historical cost earnings. This view suggests that there should be no cross-sectional association between changes in dividends and changes in current cost earnings. Finally, management discussions in annual reports often suggest that no association exists. For example, Tenneco, in its 1981 annual report, preceded the disclosure of current cost data with the remark, "the methods utilized inherently involve the use of assumptions, approximations, and subjective judgments" (p. 50).

Research in finance is divided on the determinants of dividend policy and on the relevance of dividend policy for firm value. Perhaps, as a result, the above hypotheses in the accounting literature about the association between current cost data and dividends focus on management use of current cost data for specific managerial decisions (such as capital maintenance or investment decision), and are not generally based on rigorous models of value maximization. Such models are not attempted in this study either. Instead, the competing hypotheses on the association between current cost data and dividend decisions are empirically examined.

To get robust results, this article examines three years of current cost data for 325 U.S. firms and reports the findings from four different, though somewhat related, research approaches. Firstly, an approach similar to Fama and Babiak (1968) is used to see whether the frequency of dividend changes is monotonically related to historical cost or current cost earnings changes.[1] The results (Table 1) show that changes in historical cost earnings, rather than current cost earnings, explain the *frequency* of divided changes. Secondly, the percentage changes in dividends (rather than the frequency of dividend changes) is related to the signs of historical cost and current cost earnings changes, in a one-way analysis of variance format. The data (Table 2) indicate that dividend growth rates are explained by historical cost earnings changes, consistent with the target payout (or partial adjustment) model, and not by current cost earnings changes.

Thirdly, a regression of percentage changes in dividends with percentage changes in historical cost and current cost earnings indicates (Table 3) that the coefficient for historical cost earnings is positive and significant as predicted by the target payout model while the coefficient for current cost earnings is insignificant. Finally, a test of the partial adjustment model of dividends with the addition of a current cost earnings term shows (Table 4) that the model is strongly supported but the current cost earnings coefficient is generally insignificant.

The evidence strongly supports the partial adjustment model and the

---

[1] The study by Fama and Babiak (1968) is described in the section headed Results.

target payout hypothesis, and generally shows that current cost data appear to possess little explanatory power about dividend decisions. In particular, there seems little support for the capital maintenance hypothesis. To the extent that dividend decisions can affect security returns (Blume, 1980; and Litzenberger and Ramaswamy, 1982), the evidence of lack of association between current cost data and dividend decisions is consistent with Beaver and Landsman's (1983) finding that SFAS-33 data possess little explanatory power about security returns.

In the next section, the various alternative hypotheses offered by the capital maintenance, investment opportunity, and target payout models are discussed. Sample selection is described in the third section. In the fourth section, the tests are described and the results presented. Some concluding remarks are presented in the last section.

HYPOTHESES

Theoretical arguments for the use of current cost or similar data by management for dividend decisions have focused on the ability of the enterprise to maintain its operating capacity. For example, Revsine (1981) notes that historical cost-based income data create "the illusion of prosperity," and warns that their use by management and governmental regulators may result in (physical) capital liquidation. Revsine (1973) develops the theory underlying this thinking. He argues that, under the assumption of perfect competition, current cost operating income represents "the maximum amount that the firm can distribute as a dividend and still maintain physical operations and future dividends at their existing levels" (p. 100). He also argues that the above relationship holds as an "approximation" when the perfect competition assumption is relaxed. Grant (1983), sounding a similar theme, emphasizes that managements must start using the price-adjusted data for dividend decisions, or otherwise "[they] may be returning capital, not profits, to shareholders and letting the company drift toward liquidation." As noted in the "Basis for Conclusions" section of SFAS-33, the FASB also cites similar arguments to support its current cost disclosure requirements.

Summary statistics reported in an FASB-sponsored study by Evans and Freeman (1983), based on SFAS-33 disclosures of over 500 firms, indicate that firms have indeed been paying dividends far in excess of the current cost operating earnings reported under SFAS-33. The above arguments recommending dividend reduction for such firms implicitly assume that firms were paying large dividends prior to SFAS-33 (and to SEC's ASR-190 rule) because managers and investors were unaware of inflation's effect on a firm's capital. If current cost data contain information sufficient to determine optimum capital maintenance requirements, then managers would consider this information in setting their dividend policies.[2] In particular, the capital mainte-

---

[2] This study does not, however, test whether such a change in dividend policy occurred after the first disclosures from ASR-190.

nance argument says that firms would try to pay dividends that are less in amount than current cost operating income. Since such a change in dividend level is more likely to be implemented over a period of time rather than abruptly, an implication is that increases or decreases in year-to-year dividend payments would be governed by increases or decreases in current cost income rather than historical cost income. Hence the hypothesis suggested by the capital maintenance model is:

H_0: (Capital maintenance hypothesis) Changes in dividends are positively associated with changes in current cost earnings.

Some writers have cautioned against proposing, as the capital maintenance model does, that dividends should be less than current cost operating income. Rappaport (1981), for example, argues that a firm's "maximum affordable" dividends, that is, the amount a firm can pay and still not liquidate capital, depends not on its current cost earnings *per se*, but on its growth targets, investment opportunities, and financing constraints. As noted, this is also the view expressed by ASC in SSAP-16.

That investment opportunities and dividends may be related is supported by the fact that during 1979–83, steel and construction material industries in the United States had the lowest sales growth rates and the highest dividend payout rates (dividends divided by income before nonrecurring items). By contrast, oil and gas and electronics industries had two of the highest sales growth rates and the lowest dividend payout rates.[3] While sales growth is not necessarily indicative of investment opportunities, these data do lend indirect support to the investment opportunity model.

If current cost earnings are a proxy for future investment returns, then the investment opportunity model suggests an alternative hypothesis about current cost data and dividends. If firms with increases in current cost earnings are more likely to have attractive investment opportunities than firms with decreases in current cost earnings, then the latter firms may increase their dividends and return more capital to investors for alternative uses. Note that the applicability of the investment opportunity model for the current cost-dividend relationship requires a model of how current cost earnings and future investment opportunities are related, and this is not attempted in this study. In addition, historical cost earnings and current cost earnings are generally highly correlated, and hence the information about investment opportunities is not likely to be unique to current cost earnings. Nevertheless, it is worth noting that if the investment opportunity model is valid then one would expect a negative association between current cost earnings and dividend changes, rather than the positive association as in H_0.

A different association pattern is suggested by the work of Lintner (1956), Fama and Babiak (1968) and others who have reported evidence that firms' dividend decisions are consistent with a "target" payout objective, that is, a

---

[3] Data were computed using August 1985 COMPUSTAT tape and by grouping firms according to their 2-digit SIC codes. The Spearman rank correlation between sales growth and payout was -0.363, significant at the 0.08 level.

desire to maintain a stable long-term relationship between dividends and reported historical cost earnings. In addition, firms prefer to adjust their dividend levels to the desired level over a period of time rather than abruptly. In other words, year-to-year changes in dividends are governed by the desired target payout level *and* a speed-of-adjustment factor. This so-called partial adjustment model, which is described more fully below in the section headed Results, implies that dividend changes are positively associated with historical cost earnings and the previous period's dividend level. Moreover, since the target dividend level is postulated to depend only on historical cost earnings and not on current cost data, these models predict no association between current cost earnings changes and dividend changes.

Finally, management discussions in annual reports of the importance of current cost data also suggest that a hypothesis of no association between current cost earnings and dividends may be valid. In its annual survey of corporate annual reports, Peat Marwick Mitchell (1984) found that a significant number of managements expressed doubts about the usefulness of current cost data and cautioned investors that the measurement methods were approximate. The zero incremental information content of current cost data found by Beaver and Landsman (1983) and Matolcsy (1984) also provides indirect support for this hypothesis, though their results do not necessarily rule out an association between current cost earnings and dividends since it is possible that changes in dividend policies may not affect firm value. Similar inconsistencies between managerial decision effects and firm value have been found for other accounting information——for example, accounting for foreign currency translation (Dukes, 1978; and Evans et al., 1978) and accounting for leases (Abdel-khalik, 1981).

The above discussions suggest the following alternative hypothesis:

H_1: There is no positive association betweeen current cost earnings changes and dividend changes.

The remaining sections describe empirical tests of the association between current cost earnings and dividends using current cost data from 1980 to 1983.[4] Sample selection is discussed next.

SAMPLE

Annually, *Business Week* publishes a survey of inflation accounting data for over three hundred US firms. The surveys published in 1981 through 1984 are used in this study to collect cost accounting disclosures.[5] Additional financial data, including dividends, are obtained from the COMPUSTAT tape. A sample of 325 firms is obtained by including all companies listed in the 1981

---

[4] 1980 was chosen as the first year because, though SFAS-33 became effective in 1979, uniform computation and disclosure methods with respect to current cost data became widespread only from 1980.

[5] The 1985 and 1986 surveys could not be used because of a major change in format.

Business Week survey and the July 1984 COMPUSTAT tape, except for six firms which changed their fiscal years between 1979 and 1983. The appendix provides the distribution of firms in the sample by industry. Forty-four industry groups based on 2-digit SIC codes are represented in the sample, with fifteen of them having more than five firms each.

RESULTS

In this section, the association between dividends and earnings is examined using four different approaches. The results are presented in four corresponding subsections. To facilitate the discussion, the following notations are used:

$E_{j,t}$: Historical cost earnings (of firm j, year t),

$C_{j,t}$: Current cost earnings,

$D_{j,t}$: Dividend per share (or total dividends where indicated),

Δ: Change from previous period (i.e., $\Delta E_{j,t} = E_{j,t} - E_{j,t-1}$).

%Δ: Percentage change (i.e., $\%\Delta E_{j,t} = 100 \times \Delta E_{j,t}/E_{j,t-1}$).

Frequency of Dividend Changes

A simple way to examine whether dividends are associated with current cost earnings (as postulated by the capital maintenance and investment opportunity models) is to see whether the frequency of dividend increases (or dividend decreases) depends on the *sign* of current cost earnings change. This procedure is similar to the one used by Fama and Babiak (1968, Table 1) to examine the relationship between dividend changes and historical cost earnings. They placed their firms into eight groups based on the signs (+ or −) of $\Delta E_{j,t}$, $\Delta E_{j,t-1}$, and $\Delta E_{j,t-2}$, and found a strictly monotonic relationship between the ordering of the eight groups and the frequency of dividend increases.[6] For example, firms with three consecutive earnings increases had the most frequent dividend increases and the least frequent dividend decreases. Similarly, firms with three earnings decreases had the least frequent dividend increases and most frequent decreases. They concluded that dividend increases and decreases were affected by past and current earnings changes as predicted by the target payout and particular adjustment models.

Following their procedure, firms in the sample are placed into four groups based on the signs of $\Delta E_{j,t}$ and $\Delta C_{j,t}$, with group 1 having positive changes in both E and C, group 2 having $\Delta E > 0$ and $\Delta C < 0$, group 3 having $\Delta E < 0$ and $\Delta C > 0$, and group 4 having negative values of both ΔE and ΔC. For each group, the frequency of dividend increases and dividend decreases

---

[6] See Brealey and Myers (1984), p. 335, for an excellent summary of this paper.

is calculated using dividend per share data.[7] If current cost earnings affect dividends, then the frequency of dividend increases (or decreases) should be different for groups 1 and 2 (both of which have $\Delta E > 0$ but have opposite signs of ΔC), and similarly for groups 3 and 4. Moreover, the capital mainte-nance hypothesis would predict a larger frequency of dividend increases for firms with $\Delta C > 0$ (groups 1 and 3) compared to firms with $\Delta C < 0$ (groups 2 and 4). The investment opportunity model would predict the opposite relationship.

Table 1 presents the frequencies of dividend changes for the four groups for each of the 3 years examined. It is seen that dividend increases are more frequent when historical cost earnings increase ($\Delta E > 0$) than when they decrease ($\Delta E < 0$).[8] In 1981, for example, about 80 percent of the firms with $\Delta E > 0$ increased their dividends, while only about 59 percent of the firms with $\Delta E < 0$ had dividend increases. While the overall frequency of dividend

[7] Dividend per share rather than total dividends is used in this test and in the following one because total dividends depend on changes in the number of shares outstanding, even when dividend per share is constant.

[8] To keep the discussion simple, chi-square test statistics are not reported for this test. The statistics are generally in line with the reported findings. Test statistics are reported for the next three tests.

TABLE 1 Test 1: Frequency of Dividend Changes

Panel A: 1981 Data

| | Percent of Firms with | | | |
| | Dividend | Constant | Dividend | Total |
Group	Increases	Dividends	Decreases	Firms
(1) $\Delta E > 0$, $\Delta C > 0$	80.5%	16.0%	3.5%	169
(2) $\Delta E > 0$, $\Delta C < 0$	82.5%	12.5%	5.0%	40
(3) $\Delta E < 0$, $\Delta C > 0$	58.6%	34.5%	6.9%	29
(4) $\Delta E < 0$, $\Delta C < 0$	59.3%	29.1%	11.6%	86

Panel B: 1982 Data

| | Percent of Firms with | | | |
| | Dividend | Constant | Dividend | Total |
Group	Increases	Dividends	Decreases	Firms
(1) $\Delta E > 0$, $\Delta C > 0$	75.5%	20.5%	4.0%	102
(2) $\Delta E > 0$, $\Delta C < 0$	85.0%	10.0%	5.0%	20
(3) $\Delta E < 0$, $\Delta C > 0$	65.0%	25.0%	10.0%	20
(4) $\Delta E < 0$, $\Delta C < 0$	45.1%	34.6%	20.3%	182

Panel C: 1983 Data

| | Percent of Firms with | | | |
| | Dividend | Constant | Dividend | Total |
Group	Increases	Dividends	Decreases	Firms
(1) $\Delta E > 0$, $\Delta C > 0$	49.7%	39.3%	11.0%	191
(2) $\Delta E > 0$, $\Delta C < 0$	54.2%	33.3%	12.5%	24
(3) $\Delta E < 0$, $\Delta C > 0$	38.5%	38.5%	23.0%	13
(4) $\Delta E < 0$, $\Delta C < 0$	36.0%	46.1%	17.9%	89

Note: ΔE stands for change in historical cost earnings, and ΔC stands for change in current cost earnings.

increases is smaller in 1982 and 1983, group 1 and 2 firms with $\Delta E > 0$ still have more dividend increases than group 3 and 4 firms with $\Delta E < 0$ in these years. These data are in line with Fama and Babiak's result that historical cost earnings increases are associated with dividend increases.

However, changes in current cost earnings do not explain the frequency of dividend changes. Groups 1 and 2, for example, have comparable frequencies of dividend increases and decreases in all 3 years despite differing signs of ΔC. Similarly, groups 3 and 4 have comparable frequencies of dividend increases in all 3 years. In fact, with respect to dividend increases, a result similar to Fama and Babiak's strict monotonicity result can be obtained by ordering the four groups as group 2, group 1, group 4, and group 3, that is, firms with $\Delta C < 0$ generally have more dividend increases than firms with $\Delta C > 0$. The differences between $\Delta C > 0$ groups and $\Delta C < 0$ groups, however, are not significant and hence this ordering does not necessarily support the investment opportunity model. Overall, the results in Table 1 reject the null hypothesis and support the target payout and partial adjustment models.

Dividend Growth Rates

The above procedure of examining only the frequencies of dividend changes, while illustrative, ignores the possibility that dividend *growth rates* may be associated with current cost earnings. Moreover, a simple one-way analysis of variance test can be formulated if dividend growth rate rather than frequency is defined as the dependent variable. Hence, in this test, the average dividend growth rates of firms in the four groups are calculated using the dividend per share data. Table 2 provides the average growth rates as well as the number of applicable firms in each group, for each of the three years.[9]

The growth rates in Table 2 are consistent with the frequency results in Table 1. Firms with an increase in historical cost earnings (row 1 in each 2×2 table) generally have higher dividend growth rates than firms with $\Delta E < 0$ (row 2). This is true regardless of the sign of current cost earnings change. Moreover, given the same sign of ΔE, firms with an increase in current cost earnings (column 1) do not seem to have different growth rates than firms with a decrease in ΔC (column 2). Growth rates in column 2 are smaller than column 1 data in three of the six cases and larger in the other three cases, indicating no definite pattern of influence by the current cost data.

The overall F ratio from a one-way analysis of variance is significant at the 0.001 level for 1981 and 1982 and at the 0.16 level for 1983. Hence, the hypothesis that the four groups have equal growth rates can be rejected. In addition, the above analysis indicates that the grouping based on historical cost income rather than current cost income accounts for this differential behavior among the groups. These results support the partial adjustment and

[9] Growth rate is undefined if current year dividend is non-zero and preceding year dividend is zero. This accounts for the slight difference in the frequency of firms reported in Tables 1 and 2. To control for outlier values, the maximum value of growth rates is set to 300 percent. See Frecka and Hopwood (1983) and Deakin (1976) for the need to control ratio outliers.

TABLE 2 Test 2: Dividend Growth Rates Versus Earnings Changes

Panel A: 1981 Data

	ΔC > 0		ΔC < 0		
ΔE > 0	11.99%	169	11.56%	40	
ΔE < 0	5.15%	29	5.73%	86	F Ratio = 7.21 (sig. at 0.0001 level)

Panel B: 1982 Data

	ΔC > 0		ΔC < 0		
ΔE > 0	6.54%	102	8.23%	19	
ΔE < 0	6.16%	20	−3.70%	181	F Ratio = 6.11 (sig. at 0.0005 level)

Panel C: 1983 Data

	ΔC > 0		ΔC < 0		
ΔE > 0	0.18%	190	−1.87%	24	
ΔE < 0	−7.22%	13	−5.73%	89	F Ratio = 1.73 (sig. at 0.1614 level)

Note: Data in the cells are average dividend per share growth rates. The box within each cell contains the number of firms on which the average is based. For each year given below, earnings changes and dividend growth rates are calculated with respect to the previous year. ΔE stands for change in historical cost earnings, and ΔC stands for change in current cost earnings.

target payout models and do not lend support to the null hypothesis from the capital maintenance model.

Regression of Percentage Change in Dividends and Earnings

The analysis-of-variance test reported above considers the information about the magnitude of dividend changes but ignores the information about the magnitudes of earnings changes. Instead, only the sign changes are considered in forming the four groups. Though the two-by-two tables in Table 2 are effective in highlighting the relationship between dividend and earnings changes, a regression analysis of the variables can make better use of the information about earnings magnitude changes. Hence the following cross-sectional regression is estimated for the sample of firms for each of the three years to determine the relationship between percentage changes in dividends and earnings:

$$\%\Delta D_{j,t} = \alpha_1 + \beta_1 \%\Delta E_{j,t} + \beta_2 \%\Delta C_{j,t}, \tag{1}$$

where the dependent variable is the percentage change in dividend per share. Let a_1, b_1, and b_2 be the estimated values of α_1, β_1, and β_2 respectively. (The year subscript for the coefficients has been omitted for convenience.) If current cost data provide incremental explanatory power for dividend policy, then $b_2 > 0$ would support the capital maintenance hypothesis (H_0). $b_2 < 0$ or $b_2 = 0$ would support the alternative hypothesis (H_1) of investment opportunity model or target payout model, respectively.

Regression results for this model are summarized in Table 3 for all 3 years. The coefficient of current cost earnings variable is insignificant in all 3 years. In none of the 3 years is it significant and positive as hypothesized by the capital maintenance model. In addition, the coefficient of historical cost earnings variable is positive and significant in all 3 years, consistent with the target payout model's prediction that an increase in historical cost earnings would result in an increase in dividends assuming that the target payout ratio is constant.

Bar-Yosef and Lev (1983) also studied the relationship between changes in dividends and changes in various SFAS-33 based earnings measures. Their objective was to examine the incremental information contained in current cost earnings rather than to test various dividend models as done here. They did not examine the 1981–1983 data either. Nevertheless, some comparisons between the two studies can be made. In one of their tests, they ran cross-sectional regressions of dividends with either current cost earnings or historical cost earnings, but not both. Based on R^2 values, they concluded that "historical cost earnings and dividend changes are more strongly correlated than price-adjusted earnings and dividend changes." This result is consistent

TABLE 3 Test 3: Regression of Percentage Change in Dividends versus Earnings

Year	Sample Size	a_1 (t-val)	b_1 (t-val)	b_2 (t-val)	R^2
1981	256	11.380 (13.353)	0.113 (3.678)	0.001 (0.192)	0.085
1982	256	8.556 (10.176)	0.128 (5.408)	0.005 (0.401)	0.284
1983	199	5.510 (7.764)	0.034 (1.839)	0.003 (0.284)	0.054

Note: The estimated regression is: $\%\Delta D_{j,t} = a_1 + b_1 \%\Delta E_{j,t} + b_2 \%\Delta C_{j,t}$. The dependent variable is the percentage change in dividend per share. (Results are similar when total dividends are used.) $\%\Delta E$ is the percentage change in historical cost earnings. $\%\Delta C$ is the percentage change in current cost earnings.

with the larger significance of b_1 compared to b_2 reported in Table 3. They next regressed 1980 dividends against 1979 dividends, 1980 and 1979 historical cost earnings, and 1980 and 1979 current cost earnings residuals—the last two obtained from regressing current cost earnings with contemporaneous historical cost earnings. They found that R^2 values of the regressions with current cost residuals included were little changed from R^2 values of regressions without these residuals, and hence the "incremental contribution of the price-adjusted earnings in explaining cross-sectional differences in dividend changes is evidently negligible" (p. 46). While their regression model is ad hoc, their result is somewhat consistent with Table 3's insignificant b_2 in all 3 years.

Though the positive coefficient values of historical cost earnings variable in Table 3 strongly support the target payout hypothesis, the low R^2 values and the fact that both b_1 and b_2 have the same signs in all 3 years suggests that the insignificant values for b_2 may be due to multicollinearity. For example, the correlation between $\%\Delta E$ and $\%\Delta C$ is 0.632, 0.828, and 0.788 in the 3 years, respectively. To test this possibility, the regression diagnostic procedure of Belsley, Kuh and Welsch (1980) can be used. Briefly, in this procedure the condition indexes of the regression data matrix are first computed.[10] Values of 5 to 10 or more for a condition index indicate a near dependency among the regression variables. For Table 3 regressions, the largest condition index is computed to be only 2.13 in 1981, 3.62 in 1982, and 2.91 for 1983, indicating some but not a major multicollinearity problem. Overall, the results in Table 3 confirm the finding from the first two tests that current cost earnings do not generally provide incremental explanatory power for dividend decisions.

Partial Adjustment Model

The regression relationship in equation (1) is written in a form to directly test the hypothesis being tested. However, the equation's form is not equivalent to the traditional partial adjustment model of dividends even when the current cost term is removed. In this test, the regression equation is restated to conform with the partial adjustment model, and the incremental explanatory power of current cost earnings is examined using the restated model.

Under the target payout hypothesis of Lintner (1956), total dividends paid in a year equal $kE_{j,t}$, where k is the target payout ratio. (The firm subscript is suppressed here from k because of the cross-sectional nature of the test reported below.) Hence the dividend change would be given by $\Delta D_{j,t} = kE_{j,t} - D_{j,t-1}$. However, firms generally prefer not to raise or lower dividends by the full desired difference and instead prefer a smoother transition to the desired levels. If s is the speed of adjustment to the desired level, then the partial adjustment model of dividend change gives the following equation:

---

[10] Condition indexes are based on eigen values of the data matrix, and can be computed using the COLLIN option in the SAS regression procedure.

$\Delta D_{j,t} = s(kE_{j,t} - D_{j,t-1})$. Rewriting the terms, the following regression equation is suggested by the partial adjustment model:

$$\Delta D_{j,t} = \alpha_2 + \beta_3 E_{j,t} + \beta_4 D_{j,t-1}, \tag{2}$$

where $\beta_3 = sk$ and $\beta_4 = -s$. Inclusion of the constant term is recommended by Lintner to model the fact that firms prefer not to reduce dividends.

This equation differs considerably from equation (1). The dependent variable is the difference in total dividends rather than percentage change in dividends. Also, earnings level rather than percentage change in earnings is the independent variable. To test for the incremental explanatory power of dividends, the above partial adjustment model is expanded to include a current cost earnings term, $\beta_5 C_{j,t}$, as the independent variable, and the expanded model is estimated cross-sectionally for each of the 3 years. Let a_2, b_3, b_4, and b_5 be the estimated regression coefficients. (As before, the year subscript is omitted for convenience.) Then the partial adjustment model predicts b_3 (the coefficient of E) to be positive and b_4 (the coefficient of dividend level) to be negative. Moreover, if current cost has incremental influence over target dividends as suggested by the capital maintenance hypothesis, then b_5 should be positive.

Table 4 has the estimation results of 1981, 1982, and 1983 data in panel A. Though the R^2 values of Table 4 are not directly comparable to Table 3's values because the dependent variables are of different forms, the regression results indicate, consistent with the evidence in the literature, that the partial

TABLE 4 Test 4: Partial Adjustment Model of Dividends

Panel A: Total Sample

Year	Sample Size	a_2 (t-val)	b_3 (t-val)	b_4 (t-val)	b_5 (t-val)	R^2
1981	324	−1.715 (−2.124)	0.093 (22.407)	−0.134 (−17.130)	0.004 (0.959)	0.810
1982	324	0.951 (1.146)	0.049 (8.044)	−0.066 (−6.455)	−0.005 (−1.248)	0.370
1983	317	−0.252 (−0.369)	0.026 (5.814)	−0.040 (−5.251)	0.024 (7.544)	0.726

Panel B: Firms with Positive E and C Earnings in Period t Only

Year	Sample Size	a_2 (t-val)	b_3 (t-val)	b_4 (t-val)	b_5 (t-val)	R^2
1981	266	−1.792 (−1.890)	0.088 (19.712)	−0.102 (−8.540)	−0.007 (−1.075)	0.793
1982	212	1.589 (1.850)	0.047 (6.481)	−0.040 (−3.170)	−0.014 (−2.191)	0.412
1983	215	0.087 (0.128)	0.111 (2.074)	−0.020 (−2.540)	0.035 (8.419)	0.820

Note: The estimated regression is $\Delta D_{j,t} = a_2 + b_3 E_{j,t} + b_4 D_{j,t-1} + b_5 C_{j,t}$, where the dependent variable is the difference between total dividends of period t and period $t-1$, E is historical cost earnings, D is total dividends, and C is current cost earnings.

adjustment model is superior to a simple linear relationship such as equation (1). Examining the b_3 and b_4 coefficients first, it is clear that the partial adjustment and target payout models are strongly supported by the estimated coefficients. Both coefficients are significant and have the expected signs in all 3 years. For 1981, the estimated sample-wide average values of the speed of adjustment (s) is 0.134 and the target payout ratio (k) is $0.093/0.134 = 0.694$. The coefficient of current cost earnings, however, is not significant in two of the three years examined, and has the wrong sign in one of these years. Only in 1983 is b_5 significant and positive. Thus the panel A data do not indicate a consistent positive relationship between current cost earnings and dividends. The evidence, though, is consistent with some learning effect about the relationship between current cost data and dividends. The coefficient of current cost earnings is most significant in 1983 and least significant in 1981.[11]

There is some reason to believe that the target payout model is valid only when earnings are positive. For example, firms with losses in a year would rarely have *negative* dividends (i.e., new stock issue) of k times the loss as predicted by the target payout model. Similarly, it is implausible that such negative dividends would be the target to which dividends would be adjusted as suggested by the partial adjustment model. More likely, the target dividend would be zero. Hence the equation (2), with the added current cost earnings term, is re-estimated by including only those firms for which both historical cost and current cost earnings are positive in period t. Results of this estimation are presented in panel B of Table 4. The results, however, are basically in agreement with the results in panel A, including evidence of some learning effect with respect to the use of current cost data.

CONCLUSION

The overall inference from the four test results is that current cost data possess no incremental explanatory power for dividend decisions. This is consistent with the rejection of the capital maintenance hypothesis. Moreover, since incremental explanatory power for dividend decision is *assumed* for the investment opportunity hypothesis (see the section headed Hypotheses), the results are consistent with the rejection of the investment opportunity model as well. Overall, the results in Tables 1 to 4 strongly support the target payout and partial adjustment models, though there is some evidence of learning with respect to the use of current cost data for dividend decisions when 1983 results are compared to 1981 results. The following caveats, however, apply to the results.

For current cost data based on SFAS-33 to be potentially informative for management, they must be the most timely sources of such information. The

---

[11] The constant term is least significant in 1983, consistent with the data in Table 1 indicating that firms were not reluctant to cut dividends in 1983.

tests here exclude the possibility that management may have many alternative sources of current cost data such as industry-wide performance and competitive measures, and more importantly exclude various possible sources in the financial statements themselves, such as the accounting methods used for inventory and depreciation, proportion of fixed assets to total assets, and so on, which may provide the above information. The lack of significant relationship between current cost earnings and dividends reported here may be due to the possibility that these alternative sources of data proxy for current cost information and affect the dividend decision.

Secondly, the association predicted by the capital maintenance hypothesis between changes in dividends and changes in current cost earnings may not be linear in all ranges of current cost earnings values. For example, if current cost earnings exceeded dividends in the previous period, a decline in current cost earnings this period to a level still above previous period's dividends need not lead to a decline in dividends under this hypothesis. To the extent that the hypothesis is tested in the form of a linear model, the results may be biased against accepting the hypothesis. Future research might examine this issue by focusing on a subset of firms where current cost earnings are greater than dividends in the current year and decline below current dividend levels in the subsequent year.

Thirdly, the tests of frequency and rate of dividend changes and the tests of the descriptive models of dividend decision (viz., equations 1 and 2) assume that earnings changes are the only relevant factors for dividend decisions while in fact there may be many additional firm-specific factors that may explain dividend decisions. Identification of these factors has been a focus of research in the finance literature. Though a well-defined descriptive model of dividend decisions is not available in the literature, many firm-specific factors such as maturity, size, and financial structure have been suggested as relevant descriptive variables. The tests used here exclude such variables.

The positive association between historical cost earnings changes and dividends and the positive association between historical cost earnings and current cost earnings reported in this paper suggest that researchers examining security return effects of current cost earnings disclosures may have to control for dividend changes caused by contemporaneous changes in historical cost earnings. Otherwise, they may mistake the "yield effect" resulting from the dividend changes for the security return effects of current cost disclosures.[12] Future studies on the relationship between current cost data and security returns should explicitly consider the potential related effect of changes in dividends.

---

[12] See Blume (1980) and Litzenberger and Ramaswamy (1982) for evidence on positive yield effect, i.e., a positive association between yield and risk-adjusted returns. Black and Scholes (1974) and Miller and Scholes (1982) report a no-effect evidence.

APPENDIX
Distribution of Sample Firms by Industry

SIC Code	Industry	Firms
20	Food and Beverages	25
26	Paper products	15
27	Publishing	6
28	Chemicals	41
29	Oil and gas[a]	28
30	Rubber	6
32	Construction material	7
33	Steel	13
34	Metal products	7
35	Machinery	22
36	Electrical products	35
37	Vehicle manufacturing	20
38	Instruments	10
45	Air transportation	9
51	Wholesalers	10
	Others[b]	71
	Total	325

[a] Includes SIC group 13 (oil and gas production) firms.
[b] Includes 29 industry groups with five or fewer firms.

REFERENCES

Abdel-khalik, A. R. (1981), *The Economic Effects on Leases of FASB Statement No. 13, Accounting for Leases* (Financial Accounting Standards Board, 1981).

Accounting Standards Committee (1980), "Statement of Standard Accounting Practices No. 16," *Accountancy* (April 1980), Vol. 91, pp. 97–110.

Bar-Yosef, S., and B. Lev (1983), "Historical Cost Earnings versus Inflation-Adjusted Earnings in the Dividend Decision," *Financial Analysts Journal* (March–April 1983), pp. 41–50.

Beaver, W. H., and W. R. Landsman (1983), *Incremental Information Content of Statement 33 Disclosures* (Financial Accounting Standards Board, 1983).

Belsley, D. A., E. Kuh, and R. E. Welsch (1980), *Regression Diagnostics: Identifying Influential Data and Sources of Collinearity* (John Wiley & Sons, 1980).

Black, F., and M. S. Scholes (1974), "The Effects of Dividend Yield and Dividend Policy on Common Stock Prices and Returns," *Journal of Financial Economics* (May 1974), Vol. 1(1), pp. 1–22.

Blume, M. E. (1980), "Stock Returns and Dividend Yields: Some More Evidence," *Review of Economics and Statistics* (November 1980), Vo. 62, pp. 567–577.

Brealey, R., and S. Myers (1984), *Principles of Corporate Finance* (McGraw-Hill, 1984).

Deakin, E. B. (1976), "Distributions of Financial Accounting Ratios: Some Empirical Evidence," *Accounting Review* (January 1976), Vol. 51(1), pp. 90–96.

Dukes, R. E. (1978), *An Empirical Investigation of the Effects of Statement of Financial Accounting Standards No. 8 on Security Return Behavior* (Financial Accounting Standards Board, 1978).

Evans, K., and R. Freeman (1983), "Statement 33 Disclosures Confirm Profit Illusion in Primary Statements," *FASB Viewpoints* (24 June 1983).

Evans, T. G., W. R. Folks, Jr., and M. Jilling (1978), *The Impact of SFAS No. 8 on the Foreign Exchange Risk Management Practices of American Multinationals: An Economic Impact Study* (Financial Accounting Standards Board, 1978).

Fama, E., and H. Babiak (1968), "Dividend Policy: An Empirical Analysis," *Journal of the American Statistical Association* (December 1968), Vol. 63, pp. 1132–1161.

Financial Accounting Standards Board (1979), *Financial Reporting and Changing Prices, Statement of Financial Accounting Standards No. 33* (Financial Accounting Standards Board, 1979).

Frecka, T. J., and W. S. Hopwood (1983), "The Effects of Outliers on the Cross-sectional Distributional Properties of Financial Ratios," *Accounting Review* (January 1983), Vol. 58(1), pp. 115–128.

Grant, J. L. (1983), "Inflation's Full Impact on the Bottom Line," *Business Week* (7 February 1983), p. 8.

Lintner, J. (1956), "Distribution of Incomes of Corporations Among Dividends, Retained Earnings and Taxes," *American Economic Reviw* (May 1956), Vol. 46, pp. 97–113.

Litzenberger, R. H., and K. Ramaswamy (1982), "The Effects of Dividends on Common Stock Returns: Tax Effects or Information Effects?" *Journal of Finance* (May 1982), Vol. 37(2), pp. 429–443.

Matolcsy, Z. P. (1984), "Evidence on the Joint and Marginal Information Content of Inflation-adjusted Accounting Income Numbers," *Journal of Accounting Research* (Autumn 1984), Vol. 22(2), pp. 555–569.

Miller, M. H., and M. S. Scholes (1982), "Dividends and Taxes: Some Empirical Evidence," *Journal of Political Economy* (1982), Vol. 90, pp. 1118–1141.

Peat, Marwick, Mitchell & Co. (1984), "Annual Reports of Top Companies Reflect Range of Industry Issues," *Executive Newsletter* (28 November 1984), Vol. 10(11), p. 1.

Rappaport, A. (1981), "Inflation Accounting and Corporate Dividends," *Financial Executive* (February 1981), pp. 20–22.

Revsine, L. (1973), *Replacement Cost Accounting* (Prentice-Hall, 1973).

———— (1981), "Let's Stop Eating Our Seed Corn," *Harvard Business Review* (January–February 1981), Vol. 59(1), pp. 128–134.

CHAPTER 18

International Financial Reporting Issues

With the increasing globalization of capital markets in the 1960s and 1970s, a movement began to "harmonize" international accounting practices. The International Accounting Standards Committee (IASC), a private-sector standard-setting body based in London,[1] was founded in 1973 by leading figures from the accounting bodies in nine countries. In the late 1960s, the European Economic Community, now known as the European Community (EC), began the lengthy and tortuous process of drafting directives on the contents of statutory and consolidated financial statements. The EC's Fourth and Seventh Directives on these subjects were approved in 1978 and 1983, respectively, and by 1991 the laws of all 12 member countries had been adapted to both directives.

These efforts, while unquestionably contributing to a narrowing of the differences in accounting practice among countries, nonetheless fell well short of achieving genuine comparability as between different countries' financial reporting. IASC standards, while proscribing clearly objectionable practices, allowed free choices in most of its standards. The EC directives, especially the Fourth, permitted a considerable number of optional treatments. The member countries differed as to which options they translated into national legislation, and each of the national adaptations allowed companies a range of choice in numerous areas.

The United Nations and the Organisation for Economic Co-operation and Development have also been active in the sphere of financial reporting, but the impact of their initiatives is more difficult to gauge.

---

[1] Today, the IASC claims 105 member bodies in 78 countries, representing over one million accountants in industry and commerce, public practice, academic institutions and government. The offices of the IASC are at 167 Fleet Street, London EC4A 2ES, England.

IASC standards were adopted or adapted in a number of developing countries, and were used to fashion the national agenda of subjects to be addressed in others (in New Zealand, for example). Few of the major standard-setting countries, however, altered their practices in order to adhere to IASC standards. Indeed, the IASC standards ordinarily embraced U.S. and U.K. practices, so it was not necessary for those countries' standard setters to act in response to their .issuance, other than to affirm that their national standards already reflected IASC recommendations. The London Stock Exchange has expected listed companies from non-EC countries to provide a reconciliation of their net income and owners' equity determined in accordance with their home country's standards to the results that would be obtained by using IASC standards.

In the late 1980s, the International Organization of Securities Commissions (IOSCO), at the urging of the U.S. Securities and Exchange Commission (SEC), persuaded the IASC to move to a stage beyond its harmonization program. The SEC had hoped that, if IASC standards could become more narrowly defined, replacing the free choices with "preferred" (later renamed "benchmark") standards and a limited number of allowed alternative treatments, they might one day be designated by the SEC as the standards to which foreign registrants must reconcile their net income and owners' equity determined by home country standards. At present, the SEC requires foreign registrants to reconcile to highly restrictive U.S. generally accepted accounting principles (GAAP), which apparently has served to discourage some overseas companies from entering the U.S. capital market. In order to enhance the standing of the New York capital market, the SEC seeks to promote a "level playing field," by which one set of standards could be used as the international norm for reconciliation purposes. Therefore, if the IASC standards were to become sufficiently strict to gain the SEC's approval, the New York Stock Exchange could join the London Stock Exchange in requiring a reconciliation to IASC standards.

Germany is a special case. German companies have refused to provide reconciliations to any other accounting standards. While German companies, being from an EC country, are exempt from such reconciliation on the London Stock Exchange, they would enjoy no such exemption in the United States. In 1992, the president of the New York Stock Exchange unsuccessfully sought to persuade the SEC to allow it to list German companies without the requirement that they reconcile their published figures to U.S. GAAP.[2] Finally, in March 1993, Daimler-Benz, AG, Germany's largest company, entered into an agreement with the SEC under which it would be admitted to listing on the New York Stock Exchange in return for its assurance that its financial reporting would meet the SEC's standards.[3] Daimler-Benz thus became the first German company to be traded in the New York capital market, and other major German companies and banks are expected to follow

[2] See Michael Siconolfi and Kevin G. Salwen, "Big Board, SEC Fight Over Foreign Stocks," *The Wall Street Journal* (May 13, 1992).
[3] "Daimler's SEC Pact to List Stock in U.S. May Spur Other Foreign Firms to Follow," *The Wall Street Journal* (March 31, 1993), p. A4.

suit. This is an excellent example of how access to a major capital market can provide an incentive for companies to be more forthcoming about the reporting of financial information.

Thus encouraged by IOSCO to remove many of the free choices from its standards, the IASC announced a program of slimmed-down standards in January 1989, and in July 1990 it issued a Statement of Intent for an ambitious program of reconsidering and revising its previously issued standards, with a view toward eliminating many of the free choices. It has come to be known as IASC's Comparability/Improvements project. Exposure drafts of a number of revised standards have been issued, and the IASC's 14-member board is working assiduously to complete work on most of the revised standards by the end of 1993, when IOSCO will make a decision about the acceptability of the revised standards for use in multinational securities offerings.

As mentioned in Chapter 6, the task of narrowing the range of choices is more difficult than the IASC's optimistic predictions might have suggested. Included in the IASC's Statement of Intent was a proposal that LIFO be eliminated from the set of allowed alternative treatments. There was considerable unhappiness in the United States about this prospect, since the use of LIFO is linked to income tax relief. Nonetheless, the U.S. delegation, in the spirit of international solidarity, refrained from dissenting at the board's October 1992 meeting when the status of LIFO was decided. But four other countries that also viewed LIFO through the prism of taxation—Germany, Italy, Japan, and Korea—voted against the expulsion of LIFO, and the motion was defeated. Even in the IASC's corridors, where the cause of comparability in international financial reporting finds its most articulate champions, the protection of national self-interest is not without its supporters.

Another obstacle to international harmonization is the self-interested lobbying pressure imposed on national standard setters. Such pressure serves to diminish the impact of the "accounting model" (i.e., matching or asset-liability analysis, depending on one's orientation) on the content of standards, with a consequent increase in the impact of "political" or economic consequences factors. Since there is no reason to believe that "political" factors that are dominant in one country would be similarly dominant in most other countries, international harmonization could be threatened.

A recent study by Touche Ross Europe gave an interesting perspective of the relative degrees of conservatism of different European countries' accounting practices.[4] The firm prepared alternative sets of consolidated financial statements for a multinational group according to assumptions and accounting policies most likely to be applied in each of seven European countries. The purpose of the study was to ascertain which countries' accounting practices would yield the most and least conservative renderings of profit. The principal differences were traceable to the treatments of goodwill and deferred taxation. The United Kingdom showed the highest profit, and Spain showed the lowest, as follows (expressed in million European Currency Units, Ecus):

---

[4] Andy Simmonds and Olivier Azières, *Accounting for Europe—Success by 2000 AD?* (London: Touche Ross Europe, 1989), pp. 31–42.

Country	Profits (Million Ecus)	Percent of U.K. Level
United Kingdom	192	100.0
Italy	174	90.6
France	149	77.6
Netherlands	140	72.9
Belgium	135	70.3
Germany	133	69.3
Spain	131	68.2

Clearly, the impact of different European countries' accounting practices on financial statement figures can be considerable.

In "International Accounting Rules Advance," Alison Leigh Cowan, the accounting reporter for *The New York Times*, views recent IASC developments from a U.S. perspective. Interestingly, a leading U.S. financial analyst predicts that "there's a real risk that ultimately the IASC, because of the globalization of the capital markets, could supersede the FASB."

S.E.C. Purvis, Helen Gernon, and Michael A. Diamond, in "The IASC and Its Comparability Project: Prerequisites for Success," perform an extensive analysis of countries' compliance with IASC standards. They find that some of the founder countries (Germany and Mexico) do not have a strong record of conformity with IASC standards. The authors support the harmonization movement, and they view the IASC as the vehicle promising the most success. But they warn against unenlightened efforts to lobby the IASC in support of national accounting interests, and they regard regulators, other than accounting standard setters, as being critical to the harmonization cause. Above all, the authors conclude that "the IASC must win the commitment of standard-setters and regulators in at least three major markets—the United Kingdom, the United States, and Japan—for comparability to proceed."

It falls to financial analysts to be able to "see through" the national differences in accounting and disclosure practices in order to draw meaningful comparisons between companies from different national environments. David F. Hawkins, in "Direct Transnational Financial Statement Analysis: Converting IAS to US GAAP," which appeared in an accounting bulletin published by Merrill Lynch, provides a framework for use by U.S. portfolio managers and security analysts in reconciling foreign financial statements to U.S. generally accepted accounting principles. Hawkins, a Harvard Business School professor, illustrates the application of his framework to the financial statements of Grand Metropolitan PLC, one of Britain's ten largest industrial companies.

BIBLIOGRAPHICAL NOTES

A planned series of 12 volumes dealing comprehensively with the financial reporting standards and practices of the EC countries, all to be published by

Routledge in association with The Institute of Chartered Accountants in England and Wales, has thus far yielded five volumes:

Brennan, Niamh, Francis J. O'Brien, and Aileen Pierce: *European Financial Reporting: Ireland* (1992).
Gonzalo, José A., and José L. Gallizo: *European Financial Reporting: Spain* (1992).
Scheid, Jean-Claude, and Peter Walton: *European Financial Reporting: France* (1992).
Christiansen, Merete, and Jens O. Elling: *European Financial Reporting: Denmark* (1993).
Papas, Anthony A.: *European Financial Reporting: Greece* (1993).

A guidebook on the accounting standards and practices in 21 European countries, with commentary on the political, legal and economic factors that have shaped the standards and practices, is

Alexander, David, and Simon Archer (editors): *HBJ Miller Comprehensive European Accounting Guide*, U.S. Edition (San Diego, CA: Harcourt Brace Jovanovich, Publishers, 1991). An international edition is available under the title, *The European Accounting Guide*, published by Academic Press Limited, London.

An extensive doctoral dissertation done at the Erasmus University, Rotterdam, examining harmonization efforts in the European Community, and including empirical surveys on the degree of harmonization achieved on disclosure (segmentation of net turnover) and measurement (goodwill and deferred taxation), is:

Van der Tas, L. G.: *Harmonisation of Financial Reporting: With a Special Focus on the European Community* (Rotterdam: The Author, 1992).

A collection of essays on comparative standard setting may be found in

Bromwich, Michael, and Anthony G. Hopwood (editors): *Accounting Standards Setting: An International Perspective* (London: Pitman, 1983).

Two extensive studies of Japanese financial reporting are the following:

Choi, Frederick D. S., and Kazuo Hiramatsu: *Accounting and Financial Reporting in Japan: Current Issues and Future Prospects in a World Economy* (Wokingham, Berks: Van Nostrand Reinhold (U.K.) Co. Ltd, 1987).
Cooke, T. E., and M. Kikuya: *Financial Reporting in Japan: Regulation, Practice and Environment* (Oxford: Blackwell Publishers Ltd, 1992).

Since 1987, the American Institute of Certified Public Accountants has published a series of informational booklets on the accounting profession (including accounting principles and practices) in each of about 15 countries, prepared by the technical personnel of leading public accounting firms.[5]

Coopers & Lybrand has compiled detailed summaries of accounting standards in 24 countries, with additional chapters on IASC standards and the EC's Fourth and Seventh Directives:

Coopers & Lybrand (International): *1991 International Accounting Summaries: A Guide for Interpretation and Comparison* (New York: John Wiley & Sons, Inc., 1991). (Annual updating supplements will be published.)

The U.K. firm of Coopers & Lybrand has published five booklets in which U.K. financial reporting is compared to that in each of 15 European countries:

Nobes, Christopher (compiler): *Accounting Comparisons* (London: Coopers & Lybrand/ Gee, October 1992), 5 booklets. (Booklets are also available on U.K./U.S.A./ Canada and on U.K./Japan.)

Annually, the Canadian firm of Price Waterhouse publishes a booklet entitled *Accounting Principles and Practices in Canada and the United States of America: A Survey of Significant Differences.*

The Big Six public accounting firms in the United States cooperated in an International Research Project, with each firm preparing a survey and analysis of the accounting standards and practices in eight countries (Australia, Canada, France, Germany, Italy, Japan, the Netherlands, and the U.K.) in comparison with those in the United States, in different areas as follows:

Consolidations/Equity Accounting Practices (Price Waterhouse, 1990).
Accounting for Leases (Ernst & Young, 1991).
Accounting for Income Taxes (KPMG Peat Marwick, 1991).
Accounting for Foreign Currency (Deloitte & Touche, 1991).
Employers' Accounting for Pensions (Coopers & Lybrand, 1991).
Accounting for Business Combinations, Goodwill and Other Intangibles (Arthur Andersen & Co., 1991).

A study of major issues, problems and trends relating to information disclosure by multinational corporations is

Gray, S. J., with L. B. McSweeney and J. C. Shaw: *Information Disclosure and the Multinational Corporation* (Chichester, England: John Wiley and Sons, 1984).

The proceedings from a conference held in 1985 by the OECD on accounting harmonization is

Harmonization of Accounting Standards: Achievements and Prospects (Paris: Organisation for Economic Co-operation and Development, 1986).

An indication of the role played by the United Nations' Intergovernmental Working Group of Experts on International Standards of Accounting and Reporting (ISAR) in developing guidelines for transnational corporations in the area of information disclosure and accounting practices may be found in a volume containing the record of accomplishments during ISAR's ninth session:

United Nations Centre on Transnational Corporations, *International Accounting and Reporting Issues, 1991 Review* (New York: United Nations, 1992).

A collection of essays (in Spanish) on accounting in Latin American countries, as well as in Spain and Portugal, is

Tua Pereda, Jorge (coordinador): *La Contabilidad en Iberoamérica* (Madrid: Instituto de Contabilidad y Auditoría de Cuentas, Ministerio de Economía y Hacienda, 1989).

[5] The address of the AICPA is 1211 Avenue of the Americas, New York, NY 10036-8775.

Three recent editions of textbooks/treatises on international accounting are:

Choi, Frederick D. S., and Gerhard G. Mueller: *International Accounting* (Englewood Cliffs, NJ: Prentice-Hall, second edition, 1992).

Nobes, Christopher, and Robert Parker: *Comparative International Accounting* (Hemel Hempstead, Herts: Prentice Hall International (U.K.) Ltd, third edition, 1991).

Radebaugh, Lee H., Sidney J. Gray and Jeffery Arpan: *International Accounting* (New York: John Wiley & Sons, Inc., third edition, 1993).

A major reference work on international accounting is

Choi, Frederick D. S. (editor): *Handbook of International Accounting* (New York: John Wiley & Sons, Inc., 1991).

An in-depth study of the "survival strategies" of the IASC is

Wallace, R. S. Olusegun: "Survival Strategies of a Global Organization: The Case of the International Accounting Standards Committee," *Accounting Horizons* (June 1990), pp. 1–22.

A historical study of the process of regulating financial reporting in the Netherlands, including a comparison with approaches in the United States and the United Kingdom, is

Zeff, Stephen A., Frans van der Wel, and Kees Camfferman: *Company Financial Reporting: A Historical and Comparative Study of the Dutch Regulatory Process* (Amsterdam: North-Holland, 1992).

International Accounting Rules Advance

Alison Leigh Cowan
The New York Times

After years of talk, the adoption of an internationally accepted set of accounting rules is moving toward reality.

A London-based group, the International Accounting Standards Committee, which has been working on the rules for 18 years, is finally nearing its goal.

About 80 countries, including the United States and most other industrialized nations, are watching the group's progress. Although most nations have not pledged to adopt the group's rules, their regulators have said that, if the proposals were reasonable, they would work to make them acceptable alternatives for foreign companies doing business in their countries.

The existence of an alternative set of rules is likely to put pressure on countries to move their own national rules closer to the international ones. In the United States, the Securities and Exchange Commission has been a champion of this process.

Progress in the adoption of international accounting rules has divided Corporate America between those who want to see cross-border financings made easier and those who mistrust anything that could affect their bottom lines.

Most of the rules being devised are shorter and more flexible than United States accounting standards, and some would tend to increase corporate profits while others would tend to reduce them. Either way, companies are paying attention.

"We think it's coming closer to reality," said Raymond Alleman, the controller of the ITT Corporation in New York, which made a $4,000 donation—its first—to the group this year. "I don't know if it's going to happen next year or the year after, but they're moving in the right direction."

The international rules would affect United States financial statements in different ways. For instance, while a proposed rule governing inventory costs would be kinder to corporate profits than the American version, many United States companies would pay more in taxes if forced to follow it.

Also controversial is a rule on business combinations that the international group is expected to propose next spring. This rule would shrink the loophole that the American Telephone and Telegraph Company is using to buy the NCR Corporation without having to take a $5 billion charge for goodwill. It would also give corporate acquirers no more than 20 years to take a goodwill charge, half of what is permitted under American rules.

NEED TO RAISE CAPITAL

Richard Reinhard, an associate chief accountant for the S.E.C. who has been monitoring the group's progress, said that rewriting some domestic accounting rules would be a small price to pay for international harmony and opening markets.

"If the answer is within a reasonable range of acceptable answers, we don't object," Mr. Reinhard said. "If every country thought only about what was best for itself, you might as well not make the effort."

The drive for international standards is an outgrowth of the globalization of business, with companies looking beyond their own borders for opportunities to raise money.

"That's the driving force, no question," said Arthur R. Wyatt, the London group's chairman.

Helping the international group in reaching its goal was a move in 1989 by the International Organization of Securities Commissions in Montreal.

In that year, the influential body of regulators that includes the S.E.C. dangled an enormous carrot: If the London group could whittle down the number of options in its standards and provide more guidance on applying the rules by 1992, the market regulators pledged to support the international standards in their respective markets. Today, the London group has agreed on how to narrow 21 of its 29 existing rules.

SHOPPING FOR STANDARDS

The rush by some eastern European and Latin American countries to embrace Western-style capitalism is also working in the group's favor. To attract foreign capital, these countries are shopping for accounting standards that investors of many nationalities will find acceptable. And because they have no home-grown standards to protect, these countries could give the London group the critical mass it needs for its rules to become the true international standard.

Oddly, Mr. Wyatt, the London group's chairman, was once a member of the Financial Accounting Standards Board in Norwalk, Conn., and a contender for its top job. As the board that makes most of the nation's accounting rules, the F.A.S.B. arguably is among those with the most to lose from the London group's success.

Mr. Wyatt, a 64-year-old Chicago accountant, resigned his seat on the board in July 1987, after losing in a race for the chairmanship to Dennis R. Beresford, the current chairman.

PART-TIME JOB

Shortly after Mr. Wyatt returned to Arthur Andersen's Chicago office to resume private practice, he was approached about occupying the one seat of the 14 in the international group that is reserved for an American. Two and a half years later, he became its chairman, a job that consumes about 40 percent of his time.

Since then, Mr. Wyatt has had to learn to do more with less. Though the London group was formed in 1973—coincidental with the creation of the F.A.S.B.—its 1990 budget of $750,000 was less than one-twentieth the $17 million that the F.A.S.B. spent last year. Committee members meet three times a year compared with once a week at the F.A.S.B., and the international group needs an even bigger majority than the F.A.S.B. to pass new rules.

Yet companies say they are impressed with the group's results.

"With a relatively small staff and investment, they've turned out a lot of standards that have been practical, concise and easy to read," said Susan Koski-Grafer, the assistant controller at A.T.&T.

CORPORATE SUPPORT

A.T.&T. is one of several American corporations whose donations have helped the London group expand its staff and move to larger quarters at 167 Fleet Street. Other companies, like Salomon Inc., the Exxon Corporation, the FMC Corporation, the General Electric Company and CPC International, are showing their support by pointing out in their annual reports whether their existing accounting rules conform to the proposed international standards.

If the new standards catch on, the F.A.S.B. could face its most serious challenge yet.

"Certainly, we expect to be spending more of our time on international issues over the next couple of years," Mr. Beresford, the chairman, said in a recent interview.

Already, the organization has begun weighing the accounting practices of other countries in new proposals it issues. As a test case for further cooperation, it is negotiating with the London group to rewrite the rules governing how companies calculate their earnings per share. But it is also feeling the heat.

"In the past, the I.A.S.C. waited for big countries to come up with pronouncements and then piggybacked on that," said Jeannot Blanchet, an F.A.S.B. project manager assigned to international accounting issues. "But now they're really trying to be leaders."

NEED FOR NATIONAL RULES

For all the London group's momentum, Mr. Beresford strongly believes that national rule makers like the F.A.S.B. face little immediate risk of obsolescence. "There may eventually be a diminished need for the kind of activity we have here," he said, "but I don't see that in the foreseeable future."

Even if the London group eventually dictates the standards for multinational companies doing cross-border financings, Mr. Beresford said, there would still be a role for the F.A.S.B. at home.

He pointed to a recent F.A.S.B. rule on retiree health benefits, an issue that is unique to American income statements. "In most other parts of the world, retiree health-care costs are covered by the government," Mr. Beresford said.

Others are not so sure that the F.A.S.B.'s future is guaranteed.

"I think there's a real risk that ultimately the I.A.S.C., because of the globalization of the capital markets, could supersede the F.A.S.B.," said Patricia A. McConnell, an accounting expert at the Bear Stearns Companies who shares a seat on the I.A.S.C. reserved for analysts.

She said the London group's effort to whittle down the number of acceptable alternatives in its rules "is an analyst's dream." Streamlined rules would ease cross-border comparisons of corporate performance, which have been nearly impossible in the past, she said.

"If it works," she said, "there will be a much reduced role for the F.A.S.B."

The IASC and Its Comparability Project: Prerequisites for Success

S. E. C. Purvis
University of California, Los Angeles

Helen Gernon
University of Oregon

Michael A. Diamond
University of Southern California

INTRODUCTION

As the volume of international financial operations and cross-border investments continues to surge, the need for a common language of business in financial statements is increasing in urgency. It has long been argued that different national accounting standards militate against the efficiency of international capital markets and may even impair the ability of corporations to compete effectively for capital in those markets. Barthes observed that the:

> business community is tired of differences in accounting. These differences lead to increased costs for those companies that operate and raise capital

From *Accounting Horizons* (June 1991), pp. 25–44. Reprinted by permission of the American Accounting Association and the authors. Copyright © 1991 by the American Accounting Association.

abroad and to an unlevel playing field for those international companies that are competing with one another for business opportunities.[1]

In the last three decades, standard-setters[2] and regulators[3] in different countries have grappled with the problems posed by different national standards. Several international institutions have risen to the challenge presented by the development of international accounting standards. These include the United Nations (UN), the European Community (EC), the Organisation for Economic Cooperation and Development (OECD), all governmental or quasi-governmental institutions, and the International Accounting Standards Committee (IASC), the only private standard-setter in the international arena. Two years ago, the IASC released Exposure Draft 32 (ED32), "Comparability of Financial Statements," proposing an improved set of international standards.[4] ED32 represents the culmination of a 2-year project which had been encouraged by the International Organisation of Securities Commissions (IOSCO), and stakes the IASC's claim to be the preeminent provider of international financial accounting and reporting standards.

The purpose of this article is to assess the likely compliance with ED32 and to debate the prerequisites for the success of the IASC's proposal for international accounting comparability. The next section analyzes national compliance with existing IAS's, and identifies several factors which may hinder this comparability attempt. The third section briefly reviews ED32 and discusses the likely compliance of five major countries with ED32. In the

[1] Georges Barthes, "Meeting the Expectations of Global Capital Markets." *IASC News*, Vol. 18, No. 3 (July, 1989): 1–2.

[2] *Standard-setters* are institutions or groups responsible for setting national accounting and reporting standards. These groups may be in the private sector, e.g., the Financial Accounting Standards Board (FASB) and the current Accounting Standards Committees in Canada and the United Kingdom. In some countries, these national standard-setters may be government agencies, related to government agencies, or even the government itself. For example, in Japan, the Business Accounting Deliberations Council, affiliated with the Ministry of Finance, is involved in setting accounting standards, whereas in Germany, accounting standards are set by Parliament through the Ministry of Justice. In the Netherlands, Parliament has primary responsibility (again through the Ministry of Justice), but there is also an independent, private sector Council for Annual Reporting.

[3] *Regulators* are groups or institutions with statutory authority to regulate stock exchanges, and, which, in so doing, may prescribe accounting standards and disclosure requirements. These groups also have enforcement authority to insure compliance. In many countries, the regulatory function is separated from the standard-setting function. For example, in the U.S., the Securities and Exchange Commission (SEC), while having statutory authority to set standards, has generally looked to the private sector (presently, the FASB) for the development of accounting standards. The SEC, however, has mandated disclosure requirements which apply to listed companies through regulations S-X and S-K. In other countries, the regulating body may be the same as the standard-setting body. The Swedish Accounting Standards Board is such an example.

[4] International Accounting Standards Committee (a). "Comparability of Financial Statements: Proposed amendments to International Accounting Standards 2, 5, 8, 9, 11, 16, 17, 18, 19, 21, 22, 23, and 25." *Exposure Draft 32* (London: IASC, 1989).

International Accounting Standards Committee (b). "Towards the International Harmonisation of Financial Statements: An Invitation to Comment on an Exposure Draft on the Comparability of Financial Statements." (London: IASC, 1989).

section, possible responses from different groups of countries to the IASC's move are considered. In the fifth section, prerequisites for success of the Comparability Project are reviewed. In the sixth section, the desirability of harmonization is debated. Finally, it is concluded that the IASC needs the cooperation and endorsement of standard-setters and regulators in the major markets in order to realize the aims of the Comparability Project.

REVIEW OF COMPLIANCE WITH EXISTING IAS's

In 1988, the IASC published a major survey[5] of compliance with international accounting standards (IAS) in force at that time. Member institutions were asked to indicate the extent to which national standards or practices conformed with the 25 IAS's.[6] Responses received from 54 member countries were reported in tabular form, but were not subjected to examination by the IASC. This study analyzes the IASC data from several different perspectives, including compliance by standard and by country.

Compliance by Standard

Table 1 shows the current level of compliance with existing IAS on a standard by standard basis. The numbered columns record the presence or absence of substantial conformity, as defined in the table.

The categories employed by the IASC in its questionnaire may be distinguished into conforming versus nonconforming responses (columns 1–4 and 5–6 respectively). In order to evaluate the degree of compliance with the 25 existing standards, two conformity indices were constructed. In each percentage-based index, the numerator represents the sum of all *conforming* responses (in columns 1–4). There are two possible choices for the denominator: (A) the sum of conforming and nonconforming responses (in columns 1–6), or (B) 54, the number of countries surveyed.[7] The difference between the two denominators is column 7, which represents the number of countries omitting a response, or otherwise indicating that a particular standard was not applicable. The two indices are highly correlated (Spearman's correlation coefficient, rho = .849), and strongly statistically significant (p = .0001). Note that the number of countries in column 7 increases directly with the recency of the standard. Indeed, Spearman's correlation (rho) of the standard number

---

[5] International Accounting Standards Committee. *Survey of the Use and Application of International Accounting Standards*. (London: IASC, July 1988).

[6] A complete list of international accounting standards, titles, and release dates may be found in the inside back cover of ED32.

[7] It is recognized that this coding scheme is rather generous in that it weights each category of conformity equally. It could be argued that category 4 should be assigned a lower weight than categories 1–3. Similarly, one could argue that a national standard conflicting with an IAS should receive greater weight than a non-conforming national practice. Different weights were used in a sensitivity analysis (not reported here). While the absolute scores changed according to the weights used, the relative rankings of each standard in the table were not significantly affected.

TABLE 1 Conformity with Existing Standards: Analysis by Standard

	Response Category							Conformity	Conformity
	1	2	3	4	5	6	7	Index A	Index B
Standard									
IAS 1	7	7	25	9	3	2	1	90.6%	88.9%
IAS 2	7	4	30	7	5	1		88.9%	88.9%
IAS 3	7	4	21	13	4	4	1	84.9%	83.3%
IAS 4	7	7	29	10	1			98.2%	98.2%
IAS 5	7	6	28	11	2			96.3%	96.3%
IAS 7	7	4	24	15	1	3		92.6%	92.6%
IAS 8	7	3	30	8	4	2		88.9%	88.9%
IAS 9	7	4	18	12	7	2	4	82.0%	75.9%
IAS 10	7	6	28	11	1	1		96.3%	96.3%
IAS 11	7	6	21	15	2	2	1	92.5%	90.7%
IAS 12	7	3	16	8	9	6	5	69.4%	63.0%
IAS 13	7	5	26	13	2	1		94.4%	94.4%
IAS 14	7	2	6	10	7	19	3	49.0%	49.3%
IAS 15	4	5	11	5	22		7	42.6%	37.0%
IAS 16	7	3	26	14	2		2	96.2%	92.6%
IAS 17	7	3	15	10	6	11	2	67.3%	64.8%
IAS 18	7	4	18	18	2	1	4	94.0%	87.0%
IAS 19	6	4	13	9	3	11	8	69.6%	59.3%
IAS 20	6	1	17	14	4	7	5	77.6%	70.4%
IAS 21	7	6	17	11	6	4	3	80.4%	75.9%
IAS 22	6	2	15	14	5	8	4	74.0%	68.5%
IAS 23	7	4	15	17	2	5	4	86.0%	79.6%
IAS 24	4	1	15	12	2	14	6	66.7%	59.3%
IAS 25	4	3	16	14	5	4	8	80.4%	68.5%
IAS 26	4	3	6	9	3	15	14	55.0%	40.7%
Total	160	95	480	295	93	145	82	80.5%	76.3%

Notes: The response categories are defined as follows:
  1. "IAS adopted as national standard"
  2. "IAS used as the basis for a national requirement"
  3. National requirements conform "in all material respects with IAS"
  4. National practice "generally conforms with IAS"
  5. National requirements do "not conform with IAS"
  6. "National practice does not generally conform with IAS"
  7. Not applicable[a]
The values represent the number of countries (out of 54) that selected each response category.

[a] Some countries were not assigned a response in the IASC survey results. Recent correspondence with the IASC indicates that these should be coded "Not applicable," and therefore they have been assigned to category 7.

(as a proxy for issue date) with column 7 is .746, a very high degree of association, which explains more than half of the observed variance ($r^2 = .558$).

Some of the missing responses surely reflect a lack of compliance with the standards rather than the standards' lack of relevance to the country. It is difficult to imagine that a country could argue that IAS 1 "Disclosure of

Accounting Policies" is "not applicable." Consequently, Index B is used in subsequent analyses because it more accurately reflects *active* compliance.

Conformity by Standard

An examination of Table 1 shows a high level of conformity with the first group of standards issued, but much lower levels for standards issued more recently. Both conformity indices show a strong negative correlation with the date on which each standard came into effect (Index A, rho = $-.534$, p = .006; and Index B, rho = $-.640$, p = .0006). There are (at least) two explanations for this negative relationship. First, the early standards tended to address more fundamental issues at a high level of generality, which enabled many countries to conform with a minimum of effort. As noted by Stronge,[8] "compliance with International Accounting Standards means little because of the range of permitted alternative treatments." Second, the passage of time has perhaps permitted other countries with initially nonconforming standards or practices to adopt new approaches that are in line with IAS's.

To test this suggestion, cluster analysis of the country responses by standard was performed. Clustering techniques essentially sort observations (raw data) into groups (or clusters) based on the degree of similarity that an observation bears to existing members of a cluster. The results suggest that the IASC has issued three types of standards: (1) standards issued early in the IASC's life and with which conformity was easily achieved; (2) standards issued more recently, perhaps requiring additional procedures for some countries to achieve conformity; and (3) some standards which have not been adopted by the majority of the IASC's member countries. The first group contains 12 standards (IAS 1–5, IAS 7–8, IAS 10–11, IAS 13, IAS 16, and IAS 18), which have been in effect for an average of 11.0 years and have achieved an average conformity of 92 percent. The second group contains 10 standards (IAS 9, IAS 12, IAS 17, and IAS 19–25), which have been in effect for an average of 5.7 years. Only 69 percent of the member countries have demonstrated some form of conformity with these standards. The third group contains only three standards (IAS 14–15 and IAS 26), achieving conformity in only 41 percent of the member countries. IAS 14 (segment disclosure) and IAS 15 (price-level changes), which became effective in 1983, are apparently unwelcomed by the international accounting community. IAS 26 (retirement benefits) came into effect in 1988, the year in which the data was collected.

Conformity by Country

Conformity Index B was calculated for each of the 54 countries responding to the IASC survey. The score represents the percentage of the 25 IAS's with which each country complied (i.e. the country response to the questionnaire

---

[8] Chris Stronge, "Financial Reporting: Disturbing Lack of a Common Language." *Accountant* (July 1988): 22–23.

TABLE 2 Development of Accounting Standards

Practice not yet standardized		Dependent on IASC		Independent of IASC	
Country	%	Country	%	Country	%
Abu Dhabi	96	Botswana	100	Belgium	84
Bahrain	100	Cyprus	100	Brazil	92
Dubai	100	Fiji	44	Canada	84
Greece	80	Jamaica	76	Finland	100
Kuwait	88	Malawi	88	France	76
Lesotho	72	Malaysia	72	Germany	96
Malta	100	Oman	96	Ireland	84
Saudi Arabia	96	Pakistan	92	Japan	88
Switzerland	96	Singapore	96	Mexico	76
Trinidad and		Sri Lanka	44	Netherlands	88
Tobago	100	Zimbabwe	92	Spain	84
				Sweden	88
				United Kingdom	84
				United States	100
Ghana	64			Australia	64
Hong Kong	52			Austria	68
India	44			Denmark	60
Kenya	52			Iceland	60
Morocco	56			Indonesia	72
Nigeria	52			Italy	64
South Africa	36			New Zealand	64
Taiwan	60			Norway	60
				Swaziland	52
				Tanzania	60
				Yugoslavia	68
Total 18	Av. 74.7	Total 11	Av. 81.8	Total 25	Av. 76.6

Note: The figures indicate the percentage of the 25 standards which were developed in that mode for each country. Only the predominant mode is reported.

was one of columns 1–4). While the mean conformity score was 76.3 percent, there was substantial inter-country variation. Fifteen countries have scores of 90 percent or more and five have scores lower than 50 percent, meaning that they comply with fewer than half of the existing IAS's.

There are, of course, many reasons why a country has or has not adopted an accounting treatment which conforms with IAS's. One contributing factor is the strength of the national accounting institutions, which affects the way in which standards are developed (see Table 2). Countries with weak or newly established accounting professions may lack a formalized system for developing, issuing and enforcing accounting and reporting standards. These countries were identified from IASC questionnaire categories 4 and 6, conforming and nonconforming national *practices*. For example, Trinidad and Tobago and Bahrain have no national requirements at all in the areas covered by the 25 IAS's in the survey. Other countries, such as India and Hong Kong, have national practices, but no standards, in 11 and 13 areas, respectively. Altogether, a total of 18 countries have not codified or otherwise standardized the majority of their accounting treatments (abbreviated as "unstandardized," see Table 2 column 1). On average, this group has issued standards corresponding to 5.5 of the 25 IAS's.

The other 36 countries have a formalized system for promulgating and enforcing the majority of their accounting treatments, either via national laws, via the accounting profession, or a combination of both. This group may be further subdivided into two groups, one of which includes 11 countries which rely upon the IASC for the development of standards (abbreviated as "dependent," see Table 2 column 2) and a group of 25 countries which have a strong tradition of accounting or powerful accounting institutions and typically issue standards independently of the IASC (abbreviated as "independent," see Table 2 column 3).

In developing countries, the tendency is for local accounting institutions to adopt or adapt IAS's for their own standards (IASC questionnaire categories 1 and 2, respectively). Illustrative of the dependent category are Botswana and Cyprus (both 100 percent), which have adopted the IAS's as their own. Other countries, such as Jamaica and Singapore, use the IAS's as a basis for developing their own standards. It is interesting to note that all of the countries in column 2 of Table 2 are (or have been) members of the British Commonwealth. On average, these countries have adopted or followed 20.5 of the 25 IAS's.

The independent category comprises countries which have national accounting requirements that were not developed from IAS's (i.e., IASC questionnaire categories 3 and 5). On average, these 25 countries developed requirements corresponding to the IAS's for 18.6 standards out of 25. The leading examples in this category are the United States (100 percent) and Germany (96 percent) (see Table 2, column 3). The authority underlying national accounting treatments in these countries typically predated the creation of IASC. For example, in the U.S.A., the Securities Acts of 1933 and 1934, the Committee on Accounting Procedure and the Accounting Principles Board paved the way for the Financial Accounting Standards Board (FASB), which came into being in 1973. In Germany, the Commercial Code is the major source of accounting regulation. Both countries have created national guidelines or issued standards on topics well before the IASC pronounced on these issues.

In order to test the similarity of the three country groupings (IASC-dependent, independent, and unstandardized with respect to accounting treatments), the 54 country responses (level and type of conformity with the 25 existing IAS's) were further analyzed by group. The intergroup correlations suggest that they are capturing significantly different behavior. The conformity indices of those countries which may be classified as independent of the IASC show a strong negative correlation (rho = $-.597$, p $\leq$ .001) when compared to the conformity indices of the dependent group. The indices of the unstandardized group show similar negative correlations when compared to the independent group (rho = $-.409$, p $\leq$ .002) and with the dependent group (rho = $-.488$, p $<$ .001). Each group is distinctly different from the others, as is shown by the negative correlations, all highly significant, statistically. In particular, the strong negative Spearman correlation (rho = −.597) between the dependent and independent groups evidences the wide gulf that the IASC must bridge if the Comparability Project is to be realized.

The development of accounting standards in each country (Table 2) is associated with the level of conformity with existing IASC standards (Table 1). The mean Conformity Index for the "dependent" category is 89.1 percent, with a standard deviation of 12.7 percent. By way of contrast, the mean Conformity Index for the "independent" group is substantially lower, 74.2 percent, and has a larger standard deviation, 20.3 percent, and the mean for the "unstandardized" group is 71.3 percent, with a standard deviation of 19.5 percent. The dependency scores from Table 2 were correlated with the Conformity Index B scores from Table 1 for each country, using Spearman's rho. The IASC-dependent group scores were positively associated with the Conformity Index score (rho = .382), at a high level of statistical significance (p = .001). In other words, the statistical analysis suggests that the greater the degree of dependence on the IASC, the greater the country's score on the Conformity Index. Also, as expected, the "unstandardized" group scores were negatively associated with the Conformity Index (rho = −.227) but at a marginal level of statistical significance (p = .107).

The weak and negative correlation (rho = −.170) of the "independent" group with Conformity Index B reflects the bipolar distribution of countries on this dimension. Several countries with well-established accounting professions have issued standards or passed laws at variance with existing IAS's, while others with their own standard-setting function have produced standards that are largely comparable with IAS's. Typical of the latter are Canada, France, the United Kingdom and the United States, with Conformity Index scores ranging from 84 percent to 96 percent. Remarkably, the former includes some of the founding members of the IASC, with comparatively low scores on Conformity Index B, notably Germany (28 percent) and Mexico (48 percent).

An examination of the individual country responses to the IASC survey shows that, as a group, the IASC founders demonstrate an average compliance that is fractionally worse than non-founders (75.7 percent and 76.4 percent respectively). The IASC survey respondents included 10 of the EC's 12 members. (Luxembourg and Portugal were omitted.) These countries, all in the "independent" category (except for Greece, which was "unstandardized"), obtained a mean score of 71.6 percent on Index B, which is consistent with Doupnik and Taylor's[9] observation of lower levels of conformity with IAS's within the EC. These findings pinpoint a major obstacle to the IASC's comparability quest. The cooperation of the major "independent" standard-setting groups must be obtained in order to progress.

---

[9] T. S. Doupnik and M. E. Taylor, "An Empirical Investigation of the Observance of IASC Standards in Western Europe." *Management International Review*, Vol. 25, No. 1 (1985): 27–33.

Country Patterns of Conformity

Choi[10] observed a correlation between financial disclosure and the development and efficiency of capital markets. More recently, Pratt and Behr[11] suggested that, in the case of the United States and Switzerland, differences in the standard-setting process and the types of standards promulgated may be explained in terms of differences in the "size, complexity, and diversity of capital transactions, the wide distribution of ownership and the opportunistic nature of the market participants." These contentions were examined in the context of the IASC survey data.

The country responses were subjected to two cluster analysis procedures available on SAS to ascertain whether discernible patterns of conformity existed. These two clustering techniques differ in two important ways: (1) the method used to structure initial clusters, and (2) the method of calculating similarity. When the SAS[12] CLUSTER procedure was used with the average link metric of similarity, the 54 countries were allocated to five clusters. The results are shown in Table 3. The first cluster includes all the countries that have not yet standardized their accounting practice, which may explain the low average Index B score of 66.4 percent for this cluster. Cluster 3 comprises countries which are highly dependent on the IASC and, in general, have high scores on Conformity Index B, with an average of 89.1 percent. Cluster 2 contains the countries which set standards independently of the IASC, and which have a lower level of conformity, 72.9 percent, largely attributable to the nonconforming standards of Finland, Germany, and Mexico. Countries which had medium scores on the Unstandardized Index (ranging from 36 percent to 64 percent) were in cluster 4, and those with similar scores on the Independence Index (ranging from 52 percent to 72 percent) were grouped in cluster 5. As the results of the second cluster procedure were very similar,[13]

[10] Frederick D. S. Choi, "Financial Disclosures and Entry to the European Capital Market." *Journal of Accounting Research*, Vol. 11, No. 2 (Autumn 1973): 159–175.

[11] Jamie Pratt and Giorgio Behr, "Environmental Factors, Transaction Costs, and External Reporting: A Cross-National Comparison," *International Journal of Accounting Education and Research*, Vol. 22, No. 2 (Spring 1987): 1–24.

[12] SAS Institute. "SAS Users' Guide," Version 6 (Cary, NC: SAS Institute Inc., 1989).

[13] Because cluster analysis can yield unstable results, the data was subjected to a very different cluster procedure, VARCLUS, also available on SAS. Varclus, which utilizes an oblique principal component methodology, generated four clusters. Three clusters formed under this procedure were identical to the first three clusters shown in Table 3, with the sole exception of Yugoslavia, which was placed in Cluster 2. The fourth cluster combined Clusters 4 and 5 (again with the exception of Yugoslavia). The cluster summary for this procedure is shown below:

Oblique Principal Component Cluster Analysis

Cluster	Members	Cluster Variation	Variation Explained	Proportion Explained	Second Eigenvalue
1	10	10.00	9.49	0.940	0.415
2	15	15.00	14.06	0.937	0.798
3	11	11.00	10.30	0.936	0.579
4	18	18.00	16.88	0.937	0.649

Total variation explained = 50.72   Proportion = 0.939

TABLE 3 Cluster Analysis of Responses to Standards

Cluster 1: Unstandardized	B	U	r²	Cluster 4: Unstandardized	B	U	r²
Abu Dhabi	80	96	.99	Ghana	84	64	.92
Bahrain	80	100	.99	Hong Kong	80	52	.98
Dubai	68	100	.99	India	56	44	.94
Greece	24	80	.78	Kenya	52	52	.84
Kuwait	72	88	.98	Morocco	96	56	.96
Lesotho	68	72	.91	Nigeria	100	52	.85
Malta	68	100	.99	South Africa	76	36	.82
Saudi Arabia	68	96	.99	Taiwan	76	60	.95
Switzerland	36	96	.91				
Trinidad and Tobago	100	100	.95				
Mean	66.4	92.8	.95	Mean	77.5	52.0	.91

Cluster 2: Independent	B	I	r²	Cluster 5: Independent	B	I	r²
Belgium	76	84	.99	Australia	92	64	.97
Brazil	76	92	.99	Austria	80	68	.95
Canada	96	84	.96	Denmark	80	60	.99
Finland	12	100	.61	Iceland	76	60	.98
France	84	76	.96	Indonesia	100	72	.93
Germany	28	96	.78	Italy	68	64	.94
Ireland	88	84	.98	New Zealand	80	64	.97
Japan	68	88	.99	Norway	72	60	.98
Mexico	48	76	.95	Swaziland	72	52	.99
Netherlands	84	88	.96	Tanzania	60	60	.93
Spain	96	84	.96	Yugoslavia	56	68	.93
Sweden	84	88	.99				
United Kingdom	88	84	.98				
United States	92	100	.98				
Mean	72.9	87.4	.94	Mean	76.0	62.9	.95

Cluster 3: IASC-Dependent	B	D	r²
Botswana	100	100	.96
Cyprus	100	100	.96
Fiji	60	44	.77
Jamaica	88	76	.97
Malawi	88	88	.98
Malaysia	100	72	.97
Oman	96	96	.97
Pakistan	92	92	.98
Singapore	96	96	.95
Sri Lanka	68	44	.80
Zimbabwe	92	92	.98
Mean	89.1	81.8	.94

Notes:

1. The B column denotes the country's percentage compliance with IAS's, as captured by Conformity Index B.
2. The columns headed I (Independent), D (Dependent) and U (Unstandardized) indicate each country's dominant mode of developing standards (see Table 2).
3. The r² column measures each country's degree of association with its own cluster.

there is evidence that these clusters represent different groupings on a meaningful dimension.

The clusters confirm the deep difference in country attitudes to the IASC, the IAS's and standard-setting that was highlighted by Table 2. The importance of the country differences in standard-setting is compounded by the presence of major stock exchanges (refer to Table 5). The latter are usually supervised by regulatory bodies that are independent of the accounting profession, and which may stipulate accounting treatments and specify disclosures as a condition of listing. Cluster 3 (IASC-dependent) and cluster 1 (unstandardized) each contain only one major stock exchange country (Singapore and Switzerland respectively). Eight of the world's major stock markets are located in countries appearing in cluster 2, which exhibits high IASC-independence. Three major markets operate in countries in cluster 5, which represents medium to high levels of IASC-independence. (The remaining exchange is in Luxembourg, which was not included in the IASC survey.) These findings are consistent with Choi (1973) and Pratt and Behr (1987), who noted the association between accounting disclosure and the development of capital markets.

If the IASC is to make real progress with its comparability initiative, the preceding analysis of conformity with IAS's suggests that the IASC must win the support not only of the standard-setters but also of the regulators in the countries hosting the world's major stock exchanges. At the very minimum, ED32 requires the active endorsement of the United States, Japan, and the United Kingdom, which are the three largest markets and together have 50.8 percent of the total listings on major exchanges.

COUNTRY CONFORMITY WITH ED32

The existing accounting requirements of five major countries were reviewed for conformity with ED32. Canada, France, Japan, the United Kingdom, and the United States were chosen for three reasons: (1) they were founder members of the IASC; (2) they are economically significant; and (3) they each host major stock exchanges, which together accounted for 91.1 percent of the annual turnover on major exchanges in 1986. Table 4 indicates the potential areas of conflict if ED32 in its present form were to be issued as a standard.

Revised IAS 11 eliminates the completed contract method of accounting for construction contracts, whereas the five countries currently permit this treatment. Likely to be of greater economic significance are the changes that would ensue from the adoption of revised IAS 22, which requires that positive goodwill be amortized over 5 and certainly no more than 20 years. Canada follows the American practice of a 40-year amortization period. The preferred (at the time of writing) British treatment, the immediate write-off of goodwill, would also be unacceptable.

The number of "No discussion" entries in the table is quite compelling. Some reflect an absence of a standard on a particular topic while there may be an understood practice which is not documented in country GAAP. However, a number have arisen because ED32 is breaking new ground,

TABLE 4 Current Country Compliance with Revised IAS's

Standard	Canada	France	Japan	UK	USA
IAS 2 Inventory	FIFO-Preferred LIFO-Allowed	Preferred	Possibly NIC	Preferred	FIFO-Preferred LIFO-Allowed
IAS 8 Prior Period Adjustments	Preferred	Statement disclosure may be acceptable. Footnote disclosure may not be in compliance.	Statement disclosure may be acceptable. Footnote disclosure may not be in compliance.	Preferred	Preferred
IAS 9 R & D	Preferred Capitalization-Allowed	Preferred Capitalization-Allowed	Preferred Capitalization-Allowed	Preferred	Preferred
IAS 11 Contracts	Percentage-Required Completion-NIC	Percentage-Required Completion-NIC	Percentage-Required Completion-NIC	Percentage-Required Completion-NIC	Percentage-Required Completion-NIC
IAS 16 p. 36 Fixed assets p. 47	Cost-Preferred Valuation-Allowed	Preferred	Preferred	Cost-Preferred Valuation-Allowed	Preferred
	ND	NIC	N/A	ND	ND
IAS 17 Leases	ND	ND	ND	Required	Required
IAS 18 Revenue recognition	ND	ND	ND	ND	ND
IAS 19 p. 45a Retirement Benefits	Accrued-Preferred Projected-Allowed	NIC	NIC	NIC	Preferred
p. 5	Required	ND	ND	NIC	Required
p. 45c	Required	NIC	NIC	NIC	Required

IAS 21 p. 28–30 Foreign Currency	Required	NIC	Required	Required	Required
p. 31	ND	ND	ND	ND	ND
p. 32c	Required Closing-NIC	Average-Required	NIC	Required	Required
p. 33	ND	Possibly NIC Losses-Preferred	ND	Required	Required
p. 34	ND Gains-NIC	ND	ND	ND	ND
IAS 22 Business combinations					
p. 36–38	Required Pooling-NIC	Purchase-Required	Required	Required Pooling-Possibly NIC	Purchase-Required
Positive goodwill p. 40–42	Asset-Required Life 40-NIC	Required	Required	NIC	Asset-Required Life 40-NIC
Negative goodwill	Preferred	NIC	ND	NIC	Required
Minority interests p. 45	ND	ND	ND	ND	ND
IAS 23 Capital. interest	Preferred Asset-Allowed	Expense-Preferred Asset-Allowed	Expense-Preferred Asset-Allowed	Expense-Preferred Asset-Allowed	Expense-Preferred
IAS 25 Long term investments					
p. 47 Individual	Preferred	ND	Preferred	Preferred	Preferred
	Preferred	ND	Preferred	Preferred	NIC
p. 45	ND	ND	ND	NIC	ND
p. 46	Possibly NIC	ND	ND	ND	NIC
p. 48,49	ND	ND	ND	ND	Required
p. 50	ND	ND	ND	ND	ND

NIC = Not in compliance　N/A = Not applicable　ND = Not discussed in standards particularly in the areas of foreign currency and long-term investments. The IASC has also undertaken a major project on financial instruments, which were therefore excluded from the Comparability Project.

Canada and the United Kingdom would continue to exhibit a high degree of conformity with revised IAS's, as each has only four areas of conflict. The United States has five, Japan six and France nine potential departures from revised IAS's. There will doubtless be opposition from countries whose accounting treatments are to be eliminated by ED32. While many countries are in compliance with either required, preferred, or allowed treatments, there are a number of instances where prevailing domestic practice would not conform. Even in those countries whose standards are in complete agreement with existing IAS's, major adjustments may have to be made by companies that had selected any of the 23 treatments now prohibited, and minor adjustments would be necessary to provide a reconciliation from any allowed alternative selected to the benchmark provided by the preferred treatment. If each country chooses to ignore IAS's in the area of non-compliance, little progress will be made in the quest for comparability. Perhaps the only practical way is for each country to "suffer" to some extent in the interest of achieving standards that are more comparable internationally.

THE IASC COMPARABILITY PROJECT: WHAT NEXT?

Significant accounting policies in individual countries are likely to be at variance with revised IAS's as prescribed by ED32. This raises the question of how national policy-setters and regulators will react to the Comparability Project. The responses from these groups will largely determine the future for comparable international standards. The spectrum of responses ranges from adoption of the revised IAS's, through lobbying to change the less attractive features of the proposed standards, to maintaining the status quo. Potential responses to the Comparability Project, from the most optimistic to the most pessimistic, include:

(A) IASC standards as amended by Exposure Draft 32 are adopted or incorporated in national standards by both national policy-setters and regulators.
(B) Regulators and/or national policy-setters *require* reconciliation to the IASC required or preferred standards in the primary financial statements.
(C) Regulators and/or national policy-setters encourage adoption of or reconciliation to the IASC's benchmark in supplementary financial statements or notes to the primary financial statements.
(D) There is no international movement toward adoption of the new IASC standards.

This section debates the potential responses from two groups of countries: (1) those that are dependent on the IASC for setting standards; and (2) those that set standards independently of the IASC. The third group, countries that have not yet fully standardized their accounting treatments, may move closer to the IASC or may follow the leading independent countries in their economic sphere influence.

IASC-dependent Countries

ED32 eliminates some 23 presently acceptable accounting policies. Immediate adoption of the revisions could have adverse economic consequences for companies required to comply with the revised standards. The stock market reaction to the new presentation (or new information) is unpredictable. However, if compliance with revised IAS's alters accounting income, there may be an impact on tax flows. The dependent group, which in the past required primary financial statements prepared in accordance with international generally accepted accounting principles (I-GAAP), may be reluctant to endorse full adoption of ED32. Instead, they may encourage, rather than require, conformity with IAS's, at least in the near-term, to permit companies to phase in the new standards. The creation of a transitional period also allows the accounting profession and the corporate CFOs time to debate the tax impact of these changes with national revenue authorities. Alternatively, these countries may require the preparation of secondary financial statements in accordance with I-GAAP. This approach is without tax consequences and may promote greater domestic comparability than presently obtains. However, companies are then burdened with the additional reporting requirements. A hybrid alternative would give companies the option of preparing either primary or secondary financial statements in accordance with revised IAS's. This may be a viable option in the short-run for countries like Singapore that have adopted IAS's in the past.

IASC-independent Countries

As noted earlier, these countries have strong accounting institutions and, as hosts to most of the world's major stock-markets, have well-developed regulatory functions. The response of the standard-setters and regulators in these countries is critical for the Comparability Project. If IASC standards, as revised, are adopted by many countries as their national standards, international comparability in practice would be greatly enhanced. This is especially true if countries with large capital markets adopt these standards. However, for IASC standards permitting a preferred and/or alternative treatment, domestic comparability may be somewhat inhibited, despite the reconciliation that is required for the allowed alternative in countries that currently permit only one accounting treatment. National standard-setters, if unwilling to relax their standards in such cases, may adopt the IASC's proposals piecemeal.

If IASC standards are widely adopted, it would be appropriate for the current composition of the IASC to change. National standard-setting groups, such as the FASB, and other groups currently recognized on a consultative basis, such as the UN, the OECD, or the EC, might be invited to become full members of the IASC. There arises an interesting question of the relationship between the IASC and the national standard-setting groups. If the IASC emerges as a forum for consultation, a cooperative relationship may develop. On the other hand, if the IASC becomes the primary originator of new financial accounting and reporting standards, the role of the national standard-setting groups may diminish. Daley and Mueller have argued that national standard-setters might find that they were "relegated" to "lobbying for the interests of their local constituencies at the international level."[14] The current behavior of European Community members lends support to this view. The resolution of this issue may hinge on the locus of enforcement powers.

In theory, existing IAS's apply to all public and private companies in the member countries. However, as there is no enforcement mechanism, current conformity varies greatly within this group (see cluster 2, Table 3). In our opinion, it is highly unlikely that this situation will improve with ED32. If these countries support ED32 at all, they may choose to restrict required conformity to a subset of firms in their jurisdiction. For example, in declining order of size of domain, IAS conformity may be required of (1) only listed domestic public companies; or (2) listed public companies whose securities are registered on foreign exchanges; or (3) foreign companies seeking a listing on a domestic exchange. The first case has obvious implications for national standards. The second and third cases create the possibility of dual standards if countries were to accept I-GAAP in lieu of domestic GAAP for foreign registrants. Alternatively, countries may require that foreign financial statements be supplemented by a reconciliation to I-GAAP.

A. IASC Standards Adopted as the National Standards

It could be argued that all listed public companies should use international standards. No company is purely domestic if individuals or institutions from other countries can purchase its shares. The needs of a German, Japanese, or Australian investor for adequate and accurate information, coupled with investor protection, when purchasing shares of a U.S. company on the New York Stock Exchange, should be given as much consideration as the needs of a domestic investor.

It is possible that IASC standards could be adopted as the national standards in those countries which have in the past partially or fully adopted IASC pronouncements. However, the likelihood that both national standard-setters and regulators would adopt or revise national standards to conform with IASC standards is remote in countries with strong national policy-setting groups. For example, consider the posture of the EC regulators. The Fourth Directive permits a variety of accounting treatments, whereas ED32 permits at most a choice of two. In the Brussels Conference, the Commission concluded:

---

[14] Lane A. Daley and Gerhard G. Mueller, "Accounting in the Arena of World Politics." *Journal of Accountancy*, Vol. 153, No. 2 (February 1982): 40–46, 48, 50.

The time is not ripe for future accounting directives . . . for the foreseeable future, there will be no reduction of options and no extension of the directives to cover subject areas not previously addressed.[15]

More than a decade ago, the International Federation of Stock Exchanges "recommended to its member exchanges situated in IASC countries to require as part of the listing requirements reference to the adherence to international standards of accounting."[16] No country has yet undertaken this step. Canada, a prominent exception in this regard, currently encourages companies to follow IAS's, and to disclose that fact in their annual report (Turner, 1983).[17] For example, GE Canada's 1988 annual report indicated in the Summary of Significant Accounting Policies: "These principles also conform in all material respects with International Accounting Standards on a historical cost basis." Some 100 Canadian companies, barely 9 percent of the listed companies, make such disclosures.[18] Even fewer companies in other countries disclose conformity with IAS's. A rare exception is the French company Lafarge Coppée (see its English language annual report for 1988).

B. Regulators Require Use of or Reconciliation to IASC Standards (in effect dual standards are promulgated)

Here, the regulators would require compliance with IASC standards only by foreign filers. For example, the SEC may require Mexican or Thai companies to use IASC standards if they wish to list on U.S. exchanges.

If a country does restrict the range of companies required to conform with IAS's, two tiers of financial reporting are erected. Dual standards on a single exchange pose the question of preferential treatment for international filers vis-à-vis domestic filers. (Foreign international filers on the London Stock Exchange have been permitted to file statements prepared in accordance with I-GAAP for some years.) This problem is particularly salient in countries where domestic standards may be considered more complete or more rigorous than comparable IASC standards. The dual standards issue also creates a problem for international filers in the preparation of their domestic statements. This happens to a certain extent today, and some believe that it clouds rather than clears the comparability issue, and raises questions about the "fair presentation" of any given set of financial statements.

From a preparer's point of view, this approach might result in extra costs to prepare and disseminate dual sets of financial statements, designed for the

---

[15] Federation des Experts Comptables Europeens (FEE). "The Future of Harmonisation of Accounting Standards within the European Communities." Memorandum on Commission Conference 17/18 January, 1990, dated January 19, 1990.

[16] Seymour M. Bohrer, "Harmonization of Accounting," pp. 198–205 in *Accounting for Multinational Enterprises*. Edited by Dhia D. AlHashim and James W. Robertson (Indianapolis: Bobbs-Merrill Inc., 1978).

[17] John N. Turner, "International Harmonization: A Professional Goal." *Journal of Accountancy*, Vol. 155, No. 1 (January 1983): 58–64, 66.

[18] John Kirkpatrick, "The Case for Visible Conformity." *Accountancy*, Vol. 99, No. 1121 (January 1987): 17–18.

domestic and international marketplaces. Whether this cost is great enough to offset the benefits of being able to file on various exchanges that recognize IAS's is an empirical question. At the OECD forum in 1985, representatives of Shell International and Du Pont spoke in favor of international harmonization. In their view, it "would save costs, help understanding of accounting numbers of overseas subsidiaries, open up capital markets, etc."[19] There is little concrete evidence for these beliefs. However, Eiteman and Stonehill suggest that the "recent trend for European and Japanese firms to request bond ratings by Moody's and Standard and Poor's (supports) the idea that executives may believe further disclosure may reduce the cost of debt."[20] However, it is expected that using one set of financial statements to access several exchanges at the very least would provide considerable cost savings.

This scenario raises problems of attestation. Are the revised IASC standards set forth in such a complete and detailed manner that two different preparers would arrive at the same treatment? If not, it may be difficult for auditors to issue an opinion that states the financial statements "fairly present" or present "a true and fair view."[21] Further, would the regulators accept unaudited I-GAAP financial statements? Would domestic auditors extend the domestic opinion to the international financial statements, or would a separate opinion be required?

C. Regulators Encourage the Use of or Reconciliation to IASC Standards

Countries which are in the independent group and display low levels of conformity with current IAS's, such as Germany and Mexico, are likely to do nothing, or, at the most, encourage some form of reconciliation. Members of the unstandardized group may do likewise. Optimistically, some of these may encourage the preparation of secondary financial statements, as may high conformity members of the independent group. A lower cost, and less useful alternative, would be the preparation of a statement reconciling the reported income number to the one which would have resulted if revised IAS's had been applied.

A reconciliation requirement for all filers would place a burden on preparers in countries with significant differences between domestic and I-GAAP. For example, Table 2 shows that eight of the 54 countries in the IASC survey currently do not comply with IAS 3 (consolidations), 27 are not in compliance with IAS 15 (inflation accounting), and 18 countries do not comply with IAS 26 (post-retirement benefits). Clearly, the costs of preparing a

---

[19] Rolf Rundfelt, "Views From Abroad: Europe." *Journal of Accounting, Auditing & Finance*, Vol. 9, No. 1 (Fall 1985): 85–88.

[20] David K. Eiteman and Arthur I. Stonehill, *Multinational Business Finance* (5th ed.). (Reading, Mass: Addison-Wesley, 1989).

[21] The recent issue of Statement on Auditing Standards No. 51, "Reporting on Financial Statements Prepared for Use in Other Countries," by the (US) Auditing Standards Board has heightened the U.S. auditing profession's awareness of the difficulties.

reconciliation in these countries would be significant. The legal ramifications of reporting under two standards must also be resolved. A reconciliation requirement, whether imposed on domestic or on international filers, also raises the attestation issues discussed earlier. Thus, standard-setting groups might be pressured by preparers and international audit firms to adopt at least some IASC standards in order to reduce financial statement preparation time and expense. Alternatively, the IASC might face continual pressure to permit more options, which would defeat the purpose of the Comparability Project.

The (British) Accounting Standards Committee, chaired by Mr. Renshall, has already opposed ED32's reconciliation requirement on two grounds. There was concern that the IASC would seek:

> to override the requirements of national securities exchanges. There was a danger that there would be two reconciliation statements, one from the relevant securities exchange and one from the IASC and that would not be particularly useful (quoted by Spink).[22]

Doubtless, there will be support for the ASC's position from other policy-makers. The disclosure of two sets of income and shareholders' equity amounts might prove confusing to users of the financial statements, thrusting the issue of dual standards into prominence. Whether the benefits of this reconciliation process outweigh the problems related to dual standards is an unsettled issue. However, even with the extra preparation time required for a reconciliation, international filers would most certainly benefit if IOSCO members accept a single reconciliation to I-GAAP income for access to their exchanges.

THE COMPARABILITY PROJECT: PREREQUISITES FOR SUCCESS

It would seem that there are three major obstacles which must be overcome in order for the Comparability Project to be successful. First, the member countries must be willing to cooperate with the IASC, rather than fight to promote their national interests. Second, regional efforts at harmonization must be restrained or otherwise subordinated to the IASC's endeavors. Third, the IASC must vigorously pursue its aims, and must be sufficiently funded to enable it to achieve them. These points are developed further below.

The level of cooperation among IASC members appears to be the most critical concern. If, for example, each IASC member vehemently opposes the parts of the ED32 having the greatest effect on its national standards, the IASC may be unable to go forward with the project. Alternatively, the project may be so diluted as a result of lobbying that it garners little support from

---

[22] Hazel Spink, "ASC Refuses to Yield on World Standards." (Newspaper, 1989).

bodies such as IOSCO. Such a scenario would weaken the position of the IASC and reduce its influence over the development of international standards. Some fear that the "do nothing" alternative might lead to the de facto international adoption of American standards.[19,23] Simmonds considered that:

> there are only two credible pretenders to the crown of international standards setter—US GAAP and the IASC. The case in support of US GAAP is that it is already in a commanding lead over other national alternatives. . . . its standards show the natural signs of domestic influence—including unavoidable fiscal implications that are not applicable elsewhere. . . . I question whether US standards could adequately reflect the needs of groups operating in a non-US international environment.[24]

Following Simmonds' reasoning, there may be a corps of countries that prefer the IASC to the alternative.

There are two different, but perhaps overlapping, approaches to harmonization, the first focusing on accounting practices and the second on disclosure.[25] The IASC Comparability Project has addressed measurement issues, and has not broadened the disclosure requirements. The SEC Policy Statement[26] suggests that the ultimate goal should be the development of an integrated international disclosure system and would like to see more detail in IASC standards and greater coverage of topics. IOSCO has hinted that international accounting standards might eventually be used in prospectuses of MNE offerings, provided several problems can be overcome: the elimination of most accounting choices, and increased detailed guidance contained in each statement and increased breadth of coverage of the standards as a whole. The SEC has made similar statements. FASB's current chairman indicated in a presentation to the IASC that:

> FASB would support an objective that seeks to create superior international standards that would gradually supplant national standards as the superior standards become universally accepted.[27]

As to the question of restraining regional efforts at harmonization, Choi argued that "harmonization efforts within clusters may be a more fruitful and feasible development strategy than attempts to harmonize accounting stan-

---

[23] Paul Rutteman, "Demands of a Different Environment." *Accountancy,* (October 1987): 17–18.

[24] Andy Simmonds, "Bridging the European Gap." *Accountancy,* (August 1989): 29.

[25] Philip M. Reckers and D. J. Stagliano, "International Accounting Standards: Progress and Prospects." *Survey of Business,* Vol. 16, No. 4 (Spring 1981): 28–31.

[26] Securities and Exchange Commission (SEC). "Regulation of International Securities Markets." Policy Statement (November 1988).

[27] Dennis R. Beresford, "Internationalization of Accounting Standards: The Role of the Financial Accounting Standards Board." *Financial Accounting Standards Board Status Report,* Series 065, No. 195 (June 1988): 3–6.

dards on a worldwide basis.[28] Others have warned that the present efforts[29] of the EC to harmonize accounting standards within that community "pose a serious obstacle to development of worldwide standards."[30] Similar observations have been made by McComb[31] and Choi and Mueller.[32] Damant commented, "it is bad enough having so many different national standards. The last thing which is needed is a complication of international harmonization by the establishment of regional standards."[33]

Despite the comments expressed earlier, members of the EC Commission in Brussels, such as Van Hulle,[34] see their efforts as consistent with international harmonization. Clearly, the IASC and the EC must work together to develop international standards. The current president of the Federation of European Accountants (FEE) also espoused this view.[35] Mr. Carey of the Accounting Standards Committee (ASC) said, "the UK profession's view is very clear. We believe harmonization should be through international standards and the IASC."[36] These views apparently prevailed, for the Commission Conference on accounting standards, held in Brussels in January 1990, recognized the IASC as "the appropriate forum for worldwide work in this field, and it was decided that the community would strengthen its input to IASC."[15]

Sir Henry Benson, a former IASC chairman, noted the key prerequisites of harmonization: focused leadership; reconciliation to a single set of international standards; compliance with international standards to be a requirement for stock exchange listing; national standard-setters to be on the IASC standard-setting board; greater industry involvement in standard-setting; and national accounting bodies to use disciplinary action to enforce IAS's.[37] Dur-

[28] Frederick D. S. Choi, "A Cluster Approach to Accounting Harmonization." *Management Accounting*, Vol. LXIII, No. 2 (August 1981): 17–31.

[29] For a more detailed discussion of the progress of harmonization within the European Community, see the following articles by Van Hulle:
Karel Van Hulle, (a). "The EC Experience of Harmonisation - Part I." *Accountancy*, (September 1989): 76–77. (b). "The EC Experience of Harmonisation - Part II." *Accountancy*, (October 1989): 96–99.

[30] Richard D. Fitzgerald, "International Harmonization of Accounting and Reporting." *International Journal of Accounting Education and Research*, Vol. 17, No. 1 (Fall 1981): 21–32.

[31] Desmond McComb," International Accounting Standards and the EEC Harmonization Program: A Conflict of Disparate Objectives." *International Journal of Accounting Education and Research*, Vol. 17, No. 2 (Spring 1982): 35–48.

[32] Frederick D. S. Choi and Gerhard G. Mueller, *International Accounting*. (2nd ed.) (Englewood Cliffs: Prentice-Hall Inc., 1984).

[33] David Damant, "Accounting Standards: Europe and the World." *European Accounting Focus*, (May 1989): 14–15.

[34] Karel Van Hulle, "Harmonisation of Accounting Standards Throughout the EC." *European Accounting Focus*, (Spring 1989); 11–13.

[35] IASC. "FEE address to the IASC, April 1989." *IASC News*, Vol. 18, No. 2 (June 1989).

[36] Carey, quoted in *Accountancy Age*, (August 31, 1989).

[37] J. C. Burton (ed.), *The International World of Accounting. Challenges and Opportunities*. (Reston, VA: Council of Arthur Young Professors, 1981).

ing the last decade, the IASC has worked diligently on Benson's program for harmonization, perhaps spurred by the fear that the accounting profession might lose control of setting international standards,[38] and is now poised to meet several of Benson's prerequisites if the major funding problems of the IASC can be overcome: funding structure and level of financial support.

Currently, the IASC's budget is funded by International Federation of Accountants (IFAC), which, in turn, collects membership fees from the member institutions. The IASC's effectiveness as a supplier of international accounting standards would doubtless be enhanced by restructuring the funding procedures to include direct contributions and increasing the membership fees. Without significant increases in the budget, there is little hope that the IASC can meet the challenge of providing detailed and completed international standards, without excessive reliance upon its previous pillars of support, the United Kingdom and the United States.

IS HARMONIZATION DESIRABLE?

Many professionals have questioned whether harmonization is feasible or even desirable.[39] They acknowledge that individual and institutional investors are not deterred by country boundaries in the selection of investment portfolios. Total transactions in US corporate securities for foreigners in 1988 totaled US$452.7 billion. Total transactions in U.S. securities (including treasury and government securities) amounted to US$3,579.3 billion, an increase of US$263.9 billion over 1987. U.S. investors purchased or sold a total of US$594.5 billion worth of foreign stocks and bonds in 1988.[40] Foreign direct investments into the United States increased by US$58.4 billion in 1988.[41] Similarly, institutions in search of capital are addressing the global marketplace. For example, funds raised in international capital markets totalled US$225 billion in 1986, but amounted to US$347 billion in 1989.[42] Many companies have already obtained listings on stock exchanges outside their own country.

Table 5 summarizes the relative size of the stock markets in 14 countries and their annual turnover and activity levels. While the United Kingdom has the most listings, the United States is the largest market in terms of size and turnover. However, the Tokyo Stock Exchange is a very strong second on both dimensions.

The table also indicates the percentage of listings that are "foreign." The

---

[38] J. A. Burggraaff, "IASC developments: an Update." *Journal of Accountancy*, Vol. 154 (September 1982): 104, 106–110.

[39] Richard Karl Goeltz, "International Accounting Harmonization: The Impossible and (Unnecessary?) Dream." *Accounting Horizons*, Vol. 5, No. 1 (March 1991): 85–88.

[40] U.S. Bureau of the Census. "Statistical Abstract of the United States, 110th Edition." (Washington, DC: 1990): Tables 840 and 841.

[41] Federal Reserve Bulletin. "Monetary Policy Report to the Congress." (August 1989): A55.

[42] Organisation for Economic Cooperation and Development (OECD). "Financial Statistics." (December 1990).

TABLE 5 Major Stock Exchanges in 1986

	Total Listings	Foreign Percentage	Market Size US$B	Av. size per listing US$M	Annual Turnover US$B	Activity %
Australia	1,193	2.6	78	65.4	27.0	34.6
Belgium	331	42.3	36	108.8	7.0	19.4
Canada	1,085	4.7	166	153.0	57.0	34.3
Denmark	281	2.5	*	NC	1.9	NC
France	1,100	20.5	150	136.4	56.0	37.3
Germany	673	26.9	246	365.5	136.0	55.3
Italy	184	0.0	141	766.3	45.0	31.9
Japan	1,551	3.4	1,746	1,125.7	954.0	54.6
Luxembourg	421	39.9	*	NC	*	NC
Netherlands	409	59.2	73	178.5	30.0	41.1
Singapore	317	61.5	33	104.1	5.0	15.2
Switzerland	339	57.2	132	389.4	*	NC
United Kingdom	2,613	19.6	440	168.4	133.0	30.2
United States	2,373 [a]	4.6	2,203	928.4	1,374.0 [b]	62.4
Total	12,870		5,444		2,825.9	
Mean	919.29	24.63	388.86	299.32	201.85	29.74
Std. dev.	759.65	22.43	662.25	345.14	403.01	19.90

Notes:
US$B = US$ billions
US$M = US$ millions
* = Not given in data source
NC = Not calculable
a = New York and American Stock Exchanges combined
b = NYSE only

Activity is defined as Turnover/Market size and may be viewed as a measure of market breadth.

Market size and turnover data is taken from Exhibits 10.8 and 10.9 in Eiteman and Stonehill, 1989.[20] Total listings are taken from, and the foreign percentages are derived from, data presented in the report of the Staff of the U.S. Securities and Exchange Commission to the Senate Committee on Banking, Housing and Urban Affairs and the House Committee on Energy and Commerce on the Internationalization of the Securities Market, July 29, 1987, p. II–66.

huge variation in the foreign percentage is readily discerned, with the smaller exchanges heavily dependent on foreign registrants. (For example, 61.5 percent of Singapore's and 59.2 percent of the Netherlands' listings are foreign.) However, the percentage of foreign listings on the world's busiest exchanges is still rather small (NYSE and AMEX combined, 4.6 percent; Tokyo, 3.4 percent). This lends support to the argument advanced by the Technical Committee of IOSCO that a "primary impediment to international offerings of securities is that different countries have different accounting standards."[43]

As the table confirms, there is a significant volume of foreign registrations. However, the countries with stringent listing requirements (for example, the U.S.A. and Japan) are capturing little of this market (4.6 percent and 3.4 percent, respectively, of their total listings are foreign). By way of con-

[43] Quoted in *IASC News*, Vol. 18, No. 1 (January 1989): 2.

trast, foreign registration in Singapore comprises 61.5 percent of the total. This table is significant evidence that companies seek to avoid rigorous accounting and disclosure requirements. (Saudagaran[44] has recently confirmed this finding.)

The economic consequences of this maneuvering are profound. First, the paternalistic notion, so dear to the regulators, of investor protection is completely undermined where investors can (and do) purchase securities in jurisdictions with relatively fewer requirements. Second, the financial services industry (from stockholders to analysts and beyond) is separated from market transactions that take place in Belgium or Luxembourg, for example, rather than at home, with significant loss of revenue to that sector. Third, it has been suggested that the costs of raising debt and equity in different markets is affected by the perceived rigor of the accounting policies and disclosure requirements. Fourth, there is anecdotal evidence from analysts, and others, suggesting that funds are misallocated (see Damant in Gernon, Purvis & Diamond[45]) because economic differences between investment vehicles in different jurisdictions are obscured by different financial accounting treatments and disclosure practices. Trade negotiators representing the United States, in response to initiatives from FEE, have recently acknowledged that the use of I-GAAP "would facilitate expansion of trade in services by removing barriers caused by different national accounting requirements." Accordingly, they "have proposed that the General Agreement on Trade and Services (GATS) agreement should recognize the importance of International Accounting Standards."[46] In view of these factors, we share IOSCO's view that increased comparability is an important objective, and that the IASC is the best vehicle to realize this goal.

CONCLUSION

Moulin,[47] among others, identified prerequisites for improved IAS: sufficient detail to guide interpretation; increased scope to cover key areas, including earnings per share, discontinued operations, and accounting for specialized industries; additional disclosure requirements; and standards developed with the needs of users in mind. It seems clear that ED32 does not meet all of these preconditions, yet that does not mean that the IASC's venture is a failure. The Comparability Project has narrowed the range of choices, a major criticism in the past, and has provided a forum for debate of comparability issues. The

[44] Shahrokh M. Saudagaran, "An Empirical Study of Selected Factors Influencing the Decision to List on Foreign Stock Exchanges." *Journal of International Business Studies*, Vol. 19, No. 1 (Spring 1988): 101–127.

[45] Helen Gernon, S.E.C. Purvis and Michael A. Diamond. "An Analysis of the Implications of the IASC's Comparability Project." *Topical Issues Study No. 3* (Los Angeles: SEC and Financial Reporting Institute, School of Accounting, University of Southern California, 1990).

[46] IASC. "Board Supports Commitment to International Accounting Standards." *IASC News*, Vol. 19, No. 4 (December 1990): 1.

[47] Donald J. Moulin, "Practical Means of Promoting Common Accounting and Auditing Standards." Paper presented at the 13th Annual Conference of IOSCO, Melbourne, 1988.

IASC offers an institutional means of addressing (and implementing) subsequent steps in the quest for comparability.

If global comparability of accounting standards is ever to be achieved, significant effort will have to be expended to alter the direction of accounting evolution, to emphasize international, rather than national, interests. It is important to recognize that, whatever scenarios evolve, progress toward international comparability of accounting standards is likely to be slow and will not proceed in the same direction nor at the same pace in the various IASC member countries. Changing domestic standards is a slow process; the economic, legal and professional differences among countries provide additional complexity in the international arena.

The pace of a planned evolution to comparable international accounting standards will be affected by several important factors: the responses of the national standard-setters and regulators to the Comparability Project and the extent to which the intent of the Steering Committee survives the exposure draft phase; the reaction of IOSCO and national regulators to the final version, and the extent of their subsequent support for the IASC's international standards; and the way in which future IASC standards are developed. It is essential that they be drafted with a breadth of coverage and sufficient detail to provide implementation guidance, thus promoting the comparability envisioned by the IASC and to allay the concerns of certain regulatory bodies. Even standards that require one treatment or have a preferred and allowed alternative with a reconciliation will not result in comparability if they do not provide adequate implementation guidance. The IASC Board has accepted this criticism. In its updated five-year plan, the Board has pledged to revise existing IAS's "to ensure that they are sufficiently detailed and complete and contain adequate disclosure requirements to meet the needs of capital markets and the international business community."[48]

To realize the intent of the Comparability Project will require a long-term sustained effort on the part of the IASC, which will need to increase its staff. Member countries must provide greater support, not merely in terms of financial contributions, but also in active promotion of IAS. As Kanaga observed, "if the IASC fails in its mission, the UN or regional governmental bodies will step in as the clamor grows to improve transnational reporting," (cited in Burton).[37] Finally, the IASC must win the commitment of standard-setters and regulators in at least three major markets—the United Kingdom, the United States and Japan—for comparability to proceed.

---

[48] IASC. "IASC's Five Year Plan - Update." *IASC News*, Vol. 19, No. 4 (December 1990): 3.

Editors' note: In July 1990, the IASC issued a Statement of Intent on Comparability of Financial Statements, in which it modified some of the proposals in ED32. Among other things, it said that it would no longer impose the reconciliation requirement in ED32 but would encourage enterprises to publish such a reconciliation as part of their financial statements. Capital market regulators and stock exchanges could also impose such a reconciliation requirement, so it continues to be an active issue.

Direct Transnational Financial Statement Analysis: Converting IAS to US GAAP

David F. Hawkins

Harvard University

Transnational financial statement analysis is the analysis of financial statements issued by corporations other than those domiciled in the analyst's home country. This *Accounting Bulletin* notes the increase in direct transnational financial analysis being performed by institutional investors and discusses one technical aspect of transnational financial analysis: namely, the conversion of foreign corporate income and cash flow data that conforms to International Accounting Standards (IAS) to its US generally accepted accounting principles (US GAAP) equivalent. Grand Metropolitan PLC's 1989 financial statements are used to illustrate this methodology.

This *Accounting Bulletin* is a follow-on piece to an earlier *Accounting Bulletin*[1] which described the various international accounting standards issued to date by the International Accounting Standards Committee (IASC). This earlier *Accounting Bulletin* also noted that the widespread adoption by foreign stock exchange listed companies of IAS-conforming accounting had led to a significant lowering of the historically high transnational financial statement analysis costs associated with direct investment in the equities of these companies. The principal reason given for the lower costs was that US investors who are knowledgeable about US GAAP can read, understand, analyze, and interpret IAS-conforming financial statements.[2]

From *Accounting Bulletin* #2 (September 1990), pp. 1–13, a publication of Merrill, Lynch Capital Markets. Reprinted by permission of Merrill Lynch, Pierce, Fenner & Smith, Inc. Copyright © 1990 by Merrill Lynch, Pierce, Fenner & Smith, Inc.

[1] See "Dealing With International Accounting Diversity: International Accounting Standards," *Accounting Bulletin #1*, May 1990. Copyright Merrill Lynch, Pierce, Fenner & Smith Incorporated.

[2] IAS-conforming accounting is most frequently used by companies listed on the following stock exchanges:

Australia	Hong Kong	New Zealand	Swaziland
Bahrain	Ireland	Norway	Sweden
Belgium	Jamaica	Pakistan	United Kingdom
Canada	Japan	Saudi Arabia	Zimbabwe
Dubai	Kuwait	Singapore	
France	Malaysia	Spain	

TWO SIGNIFICANT INDUSTRY TRENDS

The lowering of transnational financial statement analysis costs has contributed in part to two significant emerging trends among institutional equity investment and advisory firms. These are:

> First, a small but increasing number of primarily domestic equity investment-oriented firms are encouraging all or some of their portfolio managers and security analysts to perform direct transnational financial statement analyses of the foreign companies that their domestic investee firms compete against at home and abroad.

> Second, a growing interest among indirect transnational investors in shifting from indirect to direct transnational investing.

The contribution of this *Accounting Bulletin* to these trends is that the approach outlined to convert IAS income and cash flow data to its US GAAP equivalent *further lowers* the cost of transnational financial statement analysis.[3]

TRANSNATIONAL FINANCIAL ANALYSIS

Transnational financial statement analyses are financial analyses performed on the financial statement data of companies domiciled in countries other than the analyst's home country. Typically, the foreign companies use accounting principles, practices and formats that differ in varying degrees from those commonly followed by the analyst's home country firms. The typical transnational financial statement analysis requires a quality-of-earnings type appreciation of the foreign company's accounting policy choices, accounting practices, and business transactions; restatement of the foreign company's financial statements to conform to an accounting model selected by the analyst; analysis of the original and restated data taking into account the foreign company's business, tax, cultural, and regulatory environment; and, interpretation of the results of the analyses in light of the analytical purpose.

---

[3] Methodologies for analyzing financial statements that do not conform to all or most of the International Accounting Standards, such as those issued by the typical German listed company, will be covered in a subsequent *Accounting Bulletin*. In these cases, the cost of transnational financial statement analysis is considerably higher than the cost of transnational financial statement analysis of International Accounting Standards-conforming financial statements. Typically, these higher transnational financial statement analysis costs are incurred when examining the financial statements of companies listed on the following foreign stock exchanges:

Austria	Finland	Italy	South Africa
Brazil	Germany	Mexico	Switzerland
Denmark	Greece	Morocco	Taiwan

Sometimes direct transnational financial analyses are performed in part by computers, but more often than not the whole task is carried out by individual portfolio managers and security analysts.

In the past, among institutional equity investors the practice of performing direct transnational financial statement analyses was limited almost exclusively to direct transnational investors and their advisors. Direct transnational financial analyses by primarily domestic equity investment and research firms were seldom, if ever, performed.

The growing realization that the equity values of many U.S. companies are influenced by the competitive strengths and acquisition capabilities of their foreign competitors has changed this situation. Some purely domestic-oriented investors have responded to this equity market reality. They are asking all or some of their portfolio managers and security analysts to:

- Become competent transnational financial statement analysts;
- Expand their research coverage to include foreign firms; and
- Perform on a regular basis direct financial statement analyses of these foreign firms.

The three principal motives for this change are:

First, a belief that a full appreciation of the investment value and competitive strengths and weaknesses of most US domestic and US multinational companies requires at least an understanding of the financial condition, operating results, and acquisition capabilities of the foreign firms who are their principal competitors at home and abroad.

Second, a desire to differentiate the investment or advisory firm from its competitors. Representing to clients that the firm looks at global competition before investing in domestic equities is viewed as one way to achieve this objective.

Third, a belief that eventually the firm will have to participate in some direct transnational investing as national equity markets begin to overlap, merge, and eventually shift to a global valuation basis. Adding transnational financial statement analysis to the firm's capabilities at this time helps prepare it for the inevitable shift to direct transnational investing.

The lower cost of transnational financial statement analysis has also contributed to this emerging analytical development among institutional investors. It made it economically feasible.

PUSHING COSTS EVEN LOWER

The cost of direct transnational financial analysis can be lowered *further* by investors and analysts adopting a systematic approach to converting foreign-company financial statement data to conform to the accounting form and inputs required by the investor or analyst for equity valuation purposes.

This *Accounting Bulletin* outlines one such cost-reducing approach to restating foreign income and cash flow data that conform to all or most of the IAS to their US GAAP cash flow and net income equivalent. Grand Metropolitan's 1989 financial statements are used to illustrate this approach.

RESTATEMENT METHODOLOGY

The process for restating International Accounting Standard-conforming financial statements to a US GAAP basis is done in two principal steps. The first involves an examination and classification using a standard form of the foreign firm's accounting policies. The second requires the completion of a standard worksheet to convert the foreign company's reported net income and cash flow figures to a US GAAP basis.

When preparing restatements, it is important to remember that a complete restatement to a US GAAP basis is seldom possible. The best point of view to adopt is that "close is good enough." This perspective is acceptable, since accounting reports prepared according to US GAAP are themselves only approximations of the "truth." A corollary of this point of view is "focus on the material differences." This perspective does not mean that the areas of nonreconciliation should be ignored. Their significance must be assessed. This can be accomplished, for example, as part of the quality of earnings appraisal incorporated in the price-earnings assessment.

Another important point to keep in mind when preparing US GAAP restatements is to use restatement approaches that minimize the cost of restatement without introducing material distortions. Often, more precision can be achieved by using costly restatement methods, but the added precision is seldom worth the added cost. The best approach to restatement is "keep it simple."

STEP 1: CLASSIFY ACCOUNTING POLICIES

The first restatement step is to examine the foreign company's accounting policies. Appendix A presents an illustrative accounting policy analysis of Grand Metropolitan's 1989 financial statements[4] using the recommended methodology.

The value of this recommended accounting policy analysis is that it forces the analyst to study the foreign companies' accounting policies carefully; it alerts the analyst to problem areas; it provides a permanent record to keep

---

[4] Grand Metropolitan primarily uses United Kingdom accounting standards. These standards conform to IAS. [*Editors' note:* An important UK departure from IASC standards is the immediate charge-off of purchased goodwill against owners' equity. Under IASC (and US) standards, goodwill is to be capitalized and amortized. Later in this article, Hawkins deals with this difference between UK and US (and IASC) accounting standards.]

track of accounting changes; and, it speeds up the accounting policy review and comparison in future years. All the analyst needs to do is focus on changes in accounting policy. This reduces future analytical costs significantly.

As indicated in Appendix A, the accounting policy appraisal is reduced to writing using a three-column format. The first column lists the item being accounted for. The next column shows the foreign company's accounting policy used to recognize and measure each item. The third column indicates the comparable US GAAP accounting principles.

Within the recommended 3-column accounting policy record format, as indicated in Appendix A, the various accounting policies are divided into six categories. Assigning accounting policies to these categories focuses attention on the significant areas for restatement; provides a permanent record of the analyst's rationale for restating some items and not others; and reduces the cost of future accounting policy reviews. The six categories and their significance for restatement are:

Similar to US GAAP.   These accounting policies are similar to US GAAP and produce results equivalent to US GAAP. They do not require restatement. In making this classification, "similar" should be interpreted to mean "similar in concept and thrust to US GAAP, but not necessarily in all of the details."

No Material Difference.   These are accounting policies where the effect of the difference between US GAAP and the company's accounting policy is typically immaterial in its effect on account balances. For restatement purposes, reported account balances should be regarded as being equivalent to US GAAP.

Similar Outcome.   These are non-US GAAP accounting policies whose application leads to similar financial statement results as those that would result from the use of US GAAP. In some cases, US GAAP is restricted to one method, but in practice many outcomes result from its application. Pension accounting is a good example. All US companies follow the same method but in any one situation management can apply this method to obtain a wide range of pension expenses depending on the assumptions made. If the foreign company's non-US GAAP accounting policy produces results that probably fall within the range of outcomes possible from applying US GAAP, accept the foreign accounting practice as being equivalent to US GAAP.

Balance Sheet Effect Only.   Non-US GAAP accounting policies that only have balance sheet effects belong in this category. If the analyst's focus is on income, forget these differences.

Different Circumstances.   Accounting policies belong in this category for which there is no US GAAP equivalent. Typically, this non-US GAAP accounting reflects circumstances of a foreign company that are different from those encountered by US companies. Where there are differences between a foreign company and US companies and there is no US GAAP covering the foreign company's circumstances, accept the foreign company's treatment of the particular situation as long as the accounting reflects the reality of the circumstances. If the foreign company's accounting does not reflect the particular circumstances, if possible restate the accounting results using an accounting approach of your choice that does reflect the circumstances. The stock market probably is already making a similar adjustment.

Material Differences. These are non-US GAAP accounting practices that may result in some years in material financial statement differences between the application of the company's accounting policy and its US GAAP equivalent. The restatement should focus on these accounting differences. The accounting policies in this category will usually be accounting for business acquisitions, discontinued operations, provisions for reserves, depreciation, deferred taxes and intangible assets. Fortunately, most foreign companies following IAS-type accounting disclose enough information to reconcile the differences between most of the company's accounting policies in these areas and US GAAP.

GRAND METROPOLITAN

Grand Metropolitan's accounting policies fall into all of the above accounting policy categories.[5]

Like most IAS-conforming companies, many of Grand Metropolitan's accounting policies fall into the category "Similar to US GAAP." No adjustments to reported net income and cash flow data are required for this company's US GAAP-like accounting practices.

The most important accounting policies falling into the "Similar to US GAAP" category are the company's consolidation and related company accounting policies. If a company's policies in these two areas were not similar to US GAAP, attempts to convert its income and cash flow figures to a meaningful US GAAP basis is seldom worthwhile if material off-balance sheet operations are involved. Material profits and losses may be excluded entirely from the reported numbers. Fortunately, this is not the situation in this instance.

Again, like many other IAS-conforming companies, many of Grand Metropolitan's non-US GAAP accounting policies fall into the other three accounting categories that do not lead to material differences between the company's net income and cash flow as reported and on a US GAAP basis.

[5] These accounting classifications and the subsequent restatement of Grand Metropolitan's income and cash flow data to a US GAAP basis are solely the responsibility of the author. For more comprehensive information and research views on Grand Metropolitan, see 'Grand Metropolitan PLC," May 23, 1990, prepared by Sue Leslie, copyright Merrill Lynch, Pierce, Fenner & Smith.

These three categories are: "No Material Differences," "Similar Outcome," and "Balance Sheet Effect Only." No reported net income or cash flow adjustments need be made for these non-US GAAP accounting practices.

Since no adjustments are made for the four categories of Grand Metropolitan's accounting policies discussed above, the practice of setting up four categories might be questioned. Why not, for instance, use one category labeled "Accounting Policies Not Requiring Adjustments"? The principal reason for using four categories is to highlight and keep track of the *reasons* why no accounting adjustments are necessary.

Grand Metropolitan has one non-US GAAP accounting practice that might be assigned to the "Different Circumstances" category. The company does not depreciate its public houses ("pubs") because, as stated in the notes accompanying the 1989 financial statements:

> It is the group's policy to maintain all of its public houses to a high standard
> in order to protect their trade. Because of this, such properties maintain
> disposal values in the aggregate at least equal to their book values.

In the absence of evidence to the contrary, this is a reasonable position to take, but it is not US GAAP. A strict application of US GAAP would require depreciation of these properties. But, would it make a difference? A good case can be made for a 100-year depreciation period for these properties. On this basis, the end result of applying US GAAP depreciation accounting would be an immaterial income statement adjustment. Consequently, in line with the earlier advice to concentrate on the "material items," no US GAAP adjustment is required in this case at this time.

Five of Grand Metropolitan's non-US GAAP accounting policies are classified in the "Material Differences" category. These non-US GAAP practices shown in Appendix A are examples of material differences typically encountered when converting IAS-conforming financial statements to a US GAAP basis. The differences usually involve either noncash items, such as depreciation, contingency reserves, goodwill, intangibles, and deferred taxes; or gain and loss classifications, such as operating items, unusual items, discontinued operations, extraordinary items and cumulative accounting changes. Occasionally, restatement of revenue and expense items other than non-cash items, such as fee income and capitalized development costs, is also required to convert IAS-conforming financial reports to a US GAAP basis. No material restatements of this latter kind are required in the Grand Metropolitan situation.

Once the major non-US GAAP accounting policies have been identified, the next step is to complete the worksheet making the required adjustments to US GAAP.

STEP 2: COMPLETE THE WORKSHEET

The worksheet is designed to reflect the typical transnational financial statements analyst's cash flow and profit information objectives. The worksheet

TABLE 1 Basic Restatement Worksheet Calculation Flow Chart

Reported Results	Est. US GAAP Equivalent
Reported Net Income	Est. US GAAP Net Income
↓	↑
Reported Operating Profit After Taxes	Est. US GAAP Operating Profit After Taxes
↓	↑
Reported Operating Profit Before Taxes	Est. US GAAP Operating Profit Before Taxes
↓	↑
Reported Operating Profit Before Interest, Taxes, Depreciation and Amortization →	Est. US GAAP Operating Profit Before Interest, Taxes, Depreciation and Amortization

consists of two major sections, each of which is broken down in turn into comparable profit and cash flow subsections. Table 1 presents the worksheet's basic flow chart.

The worksheet's first major section shows the company's profits and cash flows based on its reported results. These data are important. They give the analyst a view of the company as its home country investors may see it for valuation purposes. Sometimes this is a more relevant perspective for valuation purposes than the US GAAP perspective. These data also provide a benchmark for measuring the extent of the profit and cash flow differences resulting from using non-US GAAP rather than US GAAP accounting.

The second major section of the worksheet presents the US GAAP equivalent of the profit and cash flow items shown in the first major section.

Both major subsections are broken down into comparable subsections, each of which presents the typical principal profit and cash flow information objectives of financial statement analysts.

The restatement objective of most equity investors' attempts to convert IAS-conforming financial statement data to a US GAAP basis is to determine the US GAAP equivalent of the foreign company's:

- Profits related to continuing operations. These data are important since equity values reflect in large measure a company's expected continuing stream of profits. Operating profits best measure this expectation.
- Cash flow related to continuing operations. Cash flow data is regarded by many as the best measure of corporate performance to use when comparing companies across national boundaries. It is a legitimate valuation basis and easier to compute than earnings on a comparable accounting basis. Cash flow data are used by transnational investors who rely heavily on computer-driven investment approaches.
- Net income. This all-inclusive figure when viewed over time captures the company's overall profit trends and performance.

Allocating any difference between operating profits and net income on a US GAAP basis between discontinued operations, extraordinary items, and cumulative accounting changes is seldom a restatement objective or practice of equity investors. Since equity values reflect a company's future continuing stream of earnings and this is best reflected by operating profits, the added information value of calculating the US GAAP equivalent of a foreign company's gains and losses from discontinued operations, extraordinary items, and cumulative accounting changes is very low. Simply knowing the net difference between operating profits and net income on a US GAAP basis is sufficient in most cases.

As indicated on Table 1, the basic worksheet format reflects these analytical information objectives and practices as it moves from the company's reported net income to its EBITDA cash flow based on reported data; then, to the company's EBITDA cash flow's GAAP equivalent; next, to the company's operating profit on a US GAAP basis; and, ends with the company's net income on a US GAAP equivalent. This basic worksheet format can be expanded to fit additional profit and cash flow information objectives. For example, the calculation of after-tax cash flow, such as net income plus depreciation, could be shown as a separate step in the flow. Also, a line showing operating data excluding unusual items might also be added.

GRAND METROPOLITAN

A completed basic worksheet showing Grand Metropolitan's 1989 net income, operating profit, and cash flows restated to a US GAAP basis is presented in Appendix B. The restated items listed on this worksheet are those included in the "Material Differences" category in Appendix A.

The reported profit and cash flow presented on the upper half of the worksheet are based on the company's accounting policies. These are the data that are converted to a US GAAP equivalent in the lower half of the worksheet.

The conversion of the company data to US GAAP begins with the restatement of the company's reported operating profit before interest, taxes, depreciation and amortization cash flow figure. To convert this figure to a US GAAP basis, the profits of discontinued operations must be subtracted. Grand Metropolitan, like many IAS-conforming companies, includes the profits of discontinued operations in operating income up to the time that compensation is received from the sale of the discontinued business or it is otherwise disposed of. Under US GAAP these profits are excluded from operating profits, primarily because to include them distorts the current measurement of the company's continuing stream of business profits. This accounting view of operating profit is also congruent with that of most investors.

The amount of discontinued profit included in Grand Metropolitan's operating income is disclosed in the notes to the financial statements. It consists of two items—operating profits of discontinued businesses and a gain on the sale of the property of discontinued businesses. The sum of these two items is the US GAAP adjustment.

The next step in the worksheet is to convert the US GAAP operating cash flow figure computed above to the US GAAP equivalent of Grand Metropolitan's operating profit before taxes. This is accomplished by adding back the company's reported interest and computing on a US GAAP basis its 1989 goodwill and depreciation expenses.

Grand Metropolitan charges all of the goodwill created through purchase transactions to owners' equity at the time of acquisition. This is not US GAAP, which requires goodwill to be amortized to income over a period not to exceed 40 years.

The goodwill GAAP adjustment to Grand Metropolitan's pretax operating profit shown in Appendix B is based on goodwill data disclosed in the notes accompanying the company's financial statements. These notes disclose the balance of the aggregate goodwill, net of disposals, written off against owners' equity at the beginning and end of the year. The US GAAP adjustment to goodwill is the sum of the beginning balance divided by 40 years plus half the 1989 addition divided by 40 years.[6]

Significant owned brands acquired by Grand Metropolitan after January 1, 1985, the value of which is not expected to diminish in the foreseeable future, are recorded on the balance sheet as fixed intangible assets at appraisal values determined subsequent to acquisition and independently of the business combination accounting. The costs of these brands is not charged to income. In contrast, US GAAP does not permit brand valuation. Since no expense related to intangible asset is charged to income, no adjustment is required.

Grand Metropolitan's depreciation expense is based partially on appraisal values and original cost. This combination of depreciation bases is typical of many foreign companies. The portion based on original cost conforms to US GAAP accounting for depreciation. The depreciation expense based on appraised value does not. It must be adjusted to conform to US GAAP. The first step in the adjustment process is to identify the portion of the depreciation expense based on original cost. Grand Metropolitan discloses this figure. The next step is to compute the historical cost equivalent of that portion of the total depreciation expense based on appraised values. Fortunately, Grand Metropolitan discloses the historical cost and accumulated depreciation related to the land and buildings carried at appraised values. The annual change in this historical cost accumulated depreciation account is used as a proxy for the appraised assets' depreciation on a US GAAP basis.

The next step in the worksheet procedure is the conversion of Grand Metropolitan's US GAAP-equivalent operating profit before taxes to an after-

---

[6] Grand Metropolitan discloses sufficient goodwill data to prepare a more refined estimate of the US GAAP goodwill expense. Since the more refined calculation does not produce materially different results, the lower cost calculation is used. Remember, "Keep it simple."

tax basis. This is always a difficult step to complete with confidence, since it involves a complex accounting item, a multiplicity of tax rates, and requires estimating the deferred and current tax effects of the US GAAP adjustments made to the company's reported pretax income. In the case of Grand Metropolitan, these are:

- Reduction in book depreciation from an appraised value basis to an historical cost basis;
- Addition of goodwill amortization expense; and
- Elimination of discontinued operations-related profits and gains from operating income.

In addition, Grand Metropolitan's deferred taxes determined by the non-US GAAP partial allocation method must be adjusted to a US GAAP comprehensive tax allocation basis.

The recommended procedure is to adjust first the company's reported deferred tax expense using the partial allocation approach to a comprehensive tax allocation basis. Next, recompute the company's book tax rate using the adjusted deferred tax expense. Then, apply this rate to the US GAAP pretax operating profit figure. This procedure is not particularly accurate, but it is about the best you can do under the circumstances.

A clue to the possible extent of the adjustment required to convert Grand Metropolitan's deferred taxes from a partial to a comprehensive basis is provided in the financial statements' tax note. It discloses the balance of the deferred taxes not recorded as a result of the use of the partial allocation method. The annual size and change in this unrecorded balance is used to estimate the potential US GAAP adjustment in the deferred tax expense. In the case of Grand Metropolitan, the unrecorded deferred tax liability account declined during 1989 and was £116 million at yearend. These facts suggest that any 1989 US GAAP adjustment to deferred tax expense would not be material and no adjustment is necessary. The company's book tax rate can be used to convert the US GAAP pretax profit figure to an after-tax basis. This may not necessarily be the case in future years.

The final worksheet step is to reclassify Grand Metropolitan's extraordinary gain as a discontinued operations gain, since the transactions comprising this item primarily involve discontinued operations, and to record as a discontinued operations item the discontinued operations profits and gains previously eliminated from operating profit. The company's book tax rate is used to convert this latter item to an after-tax basis.[7]

Table 2 presents a comparison of Grand Metropolitan's 1989 profit and cash flow data on an as-reported and estimated US GAAP basis. Under no circumstances should the US GAAP figures and percentage adjustments shown in Table 2 be considered indicative of future years' income and adjustment levels. Grand Metropolitan's 1989 income only included nine months of Pillsbury's earnings, and the company made significant divestitures after the

---

[7] No material unusual item adjustments are required in 1989. Since adjustments for this item may be required in future years, it is classified in the "Material Difference" category.

TABLE 2 Comparison of Selected Grand Metropolitan As-Reported and Estimated US GAAP Equivalent 1989 Income and Cash Flow Data (£ in millions)

	As reported	Estimated US GAAP Equivalent	Percentage Difference
Net income	£1,068	£1,053	-2
Operating profit after taxes	516	398	-23
Operating profit before taxes	732	556	-24
Operating profit before interest, taxes, depreciation & amortization	1,202	1,056	-12

close of the fiscal year. Also, the 1989 operating profit's US GAAP adjustment related to discontinued businesses is a one-time item.

WHY US GAAP?

Transnational financial statement analyses of foreign companies using IAS-conforming accounting are usually performed on both the company's financial results as reported and on an adjusted basis that conforms to an accounting model that the analyst believes is appropriate for the analytical purpose. The US GAAP accounting model is preferred by most US equity analysts as the accounting basis for the adjusted version of a foreign company's financial statements. This is a sensible approach, since

- US investors and analysts are comfortable working with US GAAP financial statements;
- US GAAP is designed to be useful to investors making investment decisions;
- The accounting and cash flow-related equity valuation multiples that US investors are most familiar with use US GAAP-determined accounting data;
- The number of US GAAP adjustments and their cost is reduced since US GAAP conforms to IAS, and IAS-conforming statements typically provide sufficient data to make most of the desired US GAAP adjustments; and
- The financial ratio standards US analysts are most familiar with are based on US GAAP accounting data.

While the US GAAP model is preferred by most US investors and is useful for many analytical purposes, its use should not be automatic. Alternatives to using a US GAAP-based accounting model may in some circumstances be more relevant to the analytical purpose. Also, in some cases, restatement may not be necessary. Whenever an analytical purpose requires a transnational financial statement analysis, always ask and answer the question: "Should the foreign company's financial statements be restated to an alternative accounting basis, and, if so, what should that basis be?"

APPENDIX A Illustrative Accounting Policy Classification Chart: Grand Metropolitan's 1989 Financial Statement Accounting Policies

Item	Grand Metropolitan	US GAAP
	I. Similar To US GAAP	
Consolidation	All controlled subsidiaries	All controlled subsidiaries
Investment in Related Companies	Equity method when 20–50% ownership	Equity method when 20–50% ownership
Inventories	Lower of cost or market	Lower of cost or market
Research & Development	Expense as incurred	Expense as incurred
Investments (other than in related companies)	Lower of cost or market	Lower of cost or market
Overseas Subsidiaries	Present on a uniform accounting basis	Present on a uniform accounting basis
Undistributed Foreign Profits	No deferred tax provision	No deferred tax provision necessary
Foreign Currency Income Statements	Profits & losses of overseas subsidiaries are translated into sterling at weighted average rates of exchange during the year, with year-end adjustments into sterling at the balance sheet exchange rate taken to owners' equity	Similar treatment when functional currency is non-sterling currency
	II. No Material Difference	
Interest Related To Construction Of Long-Lived Assets	Capitalize, net of any tax relief	Capitalize gross amount
Other Postretirement Benefits	Accrue over active work life of employees	Cost equal to cash paid to obtain current benefits for retirees
Leases	Leases where the lessor has all the risks & rewards of ownership are treated as finance leases. Other leases are treated as operating leases.	Classification of finance lease is based on specific criteria
	III. Similar Outcome	
Retirement Plans	Defined benefit plans charged to income on a systematic basis. Pension surpluses and deficits allocated over the expected remaining service lives of current employees. Based on actuarial methods, principally the projected unit method. Salary progression assumed.	Requires a standardized method to be followed by all companies for measuring the net periodic pension cost of defined benefit plans.

Item	Grand Metropolitan	US GAAP
	IV. Different Circumstances	
Public House Depreciation	No depreciation of owned and leased public house costs	Depreciate cost over useful life
	V. Balance Sheet Effect Only	
Unfunded Postretirement Medical Benefit Liability	Liability on balance sheet	Not recorded as a liability
Foreign Currency Balance Sheets	Translated into sterling at the balance sheet date exchange rate. Gains & losses on translation taken to owners' equity.	Similar treatment when non-sterling currencies are the functional currencies
	VI. Material Differences	
Amortization of Intangibles	Goodwill charged to shareholders' equity in year of acquisition. Purchased intangibles accounted for as fixed intangible assets (i.e. no write off unless loss in value).	Amortize over useful life or 40 years, whichever is shorter
Unusual Items	Included in extraordinary items	Included in operating income
Discontinued Businesses	Income or loss up to time of completion of sale or disposition included in operating income. Gains & losses on disposition included in extraordinary items.	Income and gains and losses from measurement date (date of adoption of plan to discontinue) reported separately as a discontinued item
Deferred Taxation	Partial tax allocation (i.e., no provision for deferred taxes made for accelerated depreciation used for tax purposes if there is reasonable evidence that such deferred tax will not be payable in the foreseeable future)	Comprehensive tax allocation required
Fixed Assets and Depreciation	Stated at cost or at professional valuation and depreciated over useful life (see IV, for treatment of public houses)	State at cost and depreciate over useful life

APPENDIX B Illustrative Restatement to US GAAP Worksheet: Grand Metropolitan 1989 Net Income, Operating Profit and Cash Flow (£ in millions)

Reported Net Income		£1,068
Extraordinary Items	£560	
Discontinued Operations	—	
Accounting Changes	—	
Minority Interest	-8	552
Reported Operating Profit After Taxes		£ 516
Current Tax Expense	113	
Deferred Tax Expense	103	216
Reported Operating Profit Before Taxes		£ 732
Interest	£280	
Depreciation	190	
Amortization—Goodwill	0	
Amortization—Intangibles	0	470
Reported Operating Profit Before Interest, Taxes, Depreciation & Amortization		£1,202
Operating Profit of Discontinued Businesses Included in Reported Operating Profit		146
Estimated US GAAP Operating Profit Before Interest, Taxes, Depreciation & Amortization		£1,056
Interest	£280	
Depreciation	162	
Amortization—Goodwill	58	500
Estimated US GAAP Operating Profit Before Taxes		£ 556
Tax Expense (29.5%)		158
Estimated US GAAP Operating Profit After Taxes		£ 398
Extraordinary Items	—	
Discontinued Operations	£663	
Accounting Changes	—	
Minority Interest	-8	655
Estimated US GAAP Net Income		£1,053